Fodor's

MEXICO

26th Edition

o Stay and Eat
udgets

ee Sights
cal Secrets

s You Can Trust

vel Publications New York, Toronto, London, Sydney, Auckland
rs.com

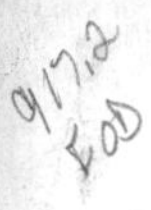

FODOR'S MEXICO

Editors: Laura M. Kidder (lead project editor); Kelly Kealy, Alexis Kelly, Margaret Kelly

Writers: Eva Ginsburg, Gerard Helferich, Michele Joyce, Marlise Kast, Maribeth Mellin, Laura Mestre, Teresa Nicholas, Rachel Nolan, Jane Onstott, Emily Schmall, Meghan Collins Sullivan, Jeffrey Van Fleet

Production Editor: Carrie Parker
Maps & Illustrations: David Lindroth, Henry Colomb, Mark Stroud, and Ali Baird, Moon Street Cartography, and Dr. Ed Barnhart, director, Maya Exploration Center (map of Palenque), *cartographers;* Bob Blake, Rebecca Baer, *map editors;* William Wu, *information graphics*
Design: Fabrizio La Rocca, *creative director;* Guido Caroti, Siobhan O'Hare, *art directors;* Tina Malaney, Chie Ushio, Ann McBride, Jessica Walsh, *designers;* Melanie Marin, *senior picture editor*
Cover Photo: (Ballet Folklorico de Mexico, Mexico City): Lindsay Hebberd/Corbis
Production Manager: Steve Slawsky

26th Edition

ISBN 978-1-4000-0491-1

ISSN 0196-5999

SPECIAL SALES

This book is available at special discounts for bulk purchases for sales pr premiums. Special editions, including personalized covers, excerpts of exi and corporate imprints, can be created in large quantities for special need information, write to Special Markets/Premium Sales, 1745 Broadway, M York, New York 10019, or e-mail specialmarkets@randomhouse.com.

AN IMPORTANT TIP & AN INVITATION

Although all prices, opening times, and other details in this book are bas mation supplied to us at press time, changes occur all the time in the trave Fodor's cannot accept responsibility for facts that become outdated or for errors or omissions. So **always confirm information when it matters,** especia making a detour to visit a specific place. Your experiences—positive and matter to us. If we have missed or misstated something, **please write to us.** W on all suggestions. Contact the Mexico editor at editors@fodors.com or c/ 1745 Broadway, New York, NY 10019.

PRINTED IN THE UNITED STATES OF AMERICA

10 9 8 7 6 5 4 3 2 1

Be a Fodor's Correspondent

Your opinion matters. It matters to us. It matters to your fellow Fodor's travelers, too. And we'd like to hear it. In fact, we need to hear it.

When you share your experiences and opinions, you become an active member of the Fodor's community. That means we'll not only use your feedback to make our books better, but we'll publish your names and comments whenever possible. Throughout our guides, look for "Word of Mouth," excerpts of your unvarnished feedback.

Here's how you can help improve Fodor's for all of us.

Tell us when we're right. We rely on local writers to give you an insider's perspective. But our writers and staff editors—who are the best in the business—depend on you. Your positive feedback is a vote to renew our recommendations for the next edition.

Tell us when we're wrong. We're proud that we update most of our guides every year. But we're not perfect. Things change. Hotels cut services. Museums change hours. Charming cafés lose charm. If our writer didn't quite capture the essence of a place, tell us how you'd do it differently. If any of our descriptions are inaccurate or inadequate, we'll incorporate your changes in the next edition and will correct factual errors at fodors.com immediately.

Tell us what to include. You probably have had fantastic travel experiences that aren't yet in Fodor's. Why not share them with a community of like-minded travelers? Maybe you chanced upon a beach or bistro or B&B that you don't want to keep to yourself. Tell us why we should include it. And share your discoveries and experiences with everyone directly at fodors.com. Your input may lead us to add a new listing or highlight a place we cover with a "Highly Recommended" star or with our highest rating, "Fodor's Choice."

Give us your opinion instantly at our feedback center at www.fodors.com/feedback. You may also e-mail editors@fodors.com with the subject line "Mexico Editor." Or send your nominations, comments, and complaints by mail to Mexico Editor, Fodor's, 1745 Broadway, New York, NY 10019.

You and travelers like you are the heart of the Fodor's community. Make our community richer by sharing your experiences. Be a Fodor's correspondent.

¡Buen Viaje!

Tim Jarrell, Publisher

CONTENTS

Fodor's Features

CONTENTS

MAPS

ABOUT THIS BOOK

Our Ratings

Sometimes you find terrific travel experiences and sometimes they just find you. But usually the burden is on you to select the right combination of experiences. That's where our ratings come in.

As travelers we've all discovered a place so wonderful that its worthiness is obvious. And sometimes that place is so unique that superlatives don't do it justice: you just have to be there to know. These sights, properties, and experiences get our highest rating, **Fodor's Choice,** indicated by orange stars throughout this book. Black stars highlight sights and properties we deem **Highly Recommended,** places that our writers, editors, and readers praise again and again for consistency and excellence.

By default, there's another category: any place we include in this book is by definition worth your time, unless we say otherwise. And we will.

Disagree with any of our choices? Care to nominate a place or suggest that we rate one more highly? Visit our feedback center at www.fodors.com/feedback.

Budget Well

Hotel and restaurant price categories from ¢ to $$$$ are defined in the opening pages of each chapter. For attractions, we always give standard adult admission fees; reductions are usually available for children, students, and senior citizens. Want to pay with plastic? **AE, D, DC, MC, V** following restaurant and hotel listings indicate whether American Express, Discover, Diner's Club, MasterCard, and Visa are accepted.

Restaurants

Unless we state otherwise, restaurants are open for lunch and dinner daily. We mention dress only when there's a specific requirement and reservations only when they're essential or not accepted—it's always best to book ahead.

Hotels

Hotels have private bath, phone, TV, and air-conditioning and operate on the European Plan (aka EP, meaning without meals), unless we specify that they use the Continental Plan (CP, with a continental breakfast), Breakfast Plan (BP, with a full breakfast), or Modified American Plan (MAP, with breakfast and dinner), or are all-inclusive (AI, including all meals and most activities). We always list facilities but not whether you'll be charged an extra fee to use them, so when pricing accommodations, find out what's included.

Many Listings

- ★ Fodor's Choice
- ★ Highly recommended
- ✉ Physical address
- ✥ Directions or Map coordinates
- Mailing address
- ☏ Telephone
- Fax
- On the Web
- E-mail
- Admission fee
- Open/closed times
- Ⓜ Metro stations
- Credit cards

Hotels & Restaurants

- Hotel
- Number of rooms
- Facilities
- Meal plans
- ✕ Restaurant
- Reservations
- Dress code
- Smoking
- BYOB

Outdoors

- Golf
- Camping

Other

- Family-friendly
- ⇨ See also
- Branch address
- ☞ Take note

Experience Mexico

Women in traditional dress holding pottery, Chiapa de Corzo, Chiapas.

WORD OF MOUTH

"[We] spent two weeks on the Yucatán Peninsula . . . fishing, diving, snorkeling in cenotes, and exploring Maya ruins and a variety of towns (Tulum, Valladolid, San Felipe, and Isla Mujeres). [We spent another] two weeks studying Spanish in San Cristóbal de las Casas in Chiapas . . . living with a host family and exploring water features, Maya ruins, and indigenous villages."

—hopefulist

www.fodors.com/community

WHAT'S WHERE

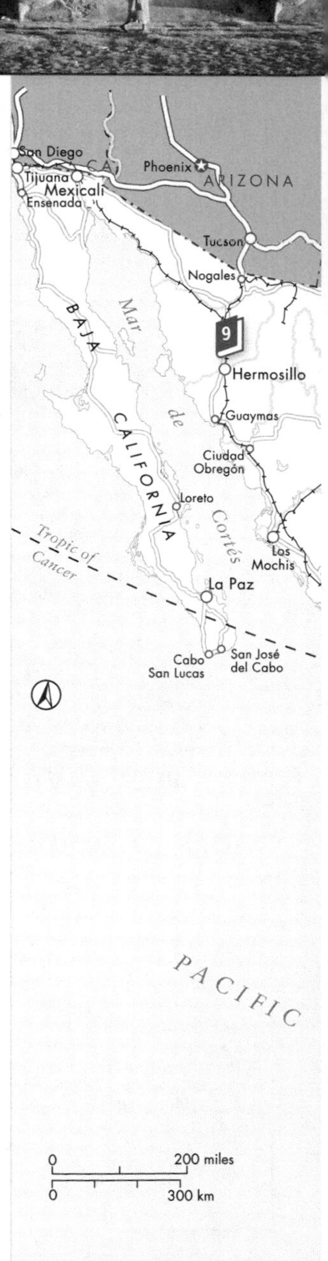

Numbers correspond to chapter numbers.

2 Mexico City. The sprawling capital Isn't for everyone (the crime, the smog), but its cultural vibrancy attracts hip globe-trotters. You can sample the city in a day or two by strolling the streets around the central square or enjoying downtown's high-rises and galleries.

3 Around Mexico City. Within a few hours of the capital are ruins, colonial towns, indigenous villages, and volcanoes. Some sights, like the ancient city of Teotihuacán, are easy day trips. Colonial Puebla and Cuernavaca, known for its lush walled gardens, are popular multiday trips.

4 San Miguel de Allende and the Heartland. San Miguel's cobbled streets and haciendas continue to inspire its colony of American artists, writers, and retirees. For a place where people actually speak Spanish, head to Zacatecas or Guanajuato. Intrepid souls can also enjoy hot springs, mountain biking, horseback riding, and hang gliding.

5 Guadalajara. Mexico's second-largest city has a Centro Histórico lined with beautiful buildings and is thoroughly modern everywhere else, which means good restaurants and happening nightlife. Guadalajara is also the capital of Jalisco State—birthplace of tequila, *charreadas* (the ubiquitous Mexican-style rodeo), and mariachi music.

6 Veracruz. Its beaches, though not as nice as Cancún's, are popular with Mexican families. Cuban-influenced, seaside Veracruz City is noteworthy, as are the ruins of El Tajín.

7 Oaxaca. This gorgeous place has it all: a lovely colonial city, ruins, crafts villages, forest-covered mountains, low-key surfer beaches, and superb Oaxaca City.

8 Chiapas and Tabasco. Isolated, jungle-swathed Chiapas is untrammeled, due in part to occasional Zapatista uprisings. What keeps it from falling off the map are the ruins of Palenque—as Mayan cities go, only Tikal in Guatemala and Copán in Honduras compare. Visit neighboring Tabasco to see the massive heads carved by the Olmecs.

9 Sonora. If you don't live close to the border, getting to Sonora, with its desert and ranchland, will likely require more effort than it's worth. Its well-maintained highways and mission route, however, make it popular with road-trippers (especially RVers).

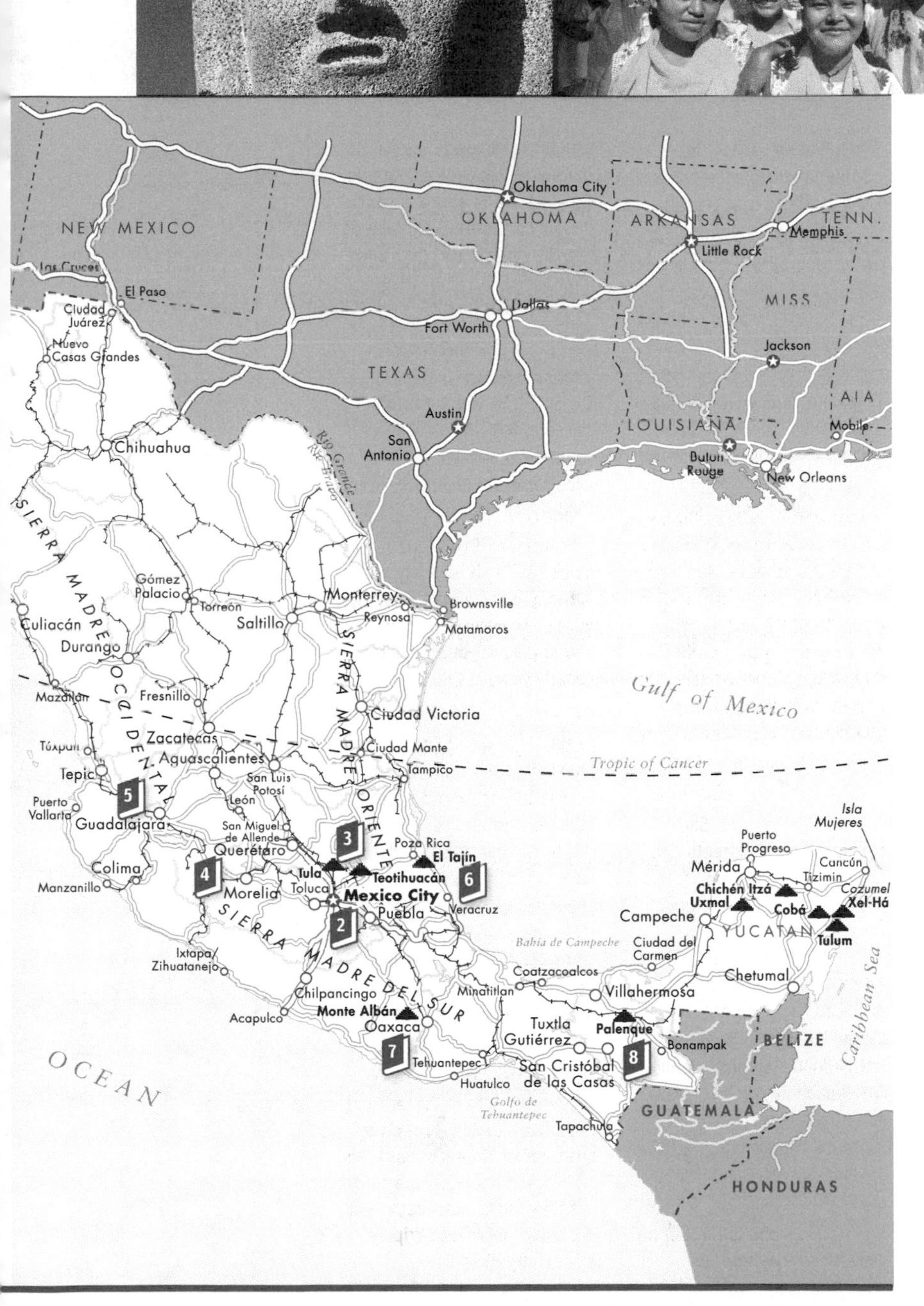

NEW MEXICO
OKLAHOMA
Oklahoma City
ARKANSAS
Little Rock
TENN.
Memphis
MISS
Jackson
ALA
Mobile
Las Cruces
El Paso
Ciudad Juárez
Nuevo Casas Grandes
Dallas
Fort Worth
TEXAS
Austin
San Antonio
LOUISIANA
Baton Rouge
New Orleans
Rio Grande
Río Bravo
Chihuahua
SIERRA MADRE OCCIDENTAL
Gómez Palacio
Torreón
Saltillo
Monterrey
Reynosa
Brownsville
Matamoros
SIERRA MADRE ORIENTAL
Culiacán
Durango
Mazatlán
Fresnillo
Zacatecas
Ciudad Victoria
Ciudad Mante
Tampico
Gulf of Mexico
Tropic of Cancer
Túxpan
Tepic
Aguascalientes
San Luis Potosí
León
Puerto Vallarta
Guadalajara
San Miguel de Allende
Querétaro
Poza Rica
El Tajín
Tula
Teotihuacán
Colima
Manzanillo
Morelia
Toluca
Mexico City
Veracruz
Puebla
SIERRA MADRE DEL SUR
Ixtapa/ Zihuatanejo
Chilpancingo
Acapulco
Monte Albán
Oaxaca
Tehuantepec
Huatulco
Golfo de Tehuantepec
OCEAN
Bahía de Campeche
Coatzacoalcos
Minatitlán
Villahermosa
Tuxtla Gutiérrez
San Cristóbal de las Casas
Palenque
Bonampak
Tapachula
Isla Mujeres
Puerto Progreso
Mérida
Cancún
Tizimín
Cozumel
Chichén Itzá
Uxmal
Cobá
Xel-Há
Tulum
Campeche
YUCATÁN
Ciudad del Carmen
Chetumal
BELIZE
Caribbean Sea
GUATEMALA
HONDURAS

WHAT'S WHERE

10 **Copper Canyon.** Many people compare the Copper Canyon (Barrancas del Cobre) to the Grand Canyon—the one that existed a century ago. Most visitors rely on a stunning 15-hour train ride to see this region, perhaps doing a day hike into the canyon.

11 **Los Cabos and the Baja Peninsula.** There are two Bajas, literally and figuratively. Baja Norte is still slightly rugged, with boulder-strewn deserts, mountain ranges, and long beaches. Baja Sur has Los Cabos and expensive spa-resorts.

12 **Puerto Vallarta and the Pacific Coast Resorts.** PV is more sophisticated than Cancún, but more laid-back than Acapulco. North of it is Mazatlán, a former spring-break spot that now attracts families and retirees. South of PV are miles of untouched beaches reached by dirt roads and linked by the port town of Manzanillo and the twin resorts of Ixtapa and Zihuatanejo.

13 **Acapulco.** This city has many draws: an undeniably gorgeous bay, hot new hotels, great restaurants, sizzling nightlife. But, of late, it's been plagued by drug cartel–related gang violence. Check the state department's Web site and inquire on Fodors.com forums before planning your trip.

14 **Cancún and Isla Mujeres.** Americans flock to Spring-Break Land for turquoise water; white, white sand; tons of water sports; and a lively environment. Yeah, it's overdeveloped, but it's also low-key in the off-season, and a few swanky lounges and hotels now offset the rowdy bars and all-inclusives. For true peace and quiet, head to Isla Mujures just across the bay.

15 **Cozumel and the Riviera Maya.** The island of Cozumel is a kinder, gentler version of Cancún. Many reefs and the 8-mi channel just off the coast make it *the* place to snorkel and dive. Playa del Carmen, a beach town on the mainland, is a hub of the Riviera Maya, a string of beaches and resorts south of Cancún.

16 **Mérida and Environs.** Chances are you've heard of Chichén Itzá. The ruins are in Yucatán State and far inland—in fact they're close enough to Cancún and Cozumel that many people prefer to do their day trips from there. But Yucatán also holds the colonial city of Mérida—one of those places that seem to cast a spell.

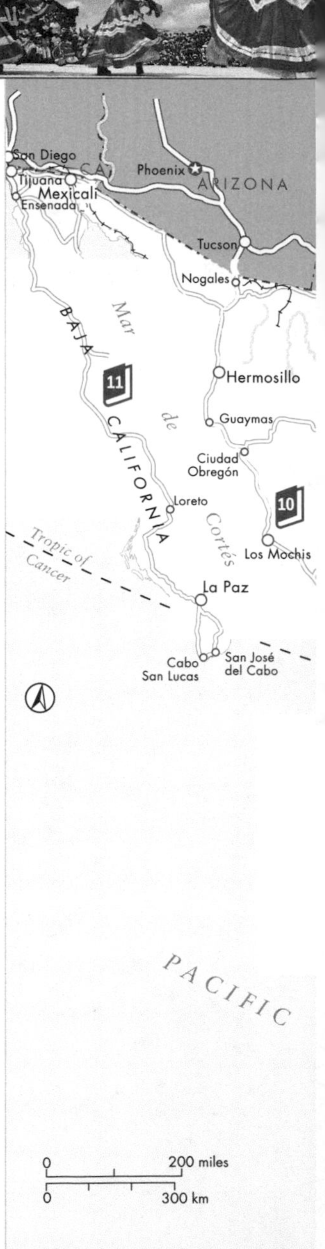

NEW MEXICO
OKLAHOMA
Oklahoma City
ARKANSAS
TENN.
Memphis
Little Rock
Las Cruces
El Paso
Ciudad Juárez
Dallas
Fort Worth
MISS.
Nuevo Casas Grandes
Jackson
TEXAS
ALA.
Austin
LOUISIANA
Mobile
Chihuahua
San Antonio
Baton Rouge
New Orleans
Rio Grande
Río Bravo
SIERRA MADRE OCCIDENTAL
Gómez Palacio
Torreón
Monterrey
Brownsville
Culiacán
Saltillo
Reynosa
Matamoros
Durango
SIERRA MADRE ORIENTE
Mazatlán
Fresnillo
Gulf of Mexico
Ciudad Victoria
Zacatecas
Ciudad Mante
Túxpan
Aguascalientes
Tropic of Cancer
Tepic
San Luis Potosí
Tampico
León
Puerto Vallarta
Guadalajara
Guanajuato
Isla Mujeres
12
San Miguel de Allende
Querétaro
Poza Rica
Puerto Progreso
El Tajín
Mérida
16
Cancún
Colima
Morelia
Tula
Teotihuacán
Tizimin
Manzanillo
Pátzcuaro
Toluca
Mexico City
Veracruz
Chichén Itzá
14
Uxmal
SIERRA MADRE DEL SUR
Puebla
Campeche
Cobá
Cuernavaca
Bahía de Campeche
Ciudad del Carmen
YUCATAN
Tulum
Ixtapa/Zihuatanejo
13
Caribbean Sea
Coatzacoalcos
Chetumal
15
Chilpancingo
Minatitlan
Villahermosa
Acapulco
Monte Albán
Oaxaca
Tuxtla Gutiérrez
Palenque
Bonampak
BELIZE
OCEAN
Tehuantepec
San Cristóbal de las Casas
Comitán
Huatulco
Golfo de Tehuantepec
GUATEMALA
Tapachula
HONDURAS

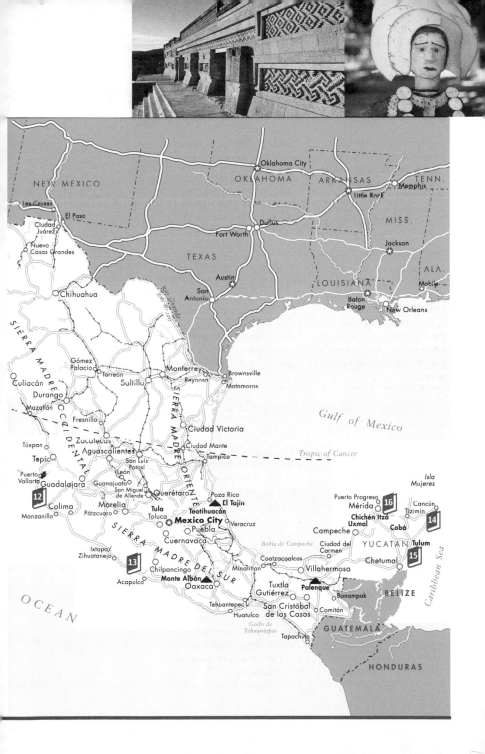

MEXICO PLANNER

Trip Planning

If you're not planning to cocoon at a beach resort, look at the country the way the tour operators do—as a collection of cultural or historical routes.

The Ruta del Vino (wine route) is a road through Baja's burgeoning wine region in the Valle de Guadalupe. The Ruta Maya (Mayan route) lets you trace Mayan history through the southeast. The Ruta de los Dioses (Route of the Gods) shows up in many itineraries, usually starting in Mexico City (and Teotihuacán), heading to Puebla and Cholula, and continuing to Veracruz City or Oaxaca City—hitting ruins all along the way.

Not ready to commit to the grand Mayan trek? Check out the Mexico Tourist Board's Web site for a list of UNESCO World Heritage Sites—picking two or three would easily focus your trip. Similarly, consider building a trip around Sectur's Pueblos Mágicos (Magical Villages), almost three-dozen well-preserved towns of historical and cultural significance.

Visitor Info

Mexico's 31 states and the Federal District (Mexico City) have tourism Web sites, though few are in English. A notable exception is the official page of the **Mexico Tourism Board** (☎ *800/446–3942 [44–MEXICO]* 🌐 *www.visitmexico.com*).

Be sure to check out **Fodors** (🌐 *www.fodors.com*) for destination information, articles, hotel and restaurant ratings, and community feedback in the forums. Other excellent English-language sites for history, travel information, and news stories include the **Mexico Channel** (🌐 *www.mexicochannel.net*), **Mexico Connect** (🌐 *www.mexconnect.com*), and **Mexico Online** (🌐 *www.mexonline.com*).

For archaeology, two sites stand above others: **Mesoweb** (🌐 *www.mesoweb.com*) and the nonprofit site **Ancient Mexico** (🌐 *www.ancientmexico.com*).

Mexico's sites have a page on the Web site for **World Heritage Sites** (🌐 *www.worldheritagesite.org/countries/mexico.html*). And **Mexico Guru** (🌐 *www.mexicoguru.com*) has interactive satellite maps of Mexico linked to destination articles.

Language-Study Programs

Mexico has many language institutes. For total immersion, most schools offer boarding with a family, but there's generally flexibility in terms of the type of lodgings and the length of your stay.

The **Academia Hispano Americana** (☎ *415/152–0349* 🌐 *www.ahaspeakspanish.com*) offers full immersion or a few hours a day, and cooking classes once a week. Many programs hold courses in Latin American studies and culture, as well as language. **AmeriSpan Unlimited** (☎ *800/879–6640* 🌐 *www.amerispan.com*), based in the United States, specializes in medical and business Spanish. Special programs include those at the **Centro de Idiomas de la Universidad Autónoma Benito Juárez** (☎ *951/514–0049 in Oaxaca,* 🌐 *www.uabjo.mx*), which holds classes in Mixtec and Zapotec as well as Spanish.

Health

The biggest health risk you're likely to face is *turista* (traveler's diarrhea), from consuming contaminated fruit, vegetables, water, or ice. Other concerns involve discomfort from air pollution (particularly in Mexico City), water pollution, sunburn, altitude, and insect bites.

According to the U.S. National Centers for Disease Control and Prevention (CDC), there's a limited risk of malaria, dengue fever, and other insect-carried or parasite-caused illnesses largely, but not exclusively, in rural and tropical coastal areas.

HEALTH PRECAUTIONS

Mexico was at the epicenter of the early 2009 H1N1 outbreak. Health clubs, nightclubs, stadiums, and many businesses in the Distrito Federal and elsewhere went dark for days, and several international air carriers suspended service to prevent the spread of the virus. By late May of that year, health alerts were lowered, precautionary measures lifted, and experts announced that it was a mild strain after all.

Check the CDC and WHO Web sites for updates on H1N1 and other health issues. Discuss risks and precautions related to infectious diseases, high altitude, and air-pollution with your doctor. Find out if you need antimalarials and/or vaccinations against typhoid, hepatitis A, or hepatitis B. Examine your health-insurance policy to see what's covered abroad. If need be, buy medical-only trip insurance. If you plan to be physically active, sign up with a medical-evacuation assistance company.

If you're traveling to areas where malaria is prevalent, don't wait until you're in Mexico to start antimalarials; the medicine needs time to get into your system. There's no vaccine to combat dengue, so your best prevention is good insect repellent, something with at least 10% DEET.

Safety

Since early 2008, violent crime—most of it drug trafficking-related—has spiked significantly in Mexico, particularly in border areas. Since then, there have been firefights in Tijuana, Ciudad Juarez, and Chihuahua City. The violence is aimed at police or members of the drug cartels, and often takes place in rough neighborhoods rarely frequented by travelers. That said, conflicts in Acapulco have brushed up against tourist areas.

Before your trip, check the news and the state department Web site for updates on both safety and health.

SAFETY RESOURCES

Mexico Ministry of Tourism (☎ *800/446–3942, 01800/903–9200 toll-free in Mexico* 🌐 *www.sectur.gob.mx*).

U.S. Department of State (🌐 *www.state.gov/travel*).

U.S. Embassy (✉ *Paseo de la Reforma 305, Col. Cuauhtémoc, Mexico City* ☎ *55/5080–2000* 🌐 *mexico.usembassy.gov/eng*).

U.S. Transportation Security Administration (🌐 *www.tsa.gov*).

TOP ATTRACTIONS

Chichén Itzá

An immense and important Mayan center, this ruined city of sun-baked pyramids and jungle-choked temples was named one of the New Seven Wonders of the World in 2007. Its proximity to Cancún sure doesn't detract from its popularity. Thousands come to the site for the vernal equinox.

Frida and Diego

Even if you're not an avid fan of Frida Kahlo's vivid and macabre paintings, retracing her and her husband Diego Rivera's steps is a great way to approach Mexico City. Frida's house, in the serene Coyoacán neighborhood, and the Museo Casa Estudio Diego Rivera y Frida Kahlo containing an impressive overview of Diego's work, provide an intimate look at the lives of these two artists.

Great Mayan Barrier Reef

Along the Caribbean Coast lies part of an immense reef system that snakes all the way to Honduras. Cozumel's marine park alone has 25 prime scuba-diving reefs, some of which are accessible to novices. Experienced divers get to see the good stuff, too: 90-foot coral pinnacles and giant sponges in all shades.

Guanajuato

As San Miguel de Allende gets all the attention and the expats (artists, poets, and writers), Guanajuato quietly enjoys its hill-ringed beauty—it's a standout in a region with no shortage of stunning colonial cities. A well-known church and a handful of offbeat sights like the mummy museum provide entertainment after you're done exploring the city's twisty streets.

Museo Nacional de Antropología

If you can't visit any of Mexico's archaeological sites, taking an English-language tour (book well in advance) at the capital's anthropology museum is the next best thing. Of course, it's an even better endeavor before or after seeing ruins. Artifacts and ethnological displays are set up so that you learn about the many pre-Hispanic and contemporary Mesoamerican cultures as well as where they once lived and often still do.

Subterranean Swimming Holes

The Yucatán Peninsula has intricate systems of underground rivers connected to the surface by sinkholes called cenotes. Swimmers can take a quick dip in the crystal-clear freshwater, while divers can explore the cave systems.

Teotihuacán

At this magnificent site you can wander along the Avenue of the Dead, puzzle over depictions of jaguars and plumed serpents, or climb the Temple of the Sun—one of the world's largest pyramids. If its steep 240 steps are too much, attempt the smaller Temple of the Moon instead. Archaeological finds in 2010 might help to shed light on the mysterious culture that built all this. Oh, yeah, and did we mention that all this is just an hour's drive from Mexico City?

Tequila Country

Jalisco State is the birthplace of Mexico's famous (infamous?) firewater. Drive 90 minutes northwest of Guadalajara and toward Puerto Vallarta to reach the town of Tequila itself. Tour museums and distilleries where José Cuervo and Herradura are made. Be sure to have a designated driver—free samples or formal tastings are part of the whole experience.

TOP EXPERIENCES

Seeing a Baby Whale Breach

Even if you only glimpse it from shore, spotting a pod of whales in the Pacific is one of Mexico's definitive experiences. If you're lucky, you'll see a mama whale teach her young one the not-so-delicate art of breaching. Baja has gray whales in its waters from December to April; in particular, Laguna San Ignacio and Bahía Magdalena on the Pacific Coast seem to sing out a siren call to grays. They come in droves to give birth or mate. Sightings are also good between Puerto Vallarta and Manzanillo.

Watching a Craftsperson at Work

How often do you get to see your mementos made right before your eyes? Many regions have rich crafts traditions, so before you settle on that refrigerator magnet or shot glass as a souvenir, visit a village where nearly every house doubles as a workshop. You'll find pottery, handwoven rugs, and delicate wood sculptures in Oaxaca's countryside, ceramics and blown glass outside Guadalajara, hammocks made to order in Mérida. You can even watch Talavera tiles being made in Puebla. Prices are often better at the source, too.

Savoring Seafood at a Beachfront Palapa

The beachfront *palapa* (thatch-roof-shelter) restaurant is ubiquitous. And there's no greater pleasure after hours of swimming or kayaking than ordering a simple meal of fish tacos with a side of rice and beans and washing it down with a *coco frío* (a cold coconut hacked open just enough to stick a straw into). No matter how much you've fallen in love with your megaresort's elaborate beachfront eatery, make sure you experience this lowbrow delight.

Destressing Simply or In Style

In the central regions you'll find *temazcales,* Mayan sweat lodges. These may be simple outbuildings at the end of a trail or reconstructed rooms inside local spas. On the other end of the spectrum are the posh spas of Los Cabos, Puerto Vallarta, and Acapulco—look for treatments that incorporate unusual local ingredients (nopales, Corona beer) and massages in oceanfront palapas. Many of these upscale spas have their own temezcal treatments, with special touches like essential oils, perfumed air, and a spa employee who helps you along your spiritual journey.

Making Your Own Mole

No dish is more mythic than mole. (It's even said that floating around somewhere in the ether is a recipe for a mole that contains 100 ingredients.) Two of Mexico's gastronomic centers—Oaxaca City and Puebla—excel at this complex sauce, though you'll find it all over. Sign up for a cooking class that starts at a local market where you'll get a crash course on Mexican produce and spices before mastering a menu full of regional specialties. We guarantee that this will be memorable.

Marveling at Mexico City from a Rooftop

It's worth spending $15 on a specialty cocktail to get your bearings in this sprawling city at the Habita Hotel's Area Bar or the W's Terrace Bar, both in the trendy Polanco neighborhood. Casa de las Sirenas restaurant also has a nice view of the historic center from its roof. The Terraza Restaurant at the Hotel Majestic, overlooking the Zócalo, offers a spectacular view and reasonably priced buffet. The Restaurante El Mayor, which overlooks the Templo Mayor, is another great place to enjoy a vista and a bite to eat.

QUINTESSENTIAL MEXICO

Day of the Dead

People across the country celebrate El Día de los Muertos, or the Day of the Dead. Some traditions, such as visiting cemeteries, setting up *ofrendas* (altars) in the home, and bestowing sugary *calaveritas* (meaning "little skulls") on children, are observed everywhere. But the holiday, held on November 1–2, will also differ depending on where you go.

In Campeche, families pilgrimage to family members' graves, remove the bones, dust them off, and carefully place them back for another year. Villagers in the most remote regions of Chiapas blanket the burial plots with marigolds, then go home to await a visit from the deceased. In Oaxaca, what begins as a meditative march to the cemetery ends with music and dancing, displays of larger-than-life puppets, and seemingly endless volleys of fireworks.

Mariachi

When Mexicans celebrate weddings, anniversaries, and *quinceañeras* (a "sweet 15" birthday bash), the music of choice is mariachi. Although this type of music hails from Jalisco State, it's popular throughout the country. You'll find men playing folk songs in concert halls, town squares, restaurants, or, as in the Mexico City suburb of Xochimilco, while floating by on flower-covered boats. Their distinctive costumes are adapted from the clothing worn by *charros,* or cowboys of the Jalisco region.

Mariachi music was born in the 19th century. Traditional melodies of various indigenous peoples were adapted to the instruments introduced by the Spanish. This is a music of contrasts, with a highly syncopated rhythm playing below a sweet and sometimes wistful melody.

Tortillas

Mexico's food varies wildly, but one item will appear on the table no matter where you are: the corn tortilla. If tortillas aren't an ingredient in your meal—they sometimes masquerade as crispy croutons in soups or as slender noodles in stews—there's always a stack of them in a basket. The average Mexican eats nearly a pound of tortillas every day.

The corn tortilla (not to be confused with the flour tortilla) was a favorite food of the Aztecs. You'll find the staple in all sizes from two inches (stuffed with beans or meat to make *gorditas*) to 10 inches or more (covered with cheese and other ingredients for pizzalike *tlayudas*). Tiny *tortillerias* crank out the goods for busy urbanites, though in villages across Mexico you'll still see women making them by hand.

Virgin of Guadalupe

The Virgin of Guadalupe, who first revealed herself to a barefoot farmer in 1531, continues to appear all over the country. Shrines to her are in quiet corners of outdoor markets and crowded corridors of bus stations. If you take a taxi, her image may be swinging on the rearview mirror.

Although she always had a following, the popularity of La Guadalupana grew when Padre Miguel Hidalgo emblazoned her image on his flag during Mexico's War of Independence. Thus she became an important religious symbol. Her enduring appeal is due to her adaptability. In the 20th century she was adopted by those demonstrating for the rights of workers, then by women who felt the sting of discrimination.

IF YOU LIKE

Diving and Snorkeling

Cozumel is still considered one of the world's premier diving destinations. Waving sea fans, anemones, moray eels, swooping manta rays, and more than 500 species of fish make their home along the **Mayan Reef.** The visibility here can reach 100 feet, so even if you stay on the surface you'll be amazed by what you can see. Thrill-seekers won't want to miss Isla Contoy's extraordinary **Cave of the Sleeping Sharks.** Here you can see otherwise fierce creatures "dozing," a bizarre response to the chemical composition of the water.

There are plenty of dive sites along the Pacific Coast. In Puerto Vallarta the best snorkeling and diving is around the offshore rock formations near **Playa Mismaloya. Punta de Mita,** about 80 km (50 mi) north of Puerto Vallarta, has at least 10 good places to snorkel and dive, including spots for advanced divers. In winter you might spot orcas or humpback whales; the rest of the year, look for manta rays, several species of eel, sea turtles, and colorful fish.

In Manzanillo the shallow waters of **Playa la Audiencia** make it a good spot for snorkeling, while an offshore wreck draws divers to **Playa la Boquita.**

At the southern tip of Baja California there are some good sites near La Paz at the coral banks off **Isla Espíritu Santo,** where you'll see parrot fish, manta rays, neons, and angelfish. **Bahía Santa María** is a great place to snorkel; fish of almost every hue swim through formations of gleaming white coral. **El Arco,** the most spectacular sight near Cabo San Lucas, is also a prime dive area.

Colonial Architecture

Before you leave **Mexico City,** make sure to take a good look at the main square. To crush the spirit of the Aztecs, Cortés built the massive Catedral Metropolitana where their temples had stood. Renaissance and baroque styles mingle in the sections completed in the 17th century, while the bell towers dating from the 18th century show a neoclassical flair.

Within a few hours of Mexico City are some of the country's finest colonial cities, including **Tlaxcala** and its supreme examples of churrigueresque architecture. The Iglesia de San Sebastián y Santa Prisca is the centerpiece of **Taxco,** one of the most perfectly preserved colonial capitals. The church is a memorable shade of pink.

The Heartland's colonial cities were financed by silver from the nearby mines. You may get lost in the labyrinthine streets of **Guanajuato,** but be sure to see La Valenciana—its altars vary in style from baroque to plateresque, the flowing lines resembling the work of a silversmith. The cathedral in nearby **Zacatecas** is thought to be the finest baroque building in Mexico. Beautifully restored mansions dating from the 18th century are the main attraction of **Querétaro.**

Perhaps the loveliest colonial capital is **Oaxaca,** known for the pale green stone used for almost all its landmarks. The architects went for baroque in most of its churches, including the Iglesia de Santo Domingo. In neighboring Chiapas the baroque facade of the cathedral in **San Cristóbal de las Casas** is painted vivid shades of red, yellow, and black—the colors seen most often in the shirts worn by indigenous women.

Ancient Cities and Ruins

Although their civilization was at its height at the time of the conquest, there are surprisingly few Aztec sites left. One of the structures that survived is the **Templo Mayor** in the middle of Mexico City. Discovered in 1978, this temple had been buried beneath a row of colonial-era houses.

Ironically, the best-preserved ruins are often the oldest. North of Mexico City is **Teotihuacán,** which thrived between AD 250 and AD 600. Its centerpiece, the Pirámide del Sol, is one of the largest pyramids ever built. So little is known about the culture that archaeologists don't even know its real name. However, the 2010 discovery of a tunnel leading to chambers containing thousands of objects beneath the site's Templo do Quetzalcóatl may change that.

Other massive monuments are in the southeastern part of the country. Overlooking Oaxaca is the Zapotec capital of **Monte Albán.** Archaeologists still debate the use of the arrow-shape structure that stands at a strange angle in the central plaza. But the people who left behind the most impressive cities were the Maya. After their civilization fell about a millennium ago, the jungle closed in around their temples, protecting them from those who would carry off their treasures.

In Chiapas you'll marvel at the elegant carvings that distinguish **Palenque,** perhaps the most awe-inspiring of these ancient cities. In the Yucatán is Mexico's most famous monument, the ancient city of **Chichén Itzá,** which is visited often, by many, but still worth a trip.

Roads Less Traveled

The Barrancas del Cobre (Copper Canyon) has grown in popularity as a tourist destination. Get off the train at Cerocahui and head down to **Urique** at the canyon's floor.

The **Mixteca** is a handsome region not far from Oaxaca City, but since the major activity here is standing slack-jawed before a massive monastery, most people leave it off their itinerary.

The **Oaxaca Coast** is stubbornly low-key despite some stirrings of development. Even the towns that get listed in all the guidebooks are no-frills compared with other resort areas, and a rental car will get you to beaches that don't have so much as a *palapa* on them.

You'll be happy anywhere in the state of Veracruz, which sees more Mexican vacationers than American tourists, but the village of **Xico,** surrounded by natural wonders, feels like a slice of a different era.

In Chiapas, Palenque is truly amazing, but you should also push on to the ruins of **Yaxchilán** on the Guatemalan border. The last hour of the trip has to be done by boat, so you definitely won't see a parking lot full of tour buses here.

And there's always road-tripping the **Baja Peninsula.** It's easy to access, with its length run through by the Carretera Transpeninsular highway, which connects many small towns you've never heard of.

GREAT ITINERARIES

DAYS 1–3: THE CAPITAL'S WONDERS AND BEYOND

Welcome to Mexico City

Can you really know Mexico if you haven't visited its dizzying capital? Once the world's largest metropolis and the primary stomping grounds of the Aztecs, the first city was razed by the conquistadors, who built the city that still stands today.

After you've settled into your hotel, head straight for the city's heart: the immense Zócalo. Highlights include the Diego Rivera murals at Palacio Nacional, the Templo Mayor, and the Catedral Metropolitana.

Next up: hop on a red Turibus for a tour of the city. If you're in a walking mood, walk up Francisco I. Madero to the Palacio de Bellas Artes and Alameda Central park. You can catch the Turibus here at the *Hemiciclo a Benito Juárez* monument on Avenida Juárez.

Logistics: When you emerge from the highly efficient immigration and customs facilities at Aeropuerto Internacional Benito Juárez, head to an official ticket counter marked TRANSPORTACIÓN TERRESTRE for a taxi. Do not purchase a ticket from other vendors or take any other taxis. A ride to a central hotel will cost about $15 and takes 30 minutes.

Beyond the Zócalo

Although the historic center of Mexico City could keep you enthralled for days, you'll enjoy visiting different *colonias,* (neighborhoods) such as the Roma and Condesa, where aging edifices mingle with trendy restaurants and bars. San Angel and Coyoacán channel colonial times with cobblestone streets, elegant homes, and lush gardens. Some of the Diego Rivera and Frida Kahlo museums are here.

Logistics: One of the easiest ways to get around the city is the Turibus, which allows you to hop on and off; it runs daily from 9 to 9. Or you can take a taxi from the taxi stands (*sitios*). Immediately state your destination to find out the fare (average $5).

Anthropology in the City

A visit to Mexico City simply isn't complete until you've set foot in the enormous Museo Nacional de Antropología, located on Paseo de la Reforma and guarded by a large sculpture of Tlaloc, the rain god.

Logistics: The museum is one of the Turibus stops. After your visit, head over to Colonia Polanco for a stroll along Avenida President Masarik, the Rodeo Drive of Mexico City, where the rich and famous dine and shop.

DAYS 4–6: ESCAPING THE CITY—EASILY

Option #1: The Pyramid of the Sun

One of the most fascinating ruins in the country is 48 km (30 mi) outside the capital: Teotihuacán and its pyramids to the Sun and Moon. If Mexico City is now one of the world's largest cities, Teotihuacán undoubtedly held that title in AD 600. A walk around these awe-inspiring grounds will give you insight into the power of the mysterious culture here. News on archaeological finds made during a 2010 excavation might make that culture less mysterious.

Logistics: Visit the famous pyramids on a guided bus tour, available through most hotels or local travel agencies.

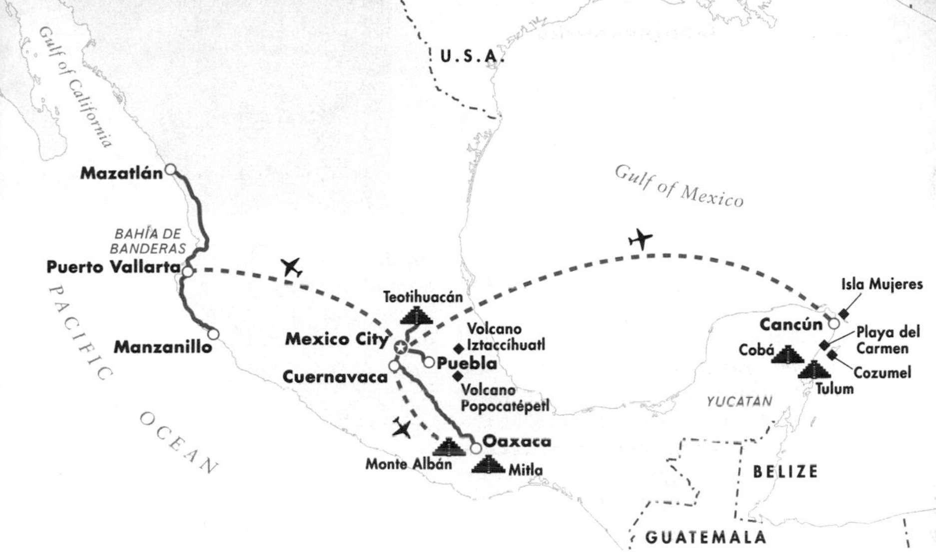

Option #2: City of Eternal Spring

An hour south is the "eternal spring" city of Cuernavaca, where Hernán Cortés once went to get a breather from the city and where the capital's residents flee to enjoy a more relaxed environment.

Logistics: One option is to rent a car and drive to Cuernavaca. It's a little more than 161 km (100 mi) round-trip on a gorgeous superhighway; consider an overnight stay. Bear in mind that you'll have to pay highway tolls. Alternatively, take a bus from the Central de Autobuses del Sur in the capital; the ride takes about 1½ hours.

Option #3: Popo, Itza, and Puebla

For a spectacular view of the snowcapped volcanoes Popocatépetl and Iztaccíhuatl, head southeast to Puebla, famed for its colonial charms, exquisite Talavera pottery, and numerous ex-convents. Nearby towns include Cholula and Cuetzalan.

Logistics: The bus ride from the capital to Puebla takes about two hours. Thanks to the frequency of buses, this makes a great one-day trip. Driving to Puebla is another easy option and will be a bit quicker. Cholula is a 15-minute cab ride from Puebla.

DAYS 7–14: MOVING ON FROM MEXICO CITY

Option #1: Oaxaca's Wonders

One hour by plane from the capital, Oaxaca is a world of culture unto itself. Observe the magnificence of the ancient Zapotec and Mixtec cultures at the Monte Albán and Mitla ruins. In the nearby villages, shop for gorgeous black pottery (*barro negro*), handwoven rugs, and *alebrijes* (colorful, carved wooden figurines). Known as "the land of the seven moles," Oaxaca is a foodie's paradise. Start off with a shot of the local *mezcal* and some fried grasshoppers.

Logistics: Low-cost airline Click Mexicana (☎ *55/5322–6262 in Mexico City* 🌐 *www.click.com.mx*) sells reasonably priced tickets between the capital and Oaxaca City. First-class buses run direct to Oaxaca from the TAPO bus station and take about 6½ hours.

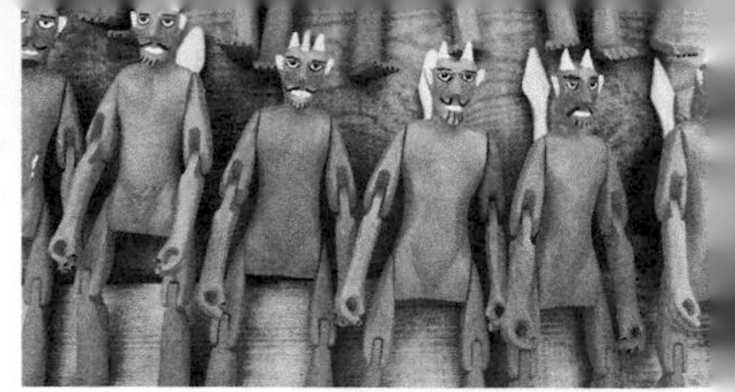

Option #2: Crazy for Cancún

If you're in the mood for sunshine and white, sandy beaches, hop on an eastbound plane, and two hours later you'll arrive at Aeropuerto Internacional Cancún. Nearby are the resorts of Cozumel, Playa del Carmen, and Isla Mujeres. Although occasionally battered by hurricanes—Wilma in 2005 was considered the strongest ever—the Riviera Maya is quick to recover. Some of Mexico's priciest resorts and spas are in the vicinity. Keep in mind that Cancún tends to draw party crowds. But there are plenty of escapes, including the nearby Mayan ruins, Tulúm and Cobá.

Logistics: Daily flights leave the capital on Aeroméxico and Mexicana. If you have the time and patience, buses depart daily from the TAPO terminal. The run takes 23 hours.

Option #3: Pacific Coast Paradise

Mexico's Pacific coast is easily accessible from Mexico City either by plane or bus. From Mazatlán to Puerto Vallarta to Zihuatanejo, the Pacific Coast is peppered with hundreds of beaches with accommodations for visitors ranging from ritzy to secluded to simple. Puerto Vallarta (PV), an elegant town on the Bahía de Banderas, is the most popular resort in the area.

Logistics: PV is 1½ hours by air from the capital and has its own airport (Aeropuerto Internacional Gustavo Díaz Ordáz). Aeroméxico, Mexicana, and Líneas Aéreas Azteca all fly from Mexico City. By bus you depart from the Terminal Norte on a 12-hour first-class bus ride.

> **TIP**
>
> For more detailed travel information, *see* the Bus Travel and Air Travel under Getting Here and Around in the Travel Smart chapter at the end of this book, as well as the Essentials information in each chapter.

WHEN TO GO

Mexico is sufficiently large and geographically diverse that you can find a place to visit any time of year. October through May are generally the driest months; during the peak of the wet season (June–September) it usually rains for a few hours daily, especially in the late afternoon. But the sun often shines for the rest of the day.

From December through the second week after Easter the resorts are the most crowded and expensive. This also holds true for July and August, school vacation months, when Mexican families fill hotels. To avoid the masses, the highest prices, and the worst rains, consider visiting during November, April, or May.

Mexicans travel during summertime school vacations, during traditional holiday periods—Christmas through January 6 (Three Kings Day), Semana Santa (Holy Week, the week before Easter), and the week after Easter—as well as during extended national holiday weekends, called *puentes*, or bridges. Festivals play a big role in Mexican national life. If you plan to travel during a major national event, reserve both lodgings and transportation well in advance.

Climate

Mexico's coasts and low-lying sections of the interior are often really hot if not actually tropical. The high central plateau, home to Mexico City, Guadalajara, and many of the country's colonial cities, tends to be springlike year-round. Days may be downright hot, however, and evenings chilly or even cold.

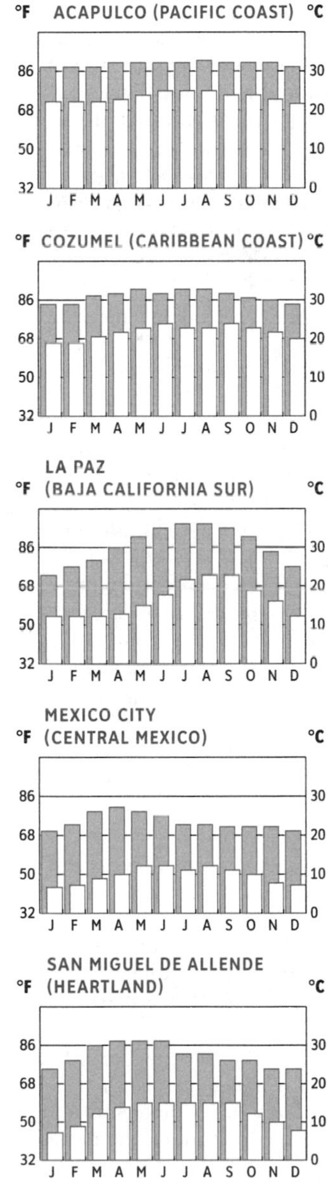

MEXICAN FLAVORS

As you travel through Mexico, you'll realize just how much today's regional dishes are shaped by what the indigenous people in the past were able to gather from their surroundings. It's the native corn, beans, tomatoes, and those essential flavors of the herbs and chilies that define Mexico's constantly evolving cuisine—a cuisine that has stayed true to its roots while absorbing influences from other parts of the world.

When the Spanish conquered this land almost five centuries ago, the foods they brought with them—fruits, grains, vegetables, cattle, poultry, sugarcane, and spices of the Far East—were grafted onto the rootstock of the local ingredients. The culinary influence from the French and Austrians was also immense. Eat in one of Mexico City's top restaurants, and you'll likely see *crepas de huitlacoche* on the menu, a delicate dish that combines French crepes with native black corn fungus.

You can enjoy this culinary fusion of ingredients and techniques throughout the country. And not just in the big-name dining establishments, but also at street vendors, market *fondas* (food stalls), and family restaurants.

Regional Variations

Most regions have their own interpretation of classic dishes, so always remember that a *tamale* eaten on a chilly early morning outside a church in San Cristóbal de las Casas, Chiapas, will be totally different from the one savored in a market in Mérida, Yucatán.

In the central region of Mexico, a delightful *mole* called *manchamanteles* (literally "tablecloth stainer") has pineapple and plantains interspersed among the pieces of chicken and pork. In Oaxaca the mole most often served is *mole negro;* in Puebla, you'll likely savor *mole poblano.* Although both the *negro* and the *poblano* varieties are black in color, sweet, and complex in flavor, the Oaxacan mole uses many chilies available only locally, as well as dried herbs as a replacement for some traditional spices.

At the huge Mercado Libertad in Guadalajara, crushed chilies and oregano coax more flavor from the bowls of earthy *pozole,* a thick pork-and-hominy soup. If you're eating pozole in Michoacán, the base will undoubtedly be a fragrant chili-red broth. Every Thursday in Acapulco you can enjoy green pozole, a variety rich with greens and ground pumpkin seeds.

And then there are the many regional varieties of *masa*-based (corn dough–based) *antojitos,* or "little cravings," such as simple *quesadillas*; *sopes,* with their crimped edges holding in a variety of fillings; and puffy *gorditas,* stuffed with cheese, chilies, or just black beans—all are relished at any time of day.

Culinary Constants

No matter the size of the town you're visiting, you can find a tiny *taquería* making fresh tortillas, then folding or rolling them around different fillings, or frying them to make crispy *tacos dorados.* If you see a large vertical skewer of thinly sliced pork topped with a juicy slice of pineapple cooking over an open fire, stop and ask for a *taco al pastor,* complete with a robust red chili salsa and chopped white onions.

On the next street corner you may find someone grilling potatoes and *chorizo,* that chili- and herb-rich Mexican sausage, for *tacos al carbón,* on top of which you can add a spirited green salsa and grilled onions.

Corn is truly the backbone of Mexico's daily food. While flour tortillas are popular in the northern border states, it is the corn tortilla that's used everywhere else. Tortillas are often used to wrap meats, stews, and moles, and to scrape up the last bites from plates and bowls; they're indispensable to the Mexican way of eating.

A coarser ground corn *masa* is used to make the savory tamales that play such an important role in commemorating special occasions. Also look for street vendors roasting or boiling field corn and serving it slathered with mayonnaise, grated cheese, and ground red chilies—a bit chewy, but definitely tasty.

Accompaniments

Where are the vegetables and salads? Think *salsas* instead. No Mexican dish is served unadorned. If it isn't cooked with a sauce, it's served with one. If the salsa isn't red, it's green, but it's always made with chilies (dried or fresh) and tomatoes or *tomatillos,* tart green fruits encased in a parchmentlike covering.

There are pickled vegetables to munch on and avocados in abundance. Both dried and fresh chilies are routinely used to encase goodies, the most famous version being *chilies en nogada*—a poblano chili filled with meat and fruit then topped with a fresh white walnut sauce studded with pomegranate seeds, together invoking the colors of the Mexican flag.

To wash all this enticing food down, you can choose one of the many local beers or any of the multihued *aguas frescas.* For more zing and a little adventure, order *michelada,* a spicy iced beer.

Yes, margaritas are imbibed in Mexico, but remember that good-quality tequila is usually enjoyed on its own, sip by sip. If you like, you can have a lick of salt, a bite of lime, or a swallow of the omnipresent chaser, *sangrita* ("little blood")—a blend of hot sauce, tomato, orange, and lime juice—to accent the underlying flavor of the maguey plant from which tequila is distilled.

Experience It All

Nowadays, especially in Mexico City, there are more and more fine restaurants translating the foods and beverages of the people into upscale cuisine, and these creations certainly are to be savored. But don't overlook the dishes that have been passed from generation to generation—perhaps a steaming bowl of *sopa de tortilla;* a warming pork-and-chicken stew called *tinga,* flavored with chorizo; or a crispy jicama-and-orange salad named *pico de gallo,* or "rooster's beak."

Experiencing the intricate weaving of the tastes and textures of these regional dishes will catapult you into a whole new world of eating enjoyment.

—By Marilyn Tausend, creator of Culinary Adventures, Inc., author of various Mexican cookbooks (including *Savoring Mexico* and *Mexicana* for Williams-Sonoma and *Cocina de la Familia), and* recipient of the Julia Child Award for Best New American Cookbook (1997).

FOOD AND DRINK PRIMER

Adobo—Combining dry chilies with vinegar, herbs, spices, and salt results in this marinade. Meat is coated with it then broiled, fried, or roasted; in some areas meat is braised in a soupy adobo.

Aguas frescas—These thirst-quenchers are made from fruits, flowers, or other more unusual ingredients and water. The most common are *agua de jamaica,* tinted scarlet from the calyxes of the hibiscus flower; *agua de tamarindo,* made from the molasses-brown pulp of tamarind pods; and the milky-white *horchata,* from ground rice, which truly tastes like a liquid rice pudding, complete with cinnamon.

Arroz—Forget about those combo plates with beans and rice. Here rice is served as a dry soup or *arroz seco,* coming before the main course. It's golden-fried and simmered in chicken broth or transformed by the addition of tomatoes for *arroz Mexicana* (red rice), *chilies poblanos* and herbs for *arroz verde* (green rice), or black beans for *arroz negro* (black rice).

Barbacoa—The traditional Sunday meal throughout much of Mexico is *barbacoa.* In the central part of the country, the roads are lined with stands selling sheep or goat covered with the spearlike leaves of the huge century plant, maguey.

Chilies—All chilies, fresh or dried, have distinctive flavors and degrees of pungency. They aren't used interchangeably, and fresh chilies have different names than their dried counterparts. The familiar *jalapeños* and *serranos* show up most often in fresh salsas. Be aware that on the Yucatán Peninsula the fruity-tasting but close-to-lethal *habanero* is the chili of choice. The similarly shaped *chili manzano,* from the highlands around Mexico City, is also made into potent salsas. The shiny, dark-green *poblano* is the favorite fresh chili for cooking. You can find it made into soups, stuffed, or sliced into *rajas* (strips). It has a distinctive taste when fresh; when dried, it's called *chili ancho,* and is an essential ingredient in *moles,* stews, and red sauces. *Chilies mulatos* are a rather chocolaty black variety of the ancho. Although there are numerous other dried chilies, from tiny *chilies pequíns* to the aromatic, smoky *chilies chipotles,* the two other most important chilies used throughout Mexico are the sharp *guajillo* and the shiny, raisin-color *pasilla.*

Chocolate—Even *Theobroma* (the scientific name of the *cacao* plant from whose seeds chocolate is made) means "food of the gods." Indeed it was considered a sacred drink by the indigenous peoples. Chocolate is still most often enjoyed as a beverage made from the roasted *cacao* beans, sugar, and often almonds. Enjoying a bowl of the hot, frothy stuff with a chunk of egg bread for dunking is an early-morning ritual. This same chocolate mixture is added to certain moles.

Frijoles—Dried beans come in an incredible variety of colors and sizes, and are served at virtually every meal. They may be refried and paired with *huevos rancheros* (fried eggs topping a crispy tortilla blanketed with a pungent tomato sauce); spread as a paste inside a puffy tortilla, where with the addition of chicken and pickled red onions it becomes a Yucatécan *panucho;* or as *frijoles de olla,* brothy beans served in a small bowl after a meal.

Mezcal and Tequila—Mezcal can be made from various types of the agave (maguey) plant; the *piña* (or heart) of the plant is buried and cooked over coals in a large

pit before being crushed, fermented, and then distilled, maintaining its distinctive smoky flavor. Oaxaca is the center of mezcal production.

Tequila can, by law, only be made from the piña of the blue agave (*Agave tequilana Weber*), which grows mainly in Jalisco. It's cooked in ovens or autoclaves (instead of a pit) before being fermented and distilled. There are two types of tequila, those made from 100% blue agave, and those made from at least 51% blue agave blended with sugars, called *mixtos*. The former are further divided into other categories: *blanco* or *plata* (white or silver); *reposado* (rested); and *añejo* (aged).

Moles and Pipianes—Discard the notion that mole is a dark chocolate-flavored sauce. In fact, only some *moles* contain chocolate, the most famous being Puebla's mole poblano. Coming from an indigenous word meaning a "concoction," mole is simply a mixture of ingredients, typically including chilies, spices, and often seeds and nuts. Although Oaxaca is often called the "Land of the Seven Moles," there are hundreds of varieties in shades of red, green, yellow, and black. *Pipianes*—thick with nuts and/or pumpkin or sesame seeds—are a similar dish.

Nopales—Cactus paddles (flat, fleshy stems of the *Opuntia* cactus) are nutritious when cooked; they're primarily used in salads or as a taco filling.

Queso—Almost without exception, Mexican cheeses are simple and made from cow's milk. The most common ones are *quesos frescos* (sometimes called *quesos ranchero*), fresh cheeses that are crumbled on top of dishes or stuffed into *chiles rellenos*. *Queso añejo* (or more properly called *queso Cotija,* for the town where it was first made) is a salty aged cheese often grated over dishes. Stringy *quesillo de Oaxaca* is rolled into balls of all sizes—good for a snack or as a melting cheese. Up north are *queso asado* and *queso Chihuahua,* which are used for such rich cheese dishes as *chilies con queso*.

Tamales—Corn *masa,* or dough, usually beaten with lard, is spread with a layer of cooked meat and a sauce of chilies and then carefully cupped in softened dry corn husks, twisted inside fresh corn or other aromatic leaves, or tenderly folded in a sheet of banana leaves before being steamed. Regional variations include the delicate banana-leaf-wrapped *tamales de mole negro* of Oaxaca; the unfilled, pyramid-shape *corundas* of Michoacán; and the *zacahuiles* of northern Veracruz, which, at 3 feet long, require special ovens to hold them. There are also sweet tamales, often distinguished by the pink or green tinting of the masa.

Tortas—Some vendors specialize in these hefty, layered, crusty-roll sandwiches (think hoagies). Although all are a satisfying and economical meal, there are two standouts. Guadalajara's *tortas ahogadas* ("drowned tortas") are crusty French rolls filled with pork and almost drowned in a fiery sauce made of *chiles de arbol*. Puebla's *cemitaa* are chewy round rolls encrusted with sesame seeds filled with your choice of many things, including shredded chicken or breaded beef cutlets, as well as avocado, Oaxacan cheese, *chiles chipotle en adobe,* and the aromatic herb *papalo*.

—Marilyn Tausend

Mexico City

2

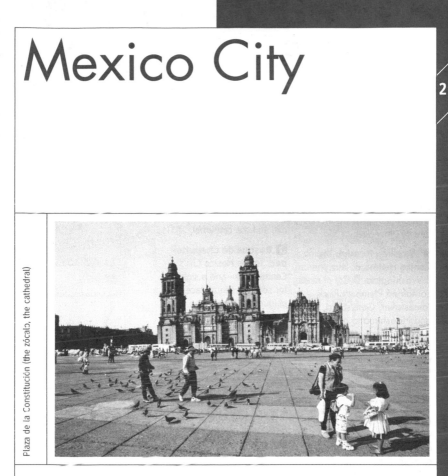

Plaza de la Constitución (the zócalo, the cathedral)

WORD OF MOUTH

"We were in Mexico City from a Tuesday until a Saturday, and, as everyone warned us, that is nowhere near enough time to do the city justice. It merely whets your appetite and makes you realize how much you have *not* been able to see. On the other hand, almost every single tourist we ran into was on a return trip to the city, and we definitely plan to make another visit. Soon."

—richnindy

www.fodors.com/community

MEXICO CITY PLANNER

Safety

Mexico City's well-publicized kidnappings have generally targeted the Mexican power elite; the average tourist isn't likely to be a victim of this type of crime. Authorities have been cracking down on taxi robberies, but policing an estimated 100,000 cabs is no easy feat. The first rule of Mexico City is *never* hail a taxi on the street, from a tourist attraction, or with your debit card in your pocket. Choose the *sitio* (stationed) cabs that operate out of stands or cabs called for by hotel or restaurant staff. The government is also phasing out VW Beetle taxis since four-door vehicles are seen as a safer option (the driver cannot access backseat passengers as easily). Avoid the two-door taxis still in service.

The Zócalo has undergone major changes, including rigorous trash pickup, a ban (sadly) on vendors and street food in the core, lots of guards, and in some places, security cameras. Major tourist areas are generally safe, but petty theft is pervasive. Pickpockets are brazen and unbelievably skilled. Recognize that Mexico City is formal, so things like big cameras, backpacks, shorts, and sandals will make you stand out.

Hot Tickets

The following should be booked well before or as soon as you get to Mexico City.

1. Reservations at the restaurants Fonda del Recuerdo, Au Pied de Cochon, and Izote.

2. Tickets to Ballet Folklórico de México. There are only three shows a week—the Sunday evening show is particularly popular.

3. An English-speaking guide for the Museo Nacional de Antropología. Call a week in advance.

4. Tickets for important soccer games at Estadio Azteca and Estadio Olímpico (get them at least a week in advance through your hotel concierge).

5. Around holidays, buy first-class bus tickets to other destinations at least a week in advance.

Travel Times

CITY	TIME BY BUS	1ST-CLASS BUS FARES	TIME BY AIR*
Guadalajara	7–8 hrs	$35	1¼ hrs
San Miguel	3½ hrs	$32	45 mins
Veracruz City	5 hrs	$28	1 hr
Oaxaca City	6½ hrs	$33	1 hr
Puerto Vallarta	12 hrs	$73	1½ hrs
Acapulco	5–6 hrs	$28	1 hr
San Cristóbal	16 hrs	$72	n/a
Villahermosa	11 hrs	$60	1½ hrs
Cancún	23 hrs	$100	2 hrs
Mérida	19 hrs	$95	1¾ hrs

*One-way airfares for nonstop flights from Mexico City generally range $150–$250.

How's the Weather?

Mexico City has a fairly mild climate all year round. The coldest and, consequently, most smog-infested months are December and January. Although it stays warm during the day, the temperature dips considerably at night during these months, so you'll need to bring a jacket.

The warmest months of the year are April and May, although it never gets too hot thanks to the capital's high altitude.

The rainy season, which brings strong downpours and causes occasional flooding, is from May to October, though you'll often have hours—and sometimes whole days—of sunshine.

How Much Time?

You could spend weeks in Mexico City—there are enough museums, restaurants, and side trips to keep even the most jaded globe-trotter occupied for a long time—but how much time you spend in the capital really depends on your expectations and your tolerance for fast-paced urban living. If you're short on time and anxious to move on to friendlier (or more scenic) climes, you can see a lot in two days, though three would be ideal.

With three days you'll have enough time to tour the historic sights, do a little museum-hopping, have more than a few fabulous meals, and spend at least part of one day on a side trip to nearby ruins (*see Chapter 3*). Hard-core city travelers will want to spend a week here to feel like they've really covered enough ground.

Money Matters

WHAT IT COSTS

	¢	$	$$	$$$	$$$$
Restaurants	under $5	$5–$10	$10–$15	$15–$25	over $25
Hotels	under $50	$50–$75	$75–$150	$150–$250	over $250

Restaurant prices are per person for a main course at dinner. Hotel prices are for two people in a standard double room in high season, including tax and service.

Health Concerns

Although Mexico (in particular, Mexico City) was the epicenter of the early 2009 H1N1 outbreak, the health alerts were lowered and things returned to normal by May. Ultimately there were more cases of and deaths from swine flu in the United States than in Mexico—or anywhere else. By June the only signs of Mexico City's flu scare were the occasional citizen wearing a mask and the antibacterial dispensers at some attractions and restaurants all over town.

To help people feel more comfortable, however, in July 2009 tourism officials implemented a plan whereby **visitors to the capital receive health-insurance coverage on check-in at any Mexico City hotel.**

Truth be told, the city's elevation and its air quality should be more of a concern to you. Initially the change in elevation may affect your breathing, sleep patterns, digestion, and alcohol tolerance. Take it easy, drink lots of water, and lay off the cocktails.

Several government initiatives have improved Mexico City's air quality. Still, if you have respiratory problems, avoid walking along busy streets during rush hour. The smog is heaviest from mid-November through January, and lightest in September and October.

2

Updated by Eva Ginsburg, Michele Joyce, Laura Mestre, Rachel Nolan, Emily Schmall

BY AND LARGE, PEOPLE HAVE the wrong idea about Mexico City. To many the name alone summons two words: crime and pollution. No doubt there are areas to be avoided, but the Distrito Federal is packed to the gills with decent people who will usually look out for one another, and for you.

Pollution summons visions of unwalkable, megahighway-filled cities jammed with cars, which this is not. The smog is real: the Aztecs built their city of Tenochtitlan in a high (7,347 feet) valley that often waits days for the air to move. But there are more than 6 million cars in the city, fewer than three for every 10 of 22-million-something inhabitants (reports vary). Truth is, those living in the capital do so more sustainably than most people in the industrialized world, at high—yet comfortable—densities (though not in high-rises), and move mostly on foot and by public transit. (If you are tempted to drive this Gordian knot of merged villages, well, we would recommend that you not.)

Most of Mexico City is aligned on two major intersecting thoroughfares: Paseo de la Reforma and Avenida Insurgentes—at 34 km (21 mi), the longest avenue in the city. Administratively, Mexico City is divided into 16 *delegaciones* (districts) and about 400 *colonias* (neighborhoods), many with street names fitting a given theme, such as rivers, philosophers, or revolutionary heroes. The same street can change names as it goes through different colonias. So most street addresses include their colonia (abbreviated as Col.). Unless you're going to a landmark, it's important to tell your taxi driver the name of the colonia and, whenever possible, the cross street.

GETTING HERE AND AROUND

Mexico City's airport, Aeropuerto Internacional de la Ciudad de México, or Aeropuerto Internacional Benito Juárez (MEX), is the country's main gateway. Many airlines fly nonstop between major U.S. cities and Mexico City.

Reaching the city center from the airport takes 20 minutes to an hour depending on traffic. ■**TIP→ If you're taking a taxi, purchase your ticket at an official airport taxi counter** marked TRANSPORTACIÓN TERRESTRE (ground transportation) or TAXI AUTORIZADO (authorized taxi); never take a *pirata* taxi (unofficial drivers hawking their services).

Within Mexico City buses are a cheap and convenient way to travel. Leaving the capital, ETN (Enlaces Terrestres Nacionales) serves cities to the west and northwest and ADO buses depart for the south. Buses depart from four outlying stations (*terminales de autobuses*): Terminal de Autobuses del Norte, going north; Terminal de Autobuses del Sur, going south; Terminal de Autobuses del Oriente, going east; and Terminal de Autobuses del Poniente, going west.

It's usually impractical to rent a car for travel within Mexico City, though it may be a good option for trips outside the city. Within the city you can also get around by *pesero* (originally six-passenger sedans, now mostly minibuses), which operate on a number of fixed routes and charge a flat rate, or by metro, which is incredibly cheap, but can be super busy at times.

Use *sitio* (stationed) taxis at stands or call for one. ⚠ **Simply do not hail taxis on the street under any circumstances.** Two reliable radio taxi companies are Servitaxi and Taximex, which accepts credit cards. If you need a cab but don't speak the Spanish necessary to call one yourself, have a hotel concierge or waiter call you a sitio taxi.

WHATS IN A NAME?

Mexico City is rarely referred to as "Mexico City" by its residents, or by anyone in Mexico for that matter. The term Mexico City is an anglicization: the official name of the city is Ciudad México; residents often refer to it as "D.F." (pronounced deh-effay), short for Distrito Federal (Federal District). On train and bus schedules and in addresses, you'll often see it listed simply as México. And elsewhere in the country, when anyone refers simply to México, they mean here.

ESSENTIALS

Bus Contacts ADO (☎ *01800/702-8000 toll-free in Mexico* 🌐 *www.ado.com.mx*). **ETN** (☎ *01800/800-0386 toll-free in Mexico* 🌐 *www.etn.com.mx*). **Terminal de Autobuses del Norte** (✉ *Av. Cien Metros 4907, Col. Magdalena de las Salina* ☎ *55/5587-1552 Ext. 102*). **Terminal de Autobuses del Oriente (TAPO)** (✉ *Ignacio Zuragoza 200, Col. 10 de Mayo* ☎ *55/5522-5400*). **Terminal de Autobuses del Poniente** (*"Observatorio"* ✉ *Río Tacubaya and Sur 122, Col. Real del Monte* ☎ *55/5271-0149 or 55/5271-0038*). **Terminal de Autobuses del Sur** (✉ *Tasqueña 1320* ☎ *55/5689-9745 or 55/5689-4987*). **Ticketbus** (☎ *55/5133-2424 or 55/5133-2444, 01800/702-8000 toll-free in Mexico* 🌐 *www.ticketbus.com.mx*).

Medical Assistance American British Cowdray (ABC) Hospital (✉ *Calle Sur 136-116, al Observatorio, Col. Las Américas* ✉ *Av. Carlos Graef Fernández 154, Santa Fe* ☎ *55/5230-8161 emergencies, 55/5230-8000 switchboard* 🌐 *www.abchospital.com.mx*). **Hospital Angeles Metropolitano** (✉ *Tlacotalpan 59, Col. Roma Sur* ☎ *55/5265-1800 for switchboard* 🌐 *www.hospitalangelesmetropolitano.com/ingles/*). **Hospital Angeles México** (✉ *Agrarismo 208, Col. Escandón* ☎ *55/5516-9900 for switchboard* 🌐 *www.hospitalangelesmexico.com*). **Hospital Español** (✉ *Ejército Nacional 613, Col. Granada* ☎ *55/5255-9600* 🌐 *www.hespanol.com*).

Rental Cars Alamo (✉ *Sheraton Hotel, Av. Paseo de la Reforma 325, Col. Cuauhtémoc* ☎ *55/5207-5541* 🌐 *www.alamo-mexico.com.mx* ✉ *World Trade Center, Montesitos 38, Primer Piso #3, Col. Napoles* ☎ *55/5900-4428*). **Avis** (✉ *Atenas 44, Col. Juárez* ✉ *Campos Eliséos 218, Col. Polanco* ✉ *Paseo de la Reforma 308, Col. Juárez* ☎ *55/5533-1336 or 55/5327-7700, 01800/288-8888 toll-free in Mexico* 🌐 *www.avis.com.mx*). **Budget** (✉ *Campos Eliséos 204, Col. Polanco* ☎ *55/5280-8974* ✉ *Atenas 40, Col. Juárez* ☎ *55/5566-8815* 🌐 *www.budget.com.mx*).

Taxis Servitaxis (☎ *55/5516-6020* 🌐 *www.servitaxis.com.mx*). **Taximex** (☎ *55/9171-8888 or 55/5634-9912* 🌐 *www.taximex.com.mx*).

Visitor and Tour Info Mexico City Tourist Office (✉ *Sala A1, Mexico City Airport, in National Arrivals* ☎ *55/5786-9002* ✉ *Nuevo León 56, at Toledo, Hipódromo Condesa* ☎ *55/5212-0260* ✉ *Terminal de Autobuses del Oriente, TAPO, Av. Calle Ignacio Zaragosa 200, Col. 10 de Mayo* ☎ *55/5784-3077* ✉ *Plaza Hidalgo 1, ground fl., Coyoacán* ☎ *55/5658-0221* ✉ *Pino 36, Col. Xochimilco,*

Barrio de San Juan ☎ *55/5676-0810 or 55/5676-8879* 🌐 *www.mexicocity.gob.mx).* **Tourism Secretariat (Federal)** (✉ *Av. Presidente Masaryk (aka Masarik) 172, Col. Polanco* ☎ *55/3002-6300, 55/5250-0027, or 800/482-9832* 🌐 *www.travelguidemexico.com).* **Tourism Secretariat (DF)** (✉ *Av. Nuevo León 56, at Laredo, Col. Condesa* ☎ *55/5212-0260).*

EXPLORING

Updated by Michele Joyce

Mexico City's principal sights fall into three areas. Allow a full day to cover each thoroughly, although you could race through them in four or five hours apiece. You can generally cover the first area—the Zócalo and Alameda Central—on foot. Getting around Zona Rosa, Bosque de Chapultepec, and Colonia Condesa may require a taxi ride or two (though the Chapultepec metro stop is conveniently close to the park and museums), as will Coyoacán and San Angel in southern Mexico City.

CENTRO HISTÓRICO AND ALAMEDA CENTRAL

The Zócalo, its surrounding Centro Histórico (historic center), and Alameda Central were the heart of both the Aztec and Spanish cities. There's a palpable European influence in this area, which is undergoing ongoing refurbishment, leaving the streets cleaner and many buildings, particularly around the Zócalo, more pleasant. Seven hundred years of history lie beneath its jagged thoroughfares. The sidewalks hum with street vendors, hurried office workers, and tourists blinking in wonder. Every block seems energized with perpetual noise and motion, though the area has lately become a bit quieter and much easier to walk. One major street, Francisco I. Madero, is now permanently closed to traffic, and several of the streets near the central plaza are also closed to cars on weekends, so the streets are free for bicyclists and pedestrians.

During the day the downtown area is vibrant with this activity. As in any capital, watch out for pickpockets, especially in crowds, and avoid deserted streets at night. The Zócalo area is quietest on Sunday, when bureaucrats have their day of rest. Shops open around 10 AM on weekends, so go earlier if you prefer to enjoy the area at its quietest. Alameda Park is quieter during the week; on weekends it's jumping with children and their parents.

TOP ATTRACTIONS

20 **Alameda Central.** Strolling around this park is a great way to break up sightseeing in the neighborhood. During the week it's quite lively. You'll be able to find a shaded bench for a few moments of rest before heading off to more museums. There are food vendors throughout the park, selling all kinds of snacks, from ice cream to grilled corn on the cob. The park has been an important center of activity since Aztec times, when the Indians held their *tianguis* (market) here. In the early days of the viceroyalty the Inquisition burned its victims at the stake here. Later, national leaders, from 18th-century viceroys to Emperor Maximilian and President Porfirio Díaz, envisioned the park as a symbol of civic pride and prosperity. In fact, the park was enjoyed exclusively by the

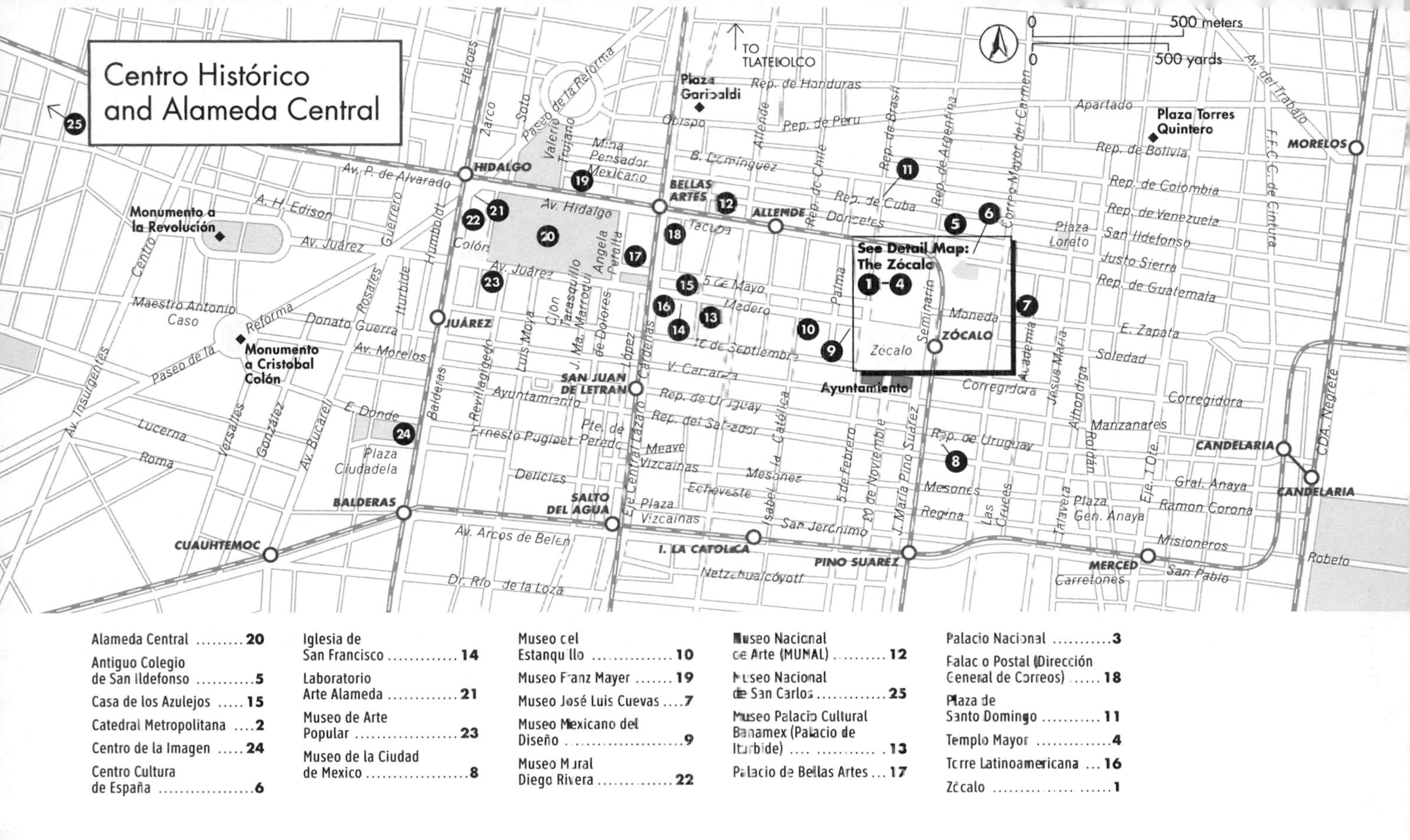

Centro Histórico
and Alameda Central
See Detail Map: The Zócalo
Alameda Central 20
Antiguo Colegio de San Ildefonso 5
Casa de los Azulejos 15
Catedral Metropolitana 2
Centro de la Imagen 24
Centro Cultura de España 6
Iglesia de San Francisco 14
Laboratorio Arte Alameda 21
Museo de Arte Popular 23
Museo de la Ciudad de Mexico 8
Museo del Estanquillo 10
Museo Franz Mayer 19
Museo José Luis Cuevas 7
Museo Mexicano del Diseño 9
Museo Mural Diego Rivera 22
Museo Nacional de Arte (MUNAL) 12
Museo Nacional de San Carlos 25
Museo Palacio Cultural Banamex (Palacio de Iturbide) 13
Palacio de Bellas Artes 17
Palacio Nacional 3
Palacio Postal (Dirección General de Correos) 18
Plaza de Santo Domingo 11
Templo Mayor 4
Torre Latinoamericana 16
Zócalo 1

wealthy during this time, and it was only open to the public after Independence. Still, *Life in Mexico,* the quintessential book on the country, describes how women donned their finest jewels to walk around the park even after Independence. Over the centuries it has been fitted out with fountains, a Moorish kiosk imported from Paris, and ash, willow, and poplar trees. A white-marble monument, *Hemiciclo a Benito Juárez,* stands on the Avenida Juárez side of the park. There's live music on Sunday and holidays. ✉ *Av. Juárez, Eje Central Lázaro Cárdenas, and Av. Hidalgo all surround plaza* Ⓜ *Bellas Artes or Hidalgo.Alameda Central.*

X-MAS MEN

The Alameda Central is particularly festive in December, when dozens of "Santas" will appear with plastic reindeer to take wish lists. Although Mexicans celebrate on the night of December 24, the tradition of giving presents—especially to children—kicks in at dawn on January 6, the Day of the Three Kings, so for about a week beforehand the Three Wise Men replace the Santas in the Alameda.

12 **Museo Nacional de Arte (MUNAL).** The collections of the National Art Museum, which include more than 800 pieces that fill a neoclassical building (designed by Italian architect Silvio Contri), span nearly every school of Mexican art, with a concentration on work produced between 1810 and 1950. On display are Diego Rivera's portrait of Adolfo Best Maugard, José María Velasco's *Vista del Valle de México desde el Cerro de Santa Isabel (View of the Valley of Mexico from the Hill of Santa Isabel),* and Ramón Cano Manilla's *El Globo (The Balloon).* Temporary exhibits are also extremely well planned and presented. ✉ *Calle Tacuba 8, Col. Centro* ☎ *55/5130–3400* 🌐 *www.munal.com.mx* *$3, free Sun.* ⏲ *Tues.–Sun. 10:30–5:30* Ⓜ *Bellas Artes or Allende.*

17 ★ **Palacio de Bellas Artes.** Construction on this colossal white-marble opera house was begun in 1904 by Porfirio Díaz, who wanted to add yet another ornamental building to his accomplishments. The striking structure is the work of Italian Adamo Boari, who also designed the post office; pre-Hispanic motifs trim the art deco facade. In fact, Boari was only present during the construction of the facade. The Revolution brought about an economic crisis, and he left the country in 1916. The opera house was not inaugurated until 1934. Inside the concert hall a Tiffany stained-glass curtain depicts the two volcanoes outside Mexico City. For an entrance fee you can see the interior, with its paintings by several celebrated Mexican artists, including Rufino Tamayo and Mexico's most famous trio of muralists: Rivera, Orozco, and Siqueiros. There are interesting temporary art exhibitions as well, plus an elegant cafeteria and a bookshop with a great selection of art books and magazines. Note that when there's no exhibition at the museum, the entry is free, and it's still worth a visit to see both the murals and the building itself. ✉ *Eje Central Lázaro Cárdenas and Av. Juárez, Alameda Central* ☎ *55/5512–2593* 🌐 *www.bellasartes.gob.mx* *Free (except for temporary exhibitions; fees vary)* ⏲ *Tues.–Sun. 10–5:45; cafeteria 11–8* Ⓜ *Bellas Artes.*

14 **Palacio Postal (Dirección General de Correos).** Mexico City's main post office building, designed by Italian architect Adamo Boari and Mexican engineer Gonzalo Garita, is a fine example of Renaissance Revival architecture. Constructed of cream-color sandstone from Teayo, Puebla, and Carrara, Italy, it epitomizes the grand imitations of European architecture common in Mexico during the Porfiriato—the long dictatorship of Porfirio Díaz (1876–1911). For many, it's one of Mexico's most splendid buildings. Downstairs, the Museo del Palacio Postal shows Mexico's postal history. ✉ *Calle Tacuba 1, at Eje Central Lázaro Cárdenas, Alameda Central* ☎ *55/5510–2999 museum, 55/5521–7394 post office* 🌐 *www.palaciopostal.gob.mx* 🎟 *Free* 🕑 *Museum Tues.–Fri. 10–5:30, weekends 10:30–3:30; post office weekdays 8–6 (stamp window open until 8), weekends 8–3:30* Ⓜ *Bellas Artes.*

TLATELOLCO

At Paseo de la Reforma's northern end, about 2 km (1.2 mi) north of Palacio de Bellas Artes, the area known as Tlatelolco (pronounced tla-tel-*ohl*-coh) was the domain of Cuauhtémoc—the last Aztec emperor before the conquest—and the sister city of Tenochtitlán. The center of Tlatelolco is the Plaza de las Tres Culturas, so named because Mexico's three cultural eras—pre-Hispanic, colonial, and contemporary—are present here: the Iglesia de Santiago Tlatelolco (1609); Colegio de la Santa Cruz de Tlatelolco (1535–36); and the modern Ministry of Foreign Affairs (1970).

16 **Torre Latinoamericana.** This is Mexico City's version of the Empire State Building. It took eight years to complete; construction began in 1948 and ended in 1956. It has 44 floors and a TV-radio tower, and weighs 25,000 tons; its mass is held up by 361 concrete pylons. You can get a great view of the city from the skyscraper's observation decks or from the cafés on floors 42, 43, and 44. On your way back down, stop in at the cafeteria and the museum (your entry fee covers this as well), which provides information on the history of the building, on the 37th floor. ✉ *Eje Central Lázaro Cárdenas 2 at Calle Madero, Alameda Central* ☎ *55/5518–7423* 🌐 *www.ociopuro.org/torre* 🎟 *$5* 🕑 *Deck daily 9 AM–10 PM* Ⓜ *Bellas Artes.*

⇨ 1 **Zócalo** 2 **Catedral Metropolitana** 3 **Palacio Nacional** 4 **Templo Mayor,** *see The Zócalo.*

WORTH NOTING

5 **Antiguo Colegio de San Ildefonso.** The college, a colonial building with lovely patios, started out in the 18th century as a Jesuit school for the sons of wealthy Mexicans. Frida Kahlo also famously studied here as an adolescent. It's now a splendid museum that showcases outstanding regional exhibitions. The interior contains murals by Diego Rivera, José Clemente Orozco, and Fernando Leal. ✉ *Calle Justo Sierra 16, almost at corner of República de Argentina, 2 blocks north of Zócalo, Col. Centro* ☎ *55/5702–6378* 🌐 *www.sanildefonso.org.mx* 🎟 *$4.50, free Tues.* 🕑 *Tues.–Sun. 10–5:30* Ⓜ *Zócalo.*

15 **Casa de los Azulejos.** This 17th-century masterpiece acquired its name, House of Tiles, from its elaborate tile work. The dazzling designs, along with the facade's iron balconies, make it one of the prettiest baroque structures in the country. The interior is also worth seeing for its Moorish patio, monumental staircase, and mural by Orozco. The house, which belonged to the Condes of the Valle de Orizaba, was not originally clad in tile. This took place a few years later, when it was covered with tiles from the nearby city of Puebla, where the fifth Countess of Orizaba spent much of her time. The building is currently occupied by Sanborns, a chain store and restaurant, and if you have plenty of time (service is slow) this is a good place to stop for a meal—especially breakfast. Many writers and journalists hang out here. There's also a store with a pharmacy, bakery, candy counter, and an ATM. ✉ *Calle Madero 4, at Callejón de la Condesa, Col. Centro* ☎ *55/5512–9820* 🌐 *www.sanborns.com.mx* ⏲ *Daily 7* AM*–1* AM Ⓜ *Bellas Artes.*

WORD OF MOUTH

"On day one we walked around the Zocalo, then took the red tourist bus for a three-hour tour. You can get on and off, but we didn't. We [loved it]—you get an overview of all the big sites and a feeling for where things are. The recorded tour was in English and very good. The only negative part was that the traffic back was very bad. Dinner at Cafe Tacuba near the Zócalo was very reasonable, with great food—we even returned there a few nights later." —PatrickSch

6 **Centro Cultural de España.** The Cultural Center of Spain is in the heart of the downtown area. It was built in an area that Hernán Cortés himself assigned to his butler, Diego de Soto, though the land changed hands many times and the current building was constructed in the 18th century, well after the years of Cortés. Temporary exhibits housed in the seven exposition rooms often highlight young artists and showcase current artistic trends. While the exhibitions are worth a look, there are also conferences and workshops held on a nearly daily basis for those who are interested in art and culture. In a fun twist, on many nights you can catch live jazz at the bar, which is favored by local twentysomethings who flock here to listen. Every weekend there are also activities for children. Check out the center's Web site for listings. ✉ *Guatemala 18, Col. Centro* ☎ *55/5521–1925* 🌐 *www.ccemx.org* 🎟 *Free* ⏲ *Tues.–Sat. 10* AM*–9* PM*, Sun. 10–4* Ⓜ *Zócalo or Allende.*

24 **Centro de la Imagen.** This pioneering photography center, housed in a former colonial tobacco-processing plant, stages the city's most important photography exhibitions, as well as occasional shows of contemporary sculpture and other art or mixed media. Photography by international artists is often grouped thematically, drawing parallels between various cultures. This is also a good place to pick up some English-language reading material—the center publishes books, catalogues, and a bilingual magazine. ✉ *Plaza de la Ciudadela 2, at Balderas, Col. Centro* ☎ *55/1450–3705* 🌐 *centrodelaimagen.conaculta.gob.mx* 🎟 *Free* ⏲ *Tues.–Sun. 11–6* Ⓜ *Balderas.*

14 **Iglesia de San Francisco.** On the site of Mexico's first convent (1524), this 18th-century structure in a French neo-Gothic style has served as a barracks, a hotel, a circus, a theater, and a Methodist temple. On Independence Day in 1856 a conspiracy was uncovered here, leading to a temporary banishment of the convent's religious folk. ✉ *Madero 7 at 16 de Septiembre, Alameda Central* ☎ *No phone* ⏲ *Daily 7* AM*–8:30* PM Ⓜ *Bellas Artes.*

21 **Laboratorio Arte Alameda.** The facade of this refurbished building from the 1950s has a colonial air, but inside is one of the most contemporary art museums in town. The name says it all: the aim of this museum is truly to be a laboratory, a place where artists let loose and engage in unbridled experimentation, collaboration, and learning. There is a space for contemporary, often experimental art, a display area for video and photographs, and a room where artists whose works are not displayed in other museums and galleries can exhibit. These are not necessarily young artists, but those who have yet to become truly established. A cafeteria provides grub, and live music often livens up the place on Thursday and Friday nights. ✉ *Dr. Mora 7, Centro Histórico* ☎ *55/5510–2793* 🌐 *www.artealameda.inba.gob.mx* 🎟 *$1.50, free Sun.* ⏲ *Tues.–Sun. 9–5* Ⓜ *Hidalgo.*

23 **Museo de Arte Popular.** This ultramodern museum is one of the best places to learn about the popular art of Mexico: you can gawk at art from 31 states in the museum's permanent collection, then buy a few pieces at the marvelous museum store. ■ **TIP→ The museum store has more unique popular art pieces than just about anywhere else in the city.** ✉ *Revillagigedo 11, at Independencia, Centro Histórico* ☎ *55/5510-2201* 🌐 *www.map.df.gob.mx* 🎟 *$4, free Sun.* ⏲ *Tues., Wed., and Fri.–Sun. 10–6, Thurs. 10–9* Ⓜ *Juárez or Hidalgo.*

8 **Museo de la Ciudad de México.** The city museum is on land that was originally owned by Juan Gutiérrez de Altamirano, Cortés's cousin. The original building was destroyed and rebuilt in 1777, and later became home to the Campeche native Joaquín Clausell (1866–1935), who arrived in Mexico City to study law, but never finished his degree because he was expatriated to Europe for his opposition to the government. While in Europe, he learned to paint, and became one of the most important impressionist painters in Mexican history. The museum displays historical objects from Mexico City, including antique maps. Clausell's studio is also open to the public, and its walls are covered with his work. ✉ *Pino Suárez 30, Col. Centro* ☎ *55/5542–0083 or 55/5542–0671* 🌐 *www.cultura.df.gob.mx* 🎟 *$2.50, free Wed.* ⏲ *Tues.–Sun. 10–6* Ⓜ *Pino Suárez.*

10 **Museo del Estanquillo.** In Mexico an *estanquillo* is a small store that sells a wide variety of items. You'll find images of colonial life in New Spain, the Mexican Revolution, political life, and other artifacts that document daily life through history to present times. Photographs of Porfirio Díaz are displayed alongside paintings and small sculptures of the *lucha libre* wrestlers. Postcards, stamps, and cartoons are also exhibited near lead miniatures that re-create an early-20th-century afternoon in the Santo Domingo plaza. Additionally, this museum houses Carlos Monsiváis's

Continued on page 48

THE ZÓCALO

It seems no matter how small a Mexican town is, it has a main square. The most famous of these plazas is Mexico City's dizzying Zócalo, the largest main square in Latin America. It's bounded on the south by 16 de Septiembre, on the north by Avenida 5 de Mayo, on the east by Pino Suárez, and on the west by Monte de Piedad.

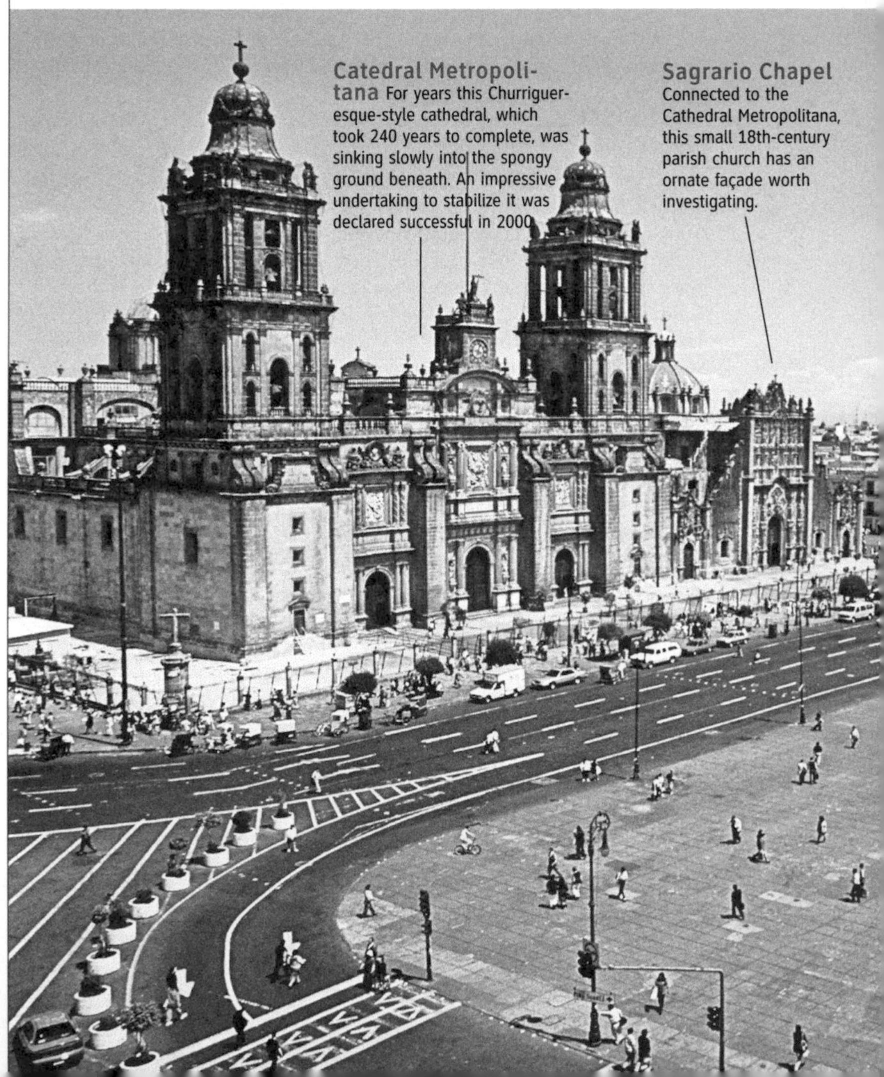

Catedral Metropolitana For years this Churrigueresque-style cathedral, which took 240 years to complete, was sinking slowly into the spongy ground beneath. An impressive undertaking to stabilize it was declared successful in 2000.

Sagrario Chapel Connected to the Cathedral Metropolitana, this small 18th-century parish church has an ornate façade worth investigating.

❶ **Zócalo** literally means "pedestal" or "base": in the mid-19th century, an independence monument was planned for the square, but only the base was built. The term stuck, however, and now the word "zócalo" is applied to the main plazas of most Mexican cities. Mexico City's Zócalo (because it's the original, it's always capitalized) is used for rallies, protests, sit-ins, and festive events. It's the focal point for Independence Day celebrations on the eve of September 16 and is a maze of lights, tinsel, and traders during the Christmas season. Flag-raising and -lowering ceremonies take place here in the early morning and late afternoon.

Mexico City's historic plaza (formally called the Plaza de la Constitución) and the buildings around it were built by the Spaniards, using local slaves. This enormous paved square occupies the site of the ceremonial center of Tenochtitlán, the capital of the Aztec empire, which

Templo Mayor and Museo del Templo Mayor
A temple dedicated to the Aztec cult of death, this ancient treasure was discovered in 1978 by unsuspecting telephone repairmen. The museum holds thousands of archaeological pieces, including an 8-ton carved stone disk depicting the moon goddess Coyolxauhqui, discovered in this very vicinity.

Palacio Nacional
Built on Moctezuma's home, this building has been rebuilt and revamped many times; today, it serves as the seat of government. Nearly 1,200 square feet of astounding murals by Diego Rivera adorn the second floor. Far above still hangs the liberty bell that was rung by Padre Hidalgo in 1810.

A SPECTACULAR VIEW OF THE ZÓCALO

If you want a break, grab a balcony seat at the Hotel Majestic's top-floor restaurant (at the corner of Madero and 5 de Febrero) and enjoy a spectacular view of the plaza below. These seats are reserved months in advance for the Independence Day celebrations, but are easily accessible when there are no events in the Zócalo.

once comprised 78 buildings. Throughout the 16th, 17th, and 18th centuries, elaborate churches and convents, elegant mansions, and stately public edificies were constructed around the square; many of these buildings have long since been converted to other uses.

The Zócalo is the heart of the Centro Histórico, and many of the neighborhood's sights are on the plaza's borders or a few short blocks away. Clusters of small shops, eateries, cantinas, and street stalls, as well as women in native Indian dress contribute to an inimitably Mexican flavor and exuberance.

❷ Catedral Metropolitana. Construction on this, the largest and one of the oldest cathedrals in Latin America, began in the late 16th century and continued intermittently throughout the next three centuries. The result is a medley of Baroque and neo-classical touches. There are five altars and 14 chapels, mostly in the ornate Churrigueresque style, named for Spanish architect José Benito Churriguera (died 1725). Like most Mexican churches, the cathedral itself is all but overwhelmed by innumerable paintings, altarpieces, and statues—in graphic color—of Christ and the saints. Over the centuries, this cathedral began to sink into the spongy subsoil, but a major engineering project to stabilize it was declared successful in 2000. The older-looking church attached to the cathedral is the 18th-century Sagrario chapel. For a small donation, tours of some of the bell towers (via an attractive, if a little tiring, staircase) are available Monday through Saturday. Inquire at the main entrance. ✉ *Zócalo, Col. Centro* ☎ *55/5512–7096* ⏲ *Daily 8–8* 🎫 *Free* Ⓜ *Zócalo.*

★ **❸ Palacio Nacional.** The grand national palace was initiated by Cortés on the site of Moctezuma's home and remodeled by the viceroys. Its current form dates from 1693, although a third floor was added in 1926. Now the seat of government, it has always served as a public-function site. In fact, during colonial times, the first bullfight in New Spain took place in the inner courtyard.

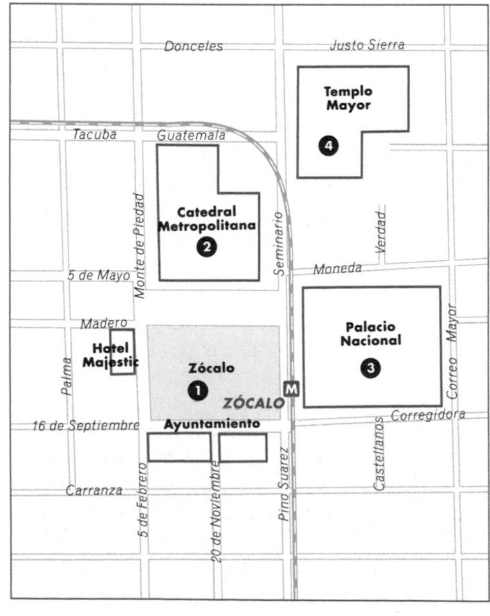

Diego Rivera's sweeping, epic murals on the second floor of the main courtyard exert a mesmeric pull. For more than 20 years, starting in 1929, Rivera and his assistants mounted scaffolds day and night, perfecting techniques adapted from Renaissance Italian fresco painting. The result, nearly 1,200 square feet of vividly painted wall space, is grandiosely entitled *Epica del Pueblo Mexicano en su Lucha por la Libertad y la Independencia* (*Epic of the Mexican People in Their Struggle for Freedom and Independence*). The paintings represent two millennia of Mexican history, filtered through Rivera's imagination. He

Seven rows of ominous stone skulls adorn one side of Templo Mayor.

painted pre-Hispanic times in innocent, almost sugary scenes of Tenochtitlán. Only a few vignettes—a man offering a human arm for sale, and the carnage of warriors—acknowledge the darker aspects of ancient life. As you walk around, you'll pass images of the savagery of the conquest and the hypocrisy of the Spanish priests, the noble independence movement, and the bloody revolution. Marx appears amid scenes of class struggle, toiling workers, industrialization (which Rivera idealized), bourgeois decadence, and nuclear holocaust. These are among Rivera's finest works—as well as the most accessible and probably most visited. The palace also houses a minor museum that focuses on 19th-century president Benito Juárez and the Mexican Congress.

The liberty bell rung by Padre Hidalgo to proclaim independence in 1810 hangs high on the central façade. It chimes every eve of September 16, while from the balcony the president repeats the historic shout of independence to throngs of citizens below. ✉ *East side of the Zócalo, Col. Centro* 🎟 *Free; you'll be asked to leave an ID at the front desk* ⏲ *Mon.–Sat. 9–4, Sun. 9–2* Ⓜ *Zócalo.*

★ Fodor's Choice **❹ Templo Mayor.** The ruins of the ancient hub of the Aztec empire were unearthed accidentally in 1978 by telephone repairmen and have since been turned into a vast archaeological site and museum. At this, their main temple, dedicated to the Aztec cult of death, captives from rival tribes—as many as 10,000 at a time—were sacrificed to the bloodthirsty god of war, Huitzilopochtli. Seven rows of leering stone skulls adorn one side.

The adjacent **Museo del Templo Mayor** housed in a discreet building designed by the influential Mexican architect Pedro Ramírez Vázquez, contains thousands of pieces unearthed from the site and from other ruins in central Mexico; they include ceramic warriors, stone carvings and knives, skulls of sacrificial victims, a rare gold ingot, models and scale reproductions, and a room on the Spaniards' destruction of Tenochtitlán. The centerpiece is an 8-ton disk discovered at the Templo Mayor. It depicts the moon goddess Coyolxauhqui, who, according to myth, was decapitated and dismembered by her brother Huitzilopochtli. Call six weeks ahead to schedule free English-language tours by museum staff in the mornings. ✉ *Seminario 8, at República de Guatemala; entrance on the plaza, near Catedral Metropolitana, Col. Centro* ☎ *55/5542–0606,* 🌐 *www.templomayor.inah.gob.mx/* 🎟 *$5* ⏲ *Tues.–Sun. 9–5* Ⓜ *Zócalo.*

An ancient stone carving at Museo Del Templo Mayor.

eclectic collection of more than 10,000 unique pieces relating to the history and popular culture of the country, though the whole of his collection cannot all be displayed at once, and is displayed on a rotating basis. One of the best-known journalists and writers in Mexico, Monsiváis, who passed away in 2010, wrote extensively on Mexican history, politics, and popular culture. The museum also has a small library, a store, and a rooftop café. ✉ *Isabel la Católica 26, at Av. Madero, Col. Centro* ☎ *55/5521–3052* 🌐 *www.museodelestanquillo.com* 🎫 *Free* 🕑 *Wed.–Mon. 10–6* Ⓜ *Zócalo or Allende.*

19 **Museo Franz Mayer.** Housed in the 16th-century Hospital de San Juan de Dios, this museum exhibits thousands of works collected by Franz Mayer, which he left to the Mexican people. The permanent collection includes 16th- and 17th-century antiques, such as wooden chests inlaid with ivory, tortoiseshell, and ebony; tapestries, paintings, and lacquerware; rococo clocks, glassware, and architectural ornamentation; and an unusually large assortment of Talavera ceramics. The museum also has more than 700 editions of Cervantes's *Don Quixote.* The old hospital building is faithfully restored, with pieces of the original frescoes peeking through. You can also enjoy a great number of temporary exhibitions, often focused on modern applied arts. ✉ *Av. Hidalgo 45, at Plaza Santa Veracruz, Alameda Central* ☎ *55/5518–2266* 🌐 *www.franzmayer.org.mx* 🎫 *$4.50* 🕑 *Weekdays 10–5, weekends 10–7* ☞ *Call 1 wk ahead for an English-speaking guide* Ⓜ *Bellas Artes or Hidalgo.*

7 **Museo José Luis Cuevas.** Installed in a refurbished former Santa Inés convent, this inviting museum displays international modern art as well as work by Mexico's enfant terrible, José Luis Cuevas, one of the country's best-known contemporary artists. The highlight is the sensational *La Giganta (The Giantess)*, Cuevas's 8-ton bronze sculpture in the central patio. It represents male-female duality and pays homage to Charles Baudelaire's poem of the same name. There is also a small collection of original Rembrandt and Picasso drawings. Up-and-coming Latin American artists appear in temporary exhibitions throughout the year. No photographs are permitted. ✉ *Academia 13, at Calle Moneda, Col. Centro* ☎ *55/5522–0156* 🌐 *www.museojoseluiscuevas.com.mx* 🎫 *$2, free Sun.* 🕑 *Tues.–Sun. 10–6* Ⓜ *Zócalo.*

9 **Museo Mexicano del Diseño.** This museum with a big gift shop and café features small expositions of contemporary Mexican design. The goals of the museum are to provide a space for design, to assist local designers, and to offer a location in which designers can make money from their craft. The expositions are shown in a back room made of brick, where you can see the old archways from Cortés's patio, which was built, in part, on top of Moctezuma's pyramid. ✉ *Francisco I. Madero 74, Col. Centro* ☎ *55/5510–8609* 🌐 *www.mumedi.org* 🎫 *$2* 🕑 *Tues.–Sun. 11–3 and 4–8* Ⓜ *Zócalo.*

⇨ 21 **Museo Mural Diego Rivera** *see Frida and Diego.*

25 **Museo Nacional de San Carlos.** The San Carlos collection, housed in a handsome, 18th-century, neoclassical stone building with a stunning open-air oval courtyard, is an important collection of European art, primarily paintings and prints, with a few examples of sculpture and

decorative arts. In small rooms off the patio the works are grouped by period and style: Gothic, Renaissance, baroque, rococo, English portraiture, neoclassicism, naturalism, romanticism, impressionism, and realism. The museum holds seminars, workshops, and extraordinary weekend classes for children. ✉ *Puente de Alvarado 50, Tabacalera* ☎ *55/5566–8085 or 55/5566–8342* 🌐 *www.mnsancarlos.com* 🎫 *$2.50, free Sun.* 🕑 *Wed.–Mon. 10–6* Ⓜ *San Cosme.*

13 **Museo Palacio Cultural Banamex (Palacio de Iturbide).** In 1780 this baroque palace—note the imposing door and its carved-stone trimmings—was built for Mariana de Berrio, a descendent of the Córdoba family, related to one of the original conquistadores. When she married a man who was said to be a poor administrator, her parents constructed this palace for her. This may have helped to preserve the resources that she brought to her marriage. The palace's name comes from Agustín de Iturbide, who stayed here only for a short time in 1822. One of the heroes of the independence movement, the misguided Iturbide proclaimed himself emperor of a country that had thrown off the Habsburg imperial yoke only a year before. He was staying here when he became emperor, though his own empire was short-lived. The house has been incarnated as a school, a café, and a hotel; it's now owned by Banamex (Banco Nacional de México), which sponsors cultural exhibitions in the atrium. ✉ *Calle Madero 17, Col. Centro* ☎ *55/1226–0281* 🎫 *Free* 🕑 *Wed.–Mon. 10–7* Ⓜ *Bellas Artes.*

11 **Plaza de Santo Domingo.** The Aztec emperor Cuauhtémoc built a palace here, where heretics were later burned at the stake during the Spanish Inquisition. The plaza was the intellectual hub of the city during the colonial era. Today its most endearing feature is the Portal de los Evangelistas, whose arcades are filled with scribes at old-fashioned typewriters filling in official forms, formatting theses, printing invitations, or composing letters. In the past, people who didn't know how to write came here for a little help. While there are still those, there are also the people who desire to keep traditions alive. At Christmastime especially, people come to have greeting cards personalized—with their greeting on the inside and return address printed on the envelopes.

The 18th-century baroque Santo Domingo church, slightly north of the portal, is all that remains of the first Dominican convent in New Spain. The convent building was demolished in 1861 under the Reform laws that forced clerics to turn over all religious buildings not used for worship to the government. ✉ *Bounded by República de Cuba, República de Brasil, República de Venezuela, and Palma, Col. Centro* ☎ *No phone* Ⓜ *Zócalo.*

BOSQUE DE CHAPULTEPEC AND ZONA ROSA

Bosque de Chapultepec, named for the *chapulines* (grasshoppers) that populated it long ago, is the city's largest park, a great green refuge from concrete, traffic, and dust. It's also home to a castle, a lake, an amusement park, the Mexican president's official residence, and five world-renowned museums. ■ **TIP→ If you have time to visit only one of Bosque de Chapultupec's museums, make it the Museo Nacional de Antropología.**

CLOSE UP

Mexico City Background

Mexico City is a city of superlatives. It is both the oldest (founded in 1325) and the highest (7,350 feet) metropolis on the North American continent. And with an estimated 22 million inhabitants it's the most populous city in the Western Hemisphere.

As the gargantuan pyramids of Teotihuacán attest, the area around Mexico City was occupied from early times by a great civilization, probably Nahuatl in origin. The founding farther south of the Aztec capital, Tenochtitlán, did not occur until more than 600 years after Teotihuacán was abandoned, around AD 750. Between these periods, from 900 to 1200, the Toltec Empire controlled the Valley of Mexico. As the story goes, the nomadic Aztecs were searching for a promised land in which to settle. Their prophecies announced that they would recognize the spot when they encountered an eagle perched on a prickly-pear cactus and holding a snake in its beak. In 1325, the disputed date of Tenochtitlán's founding, they discovered this eagle in the Valley of Mexico, the image of which is now emblazoned on the national flag. They settled on what was then an island in shallow Lake Texcoco and connected it to lakeshore satellite towns by a network of *calzadas* (canals and causeways, now freeways). Even then it was the largest city in the Western Hemisphere and, according to historians, one of the three largest cities on Earth. When he first laid eyes on Tenochtitlán in the early 16th century, Spanish conquistador Hernán Cortés was dazzled by the glistening lacustrine metropolis, which reminded him of Venice.

A combination of factors made the Spanish conquest possible. Aztec emperor Moctezuma II believed the white, bearded Cortés on horseback to be the mighty plumed serpent-god Quetzalcóatl, who, according to prophecy, was supposed to arrive from the east in the year 1519 to rule the land. Thus, Moctezuma welcomed the foreigner with gifts of gold and palatial accommodations. In return, Cortés initiated a massacre. He was backed by a huge army of Indians from other settlements such as Cholula and Tlaxcala, who saw a chance to end their submission to the Aztec empire. With these forces, the European tactical advantages of horses, firearms, and, inadvertently, the introduction of smallpox and the common cold, Cortés succeeded in erasing Tenochtitlán only two centuries after it was founded.

Cortés began building the capital of what he patriotically dubbed New Spain, the Spanish empire's colony that would spread north to cover what is now the southwestern United States and south to Panama. *Mexico* comes from *Mexica* (pronounced meh-shee-ka), which was the Aztecs' name for themselves. (Aztec is the Spaniards' name for the Mexica.) At the site of Tenochtitlán's demolished ceremonial center—now the 10-acre Zócalo—Cortés started building a church (the precursor of the impressive Metropolitan Cathedral), mansions, and government buildings. He utilized the slave labor, and the artistry, of the vanquished native Mexicans. On top of the ruins of their city, and using rubble from it, they were forced to build what became the most European-style city in North America. But instead of having the random layout of contemporary medieval cities, it followed the grid pattern of the Aztecs.

For much of the construction material the Spaniards quarried the local porous, volcanic, reddish stone called *tezontle*. The Spaniards also drained the lakes, preferring wheels and horses (which they introduced to Mexico) over canals and canoes for transport. The land-filled lake bed turned out to be a soggy support for the immense buildings that have been slowly sinking into it since they were built.

The city flourished during the colonial period, filling what is now its historic center with architectural treasures. The Franciscans and Dominicans eagerly set about converting the Aztecs to Christianity, but some indigenous customs persisted. Street vending, for instance, is a city signature even today. It is said that the conquering soldiers looked out on them in 1520 and said they had never seen such a market, not even in Rome. In 1571 the Spaniards established the Inquisition in New Spain and burned heretics at its palace headquarters, now a museum in Plaza de Santo Domingo.

It took almost three centuries for Mexicans to rise up successfully against Spain. The historic downtown street 16 de Septiembre commemorates the "declaration" of Independence. On that date in 1810, Miguel Hidalgo, father of the Catholic Church—and of a couple of illegitimate daughters—rang a church bell and cried out his history-making *grito* (shout): "Death to the *gachupines* [wealthy Spaniards living in Mexico]! Long live the Virgin of Guadalupe!" Excommunicated and executed the following year, Hidalgo is one of many independence heroes who fostered a truly popular movement, culminating in Mexico's independence in 1821. The liberty bell that now hangs above the main entrance to the National Palace is rung on every eve of September 16 by the president of the republic, who then shouts a revised version of the patriot's cry: "¡Viva México!"

Flying in or out of Mexico City you get an aerial view of the remaining part of Lake Texcoco on the eastern outskirts of the city. In daylight you'll notice the sprawling flatness of the 1,480-square-km (570-square-mi) Meseta de Anáhuac (Valley of Mexico), completely surrounded by mountains. On its southeastern side two usually snowcapped volcanoes, Popocatépetl and Iztaccíhuatl, are both well over 17,000 feet high. After a period of relative tranquillity, Popocatépetl, known as El Popo, awoke and began spewing smoke, ash, and some lava in the mid-1990s; it has remained intermittently active since then.

Sadly, the single most widely known fact about Mexico City is that its air is polluted. There's no denying the smog and nightmarish traffic, but strict legislation in recent years has led to cleaner air and, especially after the summer rains, the city has some of the clearest, bluest skies anywhere.

If the city's notoriety for smog brings Los Angeles to mind, so might the fault line that runs through the valley. In 1985 a major earthquake—8.1 on the Richter scale—took a tragic toll. The government reported 10,000 deaths, but locally it's said to be closer to 50,000. The last traces of that quake's damage have disappeared with the major renovation project in the capital's historic center, an overhaul that includes the application of the latest earthquake-resistant technology.

CLOSE UP

Take a Tour

Red double-decker, open-top buses operated by Turibus run 9–9 daily. The $14 daily pass (purchased on board) lets you get on and off as many times as desired. Two-day passes cost $21. The bus travels up and down Reforma, passes through the Centro, Plaza Río de Janeiro in the Colonia Roma, Michoacán in the Colonia Condesa (a great place to stop and eat), and Avenida Presidente Masaryk (a.k.a Masarik) in Polanco (a great stop to shop). A second circuit covers the south of the city, including the Museo de Frida Kahlo and the World Trade Center. The third, Bicentennial Route includes stops at the Plaza Garibaldi and the Monument to the Revolution. Most passengers board at the staircase of the Auditorio Nacional, just outside the Auditorio metro stop. Buses leave around a quarter past and a quarter till the hour every day except Christmas.

The Paseo por Coyoacán tourist trolleybus goes around the Coyoacán neighborhood, with a guide telling the history of the area in Spanish. It leaves from a stop opposite the Museo Nacional de Culturas Populares whenever there are enough people, so departures are irregular. It costs $4 and runs weekdays 10–5, weekends 11–6. Guided tours in English are available only for large groups; reservations are a must.

A good way to see the historic downtown—if you know some Spanish—is on the Tranvía Turístico Cultural, adorable replicas of 20-passenger trolleys from the 1920s. The 45-minute narrated tour ($4.50) includes Palacio de Bellas Artes, la Casa de los Azulejos, the Zócalo, Palacio de Iturbide, Plaza de la Constitución, Antiguo Ayuntamiento, Palacio Nacional, la Catedral and Plaza Manuel Tolsá (location of the Palacio de Minería and Museo Nacional de Arte). Trolleys depart hourly 10–5 daily from the train's offices in front of Alameda Park. There's also a night tour on Tuesday at 8 called Leyendas del Centro Histórico (Legends of the Historic Center) and a cantina tour on Thursday at 8. For the night tours, you'll need to make a reservation.

Information **National Association of Guides and Interpreters** (✉ *Serapio Rendón 95-202A, Col. San Rafael* ☎ *55/5591-0418 or 55/5592-0365*). **National Syndicate of Guides and Tourism Employees** (✉ *Ezequiel Montes 79, Col. Tabacalera* ☎ *55/5535-7787 or 55/5535-5305*). **Paseo por Coyoacán** (✉ *Av. Hidalgo 198, at Calle Allende, Coyoacán* ☎ *55/5484-4500*). **Tranvía Turístico** (✉ *Angela Peralta s/n, near Palacio de Bellas Artes, Col. Centro* ☎ *55/5491-1615*). **Turibus** (☎ *55/5141-1360 Ext. 2000 or 55/5133-2488* 🌐 *www.turibus.com.mx*).

Stores, hotels, travel agencies, and restaurants line the avenues of the touristy (with the mushrooming of fast-food spots and some tacky bars and stores, the area has lost some of its former appeal) Zona Rosa, just east of the park. There aren't many sights in Zona Rosa, so consider combining some time in the park with a meal and some shopping here. The 29-square-block area is bounded by Paseo de la Reforma on the north, Niza on the east, Avenida Chapultepec on the south, and Avenida Floréncia on the west.

Most of the buildings were built in the 1920s as two- and three-story private homes for the well-to-do. All the streets are named after European cities; some, such as Génova, are garden-lined pedestrian malls accented with contemporary bronze statuary.

You can head right to the park or start your exploration of the Zona Rosa at the junction of Reforma, Avenida Juárez, and Bucareli. The best known landmark here is the Monumento a la Independencia, also known as El Angel, which marks the western edge of the Zona Rosa. To enjoy the Zona Rosa, walk the lengths of Hamburgo and Londres and some of the side streets, especially Copenhague—a veritable restaurant row. There's a crafts market, Mercado Insurgentes, also known as Mercado Zona Rosa, on Londres. Four blocks southwest of the market, at Avenida Chapultepec, you'll come to the main entrance of the Bosque de Chapultepec.

PASEO DE LA REFORMA

Emperor Maximilian built the Paseo de la Reforma in 1865, calling it the Causeway of the Empress, for his wife, Carlotta. It was modeled after the Champs-Elysées in Paris. Its purpose was to connect the Palacio Nacional with his residence, the Castillo de Chapultepec. At Reforma's northeastern end are Tlatelolco, the Lagunilla Market, and Plaza Garibaldi, where mariachis cluster and strut. To the west, Reforma winds its leisurely way into the neighborhoods of Lomas de Chapultepec, where posh estates sit behind stone walls.

You can easily spend an hour at each Bosque de Chapultepec museum, with the exception of the Museo Nacional de Antropología, which is huge compared with its sister institutions. There you can have a quick go-through in two hours, but to appreciate the fine exhibits, anywhere from a half day to a full day is more appropriate. Tuesday through Friday are good days to visit the museums and stroll around the park. On Sunday and on Mexican holidays they're often packed with families, and if you get to the Museo Nacional de Antropología after 10 AM, you can expect to spend considerable time there, waiting.

TOP ATTRACTIONS

1 **Bosque de Chapultepec.** This 1,600-acre green space, literally the Woods of Chapultepec, draws hordes of families on weekend outings, cyclists, joggers, and horseback riders into its three sections. Its museums rank among the finest in Mexico, if not the world. This is one of the oldest parts of Mexico City, having been considered a sacred place, and inhabited by the Mexica (Aztec) tribe as early as the 13th century. Several Aztec kings had their effigies carved in stone here. The Mexica poet-king Nezahualcóyotl had his palace here and ordered construction of the aqueduct that brought water to Tenochtitlán. Ahuehuete trees (Moctezuma cypress) still stand from that era, when the woods were used as hunting preserves.

At the park's principal entrance, one block west of the Chapultepec metro station, the *Monumento a los Niños Héroes* (Monument to the

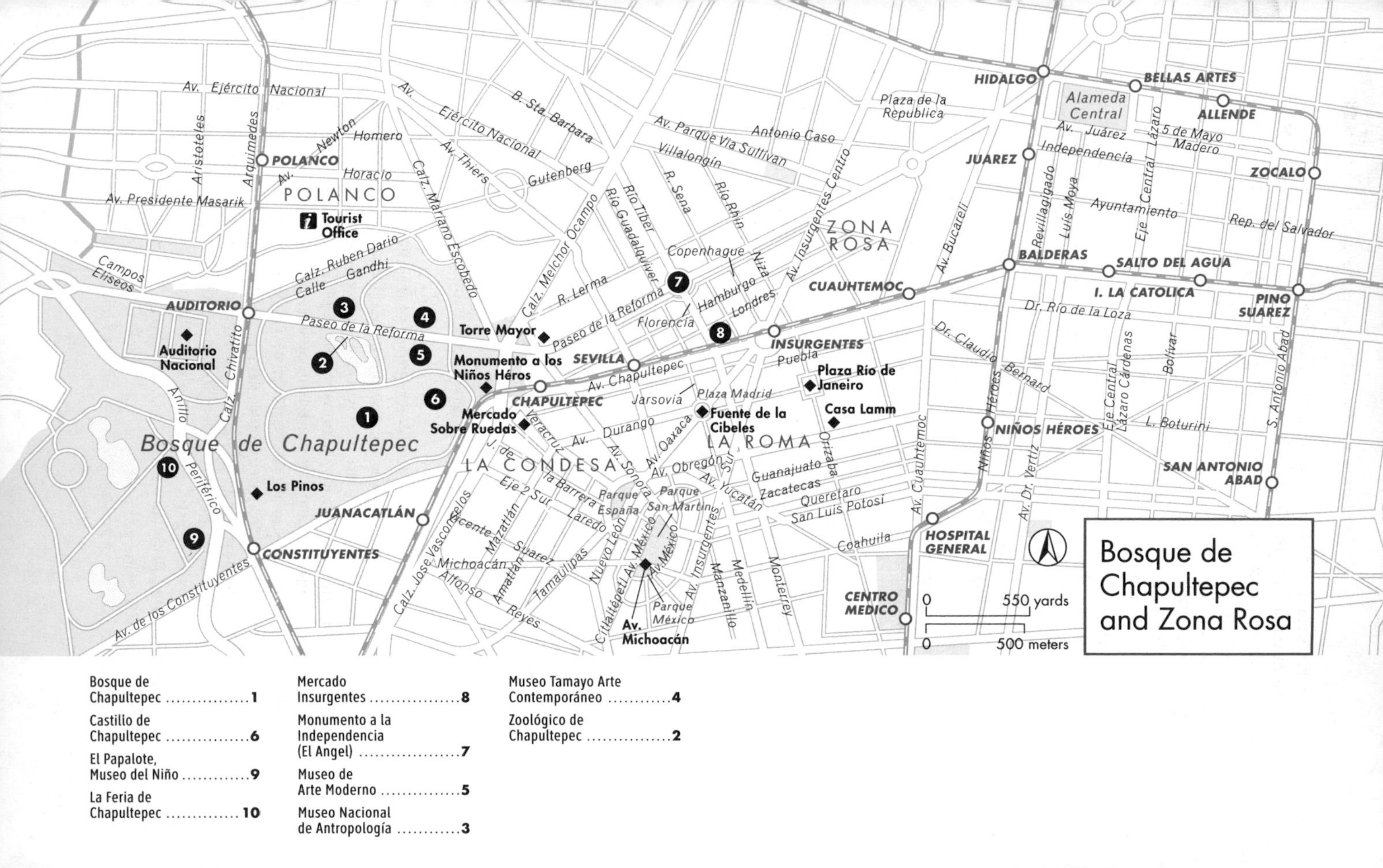

Bosque de Chapultepec and Zona Rosa
0 550 yards
0 500 meters
POLANCO
ZONA ROSA
LA ROMA
LA CONDESA
Bosque de Chapultepec
Alameda Central
Plaza de la Republica
Tourist Office
Auditorio Nacional
Torre Mayor
Monumento a los Niños Héros
Mercado Sobre Ruedas
Los Pinos
Plaza Río de Janeiro
Casa Lamm
Fuente de la Cibeles
Parque España
Parque San Martín
Parque México
Av. Michoacán
HIDALGO
BELLAS ARTES
ALLENDE
JUAREZ
ZOCALO
POLANCO
AUDITORIO
BALDERAS
SALTO DEL AGUA
I. LA CATOLICA
PINO SUAREZ
CUAUHTEMOC
INSURGENTES
SEVILLA
CHAPULTEPEC
NIÑOS HÉROES
SAN ANTONIO ABAD
HOSPITAL GENERAL
CENTRO MEDICO
JUANACATLÁN
CONSTITUYENTES
Bosque de Chapultepec 1
Castillo de Chapultepec 6
El Papalote, Museo del Niño 9
La Feria de Chapultepec 10
Mercado Insurgentes 8
Monumento a la Independencia (El Angel) 7
Museo de Arte Moderno 5
Museo Nacional de Antropología 3
Museo Tamayo Arte Contemporáneo 4
Zoológico de Chapultepec 2

Boy Heroes) consists of six asparagus-shape marble columns adorned with eaglets. Supposedly buried in the monument are the young cadets who, it is said, wrapped themselves in the Mexican flag and jumped to their deaths rather than surrender to the Americans during the U.S. invasion of 1847. To Mexicans that war is still a troubling symbol of their neighbor's aggressive dominance: it cost Mexico almost half its territory—the present states of Texas, California, Arizona, New Mexico, and Nevada.

Other sights in the first section of Bosque de Chapultepec include three small boating lakes, a botanical garden, and the Casa del Lago cultural center, which hosts free plays, cultural events, and live music on weekends. Los Pinos, the residential palace of the president of Mexico, is on a small highway called Avenida Constituyentes, which cuts through the park; it's heavily guarded and cannot be visited.

Most visitors enter through the first section of the park, near the Chapultepec metro stop, close to the Museo de Arte Moderno. This is a great place to people-watch, especially on weekends. The less crowded second and third sections of Bosque de Chapultepec contain a fancy restaurant, the national cemetery, and the grounds where Lienzo Charro (Mexican rodeo) is staged on Sunday afternoon.

6 **Castillo de Chapultepec.** The castle on Cerro del Chapulín (Grasshopper Hill) has borne witness to all the turbulence and grandeur of Mexican history. In its earliest form it was an Aztec palace, where the Mexica made one of their last stands against the Spaniards. Later it was a Spanish hermitage, gunpowder plant, and military college. Emperor Maximilian used the castle, parts of which date from 1783, as his residence, and his example was followed by various presidents from 1872 to 1940, when Lázaro Cárdenas decreed that it be turned into the Museo Nacional de Historia.

Displays on the museum's ground floor cover Mexican history from the conquest to the revolution. The bathroom, bedroom, tea salon, and gardens were used by Maximilian and his wife, Carlotta, in the 1860s. The ground floor also contains works by 20th-century muralists O'Gorman, Orozco, and Siqueiros, and the upper floor is devoted to temporary exhibitions, Porfirio Díaz's malachite vases, and religious art. ✉ *Section 1, Bosque de Chapultepec* ☎ *55/5241–3100 or 55/5061–9228* 🌐 *mnh.inah.gob.mx* 🎟 *$5, free Sun.* 🕒 *Tues.–Sun. 9–5* Ⓜ *Chapultepec.*

7 **Monumento a la Independencia.** Known as El Angel, this Corinthian column topped by a gilt angel is the city's most uplifting monument, built to celebrate the 100th anniversary of Mexico's War of Independence. Beneath the pedestal lie the remains of the principal heroes of the independence movement; an eternal flame burns in their honor. As you pass by, you may see one or more couples dressed in their wedding apparel, posing for pictures on the steps of the monument. Many couples stop off here before or after they get married, as a tribute to their own personal independence from their parents. ✉ *Traffic circle bounded by Calle Río Tiber, Paseo de la Reforma, and Calle Florencia, Zona Rosa* Ⓜ *Insurgentes.*

5 **Museo de Arte Moderno.** The Modern Art Museum's permanent collection has many important examples of 20th-century Mexican art, including works by Mexican school painters like Frida Kahlo—her *Las dos Fridas* is possibly the most famous work in the collection—Diego Rivera, José Clemente Orozco, David Alfaro Siqueiros, and Olga Costa. There are also pieces by Surrealists Remedios Varo and Leonora Carrington. ✉ *Paseo de la Reforma, Section 1, Bosque de Chapultepec* ☎ *55/5553–6233* 🌐 *www.bellasartes.gob.mx* 🎫 *$2, free Sun.* ⏲ *Tues.–Sun. 10–5:30* Ⓜ *Chapultepec.*

3 Fodor's Choice ★ **Museo Nacional de Antropología.** Architect Pedro Ramírez Vázquez's distinguished design provides the proper home for one of the finest archaeological collections in the world. Each salon on the museum's two floors displays artifacts from a particular geographic region or culture. The collection is so extensive that you could easily spend a day here, and that might be barely adequate. Explanatory labels have been updated, some with English translations, and free tours are available at set times between 3 and 6. ■ **TIP→ You can reserve a special tour with an English-speaking guide by calling the museum a week in advance, or opt for an English audio guide ($3.50) or the English-language museum guide for sale in the bookshop.**

A good place to start is in the Orientation Room, where a film is shown in Spanish nearly every hour on the hour weekdays and every two hours on weekends. The film traces the course of Mexican prehistory and the pre-Hispanic cultures of Mesoamerica. The 12 ground-floor rooms treat pre-Hispanic cultures by region, in the Sala Teotihuacána, Sala Tolteca, Sala Oaxaca (Zapotec and Mixtec peoples), and so on. Objects both precious and pedestrian, including statuary, jewelry, weapons, figurines, and pottery, evoke the intriguing, complex, and frequently bloodthirsty civilizations that peopled Mesoamerica for the 3,000 years preceding the Spanish invasion.

A copy of the Aztec ruler Moctezuma's feathered headdress (the original is now in Vienna); a stela from Tula, near Mexico City; massive Olmec heads from Veracruz; and vivid reproductions of Mayan murals in a reconstructed temple are other highlights. Be sure to see the magnificent reconstruction of the tomb of 8th-century Mayan ruler Pacal, which was discovered in the ruins of Palenque. The perfectly preserved skeletal remains lie in an immense stone chamber, and the stairwell walls leading to it are splendidly decorated with bas-relief scenes of the underworld. Pacal's jade death mask is on display nearby.

The nine rooms on the upper floor contain faithful ethnographic displays of current indigenous peoples, using maps, photographs, household objects, folk art, clothing, and religious articles. When leaving the museum, take a rest and watch the famous Voladores de Papantla (flyers of Papantla) as they swing by their feet down an incredibly high maypolelike structure just outside the museum entrance. ✉ *Paseo de la Reforma at Calle Gandhi, Section 1, Bosque de Chapultepec* ☎ *55/5286–2923 or 55/5553–6253, 55/5553–6386 for a guide* 🌐 *www.mna.inah.gob.mx* 🎫 *$5 (tickets sold until 6), free Sun.* ⏲ *Tues.–Sun. 9–7* Ⓜ *Auditorio.*

CLOSE UP

The Sun Stone

The Aztec calendar stone—the original *Piedra del Sol* (Stone of the Sun)—is in the anthropology museum's Room 7 (Sala Mexica). The 12-foot, 25-ton, intricately carved, basalt slab describing Aztec life is one of Mexico's most famous symbols. Nobel Prize–winning poet and essayist Octavio Paz immortalized the stone in his epic poem "Piedra del Sol." The stone was carved in the late 1400s; it was discovered buried beneath the Zócalo in 1790. It was originally thought to be a calendar, and, for a brief time, a sacrificial altar. In the stone's center is the sun god Tonatiuh. The rest of the carvings explain the Aztecs' idea of the cosmos: namely, that prior to their existence, the world had endured four periods (called suns) of creation and destruction. Four square panels surrounding the center image represent these four worlds and their destruction (by jaguars, wind, firestorms, and water, respectively). The ring around the panels is filled with symbols representing the 20 days of the Aztec month. Finally, two snakes form an outer ring and point to a date, 1011 AD—the date the fifth sun, or the Aztecs' current world, was created. The Aztecs believed that this fifth sun was the final sun; they believed that one day they would witness a catastrophic end of the world.

4 ★ **Museo Tamayo Arte Contemporáneo.** Within its modernist shell, the sleek Rufino Tamayo Contemporary Art Museum contains paintings by the noted Mexican artist as well as temporary exhibitions of international contemporary art. The selections from Tamayo's personal collection, which he donated to the Mexican people, making the basis for this museum's permanent collection, demonstrate his unerring eye for great art; he owned works by Picasso, Joan Miró, René Magritte, Francis Bacon, and Henry Moore. One Wednesday every month the museum has live jazz music at night. Check the Web site for dates. ✉ *Paseo de la Reforma at Calle Gandhi, Section 1, Bosque de Chapultepec* ☎ *55/5286–6519* 🌐 *www.museotamayo.org* *$1.50, free Sun.* *Tues.–Sun. 10–6* Ⓜ *Chapultepec.*

WORTH NOTING

9 **El Papalote, Museo del Niño.** Five theme sections compose this excellent interactive children's museum: Our World; The Human Body; Con-Sciencia, with exhibits relating to both consciousness and science; Communication, on topics ranging from language to computers; and Expression, which includes art, music, theater, and literature. There are also workshops, an IMAX theater (note that tickets are discounted if purchased with museum tickets as part of a package), a store, and a restaurant. Although exhibits are in Spanish, there are some English-speaking staff on hand. ✉ *Av. Constituyentes 268, Section 2, Bosque de Chapultepec* ☎ *55/5237–1773 or 55/5237–1700* 🌐 *www.papalote.org.mx* *$10* *Mon.–Wed. and Fri. 9–6, Thurs. 9–11, weekends and holidays 10–7* Ⓜ *Constituyentes.*

10 **La Feria de Chapultepec.** This children's amusement park has various games and more than 50 rides, including a truly hair-raising haunted house and

a *montaña rusa*—"Russian mountain," or roller coaster. Admission prices vary, depending on which rides are covered and whether meals are included. ✉ *Section 2, Bosque de Chapultepec* ☎ *55/5230–2121 or 55/5230–2112* 🌐 *www.feriachapultepec.com.mx* 🎫 *$5–$15* 🕐 *Tues.–Fri. 10–6, Sat. 10–7, Sun. 10–8* Ⓜ *Constituyentes.*

COLONIA POLANCO

If you want to see how Mexico's upper crust lives, head to the upscale Polanco neighborhood, just north of Bosque de Chapultepec. A mixture of residential and commercial areas with many boutiques and specialty shops, Polanco is home to some of the city's best shopping—that is, if you can afford it. The colonia is also home to Mexico's largest Jewish community, so it's not uncommon to see Orthodox Jews on the streets. As for nightlife, there are plenty of restaurants and bars, but be prepared to pay Polanco prices.

8 **Mercado Insurgentes.** Also referred to as either Mercado Zona Rosa or Mercado Londres, this is the neighborhood's large crafts market. Vendors here can be aggressive, calling you to their stalls with promises of low prices (which you may or may not find). Opposite the market's Londres entrance is Plaza del Angel, a small, upscale shopping mall, the halls of which are crowded by antiques vendors on weekends. ✉ *At Londres between Florencia and Amberes, Zona Rosa* Ⓜ *Insurgentes.*

2 **Zoológico de Chapultepec.** In the early 16th century Mexico City's zoo, in Chapultepec, housed a small private collection of animals belonging to Moctezuma II; it became quasi-public when he allowed favored subjects to visit it. The current zoo opened in the 1920s, and has the usual suspects, as well as some superstar pandas. A gift from China, the original pair—Pepe and Ying Ying—produced the world's first panda baby born in captivity (much to competitive China's chagrin). In fact, the zoo has one of the world's best mating records for these endangered animals. The zoo includes the Moctezuma Aviary and is surrounded by a miniature train depot, botanical gardens, and lakes where you can go rowing. You'll see the entrance on Paseo de la Reforma, across from the Museo Nacional de Antropología. ✉ *Section 1, Bosque de Chapultepec* ☎ *55/5553–6263 or 55/5256–4104* 🌐 *www.chapultepec.df.gob.mx* 🎫 *Free* 🕐 *Tues.–Sun. 9–4:30* Ⓜ *Auditorio.*

LA CONDESA AND LA ROMA

Next to Bosque de Chapultepec, two nearby colonias, known simply as La Condesa and La Roma, are filled with fading 1920s and 1930s architecture, sun-dappled parks, and a wide variety of eateries that cater to the city's young and trendy. The capital's elite were concentrated here at the turn of the 20th century. In the late 1990s a tide of artists, entrepreneurs, and foreigners brought a wave of energy. ■ **TIP→ La Condesa and La Roma are a must-see in spring, when the jacarandas are in bloom.**

La Condesa is the sprucer, hipper area of the two. Grittier La Roma is now home to a group of important art galleries, as well as some of the city's best cantinas, and it is becoming increasingly trendy. Many say that the Roma is on the verge of becoming the next big thing for those edgy young things who are always on the lookout.

Although it's possible to walk to Colonia Condesa from the Bosque de Chapultepec, you'd have to trek along busy, heavily trafficked roads; it's best to take a sitio taxi to the circular Avenida Amsterdam. Loop around Amsterdam until you reach Avenida Michoacán, where you can check out the boutiques and peek down the side streets. On Avenida Michoacán you'll find a sitio taxi stand—hop in for another short cab ride, this time to Colonia Roma's Plaza Río de Janeiro and more atmospheric strolling. The Condesa's nucleus is the restaurant zone (ask your taxi driver to take you to the neighborhood's *zona de restaurantes*).

CONDESA CULTURA

The **Centro Cultural Bella y Librería Fonda de Cultura Económica Rosario Castellanos** (✉ *Tamaulipas 202, at Benjamín Hill, Col. Condesa* ☎ *55/5276–7110* 🌐 *www.fondodeculturaeconomica.com*) is a Condesa cultural center. With more than 250,000 books on exhibit, it is also the largest bookstore in Mexico, complete with an art gallery and a cafeteria.

La Roma and La Condesa border each other along Avenida Insurgentes Sur, so once you're in one, the other's relatively close on foot. What could be more perfect than a morning visit to a museum or two in Bosque de Chapultepec, a late-afternoon stroll in La Roma, and dinner in La Condesa? Keep in mind that art galleries tend to close on Sunday.

LA CONDESA

TOP ATTRACTIONS

Avenida Michoacán. Restaurants, cafés, and hip boutiques radiate along and out from La Condesa's main drag, Avenida Michoacán. It's a great place for a break from a sightseeing slog—just relax at a sidewalk table and watch the hip young world go by. A snack will also fortify you for Avenida Michoacán's other main activity, shopping. The clothing stores often lean toward the trendy; Kulte, for instance, at Atlixco 118, dishes up the latest fads, as does Soho, on Avenida Vicente Suárez between Avenidas Michoacán and Tamaulipas. Along the nearby streets you'll find a good mix of temptations—everything from modern furniture to risqué lingerie.

Stop to sip coffee and flip through the magazines at **Coffee Max** (✉ *Tamaulipas 75, at Av. Michoacán, Col. Condesa* ☎ *55/5553–9562* Ⓜ *Patriotismo*). Just across the street, you can also pick up a quick slice of pizza in inventive combinations (such as ham and fig) at **Pizza Amore** (✉ *Michoacán 78, Col. Condesa* ☎ *55/5286–5126* Ⓜ *Patriotismo*).

The tacos at **El Farolito** (✉ *Altata 19, at Alfonso Reyes, Col. Condesa* ☎ *55/5515–7844* 🌐 *www.taqueriaselfarolito.com* Ⓜ *Patriotismo*) are yummy. Try the costras, in which the meat is wrapped in fried cheese before being wrapped in a tortilla. Wash it down with a delicious juice, like the mango or coconut, made fresh in the taquería.

El Péndulo (✉ *Av. Nuevo León 115, at Av. Vicente Suárez, Col. Condesa* ☎ *55/5286–9493* 🌐 *www.pendulo.com* Ⓜ *Chilpancingo*) acts as a sort of cultural center. The first of what is now a chain of bookstores is stuffed with Spanish-language books and international CDs; classical guitarists and other musicians play on weekends.

Mercado Sobre Ruedas. If you're in town on a Tuesday, stop by Avenida Pachuca, where vendors set up an inviting outdoor market between Avenida Veracruz and Juan de la Barrera from 9 to 5. Although there are many markets to visit in Mexico, this one is particularly clean and peaceful, since it's set up in a relaxed neighborhood. All tables are draped in pink plastic tablecloths, and identical cloths are hung above the tables for shade; on a sunny day the predominance of pink can be strikingly gorgeous. Vendors here sell everything from children's clothes, pirated CDs, and ceramic pots to produce, fresh flowers, and take-away food. Sometimes music groups wander between the stalls, singing and strumming their guitars for tips.

Parque México. The designer shop Carmen Rion caps Michoacán where it meets the Parque México, which has a duck pond, plus one of the city's cheapest and best taxi stands. The park used to be a racetrack, which explains the circular roads like the looping Avenida México and the occasional references to the Hipódromo (hippodrome) Condesa. From Michoacán you could also turn north on Tamaulipas and walk up a few blocks to visit smaller Parque España for a picnic or stroll. (Note that many locals refer to both parks as "Parque México," as most are unaware that the two parks are actually divided, and each has its own name.)

COLONIA ROMA

Adventurous private art galleries, independent artist-run spaces, and a rough-around-the-edges personality are the hallmarks of La Roma. Like its western neighbor La Condesa, La Roma was once an aristocratic enclave with stately homes. Now it's known for its lively cantinas, pool halls, dance clubs, and night haunts of questionable repute. Bookstores and cafés have helped transform this old neighborhood into the capital's full-blown arts district. Gentrification creeps slowly but steadily onward, though, so enjoy this up-and-comer before it becomes too respectable. ■ **TIP→ La Roma is divided into Roma Sur (south) and Roma Norte (north). Most of the action takes place in Roma Norte.**

TOP ATTRACTIONS

Casa Lamm Cultural Center. Inside this small mansion and national monument artists are nurtured and browsers are welcomed with three exhibition spaces, a library, a bookstore, a wide range of courses, a superb café, and a great restaurant that serves modern twists on Mexican classics as well as delicious international cuisine. ✉ *Av. Alvaro Obregón 99, at Orizaba, Col. Roma* ☎ *55/5525–0019* 🌐 *www.casalamm.com.mx* Ⓜ *Insurgentes.*

Galería Nina Menocal. Galería Nina Menocal specializes in work by Cuban artists. It's open weekdays 10–3 and 4–7 and Saturday 10–2, but the small staff is not always particularly welcoming to those who just want to take a look around. ✉ *Zacatecas 93, at Cordoba, Col. Roma* ☎ *55/5564–7443* 🌐 *www.ninamenocal.com* Ⓜ *Insurgentes.*

Continued on page 66

Diego Rivera mural, Palacio Nacional, Mexico City

FRIDA & DIEGO

Among Mexico's most provocative artists, Frida Kahlo and Diego Rivera had a relationship that never failed to amaze and astonish. Though they created some of Mexico's most fascinating art, it's the bizarre Beauty-and-the-Beast dynamic that has captivated the world and enshrouded both figures in intrigue. Whether you're an art historian or simply an admirer of this eccentric duo, a visit to Mexico City—where you can tour the homes they once shared, study their work, and even see the shoes they wore and beds they slept in—will compel you to delve even further into their story.

Diego Rivera and Frida Kahlo's relationship was far from placid: they were married in 1929, divorced in 1940, and then married again that same year. Together, these two colorful, larger-than-life artists have endured as vibrant characters in a singularly Mexican drama. You can connect the dots on a journey of discovery in Mexico City, where you'll find numerous sites dedicated to Frida and Diego. These include Museo Dolores Olmedo Patino, the estate of Rivera's longtime model; Museo Mural Diego Rivera; Museo de Frida Kahlo; and Estudio Diego Rivera y Frida Kahlo, which is the home that Rivera and Kahlo shared.

A gifted painter and muralist, Diego Rivera was also a political activist; many of the sumptuous murals he created in Mexico and throughout the world speak of politics, history, and the worker's struggle. Considered one of the 20th century's major artistic figures, Rivera created images—especially those rounded peasant women with braided hair, arms brimful of calla lilies—that have come to typify Mexico. Flamboyant, irreverent, and unforgettable, Frida Kahlo created arresting, and at times disturbing, works of art. Fifty-five of her 143 paintings are self-portraits, which speak of her vivaciousness and personal tragedies.

FRIDA KAHLO: A RIBBON AROUND A BOMB

Born: July 6, 1907, in Coyoacán, Mexico

Died: July 13, 1954, in Mexico City

Favorite medium: Oil paint on canvas, wood, metal, and masonite

Famous works: *Diego on My Mind; What the Water Gave Me; Tree of Hope; The Little Deer; The Two Fridas; The Broken Column; Roots;* and numerous self-portraits

Number of medical operations: 32

Pets: Monkeys, hairless dogs, parrots

Trademarks: Bright Tehuana costumes; bat-wing eyebrows; clunky, colorful jewelry

Famous lie: Kahlo often gave her birth year as 1910 because she wanted her life to begin with the Mexican Revolution.

Rumored Extramarital affairs: Communist exile Leon Trotsky; actress Dolores del Rio; painter Georgia O'Keeffe; actress Paulette Goddard; artist Isamu Noguchi

Quote: "I have suffered two accidents in my life: One in which a streetcar ran over me. The other is Diego." (Kahlo quoted in *Frida Kahlo: Torment and Triumph in Her Life and Art,* by Malka Drucker)

Frida Kahlo's hauntingly beautiful face, broken body, and bright Tehuana costumes have become the trademark of Mexican femininity. Images of her bat-wing brows, faint moustache, and clunky ethnic jewelry are as familiar in Mexico as Marilyn's pout and puffed-up white dress are in the U.S. This painter has gained international recognition since her death for her colorful but pained self-portraits.

In fact, Kahlo didn't even need to paint to make it into the history books. Controversy surrounded her two marriages to Diego Rivera, including his affair with her younger sister and her own affair with Communist exile Leon Trotsky. It's hard not to become mired in the tragic details of her life—from childhood polio to a tram accident that smashed her pelvis, and a gangrenous foot that resulted in the amputation of a leg.

But Kahlo was also a groundbreaking artist who pioneered a new expressiveness, and her unique iconography of suffering transcended self-pity to create an existential art. Kahlo was the first Latin American woman to have a painting in the Louvre; her work caused a storm in Paris in 1939 (at an exhibition entitled *Méxique*). It was André Breton who described her art as "a ribbon around a bomb."

Frida Kahlo tried hard to be as much the revolutionary as the icon of Mexican femininity. Her last public appearance was 11 days before her death on July 13, 1954, in a wheelchair at Diego's side, protesting the intervention of the United States in Guatemala.

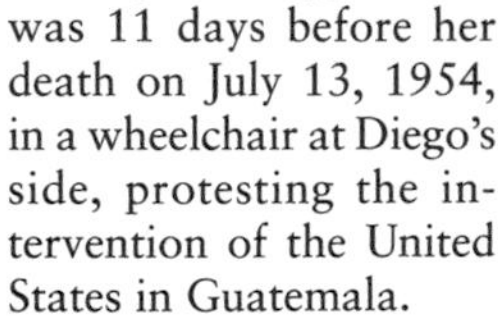

In 2007, to celebrate the 100th anniversary of her birth, there was a mega exposition of her work in Bellas Artes, in Mexico City.

Self portrait,Frida Kahlo

DIEGO RIVERA: REVOLUTIONARY WITH A PAINTBRUSH

Born: December 8, 1886, in Guanajuato, Mexico

Died: November 24, 1957, in Mexico City

Favorite process: Fresco painting

Famous works: *Night of the Rich; Detroit Industry; The Flower Carrier; A Dream of a Sunday Afternoon in Alameda Park*

Early loss: Born a twin, Rivera lost his brother before their second birthday.

Physical traits: At over 6 feet tall and 300 lbs, Rivera towered over his tiny wife.

Most incendiary moment: In 1933, Rivera was commissioned to paint a mural for the RCA building at New York's Rockefeller Center; he included Soviet leader Vladimir Lenin and the mural was destroyed a year later.

Rumored mourning: It is believed that in his intense mourning for Frida Kahlo, Rivera ate some of his wife's ashes.

Extramarital affairs: Model Dolores Olmedo and Frida Kahlo's younger sister Cristina, among many others

Quote: "Too late, I realized the most wonderful part of my life had been my love for Frida."

Diego Rivera was active both in art and politics early in his life, getting expelled from his academy for joining a student strike. In 1907 he won a scholarship to study abroad and left Mexico for Spain. He returned home briefly in 1910 and held a successful exhibition in Mexico City, at which Porfirio Díaz's wife purchased six of the 40 paintings. As auspicious as this event was, Rivera opted to return to Paris in 1911, this time falling in with the Parisian avant garde.

A trip to Italy in 1919 with fellow Mexican artist David Alfaro Siqueiros introduced Rivera to the frescos of the great Italian painters. In 1921, Rivera decided to return to Mexico with a plan to incorporate these techniques into his art—art that would be created for the enjoyment of the public. In the grand murals he created, he addressed Mexican history and humanity's future at large. Rivera's presence—and the controversy that inevitably followed him—had a profound effect on American painting and the American conception of public art. The strong Marxist themes in his work raised eyebrows wherever he went, but no controversy was greater than the one caused in 1933, when he endowed a mural commissioned by the Rockefellers for the lobby of the RCA building in Rockefeller Center with a portrait of Lenin. Rivera refused to remove the portrait from the mural, and the commission was canceled and the whole piece destroyed.

Mural Depicting Aztec Life (detail), Palacio Nacional, Diego Rivera

Despite these controversies, Rivera's work proved to be the inspiration for Franklin Delano Roosevelt's Works Progress Administration (WPA) program, which provided many unemployed artists with work during the 1930s. Rivera also continued to play a central role in the development of Mexican national art until his death in Mexico City in 1957.

The Main Sights

Above: Kitchen in Casa Azul

Museo Mural Diego Rivera. Diego Rivera's controversial mural, *Sunday Afternoon Dream in the Alameda Park*, originally was painted on a lobby wall of the Hotel Del Prado in 1947–48. Its controversy grew out of Rivera's Marxist inscription, "God does not exist," which the artist later replaced with the bland "Conference of San Juan de Letrán" to placate Mexico's Catholic population. The 1985 earthquake destroyed the hotel but not the mural, and this museum was built across the street from the hotel's site to house it. ✉ *Colón at Calle Balderas, Alameda Central* ☎ *55/5512–0754* 🌐 *www.museomuraldiegorivera.bellasartes.gob.mx* 🎫 *$1.50* ⏲ *Tues.–Sun. 10–6* Ⓜ *Hidalgo.*

Fodor's Choice **Museo de Frida Kahlo.** The Casa Azul (Blue House) where she was born in 1907 (not 1910, as she wanted people to believe) and died 47 years later, is both museum and shrine. Kahlo's astounding vitality and originality are reflected in the house, from the giant papier-mâché skeletons outside and the *retablos* (small religious paintings on tin) on the staircase to the gloriously decorated kitchen and the bric-a-brac in her bedroom. You can admire her early sketches, diary entries, tiny outfits, wheelchair at the easel, plus her four-poster bed fitted with mirror above. ✉ *Londres 247, at Calle Allende, Coyoacán* ☎ *55/5554–5999* 🌐 *www.museofridakahlo.org.mx* 🎫 *$5.50 (includes admission to Museo Diego Rivera–Anahuacalli)* ⏲ *Tues.–Sun. 10–5:45* Ⓜ *Viveros.*

Museo Casa Estudio Diego Rivera y Frida Kahlo. Some of Rivera's last paintings are still resting here on ready easels, and his denim jacket and shoes sit on a wicker chair, waiting. The museum that once was home to Diego and Frida appears as if the two could return at any moment to continue work. Architect and artist Juan O'Gorman, who designed the unique 1931 structure (essentially two houses connected by a bridge), was a close friend of Rivera. ✉ *Calle Diego Rivera, at Av. Altavista, San Angel* ☎ *55/5616–0996, 55/5550–1518, or 55/5550–1189* 🌐 *www.museoestudiodiegorivera.es.tl* 🎫 *$1, free Sun.* ⏲ *Tues.–Sun. 10–6.*

Fodor's Choice **Museo Dolores Olmedo Patiño.** In Xochimilco, on the outskirts of the city, is a superb collection of paintings by Frida Kahlo and the largest private collection of works by Diego Rivera. The museum was established by Olmedo, Rivera's lifelong model, patron, and onetime mistress. The lavish display of nearly 140 pieces from his cubist, post-cubist, and mural periods hangs in a magnificent 17th-century hacienda with beautiful gardens. This is also the place to see the strange Mexican hairless dog: Ms. Olmedo shares Rivera's passion for these creatures and keeps a few as pets on the grounds. There is a lovely small café in a glassed-in gazebo. The museum is reachable by public transportation; at the

Museo Dolores Olmedo Patino

Tasqueña metro station, catch the light rail to La Noria (*not* Xochimilco). As you exit the station, cross the street via the the stairway bridge. Walk half a block on 20 de Noviembre until you come to a traffic intersection. Without crossing the street, turn left at this intersection and continue walking down this street for two blocks. ✉ *Av. México 5843* ☎ *55/5555–1016* 🌐 *www.museodoloresolmedo.org.mx* 🎫 *$5.50, free Tues.* ⏲ *Tues.–Sun. 10–6.*

Museo Diego Rivera–Anahuacalli. Diego Rivera built his own museum for the thousands of pre-Columbian artifacts he collected over the years. The third-floor studio that Rivera did not live long enough to use displays sketches for his murals. If you visit between October and late December you'll see one of the city's finest altars to the dead in honor of Rivera himself. ✉ *Calle del Museo 150, Coyoacán, Col. San Pablo Tepetlapa* ☎ *55/5617–4310 or 55/5617–3797* 🎫 *$5.50 (includes admission to Museo de Frida Kahlo)* ⏲ *Tues.–Sun. 10:30–5 (last entry at 4:15).*

Other Sights

The **Museo Nacional de Arte (MUNAL)** in Alameda Central has Rivera's portrait of Adolfo Best Maugard. The **Museo de Arte Moderno** in Bosque de Chapultepec has Frida's *Las dos Fridas,* as well as a few of Rivera's pieces. In San Angel, the **Museo de Arte Carrillo Gil** has early murals by Rivera. And, last, but definitely not least, the **Palacio Nacional** in Centro Historico holds Rivera's epic murals, *Epic of the Mexican People in Their Struggle for Freedom and Independence*, representing two millennia of Mexican history.

Detail of *Dream of a Sunday Afternoon in the Alameda Park,* 1947-48. Hotel del Prado, Mexico City.

Galería OMR. Tucked away in a typical Colonia Roma house, with an early-20th-century stone facade and quirkily lopsided exhibition rooms, this active gallery has a strong presence in international art fairs and art magazines. It's open weekdays 10–3 and 4:30–7 and Saturday 10–2. ✉ *Plaza Río de Janeiro 54, Col. Roma* ☎ *55/5511–1179* 🌐 *www.galeriaomr.com* Ⓜ *Insurgentes.*

SAN ANGEL AND COYOACÁN

Originally separate colonial towns and then suburbs of Mexico City, San Angel and Coyoacán were both absorbed by the ever-growing capital. But they've managed to retain their original tranquillity.

You'll want to linger in these elegant sections of town, especially in Coyoacán. The Frida Kahlo and Leon Trotsky museums give intense, intimate looks at the lives of two famous people who were friends and lovers, and who breathed their personalities into the places where they lived. Allow at least an hour at each.

The other museums are much smaller and merit less time. Remember that museums close on Monday. Weekends are liveliest at the Plaza Hidalgo and its neighboring Jardín Centenario (usually referred to as *la plaza* or *el zócalo*), where street life explodes into a fiesta with balloons, clowns, cotton candy, live music, and hypnotic dancing to the sound of drums. On weekends Plaza Hidalgo hosts a crafts market.

SAN ANGEL

San Angel is a little colonial enclave of cobblestone streets, stone walls, pastel houses, rich foliage, and gardens drenched in bougainvillea. It became a haven for wealthy Spaniards during the viceroyalty period, around the time of the construction of the Ex-Convento del Carmen. The elite were drawn to the area because of its rivers, pleasant climate, and rural character, and proceeded to build haciendas and mansions that, for many, were country homes.

It's now sliced through by the busy Avenida Revolución; visitors usually focus on the area from the cobblestoned Avenida de la Paz, lined with some excellent eateries, to the Ex-Convento on Avenida Revolución, and up to the Plaza San Jacinto and its famous Saturday market.

TOP ATTRACTIONS

⇨ ⓬ **Museo Casa Estudio Diego Rivera y Frida Kahlo**, *see Frida and Diego.*

❹ **Museo de Arte Carrillo Gil.** The private collection here contains early murals by Orozco (with 50 works, this is one of the best Orozco collections you'll find anywhere), Rivera, and Siqueiros and works by modern

CULTURE ONLINE

To learn more about Mexican culture, peruse the following Spanish-language sites.

Arte Joven (🌐 *www.artejoven.com*). Directory of up-and-coming artists. **Consejo Nacional para la Cultura y las Artes** (🌐 *www.ecultura.gob.mx*). History and events calendars.

Instituto de Cultura de la Ciudad de México (🌐 *www.cultura.df.gob.mx*). Events calendars.

México Desonocido (🌐 *www.mexicodesconocido.com.mx*). Like National Geographic, all about Mexico.

TOURING SAN ANGEL AND COYOACÁN

Each of these two leafy colonial neighborhoods is accessible by subway, though you'll need to rely on at least one sitio taxi ride to cover them both in one day. San Angel is closer to the subway than Coyoacán. If you get off the metro at Miguel Angel de Quevedo and walk west down Arenal, you'll soon come to the **Monumento al General Alvaro Obregón**—the somber, gray, granite monument is a good neighborhood landmark. From there you can easily walk to all the neighborhood's sights with the exception of **Museo Casa Estudio Diego Rivera y Frida Kahlo** (though if you have the energy, that can technically be reached on foot, too). To start out from the monument, cross Insurgentes to walk up the cobblestoned, restaurant-lined Avenida de la Paz. Next cross Avenida Revolución and take the crooked street that leads upward to the left of the little park until you come to San Angel's center, **Plaza San Jacinto**.

Coyoacán is farther from the Quevedo stop, but you can reach its main attraction, **Museo de Frida Kahlo**, on foot. Most of the other sights are within walking distance of the museum, but you'll need a sitio taxi to get to **Museo del Anahuacalli**.

European artists such as Klee and Picasso; with its temporary exhibitions of contemporary international artists it's often considered the most important contemporary-art center in the city. It's a good place to learn about vanguard art. **■TIP→ This museum is considerably superior in terms of design and natural lighting to the city's better-known Museo Nacional de Arte Moderno.** ✉ *Av. Revolución 1608, at Av. Altavista, San Angel* ☎ *55/5550–1254 or 55/5550–6260* 🌐 *www.macg.inba.gob.mx* 🎟 *$1.50, free Sun.* ⏲ *Tues.–Sun. 10–6* Ⓜ *M.A. de Quevedo.*

❶ ★ **Plaza San Jacinto.** This welcoming plaza with a grisly history constitutes the heart of San Angel. In 1847 about 50 Irish soldiers of St. Patrick's Battalion, who had sided with the Mexicans in the Mexican-American War, had their foreheads branded here with the letter *D*—for deserter—and were then hanged by the Americans in this plaza. These men had been enticed to swim the Río Grande, deserting the ranks of U.S. General Zachary Taylor, by appeals to the historic and religious ties between Spain and Ireland. As settlers in Mexican Texas, they felt their allegiance lay with Catholic Mexico, and they were among the bravest fighters in the war. A memorial plaque (on a building on the plaza's west side) lists their names and expresses Mexico's gratitude for their help in the "unjust North American invasion." Off to one side of the plaza the excellent arts-and-crafts market Bazaar Sábado is held all day Saturday. ✉ *Bounded by Miramon, Cda. Santisima, Dr. Galvez, and Calle Madero, San Angel* Ⓜ *M.A. de Quevedo.*

WORTH NOTING

❷ **Centro Cultural Isidro Favela.** This 1681 mansion is one of the prettiest houses facing the Plaza San Jacinto. A huge free-form fountain sculpture—exploding with colorful porcelain tiles, shells, and mosaics—covers the eastern wall of its patio. Although it's not ranked among the city's top museums, it has a splendid collection of 17th- and 18th-century European and colonial Mexican paintings, all donated by the house's last owner, Isidro Favela. Favela also donated books and magazines to a small library behind the museum (by way of a lovely open patio) that is open to the public. Art exhibitions also rotate through. ✉ *Plaza San Jacinto 15, San Angel* ☎ *55/5616–2711* 🎟 *Free* ⏲ *Tues.–Sun. 10–5* Ⓜ *M.A. de Quevedo.*

A PLEASANT PLAZA

If you're taking a sitio taxi from San Angel, have it drop you at Plaza de Santa Catarina on Avenida Francisco Sosa. The graceful 16th-century Iglesia de Santa Catarina dominates this tiny plaza. Across the street is the Casa de Jesús Reyes Heroles—the former home of the ex-minister of education is a fine example of 20th-century architecture on the colonial model. It's now used as a cultural center. Continue east on Francisco Sosa and you'll pass Casa de Diego de Ordaz at the corner of Tres Cruces. This *Mudejar* (Spanish-Arabic) structure was the home of a former captain.

3 **Ex-Convento del Carmen.** Erected by Carmelite friars with the help of an Indian chieftain between 1615 and 1628, this church, with its domes, fountains, and gardens, was never actually a convent, despite its name. Though some locals might tell you otherwise, nuns never actually lived here. It's one of the most interesting examples of colonial religious architecture in this part of the city, and it has always been an important place for meeting and socializing. The church still operates, but part of it has been converted to Museo Regional del Carmen, with a fine collection of 16th- to 18th-century religious paintings and icons. Another museum area, the well-designed Novohispana, illustrates life in New Spain with work by early colonial artisans and trade guilds. This exhibit has a separate entrance at the back. It's also worth visiting the 12 mummified corpses tucked away in the crypt. ✉ *Av. Revolución 4, at Monasterio, San Angel* ☎ *55/5616–2816 or 55/5616–1177* 🎟 *$3, free Sun.* ⏲ *Tues.–Sun. 10–5* Ⓜ *M.A. de Quevedo.*

11 **Museo Soumaya.** This small private museum is owned by the Slim family, who own a great number of businesses, including Sanborns and Telmex. It has four rooms, each with a distinct theme. The first has an exhibit of 18th- and 19th-century Mexican portraiture, the second the art of New Spain, including 18th-century ironwork. The Julián Slim Gallery has more than 100 sculptures by Auguste Rodin in marble, bronze, terracotta, and plaster. The last room displays a collection of works from such painters as Pierre Renoir, Camille Claudelle, and Paul Gauguin. The entrance and exit halls showcase 1954 murals by Rufino Tamayo. Note that there are big plans in the works for this small museum. An ultramodern building has been designed by the Laboratory of Architecture, and is currently under construction. ✉ *Av. Revolución at Rio Magdalena, Eje 10 Sur, Plaza Loreto, San Angel* ☎ *55/5616–3731 or 55/5616–3761* 🎟 *Free* ⏲ *Sun., Mon., Wed., and Thurs. 10:30–6:30, Fri. and Sat. 10:30–8:30* Ⓜ *No stop nearby.*

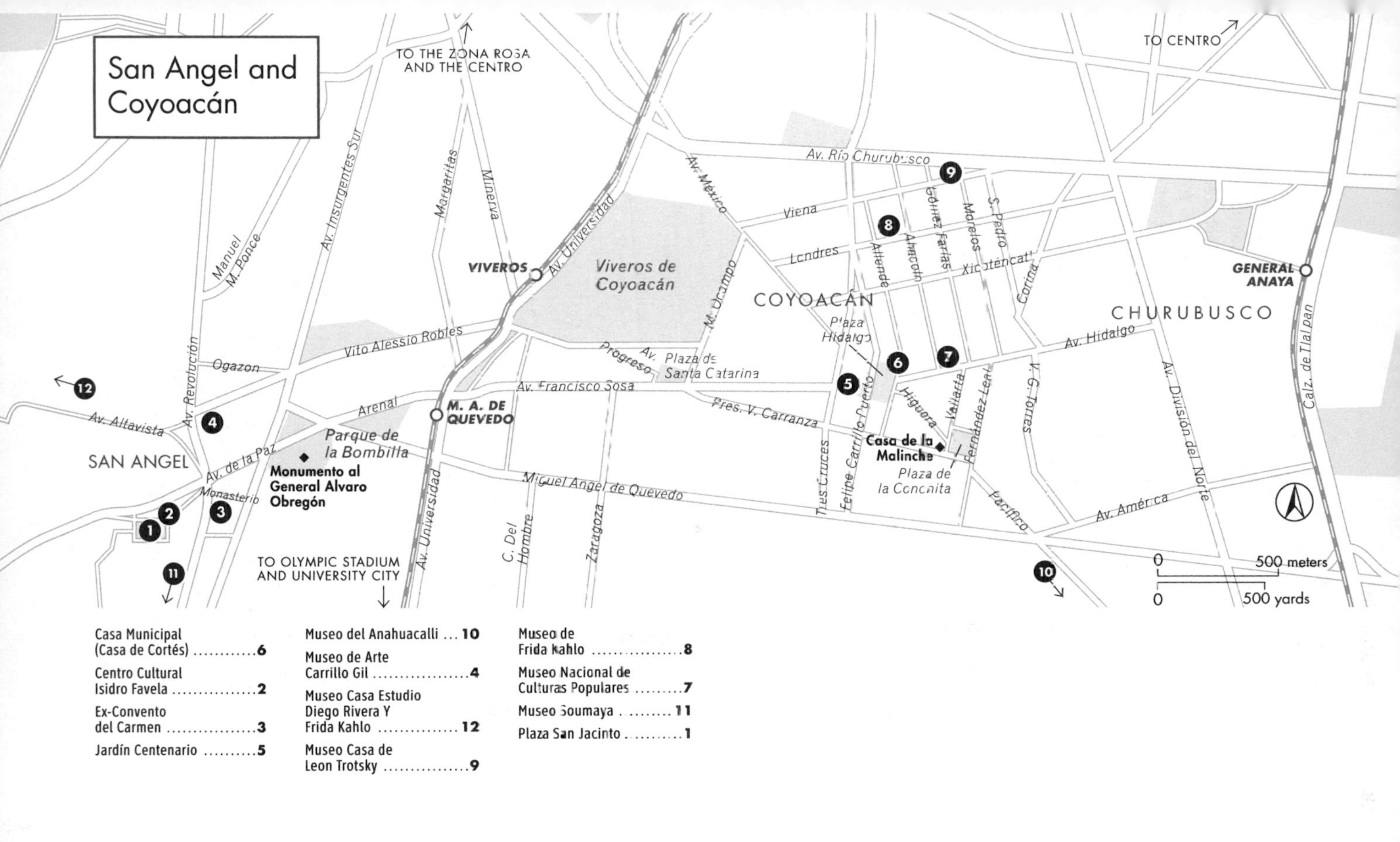
San Angel and Coyoacán
TO THE ZONA ROSA AND THE CENTRO
TO CENTRO
TO OLYMPIC STADIUM AND UNIVERSITY CITY
SAN ANGEL
COYOACÁN
CHURUBUSCO
VIVEROS
M. A. DE QUEVEDO
GENERAL ANAYA
Viveros de Coyoacán
Parque de la Bombilla
Monumento al General Alvaro Obregón
Casa de la Malinche
Plaza de la Conchita
Plaza Hidalgo
Av. Plaza de Santa Catarina
Av. Río Churubusco
Av. México
Av. Universidad
Av. Insurgentes Sur
Manuel M. Ponce
Margaritas
Minerva
Vito Alessio Robles
Ogazon
Av. Revolución
Av. Altavista
Av. de la Paz
Monasterio
Arenal
Av. Francisco Sosa
Progreso
M. Ocampo
Pres. V. Carranza
Miguel Angel de Quevedo
C. Del Hombre
Zaragoza
Viena
Londres
Allende
Abasolo
Gómez Farías
Morelos
S. Pedro
Xicoténcatl
Corina
Av. Hidalgo
Tres Cruces
Felipe Carrillo Puerto
Higuera
Vallarta
Fernández Leal
V. G. Torres
Pacífico
Av. América
Av. División del Norte
Calz. de Tlalpan
0 500 meters
0 500 yards
Casa Municipal (Casa de Cortés) 6
Centro Cultural Isidro Favela 2
Ex-Convento del Carmen 3
Jardín Centenario 5
Museo del Anahuacalli ... 10
Museo de Arte Carrillo Gil 4
Museo Casa Estudio Diego Rivera Y Frida Kahlo 12
Museo Casa de Leon Trotsky 9
Museo de Frida Kahlo 8
Museo Nacional de Culturas Populares 7
Museo Soumaya 11
Plaza San Jacinto 1

COYOACÁN

Coyoacán was founded by Toltecs in the 10th century and later settled by the Aztecs, or Mexica. Bernal Díaz Castillo, a Spanish chronicler, wrote that there were 6,000 houses at the time of the conquest. Cortés set up headquarters in Coyoacán during his siege of Tenochtitlán and kept his famous Indian mistress La Malinche here. At one point he considered making Coyoacán his capital; many of the Spanish buildings left from the two-year period during which Mexico City was built still stand.

> **LEGEND HAS IT**
>
> Coyoacán means "Place of the Coyotes." According to local legend, a coyote used to bring chickens to a friar who had saved the coyote from being strangled by a snake.

Coyoacán has had many illustrious residents from Mexico's rich and intellectual elite, including Miguel de la Madrid, president of Mexico from 1982 to 1988; artists Diego Rivera, Frida Kahlo, and José Clemente Orozco; Gabriel Figueroa, cinematographer for Luis Buñuel and John Huston; film star Dolores del Río; film director El Indio Fernández; and writers Carlos Monsiváis, Jorge Ibargüengoitia, and Nobel laureate Octavio Paz.

It's also the neighborhood where the exiled Leon Trotsky met his violent death. Coyoacán's streets buzz with activity, and it has a popular food market, the Mercado Xicotencatl. On weekends families flock to its pleasant zócalo, second in importance and popularity only to the Zócalo downtown.

TOP ATTRACTIONS

5 **Jardín Centenario.** The Centenary Gardens are barely separated from the Plaza Hidalgo (aka Jardín Hidalgo) by a narrow slow-moving road; both squares are referred to as Coyoacán's zócalo. The Jardín, with its shading trees, a fountain with two snarling coyotes, and a fringe of outdoor cafés, is the place to sit and people-watch.

The larger Plaza Hidalgo hosts children's fun fairs, amateur musical and dance performances, clowns, bubble blowers, cotton candy, and balloon sellers on weekends and national holidays. It's studded with an ornate old bandstand and the impressive Templo de San Juan Bautista, one of the first churches to be built in New Spain. It was completed in 1582, and its door has a baroque arch. On the afternoon of September 15, before the crowds become suffocating at nightfall, this delightful neighborhood zócalo is probably the best place in the capital to enjoy Independence Day celebrations. ✉ *Bounded by Calle Centenario, Av. Hidalgo, and Caballo Calco, Coyoacán* Ⓜ *Viveros.*

⇨ 8 **Museo de Frida Kahlo,** *see Frida and Diego.*

NEED A BREAK?

Cafe El Jarocho. About a block from the Jardín Centenario, Cafe El Jarocho is a great place to grab a coffee. It's been at the this corner location since 1957, originally selling coffee, mangos, and other produce from Veracruz (in Mexico, *jarocho* means "native of Veracruz"). In recent years demand has grown for its excellent coffee, and this is now a favorite spot for locals. If you're lucky enough to find a space on the outside benches on weekends,

it's a good place to watch the hip Coyoacán crowd and the vendors who set up shop here, selling jewelry and art crafts in makeshift stands on the street and on the top of their cars. There are now a few other branches, but the original is still the most popular—and the best place to get a feel for neighborhood. ✉ ***Cuauhtémoc 134, at Allende, Coyoacán*** ☎ ***55/5658-5029 or 55/5554-5418*** 🌐 ***www.cafeeljarocho.com.mx.***

WORTH NOTING

6 **Casa Municipal (Casa de Cortés).** The place where the Aztec emperor Cuauhtémoc was held prisoner by Cortés is reputed to have been rebuilt in the 18th century from the stones of his original house. Now a sandy color and topped by two coyote figures, it's used for municipal government offices; a small tourist bureau at the entrance provides maps and leaflets publicizing cultural events in the area. Usually you can wander through the wide arches to the cute tile patio. ✉ *Plaza Hidalgo 1, between Calles Carillo Puerto and Allende, Coyoacán* ☎ *55/5658-0221* ⏲ *Weekdays 8–6, weekends 8–8* Ⓜ *Viveros, then take a taxi.*

9 **Museo Casa de Leon Trotsky.** Resembling an anonymous and forbidding fortress, with turrets for armed guards, this house is where Leon Trotsky lived and was murdered. It's difficult to believe that it's the final resting place for the ashes of one of the most important figures of the Russian Revolution, but that only adds to the allure of this austere dwelling, which is owned by Trotsky's grandson. Anyone taller than 5 feet must stoop to pass through doorways to Trotsky's bedroom—with bullet holes still in the walls from the first assassination attempt, in which the muralist Siqueiros was implicated—his wife's study, the dining room, and the study where assassin Ramón Mercader (a man of many aliases) allegedly drove a pickax into Trotsky's head. On his desk, cluttered with writing paraphernalia and an article he was revising in Russian, the calendar is open to that fateful day, August 20, 1940. All informative materials are in Spanish only. ✉ *Río Churubusco 410, Coyoacán* ☎ *55/5658-8732* 🎟 *$3.50* ⏲ *Tues.–Sun. 10–5* Ⓜ *Viveros.*

⇨ 10 **Museo del Anahuacalli** *see Frida and Diego.*

7 **Museo Nacional de Culturas Populares.** A huge *arbol de la vida* (tree of life) sculpture stands in the courtyard of this museum devoted to popular culture and regional arts and crafts. Its exhibitions and events are nicely varied, including children's workshops, concerts of traditional music and dance performances. On weekends the courtyard becomes a small crafts-and-sweets market with

LA MALINCHE

Two blocks east of Plaza Hidalgo on Calle Higuera at Vallarta is a somber-looking residence called Casa de la Malinche. It was the home of La Malinche, Cortés's Indian mistress and interpreter. She aided the conquest by enabling Cortés to communicate with the Nahuatl-speaking tribes he met en route to Tenochtitlán. Today she is a reviled symbol of a traitorous xenophile—hence the term *malinchista,* used to describe a Mexican who prefers things foreign. Legend says that Cortés's wife died in this house, poisoned by the conquistador, and that it's bad luck just to walk by.

SPORTING EVENTS IN MEXICO CITY

Although the roots of *fútbol* (soccer) are probably English, a weekend afternoon game at Mexico City's colossal Estadio Azteca makes clear that this is the sport Mexicans are craziest about. Baseball has a strong following, too, as does the over-the-top *lucha libre* (wrestling).

BASEBALL

Thanks to batter-friendly thin air, baseball fans here are usually treated to slugfests at **Diablos Rojos** (✉ *Av. Viaducto Río de la Piedad, at Río Churubusco, Col. Granjas México* ☎ *55/5639–8722* 🌐 *www.diablos.com.mx*). The season runs from March to July; playoffs begin in August. Ticket prices range from $2 to $8. When purchasing tickets, you'll be asked whether you want to sit along the baseline of the home team (the Diablos Rojos) or of the visitors.

LUCHA LIBRE

Wrestling has been around since the mid-1800s, or at least the early 1900s (there is some debate about how and when it began), but it is growing more and more famous with international children's programs and movies like *Nacho Libre* (2007). Wrestlers wear masks and dress in costumes depicting good or evil (the devil against the angel, for example), and it's usually good who wins after a couple of acrobatic slams and pitches out of the ring. The discussion on whether the fights are fixed is a heated one among aficionados.

The good-guy wrestlers often become folk heroes, appear in comic books and movies, and are role models for young kids. One of the most famous wrestlers was El Santo (The Saint), whose son continues the legacy. Most wrestlers are from the barrios and the sport attracts their compatriots: it's rowdy and loud. Note that both of the arenas where you can catch the lucha are in parts of town where caution is recommended as you come and go. It's best to travel in a group; women should absolutely have a male escort. Be sure to arrange for safe transport.

Matches take place every Tuesday night at 7:30 and Friday night at 8:30 at the **Arena Mexico** (✉ *Dr. Lavista between Dr. Carmona and Dr. Lucio, Col. Doctores* ☎ *55/5588–0508 or 55/5588–0266*). Ringside seats fetch $10. Avoid hailing cabs directly outside the arena. Matches also take place at the **Arena Coliseo** (✉ *Perú 77, Col. Centro* ☎ *55/5526–1687*), the oldest arena in Mexico, every Sunday at 5.

SOCCER

Fútbol is the sport that Mexicans are most passionate about, which is evident in the size of their soccer stadium, **Estadio Azteca** (✉ *Calz. de Tlalpan 3465, Tlalpan*), the second-largest in Latin America and home of the Aguilas de América, one of Mexico's top fútbol teams. You can buy tickets outside the stadium in the south of the city on the same day of any minor game. For more important games, buy tickets a week in advance. The Pumas, a popular university-sponsored team, play at Estadio Olímpico, Avenida Insurgentes Sur at Universidad Nacional Autónoma de México, Ciudad Universitaria. Tickets sell fast for Pumas games, so the best bet is to order them through Ticketmaster online at 🌐 *www.ticketmaster.com.mx*.

some worthwhile exhibitors displaying their wares from all over the country. The museum shop stocks art books and high-quality crafts. ✉ *Av. Hidalgo 289, at Calle Allende, Coyoacán* ☎ *55/4155–0920* 🎫 *$1* 🕑 *Tues.–Thurs. 10–6, Fri.–Sun. 10–8* Ⓜ *Viveros.*

OUTSKIRTS OF MEXICO CITY

As the capital continues to expand, many attractions that used to be side trips are becoming more accessible. To the north of Mexico City stands the Basílica de Guadalupe, a church dedicated to Mexico's patron saint. It can be enjoyed in a half-day tour; if you get an early start, you could combine your visit with a jaunt to the pyramids of Teotihuacán in the afternoon.

Xochimilco (pronounced kso-chee-*meel*-coh), famous for its floating gardens, lies on the southern outskirts of the city. You can ride in gondolalike boats and get a fleeting sense of a pre-Hispanic Mexico City.

La Villa de Guadalupe. "La Villa"—the local moniker of the site of the two basilicas of the Virgin of Guadalupe, north of the Zócalo—is Mexico's holiest shrine. Its importance derives from the miracle that the devout believe occurred here on December 12, 1531: an Aztec named Juan Diego received from the Virgin a cloak permanently imprinted with her image so he could prove to the priests that he had had a holy vision. Although the story of the miracle and the cloak itself has been challenged for centuries, it is hotly defended by clergy and laity alike. As author Gary Wills observed, the story's "authority just grows as its authenticity diminishes." Every December 12, millions of pilgrims arrive, many crawling on their knees for the last few hundred yards, praying for divine favors.

Outside the **Antigua Basílica** (Old Basicila) stands a statue of Juan Diego, who became the first indigenous saint in the Americas with his canonization in 2002. The canonization of Juan Diego was wildly popular among Mexican Catholics, although a vocal minority of critics (both in and out of the Church) argued that, despite the Church's extensive investigation, the validity of Juan Diego's existence is suspect. Many critics see the canonization of this polarizing figure as a strategic move by the Church to retain its position among Mexico's indigenous population. The old basilica dates from 1536; various additions have been made since then. The altar was executed by sculptor Manuel Tolsá. The basilica now houses a museum of ex-votos (hand-painted depictions of miracles, dedicated to Mary or a saint in gratitude) and popular religious, decorative, and applied arts from the 15th through 18th centuries.

Because the structure of the Antigua Basílica had weakened over the years and the building was no longer large enough or safe enough to accommodate all the worshippers, Pedro Ramírez Vázquez, the architect responsible for Mexico City's splendid Museo Nacional de Antropología, was commissioned to design a shrine, which was consecrated in 1976. In this case, alas, the architect's inspiration failed him: the **Nueva Basílica** (New Basilica) is a gigantic, circular mass of wood, steel, and polyethylene that feels like a stadium rather than a church.

The famous image of the Virgin is encased high up in its altar at the back and can be viewed from a moving sidewalk that passes below. The holiday itself is a great time to visit if you don't mind crowds; it's celebrated with various kinds of music and dancers. Remember to bring some water with you; you'll need it in the crush.

It's best not to take the metro here. It's in a dangerous neighborhood (no need to wander around outside the complex of churches). Any local will tell you that the safest way to get here is via radio taxi or chauffer-driven car or on a tour. ✉ *Paseo de las Americas 1, Col. Villa de Guadalupe* ☎ *55/5577–6022* 🌐 *www.virgendeguadalupe.org.mx* ⏲ *Daily* 6 AM–9 PM.

⇨ **Museo Dolores Olmeda Patino,** *see Frida and Diego.*

Xochimilco. When the first nomadic settlers arrived in the Valley of Mexico, now 21 km (13 mi) south of Mexico City center, they found an enormous lake. As the years went by and their population grew, the land could no longer satisfy their agricultural needs. They solved the problem by devising a system of *chinampas* (floating gardens), rectangular structures akin to barges, which they filled with reeds, branches, and mud. They planted the barges with willows, whose roots anchored the floating gardens to the lake bed, making a labyrinth of small islands and canals on which vendors carried flowers and produce grown on the chinampas to market.

Today Xochimilco is the only place in Mexico where the gardens still exist. Go on a Saturday, when the *tianguis* (market stalls) are most active, or, though it's crowded, on a Sunday. On weekdays the place is practically deserted, so it loses some of its charm. Hire a *trajinera* (flower-painted boat); an arch over each spells out its name in flowers. As you sail through the canals you'll pass mariachis and women selling tacos from other trajineras.

For Xochimilco, take metro line No. 2 to Tasqueña; here hop on the *tren ligero* (light-rail) that continues south to Xochimilco. Expect a bit of a free-for-all outside the station, as several guides—often on bicycles—will be waiting to direct tourists to the gardens. Official tour guides, employed by the government, wear identifying tags; any other guides volunteering to take people to the gardens take them to a specific trajinera rental business that pays them for bringing in clients. You can cast your lot with a guide (official or not) or catch any bus marked XOCHIMILCO; buses usually pick up passengers right outside the train station. To walk to the nearest trajinera *embarcadero* (dock), head down Cuauhtémoc for three blocks, then make a left on Violeta. Continue on Violeta for two blocks (you'll see signs pointing toward "Belen," the embarcadero), and turn right off Violeta at Nezahualcóyotl. Alternatively, you could take a sitio taxi (up to $35). The trip should take between 45 minutes and one hour from the downtown area, depending on traffic.

MEXICO CITY'S MODERN-DESIGN MAKER

Casa Luis Barragán. As you travel through the capital, it would be nearly impossible to note all of the architectural styles, since there are just too many. Bold colors, lines, and innovative designs decorate just about everywhere you look. If you are interested in learning more about these modern-architecture nuances, visit the home of architect Luis Barragán. Yes, this museum is far from the typical tourist routes, but if you have a little extra time to spend in the city, this is a good way to do it. Barragán was an influential modernist architect on a world scale, and certainly one of the most influential architects in Mexico in the last century. This house, designated by UNESCO as a World Heritage Center, is quite an accomplishment in itself, but Barragán was also involved in much larger-scale projects that shaped the city you see today. He was instrumental in the design of the Pedregal neighborhood, in the south of the city, and Ciudad Satélite, just north of the capital. It is imperative that you call ahead, since guided tours through the museum are required. Tours are available in English; mention that you'll need English when you call, so they'll be prepared for you. ✉ *General Francisco Ramírez 14, Col. Daniel Garza* ☎ *55/5515-4908* 🌐 *www.casaluisbarragan.org* ⏲ *Weekdays 10–2 and 4–6, Sat. 10–1.*

WHERE TO EAT

Updated by Rachel Nolan

Mexico City has been a culinary capital ever since the time of Moctezuma. Chronicles tell of the extravagant banquets prepared for the Aztec emperor with more than 300 different dishes served. Today's Mexico City is a gastronomic melting pot, with some 15,000 restaurants. You'll find everything from taco stands on the streets to simple, family-style eateries and elite restaurants. The number and range of international restaurants is growing and diversifying, particularly in middle- and upper-class neighborhoods like Polanco, San Angel, La Condesa, La Roma, Lomas de Chapultepec, and Del Valle. Argentine, Spanish, and Italian are the most dominant international cuisines; however you'll also find a fair share of Japanese, Korean, Arabic, and French restaurants. Mexico City restaurants open 7–11 AM for breakfast (*el desayuno*) and 1–6 for lunch (*la comida*)—although it's rare for Mexicans to eat lunch before 2, and you're likely to feel lonely if you arrive at a popular restaurant before then. Lunch is an institution in this country, often lasting two or more hours, and until nightfall on Sunday. Consequently, the evening meal (*la cena*) may often be really light, consisting of sweet bread and coffee, traditional tamales and atole at home, or tacos and appetizers in a restaurant.

When dining, most locals start out at 9 PM for dinner; restaurants stay open until 11:30 during the week and later on weekends. Many restaurants are open only for lunch on Sunday. At deluxe restaurants dress is generally formal (jacket at least), and reservations are recommended; see reviews for details. If you're short on time, you can always head to American-style coffee shops or recognizable fast-food chains all over the city that serve the tired but reliable fare of burgers, fried chicken, and pizza. If it's local flavor you're after, go with tacos or the Mexico City fast-food staple, the *torta* (a giant sandwich stacked with the ingredients of your choice for about $2). Eating on the street is part of the daily experience for those on the go, and surprising as it may seem, many people argue that it's some of the best food in the city. Still, even locals can't avoid the occasional stomach illness, so dig in at your own risk.

Also cheap and less of a bacterial hazard are the popular *fondas* (small restaurants). At lunchtime fondas are always packed, as they serve a reasonably priced four-course meal, known as the *comida corrida,* which typically includes soup of the day, rice or pasta, an entrée, and dessert. Asian cuisine is still limited here, but you'll find some decent Japanese, Korean, and Chinese restaurants. There are few vegetarian restaurants, but you'll have no trouble finding nonmeat dishes wherever you grab a bite. Vegetarians and vegans, however, will have a more difficult time, as many dishes are often prepared using lard.

Colonia Polanco, the upscale neighborhood on the edge of the Bosque de Chapultepec, has some of the best and most expensive dining (and lodging) in the city. Zona Rosa restaurants fill up quickly on Saturday night, especially on Saturdays coinciding with most people's paydays: the 1st and 15th of each month. The same is true of San Angel, whereas the Condesa and Roma neighborhoods buzz with a younger crowd Thursday to Saturday.

CENTRO HISTÓRICO

$–$$$ MIDDLE EASTERN
Al Andalus. Lebanese restaurant Al Andalus, in a magnificent 16th-century colonial building downtown, makes some of the best Arabic food in the capital. Proximity to La Merced, the city's biggest and best market, means that the numerous menu options are made with the freshest ingredients. If you don't want to choose, order the *mesa libanesa,* a mixed platter with everything from hummus and kebbeh to lamb shwarmas. ✉ *Mesones 171, at Cruces, Col. Centro* ☎ *55/5522–2528* 💳 *AE, MC, V.*

$–$$$$ MEXICAN
Café de Tacuba. An essential, if touristy, breakfast, lunch, dinner, or snack stop downtown, this Mexican classic opened in 1912 in a section of an old convent. At the entrance to the main dining room are huge 18th-century oil paintings depicting the invention of *mole poblano,* a complex sauce featuring a variety of chilies and chocolate that was created by the nuns in the Santa Rosa Convent in Puebla. A student group dressed in medieval capes and hats serenades diners Wednesday through Sunday from 3 to 11. ✉ *Calle Tacuba 28, at Allende, Col. Centro* ☎ *55/5521–2048* 🌐 *www.cafedetacuba.com.mx* 💳 *AE, MC, V.*

$$–$$$
Círculo Vasco Español. Dating from the 1890s, this huge, high-ceiling restaurant basks in the faded glamour of the days when dictator Porfirio Díaz dined here regularly. Its founders were Basque, and though it has been run by Galicians for more than 20 years, the menu retains a Basque flavor. Look for *rueda de robalo a la donostiarra* (sea bass cooked with parsley and white wine) and a seafood buffet on weekends. A hearty breakfast, like the omelet *de rajas con queso* (with poblano chili and

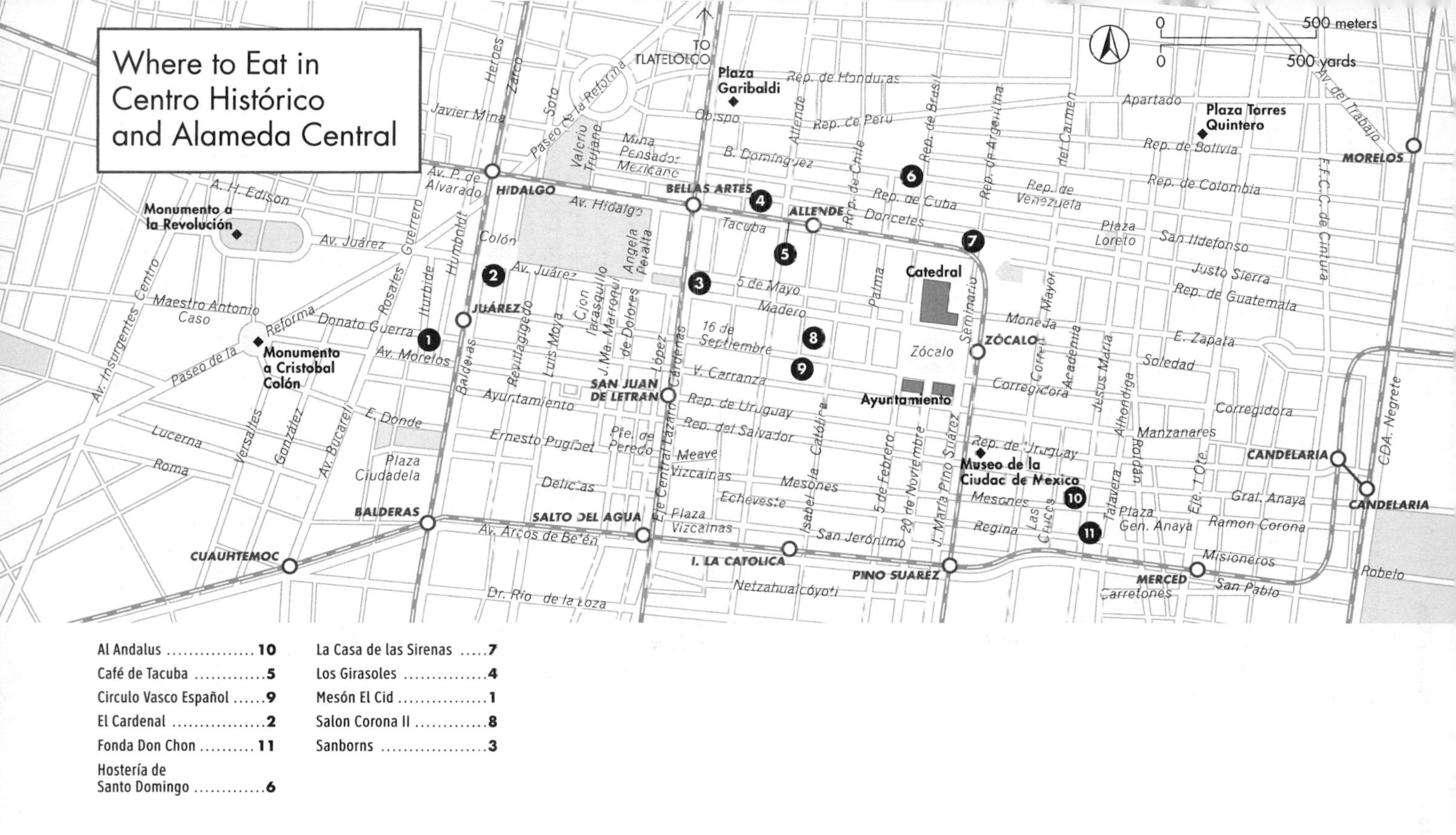

Al Andalus 10
Café de Tacuba 5
Circulo Vasco Español 9
El Cardenal 2
Fonda Don Chon 11
Hostería de Santo Domingo 6
La Casa de las Sirenas 7
Los Girasoles 4
Mesón El Cid 1
Salon Corona II 8
Sanborns 3

cheese), will set you up for serious sightseeing. ✉ *Av. 16 de Septiembre 51, Col. Centro* ☎ *55/5518–2908* ▭ *AE, MC, V* ⏲ *No dinner.*

$$$–$$$$ MEXICAN ✕ **El Cardenal.** In the ground floor of the Centro Histórico Sheraton across Juárez from the elegant Alameda, this upscale venue concentrates on food over surroundings (you could be in any luxury hotel in any city)—and how. For dinner, try one of the Oaxacan moles—colorado, rojo, or almendrado (almond). But the real treat is breakfast, replete with frothy hot chocolate, enchiladas, and fresh-baked pan dulce (a sweet Mexican pastry). ✉ *Juárez 70, Col. Centro* ☎ *55/5518–6633* ▭ *AE, MC, V.*

$–$$$ MEXICAN ✕ **Fonda Don Chon.** This unpretentious family-style restaurant, deep in a downtown working-class neighborhood, is famed for its pre-Hispanic Mexican dishes. A knowledge of zoology, Spanish, and Nahuatl helps in making sense of a menu that includes ingredients from throughout the republic. *Escamoles de hormiga* (red-ant roe) is known as the "caviar of Mexico" for its texture and costliness, but it is an acquired taste. Other exotic dishes are armadillo in mango sauce and fillet of wild boar. ✉ *Regina 160, near La Merced market, Col. Centro* ☎ *55/5542–0873* ▭ *AE* ⏲ *Closed Sun. No dinner.*

$$$–$$$$ MEXICAN ★ ✕ **Hostería de Santo Domingo.** This genteel institution near downtown's Plaza Santo Domingo has been serving colonial dishes in a delightful town house since the late 19th century. Feast on oysters in cocktail sauce, stuffed cactus paddles, hot pepper soup, and the house specialty, *chiles en nogada* (stuffed poblano chili peppers bathed in creamy walnut sauce). This is a great place for a boozy lunch, with options ranging from wine to whiskies to tequilas. The place is open for breakfast and is always full at lunch; it closes at 10 PM. ✉ *Belisario Dominguez 72, Col. Centro* ☎ *55/5510–1434 or 55/5526–5276* 🌐 *www.hosteriadesantodomingo.com.mx* ▭ *AE, MC, V.*

$–$$$ MEXICAN ✕ **La Casa de las Sirenas.** The place is the calling card here—the 16th-century mansion sits at the foot of the Templo Mayor ruins, stones from which were incorporated into the building. The atmospheric second-floor terrace is within sight and sound of numerous Indian dancers below honoring the spirits of the crumbling Aztec temples. The menu is a mishmash of international (Cornish game hen) and Mexican (cilantro soup). ✉ *República de Guatemala 32, Col. Centro* ☎ *55/5704–3225 or 55/5704–3465* ▭ *AE, MC, V* ⏲ *No dinner Sun.*

$–$$ MEXICAN ✕ **Los Girasoles.** Two prominent Mexico City society columnists own this downtown spot. Los Girasoles (which means "sunflowers") is on a lovely old square in a restored three-story colonial home. It was one of the first places to serve *nueva cocina mexicana,* and there are also pre-Hispanic delicacies such as *escamoles (ant eggs)*, *gusanos de maguey* (chilied worms), and *mini chapulines* (tiny, crispy, fried grasshoppers). Be aware that you will be charged for the bread and spreads if you eat them—it's better to wait for your more interesting main course. It closes at 9 PM on Sunday and Monday, but is open till midnight the rest of the week. ✉ *Calle Tacuba 9, Plaza Manuel Tolsá on Xicoténcatl 1, Col. Centro* ☎ *55/5510–0630* ▭ *AE, MC, V.*

$$–$$$ SPANISH ✕ **Mesón El Cid.** This alluring *mesón* (tavern) exudes Old Spain with stained-glass windows and a roaring fireplace. Weekdays, classic dishes

such as paella, spring lamb, suckling pig, and Cornish hens with truffles keep customers happy, but on Saturday night this place comes into its own with a four-course medieval banquet (starting at 9 PM), including a procession of costumed waiters carrying huge trays of steaming hot viands for $30 per person. Further entertainment is provided by a student vocal group dressed in medieval Spanish capes and hats, a juggler, and a magician. For dessert, a real winner is the *turrón* (Spanish nougat) ice cream. ✉ *Humboldt 61, Col. Centro* ☎ *55/5512–7629* ▭ *AE, MC, V* ⏲ *No dinner Sun. and Mon.*

WORD OF MOUTH

"Mexico City was amazing. It was [one of] the best family trips we have ever taken. Mexico City might be fun for couples and singles, but it is definitely made for families. The food, of course, was excellent and the people were extremely friendly." —alyssamma

¢–$$ MEXICAN ✕ **Salon Corona II.** The famous *cervezeria* (brewery) went into the restaurant business last year, with this clean, well-lighted upstairs locale overlooking one of the center's busiest pedestrian streets. The concept was to take street food indoors, clean it up, and serve it (still cheap) with a beer. The *bacalao* (salt cod) tacos are reputed to be a hangover cure. Flat-screen TVs tuned to sports are outsized by the room, and so don't dominate the place, and you can sit in the open air under the retractable roof. ✉ *Filomeno Mata 18, at Madero, Col. Centro* ☎ *55/5510–0624* ▭ *No credit cards* ⏲ *No dinner Sun.*

$–$$ MEXICAN ✕ **Sanborns.** The Casa de los Azulejos (House of Tiles) houses one the first of the Sanborns in the country. Now the popular stores-cum-restaurants owned by billionaire Carlos Slim, populate every major town in Mexico. The menu plays it safe with non-spicy Mexican dishes and international options like burgers, soups, and club sandwiches. Though the food isn't stellar, this is a popular spot among Mexicans for coffee and a snack. ✉ *Calle Madero 4, at Cinco de Mayo, Col. Centro* ☎ *55/5512–9820* 🌐 *www.sanborns.com.mx* ▭ *AE, MC, V.*

ZONA ROSA

$–$$ CONTINENTAL ✕ **Bellinghausen.** This cherished Zona Rosa lunch spot has been a capital classic for over a century. The partially covered hacienda-style courtyard at the back, set off by an ivy-laden wall and fountain, is a midday magnet for executives and tourists. A veritable army of waiters scurries back and forth serving such tried-and-true favorites as *filete chemita* (broiled steak with mashed potatoes). ✉ *Londres 95, at Niza, Zona Rosa* ☎ *55/5207–6149* ▭ *AE, DC, MC, V* ⏲ *No dinner.*

$–$$ FRENCH ★ ✕ **Bistrot Arlequin.** Here you'll find everything you would expect from a petit bistrot: an intimate environment, comforting food, good music that's not too loud, and excellent French wines. Start by ordering the house specialty, hailing from Lyon, France: fish quenelles with your choice of various sauces. A popular main dish is the *carne bourguignonne,* beef cooked in red wine and butter with bacon and mushrooms. If there's room for dessert, try the clafouti, a French custard with cherries that has a texture similar to mousse. There is no sign—go to the northeast corner of Plaza Juanacatlán and listen for people

Bellinghausen ...7
Bistrot Arlequin 2
Cheong Ki Wa ...5
El Dragón 6
Fonda El Refugio...... 10
La Lanterna 1
Los Arcos 8
Mikado 3
Tezka 9
Urbano dos22 ...4

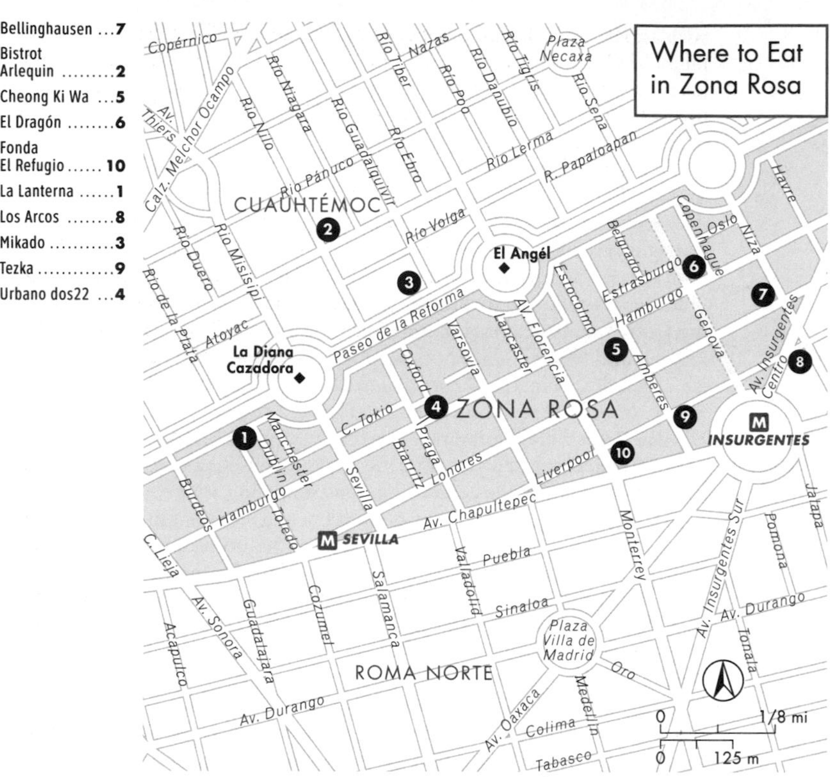

speaking French. Reservations recommended. ✉ *Río Nilo 42, at Río Lerma, Cuauhtémoc, northwest of Zona Rosa* ✣ *About 3 blocks from Angel of Independence monument* ☎ *55/5207–5616* ▭ *MC, V.*

$–$$ KOREAN ✕ **Cheong Ki Wa**. Of the many Korean restaurants cropping up in the Zona Rosa, this one ranks among the best. Parties of three or more can order the *paquetes*, complete with appetizers, tofu soup, Korean dumplings, and marinated meats. These are cooked in front of you on a grill in the middle of the table. The spice factor is normal for Mexicans, rather high for foreigners. ✉ *Amberes 41, Zona Rosa* ☎ *55/5511–6198* ▭ *AE, DC, MC, V.*

$$–$$$ CHINESE ✕ **El Dragón**. The former ambassador to China was so impressed by El Dragón's lacquered Beijing duck that he left behind a note of recommendation (now proudly displayed on one of the restaurant's walls) praising it as the most authentic in Mexico. The duck is roasted over a fruitwood fire and later brought to your table, where the waiter cuts it into thin, tender slices. Most of the cooks hail from Beijing, but they mix up their regional cuisines. ✉ *Hamburgo 97, between Génova and Copenhague, Zona Rosa* ☎ *55/5525–2466* ▭ *AE, DC, MC, V.*

$–$$$ MEXICAN ✕ **Fonda El Refugio**. Expect dishes from each major region of Mexico when you come here. Along with a varied regular menu, there are tempting daily specials; you might find a mole made with pumpkin seeds or *huachinango a la veracruzana* (red snapper bathed in a tomato sauce with capers and olives). Try the refreshing *aguas* (fresh-fruit and seed juices) with your meal and the *café de olla* (clove-flavored coffee cooked in a clay pot and sweetened with brown sugar) afterward. ✉ *Liverpool 166, at Florencia, Zona Rosa* ☎ *55/5207–2732 or 55/5525–8128* ▭ *AE, DC, MC, V.*

2

$$–$$$ ITALIAN ✕**La Lanterna.** The Petterino family has run this two-story restaurant since 1966. The locale—right on Reforma but away from the main flow of traffic—is totally cosmopolitan. The vibe is rustic northern Italian trattoria. Seating is cramped, but that just makes the place feel especially intimate. All pastas are made on the premises; the Bolognese sauce is a favorite. Raw artichoke salad, eggplant Parmesan, and filete al burro nero (steak in black butter) are all tasty dishes. ✉ *Paseo de la Reforma 458, at Toledo, Col. Juárez* ☎ *55/5207–9969 or 55/5208–9878* ▭ *AE, DC, MC, V* ⏲ *Closed Sun. and Dec. 25–Jan. 1.*

$$–$$$ MEXICAN/ SEAFOOD ✕**Los Arcos.** This chain of Pacific Coast–style seafood restaurants has branched out to six states, yet it hasn't compromised on quality. The restaurant's crowning culinary glory is the *corbina a las brasas,* a sweet fish grilled to perfection and seasoned with chipotle, soy sauce, and mustard. For some fish dishes, like the corbina and the pargo, you'll be charged by the kilogram, so don't be surprised if prices vary. ✉ *Liverpool 104, at Niza, Zona Rosa* ☎ *55/5525–4408* ▭ *MC, V.*

$–$$$ JAPANESE ✕**Mikado.** Strategically positioned a few blocks west of the U.S. embassy and close to the Japanese embassy, this spot is notable for its fairly priced sushi. A fine Japanese chef, an extensive menu, and a cheerful bustle also make Mikado a real treat. ✉ *Paseo de la Reforma 369, Col. Cuauhtémoc* ☎ *55/5525–3096* ▭ *AE, DC, MC, V.*

$$$ SPANISH ✕**Tezka.** This Zona Rosa restaurant specializing in *nueva cocina Basque* was created by legendary chef Juan Mari Arzac, who brought many of his best dishes to Mexico from his restaurant in San Sebastían, Spain. Feast on yellow tuna in a sweet and spicy sauce, or liver prepared with beer, green pepper, and malt. The starters are exquisite, especially the *caldo de xipiron* (broth of baby squid). Tezka's consistent quality can be attributed to the fact that it's a training ground for the city's best young chefs. A decent list of Spanish wines includes Cune, Vina Ardanza, and Reserva 904. ✉ *Royal Hotel, Amberes 78, at Liverpool, Col. Juárez* ☎ *55/9149–3000* ▭ *AE, DC, MC, V* ⏲ *Closed Sun. No dinner Sat.*

$$$–$$$$ CONTEMPORARY ✕**Urbano dos22.** With its zestful fusion cuisine, groovy club music, extensive bottle service, dark-leather chairs, and waitresses in black minis, this eatery adds bit of haute and soul to the Zona Rosa. Eight cuts of Angus steak and standout dishes such as tiradito de aguachile (shrimp and scallops marinated in a spicy pepper sauce) affirm that you're in a generous eatery. Desserts include artisanal sorbet and tiramisu with strawberries. ✉ *Hamburgo 222, Zona Rosa* ☎ *55/5525–4194* 🌐 *www.urbano222.com* ▭ *AE, MC, V.*

POLANCO

$$$–$$$$ FRENCH ★ ✕**Au Pied de Cochon.** Open around the clock inside the Hotel Presidente, this fashionable bistro continues to seduce well-heeled *chilangos* (as Mexico City residents are sometimes known) with high-end French classics. The roasted leg of pork with béarnaise sauce is the signature dish; the green-apple sorbet with Calvados is a delicate finish. The daily three-course set menu is $20 (Visa credit card payment only) and includes a glass of house wine; it's served at lunchtime on weekdays. ✉ *Campos Elíseos 218, Col. Polanco* ☎ *55/5327–7756 or 55/5327–7700* 🌐 *www.aupieddecochon.com.mx* *Reservations essential* 💳 *AE, DC, MC, V.*

$$$–$$$$ JAPANESE ✕ **Benkay.** The silk-clad staff includes a sake sommelier in this prestigious restaurant in the Hotel Nikko. *Kaiseki* is the specialty, a series of small, exquisite dishes. Prices are high, but you're getting the best Japanese food in the city. ✉ *Ground fl. of Nikko Hotel, Campos Elíseos 204, Col. Polanco* ☎ *55/5283–8700 Ext. 8600* 💳 *AE, DC, MC, V.*

$–$$$ ECLECTIC ✕ **Bistro Charlotte.** At lunch, regulars are greeted with hugs by Charlotte herself. The ever-changing menu is inspired, and could include anything from caramelized fig–and-Brie appetizers to bistro classics like coq au vin. By popular demand each Sunday the 11-table bistro offers a classic roast with Yorkshire pudding and horseradish sauce. Note that Charlotte closes at 6 PM to attend to her catering business, which serves visitors like Prince Charles. ✉ *Lope de Vega 341-A, Col. Polanco* ☎ *55/5250–4180* 💳 *DC, MC, V* ⏲ *Closed Sat. No dinner.*

$$$$ ARGENTINE ✕ **Cambalache.** This beef-lover's dream is popular with everyone from businessmen to young families. The low-ceiling, wood-beamed dining room is hung with nostalgic pictures of Buenos Aires. Everything is grilled, from the Argentine beef to the lamb to the whitefish in a mild chili sauce. Desserts are large and inventive—try the riff on an alfajor, a typical dulce de leche sandwich cookie. ✉ *Arquímedes 85, Col. Chapultepec Morales* ☎ *55/5280–2080 or 55/5282–2922* 💳 *AE, MC, V.*

$ MEXICAN ✕ **El Bajío.** Vivacious Carmen "Titita" Ramírez—a culinary expert who has been featured in various U.S. food magazines—attracts crowds of Mexican families and tourists to the Polanco offshoot of her famous restaurant. (The original is in the out-of-the-way, working-class neighborhood of Colonia Obrero Popular.) The labor-intensive 30-ingredient mole de Xico is a favorite; also excellent are *empanadas de plátano rellenos de frijol* (tortilla turnovers filled with bananas and beans) and crab tamales. The atmosphere is a little sleeker and more modern than the original, but still colorful and strewn with artwork. There's also a branch in the Parque Delta Shopping Center in Colonia Navarte just south of Colonia Roma. ✉ *Av. Alejandro Dumas 7, Col. Polanco* ☎ *55/5281–8245* 🌐 *www.carnitaselbajio.com.mx* 💳 *AE, MC, V.*

$$–$$$$ MEXICAN ✕ **Hacienda de los Morales.** Built in the 16th century to house a mulberry farm, this hacienda has been transformed into one of Mexico's most elegant dinner spots. The atmosphere outclasses even the food, which includes an excellent lime-crusted whitefish and standards like chiles en nogada. A violinist and pianist strike up sonatas in the back corner after 9 PM. Begin with a cocktail at the wood-and-brass tequila bar, and end with a stroll around the leafy courtyard. ✉ *Vázquez de Mella 525, Col. Del Bosque, in Polanco area* ☎ *55/5283–3054* 💳 *AE, DC, MC, V.*

$$$$ MEXICAN Fodor's Choice ★ ✕ **Izote.** Reservations here are much sought after, as cookbook author Patricia Quintana has won over celebrities and the rest of the capital with her sophisticated take on pre-Hispanic flavors. Keep an eye out for the unique fish entrées, such as shark fillet sautéed with chili,

onion, garlic, and epazote, then steamed in chicken stock and *pulque* (an Aztec-era liquor made from the maguey cactus). Tender lamb gets steamed as well, in maguey and banana leaves, after being quickly fried with chilies. Unique, delicious red mole (served with anything from shrimp to lamb shank) is consistently popular, as are the elegant tacos and tamales. ✉ *Av. Presidente Masaryk 513, at Socrates, Col. Polanco* ☎ *55/5280–1671* *Reservations essential* ▭ *AE, DC, MC, V.*

2

$$$ MEXICAN ★ ✕ **La Fonda del Recuerdo.** This popular fonda has made a name for itself with fish and seafood platters from Veracruz. Sharing their fame is the *torito,* a potent drink made from sugarcane liquor and tropical fruit juices. Every day, *jarocho* (Veracruz-style) and mariachi groups provide live entertainment. The music starts between 1 and 3 in the afternoon, and sometimes continues well into the evening. Between the torito and the music, this place is always full of good cheer. Colonia Veronica Anzures is northwest of the Zona Rosa and east of Polanco. ✉ *Bahía de las Palmas 37, at Valle de Todos Santos, Col. Veronica Anzures* ☎ *55/9112–7476 or 55/9112–7477* 🌐 *www.fondadelrecuerdo.com* ▭ *AE, MC, V.*

$$$–$$$$ MEXICAN Fodor'sChoice ★ ✕ **La Valentina.** The epitome of good taste in all things Mexican, La Valentina devotes itself to preserving and promoting traditional native cuisine. It avoids gimmicks with balanced dishes that are soft on the palate, yet fragrant, with blends of chilies, herbs, nuts, and flowers. Starters reflect specialties from across the country, from the Sinaloan Chilorio tacos to the famous *panuchos Yucatecos* (fried tortillas with Yucatán-style spiced chicken or pork). The place is hard to find, upstairs inside a mall between Calles Anatole France and La Fontaine. ✉ *Av. Presidente Masaryk 393, Col. Polanco* ☎ *55/5282–2812* ▭ *AE, MC, V.*

$$$ MEXICAN ✕ **Los Almendros.** If you can't make it to the Yucatán, try the peninsula's unusual food here. The habañero chilies, red onions, and other native Yucatecan ingredients are a delightful surprise for those not yet in the know. Traditional dishes like a refreshing lime soup share the menu with hard-to-pronounce Mayan cuisine like *cochinita pibíl*, an orange pork dish. Especially worth trying is the *pescado tikinxic*—whitefish in a mild red marinade of annatto seed and bitter-orange juice. ✉ *Campos Elíseos 164, Col. Polanco* ☎ *55/5531–6646* 🌐 *www.almendros.com.mx* ▭ *AE, MC, V.*

$–$$$ SPANISH ✕ **Loyola.** A Basque tour de force, the ample menu with unpronounceable but delicious items includes *kokotxas* (fish cheeks), tapas, black rice simmered in squid ink, oxtail, and many other regional delicacies. Great salads and wines are another welcome feature. Courteous service, stained glass, Basque coats of arms, and the cozy hum of conversation make this an excellent and authentic dining experience. A weekend buffet is $16. ✉ *Aristóteles 239, Col. Polanco* ☎ *55/5250–6756 or 55/5250–9097* ▭ *AE, MC, V* ⊙ *No dinner.*

$$$–$$$$ ARGENTINE ✕ **Rincón Argentino.** This established Argentine restaurant is known as much for its interior design as for its exquisite cuts of beef. The ceiling is painted to resemble the sky, the bar is covered by a thatch roof, and the dining areas call to mind a stone-and-wood lodge. Despite the faintly kitschy atmosphere, Rincón has one of the best steaks in town. ✉ *Av. Presidente Masaryk 177, Col. Polanco* ☎ *55/5254–8775* 🌐 *www.rinconargentino.com.mx* ▭ *AE, MC, V.*

$$$ THAI ✕ **Thai Gardens.** This is the best—indeed, the only—place for upscale Thai food. The atmosphere is calming, with Eastern art objects and a lovely indoor garden. Options are mostly limited to standbys like tofu in a green curry or pad thai rice noodles with peanut sauce. If you want to sample a little bit of everything, order the generous *menú de degustación*, which includes six appetizers, six entrées, and dessert. ✉ *Calderón de la Barca 72, between Emilio Castelar and Av. Presidente Masaryk, Col. Polanco Chapultepec* ☎ *55/5281–3850* ▭ *AE, DC, MC, V.*

LA CONDESA AND LA ROMA

$–$$$ GREEK ✕ **Agapi Mu.** Rambunctious Greek song and dance enliven this small, friendly bistro Thursday through Saturday nights. Tucked away in a cozy room of a converted home, you'll hum along as you tear into traditional dishes like *tiropitákia* (meat, cheese, and olive pastries), *kalamárea* (fried Greek-style squid), and *musaka* (lamb-and-eggplant lasagna). ✉ *Alfonso Reyes 96, between Cuatla and Cuernavaca, Col. Condesa* ☎ *55/5286–1384* 🌐 *www.agapimu.com.mx* ▭ *AE, MC, V.*

$$$–$$$$ ECLECTIC ✕ **Bellini.** Revolving slowly on the 45th floor of the World Trade Center, Bellini maintains a formal, reserved character. It's known less for the food than for the views: romantically twinkling city lights at night and a pair of volcanoes on a clear day. Despite the name, most dishes here aren't Italian but rather Mexican and international, with lobster as the specialty. For a real night out on the town, order the Canadian lobster in coriander sauce for $50 a pop. Finish in style with strawberries jubilee or crêpes suzette. Colonia Nápoles is a lovely residential neighborhood south of La Condesa and La Roma—you'll need to take a sitio (taxi stand or radio taxi) here. Monday through Saturday, the restaurant opens, oddly enough, at 1 PM—a little late for lunch. That said, it stays open till 11 PM. Sunday sees brunch from 9 AM to 2 PM; the closing time remains the same. ✉ *Montecito 38, 45th fl., Torre WTC (World Trade Center), Col. Nápoles* ☎ *55/9000–8305* 🌐 *www.bellini.com.mx* ▭ *AE, DC, MC, V.*

$–$$$ FRENCH Fodor's Choice ★ ✕ **Bistrot Mosaico.** This French-inflected local favorite serves as a second living room to a relaxed Condesa crowd. You may have to wait for a table on weekends, but one look at the handwritten chalkboard menu, and you'll be hooked. The salad of the day is always a good bet, as are quiche with fillings ranging from bacon to spinach to leek. ✉ *Av. Michoacán 10, between Avs. Amsterdam and Insurgentes, Col. Condesa* ☎ *55/5584–2932* ▭ *AE, MC, V* ⏲ *No dinner Sun.*

$$$ MEXICAN Fodor's Choice ★ ✕ **El Hidalguense.** This restaurant has mastered the art of preparing Hidalgo-style *barbacoa* (tender mutton slow-cooked over mesquite). The family has been in the barbacoa biz for nearly four decades; its Mexico City restaurant has been going strong for 15 years. Most people order the barbacoa tacos and the consommé, flavored with mutton drippings. Wash it all down with a potent glass of *pulque* (the fresh, pre-tequila, semi-fermented mulch from the heart of the agave plant). ✉ *Campeche 155, Col. Roma* ☎ *55/5564–0538* ▭ *No credit cards* ⏲ *Closed Mon.–Thurs. No dinner.*

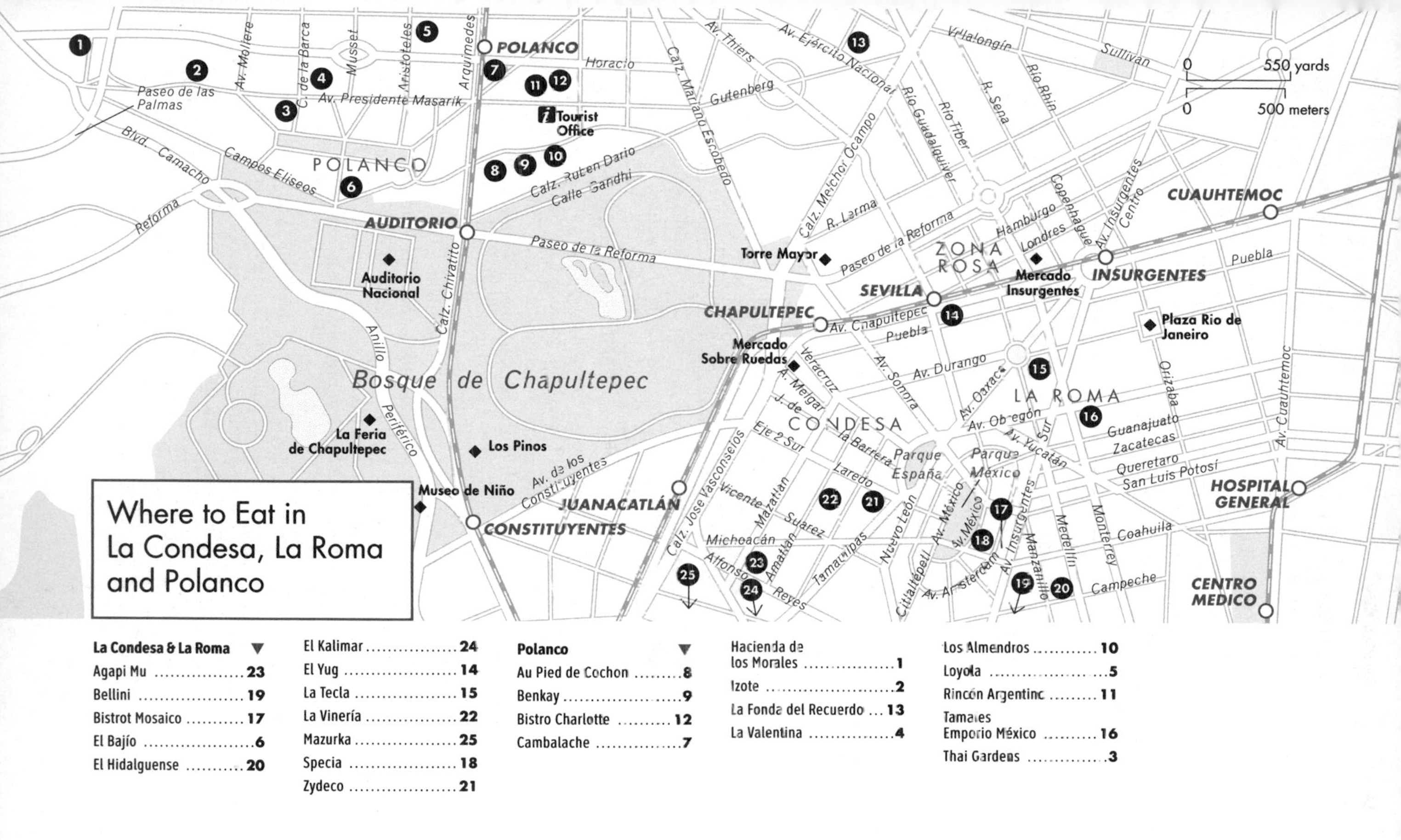

Where to Eat in
La Condesa, La Roma
and Polanco
La Condesa & La Roma ▼
Agapi Mu 23
Bellini 19
Bistrot Mosaico 17
El Bajío 6
El Hidalguense 20
El Kalimar 24
El Yug 14
La Tecla 15
La Vinería 22
Mazurka 25
Specia 18
Zydeco 21
Polanco ▼
Au Pied de Cochon 8
Benkay 9
Bistro Charlotte 12
Cambalache 7
Hacienda de los Morales 1
Izote 2
La Fonda del Recuerdo ...13
La Valentina 4
Los Almendros 10
Loyola 5
Rincón Argentino 11
Tamales Emporio México 16
Thai Gardens 3
0 550 yards
0 500 meters
POLANCO
AUDITORIO
Auditorio Nacional
Bosque de Chapultepec
La Feria de Chapultepec
Los Pinos
Museo de Niño
CONSTITUYENTES
JUANACATLÁN
CHAPULTEPEC
Mercado Sobre Ruedas
Torre Mayor
SEVILLA
ZONA ROSA
Mercado Insurgentes
INSURGENTES
CUAUHTEMOC
Plaza Rio de Janeiro
LA ROMA
CONDESA
Parque España
Parque México
HOSPITAL GENERAL
CENTRO MEDICO
Tourist Office
Paseo de la Reforma
Av. Presidente Masaryk
Paseo de las Palmas
Blvd. Camacho
Campos Eliseos
Av. Moliere
Musset
Aristoteles
Arquimedes
Horacio
Calz. Ruben Dario
Calle Gandhi
Calz. Chivatito
Anillo Periférico
Av. de los Constituyentes
Calz. Mariano Escobedo
Gutenberg
Av. Thiers
Av. Ejército Nacional
Calz. Melchor Ocampo
Río Guadalquivir
Río Tiber
R. Sena
Río Rhin
Villalongín
Sullivan
Av. Insurgentes Centro
Copenhague
Hamburgo
Londres
Puebla
Av. Chapultepec
Av. Durango
Av. Sonora
Av. Oaxaca
Av. Obregón
Av. Yucatán
Av. Cuauhtemoc
Orizaba
Guanajuato
Zacatecas
Queretaro
San Luis Potosí
Coahuila
Campeche
Monterrey
Medellín
Manzanillo
Av. Insurgentes Sur
Av. México
Av. Amsterdam
Citlaltépetl
Nuevo León
Tamaulipas
Amatlán
Mazatlán
Suarez
Vicente
Michoacán
Alfonso Reyes
Laredo
la Barrera
Eje 2 Sur
J. de
A. Melgar
Veracruz
Calz. Jose Vasconselos
Reforma

¢–$ MEXICAN ✕ **El Kaliman.** This no-frills taqueria provides the neighborhood's best taco bang for the buck. Specialties are tacos *al pastor,* adobo-soaked pork sliced from the spit and served on fresh tortillas with onion and cilantro. Try your taco "gringa style," with melted cheese, cilantro, and warm pineapple. Open late into the morning, exactly when you might need a taco. ✉ *Campeche 375, at Ensenada, Col. Condesa* ☎ *No phone* ▭ *AE, MC, V.*

$ VEGETARIAN ✕ **El Yug.** It's one of the few fully vegetarian restaurants in Mexico City. Homemade soups and main courses—from veggie burgers to chiles rellenos—come with whole-grain bread. The lunch buffet is only $4.50. Yug's sister restaurant in the Zona Rosa is open daily for breakfast, lunch, and dinner. Don't be fooled by the Roma address—the entrance is actually three doors down and around the corner on Calle Cozumel. ✉ *Puebla 326-6, Col. Roma* ☎ *55/5553–3872* ✉ *Varsovia 3-B, at Paseo de la Reforma, Zona Rosa* ☎ *55/5525–5330* ▭ *AE, DC, MC, V.*

$$–$$$ MEXICAN ★ ✕ **La Tecla.** This see-and-be-seen eatery, with branches in two of the hippest neighborhoods, is a popular veteran of Mexico City's *nueva cocina mexicana* scene. The appetizers are especially intriguing, including squash flowers stuffed with goat cheese in a chipotle sauce, and steak smothered in a sauce of *huitlacoche*—a corn fungus nicknamed the "Aztec truffle." ✉ *Av. Durango 186A, Col. Roma* ☎ *55/5525–4920* ✉ *Av. Moliere 56, Col. Polanco* ☎ *55/5282–0010* ▭ *AE, MC, V* ⊙ *No dinner Sun.*

$$$$ CONTEMPORARY ★ ✕ **La Vinería.** A welcome, grown-up addition to La Condesa, this cozy restaurant and wine bar is ideal for a private conversation and a light meal. Try the delicious *hojaldre con hongos* (mushroom pastry) or salmon in mango curry. Then indulge in a Chablis or a tasty strudel. ✉ *Av. Fernando Montes de Oca 52-A, at Amatlán, Col. Condesa* ☎ *55/5211–9020* ▭ *AE, MC, V* ⊙ *Closed Sun.*

$$–$$$ POLISH ★ ✕ **Mazurka.** The glowing reputation of this Polish restaurant shone even brighter after people got word that the establishment had served Pope John Paul II on several of his visits to Mexico City. Settle in with starters of blini with herring paste and cucumber, dill, and cream salad, as Chopin's polonaises trill in the background. The star of the menu is a crispy, oven-baked duck stuffed with bitter apple and blueberries. Or try the roasted pork with plums and applesauce. The generous Degustación del Papa (Pope's Menu) includes small portions of various entrées served to the pope and is only $21. Colonia Nápoles is south of La Condesa and La Roma, so the best bet is to take a sitio taxi. ✉ *Nueva York 150, between Calles Texas and Oklahoma, Col. Nápoles* ☎ *55/5543–4509 or 55/5523–8811* 🌐 *www.restaurantemazurka.com* ▭ *AE* ⊙ *No dinner Sun. and Mon.*

$$$–$$$$ POLISH Fodor's Choice ★ ✕ **Specia.** One taste of Specia's famous duck, and you'll think you've died and gone to heaven—the *pato tin* is a generous portion of roasted duck with an apple-based stuffing, mashed potatoes, and a baked apple bathed in blueberry sauce. Another crowd-pleaser is the mutton goulash, seasoned with paprika and tomato. At lunchtime (between 3 and 5), you'll probably have to wait for a table if you haven't made a reservation. ✉ *Amsterdam 241, at Michoacán, Col. Condesa* ☎ *55/5564–1367* ▭ *AE, MC, V.*

CLOSE UP

Cuisine Old and New

The capital may be able to sate your cravings for blini or sushi, but some of the most intriguing dining experiences stem from Mexican chefs looking forward—or far backward. Some newcomers on the restaurant scene are experimenting with established Mexican favorites; others are bringing ancient dishes out of the archives and onto the table.

Until the 15th century, Europeans had never seen indigenous Mexican edibles such as corn, chilies of all varieties, tomatoes, potatoes, pumpkin, squash, avocado, turkey, cocoa, and vanilla. In turn, the colonization brought European gastronomic influence and ingredients—wheat, onions, garlic, olives, citrus fruit, cattle, sheep, goats, chickens, domesticated pigs (and lard for frying)—and ended up broadening the already complex pre-Hispanic cuisine into one of the most multifaceted and exquisite in the world. Thus was traditional Mexican food born.

The last two decades have seen the evolution of the so-called *nueva cocina mexicana* (nouvelle Mexican cuisine) from a trend to an established and respected restaurant genre. The style emphasizes presentation and intriguing combinations of traditional ingredients with contemporary techniques. In the more serious or purist restaurants that aim to rescue recipes from the pre-Hispanic past, you can enjoy the delicate tastes of regional dishes gleaned from colonial documents and diaries, and indigenous cooking techniques such as steaming and baking. And, irrespective of fashion, market eateries sell pre-Hispanic seasonal delicacies such as crunchy fried grasshoppers and fried maguey larva.

¢–$ MEXICAN ✕ **Tamales Emporio México.** If you like tamales, this is the place. This small restaurant with traditional wood furnishings and murals serves delicious tamales, made using recipes from all over the country. Tamales come in all forms: wrapped in corn husks or wrapped in banana leaves, filled with poblano chili and cheese or with chicken and green mole. The recipe from Chiapas is exceptional, and includes green olives, almonds, prunes, egg, red pepper, chicken, and mole. These tamales are unusual in a city where the only options are often chicken with red or green salsa. Be sure to get in early, especially on weekends. The restaurant does sometimes run out of its most popular tamales, even early in the day, because tamales are a popular breakfast item. ✉ *Alvaro Obregón 154, Col. Roma* ☎ *55/5574–2078* 🌐 *www.tamales.com.mx* 🕙 *No dinner Sun.*

$–$$ CAJUN ✕ **Zydeco.** Don Bergeron, a Louisiana native and traveling chef for the state tourism office, developed the menu for Zydeco, making it a one-of-a-kind Cajun treat for Mexicans. Popular appetizers include Mississippi catfish strips and Creole crab cakes. Next up is gumbo or the pecan-crusted fish with shrimp étouffée. Live zydeco, blues, and rock acts play on Tuesday and Wednesday nights. ✉ *Tamaulipas 30, at Juan Escutia, Condesa* ☎ *55/5553–3329* 💳 *AE, DC, MC, V.*

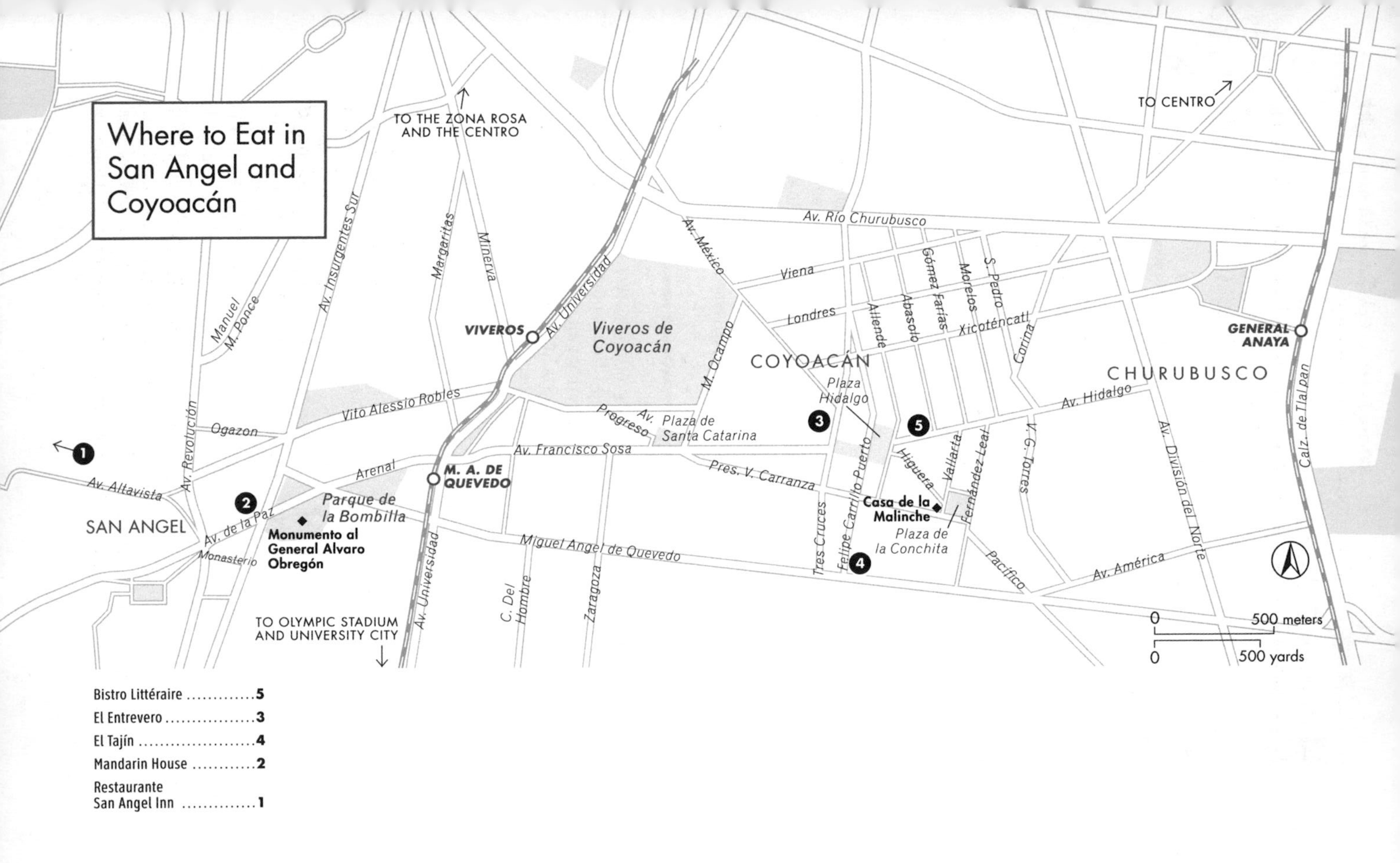
Where to Eat in San Angel and Coyoacán
TO THE ZONA ROSA AND THE CENTRO
TO CENTRO
Av. Río Churubusco
Av. México
Viena
Londres
Allende
Abasolo
Gómez Farías
Morelos
S. Pedro
Xicoténcatl
Corina
GENERAL ANAYA
CHURUBUSCO
COYOACÁN
Plaza Hidalgo
Av. Hidalgo
Calz. de Tlalpan
VIVEROS
Av. Universidad
Viveros de Coyoacán
M. Ocampo
Manuel M. Ponce
Av. Insurgentes Sur
Margaritas
Minerva
Vito Alessio Robles
Ogazon
Av. Revolución
Av. Plaza de Santa Catarina
Progreso
Av. Francisco Sosa
Pres. V. Carranza
Higuera
Vallarta
Fernández Leal
V. G. Torres
Av. División del Norte
M. A. DE QUEVEDO
Arenal
Av. Altavista
SAN ANGEL
Parque de la Bombilla
Av. de la Paz
Monasterio
Monumento al General Alvaro Obregón
Miguel Angel de Quevedo
Tres Cruces
Felipe Carrillo Puerto
Casa de la Malinche
Plaza de la Conchita
Pacífico
Av. América
C. Del Hombre
Zaragoza
TO OLYMPIC STADIUM AND UNIVERSITY CITY
0
500 meters
500 yards
Bistro Littéraire 5
El Entrevero 3
El Tajín 4
Mandarin House 2
Restaurante San Angel Inn 1

SAN ANGEL AND COYOACÁN

$$–$$$ FRENCH ★ **Bistro Littéraire.** At the far end of the French bookshop La Bouquinerie, this gem is clearly run for love, not profit. You can expect reasonable prices on both wine and food, including such dishes as aromatic escargots, couscous for two, duck confit, or *moules marinières* (mussels marinated in white wine). Unfortunately, you can also expect slow service. *Camino al Desierto de los Leones 40, Prolongación Altavista, between Avs. Insurgentes and Revolución, San Angel 55/5616–6066 AE, MC, V No dinner weekends.*

$–$$$ ARGENTINE **El Entrevero.** A Uruguayan may own this friendly eatery on the square of Coyoacán, but the menu is all about Argentine standards—the scrumptious *provoleta* (grilled provolone cheese with oregano) among them. Uruguay's Italian heritage appears on the menu as well, with excellent pizzas and gnocchi. The *crema quemada* (a version of crème brûlée) is sinful. Fair prices and a location right in the heart of Coyoacán guarantee that this place is always busy, so arrive early on weekends. *Jardín Centenario 14-C, Col. Coyoacán 55/5659–0066 AE, MC, V.*

$–$$ MEXICAN **El Tajín.** Named after El Tajín pyramid in Veracruz, this elegant lunch spot sizzles with pre-Hispanic influences. Innovative appetizers include *chilpachole,* a delicate crab-and-chili soup with epazote, while main dishes could include octopus cooked in its own ink. Prices are quite moderate for this caliber of cooking, and there's an impressive wine list to boot. Spacious and relaxing, with a garden for children to play in, the place has an excellent vibe. Ancient Huastecan faces grinning from a splashing fountain add a bit of levity to the dining experience. *Centro Cultural Veracruzano, Miguel Angel de Quevedo 687, Coyoacán 55/5659–4447 or 55/5659–5759 AE, MC, V No dinner.*

$$$ CHINESE **Mandarin House.** Standing proudly at the head of the eateries that line San Angel's cobbled Avenida de la Paz, this spacious restaurant cooks up predominantly Mandarin cuisine. The chef's specialties include Peking duck and pollo mo su (chicken with bamboo, cabbage, mushroom, and hoisin sauce). Though there's no strict dress code, you may feel comfortable in more formal dress. *Av. de la Paz 57, San Angel 55/5616–4410 or 55/5616–4434 AE, MC, V No dinner Sun.*

$$$$ MEXICAN ★ **Restaurante San Angel Inn.** Dark mahogany furniture, crisp white table linens, exquisite blue-and-white Talavera place settings, and impeccable service strike a note of restrained opulence. Start with the gazpacho, chilled on a bed of ice, and the warm bacon and spinach salad. Move on to the spicy *puntas de filete* (sirloin tips). The dessert tray, which displays everything from rich chocolate cake to creamy meringue, is a don't-miss. *Calle Diego Rivera 50, at Av. Altavista, San Angel 55/5616–0537 or 55/5616–2222 AE, DC, MC, V.*

WHERE TO STAY

Updated by Laura Mestre

Although the city is huge and spread out, most hotels are clustered in a few neighborhoods. Colonia Polanco has a generous handful of business-oriented hotels; these tend to be familiar major chains. The Zona Rosa has plenty of big, contemporary properties; it's handy to have restaurants and other services right outside the door. The pleasant tourist areas of La Roma, Coyoacán, and San Angel are still poorly furnished with accommodations, but La Condesa is a growing hot spot for notable hotels.

Business travelers tend to fill up deluxe hotels during the week; some major hotels discount their weekend rates. Many smaller properties have taken the cue and give similarly reduced rates as well. If you reserve through the toll-free reservation numbers, you may find rates as much as 50% off during special promotions.

CENTRO HISTÓRICO

$$–$$$ **Best Western Majestic Hotel.** If you're interested in exploring the historic downtown, the atmospheric, colonial-style Majestic will give you a perfect location. It's also ideal for viewing the Independence Day (September 16) celebrations, for which many people reserve a room a year in advance. Rooms have heavy wooden furniture. There is also a restaurant on the top floor with a wonderful view of the Zócalo. **Pros:** restaurant serves all kinds of well-prepared Mexican and international food, and it's hard to beat its classic tacos. **Cons:** although the front units have balconies and a delightful view, they can be noisy with car traffic until about 11 PM. ✉ *Av. Madero 73, Col. Centro* ☎ *55/5521–8600, 800/528–1234 toll-free in U.S.* 🌐 *www.majestichotel.com.mx* *80 rooms, 5 suites* *In-room: safe, Wi-Fi. In-hotel: restaurant, bar, laundry service* 💳 *AE, MC, V.*

$$ **Gran Hotel de la Ciudad de México.** Ensconced in a former 19th-century department store, this freshly renovated hotel has rooms furnished in a modern style. Its distinctive belle epoque lobby—with a striking Parisian stained-glass dome from Jacque Graber's workshop, chandeliers, gilded birdcages, and 19th-century wrought-iron elevators—is worth a visit in its own right. The Terrace breakfast restaurant overlooks the Zócalo. **Pros:** the Restaurant Plaza Mayor restaurant-bar, with some windows facing the Zócalo, is one of Mexico City's best. **Cons:** hotel often holds parties in lobby; staff can be unhelpful. ✉ *Av. 16 de Septiembre 82, at 5 de Febrero, Col. Centro* ☎ *55/1083–7700* 🌐 *www.granhotelciudaddemexico.com.mx* *60 rooms* *In-room: safe, Internet (some). In-hotel: 3 restaurants, room service, bar, gym, parking (paid)* 💳 *AE, MC, V.*

$$$ **Hilton Mexico City Reforma.** The abstract red-and-blue mural in the lobby and cantilevered gray facade add a dramatic flourish to this hotel in the historic center. Geared to conventions, everything is oversize here, from the lobby to the five food-and-beverage outlets. Plush Italian furniture, gray-green carpeting, and Spanish marble are features of the guest rooms, which come in one of four different color schemes: vanilla, gray, wine, or blue. Rooms and hallways all display old photos of the Centro Histórico. **Pros:** suites with a kichenette and dining area are available for long-term stays; walking distance to several sights. **Cons:** additional charge for Internet. ✉ *Av. Juarez 70, Col. Centro* ☎ *55/5130–5300* 🌐 *www.hiltonmexicocity.com* *458 rooms, 36 suites* *In-room: safe, Wi-Fi. In-hotel: 3 restaurants, bar, pool, gym, spa, parking (paid)* 💳 *AE, DC, MC, V.*

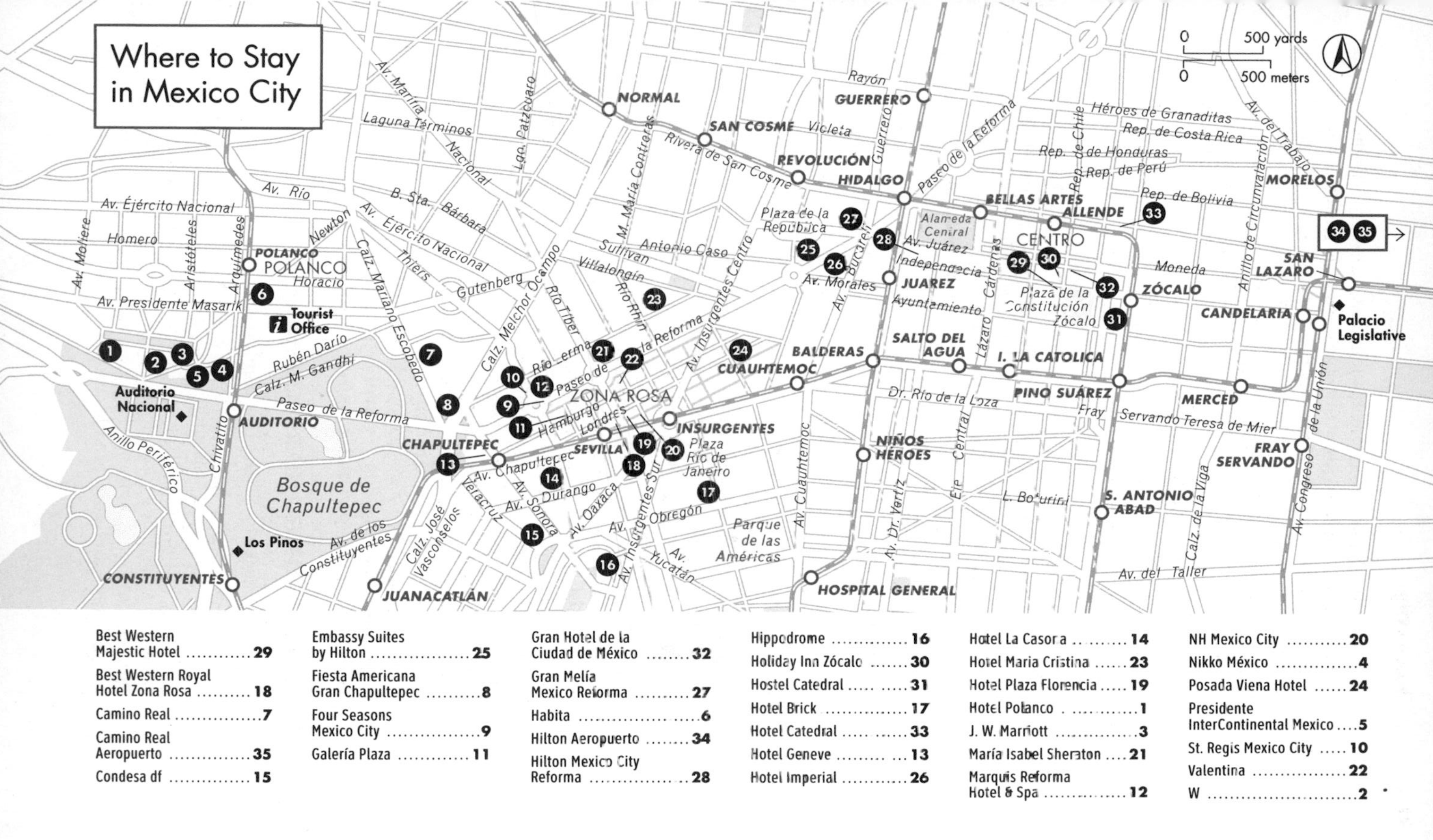

Where to Stay in Mexico City
0 500 yards
0 500 meters
NORMAL
SAN COSME
REVOLUCIÓN
HIDALGO
GUERRERO
BELLAS ARTES
ALLENDE
MORELOS
SAN LAZARO
CANDELARIA
ZÓCALO
CENTRO
JUAREZ
BALDERAS
SALTO DEL AGUA
I. LA CATOLICA
PINO SUÁREZ
MERCED
FRAY SERVANDO
S. ANTONIO ABAD
NIÑOS HEROES
HOSPITAL GENERAL
CUAUHTEMOC
INSURGENTES
SEVILLA
ZONA ROSA
CHAPULTEPEC
JUANACATLÁN
CONSTITUYENTES
AUDITORIO
POLANCO
Auditorio Nacional
Tourist Office
Los Pinos
Bosque de Chapultepec
Palacio Legislative
Alameda Central
Plaza de la República
Plaza de la Constitución Zócalo
Plaza Río de Janeiro
Parque de las Américas
Paseo de la Reforma
Av. Insurgentes Sur
Av. Chapultepec
Anillo Periférico
Anillo de Circunvalación
Best Western Majestic Hotel ... 29
Best Western Royal Hotel Zona Rosa ... 18
Camino Real ... 7
Camino Real Aeropuerto ... 35
Condesa df ... 15
Embassy Suites by Hilton ... 25
Fiesta Americana Gran Chapultepec ... 8
Four Seasons Mexico City ... 9
Galería Plaza ... 11
Gran Hotel de la Ciudad de México ... 32
Gran Meliá Mexico Reforma ... 27
Habita ... 6
Hilton Aeropuerto ... 34
Hilton Mexico City Reforma ... 28
Hippodrome ... 16
Holiday Inn Zócalo ... 30
Hostel Catedral ... 31
Hotel Brick ... 17
Hotel Catedral ... 33
Hotel Geneve ... 13
Hotel Imperial ... 26
Hotel La Casona ... 14
Hotel Maria Cristina ... 23
Hotel Plaza Florencia ... 19
Hotel Polanco ... 1
J. W. Marriott ... 3
María Isabel Sheraton ... 21
Marquis Reforma Hotel & Spa ... 12
NH Mexico City ... 20
Nikko México ... 4
Posada Viena Hotel ... 24
Presidente InterContinental Mexico ... 5
St. Regis Mexico City ... 10
Valentina ... 22
W ... 2

$$ ★ **Holiday Inn Zócalo.** This hotel couldn't have a better location—on the Zócalo and close to a gaggle of museums, restaurants, and historic buildings. You'd expect nothing less than to be in the heart of the colonial city, given that one wing of the building was once the home of Hernán Cortés. Rooms have wooden floors, wrought-iron or chunky wooden headboards, crisp white spreads, touches of red upholstery. Flat-screen TVs and pillow menus are nice touches, too. There's some atmosphere to the terrace restaurant, which has slate floors, old-fashioned wrought-iron tables, and an amazing view of the Catedral Metropolitana and Palacio Nacional. **Pros:** the location is phenomenal; really good value for the money. **Cons:** corridors are dark and narrow; public areas are very dated; food is so-so at best. *Av. 5 de Mayo 61, at Zócalo, Col. Centro 55/5130–5130 www.hotelescortes.com 105 rooms, 5 suites In-room: safe, Wi-Fi. In-hotel: restaurant, room service, bar, gym, Internet terminal, parking (paid) AE, MC, V.*

¢ **Hostel Catedral.** In the heart of downtown Mexico City, just behind the Catedral Metropolitana, this large hostel provides sunny, clean, and comfortable rooms at rock-bottom prices. The café in the entryway, which serves inexpensive pastas, sandwiches, and salads, is a great place to swap stories with fellow travelers (mostly young vacationers on a budget). The kitchen, sunroof, and TV room are also natural places to strike up a conversation. If you're on a tight budget, ask about the shared rooms. Also be sure to ask about tours and other classes available at the hostel. There are often weekly excursions and dance classes. **Pros:** central location. **Cons:** very few room amenities. *República de Guatemala 4, Col. Centro 55/5518–1726 www.hostelcatedral.com 42 rooms and dormitories In-room: no a/c, no phone, no TV. In-hotel: restaurant, laundry facilities, Internet terminal MC, V. BP.*

¢–$ ★ **Hotel Catedral.** This refurbished older hotel on a busy street in the heart of downtown is a bargain, with many of the amenities of the more upscale hotels at less than half the price. Public areas sparkle with marble and glass. Guest rooms are spacious and clean, if a little generic. You can get a room with a view of the namesake Catedral. If your room doesn't have a view, the small terrace is a great place to watch the sun set over the Zócalo. **Pros:** El Retiro bar attracts a largely Mexican clientele to hear live Latin music. **Cons:** the Catedral's bells chime every 15 minutes late into the night. *Donceles 95, Col. Centro 55/5518–5232 or 55/5521–6183 www.hotelcatedral.com 108 rooms, 8 suites In-hotel: restaurant, room service, bar, laundry service, Internet terminal, parking (free) AE, MC, V.*

MIDTOWN AND ALONG THE REFORMA

$$$ **Embassy Suites by Hilton.** This comfortable hotel right in the middle of Reforma Avenue action is perfectly located to get just about anywhere in the city fast. It is within walking distance of the Zona Rosa, and close to the Monumento a la Revolución. Both the monument (which fills up with politicians and union workers during work hours on weekdays) and Reforma surround the hotel with activity. Rooms are spacious and comfortable, furnished with queen- or king-sized

beds, marble bathrooms, and flat-screen TVs. **Pros:** there are also evening receptions with snacks and drinks, where guests can swap stories about the sights; prices are lower on weekends. **Cons:** many agree that taxis, when booked through this hotel, are much more expensive than they otherwise would be. ✉ *Paseo de la Reforma 69, Col. Tabacalera* ☎ *55/5061–3000, 01800/800–6868 toll-free in Mexico* 🌐 *www.embassysuitesmexicocity.com* *160 suites* *In-room: safe, Wi-Fi. In-hotel: restaurant, bar, pool, gym* *AE, DC, MC, V* *BP.*

2

$$$$ Fodor'sChoice ★ **Four Seasons Mexico City.** Among the most luxurious hotels in the capital, this eight-story hotel was modeled after the 18th-century Iturbide Palace—it even has a traditional inner courtyard with a fountain. Half the rooms overlook this courtyard. The rest of the hotel doesn't disappoint: rooms are adorned with palettes of light yellow, peach, and soft green, and the business center is very complete. The well-stocked tequila bar off the garden is a perfect predinner option. **Pros:** excellent cultural tours of the city are available. **Cons:** all amenities are (as expected) expensive. ✉ *Paseo de la Reforma 500, Col. Juárez* ☎ *55/5230–1818, 01800/906–7500 toll-free in Mexico* 🌐 *www.fourseasons.com/mexico* *200 rooms, 40 suites* *In-room: Wi-Fi. In-hotel: 2 restaurants, bar, pool, gym, laundry service, Wi-Fi hotspot* *AE, DC, MC, V.*

$$–$$$ **Gran Melía Mexico Reforma.** Convenient to downtown, the Stock Exchange, and the Zona Rosa, this gorgeous, if a little over-the-top, 22-floor smoked-glass behemoth answers the call of business travelers looking for location, well-appointed rooms, and high-tech business services. The lobby is certainly a great meeting place, with a brass-domed lounge, snug little corners for tête-à-têtes, and a glossy, dove-gray marble floor. Guest rooms are large, with soft blue and auburn colors, oversize TVs, and comfortable sitting areas; the executive floor features butler service. There's also a full-service spa (the largest such spa in a Mexico City hotel). **Pros:** large guest rooms; friendly staff. **Cons:** time for a refurbishment. ✉ *Reforma 1, Col. Tabacalera* ☎ *55/5063–1000* 🌐 *www.solmelia.com* *454 rooms, 35 suites* *In-room: safe, Internet (some). In-hotel: 2 restaurants, bar, gym, spa, Wi-Fi hotspot, laundry service* *AE, DC, MC, V.*

$ **Hotel Imperial.** Suiting its name, this hotel occupies a stately late-19th-century, clean, white building with a corner cupola right on the Reforma alongside the Columbus Monument. The hotel's Restaurant Gaudí serves continental cuisine with some classic Spanish selections. **Pros:** quiet elegance and personal service are keynotes of this privately owned property. **Cons:** rooms aren't terribly impressive, though—the blue furnishings could use some updating. ✉ *Paseo de la Reforma 64, Col. Juárez* ☎ *55/5705–4911* 🌐 *www.hotelimperial.com.mx* *50 rooms, 10 junior suites, 5 master suites* *In-room: safe, Internet (some). In-hotel: 2 restaurants, bar, laundry service, Internet terminal, parking (free)* *AE, MC, V.*

$ ★ **Hotel María Cristina.** This Spanish colonial–style gem is a Mexico City classic. Impeccably maintained since it was built in 1937, the building surrounds a delightful garden courtyard—the backdrop for its El Retiro bar. Three apartment-style master suites come complete with hot tubs. In a quiet residential neighborhood near Parque Sullivan, the hotel is close to the Zona Rosa. **Pros:** all in all you get a lot for your money here. **Cons:** the rooms aren't that exciting. ✉ *Río Lerma 31, Col. Cuauhtémoc* ☎ *55/5703–1212 or 55/5566–9688* 🌐 *www.hotelmariacristina.com.mx* *142 rooms, 8 suites* *In-room: no a/c (some), safe, Wi-Fi (some). In-hotel: restaurant, room service, bar, parking (free)* ▭ *AE, MC, V.*

$$$–$$$$ **María Isabel Sheraton.** Don Antenor Patiño, the Bolivian "Tin King," inaugurated this Mexico City classic in 1969, and named it after his granddaughter, socialite Isabel Goldsmith. The stunning marble lobby has gleaming brass fixtures. All guest and public rooms are impeccably maintained; the former have extra-comfy Posturepedic mattresses and goose-down pillows. Penthouse suites in the 22-story tower are extra spacious and have butler service. **Pros:** the location—across from the Angel Monument and the Zona Rosa, with Sanborns next door and the U.S. Embassy a half-block away—is prime. **Cons:** some areas need some TLC; unexpected charges. ✉ *Paseo de la Reforma 325, Col. Cuauhtémoc* ☎ *55/5242–5555* 🌐 *www.sheraton.com* *683 rooms, 72 suites* *In-room: safe, Wi-Fi. In-hotel: 3 restaurants, room service, bars, pool, tennis courts, gym, spa, laundry service, parking (paid)* ▭ *AE, DC, MC, V.*

$$$$ Fodor's Choice ★ **Marquis Reforma Hotel & Spa.** This plush, privately owned member of the Leading Hotels of the World is within walking distance of the Zona Rosa. Its striking art nouveau facade combines pink stone and curved glass. The lobby is filled with an eclectic sculpture collection selected by the owners. Rooms and suites are spacious, but dated. A floor-by-floor refresh is underway that will take guest quarters away from art deco and toward midcentury modern. The pool and gym are in glass-enclosed atriums that make you feel as if you're outdoors. The most elegant and updated of spaces is the spa, which has an extensive menu of massages, facials, and body/beauty treatments. **Pros:** spa; staff successfully blends white-glove service with personal warmth. **Cons:** lobby and rooms really do need updating; bar is a bit of a downer. ✉ *Paseo de la Reforma 465, Col. Cuauhtémoc* ☎ *55/5229–1200, 800/235–2387 toll-free in U.S.* 🌐 *www.marquisreforma.com* *125 rooms, 83 suites* *In-room: safe, Wi-Fi. In-hotel: 2 restaurants, room service, bar, pool, gym, spa, Wi-Fi hotspot* ▭ *AE, MC, V.*

$$$–$$$$ Fodor's Choice ★ **St. Regis Mexico City.** The intimate layout and bespoke service provide the ultimate sanctuary from urban chaos—despite being in one of the busiest sections of the city and in one of the tallest towers. A compellation of work by world-renowned architects, interior designers, and artists, the hotel is a stunning representation of modern elegance. The well-appointed rooms all have superb views of the city, personal butler service, and double-paned windows which eliminate almost all external noise. A cocktail on the palm tree–lined terrace of the King Cole Bar is a great way to wrap up a business meeting or relax after a day of sightseeing. At this writing, plans for a Jean-Georges Vongerichten restaurant, JG Steakhouse, are in the works. Pros: world-class spa and fitness center. Cons: almost too quiet in public areas. ✉ *Paseo de la Reforma 439, Col. Cuauhtémoc* ☎ *55/5228–1818* 🌐 *www.starwoodhotels.com/stregis* *189 rooms, 35 suites* *In-room: safe, Wi-Fi. In-hotel: restaurant, room service, bar, gym, spa, pool, laundry service, parking (paid)* ▭ *AE, MC, V.*

ZONA ROSA AND JUÁREZ

$$ **Best Western Royal Hotel Zona Rosa.** The immaculate marble lobby of the modern Royal Hotel, beloved by travelers from Spain, is filled with plants and the exuberant conversation of its guests. Spacious rooms have large bathrooms, well-equipped work areas, and interactive TV. Its Spanish restaurant, Tezka, was founded by award-winning chef Arzac, and is known for its extraordinary Basque cuisine. **Pros:** nice views if you're on one of the top floors. **Cons:** it's a Best Western property, which means that some things are more generic. ✉ *Amberes 78, Col. Juárez* ☎ *55/9149–3000* 🌐 *www.hotelroyalzr.com* *161 rooms, 1 suite* *In-room: safe, refrigerator, Wi-Fi. In-hotel: 2 restaurants, bar, gym, laundry service, parking (free)* *AE, MC, V.*

$$ **Galería Plaza.** Location gives this ultramodern hotel an edge; it's on a quiet street, but plenty of shops, restaurants, and nightspots are nearby. Service and facilities are faultless; advantages include a heated rooftop pool with sundeck, a secure underground parking lot, and a 24-hour restaurant. **Pros:** all rooms are fresh and bright, with small work areas. **Cons:** many conferences held here. ✉ *Hamburgo 195, at Varsovia, Col. Juárez* ☎ *55/5230–1717, 866/221–2961 toll-free in the U.S.* 🌐 *www.brisas.com.mx* *397 rooms, 37 suites* *In-room: safe, Wi-Fi. In-hotel: 2 restaurants, room service, bar, pool, gym, laundry service, parking (paid)* *AE, DC, MC, V.*

$$–$$$ **Hotel Geneve.** This five-story 1907 hotel, referred to locally as El Génova, has a pleasant lobby with traditional colonial-style carved-wood chairs and tables. Guest rooms are small but comfortable, with modern furnishings. The inviting Salón Jardín, part of the popular Sanborns restaurant chain, has art deco stained-glass flourishes. **Pros:** it's in the heart of the Zona Rosa. **Cons:** service and interior decoration are only so-so. ✉ *Londres 130, Col. Juárez* ☎ *55/5080–0800* 🌐 *www.hotelgeneve.com.mx* *208 rooms, 21 suites* *In-room: safe, Internet. In-hotel: 2 restaurants, room service, bar, gym, spa, laundry facilities, parking (free)* *AE, DC, MC, V.*

$$ **Hotel Plaza Florencia.** The lobby of this hotel may be weighted with heavy furniture and dark colors, but the rooms upstairs are bright, modern, and, most important, soundproofed against the traffic noise of the busy avenue below. Some large family suites are available. **Pros:** higher floors have views of the Angel Monument. **Cons:** a little dark and dated. ✉ *Florencia 61, Col. Juárez* ☎ *55/5242–4700, 01800/717–2983 toll-free in Mexico* 🌐 *www.plazaflorencia.com.mx* *134 rooms, 8 suites* *In-room: safe, Internet. In-hotel: restaurant, bar, gym, laundry service* *AE, DC, MC, V.*

$–$$ **NH Mexico City.** There's a stylish lobby cocktail lounge and a restaurant that serves excellent international cuisine. Rooms have business travelers in mind, with sober gray and green colors, Scandinavian-style furniture, and hardwood floors. **Pros:** the hotel is in the heart of Zona Rosa; has an excellent view of the neighborhood from the rooftop pool terrace. **Cons:** particularly business focused, so seems a little impersonal. ✉ *Liverpool 155, Col. Juárez* ☎ *55/5228–9928* 🌐 *www.nh-hotels.com* *267 rooms, 35 suites* *In-room: safe, Internet. In-hotel: restaurant,* *bar, pool, gym, laundry service, Wi-Fi hotspot, parking (paid)* ▭ *AE, DC, MC, V.*

$$ **Posada Viena Hotel**. Hidden away in a quiet spot three blocks from the hustle and bustle of the Zona Rosa, this hotel is convenient to restaurants, bars, and shops, but much more affordable than some of its more central counterparts. The rooms are fresh and clean, painted with slivers of bright purples, oranges, yellows, and blues. Suites, suitable for up to four people, are ideal for families. The Argentine restaurant hosts tango lessons on Saturday night and serves delicious steak dishes. **Pros:** the staff couldn't be nicer. **Cons:** elevator and hallways are a little musty. ✉ *Marsella 28, corner of Dinamarca, Col. Juárez* ☎ *55/5566–0700, 01800/849–8402 toll-free in Mexico* 🌐 *www.posadavienahotel.com* *66 rooms, 20 suites* *In-room: no a/c, Wi-Fi. In-hotel: 2 restaurants, room service, bar, laundry service, parking (free)* ▭ *AE, MC, V.*

$$$ ★ **Valentina**. The decor is minimalist and quirky: walls are awash with electric colors, the furniture is asymmetrical, the accents are futuristic. Flat-screen TVs and free Internet access in every room are nice touches. Suites on the top floor all have balconies with decent views. Pros: central location on popular cobblestone street. Cons: restaurant only serves breakfast; no bar. ✉ *Amberes 27, Col. Juárez* ☎ *55/5080–4500* 🌐 *www.room-matehotels.com* *59 rooms, 4 suites* *In-room: safe, Wi-Fi (free). In-hotel: restaurant, laundry service, gym, parking (paid)* ▭ *AE, DC, MC, V* *CP.*

POLANCO

$$$–$$$$ ★ **Camino Real**. About the size of Teotihuacán's Pyramid of the Sun, this sleek, low-slung, 8-acre megalith was designed by Mexico's modern master, Ricardo Legorreta. The whole place is one big sculpture punctuated by fountains, splashes of canary yellow and electric pink, and impressive artwork that includes Rufino Tamayo's mural *Man Facing Infinity* and a Calder sculpture. Rooms have gorgeous marble bathrooms; suites have Legoretta's signature bright yellow on one wall. The María Bonita restaurant puts a modern spin on the traditional cantina and is a great place for lunch. For dinner, consider Italian in the Bice Bistro or worldly Asian at the China Grill. Afterward, have a drink in the cool Blue Lounge, where one area is perched over water and has transparent floors. **Pros:** great architecture and art; terrific nightlife options. **Cons:** standard rooms are drab and dated; too large for some people's liking; draws many conferences. ✉ *Mariano Escobedo 700, Col. Anzures* ☎ *55/5263–8888* 🌐 *www.caminoreal.com* *667 rooms, 45 suites* *In-room: safe, Internet. In-hotel: 5 restaurants, bars, pools, gym, laundry service, parking (paid)* ▭ *AE, DC, MC, V.*

$$$ **Fiesta Americana Grand Chapultepec**. Sleek and contemporary, this stylish hotel stands opposite the Bosque de Chapultepec, close to the city's main shopping area, and five minutes from the Auditorio Nacional. Rooms are done in muted olives and browns. The spa, beauty salon, and barbershop guarantee that you will be presentable for the ultramodern Lobby Bar. **Pros:** rooms are angled to maximize views. **Cons:** many amenities cost extra. ✉ *Mariano Escobedo 756, Col. Anzures* ☎ *55/2581–1500* 🌐 *www.fiestaamericana.com* *189 rooms, 14 suites*

In-room: safe, Wi-Fi. In-hotel: restaurant, bar, gym, spa, laundry service, parking (paid) AE, MC, V.

$$$–$$$$ ★ **Habita.** Characterized by pale colors and a spalike mood, Mexico's first design hotel strikes a harmonious balance between style statements and minimalism. New Age music is piped into the rooms (you can turn it off), and bowls of limes sit by state-of-the-art TVs. Thursday to Saturday, the swanky rooftop bar attracts international celebs and chic chilangos to its open-air views, fireplace, and selection of mezcals. The Lobby Restaurant is a unique space with fantastic bistro-Mexican cuisine created by renowned chef Enrique Olvera. **Pros:** large rooms; nicely decorated; unique concept. **Cons:** hidden charges; some difference between rooms. *Av. Presidente Masaryk 201 Col. Polanco 55/5282–3100 www.hotelhabita.com 32 rooms, 4 junior suites In-room: safe, Wi-Fi. In-hotel: restaurant, bar, gym, spa, Wi-Fi hotspot, parking (free) AE, MC, V.*

$$ **Hotel Polanco.** This small favorite right off Polanco park, and not far from Chapultepec park, has many of the amenities of larger hotels, but at a much better price. Marble floors and dark-wood furniture accent the cozy lobby, which leads to five floors of tidy, carpeted rooms with cedar furnishings. **Pros:** a pleasant street-side restaurant serves out-of-the-ordinary Italian cuisine. **Cons:** rooms are tiny. *Edgar Allan Poe 8, Col. Polanco 55/5280–8082 www.hotelpolanco.com.mx 65 rooms, 6 junior suites In-room: safe, Wi-Fi. In-hotel: restaurant, room service, bar, gym, laundry service, Wi-Fi hotspot, parking (free) AE, MC, V.*

$$$$ **J.W. Marriott.** In keeping with its genteel neighborhood, this high-rise hotel has personalized service and small, clubby public areas; nothing overwhelms here. Rooms have plenty of wood and warm colors. The hotel has a well-equipped 24-hour business center and an ATM machine. **Pros:** tempting weekend rates for double rooms are around $269. **Cons:** rooms are unremarkably styled. *Andrés Bello 29, at Campos Elíseos, Col. Polanco 55/5999–0000 www.marriott.com 283 rooms, 29 suites In-room: safe, Wi-Fi. In-hotel: 2 restaurants, bar, pool, gym, spa, laundry service AE, MC, V.*

$$$–$$$$ **Nikko México.** Occupying a prime Polanco position adjacent to the Bosque de Chapultepec, this hotel is a five-minute walk from the anthropology museum. With signage and menus in Japanese, English, and Spanish, it caters especially to business travelers. It's the second-largest hotel in the city, and has marvelous views from the top-floor suites. The lobby is filled with paintings by important Mexican artists. There are also several small galleries in the hotel, including a branch of the highly regarded Galería Alberto Misrachi (*www.misrachi.com.mx*). Each room soothes with subdued earth tones and bamboolike walls; two rooms are done in Japanese style, with tatami mats. Among the restaurants is the excellent Benkay. **Pros:** considering that this is one of the most elegant places to stay in the city, weekend special rates are definitely reasonable. **Cons:** falls short in some aspects of service. *Campos Elíseos 204, Col. Polanco 55/5283–8700 www.hotelnikkomexico.com.mx 732 rooms, 24 suites In-room: safe, Wi-Fi. In-hotel: 4 restaurants, bar, tennis courts, pool, gym AE, DC, MC, V.*

$$$ **Presidente InterContinental México.** President Barack Obama stayed here on his visit in April 2009. Indeed, the InterContinental regularly hosts heads of state. The expansive atrium lobby has parquet floors; thick walls; oversized furniture; and Talavera pottery, which is showcased throughout. Rooms are contemporary and soothing in creams, beiges, and browns; those on the upper floors have panoramas that stretch for miles over the city. There are also breathtaking views near the elevator banks and from lounges on executive floors. Mexican, Asian, and Italian fare are among the cuisines featured in the six on-site restaurants, which include a branch of The Palm and the city's famous, open-round-the-clock French place, Au Pied de Cochon. All benefit from the hotel's amazing wine cellar. **Pros:** extremely professional service; women's floor with extra amenities and security; the ability to order foie gras 24/7. **Cons:** standard rooms are cramped; no on-site spa. ✉ *Campos Elíseos 218, Col. Polanco* ☎ *55/5327–7700* 🌐 *www.intercontinental.com* *661 rooms, 33 suites* *In-room: safe, Internet. In-hotel: 6 restaurants, bar, gym, laundry service, Wi-Fi hotspot, parking (paid)* *AE, MC, V.*

WORD OF MOUTH

"I was born and raised in the DF (and I'm a single woman), and both Condesa and Centro Historico are pretty safe, foreigner-friendly [neighborhoods]. I personally love Polanco. I walk around there by myself all the time and always feel safe. The Presidente Intercontinental is beautiful. While it's still a chain (not like other boutique Mexican hotels), a lot of Mexicans traveling for business and pleasure stay there. The area is a lot of fun. Think Paris with a Mexican flair. Lots of streetside cafes, upscale stores, little bars and old houses." —Carlita23

$$$$ Fodor's Choice ★ **W.** The first W hotel in Latin America grooves with sassy red, black, and white colors under colorful fluorescent lighting. It manages to be informal and chic at the same time, with the staff clad in casual black rather than the usual stiff uniforms. Guest rooms have some outside-the-box design: bathrooms are big enough for a dance, strung with hammocks, and are outfitted with pressure-point showers; sinks are placed inside the bedroom European-style. Work areas have enormous desks and ergonomic chairs; some rooms are outfitted with faxes and scanners. See and be seen in the red lobby bar or just chill in the Whiskey Bar. The Away Spa and Fitness Center has a huge pre-Hispanic *temazcal* (adobe-domed sweat lodge). **Pros:** special touches; nice place to hang out. **Cons:** more attention is paid to look than comfort. ✉ *Campos Eliseos 252, Col. Polanco* ☎ *55/9138–1800* 🌐 *www.whotels.com* *229 rooms, 8 suites* *In-room: safe, DVD, Wi-Fi. In-hotel: restaurant, bars, gym, spa, laundry service* *AE, MC, V.*

LA ROMA AND LA CONDESA

$$$ Fodor's Choice ★ **Condesa df.** It's all about the details at this hip hotel, from rooms equipped with flat-screen televisions, DVDs, and iPods to a library of coffee-table books about Mexican history and culture. Room doors are labeled with black, oversize Roman numerals in white corridors

surrounding a central courtyard, where the hotel restaurant serves a delicious mix of Mexican- and Asian-inspired cuisine. Rooms are buffered from restaurant noise at night by a foldout wall that is as impressively designed as the hundreds of other details that make a stay here a real experience. **Pros:** courtyard restaurant-bar packs in the trendy day and night, yet remains low-key; small spa on the roof, where there's also a great view of the leafy neighborhood. **Cons:** some rooms are small; some find extremely modern furnishings and accoutrements cold. ✉ *Av. Veracruz 102, Col. Condesa* ☎ *55/5241–2600* 🌐 *www.condesadf.com* *22 rooms, 18 suites* *In-room: safe, Wi-Fi. In-hotel: 2 restaurants, gym, spa* 💳 *AE, MC, V.*

$$–$$$ **Hippodrome.** Housed in a 1930s art deco building near Parque México, this boutique hotel adds some hip style to the already vibrant Condesa neighborhood. The building was remodeled by architect Nahim Dagdug and Tom Shortt. All 15 rooms are done up in browns and subdued colors with marble bathrooms. You'll settle in easy with flat-screen TVs and memory-foam beds. Despite these luxuries, some rooms still feel a little low on space. The hotel's restaurant, the Hip Kitchen, with a menu designed by Irak Roaro, serves contemporary Mexican-fusion food. **Pros:** A bonus? You can use the fashionable Qi Fitness health club just blocks away. **Cons:** rooms are little for what you're paying. ✉ *188 Avenida México, Col. Condesa* ☎ *55/5212–2110* 🌐 *www.thehippodromehotel.com* *10 rooms, 5 suites* *In-room: safe. In-hotel: restaurant, room service, gym, Wi-Fi hotspot* 💳 *AE, MC, V.*

$$$ **Hotel Brick.** A stay in this captivating boutique hotel—in a renovated brick mansion from the early 20th century—is a great way to feel completely integrated with La Roma's rich cultural heritage without giving up modern conveniences like a gym and room service. The mansion is thoughtfully decorated in an eclectic style with bohemian, modern, and traditional touches—think mannequin-bust lamps next to tree-stump coffee tables and wrought-iron doors. Guest rooms are bright, ample, and have Kiehl's bath amenities and plasma TVs. Pros: unique building. Cons: the hotel is a nightlife hotspot for locals, which means heavy crowds on weekends. ✉ *Orizaba 95, Col. Roma Norte* ☎ *55/5525–1100* 🌐 *www.hotelbrick.com* *8 rooms, 9 suites* *In-room: safe, Wi-Fi. In-hotel: 2 restaurants, room service, bar, gym, pool, spa, laundry service, parking (paid), some pets allowed* 💳 *AE, MC, V.*

$$$ **Hotel La Casona.** This captivating hotel is an elegant, understated former mansion, registered as an artistic monument by Mexico's Institute of Fine Arts. From its sunny patios to its sitting rooms, the hotel's interior conveys the spirit of the Porfiriato. The owner loves classical music, and has added such whimsical touches as a trumpet turned into a lamp in one room and a portrait of Richard Strauss in another. The two-story hotel building, with its salmon-color facade, looks out onto a quiet tree-lined street. **Pros:** no two rooms are alike, but all have hardwood floors, elegant furniture, and good-size bathtubs. **Cons:** room decoration a little tacky. ✉ *Av. Durango 280, at Cozumel, Col. Condesa* ☎ *55/5286–3001, 01800/849–8374 toll-free in Mexico* 🌐 *www.hotellacasona.com.mx* *29 rooms* *In-room: safe, refrigerator (some), Wi-Fi. In-hotel: restaurant, room service, bar, gym, laundry service, parking (paid)* 💳 *AE, DC, MC, V* 🍴 *BP.*

AIRPORT

$$–$$$ **Camino Real Aeropuerto.** This sleek hotel can be reached from the airport via a short, covered footbridge. Rooms are light and cheery and have sealed double windows to keep out airport noise. Even if you're only between flights and don't overnight, you can sit in one of the overstuffed chairs in the soothing lobby or catch a meal in the restaurants to get away from the frantic energy of the airport. **Pros:** linked to airport by walkway; a couple of services, including room service and the business center, run 24 hours, useful for travelers on odd-hours schedules. **Cons:** some rooms can be noisy. ✉ *Benito Juárez International Airport* ☎ *55/3003–0033, 01800/901–2300 toll-free in Mexico* 🌐 *www.caminoreal.com* *575 rooms, 25 suites* *In-room: safe, Wi-Fi. In-hotel: 3 restaurants, bar, pool, gym, parking (paid)* 💳 *AE, MC, V.*

$$$–$$$$ **Hilton Aeropuerto.** Cool and compact—with a distinctive gray-marble lobby and a bar with a wide-angle view of landing planes—the Hilton feels like a private club, enhanced by an attentive but unobtrusive staff. You can choose from four different views: airstrip, street, atrium, or "garden" (bamboo plants set along a concrete ledge). **Pros:** rooms come with full working gear for a traveling executive: two phone lines, modem connection, ergonomic chairs, oversized desk, and coffeemaker. **Cons:** not as swank as some Hiltons; more convenient to Terminal 1. ✉ *Benito Juárez International Airport* ✣ *At international terminal* ☎ *55/5133–0505, 800/774–1500 toll-free in the U.S.* 🌐 *www.hilton.com* *129 rooms* *In-room: safe, Wi-Fi. In-hotel: restaurant, room service, bar, gym, parking (paid)* 💳 *AE, MC, V.*

NIGHTLIFE

Updated by Emily Schmall

Condesa, Roma, Centro Histórico, Coyoacán, and Polanco stand out as Mexico City's hippest neighborhoods. If you're looking to do some bar-hopping and want to foot it, you can do so in La Condesa. The Zona Rosa has lost ground to Condesa and Polanco in the past few years, but it's still packed on Friday and Saturday nights, and everything is within walking distance. Niza, Florencia, Londres, and Hamburgo streets are teeming with bars and discos.

Night is the key word. People generally take in dinner and a show at 9 or 10 PM, head to bars or nightclubs at midnight, then find a spot for a nightcap or tacos somewhere around 3 AM. (Cantinas are the exception; people start hitting them in the late afternoon and most close by 11 PM.)

You should have no trouble getting around on your own, *but see the Safety box in the Planner at the start of the chapter about the perils of hailing cabs.* ■ **TIP→ Always take official hotel taxis or sitio (stationed) taxis; it can be expensive to bar-hop this way, but your safety is worth the cost.**

BARS AND CANTINAS

Nice bars to sit and have a few drinks in used to be hard to come by in Mexico City, but the situation is improving. The rougher cantinas are usually noisy and sometimes seedy, with an early closing time (11 PM), but the better cantinas, still full of character, are well worth a visit. The cantinas we list are fairly safe places, but women may get some stares and unwanted attention from time to time. Bars are usually open Tuesday–Saturday 8 PM–3 AM and generally don't charge a cover.

> **NIGHTLIFE TOURS**
>
> **Gray Line** organizes nightlife tours to the mariachi plaza (Plaza Garibaldi) and the Zócalo, complete with an English-speaking guide and a complimentary drink. The outings are cheaper if you have a group of 10 or more people; you should make reservations 12 hours in advance. ☎ *55/5583–5533* 🌐 *www.grayline.com.*

DANCE CLUBS

Dance emporiums in the capital run the gamut from cheek-to-cheek romantic to throbbing strobe lights and earsplitting music. Most places have a cover charge, but it's rarely more than $10. Friday and Saturday are the busiest club nights; Thursday's a good option if you'd like a bit of elbow room for dancing. The most popular clubs are open Wednesday, too. Some clubs require that reservations be made one to two days in advance if you want a table.

LIVE MUSIC

Music thrums throughout the capital, from itinerant trumpeters and drummers playing in the streets to marimba in the marketplaces. Some of the best street musicians play at popular lunchtime eateries, especially in markets. It's customary to give a tip of small change; at least a few pesos will be appreciated. Free concerts are spread throughout the city's plazas on weekends. Most Mexican music (salsa, son, cumbia, danzón) is for dancing, and you will usually find a succession of great live bands in the dance halls and nightclubs.

CENTRO HISTÓRICO

BARS

Fodor's Choice ★ **Centro Cultural de España en México.** It housed conquistadors during the 16th century; today the Centro is a Spanish cultural center for art exhibits, plays, and other events. On Thursday, Friday, and Saturday nights, starting at 10, indie, electronic, and rock bands play live music on the terrace of the bar-restaurant. ✉ *Guatemala 18, behind cathedral, Col. Centro* ☎ *55/5521–1925* 🌐 *www.ccemx.org* ⊗ *Closed Mon.*

El Puerto del Sol. Perhaps because of its proximity to the Zócalo's tourist-friendly west side, simple, traditional El Puerto del Sol always seems to be packed with Americans kicking back with its reasonably priced tequilas. ✉ *Calle 5 de Mayo 24, at Calle Palma, Col. Centro* ☎ *5512–7244.*

La Ópera. One of the city's most elegant watering holes has attracted top personalities since it opened in 1870. Don't forget to have your waiter point out the bullet hole in the ceiling allegedly left by Mexican revolutionary hero Pancho Villa. ✉ *5 de Mayo 10, at Filomeno Mata, Col. Centro* ☎ *55/5512–8959.*

Salón Corona. This popular, centrally located hangout tends to attract local artists, journalists, and photographers, and is one of the friendliest

GAY BARS IN MEXICO CITY

Gay and lesbian life in the capital is something of a contradiction. In one of the largest cities in the world—and one that has just now legalized same-sex unions—one would expect a thriving, out-and-proud community. But Mexico isn't like that, and here the gay and lesbian scene is still largely in the shadows.

Personal freedom of choice in Mexico is the companion of money, and so the majority of gays and lesbians, who lack deep pockets, live a closeted, traditional (heterosexual) family lifestyle. When gathering places do appear, they tend to be down and dirty and to be closed down by authorities or swap locations quickly.

Centro's Calle Republica de Cuba was once the closest thing (apart from the anything-goes Zona Rosa in general) D.F. had to a gay neighborhood, and its hole-in-the-wall taverns may at times once again take on that character. The spots listed below are large, well-established institutions. We suggest surfing the Web for the latest hot spots.

Cabaret La Perla. The gritty Cabaret La Perla dates from 1946, and has some of the city's best female impersonators, who sing everything from Madonna to surf punk. Friday and Saturday shows are at 11:30 PM and 1:30 AM. ✉ *República de Cuba 44, Col. Centro* ☎ *55/1997–9001.*

Patrick Miller. At this high-energy "danceteria," DJs spin '80s pop classics, disco, and techno, and the flamboyant patrons compete in theatrical dance-offs. Prepare to sweat. ✉ *Mérida 17, Col. Roma* ☎ *55/5511–5406* 🎫 *$2.50.*

joints in town. In typically fatalistic Mexican fashion, the giant photos on the wall show the clientele reacting to the 1986 World Cup at the moment defeat was snatched from the jaws of victory by the national team. ✉ *Calle Bolívar 24, at Madero, Col. Centro* ☎ *55/5512–5725 or 55/5512–9007.*

DANCE CLUB

El Pacífico. The so-called cathedral of *quebraditas* (a fast-paced country dance) showcases some of the city's most talented dancers as they toss and swing their partners to northern-style *banda* music. El Pacífico could also easily win a prize as Mexico's noisiest club. It never disappoints. ✉ *Bucareli 43, at Morelos, Col. Centro* ☎ *No phone.*

LIVE MUSIC

Circo Volador. The sound quality may not be the best, but nobody seems to be complaining at this headbangers' haven. Colonia Jamaica is 15 minutes southeast of the Centro Histórico; it's accessible via subway or sitio taxi (but we recommend sitio, which will cost about 50 pesos). ✉ *Calzada de la Viga 146, Col. Jamaica* ☎ *55/5740–9012.*

Pasagüero. Pasagüero presents a mixed bag of live indie music, art exhibits, and other cultural events. The concerts start at 10 PM on Thursday, Friday, and Saturday. For a complete listing of upcoming events, visit the Web site. ✉ *Motolinía 33, at 16 de Septiembre, Col. Centro* ☎ *55/5521–6112* 🌐 *www.pasaguero.com.*

Salón Los Angeles. A night here takes you back in time to the 1930s, with a backdrop straight out of the golden era of Mexican cinema. The grand, open dance floor swings to the rhythms of danzón and salsa. When renowned Latin musicians come to town, this is often where they perform. ✉ *Lerdo 206, Col. Guerrero* ☎ *55/5597–8847.*

Fodor's Choice ★ **Zinco Jazz Club.** Set in the vault of an art deco bank in the heart of Centro, the capital's coolest jazz joint hosts local and international acts. The intimate setting and enthusiastic audiences seem to bring out the best in performers. It's open Wednesday through Saturday; entry fee is $10 on Friday and Saturday, and free other days. ✉ *Motolonía 20, at 5 de Mayo, Col. Centro* ☎ *55/5518–6369.*

ZONA ROSA

BARS

Bar Milán. The young and the hip favor this bar. Upon entering, you need to change pesos into *milagros* (miracles), which are notes necessary to buy drinks throughout the night. The trick is to remember to change them back before last call. The bar is a 10-minute walk northeast of Zona Rosa. ✉ *Milán 18, at General Prim, Col. Juárez* ☎ *55/5592–0031.*

El Trompo. A perfect getaway spot from the Zona Rosa's loud discos and flashy nightclubs, this cantina keeps things cheap and cheerful with drink specials and upbeat music. ✉ *Hamburgo 87, at Niza, Zona Rosa* ☎ *55/5207–8503.*

DANCE CLUB

Tandem Pub. Tandem underwent a makeover of sorts several years ago when a group of local DJs transformed the otherwise quiet pub into a weekend hot spot. It's a five-minute walk north of Zona Rosa. ✉ *Río Nazas 73, Río Tigris, Col. Cuauhtémoc* ☎ *55/5525–7358.*

LA CONDESA

BARS

Fodor's Choice ★ **Black Horse.** It doesn't miss a beat with live funk, jazz, and rock groups jamming throughout the week. On the third Wednesday of each month the Horse hosts a pub quiz; the winner takes home a bottle of booze. Wednesday is Ladies Night, with great drink specials. The Web site lists all the events. For a late-night nosh, try the all-day breakfast, the curry dish, or bangers (Scottish sausage) with mashed potatoes and gravy. The Horse is an expat hangout, drawing American journalists and Fulbright scholars who live in Condesa ✉ *Mexicali 85, at Tamaulipas, Col. Condesa* ☎ *55/5211–8740* 🌐 *www.caballonegro.com.*

Celtics. Get your Guinness on at this Irish-style pub—that is, if you can push your way through the throng to reach the bar. ✉ *Tamaulipas 36, Col. Condesa* ☎ *55/5211–9081.*

★ **La Botica.** The good news? This place serves 20 varieties of mezcal; try the *pechuga* (distilled with fruit, and a chicken breast), the *añejo* (aged), or the *cremas* (liqueurs). The bad news? Mezcal isn't ordinary booze: no matter how much of a pro you are, drink shots of it like you do tequila, and you'll probably end up on the floor. If the tiny space is too crowded, order some bottles to go. ✉ *Campeche 396, at Tamaulipas, Col. Condesa* ☎ *55/5211–6045.*

Pata Negra. On weekends this Argentine-owned hot spot can get pretty crowded, so get here before 11 PM if you want a table. Most nights, when the bar thins out, local groups play acid jazz, bossa nova, and flamenco. ✉ *Tamaulipas 30, at Juan Escutia, Col. Condesa* ☎ *55/5211–5563.*

Rioma. At this basement restaurant-bar, formerly owned by Mexican film comedian Cantinflas, local and foreign DJs spin house, trance, and chill-out music. ✉ *Insurgentes Sur 377, near Michoacán, Col. Condesa* ☎ *55/5584–8540.*

Salón Malafama. Malafama takes the prize for Mexico City's hippest pool hall. Since there's often a wait for the tables, the bar area is a popular gathering spot. ✉ *Michoacán 78, at Tamaulipas, Condesa* ☎ *55/5553–5138.*

NEED A BREAK?

Neveria Roxy. After dinner or drinks, Condesa's old-style, traditional-Mexican ice-cream parlor packs in hipsters until the wee hours. ✉ ***Fernando Montes de Oca 89, Col. Condesa*** ☎ ***No phone.***

CANTINAS

El Centenario. Bar-hoppers often meet at this traditional cantina in the heart of the Condesa's restaurant zone for drinks and song before moving on to late-night haunts nearby. Tables go fast, so prepare to belly up to the bar. ✉ *Vicente Suarez 42, at Michoacán, Col. Condesa* ☎ *55/5553–5451.*

La Capital. A nouveau take on the traditional cantina, La Capital is smartly adorned with art deco furniture, and for a cantina, an unusually good dinner menu. ✉ *Nuevo León 137, at Campeche, Col. Condesa* ☎ *55/5256–5159.*

Mojito Room. If you're itching to dance on a weekday, Cuban salsa club Mojito Room is the place. Wednesday sees free salsa lessons at 8 PM, a live band, a packed dance floor, and no cover charge. ✉ *Nuevo León 81, Col. Condesa* ☎ *55/5286–6316.*

LA ROMA

BARS

Ixchel. This bar in a lovely old building is a great place for a relaxing sip. ✉ *Medellín 65, at Colima, Col. Roma* ☎ *55/3096–5010.*

La Bodeguita del Medio. At this welcoming, lively joint every surface is splashed with graffiti, making it one of the city's most intriguing spaces. Inspired by the original Havana establishment—where Hemingway lapped up mojitos—the place also serves cheap Cuban food. Another location is a short walk from Coyoacán. ✉ *Cozumel 37, at Durango, Col. Roma Norte* ☎ *55/5553–0246.*

Fodor's Choice ★

La Hija de los Apaches. This sloppy gem of a loft is part metro stop, part college-dorm commons, part debating society, and part *pulqueria*. It's run by 1950s national lightweight boxing champion and folk hero Epiphanio 'Pifas' Leyva, and serves beer and *pulque* (a drink made with the pungent sap of the agave plant) to a young, intellectual crowd that loves to sing and dance to the excellent jukebox of punk and local guacapunk (Mexican ska) classics. If you want a rowdy afternoon (the bar is usually closed by 11, and always closed on Sunday), this is the place. Note that it's technically in the Doctores neighborhood, but is really part of Roma and Insurgentes. ✉ *Dr. Claudio Bernard 149, at Dr. Liceaga, Col. Doctores* ☎ *55/4056–1648.*

La Taberna Travazares. This bar is a recent addition to the Atrio, an art gallery and cultural center. It's a quiet and pleasant place—reminiscent of a spot in New York's West Village—that serves Cosaco, one of Mexico's finest microbrews, on tap. A jazz group plays on Wednesday and Saturday nights. ✉ *Orizaba 127, at Chihuahua, Col. Roma* ☎ *55/5264–1421.*

CAUTION

Remember that the capital's high altitude makes liquor extremely potent, even jolting. Imported booze is expensive, so you may want to stick with what the Mexicans order: tequila, mezcal, cerveza, and rum, that last item usually as a Cuba libre (with Coke). If you order a bottle of hard alcohol (some clubs require this), make sure that the seal hasn't been broken before you're served, as some ill-reputed establishments have been known to sell adulterated booze. Your head will thank you the next day.

CANTINAS

El Portal de Cartagena. A fantastic old cantina, El Portal de Cartagena is ideal for a simple, long lunch and a few beers. ✉ *Chiapas 174, at Medellín, Col. Roma* ☎ *55/5264–8714 or 55/5584–1113.*

La Covadonga. This grand cantina has an antique bar and a good restaurant serving up Spanish fare. Nightly it's filled with the sound of exuberant games of dominoes. ✉ *Puebla 121, at Cordoba, Col. Roma* ☎ *55/5533–2922.*

DANCE CLUB

★ **Mama Rumba.** It's nondescript Cuban restaurant—a 10-minute cab ride from Zona Rosa—during the day, but on Wednesday through Saturday night it turns on the heat with live Latin music. It's so popular with young pleasure-seekers that you can barely move. If the Roma location is too crowded, which it usually is, a San Angel branch may give you a little more breathing room. ✉ *Querétaro 230, at Medellín, Col. Roma* ☎ *55/5264–7823.*

LIVE MUSIC

Multiforo Alicia. Multiforo Alicia headlines foreign and local indie bands playing punk, ska, surf, and garage music. In true punk-rock fashion, the space is poorly ventilated, and the sound system leaves much to be desired, but it offers a cheap night out and entertaining scene. ✉ *Cuauhtémoc 91-A, at Durango, Col. Roma* ☎ *55/5511–2100.*

POLANCO

BARS

Area. Area showcases a magnificent view of the city from a chic open-air bar and terrace atop the Habita Hotel. The lounge area near a fireplace is a great place to chill out without catching a chill. Sipping a selection from the range of mezcals on offer will also do the trick. ✉ *Av. Presidente Masaryk 201, at Arquímedes, Col. Polanco* ☎ *55/5282–3100.*

Blue Lounge. The lounge in the Camino Real Hotel, southeast of Polanco, has a sophisticated crowd and mellow music. Lighting and overall color schemes are, as you probably guessed, blue-tinged. There are several seating areas; furnishings are eclectic but are heavy on mid-century modern pieces. One area has a transluscent floor that's lit from below and set over water—very cool and blue. ✉ *Mariano Escobedo 700, Col. Nueva Anzures* ☎ *55/5263–8888 Ext. 8489.*

Ivoire. Chic and comfortable Ivoire is decorated like an upper-class home in the French countryside. Try for a spot on the top-floor terrace overlooking Parque del Reloj. ✉ *Emilio Castelar 95, at Alejandro Dumas, Col. Polanco* ☎ *55/5280–0477.*

DANCE CLUB

La Maraka. Many locals consider the merengue and salsa music played at this dance hall south of Roma to be some of the city's best. ✉ *Mitla 410, at Eje 5, Col. Narvarte* ☎ *55/5682–0636.*

LIVE MUSIC

Hard Rock Cafe. Mexico City's Hard Rock is in a 17th-century mansion and combines an intimate feel with a state-of-the-art sound system. ✉ *Campos Elíseos 278, Col. Chapultepec Polanco* ☎ *55/5327–7100 or 55/5327–7101.*

COYOACÁN

BARS

El Convento Fernández. In a former convent converted into a restaurant-bar, the sights and sounds have certainly changed over the years, but the hospitality remains the same. There's live music on Wednesday, Friday, and Saturday. ✉ *Fernández 96, at Pacífico, Coyoacán* ☎ *55/5554–4065.*

El Hijo del Cuervo. Students and hip intellectuals of all ages pack this place, thanks to an interesting mix of rock and protest music, known as *nueva canción.* It also produces the occasional theater show; cover charges vary (up to $5). ✉ *Jardín Centenarios 17, Coyoacán* ☎ *55/5658–7824* 🌐 *www.elhijodelcuervo.com.mx.*

CANTINA

La Guadalupana. This famous cantina, dating from 1932, is always packed. The wall-mounted bulls' heads add a bit of carnage to the bar's bullfighting theme. ✉ *Calle Higuera 2, Coyoacán* ☎ *55/5554–6253.*

2

LIVE MUSIC

Bulldog Café. This spot north of Coyoacán books mostly rock acts. The cover charge varies depending on the headline band; expect to pay at least $25 if a well-known group is playing. ✉ *Rubens 6, at Av. Revolución, Col. Mixcoac* ☎ *55/5054–2789.*

SHOPPING

Updated by Eva Ginsburg

The area with the highest concentration of shops is the **Zona Rosa. It's** chock-full of boutiques, jewelry stores, leather-goods shops, antiques stores, and art galleries. **Polanco,** the choice residential neighborhood along the northeast perimeter of Bosque de Chapultepec, has blossomed into a more upscale shopping area.

La Condesa and La Roma, though better known for restaurants and cafés, are sprouting designer boutiques, primarily for a younger crowd and artsy types. Jewelers, shoe shops, vintage clothes, and hip housewares stores are squeezing in as well. Most cluster along avenidas Michoacán, Vicente Suárez, Amsterdam, and Tamaulipas, in Condesa, and Alvaro Obregón and thereabouts, in Roma.

Hundreds of shops with more modest trappings and better prices are spread along the length of **Avenida Insurgentes** and **Avenida Juárez.**

CENTRO HISTÓRICO

ARCADE

Portales de los Mercaderes. This arcade has attracted merchants since 1524. It's lined with jewelry shops selling gold (often by the gram) and authentic Taxco silver at prices lower than those in Taxco, where the overhead is higher. **One of the most interesting shops, however, is** Sombreros Tardán (🌐 *www.tardan.com.mx*), **which specializes in fashionable men's hats of every shape and style. It's more or less in the middle of the arcade.** ✉ *Extending length of west side of Zócalo between Calles Madero and 16 de Septiembre, Col. Centro.*

CANDY

Dulcería de Celaya. It was founded in 1874 and has been a haven for those with a sweet tooth ever since. It specializes in candied pineapple, guava, and other exotic fruits; almond paste; candied walnut rolls; and *cajeta,* made with thick caramelized milk. These traditional sweets are not available in many other stores in Mexico City. There's another branch in La Roma. ✉ *5 de Mayo 39, Col. Centro* ☎ *55/5521–1787.*

HANDICRAFTS

Arte Mexicano para el Mundo. The location in the heart of downtown and the selection of high-quality crafts make this store a good bet if you're short on time and need to combine souvenir shopping with sightseeing. Look for silver jewelry, textiles, ceramics, and food products. Prices are generally reasonable, but, if you have a chance, check prices at some of the competition to be sure you're getting a deal. The shop's sixth-floor Puro Corazón restaurant has a great view of the Zócalo and a menu of inventive (mainly Mexican) dishes. ✉ *Monte de Piedad 11, Col. Centro* ☎ *55/5518–0300* 🌐 *www.arte-mexicano.com.mx.*

CLOSE UP

Mexican Culture by Night

The capital's nightlife often has the music, the pulse, and the flavor of Mexican traditions from other places and other times. You can watch Aztec dancers adorned in feather headdresses stomp to percussion composed 500 years ago; listen to the fiddles, accordions, and falsetto of mariachi musicians; or take a candle-lit boat ride through floating gardens.

CATCH SOME MARIACHI MUSIC

The traditional last stop for nocturnal Mexicans is **Plaza Garibaldi** in Colonia Centro, east of Eje Central Lázaro Cárdenas, between República de Honduras and República de Perú. Here exuberant, and often inebriated, mariachis gather to unwind after evening performances—by performing even more. There are roving mariachis, as well as *norteño* (country-style) musicians and white-clad *jarocho* (traditional music from Veracruz) bands peddling songs in the outdoor plaza, where you can also buy beer and shots of tequila. Beware: the alcohol sold in the outdoor square is rotgut. You'll usually find unadulterated drinks inside the cantinas or clubs surrounding the plaza, where well-to-do Mexicans park themselves and belt out their favorite songs.

The square was spruced up in the early 1990s and underwent another makeover in time for Mexico's bicentennial. New streetlamps and added security make things less sketchy than they once were. There's also a new building that houses a Mexican restaurant and galleries with displays on the history of tequila and that of mariachi. That said, **■ TIP→ it's best to either arrange your trip to Plaza Garibaldi through a tour agency or to plan on taking one of the safe sitio taxis to and fro.** It can still be a rough place at night, and leaving it for the surrounding areas can be dangerous. Although it's pretty safe to return to Centro hotels via Eje 1 Lazaro Central Cardenás, avoid other streets.

ATTEND A FLOATING GARDEN PARTY

There's probably nothing anywhere in the world like a weekend night at **Xochimilco**, the floating gardens that were the breadbasket of the Aztec city of Tenochtitlán and where you can rent a flower-bedecked trajinera, with a pilot to push it along (cost is about $16 for three hours). If you go on a warm weekend evening just before sundown, you'll witness a magical transformation. At dusk canoes pull up with candles, corn, tacos, beer, and tequila shots, and other boats bearing entire mariachi bands pole over to perform while festive locals hail you loudly from their own floating parties. It has been said before by well-traveled individuals that this could be the most magnificent and romantic place on the planet, and you will be hard-pressed to argue otherwise.

The easiest way to get here is by sitio taxi; it's a 35-minute, 90-peso ride. To get here by subway (relatively safe but potentially disorienting for non-Spanish speakers), take the No. 2 Metro (blue) line south to its end, in Tasqueña (sometimes written on signs as TAXQUEÑA), and follow the signs across the pedestrian bridge to the *tren ligero*, or light-rail. Ride it to its end, at Xochimilco (all this will take less than an hour from the Zócalo). Once in the neighborhood, simply follow the signs saying BARCOS; almost any eastward side street here will lead to a jetty.

SEE A FOLKLORIC SHOW

At **La Hacienda de Los Morales** you can watch traditional folk and Aztec dances Sunday through Friday nights, and on Sunday afternoons you can sit down to a meal with live mariachi music. The show plus dinner and two drinks costs $35. ✉ *Vazquez de Mella 525, Col. Del Bosque* ☎ *55/5207–8055.*

The world-renowned **Ballet Folklórico de México** is a visual feast of Mexican regional folk dances in whirling colors. Lavish and professional, It's one of the country's most popular shows. Performances are on Wednesday at 8:30 PM and Sunday at 9:30 AM and 7:00 PM at the magnificent Museo Nacional de Antropología (National Anthropology Museum; performances were formerly held at the Palacio de Bellas Artes, but have moved here due to restoration work at the palace). You can purchase tickets by calling Ticketmaster for prices and reservations. Hotels and travel agencies can also secure tickets. ✉ *Museo Nacional de Antropología, Paseo de la Reforma at Calle Gandhi, Section 1, Bosque de Chapultepec* ☎ *55/5529–9320 box office, 55/5325–9000 Ticketmaster* 🌐 *www.balletamalia.com.*

SAMPLE PULQUE

Salon Tenampa is the last pulqueria on what was once a square of pulquerias in a city of pulquerias. Que lastima. Pulque is the agave-heart mulch, which is turned into tequila, and capitalinos were once mad for it. The rich, nutritious beverage is something of an acquired taste, and its effects can best be compared to that of a mescaline smoothie. The mix goes bad in 24 hours, so pulque is extremely hard to get outside the capital and the state of Tequila. The salon is open Sunday through Thursday until at least 3 AM and even later on Friday and Saturday. As it's in Plaza Garabaldi, a square that can be dangerous at night and whose surrounding streets are dangerous at all times, take a sitio taxi here and back. ✉ *Plaza Garibaldi 12, Col. Centro* ☎ *55/5526–6176.*

DEPARTMENT STORE CHAINS

Upscale department store **El Palacio de Hierro** is noted for items by well-known designers and its seductive advertising campaigns. There are freestanding branches in Centro, Polanco, and La Roma, as well as anchor stores in malls such as Centro Santa Fe, Mexico's largest mall in the up-and-coming Santa Fe district. The Durango department store in La Roma is owned by the same company. ✉ *Av. 20 de Noviembre 3, Col. Centro* ☎ *55/5728-9905* 🌐 *www.elpalaciodehierro.com.mx.*

Liverpool is the largest retailer in Mexico City, and often has bargains on clothes. Look for branches in Centro and Polanco, as well as in Centro Santa Fe and elsewhere. ✉ Venustiano Carranza 92, *Col. Centro06060* ☎ *55/5262-9999 general customer service* 🌐 *www.liverpool.com.mx.*

Sanborns is a chain of minidepartment stores with some 80 branches in Mexico City, including one in almost every shopping mall. The most convenient are at Calle Madero 4 (its original store in the House of Tiles, downtown), though there are also several along Paseo de la Reforma (including one at the Angel Monument and another four blocks west of the Diana Fountain); in San Angel (on Avenida de la Revolución and Avenida de la Paz); Coyoacán (at the Jardín Centenario); and in the Zona Rosa (one at the corner of Niza and Hamburgo and another at Londres 130 in the Hotel Calinda Geneve). They carry ceramics and crafts (and can ship anywhere), and most have restaurants or coffee shops with free wireless Internet access, a pharmacy, ATMs, and periodical-book departments with English-language publications. 🌐 *www.sanborns.com.mx.*

Fonart. Under the auspices of the National Council for Culture and Arts, the *National Fund for Promoting Arts and Crafts* operates five stores in and around Mexico City, with more around the country. Prices are fixed and high, but the diverse, top-quality folk art and handcrafted furnishings represent some of Mexico's best artisans. The best location is downtown, west of Alameda Park. Major sales at near-wholesale prices are held from time to time at the main store–warehouse. ✉ *Juárez 89, Col. Juárez* ☎ *55/5521–0171main store–warehouse* ✉ *Av. Patriotismo 691, Col. Mixcoac* ☎ *55/5093–6060 or 55/5093–6061* ✉ *Av. Paseo de la Reforma 116, ground fl., Col. Juárez* ☎ *55/5328–5000 Ext. 53130 or 53089* 🌐 *www.fonart.gob.mx.*

MARKETS

La Lagunilla. Enormous La Lagunilla has been the site of trade and bartering for more than five centuries. The day to go is Sunday, when vendors set up outside to sell everything from antique paintings and furniture to old magazines and plastic toys. Dress down, and watch out for pickpockets; this is known affectionately as the Thieves' Market—local lore says you can buy back on Sunday what was stolen from your home Saturday. ✉ *Paseo de la Reforma between Comonfort and Jaime Nunó, Col. Guerrero.*

Fodor's Choice ★ **Mercado Artesanal de la Ciudadela.** This market, a 10- to 15-minute walk from the Alameda, bursts with the capital's widest range of wares and best bargains daily from about 10 to 5. We're talking about Talavera pottery, leather belts, guitars, tile-framed mirrors, hammocks, silverware, papier-mâché skeletons, rugs, trays from Olinalá, sombreros. . . . Prices are better than at most crafts markets (though you can still haggle), and so is the scene. On Saturday, enthusiasts gather across the street in Plaza de la Ciudadela at around noon to dance danzón. ✉ *Balderas and Plaza de la Ciudadela, Col. Centro.*

2

ZONA ROSA

ANTIQUES

Bazar de Antigüedades. Shopping in the line of antiques stores along a passageway at Plaza del Angel is at its liveliest on Saturday. Combine a trip here with one to the Mercado Insurgentes, the crafts market across the way, for a full day of shopping. ✉ *Between Londres and Hamburgo, opposite Mercado Insurgentes, Zona Rosa* 🌐 *www.antiguedadesplazadelangel.com.mx.*

Galería Windsor. Windsor specializes in 18th- and 19th-century antiques and Mexican historical art. ✉ *Hamburgo 224, at Praga, Zona Rosa* ☎ *55/5525–2881 or 55/5525–2996* 🌐 *www.galeriawindsor.com.mx.*

ARCADE

Plaza La Rosa. Prestigious shops and boutiques fill this modern shopping arcade. Among them are Kosiuko (🌐 *www.kosiuko.com*), with clothing that would appeal to even the pickiest hipster, and the sporting goods chain Martí (🌐 *www.marti.com.mx*). It spans the depth of the block between Londres and Hamburgo, with entrances on both streets. ✉ *Between Amberes and Génova, Zona Rosa.*

HANDICRAFTS

Artesanos de México. Browse for folk art, sculpture, and furniture in this gallery. ✉ *Londres 117, Zona Rosa* ☎ *55/5514–7455.*

MARKET

Mercado Insurgentes. This typical neighborhood market is an entire block deep, with entrances on both Londres and Liverpool. Most of its more than 200 stalls sell crafts: serapes and ponchos, baskets, pottery, silver, pewter, fossils, and onyx. Expect to pay slightly higher prices here than at the Mercado Artesanal de la Ciudadela. Combine a trip here with one to the antiques stores at Bazar de Antigüedades in Plaza San Angel across the way. It operates Monday–Saturday 10 to 7 or 7:30 and Sunday 11 to 4. ✉ *Between Florencia and Amberes, Zona Rosa.*

CONDESA

ART

Galería de Arte Mexicano (GAM). Founded in 1935, the GAM was the first place in Mexico City dedicated full-time to the sale and promotion of art (before its inception, there were no official galleries here). It has as played an important role in many Mexican art movements and continues to support the country's most important artists. GAM has

CLOSE UP

Mexico's Largest Mall

Centro Santa Fe. The largest mall in Mexico—with nearly 300 stores, a movie theater, an international exhibition center, hotels, a theme park for kids, and several restaurants—might be reason enough for you to make the trek to the Santa Fe district, about 27 km (17 mi) from Centro. Ironically what was once a garbage dump is now a wealthy area littered with modern apartment and office buildings—many of them breathtaking both in scale and design—and crisscrossed by roads so new you can practically smell the tar. It's also starting to fill up with upscale hotels and restaurants. ✉ *Av. Vasco de Quiroga 3800, Santa Fe* 🌐 *www.centrosantafe.com.mx.*

also published noteworthy books; these works and catalogs are available at the gallery bookstore. It's just west of the Condesa neighborhood, toward the southern edge of Bosque de Chapultepec. ✉ *Gob. Rafael Rebollar 43, Col. San Miguel Chapultepec* ☎ *55/5272–5696 or 55/5272–5529* 🌐 *www.galeriadeartemexicano.com.*

DESIGNER CLOTHING

Carmen Rion. Linen dresses by this Mexican designer are done in palettes and patterns that bring to mind (and sometimes incorporate) traditional Mexican textiles, embroidery, and lace. The draping and layering, however, are very contemporary. Skirts and wraps that flow elegantly—often in vertical lines—are juxtaposed with structured, sometimes architectural bodices and tops. Ties, fastenings, and jewelry are equally tantalizing, the latter often combining wood, silver, and seedpods. Rion has been recognized not only for her unique designs, but also for her ethical practices, which have included working with Mexican artisans to create her garments. ✉ *Av. Michoacán 30-A, at Parque México, Col. Condesa* ☎ *55/5264–6179* 🌐 *www.carmenrion.com.mx.*

HOME FURNISHINGS

Mob. The young and the trendy fill their homes with furniture and accessories from this shop. ✉ *Campeche 322, Col. Condesa* ☎ *55/5286–7239* 🌐 *www.mob.com.mx.*

JEWELRY

Pladi. This store sells unusual jewelry by Mexican designers, mostly in silver, glass, and stone, as well as sculpture. ✉ *Montes de Oca 47, Col. Condesa* ☎ *55/5286–1535* 🌐 *www.pladi.com.mx.*

ROMA

DESIGN

DIME. The inventory of art, design, and fashion at this small gallery-cum-shop is provided by 50, give or take, young Mexican designers. It's a great place to find original, one-of-a-kind gifts or souvenirs. Kitsch is key here: think T-shirts with quirky graphics, bags made from colorful plastic tablecloths, clothing that combines color-blocked solids and patterns (like polka dots). ✉ *Alvaro Obregón 185-B, Col. Roma* ☎ *55/2454–6790* 🌐 *www.dimetienda.com.mx.*

POLANCO

ART

Alberto Misrachi Gallery. This gallery is heavy on contemporary painting, with a smattering of sculpture, by Mexican artists, many of them well-known. Some international artists are also represented. Branches in Mexico City include a freestanding one on the Campos Elíseos and one in the Hotel Nikko. ✉ *Campos Elíseos 215, local E, Col. Polanco* ☎ *55/5281–7456 or 55/5251–7457* 🌐 *www.misrachi.com.mx.*

Juan Martín Gallery. The emphasis is on avant-garde painting, sculpture, photography, and mixed media. But exhibitions have also included things like artisanal mosaics in contemporary patterns that seemed inspired by both traditional and midcentury-modern tile works. ✉ *Dickens 33-B, Col. Polanco* ☎ *55/5280–0277 or 55/5280–8212* 🌐 *www.galeriajuanmartin.com.*

Oscar Román Gallery. Works—mostly paintings and most with a contemporary edge—by Mexican artists pack this gallery. There's also a smattering of colonial art and religious figurines. ✉ *Julio Verne 14, Col. Polanco* ☎ *55/5280–0436* 🌐 *www.galeriaoscarroman.com.mx.*

Ginocchio Galleria This gallery promotes distinguished artists from Mexico and elsewhere in Latin America. ✉ *Arquímedes 175, Col. Polanco* ☎ *55/5254–8813* 🌐 *www.ginocchiogaleria.com.*

Sergio Bustamante. The renowned artist's wild sculpture and jewelry are sold at this store and gallery in the Hotel Nikko. There's also a branch at the Presidente InterContinental hotel. ✉ *Hotel Nikko, Campos Elíseos 204, Col. Polanco* ☎ *55/5282–2638 or 55/55281–8157* 🌐 *www.sergiobustamante.com.mx*

JEWELRY

Tane. This store is is a mine of perhaps the best silverwork in Mexico—jewelry, flatware, candelabra, museum-quality reproductions of archaeological finds, and bold designs by young Mexican silversmiths. The Masaryk shop is one of several, including those in the Four Seasons and Presidente InterContinental hotels and in the upscale Centro Santa Fe. ✉ *Av. Presidente Masaryk 430, Col. Polanco* ☎ *55/5282–6200* 🌐 *www.tane.com.mx.*

MALL

Antara Polanco. One of the only outdoor malls in the city has a collection of upscale stores that includes

AVENIDA PRESIDENTE MASARYK

Polanco's Avenida Presidente Masaryk (also seen as Masarik and named for the first president of Czechoslovakia) is to Mexico City what Madison Avenue or 57th Street are to New York City. It's lined with the boutiques of such high-end international jewelers and designers as Cartier, Chanel, Burberry, Hermès and on through the alphabet to Tiffany and Ermenegildo Zegna. If you can't find a luxury name here, head north a short way to the Antara Polanco mall.

Carolina Herrera, Zara, Emporio Armani, and Marc Jacobs, as well as branches of several luxury stores that are along the Polanco neighborhood's ritzy Avenida Presidente Masaryk. ✉ *Ejército Nacional 843-B, Col. Granada* ☎ *55/5280–2954* 🌐 *www.antarapolanco.com.*

SAN ANGEL

MARKET

★ **Mercado del Sábado.** A must if you're in town on a Saturday is a visit to this market. Hundreds of vendors sell crafts, silver, wood carvings, embroidered clothing, leather goods, wooden masks, beads, *amates* (bark paintings), and trinkets at stalls on a network of cobbled streets outside the bazaar's building, a two-story colonial mansion. Inside are the better-quality—and higher-priced—goods, including *alebrijes* (painted wooden animals from Oaxaca), glassware, pottery, jewelry, and papier-mâché flowers. A patio buffet and an indoor restaurant will help you conquer hunger and thirst. ✉ *Plaza San Jacinto, San Angel.*

Around Mexico City

3

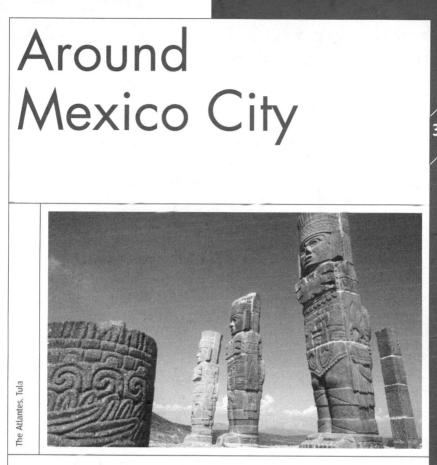

The Atlantes, Tula

WORD OF MOUTH

"[For climbing temples at Teotihuacán] a good pair of good walking shoes is better than sneakers. The only thing you really have to worry about is slipping, so go for the best traction. Do not wear flat leather soles! It can be hot, and the climb is tiring, but there are places to stop and catch your breath. Make sure to visit the Temple of Quetzalcoatl at the area known as "the citadel." It's one of the high points of Teotihuacán."

—Fra Diavalo

www.fodors.com/community

WELCOME TO AROUND MEXICO CITY

TOP REASONS TO GO

★ **Day-tripping to ancient cities:** Spend the day scrambling over ruins and pyramids and be back in Mexico City for dinner.

★ **Experiencing the great outdoors:** Some of the country's highest mountains, such as Iztaccíhuatl, offer challenging climbs for the intrepid or easier trails at their bases.

★ **The chance to eat Puebla's regional cuisine:** The city has made some important contributions to Mexico's culinary heritage, such as mole, a sauce that can use upward of 30 different ingredients, including chocolate.

★ **Getting a European vacation without having to cross the pond:** Due to its lakeside location amid pine forests, and popularity with wealthy jet-setters, Valle de Bravo has been likened to the "Switzerland of Mexico."

★ **Putting the guidebook away:** In Tlaxcala and Cuetzalan, you'll run out of sights to see in the first 15 minutes. The real joy is strolling around without an agenda.

1 Puebla and Environs. If you don't have time to visit the Heartland, colonial Puebla and its surrounding towns are a great alternative. Puebla's the hub of the region; from here you can head to the city's smaller, more peaceful counterparts, Cholula and Tlaxcala, or take a four-hour bus ride up winding mountain roads to Cuetzalan, a lovely town in the Sierra Norte.

2 Cuernavaca and Environs. This is the direction to head in if you want to find a spa or *temazcal,* a traditional sweat lodge. For centuries Cuernavaca has been the old standby for Mexicans fleeing the capital. Nearby Tepoztlán has become a center for meditation, yoga, and the like, and is cleaner and more peaceful. The ruins of Xochicalco are a good side trip from Cuernavaca.

3 Teotihuacán. These ruins are a must. The view from either of the two pyramids is worth the trip an hour north of the city alone. It's an outstanding day trip, as there's frequent bus service from the capital.

4 Valle de Bravo and Environs. Lakeside Valle de Bravo has eclipsed Cuernavaca as the weekend getaway of Mexico City's elite. It's a good spot for sports, both on and off the lake. Parque Nacional Nevado de Toluca has a bunch of trails snaking up its mountain; there's also a scenic drive if you can't make the climb.

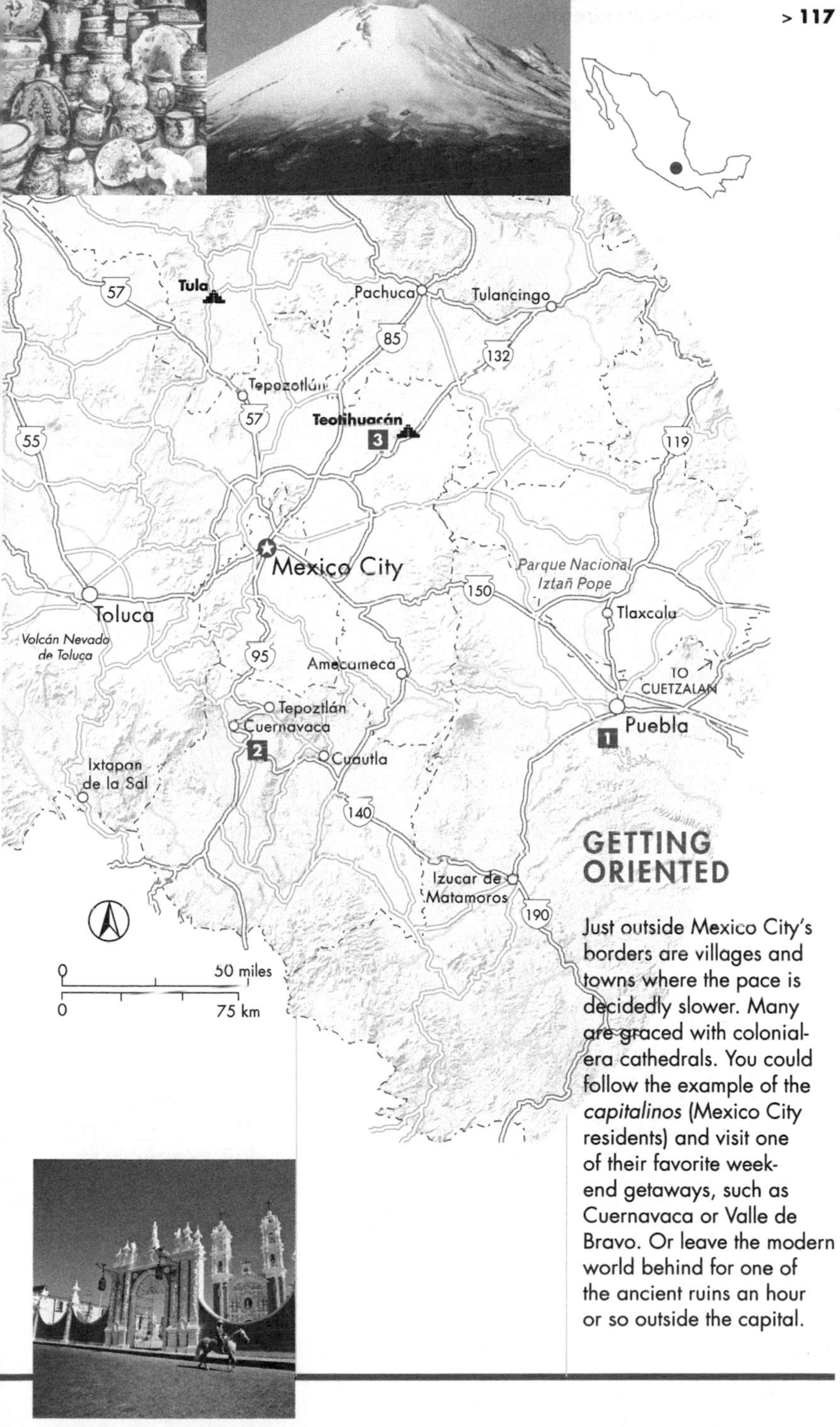

GETTING ORIENTED

Just outside Mexico City's borders are villages and towns where the pace is decidedly slower. Many are graced with colonial-era cathedrals. You could follow the example of the *capitalinos* (Mexico City residents) and visit one of their favorite week-end getaways, such as Cuernavaca or Valle de Bravo. Or leave the modern world behind for one of the ancient ruins an hour or so outside the capital.

AROUND MEXICO CITY PLANNER

Day Trips vs. Extended Stays

If you're going to Cuernavaca or Valle de Bravo, you should plan to overnight. Two nights in either city would allow you to do a side trip to the ruins of Xochicalco (from Cuernavaca) or to the Parque Nacional Nevado de Toluca (from Valle). You can visit Puebla on a day trip, but it would be a shame to rush it. Moreover, the city is lovely at night, when the buildings around the zócalo are floodlit, and the sidewalk cafés fill up. If you do overnight, spend the first day seeing the city and the next day in nearby Cholula or at the ruins of Cacaxtla. You might want to leave some flexibility in your schedule for an overnight stay at the magical Hacienda Soltepec outside of Tlaxcala.

Health Concerns

Even if you don't feel the altitude in Mexico City proper, you're bound to feel it if you head up to Cuetzalan or while attempting to climb the pyramids at Teotihuacán; take it slow and give yourself time to acclimate.

Travel Times

BY BUS FROM MEXICO CITY

CITY	TIME
Teotihuacán	1 hr
Puebla	2 hrs
Cholula	1¾ hrs
Tlaxcala	1¾ hrs
Cuetzalan	6 hrs (4 hrs from Puebla)
Valle de Bravo	2½ hrs

Note that travel times can vary greatly. Traffic snarls, especially at highway exits and tollbooths, can eat up a great deal of time. The easiest way to cut down on time in traffic, especially at city exits, is to plan on traveling when others are not. Head out of the capital early in the morning, for example.

Booking in Advance

Many of these places are popular destinations for Mexican families and may fill up fast during major holidays and festivals. Advance reservations are advised for the Christmas period and Semana Santa. On the long weekend marking Independence Day (September 16) it's often hard to get a room in Cuernavaca or Valle de Bravo. You should also make reservations if you plan to visit Cuetzalan during the town's fair during the first week of October.

WHAT IT COSTS IN DOLLARS

	¢	$	$$	$$$	$$$$
Restaurants	under $5	$5–$10	$10–$15	$15–$25	over $25
Hotels	under $50	$50–$75	$75–$150	$150–$250	over $250

Restaurant prices are per person for a main course at dinner. Hotel prices are for two people in a standard double room.

Updated by
Michele Joyce

PUEBLA, A WELL-PRESERVED COLONIAL TOWN that is the capital of the state of the same name, is a dazzling city and a destination in its own right. You can cover the city in a day trip, but you really should try to stay overnight. You could be drawn onward by nearby Cholula, with its dozens of churches, or Tlaxcala, with a pair of shady plazas perfect for spending a lazy afternoon in. Farther north in Puebla State you'll find the mountain town of Cuetzalan, with its wonderful Sunday market. If you've opted to head this way instead of hitting Teotihuacán, you can get a ruins fix at Cacaxtla.

PUEBLA

121 km (75 mi) east of Mexico City center.

The city of Puebla fairly bursts with baroque flourishes and the colors of its famed Talavera tiles. The downtown area in particular overflows with religious structures; it probably has more ex-convents and monasteries, chapels, and churches per square mile than anywhere else in the country.

The city center generally follows a tidy grid pattern. The streets are either *avenidas* or *calles*, and most are numbered. Avenidas run east (*oriente*) and west (*poniente*), while calles run north (*norte*) and south (*sur*). Odd-numbered avenidas start south of the *zócalo* (town square) and even-numbered avenidas start from the square's north side. Odd-numbered calles begin on the west of the zócalo, even-numbered calles to the east.

■ TIP→ Some of the blocks are particularly long here, so if you get tired or need to save time, hail a taxi. They're safe and should cost no more than $4 for a ride in the city center—just remember to fix the price before you set off.

GETTING HERE AND AROUND

Buses bound for Puebla depart several times an hour from Mexico City's TAPO terminal. On ADO, the most reliable company, the two-hour ride costs about $10. From Mexico City's Terminal del Sur, hourly Cristobal Colón buses cost $11. By car, trips on the toll road Route 150D take about 1½ hours; on Route 190, the scenic—and bumpy—free road, the same journey takes three hours.

■ TIP→ The double-decker Turibus (☎ 55/5563-6693 or 55/5598-6309) is a good option for exploring the city and the neighboring town of Cholula. Every day from 9 to 9, these open-topped buses follow a circuit around the city; you can board the buses at stops marked with Turibus signs.

ESSENTIALS

Bus Contacts **ADO** (☎ *55/5133-2424* 🌐 *www.adogl.com.mx*). **Cristobal Colón** (☎ *55/5544-9008 in Mexico City; 222/225-9007 in Puebla* 🌐 *www.ticketbus.com.mx*).

Currency Exchange **Caja Central** (✉ *Portal Hidalgo 6-11, Col. Centro* ☎ *222/232-9691*).

Medical Assistance **Hospital Angeles Puebla** (✉ *Av. Kepler 2143, Unidad Territorial* ☎ *222/303-6600* 🌐 *www.hospitalangelespuebla.com.mx*).

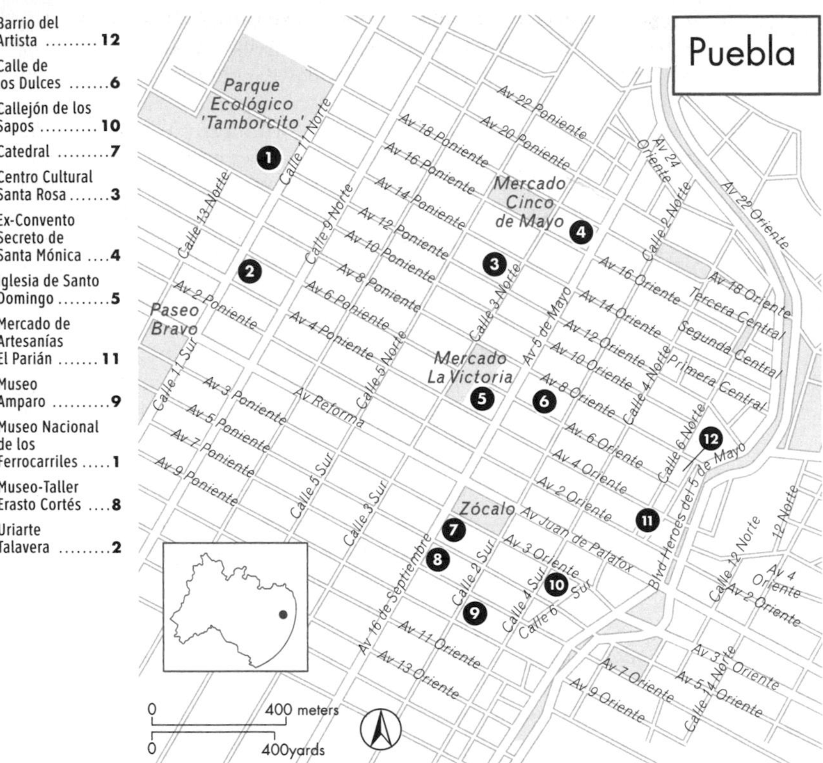

Post Office **Central Post Office** (✉ *16 de Septiembre 305, Col. Centro* 🌐 *www.sepomex.gob.mx*).

Rental Cars **Avis** (✉ *Blvd. Hermanos Serdán 104, Local 5, Col. Real del Monte* ☎ *222/249–6199* 🌐 *www.avis.com.mx*). **Hertz** (✉ *Blvd. Atlixco 307, Col. Real del Monte* ☎ *222/249–0049* 🌐 *www.hertz.com.mx*).

Visitor and Tour Info **Puebla Municipal Tourist Office** (✉ *Portal Hidalgo 14, Centro Histórico* ☎ *222/404–5008* 🌐 *www.turismopuebla.gob.mx*). **Puebla State Tourism Office** (✉ *Av. 5 Oriente 3, Centro Histórico* ☎ *222/777–1506* 🌐 *www.puebla.gob.mx*).

EXPLORING

TOP ATTRACTIONS

12 **Barrio del Artista.** Watch painters and sculptors at work in the galleries in this neighborhood. Farther down Calle 8 Norte, you can buy Talavera pottery and other local crafts from the dozens of small stores and street vendors. There are occasional weekend concerts and open-air theater performances. ✉ *Calle 8 Norte and Av. 6 Oriente* ⏲ *Daily 10–6.*

6 **Calle de los Dulces.** Puebla is famous for all kinds of homemade goodies. Calle de Santa Clara, also known as Sweets Street, is lined with shops

selling a wide variety of sugary treats in the shape of sacred hearts, guitars, and sombreros. Don't miss the cookies—they're even more delicious than they look. ⊠ *Av. 6 Oriente, between Av. 5 de Mayo and Calle 4 Norte* ⏲ *Daily 9–8.*

10 **Callejón de los Sapos.** "Alley of the Toads" cuts diagonally behind the cathedral. The attached square has an up-and-coming antiques market with all sorts of Mexican art, from elaborately carved doors to small paintings on pieces of tin offering thanks to a saint for favors. There are also cafés filled with young people listening to live music on weekend nights. ⊠ *Av. 5 Oriente and Calle 6 Sur* ⏲ *Daily 10–7.* 3

7 **Catedral.** Construction on the cathedral began between 1536 and 1539. Work was completed by Puebla's most famous son, Bishop Juan de Palafox y Mendoza, who donated his personal fortune to build its famous tower, the second-largest in the country. The altar was constructed between 1797 and 1818. Manuel Tolsá, Mexico's most illustrious colonial architect, adorned it with onyx, marble, and gold. ⊠ *Calle 2 Sur, south of zócalo* ☎ *No phone* ⏲ *Daily 7AM–12:30 and 4:15–7:30.*

5 **Iglesia de Santo Domingo.** The magnificent church of St. Dominic is famous for its overwhelming Capilla del Rosario (Chapel of the Rosary), where almost every inch of the walls and ceilings is covered with gilded carvings. Dominican friars arrived here in 1534, barely a dozen years after the Spanish conquered this region. The Capilla de la Tercera Orden (Chapel of the Third Order) was originally called the "Chapel of the Dark-Skinned Ones," named for the mixed-race population born a short time later. ⊠ *Av. 5 de Mayo at Av. 4 Poniente* ☎ *222/242–3643* ⏲ *Daily 10–6.*

11 **Mercado de Artesanías El Parián.** This market is the place for kitschy versions of such tourist souvenirs as toy guitars and colorful sombreros. Feel free to haggle. For better-quality goods, **La Casa del Artesano**, alongside the market, is the state-sponsored shop for regional craftwork. ⊠ *Av. 4 Oriente and Calle 6 Norte* ⏲ *Daily 10–7:30.*

9 ★ **Museo Amparo.** Home to the private collection of pre-Columbian and Colonial-era art of Mexican banker and philanthropist Manuel Espinoza Yglesias, Museo Amparo is one of the country's grandest museums. It exhibits unforgettable pieces from all over Mexico, including more than 2,000 pre-Hispanic artifacts. The collection includes colonial-era painting, sculpture, and decorative objects and a small modern art section notable for works by Diego Rivera, Frida Kahlo, Miguel Felguérez, and Vicente Rojo. ⊠ *Calle 2 Sur 708, at Av. 9 Oriente* ☎ *222/246–4646 or 222/229–3850* 🌐 *www.museoamparo.com* 🎫 *$3.50; free Mon.* ⏲ *Wed.–Mon. 10–6.*

WORTH NOTING

3 **Centro Cultural Santa Rosa.** The former convent houses a museum of crafts from the state's seven regions. The museum also contains the intricately tiled kitchen where Puebla's renowned chocolate mole sauce is believed to have been invented by the nuns, as a surprise for their demanding bishop. ⊠ *3 Norte 1203* ☎ *222/232–779* 🎫 *$13; free Tues.* ⏲ *Tues.–Sun. 10–5.*

CLOSE UP

Misty Mountaintops

Leaving Mexico City on Route 150D (known as the Carretera a Puebla or the Puebla Highway), you'll see Mexico's second- and third-highest peaks, Popocatépetl and Iztaccíhuatl, to your right—if the clouds and climate allow. Popo, 17,887 feet high, is the pointed volcano farther away, sometimes graced with a plume of smoke; Izta is the larger, rugged one covered with snow. Popo has seen a renewed period of activity since the mid-1990s; volcanic activity occurred in early 2008 (the mountain is still in "yellow" alert level).

As legend has it, Aztec warrior Popocatépetl was sent by the emperor—father of his beloved Iztaccíhuatl—to bring back the head of a feared enemy in order to win her hand. He returned triumphantly only to find that Iztaccíhuatl had killed herself, believing him dead. Grief-stricken, Popo laid out her body on a small knoll and lighted an eternal torch that he watches over. Each of Iztaccíhuatl's four peaks is named for a different part of her body, and its silhouette conjures up its nickname, "Sleeping Woman" (although the correct Nahuatl translation is "the white woman").

Popo is strictly off-limits for climbing, but several of Izta's rugged peaks can be explored as long as you are accompanied by recommended guides. You'll be rewarded with sublime views of Popo and other volcanoes, with the Pico de Orizaba (or Citlaltepetl) to the east and the Nevado de Toluca to the west.

■ **TIP→ Ideally, you won't need it, but the Brigada del Rescate del Socorro Alpino de México (☎ 55/5392–9299 or 044–55/1288–5920** 🌐 *www.socorroalpinodemexico.org.mx.*) **handles emergencies in the Parque Nacional Izta-Popo.**

The town of Amecameca is the most convenient base. Its tourism infrastructure is no-frills but adequate, and the offices of the national park and CONANP (✉ *Plaza de la Constitución 10-B* ☎ *597/978–3829 or 597/978–3830* 🌐 *www.edomexico.gob.mx*), the national commission for protected areas, are both here. The CONANP bureau, near the church on the zócalo, is a rich source of information on the volcanoes. It also makes guiding arrangements for climbing Izta. The best time to visit is from the end of October until May; it's bitterly cold at night in the winter months.

A cobbled road lined with olive trees and cedars leads to the hilltop Santuario del Sacromonte, a church and active seminary known for the *Cristo de Sacromonte.* The black Christ figure, made of sugarcane, is said to date from 1527; it's kept in a cavelike space behind the altar. On clear days this perch is one of the best spots for breathtaking views over Amecameca toward the volcanoes. The church is open daily 9–5. Take a bumpy track even higher up to reach the little Guadalupita chapel.

4 **Ex-Convento Secreto de Santa Mónica.** This former convent opened in 1688 as a spiritual refuge for women whose husbands were away on business. Despite the Reform Laws of the 1850s, it continued to function until 1934. It is said that the women here invented the famous dish called *chiles en nogada*, a complicated recipe that incorporates the red, white, and green colors of the Mexican flag. Curiosities include the gruesome display of the preserved heart of the convent's founder and paintings in the *Sala de los Terciopelos (Velvet Room)*, in which the feet and faces seem to change position as you view them from different angles. Note that, at this writing, the building is closed for restoration work, with no firm re-opening date. *Av. 18 Poniente 103, near Av. 5 de Mayo* *222/232–0178* *$3.30; free Sun.* *Tues.–Sun. 9:30–5:30.*

1 **Museo Nacional de los Ferrocarriles.** Occupying a train station inaugurated by President Juárez in 1869, the National Railway Museum extends a nostalgic treat. Period engines sit on the now-unused platforms, and several cars—including a caboose—can be explored. *Calle 11 Norte at Av. 12 Poniente* *222/774–0100* *www.museoferrocarriles.org.mx* *$1; free Sun.* *Tues.–Sun. 9–4:45.*

8 **Museo-Taller Erasto Cortés.** Named for Erasto Cortés Juárez, the city's most important 20th-century artist, this museum displays his vibrant engravings and portraits. It also showcases up-and-coming international artists. *Av. 7 Oriente 4, between 2 Sur and 16 de Septiembre* *222/246–6922* *Free* *Tues.–Sun. 10–5.*

2 **Uriarte Talavera.** Founded in 1824, this is one of the few authentic Talavera workshops left today. To be the real deal, pieces must be hand-painted in intricate designs with natural dyes derived from minerals. That's why only five colors are used: blue, black, yellow, green, and a reddish pink. **TIP→ English- and Spanish-language tours take place weekdays every half hour between 10 and 2 and cost $5. If you miss the tour, you can only visit the shop and the patio.** *Av. 4 Poniente 911, at Calle 11 Norte* *222/232–1598* *www.uriartetalavera.com.mx* *Mon.–Sat. 10–6, Sun. 11–5.*

WHERE TO EAT

Lunchtime is when most *poblanos* (people from Puebla) eat out, and restaurants tend to be quiet at night unless it's a Friday or Saturday. There are an increasing number of cafés and fast-food joints around the zócalo that are good for a quick bite between museum visits. At the restaurants under the *portales* (arches) you can tuck into Mexican and international fare while enjoying some prime people-watching.

$ MEXICAN **Fonda de Santa Clara.** Founded in 1965, this popular eatery has three branches in Puebla (and others in Acapulco and Mexico City). Two of the Puebla branches have great locations in the center of town. The original, near the zócalo, is cozier, but the larger newcomer at Paseo Bravo still manages a nice colonial aura. The food consists of mole, mole, and more mole, but you can also get *nopal* (prickly-pear leaf) salad, *sopa de medula* (marrowbone soup), and other hearty regional fare. *Calle 3 Poniente 307* *222/242–2659* *www.fondadesantaclara.*

CLOSE UP

A Well-Rounded Hacienda

La Hacienda de Panoaya, also known as Parque de los Venados Acariciables (pettable deer), has plenty of animals for curious kids, with ostriches, emus, and llamas as well as deer (horseback rides are also a possibility). But the menagerie is only part of the game; there are also two museums. The Museo Internacional de los Volcanes has some interesting information on volcanoes, but it's primarily a big thrill for kids, who love to scream at the recorded sound of an eruption. Meanwhile, the Museo Sor Juana Inés de la Cruz honors its namesake, a nun, scholar, and author who learned to read here and went on to produce some of the most significant poetry and prose of the 17th century. De la Cruz's intellectual accomplishments were truly exceptional in her time, as was her fervent defense of women's rights. The hacienda is a 15-minute walk out of town along the boulevard Iztaccíhuatl. ✉ *Carretera México-Cuautla, Km 58, Amecameca* ☎ *597/978–5050* 🌐 *www.haciendapanoaya.com* 🎟 *$2 (access to public/green areas); $8 (to public areas and two of three attractions, e.g., petting zoo and one museum); $10 (access to everything)* ⏲ *Zoo daily 10–5; museums weekends 10–5.*

com ✉ *Paseo Bravo, Calle 3 Poniente 920* ☎ *222/246–1919* 💳 *AE, MC, V.*

$–$$$ MEXICAN ✕ **Las Bodegas del Molino.** This restaurant's setting—an elegant 16th-century hacienda at the edge of town—is matched by its fine cuisine. If you're not sure about mole, give it a try here: the same woman has been making it since 1982, and her seductive, fruity blend will probably win you over. Romantics should book in advance a private dinner in the French Room. ■ **TIP→ After dining, you can request a tour of the fabulous premises.** ✉ *Calzada del Bosque 2, Molino de San José del Puente* ☎ *222/249–0399* 💳 *AE, MC, V.*

$$–$$$ MEXICAN ✕ **Mi Ciudad Puebla.** This longtime favorite is the place for a tasty traditional meal. The interior decoration is typical Puebla—complete with tile floors, colorful murals, and a newspaper stand inside—as is the menu. The mole is as traditional as it comes, and the *sopa poblana (a cream soup with poblano chilies, mushrooms, and corn)* is exceptional. This is also a great place to enjoy grilled meat. ✉ *Av. Juárez 2507* ☎ *222/231–5326* 💳 *AE, MC, V.*

WHERE TO STAY

$$–$$$ 🏨 **Camino Real.** Formerly a convent, this 16th-century building radiates historic character, from its luminous restored frescoes to its wooden shutters. Large white rooms have colonial antique furniture and exposed beams. The junior suite was once the convent's chapel, and the presidential suite has original 16th-century gilded furnishings and carpeting. The staff is warm and professional. **Pros:** stunning architecture; in the heart of the city; excellent service. **Cons:** pricier than nearby lodgings. ✉ *Av. 7 Poniente 105* ☎ *222/229–0909 or 222/229–0910* 🌐 *www.caminoreal.com/puebla* 🛏 *75 rooms, 9 suites* 👍 *In-room: safe, refrigerator, Internet.*

In-hotel: 2 restaurants, room service, bar, Internet terminal ⊟ *AE, DC, MC, V.*

$$$ **Casona de la China Poblana.** This marvelously renovated colonial building may no longer be a private home, but it still has the same cozy environment. Many of the original details have been preserved, but there are also modern furnishings. The central patio is home to Ekos, which serves well-prepared and beautifully presented traditional Mexican dishes and interesting international fare. Keeping watch over the dining room is a large statue of the place's namesake: China Poblana, the daughter of a Mongol king who was kidnapped and brought to Mexico. **Pros:** great restaurant; friendly service; easy walk to downtown sights. **Cons:** more expensive than nearby hotels. ✉ *4 Norte 2* ☎ *222/242–5336* 🌐 *www.casonadelachinapoblana.com* *10 rooms* *In-room: refrigerator, Wi-Fi. In-hotel: restaurant, bar, spa, Wi-Fi hotspot* ⊟ *AE, D, MC, V.*

MOLE AND MORE

Two of Mexico's most popular dishes were supposedly created in Puebla. One specialty is mole (pronounced mo-lay), a sauce with as many as 30 ingredients. The other specialty is *chiles en nogada,* green poblano chilies filled with meats, fruits, and nuts, then covered with a sauce of chopped walnuts and cream, and topped with pomegranate seeds; the colors represent the Mexican flag. Typical snacks are *pelonas,* fried rolls filled with lettuce, beef, cream, and sauce; and *cemita,* which is like a *torta* but made with a sweeter bread and filled with avocado, meat, and cheese.

$–$$ **Hotel Casa de la Palma.** In an older building, this newly renovated hotel has a great location in the center of town. Every room has been lovingly restored and individually decorated by Carlos Olea, an antiquarian who has years of experience working in Puebla. Some rooms are named for artists or animals, but the real showstopper is the room dedicated to former President Porfirio Díaz—with its high ceilings, over-the-top portraits, and original letters signed by the dictator himself. Also popular is the Suite Morisca, decorated in a Moorish style complete with tall arches and intricate wall carvings. **Pros:** wonderfully decorated; reasonable prices; friendly staff. **Cons:** not all rooms are created equal; stairs are a little steep. ✉ *3 Oriente 217* ☎ *222/246–1437* 🌐 *www.casadelapalmapuebla.com* *16 rooms* *In-room: Wi-Fi. In-hotel: gym* ⊟ *AE, MC, V* *BP.*

$ **Hotel Royalty.** This well-maintained hotel is always busy because of its popular restaurant under the *portales* (arches) on the main square. People stop by for a pleasant breakfast or lunch while watching residents go about their day. The old colonial building is an excellent choice for its central location on the zócalo; the best rooms are the junior suites. **Pros:** on the main square; bargain price. **Cons:** no air-conditioning. ✉ *Portal Hidalgo 8* ☎ *222/242–4740* 🌐 *www.hotelr.com* *34 rooms, 11 suites* *In-room: no a/c. In-hotel: restaurant, room service, bar, Internet terminal, parking (paid)* ⊟ *AE, MC, V* *BP.*

¢ **Hotel Santiago.** One of the cheaper central options, this little no-frills hotel opposite a department store is modern and clean. The double rooms have two double beds. **Pros:** unbeatable price; comfortable rooms. **Cons:** no air-conditioning. ✉ *Av. 3 Poniente 106, at 16 de Septiembre* ☎ *222/242–2860* 🌐 *www.hotelsantiago.com.mx* *37 rooms* *In-room: no a/c, Wi-fi* 💳 *MC, V.*

> **DID YOU KNOW?**
>
> Mole is such a quintessentially Mexican dish that it's common to hear that something is "más mexicano que el mole" ("more Mexican than mole"), which is like saying something is "as American as apple pie."

$$$–$$$$ **La Purificadora.** This hotel, part of the Grupo Habita chain, is without a doubt one of the hottest places to stay in Puebla. While many historic elements of this former factory have been left untouched, ultramodern materials have been used for the renovation, creating an environment full of interesting contrasts. For example, rough-hewn stone walls are paired with brushed metal and polished glass. The place has a whimsical attitude, with wonderful touches like the glass-sided rooftop pool. Rooms, decorated with sleek furnishings, are positively modern. The menu at the hotel restaurant, designed by award-winning chef Enrique Olvera, serves many traditional regional options. **Pros:** attention paid to every detail; interesting architecture; wonderful restaurant. **Cons:** can be a bit of a scene; pricier than most lodgings. ✉ *Callejon de la 10 Norte 802* ☎ *222/309–1920* 🌐 *www.lapurificadora.com* *26 suites* *In-room: safe, refrigerator, Wi-Fi. In-hotel: restaurant, room service, pool, gym, spa* 💳 *AE, MC, V.*

$$–$$$ **Mesón de Capuchinas.** Though this 17th-century building sits in the center of the city, its thick walls make it a calm, quiet sanctuary. Each spacious room has a slightly different, somewhat monastic, style. Many have beamed ceilings; some have wrought-iron bedsteads or religious icons. The suites are decorated in a more contemporary style. The restaurant ($) is especially popular at lunch. **Pros:** great service; pleasant restaurant; rooms have handsome antiques. **Cons:** street noise in the evening. ✉ *Av. 9 Oriente 16* ☎ *222/232–8088 or 222/246–6084* 🌐 *www.mesondecapuchinas.com.mx* *7 suites* *In-room: safe, Wi-Fi. In-hotel: restaurant, bar, parking (free)* 💳 *AE, MC, V* *BP.*

$$$ **Mesón Sacristía de la Compañía.** If any of the antiques that decorate your room strike your fancy, you might consider taking home a souvenir. They are all for sale. Warming touches are both figurative and literal at this converted colonial mansion; you'll be welcomed with a plate of cookies, and if it gets chilly, heaters are brought to your room. The rich colors of folk art pervade the cozy but stylish bar. The lovely restaurant ($$) serves tasty regional dishes such as *carne San Pascual* (steak with corn fungus). There is live music in the evening. **Pros:** excellent restaurant; top-notch service; good location. **Cons:** street noise in the evening. ✉ *Calle 6 Sur 304, at Callejón de los Sapos* ☎ *222/232–4513* 🌐 *www.mesones-sacristia.com* *8 rooms* *In-room: Wi-Fi. In-hotel: restaurant, room service, bar, parking (free)* 💳 *AE, MC, V* *BP.*

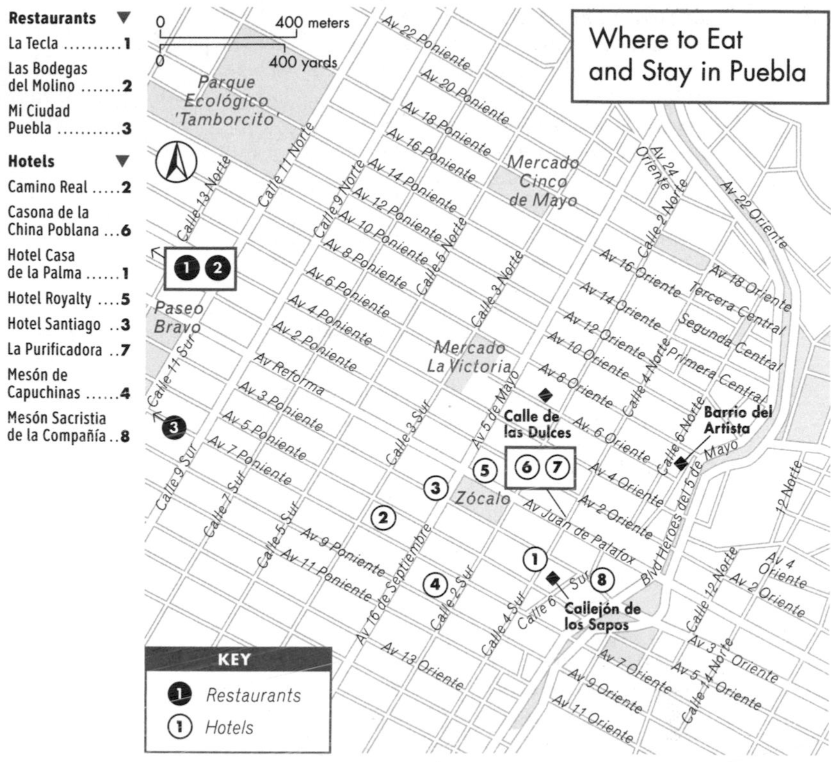

NIGHTLIFE

Puebla's nightlife centers on the bars on Avenida Juárez. **La Cantina de los Remedios** has mariachis who keep the songs coming. It's a good place for after-dinner drinks. ✉ *Av. Juárez 2504, Col. la Paz* ☎ *222/249–0843* 🌐 *www.losremedios.com.mx.*

CHOLULA

14 km (9 mi) west of Puebla via Rte. 190, 113 km (70) mi southeast of Mexico City.

Creeping out from under the shadow of Puebla, Cholula is gradually being restored to something of its former greatness. Before the Spanish conquest, the ancient settlement west of Puebla had hundreds of temples and rivaled Teotihuacán as a cultural and ceremonial center. On his arrival, Cortés ordered every temple destroyed and replaced by a church. However, the claim that Cholula has 365 church cupolas, one for every day in the year, is to be taken with a grain of salt.

GETTING HERE AND AROUND

Second-class Autobuses Unidos/Ticketbus buses depart from Mexico City's Terminal Autobuses Oriente several times daily. The two-hour ride costs $9. You may prefer to take a first-class bus to Puebla and then take a $10 taxi ride to Cholula. By car, trips from Mexico City on the toll road Route 150D take about 1½ hours; on Route 190, the scenic—and bumpy—free road, the same journey takes three hours.

ESSENTIALS

Bus Contacts Autobuses Unidos/Ticketbus (☎ *55/5133–2424* 🌐 *www.ticketbus.com.mx*).

Medical Assistance Farmacia Sagrado Corazón (✉ *Av. Hidalgo 103 B* ☎ *222/247–0398*). **Hospital General de Cholula** (✉ *Calle 2 Poniente 1504* ☎ *222/247–1800*).

Visitor and Tour Info San Pedro Cholula Tourist Office (✉ *12 Oriente at 4 Norte* ☎ *222/261–2393* 🌐 *www.vivecholula.gob.mx*).

EXPLORING

Weekends are the liveliest time to visit Cholula, when you can catch the Sunday market and some live music with dinner. The town's even busier during one of its many festivals, especially the *Feria de San Pedro,* during the first two weeks of September.

The town is divided into three municipalities; most of the major sites of interest are divided between San Pedro Cholula and San Andrés Cholula.

TOP ATTRACTIONS

Ex-Convento de San Gabriel. This impressive, huge former convent includes a trio of churches. The most unusual is the Moorish-style Capilla Real, with 49 domes. Construction began in the 1540s, and the building was originally open on one side to facilitate the conversion of huge masses of people. Fewer than 20 Franciscan monks still live in one part of the premises, so be respectful of their privacy. ✉ *2 Norte s/n, east of Cholula Zócalo* ☎ *No phone* ⏲ *Daily 10–12:30 and 4:30–6.*

Gran Pirámide. The Great Pyramid was the hub of Olmec, Toltec, and Aztec religious centers and is, by volume, the largest pyramid in the world. It consists of seven superimposed structures connected by tunnels and stairways. Ignacio Márquina, the architect in charge of the initial explorations in 1931, decided to excavate two tunnels partly to prove that *el cerrito* (the little hill), as many still call it, was an archaeological trove. When seeing the Zona Arqueológica, you'll walk through these tunnels to a vast 43-acre temple complex that was dedicated to the god Quetzalcóatl.

On top of the pyramid stands the Spanish chapel Nuestra Señora de los Remedios (Our Lady of the Remedies). Almost brought down by a quake in 1999, it has been wonderfully restored. From the top of the pyramid you'll have a clear view of other nearby churches, color-coded by period: oxidized red was used in the 16th century, yellow in the 17th and 18th centuries, and pastel colors in the 19th century. You can obtain an English-language guide for about $15. ✉ *Calz. San Andrés at Calle 2 Norte* ☎ *222/247–9081* 🎫 *$4 includes museum* ⏲ *Daily 9–6.*

WORTH NOTING

San Francisco Acatepec. Manuel Toussaint, an expert in colonial art, likened this church to "a temple of porcelain, worthy of being kept beneath a crystal dome." Construction began in 1590, with the elaborate Spanish baroque decorations added between 1650 and 1750. Multicolored Talavera tiles cover the exceptionally ornate facade. The interior blazes with polychrome plasterwork and gilding; a sun radiates overhead. Unlike that of the nearby Santa María Tonantzintla, the ornamentation hews to the standard representations of the Incarnation, the Evangelists, and the Holy Trinity. Look for St. Francis, to whom the church is dedicated, between the altarpiece's spiraling columns. ✉ *6½ km (4 mi) south of Cholula* ☎ *No phone* ⏲ *Daily 9–5.*

★ **Santa María Tonantzintla.** The exterior of this 16th-century church might be simple, but inside waits an explosion of color and swirling shapes. To facilitate the conversion of the native population, Franciscan monks incorporated elements recalling the local cult of the goddess Tonantzin in the ornamentation of the chapel. The result is a jewel of the style known as churrigueresque. The polychrome wood-and-stucco carvings—inset columns, altarpieces, and the main archway—were completed in the late 17th century. The carvings, set off by ornate gold-leaf figures of plant forms, angels, and saints, were made by local craftspeople. Flash photography is not allowed. ✉ *Av. Reforma, 5 km (3 mi) south of Cholula* ☎ *No phone* ⏲ *Daily 9–5.*

WHERE TO EAT

¢–$ MEXICAN ✕ **Güeros.** This budget eatery to the side of the portales on the zócalo is a favorite for fresh local fare. The menu includes tacos, *flautas* (tortillas rolled into tubes and deep-fried), and *pozole* (flavorful hominy soup with pork or chicken). The *tortas* (sandwiches) are stuffed with anything from breaded chicken to *riñones* (kidneys). The place stays open until around midnight. ✉ *Av. Hidalgo 101* ☎ *222/247–2188* ▭ *MC, V.*

$–$$ MEXICAN ✕ **La Lunita.** A stone's throw from the Gran Pirámide, this little eatery has bumped up its prices a bit, but it's still a good place to cool off after a sweltering afternoon in the archaeological zone. It's welcoming and cluttered with bric-a-brac. The specialty is *acamayas,* a kind of crayfish. Also available are *chilaquiles,* milkshakes, various types of mole, and meat dishes. ✉ *Av. Morelos at 6 Norte* ☎ *222/247–0011* 🌐 *www.lalunita.com* ▭ *AE, MC, V.*

¢–$$ MEXICAN ✕ **Restaurant-Bar Los Jarrones.** Simple but smart, Los Jarrones ("The Pitchers") welcomes diners with long wooden tables, comfy cushioned chairs, and white walls accented with green tiles. Starters include onion and garlic soup; the *parrillada* (a variety of grilled meats) is a popular option for sharing. A weekend breakfast buffet is served 9:30 to 1. Live music at night is loud but pleasant. ✉ *Portal Guerrero No. 7* ☎ *222/247–1098* ▭ *AE, MC, V.*

WHERE TO STAY

¢ 🏨 **Hotel Plaza Santa Rosa.** This place has the distinction of being the only hotel on the zócalo; look for the small entrance under the arches by a busy coffee shop. The rooms are comfortable, but some are depressingly dark, so ask to see a few before you settle on one. **Pros:** great location; bargain price. **Cons:** no air-conditioning. ✉ *Portal de Guerrero 5, San Pedro Cholula* ☎ *222/247–7719 or 222/247–0341* 🌐 *www.plazasantarosa.com.mx* *27 rooms* *In-room: no a/c, safe, Wi-Fi. In-hotel: restaurant, bar, Wi-Fi hotspot* ▭ *AE, MC, V.*

$$–$$$ ★ **Hotel Quinta Luna.** The elegance of this boutique hotel—a five-minute walk from the zócalo—has been crucial in putting Cholula back on the map. The restored 17th-century mansion was built around a central patio with a fountain. Immaculate rooms have natural colors, polished wood furniture and floors, and high, exposed-beam ceilings. King-size beds are wrapped in luscious, down-filled bedding and supplied with more pillows than you could possibly use. The outstanding restaurant ($–$$) creates Mexican and nouvelle dishes and is worth a visit in its own right. **Pros:** alluring gardens; comfortable rooms; elegant place. **Cons:** expensive rates; fills up far in advance. ✉ *3 Sur 702, San Pedro Cholula* ☎ *222/247–8915* 🌐 *www.laquintaluna.com* *7 suites* *In-room: safe, refrigerator, DVD, Wi-Fi. In-hotel: restaurant, bar* ▭ *AE, MC, V* *BP.*

$$ **Hotel Villa Arqueológica.** This small hotel is close enough to the pyramid to enjoy a run up all those steps before breakfast (or if you prefer, you can just enjoy the view from the hotel entrance). Rooms are simple, decorated with rustic wood furniture and brightly colored bedspreads; Mexican crafts occupy small niches in the rooms and hallways. The inviting outdoor swimming pool, surrounded by plants, is a great place to relax after a day in the warm sun. **Pros:** great location near the pyramid; reasonable rates. **Cons:** cramped rooms; no Internet connection in guest rooms. ✉ *2 Poniente 601* ☎ *222/273–7900* 🌐 *www.villasarqueologicas.com.mx* *44 rooms* *In-room: no a/c, safe. In-hotel: restaurant, bar, tennis courts, pool, Internet terminal* ▭ *AE, MC, V.*

SPORTS AND THE OUTDOORS

Club de Golf La Huerta (✉ *Prolongación 15 Sur 219, Privada Juan Blanca* ☎ *222/247–3392* 🌐 *www.lahuertagolfhotel.com*)) is a 9-hole golf course with reasonable greens fees of $50 on weekdays and $60 on weekends.

TLAXCALA

31 km (19 mi) north of Puebla, 121 km (75 mi) east of Mexico City.

Tlaxcala (pronounced tlas-*ca*-la) is a place where you may well find yourself lingering longer than you had planned, lulled by a few hours spent on the Plaza Xicohténcatl or at a café in one of the colonnades near the zócalo. The distinctive terra-cotta roofs gave the state capital the name Ciudad Roja, or Red City. Climb up to one of the hilltop churches and a sea of ruddy roofs will stretch out around you.

EXPLORING

TOP ATTRACTIONS

Cacaxtla. Tlaxcala's most famous site isn't in the town at all. At the nearby archaeological site of Cacaxtla you'll see some of Mexico's most vividly colored murals. Accidentally discovered in 1975, the main temple at Cacaxtla contains breathtaking scenes of a surprisingly vicious battle between two bands of warriors. The nearly life-size figures wearing jaguar skins clearly have the upper hand against their foes in lofty feathered headdresses.

The site, dating from AD 650 to AD 900, is thought to be the work of the Olmeca-Xicalanca people. Other paintings adorn smaller structures. The newly restored Templo Rojo, or Red Temple, is decorated with stalks of corn with cartoonlike human faces. Perhaps the most delightful is in the Templo de Venus, or Temple of Venus, where two figures are dancing in the moonlight, their bodies a striking blue.

3

On a hill about 1½ km (1 mi) north of Cacaxtla is the site of Xochitécatl, with four Classic Period pyramids. You can see both sites with the same admission ticket. Head south from Mexico City toward Puebla on Carretera Federal 119. Veer off to the right toward the town of Nativitas. Both sites are near the village of San Miguel del Milagro. ✉ *About 19 km (12 mi) southwest of Tlaxcala on Carretera Federal 119* ☎ *246/416–0477 or 246/416–0000* 🌐 *www.inah.gob.mx* 🎫 *$4.90* ⏲ *Daily 9–5.*

Palacio de Gobierno. Inside the eastern entrance to this government building north of the main square are murals by local painter Desiderio Hernández Xochitiotzin depicting Tlaxcala's pivotal role in the Spanish conquest. The city aligned itself with Cortés against the Aztecs, thus swelling the conqueror's ranks significantly. The building is open daily 9–5:30. ✉ *Plaza de la Constitución.*

Zócalo. Bordered by Calle Camargo and Avenida Juárez, Tlaxcala's main square has a gorgeously tiled bandstand shaded by graceful trees. Adjoining the zócalo at its southeast corner is another square, Plaza Xicohténcatl. Souvenir shops line its eastern edge.

WORTH NOTING

★ **Basilica de Ocotlán.** On a hill about 1 km (½ mi) northwest of the center of Tlaxcala stands the ornate Basilica de Ocotlán. You can see its churrigueresque facade, topped with twin towers adorned with the apostles, from just about everywhere in the city. The church is most notable as a pilgrimage site. In 1541 the Virgin Mary appeared to a poor peasant, telling him to cure an epidemic with water from a stream that had suddenly appeared. Franciscan monks, eager to find the source of the miracle, ventured into the forest. There they discovered raging flames that didn't harm one particular pine (*ocotlán*). When they split the tree open, they discovered the wooden image of the Virgen de Ocotlán, which they installed in a gilded altar. Many miracles have been attributed to the statue, which wears the braids popular for indigenous women at the time. Behind the altar is the brilliantly painted *Camarín de la Virgen (Dressing Room of the Virgin)* that tells the story. At the base of the hill is the appealing Capilla del Pocito de Agua Santa, an octagonal chapel decorated with images of the Virgen de Ocotlán. The faithful come to draw holy water from its seven fountains. ✉ *Calle Guridi y Alcocer* ☎ *246/465–0960 to local tourism office, which is great about giving info on the basilica* ⏲ *Daily 9–6.*

Catedral de Nuestra Señora de la Asunción. This cathedral is atop a hill one block south of Plaza Xicohténcatl. Its most unusual feature is its

Moorish-style wood ceiling beams, carved and gilded with gold studs. There are only a few churches of this kind in Mexico, as Mudejar flourishes were popular here only during the really early years after the Spanish conquest. The austere monastery is home to the Museo Regional de Tlaxcala, which displays 16th- to 18th-century religious paintings as well as a small collection of pre-Columbian pieces. A beautiful outdoor chapel near the monastery has notable Moorish and Gothic traces. ✉ *Calz. de San Francisco* ☎ *No phone* 🌐 *www.inah.gob.mx* 🎫 *Museum $3* ⏲ *Daily 10–5.*

Museo de la Memoria. To the west of Plaza Xicohténcatl is this fascinating museum with a colonial-era facade but a strikingly modern interior. By focusing on the folklore and festivals of various indigenous cultures, its displays recount the region's past and present. ✉ *Av. Independencia 3* ☎ *246/466–0791* 🎫 *$3.50; free Tues.* ⏲ *Tues.–Sun. 10–5.*

Parroquia de San José. The Parroquia de San José is cheerfully decorated in vivid shades of yellow and green. Don't miss the pair of fonts near the entrance that depict Tlaxcalan, a god of war. The church is open daily 9–6. ✉ *Av. Lira y Ortega and Calle Lardizábal.*

WHERE TO EAT AND STAY

$–$$ MEXICAN

✕ **Fonda del Convento.** In a low stone building on a tree-lined street, this unassuming café is overlooked by most travelers but is always packed with locals. The series of small dining rooms means it won't be hard to find a quiet table. The delicious traditional fare includes such dishes as chicken broth with creamy avocados and strips of cactus flambéed with bits of onion and chilies. Ask your waiter if there's *caldo de habas*, a bean soup with strips of cactus; it's not something that you find everywhere, and is quite tasty. ✉ *Calz. de San Francisco 1* ☎ *246/462–0765* 💳 *MC, V.*

$$ MEXICAN Fodor'sChoice ★

Hacienda Soltepec. Resembling an old castle, this hacienda was made famous as the backdrop for the 1955 film *La Escondida*. Converted into an elegant and welcoming hotel, it is a true gem in the middle of nowhere. Located 51 km (32 mi) from Tlaxcala, it has pristine views of the Malinche volcano. The stately restaurant ($), watched over by two stuffed bulls, serves delicious regional fare and has a cozy fireplace to warm up the chilly winter nights. It is a hive of activity on Sunday, when *poblanos* come here to lunch. Best of all, the hotel gives tours to other remote haciendas of Tlaxcala State, an eye-opener into the history of the rural region. **Pros:** marvelous building; excellent service; great volcano views. **Cons:** need a car to get around. ✉ *Carretera Huamantla-Puebla, Km 3, Huamantla* ☎ *247/472–1466 or 247/472–3110* 🌐 *www.haciendasoltepec.com* *12 rooms* *In-room: no a/c, Wi-Fi. In-hotel: restaurant, tennis courts, pool, gym, spa, parking (free)* 💳 *AE, MC, V.*

CUETZALAN

Fodor'sChoice ★

182 km (113 mi) north of Puebla, 200 km (124 mi) northeast of Mexico City.

The colonial town of Cuetzalan in the Sierra Norte region is one of the most precious and unspoiled attractions in the state of Puebla. The

Sierra Norte has been referred to as the Sierra Mágica (magical mountain range) for the mystic beliefs held by the pre-Hispanic peoples who inhabited this lush, dramatic swath of land. Cuetzalan's breathtaking landscape is etched with canyons, rushing rivers, and caves, and swaddled in dense, outsize vegetation. Because of its elevation the town is often enveloped in clouds.

At the weekly Sunday market, or *tianguis,* in the town center, local farmers come to sell and trade corn, coffee, beans, spices, and citrus fruits. Most people wear indigenous dress and chatter in Nahuatl, sizing up the cinnamon or bargaining for guavas. The character, color, and fragrant smells of this lively event are not to be missed.

GETTING HERE AND AROUND

Texcoco/Primera Plus buses make the six-hour trip from Mexico City's TAPO terminal only on weekends. The ride costs about $10. For those who wish to visit during the week, the best option is to go to Puebla and transfer to an ADO bus to Cuetzalan. The four-hour trip from Puebla costs $5.

ESSENTIALS

Bus Contacts ADO (☎ *55/5133-2424* 🌐 *www.adogl.com.mx*). **Texcoco/Primera Plus** (☎ *55/5542-8689; 01800/375-7587 toll-free in Mexico*).

Medical Assistance Hospital Integral (✉ *Miguel Alvarado 85* ☎ *233/331-0127*).

Visitor and Tour Info Dirección Municipal de Turismo Cuetzalan (✉ *Hidalgo 29* ☎ *233/331-0015* 🌐 *www.cuetzalan.gob.mx*).

EXPLORING

TOP ATTRACTIONS

Zócalo. On the town's square you'll find the Renaissance-style church, La Parroquia de San Francisco, as well as the Palacio Municipal. The bandstand and the municipal clock tower were both built in the early 20th century. As you take in the sights, vendors will try to sell you everything from flowers to napkin holders. If you are not interested in buying, sometimes saying "*no, gracias*" ("no, thank you") is not sufficient. If you want to get your point across, try "*ya compré*" ("I already bought one").

■ TIP→ Wear sturdy walking shoes and be prepared for cool and damp weather. The steep, cobblestoned streets can be dangerously slippery when the weather is misty or rainy. Happily, taxis here are extremely cheap.

WORTH NOTING

Casa de la Cultura. What was originally a coffee processing plant now houses a public library, the town archives, and a somewhat haphazard ethnographic museum, which often displays works by local artists. Opposite the building across Avenida Miguel Alvarado is Cuetzalan's daily crafts market, open from noon to 5. ✉ *Av. Miguel Alvarado 18* ☎ *No phone* 🎫 *Free* ⏲ *Daily 10–6.*

El Santuario de Guadalupe. This church shows a Gothic strain in its needle-slim tower and the pointed arch of the main door. Its common name, La Iglesia de los Jarritos (Church of the Little Pitchers) refers to its landmark spire, prettily adorned by 80 clay vessels. There is a cemetery in front of the church that is often full of vibrantly colored flowers. ✉ *Calz. de Guadalupe* ☎ *No phone* ⏲ *Daily 9–6.*

Yohualichan. About 8 km (5 mi) outside Cuetzalan lies the splendid archaeological zone of Yohualichan, founded by the Totonac around AD 400. Partly obscured from the road by an austere stone church, Yohualichan (which means "house of night") consists of a lovely hilltop grouping of administrative and ceremonial buildings, houses, plazas, and a long ball court. The easiest way to get here is to take a taxi (the ride should cost no more than $6), but *combis* (vans used for public transport) also make regular drop-offs at the top of the road that leads down to the site. To return to Cuetzalan, you can either make arrangements with your taxi driver to wait for you or walk up to the road and hail a combi or taxi. ✉ *Carretera a Santiago* ☎ *No phone* *$2* ⏲ *Tues.–Sun. 9–5.*

WHERE TO EAT

¢ CAFÉ ✕ **Café Te Cuento.** This cute cafeteria serves pies, cakes, and flans, as well as pizzas, sandwiches, beer, and a range of cocktails and liquors. It's open until 10 PM daily. ✉ *Calle Hidalgo 38* ☎ *233/331–1259* ▭ *No credit cards* ⏲ *Closed Wed.*

¢–$ MEXICAN ★ ✕ **Los Jarritos.** This cavelike restaurant might only be open three days a week, but it has unforgettable regional cuisine. Even simple items like the salsas and *frijoles* (black beans) are intensely flavored. There's an exquisite *sopa de setas* (soup of oyster mushrooms), or you could try the signature dish, *enchiladas de picadillo con mole de olla* (ground beef and raisin enchiladas with a savory local mole). ✉ *Plazuela Lopez Mateo 7* ☎ *233/331–0558* ▭ *MC, V* ⏲ *Closed Sun.–Thurs.*

¢–$ MEXICAN ✕ **Restaurante Yoloxochilt.** Just above the market, with a view of the main plaza, this plant-filled restaurant makes delicious regional cuisine served by a friendly staff. The *envueltos de mole* (chicken-filled tortillas covered in a thick, smoky mole sauce) are an excellent choice if you want to take a break from walking around the market and enjoy a snack. ✉ *2 de Abril 1* ☎ *233/331–0335* ▭ *No credit cards.*

WHERE TO STAY

$ **Hotel Casa de Piedra.** This fine hotel, with its sunny, cobblestone courtyard and appealing restaurant, tops the rest. Guest rooms have wood furniture and small balconies for views over the town or of the flourishing, overgrown yard with cackling turkeys. The staff will help you hire guides to the nearby waterfall or Yohualichan. The hotel is less than two blocks from the zócalo. **Pros:** good service; tours available; space heaters available (few hotels have them, and it can get chilly in this town at night). **Cons:** no room phones; stairs to climb. ✉ *Calle Carlos García 11* ☎ *233/331–0030* 🌐 *www.lacasadepiedra.com* *20 rooms* *In-room: no a/c, no phone. In-hotel: restaurant, parking (free)* ▭ *MC, V.*

$ **Hotel Posada Cuetzalan.** Centrally located and well established, this cheerful hotel has colorful rooms, a pair of lovely patio gardens, and a busy restaurant. The staff can help organize cave tours and horseback rides to the pyramids and local waterfalls. **Pros:** excellent location; friendly staff; nice mountain views. **Cons:** rooms facing the pool *are noisy; rooms in the back are far from the entrance.* ✉ *Zaragoza 12* ☎ *233/331–0154 or 233/331–0395* 🌐 *www.posadacuetzalan.com* *36 rooms* *In-room: no a/c. In-hotel: restaurant, bar, pool, laundry service, Internet terminal, parking (free)* 💳 *MC, V.*

CUERNAVACA AND ENVIRONS

Cuernavaca and the surrounding region have long been a playground for residents of Mexico City. Known as "City of Eternal Spring," Cuernavaca basks in springlike temperatures for most of the year, making it irresistible to the capital's elite. The area's allure has a long history: Aztec emperors came here to enjoy the weather, Cortés built a palace here on the ruins of the Aztec city he destroyed, and Emperor Maximilian retreated here when the pressures of governing a country where he was despised grew too much to bear. Nearby Tepoztlán is another popular spot, especially with outdoors enthusiasts who enjoy hiking to its famous pyramid. Like Cuernavaca, the town itself has appealing architecture and an pleasant downtown area with interesting sights for visitors.

CUERNAVACA

88 km (55 mi) south of Mexico City center.

The road to Cuernavaca will likely heighten your anticipation—you'll catch your first glimpse of the city's lush surroundings from a mountain highway, through lacy pine branches. Cuernavaca's perfect weather has made for stunning gardens. The Jardín Borda, where José de la Borda (who made his fortune in Taxco silver) died, is perhaps the most famous. It has been a private garden for centuries, and it is where Emperor Maximilian and his empress came to rest. It is now open to the public.

Undoubtedly, many of the best gardens lie behind high walls. And truth be told, Cuernavaca's growth in the last decade has weakened some of its tourist appeal. But the city still has much to recommend it. There are certainly enough museums, palaces, old churches, and other sites to see—many of them concentrated in the downtown area—to keep you busy.

GETTING HERE AND AROUND

Buses from Mexico City's Central de Autobuses del Sur depart for Cuernavaca every 10 minutes. The 1½-hour trip costs about $5.50. Both Grupo Pullman and Cristobal Colón provide regular, reliable service. To drive here, the *cuota* (toll road, Route 95D) costs about $10 but takes 1½ hours. The *carretera libre* (free road, Route 95) takes much longer, but has delightful forest scenery.

ESSENTIALS

Bus Contacts **Cristobal Colón** (☎ *55/5544–9008*). **Grupo Pullman de Morelos** (☎ *55/5549–3505 Ext. 08 in Mexico City; 777/312–6063 in Cuernavaca* 🌐 *www.pullman.com.mx*).

Continued on page 141

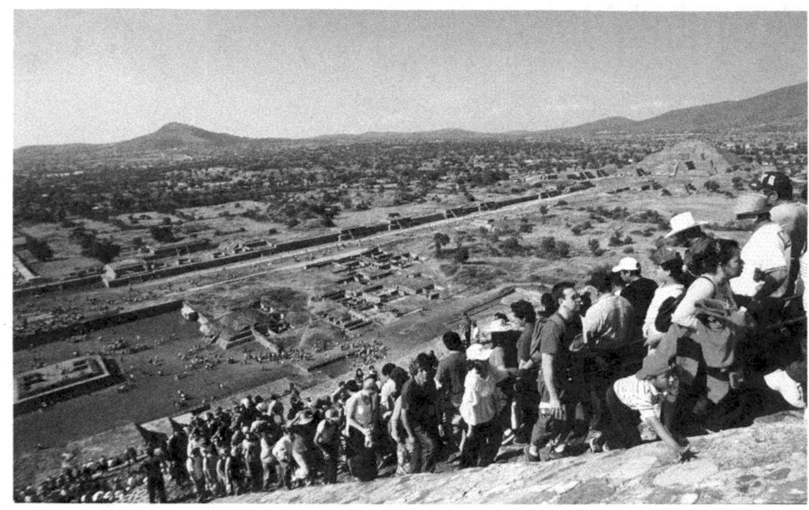

View of Avenue of the Dead from Pirámide del Sol

THE MAJOR SIGHTS

The ❶ **Ciudadela** is a massive citadel ringed by more than a dozen temples, with the ❷ **Templo de Quetzalcóatl** (Temple of the Plumed Serpent) as the centerpiece. Here you'll find detailed carvings of the benevolent deity Quetzalcóatl, a serpent with its head ringed by feathers, jutting out of the facade.

One of the most impressive sights in Teotihuacán is the 4-km-long (2½-mi-long) ❸ **Calzada de los Muertos** (Avenue of the Dead), which once held great ceremonial importance. The Aztecs gave it this name because they mistook the temples lining either side for tombs. It leads to the 126-foot-high ❹ **Pirámide de la Luna** (Pyramid of the Moon), which dominates the city's northern end. Some of the most exciting recent finds, including a royal tomb, have been unearthed here. In late 2002 a discovery of jade objects gave new evidence of a link between the Teotihuacán rulers and the Maya.

Facing the Pyramid of the Moon is the ❺ **Palacio del Quetzalpápalotl** (Palace of the Plumed Butterfly); its beautifully reconstructed terrace has columns etched with images of various winged creatures, some still with their original obsidian-set eyes. Nearby is the ❻ **Palacio de los Jaguares** (Palace of the Jaguars), a residence for priests. Spectacular bird and jaguar murals wind through its underground chambers. The stunning ❼ **Pirámide del Sol** (Pyramid of the Sun), the first monumental structure constructed here, stands in the center of the city. With a base nearly as broad as that of the pyramid of Cheops in Egypt, its size takes your breath away, often quite literally, during the climb up its west face. Deep within the pyramid archaeologists have discovered a natural clover-shape cave that they speculate may have had some connection to the city's religion.

Set amidst rich obsidian mines, the city was home to powerful rulers. The city's crafts and goods were traded with distant cities such as Tikal in Guatemala and Copán in Honduras. Not only did the people of Teotihuacán trade with foreigners, but foreigners also lived in this city which archaeologists surmise was incredibly cosmopolitan. The best artifacts uncovered at Teotihuacán are on display at the Museo Nacional de Antropologia in Mexico City. Still, the **8 Museo de la Sitio**, adjacent to the Pirámide del Sol, contains a few good pieces, such as a stone sculpture of the saucer-eyed Tlaloc, some black and green obsidian arrowheads, and the skeletons of human sacrifices arranged as they were when discovered.

More than 4,000 one-story adobe and stone dwellings surround the Calzada de los Muertos; these were occupied by artisans, warriors, and tradesmen. The best example, a short walk from the Pirámide del Sol, is called **9 Tepantitla**. Here you'll see murals depicting a watery realm ruled by the rain god Tláloc. Restored in 2002, its reds, greens, and yellows are nearly as vivid as when they were painted more than 1,500 years ago.

In 2010, a century after the first excavations were conducted, archaeologists discovered a tunnel, about 14 meters (40 feet) down, that passes below the Templo de Quetzalcóatl and is thought to have been intentionally closed off between AD 200 and 250. The tunnel leads to chambers into which thousands of objects were thrown, perhaps as an offering to rulers. Although rulers were often deified at other sites, no tombs, or even depictions of rulers, have ever been found at Teotihuacán.

ARCHAEOLOGY ACCESS

There are five entrances to Teotihuacán, each near one of the major attractions. Around these entrances there are small restaurants and vendors. If you have a car, it's a good idea to drive from one entrance to the next. Seeing the ruins will take several hours, especially if you head to the lesser-known areas. A good English-language guidebook is sold at the site. ☎ *594/956–0276* 🌐 *archaeology.la.asu.edu/teo* 🎫 *$5.10.*

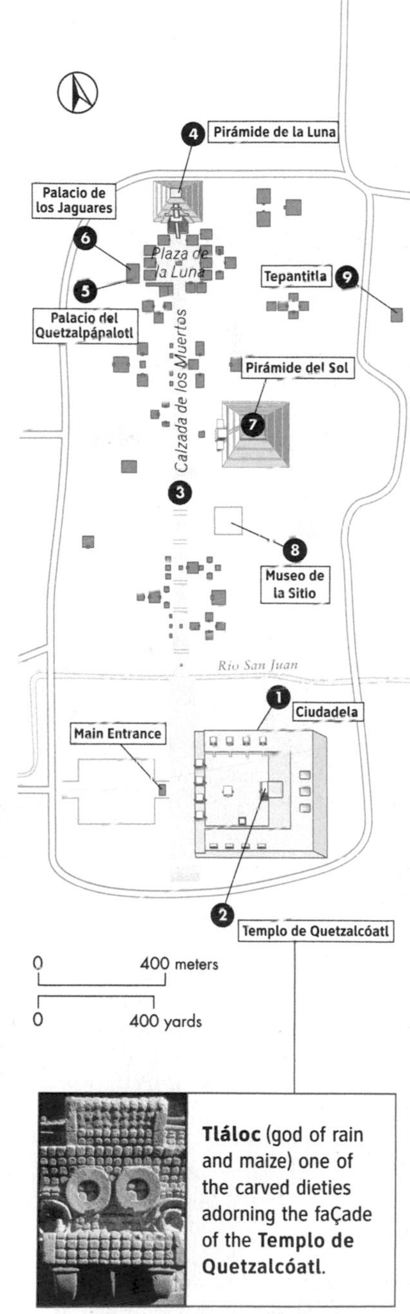

Tláloc (god of rain and maize) one of the carved dieties adorning the faÇade of the **Templo de Quetzalcóatl**.

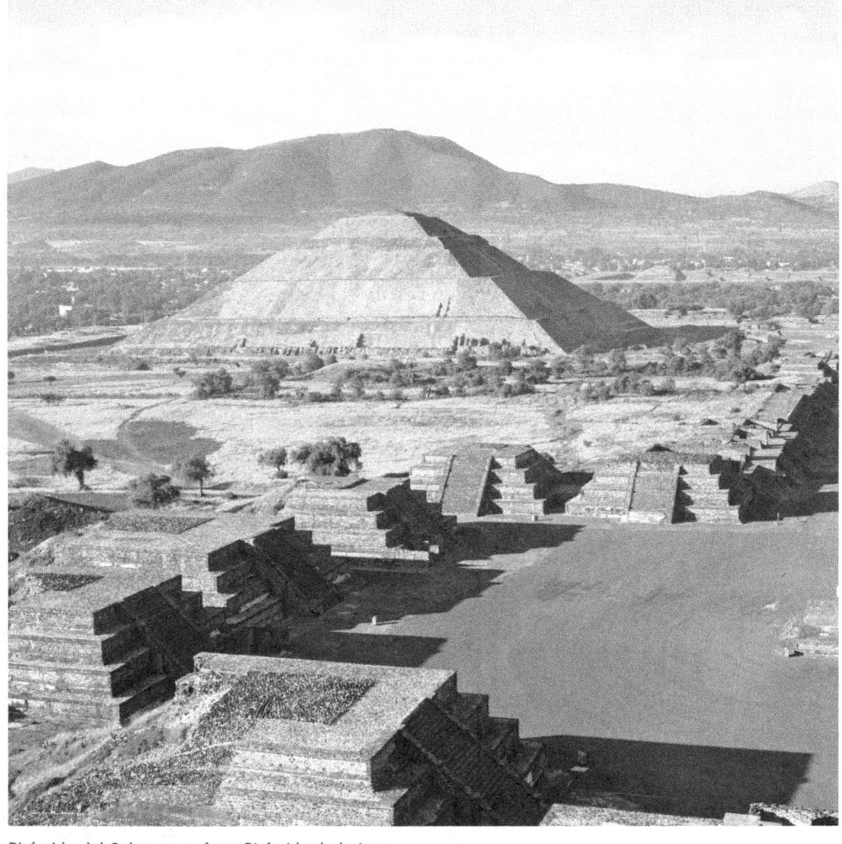

Pirámide del Sol as seen from Pirámide de la Luna

HOW TO GET HERE

50 km (31 mi) northeast of Mexico City center.

BY BUS: To get to Teotihuacán, take one of the Línea Teotihuacán buses that depart every 15 minutes from the Central de Autobuses del Norte in Mexico City. (In the bus station, look for signs marked PIRAMIDES; they don't say Teotihuacán.) The hour-long trip costs about $2.30. Buses leave Mexico City from 6 AM–6 PM. The last bus from Teotihuacán leaves at 6 PM.

Bus Companies **Autobus Teotihuacanos** ☎ 55/5587-0501.

BY CAR: To get to Teotihuacán from Mexico City, take Highway 85D, and follow the signs. In general, the ruins have free parking but the parking areas are a short walk from the sites, so be sure not to leave any valuables in your car.

Medical Assistance Hospital General de Cuernavaca "Dr. José G. Parrés" (✉ *Av. Domingo Diez s/n, Col. Lomas de la Selva* ☎ *777/311–2209 or 777/311–2210*).

Visitor and Tour Info Cuernavaca Tourist Office (✉ *Av. Morelos 187, Col. Centro* ☎ *777/314–1880* 🌐 *www.arte-cultura-morelos.gob.mx*).

EXPLORING

TOP ATTRACTIONS

Jardín Borda. The Borda Gardens, among the most popular sights in Cuernavaca, were designed in the late 18th century for Don Manuel de la Borda, son of Don José de la Borda, the wealthy miner who established the beautiful church of Santa Prisca in Taxco. The gardens were once so famous they attracted royalty. Maximilian and Carlotta visited frequently. Here the emperor reportedly dallied with the gardener's wife, called La India Bonita, who was immortalized in a famous portrait. Novelist Malcolm Lowry turned the formal gardens into a sinister symbol in his 1947 novel *Under the Volcano*. A pleasant café and a well-stocked bookstore sit just inside the gates. ✉ *Av. Morelos 271, at Hidalgo* ☎ *777/318–1038* 🎫 *$3; free Sun.* ⏲ *Tues.–Sun. 10–5:30.*

Museo Regional Cuauhnáhuac. North of the Plaza de Armas you'll find the Museo Regional Cuauhnáhuac, whose name is derived from the Aztec word for the surrounding valley, though it's also known as the Palacio de Cortés. The fortresslike building was constructed as a stronghold for Hernán Cortés in 1522, as the region had not been completely conquered at that time. His palace sits atop the ruins of Aztec buildings, some of which have been partially excavated. There are plenty of stone carvings from the area on display, but the best way to digest all this history is by gazing at the murals Diego Rivera painted between 1927 and 1930 on the top floor. ✉ *Leyva 100* ☎ *777/312–8171* 🌐 *www.inah.gob.mx* 🎫 *$4.10; free Sun.* ⏲ *Tues.–Sun. 9–6.*

Plaza de Armas. The city's most traditional square is marked by a hefty, volcanic-stone statue of revolutionary hero José María Morelos and a couple of little fountains. On weekdays the square fills with vendors from neighboring villages. On weekends it is crowded with balloon sellers, amateur painters, and stalls for crafts, jewelry, and knickknacks. To the north of the square is leafy Jardín Juárez (Juárez Garden), which hosts Sunday concerts at its bandstand. ■ **TIP→ The Tren Turístico, a wooden trolleybus that's a great way to sightsee, departs from the plaza's southeast corner, opposite the Palacio de Cortés.** ☎ *777/318–045 for tourist train info* 🌐 *www.morelosweb.com/trenturistico* 🎫 *Train: $4 weekdays, $4.50 on Fri. and weekends.*

★ **Xochicalco.** A trip to these ruins is one of the best reasons to visit Morelos State. Built by the Olmeca-Xicalanca people, the mighty hilltop city reached its peak between AD 700 and 900. It was abandoned a century later after being destroyed, perhaps by its own inhabitants.

With its several layers of fortifications, the city appears unassailable. The most eye-catching edifice is the **Pyrámide de Quetzalcóatl** (Temple of the Plumed Serpent). Carvings of vicious-looking snakes—all in the style typical of the Maya to the south—wrap around the lower level, while figures in elaborate headdresses sit above. Be sure to seek out the **Observatorio** in a man-made cave reached through a tunnel on the northern side of the city. Through a narrow shaft in the ceiling the Xochicalco astronomers could observe the heavens. Twice a year—May 14 and 15 and July 28 and 29—the sun passes directly over the opening, filling the room with light.

Stop in at the museum—a wonderfully mounted exhibit of a wide variety of artifacts from Xochicalco are on display—but note that all explanations are in Spanish.

There are dozens of other structures here, including three impressive ball courts. The site's solar-powered museum has six rooms of artifacts, including gorgeous sculptures of Xochicalco deities found nearby. ✉ *Hwy. 95D, southwest of Cuernavaca* ☎ *737/374–3092* 🌐 *www.inah.gob.mx* 🎫 *$5.10; $7 sound-and-light show on Fri. and Sat. at 7 PM, Oct.–Apr.* ⏲ *Daily 9–6; tickets sold until 5.*

WORTH NOTING

Catedral de la Asunción. Cortés ordered the construction of this cathedral, with work beginning in 1525. Like his palace, the cathedral doubled as a fortress. Cannons mounted above the flying buttresses helped bolster the city's defenses. The facade may give you a sense of foreboding, especially when you catch sight of the skull and crossbones over the door. The interior is much less ominous, though, thanks to the murals uncovered during renovations. ✉ *Hidalgo and Av. Morelos* ☎ *777/312–1290* 🎫 *Free* ⏲ *Daily 8–2 and 4–9.*

Robert Brady Museum. A museum on a quiet street south of the Plaza de Armas showcases the collection of the artist, antiquarian, and decorator from Fort Dodge, Iowa. Ceramics, antique furniture, sculptures, paintings, and tapestries fill the restored colonial mansion, all magnificently arranged in rooms painted with bright colors. Note that the building numbers on this street are out of order. The museum is just across the street from numbers 21 and 121. ✉ *Calle Netzahuacóyotl 4, between Hidalgo and Abasolo* ☎ *777/318–8554* 🌐 *www.bradymuseum.org* 🎫 *$3* ⏲ *Tues.–Sun. 10–6.*

WHERE TO EAT

$$–$$$ CONTEMPORARY

✕ Casa Tamayo. This chic restaurant has a startling view over the *barranca.* For those longing for something fresh and green, the salad of almonds and Roquefort cheese over mixed greens is a treat. A favorite main dish is the *pollo pancha,* a chicken breast filled with mozzarella and spinach in a semisweet orange sauce. Reservations are recommended on weekends. ✉ *Rufino Tamayo 26, Col. Centro* ☎ *777/312–8186* 🌐 *www.hotelcasatamayo.com* 💳 *AE, MC, V* ⏲ *No dinner Sun.*

$$$$ MEXICAN

✕ Gaia Restaurante. In an exquisite old house that once belonged to Mario Moreno, the movie star popularly known as Cantinflas, is one of the most elegant restaurants in Cuernavaca. The chef serves delicious and perfectly presented lunches and dinners, including tasty twists on old Mexican classics like *chiles rellenos* (peppers stuffed with three cheeses) and duck tacos. The *camarones crujientes con coco y nuez* (crispy shrimp with coconut and nuts) is also worth a try. A long lunch is served by the pool, which has a mosaic often attributed to Diego

CLOSE UP

Traditional Medicine Makes a Comeback

Herbal medicine remains an integral part of Mexican life, and still predominates in remote areas where modern medicines are hard to come by or are too expensive for rural laborers. Even in the capital, most markets will have distinctive stalls piled with curative herbs and plants.

The Aztecs were excellent botanists, and their extensive knowledge impressed the Spanish, who borrowed from Mexico's indigenous herbarium and cataloged the intriguing plants. Consequently, medicine remains one of the few examples of cultural practices and indigenous wisdom that have not been lost to history. Visitors to the capital can find a display of medicinal plants used by the Aztecs in the Museum of Medicine, in the former Palace of the Inquisition, at the northwest corner of Plaza Santo Domingo.

A rich variety of herbs is harvested in the 300 rural communities of the fertile state of Morelos, where *curanderos* (natural healers) flock to the markets on weekends to give advice and sell their concoctions. Stores in the state capital, Cuernavaca, sell natural antidotes for every ailment imaginable and potions for sexual prowess, lightening the skin, colic in babies, and IQ enhancement.

Chamanes (shamans) and healers abound at the weekend market in the main square of the delightful mountain village of Tepoztlán. Long known for its *brujas* (witches), Tepoztlán continues to experience a boom in spiritual retreats and New Age shops. Visitors can benefit from the healing overload without getting hoodwinked by booking a session in one of the many good *temazcales* (Aztec sweat lodges) in town.

The temazcal is a "bath of cleansing" for body, mind, and spirit; a session consists of a ritual that lasts at least an hour, ideally (for first-timers) with a guide. Temazcales are igloo-shape clay buildings, round so as not to impede the flow of energy. They usually seat 6 to 12 people, who can participate either naked or in a bathing suit. Each guide develops his own style, under the tutelage of a shaman, so practices vary. In general your aura (or energy field) is cleaned with a bunch of plants before you enter the temazcal, so that you start off as pure as possible. You will have a fistful of the same plants—usually rosemary, sweet basil, or eucalyptus—to slap or rub against your skin. You walk in a clockwise direction and take your place, and water is poured over red-hot stones in the middle to create the steam. Usually silence is maintained, although the guide may chant or pray, often in Nahuatl. The procedure ends with a warm shower followed by a cold one to close the pores.

The experience helps eliminate toxins, cure inflammations, ease pains in the joints, and relieve stress. Consequently, temazcales are growing in popularity, even drawing city executives from the capital on weekends.

—by Barbara Kastelein

Rivera. The restaurant has a great location two blocks from the Palacio de Cortés. ✉ *Blvd. Benito Juárez 102* ☎ *777/310–0031* 🌐 *www.gaiarest.com.mx* 💳 *AE, MC, V.*

$$–$$$ MEXICAN ✕ **Restaurante Casa Hidalgo.** The marvelous view of the Palacio de Cortés helped make this restaurant a big hit among the foreigners in town. The menu mixes Mexican and international foods; you might try the *filetón hidalgo* (breaded veal stuffed with Serrano ham and manchego cheese) or the *tacos con napoles* (tacos stuffed with grilled cactus). A jazz band plays on Saturday night. ■ **TIP→ Reservations are recommended on weekends—request a table on the small balcony for a great view of the Palacio just across the street.** ✉ *Jardín los Héroes, Hidalgo 6, Col. Centro* ☎ *777/312–2749* 🌐 *www.casacolonial.com* 💳 *AE, MC, V.*

WHERE TO STAY

$$$–$$$$ **Camino Real Sumiya.** Woolworth heiress Barbara Hutton built this monumental hideaway in the 1950s, after her long search for a site with excellent weather and an interesting history. The Japanese theme is pleasingly consistent, flowing seamlessly from the imposing entrance to the lobby and bar. Restaurante Sumiya, which serves international and Japanese food, is so good it draws people who aren't staying at the hotel. The rooms are in the far part of the garden for privacy, and many have sublime garden views. To reach the hotel, which is about 15 minutes south of town at Interior del Fraccionamiento Sumiya, take the Civac-Cuauhtla exit off the Acapulco Highway. **Pros:** excellent restaurant; delightful gardens; unexpected architecture. **Cons:** frequent events mob the place; prices are high. ✉ *Int. Fraccionamiento Sumiya, Col. José Parres, Jiutepec* ☎ *777/329–9888* 🌐 *www.caminoreal.com/sumiya* *157 rooms, 6 suites* *In-room: safe, refrigerator, Wi-Fi. In-hotel: 2 restaurants, bar, tennis courts, pools* 💳 *AE, DC, MC, V.*

$$$–$$$$ ★ **Hacienda San Gabriel de las Palmas.** A colorful history distinguishes this grand hacienda, built in 1529. Now it's a haven of quiet with lush gardens—disturbed only by birdcalls, the splashing of a waterfall, and the ringing of a chapel bell. If you'd like to get even more blissed-out, visit the spa, which includes a traditional temazcal. Antiques fill both the public areas and the spacious guest rooms. Outstanding Mexican food is prepared in an inviting open kitchen close to the pool. The hacienda is 35 minutes outside Cuernavaca. **Pros:** peaceful mood, easy drive to Cuernavaca and Taxco. **Cons:** far from main sites, rates are pricey. ✉ *Carretera Federal Cuernavaca–Chilpancingo, Km 41.8, Amacuzac* ☎ *751/348–0636; 01800/508–7923 toll-free in Mexico* 🌐 *www.hacienda-sangabriel.com.mx* *5 rooms, 15 suites* *In-room: no a/c (some), safe, no TV (some), Wi-Fi. In-hotel: restaurant, bar, tennis court, pools, spa, Wi-Fi hotspot* 💳 *AE, MC, V.*

$$–$$$ **Hotel Casa Colonial.** This old colonial mansion has been wonderfully restored. The rooms are individually decorated, giving them a homey quality. The best part is that you are right in the middle of downtown. You can be at any number of interesting sights in minutes. **Pros:** incredible location; pleasant accommodations. **Cons:** neighborhood is noisy on the weekends. ✉ *Netzahualcoyotl 37* ☎ *777/312–7033* 🌐 *www.casacolonial.com* *18 rooms* *In-room: Wi-Fi. In-hotel: restaurant, bar, pool* 💳 *AE, MC, V.*

$$$–$$$$ ★ **Hotel Hacienda de Cortés.** This 16th-century former sugar mill once belonged to the famed conquistador. Wandering around the gardens and discovering cascades, fountains, abandoned pillars, and sculptures is an enchanting experience, especially at dusk. Ask for a room in the old part of the building to immerse yourself in the flavor of the place. Rooms have traditional Mexican furnishings and lovely patios or balconies. The restaurant ($–$$) is within old fort walls draped with vines—it's like dining inside a ruined castle. **Pros:** historic building; romantic environment; pleasant bar. **Cons:** noisy events sometimes take over the hotel. ✉ *Plaza Kennedy 90, Col. Atlacomulco, Jiutepec* ☎ *777/315–8844* 🌐 *www.hotelhaciendadecortes.com.mx* *17 rooms, 6 suites* *In-room: safe, refrigerator, Wi-Fi. In-hotel: restaurant, bars, pool* *AE, MC, V* *BP.*

3

$$ **Hotel Posada María Cristina.** This delightful hotel, popular with foreign travelers, was constructed in the 16th century as a home for one of Cortés's soldiers. It is full of character, with plenty of alcoves, nooks, and crannies to explore. Lush gardens slope down the steep hill toward the pool. The main restaurant serves Mexican and international cuisine, while the poolside restaurant refreshes loungers with Argentine food. **Pros:** incredible location; historic building; architectural charm. **Cons:** some rooms are better than others; street noise can be a problem on weekends. ✉ *Juárez 300, Col. Centro* ☎ *777/318–2981; 777/318–5767; 01800/024–5767 toll-free in Mexico* 🌐 *www.maria-cristina.com.mx* *16 rooms, 4 suites* *In-room: Internet (some). In-hotel: 2 restaurants, bar, pool, Wi-Fi hotspot* *AE, DC, MC* *BP.*

$$–$$$ **Hotel Villa Rosa.** This extremely pink hotel has the advantage of being both extremely central and extremely tranquil. Although each room is different—you'll find everything from floral patterns to executive-friendly modernity—all have high ceilings with exposed beams and are refreshingly cool, even though only three rooms have air-conditioning. Located at the end of a cobblestone street, with a grassy garden, shaded pool area, and tiny spa, the Villa Rosa makes a good retreat, particularly midweek when prices dip. **Pros:** central location; lovely shaded pool. **Cons:** drab furnishings and design; not all rooms have air-conditioning; pricey for what you get. ✉ *2a Privada de Humboldt 6, Col. Centro* ☎ *777/312–1632 or 777/312–9225* 🌐 *www.villarosacuernavaca.com* *11 rooms* *In-room: no a/c (some), safe, Wi-Fi. In-hotel: restaurant, pool, spa* *AE, MC, V.*

$$$$ Fodor'sChoice ★ **Las Mañanitas.** An American expat opened this hacienda-style hotel in the 1950s, and it is still one of the best lodgings in Cuernavaca. The ample rooms are outfitted with traditional fireplaces, hand-carved bedsteads, hand-painted tiles in the bathrooms, and gilded crafts. The restaurant ($–$$$), with its spectacular open-air terraces and garden inhabited by flamingos, peacocks, and African cranes, is a wonderful place to spend an afternoon enjoying a leisurely meal. Sadly, the quality of the food isn't as reliable as it once was. However, you can't go wrong with traditional dishes like the well-prepared *mole poblano* or the *sopa de tortilla* (tortilla soup). **Pros:** gorgeous place; stylish rooms; brand-new spa. **Cons:** restaurant has lost a bit of its luster. ✉ *Ricardo Linares 107* ☎ *777/314–1466; 01800/221–5299 toll-free in Mexico; 888/413–9199*

🌐 *www.lasmananitas.com.mx* *25 suites In-room: safe, Internet. In-hotel: restaurant, room service, bar, pool, spa, Wi-Fi hotspot* ▭ *AE, MC, V.*

> **WORD OF MOUTH**
>
> "...[Cuernavaca's square] is very lively and full of people eating corn-on-the-cob, which seems to be the local delicacy, and cones of flavored ice, scraped from a block while you wait.... If you're at all interested in ancient Indian cultures visit Xochicalco.... If you admire Malcolm Lowry's great novel *Under the Volcano* there are a number of related sights: the Borda Gardens, certain squares, etc...." —Olo

$$$$ **Misíon del Sol.** This exclusive resort and spa was designed with body and spirit in mind, and every detail of the grounds—from the handmade adobe buildings and lush gardens to the exceptional restaurant to the pool with water that somehow feels like silk—invites its adults-only clientele to relax and enjoy. Maybe it's the beauty of the place, the magnets strategically placed under the beds to promote rest, or the massages given at the spa, but guests come from this resort and spa happy and rested. Consciousness-expanding events, from yoga and meditation classes to guest speakers like Dr. Deepak Chopra (who has spoken several times here) are always available and listed on the Web site. **Pros:** peaceful place; exceptional service; good spa treatments. **Cons:** a bit too quiet at times; not the place for families. ✉ *Av. Gral. Diego Días González 31* ☎ *777/321–0999; 01800/999–9100 toll-free in Mexico* 🌐 *www.misiondelsol.com* *40 rooms, 12 villas In-room: safe. In-hotel: restaurant, tennis court, pool, spa, Internet terminal, no kids under 18* ▭ *AE, MC, V* *BP.*

NIGHTLIFE

Cuernavaca is a great place to be after the sun goes down. Evenings are cool and agreeable throughout the year, which means people venture out to enjoy a drink or listen to live music. The bars draw an interesting mix of locals, weekenders escaping the capital, and international tourists.

Alebrije. Young people crowd the dance floor here to move to popular English- and Spanish-language tunes every Friday and Saturday night. Men pay to get in the door, while women enter for free. ✉ *Av. Plan de Ayala 405, Col. Teopanzolco* ☎ *777/322–4282.*

Juárez 4. This is *the* spot for those who are into electronic music. While there is no cover, there's a minimum amount ($10) men must spend at the bar. Women, naturally, do not have a minimum. ✉ *Blvd. Benito Juárez 4, Col. Centro* ☎ *777/312–7984.*

Taizz. Drawing a more diverse crowd than its competitors, this popular dance club, mixes its musical styles well. You'll hear everything from electronic music to the latest hits in English and Spanish. ✉ *Bajada Chapultepec 13, Col. Chapultepec* ☎ *777/315–4060.*

SHOPPING

Cuernavaca has shops for all tastes. In the downtown area, vendors are found around the zócalo and along the surrounding streets. You'll find leather shoes, embroidered blouses, beaded necklaces, and other crafts.

Some of these are produced in Cuernavaca, but others are brought in from around the country.

Librería Educal Libros y Arte Jardín Borda. The bookshop at the entrance to the Jardín Borda has quite a collection of titles, particularly on Mexico and Mexican art. Many titles are in English. ✉ *Av. Morelos 271* ☎ *777/314–3978.*

Libros y Arte. The small bookstore connected to the Palacio de Cortés sells titles on Mexican history, culture, and art, mostly in Spanish. ✉ *Leyva 100* ☎ *777/312–9933* 🌐 *www.librosyarte.com.mx.*

SPORTS AND THE OUTDOORS

With near-perfect weather, Cuernavaca is a great place for sports enthusiasts, and there are some good places to play tennis and golf. Remember that you will find more crowds on weekends.

Hacienda San Gaspar. This golf club has an impressive steel-and-glass clubhouse. The 18-hole course is surrounded by lush gardens. Greens fees are $145 on weekends and $85 on weekdays. ✉ *Av. Emiliano Zapata s/n, Col. Cliserio* ☎ *777/319–4404* 🌐 *www.sangaspar.com.*

Las Estacas. Ninety minutes from Mexico City, Las Estacas is an ideal place for a swim in a pool or in a cool, clean river born of an underwater spring. The weather here is almost always sunny, even when it's raining in Mexico City. Large stretches of grass under palm trees are great places to sunbathe. Dive classes and spa services are available. And, at this writing, the dressing rooms are being upgraded and shops are being added. Grab a juicy grilled hamburger at the restaurant. A day pass costs $23; the complex is open daily 8 to 6. ✉ *Carretera Jojutla-Tltizapán, Km 7* ☎ *734/345–0077; 55/3004–5300 in Mexico City; 777/312–4412 in Cuernavaca* 🌐 *www.lasestacas.com.*

TEPOZTLÁN

76 km (47 mi) south of Mexico City, 19 km (12 mi) northeast of Cuernavaca via Route 95D.

Surrounded by sandstone monoliths that throw off a russet glow at sunset, Tepoztlán is a magical place. No wonder it attracts practitioners of astrology, meditation, yoga, and other New Age pursuits. But you'll still find women selling homegrown produce in the lively weekend market surrounding the main square and traditional celebrations that predate the conquest.

Tepoztlán's temperatures fluctuate, from blistering around midday to bitterly cold at night. Visitors who plan an overnight stay in the winter months should bring warmer clothing and a coat.

GETTING HERE AND AROUND

Buses leave Mexico City's Central de Autobuses del Sur. Two reliable bus companies are Grupo Pullman de Morelos and Cristobal Colón. You can easily combine a trip to Cuernavaca and Tepoztlán by taking a bus to Cuernavaca and another bus or a taxi from Cuernavaca to Tepoztlán. By car, take the Mexico-Cuernavaca *cuota*, or toll highway. It costs about $10. If you want to take the free Route 95D, budget much more time.

EXPLORING

Ex-Convento Dominico de la Natividad. Rising above most of Tepoztlán's buildings is this buttressed former convent. It dates from the mid-16th century and has a facade adorned with icons dating from before the introduction of Christianity. Many of the walls, especially on the ground floor, have fragments of old paintings in earthen tones on the walls and decorating the arches. It is worth a visit just to see the building, which also houses temporary exhibits and a complete bookstore with a good selection of books, CDs, and videos. ✉ *Av. Revolución 1910* ☎ *No phone* ⏲ *Tues.–Sun. 10–5.*

★ **Pirámide de Tepozteco.** Perched on a mountaintop, this tiny temple is dedicated to either the Aztec deity Tepoztécatl or—depending on whose story you believe—Ome Tochtli, the god of the alcoholic drink pulque. The pyramid was part of a city that has not been uncovered, but was of such importance that pilgrims flocked here from as far away as Guatemala. It attracts hikers and sightseers not afraid of the somewhat arduous climb. The view over the valley is terrific. ✉ *North end of Av. Tepoztlán* 🎫 *$4* ⏲ *Daily 9:30–5:30.*

WHERE TO EAT

$–$$ MEXICAN ✕ **Axitla.** This smart establishment in the folds of the mountains is surrounded by ponds and bridges. Among the delicious concoctions are *chili jaral* (ancho chili stuffed with shredded beef and raisins) and lamb in zucchini sauce. You can dine in the pink, high-ceiling dining room overlooking the trees and river or alfresco. A lone guitar player adds to the character weekend lunchtimes. ✉ *Av. del Tepozteco 50, at road to Pyramid* ☎ *739/395–0519 or 739/395–2555* 💳 *MC, V* ⏲ *Closed Mon. and Tues.*

$–$$ MEXICAN ✕ **El Ciruelo.** You'll need to call two or three days in advance to reserve a nice seat—with a view of the pyramid—for the weekend. The rest of the tables at this casual restaurant are centered around a partially open patio. A varied menu includes chicken breast stuffed with *huitlacoche,* an exquisite inky fungus that grows on corn, and spicy shrimp tacos. There is a place for children to play on weekends. ✉ *Zaragoza 17* ☎ *739/395–1037* 💳 *AE, MC, V* ⏲ *Open daily for lunch; dinner served on Fri. and Sat. only.*

$–$$ MEXICAN ★ ✕ **Los Colorines.** Hung with colorful *papeles picados* (paper cutouts), this family-friendly restaurant serves great bean soups, stuffed chilies, and grilled meats made in an open kitchen. Special dishes include *huauzontles* (a broccoli-like vegetable you scrape from the stalk with your teeth). Note that the restaurant closes at 9:30 PM during the week; weekends it's open until 10 or until the crowd leaves. ✉ *Av. del Tepozteco 13* ☎ *739/395–0198* 💳 *No credit cards.*

WHERE TO STAY

$$$$ 🏨 **Hostal de la Luz Spa Holistic Resort.** An experiment in "holistic tourism" is making waves at the foot of the Quetzalcóatl mountains in the village of Amatlán. From the traditional adobe structure to the use of feng shui, the complex, which includes a spa, is designed to blend with the environment and soothe guests. Rooms have wicker meditation chairs set in bay-window alcoves from which to absorb the unparalleled

views. Look into package deals that include spa treatments and meals. The resort is roughly a 15-minute drive from Tepoztlán. **Pros:** secluded surroundings; excellent spa treatments. **Cons:** rather pricey; no Internet connections. ✉ *Carretera Federal Tepoztlán-Amatlán, Km 4, Amatlán de Quetzalcóatl* ☎ *739/395–3374* 🌐 *www.hostaldelaluz.com* *21 suites* *In-room: no a/c, no TV. In-hotel: restaurant, pool, spa* *AE, MC, V* *BP.*

$$ **Posada Ali.** With unobstructed views of the mountains from its rooms, this family-run inn draws many repeat customers. No two rooms are exactly alike, and all have adorable hand-hewn furniture. There's a tiny pool in back. This is not the most elegant hotel in Tepoztlán, but it is clean and inexpensive. **Pros:** family-friendly environment; lovely views. **Cons:** weekends are busy; need to reserve far in advance. ✉ *Netzahualcóyotl 2* ☎ *739/395–1971* 🌐 *www.posadaali.com.mx* *16 rooms* *In-room: no a/c. In-hotel: restaurant, pool* *No credit cards* *BP.*

$$$$ Fodor's Choice ★ **Posada del Tepozteco.** Enjoy splendid views of both the village and the pyramid as you stroll through this hotel's terraced gardens. A honeymooners' favorite, the inn is also a good place for children, with its trampoline, swings, and pair of pet rabbits. Most rooms have balconies and hot tubs, and some have terrific views of the pyramid. Make reservations for weekend stays two weeks in advance. This is also a great place to stop in for a leisurely meal on the patio, where the tables are set around a murmuring stone fountain and circled by vine-covered archways. ■ **TIP→ The weekend buffet breakfast is an excellent time to visit and enjoy the view overlooking the village, even if you are not staying at the hotel.** **Pros:** unbeatable views; excellent service. **Cons:** buffet draws big crowds; uphill walk from downtown. ✉ *Calle del Paraíso 3* ☎ *739/395–0010* 🌐 *www.posadadeltepozteco.com* *8 rooms, 12 suites* *In-room: no a/c, safe, no TV. In-hotel: restaurant, room service, bar, tennis court, pool, Wi-Fi hotspot* *AE, MC, V* *BP.*

VALLE DE BRAVO

75 km (47 mi) southwest of Mexico City.

A few hours here explains why "Valle" is often billed as Mexico's best-kept secret. The pines, clear air, and the Lago Valle de Bravo make it totally different from most people's idea—and experience—of Mexico. The nation's wealthy political and business elite keep weekend homes here, and barely a weekend goes by without a sailing regatta. It's also popular with fans of ecotourism and extreme sports.

This colonial lakeside treasure is peppered with white stucco houses trimmed with wrought-iron balconies and red-tile roofs with long eaves to protect walkers from both the rain and the glaring sun. Connected to Mexico City mostly via a two-lane, winding, mountainous road, the town is visited primarily by wealthy Mexicans—particularly weekenders from the capital—and fans of adventure tourism.

Valle was founded in 1530, but has no significant historical sights to speak of other than the St. Francis of Assisi cathedral on the town square and the church of Santa Maria, with a huge crucified black Christ on its altar. Rather than sightsee, saunter the streets and check out the bazaars, boutiques, galleries, and markets. Valle is famous for its lacelike fabrics called *deshilados* and its earthenware and hand-glazed ceramics.

The town's major festival is called Festival de las Almas; it usually occurs in the month of October and involves many old Mexican traditional games and dances as well as elaborate fireworks displays. If you plan to come during a festival, over Christmas, or on a weekend, make sure you make hotel reservations well in advance. ■ **TIP→ To avoid the crowds from the capital and nab lower hotel rates, visit during the week for a quieter experience, more suitable for those who wish to hike and enjoy the pristine views.**

GETTING HERE AND AROUND

By car, take Highway 15 toward Toluca. As the highway passes through Toluca it is called Paseo Tollocan. Look for signs on the left for Valle de Bravo. Follow Highway 142 until you reach Francisco de los Ranchos, then bear right to reach Valle de Bravo. Much of the route is a narrow, two-lane road through leafy countryside. Passing slower traffic is impossible, so expect a long ride. Buses for Valle de Bravo leave the Terminal de Autobuses Poniente, at the Observatorio metro station. Todo Valle buses leave Mexico City nearly every hour for Valle de Bravo.

ESSENTIALS

Bus Contacts **Autobuses Todo Valle** (☎ *726/262-0213*).

Medical Assistance **Farma Pronto** (✉ *Pagaza 100, on corner of Plaza Independencia at Bocanegra* ☎ *726/262-1441*). **Hospital General de Valle de Bravo** (✉ *Fray Gregorio Jiménez de la Cuenca s/n* ☎ *726/262-1646*).

Visitor and Tour Info **Mexico State Tourist Office** (✉ *Urawa 100, Gate 110, Toluca* ☎ *722/219-5190* 🌐 *www.edomexico.gob.mx*). **Valle de Bravo Turismo Municipal** (✉ *Presidencia Municipal, 5 de Febrero 100, entrance opposite bell tower* ☎ *726/262-1678*).

WHERE TO EAT

$–$$ MEXICAN ✕ **La Michoacana.** You can gaze out over the lake and the town's red rooftops at the Michoacana, which is just a short walk from the zócalo. It's one of the town's best sources of regional fare and a great place for a family meal. You can't go wrong here—all the typical Mexican plates you'll recognize are available, but the house specialties include pre-Hispanic dishes that you won't find everywhere else, such as venison, *chapulines con cebolla y chili de arbol* (toasted grasshoppers with onion and a spicy red chili sauce), and *escamoles a la mantequilla* (ant eggs lightly fried in butter). ✉ *Calle de la Cruz 100* ☎ *726/262-1625* 💳 *AE, MC, V.*

$$$ SEAFOOD ✕ **Los Veleros.** If you want seafood, skip the floating restaurants at the dock (where the food leaves much to be desired and locals say you will likely walk away with a stomachache) and head to Los Veleros, a cozy family restaurant in an old mansion just a block away, which has one of the biggest seafood selections in the region. Sit out on the terrace overlooking the splendid garden as you enjoy your meal. It's open on Friday, Saturday, and Sunday, until midnight or later, depending on

how many customers are still around. ✉ *Salitre 104* ☎ *726/262–0370* ▭ *AE, MC, V.*

$$–$$$ MEXICAN ✕ **Mozzarella Restaurant.** People spend hours enjoying their meals at this eatery in a plant-filled courtyard of the Hotel Batucada. Tables are set around a carved stone fountain. The creative plates include black rice, made with shrimp, squid, octopus, clams, and mussels, and the fresh and delicious blue salad, made with different varieties of greens, pears, grapefruit, and beets, topped off with a light blue-cheese dressing. ✉ *Bocanegra 207-A* ☎ *726/262–0480* 🌐 *www.hotelbatucada.com.mx* ▭ *AE, MC, V.*

WHERE TO STAY

$$$ **Avandaro Golf and Spa Resort.** This former country club morphed into the one of the most upscale resorts in Valle. All guest rooms have fireplaces and great views of the pine forest. If the 18-hole, par-72 golf course doesn't tempt you, perhaps a massage, facial, or yoga class at the high-tech spa will. The property is about 10 minutes from Valle de Bravo, so if you didn't come by car you'll need to take taxis into town. **Pros:** excellent service; great restaurant; excellent golf. **Cons:** far from downtown; area gets quite cold. ✉ *Vega del Río, Fracc. Avándaro* ☎ *726/266–0366; 55/5280–1532 in Mexico City* 🌐 *www.hotelavandaro.com.mx* *60 rooms* *In-room: no a/c. In-hotel: restaurant, room service, bar, golf course, tennis courts, pools, gym, spa, Wi-Fi hotspot* ▭ *AE, MC, V* *BP.*

$ **Hotel Casanueva.** This small hotel is the best option on Plaza Independencia. There are crafts in every room and hallway, in some of the most unexpected places. The terraced rooms present great views of the plaza. There are tables in the courtyard, and the hotel calls orders over to Alma Edith, the small restaurant just across the cobblestone street, which serves typical Mexican food at affordable prices. **Pros:** good service; excellent location; decorated with care. **Cons:** noisy neighborhood on weekends. ✉ *Villagrán 100, at Plaza Independencia* ☎ *726/262–1766* *8 rooms* *In-room: no a/c. In-hotel: restaurant* ▭ *No credit cards.*

$–$$ **Hotel Cueva de Leon.** This cheerful hotel on the corner of Plaza Independencia is an excellent option for its location alone. Rooms are cozy, with brightly colored bedspreads and carved headboards; some have kitschy hot tubs tucked into a corner. The restaurant ($) is by far the most enchanting on the square and has wonderful views of the town. **Pros:** downtown is steps away; pleasant restaurant. **Cons:** sparsely decorated rooms. ✉ *Plaza Independencia 2* ☎ *726/262–4062* *10 rooms, 4 suites* *In-hotel: restaurant, bar* ▭ *MC, V.*

SHOPPING

Galería Indigo. It has wonderful exhibits that really are worth a visit. The gallery is only open on weekends. ✉ *Joaquín A. Pagaza 403* ☎ *726/262–5345.*

SPORTS AND THE OUTDOORS

MOUNTAIN BIKING

Valle is ideal for mountain biking, with readily accessible trails.

Cletas Valle. Rates for bikes and helmets are extremely good at this shop, which also sells biking gadgets. Owner Carlos Mejía can recommend places to go. ✉ *16 de Septiembre 200* ☎ *726/262–0291.*

Pablo's Bikes. This is a good place to rent bikes by the hour or by the day. ✉ *Joaquín Arcadio Pagaza 103* ☎ *726/262–2595* 🌐 *www.pablosbikes.com.*

PARAGLIDING

Valle is world-famous for paragliding, and competitions are held here nearly every year. The exhilarating sport is so popular that anyone with a flat, large garden for landing in is prepared for angelitos (little angels) to appear out of the sky when winds or misjudgment cause them to miss the standard landing spots.

Vuelos Panorámicos. Across the road from the lake, Vuelos Panorámicos has certified instructors and is a good place to learn. A 30-minute tandem glide down with an instructor costs $120 (be sure to bring cash—there's a small charge if you use a credit card). Bring a jacket or windbreaker, sneakers, and a camera. ✉ *Plaza Valle* ☎ *726/262–6382* 🌐 *www.alas.com.mx.*

San Miguel de Allende and the Heartland

4

Tarascan fishermen with butterfly nets, Lake Pátzcuaro, Michoacán State.

WORD OF MOUTH

"Typically, it does not rain (much) except from June until mid-September. During those months the rain is 'regular.' Meaning that it will rain twice a week or so, commonly at night. We walk everywhere year round, rain or shine. The weather is not only not really a problem, it is one of our joys."

—alfonsogatito

www.fodors.com/community

WELCOME TO THE HEARTLAND

TOP REASONS TO GO

★ **Experiencing modern life amid colonial grandeur:** The Heartland's cities preserve the best of colonial Mexico, but they're not stuck in the past. All of the cities except Pátzcuaro appear on UNESCO's list of World Heritage Sites. Each has its own personality, restaurant scene, nightlife, and classic zócalo, usually anchored by a grand colonial church.

★ **Enjoying the outdoors:** The region's near-perfect weather, along with its farmland, hills, lakes, and river valleys afford many opportunities for day hikes, riding, mountain biking, or just sitting and soaking up the sun in one of the region's many hot springs.

★ **A calendar full of festivals:** From jazz in San Miguel de Allende to Pátzcuaro's elaborate Day of the Dead celebration, they're always partying somewhere.

★ **Staying in a hacienda:** Colonial mansions with gracious courtyards are ubiquitous in the Heartland's cities, and many have been restored into gorgeous hotels, where you can fall asleep to the strumming of guitars in a nearby plaza.

1 Zacatecas. It's slightly off the beaten track, but Zacatecas is a must. Its famed cathedral is a pink limestone masterpiece in churrigueresque style. The only cable car in the world to cross an entire city delivers you to a panoramic viewpoint. The city's not without sophistication—you can dance the night away in a disco buried in a silver mine—but its middle-of-nowhere status has kept it more on the small-town side of things than some of its sprawling sisters.

2 Pátzcuaro. An enchanting colonial town on the shores of Lake Pátzcuaro is the site of the Heartland's most important Day of the Dead celebrations and one of Mexico's most splendid zócalos. Shops sell some of the finest folk art in Mexico and honest and delicious food is turned out at humble stalls and back-alley restaurants.

3 Morelia. It doesn't have the peaceful charm of its neighbors, but Morelia's impressive Centro, with its pink limestone colonial buildings and magnificent churches, is filled with fine examples of baroque, neoclassical, and plateresque architecture.

4 Guanajuato. Tucked into a gorge and spilling across the surrounding mountainsides, this gorgeous town is made up of twisting streets and alleys and brightly colored houses. Add in church spires and the fortresslike University of Guanajuato, and it's hard to find a more visually arresting city. La Valenciana—once the greatest silver mine in the world and responsible for Guanajuato's existence—is just outside of town.

5 Querétaro. Beneath the bustling, modern exterior is an elegant colonial center. Querétaro is one of the Heartland's most historic cities, with many reminders of its past, including a wealth of extraordinary buildings, appealing plazas, and winding pedestrian walkways. Its unique combination of sophistication and relative lack of tourism make it an underrated gem of the region.

6 San Miguel de Allende. Cobblestoned streets, well-preserved rustic architecture, clear light, and mountainside vistas help to make San Miguel the most touristed town in the Heartland. There's also a thriving arts and music scene, and a renowned language and arts school. Known for its community of North American expats, San Miguel is still Mexican at heart.

GETTING ORIENTED

Also referred to as the Bajío, this area (parts of the states of Guanajuato, Querétaro, and Michoacán) really is the heartland of Mexico—geographically and historically. This is where men and women first fought and died for national independence, and where a 60-foot-high statue of Christ the King (Cristo Rey) keeps watch from atop the highest mountain in Guanajuato. The main attraction of the region is a collection of colonial cities, many former silver-and-gold-mining centers. Beyond city life, the mountains beckon intrepid bike riders, and natural hot springs invite all to relax.

SAN MIGUEL DE ALLENDE AND THE HEARTLAND PLANNER

How Much Can You Do?

Travel between the Heartland's major cities is easy; distances are (relatively) short. Even if you only have a few days, you'll still be able to see a lot.

If you have 3 days. Fly into and out of León's airport and base yourself in Guanajuato, enjoying its spectacular architecture, silver mine and church, and memorable funicular ride. Visit San Miguel de Allende on a day trip, an easy 1½-hour drive from Guanajuato.

If you have 5–6 days. Fly into León, spend the first two nights in Guanajuato, and the third night in San Miguel. Next, head south a couple of hours and stay in the bustling university town of Morelia. From there it's only an hour's drive on a superhighway to Pátzcuaro. An alternative route would begin by flying into Zacatecas and spending two nights there, then driving down to Guanajuato and spending the balance of your time there and in San Miguel, with a day trip to Morelia or Querétaro.

Getting Around

The Heartland is an accessible destination, easily reached from Mexico City or Guadalajara. A network of superhighways connects many major cities. Although it may be more fun to tour by car, there is frequent and inexpensive bus service between the region's cities.

Primera Plus, ETN, and Estrella Blanca are the major first-class lines. Aero Plus runs buses between the Mexico City and Querétaro airports. Flecha Amarilla is the second-class branch of Primera Plus, operating along the same routes. Herradura de Plata also has limited second-class service throughout the Bajío.

Tour Companies

Guanajuato **Transporte Exclusivo de Turismo** (☎ *473/732–5968*). **Transportes Turísticos de Guanajuato** (☎ *473/732–2134 or 473/732–2838*).

Heartland **Arturo Morales** (☎ *415/152–5400* 🌐 *www.tasma.info*).

Morelia **Morelia Operadores de Viajes** (☎ *443/312–8723 or 443/312–8747*).

Pátzcuaro **Francisco Castilleja** (☎ *434/344–0167*). **Miguel Angel Nuñez** (☎ *434/344–0108*).

Zacatecas **Operadora Zacatecas** (☎ *492/924–0050*). **Viajes Mazzocco** (☎ *492/922–0859*).

When to Go

The good news is that for the most part, high season is limited to Christmas, Easter, and the weeks around regional festivals. San Miguel's at its busiest in September, when it honors the Mexican Revolution and Independence; in mid-August during the International Chamber Music Festival; and in late November for the International Jazz Festival. Tourism also spikes during the Day of the Dead celebrations in Pátzcuaro on November 1–2; during Morelia's International Organ Festival in May; and during Guanajuato's International Cervantes Festival in October.

Travel Times

MEXICO CITY TO:	
San Miguel	3½ hrs
Querétaro	3 hrs
Guanajuato	5 hrs
Morelia	4 hrs
Pátzcuaro	5 hrs
Zacatecas	8 hrs

SAN MIGUEL TO:	
Querétaro	1 hr
Guanajuato	1½ hrs
León	2½ hrs
Morelia	4½ hrs
Zacatecas	3¾ hrs
Guadalajara	5½ hrs

Money Matters

Most moderate and inexpensive hotels quote prices with 17% value-added tax already included.

WHAT IT COSTS IN DOLLARS

	¢	$	$$	$$$	$$$$
Restaurants	under $5	$5–$10	$10–$15	$15–$25	over $25
Hotels	under $50	$50–$75	$75–$150	$150–$250	over $250

Restaurant prices are per person for a main course at dinner. Hotel prices are for two people in a standard double room in high season.

Safety

There has been trouble with drug cartel–related violence in Michoacán State. Stay to the more touristed areas within the state *and* within its capital, Morelia. If you are compelled to head off the path, do so with a reputable tour operator, rather than solo. For updates on the situation, check the U.S. State Department's Web site (🌐 *www.state.gov/travel*).

Weather

The Heartland has a superb climate—rarely does it get overly hot, even in midsummer, and although winter days can get nippy, especially in northern Zacatecas, they're generally temperate.

Average temperatures in Morelia range from 20°C (68°F) in May to just under 13°C (55°F) in January. Zacatecas is more extreme, with winter temperatures as low as 0°C (32°F) and snow flurries every several years, and summer highs of 28°C–30°C (81°F–85°F). Expect cool nights year-round in most of the region's cities.

The Heartland's rainy season hits between June and October and is strongest in July and August. At this time, the semiarid countryside comes to life with pink, yellow, and blue wildflowers, and the farms offer up fresh vegetables and fruits.

4

SAN MIGUEL DE ALLENDE

Updated by Teresa Nicholas and Gerard Helferich

YOU'VE HEARD THAT SAN MIGUEL de Allende is an artists' retreat, where the beauty of the surroundings, coupled with the inspired bent of those who seem to be drawn here, results in a proliferation of all things creative. There are literary readings, art shows, annual chamber music and jazz festivals, as well as yoga classes.

For travel novices, San Miguel can be a painless entry-level experience, practically free from concerns about health, safety, culture clash, and language. But even newcomers to Mexico shouldn't make the mistake of spending their whole trip here.

The city began luring foreigners in the late 1930s, when American Stirling Dickinson and prominent local residents founded an art school in this mountainous settlement. The school, now called the Instituto Allende, has grown in stature over the years—as has the city's reputation as a writers' and artists' colony. On any cobblestone street you'll run into expats of all nationalities, but particularly Americans and Canadians. Some come to study at the Instituto Allende or the Academia Hispano-Americana, some to escape harsh northern winters, and still others to retire.

San Miguel, declared a national monument in 1926 and named a UNESCO World Heritage Site in 2008, retains its Mexican characteristics. Eighteenth-century mansions, fountains, monuments, and churches are all reminders of the city's illustrious and sometimes notorious past. At the corner of Calles Hernández Macías and Pila Seca, for example, is the onetime headquarters of the Spanish Inquisition in New Spain. The former Inquisition jail stands across the way.

A great way to get your bearings is to take a spin on San Miguel's trolleybus that departs every two hours from the Municipal Tourism Office in the Jardín between 10 AM and 8 PM. The trolley's route will let you see most of the town, including a stop at the Mirador overlook, where you'll have a spectacular view of San Miguel, especially at sunset. The trolley runs daily and the fare is $5. For more information, call ☎ *415/154–5408*.

Bear in mind that the city is more than a mile above sea level, so you might tire quickly during your first few days if you aren't accustomed to high altitudes. Also, the streets are paved with rugged cobblestones, and narrow sidewalks are paved with stones that can get really slippery when wet. Most of San Miguel's sights are in a cluster downtown, which you can visit in a couple of hours.

Independence Day, celebrated on September 15 and 16, is San Miguel's biggest fiesta, with fireworks, dances, and parades; cultural events fill out the remainder of the month.

GETTING HERE AND AROUND

Querétaro (QRO) has the closest airport to San Miguel. The 45-minute drive costs less than $50 by taxi. However, the more commonly used airport is León; most travelers arrange for van pickup by Viajes San Miguel (☎ *415/152–2537* ✉ *info@viajessanmiguel.com*), for a cost of $30 and a trip of an hour and 15 minutes. Another option is San Miguel

Airport Shuttle (☎ *415/152–1999* ✉ *info@sanmigueltravelservices.com*). Primera Plus has first-class service from Mexico City's Central Norte station to San Miguel. The trip takes 3½ hours and costs \$20–\$25. First-class service by Primera Plus from Guadalajara takes 5½ hours and costs \$25–\$35. First-class bus lines such as Autobuses Americanos offer direct bus service from cities in Texas for under \$100. Driving from Mexico City to San Miguel (290 km [180 mi]) takes roughly four hours via the excellent Highway 57 (to Querétaro). San Miguel has big parking lots on Insurgentes 31 between Hidalgo and Reloj (\$1.50 an hour) and on Insurgentes 63 between Hernández Macías and Hidalgo (\$1 an hour). Some close at 8 PM. San Miguel Rent a Car has a selection of manual- and automatic-transmission vehicles.

WHERE IS IT?

For an excellent interactive map of San Miguel, with hotels, restaurants, bars, services, and more, go to 🌐 *smamap.com*; the site also has a green map of San Miguel, including bus routes, hiking trails, and a calendar of green events.

4

ESSENTIALS

Bus Contacts Autobuses Americanos (☎ *415/154–8233 in San Miguel* 🌐 *www.autobusesamericanos.com.mx*). **ETN** (☎ *01800/800–0386 toll-free in Mexico* 🌐 *www.etn.com.mx*). **Primera Plus** (☎ *415/152–0084, 01800/375–7587 toll-free in Mexico* 🌐 *www.primeraplus.com.mx*).

Medical Assistance Ambulance–Red Cross (☎ *415/152–1616*). **Fire Department** (☎ *415/152–2888*). **Hospital de la Fé** (✉ *Libramiento Manuel Zavala 12, Mesa el Malanquín* ☎ *415/152–2233 or 415/152–2320*). **Police** (☎ *415/152–0022*).

Rental Cars San Miguel Rent a Car (✉ *Codo 9, Int. 2, El Centro* ☎ *415/152–0198* 🌐 *www.sanmiguelrentacar.com*).

Visitor and Tour Info Consejo Turistico de San Miguel de Allende (✉ *Plaza Principal 10, El Centro* ☎ *415/152–0900 or 415/154-7175*).

EXPLORING

TOP ATTRACTIONS

3 **Casa de Ignacio Allende.** Constructed in 1764, this house is the birthplace of Ignacio Allende, one of Mexico's great independence heroes. Allende was a Creole aristocrat who, along with Father Miguel Hidalgo, plotted in 1810 to overthrow the Spanish regime. He was captured and executed by the Spanish Royalists in 1811. As a tribute to his brave efforts, San Miguel El Grande was renamed San Miguel de Allende in 1826. The highlight of the museum is the second floor, with period rooms and furnishings including a kitchen, chapel, parlors, and bedrooms. ✉ *Cuna de Allende 1, El Centro* ☎ *415/152–2499* 🎫 *\$3* ⏲ *Tues.–Sun. 9–5.*

4 **El Jardín.** San Miguel's heart, the plaza commonly known as El Jardín (the Garden), is where much of the town's action takes place, from political rallies and live music to dance presentations and fireworks on special occasions. You can get a real feel for the town just by sitting on

Bellas Artes 2
Biblioteca Pública 5
Casa de Ignacio Allende 3
El Charco del Ingenio 7
El Jardín 4
Iglesia de la Concepción 1
Iglesia de San Francisco 6
Instituto Allende 9
Lavaderos Públicos 8

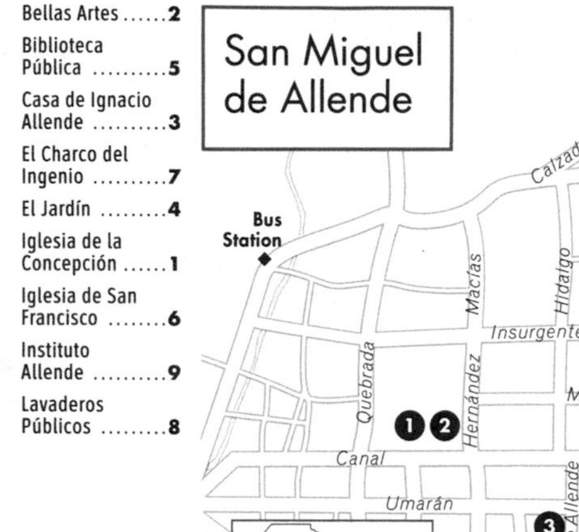

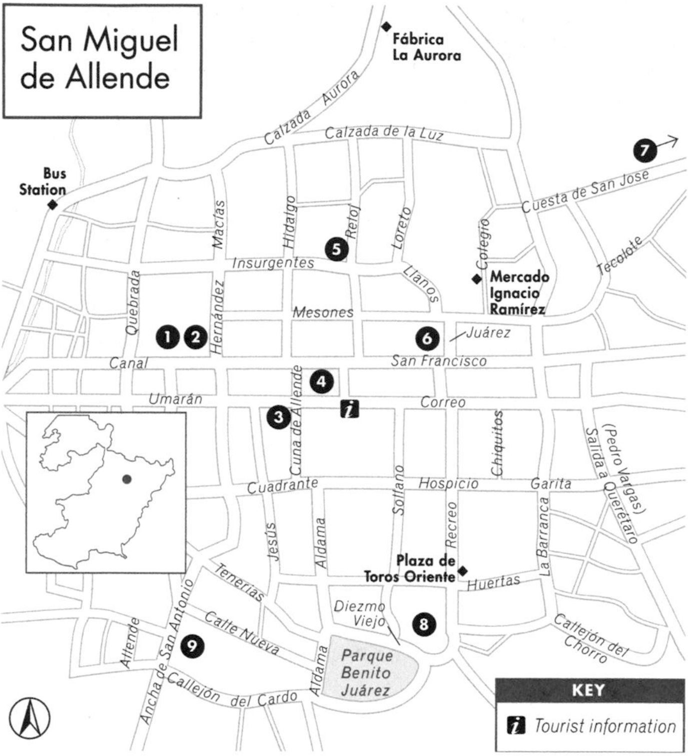

one of its wrought-iron benches, where locals and expats alike enjoy the early-morning sunshine and share some gossip before attending to the serious business of the day. The Parroquia bells toll each quarter hour, and at dusk the square fills with musicians, mothers and their kids, and teenagers taking their ritual evening stroll around the garden. ✉ *Bordered by Correo on fthe south, San Francisco on the north, Portal Allende on the west, and Portal Guadalupe on the east, El Centro.*

1 **Iglesia de la Concepción.** Just behind the Bellas Artes cultural center is this church, which has one of the largest domes in Mexico. The two-story dome (completed in 1891) and the elegant Corinthian columns and pilasters gracing its drum are said to have been inspired by Paris's dome of the Hôtel des Invalides. Ceferino Gutiérrez, the architect of La Parroquia, is credited with its design. ✉ *Calle Canal between Calles Hernández Macías and Zacateros, El Centro* ☎ *No phone.*

6 **Iglesia de San Francisco.** This church has one of Guanajuato State's finest churrigueresque facades. The term for this style refers to José Churriguera, a 17th-century (baroque) Spanish architect noted for his extravagant surface decoration. Built in the late 18th century, the church was financed by donations from wealthy patrons and by bullfight revenues. Topping the elaborately carved exterior is the image of Saint Francis of Assisi. Below, along with a crucifix, are sculptures of Saint John and

Our Lady of Sorrows. ✉ *Calle Juárez between Calles San Francisco and Mesones, El Centro* ☎ *No phone.*

NEED A BREAK?

Cafés around El Jardín offer outdoor seating under the *portales* (arcades), with the side streets closed to traffic: La Terraza, next to the Parroquia, has a big terrace perfect for people-watching; Café del Jardín in the Portal Allende is *a good* breakfast spot; Mesón de Don Tomás in the Portal Guadalupe is good any time of the day; and the Posada de San Francisco has a sunny restaurant.

WORTH NOTING

2 **Bellas Artes.** Once the Royal Convent of the Conception, this impressive cloister has been an institute for the study of music, dance, and the visual arts since 1938. It's across the street from the U.S. Consulate and has rotating exhibits and a café. Cultural events are listed on a bulletin board at the entrance. ✉ *Calle Hernández Macías 75, El Centro* ☎ *415/152–0289* *Free* *Mon.–Sat. 9–7, Sun. 10–3.*

5 **Biblioteca Pública.** Within the library's walls are a lovely courtyard café, the offices of the English-language newspaper *Atención San Miguel*, and reading rooms with back issues of popular publications and books in English. Movies are shown during the week at its Santa Ana Theater. On Sunday at noon a two-hour house-and-garden tour (about $15) of San Miguel leaves from the library. **■TIP→ Notices about such things as literary readings and yoga and aerobics classes are posted on the bulletin board in the library's entranceway.** ✉ *Insurgentes 25, El Centro* ☎ *415/152–0293* *Free* *Weekdays 10–7, Sat. 10–2.*

7 **El Charco del Ingenio.** San Miguel's botanical garden has an extensive collection of Mexican cacti and other plants collected from different parts of the country. The area is protected from encroachment by an ecological reserve of 445 acres and was visited by the Dalai Lama, who declared El Charco one of the five "zones of peace" in Mexico. A garden area will introduce you to some of the 120 varieties of agaves that grow here. **■TIP→ The reserve is huge, and has special pathways for walking, running, and mountain biking.** Twice a month it opens the *temazcales*, ritual herbal steam baths. If you're driving, turn left past the shopping center on the Salida a Querétaro and follow the signs to the main entrance. A cab will cost about $3. ✉ *Paloma s/n, above Atascadero* ☎ *415/154–4715 or 415/154–8838* 🌐 *www.elcharco.org.mx* *$3* *Daily 7 AM–8 PM.*

9 **Instituto Allende.** Since the school's founding in 1951, thousands of students from around the world have come here to learn Spanish and to take classes in the arts. The gorgeous campus, a former country estate, is open to visitors—even if you don't plan on taking any courses, the institute is a great place to spend a few peaceful hours. Take a break at El Cafecito coffee bar. The Galería La Pérgola specializes in modern Mexican art. The Institute also provides a complete travel service, hotel bookings, and cultural, adventure, and shopping tours. ✉ *Ancha de San Antonio 20, El Centro* ☎ *415/152–0226* 🌐 *www.institutoallende.com.mx* *Free* *Daily 9–9.*

4

8 **Lavaderos Públicos.** This collection of red concrete tubs above Parque Benito Juárez is a public laundry where local women gather daily to wash clothes and chat as has been done for centuries. Some women claim to have more efficient washing facilities at home, but the lure of the spring-fed troughs and the chance to catch up on the news bring them to this shaded courtyard. ✉ *Calle Diezmo Viejo at Calle Recreo, El Centro.*

BENITO JUÁREZ PARK

This fantastic park in the heart of San Miguel has ancient trees, flower-lined paths ideal for a morning jog, a basketball court, and a children's play area with swings and fun things to climb. It's on Calle Aldama in El Centro, a short stroll south from El Jardín.

WHERE TO EAT

$$ MEXICAN ✕ **Bugambilia.** A lovely location in an evocative courtyard and live music played every night make this a favorite with tourists and locals alike. Most come for the *chiles en nogada* (poblano peppers with a creamy walnut sauce) with pomegranate seeds sprinkled on top. The pechuga rellena de elote y mango (chicken breast stuffed with corn and mango) is also popular. There's a nice list of local liquors. ✉ *Hidalgo 42, El Centro* ☎ *415/154–5180* ▭ *MC, V.*

$$$ SPANISH ✕ **Café Ibérico.** Tapas are on the menu at this casual, lively restaurant and bar, which focuses on simple, fresh ingredients, some flown in from Spain. Try the sizzling chili shrimp, fried goat cheese with honey, stuffed piquillo peppers, marinated grilled octopus, and *jamon Serrano* with Tete de Moine cheese. The American chef learned the art of tapeo as a young man in Spain, and his pastry-chef wife learned her art at her French grandmother's knee. The desserts are a knockout, especially the cheesecake and crème brûlée. ✉ *Mesones 101, El Centro* ☎ *415/152–6154* 🌐 *www.cafeiberico.com.mx* ▭ *MC, V.*

$ ECLECTIC ✕ **El Pegaso.** This family-owned restaurant is known for its friendly service and casual atmosphere. It has great breakfast options, including eggs Benedict and waffles, which are available until noon to aid late risers. At lunch and dinner light fare predominates, including salads, sandwiches, and hamburgers, though the chiles en nogada are the most popular item on the menu. ✉ *Calle Corregidora 6, El Centro* ☎ *415/152–1351 or 415/154–7611* ▭ *D, DC, MC, V* ⊙ *Closed Sun.*

$ MEXICAN ✕ **El Rinconcito.** The best bargain in town is also the place for the best home-cooked Mexican food, prepared in the immaculate open-air kitchen. Along with tacos and quesadillas, try hamburgers, grilled chicken, or shrimp wrapped in bacon. ✉ *Calle Refugio Norte 7, San Antonio* ☎ *415/154–4809* ▭ *No credit cards* ⊙ *Closed Tues.*

$ FRENCH/MEXICAN ✕ **La Brasserie.** This homey bistro offers what may be the best dining value in San Miguel, with a three-course pre-fixe menu at about $11, including a glass of wine or beer. You'll start with a homemade soup or fresh salad, then choose a main course such as shrimp Provençal or arrachera, Mexican flank steak. For dessert, there are classic French favorites including flan, crepes, and chocolate mousse. La Brasserie shares space with the popular Café de la Parroquia, which

CLOSE UP

Eating Green in San Miguel

The local-food movement is alive and well in San Miguel. With several nearby farms now specializing in organic food, San Miguel has seen the addition of restaurants focusing on natural ingredients. Here are a few places to try. Café Rama (✉ *Calle Nueva 7, El Centro* ☎ *415/154–9655*) offers innovative seasonal selections with an international slant, such as Southeast Asian chicken salad and lamb shepherd's pie. Café Tapas (✉ *Margarito Ledesma 2, Colonia Guadalupe* ☎ *415/154–8131*) shares a pleasant space with Vía Orgánica, a popular organic food store, and offers salads, soups, and other light fare. El Tomato (✉ *Mesones 62, El Centro* ☎ *415/154–6390*) features Italian- and Argentine-inspired cooking including pastas, soups, and salads, with a wide vegetarian selection.

4

serves traditional Mexican fare for breakfast and lunch. ✉ *Jesús 11, El Centro* ☎ *415/152–3161* ▭ *No credit cards* ⊙ *No lunch. Closed Sun. and Mon.*

$ MEXICAN Fodor's Choice ★ ✕ **La Posadita.** Here, in the shadow of La Parroquia, you'll find some of the best-prepared traditional Mexican food in town. The guacamole is great, as are any of the enchiladas, the chiles rellenos, and the Yucatan specialty, cochinita pibil. Top it off with the homemade flan, a delicious preparation of an old standby, and wash it all down with one of the well-prepared margaritas. The sweeping countryside view from one of San Miguel's most romantic rooftop terraces is another enchantment. ✉ *Cuna de Allende 13, El Centro* ☎ *415/154–8862* ▭ *MC, V* ⊙ *Closed Wed.*

$$$ ECLECTIC ✕ **The Restaurant.** Founded in 2008 by chef Donnie Masterton, formerly of New York's Bouley, Montrachet, and Tavern on the Green, The Restaurant is where well-heeled and shabby-chic expats dine with fashionistas and movers and shakers, though they cede the pleasant vine-covered patio to wealthy Mexican visitors come the weekend. The menu emphasizes organic ingredients and changes according to the season and whatever inspires chef Masterton in the local market. Specialties include homemade ravioli with goat cheese and poblano, crab cakes with guacamole, miso-marinated Pacific salmon, sautéed salmon trout in curry brown butter, and, for dessert, panna cotta made with goat yogurt and honey. ✉ *Sollano 16, El Centro* ☎ *415/154–7877* 🌐 *www.therestaurantsanmiguel.com* ▭ *MC, V* ⊙ *Closed Sun.*

WHERE TO STAY

$$ **Casa Carmen.** Located in a colonial house with most rooms facing the large central patio, complete with plants and bubbling fountain, this family-run pension offers excellent location and value, plus a homey atmosphere. Rooms are good-sized, but the furnishings are a bit on the basic side. Prices include a full breakfast plus a family-style three-course luncheon. **Pros:** central location; good value; friendly staff. Cons: outdated furnishings; rooms facing street can **be noisy.** ✉ *Correo*

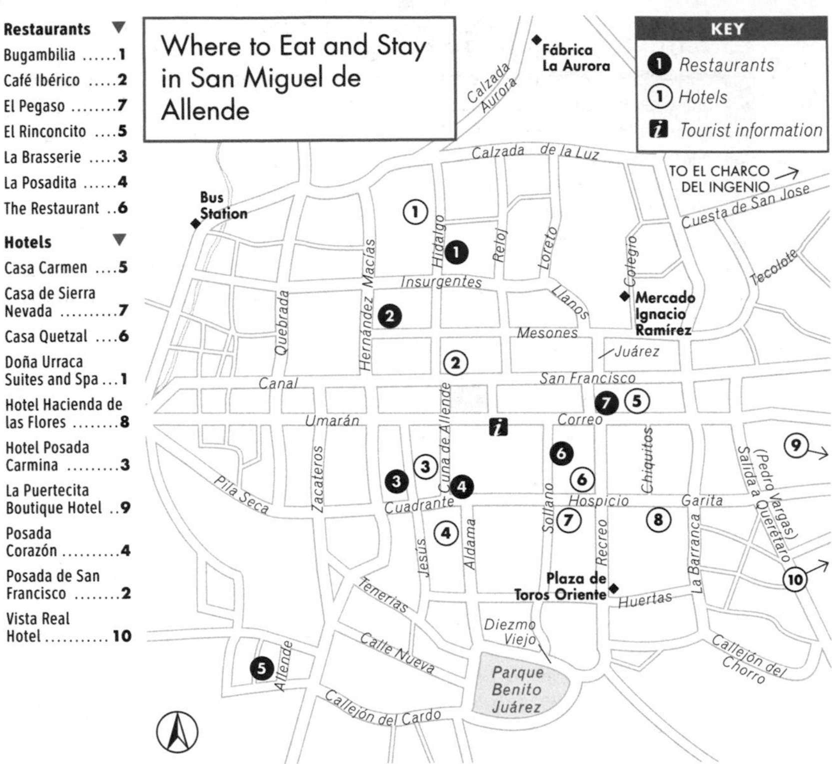

31, El Centro ☎ *415/152–0844* 🌐 *www.casacarmenhotel.com* 🛏 *11 rooms* 👍 *In-room: no a/c, no phone, no TV, Wi-Fi. In-hotel: restaurant, laundry service, Wi-Fi hotspot, some pets allowed* 💳 *No credit cards* 🍽 *MAP.*

$$$$ 🏨 **Casa de Sierra Nevada.** Built in 1580 as the archbishop of Guanajuato's residence, this elegant country-style inn still attracts ambassadors, diplomats, film stars, and other luminaries. Rooms are distributed throughout a series of small mansions. Lace curtains, handwoven rugs, and chandeliers adorn some of them; fireplaces, cozy terraces, and skylights enhance others. The hotel runs the separate **Casa del Parque,** an exquisitely restored 18th-century hacienda with five guest rooms a few minutes' walk away, on the Parque Benito Juárez; its restaurant serves refined versions of traditional Mexican dishes and has a popular Sunday buffet brunch. **Pros:** old-fashioned elegance; cooking classes and language school on grounds. **Cons:** pricey. ✉ *Calle Hospicio 42, El Centro* ☎ *415/152–7040* 🌐 *www.casadesierranevada.com* 🛏 *27 rooms, 10 suites* 👍 *In-room: a/c (some), safe, DVD, Internet. In-hotel: 2 restaurants, room service, bars, pool, spa, laundry service, Internet terminal, parking (free)* 💳 *AE, MC, V.*

$$$ ★ 🏨 **Casa Quetzal.** Three blocks from the main square, this boutique hotel offers eclectic suites, each with its own characteristic style; for example, you'll find Japanese-inspired touches in the Zen Suite and bold colors in

the Mexican-style Frida Suite. Rooms are considerably smaller; a suite is ideal even for a party of just two. A full breakfast is included with your stay. Casa Quetzal can arrange tours to Querétaro and Guanajuato, as well as horseback-riding trips to a nearby canyon. **Pros:** tranquil and homey. **Cons:** some rooms feel cramped. ✉ *Calle Hospicio 34, El Centro* ☎ *415/152–0501* 🌐 *www.casaquetzalhotel.com* *4 rooms, 6 suites* *In-room: a/c (some), safe, kitchen (some), DVD (some), no TV (some), Wi-Fi (some). In-hotel: laundry service, Wi-Fi hotspot, parking (paid), some pets allowed* *MC, V* *BP.*

$$$ **Doña Urraca Suites and Spa.** You may be startled as you step through the plate-glass entrance that transports you from a colonial city to a location with minimalist furnishings and decoration. Everything is white marble, walls are often substituted by floor to-ceiling plate glass, black marble is used for countertops, and chairs and sofas are red or white leather. **Pros:** high style. **Cons:** front rooms can be noisy; minimalist style can come off as cold. ✉ *Hidalgo 69, El Centro* ☎ *415/154–9770 or 415/154–9771* 🌐 *www.donaurraca.com.mx* *23 rooms* *In-room: no a/c, no phone, safe, refrigerator (some), DVD (some), Wi-Fi. In-hotel: pool, spa, laundry service, Wi-Fi hotspot, parking (free)* *AE, MC, V* *BP.*

$ **Hotel Hacienda de las Flores.** A plant-lined path leads up to flowering gardens and a swimming pool, one of only two hotel pools in Centro. The rooms here can be on the small side, but they're clean and comfortable, and all face the garden. The hotel is two blocks uphill from the Jardín. **Pros:** pool; garden; tranquil atmosphere. **Cons:** uphill walk; out-of-date decor in rooms. ✉ *Hospicio 16, El Centro* ☎ *415/152–1808 or 415/152–1859* 🌐 *www.haciendadelasflores.com* *5 rooms, 11 suites* *In-hotel: pool, Wi-Fi hotspot* *AE, MC, V* *BP.*

$$ **Hotel Posada Carmina.** This restored 18th-century house stands next to Ignacio Allende's home and opposite the Parroquia. A great location for sure, and the view is spectacular, but be forewarned that La Parroquia's bells might wake you up at all hours. The rooms surround a lavish courtyard, which has a lovely fountain, umbrella-shaded tables, and a plethora of vines tumbling down the stucco walls. Rooms are sparsely decorated—you won't find the profusion of folk art or bold colors that decorate many of the hotels in the region—but they don't lack comfort or amenities. You might fare better against the ever-chiming bells with one of the newer rooms toward the back. The hotel's restaurant, La Felguera, hosts live music every night of the week except Sunday. **Pros:** splendid courtyard and proximity to city center. **Cons:** street noise. ✉ *Cuna de Allende 7, El Centro* ☎ *415/152–8888* 🌐 *www.posadacarmina.com* *24 rooms* *In-room: no a/c, no phone, refrigerator (some), Wi-Fi. In-hotel: restaurant, room service, bar, laundry service, Wi-Fi hotspot, parking (free)* *MC, V* *BP.*

$$$ **La Puertecita Boutique Hotel.** Visitors seeking tranquil surroundings might choose La Puertecita for its elegant mix of colonial and modern Mexican design. The hotel is a few minutes from downtown (there's shuttle service), in a private park with waterfalls and flowering trees. The tree-house restaurant (yes, you read that correctly) La Palapa has a view of a 300-year-old aqueduct and offers a romantic backdrop

for intimate lunches and candlelit dinners. Reservations are essential, and upon making them you can create your own menu. **Pros:** romantic restaurant; tastefully decorated. **Cons:** can't walk to city center and far from nightlife. ✉ *Calle Santo Domingo 75, Col. Los Arcos* ☎ *415/152–5011* 🌐 *www.lapuertecita.com* *18 rooms, 6 suites* *In-room: no a/c, safe, kitchen (some), Wi-Fi. In-hotel: restaurant, room service, bar, pools, spa, laundry service, Wi-Fi hotspot, parking (free)* 💳 *AE, MC, V.*

HACIENDA HAVEN

If you're looking for a real getaway far from the madding crowd, book yourself into a real hacienda—Las Trancas—under an hour's drive north of San Miguel. Here you can turn back the clock and relax in vast rooms whose walls are 3 feet thick, lounge in the shade of colonnaded porticos, or roam the countryside on a pony. **Hacienda Las Trancas** ✉ *Rte. 51 at Las Trancas, north of Dolores Hidalgo* ☎ *418/182–9500* 🌐 *www.haciendalastrancas.com.*

$$$ ★ **Posada Corazón.** One of San Miguel's oldest families has opened its ranch-style home as a hotel, complete with a common area with fireplace and a library full of Mexican and international art books. Only blocks from the action of downtown, rooms here open onto lush gardens and trees. From an ample terrace with sweeping views you can enjoy an organic breakfast. One of the rooms has its own swimming pool. **Pros:** incredibly warm and accommodating staff; central location; peaceful. **Cons:** for some, may lack amenities. ✉ *Aldama 9, El Centro* ☎ *415/152–0182 or 415/152–2165* 🌐 *www.posadacorazon.com.mx* *6 rooms* *In-room: no a/c, no phone, no TV, Wi-Fi. In-hotel: room service, bar, spa, laundry service, Wi-Fi hotspot, parking (free)* 💳 *D, DC, MC, V* *BP.*

$$ **Posada de San Francisco.** This restored colonial mansion right on the Jardín was San Miguel's first hotel, in operation since 1939. However, it's not its most inspired—rooms are somewhat monastic. If you don't mind the noise, request one that faces the Jardín for a great view of La Parroquia and all the events and activities taking place in the center of town. **Pros:** reasonable price; location couldn't be more central. **Cons:** rooms are a bit dowdy; can be noisy. ✉ *Plaza Principal 2, El Centro* ☎ *415/152–7213 or 415/152–7214* 🌐 *www.posadadesanfrancisco.com* *44 rooms, 5 suites* *In-room: Wi-Fi. In-hotel: 2 restaurants, room service, bar, laundry service, Wi-Fi hotspot, parking (free)* 💳 *AE, D, DC, MC, V.*

NIGHTLIFE

Sleepy San Miguel offers a toned-down nightlife that's largely aimed at tourists and expats. The Biblioteca Pública has screenings of foreign and U.S. films. There is also an eight-screen theater in the Luciernaga shopping center east of town. Concerts, literary readings, theater, art exhibitions, and dance lessons will keep you busy. Listings appear in the English-language newspaper *Atención*, published every Friday.

You can grab a quiet after-dinner drink any night of the week in El Centro, but nightlife is truly alive Thursday through Sunday. You can quite

¿HABLA ESPAÑOL?

Ever since Stirling Dickinson and the World War II veterans came to study on the GI Bill, San Miguel has been about learning. Many come to study Spanish, and there is a good variety of schools to choose from:

Academia Hispano Americana (✉ *Mesones 4, El Centro* ☎ *415/152–0349 or 415/152–4349*)

Centro Bilingue de San Miguel (✉ *Correo 46, El Centro* ☎ *415/152–5400*)

Centro Mexicano (✉ *Orizaba 15, Col. San Antonio* ☎ *415/152–0763*)

Habla Hispana (✉ *Calzada de la Luz 25, El Centro* ☎ *415/152–0713*)

Instituto Allende (✉ *Ancha de San Antonio 22, El Centro* ☎ *415/152–0190*)

Warren Hardy Spanish School (✉ *San Rafael 6, Col. San Juan de Dios* ☎ *415/154–4017 or 415/152–4728*)

easily start (and end) your evening pub crawl on Calle Umarán. **Berlin Bar** (✉ *Umarán 19, El Centro* ☎ *415/154–9432*) is a pretty, upscale bar with an international crowd.

El Manantial (✉ *Barranca 78, El Centro* ☎ *415/110–0007*), located in what was the oldest cantina in town, offers exotic drinks such as fresh ginger martinis, and seafood tacos in an atmospheric setting.

La Azotea (✉ *Umarán 6, El Centro* ☎ *415/152–8265*), located upstairs from the Pueblo Viejo restaurant, is the most popular haunt for the well-heeled and well-dressed crowd, making for supreme people-watching and great sunset views.

La Felguera (✉ *Cuna de Allende 7, El Centro* ☎ *415/152–8888*) offers two-for-one drinks as well as live music Tuesday through Saturday, all in a gorgeous place.

La Felguera's neighbor, elegant **La Fragua** (✉ *Cuna de Allende 3, El Centro* ☎ *415/152–1144*) showcases live entertainers singing in Spanish and English.

Limerick (✉ *Umarán 24, El Centro* ☎ *415/154–8642*) is an Irish bar, complete with dart board and pool table, and attracts a young crowd.

SHOPPING

For centuries San Miguel's artisans have created crafts ranging from straw products to metalwork. Although some boutiques in town may be pricey, you can find good buys on silver, brass, tin, woven cotton goods, and folk art. Hours are erratic, but most stores open daily at around 10, shut their doors for the afternoon siesta (2 to 4 or 5), then reopen in the afternoon until 7 or 8. They're usually open for just a half day on Sunday. Most San Miguel shops accept MasterCard and Visa. Many shops are located near the Jardín.

ART GALLERIES AND HANDICRAFTS

Long known as an artists' colony, San Miguel has galleries, museums, and arty shops that line the streets near the Jardín; most close weekdays between 2 and 4 and are open weekends from 10 or 11 to 2 or 3. Two salons—at **Bellas Artes** and **Instituto Allende**—show the work of Mexican artists.

Artes de México (✉ *Calz. Aurora 47, at Dolores Hidalgo exit, Col. Guadalupe* ☎ *415/152–0764*) has been producing and selling traditional crafts for more than 40 years.

Casa Michoacana (✉ *Calzada de la Aurora 23, El Centro* ☎ *415/154–5008)*, located near Fábrica La Aurora, offers gorgeous, high-quality handicrafts from the state of Michoacán.

> **NAME THAT TUNE**
>
> For more than 30 years San Miguel has hosted August's top-notch Festival de Musica de Camara, a feast of classical chamber music that includes groups from around the globe. The International Jazz & Blues Festival takes place around the last week in November (🌐 *www.sanmigueljazz.com*). You can buy tickets for the concerts, workshops, and after-hours jam sessions individually or for the series. Call the tourist office or visit 🌐 *www.chambermusicfestival.com* for dates and details.

The two collectors behind the regional and international talent of **Galería Atenea** (✉ *Calle Jesús 2, El Centro* ☎ *415/152–0785*) have a thing for appealing watercolors and Bustamante jewelry.

For a taste of contemporary Mexican art and the whimsical folk-art paintings of Carlos Vital, stop by **Galería San Miguel** (✉ *Plaza Principal 14, El Centro* ☎ *415/152–0454*).

Galerie 19 (✉ *Jesús 19, El Centro* ☎ *415/154–9980* 🌐 *www.sanmiguelart.com*) specializes in painting, sculpture, and photography.

Kunsthaus Santa Fé (✉ *Santa Fé 22A, Col. Allende* ☎ *415/152–5608* 🌐 *www.kunsthaus.org.mx*) is a contemporary art space showing multifaceted installations—it feels more Manhattan than Mexico.

Ono (✉ *Plaza Principal 20, El Centro* ☎ *415/152–1366*) offers a pleasing assortment of handicrafts including silver, textiles, and wooden boxes and frames.

Zócalo(✉ *Hernandez Macías 110, El Centro* ☎ *415/152–0663*) sells some of the highest-quality folk art and crafts in San Miguel, collected from all over Mexico.

CLOTHING

San Miguel Shoe (✉ *Reloj 27, El Centro* ☎ No phone) features a delightful selection of inexpensive locally crafted shoes.

HOME DECOR

Guajuye (✉ *Lupita No. 2, Estacion F.F.C.C.* ☎ *415/152–7030* 🌐 *www.guajuye.com*), on the road to the railroad station, is the local glass factory, where you can pick up all sorts of handblown glassware. It also has a shop in town at Correo 11. **María Luisa Decoraciones** (✉ *Canal 40, El Centro* ☎ *415/152–0130*) has contemporary Mexican furniture, frames, household items, lamps, and art.**Rachel Horn** (✉ *Fábrica*

CLOSE UP

Fábrica La Aurora

Fábrica La Aurora. A 10-minute walk from the center of town, Fábrica La Aurora, which was established in 1902, was the principal source of fine-quality muslin in the region until competition forced its closing. Decades later, it reopened as exhibition spaces for art galleries and antique- and modern-furniture showrooms; also, many local artists have opened studios here.

The concentration of art galleries draws visitors in huge numbers. The **Generator Gallery**, complete with the Fábrica's original generator, features San Miguel artists and contemporary art. Galerie La Piccola represents two other local artists—Peter Leventhal, whose exuberant paintings are often based on classical themes, and Terra Mizwa, who creates classically inspired bronze and terracotta sculptures. **Galería Florencia Riestra** is owned by one of Mexico City's leading galleries. The folks at **Pepe Cerroblanco** are locally revered jewelry designers working with modernistic designs in silver and precious stones.

Planning to decorate? You will find inspiration from the past in the numerous antiques shops, including **Cantadora** and **La Buhardilla,** with their superb collection of Mexican colonial objets d'art. **Rachel Horn, Sisal, Atrium,** and **C.DeWayne Youts** are the showrooms of some of San Miguel's most inspired interior designers. **La Bottega di Casa** sells jacquard cottons, fine linens, Capodimonte ceramics, alabaster vases, and traditional pewter from Italy.

If you're shopped out and hungry, head for the **Food Factory** with its Old World character and comfortable sofas under a covered patio. Or pick up a snack at the outdoor **Café de la Aurora** coffee shop. ✉ *Calzada de la Aurora s/n, El Centro.*

4

La Aurora, Col. Guadalupe ☎ *415/154–8323*) is a dramatic haven of made-to-order furniture.

JEWELRY

Cerro Blanco Joyería (✉ *Fábrica La Aurora, Canal 17, Int. 109, Plaza Colonial, El Centro* ☎ *415/154–9501*) creates and crafts its own silver and gold jewelry, and will arrange a visit to its *taller* (workshop) on request.

Established in 1963, **Joyería David** (✉ *Zacateros 53, El Centro* ☎ *415/152–0056*) has an extensive selection of gold and silver jewelry, all made on the premises. Many pieces contain Mexican opals, amethysts, topazes, malachite, and turquoise.

MARKETS

Spilling out for several blocks behind the Mercado Ignacio Ramírez is the **Mercado de Artesanías.** You'll find vendors of local work at this artisans' market—glass, tin, and papier-mâché—as well as silver jewelry at bargain prices.

Mercado Ignacio Ramírez, a traditional Mexican covered market off Calle Colegio, one block north of Calle Mesones, is a colorful jumble of fresh

CLOSE UP

Outdoorsy in San Miguel

From birding and bathing to mountain biking and golfing, enjoying the outdoors around San Miguel, with its eternal spring climate, is an opportunity not to be missed.

Our favorite outdoor adventures in the region include **mountain biking and hiking,** which may be the most intimate ways to get to know the San Miguel countryside. San Miguel is on the slopes of an ancient volcano called Los Picachos (not active). Riding or walking along narrow mountain paths, you'll find oak and pine forests, bogs, marshes, and streams where migrating birds come to feed. You may come across abandoned chapels, old mining sites, and ancient, solitary haciendas, all testimonies to long-forgotten times. There are several rental outfits specializing in mountain bikes, helmets, and gloves. Expert guides offer various tours for mountain biking and hiking according to your ability. (⇨ *See Sports and the Outdoors for tour and rental information.*)

Whether you have been trekking through the mountains or trudging over cobblestones, a swim in one of San Miguel's **thermal pools** is a welcome way to relax. All the *balnearios* are a short drive out of town, on the Dolores Hidalgo Highway. Balneario Xoté, with its slides and swings, is an ideal place to take kids. Most balnearios have some facilities like snack stands.

fruits, flowers, stands, toys, and Mexican-made cassettes. Both markets are open daily from around 8 to7.

SPORTS AND THE OUTDOORS

HEALTH CLUBS

Fitness International (✉ *Salida a Celaya, next to La Mega supermarket, La Lejona* ☎ *415/120–0700* 🎫 *$6 day pass* ⊙ *Closed Sun.*) is the best-equipped gym in town. The **Club de Golf Malanquín** (✉ *Celaya Hwy., Km 3, Malanquín* ☎ *415/152–0516* ⊙ *Closed Mon.*) has a heated pool, steam baths, and 9 holes of golf, all of which are open to the public for $60 on weekdays or $90 on weekends. **Balenario Xoté** (✉ *Dolores Hidalgo Hwy., Km 5.5* ☎ *415/155–8187*) has slides and swings—perfect for kids.

HOT SPRINGS

La Gruta (✉ *Dolores Hidalgo Hwy., Km 11* 🎫 *$8* ⊙ *Closed Tues.*) has several pools, one of which is accessed via a tunnel. **Shanti San Miguel** (✉ *Highway to Los Rodriguez, Km 9* ☎ *044/415/151–8289* 🌐 *www.shantisanmiguel.com* 🎫 *$10* ⊙ *Wed.–Sun. 10–6*) offers cushy lounge chairs beside a gorgeous pool in a transcendent setting, along with spa services, yoga classes, and an international restaurant. It's a great place to get pampered.

Taboada (✉ *Dolores Hidalgo Hwy., Km 8*) has three outdoor geothermal pools, one of which is nearly Olympic-size and good for doing laps. The pools are open to the public for $8 from 8 AM to 6 PM every day but Tuesday.

YOGA

Yoga is popular in San Miguel, and there are many opportunities to practice; most classes are bilingual. Here are a few studios and their approaches.

Centro de Yoga Shakti (✉ *Ancha de San Antonio 7, San Antonio* ☎ *044/415/113–7061* features vinyasa style classes run by Tanya Kawan, who trained with Rodney Yee at Kripalu.

Yoga with Anabel (✉ *Bellas Artes, Hernández Macías 75, El Centro* ☎ *415/152–8129)* offers hatha yoga in an eclectic style.

Yoga the Iyengar Way (✉ *Terraplen 34, El Centro* ☎ *415/120–0767)*is a good bet for getting in a solid Iyengar session.

OUTDOOR ADVENTURING

Arturo Morales (☎ *415/152–5400* 🌐 *www.tasma.info*) can take you on cultural, mountain-bike, or eco-friendly hiking tours.

BICI-BURRO (✉ *Calle Hospicio 1, El Centro* ☎ *415/152–1526* 🌐 *www.bici-burro.com*) rents bikes and leads various hiking and biking tours.

Coyote Canyon Adventures (☎ *415/154–4193* 🌐 *www.coyotecanyon-adventures.com*) offers hiking, trail riding, ballooning, mountain biking, and overnight camping on its own ranch. A special weeklong trail ride goes from San Miguel to Guanajuato. Make reservations through its Web site.

MOTO-RENT (✉ *Jesús 18, El Centro* ☎ *415/152–4711 or 415/152–1080*) rents various types of equipment, including bikes, ATVs, and scooters.

SIDE TRIPS FROM SAN MIGUEL DE ALLENDE

DOLORES HIDALGO

40 km (25 mi) north of San Miguel de Allende via Rte. 51.

An easy one-hour bus ride from San Miguel de Allende's Central de Autobuses, Dolores Hidalgo is famous for its lovely hand-glazed Talavera-style ceramics, most notably tiles and tableware. Calle Puebla, a few blocks southeast of the main square, is a good place to browse, especially Artesanías JMB (✉ *Puebla 60, at the corner of Tamaulipas* ☎ *418/182–0749*), which advertises that its wares are lead-free; it also ships internationally. After shopping, stroll over to the plaza for one of Dolores's famous ice creams, including some of the most exotic flavors you'll ever taste, such as mole, avocado, beer, and corn.

It was in Dolores Hildalgo, before midnight on September 15, 1810, that local priest Miguel Hidalgo launched Mexico's fight for independence with an impassioned call to arms known as the *grito*, or "cry." Every September 15 at 11 PM, in the Zócalo in Mexico City, the Mexican president rings the bell taken from Hidalgo's church in Dolores and reads a version of the original grito—"Viva Mexico! Viva Mexico! Viva Mexico!"

EXPLORING

Once Father Hidalgo's home, **Museo Casa Miguel Hidalgo** is now a museum with copies of Hidalgo's important letters and other independence memorabilia. ✉ *Calle Puebla and Hidalgo* ☎ *418/182–0171 or 418/182–1164* 🎫 *$2.50* ⏲ *Tues.–Sat. 9–6, Sun. 9–5.*

If you're driving, you might want to make a stop at **Santuario de Atotonilco**, which is 10 minutes off the Dolores Hidalgo Highway. Named a World Heritage Site in 2008, the sanctuary was built by Father Felipe Neri de Alfaro in the 18th century. In 1810, Hidalgo and his troops stopped here to claim the banner of Our Lady of Guadalupe before their successful march on San Miguel. The small church is completely covered in murals that have earned it the title "the Sistine Chapel of Mexico." It also houses a venerated statue of Our Lord at the Column, a bloodied Christ leaning over a pedestal, which has been credited with several miracles. On Sunday there's often a market of statues, rosaries, crowns of thorns, and other religious souvenirs, and you may see pilgrims wearing bridal veils (even the men) and flagellating themselves as they enter the grounds for a week's penitence and prayer.

MINERAL DE POZOS

35 km (22 mi) northeast of San Miguel de Allende.

The captivating Sierra Gorda town of Pozos was a silver-mining center for centuries. Now it's a virtual ghost town of about 2,000 people, where you can roam the crumbling buildings, including the eerie, abandoned church. There are two hotels with restaurants on the main square; inquire at either to arrange a tour of the old mines above the city. The mines are ideal for picnicking, but if you go by yourself, be careful; some shafts are unguarded and easy to stumble into if you're not paying attention. Pozos is a 45-minute drive from San Miguel; take the highway toward Querétaro and turn on the road marked "Dr. Mora."

WHERE TO STAY

$$ **Posada de las Minas.** Located one block off the main square, this comfortable inn has bedrooms decorated in a variety of styles, from colorful Mexican folk art to elegant Victorian. Some have fireplaces, and a pool and spa are under construction. The friendly owner will also help you arrange tours to the nearby mines and tell you where to see local artisans making replicas of pre-Hispanic musical instruments. **Pros:** comfortable rooms and warm staff. **Cons:** no Wi-Fi in rooms. ✉ *Manuel Doblado 1* ☎ *442/293–0213* 🌐 *www.posadadelasminas.com* *6 rooms, 2 suites* *In-room: no a/c, kitchen (some). In-hotel: restaurant, room service, bar, bicycles, laundry service, Wi-Fi hotspot, parking (free), some pets allowed* 💳 *MC, V* 🍽 *BP.*

QUERÉTARO

63 km (39 mi; 1 hr by bus) southeast of San Miguel de Allende via Hwy. 111, 220 km (137 mi) northwest of Mexico City via Hwy. 57.

Querétaro is a modern city of about a million inhabitants, but it holds its own against the region's other colonial cities, with wide, tree-lined boulevards and wonderfully manicured parks adorned with fountains

CLOSE UP

Mexico's Beating Heart

Named for its central position, the Heartland is known for its well-preserved colonial architecture, its fertile farmland and encircling mountains, and its salient role in Mexican history, particularly during the War of Independence (1810–21). The Bajío (ba-*hee*-o), as it is also called, corresponds roughly to the state of Guanajuato and parts of Querétaro and Michoacán states.

Intense Spanish colonization of the Heartland followed the discovery of silver in the 1500s. Guanajuato was the site of the world's largest silver mine, and the Spanish conquistadors wasted no time in founding a network of towns such as Morelia, Zacatecas, and San Miguel de Allende, where they built mansions to fit their lavish lifestyles and protect their interests. Wealthy Creoles (Mexicans of Spanish descent) in Querétaro and San Miguel took the first steps toward independence from Spain three centuries later. When their efforts were discovered, two of the early insurgents, Ignacio Allende and Father Miguel Hidalgo, began in earnest the War of Independence.

Another native son, José María Morelos, rallied for independence when Allende and Hidalgo were executed in 1811. This *mestizo* (mixed race) muleskinner–turned–priest–turned–soldier nearly gained control of the land with his army of 9,000 before he was killed in 1815. Thirteen years later the city of Valladolid was renamed Morelia in his honor.

Long after the War of Independence ended in 1821, cities in the Bajío continued to figure prominently in Mexico's history. Three major events occurred in Querétaro alone: in 1848 the Mexican-American War ended with the signing of the Treaty of Guadalupe Hidalgo; in 1867 Austrian Maximilian of Habsburg, then emperor of Mexico, was executed just north of town; and in 1917 the Mexican Constitution was signed here.

The Heartland continually honors the events and people that helped shape modern Mexico. In ornate cathedrals or bucolic plazas, down narrow alleyways or atop high hillsides, you'll find monuments to—and remnants of—a heroic past. You can savor the region's historic spirit during its numerous fiestas. On a night filled with fireworks, off-key music, and tireless celebrants, it's hard not to be caught up in the vital expression of national pride.

Unlike areas where attractions are specifically designed for tourists, the Bajío relies on its historic ties and architectural integrity to appeal to travelers. Families visit parks for Sunday picnics, youngsters tussle in school courtyards, old men chat in shaded plazas, and Purépecha women in traditional garb sell their wares in crowded markets.

and statues of its heroes. Even the large factories rising around the perimeter manage to look nice.

The city draws more international executives than tourists, but it is sophisticated, with many restaurants, nightclubs, and theaters. Historically, Querétaro is notable as the former residence of Josefa Ortíz de Domínguez, popularly known as La Corregidora, who warned the conspirators gathered in San Miguel and its environs that their independence plot had been discovered. It is here that the ill-fated Emperor Maximilian made his last stand and was executed by firing squad on the Cerro de Las Campanas (Hill of Bells), and where eventually the Mexican Constitution was signed in 1917.

The city's relatively small historic center is easily viewed by walking along its *andadores* (pedestrian walkways). When you want to venture farther afield, your best bet is the *tranvías turísticos* operated by the Tourism Department located at Pasteur 4 Norte in the historic center. There are three routes: Ruta A, Maximilian's Empire, tours the city with a stop at the Cerro de Las Campanas where Emperor Maximilian was shot; Ruta B, Foundation of the City, visits historic 18th-century buildings; and Ruta C affords panoramic city views. The trolleys run daily, departing roughly every hour from 10 to 7:30. The cost is $5–$7, depending on the route. Routes A and B have wheelchair access. Museums close on Monday.

In addition to the tourist info provided below, there is also a tourist information kiosk in the Plaza de la Constitución.

■ TIP→ Querétaro is renowned for its opals, which come in red, green, honey, and fire varieties. Because some street vendors sell opals so full of water that they crumble shortly after purchase, you should make purchases only from reputable dealers.

GETTING HERE AND AROUND

Continental Airlines flies to Querétaro International Airport from Houston. Primeral Plus has first-class bus service from Mexico City's International Airport direct to Querétaro. The trip takes three hours and costs $20. Omnibus de Mexico and Primera Plus have frequent service from the Central del Norte station for $14. ETN also has first-class service from San Miguel (one hour, $6). Omnibus has frequent service from Querétaro to Zacatecas (five hours, $28). It takes about three hours to get to Querétaro from Mexico City via Highway 57.

ESSENTIALS

Bus Contacts **ETN** (☎ *01800/800-0386 toll-free in Mexico* ⊕ *www.etn.com.mx*). **Omnibus de Mexico** ☎ *01800/765-6636 toll-free in Mexico* ⊕ *www.odm.com.mx*). **Primera Plus** (☎ *01800/375-7587 toll-free in Mexico* ⊕ *www.primeraplus.com.mx*).

Medical Assistance **Hospital Angeles de Querétaro** (✉ *Bernardino del Razo 21* ☎ *442/192-3000* ⊕ *www.hospitalangelesqueretaro.com*). **Hospital San José** (✉ *Prolongación Constituyentes 302* ☎ *442/211-0080* ⊕ *www.hospitalsanjose.com*).

Visitor and Tour Info **Secretaria de Turismo del Estado** (✉ *Luis Pasteur Norte 4* ☎ *442/238-5067* ⊕ *queretaro.travel/english*).

EXPLORING

TOP ATTRACTIONS

❶ **Jardín de la Corregidora.** This plaza is prominently marked by a statue of its namesake and War of Independence heroine—Josefa Ortiz de Domínguez. Behind the monument stands the Arbol de la Amistad (Tree

of Friendship). Planted in 1977 in a mixture of soils from around the world, the tree symbolizes Querétaro's hospitality to all travelers. This is the town's calmest square, with plenty of choices for patio dining. ✉ *Corregidora at Av. 16 de Septiembre.*

❸ **Museo de Arte de Querétaro.** Focusing on European and Mexican artworks, this baroque 18th-century Augustinian monastery-turned-museum exhibits paintings from the 17th through 19th centuries, as well as rotating exhibits of 20th-century art. Ask about the symbolism of the columns and the figures in conch shells atop each arch on the fascinating baroque patio. ✉ *Allende Sur 14* ☎ *442/212–2357 or 442/212–3523* 🌐 *www.queretaro-mexico.com.mx/museo-arte* 🎫 *About $3* 🕑 *Tues.–Sun. 10–6.*

❺ **Museo Regional de Querétaro.** This bright yellow 17th-century Franciscan monastery displays colonial and European artwork in addition to historic memorabilia. There are early copies of the Mexican Constitution and the table on which the Treaty of Guadalupe Hidalgo was signed. ✉ *Corregidora Sur 3* ☎ *442/212–4888 or 442/220–2031* 🌐 *www.queretaro-mexico.com.mx/coneculta/regional.html* 🎫 *About $3* 🕑 *Tues.–Sun. 10–7.*

❻ **Plaza de la Independencia.** Also known as Plaza de Armas, this immaculate square is bordered by carefully restored colonial mansions and is especially lovely at night, when the central fountain is lighted. Built in 1842, the fountain is dedicated to the Marqués de la Villa del Villar, who constructed Querétaro's elegant aqueduct. The old stone aqueduct, with its 74 towering arches, stands at the town's east end. ✉ *Bounded by Av. 5 de Mayo on the north, Av. Libertad Oriente on the south, Pasteur on the east, and Vergara Sur on the west.*

WORD OF MOUTH

"[We stayed in Queretaro] as part of a two-city visit to Mexico. We went to witness the celebration of their Independence Day. We drove in from [Guanajuato's] León airport and found the roads and signs to be very easy to navigate. Peel back the tatter and wear, and you will unveil a charming town with wonderfully warm and friendly people." —johnb

WORTH NOTING

7 **Casa de Ecala.** Long ago, as the story goes, the palace's 18th-century owner elaborately adorned his home in a remodeling war (which he won) with his neighbor. Behind the original facade of this Mexican baroque palace are the offices of DIF, a family-services organization. You can wander the courtyard when the offices are open. ✉ *Pasteur Sur 6, at Plaza de la Independencia* ⏲ *Weekdays 9–5.*

2 **Fuente de Neptuno.** Renowned Mexican architect and Bajío native Eduardo Tresguerras built this fountain in an orchard of the San Antonio monastery in 1797. According to one story, the monks sold some of their land and the fountain along with it when they were facing serious economic problems. It now stands next to the Templo de Santa Clara. ✉ *Allende at Av. Madero.*

4 **Palacio del Gobierno del Estado.** Dubbed La Casa de la Corregidora, this building now houses the municipal government offices, but in 1810 it was home to Querétaro's mayor-magistrate (El Corregidor) and his wife, Josefa Ortíz de Domínguez (La Corregidora). La Corregidora's literary salon was actually a cover for conspirators—including Ignacio Allende and Father Miguel Hidalgo—to plot a course for independence. When he discovered the salon's true nature, El Corregidor imprisoned his wife in her room, but not before she alerted Allende and Hidalgo. Soon after, on September 15, Father Hidalgo tolled the bell of his church to signal the onset of the fight for freedom. A replica of the bell caps this building. ✉ *Northwest corner of Plaza de la Independencia* ☎ *No phone* 🎫 *Free* ⏲ *Weekdays 9–8, Sat. 8–3.*

8 **Templo de Santa Rosa de Viterbo.** This ex-convent constructed from 1727 to 1752 and attributed to the Queretano Don Ignacio Mariano de las Casas, is noteworthy for its whimsical arches and the Arab influence of its facade. Inside, the church is one of the joys of the Mexican baroque, famous for its five fantastically carved, gold-leaf altarpieces, as well as its rich paintings and statues. ✉ *Corner of Av. General Arteaga and Ezequiel Montes* ☎ *No phone* 🎫 *Free* ⏲ *Daily 10–6.*

WHERE TO EAT

¢ MEXICAN ✕**Cenaduría Blas.** Nothing fancy here, just some of the best traditional Mexican fare in the city since 1940—tacos, enchiladas, gorditas, pozole, guajalotes (sandwiches made from a hero roll and bathed in mild red sauce), homemade desserts, and wonderful agua de lima (purified water mixed with the juice of a tropical citrus fruit with a flavor all its own). Find a table among the Mexican families in the simply furnished, cavernous space and enjoy! Open for dinner and late into the night for those sampling the clubs and bars on Cinco de Mayo. ✉ *Cinco de Mayo 125* ☎ *442/212–3126* ▭ *No credit cards.*

$$ MEXICAN ✕**El Mesón de Chucho el Roto.** This restaurant, named after Querétaro's version of Robin Hood, is on the quiet Plaza de Armas. It's strong on regional dishes like goat-filled tacos and shrimp with nopal (cactus) and corundas, a kind of tamale from the neighboring state of Michoacán. The restaurant nearby at Andador Libertad #62, 1810, offers much the same fare. ✉ *Calle Pasteur 16, Plaza de Armas* ☎ *442/212–4295* ▭ *AE, MC, V.*

$ MEXICAN ✕**Fin de Siglo.** Across the street from the Teatro de la República, this sunny, colorful restaurant offers traditional Mexican cuisine such as arrachera, enchiladas queretanas (with cheese, potatoes, and cream), and pechuga fin de siglo (chicken breast filled with zucchini blossoms and cheese and topped with a zucchini-blossom sauce), all served with homemade corn tortillas hot off the comal. On weekends there's an extensive buffet luncheon. ✉ *Hidalgo 1* ☎ *442/224–2548* ▭ *AE, MC, V.*

¢ MEXICAN ✕**La Mariposa.** A wrought-iron *mariposa* (butterfly) overlooks the entrance of this cafeteria-like local favorite. Despite its plain appearance, it's the spot for breakfast, coffee and cake, or a light Mexican lunch of tacos, tamales, enchiladas, or *tortas* (sandwiches). ✉ *Angela Peralta 7, half a block from Teatro de República* ☎ *442/212–1166* ▭ *No credit cards.*

$$ MEXICAN ✕**Los Laureles.** The flower-filled grand patio in this perfectly restored hacienda just outside the city offers great outdoor dining (shaded by umbrellas). The house specialty is *carnitas,* pieces of pork stewed overnight and served with oodles of guacamole, beans, and homemade tortillas. There's live music *and* mariachis on weekends. Note that this restaurant's hours might be a little awkward for some; while technically they are open for lunch and dinner, the hours are 1 PM to 6 PM. ✉ *Carretera Querétaro–San Luis Potosí, Km 8* ☎ *442/218–1118* ▭ *AE, MC, V.*

$$$ STEAKHOUSE ✕**Restaurante Josecho.** Among the hunting trophies adorning the wood-paneled walls of this highway road stop—known as one of the best restaurants in the city—are peacocks, elk, bears, and lions. Sports fans stop here for the animated environment as well as the house specialties, which include *filete Chemita* (steak sautéed in butter with onions). Save room for the creamy coconut ice cream. A classical guitarist or pianist performs most evenings. Waiters celebrate birthdays by singing and blasting a red siren. ✉ *Dalia 1, next to Plaza de Toros Santa María* ☎ *442/216–0201* ▭ *AE, MC, V.*

WHERE TO STAY

$$$ Fodor's Choice ★ **Casa de la Marquesa.** A private home in the 18th century, it's now a handsome hotel in Querétaro's center. Each guest room is large, and has antiques, tasteful art, parquet floors, and area rugs. The main building's rooms are more elegant and expensive than those in the adjacent La Casa Azul. The restaurants serve both international and Mexican cuisine. **Pros:** uniquely decorated rooms and interesting Moorish architecture. **Cons:** not ideal for traveling families; so-so service. *✉ Madero 41 ☎ 442/212–0092 ⊕ www.lacasadelamarquesa.com 25 suites In-room: Wi-Fi. In-hotel: restaurant, room service, bar, laundry service, Wi-Fi hotspot, parking (paid) AE, MC, V.*

$$$ ★ **Gran Hotel.** On lively Plaza de la Constitución, this hotel, the largest in the historic center, brings a touch of modernity to colonial Mexico, with wide marble hallways decorated in pastel colors and hung with contemporary art. Rooms are good-sized and beautifully furnished, exuding comfort and, thanks to double-paned windows, tranquillity as well. **Pros:** central location, tranquil atmosphere. **Cons:** no restaurant or bar, though there are plenty nearby. *✉ Juárez Sur 5 ☎ 442/251–8050, 01800/702–4737 toll-free in Mexico ⊕ www.granhoteldequeretaro.com.mx 42 suites In-room: safe, kitchen (some), refrigerator, DVD, Wi-Fi. In-hotel: laundry service, Wi-Fi hotspot, parking (paid) AE, D, DC, MC, V BP.*

$$$ **Hacienda Jurica.** Families from Mexico City escape to this sprawling 16th-century ex-hacienda, part of the Brisas chain, which has topiary gardens, a horse stable, golf access, and nearly 30 acres of grassy sports fields. Antique horse-drawn carriages dot the grounds and courtyards, and the spacious earth-tone rooms have dark-wood furniture. Jurica is an upscale residential neighborhood 13 km (8 mi) northwest of the city off Highway 57. It's a good alternative to staying in the city. **Pros:** no shortage of activities; romantic restaurant. **Cons:** need a car to stay here. *✉ Paseo Jurica at Paseo del Mesón ☎ 442/218–0022, 01880/401–1100 toll-free in Mexico ⊕ www.brisas.com.mx 176 rooms, 6 suites In-room: safe, refrigerator (some), DVD, Wi-Fi. In-hotel: restaurant, room service, bar, tennis courts, pool, children's programs, laundry service, Wi-Fi hotspot, parking (free) AE, MC, V.*

¢ **Hotel Hidalgo.** This hotel is one of the best values in the city. It's in a former colonial residence—once host to Santa Ana—just a few doors down from Casa de la Marquesa. The rooms are totally simple, but they surround a lovely little courtyard. Restaurant La Llave is small and cute, serving simple Mexican food. **Pros:** interesting and long history; low prices. **Cons:** drab style. *✉ Madero 11 ☎ 442/212–0081 or 442/212–8102 ⊕ www.hotelhidalgo.com.mx 47 rooms In-room: no*

THE BARD

For a change of pace, go to the **Corral de Comedias** (*✉ Venustiano Carranza 39 ☎ 442/212–0165*), a family-run theater-in-the-round that presents mostly comedies, including Shakespeare in Spanish. It certainly helps if you speak the language, but you still get some laughs even if you don't. Purchase your tickets at the entrance.

a/c, Wi-Fi. In-hotel: restaurant, room service, bar, Wi-Fi hotspot, parking (paid) ▭ *AE, MC, V.*

$$ **Mesón Santa Rosa Hotel.** On the serene Plaza de la Independencia, this elegant property was a stopover for travelers to the north almost 300 years ago. Rooms are clustered around a placid courtyard. Lace-hung glass doors and wood-beam ceilings preserve the colonial charm in the rooms, but some modern additions like a chrome-color coffee shop at the entrance detract from the character. **Pros:** overall charm of hotel; views from rooms. **Cons:** quite old, and could use some renovations. ✉ *Pasteur Sur 17* ☎ *442/224–2623 or 442/227–0600* ⊕ *www.mesonsantarosa.com* *5 rooms, 16 suites* *In-room: safe, refrigerator, Wi-Fi. In-hotel: restaurant, room service, bar, pool, gym, laundry service, Wi-Fi hotspot, parking (paid)* ▭ *AE, MC, V* *BP.*

4

NIGHTLIFE

Every Sunday evening at 6 there's a band concert in the **Jardín Zenea**, Querétaro's main square at the corner of Corregidora and Juárez. At the tourist office you can pick up a monthly publication called *Asomarte* (in Spanish), which provides current information about festivals, concerts, and other events.

The coolest dance club, **La Viejoteca** (✉ *Andador 5 de Mayo 39* ☎ *442/224–2760*), is in the 18th-century Casa de los Cinco Patios.

Querétaro has a happening bar scene, much of it located on **Avenida Cinco de Mayo**, north of the Jardín de la Corrigadora. Stroll up the street and find your own favorite, but here are a few to get you started: Alquimia Bar (✉ *Cinco de Mayo 71* ☎ *no phone*), Nacht Bar (✉ *Cinco de Mayo 46* ☎ *442/212–9908*), Wicklow Irish Pub (✉ *Cinco de Mayo 86* ☎ *442/212–0947*).

SIDE TRIPS FROM QUERÉTARO

TEQUISQUIAPAN

58 km (36 mi) southeast of Querétaro via Hwy. 57, then Rte. 120.

Drenched in sun, bougainvillea, and flowering trees, Tequis (as the locals call it) is a pleasant stop for a day trip. Join the families from Querétaro and Mexico City who come to stroll through the main square, with its neoclassical Templo de Santa María de la Asunción, whose facade has been said to resemble swirls of cotton more than stone. Stop for lunch in one of the outdoor cafés under the arcades that front the plaza and visit the surrounding streets and the Mercado de Artesanías to shop for handicrafts. Tequisquiapan means "water of tequesquite," or salty minerals, and the town is still known for its pools and spas; most are located north of town. Check with the tourist office on the main square for directions. Tequis hosts a wine-and-cheese festival in late May and early June.

EXPLORING

Tequis has a well-deserved reputation for high-quality craftwork, from wicker baskets to opals; head to the **Mercado de Artesanías** (✉ *Calle Ezequiel Montes and Salvador Michaus* ☎ *No phone*) for woven goods, wood, ceramics, and jewelry.

HAPPY HOUR

If you have time, visit the nearby **Cavas Freixenet**, for a free guided tour of the cellars, offered daily. Afterward you can sit in the plant-filled patio and sample some of the wares. ✉ *Carretera San Juan del Río–Cadereyta, Km 40.5* ☎ *441/277–0147* 🌐 *www.freixenetmexico.com.mx.*

BERNAL

59 km (37 mi) northeast of Querétaro via Hwy. 57; turn off toward Peña de Bernal.

XILITLA

Approximately 320 km (198 mi) northeast of Querétaro.

Feel the ordinary world fade away with a trip to the decidedly off-the-beaten-path **Las Pozas** *(The Pools)*, the extraordinary sculpture garden of the late, eccentric English millionaire Edward James (1907–84). A friend to artists Dalí and Picasso and rumored to be King Edward VII's illegitimate son, James spent 20 years building 36 Surrealist concrete structures deep in the waterfall-filled Xilitla jungle. These astonishing structures are half-finished fantasy castles, gradually falling to ruin as the rain forest slithers in to claim them. The castles don't have walls, just vine-wrapped pillars, secret passageways, and operatic staircases leading nowhere.

It's a six- to seven-hour thrilling but exhausting mountainous drive to Xilitla, with hairpin turns and spectacular desert, forest, and jungle vistas. On the way to Xilitla it's well worth taking the time to stop at the five Sierra Gorda missions established by Padre Junípero Serra in the 18th century. They're a mixture of baroque styles and the local imagination of the Indians who worked on them, with angels, saints, and flora and fauna in great profusion. ■ **TIP→ Plan on staying at least two nights, as you'll want time to soak up the jungle magic.** If you choose not to drive, you can take a bus to Ciudad Valles (a 1½-hour drive from Xilitla) or fly to Tampico (a 3½-hour drive from Xilitla), and arrange ahead for the staff of Posada El Castillo to pick you up. ✉ *From Querétaro head north on Hwy. 57 toward Mexico City. Take the* PEÑA DE BERNAL *turnoff, marked on a bridge overpass and also on a smaller sign at the Cadareyta exit. Continue north through Bernal, after which the road joins Rte. 120. Take 120 through Jalpan and then on to Xilitla, just across the border in the state of San Luis Potosí. The turnoff to Las Pozas is just beyond Xilitla on the left after passing a small bridge* 🎫 *$1.50* ⏲ *Daily dawn–dusk.*

WHERE TO STAY

$–$$ **Posada El Castillo.** When he wasn't living in his jungle hut, Edward James stayed in town (a 10-minute drive away) in a whimsical house that feels like an extension of the garden structures at Las Pozas—except that it has walls. The house, El Castillo (the Castle), is now a quirky inn run by Lenore and Avery Danziger, who produced an outstanding documentary film about James that they screen for guests. Rooms are adorned with simple wooden furnishings; the best rooms have huge Gothic windows and panoramic mountain views. You can arrange to have meals here; otherwise, there are few dining options in the area. **Pros:** the story behind the place; proximity to Indian villages and outdoor activities. **Cons:** a little difficult to get to; requires some degree of roughing it. ✉ *Ocampo 105, Xilitla, San Luis Potosí* ☎ *489/365–0038* 🌐 *www.junglegossip.com/castillo.html* *8 rooms* *In-hotel: pool* *No credit cards.*

GUANAJUATO

100 km (62 mi) west of San Miguel de Allende, 365 km (227 mi) northwest of Mexico City.

Guanajuato is simply gorgeous. It spills across cliffs and hillsides down to a series of tree-shaded plazas whose sidewalk cafés and street life are unmatched in any comparably sized town in Mexico. The city's street plan is nearly inscrutable—roads never seem to end up where you'd expect, and are intersected by dozens of alleys—but getting lost for a few hours will be an adventure rather than a nuisance. You'll see gringos here than in San Miguel; the majority of tourists are Mexican.

Once the most prominent silver-mining city in colonial Mexico, Guanajuato is in a gorge surrounded by mountains at 6,700 feet. Its cobblestone streets, which are peppered with colorful houses, wind precipitously up the mountainside. The city's other distinguishing feature is a vast subterranean roadway, where a rushing river once coursed through the city.

The city was settled by wealthy land- and mine-owners, and many of its colonial buildings date back to the 18th century. Those buildings around the center of town have become museums, restaurants, hotels, and government offices. Add to this its many imposing churches, plus the green-limestone University of Guanajuato, and it's no wonder the town was named a World Heritage Site in 1988.

One thing you don't need in Guanajuato is a car. Guanajuato's streets are often clogged with traffic, and you can find yourself stuck in an exhaust-filled tunnel for up to an hour waiting for traffic to clear. It's easy and much more practical to stroll along the two main arteries, Avenida Juárez and Positos, from which you can access the main sights.

Start your exploration of Guanajuato with a ride on the funicular (behind the Teatro Juárez) up to the statue of El Pípila to get a great view of this colorful town. If you study your map, you'll be able to identify most of the important buildings, like the university, the cathedral, and the Mercado Hidalgo. This perspective may come in handy later, when the curving streets spin you around.

A walk around the center of town will take a couple of hours. Remember that most museums and the theater are closed Monday.

GETTING HERE AND AROUND

León's Guanajuato International Airport (BJX) is roughly 30 to 45 minutes west of downtown Guanajuato and a 1½-hour drive from San Miguel. It's a small airport, so the check-in desks can have long lines. Taxis to downtown Guanjuato cost about $30. If you're considering going by bus, Primera Plus and ETN have first-class service from Mexico City's Central del Norte to Guanajuato's Central Camionera (five hours, $28–$30). There is also service from San Miguel (1½ hours, $8–$12) and from San Miguel to León (2½ hours, $12).

ESSENTIALS

Bus Contacts **ETN** (☎ *01800/800-0386 toll-free in Mexico* 🌐 *www.etn.com.mx*). **Primera Plus** (☎ *01800/375-7587 toll-free in Mexico* 🌐 *www.primeraplus.com.mx*).

Medical Assistance **Ambulance–Red Cross** (☎ *473/732-0487*). **Hospital General** (☎ *473/733-1573*). **Police** (☎ *473/732-0266*).

Visitor Info **Guanajuato tourist office** (⊠ *Plaza de la Paz 16, ElCentro* ☎ *473/732-1574, 01800/848-3486 toll-free in Mexico*).

EXPLORING

TOP ATTRACTIONS

7 **Alhóndiga de Granaditas.** Previously this 18th-century grain-storage facility served as a jail under Emperor Maximilian and as a fortress during the War of Independence, where El Pípila helped the revolutionaries overcome the royalists. The hooks on which the Spanish Royalists hung the severed heads of Father Hidalgo, Ignacio Allende, and two other independence leaders still dangle on the exterior of this massive stone structure. It's now a state museum with exhibits on local history, archaeology, and crafts. ⊠ *Mendizábal 6, El Centro* ☎ *473/732–1112 or 473/732–1180* 🎫 *$4* ⏲ *Tues.–Sat. 10–6, Sun. 10–3.*

4 **Basílica Colegiata de Nuestra Señora de Guanajuato.** Painted in a striking yellow, the Basílica is an 18th-century baroque church that dominates Plaza de la Paz. Inside is Mexico's oldest Christian statue: a bejeweled 8th-century Virgin. The venerated figure was a gift from King Philip II of Spain in 1557. On the Friday preceding Good Friday, miners, accompanied by floats and mariachi bands, parade to the Basílica to pay homage to the Lady of Guanajuato. ⊠ *Plaza de la Paz, Centro* ☎ *473/732–0314* 🎫 *Free* ⏲ *Weekdays 9–1 and 4–7, Sat. 9–1.*

11 **El Pípila.** A half-hour climb or short funicular ride from downtown is this statue of Juan José de los Reyes Martínez, a young miner and hero of the War of Independence of 1810. Nicknamed El Pípila, de los Reyes crept into the Alhóndiga de Granaditas, where Spanish Royalists were hiding, and set the door ablaze. This enabled Father Hidalgo's army to capture the Spanish troops in this first major military victory for the independence forces. The monument has spectacular city views. Funiculars run daily from 10 to 8 from behind the Juárez Theater and cost about $2 round-trip. ⊠ *Carretera Panorámica, on bluff above south side of Jardín de la Unión, El Centro.*

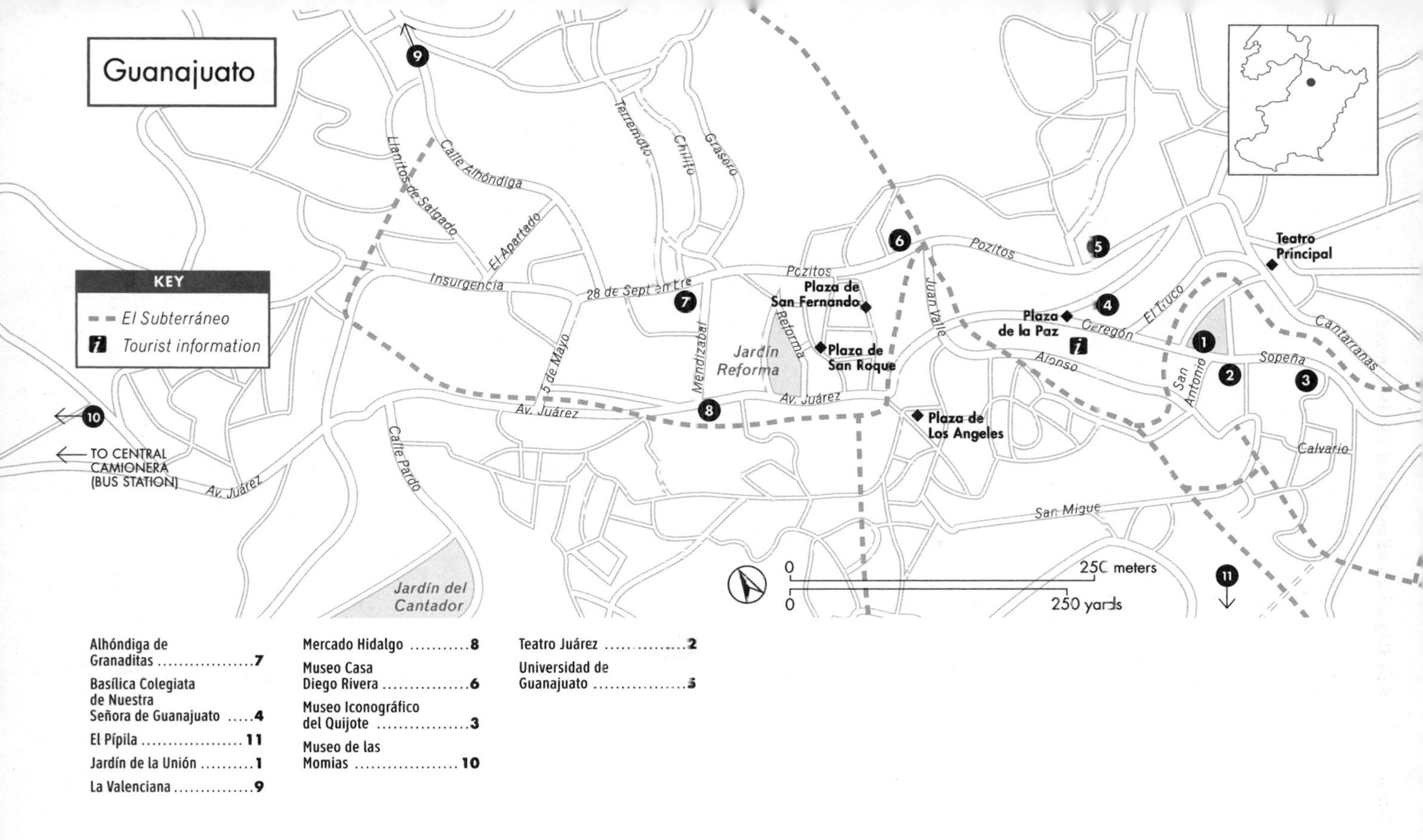

Guanajuato
KEY
El Subterráneo
Tourist information
Teatro Principal
Cantarranas
Sopeña
Calvario
San Antonio
El Truco
Oregón
Plaza de la Paz
Alonso
Pozitos
Juan Valle
Plaza de Los Angeles
Plaza de San Fernando
Plaza de San Roque
Reforma
Jardín Reforma
Av. Juárez
Mendizabal
28 de Sept en tre
Grasero
Chilito
Terremoto
5 de Mayo
El Apartado
Calle Alhóndiga
Insurgencia
Llanitos de Salgado
Calle Pardo
Jardín del Cantador
San Migue
TO CENTRAL CAMIONERA (BUS STATION)
250 meters
250 yards
0
Alhóndiga de Granaditas 7
Basílica Colegiata de Nuestra Señora de Guanajuato 4
El Pípila 11
Jardín de la Unión 1
La Valenciana 9
Mercado Hidalgo 8
Museo Casa Diego Rivera 6
Museo Iconográfico del Quijote 3
Museo de las Momias 10
Teatro Juárez 2
Universidad de Guanajuato 5

1 **Jardín de la Unión.** Guanajuato's central square is a tree-lined, wedge-shaped plaza bordered by pedestrian walkways. There are musical performances in the plaza's band shell on Tuesday evening and Sunday afternoon; at other times, groups of musicians break into impromptu song along the shaded tile walkways. Strolling mariachis will perform, too—for a price.

GO WITH A GUIDE

These tour operators give half- and full-day tours in English that typically include the Museo de las Momias, the church and mines of La Valenciana, the monument to El Pípila, the Panoramic Highway, subterranean streets, and residential neighborhoods. Night tours often begin at El Pípila and end at a dance club.

Transporte Exclusivo de Turismo (✉ *Av. Juárez at Calle 5 de Mayo, Centro* ☎ *473/732–5968*). **Transportes Turísticos de Guanajuato** (✉ *Plaza de la Paz 2, by Basílica de Guanajuato, Centro* ☎ *473/732–2134 or 473/732–2838*).

9 ★ **La Valenciana.** Officially called La Iglesia de San Cayetano and a 15-minute trek from the city center, this is one of the best-known colonial churches in Mexico. The mid- to late-18th-century pink-stone facade is brilliantly ornate. Inside are three altars, each hand carved in wood and brightly gilded, in different styles: plateresque, churrigueresque, and baroque. There are also religious paintings from the viceregal period. ■ **TIP→ Both the mine and church are included in any of Guanajuato's guided tours, and buses (marked** LA VALENCIANA**) frequently make the trip from the city center.** ✉ *Carretera Guanajuato–Dolores Hidalgo, Km 5* ☎ *No phone* 🎫 *San Cayetano mine tour about $2.50* ⏲ *Daily 9–6.*

6 ★ **Museo Casa Diego Rivera.** The birthplace of Diego Rivera contains family portraits, furniture, and works by Mexico's foremost muralist; among them are his studies for the controversial mural commissioned for New York City's Rockefeller Center. Completed in 1933, the mural's portrait of Lenin and overall Communist bent prompted Rivera's benefactors to destroy it immediately after it was displayed. The museum's upper galleries show revolving contemporary art exhibitions, often from other countries. ✉ *Calle Pozitos 47, El Centro* ☎ *473/732–1197* 🎫 *$1* ⏲ *Tues.–Sat. 10–7, Sun. 10–3.*

10 ★ **Museo de las Momias.** Mummified human corpses—once buried in the municipal cemetery off Calzada del Panteón—are on display in this unique, though run-down, museum at the town's west end; it was renovated in 1972. Until the law was amended in 1858, corpses were removed to make room for arrivals if the grave site hadn't been paid for after five years. Because of the mineral properties of the local soil, these cadavers (the oldest is almost 150 years old) were in astonishingly good condition upon exhumation. You'll need to catch a cab to get here; it's atop a steep hill. ✉ *Panteón Municipal, El Centro* ☎ *473/732–0639* 🎫 *$4* ⏲ *Daily 9–6.*

2 **Teatro Juárez.** Adorned with bronze lion sculptures and a line of large Greek muses overlooking the Jardín de la Unión from the roof, the theater was inaugurated by Mexican dictator Porfirio Díaz in 1903 with a

performance of *Aïda*. It now serves as a principal venue of the annual International Cervantes Festival. You can take a brief tour of the art deco interior. ✉ *Sopeña s/n, Centro* ☎ *473/732–0183* 🎫 *$3* ⏲ *Tues.–Sun. 9–1:45 and 5–7:45.*

MINE EXPLORATIONS

A Valenciana mine near the church has one entrance at **Bocamina de San Ramón** (✉ *Callejón de San Ramón 10*), whose $2.50 tour you might call entry-level—you just head down 66 feet, look around, and pop back up.

WORTH NOTING

NEED A BREAK?

Go to the Hotel Museo Posada Santa Fé (✉ *Jardín de la Unión 12, El Centro* ☎ *473/732-0084*) for alfresco dining at the Jardín. Try the *pozole estilo Guanajuato* (hominy soup to which you can add onions, radishes, lettuce, lime, and chili peppers).

8 **Mercado Hidalgo.** Don't miss this 1910 cast-iron-and-glass structure, designed by the one-and-only Gustave Eiffel. ■ **TIP➔ T-shirts and cheap plastic toys fill the balcony stalls, but the lower level is full of authentic local wares and colorful basketry, as well as fresh produce, peanuts, and honey-drenched nut candies shaped like mummies.** ✉ *Calle Juárez near Mendizabal, Centro* ⏲ *Daily 7 AM–9 PM.*

3 **Museo Iconográfico del Quijote.** During his imprisonment in a Spanish concentration camp in the 1930s, Spanish writer and journalist Eulalio Ferrer was so uplifted by Miguel de Cervantes's classic novel that he developed a lifelong passion for *Don Quixote*. This restored 19th-century home is a museum displaying Ferrer's collection of more than 600 pieces of art, all dedicated to the man of La Mancha. Gathered after he fled Fascist Spain for Mexico, the star-studded collection includes works by Salvador Dalí, Pablo Picasso, Jose Luis Cuevas, and Alfredo Zalce. ✉ *Manuel Doblado 1, Centro* ☎ *473/732–6721 or 473/732–3376* 🌐 *www.guanajuato.gob.mx/museo* 🎫 *$2* ⏲ *Tues.–Sat. 9:30–6:45, Sun. 9:30–2:30.*

5 **Universidad de Guanajuato.** Founded in 1732, the university was formerly a Jesuit seminary. The original churrigueresque church, **La Compañía,** still stands next door. The facade of the university, built in 1955, was designed to blend in with the town's architecture. ■ **TIP➔ If you do wander inside, check the bulletin boards for the town's cultural events.** ✉ *Lascurain de Retana 5, ½ block north of Plaza de la Paz, El Centro* ☎ *473/732–0006* 🌐 *www.ugto.mx* ⏲ *Weekdays 8–3:30.*

WHERE TO EAT

$$ MEXICAN

✕ **Casa del Conde de la Valenciana.** Across from La Valenciana is this refurbished 18th-century home whose colonial aura enhances the touristy but serviceable restaurant. Among the highlights are the *crema de aguacate con tequila* (cream of avocado with tequila) served in a bowl made of ice, tender *lomo en salsa de ciruela pasa* (pork shoulder in prune sauce), and *pollo a la flor de calabaza* (chicken with poblano chili slices and squash-blossom sauce). Round out the meal with mango ice cream served in the rind. ✉ *Carretera Guanajuato–Dolores Hidalgo,*

Km 5, La Valenciana ☎ *473/732–2550* ▭ *AE, MC, V* ⏲ *Closed Sun. No dinner.*

$ MEXICAN Fodor's Choice ★ ✕ **El Abue.** Don't let Guanajuato's twisted streets deter you from finding this little gem near the university. It's serves what is arguably the best traditional Mexican food of any restaurant in the town. The interior has a romantic, warmly lit, European vibe. Start with the margaritas, and move on to Caesar salad, one of the house specialties. The delicious chiles en nogada, topped with crunchy pomegranate seeds and filled with savory pork, are one of the best versions in Guanajuato. Even better are the enchiladas El Abue, stuffed with dried fruits and covered with Oaxacan red mole. The homemade breads and pastas are also a standout. Breakfast is on offer daily for $4.50. ✉ *Calle San José 14* ☎ *473/732–6242* ▭ *AE, MC, V.*

¢ MEXICAN ✕ **El Claustro.** El Claustro manages to strike a delicate balance: situated in a lively plaza, it captures the energy of the city while not feeling like a tourist trap. Walk into the semi-subterranean space and you'll see women making fresh tortillas—always a good sign—and the buzz of locals enjoying simple, authentic Mexican food. The specialty here is enchiladas, and the *enchiladas rojas* are particularly good. Also worth a try is the *pollo a la veracruzana* (chicken stewed with tomatoes and onions). There are three tree-shaded tables out on the plaza. ✉ *Jardín de la Reforma 13-B* ☎ *473/732–9781* ▭ *No credit cards.*

$ ITALIAN ✕ **El Gallo Pitagórico.** Huff and puff your way up the 40-plus steps to this restaurant's threshold for an exceptional view of downtown Guanajuato, as well as for the mouthwatering house specialty, *filetto Claudio* (beef fillet with olives, capers, herbs, and garlic). Save room for the velvety tiramisu. Weather permitting, have your aperitif on the terrace, which has an even more dazzling view, best as sunset tints Guanajuato's domes several different shades of gold. ✉ *Constancia 10, behind Teatro Juárez, El Centro* ☎ *473/732–9489* ▭ *MC, V.*

$ MEXICAN ✕ **El Tapatío.** One of the best-kept secrets in Guanajuato is this hole-in-the-wall across from the university whose bargain *comida corrida* at lunchtime—four courses for 50 pesos—is equally popular with students, faculty, and local workers. It starts with delicious fresh-baked bread, then continues with a starter such as *crema de verduras* (vegetable soup) with green chili, or a chipotle-spiked chicken soup. Tacos and an *antojito* (appetizer) then a meat will follow, plus dessert. The space is cute, with brick archways, knickknacks, and waiters dressed in black and white who are more friendly than attentive. ✉ *Lascuráin de Retana 20* ☎ *473/732–3291* ▭ *MC, V* ⏲ *No dinner Sun.*

$$ ITALIAN ✕ **Frascati.** This bold restaurant overlooking the city's principal plaza takes Italian cooking in Mexico to a new level in an environment that showcases both a city view and a romantic, well-lit interior. Even better are the authentic Italian dishes, from carpaccio to pastas (especially a meaty Bolognese) to thin-crust pizzas to a tender, slow-braised osso buco. Fried appetizers are delicately prepared, and the shrimp are especially delicious. The wine list is surprisingly good for Guanajuato. ✉ *Jardín de la Unión 1* ☎ *473/732–2158* ▭ *AE, MC, V.*

$ ECLECTIC ✕ **La Capellina.** This fresh fusion restaurant, in a 1673 building, is at once minimalist, eclectic, international, French-influenced, and tasty. Each dish is marked on the menu with its own nationality. A recipe for disaster? Not in the case of the shrimp *michelada*, which are beer-marinated with lemon, onion, jicama, carrots, cucumber, and serrano chili; or the *arrachera fusión,* a variation on the classic Mexican marinated steak that includes avocado, goat cheese, and a chipotle–red wine salsa. The menu includes a large selection of creative pizzas. Not everything's perfect—*guajillo* (a type of chili) salmon, for one. The wine list is fantastic, and there is live music Friday and Saturday nights. ✉ *Calle Sopeña 3* ☎ *473/732–7224* 🌐 *www.lacapellina.com* 💳 *D, DC, MC, V.*

$$ MEXICAN ★ **Las Mercedes.** Located a 10-minute cab ride above the city, this family-run restaurant with only six tables is in a private home with a panoramic view; for the full effect, be sure to reserve a table near the front. The food is "Mexican artisanal," updates of family recipes going back to the chef's grandmother (and the restaurant's namesake). The small, seasonal menu emphasizes meat and fish, including *salmón negro* served with a tangy black *mole*, and *pollo mole verde de pistacho* (chicken breast in a delicate green sauce). For dessert, don't miss the *pan de elote*, a warm corn cake topped with homemade caramel ice cream. ✉ *Calle de Arriba 6, San Javier* ☎ *473/732–7375* 💳 *MC, V* ⊗ *Closed Mon.*

$ MEXICAN ★ **México Lindo y Sabroso.** As you sit at umbrella-shaded tables in a gracious courtyard framed by bougainvillea, serenaded by Mexican music, you'll be transported back to a simpler Mexico. The margaritas are good and the menu is interesting, from a well-developed *pozole verde* (a rich soup made with hominy) to juicy *cochinita pibíl* (pork baked in banana leaf) with black beans and the traditional pickled onions. The *enchiladas México Lindo* and *enchiladas mineras* are also crowd-pleasers. The restaurant is out in the quiet residential neighborhood of Presa, above the city center, but it's worth the trip. ✉ *Paseo de la Presa 154, Presa* ☎ *473/731–0529* 💳 *MC, V.*

$ MEXICAN **Truco 7.** Totally local yet beloved by visitors, this place is the real deal, morning, noon, and night. Multigenerational Mexican families dine among a spattering of granola-crunchy tourists, all comfortably ensconced within the warm colors of the walls, wood, and endless bric-a-brac. At breakfast, egg dishes reign supreme and *enfrijoladas* (corn tortillas layered with refried beans, cheese, and sour cream) are an excellent choice. It's also hard to go wrong with the traditional lunch plates, which include lots of enchiladas and chicken dishes. It's open later than most spots in town. ✉ *Truco 7* ☎ *473/732–8374* 💳 *No credit cards.*

WHERE TO STAY

$$ **Casa del Agua.** The theme here is clearly maritime, with a light-blue color scheme, glass-covered blue tiles, and a bar called Azul. Rooms, however, are decidedly more terrestrial. Somewhat bland, with beige as the dominant color, they're not as exciting as the rest of the hotel. The views are great, though; rooms facing outward have balconies, some with stunning views, and all have a Jacuzzi. Its location just behind Jardín de la Unión puts you right within access of the square's vibrancy, but without the all the noise. **Pros:** hot tubs in room; fun bar at hotel. **Cons:** feels somewhat tired; management not always present. ✉ *Plaza de la Compañía 4, El Centro* ☎ *473/731–2257 or 473/734–1974* 🌐 *www.*

hotelcasadelagua.com.mx ⇨ *15 suites* ☝ *In-room: no a/c, safe, refrigerator (some), Wi-Fi. In-hotel: restaurant, room service, bar, laundry service, Wi-Fi hotspot, parking (paid)* ▭ *D, DC, MC, V.*

$$$ ★ **Casa Estrella de la Valenciana**. With a panoramic view near the church of La Valenciana, this American-owned house is an upmarket bed-and-breakfast—and one of the most expensive hotels in the city. Some rooms have their own Jacuzzis, and all have a terrace with a stunning view. The only downside is its distance from the city, but on the other hand it's nice to get away from the hustle and bustle. **Pros:** beautiful views; tranquillity; great breakfast. **Cons:** distance from city, which requires a 10-minute cab ride. ✉ *Callejón Jalisco 10, La Valenciana* ☎ *473/732–1784 or 866/983–8844* ⊕ *www.mexicaninns.com* ⇨ *4 rooms, 2 suites, 1 casita* ☝ *In-room: no a/c, no phone, safe, kitchen (some), DVD, Wi-Fi. In-hotel: room service, bar, pool, laundry service, Wi-Fi hotspot, parking (free), some pets allowed* ▭ *AE, MC, V* ⦿ *BP.*

$$ **Hostería del Frayle**. Formerly the Casa de Moneda, where ore was taken to be refined after leaving the mines, this quiet four-story lodging was built in 1673 and turned into a hotel in the mid-1960s. It has whitewashed plaster and wood-beam rooms arranged around a small maze of stairways, landings, and courtyards. Some rooms have excellent views of the Pípila, Teatro Juárez, and Jardín de la Unión, which is a half-block away. Make sure to dine in the adjacent restaurant, La Capellina. **Pros:** in the heart of the city; great restaurant next door. **Cons:** lots of noise late at night; drab rooms. ✉ *Calle Sopeña 3, El Centro* ☎ *473/732–1179* ⊕ *www.hosteriadelfrayle.com* ⇨ *37 rooms, 1 suite* ☝ *In-room: no a/c, safe. In-hotel: parking (free)* ▭ *AE, MC, V* ⦿ *BP.*

$$ **Hotel Luna**. Right on the Jardín de la Unión, this hotel is a great bet—as long as you get an exterior-facing room. Those on the interior feel small, dark, and dingy, but the ones facing out are full of life, especially when the light hits their shiny chandeliers. The whole hotel has a quirky, ironic quality to it, mixing faux-sleazy dim red lights with old colonial grandeur. The lively bar turns into more of a straight-up cantina late at night. **Pros:** cheeky style; supreme people-watching. **Cons:** some rooms are a bit dark; not a place for those who like to retire early. ✉ *Plaza Principal at Jardín de la Unión 8, El Centro* ☎ *473/732–9720* ⊕ *www.hotelluna.com.mx* ⇨ *19 rooms, 2 suites* ☝ *In-room: no a/c, Wi-Fi. In-hotel: restaurant, bar, laundry service, Wi-Fi hotspot* ▭ *D, DC, MC, V* ⦿ *BP.*

$$ **Hotel Museo Posada Santa Fé**. This colonial-style inn at the Jardín de la Unión—the best location in town—has been in operation since 1862. Large historical paintings by local artist Don Manuel Leal hang in the wood-paneled lobby. Rooms are a bit drab, with barely adequate bathrooms. Rooms facing the plaza can be noisy, but have the best views; quieter rooms face narrow alleyways, and sometimes look onto Guanajuato's twisting roads. The hotel's restaurant is great for late-night snacks. **Pros:** great location, and not too noisy if you get the right room. **Cons:** some rooms face hallways and have privacy issues; bathrooms are small and lacking in amenities. ✉ *Plaza Principal at Jardín de la Unión 12, El Centro* ☎ *473/732–0084* ⇨ *36 rooms, 8 suites* ☝ *In-*

room: no a/c, Wi-Fi. In-hotel: restaurant, room service, bar, laundry service, Wi-Fi hotspot, parking (free) ▭ *AE, MC, V* 🍽 *BP.*

$$$ Fodor's Choice ★ **Hotel Refugio Casa Colorada.** The spectacular onetime residence of former president Luis Echeverría sits atop one of the highest bluffs in town, with possibly the best views of Guanajuato. The whole building is surrounded by an impressive cactus garden. Each elegantly decorated suite is spacious, with restrained colonial touches; they have bathrooms tiled with local ceramics, floor-to-ceiling windows with views over the town, and small balconies. The Presidential Suite has a sunken tub and a telescope to complement its floor-to-ceiling picture window. The restaurant offers indoor and outdoor dining on a spacious terrace overlooking the town. **Pros:** relatively new building; doting service. **Cons:** not close to city center. ✉ *Cerro de San Miguel 13, Col. Loma de Pozuelos* ☎ *473/732–3993 or 473/734–1151* 🌐 *www.hotelesrefugio.com* ⇆ *6 suites* ♢ *In-room: safe, kitchen, Wi-Fi. In-hotel: restaurant, room service, bar, laundry service, Wi-Fi hotspot, parking (free)* ▭ *MC, V.*

$$ ★ **La Casa de Espíritus Alegres Bed and Breakfast.** Folk art lovers are drawn to this "house of happy spirits" for its collection of crafts. Owned by a California artist, the lovingly restored hacienda (circa 1700) has thick stone walls and serene, almost jungle-like grounds covered with bougainvillea and calla lilies. Hand-glazed-tile baths, fireplaces, and private terraces are standard with each room, but otherwise, all rooms are unique. Marfil is a 15-minute drive from the center of town—frequent buses are available. Taxi drivers may be unfamiliar with the hotel, so come prepared with directions. **Pros:** uniquely and creatively decorated suites; warm staff and complimentary breakfasts. **Cons:** hard to find, and driveway is difficult to maneuver. ✉ *La Ex-Hacienda La Trinidad 1, Marfil* ☎☎ *473/733–1013* 🌐 *www.casaspirit.com* ⇆ *5 rooms, 3 suites* ♢ *In-room: no a/c, no phone, no TV, Wi-Fi. In-hotel: bar, laundry service, Wi-Fi hotspot, parking (free), no kids under 10* ▭ *MC, V* 🍽 *BP.*

$$$$ ★ **Quinta Las Acacias.** It would be hard to argue that the Frida Kahlo suite here, perched as it is above Guanajuato with a full Jacuzzi, relaxing living room, two large-screen TVs, and an enormous bathroom—is not the single best room in town. This boutique hotel, which opened in 1998, offers modern, Mexican-style rooms that are handsomely decorated. It's an utterly relaxing place, though you should venture elsewhere for meals. **Pros:** enchanting and spacious rooms; incredibly comfortable. **Cons:** it's a bit of a trip to town. ✉ *Paseo de la Presa 168, La Presa* ☎ *473/731–1517* 🌐 *www.quintalasacacias.com* ⇆ *7 rooms, 10 suites* ♢ *In-room: safe, DVD, Wi-Fi. In-hotel: restaurant, room service, bar, laundry service, Wi-Fi hotspot, parking (free), no kids under 12* ▭ *AE, MC, V* 🍽 *BP.*

NIGHTLIFE

BARS

There are a number of pricey bars right on the main plazas, such as Jardín de la Unión, that attract more than a few tourists because of their unparalleled people-watching opportunities.

A good plaza-side perch is **Bar Luna** (✉ *Jardín de la Unión 8,* ☎ *473/734–1864*), part of the hotel by the same name. It's open late into the evening. Indoors it's got cheeky design, and outdoors it's got a great crowd.

For an authentic Mexican cantina experience, **El Incendio** (✉ *Cantarranas 15* ☎ *No phone*) is open until 4 AM and comes complete with swinging doors, gruff old men downing beer after beer, and an exposed urinal on one wall. If you're a woman, it's best to come accompanied.

Calle Sopeña hops with nighttime activity, thanks in part to interesting spots like **La Capellina** (✉ *Sopeña 3, El Centro* ☎ *473/732–7224*); restaurant by day, bar by night, La Capellina does great drinks and hosts live music ranging from Latin jazz to blues.

EATING ON THE GO IN PRESA

If you're staying in the Presa neighborhood, you should walk along Paseo de la Presa into the city. You'll pass a number of food carts in Parque Florenceio Antillón, all selling great food at even better prices. Fish ceviche tostadas are astoundingly fresh; you might also find savory tacos *al pastor* (pork), with tortillas made in front of you on a comal, a large, often cast-iron, plate. It's better to make this walk into the city than out—going back to Presa is all uphill, perfect for a taxi.

La Oreja de Van Gogh (✉ *San Fernando 24* ☎ *473/732–0301*) has reasonably priced drinks and perfect seating near sidewalks filled with late-night revelers. There's a larger branch at Plaza de la Unión with similar offerings.

An old-school cantina worth its salt is **Los Barrilitos** (✉ *Juárez 180, on corner of Callejón del Cañón Rojo, Jardín de la Unión* ☎ *No phone*). It's an absolute classic, with long, fluorescent lights and a sign reading PELIGRO: HOMBRES BEBIENDO (Danger: Men Drinking). Unusual for a cantina, there's a fine selection of top-end tequilas, including the sweet, smooth Cazadores Reposado.

Geared toward an older, quieter crowd, **Puerta del Sol** (✉ *Sopeña 14* ☎ *No phone*) offers a romantic environment complete with *peñas* (traditional folk music performances)—best enjoyed over some tequila.

CLUBS

Students gather for drinks and salsa dancing (including classes) at **El Café** (✉ *Sopeña 10, El Centro* ☎ *473/732–2566*).

★ Calle Sopeña is one of the hottest streets on weekend nights. **La Dama de las Camelias** (✉ *Calle Sopeña 32* ☎ *473/732–7587*), with its dingy-hip furnishings and longtime regulars, manages to stay unpretentious while pulling off its dive-bar-meets-vaudeville theme. You'll find everyone from twentysomethings to sixtysomethings hitting the dance floor for salsa and cumbia. It's open until 4 AM.

The crowd often takes to singing at **Rincón del Beso** (✉ *San Miguel, corner of Manuel Doblado* ☎ *473/732–5912*).

FESTIVALS

Guanajuato is completely mobbed each fall for the **Festival Internacional Cervantino** (*International Cervantes Festival* ✉ *Plaza de San Francisquito 1, El Centro* ☎ *473/731–1150 or 473/731–1161* 🌐 *www.festivalcervantino.gob.mx*). For nearly three weeks each October, world-renowned actors, musicians, and dance troupes perform nightly at the Teatro Juárez and other local venues. Plaza San Roque, a small square near the Jardín Reforma, hosts a series of Entremeses Cervantinos—swashbuckling one-act farces by classical Spanish writers, such as Cervantes. Grandstand seats require advance tickets, but crowds often gather by the plaza's edge to watch for free. Guanajuato's nightlife also reaches a peak during the festival, and revelers from different parts of Mexico walk through the city streets and display their regional pride by jumping up and down and chanting the name of their hometown. If you're going to be among the hundreds of thousands who attend the festivities annually, contact the Festival Internacional Cervantino office well in advance to secure tickets for top-billed events, or contact Ticketmaster. However, if you're not a fan of elbow-to-elbow crowds morning, noon, and night, you should avoid the festival.

4

FOLK MUSIC

Thursday, Friday, Saturday, and Sunday between 8 and 9 PM, **Callejoneadas** (mobile musical parties) begin in front of Teatro Juárez on Calle Sopeña, in the center of town. These quintessential, traditional tours are led by a group of student-minstrels, in full-out period costumes, who roam the narrowest streets of Guanajuato—the callejones—while strumming stringed instruments and singing folk songs, followed by the mass of paying customers, tourists from both Mexico and abroad. For a small fee you can travel with the group while enjoying an alcoholic beverage of sorts. (It's usually some bad combination of grape drink and firewater—so we recommend bringing your own.) The important thing is to try to get in a smaller group in order to keep up and hear the commentary—which is in Spanish only. You'll see people selling tickets around the theater, and you should ideally pay no more than 100 pesos per person. A fun part of your night will be stopping on the Callejón del Beso, a street so narrow it's said that a kiss could be exchanged between secret lovers on top-floor balconies. Bundle up on cold nights; the tours last up to two hours.

THEATER

Even when it's not festival season, Guanajuato still has drama, dance, and musical performances at **Teatro Juárez** (✉ *Sopeña s/n, El Centro* ☎ *473/732–0183*).

SHOPPING

Artesanías Vázques (✉ *Cantarranas 8* ☎📠 *473/732–5231*) has Talavera ceramics from Dolores Hidalgo. Browse the painterly, old-style majolica ceramics at **Capelo** (✉ *Ponciano Aguilar 25* ☎ *No phone*).

Casa del Conde de la Valenciana (✉ *Carretera Guanajuato–Dolores Hidalgo, Km 5, La Valenciana* ☎ *473/732–2550*), in addition to being a restaurant, specializes in brass, tin, ceramic, and wrought-iron home decorations from Mexico and Africa. **La Casa del Quijote** (✉ *Sopeña 17* ☎ *473/732–8226*) has a huge selection of crafts from all over Mexico, emphasizing jewelry and pottery. A good place for ceramics is **La Cruz** (✉ *Cerro de la Cruz* ☎ *473/732–9037*). **La Florecita** (✉ *Sopeña 13* ☎ *473/732–1398*) features Mexican handmade fabrics, including blouses and shawls. **Mayólicas Santa Rosa** (✉ *Carretera Guanajuato–Dolores Hidalgo, Km 13* ☎ *473/102–5017*) has lovely Santa Rosa ceramics.

GO WITH A GUIDE

Viajes Mazzocco, a well-established travel agency and the local American Express representative, gives tours of the city center, the Eden mine, the Teleférico, La Bufa, and the Quemada ruins. Ask in advance for an English-speaking guide.

Operadora Zacatecas also gives tours of the city center and other sites.

Operadora Zacatecas (✉ *Av. Hidalgo 630* ☎ *492/924–0050*). **Viajes Mazzocco** (✉ *Blvd. Lopez Portello 746* ☎ *492/922–0859* 🌐 *www.viajesmazzocco.com*).

Some jewelry and regional knickknacks are sold at the **Mercado Hidalgo** (✉ *Calle Juárez near Mendizabal, El Centro* ☎ *No phone*). Shops around Plaza de la Paz and Jardín de la Unión and in Calle Sopeña sell ceramics, woolen shawls, and sweaters. Book fairs are held on shady Plaza de San Fernando. Street vendors and shops clustered near La Valenciana and La Valencia sell silver.

ZACATECAS

300 km (186 mi or 3½ hrs by car) northwest of San Miguel, 250 km (155 mi) northwest of Guanajuato, 350 km (217 mi) northwest of Querétaro, 600 km (373 mi) northwest of Mexico City via Hwy. 57.

Although Zacatecas, high up at nearly 8,000 feet, was once the world's largest silver-producing city, it's relatively undiscovered by foreigners. Designated a UNESCO World Heritage Site in 1993, this extraordinary town is often labeled the "pink city," since most of its 17th- and 18th-century buildings were built of local pink limestone.

As a state capital with a population of 135,000, Zacatecas toes the line between city and town. There are some good restaurants and museums, and nightlife includes partying in an old silver mine deep underground. Each year during the Festival Cultural de Zacatecas, the city comes alive with dance, theater, music, and art.

Most town-center attractions are accessible on foot, although you may want a taxi to visit farther-flung sights like the Cerro de la Bufa, a dramatic limestone outcropping visible from most strategic points in town. There's an efficient and inexpensive bus system with clearly marked buses and 30¢ rides. The city's principal avenues such as López Velarde and González Ortega often change names as they proceed through the town, and the traffic is divided by islands decorated with carved limestone vases and lampposts, occasional statues, and ornate fountains.

We suggest you get your bearings first on the Tranvía Turístico, a trolley bus that departs on the hour from 10 AM to 9 PM daily in front of the cathedral. The 45-minute tour costs $5.

LOCAL BREW

To sample the local mezcals, you can go to **La Casa Zacatecana de Mezcal** (✉ *Av. Hidalgo 729* ☎ *492/925-4665*) which has a good selection, ranging from young platas to venerable añejos.

GETTING HERE AND AROUND

The Zacatecas La Calera airport (ZCL) is 29 km (18 mi) north of town. Aeromar flies from Mexico City to Zacatecas. Mexicana has direct flights from Chicago (though at this writing, Mexicana is reorganizing; check this route's availability before planning travel). Taxis from the airport into town cost around $17; the Aerotransportes shuttle service costs about the same. The Zacatecas bus depot is a couple of miles southwest of the town center. Omnibus de México and Estrella Blanca make the 5½-hour trip between Querétaro and Zacatecas ($27). There are no direct buses from San Miguel de Allende, but you can take a bus to Querétaro and transfer, or drive from there on excellent state highways in less than four hours.

ESSENTIALS

Bus Contacts **Estrella Blanca** (☎ *01800/507-5500 toll-free in Mexico* 🌐 *www.estrellablanca.com.mx*). **Omnibus de Mexico** (☎ *01800/765-6636 toll-free in Mexico* 🌐 *www.odm.com.mx*).

Medical Assistance **Farmacia Issstezac** (✉ *Tacuba 140* ☎ *492/924-0690*). **Hospital General** (✉ *Paseo García Salinas 707* ☎ *492/923-3000*). **Police** (☎ *492/922-0180*). **Red Cross** (☎ *492/922-3005*).

Visitor and Tour Info **Zacatecas Tourist information office** (✉ *Av. Hidalgo 403* ☎ *492/922-6751 or 492/922-3426* 🌐 *www.turismozacatecas.gob.mx*).

EXPLORING

TOP ATTRACTIONS

5 **Catedral de Zacatecas.** This is one of Mexico's finest interpretations of baroque style. It has three facades—the principal one dedicated to the Eucharist is best viewed from 2 to 6 PM, when the afternoon sun lights up the deeply sculpted reliefs. ✉ *South side of Plaza de Armas on Av. Hidalgo* ☎ *492/922-6211* ⏲ *Mon.–Sat. 6:30–1 and 5–9, Sun. 6:30–3 and 5–10.*

7 **Cerro de la Bufa.** Pancho Villa's definitive battle against dictator Victoriano Huerta occurred on this rugged hill, now a city landmark, in June 1914. The spacious Plaza de la Revolución, paved with three shades of pink Zacatecas stone, is crowned with three huge equestrian statues of Villa and two other heroes, Felipe Angeles and Panfilo Natera. You can have your photo taken dressed up like Pancho Villa (complete with

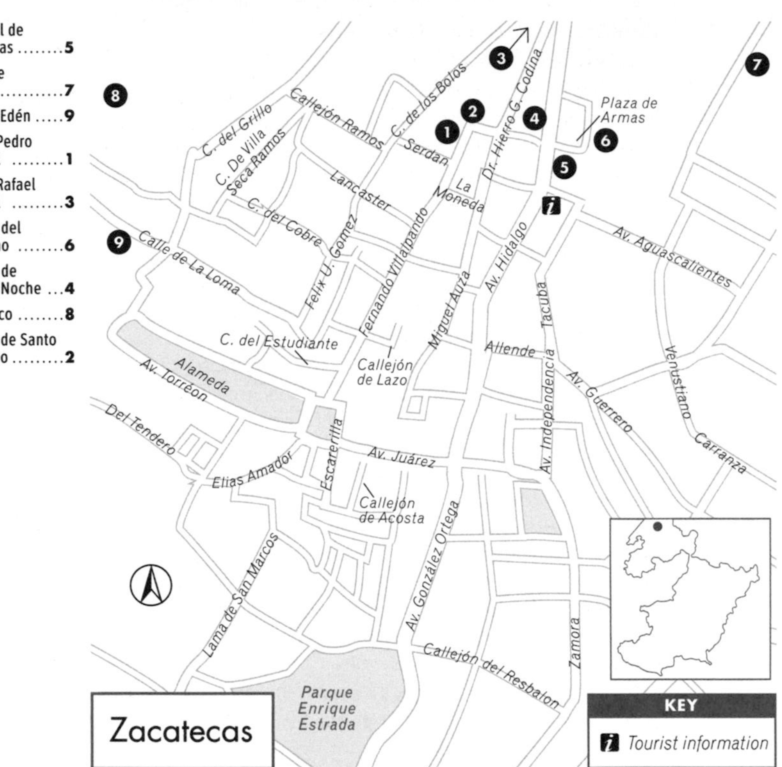

antique rifle) and a soldadera companion with outfits supplied by an enterprising young man. A walk up to the observatory gets you the best view of Zacatecas. Also on-site are the Sanctuario de la Virgen de Patrocinio, a chapel dedicated to the city's patron, and the **Museo de la Toma de Zacatecas** (☎ *492/922–8066* 🎟 *$2* ⏲ *Daily 10–5*), which has 10 rooms of historic objects such as guns, newspapers, furniture, and clothing from the days of Pancho Villa. ✉ *If driving, follow Av. Hidalgo north from town to Av. Juan de Tolosa; turn right and continue until you come to a fountain; take right off retorno (crossover) onto Calle Mexicapan, which leads to Carretera Panorámica. Turn right to signposted Carretera La Bufa, which leads to top of hill* ☎ *Museum 492/922–8066* 🎟 *$2* ⏲ *Daily 10–5.*

9 **Mina El Edén.** From 1586 until 1960 this mine supplied Zacatecas with most of its silver. Tours are in Spanish, but you'll have no trouble imagining what life was like for a miner once you're riding in the open mine train down into the underground tunnels. Wear sturdy shoes and bring a sweater. Among the train's stops is a discotheque—Club La Mina—which you should definitely revisit at night during its operating hours. There's a small gift shop at the entrance, and another inside the mine at the museum, where you can see examples of different minerals and fossils. ✉ *Entrance on Jaime Dovali off Av. Torréon beyond Alameda*

García de la Cadena ☎ *492/922–3002* 🎫 *$6* ⏲ *Daily 10–5.*

3 ★ **Museo Rafael Coronel.** Concealed by the Ex-Convento de San Francisco's mellow, pink, 18th-century facade is a rambling structure of open, arched corridors, all leading through garden patios to rooms that exhibit, on a rotating basis, 3,000 of the museum's 10,000 *máscaras* (masks). These representations of saints and devils, wise men and fools, animals and humans were once used in Mexican regional festivals. The museum also has a remarkable display of puppets, pre-Hispanic art, photography, and paintings. It's northeast of the town center, toward Lomas del Calvario. ✉ *Off Vergel Nuevo between Chaveño and Garcia Salinas* ☎ *492/922–8116* 🎫 *$3* ⏲ *Thurs.–Tues. 10–5.*

MARCHING MADNESS

Among the charms of Zacatecas is its *tambora,* a musical parade led by a *tamborazo,* a local band that shatters the evening quiet with merriment. It's also known as a *callejoneada* (*callejón* means "alley"), and everyone along the way either joins in or cheers from balconies and doorways. During the December *feria* (festival), the tamborazos serenade the Virgin of Zacatecas by playing night and day.

8 Fodor's Choice ★ **Teleférico.** The only cable car in the world to cross an entire city, the Teleférico runs from Cerro del Grillo (Cricket Hill) above the Mina Edén to Cerro de la Bufa. Though it crosses at the narrowest point, it showcases the city's magnificent panorama and baroque church domes and spires. It's worth the cost to get the ride up to Cerro de la Bufa, which is quite a climb otherwise. ✉ *Cerro del Grillo station: off Paseo Díaz Ordaz, a steep walk from Plaza de Armas* ☎ *492/922–5694* 🎫 *$2* ⏲ *Daily 10–6, except when there are high winds.*

WORTH NOTING

1 **Museo Pedro Coronel.** Originally a Jesuit monastery, this building was used as a jail in the 18th century, and is now a museum that exhibits the work of Zacatecas artist and sculptor Pedro Coronel. Also on display is his extensive collection of works by Picasso, Dalí, Miró, Braque, and Chagall, among others, as well as art from Africa, China, Japan, India, Tibet, Greece, and Egypt. ✉ *Centro s/n at Plaza Santo Domingo* ☎ *492/922–8021 or 492/924–2663* 🎫 *$3* ⏲ *Fri.–Wed. 10–5.*

4 **Palacio de la Mala Noche.** Across from the downtown plaza is a national monument: two 18th-century colonial buildings with lacy ironwork balconies, built from native pink stone. One is a municipal building known as the Palace of the Bad Night, which, according to legend, was the home of a silver-mine owner. The mine had failed, so, left with only enough funds to pay his workers' final wages, he went to pray at the cathedral. On the way home he ran into a woman whose son was sick and gave her everything he had. Early the next morning loud banging on the door seemed to herald his doom, but upon opening the door he was instead informed that the mine workers had found the richest gold vein ever seen in these parts. ✉ *Av. Hidalgo 639* ☎ *No phone* 🎫 *Free* ⏲ *Weekdays 9–3 and 5–7.*

6 **Palacio del Gobierno.** The Governor's Palace is an 18th-century mansion with verdant courtyards and, on the main staircase, a poignant mural by António Pintor Rodríguez that depicts the history of Zacatecas. ✉ *East side of Plaza de Armas* ☎ *No phone* 🎫 *Free* ⏲ *Weekdays 9–3 and 5–7.*

2 **Templo de Santo Domingo.** This 18th-century Jesuit church has an ornamented facade and an opulent interior with religious paintings. In the sacristy is an extensive collection of religious art. ✉ *Av. Fernando Villalpando at Plaza Santo Domingo* ☎ *No phone* 🎫 *Free* ⏲ *Daily 10–4:30.*

GOURMET STOP

San Patricio Caffé on Avenida Hidalgo 403 serves the most elaborate gourmet coffee and tea in Zacatecas. Within an airy, elegant courtyard tucked behind one of the city's most bustling streets, the café is littered with lacquered-wood furniture and delightful imported goodies.

WHERE TO EAT

$ CAFÉ ✕ **Café y Nevería Acrópolis.** This diner is trimmed with paintings and sketches given to the owner by famous people who've eaten here, including a small acrylic by Rafael Coronel. Sip a strong Turkish coffee while watching the locals flood in for breakfast. The *chilaquiles verdes* (fried tortilla strips smothered in tangy green sauce and white cheese) comes with a basket of pastries and bread. Mild *enchiladas zacatecanas* are filled with cheese, onion, and chili, and topped with cream. Traditional café fare like hamburgers, sandwiches, and fruity shakes is available for lunch. ✉ *Av. Hidalgo at Plazuela Candelario, in Mercado González Ortega, alongside cathedral* ☎ *492/922–1284* 💳 *MC, V.*

$ MEXICAN ✕ **El Recoveco.** There are 25 steaming plates of traditional Mexican dishes to choose from at this rustic, full-buffet diner. Lunch will likely include Spanish rice, beans, *pollo en mole* (chicken in mole sauce), fresh salads, and *aguas frescas* (fruit water). Prices are reasonable: around $6 for all-you-can-eat lunch, $5 for breakfast. ✉ *Av. Torréon 513, in front of Alameda* ☎ *492/924–2013* 💳 *MC, V.*

¢ MEXICAN ✕ **Gorditas Doña Julia.** Much loved by locals, Doña Julia makes dozens of varieties of *gorditas* day and night—it seems there's nary an hour when the place isn't full of people, in part because of the rock-bottom prices. In the wide-open entrance to the simple shop, you'll watch a woman shaping your fresh tortilla with her hands before putting it on the open fire. Many fillings are available, such as delicious regional specialties like beef tongue, rice with mole, *rajas con queso* (chili strips with cheese), and cactus. There are other locations around the city. ✉ *Av. 5 de Mayo in Col. Guadalupe and Hidalgo 409 in El Centro* ☎ *492/923–7955* 💳 *No credit cards.*

WHERE TO STAY

$ 🏨 **Hostal del Vasco.** For an authentic Zacatecano hotel, consider this clean, quiet place. The spacious brown-carpeted suites have dark antiques; some are equipped with a small kitchen (but no cookware). Sprawling plants and singing birds—Pepe the parrot leads the choir—enliven the two-story interior courtyard. There's also a breakfast room. **Pros:** kitchens in rooms; live birds. **Cons:** rooms are dark and have thin walls. ✉ *Alameda and Velasco 1* ☎📠 *492/922–0428* 🌐 *www.hostaldelvasco.com.mx* *13 rooms, 6 suites* *In-room: no a/c, kitchen (some), DVD, Wi-Fi. In-hotel: bar, laundry service, Wi-Fi hotspot, parking (free), some pets allowed* 💳 *AE, MC, V.*

$$ **Hotel Emporio.** The 18th-century pink-stone facade of this lovely old colonial building faces the Plaza de Armas and the cathedral. During festival season, rooms looking onto the plaza are within earshot of late-night and early-morning tamborazo music. That said, you'll get a great view of the festivities from your small balcony. **Pros:** extremely friendly staff; within walking distance of sights. **Cons:** restaurant not the best; some rooms are noisy. ✉ *Av. Hidalgo 703* ☎ *492/925–6500* 🌐 *www.hotelesemporio.com* *86 rooms, 27 suites* *In-room: safe, DVD, Wi-Fi. In-hotel: restaurant, room service, bar, gym, laundry service, Wi-Fi hotspot, parking (paid)* 💳 *AE, MC, V.*

$$$ ★ **Hotel Santa Rita.** This shiny, modern hotel, with its prime location on Avenida Hidalgo, has taken the city by storm. A marble staircase leads up to the first floor, past gleaming glass structures. Rooms are top-of-the-line, simple and sleek, with dark-wood floors, lovely bathrooms, and, in some cases, terraces that open onto terrific views of the city. The restaurant isn't as exciting. **Pros:** good-looking hardwood floors in rooms; lots of privacy on balconies. **Cons:** poor restaurant. ✉ *Av. Hidalgo 507* ☎ *492/925–1194* 🌐 *www.hotelsantarita.com* *30 rooms, 4 suites* *In-room: safe, Wi-Fi. In-hotel: restaurant, room service, gym, spa, laundry service, Wi-Fi hotspot, parking (paid)* 💳 *AE, D, DC, MC, V* *BP.*

$$ **Mesón de Jobito.** Once an early-19th-century apartment building, this hotel is absolutely sprawling, with courtyard upon courtyard giving way to more rooms than you imagined could exist here. There are two levels of guest rooms, all of which are done in tasteful, if somewhat bland, furnishings. The Mesón's placement on a little plaza set back from and above the street enhances its tranquil quality. **Pros:** sprawling, village-like character; bright, festive colors. **Cons:** rooms are a bit drafty; some steep uphill walking to hotel's plaza. ✉ *Jardín Juárez 143* ☎ *492/924–1722* 🌐 *www.mesondejobito.com* *26 rooms, 26 suites* *In-room: safe, Wi-Fi. In-hotel: 2 restaurants, room service, bar, laundry service, Wi-Fi hotspot, parking (free)* 💳 *MC, V* *BP.*

$$$$ Fodor's Choice ★ **Quinta Real.** This is one of the world's more curious hotels: it's built around Mexico's first *plaza de toros* (bullring), which is the second-oldest in the Western Hemisphere. Pastel fabrics complement dark, traditional furniture in the large, bright, and plush rooms. Some of the former bull pens are part of the

WORD OF MOUTH

"I'm actually wearing a Zacatecas T-shirt as I write this. We visited [the city] a few years back and enjoyed it quite a bit. A couple of nights is probably enough. We stayed at the Quinta Real which used to be a bull ring and loved the hotel. The restaurant there is very good too."
—Otis_B_Driftwood

4

bar, which is a great place to unwind; candles supply the lighting, and there are cozy corners. Two levels of the spectator area make up an outdoor café. The formal restaurant ($$–$$$) offers continental cuisine and an awesome view of the bullring and the aqueduct beyond. **Pros:** bar in a bullring; decent restaurant. **Cons:** sometimes the space is overrun by events; pricey; some distance from the Centro. ✉ *Av. Ignacio Rayón 434, to side of aqueduct* ☎ *492/922–9104 or 492/922–9107* 🌐 *www.quintareal.com* *36 rooms, 13 suites* *In-room: safe, refrigerator, DVD, Wi-Fi. In-hotel: restaurant, room service, bar, gym, spa, laundry service, Wi-Fi hotspot, parking (free)* *AE, MC, V.*

SHOPPING

Opposite the east end of Plaza de Armas is **La Cazzorra** (✉ *Av. Hidalgo 713* ☎ *492/924–0484*), a collectibles shop with authentic antiques, books about Zacatecas, Huichol art, *rebozos* (traditional woven wraps), and a fine selection of jewelry from the local silver factory. The owners are a good source of information about the city.

NIGHTLIFE

BARS

Stroll along Avenida Hidalgo to survey the bars and dance clubs.

Fodor's Choice ★ Remember—whatever happens in **La Mina Club** (✉ *La Mina Edén* ☎ *492/922–3002*) stays more than 1,000 feet underground. This is the world's only nightclub in a mine. DJs spin modern dance music—don't expect salsa and merengue—while revelers admire the toxic waters deep below through glass floors. It's open Thursday through Saturday nights 10 PM–3 AM, with a cover charge of around $12.

★ The **Quinta Real** (✉ *Av. Ignacio Rayón 434* ☎ *492/922–9104*) is one of Mexico's most unusual and romantic bars, a candlelit haunt literally built into the old bullring.

SIDE TRIP FROM ZACATECAS

ZONA ARQUEOLÓGICA LA QUEMADA

50 km (31 mi) southwest of Zacatecas on Hwy. 54, 3 km (2 mi) off highway.

By the time the Spaniards arrived in the 16th century, this ancient city was already a ruin. The site's original name, Chicomostoc, means "place of the seven tribes." It was previously believed that seven Native American cultures had occupied the area, one community building atop the other. The principal draw is a group of rose-color ruins containing 11 massive round columns built of the same small slabs of rock. Interesting artifacts are housed in the site's impressive museum. To get here, take a bus toward Villanueva, get off at the entrance to La Quemada, and walk 3 km (2 mi). The bus ride takes about an hour. Alternatively, take a taxi or guided tour. ☎ *492/922–5085* *$3* *Site and museum daily 9–5.*

MORELIA

200 km (124 mi) southwest of San Miguel, 302 km (188 mi) west of Mexico City, 50 km (31 mi) northeast of Pátzcuaro.

WILLY WONKA WISHES

Morelia has the delicious distinction of being the candy capital of Mexico. So popular are the sweets that the city has an entire market devoted to candy, called the Mercado de Dulces.

Morelia is Michoacán State's capital—its long, wide boulevards and earth-tone colonial mansions earned it its status as a UNESCO World Heritage Site. Founded in 1541 as Valladolid (after the Spanish city), it changed its name in 1828 to honor José María Morelos, the town's most famous son. The legendary mule skinner–turned–priest led the battle for independence after its early leaders were executed in 1811.

Morelia's streets are almost always clogged with traffic, so it's best to see the city on foot—an easy task given the proximity of most sites to the zócalo. The city's well-preserved colonial buildings are today's offices, museums, shops, restaurants, and hotels. The magnificent 17th-century aqueduct, with its 253 arches, still carries water into the city. Lately, the city has become a hotbed for international students.

Finding your way around Morelia can be a challenge, as street names change frequently, especially on either side of Avenida Madero, the city's main east–west artery. Buses run the length of Avenida Madero.

Morelia is always more fun if you start with a trip on the Tranvía (city sightseeing bus) that departs from in front of the cathedral. It offers tours of the city with stops at various spots, including the Museo del Dulce, where you can see a demonstration of how the city's delicious confections are made.

GETTING HERE AND AROUND

Aeropuerto Internacional General Francisco J. Mujica (MLM) is 24 km (15 mi) north of Morelia. Taxis from the airport into town cost around $35. Aeroméxico and Aeromar fly from Mexico City to Morelia. For bus service, Primera Plus, ETN, and Herradura de Plata run to Morelia from Mexico City (five–six hours, $25–$30); Primera Plus goes to San Miguel via Celaya (3½ hours, $15). Bus trips from Morelia to Pátzcuaro take one hour and cost $7.

ESSENTIALS

Bus Contacts ETN (☎ *01800/800–0386 toll-free in Mexico* ⊕ *www.etn.com.mx*). **Primera Plus** (☎ *01800/375–7587 toll-free in Mexico* ⊕ *www.primeraplus.com.mx*).

Medical Assistance Ambulance–Red Cross (☎ *443/314–5073 or 443/314–5025*). **Hospital de la Cruz Roja** (✉ *Ventura Puenta 27* ☎ *443/314–5151*). **Hospital Memorial** (✉ *PeriféricoPaseo de la República 2111* ☎ *443/315–1099*).

Visitor and Tour Info Secretaría Estatal de Turismo (✉ *Av. Tata Vasco 80* ☎ *800/450–2300*).

EXPLORING

TOP ATTRACTIONS

2 **Catedral.** Morelia's cathedral is a majestic structure built between 1640 and 1744. It's known for its 200-foot baroque towers, which are among Mexico's tallest, and its 4,610-pipe organ. ✉ *Av. Madero between Plaza de Armas and Av. Morelos* ☎ *No phone* 🎫 *Free.*

5 **Mercado de Dulces.** If you have a sweet tooth, don't miss Morelia's candy market. All sorts of local sweets are for sale, such as *ate* (a candied fruit) and *cajeta* (heavenly caramel sauce made from goat's milk). Wooden knickknacks, cheap jewelry, and handcrafted acoustic guitars are among the nondigestible crafts. ✉ *Av. Madero Ponente at Av. Valentín Gómez Farías* ☎ *No phone* ⏲ *Daily 10–9.*

10 **Museo de Arte Contemporáneo.** On a lovely property a stone's throw from both the aqueduct and the Bosque Cuauhtémoc, this late-19th-century summer home is now Michoacán's principal contemporary-art museum. The permanent collection has work by famed muralist, lithographer, and illustrator Alfredo Zalce, a Pátzcuaro native. Some of Mexico's leading contemporary artists have temporary exhibitions here. Dance, cinema, theater, and music performances are held regularly in the small auditorium. ✉ *Av. Acueducto 18* ☎ *443/312–5404* 🎫 *Free* ⏲ *Weekdays 10–8, weekends 10–6.*

4 **Museo del Estado.** Across from a small plaza with statues of Bishop Vasco de Quiroga and Spanish writer Miguel de Cervantes, this history museum is in a stately mansion that was previously home to the wife of Agustín de Iturbide, Mexico's only native-born emperor. Among the 18th-century home's highlights is a complete Morelia pharmacy from 1868. On display are regional archaeological artifacts and exhibits about mining and indigenous culture. ✉ *Guillermo Prieto 176* ☎ *443/313–0629* 🎫 *Free* ⏲ *Weekdays 9–2 and 4–8, weekends 10–6.*

6 **Museo Regional Michoacano.** Formerly an 18th-century palace, the museum traces Mexico's history from its pre-Hispanic days through the Cardenista period, which ended in 1940. President Lázaro Cárdenas, a native of Michoacán, was one of Mexico's most popular leaders because he nationalized the oil industry and supported other populist reforms. On the ground floor is an art gallery, plus archaeological exhibits from Michoacán. Upstairs is an assortment of colonial objects, including furniture, weapons, and religious paintings. ✉ *Allende 305* ☎ *443/312–0407* 🎫 *$3, free Sun.* ⏲ *Daily 9–5.*

NEED A BREAK?

When you've finished your tour of the Museo Regional Michoacano, walk across the street to the colonial stone *portales* (arcades). On one side of the square, the portales are lined with popular sidewalk cafés. For a sandwich, guacamole with chips, or juices, coffees, and teas, try Best Western Hotel Casino (✉ *Portal Hidalgo 229* ☎ *443/313–1328*).

11 **Parque Zoológico Benito Juárez.** This is the largest zoo in Mexico, with more than 3,800 wild animals. It also has the largest aviary in Latin America. This is a great place to take the kids, and there's an espe-

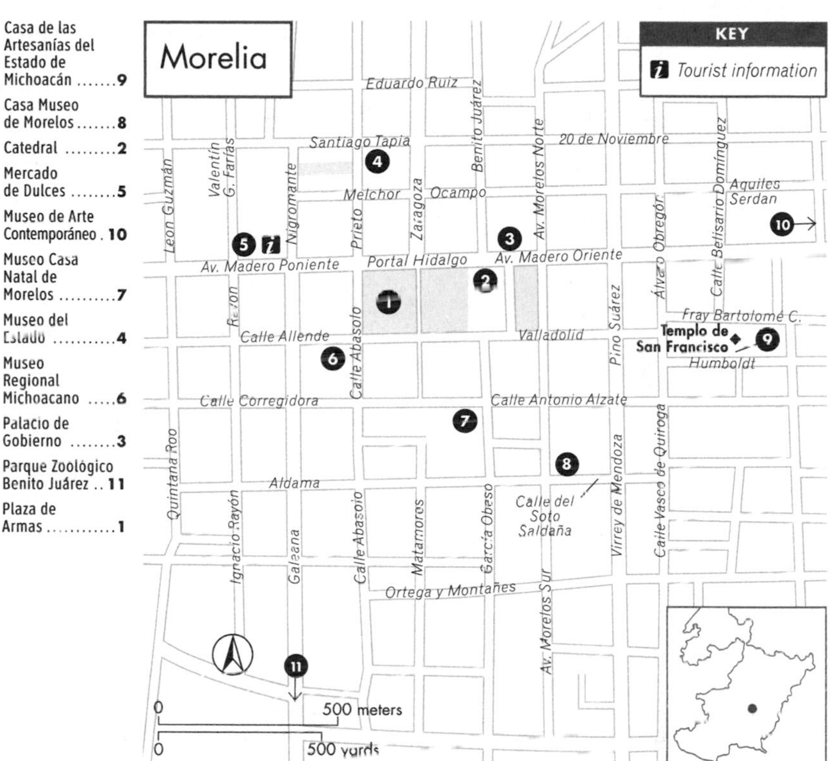

cially exciting nighttime tour. ✉ *Calzada Juárez s/n* ☎ *443/299–3522 or 443/299–3610* 🎟 *Entrance $2, packages available* ⏲ *Daily 9:30–5.*

❶ **Plaza de Armas.** During the War of Independence, several rebel priests were brutally murdered on this site, and the plaza, known as Plaza de los Mártires, is named after them. Today sweethearts stroll along the tree-lined walks, friends chat under the silver-domed gazebo, and painters exhibit their work on sunny days. ✉ *Bounded on the north by Av. Madero, on the south by Allende, on the west by Abasolo, and on the east by the cathedral.*

WORTH NOTING

❾ **Casa de las Artesanías del Estado de Michoacán.** In the 16th century, Vasco de Quiroga, the bishop of Michoacán, helped the Purépecha Indians develop artistic specialties so they could be self-supporting. At this two-story museum and store you can see the work that the Purépechas still produce: copper goods from Santa Clara del Cobre, lacquerware from Uruapan, straw items and pottery from Pátzcuaro, guitars from Paracho, fanciful ceramic devil figures from Ocumicho. Some of these items are showcased on the two main floors around the courtyard of the Museo Michoacana de las Artesanías, and artists demonstrate how they are made. ✉ *Fray Juan de San Miguel 129* ☎ *443/312–2486* 🎟 *Free* ⏲ *Mon.–Sat. 9–8, Sun. 9–3:30.*

8 **Casa Museo de Morelos.** What is now a two-story museum was acquired in 1801 by José María Morelos and was home to generations of the independence leader's family until 1934. It exhibits family portraits, various independence-movement artifacts (including a camp bed used by Ignacio Allende), and the blindfold Morelos wore at his execution. ✉ *Av. Morelos Sur 323* ☎ *443/313–2651* 🎟 *$3* ⏲ *Tues.–Sat. 9–5, Sun. 9–4.*

7 **Museo Casa Natal de Morelos.** José María Morelos's birthplace is now a national monument and library, with mostly literature and history books (as well as two murals by Morelian Alfredo Zalce). Visit the courtyard in back, where a marker and an eternal flame honor the fallen hero. ✉ *Corregidora 113* ☎ *443/312–2793* 🎟 *Free* ⏲ *Daily 9–8.*

3 **Palacio de Gobierno.** Notable graduates of this former Tridentine seminary, built in 1770, include independence hero José María Morelos, social reformer Melchor Ocampo, and Mexico's first emperor, Agustín de Iturbide. In the 1960s local artist Alfredo Zalce painted the striking murals (on the stairway and second floor), which depict dramatic, often bloody scenes from Mexico's history. ✉ *Av. Madero 63* ☎ *443/312–2032* 🎟 *Free* ⏲ *Daily 9–3 and 6–9.*

WHERE TO EAT

$$$ ECLECTIC Fodor's Choice ★

✕ **Fonda Las Mercedes.** A dramatic, narrow entrance lined with stone pillars topped with geodes—round rocks collected from the surrounding countryside—lead into this restored colonial mansion's plant-filled stone patio and covered atrium. The bar and ceiling are covered in vines, and paintings hang everywhere else. Offerings from the eclectic menu include numerous soups plus various kinds of crepes. The chicken *a la portuguesa* is stuffed with cheese, rolled in bacon, and cooked in a white-wine sauce—it's quite memorable. ✉ *León Guzmán 47* ☎ *443/312–6113* 💳 *AE, MC, V.*

$$ MEXICAN ★

✕ **La Azotea.** This restaurant overlooking the cathedral might not have the best food in Morelia, but it has the most iconic view, with hip, white lounge cushions to boot. You can dine indoors or out—both provide the stunning panorama. The menu is pricey and a bit stuffy, but not offensively so—its core is formed by Mexican dishes with some fusion touches. The tequila list is overpriced but excellent. ✉ *Hotel Los Juaninos, Morelos Sur 39* ☎ *443/312–0036* 💳 *AE, MC, V.*

$$ MEXICAN

✕ **La Casa del Portal.** This restaurant overlooking the Plaza de Armas has a focus on local dishes. Covered in a red sauce, *corundas* are topped with chopped pork, cream, queso fresco, and chili poblano strips. Don't miss the *arrachera Valladolid,* a slice of skirt steak with *nopales* (sliced and steamed cactus), guacamole, and beans. ✉ *Guillermo Prieto 30* ☎ *443/313–4899* 💳 *AE, MC, V.*

$$ MEXICAN

✕ **Los Mirasoles.** This restaurant is in a marvelously restored, plant-filled 17th-century mansion. Specialties include the full range of local dishes as well as Argentine-style massive steaks. Salads, pastas, and homemade soups round out the menu. The bar resembles a cozy living room; copper trays serve as tables, and the painted, domed ceilings resemble the sky. The wine list includes a selection of Mexican wines. ✉ *Av. Madero Poniente 549* ☎ *443/317–5775 or 443/317–5777* 🌐 *www.losmirasoles.com* ▭ *AE, D, DC, MC, V* ⊗ *No dinner Sun.*

¢ MEXICAN ✕ **Taquería Pioneros.** Even though it's far from the city center, the tables at this positively plain taco shop are packed at lunch. People come for the delicious grilled meats, prepared Michoacán style, with salsas and mountains of fresh, hot tortillas made on-site. The *pionero* (beef, ham, bacon, onions, and cheese, all grilled) is the only option served in a half portion, which is plenty for most appetites. ✉ *Aquiles Serdán 7, at Morelos Norte* ☎ *443/313–4938* ▭ *No credit cards.*

TO TASTE

Morelia's restaurants serve some of Michoacán's tastiest dishes: *sopa tarasca* (a black-bean soup with cream and cheese), corn products such as *huchepos* (sweet tamales) and *corundas* (savory triangular tamales with cream and salsa), and game such as rabbit and quail.

4

WHERE TO STAY

$$ **Hotel Posada de la Soledad.** A private mansion built in the 17th century is now an alluring hotel one block from the Plaza de Armas. In the original section, rooms surround an elegant patio with a large fountain and massive bougainvilleas. Smaller, plainer, and quieter rooms are in the newer section. **Pros:** inexpensive, with a relaxing patio where you'll forget all about city noise. **Cons:** rooms on Calle Ocampo get traffic noise. ✉ *Ignacio Zaragoza 90* ☎ *443/312–1888 or 01 800/716–0189* 🌐 *www.hsoledad.com* *47 rooms* *In-room: no a/c, safe, Wi-Fi. In-hotel: restaurant, bar, laundry service, Wi-Fi hotspot, parking (free)* ▭ *AE, MC, V* *BP.*

$$$ Fodor's Choice ★ **Hotel Virrey de Mendoza.** Built in 1565 for a Spanish nobleman, this downtown hotel radiates the aura of a bygone era. A massive stained-glass skylight casts a warm glow over an elegant lobby lounge fitted with an enormous stone fireplace and cushy black-leather couches. Guest rooms have dark colonial-style furnishings, lace curtains, soaring ceilings, creaking hardwood floors, and bathrooms with porcelain tubs. ■ **TIP→ Make sure to get a room with a window facing outdoors, as some face only the lobby.** **Pros:** possible celebrity sightings; lobby complete with piano player on occasion. **Cons:** it's noisy sometimes, and there are problems related to the age of building. ✉ *Av. Madero Poniente 310* ☎ *443/312–0633 or 443/312–0045* 🌐 *www.hotelvirrey.com* *40 rooms, 15 suites* *In-room: Wi-Fi. In-hotel: restaurant, room service, bar, laundry service, Wi-Fi hotspot, parking (free)* ▭ *AE, MC, V* *BP.*

$$$ ★ **Villa Montaña Hotel & Spa.** French count Philippe de Reiset fitted this villa with all the trappings of a wealthy Mexican estate. High above Morelia in the Santa María hills, its five impeccably groomed acres are studded with stone sculptures. Each unit has at least one piece of antique furniture, and most have a fireplace and private patio. The hotel's restaurant serves North American, French, and Mexican cuisine; from its huge windows you'll have a marvelous view of Morelia, especially at night. Children under eight are discouraged from dining in the

restaurant. **Pros:** supreme relaxation and creature comforts. **Cons:** distance from city; mediocre restaurant. ✉ *Patzimba 201* ☎ *443/314–0231* 🌐 *www.villamontana.com.mx* *13 rooms, 25 suites* *In-room: safe, Wi-Fi. In-hotel: restaurant, room service, bar, tennis court, pool, gym, laundry service, Wi-Fi hotspot, parking (free)* 💳 *AE, MC, V.*

NIGHTLIFE

BARS

Don't miss the trendy **Bar de Los Juaninos** (✉ *Morelos Sur 39* ☎ *443/312–0036*), in open air atop the Hotel de Los Juaninos, for the best view of Morelia's cathedral, and proper cocktails to complement it. The bar pushes champagne, too, and it has a great tequila selection—even if it is a bit overpriced.

Live music is played at **La Porfiriana** (✉ *Calle Corregidora 694* ☎ *443/312–2663*) every night from 10:30 PM to 3 AM.

FOLK MUSIC

Morelia has many lively folk-music clubs in gorgeous downtown locations. **Colibrí** (✉ *Galeana 36* ☎ *443/312–2261*) has Latin American folk music every night from 10 PM to 2 AM.

El Rincon de los Sentidos (✉ *Av. Madero Poniente 485* ☎ *443/312–2903*) is one of the best-loved places in town for predinner drinks in comfy chairs, and is popular with students who like trova music (about love and protest). There are cute hanging paper lamps upstairs, and live music downstairs Wednesday through Sunday. Just stay away from hot-tequila-and-mint cocktails. It's open daily from 8 PM to midnight.

SIDE TRIP FROM MORELIA

SANTUARIO DE MARIPOSAS EL ROSARIO

Approximately 115 km (71 mi) east of Morelia.

Fodor's Choice ★ One hundred million monarch butterflies migrate annually from the United States and Canada to winter in the easternmost part of Michoacán, near Mexico State's border. A visit to the Santuario de Mariposas el Rosario between early November and early March is an awesome experience. The sanctuary's pine forest is so caked with orange-and-black butterflies it looks like it's on fire. Listen closely and you'll hear the rustle of millions of wings beating. ■ **TIP→ The hike to the groves is a steep climb, and the high altitude (10,400 feet) will require that you take it slowly.**

This day trip takes about 10 hours, but it's absolutely worth the effort. We suggest you don't drive yourself, but catch a guided tour in Morelia. ✉ *Hwy. 15 east to Zitácuaro, then take the marked but unnumbered road north to Angangueo, and on to sanctuary entrance* ☎ *No phone* *$3* *Daily 10–5.*

FESTIVALS

Each May the **International Organ Festival** is celebrated in the cathedral, giving voice to its outstanding 4,610-pipe organ. The Festival Internacional de Música, featuring baroque and chamber music, is held the last two weeks of November (see 🌐 *www.festivalmorelia.com.mx*).

PÁTZCUARO

50 km (31 mi) southwest of Morelia.

Founded in the 16th century on the shores of the tranquil Lake Pátzcuaro, this town remained largely undisturbed for several centuries until it was "discovered" by international and Mexican tourists. The town's founder was Bishop Vasco de Quiroga, who implemented a plan whereby area villages were assigned a different skill, and to this day their descendants have continued this tradition: artisans in nearby Paracho produce excellent guitars; those in Tzintzuntzán are known for their green-glazed pottery; hand-beaten copper plates and vases come from Santa Clara; lacquerware from Quiroga; fanciful *catrinas* (high-society ladies with the face of a skeleton) from Capula; and the finest *rebozos* (shawls) are handwoven in Nurío.

Many of Pátzcuaro's principal sights are near the Plaza Vasco de Quiroga and Plaza Bocanegra in the center of town. Lake Pátzcuaro, which you must surely visit, is a 10-minute cab ride from the center of town. Note that the archaeological areas are closed on Monday. If you want to visit the surrounding villages you can hire taxis. Trails near Pátzcuaro wind up to nearby hilltops for great views across town and the countryside.

■ TIP→ On November 1 the town is inundated with tourists en route to Janítzio, an island in Lake Pátzcuaro, where one of Mexico's most elaborate Day of the Dead graveyard ceremonies takes place. Many younger people take the journey to the village of Tzintzuntzán, where for them Day of the Dead festivities are focused primarily on imbibing.

GETTING HERE AND AROUND

Primera Plus has first-class buses to Pátzcuaro from Mexico City (six hours, $30) and Morelia (one hour, $7). From Morelia the excellent, free superhighway to Pátzcuaro takes just over an hour. From Mexico City, the Mexico City–Guadalajara tollway cuts driving time to Pátzcuaro to four and a half or five hours. There are no rental outlets in Pátzcuaro.

ESSENTIALS

Bus Contacts **Primera Plus** (☎ *01800/375–7587 toll-free in Mexico* 🌐 *www.primeraplus.com.mx*).

Medical Assistance **Hospital General** (✉ *Romero s/n* ☎ *434/342–0285*). **Police** (☎ *434/342–0004*).

Visitor and Tour Info **Departamento de Turismo** (✉ *Ahumada 13* ☎ *434/342–1214*).

EXPLORING

TOP ATTRACTIONS

3 **La Basílica de Nuestra Señora de la Salud.** Vasco de Quiroga began this church in 1554, and throughout the centuries others—undaunted by earthquakes and fires—took up the cause and eventually completed it in honor of the Virgin of Health. Near the main altar is a statue of the

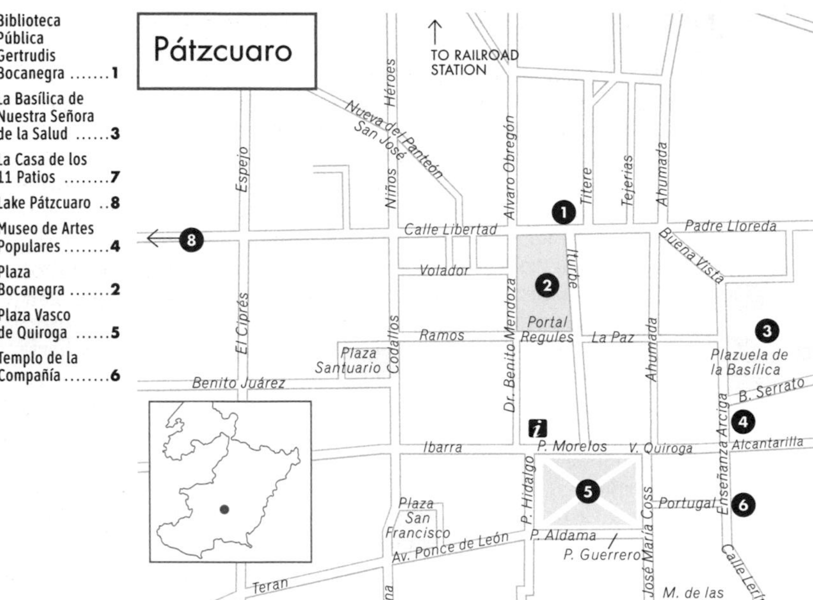

Virgin made of derivatives of cornstalks and orchids. Several masses are held daily; the earliest begins shortly after dawn. Out front, Purépecha women sell hot tortillas, herbal mixtures for teas, and religious objects. ✉ *Enseñanza Arciga, near Benigno Serrato* ☎ *434/342–0055.*

7 ★ **La Casa de los 11 Patios.** A maze of shops featuring Purépecha handiwork is housed in this former 18th-century convent. As you meander through the shops and courtyards, you'll encounter weavers producing large bolts of cloth, artists working with black lacquerware trimmed with gold, vendors selling woven hats and place mats, and seamstresses embroidering blouses. ✉ *Madrigal de las Altas Torres s/n* ⏲ *Daily 10–2 and 4–8; some shops close Mon.*

8 **Lake Pátzcuaro.** The tranquil shores of Lake Pátzcuaro are a 10-minute cab ride from downtown. There are two different *muelles* (docks) from which you can catch a boat to Janítzio, but you should head to the central muelle, which offers far more service. Before or after your trip, stop at one of the lakeside restaurants, which serve fresh *pescado blanco* (whitefish) and other local catches. Wooden launches with room for 25 people (but that rarely take that many) depart for Janítzio and the other islands daily 9–5. Purchase round-trip tickets for $4 at a dockside office (prices are controlled by the tourist department).

It is absolutely worthwhile to visit La Pacanda—far more worthwhile, in fact, than Janítzio, the largest of Lake Pátzcuaro's five islands. La Pacanda is a quiet and peaceful island: amazing flowers abound, cows laze about, and the few inhabitants of the island go about their daily activities—which do not include trying to sell you garish souvenirs. La Pacanda might be even more idyllic than tiny Yunuen, but you won't want to stay more than an hour or so. At Yunuen, on the other hand—which also provides a clear picture of island life—you can arrange an overnight stay in simple yet clean visitor cabins.

2 **Plaza Bocanegra.** The smaller of the city's two squares (it's also called Plaza Chica), this is Pátzcuaro's commercial center. Bootblacks, pushcart vendors, and bus and taxi stands are all in the plaza, which is embellished by a statue of the local heroine, Gertrudis Bocanegra. Nearby, a large outdoor mercado sprawls along Libertad and its side streets. At times the road is so crowded with people and their wares—fruit, vegetables, beans, rice, herbs, and other necessities of daily life—that it's difficult to walk. If you press on for about a block, you'll see an indoor market to your left filled with more produce; large, hanging slabs of meat; hot food; cheap trinkets; and locally made wool garments. ✉ *Bounded by Av. Libertad on the north, Portal Regules on the south, Benito Mendoza on the west, and Iturbe on the east.*

5 **Plaza Vasco de Quiroga.** A tranquil courtyard girded by towering, century-old ash and pine trees and 16th-century mansions (since converted into hotels and shops), the larger of the two downtown plazas commemorates the bishop who restored dignity to the Purépecha people. During the Spanish conquest, Nuño de Guzmán, a lieutenant in Hernan Cortés's army, committed atrocities against the local population in his efforts to conquer western Mexico. He was eventually arrested by the Spanish authorities, and in 1537 Vasco de Quiroga was appointed bishop of Michoacán. To regain the trust of the indigenous people, he established model villages in the area and promoted the development of *artesanía* (crafts) commerce among the Purépecha. Quiroga died in 1565, and his remains were consecrated in the Basílica de Nuestra Señora de la Salud. ✉ *Bounded by Quiroga, Av. Ponce de León, Portal Hidalgo, and Dr. José María Coss.*

Fodor's Choice ★

6 **Templo de la Compañía.** Michoacán's first cathedral was begun in 1540 by order of Vasco de Quiroga and completed in 1546. When the state capital was moved to Morelia some 20 years later, the church was taken over by the Jesuits. It remains much as it was in the 16th century. Moss has grown over the crumbling stone steps outside; the dank interior is planked with thick wood floors and lined with bare wood benches. ✉ *Lerín s/n, east end of Portugal* ☎ *434/342–3083* ⏲ *Daily 8–6.*

WORTH NOTING

1 **Biblioteca Pública Gertrudis Bocanegra.** Juan O'Gorman painted a vast mural depicting the history of the region and of the Purépecha people in the back of this library in 1942. At the bottom right is Gertrudis Bocanegra, a local heroine who was shot in 1814 for refusing to divulge the revolutionaries' secrets to the Spaniards. The Biblioteca is on a lively plaza. ✉ *North side of Plaza Bocanegra* ☎ *434/342–5441* ⏲ *Daily 9–6:30.*

4 **Museo de Artes Populares.** The 16th-century home of the Colegio de San Nicolás Obispo now displays colonial and contemporary crafts, such as ceramics, masks, lacquerware, paintings, and ex-votos in its many rooms. Behind this building is a *troje* (traditional Purépecha wooden house) braced atop a stone platform. ✉ *Enseñanza Arciga* ☎ *434/342–1029* 🎟 *$3* ⏲ *Tues.–Fri. 9–6:30, weekends 9–4:30.*

NEED A BREAK?

Before heading to Lake Pátzcuaro, sit in Plaza Vasco de Quiroga and savor the rich Michoacán ice cream available under the portals on the west side of the plaza. Or sip a Doña Paca cappuccino with *rompope* (spiked eggnog) at the café in front of Mansión Iturbe.

GO WITH A GUIDE

Guide **Francisco Castilleja** (✉ *Centro Eronga, Profr. Urueta 105* ☎ *434/344-0167*) knows a lot about pre-Hispanic philosophy, history, archaeology, and medicinal herbs. He speaks fluent English, German, French, and Spanish. Guide and anthropologist **Miguel Angel Nuñez** (☎ *434/344-0108*) specializes in off-the-beaten-path visits to indigenous communities as well as local sights. He speaks Spanish, English, and German.

WHERE TO EAT

$$ MEXICAN ✕ **Doña Paca.** At this terrific family-run restaurant you'll find some of the best examples of local cuisine. Look for the fish specials and the triangular tamale-like corundas with cream sauce, which are also great for breakfast. There are also several good coffee concoctions. ✉ *Hotel Mansión Iturbe, Portal Morelos 59* ☎ *434/342–0368* 💳 *AE, MC, V.*

$ MEXICAN ★ ✕ **El Patio.** It's possible to duck into this low-key restaurant at midday to grab a strong cappuccino or glass of Mexican wine. Try the *pechuga de pollo* (chicken breast) stuffed with *huitlacoche*. For a snack go for a plate of quesadillas with a side order of guacamole. Breakfast is also served. ✉ *Plaza Vasco de Quiroga 19* ☎ *434/342–0484* 💳 *MC, V.*

$$ ECLECTIC ✕ **El Primer Piso.** On warm nights you can watch activities in the Plaza Vasco de Quiroga from a balcony table at this second-floor restaurant. The brightly colored interior is warm and inviting, and the eclectic menu provides a break from typical Pátzcuaro fare: try the pear salad with goat cheese, walnuts, and watercress, or the white-chocolate mousse with blackberries and melon cream. ✉ *Plaza Vasco de Quiroga 29* ☎ *434/342–0122* 💳 *MC, V* ⏲ *Closed Tues.*

$$ ARGENTINE ★ ✕ **El Viejo Gaucho.** Join the crowd for a festive night of live music from North, Central, and South America. Try the *churrasco Argentino* (seasoned steak) and don't forget to top it with *chimichurri* (an Argentine sauce made with fresh herbs and olive oil). Seasoned chicken on the grill is tasty, too. Most main courses are pseudo-Argentinian, but there are also pizza, hamburgers, and french fries. ✉ *Iturbe 10* ☎ *No phone* 💳 *AE, MC, V* ⏲ *Closed Sun. No lunch.*

$$ CONTEMPORARY ✕ **Priscilla's.** Though the prices would suggest a more humble dining experience, this is a first-class restaurant with excellent service in La Mansión de los Sueños. The style is traditional, with handcrafted wood furnishings made by local artisans. The international menu has

numerous fish and pasta dishes. Not to be missed is the cheesecake that melts in your mouth—Priscilla swears it is fat and sugar free! Breakfast is also served. ✉ *Ibarra 15* ☎ *434/342–5708* ▭ *AE, MC, V.*

WHERE TO STAY

$$ ★ **Hacienda Mariposas Resort & Spa.** A friendly, bilingual staff and terrific restaurant are just some of the amenities at this getaway just outside of Pátzcuaro; the place is surrounded by tens of acres of forest. It also offers horseback-riding trips, along with other eco-adventures, and even a food tour of the Purépecha region. Guest rooms have fireplaces and beds topped with down comforters, plus CD players. Transportation to and from Pátzcuaro is included. **Pros:** comfortable beds; good for families with young children. **Cons:** far from city center. ✉ *Santa Clara del Cobre Hwy., Km 3* ☎ *443/333–0762 or 434/342–4728* 🌐 *www.haciendamariposas.com* *16 rooms, 3 suites* *In-room: no a/c, refrigerator (some), DVD. In-hotel: restaurant, room service, bar, gym, spa, children's programs, laundry service, Internet terminal, parking (free), some pets allowed* ▭ *AE, MC, V* 🍽 *BP.*

$$ ★ **Hotel Ixhi.** This rustic lodge is up a winding road about 10 minutes outside of Pátzcuaro, but it's worth the bumpy ride for the stunning views of the lake (from atop El Estribo, rising far above the city) and Janítzio Island. There's also a small patio strung with hammocks. Some rooms have private terraces and kitchens; all rooms vary in size. This is a great value; reserve well in advance, as yoga groups sometimes take over the entire estate. **Pros:** breathtaking views of lake; inviting communal dining room. **Cons:** away from city, up a steep road; fills up easily. ✉ *Subida al Estribo Grande 48; head out to periférico and follow signs to Estribo* ☎ *434/342–6807* *4 rooms, 54 suites* *In-room: no a/c, safe, kitchen (some), Wi-Fi. In-hotel: restaurant, room service, bar, laundry service, Wi-Fi hotspot, parking (free), some pets allowed* ▭ *No credit cards* 🍽 *CP.*

$$ **Hotel Posada La Basílica.** On some mornings strains from Mass at the neighboring Basílica de Nuestra Señora de la Salud filter softly into this inn. The 17th-century building has comfortable, individually decorated rooms, some with fireplaces. Thick wood shutters cover floor-to-ceiling windows, large wooden beams grace the ceilings, and walls are trimmed in hand-painted colonial designs. **Pros:** fireplaces in rooms; wonderful beds; remarkable view. **Cons:** some noise problems. ✉ *Enseñanza Arciga 6* ☎ *434/342–1108* 🌐 *www.posadalabasilica.com* *9 rooms, 3 suites* *In-room: no a/c, Wi-Fi. In-hotel: restaurant, room service, bar, laundry service, Wi-Fi hotspot, parking (free)* ▭ *AE, MC, V.*

$$ Fodor's Choice ★ **La Casa Encantada.** The appealing Casa Encantada is a magnificent hotel built into a 17th-century mansion just off Pátzcuaro's main plaza. The enormous suites, which surround a courtyard with a garden and fountain, are some of the city's biggest. Though rented by the night, they're more like apartments than hotel rooms; most have kitchens and/or dining areas. Note that children under the age of 12 are discouraged from staying at the hotel. **Pros:** incredibly cheery rooms; superb grounds. **Cons:** not ideal for families; not all staff proficient in English. ✉ *Dr. José María Coss 15* ☎ *434/342–3492* 🌐 *www.lacasaencantada.com* 9

Continued on page 214

The Day of the Dead is celebrated with much fanfare throughout Mexico, but the island of Janítzio in Lake Pátzcuaro has been singled out for its elaborate ceremonies. Although onlookers outnumber mourners, and all-night partying has replaced quiet remembrance, the rituals—both playful and poignant—still shine through. The festivities start on November 1st and end the next day, but half the fun of this holiday is being here for the events leading up to it.

WAKING THE DEAD IN PÁTZCUARO

Well before the last day of October, Pátzcuaro's main plaza is jam-packed with tents selling the candy skulls and other materials needed to decorate graves. There are also concerts and exhibitions in town prior to November 1.

Sugar skulls to celebrate the Day of the Dead.

The area's large indigenous population is to thank for making these Day of the Dead celebrations so elaborate and important. Day of the Dead originated with the Tarascan (or P'urhépecha as they're known today) Indians, and the group still has many descendants in the area. The Tarasco people believed that the dead could pay a visit to their loved ones once a year. They also believe that Curicaueri, the fire god, and his brothers founded the towns along the lake and thus they are descended from these ancestor gods.

THE CEREMONY November 1–November 2

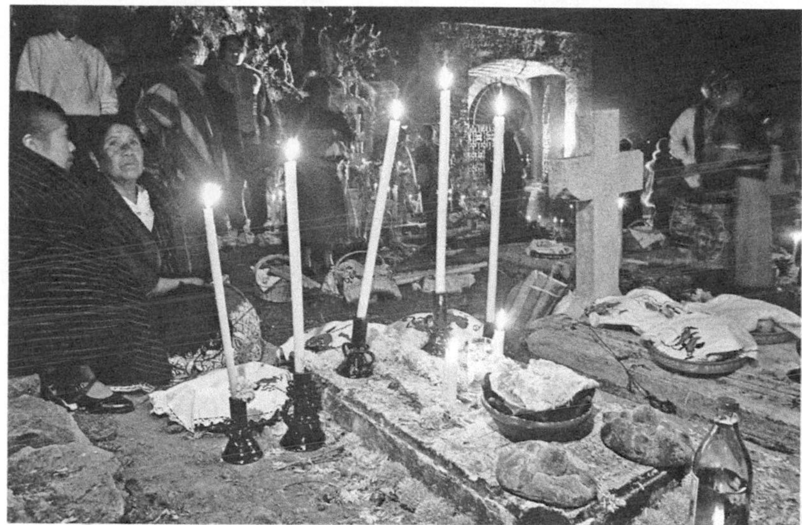

Day of the Dead celebration, Janítzio Island.

Along with decorating the graves, many families display *ofrendas* (offerings) in their homes and businesses. By **October 31st**, nearly all the houses and shops in Pátzcuaro and Janítizio have been decorated in some way. Ofrendas can include candy skulls, papier-mâché skeletons, candles, food and liquor, cigarettes, toys (for deceased children), and *cempasúchil* (yellow marigolds).

On the 31st the docks are packed with families going to and from the island, bringing supplies and decorations to gravesites or picking up items in Pátzcuaro to complete their ofrendas.

The celebration officially gets started at the crack of dawn on November 1st. P'urhépecha Indians have a ceremonial duck hunt; the ducks that are caught are cooked and incorporated into cemetery ofrendas later that night.

From 5 AM to 9 AM, the deceased children are honored in the ceremony of the *angelitos* (little angels). At 5 the church bells start ringing as a call for both the spirits of the children and the relatives honoring them. Mass begins in Janítzio's small chapel at 6. When mass is done, the women and children of the families go to the graveyard, where they clean the tombstones (sometimes no more than a wooden cross) and place their ofrendas around the graves. More people filter into the cemetery. If a family is participating in

Handmade skeletons—a common symbol.

(above) Colorful and haunting figurines.
(left) Townspeople tending to graves.

its first Day of the Dead ceremony, they might bring a band with them as they make their procession from house to graveyard. Prayers, chanting, music, and incense fill the air until the ceremony ends around 9 AM.

The ceremony for deceased adults won't take place until midnight, so the rest of the day is spent preparing for it and setting up a stage for the ceremonial dances that will precede the nighttime festivities.

There are two main dances performed before the **midnight vigil** begins. The *Danza de los Viejitos* (Dance of the Little Old Men), is performed by children dressed up as old peasant men. The children attempt to appear bent over with age as they complete this intricate dance. The *Pescado Blanco* (White Fish) dance is an act of homage to the lake, as fishing is this village's most important source of income.

At midnight, processions head back into the graveyard to honor the adults who have passed away. The church bells ring all night long, while families sit by the graves, some praying and chanting, some just sitting silently. Candles and incense are lit. At dawn the ceremony is concluded with a reading from the Bible, after which families collect their offerings and head home.

THE RITUALS OF DEATH

- Townspeople will pitch in to decorate the graves of people with no surviving relatives.
- Incense is burned because the aroma is thought to help guide the spirits to the ofrendas.
- Ofrendas will often include the deceased's favorite foods, along with traditional foods, the most common of which are *calabaza en tacha,* a sweet pumpkin dessert; some kind of tamal; and *pan de muerto,* a sweet bread that's actually European in origin (though the Spanish never shaped their altar breads into skulls, teardrops, crosses, human figures, and animals).
- Families often construct wooden arches decorated with cempasúchil as part of their cemetery ofrendas. For the first three years after a person's death, this arch is made by the person's godparents, who present it to the parents of the deceased on November 1.

(top) Decorated sugar figurines.
(above) A hearty offering.
(left) Laughing cartoon skeletons.

TIPS

The first rule of attending Day of the Dead ceremonies is to book way in advance. Some hotels are booked solid up to a year early, but booking six months ahead should still leave you with some choices.

If you don't like crowds (or a certain level of commercialism), don't bother with Janítzio. Instead, inquire at the tourist office about other towns in the area that have similar festivities. Note that the lakeside village of Tzintzuntzan will be nearly as crowded as Janítzio, and with a livelier crowd.

rooms, 3 suites ♿ *In-room: no a/c, no phone, kitchen (some), Wi-Fi. In-hotel: laundry service, Wi-Fi hotspot, parking (free), some pets allowed* ▭ *No credit cards* 🍽 *BP.*

$$$$ Fodor's Choice ★ **La Mansión de los Sueños.** Priscilla Ann Madsen's dream of owning a hotel in Pátzcuaro came true when she found this 17th-century mansion. Now completely restored, each of the rooms and suites is decorated with original hand-painted murals and a mixture of traditional and modern furnishings; fireplaces make some of them extra cozy. One room even has its own patio and Jacuzzi. There are three interior patios and surrounding gardens. **Pros:** fireplaces in some rooms; incredibly comfortable beds. **Cons:** on the pricey side. ✉ *Ibarra 15* ☎ *434/342–5708* 🌐 *www.prismas.com.mx* *10 suites, 2 master suites* ♿ *In-room: no a/c, refrigerator (some), Wi-Fi. In-hotel: 2 restaurants, room service, bar, spa, laundry service, Wi-Fi hotspot, parking (paid)* ▭ *AE, MC, V* 🍽 *BP.*

FOOD FOR THOUGHT

Pátzcuaro restaurants specialize in seafood, such as whitefish, *trucha* (trout), and *charales* and *boquerones* (two small, locally caught fish served as appetizers). Many focus on local Purépecha dishes, such as sopa tarasca, a delicious black bean soup. Since lunch is the big meal of the day, many dining establishments are shuttered by 9. For the city's best tortas, tacos, tamales, and carnitas, head straight to the market (called the Mercado, on Calle Libertad, just west of the Biblioteca) and browse its stalls. Grab one of the simple plaza tables, take in the nighttime bustle, and dig in.

$$ ★ **Mansión Iturbe.** Stone archways ring plant-filled courtyards in this 17th-century mansion. Rooms, with large wood-and-glass doors, are partially carpeted. Bicycles are lent to guests for a few hours per stay; every fourth night is free, and breakfast is included—except during high season. The owners are an excellent source of information regarding Pátzcuaro and the surrounding areas. Be sure to check out the restaurant, Doña Paca, and its tasty coffee drinks. **Pros:** friendly staff; wonderful coffee bar. **Cons:** rooms can get cold. ✉ *Portal Morelos 59* ☎ *434/342–0368* 🌐 *www.mansioniturbe.com* *12 rooms* ♿ *In-room: no a/c, no phone, safe, Wi-Fi. In-hotel: 2 restaurants, bar, bicycles, laundry service, Wi-Fi hotspot, parking (free)* ▭ *AE, MC, V* 🍽 *BP.*

NIGHTLIFE

FOLK DANCE

The **Danza de los Viejitos** is a widely known regional dance performed with mariachi music during Thursday and Saturday dinner (at 9 PM) at **Hotel Posada de Don Vasco** (✉ *Av. Lazaro Cardenas 450* ☎ *434/342–0227*) for about $13 (includes buffet dinner). On weekends dancers perform the Dance of the Old Men for tips in the plaza and outside the boarding area to Janítzio.

LIVE MUSIC

For a night of live music, head to **El Viejo Gaucho** (✉ *At Mansion Iturbe, Portal Morelos 59* ☎ *434/342–0368*) to hear some covers of American pop tunes as well as Mexican folk songs.

SHOPPING

Pátzcuaro has some of Mexico's finest folk-art shopping. There are good deals at the stalls outside the Basílica and the marketplace off Plaza Bocanegra.

Artesanías Mojiganga (✉ *Plaza Vasco de Quiroga 29* ☎ *434/342–4695*), an intimate group of stores, offers a variety of ceramics, clothing, and folk art. Since 1898 the family-run **Chocolate Casero Joaquinita** (✉ *Enseñanza Arciga 38* ☎ *434/342–5607*) has been concocting delectable homemade cinnamon-spiced hot-chocolate tablets. Don't miss the stands in front of the Basílica and at the daily mercado west of Plaza Chica for inexpensive local crafts. **Mantas Tipicas** (✉ *Dr. José María Coss 5* ☎ *434/342–1324*) sells hand-loomed tablecloths, place mats, and napkins, as well as curtain and cushion fabric.

★ Visit the doorway of Jesús García Zavala at **Platería García** (✉ *Enseñanza Arciga 28* ☎ *No phone*) for hand-worked silver Purépecha jewelry in the pre-Columbian tradition. **Santa Teresa Velas y Cirios** (✉ *Portugal 1* ☎ *434/342–4997*) sells handmade candles.

SIDE TRIPS FROM PÁTZCUARO

17 km (10½ mi) northeast of Pátzcuaro.

When the Spanish arrived to colonize the region in the 16th century, some 40,000 Purépecha lived in this lakeshore village, which they called "place of the hummingbirds." The ruins of the pyramid-shape temples, or *yacatas*, in the ancient capital of the Purépecha kingdom, still stand and are open to the public. There is also a 16th-century Franciscan monastery where Spanish friars attempted to convert the Indians to Christianity, with what are said to be the oldest olive trees in the Americas. The village is still known for the straw and ceramic crafts made by the Purépecha Indians and sold in the market on the main street. The bus marked Quiroga takes a half hour to get from Pátzcuaro's Central Camionera to Tzintzuntzan.

Guadalajara

Palacio de Gobierno, Guadalajara

WORD OF MOUTH

"We took a bus into Guadalajara for a day and then a taxi back to Tlaquepaque. We were glad we were staying there as Guadalajara was big and busy. One day we hired a driver to take us and pick us up in Ajijic, the cute little town where a friend lives. She showed us some of her town; we had a nice lunch and walked along lake Chapala."

—judi

www.fodors.com/community

WELCOME TO GUADALAJARA

TOP REASONS TO GO

★ **The chance to see murals by Orozco:** Titanic works by this distinguished artist adorn several buildings.

★ **Shopping for crafts at the source:** Master craftsmen practice their art in the suburbs of Tonalá and Tlaquepaque.

★ **Experiencing the most Mexican of Mexican traditions:** Jalisco State is the land of tequila, mariachi, and *jarabe tapatío* (the hat dance).

★ **Varied excursions:** Close to the city are Mexico's largest lake and the town of Tequila, the birthplace of the country's famous firewater.

★ **Visiting the site of pre-Hispanic ruins:** Los Guachimontones, in the foothills of Tequila Volcano, is redefining western Mexico's archaeological past.

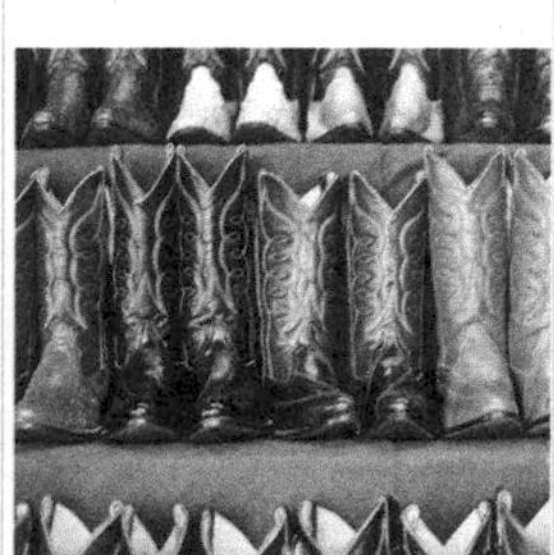

1 Zapopan. Zapopan is a high-end suburb enveloping Guadalajara's west side. The town is full of tony shopping malls and residential areas which sometimes stretch into impoverished fringe neighborhoods. It's also home to Jalisco's most revered religious icon, the four-century-old Virgin of Zapopan, housed in the main plaza's beautiful cathedral.

2 Tonalá. A formerly independent village swallowed by the city, Tonalá retains a small-town aura in its center and is home to some of Mexico's most celebrated claysmiths and glass blowers, many of whom open their workshops to visitors.

3 Tlaquepaque. The metropolitan area's tourist and handicraft magnet is Tlaquepaque, a district of shops, restaurants and bed-and-breakfasts on the southeast side of Guadalajara's sprawl.

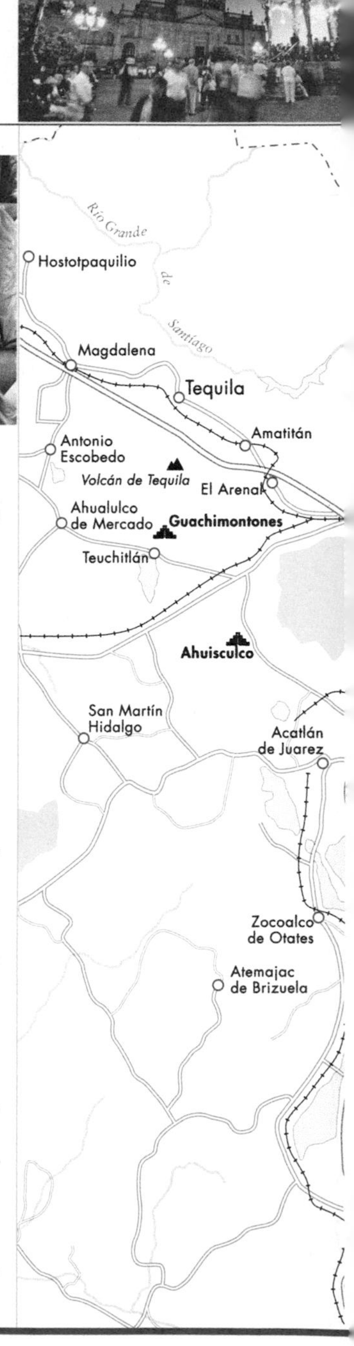

GETTING ORIENTED

Guadalajara rests on a mile-high plain of the Sierra Madre del Occidente, surrounded on three sides by rugged hills and on the fourth by the spectacular Barranca de Oblatos (Oblatos Canyon). Mexico's second-largest city has an official population of about 4 million, though most estimates put the number of residents of the metro area closer to double this number, and is the capital of the western state of Jalisco. There's a mishmash of terrain here: pine-forest mountain ranges, semi-deserts, and coastal mangrove swamps.

GUADALAJARA PLANNER

Stay A While!

Guadalajara's hotel operators and tourism officials regularly lament the fact that foreign tourists average just two days in their city. Rightly, they point out that visitors can spend at least a week in and around the City of Roses. Unless you've got afterburners on your shoes, it will take at least three days to do justice to the historic district and the artisan hubs of Tonalá and Tlaquepaque, and to savor the region's unique food, drinks, and festivals.

Booking in Advance

Major hotels are rarely booked to capacity, so finding a room at the last minute in Guadalajara is not usually problematic. But plan ahead, just in case. During the winter low season some hotels slash rates considerably, making this a good time to visit. Make reservations well in advance if you're planning on staying at a smaller establishment.

Hotel Tips

Many hotels are on busy intersections, in which case rooms higher up or in the interior tend to be less noisy. Some hotels have windows that won't open, so ask for a room with a balcony if fresh air is important to you.

Festivals and Special Events

Guadalajara's major events include the Encuentro Internacional del Mariachi y la Charrería, a mariachi gathering that takes place from the last days of August through the first week in September, with events downtown in the historic district. Highlights are the inaugural parade and an outdoor gala in Plaza Liberación. The following month brings las Fiestas de Octubre country fair, with nightly live music and other events in the *palenque* (fairground). A 10-day book fair starting in November attracts literary giants from Spanish-speaking countries and others from around the world.

To Rent or Not to Rent?

Driving in Guadalajara isn't for the faint of heart. Sure, Tapatío drivers are tamer than those in Mexico City, but traffic can still be wild. You are taking your life in your hands if you try the bus system. Taxis are cheap and your best bet in the city; if you plan on exploring outlying regions by yourself, renting a car is the best option. You can also hire a driver who specifically does day trips or bargain with a taxi driver.

If the Beach Beckons

You won't find any beaches in Guadalajara, but the city is only a 4½-hour drive (or 5-hour bus ride) from Puerto Vallarta, the hub of the Pacific Coast Resorts. The smaller, less touristy beaches of Sayulita and Manzanillo are even closer at about a 3½-hour drive. With a little planning, these completely different destinations can be combined.

Safety and Health Concerns

While Guadalajara is a relatively safe place, it still has crime, like all major cities. The best advice? Be aware of your surroundings at all times. If possible, avoid ATMs at night and be watchful of anyone following you from a bank. Try not to walk around alone at night. And, if possible, attempt to get taxis from a *sitio* (taxi stand) rather than flagging them down on the street.

While the H1N1 virus is thought to have developed in Mexico City, you are no more at risk of catching the virus in Mexico than in the United States. Take normal precautions like washing your hands and avoiding touching your face. You'll see antiseptic hand gel placed in key locations across Guadalajara, including in malls, restaurants and tourist attractions. Guadalajara has experienced a growing number of dengue fever cases, a virus contracted from mosquitoes that has seen an increasing number of outbreaks in many Latin and South American countries. The best protection is to wear long sleeves and pants during cooler times, and to use insect repellent containing DEET.

Where to Stay

Tourists often opt to stay in colonial-style hotels in the Centro, which is convenient to many of Guadalajara's sights. For a lovely stay in the historic district of Guadalajara, the refined and quiet Hotel de Mendoza is your best bet. But Guadalajara is a sprawling city, so chances are you'll have to take taxis or public transportation at some point regardless of where you stay during your visit. Modern business hotels in the Providencia, Plaza del Sol, and Minerva neighborhoods beckon both work and pleasure travelers alike. For a real treat, stay at the plush Quinta Real near Fuente Minerva.

WHAT IT COSTS IN DOLLARS

	¢	$	$$	$$$	$$$$
Restaurants	under $5	$5–$10	$11–$15	$16–$25	over $25
Hotels	under $50	$50–$75	$76–$150	$151–$250	over $250

Restaurant prices are for a main course excluding tax and tip. Hotel prices are for two people in a standard double room in high season.

How's the Weather?

Guadalajara is said to have one of the most pleasing climates in the world. For most of the year daytime temperatures hover in the low eighties and the nights are clear and cool. The city is susceptible to bouts of dry heat in May and June, when the temperature can surge to 38°C (100°F). Afternoon and evening downpours occurring July through early October douse the heat (and bring air pollution to its lowest annual levels), but turn streets into rivers. Temperatures in the mornings and nights are cooler from November to early February (lows may plunge into the 40s).

Whatever the weather in Guadalajara, the most pleasing pastimes include exploring the city's charms on foot (during the rainy season, bring an umbrella or a raincoat, or simply time it right and plan to be indoors—perhaps sipping margaritas—during the afternoon downpours).

What to Pack

Guadalajara is a casual city, though you rarely see locals in shorts. Bring clothes for a warm climate, but be sure to toss a sweater or two into your suitcase for chilly nights. Some of the more posh restaurants will demand your Sunday best, so make sure you bring something presentable.

Updated by Meghan Sullivan

THE GUADALAJARA REGION'S MUST-SEE SIGHTS can be found in four major areas: Guadalajara city itself, Zapopan, Tlaquepaque, and Tonalá. Each can each be navigated on foot in a few hours, hitting the major sites, though to get a good feel for these places one must devote at least a day to each—and more to Guadalajara city.

In Guadalajara city, the historic Guadalajara Centro houses many of the city's key tourist attractions, but several of the surrounding neighborhoods are also worth a visit. In Zona Minerva, due west of the Centro; Plaza del Sol, southwest; and Providencia, northwest, you'll find modern hotels, boutique shops, and some of the city's best cafés, bars, and restaurants. Sample the Zona Minerva district, for example, by strolling down the Avenida Juarez–Avenida Vallarta corridor; Avenida Vallarta is closed to vehicular traffic from 8 AM to 2 PM every Sunday for Via Recreativa, where locals and tourists gather to walk or bike.

GETTING HERE AND AROUND

If you're flying here, Aeropuerto Internacional Libertador Miguel Hidalgo is 16½ km (10 mi) south of Guadalajara. It's a 30 minute drive to Guadalajara, but the trip can be delayed in either direction by slow-moving caravans of trucks and weekend traffic. A taxi from the airport into the city costs around $20. The seven- to eight-hour bus ride (it takes 5 hours by car) between Guadalajara and Mexico City usually costs $40 and is generally efficient and comfortable. Many lines have large recliners, offer a snack and beverage, and provide free wireless Internet service. Estrella Blanca, ETN, Primera Plus, and Transportes al Pacifico have many daily departures. Toll highway 15D is the safest and quickest route between Mexico City and Guadalajara.

ESSENTIALS

Bus Contacts **Estrella Blanca** (☎ *55/5729–0807 from Mexico City, 33/3619–2309;* 🌐 *www.estrellablanca.com.mx*). **ETN** (☎ *33/3600–0477; 33/3770–3777; 01800/360–4200 toll-free in Mexico* 🌐 *www.etn.com.mx*). **Primera Plus** (☎ *33/3600–0014; 01800/375–7587 toll-free in Mexico* 🌐 *www.primeraplus.com.mx*). **Transportes al Pacificio** (☎ *33/3668–5920* 🌐 *www.tap.com.mx*).

Internet **Compu-Flash** (✉ *Calle Priciliano Sánchez 402, Centro Histórico* ☎ *33/3614–7165*). **La Vaca Loca** (✉ *Juárez 145, Tlaquepaque* ☎ *33/3838–6860*).

Medical Assistance **Hospital San Javier** (✉ *Av. Pablo Casals 640, Col. Providencia, Zona Minerva* ☎ *33/3669–0222*).**Hospital Puerta De Hierro** (✉ *Av. Empresarios 150,* Col. Puerta de Hierro, *Zapopan* ☎ *33/3669–0222; 01800/263-CMPDH toll free in Mexico*).

Post Office **Main Post Office** (✉ *Av. Alcalde 500, Centro Histórico* ☎ *33/3614–4770*).

Rental Cars **Alamo** (✉ *Av. Niños Héroes 982, south of Centro Histórico* ☎ *01800/849–8001 toll-free in Mexico; 33/3688–8078 at airport* 🌐 *www.alamo-mexico.com.mx*). **Avis** (✉ *Hilton, Av. de las Rosas 2933, Rinconda del Bosque* ☎ *33/3671–3422; 33/3688–5784 at airport* 🌐 *www.avis.com.mx*). **Budget** (✉ *Hotel Misión Carlton, Av. Niños Héroes 125, at Av. 16 de Septiembre, Centro Histórico* ☎ *01800/700–1700 toll-free in Mexico; 33/3688–5216 at airport* 🌐 *www.budget.com.mx*).

OPEN-AIR BUSES

The **Tapatío Tour** (✉ *Morelos 231, Centro Histórico* ☎ *33/3613–0887; 33/3614–7430; 01800/001–1827 toll free in Mexico* 🌐 *www.tapatiotour.com/*) is an easy way to get an overview of the city and its history. The open-air double-decker buses leave every 30 minutes from Rotunda de los Jalisciences Ilustres (to the left of the cathedral) and cost 90 pesos (less than $9) per person. The one-hour tour is narrated in six different languages via headphones. The English version is informative, though the Texas accent and minor slip-ups of the narrator can provide unintended humor. Don't forget to bring a hat if you intend to sit up top, as the sun can be strong. In addition to the city tour, the group offers a trip to Tlaquepaque, where they drop you off to wander. You can take any of their buses back depending on how long you want to stay; they depart from the drop-off point about every 30 minutes.

5

Visitor and Tour Info **Guadalajara Municipal Tourist Office** (✉ *Morelos 1596, Centro Histórico* ☎ *33/3668–1600*). **Jalisco State Tourist Office** (✉ *Calle Morelos 102, Centro Histórico* ☎ *33/3668–1600; 01800/363–2200 toll-free in Mexico* 🌐 *visita.jalisco.gob.mx* ✉ *Palacio de Gobierno, Av. Corona 31, Centro Histórico* ☎ *33/3668–1601 Ext. 34730* ✉ *Calle Madero 407-A, 2nd fl., Chapala* ☎ *376/765–3141*). **Tlaquepaque Municipal Tourist Office** (✉ *Calle Morelos 288, top fl., Tlaquepaque* ☎ *33/3662–7050 Ext. 2319*). **Tonalá Municipal Tourist Office** (✉ *Av. de los Tonaltecas Sur 140, Tonalá* ☎ *33/3284–3092 or 33/3284–3093*). **Tourist Board of Zapopan** (✉ *Calle Eva Briseña s/n, next to Basilica, Zapopan* ☎ *33/3818–2200 Ext. 1102 or 1103* 🌐 *www.zapopan.gob.mx*).

EXPLORING

CENTRO HISTÓRICO

The downtown core is a mishmash of modern and old buildings connected by a series of large plazas, four of which were designed to form a cross when viewed from the sky, with the cathedral in the middle. Though some remain, many colonial-era structures were razed before authorities got serious about preserving them. Conservation laws, however, merely prohibit such buildings from being altered or destroyed; there are no provisions on upkeep, as plenty of abandoned, crumbling buildings indicate.

Must-visit sights include the Palacio del Gobierno and the Instituto Cultural Cabañas; both have phenomenal murals by José Clemente Orozco. Even if you're not in the mood to shop, you should experience the bustling Mercado Libertad. Explore the district in the morning if you dislike crowds; otherwise, you'll get a more immediate sense of Mexico's vibrant culture if you wait for street performers and vendors to emerge around the huge Plaza Tapatía in the afternoon.

Allot at least three hours for the Centro, longer if you really want to absorb the main sights and stroll along the pedestrian streets.

TOP ATTRACTIONS

1 **Catedral.** Begun in 1561 and consecrated in 1618, this downtown focal point is an intriguing mélange of baroque, Gothic, and other styles. Its emblematic twin towers replaced the originals, felled by the earthquake of 1818. Ten of the silver-and-gold altars were gifts from King Fernando VII for Guadalajara's financial support of Spain during the Napoleonic Wars. Some of the world's most magnificent *retablos* (altarpieces) adorn the walls; above the sacristy (often closed to the public) is Bartolomé Esteban Murillo's priceless 17th-century painting *The Assumption of the Virgin*. In a loft above the main entrance is a magnificent 19th-century French organ. ⊠ *Av. 16 de Septiembre, between Av. Hidalgo and Calle Morelos, Centro Histórico* ☎ *33/3614–5504; 33/3614–3058* 🎫 *Free* ⏲ *Daily 8–8.*

7 Fodor's Choice ★ **Instituto Cultural Cabañas.** Financed by Bishop Juan Ruiz de Cabañas and constructed by Spanish architect-sculptor Manuel Tolsá, this neoclassical-style cultural center, also known as Hospicio Cabañas, was originally opened in 1810 as a shelter for widows, orphans, and the elderly. The Instituto's 106 rooms and 23 flower-filled patios now house art exhibitions (ask for an English-speaking guide). The main chapel displays murals by José Clemente Orozco, including *The Man of Fire,* his masterpiece. In all, there are 57 murals by Orozco, plus many of his smaller paintings, cartoons, and drawings. Kids can wonder at the murals, some which appear as optical illusions, and investigate the labyrinthine compound. The center, named a UNESCO World Heritage Site in 1997, is closed Monday. ⊠ *Calle Cabañas 8, Centro Histórico* ☎ *33/3818–2800* 🎫 *$7; free Tues.* ⏲ *Tues.–Sun. 10–6.*

5 **Museo del Periodismo y de las Artes Gráficas.** Guadalajara's first printing press was set up here in 1792; in 1810 it printed the first 2,000 copies of "El Despertador Americano," which impelled would-be Mexicans to join the War of Independence. You can see historic newspapers, printing presses, and recording equipment in this mansion, known as the Casa de los Perros for the two wrought-iron *perros* (dogs) guarding its roof. The permanent collection, opened in 1994, isn't as exciting as the traveling exhibitions of local and national press, art, and photography, which are usually on the top floor. ⊠ *Av. Alcalde 225, between Calle Reforma and Calle San Felipe, Centro Histórico* ☎ *33/3613–9285 or 33/3613–9286* 🎫 *$1* ⏲ *Tues.–Sat. 10–6, Sun. 10–3.*

3 **Museo Regional de Guadalajara.** Constructed as a seminary and public library in 1701, this has been the Guadalajara Regional Museum's home since 1918. First-floor galleries contain artifacts tracing western Mexico's history from prehistoric times through the Spanish conquest. Five 19th-century carriages, including one used by General Porfirio Díaz, are on the second-floor balcony. There's an impressive collection of European and Mexican paintings. ⊠ *Calle Liceo 60, Centro Histórico* ☎ *33/3614–9957* 🎫 *$3.50* ⏲ *Tues.–Sat. 9–5:30, Sun. 9–4:30.*

10 ★ **Palacio de Gobierno.** The adobe structure of 1643 was replaced with this churrigueresque and neoclassical stone structure in the 18th century.

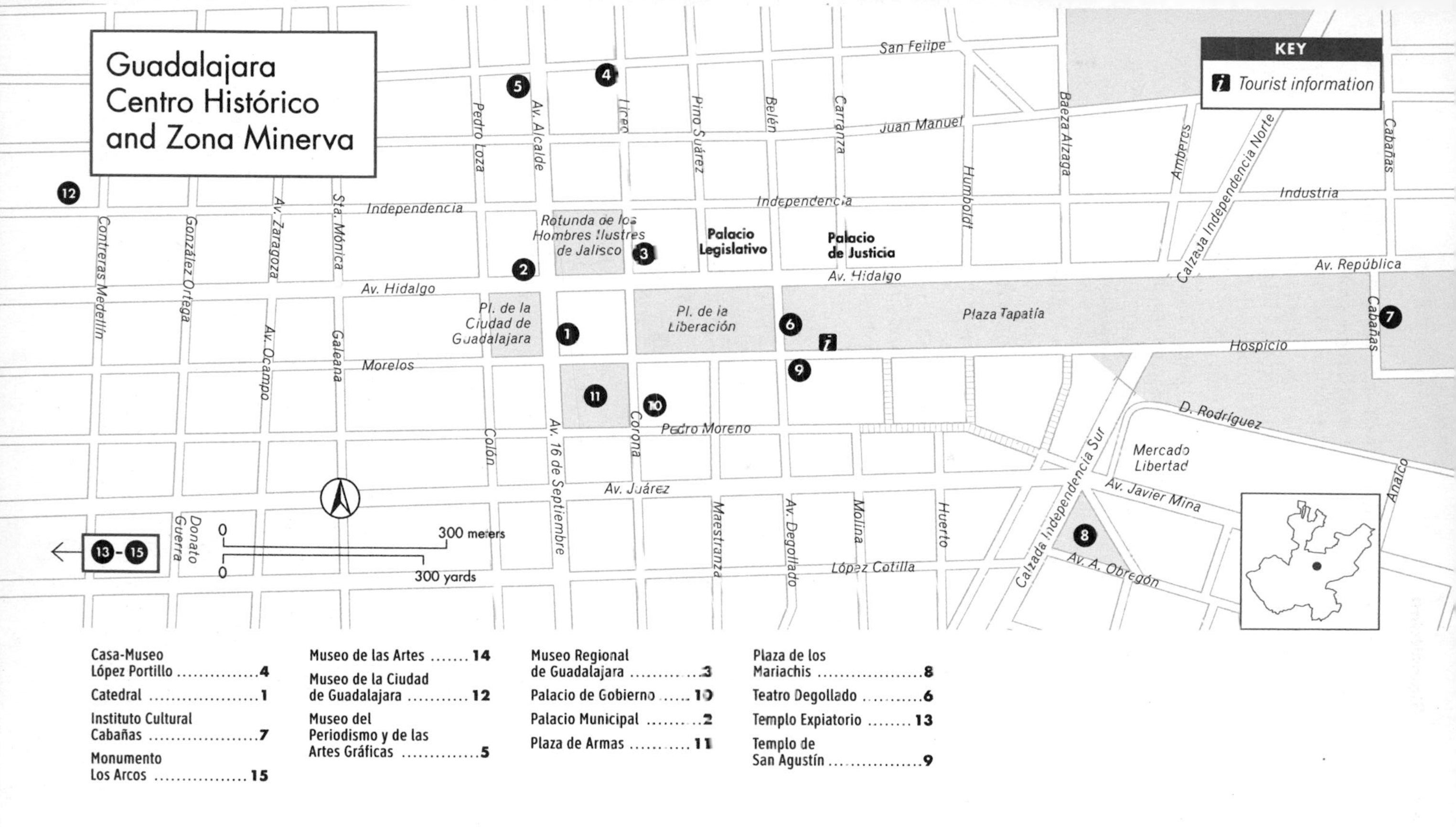

Guadalajara Centro Histórico and Zona Minerva
KEY
Tourist information
San Felipe
Juan Manuel
Independencia
Av. Hidalgo
Morelos
Av. Juárez
López Cotilla
Hospicio
Plaza Tapatía
Pl. de la Liberación
Pl. de la Ciudad de Guadalajara
Rotunda de los Hombres Ilustres de Jalisco
Palacio Legislativo
Palacio de Justicia
Mercado Libertad
D. Rodríguez
Av. Javier Mina
Av. A. Obregón
Calzada Independencia Sur
Calzada Independencia Norte
Av. República
Industria
Cabañas
Analco
Amberes
Baeza Alzaga
Humboldt
Carranza
Belén
Pino Suárez
Liceo
Av. Alcalde
Pedro Loza
Sta. Mónica
Av. Zaragoza
González Ortega
Contreras Medellín
Galeana
Av. Ocampo
Donato Guerra
Colón
Av. 16 de Septiembre
Corona
Pedro Moreno
Maestranza
Av. Degollado
Molina
Huerto
300 meters
300 yards
13 - 15

Within are Jalisco's state offices and two of José Clemente Orozco's most passionate murals, both worth the visit alone. One just past the entrance depicts a gigantic Father Miguel Hidalgo looming amid figures representing oppression and slavery. Upstairs, the other mural (look for a door marked CONGRESO) portrays Hidalgo, Juárez, and other Reform-era figures. ✉ *Av. Corona 31, between Calle Morelos and Pedro Moreno, Centro Histórico* ☎ *33/3668–1800* 🎫 *Free* 🕘 *Daily 9–8.*

6 ★ **Teatro Degollado.** Inaugurated in 1866, this magnificent theater was modeled after Milan's La Scala. The refurbished theater preserves its traditional red-and-gold color scheme, and its balconies ascend to a multitier dome adorned with Gerardo Suárez's depiction of Dante's *Divine Comedy.* The theater is home to the Jalisco Philharmonic. ✉ *Av. Degollado between Av. Hidalgo and Calle Morelos, Centro Histórico* ☎ *33/3614–4773* 🎫 *$8–$35* 🕘 *Hours vary.*

9 **Templo de San Agustín.** One of the city's oldest churches has been remodeled many times since its consecration in 1573, but the sacristy is original. The building to the left of the church, originally an Augustinian cloister, is now the University of Guadalajara's Escuela de Música (School of Music). Free recitals and concerts are held on its patio. ✉ *Calle Morelos 188, at Av. Degollado, Centro Histórico* ☎ *33/3614–5365* 🎫 *Free* 🕘 *Daily 9–11:30 and 5–8.*

WORTH NOTING

4 **Casa-Museo López Portillo.** For a taste of how the wealthy *jalisciense* (citizens of Jalisco) once lived, visit the former digs of Guadalajara's López Portillo family. The brood included writers and politicians, such as an early-20th-century Jalisco governor and his grandson, José López Portillo, Mexico's president from 1976 to 1982. The stunning collection of 17th- through 20th-century European furniture and accessories is a big hit with antiques lovers. (A former museum administrator was so enamored that she allegedly took home some goblets.) ✉ *Calle Liceo 177, at Calle San Felipe, Centro Histórico* ☎ *33/1201–8720* 🎫 *Free* 🕘 *Tues.–Sat. 10–5, Sun. 10–3.*

2 **Palacio Municipal.** Inside City Hall are murals of the city's founding, painted by Guadalajara native Gabriel Flores. If you visit, take the convenient (though technically unaffiliated) one-hour guided tram tours of Guadalajara's historic center (50 pesos), which depart from Plaza Guadalajara across the street every hour between 10 and 6. Headsets with taped tours in English and Spanish are available. ✉ *Av. Hidalgo at Av. Alcalde, Centro Histórico* ☎ *No phone* 🎫 *Free* 🕘 *Daily 9* AM*–8* PM.

11 **Plaza de Armas.** The State Band of Jalisco and the Municipal Band sometimes play at the bandstand on Tuesday around 6:30 PM. ✉ *Av. Corona between Calle Morelos and Pedro Moreno, across from Palacio de Gobierno, Centro Histórico.*

8 **Plaza de los Mariachis.** This small, triangular plaza south of the Mercado Libertad was once the ideal place to tip up a beer and experience the most Mexican of music. The once-placid spot is now boxed in by a busy street, a market, and a run-down neighborhood. It's safest to visit in the day or early evening; mariachi serenades start at about $15 a song. Use

PUBLIC TRANSPORT

Though not always convenient to where you need to go, Guadalajara's underground *tren ligero* (light-rail train) system is clean, safe, and efficient. Line 1 runs north–south along Avenida Federalismo from the Periférico (city beltway) Sur to Periférico Norte, near the Benito Juárez Auditorium. Line 2 runs east–west along Juárez from Tetlán in eastern Guadalajara to Avenida Federalismo. Lines 1 and 2 form a "T," meeting at the Juárez station at Parque Revolución, at the corner of Avenida Federalismo and Avenida Juárez. Trains run every 10 minutes from 5 AM to about 10:30 PM; a token good for one trip costs about 20¢.

In addition, the somewhat controversial Macrobus (🌐 *www.macrobus.gob.mx*), a new bus system with separate (and thus faster than regular traffic) road lanes, started running its first line in March 2009 along Calzada Independencia; at this writing, service on two more lines should be available by late 2010. The buses, some running express, provide service Monday–Saturday from 5–11 and Sunday 6–11. Cost varies depending on the type of card you buy; the average is 50 cents per ride.

the pedestrian overpass from the south side of Plaza Tapatía to avoid heavy traffic. ✉ *Calz. Independencia Sur, Centro Histórico.*

ZONA MINERVA

Also known as Zona Rosa (Pink Zone), this district west of the Centro Histórico is arguably the pulse of the city. At night a seemingly endless strip of the region's trendiest restaurants and watering holes lights up Avenida Vallarta east of Avenida Enrique Díaz de León. Victorian mansions, art galleries, a striking church, and two emblematic monuments—the Fuente Minerva (Minerva Fountain) and the Monumento Los Arcos—are scattered throughout the tree-lined boulevards.

The best way to get here from the Centro is by cab. Museo de las Artes requires two hours when all its exhibits are open. Budget an hour for the Templo Expiatorio across the street.

You can cover the relatively small Museo de la Ciudad in an hour. The larger Museo de las Artes, a 10-minute walk west, requires two hours when all its exhibits are open. Budget an hour for the Templo Expiatorio across the street. The Monumento Los Arcos and the Fuente Minerva are quick stops.

TOP ATTRACTIONS

14 **Museo de las Artes.** The University of Guadalajara's contemporary-art museum is in this exquisite early-20th-century building. The permanent collection includes several murals by Orozco. Revolving exhibits have contemporary works from Latin America, Europe, and the United States. ✉ *Av. Juárez 975, Centro Histórico* ☎ *33/3134–1664* 🌐 *www.museodelasartes.udg.mx* 🎫 *Free* 🕐 *Tues.–Fri. 10–6, weekends 10–4.*

13 **Templo Expiatorio.** The striking neo-Gothic Church of Atonement is Guadalajara's most breathtaking church. Modeled after Italy's Orvieto

MASKED CRUSADERS

Even if you are not a WWE wrestling fan, attending a **Lucha Libre** ⊠ *Mediano 67,* ☎ *33/3617-3401)* match in Guadalajara is an option few can pass up. But this unique experience is not for the easily offended: while watching the matches between masked heroes and villains, spectators scream obscenities and other uncouth sayings—in Spanish and good fun, of course—at the wrestlers and other spectators. It's about $10 for a ticket to a night of matches, held on Tuesday and Sundays, if you want a seat with the "rich" crowd, or $2 to stand in the balcony with the "poor." Kids tickets cost $1. Alternatively, the local bar chain **Red Pub** ⊠ *Bernardo de Balbuena 145,* ☎ *33/3616-3474)* offers group trips to the matches for $8, including ticket price, a rather rambunctious bus ride to the event and a beer. Call in advance for reservations.

Cathedral, it has phenomenal stained-glass windows—observe the rose window above the choir and pipe organ. ⊠ *Calle Díaz de León 930, at Av. López Cotilla, Centro Histórico* ☎ *33/3825–3410* 🎫 *Free* 🕒 *Daily 6:30* AM*–10:30* PM.

WORTH NOTING

15 **Monumento Los Arcos.** The double arches of this monument span Avenida Vallarta, a block east of Fuente Minerva. Reminiscent of the Arc de Triomphe, the neoclassical structure has an intriguing mural inside and a winding stairway to the roof, where there's a view of the fountain and the avenue below. Enter through the south leg, where there's a small tourist office. ⊠ *Av. Vallarta 2641, at Lopez Mateos Sur, Zona Minerva* ☎ *33/3615–1182* 🎫 *Free* 🕒 *Weekdays 9–6; Sat. and Sun 9-3.*

12 **Museo de la Ciudad de Guadalajara.** Rooms surrounding the tranquil interior patio of this bi-level colonial mansion contain artwork, artifacts, and documents about the city's development from pre-Hispanic times through the 20th century. Exhibits are labeled in Spanish only; English-language materials should be available at the entrance or in the library upstairs. ⊠ *Calle Independencia 684, Zona Minerva* ☎ *33/1201–8712* 🎫 *50¢* 🕒 *Tues.–Sat. 10–5, Sun. 10–2.*

ZAPOPAN

Mexico's former corn-producing capital is now a municipality of wealthy enclaves, modern hotels, and malls surrounded by hills of poor communities (as is much of metropolitan Guadalajara). Farther out, some farming communities remain. The central district, a good 25-minute cab ride from downtown Guadalajara, has two worthwhile museums, an aged church that's home to the city's most revered religious icon, and a pedestrian corridor punctuated by restaurants and watering holes popular with young Tapatíos. The neoclassical city hall building on the north side of the plaza has occasional art exhibits upstairs.

CLOSE UP

Guadalajara Background

The conquistadors had a difficult time founding Guadalajara. A decade of Indian uprisings and Spanish crown interference caused the capital of sprawling Nueva Galicia to shift locations three times before it reached its present perch in 1542. According to popular legend, the founding occurred behind downtown's Teatro Degollado. (A plaza behind the theater commemorates the event.) Guadalajara's name comes from a similarly named Spanish city; the word is Arabic in origin meaning "river of rocks."

Often cut off from the capital during the rainy season, Guadalajara developed independently, with the Catholic Church as its dominant social and political influence. Miguel Hidalgo's final battlefield defeat in the War of Independence from Spain—which eventually ended nearly 300 years of Spanish rule—took place here in 1811. It was briefly the capital of Mexico from 1856 to 1857, during the tumultuous reform period. Later, the city had a tardy start in the Mexican Revolution, taking up arms four years after it began in 1910.

When anti-clerical president Plutarco Elías Calles effectively criminalized Catholicism in 1926, Jalisco-area Catholics launched an armed rebellion against the government. During the bitter *Cristero* war, many priests were executed. In recent years several dozen *Cristero* martyrs have been canonized by the Vatican, a great source of pride for Guadalajara's Catholics.

Some of Zapopan's attractions are separated from its downtown area and best reached by taxi. Save money by catching Bus 275 or a northbound Tur. ■ **TIP→ Catch the Tur at Alcalde and San Felipe for 9 pesos and get off at the corner of Circunvalación and Avenida Laureles.** Alternatively, take the light-rail to Avila Camacho (Line 1), cross the street, and catch Bus 631.

An afternoon is adequate for downtown Zapopan's major sights. Spend 20 minutes at the basilica, about an hour each at the Huichol Museum and the Art Museum of Zapopan, and 15 minutes at City Hall. If you have more time, check out the market, which is across the plaza and beside City Hall, and a couple of surrounding churches before grabbing a drink or a bite on pedestrian-only Calle 20 de Noviembre or at one of the quaint restaurants or bars around the corner on Javier Mina.

TOP ATTRACTIONS

★ **Basílica de Zapopan.** This vast church with an ornate plateresque facade and *Mudejar* (Moorish) tile dome was consecrated in 1730. It's home to the Virgin (or Our Lady) of Zapopan: a 10-inch-high, corn-paste statue venerated as a source of many miracles. Every October 12 more than a million people crowd the streets around the basilica, where the Virgin is returned after a five-month tour of Jalisco's parish churches. It's an all-night fiesta capped by an early-morning procession. ✉ *Av. Hidalgo at Calle Morelos, Zona Zapopan Norte* ☎ *33/3633–6614* 🎟 *Free* ⏲ *Daily 7 AM–9 PM.*

Museo de Arte de Zapopan. Better known by its initials, MAZ, the large and modern Art Museum of Zapopan is Guadalajara's top contemporary-art gallery. The museum regularly holds expositions of distinguished Latin American painters, photographers, and sculptors, as well as occasional international shows. ✉ *Andador 20 de Noviembre 166, at Calle 28 de Enero* ☎ *33/3818–2575* 🌐 *www.mazmuseo.com* 🎫 *$1, free Tues.* ⏲ *Tues.–Sun. 10–6.*

★ **Museo Huichol Wixarica de Zapopan.** The Huichol Indians of northern Jalisco and neighboring states of Zacatecas and Nayarit are famed for their fierce independence and exquisite beadwork and yarn "paintings." This small museum has rather hokey mannequins wearing the intricately embroidered clothing of both men and women. Bilingual placards explain the Huichol religion and worldview. The gift shop sells a small inventory of beaded items, prayer arrows, and god's eyes. ✉ *Av. Hidalgo 152, Centro Histórico Zapopan* ☎ *33/3636–4430* 🎫 *2 pesos* ⏲ *Mon.–Sat. 9:30–1 and 3–6, Sun. 10–2.*

TLAQUEPAQUE

Local arts and handicrafts fill the showrooms and stores in this touristy town where you'll find carved wood furniture, colorful ceramics, and hand-stitched clothing, among other goods. Pedestrian malls and plazas are lined with more than 300 shops, many run by families with generations of experience. One of Guadalajara's most exceptional museums, which draws gifted artists for its annual ceramics competition in June, is also here.

But there's more to Tlaquepaque than shopping. The downtown area has a pleasant square and many pedestrian-only streets, making this a good place to take a stroll, even if you're not interested in all the crafts for sale. There are several good restaurants, some with outdoor seating perfect for people-watching.

■ **TIP→ Many tourists come to Tlaquepaque via the Tapatío Tour, an open-air bus that leaves from Guadalajara's historic center.**

TOP ATTRACTIONS

3 **Museo del Premio Nacional de la Cerámica Pantaleon Panduro.** The museum is named after Pantaleon Panduro, who's considered the father of modern ceramics in Jalisco. On display are prizewinning pieces from the museum's annual ceramics competition, held every June. It's possibly the best representation of modern Mexican pottery under a single roof. You can request an English-speaking guide. ✉ *Calle Priciliano Sánchez 191, at Calle Flórida* ☎ *33/3562–7036* 🎫 *Free* ⏲ *Tues.–Sat. 10–6, Sun. 10–3.*

Fodor's Choice ★

1 **Museo Regional de la Cerámica.** The frequently changing exhibits at the Regional Museum of Ceramics are in the many rooms surrounding a central courtyard. Track the evolution of ceramic wares in the Atemajac Valley during the 20th century. The presentation isn't always strong, but the Spanish-language displays discuss six common processes used by local ceramics artisans, including *barro bruñido,* which involves polishing large urns with smoothed chunks of the mineral pyrite. Items

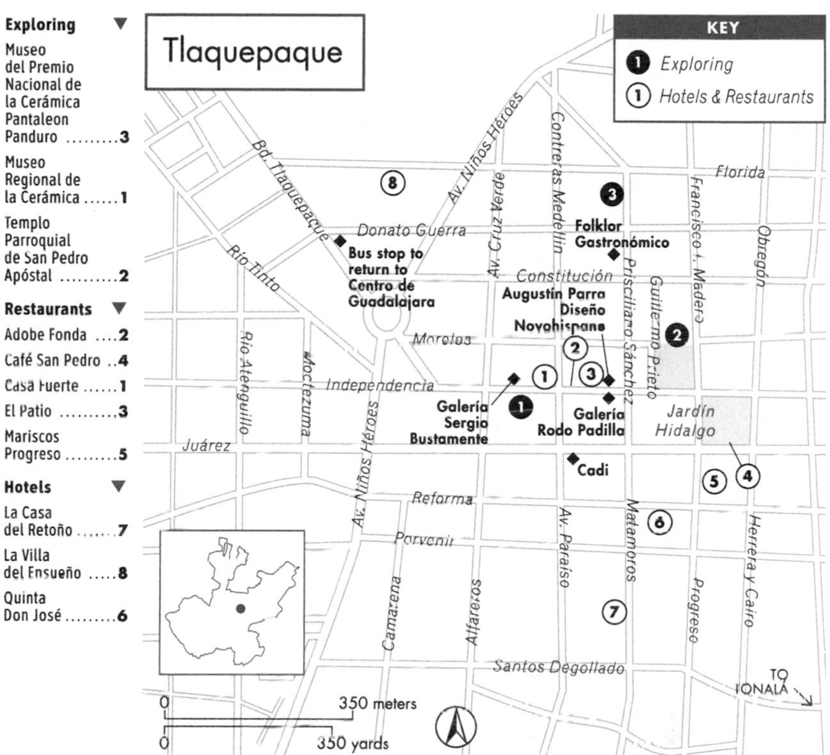

in the gift shop are surprisingly uninteresting. ✉ *Calle Independencia 237, at Calle Alfareros* ☎ *33/3635–5404* 🌐 *www.artesanias.jalisco.gob.mx/ubicacion.html* 🎫 *Free* 🕐 *Tues.–Sun. 10–6.*

2 **Templo Parroquial de San Pedro Apóstal.** Franciscan friars founded this tiny parish church during the Spanish conquest and named it after the apostle San Pedro de Analco. Adhering to the Mexican custom of adding the name of its patron saint to the town's name, Tlaquepaque was officially changed to San Pedro Tlaquepaque in 1915. The altars of Our Lady of Guadalupe and the Sacred Heart of Jesus are carved in silver and gold. ✉ *Calle Guillermo Prieto at Calle Morelos, bordering main plaza* ☎ *33/3635–1001* 🕐 *Mon.–Fri. 9–1:30 and 4:30–8; Sat. 9–1.*

NEED A BREAK?

Local mariachis will treat you to a song or two as you sip margaritas at El Parián, an enormous, partially covered conglomeration of 17 cantinas, diagonally across from the main plaza. Once a marketplace dating from 1883, it has traditional *cazuela* drinks, which are made of fruit and tequila and served in ceramic pots. It's worth visiting for the atmosphere; the food is average and overpriced. ✉ ***Jardín Hidalgo*** ☎ ***No phone.***

TONALÁ

Among the region's oldest pueblos is bustling Tonalá, a unique place filled with artisan workshops small and large. Although it's been swallowed by ever-expanding Guadalajara, Tonalá remains independent and industrious. More geared to business than pleasure, it doesn't have the folksy character of nearby Tlaquepaque. There's a concentration of stores on Tonalá Ave. and Avenida de los Tonaltecas, the main drag into town, and many more shops and factories can be found spread throughout Tonalá's narrow streets. And while the town and shops may not be as quaint or as touristy as Tlaquepaque, this is where you'll find the best bargains, since most local goods—from furniture to glassware and ceramics—are made here. Most stores are open daily from 10–5. On Thursday and Sunday, bargain-price merchandise is sold at a street market packed with vendors from 9 AM to 5 PM).

■ TIP→ The town has unusually long blocks, so wear your most comfortable walking shoes.

TOP ATTRACTIONS

4 **Tonalá crafts market.** This cramped market is *the* place for local goods. Vendors set up ceramics, carved wood, candles, glassware, furniture, metal crafts, and more each Thursday and Sunday (roughly from 9 to 5). Look for *vajilla* (ceramic place settings), but note that the more high-end ceramic offerings are at more formal stores. ✉ *Av. Tonaltecas at Calle Benito Juárez* ☎ *No phone.*

Fodor's Choice ★

WORTH NOTING

2 **Artesanías Erandi.** This is the showroom of one of Tonalá's biggest ceramics exporters. If you want to see how the pieces are made, the staff will gladly direct you to one of two nearby workshops. ✉ *Av. López Cotilla 118* ☎ *33/3683–0253* 🌐 *www.erandi.com* ⏲ *Weekdays 10–7, Sat. 10–2.*

3 **El 7.** Tonalá native J. Cruz Coldívar Lucano, who signs his work and named his shop El 7 (*el siete*), makes striking hand-painted clay masks and other wall hangings. His work has been exhibited throughout the Americas as well as in Europe, and the Spanish royal family owns some of his pieces. His studio is several long blocks from the plaza on Privado Alvaro Obregón, off the main avenue of the same name. ✉ *Privado Alvaro Obregón 28* ☎ *33/3683–1122* ⏲ *Mon.–Sat. 9–6, Sat. 9–3.*

1 **cristacolor.** An excellent place to buy glassware ranging from water pitchers and sets of tequila tasters to ceiling lights, you can also get a glimpse of the glass-blowers working their magic in the factory attached to the store. ✉ *Av. Tonaltecas 200* ☎ *33/3683-0661; 33/3683-0665* 🌐 *www.cristacolor.com.mx* ⏲ *Open daily 10–6.*

5 **La Casa de Salvador Vásquez Carmona.** On a small patio behind his home, Carmona molds enormous ceramic pots and glazes them with intricate designs. Despite posted store hours, the artist's workshop is also his home, and he's willing to receive customers most any time. ✉ *López Cotilla 328, west of Av. de los Tonaltecas* ☎ *33/3683–2896* ⏲ *No set hours: Call ahead to arange a visit.*

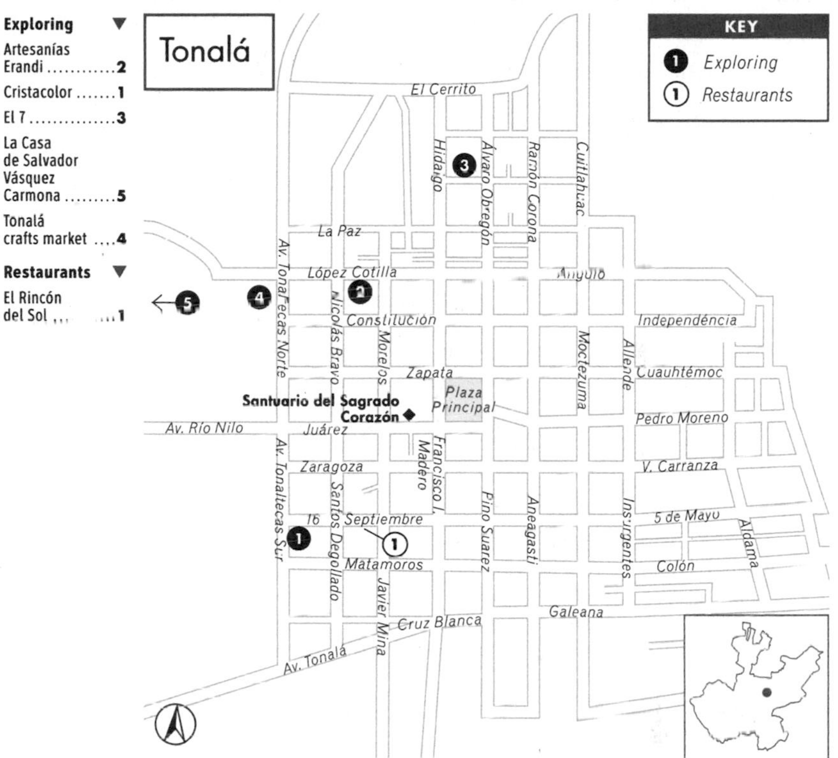

ELSEWHERE IN GUADALAJARA

North of the Centro is Zona Huentitán, which has a zoo and a canyon with decent hiking. Get to this neighborhood by cab or the northbound Trolley 600 on Calzada Independencia. The zoo is a 20-minute cab ride, more by bus because you have to walk to the entrance. To avoid crowds, go to the Barranca de Oblatos in the late morning. South of the Centro, at the confluence of 16 de Septiembre, Calzada de Independencia, and Avenida Washington, is the old train station, where the Tequila Express train departs.

TOP ATTRACTIONS

Zoológico Guadalajara. On the edge of the jagged Barranca de Huentitán, the city's zoo has more than 1,500 animals representing 360 species. In addition to the tropical birds and big cats in Mexico, you'll see rhinos, polar bears, camels, and other exotic creatures. There are two aviaries, a kids' zoo, and a herpetarium with 130 species of reptiles, amphibians, and fish. ✉ *Paseo del Zoológico 600, off Calz. Independencia, Zona Huentitán* ☎ *33/3674–4488* 🌐 *www.zooguadalajara.com.mx* *$4 admission only, $8 including train tour* ⏲ *Wed.–Sun. 10–5.*

Parque Barranca Oblatos Huentitán. Known as "La Barranca" or "The Gorge," the multipronged 2,000-foot-deep Oblatos Canyon has hiking trails and the narrow Cola de Caballo waterfall, named for its horsetail shape. A portion of the canyon complex called Barranca de Huentitán (Huentitán Canyon) has a steep, winding, 5-km (3-mi) trail to the river below. The trails are less strenuous at the entrance. Both areas can be crowded mornings and weekends. Take a northbound electric bus from in front of the Mercado Libertad and get off at Parque Mirador Independencia if you're interested only in the view. *www.guadalajaraparks.udg.mx/huentitan/index.html* *Free* *Daily 6–7.*

WHERE TO EAT

The most popular international restaurants are scattered about west Guadalajara, but some of the best Mexican food is near the main attractions in downtown Guadalajara, Tlaquepaque, and Tonalá.

If sitting down to a meal before 8 PM, you may find you don't need reservations—and you might even have the restaurant to yourself. By around 10 PM, the locals will start filling up the place, and reservations become a must. Good food tends to be very low-priced compared to comparable food in the States, even at the best restaurants in town. A main course is $6 to $15, and alcoholic beverages start at $2. Some of the best food in the city can be found at smaller taco shops and stands, where you can come away full having spent under $5 for four tacos and a soda. It's important to be careful when eating food from street vendors, however; the best sign of a stand worth trying is a long line of locals waiting to order.

CENTRO HISTÓRICO

$ MEXICAN ★ **Birrería las 9 Esquinas**. Mexican families and well-informed travelers come here for specialties, like lamb *birría,* that are readied in full view in the vibrantly colored hacienda-style kitchen. The restaurant is on a plaza in one of Guadalajara's oldest neighborhoods, the Nine Corners, so called for its intersecting streets. *Colon 384, corner of Galeana, Centro Histórico* *33/3613–6260* *www.las9esquinas.com* *No credit cards.* *daily; closes 7:30 PM Sun.*

$ MEXICAN Fodor'sChoice ★ **La Chata**. At high meal times, travelers will find lines of locals and tourists alike extending out the door of this traditional Mexican restaurant in El Centro. While the decor is plain, the food is the best in the city. Items worth testing include the *queso fundido* (cheese fondue) and the enchiladas. If you're staying in West Guadalajara, there's a second restaurant at 405 Terranova in Providencia. *Corona 126, between Avs. López Cotilla and Juárez, Centro Histórico* *33/3613–1315* *www.lachata.com.mx* *No credit cards.*

$$ MEXICAN ★ **La Fonda de San Miguel**. La Fonda, in a former convent, is perhaps the Centro's most exceptional eatery. Innovative, high-end Mexican dishes are presented in a soaring courtyard, the middle of which is dominated by a stone fountain and hung with a spectacular array of shining tin stars and folk art from Tlaquepaque and Tonalá. Relish the freshly made tortillas with the *molcajete,* a steaming stew of chicken, seafood, or beef that comes in a three-legged volcanic stone bowl. *Camarones*

Continued on page 237

With about 5,000 artisans apiece, the suburbs of Tlaquepaque and Tonalá might produce more crafts per square foot than any other place in Mexico. A mere 15–20 minute cab ride from downtown Guadalajara, the twin towns attract droves of shoppers from the city.

POTTERY AND CERAMICS IN TLAQUEPAQUE & TONALÁ

Tonalá Pottery by Antonio Ramirez

Tlaquepaque, which has upscale shops and galleries in converted haciendas, stylish restaurants, and a core of pretty pedestrian-only streets, is the more popular of the two and is actually getting a bit touristy from all the attention. But it hasn't turned into a total theme park just yet and it's still a pleasant place to stroll around and have a leisurely meal in between ducking into stores. Tonalá is less walking-friendly, less wealthy (think dusty cobblestone streets and adobe houses), and less touristy. It does get very busy on Thursday and Sunday, when most of the town is engulfed in a street market. If you can stand the crowds, you'll find bargain prices at these markets. There are more workshops and factories in Tonalá than shops or galleries—a lot of what's produced here ends up in Tlaquepaque—but many are open to the public. Also, the prices are a bit cheaper here, and you'll be able to commission custom work, often directly from the artisans.

Though you might also find glasswork, clothing, leather goods, and hand-carved wood furniture in both towns, they are really known for their pottery and ceramics. The Tonaltecan indians are responsible for Tlaquepaque's craft legacy; they were producing their distinctive decorated pottery as early as the mid-16th century. Tonalá's pre-Hispanic pottery came from the Atemajac Valley indians. Eleven different types of pottery and ceramics are still produced here. Just over 20 molding and firing techniques—most of them centuries old—are used to create the intricately painted flatware and whimsical figures.

Despite the long tradition of art in these towns, many master artisans are struggling to survive, especially in Tonalá. A trip to one of their workshops could be something your grandchildren will only hear about. To arrange studio tours, contact the Municipal Tourist Offices (33/3562–7050, ext. 2318 in Tlaquepaque, 33/3284–3093 in Tonalá) in either town at least a day in advance of your visit.

CLOSE-UP ON CERAMICS

BARRO BRUÑIDO

Polished with pyrite stones, the plates, vases, and figurines typical of this technique are bluish-gray with orange, blue, and white decorations of animals and nature scenes.

BANDERA

Red clay and white and green paint—the three colors of Mexico's *bandera* (flag)—are employed in this nationalistic pottery. However, these days green is missing from many contemporary pieces because the copper oxide used to produce the paint is increasingly rare.

TALAVERA

The colorful tiles and dinnerware of Mexico's best-known ceramics will be among the first things to catch your eye in Tlaquepaque and Tonalá. The technique is actually imported from Puebla, a central Mexican state.

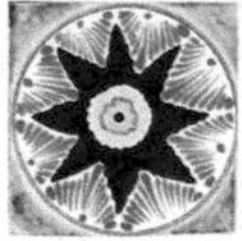

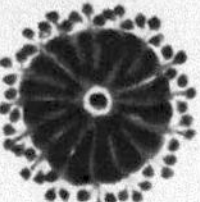

PETATILLO

The complexity of this pottery is likened to a handmade *petate* (straw mat). A single piece can require 20 days' labor and may pass through a dozen artisans' hands. Expensive as it is elaborate, *petatillo* is probably Tonalá's most endangered art form.

CANELO

Made from dirts that contribute to its cinnamon (*canelo*) coloring, these earth-toned pots are used as water-storing vessels.

POLICROMADO

Tlaquepaque's hallmark technique is the centuries-old *policromado* (from "polychrome," made using many colors), in which figurines and nativity scenes are popular.

CLOSE UP

Slowly Shaking Off Stereotypes

Guadalajarans have begun to come into their own. Called *Tapatíos* (a name possibly derived from the Nahuatl word *tlapatiotl*, a pre-Hispanic measure of payment), Guadalajarans admit to a long-standing rivalry with *chilangos*, a mildly derogatory term for Mexico City natives. Decades of official neglect from the government have made this derision commonplace in the "provinces," the term used by capital dwellers to refer to the country outside of Mexico City. As Mexico's second city, the provincial stereotype dogs Guadalajara. Despite having a population of 4.1 million (with several million more living in the greater metro area), Guadalajara lacks the plethora of culture synonymous with the D.F. (for *Distrito Federal*, or Mexico City). Major art expositions rarely open here, in part due to a dearth of galleries and energetic curators. Plans for a new Guggenheim museum in Guadalajara recently fell through due to the economic downturn. But a large, vocal gay community is steadily establishing a niche with bars and other establishments. And non-Catholic congregations hold celebrations with little protest from the public, which is more than 90% Catholic. And while most touring musicians choose the capital for their Mexico stops, more mainstream groups (The Killers, Alanis Morissette, and Peter Gabriel all played shows in 2009) are dropping in on the Tapatíos.

en mole (shrimp in mole) is another good dish. There's piano or saxophone music every evening except Monday. Piano music accompanies a breakfast buffet 8:30–noon on Saturday and Sunday. ✉ *Donato Guerra 25, Centro Histórico* ☎ *33/3613–0809* 🌐 *www.lafondadesanmiguel.com* 💳 *AE, MC, V* 🕓 *Closes at 6* PM *Mon. and 9* PM *Sun.*

$$ MEXICAN ✕ **La Rinconada.** In a dazzling green-tiled courtyard, this fine restaurant specializes in steak and seafood. The arrachera is good and the *camarones al mojo de ajo* (shrimp with garlic and butter) are even better. Named after the corner building it occupies, the grand old restaurant has appeared in sundry Mexican movies and TV comedies. ✉ *Calle Morelos 86, at Plaza Tapatía, Centro Histórico* ☎ *33/3613–9925* 💳 *MC, V* 🕓 *Closed Sun.*

WEST GUADALAJARA

$$$ ECLECTIC Fodor's Choice ★ ✕ **Cocina 88.** Teeming with a crowd of well-dressed local yuppies and business travelers every night of the week, this hip restaurant housed in a converted 90-year-old mansion not only serves fresh, wonderfully prepared steaks and seafood, it also provides a unique experience. If you arrive at gringo time, before 9 PM, you'll likely encounter the owner, Enrique, a character who likes to show off the wine store and food selections, which you can choose yourself in the front kitchen area. Ask him if he can make a sampler plate. Margaritas come complete with their own miniature bottles of Don Julio. And if you plan to return during your trip, you can buy a bottle of tequila or other liquor and store the leftovers in the wine cellar to await your next visit. ✉ *Av. Vallarta 1342,*

TASTE OF THE TOWN

Tapatíos love foreign eats, but homegrown dishes won't ever lose their flavor. The trademark local meal is *torta ahogada,* literally a "drowned sandwich." Generally consisting of chopped or shredded pork, though sometimes chicken, the entire sandwich, crunchy roll and all, is dipped in a flavorful tomato sauce—so grab a handful of napkins before you dig in. Other favorites are *carne en su jugo* (beef stew with bacon bits and beans), *birría* (hearty goat or lamb stew), and *pozole* (hominy and pork or chicken in tomato broth). Seafood is popular, and is available in trendy restaurants as well as at stands. Try a beverage favorite of Tapatíos while you're at it—local alcoholic drinks include palomas (tequila and Squirt) and micheladas (beer with lime and salt). Teetotalers should opt for one of the delicious aguas frescas.

Zona Minerva ☎ 33/3827–5996 or 33/3827–5998 🌐 www.cocina88.com ▭ AE, MC, V.

$$ TAPAS ✕ **Hemingway's.** This small, open-air bistro in the busy Providencia neighborhood is packed with locals every night of the week. The friendly Chilean owner, who speaks English well, offers a menu of tapas and mains that look as good as they taste. Nightly specials are worth trying as well. The selection of wines, many from Chile and Argentina, is both reasonably priced and very good. ✉ *José María Vigil 2854 at Ruben Dario, Col. Providencia ☎ 33/3641–4614 ▭ No credit cards. ⏲ Mon.–Sat. 1–11:30. Closed Sun.*

$ ITALIAN ✕ **Il Diavolo.** While Guadalajara feels like an international city in its plethora of food options, the town's pizza generally leaves much to be desired. But this small, casual eatery bucks the trend. Try one of the brick-oven choices from the menu, or have the always-interesting special of the day. Make a reservation or eat at off times, otherwise you could be waiting up to two hours for a table. ✉ *Av. Terranova 1189, Col. Providencia ☎ 33/3640-0785 ▭ No credit cards ⏲ Mon.–Sat. 1–12, Sun. 1–6.*

$ MEXICAN ✕ **Karne Garibaldi.** In the *1996 Guinness Book of World Records,* this Tapatío institution held the record for world's fastest service: 13.5 seconds for a table of six. Lightning service is made possible by the menu's single item: *carne en su jugo,* a combination of finely diced beef and bacon simmered in rich beef broth and served with grilled onions, tortillas, and refried beans mixed with corn. Don't be put off by the somewhat gritty area surrounding the restaurant at the original location on Calle Garibaldi. There also are three other locations in Zapopan. ✉ *Calle Garibaldi 1306, Zona Minerva ☎ 33/3826–1286 🌐 www.karnegaribaldi.com.mx ▭ AE, MC, V ✉ Mariano Otero 3019, Zona Plaza del Sol, Zapopan ☎ 33/3123–2607 ✉ Av. Vallarta 3959, Jardines del los Arcos, Zapopan ☎ 33/3621–1600 ✉ Plaza Galerias, Vallarta Norte, Zapopan ☎ 33/3165–2042.*

$$$ ARGENTINE ✕ **La Estancia Gaucha.** Tapatíos adore Argentine cuisine, and come to this first-rate steak house for its no-nonsense cuts, including the *churrasco*

estancia (rib eye) and the *bife de chorizo* (essentially New York strip steak). Savor the empanadas and Sunday lunch's homemade ravioli. ✉ *Av. Niños Héroes 2860, between Arcos and Lopez Mateos, Zona Minerva* ☎ *33/3122–6565 or 33/3122–9985* ▭ *AE, MC, V* ⊙ *Daily 1–midnight. No dinner Sun.*

$$$ ARGENTINE ✕ **La Matera.** The steak at this popular Argentine restaurant is some of the best in the city—and you can't go wrong with the arrachera (flank steak) or the rib eye. The noisy dining room draws a mix of date-night pairs, business groups, and friends celebrating life; reservations are a must no matter the time of day. ✉ *Av. México 2891, Col. Vallarta Norte* ☎ *33/3616–1626* ▭ *AE, MC, V.*

$$ ITALIAN ★ ✕ **La Moresca.** While this modern Italian restaurant comes alive at night when it turns into a hip martini bar, don't pass up a meal before partaking in the revelry. It has the best Italian food in town. The twentysomething Tapatíos like to take their dates here for delicious pasta and pizza dinners and stick around for the scene that follows. Birthday gatherings are common, too, as are simple be-seen excursions. However you do it, this place is Guadalajara at its trendiest, including music played at decibel levels that can sometimes make conversation difficult. Luckily, the Italian kitchen is up to the task. ✉ *Av. López Cotilla 1835, Zona Minerva* ☎ *33/3616–8277* ▭ *AE, MC, V* ⊙ *Closed Sun.* ✉ *Blvd. Puerto de Hierro 4965, Plaza Andares, Zapopan.*

$$$ MEXICAN ✕ **La Tequila.** If you can't make it to the village of Tequila, here's the next best thing: a friendly restaurant with spirit that serves traditional Mexican fare, including *molcajete* (meat or seafood stew served in a stone bowl), tortilla soup, beef tenderloin with three-chili sauce, and a variety of fish dishes.This spot has a separate menu for its more than 150 choices of the fiery liquor that give the restaurant its name. Antique photos of tequila distilleries and bilingual plaques explaining tequila's history line the brick walls, and copper distilling casks sit behind glass. Waiters make guacamole and salsa at your table, and offer suggestions if you are up for trying a variety of tequilas. A complimentary sorbet served in a tasting glass caps off the meal. ✉ *Av. México 2830, Col. Providencia* ☎ *33/3640–3110; 33/3640–3440* 🌐 *www.latequila.com* ▭ *AE, MC, V* ⊙ *Mon.–Sat. 1* PM*–midnight; closes at 6* PM *Sun.*

$$$ MEXICAN ★ ✕ **Sacromonte.** Elegant atmosphere, decor, and dishes make for a wonderful dining experience. This isn't the choice if you're looking for an atmosphere that feels Mexican—a significant portion of the other diners will likely be other English-speaking visitors—but the food's delicious anyway. The waiters offer menus in Spanish and in English. If you're into trying local favorites, this is the place to order *la lengua*—the beef tongue—or the chicken mole, which has a sweet twist. The pork loin and barbecue ribs are also worth a taste. For dessert, order the flan with *cajeta* (a local soft caramel sauce); it's homemade—literally made in someone's house and delivered nightly to the restaurant. One waiter's wife claims it's the best she's had. ✉ *Pedro Moreno 1398, Col. Americana* ☎ *33/3825–5447* ▭ *MC, V* ⊙ *No dinner Sun.*

$$$ MEXICAN ✕ **Santo Coyote.** While the food here is good, it simply can't compete with the environment, which has so much Disneyesque charm—think faux waterfalls, colorful folk art, and hanging lanterns—that you may

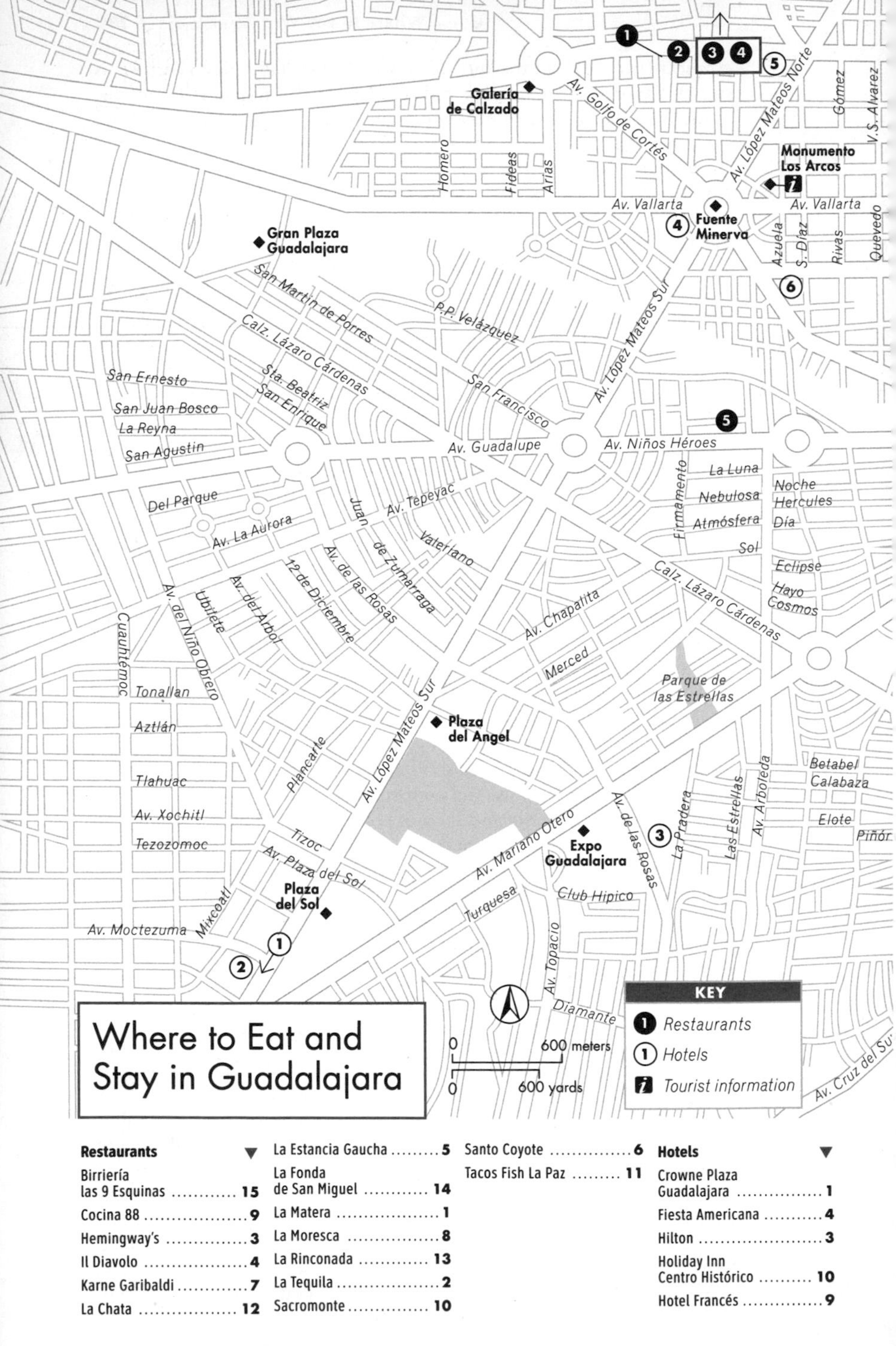

Where to Eat and Stay in Guadalajara

Restaurants

Birriería las 9 Esquinas 15
Cocina 88 9
Hemingway's 3
Il Diavolo 4
Karne Garibaldi 7
La Chata 12
La Estancia Gaucha 5
La Fonda de San Miguel 14
La Matera 1
La Moresca 8
La Rinconada 13
La Tequila 2
Sacromonte 10
Santo Coyote 6
Tacos Fish La Paz 11

Hotels

Crowne Plaza Guadalajara 1
Fiesta Americana 4
Hilton 3
Holiday Inn Centro Histórico 10
Hotel Francés 9

SEE CENTRO HISTÓRICO INSET BELOW
Centro Magno
CENTRO HISTÓRICO
Plaza Tapatía
Instituto Cultural Cabañas
Mercado Libertad
300 meters
300 yards

forget you're in Guadalajara. There's an elegant terrace filled with plants and trees. Start with chips and a delicious salsa prepared tableside to your spice specification, along with a margarita. ✉ *Calle Lerdo de Tejada 2379, Col. Americana* ☎ *33/3616–6978* 🌐 *www.santocoyote.com.mx* 💳 *AE, MC, V.*

$ MEXICAN ✕ **Tacos Fish La Paz.** There's always a long line at this simple corner fish taco stand. An extensive condiment bar offering various salsas and other tasty extras is available to top your choice of fish, shrimp, or crab tacos. The aguas frescas, including the horchata, a milky drink often including sugar, cinnamon, and vanilla, are delicious. ✉ *Av. La Paz at Donato Guerra, Col. Americana* ☎ *No phone* 💳 *No credit cards.*

ZAPOPAN

$ MEXICAN ★ ✕ **Doña Gabina Escolastica.** Colorful, festive paper cutouts hang from the ceiling of this two-story space. Each table is unique, painted a different shade from the one next to it, with booth backs designed in the form of people, faces and all. The fun-filled atmosphere and decor would be the highlight of this spot in the historic center if the food were not so good. Try the pozole, soup enough for a meal in itself. The enchiladas—you can choose pork, cheese, or chicken filling—and the tostadas also are delicious. ✉ *Javier Mina 237, Centro Historico, Zapopan* ☎ *33/3833–0883* 💳 *No credit cards* ⏲ *Tues.–Sat. 7–11, Sun. 2–10.*

$$$ SEAFOOD ✕ **El Farallón de Tepic.** Out in the open air and beneath a bright-blue awning, this restaurant on the outskirts of Zapopan specializes in fresh *pescado*—usually red snapper, sea bass, or another equally mild fish—grilled with garlic or butter, in classic tomato sauce, breaded, or stuffed with seafood and cheese. The pescado *sarandeado* (whole barbecued fish stuffed with vegetables) is worth the 30-minute wait. Go with the homemade flan for dessert. ✉ *Av. Niño Obrero 560, Col. Jardines de San Ignacio, Zapopan* ☎ *33/3121–2616* 🌐 *www.elfarallondetepic.com.mx* 💳 *AE, MC, V* ⏲ *Daily 11–6.*

TLAQUEPAQUE

There are many good restaurants in Tlaquepaque's enchanting town center, but be forewarned that almost all of them cater to daytime visitors and close by 8 PM. Don't expect a relaxing late-night meal in this town.

$$ MEXICAN ✕ **Adobe Fonda.** Set in the courtyard of a housewares-and-textiles shop, Adobe Fonda's biggest strength is its cuteness. The menu consists of delicious fusion dishes, including macaroni and cheese with a twist and molcajetes. Lamps supply the low, romantic lighting, while oversize wicker and *equipale* (pigskin) chairs add some local color. ✉ *Francisco de Miranda 27 Tlaquepaque* ☎ *33/3657–2792* 💳 *AE, MC, V* ⏲ *Sun.–Fri. noon–6, Sat. noon–7.*

¢ CAFÉ ★ ✕ **Café San Pedro.** Jazzy music emanates from this popular coffeehouse. Grab a table on the sidewalk or in the cozy dining room. The glass dessert case shows off dozens of different cakes and pies; ask which were made that day, as this huge variety means that some sit for awhile. There's a really long list of coffee drinks (including the Spanish *café* *cortado*, which is espresso with a shot of hot milk) and a sandwich maker at the back who will indulge desires beyond sweets and caffeine. ✉ *Av. Juárez 85, Tlaquepaque* ☎ *33/3639–0616* ▭ *MC, V* ⊙ *Daily 8:30* AM*–10:30* PM.

> **WORD OF MOUTH**
>
> "I'm in Guadalajara and love going to Cafe San Pedro in Tlaquepaque. It's right in the 'portales,' with a quaint setting in a picturesque arts and crafts village, great coffee, great sandwiches and good people. What else could one ask for?" —AlbertM

$$ MEXICAN ★ ✕ **Casa Fuerte.** Relax with tasty Mexican dishes at the tables along the sidewalk or under the palms and by the fountain on the patio. You'll be tempted by the tables scattered around the sidewalk, but before you decide, take a peek at those in the oversize garden patio surrounding a magnificent old tree. Try the house specialty: chicken stuffed with *huitlacoche* (a corn fungus that's Mexico's answer to the truffle) and shrimp in tamarind sauce. Live musicians accompany *comida* (2:30 to 6 PM, approximately) every day except Monday. ✉ *Calle Independencia 224, Tlaquepaque* ☎ *33/3639–6481 or 33/3639–6474* ▭ *AE, MC, V* ⊙ *Daily noon–8.*

$$ MEXICAN ✕ **El Patio.** El Patio's focal point is its inviting courtyard brimming with wrought-iron tables. For starters, try the guacamole and powerful margaritas. Order carefully for your mains, as some options are better than others. Sweet, flavorful *chiles en nogada* are a good pick; *mole enchiladas* are a wise choice as well. Don't be tempted by the interesting preparations of fish—they fall short of expectations. Lively mariachi musicians or romantic trios play most days during the midday meal. Note that this is one of a handful of restaurants in Tlaquepaque to serve during dinner hours. ✉ *Independencia 186 Tlaquepaque* ☎ *33/3635–1108* 🌐 *www.elpatio.com.mx* ▭ *AE, MC, V* ⊙ *Daily 9–9.*

$$ SEAFOOD ★ ✕ **Mariscos Progreso.** There's always one in every neighborhood: the place all the locals crowd into, leaving everything else deserted. In this case they come for seafood, from wonderfully fresh *ceviche de pescado*, served as a tostada, to a tender octopus cocktail. For your main course, don't even look at the menu—go straight for the *huachinango* (red snapper), or other catch of the day, served *a la leña*. This preparation involves coating the fish in butter and heavy spices, wrapping it in foil, and grilling it over an open fire. There's a good tequila selection here, too. ✉ *Progreso 80 Tlaquepaque* ☎ *33/3639–6149 or 33/3657–4995* ▭ *AE, MC, V* ⊙ *Daily 11–7.*

TONALÁ

$ MEXICAN ✕ **El Rincón del Sol.** A covered patio invites you to sip margaritas while listening to live trova (romantic ballads). Musicians play Tuesday to Friday evenings between 7 and 9, and on weekends during the leisurely lunch hour (roughly 3 to 5). Try one of the steak or chicken dishes, the burrito, or the classic *chiles en nogada* in the colors of the Mexican flag. The staff is friendly and helpful. ✉ *Av. 16 de Septiembre 61, Tonalá* ☎ *33/3683–1989 or 33/3683–1940* ▭ *MC, V.*

WHERE TO STAY

Choosing a place to stay is a matter of location, price, and comfort. Tourists are often drawn to the Centro, where colonial-style hotels are convenient to the historic center and other sights. But hotels in the center tend to be a bit run-down, and don't offer the amenities available at those further west. Businesspeople and those looking for more modern digs head for the area around Avenida López Mateos Sur, a 16-km (10-mi) strip extending from the Minerva Fountain to the Plaza del Sol shopping center, or Avenida Americas in Providencia, where they can take advantage of newer facilities and four-star comforts. Several hotels, like the polished Hilton, are near the Expo Guadalajara convention center.

CENTRO HISTÓRICO

$$ **Holiday Inn Centro Histórico.** This branch of the reliable international chain sits in the heart of historic Guadalajara. Though the hotel's public areas could use some updating, it has a grand entrance—with a restaurant and a men's shop—leading guests up to the check-in area. Rooms have nice touches like plasma TVs; the bathrooms have glassed-in showers, but no tubs. The breakfast buffet is a good deal, and the restaurant serves national and international dishes. **Pros:** helpful business center; free Wi-Fi in rooms and public spaces; some free items in the minibar. **Cons:** no heat; small, old gym; no pool. ✉ *Av. Juárez 211, Centro Histórico* ☎ *33/3560–1200* 🌐 *www.holidaycentrogdl.com* *45 rooms, 45 suites* *In-room: safe, Wi-Fi. In-hotel: restaurant, room service, bar, laundry facilities, laundry service, Internet terminal, Wi-Fi hotspot, parking (free), no-smoking rooms* *AE, MC, V.*

$$ **Hotel de Mendoza.** Elegant with its postcolonial architecture, this hotel is on a calm side street a block from Teatro Degollado. Hand-carved furniture and doors and wrought-iron railings adorn the public areas and the rooms. Standard rooms are small, making suites worth the extra cost. Balconies overlook the courtyard pool from some rooms. **Pros:** great location; comfortable rooms. **Cons:** standard rooms lack tubs; most rooms don't have balconies. ✉ *Calle Venustiano Carranza 16, Centro Histórico* ☎ *01800/361–2600 toll-free in Mexico; 33/3942–5151* 🌐 *www.demendoza.com.mx* *86 rooms, 18 suites* *In-room: safe, Wi-Fi. In-hotel: restaurant, pool, gym, Internet terminal, Wi-Fi hotspot, parking (paid)* *AE, MC, V.*

$ **Hotel Francés.** Dating from 1610, Guadalajara's oldest hotel is a national monument. While the run-down entrance to the hotel may scare you away, stone columns and colonial arches girdle a lovely three-story atrium lobby and dining area, with a marble fountain. However, the interior charm ends outside the guest rooms, where threadbare linens, tiny dingy bathrooms, and thin walls are serious drawbacks—music from the downstairs bar (there's a mariachi band in the lobby bar from 7 to 10 every Friday) will keep you up all night if you're in the wrong room. Rooms facing Calle Maestranza have tiny 17th-century balconies, as well as street noise. **Pros:** great downtown location; interesting period architecture; friendly staff; some rooms have Jacuzzis.

Cons: on a noisy street; tired furnishings. ✉ *Calle Maestranza 35, Centro Histórico* ☎ *33/3613–1190; 01800/718–5309 toll-free in Mexico* 🌐 *www.hotelfrances.com* 50 *rooms, 10 suites* *In-hotel: restaurant, bar, Wi-Fi hotspot, parking (free)* *AE, MC, V.*

$ Fodor's Choice ★ **Hotel Morales.** After being abandoned for 30 years, this downtown hotel—originally a 19th-century rooming house—has been transformed into one of the city's most luxurious lodgings. No wonder it's the choice of celebrities, ranging from movie stars to soccer heroes. Demure guest rooms have crown moldings, blond-wood floors, and gold-and-beige furnishings with an Old World style. Café tables on the rooftop terrace make for a casual retreat. The lobby and restaurant are much more formal. **Pros:** relaxed elegance; double-paned windows keep out the noise. **Cons:** lobby restaurant isn't cozy; no Wi-Fi in rooms. ✉ *Ave. Ramón Corona 243, Centro Histórico* ☎ *33/3658–5232* 🌐 *www.hotelmorales.com.mx* *59 rooms, 7 suites* *In-room: safe, Wi-Fi (some; first floor only). In-hotel: restaurant, parking (free)* *AE, MC, V.*

5

ZONA MINERVA

$$ ★ **Fiesta Americana.** The dramatic glass facade of this high-rise faces the Minerva Fountain and Los Arcos monument. Four glass-enclosed elevators ascend dizzyingly above a 14-story atrium lobby to the guest rooms, which have dignified modern furnishings, small marble bathrooms with bathtub, and, for the most part, arresting views (rooms 1211 through 1217 have the absolute best). The lobby bar has live music every night. Executive-floor rooms come with continental breakfast and canapes, and there's a fully equipped business center. **Pros:** airport shuttle (fee); 24-hour room service; ample parking; nice bathroom amenities; AAA discount. **Cons:** some rooms have unpleasant views of roof and generators; no swimming pool. ✉ *Av. Aurelio Aceves 225, Col. Vallarta Poniente, Zona Minerva* ☎ *33/3818–1400* 🌐 *www.fiestamericana.com.mx* *309 rooms* *In-room: Wi-Fi. In-hotel: restaurant, bar, gym, laundry service, Internet terminal, Wi-Fi hotspot, parking (paid), no-smoking rooms* *AE, DC, MC, V.*

$$ ★ **Hotel Plaza Diana.** At this modest hotel two blocks from the Minerva Fountain the rooms are on the small side. One suite has a sauna. Stay on the upper floors in the rear for the quietest rooms. The expansive, café-style restaurant specializes in Argentine-style cuts of beef. The huge indoor pool is good for swimming laps. **Pros:** free Internet; heated indoor pool; free airport shuttle. **Cons:** gym is on the small side. ✉ *Av. Agustín Yáñez 2760, Zona Minerva* ☎ *33/3540–9700; 01800/248–1001 toll-free in Mexico* 🌐 *www.hoteldiana.com.mx* *127 rooms, 24 suites* *In-room: safe, Wi-Fi. In-hotel: restaurant, room service, bar, pool, gym, Internet terminal, Wi-Fi hotspot* *AE, DC, MC, V.*

$$$ ★ **Quinta Real.** Stone-and-brick walls, colonial arches, and objets d'art fill this luxury hotel's public areas. Suites are plush, though on the small side, with neocolonial-style furnishings, original art, and faux fireplaces. Master suites have separate seating areas with love seats and marble-top desk. For a bit more, the Grand Class suites have luxurious touches like round whirlpool tubs. You can arrange in-room massages from one of two nearby spas. The wood-floor gym is outfitted with the

latest equipment and plasma-screen TVs. **Pros:** elegant rooms; stately grounds; in-room spa services. **Cons:** pricey rates; no on-site spa. ✉ *Av. México 2727, at Av. López Mateos Norte, Zona Minerva* ☎ *33/3669–0600; 866/621–9288 toll-free from U.S.; 01800/500–4000 in Mexico* 🌐 *www.quintareal.com* ↩ *76 suites* ♿ *In-room: safe, Internet. In-hotel: restaurant, bar, pool, gym, laundry service, Internet terminal, Wi-Fi hotspot, parking (free), no-smoking rooms* ▭ *AE, MC, V.*

WORD OF MOUTH

"My first choice of Guadalajara hotel is the Quinta Real. This is possibly the finest hotel in Mexico. Their philosophy is to fill ALL your needs, wants, and desires. You will NEVER hear 'no' at this fine hotel. We honeymooned there in '98 and return to Suite 45 every time we can. It includes a living, desk, dining, and bedroom area. If it is too pricey, check Hotel Mendoza, a good hotel just steps from the main plaza." —Stewbear

$$$$ Fodor's Choice ★ **Villa Ganz.** Staying in this neighborhood full of restaurants and nightlife yet away from the gritty historic center might be just the ticket. But location is just one of the many virtues of this gracious mansion. We loved the spacious rooms, the hunting-lodge-like sitting area with fireplace, and a candlelit, tree-shaded garden that will make you want to book an extended stay. Private dinners in the garden can be arranged in advance, and make for Guadalajara's most romantic dining. **Pros:** great location; inviting patios; free early-evening wine and canapes. **Cons:** suites must be paid in full when booked; high-season cancellations charged tax as well as 100% of room fee. ✉ *Av. López Cotilla 1739, Zona Minerva* ☎ *33/3120–1416* 🌐 *www.villaganz.com* ↩ *9 suites* ♿ *In-room: safe, Wi-Fi (some). In-hotel: bar, Wi-Fi hotspot, no kids under 12* ▭ *AE, MC, V* 🍽 *CP.*

ZONA PLAZA DEL SOL-CHAPALITA

$$ **Crowne Plaza Guadalajara.** Gardens encircling the pool add a bit of nature to this family-friendly hotel. A mix of antiques and reproductions fills the public spaces. Rooms, recently renovated, provide marble baths with small tub, hair dryer, iron and ironing board, and natural lighting; those in the tower have city views. (Ask for a room near the back; those near the playground can be noisy.) Some rooms have a "Sleep Advantage" program, whose amenities include hypoallergenic furnishings, special pillows, and eye masks. Packages including breakfast are available. **Pros:** free coffce in rooms; pets accepted; car rental and travel agency on-site; La Fuente Restaurant opens at 6:30 AM. **Cons:** far from downtown. ✉ *Av. López Mateos Sur 2500, Zapopan* ☎ *33/3634–1034; 01800/009–9900 toll-free in Mexico* 🌐 *www.cpguadalajara.com.mx* ↩ *294 rooms, 5 suites* ♿ *In-room: safe, Wi-Fi. In-hotel: 2 restaurants, room service, bar, pool, gym, laundry service, Wi-Fi hotspot, parking (paid), no-smoking rooms* ▭ *AE, DC, MC, V.*

$$ ★ **Hilton.** Adjacent to the Expo Guadalajara convention center is one of the city's top business hotels. President Obama stayed here when he visited Guadalajara in the summer of 2009. Among the Hilton's many business services are a multilingual staff, a business center, and an

executive floor (with free breakfast in a private dining area). The fitness center was renovated in 2007. At breakfast you'll rub elbows with local business executives at the popular Vitrales restaurant. **Pros:** 24-hour room service; super-comfortable beds with down duvets; barber shop and florist on premises. **Cons:** very little within walking distance, so you'll need transportation unless you only plan to go to the expo center. ✉ *Av. de las Rosas 2933, Zona Plaza del Sol* ☎ *33/3678–0505; 01800/003–1400 in Mexico; 800/445–8667* 🌐 *www.guadalajara.hilton.com* *450 rooms, 26 suites* *In-room: Internet, Wi-Fi. In-hotel: 2 restaurants, bar, pool, gym, spa, parking (paid), no-smoking rooms* *AE, DC, MC, V.*

$$$ **Presidente InterContinental.** With its mirrored facade and 12-story atrium lobby, this bustling hotel attracts a sophisticated business clientele. For the best city view, request a room on an upper floor facing the Plaza del Sol shopping center. A Tane silver shop is one of the many on-site stores, and the 24-hour health club is one of the city's best. **Pros:** 24-hour business center; impressive gym; heated pool. **Cons:** on a busy corner; walking distance to nothing except the mall; bed choices are one king or two twins only. ✉ *Av. López Mateos Sur 3515, at Moctezuma, Zona Plaza del Sol* ☎ *33/3678–1234 or 888/424–6835* 🌐 *www.ichotelsgroup.com* *409 rooms* *In-room: safe, Internet, Wi-Fi. In-hotel: 2 restaurants, bar, pool, gym, laundry service, Internet terminal, Wi-Fi hotspot, parking (paid)* *AE, DC, MC, V.*

5

COLONIA PROVIDENCIA

$$ **Fiesta Americana Guadalajara Country Club Grand.** With its event space and modern look, this busy, upscale 22-story hotel serves business types and tourists alike. The hotel's corner rooms featuring a wall of windows allow for the best city views—though the scenes from the gym and the Grand Club floor café also can't be beat. The hotel's 4 Estaciones restaurant offers contemporary Mexican cuisine; a piano player makes an appearance from 11 AM to noon each day. Barguero is an option for cocktails and snacks from 5 PM into the late evening. For some additional relaxation, the spa offers services from massages to pedicures and hair styling. **Pros:** gym with a view; reasonably priced spa treatments on site. **Cons:** standard rooms with two double beds are tight on space, parking costs $8 day, Internet/Wi-Fi charge is about $15/day or $5 an hour ✉ *Av. Americas 1551Col. Providenica* ☎ *33/3648-3500* 🌐 *www.fiestamericanagrand.com* *208 rooms* *In-room: safe, mini-bar, Wi-Fi. In-hotel: restaurant, bar, gym, business center, spa, parking (paid)* *AE, DC, MC, V.*

$$$ **NH Hoteles Guadalajara.** This brand-new minimalist, modern hotel opened in October 2009. Rooms on the top floors of the east-facing side have views of downtown beyond the greens of the city's exclusive golf club. Rooms are modern, with plush bed coverings, trendy furniture, and wood floors. The hotel has its own lobby restaurant and bar, nhube, and two independent fine dining establishments were set to open by early 2010: La Estancia Gaucha and Olio Bistro. One of the city's finest steak restaurants, La Portena, is positioned directly across the street. For a taste of home, several American chains, including Starbucks

and Applebees, are a few steps out the front door. Packages including breakfast are available. **Pros:** gym, free Internet in lobby café, parking costs less than $3 a day **Cons:** wireless Internet charge is about $10 a day. ✉ *Calle Sao Paulo 2334, Esq. Av. Americas, Col. Providencia* ☎ *33/3648–9500* ✉ *nhguadalajara@nh-hotels.com* *137 rooms, 3 suites* *In-room: minibar, safe, In-hotel: restaurant,24-hour room service, bar, gym, parking (paid), business center* ▭ *AE, DC, MC, V.*

TLAQUEPAQUE

$$ **La Casa del Retoño.** On a quiet street several blocks from the shopping district is this B&B. Rooms are made of painted cinder block, but are clean and cheerful. Rooms in the back overlook a large but uninspired garden, while the ones upstairs have small private terraces. There's an open-air reading area, and complimentary continental breakfast is served in the courtyard. **Pros:** quiet neighborhood; private terraces in some rooms. **Cons:** smallish rooms; lackluster garden. ✉ *Matamoros 182, Tlaquepaque* ☎ *33/3639–6510 or 33/3635–7636* ⊕ *www.lacasadelretono.com.mx* *8 rooms, 1 suite* *In-room: Wi-Fi. In-hotel: Internet terminal, Wi-Fi hotspot* ▭ *AE, MC, V* *CP.*

$$ **La Villa del Ensueño.** A 10-minute walk from Tlaquepaque's center, this intimate B&B is near lots of shopping. The restored 19th-century hacienda has thick, white adobe walls, exposed-beam ceilings, and plants in huge unglazed pots. Smokers should request a room with private balcony; smoking isn't allowed anywhere inside the hotel. Room rates include a full, hot breakfast. **Pros:** hot tub; take-out food available from adjacent Mexican restaurant; friendly staff. **Cons:** only junior suites have bathtubs. ✉ *Florida 305, Tlaquepaque* ☎ *33/3635–8792* ⊕ *www.villadelensueno.com* *16 rooms, 4 suites* *In-room: refrigerator (some), Wi-Fi. In-hotel: restaurant, bar, pools, parking (free), no-smoking rooms* ▭ *AE, MC, V* *BP.*

$$ **Quinta Don José.** One block from Tlaquepaque's main plaza and shopping area, this B&B has a great location. Natural lighting and room size vary; suites face the pool and are spacious but a bit dark. There's remarkable tile work in the master suite. Hearty continental breakfasts—with fruit, cereal, toast, and sweet breads plus juice and coffee—are served in an inner courtyard and are included in the room rate. Tasty pizzas are baked in the brick oven at the hotel's Mexican-Italian restaurant (closed Monday). If you stay three nights or more, they'll shuttle you to and from the airport or bus station. **Pros:** central location; friendly staff who speak excellent English; free calls worldwide; free Wi-Fi; free parking. **Cons:** pool is chilly; some rooms are small. ✉ *Calle Reforma 139, Tlaquepaque* ☎ *33/3635–7522; 01800/700–2223 toll-free in Mexico; 866/629–3753 in U.S. and Canada* ⊕ *www.quintadonjose.com* *18 rooms* *In-room: Wi-Fi (some). In-hotel: restaurant, bar, pool, laundry service, Internet terminal, Wi-Fi hotspot* ▭ *AE, MC, V* *BP.*

NIGHTLIFE

With the exception of a few well-established nightspots like La Maestranza, downtown Guadalajara quiets down relatively early. The existing nightlife centers around Avenida Vallarta, favored by the well-to-do under-30 set; Avenida Patria, full of bars for young people who party until early in the morning; or the somewhat seedy Plaza del Sol. Bars in these spots open into the wee hours, usually closing by 3 AM. Dance clubs may charge a $15–$20 cover, which includes an open bar, on Wednesday and Saturday nights. Dress up for nightclubs; highly subjective admission policies hinge on who you know or how you look. The local music scene is less formal and centers around more intimate digs.

OCIO

For the latest listings, grab a *Público* newspaper on Friday and pull out the weekly Ocio cultural guide.

5

BARS

Der Krug Braühaus (✉ *Miguel de Cervantes 15, at Morelos, Col. Americana* ☎ *33/1057–8386*) is the most authentic German-style beer hall in the city. Despite closing at 1 AM, it's attracting a young and hip crowd, some of whom come to nibble the beer-marinated pork chops.

One of Guadalajara's hot spots, **I Latina** (✉ *Av. Inglaterra 3128, at López Mateos, Col. Vallarta Poniente, Centro* ☎ *33/3647–7774*) is where you will spot a cool, upscale local and international crowd having cocktails.

★ Appealing and unpretentious, **La Fuente** (✉ *Calle Pino Suarez s/n, at Hidalgo, Centro Histórico* ☎ *No phone* ⊗ *Closed Mon.*) opened in this location in 1950. The cantina draws business types, intellectuals, and blue-collar workers, all seeking cheap drinks, animated conversation, and live music. Above the bar, look for an old bicycle. It's been around since 1957, when, legend has it, one of a long list of famous people (most say it was the father of local newspaper baron Jesús Álvarez del Castillo) left the bike to pay for his drinks. The bar opens at 8—arrive soon after to avoid crowds.

For some local color, stop at **La Maestranza** (✉ *Calle Maestranza 179, between López Cotillo and Madero, Centro Histórico* ☎ *33/3613–5878*), a renovated 1940s cantina full of bullfighting memorabilia.

LIVE MUSIC

★ **Rusty Trombone** (✉ *Lerdo de Tejada 2166, Col. Americana* ☎ *33/3630–2294*) is a great place to relax and enjoy a variety of hip bands.

Music lovers in their '30s and '40s head to **Barba Negra** (✉ *Calle Justo Sierra 2194, Col. Americana* ☎ *33/3673–3802*) to listen to alternative rock in Spanish and English.

El Teu LLoc (✉ *López Cotillo 570, Col. Americana* ☎ *33/3586–5262*) is a small, artsy venue featuring contemporary bands.

Sun, surf and sand rule **Wall Street** (✉ *Av. Americas 1419, Col. Providencia* ☎ *33/3817–1743*), a spring break–themed bar and dance club drawing crowds of 20-somethings and featuring live music, including pop, ska, and rock.

DANCE CLUBS

Bossé (✉ *Av. Patría 1600, Col. Agraria* ☎ *33/3848–9395*) keeps people dancing into the wee hours of the night with a rotating selection of top DJs; the crowd is young.

Cherry Lobby (✉ *Jorge Alvarez de Castillo 1034, Glorieta Colon* ☎ *33/3817–1129*) is a large club that draws groups of friends in search of dance music, including techno, pop, rock, and electronica.

Salón Veracruz (✉ *Calle Manzano 486, behind Hotel Misión Carlton, Centro Histórico* ☎ *33/3613–4422*) is a spartan, old-style dance hall where a 15-piece band keeps hoofers moving to Colombian *cumbia;* Dominican merengue; and *danzón,* a waltzlike dance invented in Cuba. It's open Wednesday to Sunday 9:30 PM–3:30 AM, and Sunday 6 PM–2 AM; cover is about $6.

PERFORMANCES

After a brief stint at the newer Teatro Diana, the internationally acclaimed **Ballet Folclórico of the University of Guadalajara** has returned to perform its traditional Mexican folkloric dances and music in the Teatro Degollado most Sundays at 12:30 PM; tickets are $5–$25. ✉ *Calle Belén s/n* ☎ *33/3614–4773* 🌐 *www.ballet.udg.mx.*

Large-scale theater, dance, and musical performances occasionally take place on a patio at the **Instituto Cultural Cabañas** (✉ *Calle Cabañas 8, Centro Histórico* ☎ *33/3818–2800 Ext. 31016*). The Tolsá Chapel hosts more intimate events. Traveling art exhibitions stop here, and affordable, long-term art courses are provided.

Orquesta Filarmónica de Jalisco. Though it's among Mexico's most poorly paid orchestras, the state-funded philharmonic manages remarkably good performances (usually pieces by Mexican composers mixed with standard orchestral fare). When in season (it varies), the OFJ performs Sunday afternoons and Wednesday and Friday evenings at Teatro Delgollado. On the facing plaza, they hold an annual outdoor performance that helps kick off September's Mariachi Festival. ☎ *No phone* 🌐 *www.ofj.com.mx* 🎟 *$8–$35.*

★ **Teatro Degollado.** Guadalajara's most traditional performing-arts venue is a nearly 150-year-old theater that's subject to constant renovation. If it's open to the public when you're there, however, it's worth a look inside. ✉ *Calle Degollado between Av. Hidalgo and Calle Morelos, Centro Histórico* ☎ *33/3614–4773.*

Affiliated with the University of Guadalajara, **Teatro Diana** (✉ *Av. 16 de Septiembre 710, Centro* ☎ *33/3614–7072* 🌐 *www.teatrodiana.com*) is Guadalajara's most modern theater. If you don't speak Spanish, see a ballet or flamenco show in which actions speak louder than words.

SHOPPING

Tapatíos love shopping at outlet malls *north* of the border. Nevertheless, the city supports a swath of modern malls, and most double as gathering spots with their restaurants and theaters. The Centro Histórico is packed with shops as well as ambulatory vendors, who compete with pedestrians for sidewalk space. You'll find the most products under one roof at labyrinthine Mercado Libertad, one of Latin America's largest markets. Tlaquepaque and Tonalá are arts-and-crafts meccas. Shoe stores and silver shops are ubiquitous in Guadalajara.

Stores tend to open Monday–Saturday from 10 or 11 until 8, and Sunday 10–2; some close during lunch, usually 2–4 or 2–5, and others close on Sunday. Bargaining is customary in Mercado Libertad, and you can talk deals with some crafts vendors in Tlaquepaque and Tonalá. The ticketed price sticks just about every where else, with the exception of antiques shops.

Neighborhood street markets, called tianguis, also abound in Guadalajara. They take place at various times throughout the week, with a larger share on Sunday morning. Some focus on specific items like antiques or art, but many have a variety of vendors selling everything from chicken, homemade mole sauce, and fruits and vegetables to flowers, clothing, and housewares.

LOCAL HAUNTS

Locals stop at the Mercado Corona, due west of the Palacio Municipal, to pick up fresh produce and meat. The streets north of the market have similar goods, dry merchandise, and school supplies. The Medrano district, starting a block south of the Plaza de los Mariachis and continuing east along Calle Obregón into eastern Guadalajara's nether reaches, is a favorite Tapatío shopping haunt. Though they're short on touristy goods, venturing into these parts is like entering the city's central nervous system.

5

MARKETS

Tonalá's crafts market, Tlaquepaque crafts and housewares shops, and Mercado Libertad are the region's top marketplaces. Allot yourself plenty of time and energy to explore both. El Trocadero is a weekly antiques market at the north end of Avenida Chapultepec. Feel free to drive a hard bargain.

Antiquers come out of the woodwork every Sunday 10–5 to sell their wares—including European flatware, Mexican pottery, and larger pieces—at **El Trocadero** in the antiques district. ✉ *Av. Mexico at Av. Chapultepec, Zona Minerva* ☎ *No phone.*

Mercado Libertad. Better known as San Juan de Dios, this is one of Latin America's largest covered markets. Its three expansive floors, with shops organized thematically, tower over downtown's east side. Fluctuating degrees of government intervention dictate the quantity of contraband electronics available. Avoid the food on the second floor unless you have a stomach of iron. Be wary of fakes in the jewelry stores. The market opens Monday–Saturday 10–8, but some stores close at 6; the few shops open on Sunday close by 3. ✉ *Calz. Independencia Sur; use pedestrian bridge from Plaza Tapatía's south side, Centro Histórico* ☎ *No phone.*

SPECIALTY SHOPS

ART AND HANDICRAFTS

Influenced by the florid baroque style of 17th-century New Spain, artist Agustín Parra crafts everything from ornate tables and doors to religious icons at **Agustín Parra Diseño Novohispano** (✉ *Calle Independencia 154–158, Tlaquepaque* ☎ *33/3657–8530* 🌐 *www.agustinparra.com.mx/*

Cadi (✉ *Juárez 174, Tlaquepaque* ☎ *33/3343–3682*) sells awesome stained-glass lamps and other decorative items for the home.

Ana Lucia Pewter (✉ *Ave. Tonalá 230, Tonalá* ☎ *33/3683–2794* 🌐 *www.analuciapewter.com*) sells beautiful locally made pewter items—from decorative tableware to picture frames—at ridiculously low prices.

Arte Jimenez (✉ *Cruz Blanca 264-F, Tonalá* ☎ *33/3690–8509* 🌐 *www.artejimenez.com*) is a unique shop specializing in decorative art made from fired copper and other metals.

El antiQuario Magazine evaluates antiques, art, and folk art online at 🌐 *www.elantiquario.com*. It's a great resource when you're deciding where to shop for ceramics, textiles, wrought iron, and rustic furniture.

Fodor's Choice ★ Sergio Bustamante's work is in galleries around the world, but you can purchase his sculptures of human, animal, and fairy-tale creatures in bronze, ceramic, or resin for less at **Galería Sergio Bustamante** (✉ *Calle Independencia 238, Tlaquepaque* ☎ *33/3639–5519, 33/3657–8354, or 33/3659–7110*) You'll also find his designs in silver- and gold-plated jewelry. Don't expect a bargain, however; most pieces range from hundreds to thousands of dollars.

The government-run **Instituto de la Artesanía Jalisciense** (✉ *Calz. González Gallo 20, at Calz. Independencia Sur, Centro Histórico* ☎ *33/3030–9090*), on the northeast side of Parque Agua Azul, has exquisite blown glass and hand-glazed pottery typical of Jalisco artisans. Prices are fixed here.

For whimsical statues, head to **Rodo Padilla** (✉ *Independencia 139, Centro, Tlaquepaque* ☎ *33/3657–3712*) The shop is full of the local artisan's hand-sculpted ceramic and metal pieces. His subjects range from older couples riding bikes to entire families crammed into cars.

CLOTHING

In a stylish Victorian mansion, the boutique of **Alberto Rodríguez** (✉ *Av. Vallarta 1300, Zona Minerva* ☎ *33/3827–2871*) displays wild and refined gowns by one of the region's top designers.

Designer **Alejandro Julian Nuñez** (✉ *Ignacio Ramirez 93, Zona Minerva* ☎ *33/3825–7464*) creates casual and semiformal clothing from *manta* (a sturdy cotton), hand embroidered with Huichol motifs.

Make a splash at Halloween dressed up as a mariachi or charro (Mexican cowboy) with a big leather belt and extra-wide-brim hat. You can thumb through an extensive selection of authentic charro gear at **El Charro** (✉ *Local 30, Av. López Mateos Sur 2375 [Plaza del Sol mall]* ☎ *33/3122–5148* ✉ *Av. Juárez, Centro* ☎ *33/3614–7599*).

SILVER AND JEWELRY

Eréndira Contis (✉ *La Gran Plaza Mall, Av. Vallarta 3959, Zapopan* ☎ *33/3123–1254*), specializing in nuptial jewelry, stands out in a city that's rife with jewelry offerings. Contis and Lewis Kant display modern Mexican art, as well as their own sculptures, and craft unique pieces from gold, silver, and precious stones.

Mercado Libertad has silver at great prices, but not everything that glitters there is certifiably silver. A safer, albeit pricier, bet is the shops along Avenida República in downtown Guadalajara, where there are more than 400 jewelers. **Centro Joyero República** (✉ *Av. República 20, Centro* ☎ *33/3617–7070*) is a safe bet for good authentic silver. Finally, for quality jewelry, check out **Tapatío Centro Joyero** (✉ *Av. República 70, Centro* ☎ *33/3617–1701*).

5

SPORTS AND THE OUTDOORS

GOLF

Clubs are less crowded on Wednesday and Thursday; all rent equipment for around $20 to $30. Golf carts typically cost around $40. Guadalajara's top golf clubs—El Cielo and Santa Anita—are technically for members only, but hotels can get you in.

Atlas Country Club (✉ *Carretera Guadalajara–Chapala, Km 6.5, El Salto* ☎ *33/3689–2620*) is an 18-hole, par-72 course designed by Joe Finger that's on the way to the airport. Greens fees are about $92 on weekdays, and $104 on weekends and holidays.

The private **El Cielo Country Club** (✉ *Paseo del Cielo 1, Zapopan* ☎ *33/3684–4436*), on a hill outside town, is an 18-hole, 6,765-yard, par-72 course blissfully removed from the city's din and with challenging holes and water features. For non-members it's $115 for 18 holes, including cart.

Las Cañadas Country Club (✉ *Av. Bosques San Isidro 777, Zapopan* ☎ *33/3685–0512 or 33/3685–0412*) is a rolling, 18-hole course in an exclusive area of Zapopan. Greens fees are $60–$80.

HEALTH CLUBS

Gold's Gym (✉ *Av. Xóchitl 4203, Zona Plaza del Sol* ☎ *33/3122–6541* ✉ *Av. México 3370, Local Ancla 1–A PB, Col. Monraz* ☎ *33/1201–1485 or 33/1201–1486* 🌐 *www.goldsgymmexico.com*) has two locations. Day passes are $8 at both. Weekday hours are 6 AM–11 PM at both; the Plaza del Sol location (which has a pool) is open 9–5 on weekends, while the Colonia Monraz location, near Plaza México, is open 7–3 on Saturday and is closed on Sunday.

The health club at the **Presidente Inter-Continental** (✉ *Av. López Mateos Sur 3515, Zona Plaza del Sol* ☎ *33/3678–1227*), open daily 5:30 AM–11 PM (pool open 7 AM–10 PM), admits non-guests for about $15 per day.

TENNIS

The court at the **Camino Real** (✉ *Av. Vallarta 5005, Zona Minerva* ☎ *33/3134–2424*) opens daily 7 AM–10 PM, and costs $14 an hour during the day and $19 at night. Reservations are essential.

SIDE TRIPS FROM GUADALAJARA

An hour's drive in just about any direction from Guadalajara will bring you out of the fray and into the countryside. Due south is Lake Chapala, Mexico's largest lake, featuring the cute waterside village of Ajijic—think copious bougainvillea and cobblestone roads. Tequila, where the infamous firewater is brewed, is west of Guadalajara. Teuchitlán, just south of Tequila, is the jumping-off point for a visit to the stellar Guachimontones ruins; go now, as they're growing in fame and popularity daily. Ajijic makes for a nice overnight jaunt, while Tequila and Teuchitlán are great for day-trippers.

TEQUILA

56 km (35 mi) northwest of Guadalajara.

As you leave the bustle of Guadalajara to head west, the entire landscape changes; suddenly, the land is peppered with the distinctive blue-green color of agave. As you near Tequila, families are selling 100% blue agave tequila in plastic bottles for astoundingly low prices. For an in-depth look at how Mexico's most famous liquor is derived from the spiny plant that grows in fields alongside the highway, stop by this tiny village.

GETTING HERE AND AROUND

The drive to tequila country is a straightforward and easy trip: head west from Guadalajara along Avenida Vallarta for about 25 minutes until you hit the toll road junction (it will say Puerto Vallarta Cuota). The whole trip takes about an hour by car. Either take the toll road (*cuota*) or the free road (*libre*) toward Puerto Vallarta. The toll road is faster, safer, and costs about $10. You can also catch a bus to Tequila from the Antigua Central Camionera (Old Central Bus Station), northeast of the Parque Agua Azul on Avenida Dr. R. Michel, between Calle Los Angeles and Calle 5 de Febrero. Buses marked AMATITÁN-TEQUILA are easy to spot from the entrance on Calle Los Angeles.

TRAIN Another option is to take the Tequila Express train from Guadalajara to Tequila and back for about $80. One of the few passenger trains left in Mexico takes guests on an all-day tour starting and ending with free canned-tequila mixed drinks (like palomas and sangrita), accompanied by mariachi music. Upon arrival in Tequila, the tour takes visitors to a distillery to learn about the process of making the liquor; the day includes tastings at the distillery, a show of traditional Jalisco dancing and music, and a delicious all-you-can-eat-and-drink Mexican buffet.

TOURS Tours of the city that include stops at distilleries and agave fields are available from two providers found under the porticos to the left of the cathedral. Tranvias Turisticos De Tequila leaves every 30 minutes daily, 10–4:30, except for Tuesday; the $8 tour lasts 2 hours. Servi-Tours Agave Azul offers three different tours every 30 minutes that range from $7 to $11, adding additional stops and time—from 1½ to 2 hours—depending on what level you choose.

RUMOR HAS IT

It's believed that centuries ago the Tiquila, a small Nahuatl-speaking tribe, discovered the fermenting powers of the agave heart's juice. When distilled (an innovation introduced after the Spanish arrived in the 16th century), the fermented liquid turns into the heady liquor, which can be legally named tequila only when cultivated and distilled in this and a few other regions of Mexico.

5

ESSENTIALS

Train Tequila Express (☎ *33/3880–9090 Ext. 2099* 🌐 *www.tequilaexpress.com.mx*).

Tours Servi-Tours Agave Azul (☎ *37/47420851*)**Tranvias Turisticos De Tequila** (☎ *33/1299–7536*).

EXPLORING

Opened in 1795, the **José Cuervo Distillery** (✉ *Calle José Cuervo 73* ☎ *37/4742–2442*) is the world's oldest tequila distillery. Every day, 150 tons of agave hearts are processed into 80,000 liters of tequila here. Tours are given daily every hour from 10 to 4. The tours at noon and 3 PM are in English, but English-speakers can often be accommodated at other times. The basic tour, which includes one margarita cocktail, costs $8. It's $12 for tours with a few additional tastings as well as an educational catalog, or $20 if you want to add special reserve tequilas to your tasting. Tours including round-trip transportation can be arranged through the major hotels and travel agencies in Guadalajara. This is a good deal, including several tequila tastings, a complimentary margarita, and time for lunch for about $22. Call 33/3343–4481 at least a day in advance to make arrangements. ■ **TIP→ Make sure to ask the guide for coupons for an additional margarita, as well as discounts at an area restaurant and in the gift shop.**

The **Museo Nacional del Tequila** (✉ *Calle Ramon Corona 34* ☎ *37/4742–0012; ask for the museum*) is open weekdays 9 to 4 ($1). The gallery sometimes hosts exhibits by local artists.

The **Sauza Museum** (✉ *Calle Albino Rojas 22* ☎ *37/4742–0247*) has memorabilia from the Sauza family, a tequila-making dynasty second only to the Cuervos. The museum opens daily 10–3. Admission costs about 50 cents; for this low price they offer tours in English as well as Spanish, depending on the needs of the crowd.

For a visit to where Herradura tequila is made, go to **San José del Refugio** (✉ *Comercio 172, Amatitán* ☎ *33/3942–3900* 🌐 *www.herradura.com*). It's a spectacular old hacienda where you can see workers' quarters from

CLOSE UP

The Struggle of the Huichol

The Huichol (WEE-chol) Indians' true name is Wirraritari, or "people who populate places of thorny plants." It's a fitting name for this hardy and reclusive group, whose independence has helped them preserve their traditions better than many of Mexico's native communities. (As a measure of their isolation, some Huichol communities only had electricity installed in 2003.) To outsiders, the most notable among Huichol traditions is the use of peyote, a hallucinogenic cactus fruit, in complex spiritual ceremonies. Huichol artists also create remarkable "paintings" by pressing colorful beads or yarn onto wood molds smeared with sap.

The Huichol fiercely resisted Spanish—and later Mexican—intrusion; nowadays most live in northern Jalisco, southern Nayarit, and Zacatecas, in a remote 592,800-acre reservation established in 1953. In recent years, however, the ownership and boundaries of some Huichol lands, much of it rented out to farmers and cattle breeders, have come under dispute. The conflict hasn't been peaceful, with allegations of human rights violations perpetrated by Nayarit police as well as by the current "tenants." In the mid-1990s, after a long investigation, Mexico's Human Rights Commission (CEDH) corroborated many of the Huichol allegations, and a recent constitutional amendment affirmed the autonomy of the Huichol and other indigenous communities within Mexico. But problems continue—there remains intense pressure to develop some Huichol lands, and the Mexican Army, in its highly visible war on drugs, has arrested Huichol coming back from religious pilgrimages in the San Luis Potosi desert, where they collect peyote.

long ago. The tour ends with a tasting of some of the different tequilas you can purchase in the gift shop. Tours are scheduled during weekdays on the hour from 9 to 3. Just to be safe, call ahead for reservations.

WHERE TO EAT

$ MEXICAN ✕ **Fonda Cholula.** This typical Mexican restaurant owned by José Cuervo serves up decent quesadillas and other local favorites without leaving your wallet empty. The margaritas are not bad, either. ✉ *Ramon Corona 55* ☎ *37/4742–1079* ⏲ *Daily 12–6, except Christmas and New Year's Day.*

TEUCHITLÁN

50 km (28 mi) west of Guadalajara.

Teuchitlán itself isn't much to see: a small Mexican town like many others, with a few small eateries surrounding a central plaza. But its main draw, the mysterious Guachimontones Ruins, are growing in popularity and preservation efforts are moving apace. Near the ruins, there are nice lakeside restaurants with decent food and better atmosphere than in town; spending some time here after seeing the ruins makes for a lovely afternoon.

GETTING HERE AND AROUND

To get to Teuchitlán from Guadalajara, drive west out along Avenida Vallarta for 25 minutes to the toll-road junction to Puerto Vallarta, then take the free (*libre*) Route 70 toward Vallarta. Head west along Route 15 for a couple of miles; then turn left onto Route 70 and continue until you reach the town of Tala. Two kilometers (1 mi) past the sugar mill, turn right onto Route 27. Teuchitlán is 15 minutes from the last junction. If you prefer not to drive yourself, it's also possible to hire a car from Guadalajara.

EXPLORING

Guachimontones Ruins. For decades, residents in this sleepy village of sugarcane farmers had a name for the funny-looking mounds in the hills above town, but they never considered the Guachimontones to be more than a convenient source of rocks for local construction projects. Then in the early 1970s an American archaeologist asserted that the mounds were the remnants of a long-vanished, 2,000-year-old community. It took Phil Weigand nearly three decades to convince authorities in faroff Mexico City that he wasn't crazy. Before he was allowed to start excavating and restoring this monumental site in the late 1990s, plenty more houses and roads were produced with Guachimonton rock—and countless tombs were looted of priceless art.

This UNESCO World Heritage Site is most distinctive for its sophisticated concentric architecture—a circular pyramid surrounded by a ring of flat ground, surrounded by a series of smaller platforms arranged in a circle. The "Teuchitlán Tradition," as the concentric circle structures are called, is unique in world architecture. While little is known about the ancient settlement, Weigand believes the formations suggest the existence of a pre-Hispanic state in the region, whereas it was previously held that only socially disorganized nomads inhabited the area at the time. Similar ruins are spread throughout the foothills of the extinct Tequila Volcano, but this is the biggest site yet detected.

Until late 2009, visitors had to find their way to the ruins by asking locals and driving up a hill on an unmarked dirt road. But construction of a large visitor center and museum was nearing completion at this writing, and there are now signs along the highway and through the town of Teuchitlán directing visitors to the site.

WHERE TO EAT

$$ MEXICAN

✕ **Restaurant Montecarlo.** This outdoor restaurant is one of a handful of eateries along the lakeside in Teuchitlán. While not fancy, it offers a variety of Mexican dishes, including fish, molcajetes, and fajitas, and provides a grand view of the lake teeming with fish and birds—including herons and pelicans. There's also a fish pond where kids can borrow a homemade rod for some catch and release. As you turn into the street, don't feel pressured by the parking attendants at the other restaurants who will make attempts to get you into their locales. ✉ *Carretera Guadalajara–Tala-San Marcos, Km 49* ☎ *38/4733–0257.*

AROUND LAGO DE CHAPALA

48 km (30 mi) southeast of Guadalajara.

Mexico's largest natural lake is a one-hour drive southeast of Guadalajara. Surrounded by jagged hills and serene towns, Lake Chapala is a favorite Tapatío getaway and a haven for thousands of North American retirees. The name probably derives from Chapalac, who was chief of the region's Taltica Indians when the Spaniards arrived in 1538.

The area's main town, Chapala, is flooded with weekend visitors, and the pier is packed shoulder-to-shoulder most Sundays. Its *malecón* is often packed with local families and couples on weekends. Eight kilometers (5 mi) west is Ajijic, a picturesque village that's home to the bulk of the area's expatriates. Farther west, San Juan Cosalá is popular for its thermal-water pools.

WATER LEVELS

Fifty miles wide but less than 30 feet deep when full, Lake Chapala is the vestige of an ancient inland sea. It's at the tail end (in geological terms) of a natural death from millennia of silt accumulation. This drying process has been accelerated in recent decades by overexploitation of the Lerma River feeding the lake. In 2002, Lake Chapala plummeted to an average depth of 4 feet, exposing a mile of lake bed stretching from the Chapala pier. Several years of heavy summer rain brought the lake back to near pre-2002 water levels, but what once was a clean place to enjoy lake activities is now much less pristine.

GETTING HERE AND AROUND

Driving from Guadalajara, take Avenida Lázaro Cárdenas or Dr. R. Michel to Carretera a Chapala. The trip takes about an hour. The Carretera a Chapala is the quickest route to Chapala and Ajijic.

Autotransportes Guadalajara Chapala (☎ *33/3619–5675*) serves the lakeside towns for about $4. It's 30 minutes to Chapala and another 15 minutes to Ajijic; there are departures every half hour from 6 AM to 9:30 PM. Make sure you ask for the *directo* (direct) as opposed to *clase segunda* (second-class) bus, which makes frequent stops along the highway en route.

CHAPALA

45 km (28 mi) south of Guadalajara.

Chapala was a placid weekend getaway for aristocrats in the late 19th century, but when then-president Porfirio Díaz got in on the action in 1904, other wealthy Mexicans followed suit. More and more summer homes were built, and in 1910 the Chapala Yacht Club opened. Avenida Madero, Chapala's main street, is lined with restaurants, shops, and cafés. Three blocks north of the promenade, the plaza at the corner of López Cotilla is a relaxing spot to read a paper or succumb to sweets from surrounding shops. The Iglesia de San Francisco (built in 1528), easily recognized by its blue neon crosses on twin steeples, is two blocks south of the plaza.

On weekends Mexican families flock to the shores of the (for now, at least) rejuvenated lake. Vendors sell refreshments and souvenirs, while lakeside watering holes fill to capacity.

CAUTION

On both ends of the highway are precarious hilly stretches. Care should be taken while returning to Guadalajara from Chapala on Sunday night, when the largely unlighted highway fills with tipsy drivers.

WHERE TO EAT AND STAY

$$ MEXICAN **Restaurant Cazadores.** This grandly turreted brick building was once the summer home of the Braniff family, former owners of the defunct airline. The menu includes slightly overpriced seafood and beef dishes. The house specialty is *chamorro*, pork shank wrapped in banana leaves. A patio overlooks the boardwalk and is inviting in the evening. *Paseo Ramón Corona 18 376/765–2162 AE, MC, V Closed Mon.*

$$ **Hotel Villa Montecarlo.** Built around a Mediterranean-style villa nearly a century old, this hotel has well-maintained grounds with plenty of places for picnics or for the kids to play. One of the two swimming pools (the biggest in the area) is filled with water from the nearby hot springs; it's usually open only on weekends and holidays. The simple, clean rooms all have patios or terraces. Popular with Mexican families, the hotel has packages that are often good deals. For about $20 more than a standard room you can get a suite with larger terrace or balcony, a kitchenette, and king-size bed. **Pros:** huge pools; extensive grounds; outdoor dining under a flowering tree. **Cons:** can be noisy. *Av. Hidalgo 296, about 1 km (½ mi) west of Av. Madero 37/6765–2024 www.hoteles.udg.mx/montecarlo 45 rooms, 2 suites In-room: no a/c. In-hotel: restaurant, bar, tennis courts, pools, laundry service, parking (free) AE, MC, V.*

$$ ★ **Lake Chapala Inn.** Three of the four rooms in this restored mansion face the shore; all have high ceilings and whitewashed oak furniture. Rates include an English-style breakfast (with a continental breakfast on Sunday). **Pros:** solar-heated lap pool; English-speaking host; sunny reading room. **Cons:** dated furnishings; square tubs not conducive to long soaks. *Paseo Ramón Corona 23 37/6765–4786 or 37/6765–4809 www.chapalainn.com 4 rooms In-room: no a/c, Wi-Fi. In-hotel: restaurant, pool, laundry service, Wi-Fi hotspot, parking (free) No credit cards BP.*

AJIJIC

8 km (5 mi) west of Chapala, 47 km (30 mi) southwest of Guadalajara.

Ajijic has narrow cobblestone streets, vibrantly colored buildings, and a gentle pace—with the exception of the considerably trafficky main highway through the town's southern end. The foreign influence is unmistakable: English is widely (though not exclusively) spoken, and license plates come from far-flung places like British Columbia and Texas.

The Plaza Principal (also known as Plaza de Armas) is a tree- and flower-filled central square at the corner of Avenidas Colón and Hidalgo. The

Iglesia de San Andrés (Church of St. Andrew) is on the plaza's north side. In late November the plaza and its surrounding streets fill for the saint's nine-day fiesta. From the plaza, walk down Calle Morelos (the continuation of Avenida Colón) toward the lake and browse the boutiques. Turn left onto Avenida 16 de Septiembre or Avenida Constitución for art galleries and studios. Northeast of the plaza, along the highway, the hub of local activity is the soccer field, which doubles as a venue for concerts.

WHERE TO EAT

$$ ARGENTINE ✕ **Ajijic Tango**. Considered one of the top, if not the top, restaurants in Ajijic, this Argentine favorite sees locals and tourists waiting in a line down the block to get inside. Many go for the *arrachera* (flank steak), lamb, or carpaccio. Reservations are a must on weekdays—but the eatery doesn't take them on weekends, so get there early. ✉ *Calle Morelos 5* ☎ *37/6766–2458* 🌐 *www.ajijictango.com* 💳 *MC, V* ⏲ *Wed.–Sat. and Mon. 12:30–10, Sun. 12:30–6.*

$–$$ GERMAN ✕ **Johanna's**. Come to this intimate bit of Bavaria on the lake for German cuisine like sausages and goose or duck pâté. Main dishes come with soup or salad, applesauce, and cooked red cabbage. For dessert indulge in plum strudel or blackberry-topped torte. Come on the early side, though; this restaurant closes at 8 PM. ✉ *Carretera Chapala–Jocotepec, Km 6.5* ☎ *37/6766–0437* 💳 *No credit cards* ⏲ *Closed Mon.*

$$ ECLECTIC ✕ **La Bodega de Ajijic**. Eat on a covered patio overlooking a grassy lawn and a small pool at this low-key restaurant. In addition to Mexican standards, the menu has Italian dishes such as pastas; the food here is a bit meager and overpriced. Still, service is friendly, and there's live music—ranging from Mexican pop and rock to blues, jazz, guitar, and harp—most nights. It opens at 8 AM, in time for breakfast, every day but Thursday, when it opens later. ✉ *Av. 16 de Septiembre 124* ☎ *376/766–1002* 💳 *AE, MC, V.*

$$ ECLECTIC ✕ **Number 4**. This trendy two-level outdoor restaurant on one of Ajijic's charming side streets offers beautifully presented dishes, many with an Asian twist. Diners can sit in the modern interior or chose to enjoy the upstairs patio, surrounded by trees and the night sky. Fabulous live piano music accompanies lunch Saturday and Sunday, and there's live music nightly. The bar offers special concoctions, such as a cranberry mandarin martini. ✉ *Donato Guerra 4* ☎ *37/6766–1360; 416/907-0609 in U.S. and Canada* 🌐 *www.number4.com.mx* 💳 *MC, V* ⏲ *Hours fluctuate seasonally.*

WHERE TO STAY

$–$$ 🏨 **Casa Blanca**. Gracious gardens, tinkling fountains, bright colors, and arched windows give the traveler a sense of sleeping in a Mexican hacienda while also enjoying the comforts of home. The hotel's basic rooms are cheerful and tastefully decorated with blond-wood furnishings, and the grounds include two patios for guest use. A small, upscale bar provides drinks of your choice, a few quick food options, and flat-screen TVs for watching sports games. Continental breakfast is included, and four of the eight rooms have a kitchenette. **Pros:** full of character; manicurist and massage therapist by reservation; complementary shoe shine; on-site Internet service. **Cons:** small rooms. ✉ *Calle 16 de Septiembre*

29, Centro ☎ *376/766–4440 or 800/436–0759* 🌐 *www.casablancaajijic.com* *8 rooms* *In-room: kitchen (some). In-hotel: bar, Internet terminal, Wi-Fi hotspot* *AE, MC, V* *CP.*

$$ ★ **La Nueva Posada.** The well-kept gardens framed in bougainvillea define this inviting inn. Rooms are large, with high ceilings and local crafts. Villas share a courtyard and have tile kitchenettes. The bar has jazz or Caribbean music some weekend evenings. Out in the garden restaurant strands of tiny white lights set the mood for an evening meal. **Pros:** uniquely decorated, airy rooms; great restaurant; discounts given for paying with cash. **Cons:** TVs in rooms are small. ✉ *Calle Donato Guerra 9* *A.P. 30, 45920* ☎ *37/6766–1344* 🌐 *www.hotelnuevaposada-ajijic.com* *19 rooms, 4 villas* *In-room: TV. In-hotel: restaurant, bar, pool, laundry service* *MC, V* *BP.*

NIGHTLIFE

La Bodega de Ajijic (✉ *Calle 16 de Septiembre 124* ☎ *376/766–1002* *$3 cover Fri. and Sun.*) has dancing on weekends, and live guitar the rest of the week. It's closed Thursday.

The rambling, hacienda-style **Vieja Posada** (✉ *Calle Morelos 1* ☎ *376/766–0744*) is a popular spot for live Latin and tropical music, usually twice a week on Tuesday (7 to 10) and Saturday (9 to 1).

SHOPPING

Ajijic's main shopping strip is Calle Morelos, but there are many galleries and shops east of Morelos, on Avenida 16 de Septiembre and Calle Constitución.

Artesanía Huichol (✉ *Calle Donato Guerra 18* ☎ *376/766–5125*) sells Huichol artwork.

Actually a women's co-op, **Creaciones del Lago** (✉ *Calle Ramón Corona 11* ☎ *376/766–1292*) sells knitted, embroidered, and crocheted items.

Mi México (✉ *Calle Morelos 8* ☎ *376/766–0133*) sells a lovely selection of women's clothing, jewelry, and crafts.

SPORTS AND THE OUTDOORS

The **Rojas family** (✉ *Paseo de los Caballos and Calle Los Carriles* ☎ *376/766–4261*) has been leading horseback trips for more than 30 years. A ride along the lakeshore or in the surrounding hills costs around $8 an hour.

5

SAN JUAN COSALÁ

2 km (1 mi) west of Ajijic, 50 km (31mi) southwest of Guadalajara.

San Juan Cosalá is known for its thermal-water spas along Lago de Chapala.

Tlalocan Spa at the **Hotel Balneario San Juan Cosalá** (✉ *Calle La Paz Oriente 420, at Carretera Chapala–Jocotepec, Km 13* ☎ *38/7761–0302* 🌐 *www.hotelspacosala.com*) gives reasonably priced massages as well as facials, reflexology, manicures, and other treatments. The water park has several large mineral-spring-fed swimming pools and two wading pools; admission is about $10. The park has barbecue grills and Wi-Fi, so put up your feet and stay awhile—even overnight; the hotel is nice and reasonably priced. Weekends are crowded with *Tapatío* families.

WHERE TO STAY

$$ **Hotel Villa Bordeaux.** This adults-only hotel is operated by the same people as the Hotel Balneario. Rooms are small but pleasing, with brick walls and high ceilings. This is a smaller, more subdued, and more tranquil option than Villas Buenaventura Cosalá. A stay here gets you access to the water park for free. **Pros:** tranquil environment; good restaurant. **Cons:** crowded on weekends; small rooms. ✉ *Calle La Paz Oriente 418, at Carretera Chapala–Jocotepec, Km 13* ☎ *387/761–0494* *11 rooms* *In-room: no a/c. In-hotel: restaurant, pool, gym, spa, no kids under 18* ▭ *MC, V.*

$$ **Villas Buenaventura Cosalá.** You can relax for free in the hotel's outdoor thermal pools or rent time in the private hot tubs or private pools. The large one- and two-bedroom suites are clean, if a bit sterile. The grounds are filled with sculptures. On many weekends during high season the hotel requires a two- or three-night minimum stay, but likely as not the third night is free, which is a real bonus. Choose a unit with or without Jacuzzi and kitchenette. **Pros:** spa-like mood; easy drive from Guadalajara. **Cons:** noisy children sometimes disturb the peace. ✉ *Carretera Chapala–Jocotepec, Km 13.5* ☎ *387/761–0202 or 387/761–0303* 🌐 *www.hotelvbc.com* *19 suites* *In-room: no a/c, kitchen (some). In-hotel: restaurant, pools* ▭ *MC, V.*

Veracruz

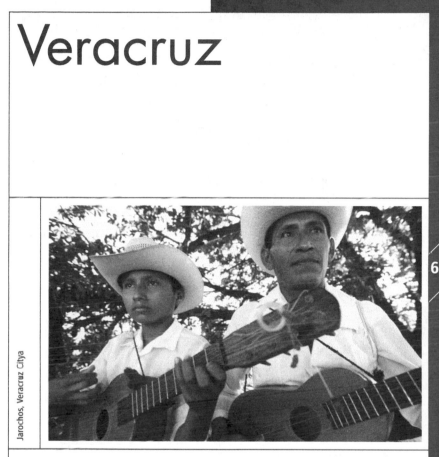

Jarochos, Veracruz Citya

WORD OF MOUTH

"I think Veracruz is a very nice port where you can get excellent food . . . the beach isn't beautiful but that's to be expected (this is the Gulf of Mexico, not the Caribbean). There are a lot of small towns nearby that can make a visit even more interesting. The downtown area is full of life so you should get some flavor of local traditions (danzón, for example)."

—mch

WELCOME TO VERACRUZ

TOP REASONS TO GO

★ **Taking the road less traveled:** Mexicans love to vacation in this state, but it's off the radar for most foreigners.

★ **Dining on amazing seafood:** Try it a la *vera-cruzana,* sautéed with tomatoes, onions, garlic, and usually green olives.

★ **Experiencing little-known ruins:** The ruins of El Tajín, which flourished from the early 9th to the early 13th centuries, are some of the most magnificent in Mexico.

★ **Watching men fly:** Paplanta's *voladores* spin from the top of an 82-foot pole in a breathtaking Totonac ceremony that makes bungee jumping look tame.

★ **Joining in the *danzón*:** This stately dance from Cuba is a cornerstone of Veracruz's eclectic culture.

1 Northern Veracruz. Built by the Totonac, the magnificent ruins of El Tajín are the best reason to travel to northern Veracruz. The coastal plains that make up this part of the state are filled with vanilla vines and orange and mango groves, giving the city of Papantla its sweet scent.

2 Central Veracruz. If you head inland, you'll meet the Sierra Madre Oriental mountain range, with its stunning 18,400-foot Pico de Orizaba. In the foothills you'll find the state capital Xalapa, a laid-back university town that's also a great base for river-rafting explorations.

3 Veracruz City. Still one of the country's busiest ports, Veracruz City isn't afraid of hard work. But when evening falls the people of this graceful colonial capital let loose and head to the city's parks, which are filled with music and dancing.

4 Southern Veracruz. This Is a favorite vacation spot for Mexican families. Along with beaches, you'll find crystalline lakes tucked among gently rolling hills. The most famous is Lago Catemaco, whose shores are lined with small boats waiting to take you out on an excursion.

GETTING ORIENTED

Veracruz State is a long, slim crescent bordering the Gulf of Mexico, about five hours east of Mexico City. The port city of Veracruz is a big draw to the region and the logical jumping-off place. Although the beaches aren't quite the white-sand wonders of the Yucatán, they're cheerful and vibrant. Moreover, the state harbors pockets of colonial history, as well as some fascinating archaeological sites.

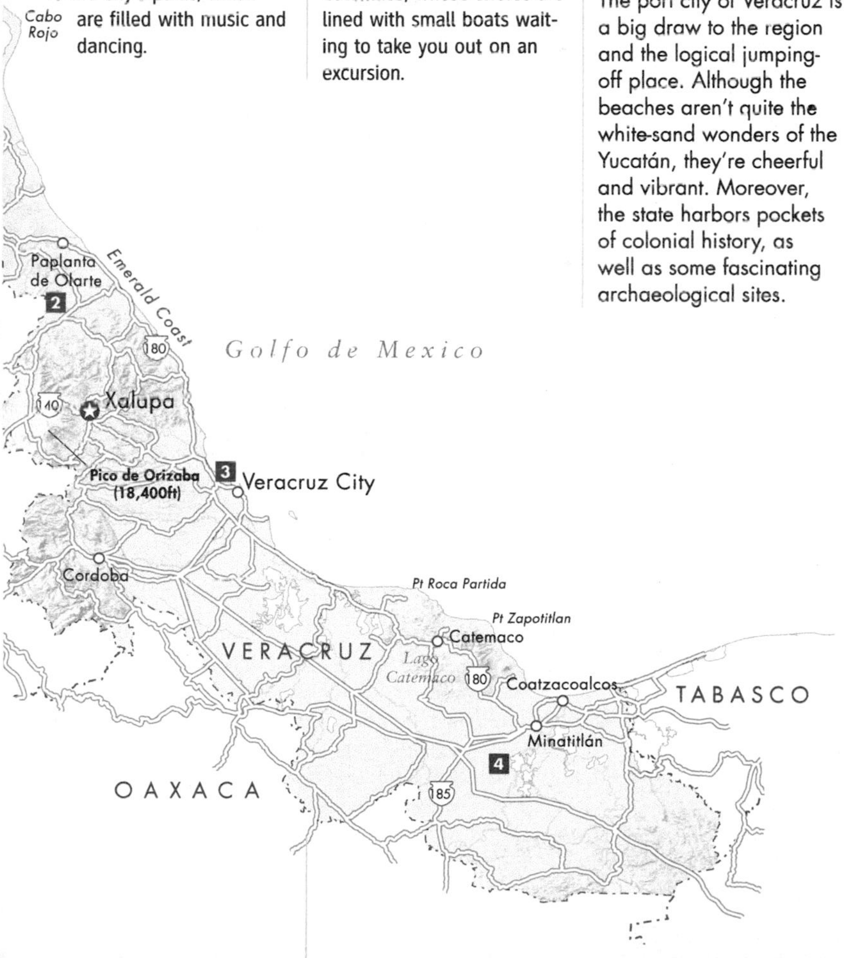

Cabo Rojo
Paplanta de Olarte
2
Emerald Coast
180
Golfo de Mexico
140
Xalupa
Pico de Orizaba (18,400ft)
3 Veracruz City
Cordoba
Pt Roca Partida
Pt Zapotitlan
Catemaco
VERACRUZ
Lago Catemaco
180
Coatzacoalcos
TABASCO
Minatitlán
4
OAXACA
185

VERACRUZ PLANNER

Dancing in the Streets

A great time to visit Veracruz City is during Carnaval, the region's major pre-Lenten bash held the week before Ash Wednesday. There are daily parades; musicians roam the city playing salsa and merengue; and couples literally dance in the streets.

In Tlacotalpan, locals worship the Virgin of the Candelaria. This patron saint of fishermen is officially honored on February 2, but the fiesta, which includes a flotilla of boats and the running of the bulls, begins January 31, lasting 10 days.

Even the smallest of villages has its fiestas. A vanilla festival in Papantla draws people every March. Coatepec, in the heart of coffee country, celebrates the bountiful bean in May. Xico is known for its raucous festival celebrating Mary Magdalene, the town's patron saint, that begins on July 16. On July 26 Xalapa celebrates the Fiesta de Santiago Apóstol with fireworks. If you're in Tlacotalpan September 27 to 29, you can take a peek at the Fiesta de San Miguelito, honoring Saint Michael. On September 30, Coatepec marks the Fiesta de San Jerónimo by constructing huge arches decorated with flowers.

Where to Start?

Your first stop will probably be Veracruz City. It's a great base for exploring the region, because many of the prettiest colonial-era towns, including La Antigua and Tlacotalpan, are within easy driving distance. There are also a few interesting ruins in the vicinity, such as Cempoala and Tres Zapotes. Veracruz City is about five hours from Mexico City and six hours from Oaxaca, so a trip by car or bus is feasible.

But if you are headed to the fascinating ruins of El Tajín, you might want to choose Xalapa as your base. The state's capital is cool and comfortable throughout the year, unlike most other parts of the region. From here you can also explore atmospheric mountain villages such as Coatepec and Xico and enjoy booming adventure tourism on the rivers of Jalcomulco.

Safari Camp Fun

Based in Jalcomulco, outside of Xalapa, Expediciones Mexico Verde (☎ *279/832–3730 or 279/832–3734, 01800/362–8800 toll-free in Mexico* 🌐 *www.mexicoverde.com*) runs adventure excursions out of their lovely, riverside ecotourism site. Raft, hike, run the challenge course, or just relax by the pool with good food and a cold cerveza.

Booking in Advance

You'll have to book in advance if you plan on staying in any of the towns during Christmas, Easter, or any festivals, particularly during Veracruz City's Carnaval.

It's always a good idea to do your research when you are planning your trip; check out the online forum at 🌐 www.fodors.com, where travelers weigh in on anything from hotel bathrooms to the best ice cream in town.

How's the Weather?

In Veracruz City and along the coast, the weather is hot and humid throughout the year. The rainy season runs from April to November, though the heaviest rains fall between June and September. Most storms are in the afternoon, clearing up by the early evening. There isn't quite as much rain in the arid areas in the northern part of the state.

Xalapa and the surrounding towns are high in the mountains, so they're usually cooler than coastal communities.

Keep in mind the possible range of temperatures if you are planning a trip to Pico de Orizaba, the highest mountain in Mexico, and its surrounding woodlands.

Savoring la Música de Veracruz

African- and Caribbean-influenced music fills the streets in this port city; the *son Jarocho* ("Veracruz sound"), centered on strings and percussion, is a regional variation of Mexican *sones*. To get a sampling of all the types of music in Veracruz, join the crowds swirling about the *zócalo* (main plaza). Inevitably, strolling mariachis and teams on marimbas (wooden xylophones) will be performing for people in the cafés. But for romance, nothing compares to the bands playing late into the night in Parque Zamora. Men blot their brows with crisp handkerchiefs, and women wave fans they had hidden in their bosoms. Everyone is willing to suffer the heat for the spirit of the *danzón,* the sultry dance brought to Mexico in 1879 by Cubans.

Money Matters

WHAT IT COSTS IN DOLLARS

	¢	$	$$	$$$	$$$$
Restaurants	under $5	$5–$10	$10–$15	$15–$25	over $25
Hotels	under $50	$50–$75	$75–$150	$150–$250	over $250

Restaurant prices are per person for a main course at dinner. Hotel prices are for two people in a standard double room.

Experiences

Soaking up the mood isn't difficult in Veracruz City. When you take a late-afternoon stroll through the cobblestone streets near the zócalo or along the breezy waterfront walk of the Paseo del Malecón, you'll be joining locals doing just the same. Stopping for an ice-cream cone or a steaming cup of *lechero* (coffee with milk) is a must. If eating seafood is a passion, don't miss the open-air Mariscos Villa Rica Mocambo, arguably one of the best seafood restaurants in the country. The Acuario de Veracruz, one of the largest aquariums in Latin America, displays tiger sharks, manatees, and sea turtles, and even allows you a dip with the sharks in their immersion tank.

Elsewhere in the state, you won't want to miss exploring the ruins at Cempoala and El Tajín (get there in time to see the voladores who entertain the crowds at midday). There are plenty of colonial villages worth exploring, like La Antigua with its narrow rope bridge and Tlacotalpan with its rows of handcrafted rocking chairs. In Catemaco, a lovely lakefront town, you can ward off evil spirits with a visit to local witches and ward off wrinkles with a mineral mud mask.

6

VERACRUZ CITY

Updated by Michele Joyce

THE LIVELY PORT CITY OF Veracruz, 345 km (214 mi) east of Mexico City, might not be the city that never sleeps, but it *is* a city that gets barely any rest. People listen to music in the squares until late at night, then sip coffee in the sidewalk cafés early the next morning. The exuberance of *jarochos,* as the city's residents are known, does not falter even in the broiling midday heat.

In 1519 Cortés landed in La Antigua, a slip of a place on the Río Huitzilapan some 25 km (16 mi) north, but it was Veracruz that became the major gateway for the Spanish settlement of Mexico. Its name, also given to many other communities throughout Latin America, means "true cross." Pirates frequently attacked the steamy coastal city, and their battles to intercept Spanish goods add a swashbuckling edge to the history of the oldest port in the Americas. The Spanish brought thousands of African slaves to Veracruz; later, Cuban immigrants flooded the town.

Today Veracruz is still one of the most important ports in Mexico, and you'll immediately sense its extroverted character. Huge cargo ships, ocean liners, and fishing vessels crowd its harbor, and the waterfront Paseo del Malecón is always buzzing with strolling couples and sailors with a few hours to kill. In the evening at the zócalo, the sound of marimbas floats through the air.

The city is actually two towns: the historic port of Veracruz and the fishing village of Boca del Río. These communities have fused into one, linked by 10 km (6 mi) of businesses geared toward tourists. The hotels in Veracruz have more charm, but those in Boca del Río, especially along the beaches near Playa Mocambo, have sun and sand. A visit to one of the seafood restaurants in Boca del Río is a must.

GETTING HERE AND AROUND

Most flights connect through Mexico City, and there are several daily nonstop flights between Veracruz and Monterrey, plus daily flights to Mérida and Cancún. Aeropuerto Internacional Heriberto Jara Corona is a clean, bright facility about 8 km (5 mi) south of downtown Veracruz. A cab ride between the airport and the city center costs $14 and takes roughly half an hour. Buy a ticket inside the airport for a fair price.

Though no city bus serves the airport, you can take a bus into and, for the most part, around the city. The most convenient way to purchase bus tickets is through Ticketbus. The bus company ADO has the most buses heading to Veracruz. The trip from Mexico City costs about $24 and takes about five hours. UNO, the deluxe bus line, also serves this route. The highways throughout the state are generally in really good condition, making renting a car a good way to see this long, slender state. From Mexico City you can reach Veracruz in about five hours on Carretera 150-D.

Tranvía La Bamba y La Marimba has double-decker tour buses that travel around the city in about 40 minutes. Though its recorded explanations are in Spanish, the tour is a good way to get your bearings, see downtown and the malecón, and listen to the local music (including songs like "La Bamba") that plays between explanations. Buses, which run 10–5 daily, leave about every hour and cost $1.50; catch them across from the Café la Parroquia, on the Paseo del Malecón in front of the Plaza de las Artesanías Miguel Alemán. Note that some buses are labeled TRANVIAS DEL MALECÓN.

The 90-minute city tour on red Turibus double-deckers takes in downtown and residential neighborhoods. Stops all over the city are marked with TURIBUS signs, and you can buy a ticket at any one of them and hop on and off as you like. Buses run daily 10–5 about every 90 minutes (there's no timetable posted at stops, though, so you won't know how long you'll have to wait till the next bus). The cost is $8.

ESSENTIALS

Bus Contacts **Ticketbus** (☎ *800/702–8000* 🌐 *www.ticketbus.com.mx*).

Currency Exchange **Bancomer** (✉ *Av. Juárez at Av. Independencia* ☎ *229/989–8000 or 229/989–8018* 🌐 *www.bancomer.com*). **Casa de Cambio Puebla** (✉ *Av. Juárez 112* ☎ *229/931–2450*).

Internet **NetChatBoys** (✉ *Calle Lerdo 369, between Avs. 5 de Mayo and Madero* ☎ *No phone*).

Medical Assistance **Hospital Regional de Veracruz** (✉ *20 de Noviembre s/n* ☎ *229/931–7857*). **Veracruz Cruz Roja** (☎ *229/937–5500*). **Police** (☎ *229/938–6599*).

Rental Cars **Alamo** (✉ *Aeropuerto Internacional Heriberto Jara Corona* ☎ *229/938–3700* 🌐 *www.alamo.com*). **Avis** (✉ *Aeropuerto* ☎ *229/934–9623* 🌐 *www.avis.com*). **Budget** (✉ *Aeropuerto* ☎ *229/939–2705* 🌐 *www.budget.com*). **Dollar** (✉ *Aeropuerto* ☎ *229/938–7878*).

Visitor and Tour Info **Tranvia La Bamba y La Marimba** (☎ *229/229–5533*). **Turibus** (☎ *229/937–4268*). **Veracruz Tourist Office** (✉ *Palacio Municipal, Planta Baja, Zaragoza and Lerdo s/n* ☎ *229/200–2217 or 229/200–2253*)

6

EXPLORING

TOP ATTRACTIONS

6 **Acuario de Veracruz.** Veracruz is home to one of Latin America's biggest and best aquariums. One tank alone has 2,000 species of marine life native to the Gulf of Mexico, including manta rays, barracudas, and sea turtles. Other tanks display tiger sharks and gentle manatees that enjoy interacting with the crowds. The entry also has a space where birds, including toucans, fly freely. Kids love the touch tanks. A guided immersion tank ($7 adults; $3.50 kids) provides daring visitors the chance to go nose to nose with the sharks. ✉ *Plaza Acuario, Blvd. Manuel Ávila Camacho s/n* ☎ *229/931–1020 or 229/932–8006* 🌐 *www.acuariodeveracruz.com* *$6 general* ⏲ *Mon.–Thurs. 9–7, Fri.–Sun. 9–7:30.*

Fodor's Choice ★

5 **Baluarte de Santiago.** The small fortress is all that's left of the old city walls. Like the Fuerte de San Juan de Ulúa, the colonial-era bulwark was built as a defense against pirates. The 1635 structure is impressively

Acuario de Veracruz **6**
Baluarte de Santiago **5**
Fuerte de San Juan de Ulúa **7**
Museo de la Ciudad **4**
Museo Histórico Naval **3**
Paseo del Malecón **2**
Zócalo **1**

solid from the outside, with cannons pointed toward long-gone marauders. Inside is a tiny museum that has an exquisite exhibit of pre-Hispanic jewelry—Spanish plunder, no doubt—discovered by a fisherman in the 1970s. ✉ *Calle Francisco Canal between Av. Gómez Farías and Av. 16 de Septiembre* ☎ *229/931–1059* 🌐 *www.inah.gob.mx* 🎫 *$4.10* 🕓 *Tues.–Sun. 10–4:30.*

7 ★ **Fuerte de San Juan de Ulúa.** During the viceregal era Veracruz was the only east coast port permitted to operate in New Spain and, therefore, was attacked by pirates. This unique coral-stone fort, the last land in Mexico to be held by the Spanish Royalists, is a monument to that era. The moats, ramparts, drawbridges, prison cells, and torture chambers create a miniature city. Fortification began in 1535 under the direction of Antonio de Mendoza, the first viceroy of New Spain. A few centuries later it was used as a prison, housing such prominent figures as Benito Juárez. After independence it was used in unsuccessful attempts to fight off invading French and Americans. You can explore the former dungeons, climb up on the ramparts, and wander across grassy patios. A tiny museum holds swords, pistols, and cannons, but signs are in Spanish only. Guides wander around in the site until about 3 PM—an English-speaking guide will charge around $25 per group. The fort is connected to the city center by a causeway; a taxi here should cost

about $5. ✉ *Via causeway from downtown Veracruz* ☎ *229/938–5151* 🌐 *www.sanjuandeulua.com.mx* 🎫 *$4.10* ⏱ *Tues.–Sun. 9–4:30.*

2 **Paseo del Malecón.** Everyone seems to come here at night, from cuddling young couples in search of a secluded bench to parents with children seeking the best place for ice cream. **■ TIP➜ Drop by during the day and you'll find boats that will take you out into the harbor for about $5 per person.** ✉ *Northern extension of Calle Molina.*

1 **Zócalo.** Also known as the Plaza de Armas, this square has distinctive *portales* (colonnades) and bells that compete for your attention. The hands-down winners are the deafening chimes of the Catedral de Nuestra Senora de la Asunción, which sits on the square's southwest corner. It dates from 1721. The runners-up are the bells of the 1635 Palacio Municipal, which have a fainter but no less insistent tune. The tower originally did double duty as a lighthouse. ✉ *Av. Independencia between Calle Lerdo and Calle Zamora.*

WORTH NOTING

4 **Museo de la Ciudad.** This museum in a lovely colonial-era building tells the city's history through artifacts, displays, and scale models. Also exhibited are copies of pre-Columbian statues and contemporary art. There are no explanatory materials in English, however. ✉ *Av. Zaragoza 397, at Calle Esteban Morales* ☎ *No phone* 🌐 *www.amiweb.com.mx/mc Icultura@veracruz-puerto.gob.mx* 🎫 *$3* ⏱ *Tues.–Sat. 10–6, Sun. 10–3.*

3 **Museo Histórico Naval.** In an impressive set of buildings that once housed navy officers, the Naval History Museum tells how the country's history was made on the high seas. Veracruz has been dubbed the city that was *cuatro veces heróica*, or "four times heroic," for its part in defending the country against two attacks by the French and two by the Americans. The museum tells of those wars, as well as the life of revolutionary war hero Venustiano Carranza. Explanatory materials are in Spanish only. ✉ *Av. Arista between Av. 16 de Septiembre and Av. Landero y Coss* ☎ *299/931–4078* 🎫 *Free* ⏱ *Tues.–Sun. 10–5.*

NEED A BREAK?

There are always lines out the door at Neveria Güero Güero Güera Güera (✉ *Calle Zamora 15, at Av. Landero y Coss* ☎ *229/932–0582* 🌐 *www.gueroguero.com*), where you can get a huge cup of *cacahuate* (peanut), *fresa* (strawberry), or more than a dozen other flavors of ice cream for only a buck. Locals say the name came about when the owner used to shout *güero* and *güera*, meaning blond-haired man or woman, to catch the attention of passing foreigners.

BEACHES

Veracruz City's beaches are not particularly inviting, being on the brownish side of gold, with polluted water. Decent beaches with paler, finer sand begin to the south in **Mocambo**, about 7 km (4½ mi) from downtown, and get better even farther down. The beach in front of the Fiesta Americana hotel is particularly well maintained. (Although it may appear to be claimed by the hotel, it's public.)

CLOSE UP

Veracruz Background

Veracruz has been a hub for more than 3,000 years. The Olmec thrived here between 1,200 BC and ADguay900, though there are few surviving examples of Olmec architecture. Instead, they're best remembered for the massive carved stone heads, a few of which are in the archaeological museum in Xalapa.

The Olmec were replaced by the Totonac, whose last legacy is the city of El Tajín in the northern part of the state, near present-day Papantla. Although you'll see architectural influences from other cultures—notably the Maya—El Tajín is unlike anywhere else. The style is typified by the hundreds of indentations in the Pyramid of the Niches. This city remained powerful until about AD 1200, when it was abandoned. Archaeologists speculate that it had grown too large to support its population.

Later Totonac cities include Cempoala, which was occupied at the time of the Spanish conquest. Its residents, who had been forced to pay tribute to the more powerful Aztecs, formed an alliance with the Spanish and helped them establish their first town in the New World, called La Villa Rica del la Vera Cruz. It was near present-day Veracruz. The Totonac also embraced Catholicism, and by 1523 the Franciscans were preaching to the population.

During the colonial period, which lasted until the early 19th century, Veracruz was the most important port in the New World. Invaders laid siege to the city time and time again. Veracruz is known as the "city four times heroic" because it repeatedly resisted invasion—first the French during the "Pastry War" in 1838, then the Americans during the Mexican-American War in 1847, the French again in 1866, then the Americans again in 1914.

About 4 km (2½ mi) south of Playa Mocambo is **Boca del Río**, a small fishing village at the mouth of the Río Jamapa that is quickly getting sucked into Veracruz's orbit. A taxi from the city center costs about $4. **Mandinga** is 8 km (5 mi) south of Boca del Río, and is less frequented by tourists. ■ **TIP→ Tread carefully if you don a pair of flip-flops (chanclas) to do your exploring. If it's wet, the pavement downtown can be dangerous.**

WHERE TO EAT

In addition to the restaurants around the zócalo, you'll want to head to Boca del Río. Many restaurants here are modest, but serve some of the finest seafood in this part of the country. If you'd like to eat with the locals, try the Mercado Hidalgo for breakfast or lunch; it's a 10-block walk south from the zócalo. ■ **TIP→ Seafood lovers can get a quick fix at the fish market, a mint-green building at the corner of Avenida Aquiles Serdán and Avenida Landero y Coss.**

CENTRO HISTÓRICO

$$$ ARGENTINE **✕ Che Tango.** For a hearty meal after a day at the aquarium, pop around the corner to this casual yet elegant Argentine restaurant. Select your cut of rib eye, tenderloin, or strip steak from the selection that's brought to your table, and tell your bow-tied waiter how you'd like it cooked. While it sizzles, nibble one of the flaky empanadas topped with *chimichurri* (sauce made with olive oil and parsley). Try the house cocktail, Rosita (made with anise). ✉ *Av. 16 de Septiembre 1938, at Calle Enríquez, Col. Flores Magón* ☎ *229/932–1745 or 229/932–1756* 🌐 *www.chetango.com.mx* ▭ *AE, MC, V* ⏲ *No breakfast.*

$$–$$$ STEAKHOUSE **✕ El Gaucho.** The scent of sizzling steaks and a giant neon cowboy draw meat lovers to this cavernous ranch-style restaurant morning, noon, and night. The epic menu lists nearly 100 dishes—from spicy chorizo hot off the grill to tongue sautéed with tomatoes and onions. Or try the shrimp stuffed with peppers and wrapped in bacon. The house specialty drink, *jarra de clericot* (red wine with melon and pineapple), is delicious. The place opens at 7 AM for breakfast. ✉ *Av. Bernal Díaz del Castillo 187, at Calle Colón* ☎ *229/935–0411* 🌐 *www.elgaucho.com.mx* ▭ *AE, MC, V.*

6

$ CAFÉ **✕ Gran Café de la Parroquia.** A leisurely stint here in the sun, watching ships unloading their cargo, is what Veracruz is all about. This family restaurant was so popular it split off into side-by-side establishments run by two brothers. The menus are nearly identical, both serving renowned *traditional lechero*. The milk is flamboyantly poured from silver jugs at a great height by a server. Visit the Gran Café closest to Hotel Emporio for classic *picadas y gordas* (puffy, deep-fried tortillas with beans, onion, mole, and cheese). **■ TIP→ Try for a sidewalk table under the arches, if you can withstand the competing marimbas and the appeals of women selling crafts.** ✉ *Paseo de Malecón between Hawaii Hotel and Hotel Emporio* ☎ *229/932–2584 or 299/932–1855* 🌐 *www.grancafedelaparroquia.com* ▭ *AE, MC, V.*

$ CAFÉ ★ **✕ Gran Café del Portal.** Sit in a shady arcade, near the live music, or in a dining room with copper columns and beamed ceilings at this famous café, which was opened as a candy shop in 1824. The menu has lots of dishes from Veracruz, including a delicious *huachinango a la veracruzana* (red snapper simmered in tomatoes, onions, garlic, green olives, and capers). The $8 weekday lunch special includes a soup or salad and a meat dish. The Gran Café del Portal has an ongoing rivalry with the Gran Café de la Parroquia as to which place serves the real lechero—here white-jacketed waiters bring you one kettle of strong coffee and another of hot milk, and let you do the mixing. ✉ *Av. Independencia 1187, across from cathedral* ☎ *229/931–2759* ▭ *MC, V.*

$ SEAFOOD **✕ Palapa Reyna.** Playa de Hornos, a popular stretch of sand south of the Acuario de Veracruz, is lined with thatch-roof seafood shacks. They all serve basically the same thing: fish cooked any way you like it. This place, with a giant neon sailfish positioned on the roof, is among the closest to the aquarium and one of the best. Grab a table in the open-air dining room or one under an umbrella along the surf. ✉ *Playa de Hornos* ☎ *No phone* ▭ *No credit cards.*

CLOSE UP

Happiness in a Seafood Shack

Some of Mexico's most delicious dishes come from Veracruz. The emphasis is on *pescado* (fish) and *mariscos* (shellfish). Some of the best places to eat in the region are the family-run seafood shacks you often find lining the beaches. Just ask for the *platillo del día.* This "dish of the day" is always fresh and served with a flourish.

Many specialties show the influence of the Spanish and African communities of nearby Cuba, including the state's signature dish, *huachinango a la veracruzana* (red snapper in the Veracruz style, which means it's simmered in tomatoes, onions, garlic, green olives, and capers). Another dish with a similar influence is *salpicón de jaiba,* a spicy crabmeat salad usually prepared with tomatoes, capers, and peppers. Other dishes reflect African ties in their use of beans, plantains, yucca, taro, and white sweet potatoes.

Peanuts are used a lot as well. They appear in such classics as *puerco encacahuatado* (pork in peanut sauce) and the bracing *salsa macha,* made by grinding peanuts with garlic, chilies, and olive oil. You'll also find peanut ice cream all over the state, as well as other *nieves* made with mangos, papayas, and other local fruits. Other sweet temptations include *buñuelos veracruzanos,* golden doughnuts dipped in a sugar and cinnamon mix.

Look out for the charge of *toritos* (little bulls), a heady alcoholic punch made with cane liquor, milk, and tropical-fruit pulp or peanuts.

BOCA DEL RÍO

$$$ STEAKHOUSE ✕ **Cacharrito.** The cowhides decorating the walls let you know exactly what's on the menu at this longtime favorite. Start off with Argentine-style empanadas (stuffed with beef, naturally), then move on to the grilled short ribs. If you have a hankering for the enormous rib eye, call at least three hours ahead. The impressive wine list includes selections from Argentina, Chile, and Spain, as well as a respectable representation from Mexico. ✉ *Blvd. Adolfo Ruíz Cortines 15, Boca del Río* ☎ *229/935–9246* ▭ *MC, V.*

$ ITALIAN ✕ **Il Veneziano.** This two-story family restaurant has a large indoor fish tank, a play area for children, and shaded tables on a white patio. The menu includes salads, pastas, meat dishes, and thin-crust pizzas. The *cuatro formaggi* pizza with mozarrella, blue cheese, Gruyère, and provolone cheeses is heavenly, especially with chimichurri sauce. The insalata golosa, a large salad served with a zesty house dressing, Gruyère cheese, bacon, and crushed nuts, is especially tasty. ✉ *Blvd. Ávila Camacho 1015, Boca del Río* ☎ *229/927–2481 or 229/927–2482* 🌐 *www.ilveneziano.com.mx* ▭ *MC, V.*

$–$$ SEAFOOD ★ ✕ **Pardiño's.** The Guinness Book of World Records honored the founder of this friendly seafood restaurant for dreaming up the world's longest seafood-stuffed fillet of fish, which was once prepared in the street along the waterfront. You can find smaller, but equally scrumptious concoctions and live midday music at this open-air dining room. Especially popular are the *camarones Pardiños* (juicy shrimp stuffed with manchego cheese and wrapped in bacon) and *ostiones a la diabla gratinados* (spicy oysters topped with grated cheese). Dishes like cheese-stuffed plantains satisfy vegetarians. ✉ *Calle Zamora 40, Boca del Río* ☎ *229/986–0135* ▭ *AE, MC, V.*

$$$ SEAFOOD **Villa Rica.** Though it's tucked away in Boca del Río, this open-air eatery is one of city's most popular seafood restaurants. Specialties include mussels, grouper, crab claws, and octopus prepared as you wish. For those who relish spicy food, the *ostiones enchilpayados* (in cream and chipotle chili) are a cut above the rest. **■ TIP→ Popular bands play Thursday through Sunday from 3 to 7, so you may need a reservation on those days.** ✉ *Calz. Mocambo 527, Boca del Río* ☎ *229/922–2113 or 229/922–3743* 🌐 *www.villaricamocambo.com.mx* ▭ *AE, MC, V.*

WHERE TO STAY

CENTRO HISTÓRICO

$$–$$$ ★ **Gran Hotel Diligencias.** The 2003 renovations of this 18th-century building into a stately hotel transformed the entire Centro Histórico: it lends elegance to the laid-back zócalo. Locals grumble that the decorations in the rooms lack any trace of Veracruz, but all you have to do is throw open the French doors to enjoy warm winds blowing through the palm trees and marimba bands in the square below. The second-floor terrace, which surrounds a small pool, is a great place to escape the heat. **Pros:** romantic architecture; nice terrace. **Cons:** bland design. ✉ *Av. Independencia 1115* ☎ *229/923–0280* 🌐 *www.granhoteldiligencias.com* *117 rooms, 4 suites* *In-room: Wi-Fi. In-hotel: restaurant, room service, bar, pool, gym, laundry service, Internet terminal, Wi-Fi hotspot, parking (free)* ▭ *AE, MC, V.*

$$ **Hawaii Hotel.** You can't miss this hotel, because its profile resembles an arrow pointing straight up. It's also one of the best deals in town. Rooms are impeccably maintained, and the eager-to-please staff makes sure you have a map of the city on arrival and a bag of local coffee to take home. **Pros:** friendly staff; close to waterfront; some rooms have nice views. **Cons:** slightly tacky architecture. ✉ *Paseo del Malecón 458* ☎ *229/989–8888* 🌐 *www.hawaiihotel.com.mx* *30 rooms* *In-hotel: Internet. In-hotel: restaurant, room service, pool, laundry service, parking (free)* ▭ *AE, MC, V.*

$$$ **Hotel Imperial.** Built in 1793 first as an elegant mesón, this hotel facing the zócalo has lots of charm. The wrought-iron elevator, brought from France in 1904, was, together with the one in the Chapultepec Palace in Mexico City, one of the first in Latin America. Though a bit dated, rooms have a certain elegance; many have balconies on the square. **Pros:** retains historical charm. **Cons:** the plaza in front is where the locals enjoy music in the evening. ✉ *Av. Miguel Lerdo 153, near Av. Independencia* 🌐 *www.hotelimperialveracruz.com* ☎ *229/932–4508* *54 rooms* *In-hotel: restaurant, room service, bar* ▭ *AE, MC, V.*

$$–$$$ **Hotel Ruiz Milán.** Rooms in this waterfront high-rise are completely up-to-date. You'll want to spend a few more dollars to look out over the ocean. The inviting, cool, marble-floor lobby is usually crowded with business executives closing a deal. **Pros:** modernized downtown business-class hotel. **Cons:** some rooms are noisy at night, a little pricey.

✉ *Paseo del Malecón 432* ☎ *229/932–6707or 229/932–5707* 🌐 *www.ruizmilan.com* 92 *rooms* *In-room: safe. In-hotel: restaurant, room service, pool, Wi-Fi hotspot, parking (free)* 💳 *AE, MC, V.*

$$ ★ **Meson del Mar**. In an enchanting colonial-era building with long corridors and graceful arches, the Meson del Mar is an intimate hotel near the waterfront. A staircase leads up to a breezy patio where you have a view over the rooftops. Exposed-wood beams and tile floors in the guest rooms recall a more gracious era. Rooms facing the busy street have double-paned windows that keep out most noise. Gandara, the open-air restaurant, serves a wide variety of fish dishes. **Pros:** good on-site restaurant; can be a good value. **Cons:** though they provide good service; many staffers don't speak English. ✉ *Calle Estaban Morales 543* ☎ *229/932–5043* 🌐 *www.mesondelmar.com.mx* *13 rooms, 7 suites* *In-room: safe, Wi-Fi. In-hotel: restaurant, bar, Internet terminal* 💳 *MC, V.*

$$ **Villa del Mar**. Across from one of the nicer sections of the downtown beach, this hotel lets you enjoy the sun of Veracruz without the scene of Boca del Río. As you might guess when you see the small playground, it caters mostly to families. The spacious rooms surround a garden with a tennis court, swimming pool, and hot tub. **Pros:** strong a/c; lots of hot water. **Cons:** some a/c makes noise; motel-like rooms. ✉ *Blvd. Manuel Ávila Camacho 2431, at Calle Bartolomé de las Casas* ☎ *229/989–6500* 🌐 *www.hotel-villadelmar.com* *92 rooms, 4 suites* *In-hotel: restaurant, bar, tennis court, pool, laundry service, parking (free)* 💳 *AE, MC, V* 🍽 *BP.*

BOCA DEL RÍO

$$$ **Balajú**. This hotel close to the aquarium is a good bargain. Rooms, all of which have ocean views, are spacious and furnished with modern furniture, including flat-screen TVs. Suites also have large sitting areas, a refrigerator, and a small kitchen. **Pros:** good value; up-to-date. **Cons:** small pool is just off the lobby, in a particularly public area. ✉ *Blvd. Manuel Ávila Camacho 1371, at Mina, Col. Flores Magón* ☎ *229/201–0808* 🌐 *www.balaju.com* *66 rooms, 2 suites* *In-hotel: restaurant, room service, pool, laundry service, parking (free), Wi-Fi* 💳 *AE, MC, V.*

$$$ **Crowne Plaza Torremar**. The lobby in this high-rise on Playa Mocambo is adorned with glass sculptures. Many of the rooms face the ocean, and the suites also have small balconies. The poolside fountain and the activities in the play area make this a good bet for families traveling with young children. It's across from Las Americas mall. **Pros:** nice pool complex; care taken in decorating. **Cons:** doesn't feel as if you're in Mexico. ✉ *Blvd. Adolfo Ruíz Cortines 4300, Playa Mocambo* ☎ *229/989–2100* 🌐 *www.crowneplaza.com* *211 rooms, 18 suites* *In-room: safe. In-hotel: restaurant, room service, bar, pools, gym, children's programs (ages 3–11), laundry service, Wi-Fi hotspot, parking (free)* 💳 *AE, MC, V.*

$$$ **Fiesta Americana**. This splashy hotel reclines on the soft sand at Playa Costa de Oro. Its marble corridors all seem to lead to the giant serpentine pool, maze of bridges, and lush gardens facing the ocean. The brightly colored rooms all overlook the beach. You have access to a

9-hole golf course 20 minutes away. Note that quoted prices often include breakfast; let them know your preference. **Pros:** the best business facilities in Veracruz. **Cons:** expensive for what you get, especially when compared to other, more affordable hotels. ✉ *Blvd. Manuel Ávila Camacho s/n, at Fracc. Costa de Oro* ☎ *229/989–8989 or 800/343–7821* 🌐 *www.fiestaamericana.com.mx* *211 rooms, 23 suites* *In-room: safe. In-hotel: 3 restaurants, room service, bars, tennis court, pool, diving, children's programs (ages 4 and up), Internet terminal, Wi-Fi hotspot, parking (free)* 💳 *AE, MC, V.*

$$–$$$ **Hotel Lois.** A sophisticated creamy-white facade has replaced the purple exterior; the *Jetsons*–esque lobby is now dressed with leather furniture. Though it's lost its personality, Lois is still a good budget option. Guest rooms have subdued pastels; spend a bit more for one with a hot tub. **Pros:** bar is *the* place for salsa dancing. **Cons:** on a busy street; rooms are small and a little dated. ✉ *Blvd. Adolfo Ruíz Cortines 10* ☎ *229/937–7031 or 229/937–8290* 🌐 *www.hotelluis.com.mx* *107 rooms, 17 suites* *In-room: safe, Internet, Wi-Fi. In-hotel: restaurant, room service, bars, pool, gym, children's programs (ages 3–9), parking (free)* 💳 *AE, MC, V.*

6

NIGHTLIFE

Plenty of cantinas are scattered around this port city. Walk down Mario Molina from the Paseo del Malecón to find a handful of the most popular. There are also plenty of beachfront bars in Boca del Río.

It's no surprise that people gravitate toward the zócalo, which is full of marimba artists, mariachi bands, and guitar players. Grabbing a table at a sidewalk café along the park's northern edge gives you a front-row seat, but it also means that every musician will approach you to play you a song for a few dollars. Friday and Saturday nights at 7 PM locals perform traditional dances on a makeshift stage.

Fodor's Choice ★ If you'd like to learn a few local steps, the **Instituto Veracruzano de la Cultura** (*Veracruz Cultural Institute* ✉ *Calle Canal at Av. Zaragoza* ☎ *229/931–6967 or 229/931–6962* 🌐 *www.culturaveracruz.ivec.gob.mx*) provides danzón classes.

A few nights a week, men in dapper hats and women with fans dance the danzón at **Parque Zamora.** It's a magical evening, as the couples swirl around a Victorian bandstand. The types of performances, locations, and times vary every month, so stop by the tourist office in the zócalo for a current schedule.

CATCH THE SOUNDS

For live music, hit the streets and follow your ears—to the zócalo and beyond. Here's a rundown of what's playing and where:

Parque Álvaro Obregón: jazz and bossanova; Saturday at 8 PM.

Paseo del Malecón: son Jarocho at 7 PM.

Plazuela de la Campana: danzón and other music; Wednesday to Saturday at 7 PM.

Plazuela de la Lagunilla: son Jarocho; Thursday at 7 PM.

Zócalo: Different kinds of music different days of the week at 7 PM or at 8 PM.

DANCE AND MUSIC CLUBS

Dance clubs are plentiful along the waterfront. Most are packed Friday and Saturday nights with a young, largely local crowd. The popular basement club at Hotel Lois has live music Thursday through Sunday.

For Cuban rhythms downtown, head to the unpretentious **El Rincón de la Trova** (✉ *Plazuela de la Lagunilla 59* ☎ *No phone*), where people of all ages gather Thursday through Saturday. **Kachimba** (✉ *Blvd. Manuel Ávila Camacho at Médico Militar, Boca del Río* ☎ *229/927–1980*) is a great spot for live Cuban music. It's open Thursday to Sunday.

SHOPPING

Browsing street stands and markets for small treasures is the way to shop here. Items made from shell make great souvenirs, as do guayabera shirts. Indeed, Veracruzanos have wholeheartedly adopted these famous embroidered *tops* (sometimes called wedding shirts) from the neighboring Yucatán. They're comfortable and lightweight, made of either cotton or linen (the linen ones are nicer). Oh, and don't tuck your guayabera into your pants.

With its sizable Cuban population, Veracruz does a brisk business in cigars. Around **Plaza de Armas** and throughout the zócalo there are plenty of street-side stands that specialize in both Mexican and Caribbean tobacco. For the largest variety, try the small kiosk on **Avenida Independencia**, in front of Gran Café del Portal; it sells Cohibas for less than a buck.

MARKETS

For a slice of Mexican life, head to the wildly vibrant **Mercado Hidalgo** (✉ *Bounded by Calles Cortés, Soto, Madero, and Hidalgo* ☎ *No phone*), where you'll find artful displays of strawberries and chilies beside platters of cow eyeballs and chicken feet.

Stands lining the **Paseo del Malecón** sell ocean-related items: seashells and the beauty creams and powders derived from them; Coatepec coffee; T-shirts; and tacky stuffed frogs, iguanas, and armadillos.

The **Plaza de las Artesanías Miguel Alemán** market on the Paseo de Malecón purveys high-quality goods, including leather and jewelry, with high prices to match. It's open daily 11 to 8.

SPECIALTY SHOPS

El Mayab (✉ *Calle Zamora 78, at Av. Zaragoza* ☎ *229/932–1435*) has a selection of machine-produced guayaberas, which go for less than the hand-embroidered variety.

The family-run **Guayaberas Fina Cab** (✉ *Av. Zaragoza 233, between Calles Arista and Serdán* ☎ *229/931–8427*) has high-quality hand-stitched shirts and dresses with embroidery that ranges from basic interlocking cables to elaborate floral designs.

Libros y Arte (✉ *Callejón Portal de Miranda 9, at Gutierrez Zamora* ☎ *229/932–6943* 🌐 *www.educal.com.mx*), near the zócalo, has a wonderful collection of books, including coffee-table volumes on the art and architecture of Veracruz, Mexican music, and plenty of maps and travel guides.

CLOSE UP

Night Moves

The air is hot and humid, even though the sun has already set on the delightful port city of Veracruz. Elderly couples seated on the wrought-iron benches around Parque Zamora barely move, hoping that inactivity will bring some relief. A conductor lifts a languid baton that rouses a group of musicians to life. The sound they make isn't quite in tune, but it is as rich as honey and as radiant as the summer evening. The couples listen for a few moments, then stroll to the bandstand. Men in crisply ironed shirts and dapper straw hats hold out their hands to women in straight skirts and blouses embroidered with birds and flowers. When they begin to dance, there's barely any movement above the waist, just subtle hip movements and the occasional fancy footwork. It's a dance designed for a tropical night.

This is the *danzón*, a languorous dance brought to Mexico in 1879 by Cubans fleeing their country's Ten Years' War. These refugees ended up living outside the city walls (only aristocrats were allowed to live inside), but the sons of the Mexican elite, looking for thrills, sneaked into the poor neighborhoods at night, and eventually introduced the danzón to high society. Sensuous compared with the stiff dances that were the norm then, the danzón was at first considered scandalous. But soon it won over its detractors and became the most popular dance in Veracruz. It still fills dance halls throughout the city. You can see people of all generations dancing in Parque Zamora every Sunday evening. While their parents and grandparents glide around the bandstand, children practice their steps off to the side.

The city's unique heritage is also evident in its music, swayed by African and Caribbean rhythms. The *son Jarocho* is one of seven different regional variations of Mexican *sones*. These songs, livelier than the danzón, can be in 4/4 or 6/4 time. Doubtless the best-known one is "La Bamba," which originated here and dates back to the 17th century. Although the most famous version of the song was released by Richie Valens in 1958, there are more than 300 other recordings. Traditionally, the *cantadores* (singers) have been both singers and wordsmiths, creating endless *coplas* (verses) for well-known songs. Between numbers they continue to entertain the audiences, telling jokes and gently ribbing the other musicians.

The son Jarocho centers on strings and percussion. Three instruments are in every ensemble: *arpa* (harp), *jarana* (a 6- or 10-string guitar), and *requinto* (a small rhythm guitar). Musicians energize audiences with their vigorous strumming. A young woman often accompanies them, performing flamenco-like steps in a frilly frock. The *tarima* (wooden dance platform) where dancers pound out the rhythms becomes another essential instrument.

Two other sones are commonly heard. In the son Huasteca, named for the region along the northeastern coast of Mexico, violins often take the melody. If trumpets are added, you are probably hearing *son jalisciense*. This type of son hails from Jalisco, a state along the southwestern coast.

—Mark Sullivan

SPORTS AND THE OUTDOORS

BOATING

You can easily charter a *lancha* (boat) to take you to nearby islands like Isla Verde and Isla de los Sacrificios. ■**TIP→ The best place to find one for a spur-of-the-moment outing is along the Paseo del Malecón.** Expect to pay about $5 per person. Longer trips to nearby Isla Verde (Green Island) and Isla de Enmedio (Middle Island) leave daily from the shack marked PASEO EN LANCHITA near Plaza Acuario. If you want to call ahead, contact the friendly folks at **Amphibian** (✉ *Calle Lerdo 117* ☎ *229/931–0997* 🌐 *www.amphibianveracruz.com*).

DIVING

The waters near Veracruz are home to nearly two dozen reefs. **Mundo Submarino** (✉ *Blvd. Manuel Ávila Camacho 3549* ☎ *229/980–6374* 🌐 *www.mundosubmarino.com.mx*) has diving lessons for newcomers to experts. The company also conducts dives to nearby reefs. **Tridente** (✉ *Blvd. Manuel Ávila Camacho 165-A* ☎ *229/931–7924*) conducts diving trips for around $70 per person; the price includes gear and instruction. If you want to snorkel, the cost is only $23.

WHITE-WATER RAFTING

On trips led by **Rio Aventura** (✉ *Calle Urano 784, Boca del Río* ☎ *229/130–2759 or 229/121–6942* 🌐 *www.rioaventura.com.mx*), you can combine rafting with other sports.

SIDE TRIPS FROM VERACRUZ CITY

LA ANTIGUA

25 km (16 mi) northwest of Veracruz City, 75 km (47 mi) southeast of Xalapa.

This sleepy village was the conquistadors' capital for 75 years. It was given its name ("The Old Town") when the Spaniards abandoned it in 1599, upon founding Veracruz City. A small community still lives here, however, and they're justifiably proud of the town.

GETTING HERE AND AROUND

La Antigua is roughly half an hour north of Veracruz, off Carretera 180. A Xalapa-bound AU bus from the second-class bus station will cost you $1.50 each way; it will drop you off about a 15-minute stroll from La Antigua. Enjoy the walk littered with fat iguanas sunning themselves and speedy lizards darting along the road. Be prepared to flag down a bus on your way back to Veracruz.

EXPLORING

Although locals call it **Casa de Cortés** (✉ *Av. Independencia at Calle Ruiz Cortés*), the 16th-century customs house actually had nothing to do with the conquistador. Little is left of the structure, which once housed 22 rooms surrounded by a huge courtyard. Its crumbling masonry has been reclaimed by clinging vines and massive tree roots.

Heading toward the river on Calle Ruiz Cortés you'll see a tree with tentacle-like branches blocking the road. This is the **Ceiba de la Noche**

Feliz *(Tree of the Happy Night)*. It's said the river once extended to this tree and that Cortés tied his boats here when he arrived.

La Antigua also has the first church of New Spain, the diminutive **Ermita del Rosario** (✉ *Av. Independencia at Calle Elodia Rosales*). The little white stucco structure has been restored (and enlarged) many times over the years. The oddly placed arch in the middle of the church was actually once the facade. You can see that two windows near the altar were originally doors.

WHERE TO EAT

$$ SEAFOOD ✕ **Las Delicias Marinas**. All roads in La Antigua seem to lead to this riverfront restaurant, a favorite for years. The huge arches facing the water are hung with nets full of cardboard fish. Try the shrimp cocktail or the *cazuela de mariscos,* a seafood stew filled with shrimp, crab, octopus, and mussels in a spicy green sauce. Afternoons at 1:30 and 6:30 there's marimba music, and on weekends the musicians are joined by dancers. ✉ *On the Río Huitzilapan* ☎ *296/971–6038* ⊕ *www.lasdeliciasmarinas.com.mx* ▭ *MC, V.*

■ TIP→ Stop by a street stand for a typical treat: cocadas, toasted balls of coconut and pineapple prepared with sugar and vanilla.

SPORTS AND THE OUTDOORS

You can take a leisurely boat ride up the **Río Huitzilapan** *(Hummingbird River)*. There are more than a dozen covered boats under the Puente Colgate, a narrow, bouncy rope bridge. Captains charge $5 per person for a cruise up the river while they re-create the scene when La Antigua was the hub of Nueva España. Ask your guide to show you where Cortés kept his ships. Now a valley of sand dunes, it's a fun place for both kids and adults to explore.

CEMPOALA

42 km (26 mi) northwest of Veracruz City.

Cempoala (sometimes spelled "Zempoala") was the capital of the Totonac people. The name means "place of 20 waters," after the sophisticated Totonac irrigation system. When Cortés arrived here under the cover of night, the plaster covering of the massive **Templo Mayor** (Main Temple) and other buildings led him to believe the city was constructed of silver. Cortés placed a cross atop this temple—the first gesture of this sort in New Spain—and had Mass said by a Spanish priest.

The city's fate was sealed in 1519 when Cortés formed an alliance with the Totonac leader. Chicomacatl—dubbed "Fat Chief" by his own people because of his enormous girth—was an avowed enemy of the more powerful Aztec, so he decided to fight them alongside the Spanish. The alliance greatly enlarged Cortés's army, and encouraged the Spaniard to march on Mexico City and defeat the Aztec. The strategic move backfired, however. The Totonac could protect themselves against the Spanish swords, but were powerless against the smallpox the invaders brought with them. The population was devastated.

Upon entering the ruins, you'll see **Círculo de los Gladiadores,** a small circle of waist-high walls to the right of center. This was the site of contests between captured prisoners of war and Totonac warriors: each prisoner was required to fight two armed warriors. One such prisoner,

6

the son of a king from Tlaxcala, won the unfair match and became a national hero. His statue stands in a place of honor in Tlaxcala. Another small structure to the left of the circle marks the spot where an eternal flame was kept lighted during the Totonac sacred 52-year cycle.

At the **Templo de la Luna** (Temple of the Moon), to the far left of Templo Mayor, outstanding warriors were honored with the title "Eagle Knight" or "Tiger Knight" and awarded an obsidian nose ring to wear as a mark of their status. Just to the left of the Moon Temple is the larger **Templo del Sol** (Temple of the Sun), where the hearts and blood of sacrificial victims were placed. Back toward the dirt road and across from it is the **Templo de la Diosa de la Muerte** (Temple of the Goddess of Death), where a statue of the pre-Hispanic deity was found along with 1,700 small idols.

There's a small museum near the entrance that contains some of the minor finds the site has yielded. Well-trained guides offer their services, but tours are mainly in Spanish. Voladores from Papantla usually give a performance here on weekends. To get here from Veracruz, drive 42 km (26 mi) north on Carretera 180, past the turnoff for the town of Cardel. Cempoala is on a clearly marked road a few miles farther on your left. If you are coming by bus, take an ADO bus to Cardel. The terminal for Autotransportes Cempoala buses is at the corner of Calle José Azueta and Avenida Juan Martinez, two blocks from the ADO station. A ride directly to the site costs about 80¢ each way. ☎ *No phone* 🌐 *www.inah.gob.mx* 🎟 *$3.40* ⏲ *Daily 10–6.*

CENTRAL VERACRUZ

The land of Central Veracruz is varied and gorgeous. It's here that you'll find coffee plantations, Mexico's highest mountains, rapids, and even a few sets of ruins. It also holds the state's second-most-important (and talked about) city, Xalapa, a sophisticated university town that's perched on a mountainside. Xalapa is the hub of culture and modernity in this area, and is a good base for exploring the small coffee towns of Coatepec and Xico.

XALAPA

100 km (62 mi) northwest of Veracruz City.

A ceremonial center for the Aztec when Cortés swept through the region, Xalapa is still a city of great importance. Take one look at the impressive Palacio de Gobierno and you know this is a political powerhouse. The presence of the Universidad Veracruzana ensures that Xalapa is a cultural capital as well. Its state theater attracts performers from around the world. In addition, Xalapa is also an agricultural center. This mixed background means that in any café you might find farm workers with their machetes, government workers shouting into cell phones, and students tapping away on laptops.

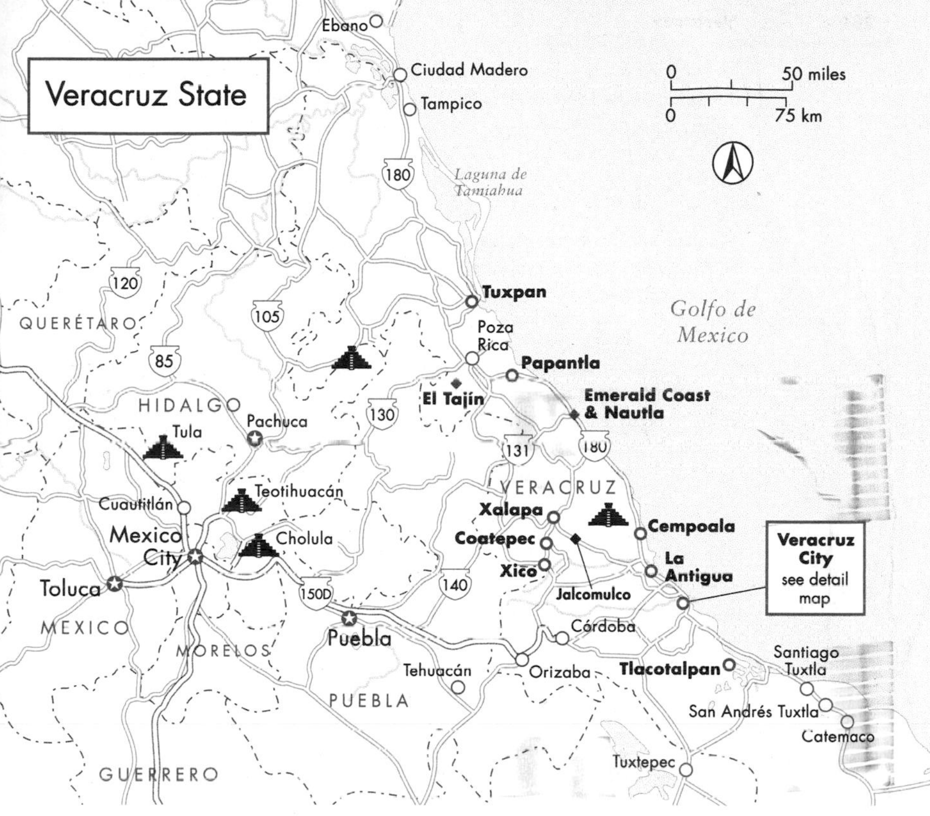

Xalapa is on the side of a mountain between the coastal lowlands and the high central plateau. More than 4,000 feet above sea level, the city enjoys cool weather the entire year. But the city also has unpredictable weather changes—sun, rain, and fog are all likely to show themselves over the course of a day. Bring an umbrella and a jacket with you, even if there's not a cloud in the sky.

Much of the city seems to have been built without a plan, and that's the source of its charm. The hills here pose intriguing engineering problems, and major avenues tend to make sharp turns, following the landscape rather than adhering to the strict grid system so beloved by the Spanish. In some places the twisting cobblestone streets are bordered by 6-foot-high sidewalks to compensate for sudden sharp inclines. Locals refer to the city as a *plato roto* (broken dish) because of its layout.

GETTING HERE AND AROUND

Xalapa's bus station, called CAXA (the Centro de Autobuses de Xalapa), is 2 km (1 mi) east of downtown on Avenida Lázaro Cárdenas, just off Avenida 20 de Noviembre. ADO runs several buses an hour between Veracruz and Xalapa. The trip takes two hours and costs about $6. If you're driving, Carretera 140, which branches off Carretera 150-D, leads from Veracruz City to Xalapa. Pay extra attention when driving in Xalapa, as getting lost is a real possibility.

ESSENTIALS

Bus Contacts ADO (🌐 *www.ado.com.mx*).

Ticketbus (☎ *800/702–8000* 🌐 *www.ticketbus.com.mx*).

Medical Assistance Angeles Verdes (☎ *078*). **General Emergencies** (☎ *066*). **Xalapa Cruz Roja** (☎ *228/817–8158*). **Police** (☎ *228/818–1810*).

Visitor and Tour Info Xalapa Tourist Information Booth (✉ *Calle Enríquez 14* ☎ *No phone*). **Xalapa Tourist Office** (✉ *Blvd. Cristóbal Colón 5, Jardines de las Animas* ☎ *228/812–7585* 🌐 *www.xalapa.gob.mx*).

EXPLORING

The city's contemporary-art museum, **Galeria de Arte Contemporáneo de Xalapa**, housed in a restored colonial-era building, has temporary exhibits, primarily with paintings, by regional artists. There are also frequent evening theater, dance, and films events. Many of these are free and advertised on the Web site as well as in the gallery's monthly schedule that you can pick up at the gallery. ✉ *Xalapeños Illustres 135 and Arteaga* ☎ *228/818–9198* 🌐 *www.culturaveracruz.ivec.gob.mx* 🎫 *Free* ⏲ *Tues.–Sun. 10–6.*

Fodor's Choice ★ Xalapa's **Museo de Antropología** is second only to the archaeological museum in Mexico City. Its collection of artifacts covers the three main pre-Hispanic cultures of Veracruz: Huasteca, Totonac, and most important, Olmec. It's filled with magnificent Olmec stone heads, carved stelae and offering bowls, terra-cotta jaguars and cross-eyed gods, and cremation urns in the form of bats and monkeys. Especially touching are the life-size sculptures of women who died in childbirth (the ancients elevated them to the status of goddesses). Written explanations appear only in Spanish, but bilingual guides are available. The museum is about 3 km (2 mi) north of Parque Juárez. ✉ *Av. Xalapa s/n* ☎ *228/815–0920 or 228/815–0708* 🌐 *www.uv.mx/max* 🎫 *$4* ⏲ *Tues.–Sun. 9–5.*

The gorgeous central square, called **Parque Juárez**, has the neoclassical Palacio de Gobierno on one side and the neocolonial Palacio Municipal on another. At first glance Parque Juárez seems like any park, but a café and art galleries reside below. Between the palaces is the Catedral de Xalapa, dating from 1772. If it looks a little crooked from the outside, wait until you step inside. A chapel juts out at an odd angle, making the whole place seem askew.

WHERE TO EAT

$–$$ STEAKHOUSE ✕ **Asadero Cien.** Locals recommend this steak house with large windows, high ceilings, and white linens, so the place is often crowded. The steaks and tacos are all tasty, served with roasted green onions and plenty of salsas. Out back there's a playground with tables where parents can enjoy a coffee and dessert while kids can run around. ✉ *Av. Ávila Camacho 118, Col. Centro* ☎ *228/818–9545* 🌐 *www.asaderocien.com.mx* 💳 *AE, MC, V.*

$ MEXICAN ✕ **La Casa de Mamá.** The antique furnishings and lazily turning ceiling fans almost succeed in giving this popular restaurant the vibe of an old-fashioned hacienda, but the insistent street noise reminds you that you're in a busy capital city. Never mind: you'll be focusing on the generous portions of charcoal-broiled steaks and the succulent shrimp and fish dishes, served with *frijoles charros* (black beans cooked in a spicy sauce). ■ **TIP→ The place is known for its desserts, which include flan with caramel and bananas flambéed in brandy.** ✉ *Av. Manuel Ávila Camacho 113* ☎ *228/817–3144* ▭ *AE, MC, V* ⊙ *No dinner Sun.*

NAME GAMES

As with most places in Mexico, Xalapa (pronounced ha-LA-pa) has had many names over the years. The current name is a slight variation on Xallapan, the name chosen when four neighboring villages decided to pool their otherwise meager resources. You'll sometimes see the name of the city spelled "Jalapa," which is the Hispanic version of the name used by the Nahuatl people, the original inhabitants of the region. Residents of Xalapa call themselves *xalapeños.*

$ MEXICAN ✕ **La Casona del Beaterio.** In contrast to the ho-hum meals served at the other cafeterias lining Avenida Zaragoza, La Casona del Beaterio dishes up fine local fare. The restaurant's two spacious rooms, surrounding a courtyard garden with a fountain, have stained-glass windows and plenty of hanging plants. Breakfast specials are a steal, but the house specialty—*cazuela de mariscos*—draws the crowds. This is java country, so the menu has a dozen different coffee and espresso concoctions. ✉ *Av. Zaragoza 20* ☎ *228/818–2119* ▭ *AE, MC, V.*

$$–$$$ MEXICAN ✕ **La Estancia de los Tecajetes.** For fine regional dishes prepared with a dash of creativity, try this rustic restaurant overlooking the tropical Parque Los Tecajetes. Inside it's cozy, always buzzing with diners feasting on *cecina* (paper-thin beef fillet) with slices of avocado, and *crepas poblanas* (crepes filled with chicken or spinach and topped with poblano chilies). The restaurant is tucked into a small strip mall, so it's tricky to find. ✉ *Plaza Tecajetes, Av. Manuel Ávila Camacho 90* ☎ *228/818–0732* 🌐 *www.xalapamio.com/lostecajetes.htm* ▭ *MC, V* ⊙ *No dinner Sun.*

$ ECLECTIC ✕ **La Fonda.** The entrance to this second-floor restaurant is hidden on a small pedestrian walkway off Calle Enríquez, a block from Parque Juárez. Bright streamers, baskets of paper flowers, and paintings enliven the little cluster of dining rooms. Breakfast starts at 8 AM, and includes delicious Mexican dishes like mole and *chilaquiles*, toasted tortillas in a spicy sauce. Lunch features hearty northern Veracruz fare. Delicious *nopales* (cactus strips) and chipotle chilies are essential elements of almost every dish. ■ **TIP→ The three-course lunch special costs between $3 and $5—such a deal.** You can stop by for an early dinner, but the restaurant closes at 5:30. ✉ *Callejón del Diamante 1, at Calle Enríquez* ☎ *228/818–7282* ▭ *No credit cards* ⊙ *Closed Sun. No dinner.*

$ FRENCH ★ ✕ **Le Bistrot San José.** You won't need your phrase book to translate such well-known French dishes as chicken with Roquefort at this adorable little bistro. Sip a crisp Bordeaux (there are several on the reasonably priced wine list) as you nibble the perfectly prepared pâté. Locals drop by to taste the city's only chocolate mousse and crème brûlée. On the gracefully crumbling walls of this colonial-era building hang etchings of Parisian sights. The back dining room, more intimate than the one facing the street, looks out on a flower-filled courtyard. ✉ *Herrera and Miguel Palacios 1* ☎ *228/812–8267* ▭ *MC, V.*

6

$–$$ SPANISH ✕ **Restaurante Casino Español.** Bullfighting posters and mirrors in elaborate frames are some of the things that make stepping into this restaurant a little like stepping back in time. Main dishes include *róbalo a la cazuela* (sea bass in a tomato-based sauce with shrimp). The daily prix-fixe menu consists of a soup, a plate of pasta or rice, and an entrée. Sunday sees a tasty paella. ✉ *Zamora 14* ☎ *228/817–7586* ▭ *MC, V* ⊗ *No breakfast.*

WHERE TO STAY

$$$ **Fiesta Inn Xalapa.** This brick-red hotel is a 10-minute drive from the center of town, but it has hard-to-find (for Xalapa) amenities like a swimming pool. The modern guest rooms in the three-story, colonial-style structure get plenty of morning sunlight. **Pros:** restaurant buffet has great variety. **Cons:** a bit out of the way. ✉ *Carretera Xalapa–Veracruz, Km 2.5, Fracc. Las Animas* ☎ *228/841–6800 or 800/504–5000* ⊕ *www.fiestainn.com* *119 rooms, 3 suites* *In-room: safe, Wi-Fi. In-hotel: restaurant, room service, bar, pool, gym, laundry service, Internet terminal, Wi-Fi hotspot, parking (free)* ▭ *AE, MC, V.*

$$–$$$ **Hotel Xalapa.** The lobby full of people shouting into cell phones is a giveaway that this is the city's best business hotel. It's on a hill high above Parque Los Tecajetes, so there's a nice view, but you'll need to take taxis back and forth into town. **Pros:** rooms are large, sunny, and quiet. **Cons:** building is less than good-looking, the disco can be loud. ✉ *Victoria at Bustamante, Zona Centro* ☎ *228/818–2222 or 228/817–7064* ⊕ *www.hotelxalapa.com.mx* *170 rooms, 28 suites, 2 villas* *In-room: Wi-Fi (some). In-hotel: 2 restaurants, room service, bar, pool, laundry service, Wi-Fi hotspot, parking (free)* ▭ *AE, MC, V.*

$ ★ **Mesón del Alférez.** A royal lieutenant of the Spanish viceroy lived in this colonial house some 200 years ago. Now it's a gem of a small hotel, restored with earthenware tiles, rustic wood beams, and lime-pigment washes on the walls. Rooms surround three small bougainvillea-covered courtyards and have lovely hand-carved wood headboards, Talavera lamps, and hand-loomed bedspreads. Mesón's friendly, dedicated founders have also opened additional hotels in Xalapa and Coatepec, which can be found at the Web site below. **Pros:** intriguing history, boutique character. **Cons:** some rooms are quite small. ✉ *Sebastián Camacho 2, at Av. Zaragoza* ☎ *228/818–6351 or 228/818–0113* ⊕ *www.pradodelrio.com* *15 rooms, 6 suites* *In-room: safe. In-hotel: restaurant, room service, laundry service, Internet terminal, parking (free)* ▭ *MC, V* *CP.*

¢–$ **Posada Del Virrey.** On the plus side, this colonial-style hotel is a short walk north of Parque Juárez. Unhappily, that walk is mostly uphill, perhaps a reason why the rates are so reasonable. The rooms are simple and quiet, but some are on the small side, so look at a few before you decide. **Pros:** nicely decorated. **Cons:** walk uphill wouldn't be easy for some. ✉ *Dr. Lucio 142, Col. Centro* ☎ *228/818–6100* ⊕ *www.posadadelvirrey.com.mx* *40 rooms* *In-hotel: restaurant, room service, bar, laundry service, Internet terminal, parking (free)* ▭ *AE, MC, V.*

¢ **Posada María de San Francisco.** Surprisingly plush, but small and somewhat crowded, rooms are set around two flower-filled courtyards with worn patio furniture at this budget hotel. Its location a few blocks north of Parque Juárez is ideal. The Mexican restaurant at the hotel entrance specializes in churros and is a comfortable place to have a snack and relax. **Pros:** great deal. **Cons:** steep walk up a hill from the park; many rooms are only accessible by stairs. ✉ *Calle Claviero 17* ☎ *228/817–3390* 🌐 *www.hotelrealdecortes.com* *19 rooms* *In-room: Wi-Fi. In-hotel: restaurant, bar* 💳 *MC, V.*

NIGHTLIFE

BARS

East of the center are many of the city's most popular bars. If you're in the mood for live music, **Barlovento** (✉ *Av. 20 de Noviembre Oriente 641* ☎ *228/817–8334*) heats up with a salsa beat Wednesday through Saturday. A coffee shop by day, cute **Café Lindo** (✉ *Primo Verdad 21* ☎ *228/841–9166*) transforms itself into a bar at night. There's live music most evenings, usually a trio crooning Mexican music.

La Corte de los Milagros (✉ *Av. 20 de Noviembre Oriente 522* ☎ *228/812–3511*) is a relaxing haunt where you can listen to Cuban-style ballads. It's open Wednesday through Saturday. **Vertice** (✉ *Av. Murillo Vidal at Calle Zempoala* ☎ *No phone*) is one of the few bars where you can have a conversation. There's music Tuesday through Thursday.

6

DANCE CLUBS

The major thoroughfares west of Parque Juárez are where you'll find most of the dance clubs.

With music so loud that it rattles the windows of passing cars, the video bar **Boulevard 93** (✉ *Av. Manuel Ávila Camacho 93* ☎ *No phone*) is popular with college students. It's open Tuesday through Sunday.

La Quimera (✉ *Blvd. Adolfo Ruíz Cortines 1* ☎ *228/812–3277*) throbs with dance music Wednesday through Saturday nights.

SHOPPING

Mexico's finest export coffee is grown in this region, specifically in the highlands around the gorgeous colonial towns of Coatepec and Xico, less than 10 km (6 mi) from Xalapa. Shops selling the prized *café de altura* (coffee of the highlands) abound.

Cafécali (✉ *Callejón del Diamante 2* ☎ *228/818–1339*) serves a wide selection of excellent coffees at good prices. **Café Colón** (✉ *Calle Primo Verdad 15, between Avs. Zaragoza and Enríquez* ☎ *228/817–6097* ⏲ *Mon.–Sat. 9–8, Sun. 10–1*) sells 20 varieties of coffee for about $2.50 a pound.

Callejón del Diamante, also known as Calle Antonio M. Rivera, is a captivating pedestrian street with vendors hawking inexpensive jewelry, handwoven baskets, and fleece-lined slippers.

The **Mercado Jaureguí** (✉ *Av. Revolución and Calle Altamirano*), open daily, is an indoor bazaar with everything from jewelry, blankets, and fresh vegetables to some rather dubious-looking natural "healing" potions and supposedly aphrodisiacal body pastes.

SPORTS AND THE OUTDOORS

HIKING AND CLIMBING

An option for climbing is the magnificent **Parque Nacional Cofre de Perote**, where the centerpiece is the 14,022-foot extinct volcano. A road leads almost to the summit, so you can either plan a day trip or stay for several days. The park is about 50 km (31 mi) west of Xalapa. In Xalapa, **Veraventuras** (✉ *Santos Degollado 81-8* ☎ *228/818–9779* 🌐 *www.veraventuras.com.mx*) runs biking and hiking trips in nearby national parks.

WHITE-WATER RAFTING

With access to six rivers for white-water rafting, Veracruz is an established mecca for the sport in Mexico. The rivers drain the steep slopes rising up to the flanks of Pico de Orizaba, and are the usual tropical-storm drains: wide valley floors with shoal-like rapids at every twist and turn. The rafting season runs from August to November.

The **Río Antigua** has five runs, all classed at level IV or under. Not far from the Río Antigua, the **Río Actopan** is an amazing Class III stream. For pure white-water fun, the **Río Pescados** is the best run in the area. In the rainy season it has some rapids on the high side of Class IV, but mostly the rapids are Class III. Tight turns against the towering cliffs make for some great splatting. Base camps with tents, rafting equipment, and dining facilities are near the river at Jalcomulco, 42 km (26 mi) southeast of Xalapa.

With **Amigos del Río** (✉ *Calle Chipancingo 205, Xalapa* ☎ *228/815–8817* 🌐 *www.amigosdelrio.com.mx*) you can choose trips based on skill level, from newcomer to expert. **Expediciones México Verde** (✉ *Av. Murillo Vidal 133, Xalapa* ☎ *279/832–3734* 🌐 *www.mexicoverde.com*) organizes various rafting excursions—from day trips to multiday programs—to Río Pescados, Río Actopan, and other rivers. Most guides speak English. The company also provides an array of adventure sports and group programs.

> **NEW HEIGHTS**
>
> The 18,400-foot **Pico de Orizaba,** Mexico's highest mountain, will virtually become your traveling companion in Veracruz State—you'll feel as though you see it at every turn. The Aztecs called the volcano Citlaltépetl, or Star Mountain, because under the full moon the snowy peak looks like a star. Woodlands spread along its flanks, with a glacier shining above. Tour operators in Xalapa organize climbs to the summit in the dry season, from November to March. Orizaba is 53 km (33 mi) south of Xalapa.

COATEPEC

8 km (5 mi) south of Xalapa on Carretera 7.

The air is cool and refreshing in Coatepec. Residents call their town the *capital mundial del café* (coffee capital of the world), as the climate is perfect for growing the sought-after *altura pluma* (mountain-grown) coffee. You'll see bushes with bright red berries on every available scrap of land. The heady scent of roasting beans wafts across the main square. Locals are so immersed in coffee culture that many swear they can distinguish a cup made with beans from Coatepac from one made with beans grown in nearby Xico.

Coatepec, from the Nahuatl phrase Coátl-Tepetl-C ("in snake hill"), was founded as a villa in 1848, officially became a city in 1886, and grew during the coffee boom years of the early 20th century. The mansions along its elegant streets are pinned with ornate balconies; take a peek inside and you'll see gorgeous courtyards overflowing with greenery.

GETTING HERE AND AROUND

Getting to Coatepec is easy. Take any of the shuttle buses marked XICO that leave from a traffic circle on Calle Allende, a few blocks west of Parque Juárez in Xalapa. The 10-minute ride costs less than $1.

EXPLORING

The wealth of Coatepec town is apparent in its gilt-covered churches. Across from the main square, the 18th-century **Parroquia San Jerónimo** (✉ *Calle 5 de Mayo at Calle Jiménez de Capillo*) has low arches trimmed with gold leaf.

The **Santuario de Nuestra Señora de Guadalupe** (✉ *Calle Aldama at Calle Hidalgo*) hardly has a surface that isn't covered with some precious metal. Make sure to take a look at the dome, which is cleverly painted to look much taller than it actually is.

6

WHERE TO EAT

¢–$ MEXICAN ✕ **Arcos de Belem.** Bricked arches beckon you to enter this warm, family-run restaurant where murals of Coatepec's landscape adorn the walls. With simple, classic Mexican dishes, these folks have been drawing fans for more than 50 years. Anticipating your hunger, *totopos* (tortilla chips and salsa) or sweet breads are delivered to your table as you sit down. The *mole* is a specialty, and children love the *zopilotas* (fried tortillas topped with beans and cheese). Stop in for breakfast or a big dinner, but don't forget a cup of Coatepec's world-famous coffee. Also keep an eye out for the children's second-floor play area. On Friday and Saturday evenings there's live music. ■ **TIP→ Ask for the sought-after open-air window seating on the second level.** ✉ *Miguel Lerdo 9* ☎ *228/816–5265* 💳 *MC, V* ⏲ *Closed Sun.*

$ MEXICAN ✕ **Los Tucanes.** This comfortable restaurant has a varied regional menu. Seafood is a specialty, particularly local trout, which is made in 20 different ways. The *acamayas*, or river lobsters, prepared with garlic are delicious; and the grilled beef and regional chorizo is also a great option. A large backyard has a couple of swing sets, and there's occasionally a big inflated castle where the kids can jump around. ✉ *Santos Degollado 23* ☎ *228/816–5434* 🌐 *www.tucanabotana.com* 💳 *No credit cards.*

WHERE TO STAY

¢ **Camino Real de Marqués Hotel.** A cheerful, yellow colonial building—just three blocks from the zócalo—houses this inexpensive hotel. Rooms are centered around an interior patio, and are simple but cheerful with bright paint schemes and fabrics. All rooms have TV and Wi-Fi. **Pros:** within walking distance of all downtown sites; reasonably priced. **Cons:** rooms are somewhat plain. ✉ *Flores Bello 68* ☎ *228/816–1891* 🌐 *www.realdelmarques.net* *32 rooms* *In-room: Wi-Fi. In-hotel: restaurant* 💳 *MC, V.*

$$ Fodor's Choice ★ **Posada Coatepec.** Once the home of a coffee baron, this 19th-century mansion—a 15-minute drive from Xalapa—is now a luxury hotel. The lobby, decorated with a fine collection of period antiques, feels like the entrance to a private home. Rooms have original tile floors, beamed ceilings, and heaters for Coatepec's often chilly weather. Stained-glass windows bathe the restaurant in warm reds and yellows. The posada can arrange coffee plantation tours and river excursions. **Pros:** darling place to stay; coffee plantation tours. **Cons:** staff can seem uncaring at times. ✉ *Calle Hidalgo 9* ☎ *228/816–0544* 🌐 *www.posadacoatepec.com.mx* *7 rooms, 15 suites, 1 villa* *In-hotel: restaurant, room service, bar, pool, laundry service, Wi-Fi hotspot, parking (paid)* 💳 *AE, MC, V.*

SHOPPING

The friendly folks at the **Café de Avelino** (✉ *Calle Aldama between Calle Constitución and Calle Morelos* ☎ *228/816–3401*) will show you how the experts rate the beans.

XICO

★ *19 km (12 mi) south of Xalapa, 11 km (7 mi) south of Coatepec.*

If you close your eyes and try to imagine the ideal Mexican small town, you'd probably come up with something surprisingly close to Xico. In many ways this village seems untouched by time: donkeys hauling burlap sacks of fresh beans clip-clop along the cobblestone streets followed by local coffee harvesters, machetes tied to their waists with red sashes. Adding to this back-in-time beauty is the fact that the town is often surrounded by mist.

The village is also known for its raucous nine-day festival in July that celebrates the town's patron saint, Mary Magdalene.

GETTING HERE AND AROUND

To get to Xico from Xalapa, take one of the shuttle buses marked XICO that leave from a traffic circle on Calle Allende, a few blocks west of Parque Juárez. The 20-minute ride costs less than $1.

EXPLORING

Xico is known for its natural wonders, notably the **Cascada de Texolo**, a majestic waterfall set in a deep gorge of tropical greenery. The lush area surrounding the falls is great for exploring; paths lead through forests of banana trees to smaller cascades and crystal-blue pools, perfect for a refreshing swim. There's also a steep staircase that will take you from the observation deck to the base of the falls.

The falls are about 3 km (2 mi) from the center of town. To reach them, start from the red-and-white church where Calle Zaragoza and Calle Matamoros meet and follow the cobblestone street downhill, bearing right when you reach the small roadside shrine to the Virgin Mary. Continue through the coffee plantations, following the signs for LA CASCADA until you reach the main observation deck. ■ **TIP→ It's a long walk, so if it's a hot day you might want to take a taxi from the main square.** Entry is free, though there's a small fee for parking.

The petite **Parroquia de Santa María Magdalena** (✉ *Calle Benito Juárez at Calle Lerdo*), at the end of Avenida Hidalgo, was built on the highest spot in town, so you have to climb some steep stairs to get to the entrance. Behind the altar is a traditional depiction of the crucifixion with Mary Magdalene, showing a bit more shoulder than usual, lying prostrate beneath the cross. A more demure statue of her is dressed in a different outfit for every day of the festival in her honor. The small museum behind the church has a display of her ensembles.

WHERE TO EAT AND STAY

$ MEXICAN **El Mesón Xiqueño.** A macaw named Paco greets you with "Hola, Paco!" when you enter this delightful courtyard restaurant. Huge wagon wheels remind you that horse-drawn carts once brought all the coffee grown here to market. The kitchen's emphasis is on local cuisine, so start with *brujitas xiqueñas,* the "little witches" that are actually pockets of fried corn filled with "beans bewitched by avocado." Main dishes include *cecina xiqueña,* which is seasoned beef pounded flat and grilled, and—obviously—moles. All dishes that have been invented at the hotel are marked on the menu with the restaurant's logo. ✉ *Av. Hidalgo 148* ☎ *228/813–0781* ▭ *MC, V.*

¢–$$ **Hotel Coyopolan.** Overlooking the Río Coyopolan, this two-story hotel couldn't have a better location. From the colonial-style building you can hear the river spill into a few small waterfalls. Rooms are small, but cheerfully decorated with local handicrafts. The open-air restaurant, La Molienda ($), serves fresh river fish. There's also a satisfying selection of beef and chicken dishes. **Pros:** fantastic location; pitter-patter of river is totally relaxing. **Cons:** like many of the hotels around here; rooms are tiny. ✉ *Calle Venustiano Carranza Sur s/n* ☎ *228/813–1266* ⊕ *www.coyopolan.com* *14 rooms* *In-room: no phone. In-hotel: restaurant, Wi-Fi hotspot* ▭ *MC, V.*

■ TIP→ Wash down your meals in Xico with a shot of local liquor. Try the creamy torito de cacahuate (peanut), morita (blackberry), or verde (technically this means "green," but in this case signifies herb) varieties.

SHOPPING

You can find just about anything along Calle Hidalgo, but the one thing not to leave without is mole. **Derivados Acamalín** (✉ *Av. Hidalgo 150* ☎ *288/813–0713*) is famous for its moles, as you can tell by the photos on the walls of celebrities who have dropped by for a taste, but they also produce bottles of local liquors.

Xinqeño (✉ *Av. Hidalgo 174* ☎ *228/813–0713*) is a little shop that sells its own brand of mole made from a wonderful recipe. Both this branch and the one on the Carretera Coatepec (near the entrance to town), sell the same thing.

NORTHERN VERACRUZ

North of Veracruz and Xalapa are a mishmash of sights. The biggest reason to head this way is El Tajín, one of the most impressive sets of ruins in all of Mexico. You can visit El Tajín on side trips from Veracruz (4 hours) or Xalapa (2½ hours), but if you use the hillside vanilla-growing town of Papantla (20 minutes from the ruins) as your base, you'll be able to see the spectacle of the *voladores.* Also nearby, north of El Tajín, is the coastal town of Tuxpán, a peaceful pit stop on the drive up the coast.

PAPANTLA

250 km (155 mi) northwest of Veracruz.

Set on a steep hillside, Papantla is in the center of a vanilla-producing region. Products made from that particular bean, from candies to liqueurs, are sold everywhere; a big vanilla festival draws people to the town every March. The rest of the year, this dusty village goes about its business. Totonac men in flowing white shirts and pants lead their donkeys through the streets, and young couples smooch underneath palm trees that ring the zócalo. Papantla is the home of the *voladores,* who twirl off an 82-foot pole in front of the town's ornate cathedral.

GETTING HERE AND AROUND

If you're driving, Carretera 130 from Mexico City leads past Poza Rica to Papantla; from Veracruz City, Carretera 180 leads north to Papantla. If you'd prefer the bus, Papantla's station, on Calle Benito Juárez at Calle 20 de Noviembre, is served only by ADO. There's service half a dozen times a day from Veracruz; the ride takes three to four hours and costs $12, and at least four buses a day to Papantla from Xalapa (3¾ to 4¼ hours, $13).

ESSENTIALS

Bus Contacts **ADO** (🌐 *www.ado.com.mx*). **Ticketbus** (☎ *800/702-8000* 🌐 *www.ticketbus.com.mx*).

Currency Exchange **Banamex** (✉ *Calle Enríquez 102* ☎ *784/842-1766* 🌐 *www.banamex.com.mx*).

Medical Assistance **Angeles Verdes** (☎ *078*). **Clínica del Centro Médico** (✉ *Calle 16 de Septiembre 12, Zona Centro* ☎ *784/842-0082*). **General Emergencies** (☎ *066*). **Papantla Cruz Roja** (☎ *784/842-0126*). **Police** (☎ *784/842-0075*).

Visitor and Tour Info **Papantla Tourist Office** (✉ *Calle Azueta at Calle Artes* ☎ *784/842-3837*).

EXPLORING

★ From the town square you'll see a giant statue honoring the voladores looking down on the city. Whether he's playing to the people below or the gods above is unclear, but he's certainly got the best view in town. Behind this statue and next to the cathedral you'll find Calle Centenario. Following this street, wind your way up to El Monumento al Volador to enjoy a lovely mural and a gorgeous view of the city below.

WHERE TO EAT

$–$$ SEAFOOD ✕ **La Choza de Lucy**. This casual restaurant, with a small swing set and a couple of children's toys in front, under two connected palapa (thatched) roofs, is the kind of place where locals might linger over a meal for hours at a time. Meals begin with corn chips, delicious molelike paste that they call chili de mole, and a fish sauce. The *pescado al mojo de ajo* (fried with garlic) is delicious; they also serve other fresh and tasty seafood plates. ✉ *16 de Septiembre 829, at Calle Azteca, Barrio del Zapote, Col. Centro* ☎ *784/842–4980* 💳 *AE, MC, V.*

$ MEXICAN ✕ **Restaurante Bar Plaza Pardo.** From the balcony of this cheerful second-story restaurant you'll have a great view of the goings-on in the zócalo. Brightly colored cloths adorn the tables, where house specialties—including *cecina con enchiladas* (salted beef with spicy enchiladas) and *rellenos al gusto* (green chilies stuffed with chicken, cheese, or beef)—are served by the friendly staff. There's free Wi-Fi for diners, so you if you bring your laptop you can check your e-mail while you eat. ■ **TIP→ Many people stop here for a breakfast of enchiladas and refried beans before heading to El Tajín** ✉ *Enríquez 105, Col. Centro* ☎ *784/842–0059* 💳 *MC, V.*

¢–$$ MEXICAN ✕ **Sorrento.** With dozens of dishes on the menu, this open-air restaurant is the most popular in Papantla. It's always crowded with locals who come to enjoy the reasonably priced seafood and to catch a few minutes of a *telenovela* (soap opera) on the giant TV set. The *platillo mexicano,* a selection of regional appetizers, is big enough for two. ✉ *Enríquez 105, Col. Centro* ☎ *784/842–0067* 💳 *No credit cards.*

WHERE TO STAY

¢–$ **Hotel Campestre Tajín.** Just a short distance from the Archaeological Zone of El Tajín, this former hacienda has been converted to a hotel. Rooms are simple, but each is different, and many have carved classic wood furniture, plenty of space, and large windows. Public areas, including a garden and large pool, are lovely. **Pros:** closest you can get to the ruins; away from the noise of town; wonderful green areas, large pool. **Cons:** no phone; no Internet access; no elevator (many rooms only accessible by stairs). ✉ *Km 17.5, Carretera Poza Roca–San Andres* ☎ *784/842–8271* *31 rooms* *In-hotel: restaurant, bar, pool, parking (free)* 💳 *No credit cards.*

¢ **Hotel Provincia Express.** Stay in the heart of things at this hotel, which is up a flight of steps from the main square. Many of the modern rooms have little balconies with views of the mountains. Rooms in front tend to be a bit noisy, so if you're a light sleeper, ask for one in the back. **Pros:** the staff couldn't be friendlier. **Cons:** some rooms are noisy. ✉ *Enríquez 103, Col. Centro* ☎ *784/842–1645 or 784/842–4213* *16 rooms, 4 suites* *In-hotel: restaurant, bar, laundry service, Internet terminal, Wi-Fi hotspot* 💳 *MC, V.*

$–$$ **Hotel Tajín.** The trick at this hillside hotel is getting the right room; the dozen or so rooms with views of the town are the best, but check the mattress for firmness and be sure to specify whether you want air conditioning, before you settle in. All rooms are spic-and-span though the décor feels dated and a little stark. Although the staff does not speak English, they go out of their way to figure out what you need and deliver it promptly. **Pros:** thoughtful staff; clean and inexpensive rooms. **Cons:** you might have to do some room testing before you settle; design is uninspired; on a street that is often busy and loud. ✉ *Domínguez 104, at Nuñez, Col. Centro* ☎ *784/842–0121* 🌐 *www.hoteltajin.com.mx* *59 rooms, 13 suites* *In-hotel: restaurant, pool, laundry service, parking (free)* 💳 *MC, V.*

Continued on page 296

THE FLIGHT OF THE VOLADORES

Like most things in Mexico, this story begins with a legend: Centuries ago a long drought had withered the crops of the Totonac people. Some of the elders decided that the only solution was to find a way to send a message to the gods about their plight. But how to attract their attention?

The sages sent five young men out into the woods in search of the tallest tree they could find. When they returned with the tree, its trunk was stripped of branches and stood on end. Four of the young men adorned their bodies with feathers so they would fool the gods into thinking they were birds and whirled around the tree, suspended from vines. The fifth played a song on the flute that resembled a bird's mournful song.

Their plan must have worked, because *voladores* (which means "the ones who fly") continue to perform versions of this ritual all over Mexico. It's a source of pride for the Totonac people, many of whom still live near the town of Papantla, because it's one of the few traditional practices that managed to survive despite the attempts of the Spanish to wipe out all native customs.

The voladores take their task very seriously, studying for years before they can participate. After all, they are learning to fly.

This ritual was originally performed only once every 52 years, to celebrate the beginning of a new calendar. Today it can be witnessed weekly in Papantla and multipe times daily at the archaeological site of El Tajín.

HOW THEY TAKE TO THE SKY

THE RITUAL BEGINS when the *caporal*, or captain, leads the four voladores to the pole which is 82 feet high. Red sashes over their shoulders represent wings; their conical hats resemble the crests of birds.

THE FIVE dance around the pole several times before ascending the pole, keeping their heads down as a sign of respect to the gods.

THE FOUR VOLADORES seat themselves on a square wooden frame suspended from the top of the pole, each facing a different cardinal direction. The caporal stands on top of the 82-foot pole, with nothing to steady himself.

THE CAPORAL JUMPS on the pole several times. He turns to the east, bending so far backward that his torso is parallel to the ground, then he shifts his position and leans forward. He repeats these moves three more times, rotating to face the points of the compass. As if this weren't difficult enough, he accomplishes these feats while playing a hide-covered drum and a three-holed flute.

AFTER THE CAPORAL FINISHES his dance, the wooden frame starts to spin. The voladores each drop backwards from the side of the platform facing east—where the sun rises and the world awakes—held aloft only by a rope tied around their waists. They throw their arms out to their sides, resembling a quartet of birds in flight.

THEY TWIST LEFT for 13 full rotations each. Between them, the flyers circle the pole 52 times, representing the sacred 52-year cycle of the Totonacs (the Maya calendar had the same 52-year cycle).

THE RITUAL takes about 30 minutes. Offering a $2 (per viewer) tip is appropriate.

SHOPPING

The teeming **Mercado Miguel Hidalgo** (✉ *Av. 20 de Noviembre*), half a block downhill from the main square, sells Totonac costumes, carvings, baskets, and shoulder bags. It's a daily market, but is much busier on weekends. The real draw is vanilla, the region's chief product, which is sold in every conceivable form. Especially lovely are flowers made from the dried vanilla pods.

EL TAJÍN

13 km (8 mi) west of Papantla.

Fodor's Choice ★

The extensive ruins of **El Tajín**—from the Totonac word for "thunder"—express the highest degree of artistry of any ancient city in the coastal area. The city was hidden until 1785, when a Spanish engineer happened upon it. Early theories attributed the complex, believed to be a religious center, to a settlement of Mayan-related Huasteca, one of the most important cultures of Veracruz. Because of its immense size and unique architecture, scholars now believe it may have been built by a distinct El Tajín tribe with ties to the Maya. Although much of the site has been restored, many structures are still hidden under jungle.

El Tajín is thought to have reached its peak between AD 600 and 1200. During this time hundreds of structures of native sandstone were built here, including temples, double-storied palaces, ball courts, and houses. But El Tajín was already an important religious and administrative center during the first three centuries AD. Its influence is in part attributed to the fact that it had large reserves of cacao beans, used as currency in pre-Hispanic times.

Evidence suggests that the southern half of the uncovered ruins—the area around the lower plaza—was reserved for ceremonial purposes. Its centerpiece is the 60-foot-high **Pirámide de los Nichoes** (Pyramid of the Niches), one of Mexico's loveliest pre-Columbian buildings. The finely wrought seven-level structure has 365 coffers (one for each day of the solar year) built around its seven friezes. The reliefs on the pyramid depict the ruler, 13-Rabbit—all the rulers' names were associated with sacred animals—and allude also to the Tajín tribe's main god, the benign Quetzalcóatl. One panel on the pyramid tells the tale of heroic human sacrifice and of the soul's imminent descent to the underworld, where it is rewarded with the gift from the gods of sacred *pulque,* a milky alcoholic beverage made from cactus.

Just south of the pyramid is the I-shape **Juego de Pelotas Sur** (Southern Ball Court). This is one of more than 15 ball courts, more than at any other site in Mesoamerica, where the sacred pre-Columbian ball game was played. The game is somewhat similar to soccer—players used a hard rubber ball that could not be touched with the hands, and suited up in pads and body protectors—but far more deadly. Intricate carvings at certain ball courts indicate that games ended with human sacrifice. It's believed that the winner of the match won the opportunity to ask a question of the gods in exchange for his sacrifice. Depending on the importance of his question, his sacrifice could be anything from minor body mutilation to his very life. It is surmised that the players involved in these sacrificial games were high-ranking members of the priest or warrior classes.

To the north, **El Tajín Chico** (Little El Tajín) is thought to have been the secular part of the city, with mostly administrative buildings and the elite's living quarters. Floors and roofing were made with volcanic rock and limestone. The most important structure here is the **Complejo de los Columnos** (Complex of the Columns). The columns once held up the concrete ceilings, but early settlers in Papantla removed the stones to construct houses. If you're prepared to work your way through the thick jungle, you can see some more recent finds along the dirt paths that lead over the nearby ridges.

You can leave bags at the visitor center at the entrance, which includes a restaurant and a small museum that displays some pottery and sculpture and tells what little is known of the site. Excellent guided tours are available in English and Spanish and cost about $20 per group. A performance by some voladores normally takes place at midday and sometimes up to five times daily. ■**TIP→ Start early to avoid the midday sun, and take water, a hat, and sunblock.** To get here, take a shuttle bus. Head down Calle 20 de Noviembre until you hit Calle Francisco Madero. Cross the street and wait in front of the gas station for an EL TAJÍN shuttle bus. The $1 trip takes about 20 minutes. ☎ *784/842–8354* 🌐 *www.inah.gob.mx* 🎫 *$4.80* ⏲ *Daily 9–5.*

6

COSTA ESMERALDA (EMERALD COAST)

175 km (109 mi) northwest of Veracruz.

Covering 35 km (23 mi) of coastline along the Gulf of Mexico between Nautla and Papantla, Costa Esmeralda's clean wide beaches and calm waters are popular with beachgoers and fishermen alike. Here Highway 180 is lined with small restaurants and stands selling fresh pineapples, oranges, and cheese. It's also peppered with campgrounds and hotels taking advantage of the amazing beachfront.

WHERE TO STAY

$$–$$$ ★ **Azúcar.** Azúcar specializes in barefoot luxury, and many of the guests are honeymooners. Thatch-roof bungalows gather invitingly around a sunken pool overlooking waves crashing 20 feet away. Private open-air seating allows you to take in the ocean view from a daybed of plush pillows or a colorful hammock. Private outdoor showers, straw hats, and whimsical furniture lend a sense of fun, while flat-screen TVs and pristine white rooms provide touches of elegance. An optional package for a minimum of four people includes two nights, one dinner, airport transfers, and round-trip travel from Mexico City on a Cessna 206. The hotel also arranges trips to El Tajín. **Pros:** nice touches for a reasonable rate; wonderful seafood restaurant; great service; no children under 14 allowed. **Cons:** some details that would make your stay more seamless are overlooked; no children under 14 allowed. ✉ *Carretera Federal Nautla–Poza Rica, Km 83.5* ☎ *232/321–0678* 🌐 *www.hotelazucar.com* *20 suites* *In-hotel: restaurant, room service, bar, pool, spa, beachfront, laundry service, parking (free)* 💳 *AE, MC, V.*

$$ **Istirincha.** As it's beyond the strip of hotels along the highway, this sprawling property is more private, with wonderful gardens to explore, a small area with crocodiles that you can study from behind a fence, and a pleasant beach that few other than fellow guests hang out on. The hotel can arrange bike and horseback rides. **Pros:** inexpensive rooms; secluded gardens and beach. **Cons:** you need a taxi to explore the area from here. ✉ *Carretera Federal Nautla–Cardel, Km 102* ☎ *235/317–4201* 🌐 *www.hotelistirincha.com* *40 rooms* *In-hotel: restaurant, tennis court, pool, laundry service, Wi-Fi hotspot* ▭ *MC, V.*

$$$ **Suspiro Hotel.** This well-designed, whitewashed hotel is the most elegant along the strip. Each spacious room has a TV, DVD player, and balcony overlooking the hotel pool, which is just off the beach. White walls and white linens contrast with a few pieces of dark-colored furniture. The hotel has a DVD library and a palapa with video games, a pool table, and board games like chess and Scrabble. The small third-story bar, overlooking the water, hosts karaoke on Friday and Saturday. **Pros:** pleasant, comfortable rooms, all with ocean views. **Cons:** no Internet access, high prices. ✉ *Carretera Federal Nautla–Poza Rica, Km 83.5* ☎ *232/321–0835* 🌐 *www.hotelsuspiro.com* *12 rooms* *In-room: safe. In-hotel: restaurant, bar, pool, spa, parking (free)* ▭ *MC, V.*

TUXPAN

89 km (55 mi) north of Papantla, 309 km (192 mi) northwest of Veracruz.

A peaceful riverside town with a tangle of twisting streets, Tuxpan—almost as often referred to as Tuxpam—is a pleasant place to stop if you're driving along the coast. In the evening you'll find people strolling beneath the palms along the waterfront promenade and watching the sun set over the water. Running parallel to the river, busy Avenida Juárez is lined with restaurants, hotels, and shops.

GETTING HERE AND AROUND

The most popular form of public transportation is the fleet of baby-blue *lanchas* (small motorboats) that carry commuters across the Río Tuxpan. A round-trip journey from any of the docks along the river costs about 40¢.

ADO buses also shuttle between Veracruz and Tuxpan several times a day; it's a four-hour to six-hour trip, and costs about $15. Tuxpan has a small bus terminal east of downtown on Calle Rodriguez.

ESSENTIALS

Currency Exchange **Banamex** (✉ *Av. Juárez at Calle Corregidora, Tuxpan* ☎ *783/834–3868* 🌐 *www.banamex.com.mx*).

Emergency Numbers **Centro Médico de Tuxpan** (✉ *Av. Cuauhtémoc 82* ☎ *783/834–7400*). **Tuxpan Cruz Roja** (☎ *783/834–0158*). **Police** (☎ *783/834–0252*).

Visitor and Tour Info **Tuxpan Tourist Office** (✉ *Av. Juárez 20* ☎ *783/834–0322 Ext. 125*).

EXPLORING

Across the river from downtown is the grandly named **Museo Histórico de la Amistad México–Cuba** *(Historical Museum of the Mexico-Cuba Friendship)*. This one-room house, bare save for black-and-white photos and a few threadbare uniforms, is where Fidel Castro lived for a time while planning the overthrow of Fulgencio Batista. To get here from the dock, walk three blocks south to Calle Obregón, then head west for several blocks until you reach the end of the street. ✉ *Calle Obregón* ☎ *No phone* 🎫 *Free* ⏲ *Weekdays 9–7.*

Avenida Juárez leads to **Parque Reforma**, where more than 100 tables are set beneath trees clipped into perfect cubes. As the sun goes down, noisy birds roost here and young couples buy ice cream from carts or slip off to secluded benches. The park has a memorial to Fausto Vega Santander, a member of the 201st Squadron of the Mexican Air Force and the first Mexican to be killed in combat during World War II.

BEACHES

Tuxpan's main attraction is the miles of beaches that begin 7 km (4½ mi) east of town.The first and most accessible beach from Tuxpan is **Playa Tuxpan**. The surf here isn't huge, but there's enough action to warrant breaking out your surf- or Boogie board. There are inexpensive hotels and restaurants along the beach, and many have bathrooms and showers that you can use for a dollar or two. Of the open-air restaurants along Playa Tuxpan, the most established is El Arca, which has a branch at the main beach entrance called El Velero. Both have an extensive menu of freshly caught seafood, and fresh coconuts.

6

WHERE TO EAT

¢–$ SEAFOOD ✕ **Barra de Mariscos.** Don't be fooled by the white plastic tables and chairs—the seafood at this open-air eatery easily rivals that at fancier places in town. Hunker down with a cold beer and a bowl of *sopa de ostión* (a spicy oyster stew), then move on to *pulpo encebollado* (octopus cooked with onions, butter, and garlic) or the house specialty, *camarones a la diabla* (a spicy concoction of grilled shrimp and chilies). You may be tempted to make a meal of the chips and salsa. ✉ *Av. Juárez 44, at Calle Ortega* 💳 *No credit cards.*

$$ SEAFOOD ✕ **El Atracadero.** This restaurant, floating on the Río Tuxpan but linked to the land with rope and a small bridge, is hands down the most elegant place to eat in town. The interior is relaxed, with exposed wood beams, a backlit bar, and large windows looking out on the water. The Spanish owners are famous for their paella Valenciana, and there are a number of seafood and beef dishes to chose from as well. The bar is well stocked, with wines and liquors from all over the world. ✉ *Río Tuxpan, between Zozimo Pérez and Hernández y Hernández* ☎ *783/835–5166* 💳 *AE, MC, V* ⏲ *No breakfast.*

$–$$ STEAKHOUSE ✕ **Restaurant Safari Steak House.** This popular steak house is a great place to enjoy a meal on a sunny day. There's a nice outdoor dining area with plants as well as toucans and other birds in cages. The menu has large tasty salads, including the so-called Kenya salad, with lettuce, nuts, pear, grapes, spinach, and Brie. Try the *puntas de filete a la Mexicana* (tenderloin tips with a red Mexican sauce served with rice and beans). ✉ *Blvd. Jesús Reyes Heroles 35* ☎ *783/834–1070* 💳 *MC, V.*

WHERE TO STAY

$ ★ **Hotel Florida**. This place certainly earns its name—tropical flora tumbles from the balconies. The art deco–style structure, dating from 1940, has gracefully curved windows on the corner overlooking the town's elegant church. The rooms are, for the most part, spacious and sunny. Some have better views than others, so ask to see a few before you decide. El Quijote, which dominates the ground floor, has excellent seafood. **Pros:** quality restaurant; nice landscaping. **Cons:** rooms can vary, so checking around is a must. ✉ *Av. Juárez 23, at Calle Garizurieta* ☎ *783/834–0222 or 783/834–0602* 🌐 *www.hotel-florida.com.mx* *75 rooms* *In-room: Wi-Fi. In-hotel: restaurant, room service, bar, laundry service, Wi-Fi hotspot, parking (free)* *DC, MC, V.*

$–$$ **Hotel May Palace**. The most luxurious lodgings in Tuxpan are at this modern hotel overlooking Parque Reforma. The five-story building—which qualifies as a high-rise here—is frequented by business executives who meet for drinks in the small video bar or for dinner in the pleasant restaurant. The rooms, all painted in neutral shades, have views of the river. It's not hard to relax by the sparkling rooftop pool. **Pros:** a good place to hang out. **Cons:** geared toward business travelers. ✉ *Av. Juárez 44* ☎ *783/834–8882* 🌐 *www.hotelmaypalace.com* *70 rooms, 4 suites* *In-room: Wi-Fi. In-hotel: restaurant, room service, bar, pool, gym, laundry service, Wi-Fi hotspot, parking (free)* *AE, MC, V.*

$$$ **Hotel Riviera de Tuxpan**. One of the town's most modern hotels is in a three-story structure across from the Río Tuxpan. Spacious rooms don't have much personality (they're decorated with simple wooden furniture and neutral colors), but they do have a/c, Wi-Fi, and cable TV. Many rooms also have good views. **Pros:** up-to-date. **Cons:** lacks personality. ✉ *Blvd. Jesús Reyes Heroles 17* ☎ *783/834–8123 or 783/834–5349* 🌐 *www.bestwestern.com.mx* *47 rooms* *In-room: Wi-Fi. In-hotel: restaurant, Internet terminal, parking (free)* *AE, MC, V.*

SPORTS AND THE OUTDOORS

For scuba diving, head to Isla Lobos (Island of the Wolves), a protected eco-reserve that shares its space with a military outpost and a lighthouse. In the shallow water offshore are a few shipwrecks and colorful reefs with puffer fish, parrot fish, damselfish, and barracuda. Generally, the best time to dive is between May and August.**Aqua Sport** (✉ *Carretera la Playa, Km 8.5* ☎ *783/837–0259*), west of Playa Tuxpan, arranges diving trips to Isla Lobos. Single-tank dives for groups of four or more cost around $80 per person; a single person can expect to pay $160.

SOUTHERN VERACRUZ

Southern Veracruz has some dramatic sights, both natural and manmade. Tlacotalpan is a tropical port city of waning importance, but its brightly colored buildings and well-preserved colonial architecture make it a lovely place to kick back for a few days. Farther south along the coast the land meets the sea quite dramatically in a trio of towns known as Los Tuxtlas, which cling to the hillside above the water. One of the towns, Catemaco, is also home to an immense lake that is a favorite spot with vacationing Mexicans.

TLACOTALPAN

★ *90 km (56 mi) south of Veracruz.*

The name Tlacotalpan is of Nahuatl origin and means "in the middle of the earth," referring to the settlement's location on what was then an island. Once a prosperous port city, Tlacotalpan, now more run-down, still charms with rustic, century-old houses, all in colors that might have been inspired by a candy shop.

GETTING HERE AND AROUND

Getting to Tlacotalpan by car is a snap: simply take Carretera 180 south from Veracruz, then head west on Ruta 175 after you pass Alvarado. If you are traveling by bus, there's a twice-daily ADO bus costing about $7 each way. You can also take the more frequent TRV buses departing from the second-class terminal for a bit less. **■TIP→ Caution: This can be a painfully slow option, as these also serve as local buses and school buses.**

EXPLORING

The massive orange-trimmed church on the north side of Plaza Zaragoza is the **Capilla de la Candelaria**, constructed in 1779. It houses the town's patron saint, the Virgen de la Candelaria. The saint is honored each year with a festival that runs from January 31 to February 9; a parade with hundreds of horses is followed by the running of the bulls through the streets. The most famous image of the festival is a statue of the Virgin Mary drifting down the river, followed by a flotilla of little boats. The buildings in Plaza Zaragoza are helpfully marked with snippets of history printed in Spanish and English.

The neoclassical **Casa de Cabildo**, which houses all the governmental offices, is painted vivid shades of red and green. The huge arch in the center of the building leads to the old port, and all newcomers once passed through this portal.

Several other churches are scattered around Tlacotalpan, but none are more delightful than the diminutive **Iglesia de San Miguel Arcangel**. Known to locals as San Miguelito (Little Saint Michael), the whitewashed structure, constructed in 1785, was once a parish church reached by crossing a little bridge. If you're in town September 27 to 29, you can take a peek at the Fiesta de San Miguelito. The church is about three blocks north of Plaza Zaragoza.

Museo Casa Lara (✉ *Calle Gonzalo Aguirre Beltrán 6* ☎ *288/884–2166* 🎫 *$2, $1 more for use of video* ⏲ *Daily 10–2 and 3–7*) is filled with photographs and other items that belonged to Augustín Lara, a musician and movie star. Look for stills from films such as *Los Tres Bohemios* and *Los Tres Amores de Lola*. The best reason to visit, though, is the chance to poke around a lovely colonial-era home.

Two tiny museums vie for your attention. On Plaza Hidalgo, diagonally across from Plaza Zaragoza, **Museo Salvador Ferrando** (✉ *Calle Manuel Alegre 6* ☎ *288/884–2385* 🎫 *$1* ⏲ *Tues.–Sun. 10:30–4:30*) displays furniture and other objects from the 19th century.

6

The Casa de Cabildo faces **Plaza Zaragoza**, the town's main square. In the square's shady center you'll find a bandstand decorated with ornamental lyres.

WHERE TO STAY

$$ **Casa del Rio Hotel**. The only hotel in town on the Río Papaloapan is in a 19th-century house that's considered a historic monument. Rooms are simple, with beige ceramic floors and white bedcovers. The joys here are in the details: linens are high quality, towels are fluffy, and service is extremely attentive. Owners Francisco and Elena speak English quite well; other staffers have a harder time but always make an effort. You can rent bikes and arrange rafting trips through the hotel. **Pros:** excellent service; nice touches; prime location. **Cons:** some rooms don't have a view; mosquitoes are a problem at some times of the year. ✉ *Miguel Z. Cházaro 39* ☎ *288/884–2947* 🌐 *www.casadelrio.com.mx* *6 rooms* *In-room: Wi-Fi. In-hotel: restaurant, bicycles* 💳 *MC, V.*

¢–$ **Posada Doña Lala**. A staircase decorated with hand-painted tiles leads you up to the second-floor rooms at this bright pink hotel. Ask for one of the spacious rooms facing the street so you can look out over the rooftops. Don't miss a meal at the seafood restaurant ($), which has tables in the beamed-ceiling dining room or on a shady porch. **Pros:** no matter where you sit, there's a river view. **Cons:** could use some updating. ✉ *Av. Venustiano Carranzo 11* ☎ *288/884–2580* 🌐 *hoteldonalala.com* *32 rooms, 5 suites* *In-hotel: restaurant, Internet terminal* 💳 *AE, MC, V.*

SHOPPING

The famous *sillón tlacatalpeño*—a wooden rocking chair with a woven seat and back—is one way locals beat the heat. Purchase a full-size love seat or a doll-size miniature at **Casa Artensenal de Tlacotalpan** (✉ *Plaza Zaragoza* ☎ *288/884–2990*). Doña Rafaela Murillo's shop, housed in a building that once served as the town's prison, also carries various objects made of carved wood, including fanciful animals and birds.

Galería Vives (✉ *Av. Venustiano Carranzo 11* ☎ *288/884–3070*) carries lacy garments and monogrammed handkerchiefs.

Oaxaca

Local handcraft shop, Oaxaca City

7

WORD OF MOUTH

"My favorite [place] is probably Oaxaca. Fascinating city. Great architecture. Some of the best food in the country. Strong indigenous culture. You could spend hours just in the market. Charming zocalo—another place where you could spend hours. And then there's Monte Alban, just outside the city—a very large archeological site built on top of a mountain."

—robertino

www.fodors.com/community

WELCOME TO OAXACA

TOP REASONS TO GO

★ **Sampling everything:** Oaxaca State is a best-of-Mexico sampler: ruins, colonial cities, beaches, crafts, and gorgeous scenery.

★ **Eating Oaxacan food:** Think cheese, mole, empanadas, tamales, soups, and rich hot chocolates. Be sure to try Oaxaca's specialty spirit, *mezcal,* which is made from dozens of types of agave (unlike tequila, which is made exclusively from blue agave).

★ **Craft-shopping at the source:** The villages around Oaxaca City actually produce many of the crafts you see in markets all over Mexico.

★ **Experiencing a coastal frontier:** The Oaxaca coast is the most unexplored and undeveloped of Mexico's shorelines.

★ **Visiting a mountaintop city:** Monte Albán, built by the Zapotecs, is one of the country's most important ruins.

1 Oaxaca City. The capital of the region is a particularly pretty colonial city. It has tree-shaded parks, cobblestone streets, and brightly colored buildings, as well as fantastic restaurants. It's a small city—the main sights are easily covered on foot.

2 The Valles Centrales. There are dozens of crafts villages and mezcal makers in the valleys surrounding Oaxaca City. In every direction are archaeological sites, the main ones being Mitla and Monte Albán. The countryside here is simply magnificent: a few main roads take you through miles of farmland.

GETTING ORIENTED

Oaxaca is in one of three adjacent valleys encircled by the majestic Sierra Madre del Sur. Mexico's fifth-largest state is bordered by Chiapas to the east, Veracruz and Puebla to the north, and Guerrero to the west. Southern Oaxaca State is blessed with 509 km (316 mi) of Pacific coast line. By the way, it's pronounced *wah-hah-ka.*

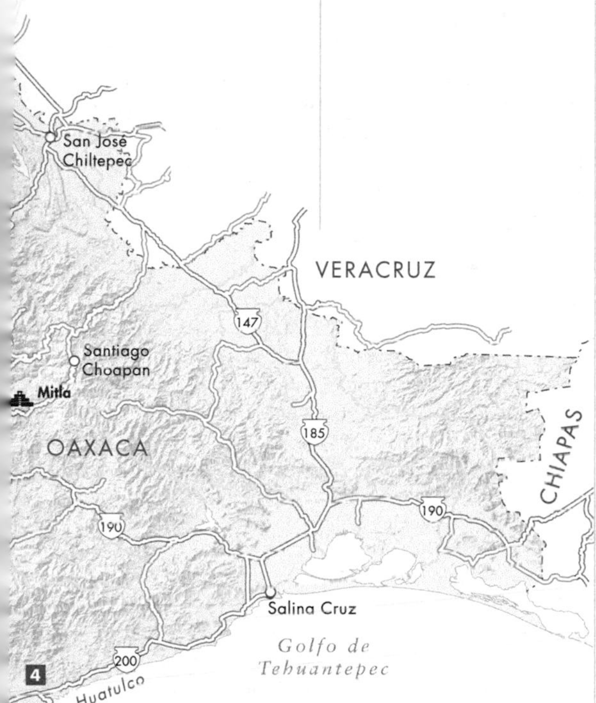

3 The Mixteca. This region, northwest of Oaxaca City, is one of the least-explored parts of the state. You'll find pine-covered hills, tiny villages that survive on subsistence farming, and a series of colossal, partially reconstructed monasteries.

4 Oaxaca Coast. The coast is fairly remote, and it is strikingly exquisite. Puerto Escondido is surfer territory, though fancier digs are starting to pop up. Bahías de Huatulco is mostly a nature reserve, though the government is trying to transform the rest into another Cancún. Midway between the two are a few tiny beach villages, including the up-and-coming paradises of Zipolite, Mazunte, and San Agustinillo.

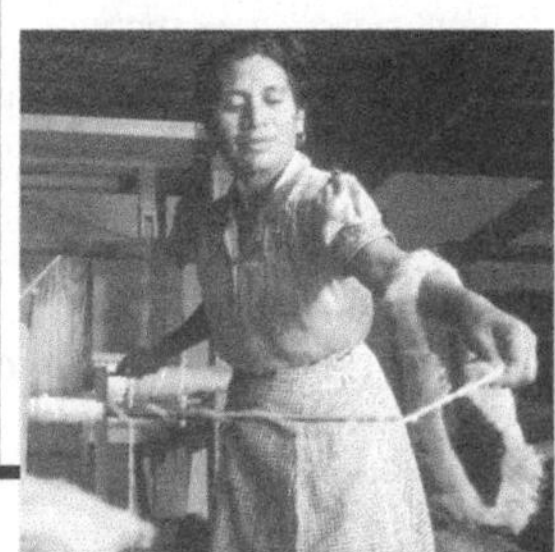

OAXACA PLANNER

How Much Can You Do?

The region may not look that big on paper, but tackling both city and coast in less than a week isn't possible without exhausting yourself. Driving from Oaxaca City to Puerto Escondido, for example, takes a minimum of seven hours. Flying is time-consuming and expensive. If your time is limited, choose either the city and its surroundings or the coast.

How's the Weather?

Oaxaca City lies in a valley at an altitude of 5,000 feet. The city's easygoing personality is complemented by year-round spring temperatures, although days can get quite hot even in winter. Evenings can be chilly, so make sure to bring a light jacket.

Rainy season runs from July to October, September being the wettest month. Generally you can count on clear mornings, with clouds and showers usually arriving in the late afternoon.

The Oaxacan coast lies well within the tropics, so it's always hot and often humid.

Tours and Excursions

Dozens of Oaxaca City operators lead half- and full-day city tours or trips to outlying market villages, half-day excursions to Monte Albán, and full-day journeys to Mitla.

Hiking and mountain-biking excursions are popular, as are treks to waterfalls and soaks in hot springs. More adventurous (and fitter) travelers can explore the remote mountain villages of the Mixteca and Sierra Norte, camping or staying in simple cabins.

Bicicletas Bravo (✉ *Calle Garcí Vigil 409, at Calle Allende, Centro Histórico* ☎ *951/516–0953*) leads trips as short as a few hours and as long as a few days into the countryside. You can also rent a bike and set out on your own. This cost is $10 an hour, but you can get discounts for renting by the day or week.

Bicicletas Pedro Martínez (✉ *Aldama 418, Centro Histórico* ☎ *951/514–5935* 🌐 *www.bicicletaspedromartinez.com*) leads hiking and biking tours in the Central Valley or Puerto Escondido. Custom tours are available, too. A two-person four- to six-hour tour costs about $75; with more people, the per-person price drops.

Expediciones Sierra Norte (✉ *Calle M. Bravo 210, Centro Histórico* ☎ *951/514–8271* 🌐 *www.sierranorte.org.mx*) has one- to five-day hiking and biking trips into the Central Valley and the Sierra Norte. You either camp or stay in simple cabins. Costs start at $48 for one-day excursions.

TierrAventura (✉ *Calle Abasolo 217, Centro Histórico* ☎ *951/501–1363* 🌐 *www.tierraventura.com*) has everything from one-day trips to local villages ($65 to $90) to four-day excursions to the coast ($330 to $400). Expect to see some villages far off the beaten path.

Turismo El Convento De Oaxaca (✉ *Calle 5 de Mayo 300* ☎ *951/516–5791* 🌐 *www.oaxacaexperts.com*) operates out of the Camino Real hotel and gives reliable tours with English speaking guides. Four-hour Monte Albán trips cost $18; eight-hour outings include trips to other sites and cost $30. Half-day trips to Mitla also visit El Tule and Teotitlán and cost $18. Excursions to area villages and markets can also be arranged. Rates include transport to and from the Camino Real or other Oaxaca City hotels.

Cooking Classes

Oaxaca is known as "the land of seven moles." You may sample a mole made with sesame seeds one day, then a pineapple- or banana-inspired mole the next. Other favorite dishes include *jicuatote,* a sweet milky dessert flavored with cloves and cinnamon, and *chapulines,* seasoned and fried grasshoppers, which are said to charm you into returning to Oaxaca.

Whether you want to master a mole or be an expert on the multicolor chili peppers at the local market, cooking courses are a great way to immerse yourself in Oaxacan culture.

The most exclusive course is by Casa Oaxaca's **Alejandro Ruiz** (☎ *951/514–4173 or 951/516–9923* 🌐 *www.casaoaxaca.com.mx*), whose take on Nuevo Mexicano cooking is the best in the city.

The cooking classes at **Casa Crespo** (☎ *951/514–1102* 🌐 *www.casacrespo.com*) begin with a visit to the market and end four hours later with a delicious meal.

Casa Sagrada (☎ *951/516–4275 or 310/455–6085* 🌐 *www.casasagrada.com*), in the Central Valley town of Teotitlan, gives half-day or weeklong classes that focus on Zapotec specialties.

Susana Trilling's **Seasons of My Heart Cooking School** (☎ *951/508–0946* 🌐 *www.seasonsofmyheart.com*), in the Etla Valley, provides half-day, full-day, weekend, and week-long classes as well as culinary tours.

Pilar Cabrera (☎ *951/516–5704* 🌐 *www.laolla.com.mx*), proprietor of La Olla restaurant, gives private or group classes in which you prepare a five-course meal. If you take private lessons, you choose which to prepare, and classes usually start with selecting ingredients at a market.

Money Matters

WHAT IT COSTS IN DOLLARS

	¢	$	$$	$$$	$$$$
Restaurant	under $5	$5–$10	$10–$15	$15–$25	over $25
Hotel	under $50	$50–$75	$75–$150	$150–$250	over $250

Restaurant prices are per person for a main course at dinner. Hotel prices are for two people in a standard double room.

Village Stays

You can experience village life by staying at a tourist *yu'u,* a Zapotec word meaning "tourist house." Developed by the state tourism board, these lodgings scattered throughout the communities of the Valles Centrales, the Mixteca, and other areas around Oaxaca City are the ultimate budget options, costing as little as $8 per person per night.

Not all *yu'us* are created equal. The older ones, in villages such as Santa Ana del Valle, are in concrete-block buildings painted a vivid shade of green. Newer places in villages like Benito Juárez are more comfortable—accommodations in four rooms in a main building house between three and nine people; six cabins accommodate two or three people.

You can cook your own meals or arrange for a local cook. Activities include horseback riding, mountain-bike trips, and temazcal (an adobe sweat lodge used by the indigenous people). Facilities in nearby villages, such as San Antonio Cuajimoloyas, have a similar range of activities.

Volunteers at the **Tourist Yu'u Project** (✉ *Calle Murguía 204, at Calle 5 de Mayo, Centro Histórico* ☎ *951/516–0123*), in the state tourism office, can show you photos of and provide fact-sheets on each yu'u. They can also make reservations for you.

OAXACA CITY

450 km (280 mi) southeast of Mexico City on toll road 135D, 389 km (242 mi) southwest of Veracruz on Hwys. 185 and 190.

Updated by Jeffrey Van Fleet

With its magical concoction of sights, smells, and sounds both ancient and modern, this mountain-ringed city of about 400,000 people, officially called Oaxaca de Juárez, embodies the bundle of contrasts that is modern Mexico. You'll hear the singsong strains of Zapotec, Mixtec, and other indigenous languages in the markets, Spanish rock in the bars and restaurants, and hip-hop in English blaring from passing cars. Affluent families sip tea or tequila in classy restaurants; out on the streets, men, women, and children of significantly more modest means sell pencils, sweets, and ears of delicious grilled *elote* (corn).

The Centro Histórico is a pastel collage of colonial- and Republican-era mansions, civic edifices, and churches. The colonial heart is laid out in a simple grid, with all the attractions within a few blocks of one another. Most streets change names when they pass the zócalo (town square); for example, Calle Trujano becomes Calle Guerrero as it travels from west to east. Only the two major east–west arteries—Avenida Morelos and Avenida Independencia—keep their names.

GETTING HERE AND AROUND

Oaxaca City's Aeropuerto Internacional Benito Juárez (OAX), 8 km (5 mi) south of town, is the region's main hub. Continental Express flies from Houston. ■**TIP→ Note that the airport closes at 11 PM no matter what; avoid late-night arrivals, which, if delayed, can be diverted to other cities because of the policy.** At the airport, metered taxis are plentiful—fares to the city center are around $15.

Deluxe buses make the six-hour nonstop run from Mexico City to Oaxaca. There are two bus terminals: the first-class station serves long-distance destinations, while the second-class station serves the Central Valley. There's bus service within the city, but you probably won't need to use it, as most major sights are within walking distance of one another, and cabs are cheap and easy to come by.

You won't need a car to get around Oaxaca City; however, if you're planning several excursions into the countryside a car is incredibly useful, and you can just park it at your hotel while you're in town.

ESSENTIALS

Airlines Continental (☎ *01800/900–5000 toll-free in Mexico*). **Mexicana** (☎ *01800/801–2010 toll-free in Mexico*).

Bus Contacts First-class terminal (✉ *Calz. Niños Héroes de Chapultepec 1036, at Calle Emilio Carranza* ☎ *951/513–0529*). **Second-class terminal** (✉ *Prolongación de Trujano at the Periférico* ☎ *951/516–1218*).

Medical Assistance General Emergencies (☎ *066*). **Hospital Reforma** (✉ *Reforma 613, Centro Histórico* ☎ *951/516–0989, 951/516–6090, or 951/516–6100*).

Visitor and Tour Info State Tourism Office (✉ *Calle Murguía 206, at Calle 5 de Mayo, Centro Histórico* ☎ *951/516–0123* ⊕ *www.aoaxaca.com* ✉ *Av. Juárez*

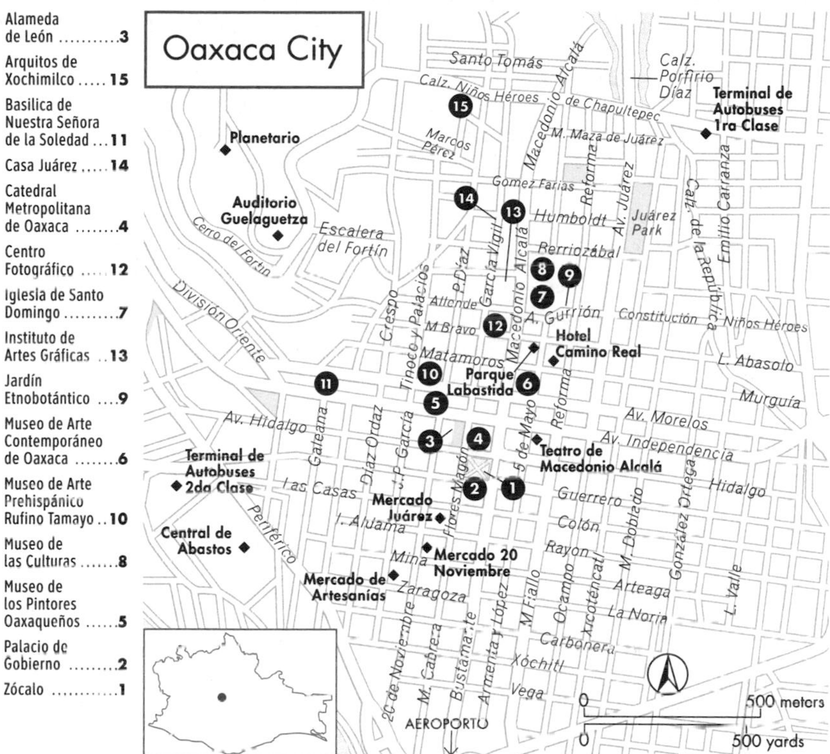

703, Centro Histórico ☎ 951/516–0123 ✉ Museo de los Pintores Oaxaqueños, Av. Independencia 607, Centro Histórico ☎ 951/516–0123).

EXPLORING

TOP ATTRACTIONS

❹ **Catedral Metropolitana de Oaxaca.** Begun in 1544, the cathedral was destroyed by earthquakes and fire and not finished until 1733. It honors the Virgin of the Assumption, whose statue can be seen on the facade above the door. The chapel at the back of the church and to the left of the altar houses the revered crucifix of El Señor del Rayo (Our Lord of the Lightning Bolt), the only piece to survive a fire that started when lightning struck the thatch roof of the original structure. There's no clapper in the bell, supposedly because it started to ring on its own accord back in the 18th century. A recent scrubbing has made this a contender for the city's most gorgeous church. The inside, however, remains sterile. ✉ *Av. Independencia 700, Centro Histórico* ☎ *951/516–4401* ⏲ *Daily 7–7.*

❼ **Fodor'sChoice ★** **Iglesia de Santo Domingo.** With a 17th-century facade framed by two domed bell towers and an interior that's an energetic profusion of white and real gold leaf (typical of the Mexican baroque style), Santo

Domingo is Oaxaca's most brilliantly decorated church. The interior of the dome is adorned with more than 100 medallions depicting various martyrs. **■TIP→ Look up at the ceiling just inside the front door to see a gilded rendering of the family tree of Santo Domingo. If you stop by as the sun sets in the afternoon, the light playing on the ceiling is the best show in town.** ⊠ *Plaza Santa Domingo, Macedonio Alcalá at Adolfo Gurrión, Centro Histórico* ☎ *951/516–3720* ⊙ *Mon.–Sat. 7–1 and 4–7:30, Sun. 7–1 and 4–7.*

NEED A BREAK?

Oaxaca is known for its coffee shops, and a stop at one of them is a great way to break up an afternoon of sightseeing. Coffee Beans (⊠ *5 de Mayo 400C, between Absolo and Constitución, Centro Histórico* ☎ *951/162–7171*) is a cozy, two-floor space near Santo Domingo church with yellow walls and local art, open from 8 in the morning until 11 at night. The coffee is local, organic, and delicious.

9 **Jardín Etnobotánico.** This sprawling botanical garden inside the massive walls of the Ex-Convento de Santo Domingo was the first of its kind in the Americas. Many plants that are now known throughout the region were first cultivated here. Species found only in Oaxaca are on display, including many varieties of cactus. Two-hour-long English-language tours are conducted on Tuesday, Thursday, and Saturday at 11 AM. Spanish-language tours are on Friday and Saturday at 10 AM. You must take a tour to gain admission, and tours fill up quickly, so sign up as early as you can. Afterward you can roam the grounds. ⊠ *Calle Gurrión Adolfo and Calle Reforma, enter on Calle Reforma, Centro Histórico* ☎ *951/516–7672* *English tour $10, Spanish tour $5* ⊙ *Daily 10–5.*

6 ★ **Museo de Arte Contemporáneo de Oaxaca.** Although it's in a lovely colonial residence, MACO houses changing exhibitions of contemporary art. Inaugurated by graphic artist Francisco Toledo, the museum has in its collection quite a few of his etchings, though they're not always on display. Be sure to check out the front gallery on the second floor, which displays fragments of frescoes that once decorated the walls of this old mansion. Signs are in Spanish only. ⊠ *Calle Macedonio Alcalá 202, at Av. Morelos, Centro Histórico* ☎ *951/514–1055* ⊕ *www.museomaco.com* *$2; free Sun.* ⊙ *Wed.–Mon. 10:30–8.*

10 ★ **Museo de Arte Prehispánico Rufino Tamayo.** You'll find a wonderfully displayed collection of pre-Hispanic pottery and sculpture at this carefully restored colonial mansion. The courtyard, dominated by a fountain guarded by a quartet of stone lions, is shaded with pink and white oleanders. Originally this was the private collection of the painter Rufino Tamayo. Especially interesting are the tiny figurines of women with children from Guerrero, some perhaps dating from more than 3,000 years ago, and the smiling ceramic figures from Veracruz. ⊠ *Av. Morelos 503, at Calle Porfirio Díaz, Centro Histórico* ☎ *951/516–4750* *$3.50* ⊙ *Mon. and Wed.–Sat. 10–2 and 4–7, Sun. 10–3.*

8 Fodor's Choice ★ **Museo de las Culturas.** This gorgeous museum is laid out in a series of galleries around the cloister of the labyrinthine Ex-Convento de Santo Domingo. On the ground floor are temporary exhibits and a collection of antique books. On the second floor you'll find rooms dedicated to

Oaxacan music, medicine, indigenous languages, and pottery. More than a dozen other salons have been organized chronologically. ■ **TIP→ Here you'll find such Monte Albán treasures as the stunning gold jewelry from Tomb 7.** Signage is in Spanish only, but English-language audio tours are available. Several lovely second-floor balconies have views of the botanical garden. The on-site shop has a wonderful collection of books, including coffee-table volumes on the art and architecture of Oaxaca. There are also plenty of maps and travel guides. ✉ *Plaza Santa Domingo, Macedonio Alcalá at Adolfo Gurrión, Centro Histórico* ☎ *951/516–2991* 🌐 *www.inah.gob.mx* 🎫 *$4* 🕐 *Tues.–Sun. 10–8, last entrance at 6:15.*

> **WORD OF MOUTH**
>
> "The first time I saw the zocalo in Oaxaca, I found myself thinking, "Now this is the Mexico I've imagined." —Fra_Diavolo

5 **Museo de los Pintores Oaxaqueños.** Even though it occupies a colonial-era building, the Museum of Oaxacan Painters isn't interested in simply reveling in the city's glorious past. Instead, this small gallery finds connections between the past and present, subtly linking Miguel Cabrera's 18th-century religious paintings, which incorporated a few dark-skinned cherubs, to 20th-century portrayals of indigenous people in works by Rodolfo Morales. ✉ *Av. Independencia 607, at Calle García Vigil, Centro Histórico* ☎ *951/516–5645* 🎫 *$2* 🕐 *Tues.–Sun. 10–8.*

1 **Zócalo.** During the day it seems as if everyone passes through Oaxaca's shady main plaza, with its wrought-iron benches and matching bandstand. At night mariachi and marimba bands play under colonial archways or in the bandstand. It's a historic and truly beloved spot: when McDonald's tried to open a branch on its east side in late 2002, grassroots opposition led by painter Francisco Toledo brought the project to a halt. There's marimba music almost every night on the west side of the square (in front of Del Jardín restaurant). On Sunday, the state marching band often strolls around the plaza at noon. ✉ *Bounded by Portal de Clavería on the north, Portal del Palacio on the south, Portal de Flores on the west, and Portal de Mercaderes on the east, Centro Histórico.*

WORTH NOTING

3 **Alameda de León.** This shady square, a bit smaller than the zócalo, is bordered by the massive cathedral on one side and the expertly restored post office on the other. Locals gossip on wrought-iron benches or read the newspaper while their children chase pigeons and blow bubbles. ✉ *Bounded by Av. Indepedencia, Av. Hidalgo, Calle 20 de Noviembre, and Calle Flores Magon, Centro Histórico.*

15 **Arquitos de Xochimilco.** These stone arches were part of the 18th-century aqueducts that carried water into the city. Through many of the arches you'll find twisting streets or secluded plazas. It's a pretty section of the city for a stroll, far from the crowds in the Centro Histórico. The arches are a 5- to 10-minute walk north of Santo Domingo church. Follow Calle Garcia Vigil north; the arches are north of Calle Cosijopi.

⑪ **Basílica de Nuestra Señora de la Soledad.** This baroque basilica houses the statue of the Virgin of Solitude, Oaxaca's patron saint. According to legend, a mule that had mysteriously joined a mule train bound for Guatemala perished at the site of the church; the statue was discovered in its pack, and the event was construed as a miracle—one commemorated by this church, which was built in 1682. Many Oaxaqueños are devoted to the Virgin, who is believed to have more than the usual facility for healing and miracle working. In the 1980s thieves removed her jewel-studded crown; she now has a replica of the original and a glass-covered shrine. Take a look at the chandeliers inside; they're held aloft by angels. ✉ *Av. Independencia 107, at Calle Victoria, Centro Histórico* ☎ *951/516–5067* ⏲ *Daily 7–2 and 4–7.*

NEED A BREAK?

In front of the Basílica de Nuestra Señora de la Soledad is a tiny park called Jardín Socrates, where half a dozen stands sell ice cream. The hands-down favorite is Nevería El Niagara (✉ *Av. Independencia and Calle Victoria, Centro Histórico* ☎ *No phone*). Flavors include *rosas* (roses), *elote*, and the slightly bitter *leche quemada* (burned milk). Wrought-iron tables and chairs and lots of shade make this plaza a great place to get out of the sun for a few minutes.

⑭ **Casa Juárez.** After he was orphaned, 12-year-old Benito Juárez, the future Mexican president and the first indigenous one, walked to Oaxaca from his village in the mountains. He was taken in by a bookbinder named Antonio Salanueva, whose colonial-era home is now a small museum honoring the president. A carefully restored workshop as well as a kitchen, dining room, and bedroom give you a peek at 19th-century Oaxacan life. ✉ *Calle García Vigil 609* ☎ *951/516–1860* 🌐 *www.inah.gob.mx* 🎟 *$3* ⏲ *Weekdays 10–6, weekends 10–5.*

⑫ **Centro Fotográfico Álvarez Bravo.** This small gallery and study center is named for the self-taught Mexico City photographer Manuel Álvarez Bravo (he won his first photographic competition here in Oaxaca). Exhibitions change every month or two. ✉ *Calle M. Bravo 116, at Calle García Vigil, Centro Histórico* ☎ *951/516–9800* 🎟 *Free* ⏲ *Wed.–Mon. 9:30–8.*

⑬ **Instituto de Artes Gráficas de Oaxaca.** This small but interesting gallery has constantly changing exhibits of graphic art and design, including some extremely big names in the national and international communities. ✉ *Calle Macedonio Alcalá 507, Centro Histórico* ☎ *951/516–2045* 🎟 *Free* ⏲ *Wed.–Mon. 9:30–8.*

② **Palacio de Gobierno.** The 19th-century neoclassical state capitol is on the zócalo's south side. A 1988 fresco by Arturo García Bustos wraps around the stairwell. In it, altars to the dead, painters of codices, fruit sellers, gods, and musicians crowd together to catalog the customs and legends of Oaxaca's indigenous people. At the top, on the left side of the mural, note the *apoala* tree, which, according to Mixtec legend, bore the flowers from which life sprang. If there's a protest in front of the building—and there occasionally is—it will be closed to visitors. ✉ *Portal del Palacio, Centro Histórico* ☎ *951/516–0677* ⏲ *Daily 9–8.*

WHERE TO EAT

CENTRO HISTÓRICO

$$$ MEXICAN Fodor'sChoice ★

Casa Oaxaca. Chef Alejandro Ruiz is behind some of the most creative food in southern Mexico—rack of lamb in pineapple-and-vanilla sauce and venison tamales with mole are just a few examples. Wild game is featured heavily on the menu, though the kitchen also has a way with red snapper. Not one course falls short here: appetizers incorporate local herbs and greens, and desserts such as a guava tart with rose-petal sorbet perfectly balance citrus and sweetness. The specialty cocktails are excellent, especially the sangria. The room is modern, open, airy, with white stucco walls, simple wooden tables and chairs, and a beamed ceiling. It's casual and effortlessly romantic. The restaurant shares a building with one of the finest art galleries in town, Galería Quetzalli, so you can browse after you eat. ✉ *Calle García Vigil 407Oaxaca* ☎ *951/516–8889 or 951/516–8531* 🌐 *www.casaoaxaca.com.mx* 💳 *AE, MC, V.*

$ MEXICAN

Catedral. This restaurant takes up the entire first floor of a colonial house. You can dine beneath the arches or in the sun next to a fountain. Popular dishes include mushroom soup flavored with *epazote* (a pungent local herb), chicken with *salsa de flor de calabaza* (pumpkin-blossom sauce), and a superbly prepared *lechón* (suckling pig). Sunday sees a buffet from 2:30 to 7. ✉ *Calle García Vigil 105, at Av. Morelos* ☎ *951/516–3285* 🌐 *www.restaurantecatedral.com.mx* 💳 *AE, MC, V* ⏲ *Closed Tues.*

$$ MEXICAN

Como Agua Pa' Chocolate. Inspired by the book *Like Water For Chocolate*, this second-story restaurant wears its heart on its sleeve. The pale yellow walls are covered with quotations about food, including, "To table and to bed you need call only once." The food is equally romantic, with a whole section of the menu dedicated to foods like quail in rose-petal sauce (a dish inspired by the book). The best choice, however, is the *espejo de moles* (a sampler of five different moles over chicken). The tables on the balcony overlooking the Alameda are the best in the house. ✉ *Calle Hidalgo 612, facing Alameda* ☎ *951/516–2917* 🌐 *www.comoaguapachocolate.com* 💳 *MC, V.*

$ MEXICAN

El Mesón Oaxaqueño. This storefront restaurant is on the west side of the zócalo, so it's surprising that it doesn't draw more tourists; rather, it's popular with locals who come for the steaks. If you're hungry, you can opt for the buffet; otherwise, order à la carte from the many taco options. For a sugar fix, have a cup of Oaxacan hot chocolate and a slice of nut or cheese pie. ✉ *Av. Hidalgo 805, at Calle Valdivieso* ☎ *951/516–2729* 💳 *MC, V.*

$ MEXICAN

La Biznaga. The food at this courtyard café is traditional—except a few touches here and there that make it seem you've stumbled on some unknown cuisine. There's the standard beef smothered with mole, for example, but this version adds the pungent flavor of goat cheese. And the ice cream for dessert comes in tantalizing flavors, such as mezcal. A retractable screen above the courtyard makes this a great retreat even on a rainy day. The cocktails here are good, too—it's a great place to sample mezcals. ✉ *Calle García Vigil 512* ☎ *951/516–1800* 💳 *MC, V* ⏲ *No dinner Sun.*

$$ MEXICAN ✕ **La Olla.** The service is a bit distracted at chef Pilar Cabrera's combination gallery-café, so you'll have plenty of time to admire the works by local artists that adorn the walls. The food makes up for any shortcomings, however. Start with the *tlayuda azteca,* a Mexican-style pizza topped with chicken, avocados, and stringy Oaxacan cheese. The sampler plate includes everything from strips of beef to seasoned pork to *chapulines*. They also serve a different *comida corrida*, or prix-fixe menu, every afternoon for 75 pesos. ✉ *Calle Reforma 402-1* ☎ *951/516–6668* 🌐 *www.laolla.com.mx* 💳 *AE, MC, V* ⏲ *Closed Sun.*

$$ MEXICAN ★ ✕ **Los Danzantes.** Named for the dancing figures carved in stone at the nearby ruins of Monte Albán, this restaurant fuses the new and the old with dishes such as *hierba santa asada,* a local leaf stuffed with goat cheese and Oaxacan cheese; and ravioli with *huitlacoche* (corn fungus) in one sauce of squash flower and another of green chili and cream. The three-story earth-color walls, consisting of triangular columns of rough stone, are reflected in a pool that takes up about half the open-air space. The service is perfectly attentive. Expect to dine exclusively in the company of other tourists. ✉ *Calle Macedonio Alcalá 403* ☎ *951/501–1184* 🌐 *www.losdanzantes.com* 💳 *AE, MC, V.*

$ SEAFOOD ✕ **Marco Polo.** Local families and expats in the know come here for a seafood fix. The ceviches are delicious, as are the whole-fried-fish platters and the shrimp specials. Margaritas, too, are best-in-class, and a wonderful baked banana dessert comes with condensed milk, cream, and rummy eggnog. The original branch, where you can enjoy your meal out in a lovely, fern-shaded garden, is a breakfast-and-lunch-only place, closing at 6 PM. Another branch on Cinco de Mayo isn't quite as cute, but it is open until 9 PM every day except Sunday. ✉ *Pino Suárez 806, across from Llano* ☎ *951/513–4308* 💳 *AE, MC, V.*

$$$ CONTEMPORARY ★ ✕ **Temple.** Where did Mexican chefs learn how to make such pillow-soft gnocchi tossed with cherry tomatoes, red cabbage, and Serrano ham? This chic little eatery—more Central Park than Centro Histórico—dares to be different, and actually succeeds in the process. Although you can find some favorite local dishes on the menu, the kitchen's focus is contemporary cuisine with Oaxacan flair, like the squash-blossom soup sprinkled with tangy goat cheese. Tapas are available at the bar all day. Sometimes there's live jazz in the evening. ✉ *Calle García Vigil 409A* ☎ *951/516–8676* 🌐 *www.temple.com.mx* 💳 *MC, V.*

$ MEXICAN ★ ✕ **Zandunga.** A shabby-chic handful of wooden tables dressed in bright paisley cloths, Zandunga is the quintessential corner café. It fills up with local families who come to sample hearty and simple dishes from the *istmo,* the southeastern part of the state around the town of Tehuantepec. The *estofado,* a savory beef stew, is recommended; start off with the sampler plate of typical regional snacks, which comes with *totopos* (crunchy tortillas that originated on the isthmus). Daily specials may include a mole for good measure. Wash it all down with a tangy tea made from hibiscus blossoms. ✉ *Calle García Vigil at Calle Jesús Carranza* ☎ *951/516–2265* 💳 *MV, V* ⏲ *Closed Sun.*

CLOSE UP

On the Menu in Oaxaca

Food isn't taken lightly in Oaxaca. Traditional recipes, many of which predate the arrival of the Spanish, are passed from generation to generation. Sisters argue over who makes the most authentic version of Grandmother's mole.

Oaxacans don't like change, which may be why restaurants like El Naranjo and Los Danzantes that serve updated versions of classic dishes are inundated by foreigners and ignored by locals. You can imagine the outcry when McDonald's announced it was going to open a restaurant on the zócalo. It didn't take long for the company to rethink its plans.

When it comes to sampling Oaxaca's cuisine, do as the locals do. Oaxaca's markets—and inexpensive eateries near them—are among the most interesting places to sample any of the following regional specialties.

Although the name sounds like an elegant dish, **chapulines** are nothing more than fried grasshoppers seasoned with salt, tangy chili, and a pinch of lime. You find them everywhere from the fanciest restaurant to the humblest vendor's cart. All sizes of grasshoppers are available, depending on the season; the large ones go down a bit easier if you remove the legs first. According to local lore, one taste will charm you into returning to Oaxaca.

The sweet, white gelatinous dessert called **jicuatote** is made with milk, cloves, cinnamon, and cornmeal. It's served in tubs or cut into cubes, and is usually colored red on top.

Although you'll find versions of this sauce everywhere in Mexico, **mole** is to Oaxaca as baked beans are to Boston. There are seven major kinds of moles, so many restaurants ladle out a different one every day of the week. If you've had mole back home, it was probably *mole oaxaqueña.* Also known as *mole negro,* or black mole, it's the standard-bearer. It gets its sweetness from chocolate and its fire from peppers, and is featured in every kind of dish.

Another favorite is *manchamanteles,* which translates as "tablecloth stainer" (it's not as thick as other moles, so it spills easily). Moles aren't always a deep, rich brown. *Verde* is green, *amarillo* is a dark, reddish yellow, and *coloradito* can be different shades of red.

Say cheese, or rather **quesillo.** The stringy cow's-milk cheese made in and around Oaxaca is soft and nutty. It ends up in many dishes, even those that have nothing to do with Mexico. Hint: that's not mozzarella on your pizza.

Made from the flowers and seeds of the cacao tree, **tejate** is sweetened with corn, coconut milk, sugar, and spices. The result—white clumps suspended in brown liquid—is served in a painted gourd bowl. The concoction may look deadly, but it's actually tasty *and* nutritious.

The huge, flat tortillas called **tlayudas** are spread with refried beans and topped with cheese, salsa, and, if you like, strips of chicken or pork. They're halfway between soft tortillas and crispy tostadas, and they're hard to eat delicately. Put away the knife and fork and break off a piece.

ELSEWHERE IN OAXACA CITY

$ MEXICAN **El Biche Pobre.** This little restaurant east of Parque Paseo Juárez is packed with locals—sometimes there's not a tourist in sight—who appreciate the traditional fare like *enchiladas suizas* (with sour cream) and the prices. It's a 10-minute walk from the zócalo. You'll know you're there when you spot the huge green eyes painted on the side of the building. ✉ *Calzado de la República 600, at Calle Hidalgo, Jalatlaco* ☎ *951/513–4636* ▭ *MC, V.*

> **WORD OF MOUTH**
>
> "One of my most favorite things was taking a cooking class in traditional Mexican food (definitely NOT TexMex). I thoroughly enjoyed the day of shopping at the local market, cooking, and—most of all—eating. We made a traditional mole that had 22 ingredients!"—hsmithcr

$$ MEXICAN **El Colibrí.** A neon sign bearing the namesake hummingbird draws you to this little cafeteria. Mothers who have packed their kids off to school and cell-phone-toting business executives favor this place, perhaps for its free refills of super-hot coffee and the extensive menu of Mexican favorites. If you're homesick, you can always order a burger with fries. While you wait, browse in the gift shop. The restaurant is across from the ADO bus station, making it a great escape from the crowded waiting area. ✉ *Calz. Niños Héroes de Chapultepec 903, Colonia Reforma* ☎ *951/515–8087* ▭ *AE, MC, V.*

$$ MEXICAN ★ **La Escondida.** An outdoor lunch buffet, from 1:30 to 6:30, is a great reason to venture outside the city to this restaurant 3 km (2 mi) east of Oaxaca on the road to Mitla. Waiters bring you a welcome cocktail and a typical appetizer, such as *taquitos de pollo* (small tacos filled with chicken) or *memelas* (fried discs of cornmeal topped with goodies). You then select from more than 70 Mexican dishes, including several kinds of meat fresh from the grill. You can linger here, listening to wandering mariachi and marimba musicians—and let the kids loose on the small playground. ✉ *Carretera a San Agustín Yatareni, Km 7, San Agustín Yatareni* ☎ *951/587–5550* 🌐 *www.restaurantelaescondida.com.mx* ▭ *AE, MC, V* ⏲ *No dinner.*

WHERE TO STAY

CENTRO HISTÓRICO

$$–$$$$ ★ **Camino Real Oaxaca.** This breathtaking 16th-century building—the former Convento de Santa Catalina de Siena—is one of the city's landmarks. Around every corner is a discovery: a rear patio holds the covered *pileta,* a circle of stone basins where the nuns did laundry. The lavish breakfast buffet, which you can enjoy even if you're not a hotel guest, is served under the arches in what was the convent's kitchen. The grassy courtyard where mariachis play is a great spot for a margarita. Staffers are crisp and professional, and always ready with directions or advice—as you'd hope they would be, given the audacious prices. Guest or not, consider signing up for the free 40-minute tour of this historic building. It departs from the lobby on Wednesday, Thursday, and Friday at 5 PM. **Pros:** historic building; lovely courtyard and pool area; excellent service. **Cons:** excessively pricey; exterior rooms get street noise;

Restaurants ▼
Casa Oaxaca **5**
Catedral **11**
Como Agua Pa' Chocolate **12**
El Biche Pobre ... **4**
El Colibrí **1**
El Mesón Oaxaqueño **13**
La Biznaga **7**
La Escondida **2**
La Olla **6**
Los Danzantes ... **9**
Marco Polo **3**
Temple **10**
Zandunga **8**

Hotels ▼
Camino Real Oaxaca **7**
Casa Cid de León **8**
Casa de las Bugambilias **6**
Casa de Sierra Azul **15**
Casa del Sótano **10**
Casa Oaxaca **9**
Casa Raab **3**
Hac. Los Laureles **2**
Hostal de la Noria **14**
Hotel Casona del Llano **4**
Hotel Cazomalli **16**
Hotel La Provincia **12**
Hotel Marqués del Valle **13**
Las Azucenas .. **11**
Las Mariposas ... **5**
Oaxaca Ollin **1**

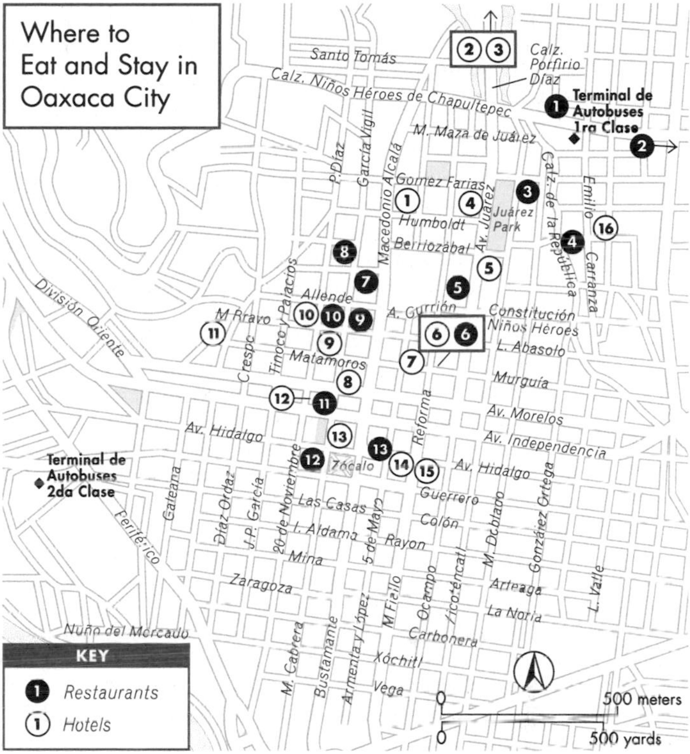

Where to Eat and Stay in Oaxaca City

KEY
Restaurants
Hotels

some rooms are dark and small. ✉ *Calle 5 de Mayo 300* ☎ *951/501–6100* 🌐 *www.caminoreal.com/oaxaca* ⇨ *84 rooms, 7 suites* ♨ *In-room: refrigerator, safe. In-hotel: restaurant, room service, bars, pool, laundry service, Wi-Fi hotspot, Internet terminal* ▭ *AE, D, DC, MC, V.*

$$$ **Casa Cid de León.** Your host, poet Lety Ricárdez, lets you know immediately that this mansion in the center of town, furnished with a memorable collection of objets d'art, is "your home." Pass through a wrought-iron gate to reach two of the suites, then climb a twisting stone staircase to find the other two. Ask for the Bella Epoca suite, where everything seems to come in threes: three rooms with three sets of French doors that lead to three balconies—there are even three crystal chandeliers. The bath has a deep whirlpool tub and towels tied with silk ribbon. The rooftop dining room and café has views of all the city's landmarks. **Pros:** romantic rooms; central location; friendly owner. **Cons:** on the pricey side. ✉ *Av. Morelos 602, at Calle García Vigil* ☎ *951/514–1893 or 951/516–0414* 🌐 *www.casaciddeleon.com* ⇨ *4 suites* ♨ *In-hotel: restaurant, room service, bar* ▭ *AE, MC, V* 🍽 *CP.*

$$ **Casa de las Bugambilias.** This bed-and-breakfast houses La Olla restaurant, and it's run by the same person, chef-personality Pilar Cabrera. Every room is different, but they're all brightly painted and comfortably outfitted. Some rooms have little terraces or patios. All rooms are no-smoking. **Pros:** nice roof deck; great breakfasts; gorgeous tiled tubs in many rooms; two-course breakfasts and cooking classes are available. **Cons:** some rooms are small; a bit expensive; resident cat bad for those with allergies. ✉ *Reforma 402* ☎ *951/516–1165 or 866/829–6778 in North America* 🌐 *www.lasbugambilias.com* *8 rooms, 1 suite* *In-room: safe, Wi-Fi. In-hotel: restaurant, bar, spa, laundry service, Internet terminal* 💳 *MC, V* *BP.*

$$ **Casa de Sierra Azul.** The central courtyard in this colonial-era mansion is certainly memorable, with lush vines tumbling down over stone arches. Other touches of note include a wrought-iron gate and leaded-glass windows. Each room is different, so look at a few before you decide; one thing they have in common are the extremely high ceilings. **Pros:** nice courtyard; good location. **Cons:** a bit pricey. ✉ *Av. Hidalgo 1002, at Calle Fiallo* ☎ *951/514–8412* 🌐 *www.hotelcasadesierrazul.com.mx* *9 rooms, 5 suites* *In-room: no a/c (some), Wi-Fi. In-hotel: restaurant, laundry service, Internet terminal* 💳 *AE, MC, V.*

$$ **Casa del Sótano.** From this hillside hotel's sunny terrace you can contemplate the Iglesia de Santo Domingo. You can also catch a glimpse from some of the wrought-iron balconies of the top-floor rooms. Inside are arched doorways, vaulted ceilings, and cool tile floors. In secluded courtyards you'll find fountains, gardens, and pools, but the best place in the whole hotel is the terrace, with an amazing city view. **Pros:** great terrace; friendly staff; nicely decorated rooms; no-smoking rooms. **Cons:** rooms are a little cramped and dark; attracts many tour groups. ✉ *Tinoco y Palacios 414* ☎ *951/516–2494* *23 rooms, 1 suite* *In-room: no a/c (some), DVD (some). In-hotel: restaurant, bar, Internet terminal, Wi-Fi hotspot, parking (free)* 💳 *MC, V.*

$$$ Fodor's Choice ★ **Casa Oaxaca.** A trio of imaginative Europeans poured their hearts and souls into this chic B&B. Their house combines traditional materials like adobe and cantera stone with minimalist sensibilities. The result is a masterpiece where gleaming white colonnades lead you to your room. Each room is different; some have little sunrooms overlooking the indigo-tile pool; others have sitting areas where you can enjoy a cocktail. Put yourself in the hands of a spiritual healer who will guide you through the cleansing experience of *temazcal* in the small poolside hut. **Pros:** spacious rooms; unique furnishings; great restaurant; cooking classes with top chef; airport shuttle. **Cons:** books up quickly; some rooms are dark. ✉ *Calle García Vigil 407* 📫 *Casa Oaxaca, Calle Garcia Vigil 407, Oaxaca 68000* ☎ *951/514–4173* 🌐 *www.casaoaxaca.com.mx* *7 rooms, 2 suites* *In-hotel: Wi-Fi. In-hotel: restaurant, room service, bar, pool, laundry service, Internet terminal, parking (free), no kids under 12* 💳 *AE, MC, V* *CP.*

$$–$$$ **Hostal de la Noria.** The rooms in this restored colonial mansion two blocks west of the zócalo have unique, homey touches; in some rooms it's carved wooden headboards, in others wrought-iron or hammered tin ones. All the rooms wrap around an adorable courtyard with a flower-filled fountain; surrounding it are tables topped with lacy umbrellas. Chicken mole and fish fillets steamed in a mezcal sauce top the list of favorites at the Restaurante Asunción ($–$$). **Pros:** nice courtyard; excellent restaurant. **Cons:** pricey; needs some updating; some street noise. ✉ *Av. Hidalgo 918* ☎ *951/501–5400* 🌐 *www.lanoria.com* *48*

rooms, 4 suites ♿ *In-room: Wi-Fi. In-hotel: restaurant, room service, bar, pool, laundry service, parking (free)* 💳 *AE, MC, V.*

$$$–$$$$ ★ **Hotel La Provincia.** With its classic central courtyard, beamed ceilings, and colonial charm, La Provincia fulfills the expectations of those looking for a bit of Old Mexico. But it's also one of the city's most modern hotels: rooms have carved-wood furnishings and colorful tile floors *and* flat-screen TVs, among other modern amenities. The location—equidistant from the zócalo and Santo Domingo church—is unbeatable. It's on a busy street, but you'd never know it by the quiet in the courtyard and rooms. Note that all but one of the double rooms have king-size beds, and the room with a double bed is discounted, so reserve it in advance if you are interested in saving. **Pros:** relaxing vibe; delightful rooftop terrace; friendly staff. **Cons:** rooms don't get much natural light; pricey; understated interior design. ✉ *Calle Porfirio Díaz 108* ☎ *951/514–0999 or 01800/506–2824 toll-free in Mexico* 🌐 *www.hotellaprovincia.com.mx* *15 rooms, 3 suites* ♿ *In-room: no phone, safe, Wi-Fi. In-hotel: restaurant, room service, bar, laundry service, Internet terminal, parking (free)* 💳 *MC, V.*

YOGA

In addition to the regular yoga classes, **Casa del Ángel** (✉ *Jacobo Dalevuelta 200, Col. Centro* ☎ *951/518–7167* 🌐 *www.casadelangel.com.mx*) offers massage; classes for moms, babies, and children; tai-chi, and meditation. An hour-long massage will cost you about $30; a yoga class will set you back around $8

Alosja Yoga (✉ *Rufino Tamayo 810, Centro Histórico* ☎ *951/158–9853* 🌐 *www.alosjayoga.com*) Alosja Van Leeuwen has been teaching yoga for about 15 years in Holland and Mexico. She offers private classes, group classes, and yogatherapy for back problems. Classes are $8.

$$ **Hotel Marqués del Valle.** Taking up almost the entire northern edge of the zócalo, this hotel puts Oaxaca at your doorstep, all the while maintaining a polished and classy personality. Many rooms have views of the Palacio de Gobierno or the Catedral Metropolitana. If you splurge a bit, you can reserve a room with French doors leading out to a small balcony. Rooms are cozy, although not as atmospheric as at most other hotels in town. The open-air restaurant facing the main square has become extremely popular; you can grab a table right in the middle of life on the plaza. **Pros:** on the main square; friendly staff; clean and comfortable rooms. **Cons:** noisy location; pricey rates; utilitarian rooms. ✉ *Portal de Clavería s/n* ☎ *951/514–0688 or 01800/849–9936 toll-free in Mexico* 🌐 *www.hotelmarquesdelvalle.com.mx* *95 rooms* ♿ *In-room: no a/c (some), safe, Wi-Fi. In-hotel: restaurant, room service, bar, laundry service, Internet terminal* 💳 *AE, MC, V.*

$ **Las Azucenas.** This intimate hotel occupies a wonderfully restored old home near the Basilica de la Soledad. You can spot that church, and at least half a dozen others, from the plant-filled terrace. The most private room is secluded on the second floor. The others are just as cozy, but one has a skylight rather than a window. Ask for a tiny *tele* (TV) at the reception desk if you can't bear to miss the evening news. **Pros:**

7

cheerful rooms; nice roof deck; good value. **Cons:** out-of-the-way location; booked far in advance; mediocre breakfasts. ✉ *Calle Martiniano Aranda 203, at Matamoros* ☎ *951/514–7918 or 01800/717–2540 toll-free in Mexico, 800/882–6089* 🌐 *www.hotelazucenas.com* *10 rooms* *In-room: no phone, no TV, Wi-Fi. In-hotel: room service, laundry service, Internet terminal* 💳 *MC, V.*

¢–$ **Las Mariposas.** María Teresa Villarreal, the owner and operator of this pleasant little place, proudly shows off her restored colonial-style home. It's not fancy, but the lived-in feeling suits most people just fine; in fact, there are long-term guests from time to time. You can mingle with other guests on the open patio gladdened with laurel and lemon trees. Those staying in standard rooms share a brightly colored outdoor kitchen, while those who have booked studios get kitchenettes with coffeemakers and other essentials. **Pros:** great value; helpful hosts. **Cons:** furnishings are simple; studios are cramped; noise from inner courtyard. ✉ *Calle Pino Suárez 517* ☎ *951/515–5854* 🌐 *www.lasmariposas.com.mx* *14 rooms, 6 suites* *In-room: no a/c, no phone, safe, kitchen (some), Wi-Fi. In-hotel: Internet terminal* 💳 *MC, V* *BP.*

NORTH OF CENTRO HISTÓRICO

$–$$ **Hotel Casona del Llano.** This tidy hotel across from Parque Paseo Juárez (El Llano) caters mostly to Mexican travelers. Although part of the hotel is in a converted mansion, the basic rooms are devoid of colonial character. They are, however, clean and comfortable, and most face a small courtyard garden. The restaurant is popular with locals for lunch and weekend brunch. Staffers are quite friendly, but few of them speak fluent English. **Pros:** good value; authentic restaurant; off the tourist track. **Cons:** basic rooms; 10-minute walk to main square; some noise during the day. ✉ *Av. Juárez 701, Jalatlaco* ☎ *951/514–7703* *28 rooms* *In-room: no a/c, Wi-Fi. In-hotel: restaurant, laundry service, parking (free)* 💳 *MC, V.*

$ **Hotel Cazomalli.** Even the baked-earth floor tiles shine at this sleepy little hostelry, whose name means "house of tranquility." It's a cobblestone district close to Parque Juárez. Clean, quiet rooms have pale pine furnishings and handwoven fabrics. Sliding doors lead to sunny patios. Friendly owner Marina Flores is happy to help arrange trips to nearby sights. **Pros:** nice views from rooftop; hosts can help book tours; quiet location. **Cons:** small bathrooms; 10-minute walk to main square. ✉ *Calle El Salto 104, at Calle Aldama, Jalatlaco* ☎ *951/513–8605* 🌐 *www.hotelcazomalli.com* *18 rooms* *In-room: no a/c, safe, no TV, Wi-Fi. In-hotel: laundry service, Internet terminal, Wi-Fi hotspot* 💳 *MC, V.*

$$ Fodor's Choice ★ **Oaxaca Ollin Bed & Breakfast.** On a quiet street near Santo Domingo church, Oaxaca Ollin feels like a well-kept secret. Two small buildings surround a patio with a pool. Cheerful rooms have lovely tiled bathrooms and traditional touches like headboards carved with elaborate calla-lily designs and wooden armoires instead of closets. Rooms on the top floor have small balconies with wrought-iron furniture. Breakfast includes plenty of fresh fruit and pastries and tasty regional dishes. The staff is unfailingly friendly, and the tours they arrange of the city and crafts villages come highly recommended. All rooms and interior areas

are no-smoking. **Pros:** peaceful environment; lovely rooms; relaxing rooftop terrace. **Cons:** rooms aren't terribly spacious; some steps to climb. ✉ *Quintana Roo 213, Jalatlaco* 📭 *Oaxaca Ollin Bed & Breakfast, Quintana Roo 213, Oaxaca 68000* ☎ *951/514–9126* 🌐 *www.oaxacabedandbreakfast.com* *10 rooms* *In-room: no a/c, no phone, safe, no TV, Wi-Fi. In-hotel: pool, laundry service, Internet terminal, Wi-Fi hotspot, no kids under 12* 💳 *AE, MC, V* 🍽 *BP.*

ELSEWHERE IN OAXACA CITY

$$ ★ **Casa Raab.** A fantasy villa buried in the wooded hills about 30 minutes north of the city center, Casa Raab is ideal for traveling groups. You can rent rooms in the main house, or take over a casita that's perfect for a family of four. Hiking trails surround the house, which has breathtaking mountain views. You'll feel part of the family as you eat meals together in the dining room. Owner Tony Raab produces his own artisanal mezcal, grows his own agave plants, and helps to organize excursions. To really get around, though, you need to rent a car. **Pros:** convenient base for valley excursions; friendly host; great for families. **Cons:** far from city center; no meals on Sunday; not great option for single travelers. ✉ *Camino Seminario s/n, San Pablo Etla* 📭 *Apartado 1528, Oaxaca 68000* ☎ *951/520–4022* 🌐 *www.casaraab.com* *6 rooms* *In-hotel: restaurant, bar, pool* 💳 *MC, V.*

$$$–$$$$ **Hacienda Los Laureles.** About a 20-minute drive north of Oaxaca's historic center, this hotel is a cool, quiet oasis. The spa, which has a hot tub, massage, and traditional temazcal steam baths, will help you regain your inner balance. Staff members can assist in arranging horseback excursions, bicycle rides, or ecological tours to the nearby mountains. All rooms are no-smoking. **Pros:** in a residential neighborhood; beautiful grounds; nice spa. **Cons:** far from historic center; not many restaurants or shops nearby. ✉ *Av. Hidalgo 21, San Felipe del Agua* ☎ *951/501–5300* 🌐 *www.hotelhaciendaloslaureles.com* *18 rooms, 9 suites* *In-room: safe, Wi-Fi. In-hotel: restaurant, room service, bar, pool, gym, spa, laundry service, parking (free)* 💳 *AE, MC, V.*

7

NIGHTLIFE

The Centro Histórico has a small but lively nightlife scene, though the crowd at most bars is definitely young. The streets directly south of Santo Domingo church have plenty of thumping dance clubs, and many people just wander until they find one that's playing music they like. The best place to start any evening is at the zócalo—cafés serve drinks and snacks, and mariachis and other performers roam the square, sometimes inspiring revelers to dance.

BARS

Café Central. It's a superhip spot that screens art flicks, hosts concerts and plays, and brings in the occasional DJ for late-night dancing. The music ranges from folk to jazz to hip-hop. There's no cover on Wednesday and Thursday, but on weekends it goes as high as $6. ✉ *Hidalgo 302, Centro Histórico* ☎ *No phone* 🌐 *cafecentraloaxaca.blogspot.com.*

Comala. Bring a flashlight to read the menu at this dimly lighted café. A mostly young, mostly local crowd sips amusingly titled drinks (try the

Dr. Pepe—beer, tequila, amaretto, and coffee liqueur) and chills out to the latest indie-rock sensations. Although the red walls adorned with crosses and gargoyles suggest a Goth crowd, it attracts more young professionals than creatures of the night. ✉ *Allende 109, across from Santo Domingo church, Centro Histórico* ☎ *No phone.*

Freebar. Its dim rooms and loud alternative music make it popular with young people who pack the place even during the week. ✉ *Calle Matamoros 100, at Calle García Vigil, Centro Histórico* ☎ *No phone.*

La Cucaracha. For $10 you can taste four tequilas or five mezcals. There's a dark, cool, colonial vibe to the cozy performance space, where you'll be serenaded with a romantic *peña* (solo-guitar folk singing). Weekends see dancing in a room so tiny that tables are on a narrow catwalk above it. ✉ *Calle Porfirio Díaz 301A, at Matamoros, Centro Histórico* ☎ *951/501–1636.*

Fodor's Choice ★ **La Nueva Babel.** It's about as big as a breadbox, but somehow manages to accommodate performers—from lone poets or guitarists to jazz trios or multigenerational *son jarocho* groups. The crowd, a mix of locals and tourists, is attentive and enthusiastic. ✉ *Calle Porfirio Díaz 224, at Calle Matamoros, Centro Histórico* ☎ *No phone.*

CANTINAS

Bastions of macho men and strong spirits, cantinas traditionally aren't places for women. The cantinas in the Centro Histórico tend to be a bit less rough, but single women should still think twice about going in alone.

La Casa del Mezcal. The place has been around since 1935. Push aside its swinging doors for a classic cantina experience that's diminished only slightly by a large TV (or two). La Casa prides itself on its stock of *tobala,* a cousin of tequila made from wild agave. ✉ *Calle Flores Magón, between Calles Las Casas and Aldama, Centro Histórico* ☎ *No phone.*

La Farola. La Farola is bit calmer than La Casa del Mezcal, but no less classic. It's been serving drinks to locals since 1916—and some of the patrons, it seems, might have been there when the joint opened up. ✉ *Calle 20 de Noviembre, between Calles Las Casas and Trujano, Centro Histórico* ☎ *951/516–5352.*

DANCE CLUBS

Candela. You can dance to live salsa music every night at the most popular club in town. ✉ *Calle Murguía 413, at Calle Pino Suárez, Centro Histórico* ☎ *951/514–2010.*

La Tentación. One of the city's most venerable watering holes has salsa, merengue, and cumbia dancing on its terrace nightly beginning at 10. ✉ *Calle Matamoros 101, at Calle García Vigil, Centro Histórico* ☎ *951/514–9521* 🌐 *www.latentacion.com.mx.*

FOLK MUSIC AND DANCE

Casa de Cantera. Every evening the rather drab Casa de Cantera transforms itself into the colorful Casa de Guelaguetza. It's a mesmerizing show, with lots of music and traditional dancing. Things get started nightly at 8:30, and the cover charge is $18. ✉ *Murguiá 102, Centro*

CLOSE UP

Mezcal's Mysteries

There are two big myths about mezcal, the distilled pride of Oaxaca. The first is that a bottle of it always contains a worm. This is true only of the low-grade, mass-produced mezcals, which use the worm as a marketing gimmick.

The second myth is that mezcal is a less-refined version of tequila. Quite the contrary: while tequila is only distilled from the blue agave plant, cooked in steam chambers, and generally made in industrial-sized batches, mezcal is made from dozens of varieties of agave, roasted over a wood fire in a traditional earth pit, distilled, and usually made in small quantities by small producers. The result is a soft, smoky, and complex liquor—one meant to be slowly sipped and savored.

A 2005 law imposed a set of standards on mezcal production, including the certification process. The law's intent was to weed out producers who mixed their mezcal with cane alcohol, but the side effect has been to impose considerable costs on producers, reducing quantities and raising prices. That said, you now know just what you're getting when you see a certified *reposado* (aged 2 months–1 year in oak barrels), *añejo* (aged 1–3 years), and *extrañejo* (aged more than 3 years). Some are aged even more than that, like the 10-year-old Joya.

You can sample mezcal in many bars, restaurants, and shops. One brand to look for is El Señorio, which makes a nice reposado. Tobalá and Del Maguey are small artisan producers. Benevá, a large producer, is pretty good, too, and certainly easy to procure—it has several outlets around town (there's one at Calle Macedonio Alcalá 402) and a tasting room and shop on the road to Mitla.

La Cava (✉ *Gómez Farías 212-B, 2 blocks east of Calle Alcalá, Centro Histórico* ☎ *951/515–2335* 🌐 *www.losdanzantes.com* ⏲ *Closed Sun.*), affiliated with Los Danzantes restaurant, sells a variety of quality mezcals along with regional wines and hand-rolled cigars.

Histórico ☎ *951/514–7585 or 951/514–9522* 🌐 *www.casadecantera.com.*

Camino Real Oaxaca. On Friday night this place hosts a two-hour regional dance show that's considered the best in town. The $45 admission includes a buffet dinner (7 PM) and the show (8 PM) in the former convent's 16th-century chapel. Make reservations. ✉ *Calle 5 de Mayo 300, Centro Histórico* ☎ *951/501–6100* 🌐 *www.caminoreal.com/oaxaca.*

Hotel Monte Albán. The Monte Albán has nightly dance shows beginning at 8:30 PM. Admission is about $10. ✉ *Alameda de León 1, Centro Histórico* ☎ *951/516–2330.*

SHOPPING

Don't despair if you can't make it out of town to visit Oaxaca Valley's crafts villages—you'll find all the goods here, in high-end boutiques, artist collectives, and touristy markets. And Oaxaca's art scene isn't just about rural customs—boutiques and galleries clustered around the pedestrian streets south of Santo Domingo church sell modern works from local ceramists and painters.

You'll also find several good books and music shops and quite a few jewelry stores. Several mercados sell packaged foods like Oaxacan chocolate and cheese and jars of mole.

> **CELEBRATE**
>
> One of Oaxaca's major celebrations is the Guelaguetza, a Zapotec word for "offering" or "gift." It's generally held on the last two Mondays in July. Delegations of traditional dancers from throughout the state perform in authentic costumes at the Auditorio Guelaguetza.

ART GALLERIES

★ **Galería Indigo.** Climb the grand staircase to reach a lovely gallery in an enormous restored mansion. Ceramics, graphics, paintings, and other fine art from talented artists from Oaxaca and beyond are for sale. ✉ *Calle Allende 104, Centro Histórico* ☎ *951/514–3889* 🌐 *www.galeriaindigo.com.*

Galería Quetzalli. Here you can see the latest from Oaxaca's most famous artist, Francisco Toledo, as well as many other well-respected contemporary artists. Of course, these are some of the most expensive works in town, but the browsing is free. ✉ *Constitución 104-1, Centro Hístorico* ☎ *951/514–2606* 🌐 *www.galeriaquetzalli.com.*

BOOKS

Amate Books. This is the bookstore you wish you had found before your trip. Hundreds of books, most of them in English, cover topics from the country's cuisine to its couture. There's also a great travel-guide section. ✉ *Calle Macedonia Alcalá 307, Centro Histórico* 🌐 *www.amatebooks.com* ☎ *951/516–6960.*

Librería Grañén Porrúa. It sells books in English as well as Spanish and has CDs and high-end gifts. There's a café as well. ✉ *Calle Macedonia Alcalá 104, Centro Histórico* ☎ *951/516–9901* 🌐 *www.libreriagp.com.*

CHOCOLATE

Chocolate Mayordomo. Oaxaca is famous for its chocolate—most of all for its hot chocolate. This shop near the market is arguably the best around; they grind their own chocolate together with the trademark Mexican cinnamon. You can also buy mole here. ✉ *Calle Colón at Calle Flores Magón, Centro Histórico* ☎ *951/516–3807.*

HANDICRAFTS

Artesanías Chimalli. Sort through an excellent selection of crafts, including painted copal-wood animals with comical expressions, at this shop. ✉ *Calle García Vigil 512-C, Centro Histórico* ☎ *951/514–2101.*

★ **Blackbox.** Young designers work with local (often organic) materials to create the contemporary home accessories sold at this hip crafts store. Wool rugs from Teotitlan de Valle eschew traditional stripes for paint-splatter designs. Handcrafted paper from Etla is used to create molded lamp shades. The store also sells shirts, bags, and jewelry. ✉ *Cinco de Mayo 412, between Absolo and Constitución, Centro Histórico* ☎ *No phone* 🌐 *www.la-blackbox.com.*

Jarciería El Arte Oaxaqueño. In business since 1961, this shop has a small but good assortment of stamped-tin products, whimsical earrings, as well as animals and skeletons carved of featherlight wood. Prices are totally reasonable. ✉ *Calle Mina 317, at J.P. García, Centro Histórico* ☎ *951/516–1581.*

★ **La Mano Mágica.** This magical shop features the works of Arnulfo Mendoza, a top weaver. His rugs, made using hand-dyed silk and wool, have incredibly intricate designs. It's no wonder that some of his larger pieces sell for several thousand dollars. There's also a gallery showing the works of many Oaxacan artists. ✉ *Calle Macedonio Alcalá 203, Centro Histórico* ☎ *951/516–4275* 🌐 *www.lamanomagica.com.*

SHOPPING KNOW-HOW

If you think you'll be buying more folk art than you can carry home, get receipts showing that you've paid the 17% sales tax on all purchases. This will allow you to send your purchases home without having to pay extra for them. Check out the high-end shops on Calle Macedonio Alcalá first; then compare prices and quality with the items you find in the markets or in the pueblos where artisans live and work. Note that some stores are closed Sunday; many also close for an hour or two at midday.

Los Baules. There's much to discover at this shop, the best place in town to stop if you're interested in regional clothing. Look for embroidered huipiles, blouses, and dresses. The designs are representative of different local indigenous groups, and in many cases the quality is beyond what you will find anywhere else. In some cases, Remigio, the shop owner, has provided textile workers with imported silks to make extraordinary dresses. Some of the dresses that are only available here sell for hundreds and are perfect for formal occasions. ✉ *Macedonio Alcalá 403, Centro Histórico* ☎ *951/501–0552.*

★ **Mujeres Artesanas de las Regiones de Oaxaca.** You'll support the women artists' co-op by shopping at this huge warren of shops often referred to as MARO. The selection and quality are excellent, the prices are reasonable, and it's open daily. ✉ *Calle 5 de Mayo 204, Centro Histórico* ☎ *951/516–0670.*

JEWELRY

The streets west of Mercado 20 de Noviembre between Trujano and Mina are crowded with jewelry shops. Most sell 10- and 12-karat gold. Calle Macedonia Alcalá has become the place for cutting-edge designs.

Oro de Monte Albán. The three Centro Histórico locations of this shop are within spitting distance of each other. They sell gold and silver reproductions of pre-Columbian jewelry found in the tombs of royalty at Monte Albán. There's also a shop at the archaeological site. ✉ *Calle Macedonio Alcalá 403* ☎ *951/514–3813* 🌐 *www.orodemontealban.com* ✉ *Calle Macedonio Alcalá 503* ☎ *951/516–4224* ✉ *Calle Macedonio Alcalá and Calle Bravo* ☎ *951/516–1812..*

SIDE TRIP TO THE VALLES CENTRALES

> **HIT THE ROAD**
>
> An alternative to the bus is a *colectivo* (shared taxi). The fare will be more than what you'd pay for the bus, but the convenience might be worth it. Colectivos leave from Oaxaca City's second-class bus station. Destinations are clearly posted on windshields; if you don't see the village you want, look for a taxi going to the nearest major town on the same route (i.e., Mitla or Ocotlan) and ask the driver if he stops along the way.

You could easily fill a week visiting the dozens of villages spreading south and east of Oaxaca City. Looking for colonial-era splendor? There are delightful squares dominated by graceful churches in Ocotlán and Santa Ana del Valle, to name but two. Unique crafts? San Bartolo Coyotepec is known for its beautiful *barro negro,* or black pottery, made without the benefit of a pottery wheel, while in Teotitlán del Valle the streets are lined with shops selling *tapetes,* the woven wool rugs that are known all around Mexico. Colorful markets? Take your pick. There are outdoor markets each day of the week, and each is different. In Zaachila, for example, you could pick up some animals—either small carvings or the real thing. Best of all, most markets are geared toward locals, so they don't sell the typical tourist wares, giving you a real sense of each village.

And don't forget the striking ruins of cities built by the Zapotec. The must-see on everyone's itinerary is Monte Albán, one of the country's most impressive ancient cities. Its proximity to the city makes it a destination for busloads of tourists. If you want to escape the crowds, head to some of the ruins that are less crowded, especially Dainzú and Yagul, where you'll probably have the place to yourself.

Planning a trip to the Valles Centrales is a snap. Many of the most popular sights are along or just off Carretera 175 (to Ocotlán), Carretera 131 (to Zaachila), or Carretera 190 (to Mitla). This makes it easy to visit two or three villages in a morning or afternoon. Renting a car is an easy and delightful way to cover the distances. Buses bound for Zaachila or other villages along Carretera 131 depart from the terminal run by Añasa on Calle Libertad at Calle Arista; those bound for Ocotlán and other points along Carretera 175 depart from the terminal run by Estrella del Valle on Calle Armenta at Calle Lopez. Distances are short: it takes 20 minutes to get to Monte Albán, San Bartolo Coyotepec, or Atzompa; 30 minutes to Zaachila; 45 minutes to Ocotlán.

■ **TIP→ Most villages don't have ATMs, so get cash before you leave Oaxaca City. Bring smaller bills, as vendors often can't change larger ones.**

MONTE ALBÁN

10 km (6 mi) southwest of Oaxaca City.

Fodor's Choice ★ Southwest of Oaxaca City, a narrow, twisting road leads up to the mountaintop city of the "cloud people," **Monte Albán**. Seeing this massive ancient metropolis is a mystical experience, especially if you are

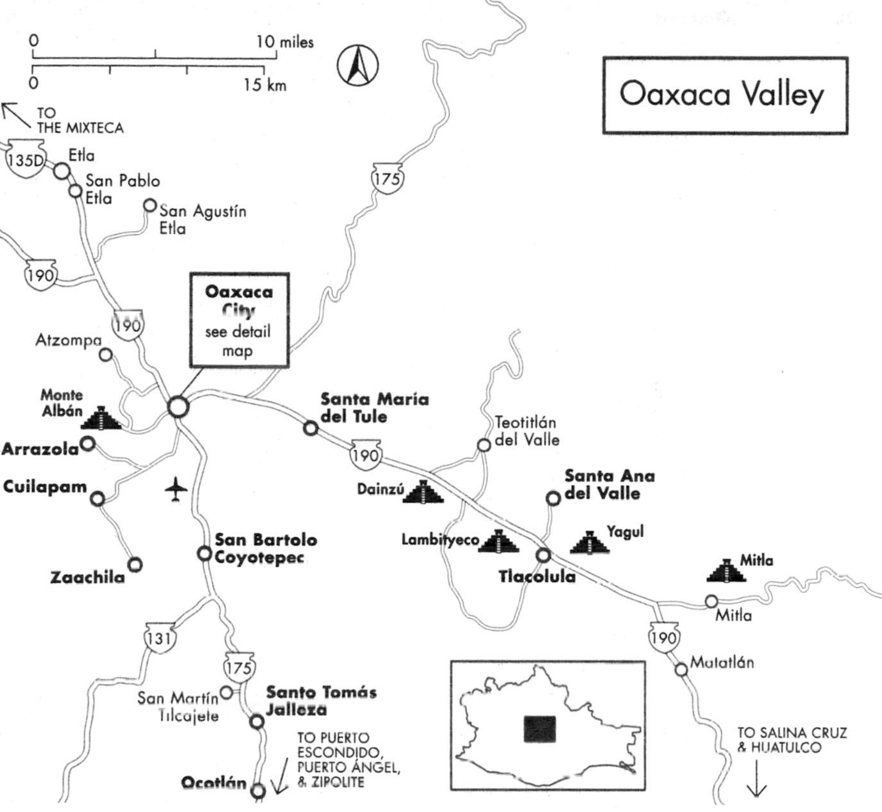

lucky enough to find one or more of the tombs open. South of the city lies a string of crafts villages. Atzompa, known for its green-glaze pottery, is a popular stop. It's on the road to Monte Albán, as is San Bartolo Coyotepec, where you'll find gorgeous black pottery.

The massive temples of Monte Albán, perched atop a mesa, make this one of the country's most spectacular archaeological sites. This vast city was home to more than 30,000 Zapotec. Despite its size, experts estimate that only about 10% of the site has been uncovered. Digs are sporadic, taking place whenever the budget permits.

Monte Albán overlooks the Oaxaca Valley from a flattened mountaintop 5,085 feet high; the views are breathtaking. Either the Zapotec or their predecessors leveled the site around 600 BC. The varying heights of the site follow the contours of distant mountains. The oldest of the four temples is the **Galería de los Danzantes,** or the Dancers' Gallery, so named for the elaborately carved stone figures that once covered the building. Most of the originals are now in the site museum, but you can still see some in the temple. Experts are unsure whether the nude male figures represent captives, warriors, or some other group; the theory that they were dancers has been discarded because some appear to be bound.

The Zapotec constructed most of the buildings along a north–south axis, except for the so-called **Observatorio** (Observatory). The arrow-shape structure is set at a 45-degree angle, pointing toward the southwest. It's thought to have been an observatory, as it's more closely aligned with the stars than with the Earth's poles.

NAMING IT

Most villages have two-part names, most often names imposed by the Spanish (usually a saint's name) followed by a traditional name. Therefore, a town like Atzompa is actually Santa María Atzompa. It's rare to hear locals use the full name. It might, however, appear on regional maps.

The **Juego de Pelota,** or ball game, was played in the well-excavated court. Hips, shoulders, knees, and elbows were probably used to hit a wooden or rubber ball. The details of these games are sketchy, but there's speculation that they were a means of solving disputes between factions or villages, of celebrating the defeat of a rival, or of worshipping the gods. Although human sacrifice is thought to have been connected with the ball game in certain parts of Mesoamerica, there's no evidence that it happened in Monte Albán.

No one knows for sure whether the Zapotec abandoned the site gradually or suddenly, but by AD 1000 it stood empty. Years afterward the Mixtec used Monte Albán as a lofty necropolis of lavish tombs. More than 200 tombs and 300 burial sites have been explored. The most fantastic of these, **Tumba 7,** yielded a treasure unequaled in North America. Inside were more than 500 priceless Mixtec objects, including gold breastplates; jade, pearl, ivory, and gold jewelry; and fans, masks, and belt buckles of precious stones and metals. The tomb is north of the parking lot but is seldom open.

At Monte Albán you'll find a small site museum with a gift shop. The cafeteria isn't half bad, and has a great view of the valley; sadly, it closes with the rest of the site at 5 PM.

Direct buses serving Monte Albán depart from the Hotel Rivera del Ángel (✉ *Calle Mina 518* ☎ *951/516–6666 or 951/516–0666*) in Oaxaca City hourly on the half-hour from 8:30 to 3:30; the last bus back is at 6 PM. The round-trip fare is about $4; to stay longer than two hours you must pay a small surcharge (you can decide once you're on-site). The road to Monte Albán is west of Oaxaca City and is very easy to follow: the trip takes 10 to 15 minutes. ☎ *951/516–1215* 🌐 *www.inah.gob.mx* *$4* *Daily 8–5.*

EN ROUTE

Take some time to wander the few main streets of unimposing **Santa María Atzompa,** 8 km (5 mi) northwest of Oaxaca City on the way to Monte Albán. Its inhabitants produce the traditional green-glaze plates, bowls, and cups that people use on a daily basis all over Mexico. Some potters sell fanciful clay pots and vases in an eye-popping range of colors. You can visit workshops, often in people's homes. More convenient (although the quality of work can be disappointing) is the Mercado de Artesanías (Handicrafts Market) open daily from 8 to 7. The easiest way to see Atzompa is on a tour of Monte Albán, as it is on the

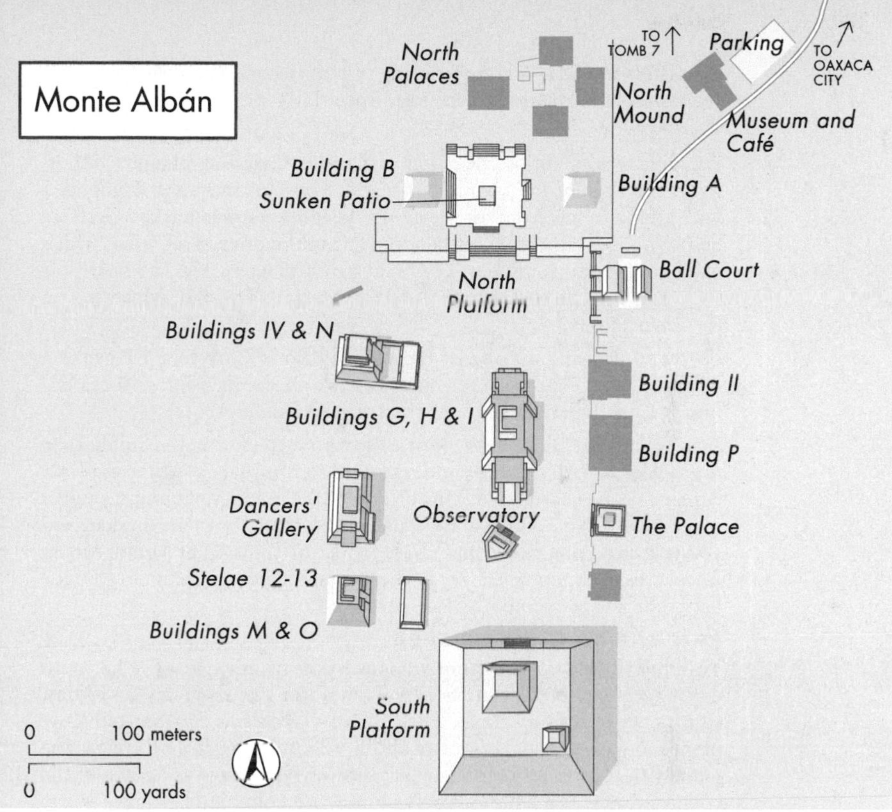

way. You can also take a taxi from anywhere in the city or a bus from Oaxaca's second-class terminal.

ARRAZOLA

A string of villages are off Carretera 131, which runs south from Oaxaca City. About 12 km (8 mi) southwest of the city is Arrazola, where you'll find the delightful *alebrijes* (angels, devils, and all sorts of creatures carved out of light, porous copal wood). These brightly colored figures, from tiny to tremendous, are decorated with dots, squiggles, and other artful touches. This craft was developed by Arrazola's best-known artist, Don Manuel Jiménez, and almost everyone in town has jumped on the bandwagon. As you wander along the streets, some people may invite you into their homes to see their work.

CUILAPAM

About 4 km (2½ mi) beyond the turnoff for Arrazola you'll come to the dusty little town of Cuilapam.

The roofless ruins of a church and monastery called the **Ex-Convento de Santiago Apóstol** is Cuilapam's claim to fame. The long, narrow church was begun in 1535 but never finished. Columns that would have supported the roof still stand ready. Vincente Guerrero, one of the heroes of the country's battle for independence, was executed in the adjacent monastery in 1831. A large painting of him is in the room where he was sequestered. Admission to the site, open daily 9–5, is $3.

ZAACHILA

Zaachila was an important center of Zapotec civic and religious authority at the time of the Spanish invasion. On Thursday, oxcarts loaded with alfalfa or hay head for the area's busiest livestock market. Get here before noon, or there won't be a pig left in the poke. The town, which is 17 km (11 mi) southwest of Oaxaca on Carretera 131, is known for its stately church, the Temple de Santa María Natividad, which sits on the main square.

To get to Zaachila or any of the villages along Carretera 131, take a bus from the second-class terminal or from a terminal for the Añasa bus line at Calle Libertad 1215, at the corner of Calle Arista.

Just behind the Temple de Santa María Natividad is the small **Zona Arqueológica**, with a pair of underground tombs that are fun to explore. A pair of eerie carved owls guards one of the graves containing a noble named Lord Nine Flower. He was buried along with an unidentified young man among riches that rivaled those of Tumba 7 at Monte Albán. These treasures, however, are in the archaeological museum in Mexico City. The site is open daily 9–5. Admission is $3.

SAN BARTOLO COYOTEPEC

Three of the most interesting villages in the Valles Centrales lie south of Oaxaca City on Carretera 175. They share a market day on Friday, so it's easy to visit all three. The first you'll reach is San Bartolo Coyotepec, bisected by the highway about 12 km (8 mi) from the city. The name Coyotepec, a Nahuatl word, literally translates as "place of the coyotes." Across from the stately church is a colonnaded square where you can buy the fragile, unglazed black ceramics for which the town is deservedly famous.

Keep an eye out for the **Alfarería Doña Rosa** (✉ *Calle Juárez 24* ☎ *951/551–0011*), a workshop named for the woman who invented the technique for giving the pottery its distinctive gloss. The revered craftswoman died in 1980, but her descendants continue making pottery the old-fashioned way. The workshop, where shelves upon shelves with items for sale line a small courtyard, is open daily 9–6.

SANTO TOMÁS JALIEZA

About 20 km (12 mi) south of Oaxaca City, Santo Tomás Jalieza sits alongside a small road off Carretera 175. Women here make belts, sashes, and other woven goods on small back-strap looms. The prices in the village are quite reasonable.

OCOTLÁN

Revered for its handcrafted knives and machetes, Ocotlán is a large town, 30 km (18 mi) south of Oaxaca on Carretera 175, with a beautifully restored church and monastery on a handsome main plaza. Buses from the second-class station depart for Ocotlán and the surrounding villages every 15 minutes or so. You can also take an Estrella del Valle bus from the terminal at the corner of Calle Armenta and Calle Lopez.

Continued on page 334

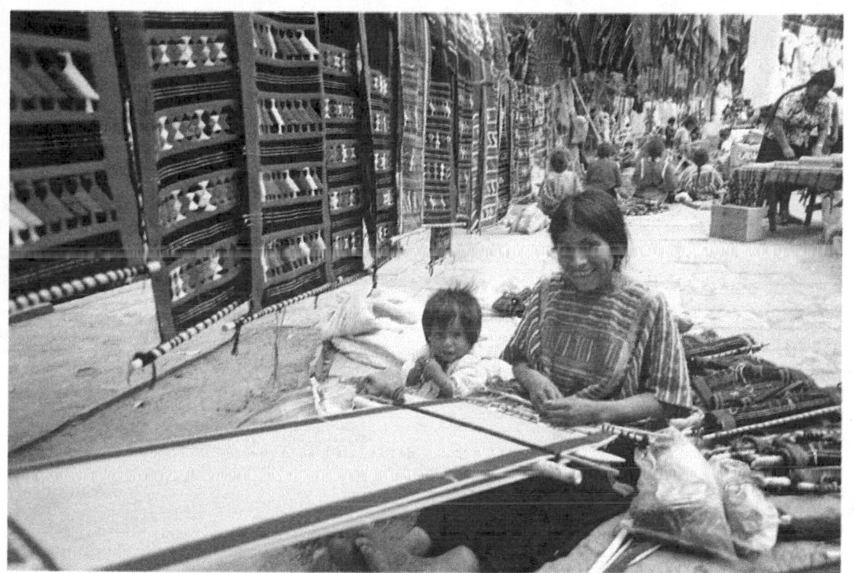

OAXACA VALLEY MARKETS

With markets open most days of the week, choosing which ones to visit may seem like a daunting task. You'll find something interesting at every Oaxaca market; however, there are a few markets you shouldn't miss. Those listed here have the unbeatable combination of beautiful settings and varied, high-quality goods.

Tlacolula, east of Oaxaca City, has a sprawling Sunday market that draws villagers from around the region. Although not specifically targeted at tourists, it has plenty of crafts, including woven blankets from nearby Teotitlán del Valle and Santa Ana del Valle.

On Thursday you should head to **Zaachila**, south of Oaxaca City. Beautiful pottery is on display in outdoor stalls in the shade of a stately church. The neighboring villages of **Ocotlán** and **San Bartolo Coyotepec** have markets on Friday, and it's easy to travel to both. Look for lovely ceramic figurines and black earthenware vases. And on Saturday there's no need to go anywhere—the best market is the Central de Abastos right in **Oaxaca City. Mitla** also has a market on Saturday.

Most tour companies offer excursions to the nearby craft villages, often combining them with visits to archaeological sites such as Monte Albán or Mitla. However, being part of a clump of tourists arriving in an air-conditioned bus that's bigger than most local dwellings may make you feel more like an invader than a visitor. Exploring the villages on your own is no problem at all. All are easily reachable by car via well-maintained roads. You can also take one of the frequent local buses that depart from the first- or second-class bus terminals. A round-trip ticket will cost $2. Hiring a taxi to take you around is a more expensive option, but you'll still be left with plenty of shopping money.

MARKET SCHEDULE	
Thursday	Zaachila
Friday	Ocotlán and San Bartolo Coyotepec
Saturday	Oaxaca City and Mitla
Sunday	Tlacolula

CITY SHOPPING

There's no need to venture far to find interesting markets. Several are right in Oaxaca City. The largest and oldest market is held at the **Central de Abastos** (literally the "Center of Supplies") on the southwestern edge of downtown. Saturday is the traditional market day, but the enormous covered market swarms daily with thousands of buyers and sellers from Oaxaca and the surrounding villages. Along with mounds of multicolored chiles and herbs, piles of tropical fruit, electronics, and bootleg CDs, you'll find intricately woven straw baskets, fragile green-and-black pottery, and colorful *rebozos* (shawls) of cotton and silk. Don't burden yourself with lots of camera equipment or bags; and keep an eye out for pickpockets and purse-slashers. Polite bargaining is expected.

Close to the zócalo, the spectacular daily **Mercado Benito Juárez** (✉ Between Calles 20 de Noviembre and Miguel Cabrera at Las Calas, Centro Histórico) has stalls selling *moles,* chocolates, fruits and vegetables, and much more. The bulky brick building teems with clothing, arts, and crafts. It's mostly locals that you'll find chowing down amid the lively stalls of the daily **Mercado 20 de Noviembre** (✉ Between Calles 20 de Noviembre and Flores Magón at Calle Aldama, Centro Histórico), across the street from the Mercado Benito Juárez. No prices are listed, but rest assured that this will be your cheapest meal in Oaxaca. For textiles, don't miss the **Mercado de Artesanías** (✉ Calle J.-P. García, near Calle Ignacio Zaragoza, Centro Histórico), a great place to shop for handwoven and embroidered clothing from Oaxaca's seven regions. This is also the place to find the handmade *huipiles* (short, blouses, often made of velveteen) worn in the Isthmus of Tehuantepec.

TYPES OF CRAFTS

ALEBRIJES

Perhaps Oaxaca's most amusing pieces are the angels, devils, Day-of-the-Dead skeletons, and fanciful creatures carved out of light, porous copal wood. These figures, from tiny to tremendous, are decorated with dots, squiggles, and other artful touches. Found in Arrazola.

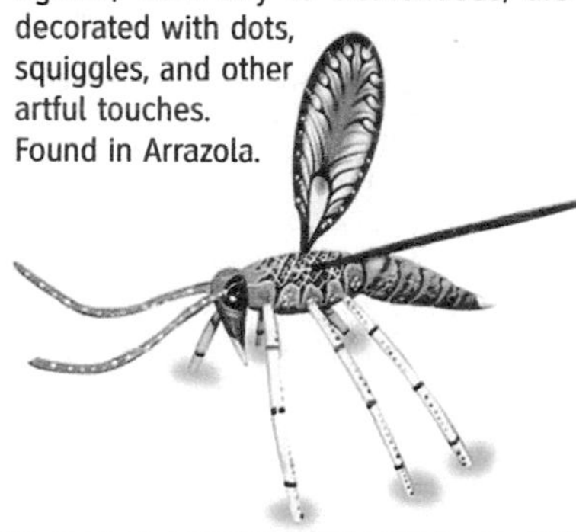

POTTERY

This tan or green-glazed pottery is made with a very simple wheel (a plate balanced on a round rock or overturned saucer). The technique of adding bits of small clay to items as decoration is called *pastillaje*. Though some artists keep their creations plain, others use multicolor glazes to add more flourishes. Found in Aztompa, Ocotlán.

TAPETES

Woven wool rugs (often with geometric patterns) are made on treadle (pedal-operated) looms. Found in Teotitlán del Valle, Santa Ana del Valle, and Tlacolula (on market day).

BARRO NEGRO

Shiny, lightweight black pottery, made without the benefit of a pottery wheel and fired in pit-kilns. Found in Zaachila, San Bartolo Coyotepec, Ocotlán. Pack it with care!

WOVEN GOODS

Though the *tapetes* are more iconic, you'll also find belts, sashes, and other woven items. Unlike the tapetes, these are done on back-strap looms. Found in Santo Tomás Jalieza.

BASKETRY

Woven with palms fronds and reeds, baskets often bear geometric designs in bright colors like magenta, green, and purple. The Mixteca villages produce the most of these crafts, but they're also in abundance in Villa de Etla, northwest of Oaxaca City.

It costs about $1 each way. Or catch a taxi for about $1.50 each way; the ride is 35 minutes.

> **WORD OF MOUTH**
>
> "I visited the village of Arrazola. Even though it was a very cool overcast day, it's such a pleasant, friendly town that it was a delight to walk around for a couple of hours." —Bixaorellana

In a painstakingly restored monastery is the **Fundación Cultural Rodolfo Morales** (✉ *Morelos 108* ☎ *951/571–0952 or 951/571–0198* ⌚ *Daily 10–3 and 5–8*), funded by the village's most famous resident, the late artist Rodolfo Morales. There are exhibits of religious art from the monastery, as well as some of the master's own work.

★ Near the entrance to Ocotlán the **workshops of the Águilar sisters** are brimming with distinctive figurines fashioned from red clay. The sisters, now elderly, might be there to show you around their adjoining workshops. If not, one of their children or grandchildren will. Their shops are clustered near each other on the road, so it's easy to go from one to the next. You can find these figures in the markets and shops of Oaxaca City, but at extremely inflated prices.

MITLA AND THE TEXTILE VILLAGES

It gets far fewer visitors, but Mitla is, in many ways, as impressive as Monte Albán. Here you'll find splendid stonework that is referred to as *greca* because it resembles that of the ancient Greeks. You'll also see walls painted a striking shade of red, a reminder that when inhabited, these cities were not just the bare stone associated with the ruins. Other worthy archaeological sites along Carretera 190, the newly resurfaced highway to Mitla, are Lambityeco and Yagul.

Carretera 190 is also the road to the great textile town of Teotitlán del Valle, where house after house is set up as a workshop where both men and women work on back-strap looms. Prices can be high, but the workmanship justifies it. Nearby Santa Ana del Valle has weavings at lower prices.

Buses bound for villages east of the city depart from the second-class terminal in Oaxaca City, across the street from the Central de Abastos.

MITLA

Fodor's Choice ★ **Mitla**, 46 km (27 mi) southeast of Oaxaca, expanded and grew in influence as Monte Albán declined. Like its predecessor, Mitla is a complex started by the Zapotec and later taken over by the Mixtec. Unlike Monte Albán, Mitla's attraction lies not in its massive scale, but in its unusual ornamentation; the stonework depicts mesmerizing abstract designs with a powerful harmony. The striking architecture, which dates as late as the 1500s, is almost without equal within Mexico thanks to the exquisite greca workmanship on the fine local volcanic stone, which ranges in hue from pink to yellow.

The first structure you enter is the Grupo del Norte, where the Spanish settlers built Mitla's Catholic cathedral literally on top of the Zapotec structure, integrating the foundation. It's comparable to having the history of Oaxaca laid out before you in one building—truly remarkable. Mitla's name comes from the Nahuatl word *mictlan,* meaning "place of the dead." Don't expect to see anything resembling a graveyard, however; the Zapotec and Mixtec typically buried their dead under the entrance to the structure where the deceased resided.

There are a few underground tombs in the impressive Grupo de las Columnas (Group of the Columns), the main section of the ruins that are fun to climb down into. In that group is also the palace that forms the most striking architectural achievement of Mitla.

The journey on Carretera 190 takes about 50 minutes. If you haven't rented a car, you can catch a *colectivo* at the side of Oaxaca City's second-class bus station or along the road to Mitla—or hire a cab or car through your hotel to take you on a day trip to Mitla (and perhaps a mezcal distillery as well). The ruins are in the midsize town of Mitla, which has many small restaurants along with a beautiful church that practically dwarfs the ruins. There's a small market area adjacent to the parking lot with public restrooms and snack and souvenir vendors. *951/568–0316 www.inah.gob.mx $3 Daily 8–5.*

WHERE TO STAY

$–$$ **Don Cenobio.** What was for a long time just a restaurant and convention center is now the top lodging choice in Mitla. Owner Alfonso Moreno Díz has lovingly restored his grandfather's estate, and it's a remarkable place to stay, complete with an inner courtyard that has a solar-heated pool, an orange-tree-shaded garden bar, and a play structure for kids. Rooms could hardly be cheerier—everything is saturated with color—with intricately carved furniture brightly painted with flowers and fruits. Some doubles have private terraces over the garden—definitely ask for one. Rates are discounted Sunday–Thursday. The restaurant ($) is worthwhile in its own right; don't pass up the *pollo relleno con quesillo y huitlacoche* (chicken stuffed with Oaxacan cheese and corn fungus) or the local version of mole negro. **Pros:** great restaurant; good base for exploring the area. **Cons:** off the beaten path. *Av. Juárez 3, Col. Centro 951/568–0330 www.hoteldoncenobio.com 19 rooms, 3 suites In-hotel: no phone (some), no TV (some), Wi-Fi (some). In-hotel: restaurant, bar, pool, Wi-Fi hotspot, Internet terminal V.*

SANTA MARÍA DEL TULE

About 14 km (9 mi) east of Oaxaca on Carretera 190, the hamlet of Santa María del Tule is known for **El Tule**, the huge cypress tree that towers over the lovely colonial-era church behind it. Thought to be more than 2,000 years old, it's one of the world's largest trees, with roots buried more than 60 feet in the ground and a canopy arcing some 140 feet high. It has an estimated weight of nearly 640,000 tons; it would take 35 adults to embrace the trunk. In front of the church is a pleasant garden with animal-shape topiaries. The fee to enter the grounds is 25¢. At informal outdoor eateries in the tree's shadow, local ladies tend large griddles, serving *atole* (a nutritious drink of ground cornmeal or rice), soups, and snacks.

Continued on page 340

THE MIXTECA MONASTERIES

Templo y Exconvento de Santo Domingo de Guzmán (16th Century), Yanhuitlán (above and right)

The Mixteca, a rugged region northwest of Oaxaca City, has some of the state's most dramatic scenery. Driving up you'll see more pine-covered hills than people. In the evening, fog creeps into the many valleys here. The Mixteca is a great day trip from Oaxaca City, but the region attracts very few tourists. This may soon change, however, when the extensive restoration of the region's stunning Dominican monasteries is completed. These enormous, ornate structures would be a sight to behold in any city, but are all the more striking here—out in the middle of nowhere—dwarfing the tiny villages that sustain them.

Dominican friars swept through this region soon after the Spanish conquest, employing local labor to construct churches. The Mixteca people were known for their work with gold and precious stones, so these structures are as opulent as any of the churches in Oaxaca City. The same indigenous people that helped build the monasteries were not allowed inside them for worship, so each has *capillas abiertas* (open chapels) that allowed priests to minister to the vast crowds forced to stand outside. The thick, stout walls of the monasteries were built to withstand earthquakes—with mixed success. For several churches, an important part of the restoration process has been reinforcing the original walls with steel supports.

Ironically, smallpox brought to the region by the Spanish eventually killed most of the indigenous Mixteca worshipers, leaving the churchyards empty. Not all monasteries were completely abandoned, though. In many cases, the congregations, too poor to repair the churches themselves, have continued services for years while the churches crumble around them. Today, you'll often find Sunday mass going on amid the construction.

Mexico's National Institute of Anthropology and History (INAH) has been working in conjunction with local conservation groups and outside engineering firms to restore key monasteries since the early 1990s; some projects are still underway and may take years to complete.

TEMPLO DE LA ASUNCIÓN, Nochixtlán
Dominating the town is the 19th-century Templo de la Asunción, in the main square. The interior is especially elegant, with a five-tier chandelier hanging from the dome. Follow the signs to El Centro.

TEMPLO Y EXCONVENTO DE SAN JUAN BAUTISTA, Coixtlahuaca
Coixtlahuaca's monastery may be the most "ruined" of them all, but it has perhaps the best preserved of the Dominican churches in the region. Vivid reds, greens, and blues still cling to the ribs on the vaulted ceiling, wind around the windows, and climb up the columns. Just inside the front doors, you'll find a large chapel dedicated to the Virgen de Guadalupe. The church's patron saint stands guard over the intricately carved retablo, and you can get close enough to the altarpiece to appreciate the delicate work. Outside, the bright red paint that once enlivened the now-demure white facade shows through cracks in the plaster. Be sure to check out the lovely courtyard garden. Though there aren't any set hours, the monastery is often open.

★ TEMPLO Y EXCONVENTO DE SANTO DOMINGO DE GUZMÁN, Yanhuitlán
This towering 16th-century structure and its adjoining monastery appear even larger because they sit on a hill overlooking the village. The massive wooden doors face away from the village's main square.

Where to Eat in Nochixtlán

✕ **Restaurante Claudla.** Half a block from the main square is this no-frills restaurant, which serves up surprisingly good food. Take a seat at one of the long tables as members of the owner's extended family watch soap operas on the tiny television. You can even check your e-mail while you wait. ✉ *Porfirio Díaz between Allende and Benito Juarez* ☎ *No phone* 💳 *No credit cards.*

The church's sheer size is its most stunning feature; its vaulted ceiling soars to almost 25 meters (82 feet). The gold-leaf retablo behind the main altar has five levels, each depicting various saints. Santo Domingo, of course, stands alone at the top. Some of the paintings on this retablo are by the Spanish master Andrés de la Concha. Don't miss the *mudéjar* (Moorish) designs in the wooden ceiling of the choir. The handsome 18th-century pipe organ was restored in 1998.

The site is being restored at a decent clip. At this writing, the church was closed and scaffolded, but the monastery was open—a stunning cobblestoned inner courtyard has been completed and beautifully stuccoed. 🎫 *$3 to view the interior* ⏲ *Tues.–Sun. 10–5*

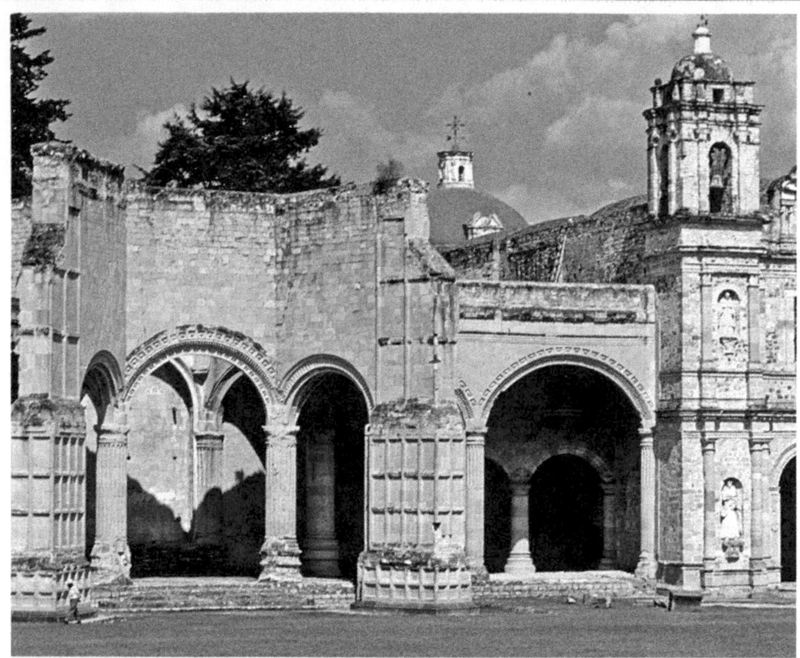

Templo y Exconvento de San Pedro y San Pablo, Teposcolula (1538)

TEMPLO Y EXCONVENTO DE SAN PEDRO Y SAN PABLO, Teposcolula
This sanctuary is one of the most impressive in the region and remains much as it was when it was built in 1538. The only major change is that the gilded retablo behind the main altar has been replaced by one with the neoclassical design that was popular in the 19th century. (You can still see the original to the left side of the main altar.)

The front of the church, which faces away from the town, is the location of its most impressive feature—a meticulously restored open chapel. The roof resembles the vaulted ceiling inside the sanctuary, but between the ribs it's open to the sky. Make sure to take a close look, as the underside is studded with gleaming gold medallions. The sprawling churchyard was meant to hold thousands of Mixteca worshippers. Inside is a pleasant rose garden ringed by small rooms. Here you'll find many unlabeled paintings by Andrés de la Concha, also responsible for many of the works on the main altar at the Templo y Exconvento de Santo Domingo de Guzmán in Yanhuitlán. Upstairs are a few restored monks' cells. Admission ($3) is charged only if someone is at the door. It's open daily from 10–6.

The other interesting structure in Teposcolula is the Casa de la Cacica, which means the "House of the Priestess." The Spanish built this stone building for a Mixteca leader, hoping that her presence would convince others to move to the village. The casa, on the road across from the church's main gate, is currently being restored.

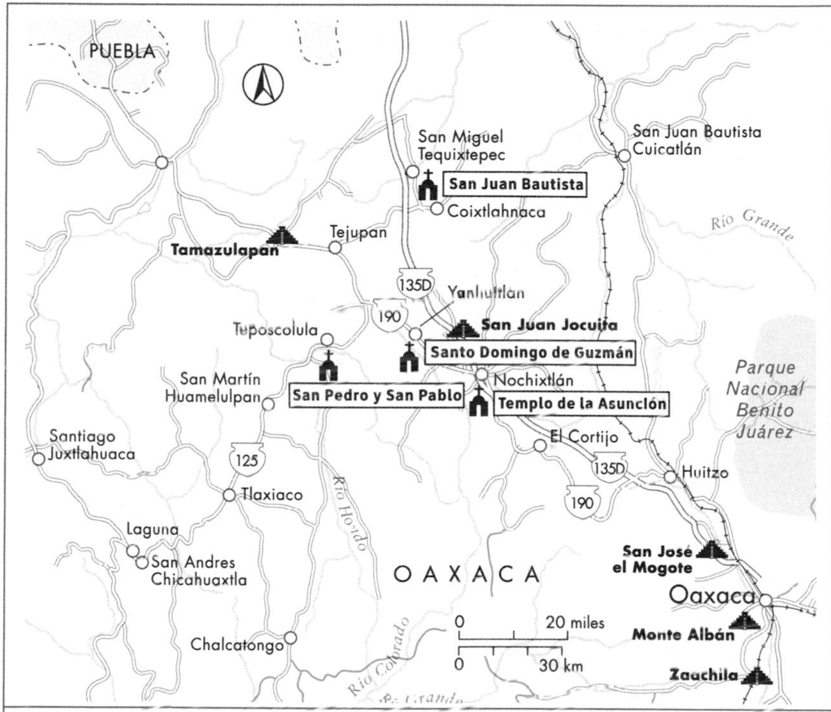

HOW TO GET THERE

BY BUS: Buses bound for Nochixtlán depart daily at 7 AM, 8 AM, and 1 PM from Oaxaca's first-class terminal. From Nochixtlán you can get connections or shared taxis to outlying monasteries, but it's easier to drive. Trips take 1 to 1½ hours.

BY CAR: Carretera 190 has a maddening amount of speed bumps, inexplicably placed in areas where there's nothing for miles but cattle. If you see a sign that says TOPE, slow down immediately or you're in for a nasty jolt. Unfortunately, many aren't marked. You'll do yourself a favor if you spring for the tolls along beautifully paved Carretera 135D. Spending the $6 gets you less traffic, fewer potholes, no speed bumps and a better view of the countryside. Secondary roads have some potholes, but are generally in good shape.

Nochixtlán: Located where Carreterra 190 and Carreterra 135D meet, Nochixtlán is the gateway to the Mixteca. The trip from Oaxaca City takes 1 hour.
Coixtlahuaca: About 35 km (22 mi) north of Nochixtlán; go up main road and turn right on Av. Independencia.
Yanhuitlán: To get to Yanhuitlán, take Carretera 190. It's about 18 km (11 mi) west of Nochixtlán and 37 km (23 mi) south of Tamazulapan.
Teposcolula: About 32 km (20 mi) or 30–40 min. from Yanhuitlán. To get here, head west on Carretera 190, then south on Carretera 125. Bypass the first set of church ruins you on 125—Teposcolula is much farther on.

THE ELIXIR

Mitla and its surroundings are home to dozens of mezcal distilleries, almost all of which sell directly to consumers and some of which run tours. American Ron Cooper is one of the most accomplished mezcal exporters in the business; his **Del Maguey** (✉ *Macedonio Alcalá 403* ☎ *951/501-2374* 🌐 *www.mezcal.com*) bottles contain mezcal sourced from extremely traditional artisanal producers in the countryside. They're prized across America, commanding upward of $70 a bottle. You can visit Cooper's bottling plant and tasting room by appointment, or, for a fee, Ron will take you on a fascinating insider's tasting tour of the region, where you'll meet the old-school producers themselves.

Mezcal Benevá (✉ *Carretera Oaxaca–Istmo Carretera 190, Km 42.5, San Pablo Villa de Mitla* ☎ *951/514-7005* 🌐 *www.mezcalbeneva.com*), at the Rancho Zapata restaurant complex, is a short drive out of the town of Mitla toward Oaxaca. Take a guided tour through the mezcal distilling process; during one part, a horse walks around in circles, stomping on the cooked agave. Benevá's mezcals are also notable, especially their five-year-old gran reserva.

Another American, Doug French, makes **Scorpion Mezcal** (☎ *951/511-5701* 🌐 *www.scorpionmezcal.com*). His tasting room is still in development, but his range of mezcals is exported as well.

DAINZÚ

The first archaeological site to the east of Oaxaca is **Dainzú**, about 20 km (12 mi) from the city. It dates as far back as 600 BC. Here you'll find some carvings that may remind you of the Dancers' Gallery at Monte Albán; these, however, depict a ball game.

The most spectacular sights are the well-restored ball court and the Tumba del Jaguar (Tomb of the Jaguar), with the fearsome head of a jaguar perched above the door. Pre-Columbian pottery shards litter the ground all over, evidence that this is a site that, unlike Monte Albán or Mitla, is still in the earlier stages of excavation. You'll likely have it to yourself, too. The grass-covered ruins are particularly pretty in the late-afternoon light. Note that there are no facilities here. Keep an eye out for the turnoff, because it's poorly marked; arriving from Oaxaca City, it's right before an overpass. ✉ *Off Carretera 190* ☎ *No phone* 🌐 *www.inah.gob.mx* 🎫 *$3* ⏲ *Daily 8–6.*

TEOTITLÁN DEL VALLE

Giant rug looms sit in the front rooms of many houses in Teotitlán del Valle, 30 km (18 mi) southeast of Oaxaca, just off Carretera 190. Although many rug shops are clustered right off the highway, be sure to drive all the way into town, where there are many more workshops.

The 17th-century **Templo de la Preciosa Sangre de Cristo** (✉ *Calle Hidalgo, 1 block east of Calle Juárez*) towers over the main square. Some parts of the facade have been scraped away to reveal stones carved with Zapotec designs that were used during the building of the church.

WHERE TO EAT

¢ MEXICAN **Tlamanalli.** For a memorable lunch of authentic regional food, head to this eatery in a handsome colonial-style building. Zapotec dishes such as *guisado de pollo* (a rich chicken stew) are so good that Tlamanalli has been featured in several food magazines. Get here early, as it isn't open for dinner. *Av. Juárez 39* *951/524–4006* V *Closed weekends. No dinner.*

SANTA ANA DEL VALLE

The tiny weaving town of Santa Ana del Valle is less well known than Teotitlán but also worth visiting; prices here are often cheaper. The turnoff is 31 km (19 mi) from Oaxaca on Carretera 190.

The tiny **Museo Shan-Dany** (*Plaza Cívica* *951/568–0373* *$1* *Daily 10–2 and 3–6*) has some interesting exhibits about the archaeological sites scattered around the area. Of particular note are several incense burners bearing the likeness of Cocijo, the Zapotec god honored at a temple in Lambityeco.

TLACOLULA

Although most often visited during its bustling Sunday market, Tlacolula, 31 km (19 mi) east of Oaxaca on Carretera 190, makes an interesting stop midweek. While you're here, visit the baroque-style Capilla del Santo Cristo, a chapel dating from the 16th century. ■ TIP→ **There are many inexpensive and tasty places in town, so it's a good place to stop for food on the way between Oaxaca and Mitla.**

7

LAMBITYECO

Lambityeco was built as the civilization of nearby Mitla was waning. The city flourished until AD 750, when it was abandoned. Many archaeologists believe the inhabitants moved to the better-protected city of Yagul. The Palacio de los Racoqui, or Palace of the Lords, is the last of six larger and larger temples built on top of each other. Here you'll see a pair of carvings of a nobleman and his wife. Between these carvings is the tomb where they were buried. Nearby is the Palacio de Cocijo, dedicated to its namesake, a Zapotec god. A pair of carvings depict the rain god wearing an impressive headdress. The site is clearly visible from the highway, but for some reason there's no sign. *Off Carretera 190* *No phone* *$3* *Daily 8–5.*

YAGUL

The ruins at **Yagul** aren't as elaborate as those at Monte Albán or Mitla, but their position atop a hill makes them worth a visit. This city, which is 36 km (22 mi) southeast of Oaxaca off Carretera 190, was predominantly a fortress protecting a group of temples. The Palacio de los Seis Patios (Palace of the Six Patios), a maze of hallways leading to hidden courtyards, is fun to explore.

If you find the eerie Tumba Triple (Triple Tomb) locked, give the guard $1 or so to open it for you. He may even let you borrow a flashlight to get a good look at the spooky carved skulls. Follow the steep trail that starts near the parking lot for a good hike and great views over the valley and ruins. The site has restrooms, but no other facilities. *951/516–0123* *$3* *Daily 8–5.*

THE OAXACA COAST

Oaxaca's 520-km (322-mi) coastline is one of Mexico's last Pacific frontiers. The town of Puerto Escondido has long been prime territory for international surfers. Its pedestrian walkways, crowded with open-air seafood restaurants, shops, and cafés, are indeed lively, but also incredibly relaxed. Fishing boats pull double duty as water taxis, ferrying folks to lovely scallops of sand up the coast. Across the highway, the "real" town above provides a look at local life and a dazzling view of the coast.

Midway between Puerto Escondido and Huatulco, tiny Puerto Ángel has a limited selection of unpolished hotels and funky bungalows tucked into the hills. The growing number of accommodations in nearby beach burgs such as Zipolite and Mazunte has seduced some of Puerto Ángel's previously faithful sun-lovers.

Huatulco covers 51,900 acres, 40,000 of which are dedicated as a nature reserve. The focal point of the development, masterminded in the 1980s by the government's tourism office, is a string of nine sheltered bays that stretch across 35 km (22 mi) of stunning coast. The first in this necklace is Conejos, which has Huatulco's most luxurious private villas and two boutique hotels. The town of La Crucecita, built to house the construction crews working on area developments, has the requisite plaza with a Catholic church as well as a thriving market, small shops, budget and moderately priced hotels, and plenty of restaurants.

Bahía Tangolunda is home to Huatulco's most exclusive hotels, whereas Santa Cruz has midrange hotels as well as a marina and a cruise-ship terminal. Development of Bahía Chahué has begun with an 88-slip marina, a luxury spa, and a few small hotels. A parking lot makes the beach accessible, and a public beach club has changing rooms, a restaurant, and a swimming pool. A Best Western and a few other small hotels, bars, and restaurants are near this bay, but most are across the highway on Boulevard Benito Juárez.

No matter where you hole up along Mexico's southern Pacific coast, you'll find that it's all about the beach, the water, and the waves. Surfers and bodysurfers whoop it up at Zicatela and less famous breaks; snorkelers hug rocky coves in search of unusual specimens; and divers share the depths with dolphins, rays, eels, and schools of fish instead of shoals of other humans. Friendly locals, superb vistas, and first-rate beaches combine to make Oaxaca's coast a stunner.

PUERTO ESCONDIDO

310 km (192 mi) south of Oaxaca City.

Puerto Escondido was the first beach resort on the *carretera costera* (coastal highway), and it remains the most popular. Playa Zicatela is famous for its waves, drawing surfers from around the world. A few ritzier cliff-top hotels have brought in more of the older set, but the steady presence of the surfing community means that even as the town continues to gentrify, it maintains a relaxed, hippie-ish vibe.

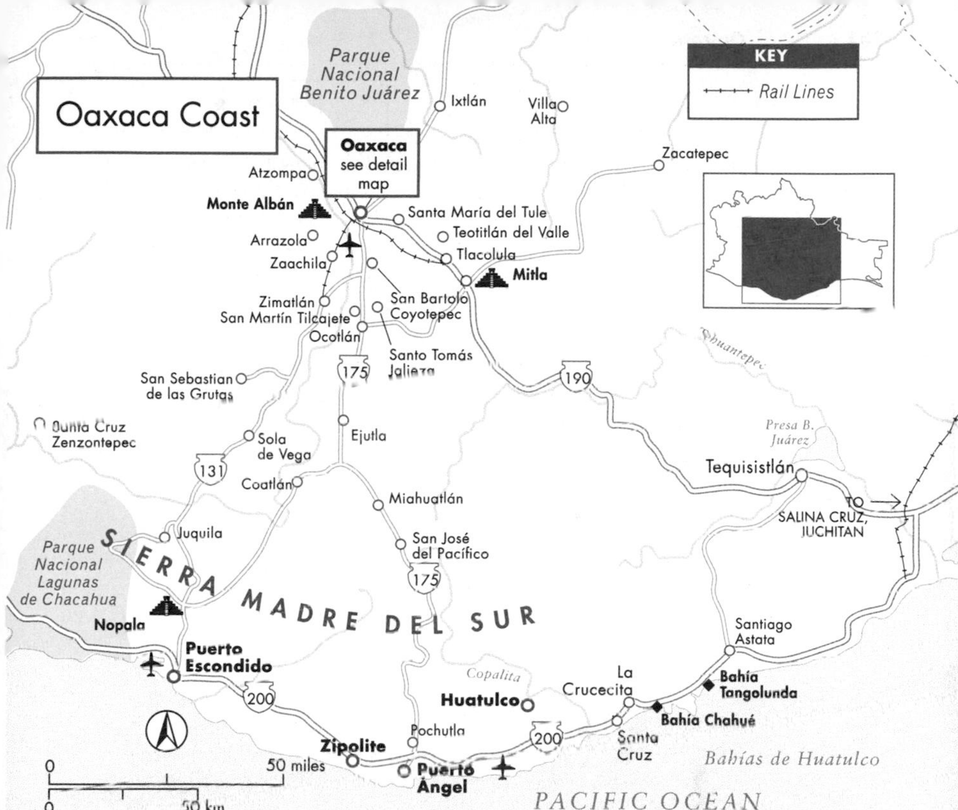

Beyond Zicatela's beachfront bars and dreadlocked denizens there are marvelous swimming beaches to the west that are popular with Mexican families. Several nearby nature preserves and a few coffee farms provide the best day-tripping opportunities, as there isn't much else in these parts besides beaches, beaches, and more beaches.

El Adoquín, the part of Avenida Pérez Gasga that's reserved for pedestrians, runs right through the center of the town. This area is most popular with Mexican families. You'll find plenty of inexpensive shops, restaurants, and hotels along the four blocks.

Northwest of El Adoquín, overlooking the sea from atop adobe-color cliffs, are the Carrizalillo, La Rinconada, and Bacocho neighborhoods. These are the most up-and-coming areas of Puerto Escondido, but for now they're still quiet, and the people who stay here like it that way. The hotels, most of them upscale, cater to families.

Along Boulevard Benito Juárez are some of the town's best restaurants. Oh, and if you were wondering why this street is as wide as a runway, it used to be the airport.

GETTING HERE AND AROUND

Aeropuerto Puerto Escondido (PXM) is a 10-minute taxi ride from town; most flights from the States connect in Mexico City. You can fly direct from Oaxaca City, but it's usually pretty pricey.

Direct bus service from Oaxaca City is available on several first-class lines. ADO has several first-class buses per day leaving from Oaxaca's first-class bus terminal. Estrella del Valle has buses leaving from Oaxaca City to Puerto Escondido about four or five times daily.

TAKE A TOUR

Lalo Ecotours (☎ *954/588–9164* 🌐 *www.lalo-ecotours.com*) runs guided trips to Laguna Manialtepec including bird-watching tours with Canadian ornithologist Michael Malone.

If you drive from Oaxaca City, there are two routes. The most direct is Carretera 131 (which turns off Carretera 175 south of Oaxaca City) and goes straight to Puerto Escondido (6½–7 hours). However, it's a winding, narrow, two-lane road. Alternatively, you can take slightly less hair-raising Carretera 190 to Salina Cruz, where you pick up Carretera 200 to Puerto Escondido (8–9 hours). Don't drive either route at night.

Taxis in Puerto Escondido start at $2 for a ride from one end of town to another (say, from the Adoquín to Fraccionamiento Bacocho). Renting a car isn't necessary unless you want to explore beaches outside of town. It can be difficult to find a car, as the major agencies aren't well represented. Ask your hotel if it can arrange a rental.

ESSENTIALS

Medical Assistance **International Friends of Puerto Escondido** (☎ *44954/540–3816* 🌐 *www.ifope.com*). **Puerto Escondido Hospital** (✉ *UMQ, Av. Oaxaca 720* ☎ *954/582–1288*) is the town's largest hospital. **Police** (☎ *954/582–0498 in Puerto Escondido*). **Red Cross** (☎ *954/582–0550*). The **Tourist Police** (☎ *954/582–3343*).

Rental Cars **Económica Rent-a-Car** (✉ *Calle Brisas s/n, just off Hwy. 200* ☎ *954/582–2579* 🌐 *www.economica.com.mx*).

Visitor and Tour Info **Puerto Escondido Tourism Office** (✉ *Blvd. Benito Juárez s/n, Fracc. Bacocho* ☎ *954/582–0175* ✉ *Av. Pérez Gasga s/n, at Marina Nacional* ☎ *No phone*). **Viajes Dimar** (✉ *Av. Pérez Gasga 905* ☎ *954/582–1551 or 954/582–0734* ✉ *Calle del Morro s/n, Playa Zicatela* ☎ *954/582–2305*).

EXPLORING

★ **Laguna de Manialtepec.** One of the easiest day trips from Puerto Escondido is the wildlife preserve of this lagoon, about 14 km (9 mi) from the center of town. It's a birder's paradise, with pelicans, hawks, hummingbirds, and spoonbills in the surrounding mangrove forests. Although an inexpensive half-day tour from Puerto Escondido is the most convenient way to visit, you can also drive or take public transportation and hire a boatman to the lagoon's beaches and restaurants.

Laguna de Ventanilla. Tour operators often combine a trip to Playa Mazunte and its sea-turtle center with a visit to Laguna de Ventanilla to see resident and migratory species of birds, as well as crocodiles. The cost of the all-day tour starts at $20 per person. Alternatively, arrange a 1½-hour tour of Laguna de Ventanilla directly from boat owners at the lagoon's entrance about five minutes west of the Centro Mexicano de la Tortuga. Arrive any day between 8 AM and 4 PM and you should be able find someone to take you around.

Parque Nacional Laguna Chacahua. About 74 km (46 mi) west of Puerto Escondido is Chacahua Lake National Park. You can tour the lagoon in a small motor launch, watching the birds that hunt among the mangroves. The bird population is biggest during the winter months, when migratory species arrive from the frozen north. Most tours from Puerto Escondido include a visit to a crocodile farm and an hour or two on the beach at Cerro Hermoso.

Temazcalli. If you want a bit of pampering, cleanse your body and soul at this spa, which claims its treatments combine the energy of wood, fire, rock, and medicinal herbs. They still use pre-Columbian techniques, so it's a true cultural experience. Choose a private scented steam ($12 each for two people) or a ritualistic group cleansing; the latter involves chants and prayers. Or opt for a good old-fashioned massage with scented oils. ✉ *Av. Infraganti at Calle Temazcalli, Col. Lázaro Cárdenas* ☎ *958/582–1023* 🌐 *www.temazcalli.com.*

BEACHES

Playa Bacocho. High red cliffs serve as the backdrop for this beach west of town. It's ringed by upscale housing and hotel developments as well as some inviting bars, discos, and restaurants. ■ **TIP→ Avoid swimming here. Although the waves aren't fierce, the rip currents are strong, especially along the east side of the bay. There aren't any lifeguards.** For most visitors, Playa Bacocho is good for playing in the sand, long walks, and sunsets. Two beach clubs have restaurant and bar service, swimming pools, showers, and shade; access is about $5. Security guards on three-wheelers patrol during the day, but it's not recommended to walk on this lonely stretch of sand at night.

Fodor's Choice ★ **Playa Carrizalillo.** In a region full of beautiful beaches, Playa Carrizalillo can still take your breath away. The high cliffs that surround it ensure that it's never too crowded. The aquamarine water here is clean, clear, and shallow—perfect for swimming and snorkeling, especially around the rocks that frame the beautiful cove. Sometimes there are waves large enough to be appropriate for beginning surfers. A handful of palm-thatched restaurants rent snorkeling equipment and serve food and drinks. It's a two-minute drive or 35-minute walk from the center of town; a small sign indicates where to turn onto the unpaved road. It's about 150 steps down from the parking area, but the steep stone staircase is well maintained.

Playa Manzanillo. Of Puerto Escondido's seven beaches, Playa Manzanillo, which rings Puerto Angelito, is one of the safest for swimming. It's also one of the best for snorkeling, with a sandy ocean floor, some rock and coral formations, and calm, clear water. You can reach this beach on foot (a 15-minute walk west of town), by taxi (less than $2 per ride), or by boat ($3 per person one-way) from Playa Marineros. There's a short staircase down to the beach that is difficult for some people to navigate. Informal snack shops selling juices, sodas, and beer—and, when available, fresh fish and oysters—rent snorkeling equipment and Boogie boards for $4 per hour. You can use their showers and rustic bathrooms for a small fee. The beach is lined with lounge chairs and can get quite crowded on weekends.

Playa Marineros. This beach abuts Playa Principal; the only thing separating the two is a tiny freshwater lagoon (the mouth of Río Rigadillo), which trickles onto the sand. Skiffs can be hired out for fishing or dolphin- or turtle-seeking expeditions, or as water taxis to nearby beaches. ■ **TIP→ Beginning to intermediate surfers can catch some waves near the east side of the bay.** Lifeguards keep watch from several towers.

Playa Principal. Meeting up with Playa Marineros at the mouth of Río Rigadillo, this strip of medium-coarse beige sand runs parallel to Avenida Pérez Gasga. There are restaurants and hotel bars where you can retreat from the sun and treat yourself to a cool drink. The sand is clean and soft near the shore, but somewhat hard and brown near the palm trees and shrubs that line the beachfront businesses. The beach is popular with Mexican families. Umbrellas can be rented for a minimal daily fee.

THE OYSTER GUY

Most days on Playa Manzanillo, from morning until about 5 PM, you can buy a dozen unbelievably fresh oysters on the half shell for about 50 pesos from a purveyor who shucks them for you right out of the bucket. He's usually set up at the far end of the beach (if you're facing the water, walk to your right), next to an elevated fish restaurant, and there's an informal agreement whereby you can eat your oysters at one of their tables, squeezing on lime and chili to your heart's content. There may not be a better food experience in Puerto Escondido.

Playa Puerto Angelito. Don't confuse the delightful cove of Puerto Angelito, home to both the eponymous beach as well as equally lovely Manzanillo Beach, with the small port town south of Puerto Escondido. Ten steps from the street put you on the white sand of Playa Puerto Angelito, where the shallow depth of the water gives it a luminous, green-blue tint. It's a good spot for swimming, snorkeling, and diving, though the number of boats moored close to shore sometimes shrinks the swimming area considerably. ■ **TIP→ While swimming, beware of water taxis and skiffs offering fishing and sightseeing.** Many thatch-roofed restaurants here serve simple fare in the shade and rent snorkels and umbrellas—the latter cost $6 whether you sit for 10 minutes or all day. Things get quite crowded on holidays and weekends.

★ **Playa Zicatela.** One of the world's top surfing beaches, Zicatela has cream-colored sands that are battered by the mighty Mexican Pipeline. In the third week of November international surfing championships are held here (followed by the even more popular bikini contest). Regardless, the beach is just about always filled with sun-bleached aficionados of both sexes intent on serious surfing. Huts right on the sand serve refreshments sporadically, but Calle del Morro, Zicatela's main street, is lined with hotels and restaurants providing shade and sustenance on a more regular basis. There are often lifeguards on duty. ■ **TIP→ Even when the waters appear calm, the undertows and rip currents can be deadly. If you have any doubts about your prowess, settle for watching the surfers.**

You can get a sort of real-time view of the waves at Playa Zicatela online at: www.puertoescondidoinfo.com/puertocam.html

WHERE TO EAT

There are many bars along Playa Zicatela and Playa Principal with beachside tables under palapas; most of those serving food have a predictable menu of basic shrimp, octopus, and fish dishes. The best choice at these places is usually the whole fried fish, often *mojarra,* generally served with a side of rice and salad. These restaurants change with such frequency that it's best to just scout them out and pick the one that has the most local customers that day.

OFF THE BEATEN PATH

Playa Agua Blanca is about 30 minutes east of Puerto Escondido, at Km 172 of the road toward Puerto Ángel. You'll see a sign for Agua Blanca pointing down a gravel road. At the end of this road is a pristine beach with soft white sand and a few rocks along the coastline. The only other people here will be locals, and you should join them underneath a palapa to eat fresh oysters. Or enjoy a full lunch at any of the shady *comedores* that dot the beach.

PLAYA ZICATELA

$$ MEXICAN ✕ **Banana's.** Although this open-air restaurant looks touristy, and its surfer clientele might set off warning bells, the Mexican food is remarkably consistent. Add to that friendly service, and the unusually late opening hours—you can sit down for dinner at 11:45 PM— and you've got a winning formula. *Enfrijoladas,*a satisfying mix of black beans, tortilla, and cheese usually served for breakfast, are served all day. The *chiles rellenos,* stuffed with *picadillo* (ground beef), are undeniably delicious. ✉ *Calle del Morro s/n* ☎ *954/582–0005* ▭ *MC, V.*

$ MEXICAN ✕ **El Sorbo.** This beachfront restaurant is a bit more upscale than its competition, with its wooden furniture, flickering candlight, and decent wine list. The focus is on seafood, with various preparations of fish and shrimp, but the Spanish-style paella is the best thing coming out of the kitchen. Try the *paella especial,* with chicken, chorizo, mussels, shrimp, squid, and crab. Wash it all down with sangria. ✉ *Calle del Morro s/n* ☎ *954/588–5910* ▭ *No credit cards.*

$ ITALIAN ✕ **La Casa de la Pasta.** This tiny restaraunt, just next door to the Hotel Papaya Surf, serves a surprising variety of handmade pastas: lasagna, cannelloni, manicotti, ravioli, gnocchi, fettucini, agnolotti, taglarini, pappardelle. There are also tasty pizzas, which you can wash down with a cold smoothie. In high season, the place fills up early for dinner, but it's worth the wait. ✉ *Av. Pérez at Andador Unión* ☎ *954/582–3322* ▭ *No credit cards.*

$$ SEAFOOD ✕ **Shiva.** The terrace of this elegant, modern, beachfront restaurant at the southern end of Playa Zicatela is a great place to watch the sun set over the water. From here you can see the entire stretch of beach, watch the surfers, and enjoy the Mongolian grill. Select your ingredients and watch them grill it for you. There's a bar as well. ✉ *Calle del Morro s/n at Av. Bajada de las Briasa* ☎ *954/582–1995* ▭ *MC, V.*

PLAYA PRINCIPAL AND EL ADOQUÍN

$$ ITALIAN

La Galería. Every inch of wall space at this open-air restaurant on the west end of the Adoquín is filled with paintings. And every inch of your small, square table will be covered by platters of homemade pasta, like tortellini, ravioli, and lasagna. Pizzas are also popular; try the one with eggplant, garlic, mushrooms, and basil. Though the service isn't great, the brick-and-stone floors and red tiles peeking through the rafters make for a pleasant environment. The restaurant features a traditional Mexican breakfast for $4. *Av. Pérez Gasga s/n, across from tourist booth 954/582–2039 Calle del Morro s/n No credit cards.*

$$ SEAFOOD

Los Crotos. This seafood specialist is romantically set right in front of the lapping waves, and the whole fish (mostly red snapper) coming out of the kitchen is fresh and delicious. Throw in cold beer, and it's hard to go wrong. *Av. Pérez Gásga s/n 954/582–0025 AE, MC, V.*

LA RINCONADA AND BACOCHO

$ MEXICAN ★

La Torre. It's a casually elegant place that's popular with travelers in the know and locals who would rather keep it a secret. The location at the far end of Boulevard Benito Juárez doesn't seem to deter anyone. Steaks are available anytime, but the *costillas de cerdo* (pork ribs) are on the menu only on Friday. On pleasant evenings there's no better place to sit than beside the fountain in the garden. *Blvd. Benito Juárez 427, La Rinconada 954/582–1119 MC, V Closed Mon. No lunch.*

PLAYA PUERTO ANGELITO

$ SEAFOOD

La Escondida. All of the seafood at this local favorite is fresh and reasonably priced. You can eat on the beach or under a palapa on a hill a bit above the beach. The *vuelve a la vida* (return to life) seafood cocktail is particularly recommended as it has many types of clams as well as shrimp, abalone, squid, and crab. Cabañas are available if you want to take a nap after lunch, and you can arrange for a fishing trip or a dolphin- or whale-watching excursion. *Calle del Morro s/n 954/111–8414 No credit cards.*

WHERE TO STAY

PLAYA ZICATELA

$–$$

Arco Iris. Private verandas hung with hammocks (available for a small fee) are standout amenities at this three-story hotel on Playa Zicatela. There's also a large swimming pool, a movie room, and a second-floor restaurant that serves many vegetarian dishes. The laid-back vibe and easy beach access make up for shortcomings such as the slightly worn furnishings and dated exterior. **Pros:** nice views; good restaurant; friendly aura. **Cons:** needs updating; noise from neighboring bars. *Calle del Morro s/n, across from Playa Zicatela 954/582–0432 www.hotel-arcoiris.com.mx 32 rooms, 4 suites In-room: no a/c, no phone, no TV (some), Wi-Fi. In-hotel: restaurant, bar, pools, gym, beachfront, laundry service, Internet terminal, parking (free) MC, V.*

$$–$$$

Casa de las Iguanas. You can sign up for surf lessons at this contemporary hotel on Playa Zicatela's best section for surfing. Rooms are decorated with simple Mexican crafts; some have cute outdoor patios with small log bridges leading up to them, while others have balconies and hammocks. There's a lounge area where you can watch the evening sunset and chat about surfing with other guests. **Pros:** beautiful view from the bar-lounge. **Cons:** pricey rooms; sleepy staff not that helpful. ✉ *Av. Bajada de las Brisa, Col. Santa María. Zicatela* ☎ *954/582–1995* 🌐 *www.casadelasiguanas.com* *14 rooms, 1 apartment* *In-room: kitchen (some), safe, Wi-Fi. In-hotel: restaurant, room service, bar, pool, laundry service, Internet terminal, parking (free)* *MC, V.*

$$–$$$ **Hotel Ines.** Spacious suites are in four buildings surrounding a small plaza with a pool and Jacuzzi. Although the suites are all different, the decor in some is a little dull. Opt for a suite with a balcony and an ocean view. The restaurant is a selling point: you can order anything from a simple quesadilla to extremely well-prepared *tampiqueña* (thinly sliced beef served with guacamole, chili, rice, and beans). **Pros:** variety of rooms and price ranges; close to bars and clubs; great dive shop. **Cons:** gets crowded in high season; standard rooms with little imagination. ✉ *Calle del Morro s/n, at Blvd. Zicatela* ☎ *954/582–0792* 🌐 *www.hotelines.com* *59 rooms, 2 suites, 8 bungalows* *In-room: no a/c (some), kitchen (some), Wi-Fi (some). In-hotel: restaurant, room service, bar, pool, laundry service, Internet terminal, Wi-Fi hotspot, parking (free)* *AE, MC, V.*

$$–$$$ **Hotel Santa Fe.** An impressive archway leads you to the Santa Fe, a hotel that feels more like a small village. A cluster of colonial-style buildings in pastel shades is surrounded by well-tended gardens filled with brilliant red hibiscus. You can catch a glimpse of the surf from the balcony of your room or bungalow. The restaurant ($–$$), known for its vegetarian food, is a great spot to sip a beer and watch the sun set. **Pros:** good restaurant; nice pool; excellent location. **Cons:** standard rooms are pricey; some areas need updating; staff not that helpful. ✉ *Calle del Morro s/n, at Blvd. Zicatela* ☎ *954/582–0170 or 01800/712–7057 toll-free in Mexico, 888/649–6407* 🌐 *www.hotelsantafe.com.mx* *60 rooms, 2 suites, 8 bungalows* *In-room: kitchen (some), refrigerator (some), Wi-Fi. In-hotel: restaurant, room service, bar, pool, laundry service, Internet terminal, parking (free)* *AE, MC, V.*

$$ **Tabachín.** Well-stocked kitchenettes, shelves filled with books, and an assortment of clocks, vases, and other gewgaws make the studios here feel homey. Given the location a block from Playa Zicatela, the spaciousness and comfort of the rooms, and a breakfast from the vegetarian restaurant featuring an astounding array of choices, the room rates are quite low. The English-speaking staff is helpful in aiding guests with travel arrangements. **Pros:** some rooms have great views; delicious breakfasts; friendly staff. **Cons:** not right on the beach; no pool. ✉ *Calle de Morro s/n, Playa Zicatela* ☎ *954/582–1179* 🌐 *www.tabachininfo.com* *6 apartments* *In-room: safe (some), kitchen, Wi-Fi. In-hotel: restaurant, laundry service, Internet terminal* *MC, V* *BP.*

$–$$ **Villa Belmar.** The Belmar's array of arches, domes, and cupolas—done in Mediterranean white and blue—give it the appearance of a crazy and secluded castle. The one-bedroom apartments and comfortable double rooms attract a mix of people, although the place has a lonely aura, often with no guests in sight. Many accommodations have balconies from which to admire Playa Zicatela. You can rent by the day in high season and by the week or the month at other times. **Pros:** rooftop pool with views; away from busy Calle Morro. **Cons:** not right on beach; rooms are nothing fancy. ✉ *Calle Belmar s/n, Playa Zicatela* ☎ *954/582–0244* 🌐 *www.villabelmar.com* 32 *rooms, 6 suites* *In-room: kitchen (some), refrigerator, Wi-Fi. In-hotel: restaurant, pool, Wi-Fi hotspot, parking (free), some pets allowed* 💳 *MC, V.*

PLAYA PRINCIPAL AND EL ADOQUÍN

$ **Villa Roca Suites.** The only downside here appears to be the absence of a pool. But because the boutique hotel—which looks a little like a sand castle—is right on the beach, you can have your toes in the water in no time. A bright color scheme and minimalist decorating give rooms a spacious tropical quality. Two upstairs rooms have large shaded patios overlooking the beach. Rooms on the street side tend to be noisy. **Pros:** close to beaches; restaurants and shops; views of Playa Principal. **Cons:** no pool; in a less-than-glamorous area. ✉ *Av. Pérez Gasga 602, El Adoquín* ☎ *954/582–3525* *7 suites* *In-hotel: beachfront, parking (free)* 💳 *MC, V.*

LA RINCONADA AND BACOCHO

$$ **Hotel Aldea del Bazar.** Like a mirage, this sparkling white hotel sits high on a bluff above the calm waters of Playa Bacocho. The rooms overlook the surf or the manicured lawns. All have tasteful little sitting areas with low couches covered in brightly colored pillows. The Maya temazcal eucalyptus sauna will help you relax before heading to dinner at the restaurant, which is done up like a storybook Moorish palace. It's a bit bizarre, but it's fun, too. **Pros:** pleasant rooms; relaxing sauna; car-rental service. **Cons:** need a car to get around; design doesn't evoke Mexico. ✉ *Blvd. Benito Juárez 7, Fracc. Bacocho* ☎ *954/582–0508; 01800/012–3094 toll-free in Mexico* 🌐 *www.aldeadelbazar.com* *47 rooms* *In-hotel: restaurant, room service, bar, pool, spa, beachfront, laundry service, parking (free)* 💳 *AE, MC, V.*

$$$ **Suites La Hacienda.** These sparkling, French country–style accommodations, owned by a Parisian interior designer, are pristine and comfortable. Each one- or two-story apartment feels like a private home, with fresh flowers, a sprinkling of carefully chosen antiques, and blue-and-white Mexican tiles. The kitchenettes are sizable, and the patio restaurant serves one or two dishes for dinner daily during high season (December–March and Easter) and with advance notice at other times. The hotel is a five-minute walk from Playa Carrizalillo, a good beach for swimming. **Pros:** handsomely decorated; really close to beach. **Cons:** need car to get around; maximum of three people in a room. ✉ *Calle Atunes 15, La Rinconada* ☎ *954/582–0279* 🌐 *www.suiteslahacienda.com* *7 apartments* *In-room: kitchen, Wi-Fi. In-hotel: restaurant, pool, laundry service* 💳 *AE, MC, V.*

$$$ ★ **Villas Carrizalillo.** Perfect for those in search of a little solitude, these private, tile-roof villas cling to a cliff above the gorgeous beach for which they were named; you descend to the idyllic beach via a steep staircase. The villas range in size from a small studio to a three-bedroom abode with a private yard. A favorite, called the Puebla, has two bay-view balconies. The road out to the secluded property is dark; this is not the spot for those who want to go into town at night, although the strip of establishments at nearby La Rinconada is burgeoning. **Pros:** good value; nicely decorated rooms; direct access to one of the area's

best beaches. **Cons:** need a car to get around; no air-conditioning in some rooms. ✉ *Av. Carrizalillo 125, Carrizalillo* ☎ *954/582–1735* 🌐 *www.villascarrizalillo.com* *12 apartments* *In-room: no a/c (some), no phone, kitchen (some), no TV, Wi-Fi. In-hotel: restaurant, bar, pool, beachfront, water sports, bicycles, laundry service, parking (free)* 💳 *MC, V.*

NIGHTLIFE

You won't have trouble finding the party in Puerto Escondido. The best part about the whole scene is how low-key it is. Have drinks in the restaurants lining the Adoquín or head to Playa Zicatela and find a beach bar overlooking the ocean.

BARS

Red is the color theme at **Bar Fly** (✉ *Calle del Morro s/n* 🌐 *www.barfly.com.mx*); grab a seat on a red couch, surrounded by red walls, and relax. It's upstairs from Banana's restaurant. Set under a dramatic dome, **Casa Babylon** (✉ *Calle del Morro s/n* ☎ *No phone*) is certainly the most beautiful bar near Playa Zicatela. While you nurse your beer, you can challenge friends to a game of Scrabble or Monopoly. It's near Hotel Arco Iris.

For spirited live entertainment, stop by **Son y La Rumba** (✉ *Calle del Morro s/n* ☎ *954/582–3709*). Owner Mayka sings and plays guitar almost every night, but you never know who will drop in to jam with her—maybe a well-known classical violinist or a flamenco guitarist. **Wipe Out** (✉ *Av. Pérez Gasga* ☎ *954/582–2302*) is a multilevel dance club that goes until the wee hours of the morning.

7

SHOPPING

The town's sprawling market, **Mercado Benito Juárez**, is a long walk (but a short cab ride) from the beaches. It's worth checking out, especially on the market days, which are Wednesday and Saturday. Look for black pottery and finely woven textiles.

SPORTS AND THE OUTDOORS

Puerto Escondido's good-looking coves aren't as deserted as they seem. Fishermen lead angling expeditions as well as sightseeing trips for spotting turtles and dolphins, and the area's not bad for diving and snorkeling.

DIVING AND SNORKELING

Deep Blue Dive (✉ *Calle del Morro s/n, at the Hotel Ines, Playa Zicatela* ☎ *954/582–0792* 🌐 *www.mexico-scubadive.com*) This PADI certified team knows the area well, and provides dive certification, gear rentals, and whale- and dolphin-watching tours. A two-tank dive costs $60.

Puerto Dive Center (✉ *El Adoquín and Andador Libertad, at Hotel Mayflower* ☎ *954/102–7767* 🌐 *www.puertodivecenter.com/*) has rentals and dive tours. A two-tank dive costs about $65.

FISHING

The most common catches off Puerto Escondido are swordfish, marlin, tuna, and dorado. Fiestas de Noviembre, when anglers compete for prizes, is held the entire month of November. Prices for fishing tours run around $35 to $40 an hour, with a minimum of three hours (four people maximum). ■ **TIP→Many local fishermen expect to keep your catch as partial payment for their services, so discuss this with the captain ahead of time.** **Omar's Sportfishing** (✉ *Playa Puerto Angelito* ☎ *954/559–4406*) will take you out on a four-hour tour of the best fishing spots for about $160 for up to four people. They also have dolphin-watching tours that last about two to three hours and cost $35 per person.

SURFING

Playa Zicatela is the best place to hang ten in Puerto Escondido. ■ **TIP→If you want to take surfing lessons, one of your best sources of information is the lifeguard at the beach.** The going rate for lessons is $30 an hour, including the board. You can buy beachwear at **Mexpipe** (✉ *Calle del Morro s/n, across from Playa Zicatela* ☎ *954/582–2288* 🌐 *www.mexpipe.com*). The staff is also happy to give lessons for $30 per hour. Canadian Paul Yacht sells and rents surfboards for $14 a day at **P. J.'s** (✉ *Calle del Morro s/n, at Bajada Las Brisas* ☎ *954/582–0759*).

ZIPOLITE

Fodor's Choice ★

60 km (37 mi) east of Puerto Escondido, 3 km (2 mi) west of Puerto Ángel.

Zipolite lovers like to brag that this beach is what Puerto Escondido was 20 years ago, but that mantra doesn't even do justice to Zipolite's singular charm. No longer dismissed as just the home of a nudist beach, the town now has delicious international food and creative cocktails served in some of Mexico's most beautiful beachfront environments. When you're not sipping a cocktail or soaking up the sun, you can choose from activities such as yoga or fishing on this idyllic stretch of sand just west of Puerto Ángel.

What actual sights to see are in Mazunte, a beach community about 8 km (5 mi) west of Zipolite. Many people come to see the turtle museum. Indeed, the turtle has been a part of Mazunte's history for a long time—the word "mazunte" itself evolved from the Nahuatl word *maxontetia*, which means "please lay eggs." Mazunte also has affordable hotel options.

Between Zipotle and Mazunte is San Augustinillo, an area with several hotels as well as a fantastic, swimmable beach (just mind the sometimes strong currents) and good fishing. Body boarders and surfers find it is easier to surf here than in nearby Zipolite.

In general, though, the whole area has displayed a remarkable resistance to any kind of high-rise development, or even any establishments that provide air conditioning or hot water. Don't expect to use a credit card anywhere, and the nearest ATM is 20 minutes away in Pochutla—the closest thing to a regional hub with amenities like banks and supermarkets. Perhaps these are the reasons for the alluring sense of isolation.

GETTING HERE AND AROUND

From Puerto Escondido, Zipolite is easily reached via Highway 200. From Puerto Ángel, hail a taxi for the 10-minute journey.

EXPLORING

The **Centro Mexicano de la Tortuga** is at Playa Mazunte. The local economy was based on catching the *golfina* (olive ridley) turtle until the government put a ban on turtle hunting in 1990. Poachers aside, Mazunte is now devoted to protecting the species. Four of the world's eight species of marine turtles come to lay their eggs on Oaxaca's shores. July through September is peak nesting season. A dozen aquariums are filled with the turtles that flourish here: green turtles, hawksbills, leatherbacks, and olive ridleys. Tour guides give explanations in English and other languages. ✉ *Carretera Puerto Ángel–San Antonio Mazunte, Km 10* ☎ *958/584–3376* *$2* ⏲ *Tues.–Sat. 10–4:30, Sun. 10–2:30.*

Cosméticos Naturales de Mazunte, an association of natural cosmetic producers in Mazunte, began in 1996 with a group of mostly women and funding from The Body Shop. You can find natural cosmetics made with ingredients like coconuts, peanuts, and seaweed. The process of making the cosmetics is also natural; set up a tour to see how it works. ✉ *Paseo del Mazunte s/n* ☎ *958/583–9656.*

BEACHES

★ **Playa Mazunte.** Eight km (5 mi) west of Zipolite, Mazunte is a stunning stretch of soft sand with a few simple seafood restaurants and low-key accommodations (though there are fewer than at Zipolite). The surf is rougher here than at Playa San Agustinillo, and attracts bodyboarders.

Playa San Agustinillo. This divine stretch of sand between Zipolite and Playa Mazunte is backed by exuberant vegetation and elegant coconut palms. It's somewhat safe for swimming, although the current can be strong. As on neighboring beaches, vendors roam the sand selling cool drinks and grilled fish, and restaurants and rustic accommodations at the back of the beach provide shade from the strong sun.

■ TIP→ Be careful at the beaches here. The undertow is extremely strong and rip currents are unpredictable.

WHERE TO EAT

ZIPOLITE

$$ MEXICAN **✕ La Providencia.** Many locals consider this the best restaurant in town. Expect creative takes on traditional Mexican dishes, like shrimp covered in coconut and served with a mango sauce, and tasty chiles rellenos (cheese-, meat-, and fish-stuffed chilies). Wander around before sitting down; there are several seating areas, including a plant-filled, thatch-roofed patio. ✉ *Segunda Calle s/n, Col. Centro* ☎ *958/100–9234* 🌐 *zipolitedesdeadentro.blogspot.com* *Reservations essential* 💳 *MC, V* ⏲ *No lunch.*

$$ ITALIAN ★ **✕ Posada México.** Palapas, candles, and lounge furniture make the vibe at this beachside extravaganza extremely romantic. The Italian chefs do justice to their country's cuisine—a true rarity in Mexico. Most remarkably authentic are the skillfully seared brick-oven pizzas and the addictive bread that comes out of the same oven. ✉ *Colonía Roca Blanca* ☎ *958/584–3194* 🌐 *www.posadamexico.com* 💳 *No credit cards* ⏲ *Closed Tues.–Wed.*

SAN AUGUSTINILLO

$ ITALIAN **La Termita**. This Italian-style restaurant serves pizzas and Argentinian empanadas baked in a wood-burning oven. The bar and the restaurant are under one big palapa, and there are small palapas with individual tables on the beach. For a light lunch, consider the deli-meat platter or a selection of Italian cheeses. There are also five clean, ocean-view guest rooms available. *Domicilio Conocido 958/107–8135 www.posadalatermita.com No credit cards No lunch.*

MAZUNTE

$$ ECLECTIC **El Armadillo**. It's in a jungly area of Mazunte, on a closed street and so hidden away that you could easily pass right by. But do make an effort to come here, even if you have to stop and ask for directions. The food at this restaurant—owned by Betty (from France) and Raúl (from Mexico City)—is a surprise. Cold beet soup with ginger and fresh fish fillet with a seafood-and-bacon sauce are standouts, as is the fresh-baked bread (you can get it to go). The restaurant also serves as an art gallery, with paintings covering the walls and a sizable sculpture collection. El Armadillo is a great place to wrap up your day, sipping wine on the patio surrounded by nature and art. *Callejon del Armadillo s/n, Camino a la Playa Rinconcito, Playa Mazunte No phone MC, V.*

WHERE TO STAY

ZIPOLITE

$–$$ **El Alquimista**. The Mediterranean-style bungalows are on a hillside at the extreme end of the beach and just steps from the sand. Each has a terrace with a lovely ocean view and a hammock. Rooms are tastefully furnished with beige linens, floral pillows, and rustic wooden furniture. The restaurant serves Mediterranean foods including pizzas from a wood-burning stove and grilled meats. Note that the beach in front of the hotel is popular among nudists. **Pros:** great location; comfortable rooms. **Cons:** pricier than other places; nudist beach not everyone's cup of tea. *Calle del Amor 94 958/587–8961 www.el-alquimista.com 16 bungalows In-room: a/c (some), no phone. In-hotel: laundry service, Wi-Fi hotspot MC, V.*

$$$ **La Loma Linda**. Yoga instructor Bridgette Longueville's escapist hotel has rustic yet modern rooms with private open-air showers. The spacious patios have hammocks and are like a second room. Yoga classes, open to the public, are held most mornings at 9:30. **Pros:** excellent beach views from rooms and restaurant; private patios. All rooms here are no-smoking. **Cons:** lots of stairs on the property; few on-site amenities. *Domicilio Conocido No phone www.lalomalinda.com 8 rooms In-room: no TV, Wi-Fi. In-hotel: restaurant, Wi-Fi hotspot No credit cards.*

SAN AUGUSTINILLO

$$ **Cabañas Punta Placer**. All the bungalows at this small hotel have beautiful ocean views and well thought-out decorative details like stone floors in the bathrooms and colorful hammocks on private terraces. The buildings themselves are arranged like a small village on the beach, and there's a small restaurant, where Claire and David, the French couple who run the place, make you feel right at home. **Pros:** on the

beach; walking distance to everything. **Cons:** no pool; no phone, making it difficult to contact. ✉ *Domicilio Conocido* ☎ *No phone* 🌐 *www.puntaplacer.com* *8 rooms* *In-room: safe, Wi-Fi. In-hotel: restaurant* ▭ *No credit cards.*

$$–$$$ **Casa Pan de Miel.** The elegant French Mediterranean–style rooms are spacious and thoughtfully equipped with everything from small kitchens to Wi-Fi. The lounge and restaurant, under a big palapa, have cushy sofas and hammocks, and the small infinity pool overlooks the ocean. Note that the hotel is a challenging (read: hilly) 20-minute walk, or about a third of a mile, west of San Agustinillo. Also because of its cliffside location, children under 18 aren't allowed. **Pros:** comfortable rooms; great restaurant; private. **Cons:** pricey; public spaces feel a little tight; somewhat isolated location. ✉ *Cerrada del Museo de la Tortuga* ☎ *958/584–3509* 🌐 *www.casapandemiel.com* *8 rooms* *In-room: safe, kitchen, refrigerator, Wi-Fi. In-hotel: restaurant, pool, no kids under 18* ▭ *MC, V.*

MAZUNTE

¢ **Posada Ziga.** On a cliff above the beach, this hotel is made up of three buildings with simply furnished rooms. Some rooms have a nice ocean view and a private bathroom. For a $10–$20 discount, choose one of the six rooms with a shared bathroom. These rooms are some of the least expensive around, making the hotel really popular with young people. The small restaurant on an open-air deck overlooking the beach serves Oaxacan dishes. **Pros:** great price; nice ocean views. **Cons:** no TV or a/c; long stairway to beach. ✉ *Domicilio Conocido* ☎ *No phone* 🌐 *www.posadaziga.com* *14 rooms, 8 with bath* *In-room: no a/c, no TV. In-hotel: restaurant* ▭ *No credit cards.*

7

PUERTO ÁNGEL

9 km (5.5) east of Zipolite, 81 km (50 mi) southeast of Puerto Escondido, 48 km (30 mi) west of Huatulco.

The state's leading seaport 100 years ago, Puerto Ángel is today simply a tiny town on a small, somewhat buggy bay. Most hotels are away from the beach, either tucked into a canyon or perched above the bay. The town is a good base for visiting smaller communities like Mazunte, as it has a few more services (including ATMs), though not many. The beaches in town are unspectacular; there are really alluring beaches in nearby coves, and it's easy to hire water taxis to explore them.

GETTING HERE AND AROUND

Puerto Ángel, east of Zipolite, is easily reached by car or taxi from Huatulco via Highway 200. Frequent buses connect Puerto Escondido, Puerto Ángel, and Huatulco, making a pit stop at the inland town of Pochutla. Taxis in Pochutla make the 20-minute ride to Puerto Ángel. Some bus and van service from Oaxaca City takes Highway 175 directly to Pochutla, but this trip is far less comfortable than taking first-class service on longer routes to Puerto Escondido or Huatulco.

BEACHES

Playa La Boquilla. About 2 km (1½ mi) east of Puerto Ángel, 400-foot-long La Boquilla can be reached by a dirt road from Highway 200 (recommended only if you have a rugged vehicle), but it's better to come by boat from Puerto Ángel. All boats are privately run, so prices vary. That said, $12 for the 20-minute ride is typical. Shallow and clear water make this a good spot for snorkeling as well as swimming. There are few services on this beach, though there's a restaurant that's open during high season.

Playa Panteón. The most popular swimming and sunning beach in Puerto Ángel proper, this 660-foot-long, brown-sand beach has calm, waveless water, which makes it great for swimmers and children. A walkway past the oceanfront *panteón* (cemetery) links it with Playa Principal, Puerto Angel's main beach. Ask about boat services at the informal restaurants along the beach.

Playa Principal. This is Puerto Ángel's main beach, closest to the town. It's busy, starting in the morning when fishing boats arrive with the day's catch. There are restaurants running along the beach.

WHERE TO EAT AND STAY

$$–$$$ **Bahía de la Luna.** This collection of thatch-roof bungalows is the only accommodation on beautiful La Boquilla beach, a water-taxi ride away from Puerto Ángel. There's no hot water and limited electricy, but rooms, though simple, are a tad more chic than those at some hotels in Mazunte or Zipolite. Note that some units are on the hillside, and paths are steep. There's nothing to do here but lie on the beach or snorkel, but the hotel can arrange tours to natural areas and nearby beaches and towns. **Pros:** on a superb beach with abundant marine life; quiet location. **Cons:** need to take expensive water-taxi ride to and from Puerto Ángel; no other facilities on beach; basic accommodations; kind of pricey in high season. ✉ *Playa la Boquilla* ☎ *958/589–5020* 🌐 *www.bahiadelaluna.com* *11 bungalows* *In-room: no a/c, kitchen (some), no phone, no TV. In-hotel: restaurant* *No credit cards.*

$–$$ **La Buena Vista.** The rooms on the top level of this hillside hotel have great bay views and the best breezes. Some have balconies; others have terraces hung with colorful hammocks. None have hot water or much of anything that could be called an amenity; all beds have mosquito netting. The third-floor restaurant has one of the most dependable kitchens in town, although the service lags when there's a crowd. Most rooms are accessed by climbing lots of stairs. **Pros:** nice views; inviting rooms; lovely pool area. **Cons:** steep stairs; away from beach. ✉ *Calle la Buena Compañía* ☎ *958/584–3104* 🌐 *www.labuenavista.com* *23 rooms* *In-room: no a/c, no phone, no TV. In-hotel: restaurant, pool* *AE, D, MC, V.*

HUATULCO

277 km (172 mi) south of Oaxaca City, 111 km (69 mi) east of Puerto Escondido, 48 km (30 mi) east of Puerto Ángel.

Development in the breathtaking Bahías de Huatulco (Bays of Huatulco) continues to march forward. Four of the nine bays have been developed, but only Bahía Tangolunda, with its golf course and luxury hotels, has the look of a resort.

If you have a car, you can drive to one of several undeveloped bays and play Robinson Crusoe to your heart's content. Boat tours are a good way to explore. Standard four- to eight-hour trips—depending on how many bays you visit—might include a lunch of freshly caught fish. Fishing, diving, and snorkeling tours visit the beaches and reefs.

TAKE A TOUR

Bahías Plus (✉ *Calle Carrizal 704, La Crucecita* ☎ *958/587-0932* 🌐 *www.bahiasplus.com*) offers tours to Puerto Ángel ($25) and coffee plantations ($45) and bay cruises ($30). **Paraíso Huatulco** (✉ *Calle Ceiba 202, La Crucecita* ☎ *958/587-2878* 🌐 *www.paraisohuatulco.com* ✉ *Barceló Hotel, Blvd. Benito Juárez, Bahía Tangolunda* ☎ *958/581-0051*) has daylong bay cruises ($20), four-wheeler tours ($45), coffee plantation tours ($40), and overnight tours to Oaxaca City by bus or air ($550). Prices are slightly higher at the Barceló branch.

GETTING HERE AND AROUND

Aeropuerto Bahias de Huatulco (HUX) is 16 km (10 mi) from Bahía Tangolunda. Continental Express flies from Houston. Otherwise, all domestic connections go through Mexico City.

By car from Oaxaca City, take Carretera 190 to Salina Cruz, where you pick up Carretera 200 to Huatulco. The trip takes seven to eight hours. First-class buses follow the same route and depart from Oaxaca City daily. Driving to Puerto Escondido takes about two hours.

Taxis are plentiful, especially in La Crucecita, and start at $4 from the center of town to the beaches. Many major car-rental agencies have kiosks at the airport, though renting a car isn't necessary unless you want to explore beaches outside of town. Scooter rental is a popular alternative, and there are vendors near the large resorts.

ESSENTIALS

Airlines **Continental** (☎ *01800/900-5000 toll-free in Mexico*).

Medical Assistance **Central Médica Huatulco** (✉ *CMH, Av. Flamboyan 205* ☎ *958/587-0104*). **Police** (☎ *958/587-1180*).

Rental Cars **Plaza Huatulco Rent** (✉ *Blvd. Benito Juárez s/n, at Hotel Plaza Huatulco, Bahía Tangolunda* ☎ *958/581-0371*).

Visitor Info **Huatulco Tourism Office** (✉ *Blvd. Benito Juárez s/n, Bahía Tangolunda* ☎ *958/581-0176* 🌐 *www.baysofhuatulco.com.mx*).

EXPLORING

La Crucecita. It's off Carretera 200 and is the place in Huatulco that most closely resembles a real Mexican town. The central plaza has a church whose interior is covered with naive frescoes; on the ceiling is a fresco of what locals claim is the world's largest Madonna. You can dine, hang out at a bar or sidewalk café, and browse in boutiques. You'll also find banks, a modern bus station, and Internet cafés here.

7

BEACHES

Bahía Chahué. The beach parking lot has a lookout point, and the marina has 88 slips, though other services aren't yet in place. You'll find a swimming pool, changing rooms, a restaurant, and shaded lounge chairs at the public beach club. Though several hotels, shops, and restaurants (serving mostly lunch and dinner) are near the main road, Boulevard Benito Juárez, the area is still being developed. Internet access isn't yet available anywhere. The beach itself has a negative reputation: people reportedly drown here more than conditions seem to warrant. **Xquenda Spa** (⊠ *Blvd. Bugambilia s/n, Bahía Chahué* ☎ *958/583–4448*) has a lap pool, tennis court, and gym, and provides massages, facials, and some spa treatments.

Bahía Santa Cruz. This bay was once home to a 30-family fishing community until development forced everyone to move elsewhere. Today the bay is a nice spot for swimming and snorkeling, although Jet Skis make a lot of noise on busy weekends and holidays. You can arrange boat tours and fishing trips at the marina. Dine on the beach, mingle with the locals in the central zócalo, or sip a cool drink or cappuccino in Café Huatulco, right in the middle of the plaza where the traditional kiosk should be.

Bahía Tangolunda. The Huatulco of the future is most evident here, where the poshest hotels are in full swing and the sea—in high season—is abob with sightseeing *lanchas* (small motorboats), kayaks, and sailboats. The site was chosen by developers because of its five magnificent beaches. Although there's a small complex with shops and restaurants across from the entrance to the Barceló hotel on Boulevard Benito Juárez, most of the shopping and dining is in the towns of Santa Cruz and La Crucecita, each about 10 minutes from the hotels by taxi or bus. By law, all beaches in Mexico are public, but Tangolunda hoteliers are notorious for shooing away nonguests from their stands of sand.

Playa Entrega. If you're looking for the best fishing and water sports in the area, head to this beach, west of Bahía Santa Cruz, where dozens of fishermen aren't shy about offering their services from the moment you set foot in the sand. It's a great place to go out on a fishing boat in the early morning (negotiate a price with one of the captains on the beach); when you come back to Playa Entrega, have one of the little seafood restaurants on the beach, such as Restaurant Arrecife, cook up your catch. Lobster fishing is another option, as are snorkeling and kayaking.

WHERE TO EAT

LA CRUCECITA AND BAHÍA SANTA CRUZ

$$$ SEAFOOD ★ ✕ **Doña Celia**. At this waterfront restaurant you can sit at a table right on the beach and enjoy the house specialty: lobster burritos. Chef-owner Celia Enríquez Gutiérrez's ceviche is absolutely divine. The service is friendly and informal—this place is more popular with locals than tourists, and as such, has a more authentic character than some of the competition in the area. ⊠ *Bahía Santa Cruz* ☎ *958/587–0128* ▭ *MC, V.*

$ SEAFOOD ✕ **El Pata**. Just two blocks from the plaza, this local favorite family restaurant serves traditional seafood dishes at reasonable prices. Try one of the seafood cocktails, perhaps with shrimp or with shrimp, octopus, and oysters. El Pata is also one of the few sit-down restaurants that serves dinner after 10 PM. ✉ *Chacah 204, La Crucecita* ☎ *958/587–2156* ▭ *MC, V.*

WORD OF MOUTH

"The beaches in Huatulco are probably the most beautiful and dramatic by far. Gorgeous views with rocky coastline and then sandy beaches. Some of the beaches are small and deserted and some are larger and more crowded." —luv2travelnmex

$$ ECLECTIC **✕ L'échalote.** The restaurant in the Posada Edén Costa is widely considered the best in Huatulco. Its menu is certainly more varied than the competition, with French, Mexican, Italian, and Mediterranean dishes—all well prepared. The *huachinango en crema de poro* (red snapper with a creamed leek sauce) is wonderful, the almond-paste ice cream memorable. ✉ *Calle Zapoteco s/n, Bahía de Chahué* ☎ *958/587–2480* ▭ *MC, V* ⊙ *Closed Mon.*

$ MEXICAN **✕ Los Portales.** As one of the more authentic taquerías in a resort town catering to visitors, Los Portales serves traditional tacos as well as some more interesting options. Tacos *al pastor* are tasty, especially when accompanied by one of the tropical drinks from the menu. You can have a sit-down meal here after 10 PM, a rarity in the area. ✉ *Av. Bugambilia, at corner of Calle Guamuchil, La Crucecita* ☎ *958/587–0070* ⊕ *www.losportaleshuatulco.com* ▭ *MC, V.*

$$ MEXICAN **✕ Onix.** A second-story restaurant that overlooks the activity of La Crucecita's zócalo, Onix is emblematic of the high-concept development that has sprung up around Huatulco to complement its luxury resorts. Options on the ambitious menu include filet mignon with chipotle on a fried tortilla or tostadas with smoked oysters, chipotle, and guacamole. The wine selection is better than average. ✉ *Av. Bugambilia 603, at Calle Guamuchil, La Crucecita* ☎ *958/587–0520* ▭ *MC, V.*

$$ MEXICAN **✕ Sabor de Oaxaca.** This narrow, open-fronted but under-ventilated restaurant across from the main plaza is popular with Mexican tourists. Learn the ABCs of Oaxacan cooking by trying one of the massive sampler plates (enough for two or three people). You can go as far as cactus soup or crunchy grasshoppers (in season, which, by the way is generally consider to be May through July). The pork *enmolada* (in a chili sauce) is a showstopper, gently spicy and deeply marinated. It's open until 11 PM, so this is a good place for a late-night snack. ✉ *Calle Guamuchil 206, La Crucecita* ☎ *958/587–0060* ▭ *MC, V.*

BAHÍA TANGOLUNDA

$$$ ECLECTIC **✕ Azul Profundo.** Sky-high prices are justified by the sky of stars above your head as you dine at this romantic bay-side restaurant. Hanging lanterns, a glowing blue pool, and a sleek lounge complete the scene. The menu is ambitious and international, highlighting lobster, shrimp, and fish tartare. Reservations are essential, but you can also come just for a cocktail without a reservation. ✉ *Camino Real Zaashila, Calle Benito Juárez* ☎ *958/583–0300* ✍ *Reservations essential* ▭ *AE, DC, MC, V.*

$$ MEXICAN **✕ Don Porfirio.** You can grab a table in the dining room or out on the covered patio near the busy road. There's a good variety of Mexican dishes, such as grasshoppers fried with chili and garlic, as well as

7

less challenging dishes such as tequila-marinated kebabs. The show is as important as the food here: waiters often dress in costumes, and are encouraged to joke and interact with diners. Steaks and shrimp are cooked on the outdoor grill, and several dishes arrive flaming at your table. Because it's popular with groups, it can be noisy, but it's almost always fun. ✉ *Calle Benito Juárez s/n, Zona Hotelera Tangolunda, across from Dreams Huatulco Resort & Spa* ☎ *958/581–0001* ▭ *MC, V.*

WHERE TO STAY

LA CRUCECITA AND BAHÍA SANTA CRUZ

$$$ **Hotel Villas Coral.** All the rooms here have private terraces with ocean views, and Playa Arrocito, about a five-minute walk from the hotel grounds, is calm and good for swimming. The hotel itself seems to breathe a really calm vibe. Rooms are clean and comfortable, albeit with simple furnishings and linens. The excellent service, the shady pool, the tasty restaurant, and the yoga classes make this a great place to relax. **Pros:** it is in the middle of La Crucecita; near restaurants. **Cons:** far from the beach. ✉ *Paseo el Arrocito Lote 8, Manzana 2* ☎ *958/581–0500* 🌐 *www.hotelvillascoral.com* *16 rooms, 6 suites, 4 villas* *In-room: kitchen (some), refrigerator (some). In-hotel: restaurant, pool, laundry service, Internet terminal, Wi-Fi hotspot* ▭ *MC, V.*

$ Fodor's Choice ★ **Misión de los Arcos.** Everything about this hotel is luxurious—except for the rates. Each room of this Mediterannean-style hotel is different, but all have adobe-style rounded walls, a soothing beige-on-bone color scheme, and a minimalist approach to interior decoration. The honeymoon suite has a huge garden patio filled with plants, a wrought-iron table and chairs, and a fountain. The youthful owner works out with half the town in the popular on-site gym. He and his wife cater to their guests, many of them Mexican businesspeople, in a way that virtually guarantees return business. The restaurant is the toast of the town. **Pros:** great value; air-conditioned rooms; friendly staff. **Cons:** away from the beaches; rooms are a little sparse; some bathrooms are small. ✉ *Calle Gardenia 902, La Crucecita* *Mision de los Arcos, Calle Gardenia 902, La Crucetita, Huatulco 70989* ☎ *958/587–0165* 🌐 *www.misiondelosarcos.com* *14 rooms* *In-room: no phone, Wi-Fi. In-hotel: restaurant, pool, gym, laundry service* ▭ *AE, MC, V.*

BAHÍA TANGOLUNDA

$$$ **Barceló Huatulco Beach.** You'll have bay views from the balcony of any room in this resort, which spans the shore of gorgeous Bahía Tangolunda. Red-tile roofs on the low-slung buildings add a touch of Mediterranean elegance. This is an all-inclusive, so you'll have free use of most water-sports equipment; dive masters are on hand with all the necessary equipment, for an extra charge. With an excellent beachfront location near the golf course, many activities for kids and adults, and large meeting rooms, this hotel is attractive for both families and corporate events; you'll find you have no reason to leave. At night candles flicker in the glamorous Casa Real restaurant. The food is northern Italian; reservations are essential. **Pros:** great location; lots of amenities; quiet and laid-back. **Cons:** property is a bit dated; staff can be hard to find. ✉ *Blvd. Benito Juárez* ☎ *958/581–0055* 🌐 *www.barcelohuatulco.*

com *346 rooms, 5 suites* *In-room: refrigerator, safe, DVD (some), Wi-Fi (some). In-hotel: 4 restaurants, room service, bars, tennis courts, pools, gym, beachfront, diving, water sports, children's programs (ages 5–12), laundry service, parking (free), Internet terminal, Wi-Fi hotspot* *AE, MC, V* *AI.*

$$–$$$ ★ **Camino Real Zaashila.** The brilliant blue free-form pool with built-in lounge chairs around its rim creates an irresistible centerpiece for this gleaming white resort. Rooms are an adept mix of modern amenities and more rustic-looking elements like hand-painted bathroom shelves and armoires. Waterfalls punctuate the property's 27 acres, and a dreamy nature walk runs from one end of it to the other. The elegant yet casual Chez Binni looks out past the pool to the ocean. Even closer to the water is Azul Profundo, which sits right on the beach. **Pros:** splendid beach; lovely pool area; lush grounds. **Cons:** fewer amenities than bigger resorts; some rooms are noisy; attracts tour groups. *Blvd. Benito Juárez Lote 5* *958/581–0460; 01800/901–2300 toll-free in Mexico; 800/722–6466* *www.caminoreal.com/zaashila* *120 rooms, 28 suites* *In-room: refrigerator, safe. In-hotel: 3 restaurants, room service, bars, tennis court, pools, beachfront, Internet terminal, parking (free)* *AE, DC, MC, V* *CP.*

$$$$ **Dreams Huatulco Resort & Spa.** The emphasis at this resort is on non-stop activity; there's a kids' club to entertain the youngsters while the grown-ups play tennis or relax by the pool. The rate includes most outdoor activities—a good deal if you want to do more than just work on your tan. The light-filled guest rooms have plenty of space in which to spread out. During the low season, Dreams allows nonguests to spend the day or evening on the property—with unlimited food, drink, and activities—for a per-person rate of $90 all day. **Pros:** nice beachfront; excellent service; good for families. **Cons:** not as tranquil as other spots; a bit pricey. *Blvd. Benito Juárez 4* *958/583–0400; 800/237–3267 toll-free in North America* *www.dreamsresorts.com* *420 rooms* *In-room: DVDs, refrigerator, safe, Wi-Fi. In-hotel: 6 restaurants, room service, bars, tennis courts, pools, gym, beachfront, Internet terminal, children's programs (ages 3–12)* *AE, MC, V* *AI.*

$$–$$$ **Las Brisas.** Only the spacious, minimalist suites of this sprawling complex have balconies, but most rooms have wonderful ocean views. Divided into four different areas that are romantically named for the mountains, stars, clouds, and sea, the rooms are far from the hustle and bustle of the main building. The complex is the size of a small village, and you get around in a fleet of hotel-operated trams. And don't miss the fresh watermelon juice at any one of the several restaurants. **Pros:** nice beach; good snorkeling; great staff. **Cons:** property is considerably spread out; all-white design is boring; few rooms have balconies. *Blvd. Benito Juárez s/n* *958/583–0200 or 888/559–4329* *www.brisas.com.mx* *339 rooms, 135 suites* *In-room: refrigerator, safe. In-hotel: 4 restaurants, room service, bars, tennis courts, pools, gym, spa, beachfront, water sports, laundry service, Wi-Fi hotspot, parking (free)* *AE, MC, V.*

$$$$ ★ **Quinta Real.** This hilltop resort, with its trademark double-dome design, takes luxury to almost excessive heights. Each suite has white

leather furniture, stained concrete floors, exquisite handwoven tapestries, a hot tub, and a terrace with an ocean view. Eight corner suites have plunge pools, and a few are equipped with telescopes for dolphin- and stargazing. Golf carts take you to and from the beach, which is a long walk from the hotel. **Pros:** elegant aura; great views; pretty pool area. **Cons:** notably expensive; not directly on beach. ✉ *Blvd. Benito Juárez 2* ☎ *958/581–0428; 01800/500–4000 toll-free in Mexico; 866/621–9288* 🌐 *www.quintareal.com* *28 suites* *In-room: safe. In-hotel: 2 restaurants, bars, tennis court, pools, spa, laundry service, parking (free)* 💳 *AE, MC, V* *CP.*

NIGHTLIFE

One of the most intimate and personable bars in the area is also the oldest. **La Crema** (✉ *Av. Carrizal 503, La Crucecita* ☎ *958/587–0702 or 958/587–2182*) serves well-mixed cocktails such as the venerable mai tai. A mix of canned tunes provides the beat: rock, lounge music, ranchera, and other Mexican music. There's dancing after 10 PM.

Styled after a Miami club, **La Papaya** (✉ *Bahía Chahué* ☎ *958/583–4911*) is an enormous venue open to the stars. Patrons eat, drink, and dance while bathing-suit-clad women swim in giant aquariums up front.

Noches Oaxaqueñas (✉ *Zona Hotelera Tangolunda, at Don Porfirio restaurant* ☎ *958/581–0001*) has a folkloric show with music and dances from Oaxaca and other Mexican states.

SHOPPING

La Probadita (✉ *Bugambilia 501, at Chacah, La Crucecita* ☎ *958/587–1641* 🌐 *www.laprobadita.com.mx*) is a little store where you can buy souveniers, and try a taste of tequilas and mezcales that you can also take home with you. **Mantelería Escobar** (✉ *Av. Cocotillo 217, La Crucecita* ☎ *958/587–0532*) is a family-run workshop where you can purchase bedspreads, curtains, tablecloths, and place mats. Custom items can usually be produced in two to seven days, so plan ahead.

La Crucecita's **Mercado Municipal** (*Municipal Market* ✉ *Calle Guanacaste s/n, between Bugambilia and Carrizal, La Crucecita* ☎ *No phone*) is a fun place to shop for postcards, leather sandals, and souvenirs amid mountains of fresh produce. The **Museo de Artesanías Oaxaqueñas** (✉ *Calle Flamboyan 216, La Crucecita* ☎ *958/587–1513*) is really a store, not a museum, where you can find handicrafts produced throughout the state: woven tablecloths, chunky pottery, and colorful rugs. Artisans are occasionally on hand for demonstrations.

SPORTS AND THE OUTDOORS

FISHING

Arrange sportfishing trips with the **Sociedad Cooperativa Tangolunda** (✉ *Santa Cruz Marina* ☎ *958/587–0081*), the boat-owners' cooperative at the marina on Bahía Santa Cruz. These people are the original inhabitants of this area (they were forceably relocated when the resort was built), so they know the waters well. Prices are more competitive than those of the larger agencies. Fishing costs about $35 an hour (three-hour minimum with a maximum of four people). The group also runs bay tours for about $35 per person. It's also easy to get a fishing expedition going at Playa Entrega.

GOLF

Bahía Tangolunda's challenging 18-hole golf course, the **Campo de Golf Tangolunda** (✉ *Blvd. Benito Juárez and Blvd. Tangolunda, Bahía Tangolunda* ☎📠 *958/581–0037*), was designed by noted Mexican landscape architect Mario Schjetnan. The greens fees are $45 for 18 holes; carts rent for $23.

SCUBA DIVING

Eagle rays, green moray eels, and, in winter, gray whales are frequently spotted in 13 different dive sites near Huatulco. The average price for area dives is $45 for a one-tank dive, $75 for two tanks.

Buceo Sotavento (✉ *Flamboyant 310, Plaza Oaxaca Local 18, La Crucecita* ☎ *958/587–2166*) is operated by PADI-certified instructor Hector Lara Ocampo, who has been diving in the area for years. He offers dives, scuba certifications, snorkeling tours, and rafting trips, and he has an expertise in local fauna that can't be beat. A two-tank dive costs about $85.

The PADI-certified dive masters at **Hurricane Divers** (✉ *Bahía Santa Cruz* ☎ *958/587–1107* 🌐 *www.hurricanedivers.com*) are well regarded and specialize in services including equipment repair, diving certification, and safety courses. Night dives and multiple-day packages are also available, as well as snorkeling trips; note that they are closed on Sunday.

7

Chiapas and Tabasco

Temple of the Assumption, Cupilco, Tabasco

8

WORD OF MOUTH

One full day at the ruins in Palenque (do stop at the museum there!) is enough. You might also enjoy the waterfalls between San Cristobal and Palenque - Misol Ha, Agua Clara, and Agua Azul. Do be prepared: Parts of the road between San Cristobal and Palenque are vertiginous.

—kja

www.fodors.com/community

WELCOME TO CHIAPAS AND TABASCO

TOP REASONS TO GO

★ **Taking in mist-covered ruins:** Much of the enormous complex of Palenque has yet to be excavated, so you can see how thoroughly the jungle claimed them.

★ **A pleasant stay in a little-visited colonial town:** Lovely colonial architecture, the excellent Museo Na Bolom, and nearby San Juan Chamula make San Cristóbal de las Casas an important stop.

★ **An exotic boat trip:** Go by water up the Río Usumacinta to see the Mayan city of Yaxchilán surrounded by magnificent 100-year-old ceiba trees.

★ **The chance to see a breathtaking canyon:** Cliffs rise to 3,500 feet at their highest point in the Cañón del Sumidero.

★ **Convening with history:** Wander through the trees around massive stone heads left behind by the Olmecs at the Parque-Museo La Venta.

1 San Cristóbal de las Casas. A handsome highland town in a valley where pine forests are interspersed with vegetable fields, San Cristóbal straddles two worlds. Here indigenous women with babies tied tightly in colorful shawls share the main square with teenagers on cell phones. Graceful colonial-era buildings house shops selling DVD players.

2 Tuxtla Gutiérrez and Chiapa de Corzo. The capital of Chiapas, hard-working Tuxtla Gutiérrez, isn't a destination in itself. You're better off staying in the village of Chiapa de Corzo closer to the stunning Cañón del Sumidero.

3 The Road to Palenque. Winding through the mountains, this road leads to many interesting sights, including waterfalls, the inspiring ruins of Toniná, and small villages where people still wear traditional dress.

4 Palenque and Environs. One of the jewels of the Mayan civilization, the ancient city of Palenque sits shrouded with mist. Nearby are two other equally fascinating ruins, Bonampak and Yaxchilán. Palenque Town makes a good base for all explorations.

5 Tabasco. Tabasco has lakes, lagoons, caves, and wild rivers that surge through the jungle. Most people who visit Tabasco's capital, Villahermosa, are traveling for business (this is oil country), but the city has an excellent museum and a collection of massive Olmec heads and altars.

6 Southeastern Chiapas. One of the most beautiful parts of Mexico, Selva Lacandona has the Western Hemisphere's second-largest remaining rain forest. For centuries this has been the homeland of the Lacandón, a people descended from the Maya.

GETTING ORIENTED

Chiapas is Mexico's southernmost state. And if the villages here resemble those of the Guatemalan Highlands, it's because Guatemala lies just beyond the eastern border. To the west lies Oaxaca, and to the south is one of Mexico's last stretches of relatively undeveloped coastline. Inland, mountain roads are full of hairpin turns hugging the edges of ravines. To the north is the mostly flat, pastoral state of Tabasco.

CHIAPAS AND TABASCO PLANNER

A Little Reassurance and Advice

Although Chiapas and Tabasco are off-the-beaten path for Americans, they are not for other travelers, so you can be assured of finding the necessary travel services, such as banks, hotels, Internet cafés, and tourist offices. San Cristóbal is especially geared toward travelers. The only places you won't find such businesses are the indigenous villages. Most tourist offices will give you maps that fold up small enough to fit into a pocket or purse.

Bus and car travel throughout the region are options for exploring; use caution, try not to drive after dark, and watch out for slick roads during the rainy season. If twisting mountain roads aren't for you, air travel is an alternative, though it won't take you to the small towns or ruins. Tuxtla and Villahermosa have airports, handling predominantly domestic flights.

If you're looking for the ideal hub for exploring Chiapas, consider San Cristóbal. Whatever you do, you won't want to miss seeing surrounding ruins, notably the Mayan city of Palenque.

The Great Outdoors

If you'd rather be climbing ruins than hanging out in colonial cities, you've come to the right place. Fly to Tuxtla Gutiérrez and head first to the impressive Cañón del Sumidero. Then head over to San Cristóbal on the brand-new toll road and use it as your base for exploring the nearby villages of San Juan Chamula and Zinacantán. When you're done in San Cristóbal, start along the Road to Palenque. From your hotel in Ocosingo, you can arrange horseback-riding trips to the ruins of Toniná or you can hit the stunning jungle waterfalls of Agua Azul before landing in Palenque Town. End with a day or two at Palenque.

The Pros of Hiring a Pro

Even if you usually turn your nose up at the thought of joining a tour group, Chiapas is a place where you should reconsider. If you want to see the isolated ruins at Bonampak and Yaxchilán, it's far easier to take a tour from Palenque Town. (The nearby ruins of Palenque are another matter—there's no need to join a tour.) And if you want to see the villages near San Cristóbal, by all means book a tour with a reputable guide. Going to a village like San Juan Chamula with a local means you'll get an insider's perspective and perhaps even be invited into someone's home. If you show up alone, you may get nothing but suspicious stares.

Regional Specialties

Stopping for a bite to eat or a bit of shopping can create memorable experiences. Favorite dishes include *cochinito horneado* (smoked pork), tamales, delicious white cheese, and *pejelagarto,* a fish that makes up for its unattractive appearance with a sweet flavor. You can also spend time combing open-air markets for hats, leather goods, and embroidered cloth, not to mention beautifully crafted jewelry featuring local amber.

Safety

Although travel in the area is reasonably safe, at this writing the U.S. State Department was advising visitors to exercise caution in Chiapas because of the presence of armed civilian groups in some areas, especially rural areas east of Ocosingo. Although none of the sporadic confrontations has been near a main tourist destination, armed men did take over one guest ranch near Ocosingo in 2003. There have been no major incidents since that time, however. Review the information on the U.S. State Department Web site at *travel.state.gov/travel* for an update on the situation before you go. Always carry your tourist card and passport even on day trips throughout the region. It's best not to stay out after dark. If you're a first-time visitor, you may be more comfortable taking tours of the region—especially if you don't speak Spanish. Throughout all of Chiapas, the number to call in case of emergency is 066. Ask for an operator who speaks English.

What to Pack

Leave room in your luggage for souvenirs. Chiapas is a great place to buy crafts such as embroidered clothing, amber jewelry, and pottery. Carry your own tissue, as toilets at some of the ruins may not be fully equipped, though most are quite clean.

Money Matters

Many, though not all, hotels quote prices that already include the 17% tax. This is especially true of budget and moderately priced lodgings. Be sure to ask about this when you're quoted a price.

WHAT IT COSTS IN DOLLARS

	¢	$	$$	$$$	$$$$
Restaurants	under $5	$5–$10	$10–$15	$15–$25	over $25
Hotels	under $50	$50–$75	$75–$150	$150–$250	over $250

Restaurant prices are per person for a main course at dinner. Hotel prices are for two people in a standard double room.

How's the Weather?

In the highlands around San Cristóbal de las Casas the weather is cool and comfortable throughout the year—the average high is 20°C (68°F). Bring a sweater or jacket for the evening, as temperatures can fall drastically after the sun sets. (Men in San Juan Chamula wear woolly black cloaks to ward off the cold.) September is the peak of the rainy season, which officially starts in August and can run until early October. In the coastal lowlands, including Palenque and Villahermosa, it is always hot and humid. Temperatures peak in May and June at about 31°C (88°F). The sun is extremely strong, so make sure to bring a hat and plenty of sunblock.

Thanks to the warm weather and spectacular landscape, restaurants, cafés, and even hotel lobbies are often outdoors; if not, the doors and windows are wide open. Therefore, a comfortable and casual style reigns at most establishments, and the only rule to live by is long pants—and maybe even some repellent—for evening outings, to help protect you from hungry insects.

SAN CRISTÓBAL DE LAS CASAS

Updated by Jeffrey Van Fleet

From the looks of this thoroughly charming city you'd never know that Chiapas is one of Mexico's poorest regions or that it was the locus of the 1994 Zapatista rebellion. San Cristóbal is the perfect hub for exploring the region's towns, lakes and rivers, and archaeological sites; a smart choice would be to make this your home base for a week or longer. In addition to admiring the town's colorful facades, budget some time to visit the market, peek into a few churches, and enjoy a cup of locally grown coffee in a shady courtyard. No itinerary is complete without a trip to the indigenous villages, such as San Juan Chamula, outside of San Cristóbal.

The town's cool climate is a refreshing change from the sweltering heat of the lowlands. On chilly evenings wood smoke scents the air, curling lazily over the red-tile roofs of small, brightly painted stucco houses. The sense of the mystical here is intensified by the fog and low clouds.

San Cristóbal is laid out in a grid pattern centered on the zócalo (town square). When walking around, remember that street names change on either side of this square: Calle Francisco Madero to the east of the square, for example, becomes Calle Diego de Mazariegos to the west. The town was originally divided into *barrios* (neighborhoods), but they now blend together into a city center that's easy to negotiate.

In colonial times indigenous allies of the Spaniards were moved onto lands on the outskirts of the nascent city. Each barrio was dedicated to an occupation. There were Tlaxcala fireworks manufacturers in one part of the town and pig butchers from Cuxtitali in another. Although specific divisions no longer exist, some of the local customs have been kept alive. For example, each Saturday certain houses downtown will put out red lamps to indicate that homemade tamales are for sale.

GETTING HERE AND AROUND

The region has airports in every major city, but they mostly handle domestic flights. If you want to fly here from the United States, your best bets are the daily flights between Houston and Tuxtla Gutiérrez on Continental Express. Otherwise you're going to connect in Mexico City or another hub. Aeropuerto San Cristóbal, 15 km (9 mi) northwest of downtown, receives no commerical air traffic. ADO GL buses travel between San Cristóbal and Tuxtla many times a day; travel time is just under two hours. Chiapas is a big state, but there are few major highways. Carretera 190 goes east from Tuxtla through Chiapa de Corzo to San Cristóbal before continuing southeast to the Guatamalan border. There is, however, a brand-new toll road that links Tuxtla and San Cristóbal—it's a much quicker alternative to 190.

ESSENTIALS

Bus Contacts **ADO GL** (🌐 *www.adogl.com.mx* ✉ *Real de Guadalupe 5* ☎ *01800/702–8000*). **San Cristóbal Bus Terminal** (*Estación Cristóbal Colón* ✉ *Av. Insurgentes and Blvd. Juan Sabines Gutiérrez* ☎ *967/678–0291*).

Currency Exchange **Agencia de Cambio Lacantún** (✉ *Calle Real de Guadalupe 12-A* ☎ *967/678–2587*). **Banamex** (✉ *Av. Insurgentes 9* ☎ *967/678–0540 or 967/678–2878* 🌐 *banamex.com.mx*).

Medical Assistance **Hospital General de San Cristóbal** (✉ *Av. Insurgentes 24* ☎ *967/678–0770*). **Policía Federal de Caminos (Federal Highway Police)** (✉ *Eje Vial 2, #20* ☎ *967/678–6466*).

Visitor Info **San Cristóbal Municipal Tourist Office** (✉ *Palacio Municipal, ground fl., on zócalo* ☎ *967/678–0665*). **San Cristóbal State Tourist Office** (✉ *Av. Miguel Hidalgo 1, 2nd fl., ½ block from zócalo* ☎ *967/678–6570 or 967/678–1467*).

EXPLORING

TOP ATTRACTIONS

3 **Arco del Carmen.** San Cristóbal's first skyscraper, this elegant tower was constructed in 1597 in the *Mudejar* (Moorish) style that was popular at the time in Spain. Note the graceful way the three-story-high arch is reflected in the smaller windows on the second and third levels. The tower, which once stood alone, is now connected to the Templo del Carmen. ✉ *Av. Hidalgo, at Calle Hermanos Domínguez.*

8 **Café Museo Café.** The smell of freshly brewed coffee may be enough to draw you into this three-room museum. The well-executed displays about the local cash crop will be enough to keep you here. Chiapas is the country's biggest producer of coffee, harvesting almost as much as Oaxaca and Veracruz combined. Although indigenous people were exploited for centuries by wealthy landowners, they now produce more than 90% of the region's coffee. The captions are in Spanish, but there are handouts in English. When you're finished with the museum, head to the central café for a taste of rich *cafe chiapaneco.* ✉ *Calle María Adelina Flores 10, between Av. General Utrilla and Av. Dominguez* ☎ *967/678–7876* 🎫 *$1.80* ⏲ *Mon.–Sat. 7* AM*–10* PM.

2 **Catedral de San Cristóbal.** Dedicated to San Cristóbal Mártir (St. Christopher the Martyr), this cathedral was built in 1528, then demolished, and rebuilt in 1693, with additions during the 18th and 19th centuries. Note the classic colonial features on the ornate facade: turreted columns, arched windows and doorways, and beneficent-looking statues of saints in niches. The floral embellishments in rust, black, and white accents on the ocher background are unforgettable. Inside, don't miss the painting *Nuestra Señora de Dolores* (*Our Lady of Sorrows*) to the left of the altar, beside the gold-plated *Retablo de los Tres*

TRANSPORT TIP

To avoid bus stations altogether, take one of the Ford Econoline vans directly across from Estación Cristóbal Colón. They leave for Tuxtla and Ocosingo as soon as they fill up, which is about every 20 minutes. A trip should cost less than $4 per person. Note that these vans can be incredibly uncomfortable, as drivers pack in as many people as possible. A van designed to hold 12, for example, might depart with 16 or 18 people.

CLOSE UP

Chiapas and Tabasco Background

As early as 1000 BC, Chiapas was in the domain of the Maya, along with Guatemala, Belize, Honduras, and much of Mexico. The Maya controlled the region for centuries, constructing colossal cities like Palenque, Toniná, and Yaxchilán in Chiapas. These cities flourished in the 7th and 8th centuries, then were mysteriously abandoned. The rain forest quickly reclaimed its land.

In 1526 the Spaniards, under Diego de Mazariegos, defeated the Chiapan people in a bloody battle. Many were said to have leaped into the Cañón del Sumidero rather than submit to the invaders. Mazariegos founded a city called Villareal de Chiapa de los Españoles two years later. For most of the colonial era, Chiapas, with its capital at San Cristóbal, was a province of Guatemala. Lacking the gold and silver of the north, it was of greater strategic than economic importance.

Under Spanish rule, the region's resources became entrenched in the *encomienda* system, in which wealthy Spanish landowners forced the locals to work as slaves. "In this life all men suffer," lamented a Spanish friar in 1691, "but the Indians suffer most of all." The situation improved only slightly through the efforts of Bartolomé de las Casas, the bishop of San Cristóbal, who in the mid-1500s protested the torture and massacre of the local people; these downtrodden protested in another way, murdering priests and other *ladinos* (Spaniards) in infamous uprisings.

Mexico, Guatemala, and the rest of New Spain declared independence in 1821. Chiapas remained part of Guatemala until electing by plebiscite to join Mexico on September 14, 1824—the date is still celebrated throughout Chiapas as the Día de la Mexicanidad (Day of Mexicanization). In 1892, because of San Cristóbal's allegiance to the Royalists during the War of Independence, the capital was moved to Tuxtla Gutiérrez.

Tabasco was dominated between 1200 and 600 BC by the Olmec, who left behind the massive heads found in Villahermosa and the surrounding area. Cortés landed here in 1519, quickly subduing the local people and taking control of the region. The Maya continued to resist Spanish domination, but they were finally defeated in 1540. One of Mexico's smaller states—only 20,853 square km (12,960 square mi)—Tabasco was of minor importance until the beginning of the 20th century, when oil was discovered off its coast in the Gulf of Mexico. You won't find much evidence of Tabasco's turbulent past today; the spirit that prevails here, at least in modern Villahermosa, Tabasco's capital, is one of commerce.

Reyes (*Altarpiece of the Three Kings*); the Chapel of Guadalupe in the rear; and the gold-washed pulpit. ✉ *Calle Guadalupe Victoria at zócalo* ⏲ *Daily 9–2 and 4–7.*

5 ★ **Mercado Municipal.** This municipal market occupies an eight-block area. Best visited early in the morning, especially on the busiest day, Saturday. The market is the social and commercial center for the indigenous groups from surrounding villages. Stalls overflow with medicinal herbs, fresh flowers, and bundles of wool, as well as the best coffee in

the region for less than $3 a pound. Be careful here, as robberies are common. If you must bring your camera, ask before photographing people. ✉ *At Avs. General Utrilla, Nicaragua, Honduras, and Belisario Domínguez* ⏲ *Daily 7–3.*

7 **Museo de la Medicina Maya.** Few travelers venture here—a shame, because the Museum of Mayan Medicine is fascinating. Displays describe the complex system of medicine employed by the local indigenous cultures. Instead of one healer, they have a team of specialists who are called on for different illnesses. The most interesting display details the role of the midwife, who assists the mother and makes sure the child isn't enveloped by evil spirits. The museum is about 1 km (½ mi) north of the Mercado Municipal. Taxis are plentiful. ✉ *Av. Salomon González Blanco 10 (an extension of Av. General Utrilla)* ☎ *967/678–5438* 🌐 *www.medicinamaya.org* 🎫 *$2* ⏲ *Daily 10–5.*

6 **Museo Na Bolom.** It's doubtful whether any foreigners have made as much of an impact on San Cristóbal as did the European owners of this home-turned-library-museum-restaurant-hotel. Built as a seminary in 1891, the handsome 22-room house was purchased by Frans and Gertrude (Trudi) Blom in 1950. He was a Danish archaeologist, she a Swiss social activist; together they created the Institute for Ethnological and Ecological Advocacy, which carries on today. It got its name, Na Bolom (House of the Jaguar), from the Lacandón Maya with whom Trudi worked: Blom sounds like the Mayan word for jaguar. Both Frans and Trudi were great friends of the indigenous Lacandón, whose way of life they documented. Their institute is also dedicated to reforestation.

Fodor's Choice ★

Both Bloms are deceased, but Na Bolom showcases their small collection of religious treasures. Also on display are findings from the Classic Mayan site of Moxviquil (pronounced mosh-vee-*keel*), on the outskirts of San Cristóbal, and objects from the daily life of the Lacandón. Trudi's bedroom contains her jewelry, collection of indigenous crafts, and wardrobe of embroidered dresses. A research library holds more than 10,000 volumes on Chiapas and the Maya. Tours are conducted daily in English and Spanish at 11:30 and 4:30.

Across from the museum, the Jardín del Jaguar (Jaguar Garden) store sells crafts and souvenirs. Look for the thatch hut, a replica of local Chiapan architecture. It consists of a mass of woven palm fronds tied to branches, with walls and windows of wooden slats, and high ceilings that allow the heat to rise. The shop here sells Lacandón crafts, as well as black-and-white photos taken by Trudi.

Revenue from Na Bolom supports the work of the institute. You can arrange for a meal at Na Bolom even if you don't stay at the hotel. In addition, the staff is well connected within San Cristóbal and can arrange tours to artisans' co-ops, villages, and nature reserves that are off the beaten path. ✉ *Av. Vicente Guerrero 33, at Calle Comitán* ☎ *967/678–1418* 🌐 *www.nabolom.org* 🎫 *Museum $3.50, tour $4.50* ⏲ *Daily 10–6. Tours daily 4:30, library weekdays 1–4, store Mon.–Sat. 10–6.*

10 **Museo Sergio Castro.** Passing by this slightly ramshackle colonial-era house, you'd never guess it was one of the city's best museums. It's also

★

8

TRAVEL BY TOUR

Gabriela Gudiño Gual (☎ *967/678-4223*) is a reliable private tour guide who specializes in history and indigenous peoples. Participants travel by van to local villages.

iPod Tours (☎ *967/631-6367* 🌐 *www.ipodtours.com.mx* ⏲ *Daily 9–2, 5–8*) provides travelers a free iPod loaded with information on self-guided walking tours, and a map. Note that for the moment you don't have to pay, since they are just beginning to promote their services, but you will need to leave your passport in exchange for the iPod. In the future, they will charge, but there's no word yet on exactly how much or when.

Otisa Travel Agency (☎ *967/678-1933* 🌐 *www.otisatravel.com*) gives daily guided tours to the Cañón del Sumidero, Palenque, Yaxchilán, and Bonampak. Horseback-riding trips are also available.

Pepe Santiago (☎ *967/678-1418*), a Lacandón native associated with Museo Na Bolom since childhood, leads tours daily to San Juan Chamula, Zinacantán, and San Nicolás Buenavista. (Pepe's name is a veritable ticket to acceptance in the more remote regions of Chiapas.) The group leaves Museo Na Bolom promptly at 10 AM (they suggest arriving at 9:45) and returns around 3; it's well worth the $20 per person price. Pepe's sister, Teresa Santiago Hernández, also leads tours.

Raúl and Alex (☎ *967/678-3741 or 967/678-9141*) really know their stuff; their tours leave every day at 9:30 AM from the cross in front of the cathedral in the zócalo, returning around 2 for $15. You'll visit San Juan Chamula and Zinacantán; the cultural commentary is particularly insightful.

Transportadora Turística Trotamundos (☎ *967/678-7021* 🌐 *www.turisticatrotamundos.com*) is an experienced tour provider that hosts daily tours from San Cristóbal de las Casas to the Cañón del Sumidero, as well as tours to sites including Palenque and Bonampak.

Turísitica del Grijalva (☎ *961/600-6402*) has boat tours and tours through the Cañón del Sumidero area that last from 2 to 2½ hours and cost $15 per person.

Viajes Chinkultik (☎ *967/678-0957*) has trips around the city and beyond, but the company's three-day trip to Laguna Miramar is especially recommended. All food, transportation, tents, and even porters (it's a three-hour walk to the lake) are included in the price of $200 per person. They can also tailor tours to your available time and interests.

one of the hardest to get into—you need to call ahead for an appointment. But the effort is well worth it. Sergio Castro's collection of colorful clothing from the villages surrounding San Cristóbal is unparalleled. He explains how different factors—geography, climate, even the crops grown in a certain area—influenced how locals dressed. In explaining their dress, he is explaining their way of life. Each ribbon hanging from a hat, each stitch on an embroidered blouse has a meaning. Castro has spent a lifetime working with indigenous peoples; he currently runs a clinic to treat burn victims. Many of the ceremonial costumes were given to him as payment for his work in the communities. Castro gives

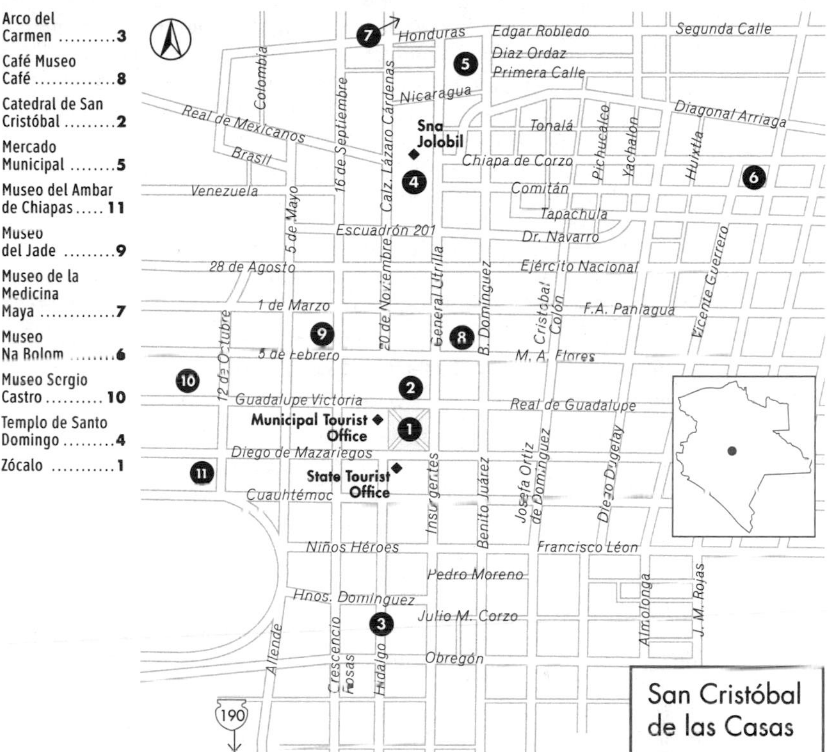

tours in English, Spanish, Italian, and French. ✉ *Calle Guadalupe Victoria 38* ☎ *967/678–4289* 🌐 *www.yokchij.org* *Donation suggested* ⏲ *Call for an appointment.*

4 **Templo de Santo Domingo.** This three-block-long complex houses a church, a former monastery, a regional history museum with a great deal to see, and the Templo de la Caridad (Temple of the Sisters of Charity). A two-headed eagle—emblem of the Hapsburg dynasty that once ruled Spain and its American dominions—broods over the pediment of the church, which was built between 1547 and 1569. The pink stone facade (which needs a good cleaning) is carved in an intensely ornamental style known as Baroque Solomonic: saints' figures, angels, and grooved columns overlaid with vegetation motifs abound. The interior has lavish altarpieces, an exquisitely fashioned pulpit, a sculpture of the Holy Trinity, and wall panels of gilded, carved cedar—one of the precious woods of Chiapas that centuries later lured Tabasco's woodsmen to the highlands surrounding San Cristóbal. At the complex's southeast corner you'll find the tiny, humble Templo de la Caridad, built in 1715 to honor the Immaculate Conception. Its highlight is the finely carved altarpiece. Indigenous groups from San Juan Chamula often light candles and make offerings here. (Do *not* take photos of the Chamulas.)

★ The Ex-Convento de Santo Domingo, adjacent to the Santo Domingo church, now houses **Sna Jolobil**, an indigenous cooperative that sells local weavings of a high quality that you won't find elsewhere. These wall hangings and other articles are truly of museum quality, and are priced accordingly. The shop is open Monday–Saturday 9–2 and 4–6.

The small **Centro Cultural de los Altos** (*Highlands Cultural Center* ☎ *967/678–1609*), also part of the complex, has a permanent exhibition of historical items and documents related to San Cristóbal and the surrounding villages. With the price of admission you can wander around the courtyards of the old monastery. It's open daily 9–6; closed Monday. Admission is $4.10, or free on Sunday. ✉ *Av. 20 de Noviembre s/n, near Calle Guatemala.*

NEED A BREAK?

On a block closed to traffic, La Casa de Elisa (✉ *Av. Hidalgo 11* ☎ *967/674-0880*) is one of the few cafés with sidewalk seating. You're just a stone's throw from the main square and the coffee's great.

1 **Zócalo**. The square around which this colonial city was built has in its center a gazebo used by marimba musicians most weekend evenings at 8. You can have a coffee on the ground floor of the gazebo; expect to be approached by children and women selling bracelets and other wares. Surrounding the square are a number of 16th-century buildings, some with plant-filled central patios. On the facade of the Casa de Diego de Mazariegos, now the Hotel Santa Clara, are a stone mermaid and lions that are typical of the plateresque style—as ornate and busy as the work of a silversmith. The yellow-and-white neoclassical Palacio Municipal (Municipal Palace) on the square's west side was the seat of the state government until 1892. Today it houses a few government offices, including the municipal tourism office. ✉ *Between Avs. General Utrilla and 20 de Noviembre and Calles Diego de Mazariegos and Guadalupe Victoria.*

WORTH NOTING

11 **Museo del Ambar de Chiapas**. Next to the graceful Ex-Convento de la Merced, this museum has exhibits showing how and where amber is mined, as well as its function in Mayan and Aztec societies. You'll see samples of everything from fossils to recently quarried pieces to sculptures and jewelry. Labels are in Spanish only; ask for an English-language summary. The volunteer staff can explain how to distinguish between real amber and fake. ✉ *Plazuela de la Merced, Calle Diego de Mazariegos s/n, Col. Centro* ☎ *967/678–9716* 🌐 *www.museodelambar.com.mx* 🎫 *$2* 🕒 *Tues.–Sun. 10–2 and 4–7.*

9 **Museo del Jade**. Jade was prized as a symbol of wealth and power by Olmec, Teotihuacán, Mixtec, Zapotec, Maya, Toltec, and Aztec nobility, and this museum shows jade pieces from different Mesoamerican cultures. The most impressive piece is a reproduction of the sarcophagus lid from Pakal's tomb, at Palenque. ✉ *Av. 16 de Septiembre 16, Col. Centro* ☎ *967/678–1121* 🎫 *$3* 🕒 *Mon.–Sat. 9 AM–9:30 PM, Sun. 9–5.*

WHERE TO EAT

$ STEAKHOUSE **Balam Centro**. This steak house and bar, open from 2 PM until midnight, serves Mexican food in a casually elegant environment. The decor might make you feel that you're in New York or San Francisco. Tables have comfortable, cushioned chairs, the walls are decorated with abstract art, and the strong lighting on the paintings is what gives light to the whole restaurant. Tables are covered with simple white tablecloths. The *jugo de carne* (a savory beef broth) and the *mollejas de res* (beef sweetbread) are great options. Save room for the Brie-and-blackberry dessert. It's a mixture of lightly fried cheese and fresh blackberries and is a delicious end to the meal. *Andador Miguel Hidalgo 1-A, Col. Centro 967/631–6728 MC, V.*

$$ MEXICAN **El Fogón de Jovel**. El Fogón de Jovel, spread across a lovely colonial courtyard, strikes a balance: it caters to tourists but is still popular with locals. Order the *parrillada chiapaneca* for a sampling of regional specialties of Chiapas. They also serve a large selection of tamales, such as the *tamal untado,* which is stuffed with chicken and mole. In keeping with local ways, they serve a margarita made with *posh* (the local firewater). *Av. 16 de Septiembre 11, Col. Centro 967/678–1153 www.fogondejovel.com No credit cards.*

$ MEXICAN **El Titanic**. The name "Titanic" may refer to the amount of food you'll get at this restaurant on the edge of the city. Sit down and just say "surtido," and you'll be brought a sampling of obscure local specialties, often including unusual parts of the pig. The food doesn't stop coming. You'll enjoy multiple courses in rapid succession, ranging from lengua (tongue) to the more pedestrian pollo en mole (chicken in mole). The out-of-the-way location has kept the place supremely local (you'll want to go by car or taxi), and you'll probably be the first foreign visitor in weeks. *Calle Tabasco 1, Barrio de San Ramón 967/678–4972 No credit cards.*

8

$ MEXICAN ★ **Emiliano's Moustache**. It's named for revolutionary hero Emiliano Zapata, which explains why sombreros and rifles are the main decorations. The place is filled with locals, who appreciate the good-natured kitsch, which sometimes includes a sequin-clad entertainer. The tortillas here are made fresh by hand throughout the day, so the taco platters are especially good (try one of the big combinations, or the regional specialties on the table tents). It's a good place to stop for lunch (there are cheap specials), or late in the evening (the dining room is open until 1 AM). Take a seat under the huge wrought-iron chandelier or in the dark upstairs bar. *Av. Crescencio Rosas 7, at Calle Diego de Mazariegos, Col. Centro 967/678–7246 MC, V.*

$ MEXICAN **Expendio de Café Fino**. This small café, which is just across the street from the main plaza, has some outdoor seating under its archways and a pleasant interior with high ceilings and plenty of fresh air. You can enjoy a meal here as you watch the people go by—they are open from breakfast through dinner. The *sopa de tortilla* (tortilla soup) and enchiladas are both tasty options. They sell regional fresh bread, muffins, and delicious coffee all day. *20 de Noviembre 8, Col. Centro 967/674–5783 Plaza 31 de Marzo 1, Col. Centro 967/674–0125 MC, V.*

CHIAPAS CHOW

Chiapas cuisine is influenced by the region's heritage, so many of the dishes have been around since the days of the Maya. It's not Mexico's most impressive food region, but some distinctive flavors come from such herbs as *chipilín* and a leaf called *yerba santa* (or *mumu*, as it's known by locals). Don't pass up the *cochinito horneado* (oven-baked pork) or the many local variations of tamales. Wash it all down with *atole* (a cornmeal drink).

$$ CAFÉ ✕ **La Paloma.** Cozy and relaxing, this café is inside a former home of city founder Diego de Mazariegos. But that doesn't mean it's a musty museum. It's surprisingly modern, with a curved bar surrounded by vegetation. Start with *sopa de flor de calabaza* (squash flower soup) or *ensalada de nopalitos* (cactus salad), then move on to the tongue-twisting *albóndigas enchipotladas* (meatballs in chili sauce). There's live music every night at 9:30. ✉ *Calle Hidalgo 3, ½ block south of zócalo, Col. Centro* ☎ *967/678–1547* ▭ *MC, V.*

$ CAFÉ ✕ **Madre Tierra.** In an old house with a pleasant patio, this vegetarian restaurant is a favorite of locals and tourists. Almost everything on the menu is homemade, including the daily baked bread. For breakfast, you can't miss with their muffins and fruit salad with fresh yogurt. You also can't beat the fresh pastas and pizzas or their soups and salads. Going on a day trip? You can buy pizzas, breads, muffins, and preserves to go. ✉ *Av. Insurgentes 19, Barrio de Santa Lucía* ☎ *967/678–4297* ▭ *No credit cards.*

$ ASIAN ✕ **Mayambé.** Brightly colored fabrics hang on the walls and from the rafters at this notable, if overrated, Pan-Asian restaurant. Grab a seat in the covered courtyard (sit closer to the fireplace if the night is a bit nippy). The expansive menu, which tends to overreach in places, includes the Vietnamese-style *platillo vietnamita* (tofu, shrimp, or chicken sautéed with peanuts, cashews, and bits of chili and coconut, and served with sweet coconut rice). *Mayambé* is a good option for vegetarians, who will enjoy the Indian vegetable, rice, and lentil dishes, although sticklers for authentic Thai will be sorely disappointed. Cocktails are weak and overly sweet. ✉ *Calle Real de Guadalupe 66, Col. Centro* ☎ *967/674–6278* ▭ *No credit cards.*

$$ MEXICAN ✕ **Na Bolom.** Just off the old-fashioned kitchen, this dining room looks much as it did when archaeologists Frans and Trudi Blom did their research here on San Cristóbal. Today the communal, oak dining table is shared by volunteers, artists, scholars, and travelers. A hearty breakfast is served from 7 AM to 1 PM, and a five-course dinner is served at 7 PM sharp. Don't expect much local cuisine; the menu focuses more on such rib-sticking dishes as beef stew or roasted chicken. Make sure to call several hours ahead for a reservation. ✉ *Av. Vicente Guerrero 33, at Calle Comitán, Barrio el Cerrillo* ☎ *967/678–1418* 🌐 *www.nabolom.org* ▭ *MC, V.*

¢ VEGETARIAN ✕ **Papalotl La Casa del Pan.** The scent of freshly baked bread is the first thing you'll notice, tempting you to skip the restaurant altogether and just grab a few of the warm rolls and a jar of locally made preserves. But the House of Bread serves a fabulous, if leisurely, breakfast. For lunch, try the tasty *tamales chiapanecos* (with a spicy cheese filling) or the mild chilies stuffed with corn and herbs. Round out your meal with bean soup and one of the best salads in town. ✉ *Calle Dr. Navarro 10, at Av. Belisario Domínguez, Col. Centro* ☎ *967/678–5895* 🌐 *www.casadelpan.com* 💳 *MC, V* ⏲ *Closed Mon.*

$ PIZZA ✕ **Pizzería el Punto.** The pizzas at this small, simple restaurant—half a block from the Convento de Santo Domingo—are tasty and hot out of a wood-burning oven. The margarita pizza, with gouda, chihuahua, and manchego cheeses is excellent. Save room for the moist and delicious tiramisu. ✉ *Calle Real de Guadalupe 47, Col. Centro* ☎ *No phone* 🌐 *www.pizzeriaelpunto.com* 💳 *No credit cards.*

$$ SWISS ✕ **Restaurant L'Eden.** People rave about the dishes—especially the steaks—at this chalet-style restaurant in the Hotel El Paraíso. The interior has eight candlelit tables and a cozy fireplace. Swiss delights include classic *raclette* and several different types of fondue. The service is doting but not distracting. The intimate bar is known for its creative, strong cocktails. ✉ *Calle 5 de Febrero 19, Col. Centro* ☎ *967/678–0085* 💳 *AE, MC, V.*

$ MEXICAN ✕ **TierrAdentro.** This big, airy Zapatista-affiliated café is in an interior patio. It's a great place to linger over a cup of coffee or enjoy the simple prix-fixe meal (there are plenty of vegetarian options) that includes juice, soup, a main plate, and rice. You can even check your e-mail while you're there. The restaurant is surrounded by small boutiques, including Nail Ch'en, where you can buy neat handmade blouses, and Mono de Papel, where you can find books and magazines (with some titles in English), including several titles on the Zapatista movement. You can also buy a T-shirt with the image of Subcomandante Marcos. ✉ *Calle Real de Guadalupe 24, Centro* ☎ *967/674–6766* 💳 *MC, V.*

8

WHERE TO STAY

$$ **Casa de los Arcángeles.** This small hotel is beautiful—and feels every bit as modern as it is (opened in mid-2006), though its architecture is more of a nod toward tradition. Seven suites surround the evocative open-air restaurant in the hotel's courtyard, which is candlelit by night. Rooms have shiny hardwood floors and bright colors. **Pros:** not having to deal with the problems that can be found in older; historic hotels (like shoddy plumbing). **Cons:** lacks a bit of San Cristóbal's colonial vibe. ✉ *Calle Cuauhtémoc 4, Col. Centro* ☎ *967/678–1531* 🌐 *www.casadelosarcangeles.com.mx* *7 suites* *In-room: safe, Wi-Fi. In-hotel: restaurant, room service, bar, spa* 💳 *MC, V.*

$$ Fodor's Choice ★ **Casa Felipe Flores.** Breakfast in this restored 18th-century mansion is served in a courtyard or in the antiques-filled dining room. It's such a nice way to start the day that you might find yourself lingering until it's time for lunch. David and Nancy Orr, the friendly owners, are happy to share their knowledge of San Cristóbal. Each guest room has a handsome wardrobe, a fireplace, and an old-fashioned bed with carved headboard. Bathrooms have whimsical hand-painted tiles. The view from the rooftop terrace, to which residents of the cozy and inexpensive Room 5 have access, is one of the city's best. **Pros:** well-run; wonderful view. **Cons:** rooms facing the street can be noisy. ✉ *Calle Dr.*

Felipe Flores 36, Col. Centro ☎ *967/678–3996* 🌐 *www.felipeflores.com* *5 rooms* *In-room: Wi-Fi. In-hotel: restaurant, bar, laundry service* *No credit cards* *BP.*

$$–$$$ **Casa Mexicana**. A pond filled with flowers is one of the many touches that make this hostelry in a restored colonial mansion stand out. Glass ceilings in the lobby and atrium make for beautiful lighting. A lovely newer wing across the street, also in a colonial home, has a colonnaded courtyard and large, quiet rooms painted light colors and filled with tasteful photographs of San Cristóbal. The restaurant, which surrounds a courtyard with banana trees, serves international dishes. **Pros:** pond and glass ceilings are extremely cool. **Cons:** lots of groups stay here and can be better accommodated than other guests. ✉ *Calle 28 de Agosto 1, at Av. General Utrilla, Col. Centro* ☎ *967/678–0698* 🌐 *www.hotelcasamexicana.com* *52 rooms, 2 suites* *In-room: Wi-Fi. In-hotel: restaurant, room service, bar, laundry service, parking (free)* *AE, MC, V.*

$$ **Casa Vieja**. Dating from 1740, this colonial-era house has been declared a historical monument. Graceful colonnades separate three interior courtyards. Most of the simple guest rooms have large windows overlooking the courtyard or corridors; a few rooms on the second floor have views of the mountains. The restaurant, Doña Rita, sits among the elegant columns on one of the porches. The hotel is three blocks east of the zócalo. **Pros:** fantastically historic; reasonably priced. **Cons:** service can be iffy. ✉ *Calle María Adelina Flores 27, Barrio de Guadalupe* ☎ *967/678–6868* 🌐 *www.casavieja.com.mx* *36 rooms, 4 suites* *In-room: Wi-Fi. In-hotel: restaurant, room service, bar, laundry service, parking (free)* *AE, MC, V.*

¢–$$ **Hotel El Paraíso**. High, beamed ceilings ennoble the guest rooms in this inviting late-19th-century building that once was a hospital. Most of the rooms wind around a central courtyard. For more solitude, request one of two rooms in the exterior courtyard. The lounge overlooks a plant-filled patio where breakfast is served. You're just a block from the town's shopping strip. **Pros:** good breakfasts; boutiquey character. **Cons:** rooms are fairly petite. ✉ *Calle 5 de Febrero 19, Col. Centro* ☎ *967/678–0085* 🌐 *www.hotelposadaparaiso.com* *14 rooms* *In-room: safe. In-hotel: restaurant, room service, bar, laundry service* *AE, MC, V.*

¢ **Hotel Hacienda San Cristóbal**. This intimate hotel, formerly called the Hotel Hacienda Los Morales, is made up of small orange buildings separated by stairs and plants, giving most of them a private feeling. The rooms themselves are simple, with rustic furniture, but each room comes equipped with a fireplace, and the rooftop views of the city more than make up for its simpleness. These might be the best hotel views in town. **Pros:** two blocks from downtown; great views of town rooftops. **Cons:** you'll need to take the stairs to access the hotel, more to access rooms; some rooms have better views of town and more privacy than others. ✉ *Av. Ignacio Allende 1, Col. La Merced* ☎ *967/678–1472* 🌐 *www.hotelhaciendalosmorales.com* *45 rooms* *In-room: Internet. In-hotel: restaurant, parking (free)* *No credit cards.*

$$$–$$$$ **Hotel Parador San Juan de Dios.** In San Cristóbal's oldest neighborhood, the adobe and stone building—with Spanish tiles dating from the 17th to the 19th century—that houses this hotel was originally a farm-and-wheat mill. The guest rooms are eclectically decorated with ornately framed mirrors, modern sculptures, oriental rugs, antique furniture, and Mexican colonial paintings. **Pros:** the upscale cuisine at the restaurant is excellent. **Cons:** far from downtown. ✉ *Calzada Roberta 16, Col. 31 de Mayo* ☎ *967/678–1167* 🌐 *www.sanjuandios.com* *12 rooms* *In-hotel: 2 restaurants, room service, pool, parking (free)* *AE, MC, V.*

$$ **Hotel Posada Real de Chiapas.** Striking indigenous weavings fill the hotel's rooms, which are dedicated to the theme of textiles of Chiapas. Guest rooms are quite clean, spacious, and filled with wrought-iron furniture along with tasteful, colorful weavings; some even have balconies. There's also a lovely interior patio that has been adapted for dining; it's a pleasant place to enjoy a meal and relax. **■ TIP→ Interior rooms are quieter at night, as they get less street noise. Pros:** if you enjoy indigenous art, there's no better place for you. **Cons:** some rooms are better looking than others, and some get more street noise than others, so you might have to tour a few before deciding. ✉ *Francisco Madero 19, Col. Centro* ☎ *967/678–0928 or 01800/701–3611 toll-free in Mexico* 🌐 *www.hotelchiapas.com.mx* *30 rooms, 2 suites* *In-hotel: restaurant, room service, bar, Wi-Fi hotspot, Internet terminal, parking (free)* *AE, MC, V* *CP.*

$$ ★ **Na Bolom.** The rooms here aren't just named for local indigenous communities; they are filled with pictures and books detailing those lives (and the lives of archaeologists Frans and Trudi Blom), as well as examples of their weavings and pottery. The rooms in the colonial house have touches like corner fireplaces. Na Bolom may be a 15-minute walk from the center of town, but it's so pleasant you might not want to go anywhere. Book well in advance, and ask for a room with a garden view. **Pros:** much knowledge can be garnered from a simple stay. **Cons:** it's a bit of a walk into the happening part of town. ✉ *Av. Vicente Guerrero 33, at Calle Comitán, Barrio el Cerrillo* ☎ *967/678–1418* 🌐 *www.nabolom.org* *16 rooms* *In-room: no a/c, no TV, Wi-Fi. In-hotel: restaurant, parking (free)* *AE, MC, V.*

$$ **Posada Diego de Mazariegos.** This old-fashioned hotel—really two perfectly preserved 18th-century colonial homes—has beautiful courtyards, gardens, and sunlit nooks throughout. Rooms have high ceilings and wide windows; some have fireplaces. Ask for one of the rooms that number in the 300s, which are in an older wing and have high wood-beam ceilings as well as working charcoal stoves. The bar, reached through a set of swinging doors, stocks more than 175 brands of tequila. **Pros:** rooms are simple, but many have extra touches. **Cons:** a little more care could be given to such things as the bed linens. ✉ *Calle 5 de Febrero 1, at Av. General Utrilla, Col. Centro* ☎ *967/678–0833* 🌐 *www.diegodemazariegos.com* *70 rooms, 6 suites* *In-room: Wi-Fi. In-hotel: restaurant, room service, bar, laundry service, Internet terminal, parking (free)* *AE, MC, V.*

¢ **Posada San Cristóbal.** The large rooms in this grand old building a block from the main plaza have high ceilings, antique furniture, and

8

heavy French doors. Most rooms have small balconies. Enjoy the patio, with its cheery walls, blue-and-white tiles, and white wrought-iron furniture. **Pros:** rooms are spacious. **Cons:** traffic noise. ✉ *Av. Insurgentes 3, Col. Centro* ☎ *967/678–6881* *18 rooms* *In-room: no a/c, no phone. In-hotel: restaurant, room service, bar, laundry service* ▭ *MC, V.*

$$ **San Marcos Hotel.** This hotel, opened in 2009, is a centrally located two-story hotel that's full of delightful, old-fashioned detail. The wooden floors (in some rooms), ceramic-tile flooring in public areas and balconies, folk art, and wide spaces will make your stay exceedingly comfortable. The suites, particularly Suite 203, are large enough to comfortably accommodate six people in one king size bed and two double beds. **Pros:** everything is brand-new; comfortable spaces; accessible prices (the suites are a surprising bargain). **Cons:** a few blocks walking to the downtown area. ✉ *Calle Crescencio Rosas 21, Barrio San Antonio* ☎ *967/116–0519* 🌐 *www.hotelsanmarcossc.com* *28 rooms, 4 suites* *In-room: Wi-Fi. In-hotel: restaurant, room service* ▭ *MC, V.*

NIGHTLIFE

BARS

Café Bar Revolución (✉ *Av. 20 de Noviembre at Calle Primero de Marzo, Col. Centro* ☎ *967/678–6664*) serves great breakfasts and lunches, in addition to having a number of good drink specials. Most nights see live jazz, rock, or ska performances.

Looking for a more sedate scene? Try **Casa Raíz** (✉ *Niños Héroes 8, Col. Centro* ☎ *967/674–6577*), a sophisticated bar two blocks south of the main square. The music here is jazz, and the bands put on quite a show. There's also a menu of light fare.

In Hotel Santa Clara, **Cocodrilo** (✉ *Av. Insurgentes 1, Col. Centro* ☎ *967/678–1140*) is a laid-back tavern that hosts rock and salsa bands most nights from 9:30 to midnight. Windows in the front overlook the zócalo.

Someone must have bribed the fire marshal, because **El Circo** (✉ *Av. 20 de Noviembre at Calle Primero de Marzo, Col. Centro* ☎ *No phone*) packs in more people than you'd think possible. The draw at this one-room establishment is the string of excellent rock bands.

Popular for years, **Latino's** (✉ *Calle Francisco I. Madero 23, at Av. Benito Juárez, Col. Centro* ☎ *967/678–9927* 🌐 *www.latinosclub.com*) showcases live salsa, merengue, cumbia, or other tropical music after 8 PM and until 3 AM every night but Sunday; cover is $3.

Tequila enthusiasts shouldn't miss **Posada Diego de Mazariegos's** (✉ *Calle 5 de Febrero 1, at Av. General Utrilla, Col. Centro* ☎ *967/678–0833*) Tequilazoo, which has more than 175 tequilas on hand, all served in simple shot glasses.

Salón Mundial (✉ *20 de Noviembre 7, Col. Centro* ☎ *967/678–7917*) is where young people come to listen to live jazz music; the cover is 15 pesos, and they are open until 3 AM.

CLOSE UP

A Voice of Many Voices

In the early hours of January 1, 1994, while most of Mexico was sleeping off the New Year's festivities, the Zapatista National Liberation Army (EZLN) surprised the world when it captured San Cristóbal de las Casas and several surrounding towns, demanding land redistribution and equal rights for Chiapas's indigenous peoples.

The Zapatista triumph was short-lived. The mostly Tzotzil and Tzeltal troops soon departed, and on January 12 President Carlos Salinas de Gortari called for a cease-fire. According to government figures, 145 lives were lost during the 12-day struggle. But hundreds have been killed in years of clashes between rebel supporters and paramilitary groups; thousands have been displaced.

Many factors led to the uprising. Centuries of land appropriation repeatedly uprooted Chiapas's Mayan-descended groups. Also, despite its natural resources (Chiapas provides nearly half of Mexico's electricity and has oil and gas reserves), the state's indigenous residents suffer high rates of illiteracy, malnutrition, and infant mortality.

In 1995 President Ernesto Zedillo sent troops into the Lacandón jungle to capture the Zapatista leadership, including charismatic leader Subcomandante Marcos. The ambush failed. The following year negotiations with the rebels resulted in the San Andrés Accords, which called for a constitutional amendment recognizing indigenous cultural rights and limited autonomy. President Zedillo instead pursued a policy of low-intensity warfare—often in the name of "development" or "reforestation."

The disastrous results include the massacre of 45 unarmed Zapatista supporters by paramilitary forces in the village of Acteal, Chenalho, in December 1997.

During his presidential campaign, Vicente Fox insisted that he could resolve the Zapatista conflict in 15 minutes; during his inaugural address he announced that he was ordering partial troop withdrawals and would submit legislation based on the San Andrés Accords. In turn, Marcos announced three conditions for the restoration of negotiations—further military withdrawals, the release of Zapatista prisoners, and implementation of the accords. The first two have been achieved. Fox, however, continues to be engaged in a media war with Marcos. In early 2001 a Zapatista caravan traveled to the capital to demand negotiations.

Fox, who welcomed the Zapatistas to the capital, has come under attack from members of the Institutional Revolutionary Party (PRI) as well as members of his own National Action Party (PAN). Not everyone is convinced of the Zapatistas' noble motives. In February 2003 a group of Zapatistas chased out the American owners of a guest ranch not far from the archaeological ruins of Toniná. Even though the resulting publicity continues to put a dent in tourism, the state government continues to decline to intervene, saying a heavy-handed approach would backfire. Around the same time, a group of Zapatistas reportedly detained, for a few hours, tourists on a kayaking trip along the Río Jatate. Whether these are isolated incidents or a series of ongoing events remains to be seen.

CAFÉS

With more than a dozen organic javas on the menu, it's not surprising that **La Selva Café** (✉ *Av. Crescencio Rosas 9, at Calle Cuauhtémoc* ☎ *967/678–7244*) is always filled with people. It's a big space, so there are plenty of quiet corners, and there's free Wi-Fi.

At **Namandí Café y Crepas** (✉ *Diego de Mazariegos 16/C, Col. Centro* ☎ *967/678–8054*) the coffee is local and organic, and there's free Wi-Fi.

FOLK PERFORMANCES

The elegant **Teatro Hermanos Domínguez** (✉ *Diagonal Hermanos Paniagua s/n, just outside city limits, Barrio de Fátima* ☎ *967/678–3637*) is a five-minute taxi ride from downtown, and features programs such as folkloric dances from throughout Latin America.

AMBER ADVICE

A good rule of thumb is that stores usually sell real amber, whereas street vendors commonly have the fakes, although there's some crossover. Moreover, amber that looks too perfect—a really smooth finish, uniform background, flora and fauna that are too neatly arranged—is probably fake. If you're about to drop a lot of cash on a piece and you want a foolproof test, rub the stone vigorously with a soft cloth; this should create enough static to pick up a small piece of paper.

SHOPPING

Look for the elaborately crafted textiles from communities surrounding San Cristóbal; they incorporate designs that have been around for millennia. San Cristóbal's market, although scenic, generally sells more produce than arts and crafts. The shops on Avenida General Utrilla, south of the market, have a large selection of Guatemalan goods, the price and quality of which may be lower than Mexican wares. Check merchandise carefully.

Shops are generally open Monday–Saturday 9–2 and 4–8. Indigenous women and children will often approach you on the streets with amber jewelry (mostly fake), woven bracelets, and dolls.

ARTS AND CRAFTS

The range of crafts in San Cristóbal extends far beyond those made by indigenous groups. **Arte Sandía** (✉ *Calle 20 de Agosto 6, Col. Centro* ☎ *967/678–4240*) has a wonderful array of housewares, including plates and dishes covered with the store's namesake watermelon. (It's a popular subject in this country, as the watermelon has the three colors of the Mexican flag.)

Artesanías Chiapanecas (✉ *Calle Real de Guadalupe 46C, at Av. Diego Dugelay, Col. Centro* ☎ *No phone*) has an excellent selection of embroidered blouses, *huipiles* (a kind of Mayan tunic or dress), tablecloths, and bags.

The government-run **Casa de las Artesanías** (✉ *Calle Niños Héroes s/n and Av. Hidalgo, Col. Centro* ☎ *967/678–1180*) sells wooden toys, ceramics, embroidered blouses, bags, and handwoven textiles from throughout the state. You'll also find honey, marmalade, and locally made liqueurs.

Casa Penagoes (✉ *Calle Real de Guadalupe 50, Col. Centro* ☎ *967/678–1126*) has an eye-popping collection of colorful clothing from indigenous groups.

Chocolatería Kakao Natura (✉ *Pedro Moreno 2-A, Col. Centro* ☎ *967/116–0954*) is stocked with fresh chocolates made from scratch on site (from the grinding of the cacao itself!).

El telar (✉ *Inside Hotel Rincón del Arco, Calle 28 de Agosto 5, Col. Barrio del Cerrillo* ☎ *967/678–3413*) specializes in hand-woven bed coverings, which are exquisite and unique souvenirs.

Iconos Mayas (✉ *Calle Real de Guadalupe 24, Col. Centro* ☎ *967/116 0599*) carries beautiful weavings, especially shawls, produced by the renowned El Camino, a nonprofit group that supports women weavers and their families. You can make an appointment to see a wider selection of El Camino's weavings by e-mail (✉ *elcaminodelosaltos@gmail.com*).

Perhaps the most memorable shop is **Nemizapata** (✉ *Calle Real de Guadalupe 57, Col. Centro* ☎ *967/678–7487*), which stocks crafts from local villages. Many of these communities were sympathetic to the Zapatista cause, which is reflected in the art. Most interesting are the *servietas* (cloth napkins) with hand-embroidered portraits of rebel leaders.

★ Among its excellent selection of wares, **Sna Jolobil** (✉ *Ex-Convento de Santo Domingo, Calz. Lázaro Cárdenas 42, Col. Centro* ☎ *967/678–7178*), the regional crafts cooperative of 800 weavers from 20 indigenous communities, has hand-dyed wool sweaters and tunics, embroidered pillow covers, and pre-Hispanic-design wall hangings. The name means Weaver's House in the Tzotzil language.

Talabartería (✉ *Diego Dugelay 56, Col. Revolución* ✉ *Av. Colombia 3, Col. Barrio de Mexicanos* ☎ *967/678–1258*), a small, crowded store, specializes in leather bags, hats, belts, and leather folders. You can also custom order a belt made from thick leather, a purse, or case just the right size for your iPod or cell phone.

Taller Leñateros (✉ *Calle Flavio A. Paniagua 54, Barrio de Guadalupe* ☎ *967/678–5174* ⊕ *www.tallerlenateros.com*), a unique indigenous co-op in an old colonial San Cristóbal home, sells top-quality crafts and lets you observe artisans at work. Look for handmade journals, boxes, postcards, and writing paper fashioned from plants.

BOOKS

Sharing a courtyard with several other shops, **Chilam Balam** (✉ *Casa Utrilla 3 and Calle Dr. Navarro, Col. Centro* ☎ *967/678–0486*) has travel, archaeology, and art books about Mexico. There are some titles in English. Just off the main square, **La Pared** (✉ *Av. Hidalgo 2, Col. Centro* ☎ *967/678–6367*) is popular with travelers. There are maps and guidebooks available.

Librería Soluna (✉ *Calle Real de Guadalupe 13-B, Col. Centro* ☎ *967/678–6805*) has a good selection of guidebooks, as well as English language books on history and culture in and around Chiapas.

CLOSE UP

Shopping in Chiapas

The weavers of Chiapas produce striking embroidered blouses, *huipiles*, bedspreads, and tablecloths. Other artisans create leather goods, homemade paper products, and painted wooden crosses. Lacandón bows and arrows and reproductions of the beribboned ceremonial hats worn by Tzotzil indigenous leaders also make interesting souvenirs.

Chiapas is one of the few places in the world that has amber mines, so finely crafted jewelry made from this prehistoric resin is easy to find in San Cristóbal—as are plastic imitations sold by street vendors. San Cristóbal is also known for the wrought-iron crosses that grace its rooftops. Although many of the iron-working shops have closed, you can still find the crosses in a few old-fashioned stores. Tuxtla Gutiérrez and Palenque, although not known for crafts, have a few shops selling quality folk art from throughout the state.

JEWELRY

In the last few years Calle Real de Guadalupe has transformed itself into the place to go for amber. Nearly a dozen shops line this narrow street off the main square. **Emili Ambar** (✉ *Calle Real de Guadalupe 26, Col. Centro* ☎ *967/678–8789*) makes up for its diminutive size with a helpful staff. Here you'll find a small selection of amber often with an insect suspended inside.

Jewelry here isn't limited to amber. For a look at pieces using a certain green stone, visit **Jades y Joyas** (✉ *Av. 16 de Septiembre, Col. Centro* ☎ *967/678–2550*). You'll find other store branches inside the Casa del Jade Museum, and the Holiday Inn, Fiesta Inn, and Crowne Plaza hotels. **Sensaciones** (✉ *Calle Hidalgo 4, Col. Centro* ☎ *967/631–5580*) carries jewelry made of turquoise and other stones in funky designs.

Tierra del Ambar (✉ *Calle Real de Guadalupe 16 and 28, Col. Centro* ☎ *967/678–0139*) has two storefronts not far from each other. The original pieces by Philippe Catillon are lovely.

SPORTS AND THE OUTDOORS

HORSEBACK RIDING

A horseback ride into the neighboring indigenous villages is good exercise for mind and body. Most hotels can arrange trips, or you can contact **Viajes Chinkultik** (✉ *Calle Real de Guadalupe 34, Col. Centro* ☎ *967/678–0957*). Bilingual guides lead five-hour horseback rides to San Juan Chamula and Zinacantán; the cost is about $12 per person.

YOGA

Shaktipat (✉ *Niños Héroes 2, Interior 6, Col. Centro* ☎ *967/107–2448* 🌐 *www.shaktipat-yoga.org*) holds Hatha yoga, yoga for kids, dance, and meditation classes. Check the Web site for class schedules in both Spanish and English.

SIDE TRIPS FROM SAN CRISTÓBAL

Surrounding San Cristóbal are many small villages celebrated for the exquisite colors and embroidery work of their inhabitants' clothing. San Juan Chamula and Zinacantán are traditional villages well worth exploring. Seeing them on your own is a possibility; taxis and colectivos (vans) depart from near the market in San Cristóbal. To get the most out of the experience, go with a knowledgeable guide.

SAN JUAN CHAMULA

12 km (7½ mi) northwest of San Cristóbal de las Casas.

Celebrated for its religious and cultural traditions, San Juan Chamula is one of the most fascinating highland villages. The Chamulas, a subgroup of the Tzotzils, are descendants of the Maya. More than 80,000 Chamulas live in hamlets throughout the highlands north and west of San Cristóbal; several thousand of them live in San Juan Chamula. Almost all adults wear traditional dress—men often don dark tunics, while women wear embroidered blouses over wool skirts.

A fiercely independent people, the Chamulas fought against the Spanish beginning in 1524. They are also fiercely devout—practicing a religion that's a blend of Catholic and Mayan practices—a trait that has sometimes pitted some members of the community against others. In the past 30 years, thousands who have converted to other religions have been forced to abandon their ancestral lands.

GETTING HERE AND AROUND

To get to San Juan Chamula from San Cristóbal, head west on Calle Guadalupe Victoria, which veers to the right onto Ramón Larrainzar. Continue 4 km (2½ mi) until you reach the entrance to the village.

EXPLORING

Fodor's Choice ★

Life in San Juan Chamula revolves around the **Iglesia de San Juan Bautista**, a white stucco building whose doorway has a simple yet lovely flower motif. The church is named for Saint John the Baptist, who here is revered even above Jesus Christ. There are no pews inside, because there are no traditional masses. Instead, the floor is strewn with fragrant pine needles, on which the Chamulas sit praying silently or chanting while facing colorfully attired statues of saints. Worshippers burn dozens of candles of various colors, chant softly, and may have bones or eggs with them to aid in healing the sick. Each group of worshippers is led by a so-called "traditional doctor" (they don't like being called shamans), whose healing process may involve sacrificing a live chicken and always involves drinking Coca-Cola or other sodas; it is thought that the carbonation will help one to expel bad spirits in the form of a burp, and you'll see rows of soda bottles everywhere.

Before you enter, buy a $2 ticket at the tourist office on the main square. Taking photographs and videos inside the church is absolutely prohibited. Some tourists trying to circumvent this rule have had their film confiscated or their cameras smashed. Outside the church, cameras are permitted, but the Chamulas resent having their picture taken except from afar. The exception are the children who cluster around the church

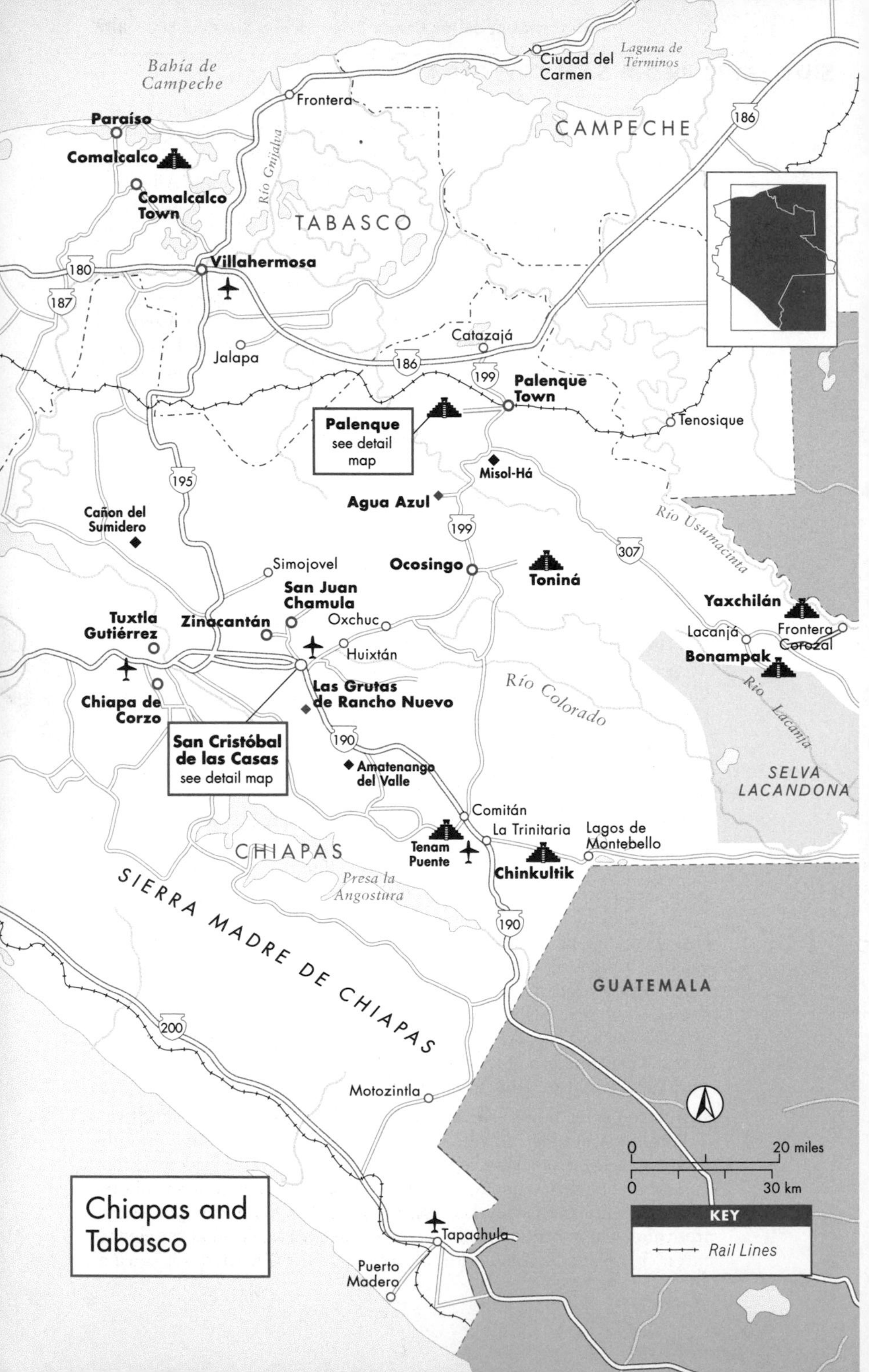

Bahía de Campeche
Laguna de Términos
Ciudad del Carmen
Frontera
CAMPECHE
186
Paraíso
Comalcalco
Comalcalco Town
Río Grijalva
TABASCO
180
Villahermosa
187
Catazajá
Jalapa
186
199
Palenque Town
Palenque
see detail map
Tenosique
Misol-Há
195
Agua Azul
Cañon del Sumidero
199
Río Usumacinta
307
Simojovel
Ocosingo
Toniná
San Juan Chamula
Yaxchilán
Tuxtla Gutiérrez
Zinacantán
Oxchuc
Lacanjá
Frontera Corozal
Huixtán
Bonampak
Las Grutas de Rancho Nuevo
Río Colorado
Río Lacanja
Chiapa de Corzo
190
San Cristóbal de las Casas
see detail map
Amatenango del Valle
SELVA LACANDONA
Comitán
La Trinitaria
Lagos de Montebello
Tenam Puente
CHIAPAS
Chinkultik
Presa la Angostura
SIERRA MADRE DE CHIAPAS
190
GUATEMALA
200
Motozintla
0
20 miles
0
30 km
KEY
Rail Lines
Tapachula
Puerto Madero
Chiapas and Tabasco

posing for pictures for money—they expect a $1 tip. ✉ *Plaza Central, Col. Centro* ⏱ *Daily 8–1 and 4–7.*

On the hill above the Iglesia de San Juan Bautista are the ruins of the **Iglesia de San Sabastián**. This church was built with stones from the Mayan temple that once stood on the site. Surrounding it is the old cemetery, an especially colorful place on the Day of the Dead.

Near the Iglesia de San Juan Bautista is the small museum called **Ora Ton**. Inside are examples of traditional dress, exhibits of musical instruments, and photos of important festivals. Admission is with the same ticket you bought for the church. ✉ *Calle Cementerio s/n, Col. Centro.*

LOCAL GUIDES

As with the other surrounding villages, most visitors choose to see Chamula with the help of a guide, whose connections and explanations can make all the difference. Among the most recommendable are Raúl and Alex *San Crist ó bal tours*. The best day to visit is on a Sunday, when the town's indigenous council sits out on the main plaza in traditional dress and performs its duties as an informal civil court and governing body.

ZINACANTÁN

4 km (2½ mi) west of San Juan Chamula, 10 km (7½ mi) northwest of San Cristóbal de las Casas.

The village of Zinacantán is even smaller than San Juan Chamula. The men wear bright pink tunics embroidered with flowers; the women cover themselves with bright pink shawls. If you visit the homes of back-strap-loom weavers along the main street you are welcome to take photos. Otherwise, cameras are frowned upon.

GETTING HERE AND AROUND

Zinacantán is reached via a paved road just outside of San Cristóbal. From San Cristóbal, take the Tuxtla road about 8 km (5 mi) and look for the signed turnoff on your right.

EXPLORING

The **Iglesia de San Lorenzo**, on the main square, at first looks much more traditional than the church in San Juan Chamula, and it is; services are basically Catholic and are performed in Spanish—not the native language. But look closely and you will notice odd little touches, like ceramic representations of animals sacred to the Maya scattered about. Admission is about 50¢.

The **Museo Ik'al Ojov**, on the street behind the church, is in a typical home and displays Zinacantán costumes through the ages. ☎ *No phone* 🎫 *Donation suggested* ⏱ *Tues.–Sun. 9–5.*

LAS GRUTAS DE RANCHO NUEVO

13 km (8 mi) south of San Cristóbal off Carretera 190.

GETTING HERE AND AROUND

To get here, catch a Teopisca-bound microbus at Boulevard Juan Sabines Gutiérrez, across from the San Diego church, in San Cristóbal. Make sure to tell the driver to let you off at the "grutas." Get off at the signed entrance, and walk about 1 km (½ mi) along the dirt road. Or catch a

CLOSE UP

People and Culture

In Chiapas you'll still find remote clusters of grass-roofed huts and cornfields planted on near-vertical hillsides. Things haven't changed much in centuries. Women still wrap themselves in traditional deep-blue shawls and coarsely woven wool skirts, and sunburned children sell fruit and flowers by the road. The region has nine distinct linguistic groups, most notably the highland-dwelling Tzotzils and the Tzeltals, who live in both highland and lowland areas. In more isolated regions, many villagers speak only their native language. In the past few years many more of the state's 4,224,800 residents have moved to the cities in search of work.

The 1,889,370 residents of Tabasco are much better off than their counterparts in Chiapas, because of the presence of the petroleum industry. Villahermosa, the capital, is a sprawling metropolis that looks forward, not back. But the people here haven't completely forgotten the past. The Parque-Museo La Venta, an open-air museum filled with stone heads carved by the Olmec people, is a place of pride for the residents.

taxi from town for about $6. For about twice that price the driver will wait while you explore the caves.

EXPLORING

Spectacular limestone stalactites and stalagmites are illuminated along a 2,475-foot concrete walkway inside the labyrinthine caves known as **Las Grutas de Rancho Nuevo** (or Las Grutas de San Cristóbal), which were discovered in 1960. Kids from the area are usually available to guide you for a small fee. You can rent horses ($5 per half hour) for a ride around the surrounding pine forest, and there's a small restaurant and picnic area. Many tour operators offer trips here. The caves are also a quick taxi ride from town. ☎ *No phone* 🎫 *$1 per car plus 50¢ per person* ⏲ *Daily 9–4:30.*

TUXTLA GUTIÉRREZ AND CHIAPA DE CORZO

Rare for most states, Chiapas's bustling capital, Tuxla Gutiérrez, is not a destination itself, but you may find yourself staying here if you want to see the spectacular Cañón del Sumidero. Or head to the small, adorable town of Chiapa de Corzo.

TUXTLA GUTIÉRREZ

85 km (53 mi) northwest of San Cristóbal.

In 1939 writer Graham Greene characterized Tuxtla Gutiérrez as "not a place for foreigners—the new ugly capital of Chiapas, without attractions." The accuracy of that bleak description is slowly fading, but most people still only pass through Tuxtla on their way to Oaxaca to the west or San Cristóbal de las Casas to the east. But the capital has what is probably Mexico's most innovative zoo. It's also close to the Cañón del Sumidero, making this a good base for exploring the area. There's also a lively, up-and-coming area around Poniente 15, filled with good restaurants and nightlife.

Tuxtla's first name derives from the Nahuatl word *tochtlan,* meaning "abundance of rabbits." Its second name honors Joaquín Miguel Gutiérrez, who fought for the state's independence from Spain and incorporation into the newly independent country of Mexico. The town became the state capital in 1892, taking the honor away from San Cristóbal.

To get your bearings, stay on Avenida Central, which becomes Boulevard Belisario Domínguez as it heads west.

GETTING HERE AND AROUND

Tuxtla Gutiérrez's Aeropuerto Ángel Albino Corzo (TGZ) is 15 km (9 mi) south of town near Chiapa de Corzo. Continental Express flies from Houston. Otherwise, you'll connect in Mexico City. Taxis from the airport cost $15. Expreso Azul first-class buses leave from Tuxtla and go to San Cristóbal, Ocosingo, and Palenque. Luxury buses run by UNO leave from a smaller terminal across the street. Chiapas is a big state, but there are few major highways. Carretera 190 goes east from Tuxtla through Chiapa de Corzo to San Cristóbal before continuing southeast to the Guatamalan border. There are plenty of hairpin curves, especially between Chiapa de Corzo and San Cristóbal. There is, however, a brand-new toll road that links Tuxtla and San Cristóbal—it costs about $3.80, and it's a much quicker alternative to 190.

ESSENTIALS

Airlines Continental (☎ *01800/900-5000 toll-free in Mexico*).

Bus Contacts Expreso Azul (✉ *Av. 5a Norte Poniente 318* ☎ *961/612-9350* 🌐 *www.autobusesaexa.com.mx*). **UNO** (✉ *Av. 2a Poniente Norte and Calle 2a Poniente Norte* ☎ *961/611-2744*). **Tuxtla Gutiérrez Bus Terminal** (*Estación Cristóbal Colón* ✉ *Av. 2a Poniente Norte 268* ☎ *961/612-2624*).

Currency Exchange Banamex (✉ *Av. 1a Sur Oriente 141* ☎ *961/612-0077*).

Medical Assistance Centro Médico Metropolitano de Tuxtla Gutiérrez (✉ *1a Oriente 847* ☎ *961/612-3041*). **Policía Federal de Caminos (Federal Highway Police)** (✉ *Av. Academia de Policías 295* ☎ *961/614-3235*).

Rental Cars Budget (✉ *Aeropuerto Terán* ☎ *961/615-0672* 🌐 *www.budget.com*). **Hertz** (✉ *Aeropuerto Terán* ☎ *961/153-6074* 🌐 *www.hertz.com* ✉ *Hotel Camino Real, Av. Belisario Domínguez 1195* ☎ *961/615-5348*).

Visitor Info The **Tuxtla Gutiérrez Municipal Tourist Office** (✉ *Calle Central Norte and Av. 2a Norte Oriente* ☎ *961/612-5511* ⏲ *Weekdays 8-8, Sat. 8-1*).

EXPLORING

The gleaming white **Catedral de San Marcos** (✉ *Av. Central at Calle Central* ☎ *961/612-0939*) sits across from the sprawling Parque Central. Founded in the second half of the 16th century, the modern structure shows some colonial touches. The tower has 98 bells that ring every hour as mechanical figurines resembling the apostles appear above. It's open daily 9:30–2 and 4:30–7:30.

8

Marimba music is popular in Tuxtla. As its name suggests, the **Jardín de la Marimba** (✉ *Av. Central Poniente at 8a Calle Poniente Sur*) hosts marimba bands every evening between 7 and 9.

Northeast of Parque Central, the leafy Parque Madero is a wide swath of greenery in a city mostly covered in concrete. It's home to the **Museo Regional de Chiapas.** One room focusing on archaeology has an excellent display of pre-Columbian pottery, while the other on history takes over after the arrival of the Spanish. A standout is an octagonal painting of the Virgin Mary dating from the 17th century. Sadly, all the captions are in Spanish. ✉ *Calzado Hombres Illustres 350, at Calle 11a Oriente* ☎ *961/612–8360* 🎫 *$3* ⏲ *Tues.–Sun. 9–4.*

TRAVEL BY TOUR

Viajes Miramar (✉ *Hotel Camino Real, Blvd. Belisario Domínguez 1195* ☎ *961/617–7777 Ext. 7230* 🌐 *www.viajesmiramar.com.mx*) gives city tours of Tuxtla Gutiérrez for about $10. It also has a five-hour tour that allows you to see the Cañón del Sumidero from the ridge above and from a boat on the river below. The cost is $75 for up to four people.

★ All the animals at the **Zoológico Regional Miguel Álvarez del Toro,** known to locals as ZooMAT, are native to Chiapas. You'll find more than 100 species in settings designed to resemble their natural habitats, including jaguars, black panthers, tapirs, iguanas, and boa constrictors. Rather than sit in cages, spider monkeys swing from trees. Birders will be excited to see the rare resplendent quetzal at close quarters. Many animals from this zoo have been sent to other zoos around the world. ✉ *Calz. Cerro Hueco s/n, southeast of town off Libramiento Sur* ☎ *961/614–4701* 🎫 *$2* ⏲ *Tues.–Sun. 8:30–4:30.*

WHERE TO EAT

$$$ ARGENTINE ✕ **Caminito.** The presence of an authentic Argentine steak house is a sign that Tuxtla may be becoming a cosmopolitan city. The dark, elegant room is appropriate for the serious meat and wine list, which includes good Argentine and Mexican selections. Rich, tender *mollejas* (sweetbreads) are a good bet for starters. The steaks are grilled by *parrilleros* (grill masters) in the front of the restaurant. ✉ *Av. Central Poniente 1440* ☎ *961/614–7148* 💳 *MC, V.*

$$$$ SPANISH ✕ **El Asador Castellano.** Spanish dishes are the specialty at this lovely little restaurant west of the center. The most popular dish is *lechón a la segoviana* (succulent baby pig), which is considered a regional specialty, and this is a great place to try it. The wine list favors Spanish wines hard to find in Mexico City, let alone Chiapas. The restaurant itself is hard to find, as it's behind a bank. ✉ *Blvd. Belisario Domínguez 2320-A* ☎ *961/602–9000* 💳 *AE, MC, V* ⏲ *No dinner Sun.*

$ STEAKHOUSE ✕ **La Carreta.** The scent of sizzling steak wafts from the door of this open-air restaurant. Portions are huge; the mixed grill for two, four, or six people comes with beans, tortillas, and salsa—a super deal. A beautiful wooden staircase leads to the second-floor terrace that overlooks the marimba players who entertain most afternoons. To see the floor show on Friday and Saturday nights, book in advance. ✉ *Blvd. Belisario Domínguez 703* ☎ *961/602–5518* 💳 *AE, MC, V.*

$$$ MEXICAN ★ **Las Pichanchas.** This downtown spot has an outstanding variety of regional dishes, including *pechuga jacuané* (chicken breast stuffed with black beans and smothered with an herb sauce). Red-sashed waiters hoot and holler when someone orders *pompo,* a punch made with mineral water, pineapple juice, lemon juice—and lots of vodka. The big draw is live marimba music in the afternoon and evening. From 9 PM to 10 PM folk dancers take to the floor. There's a playground in the rear. *Av. Central Oriente 837* *961/612–5351* *AE, MC, V.*

WHERE TO STAY

$$ **Best Western Palmareca.** On the outskirts of town, Best Western Palmareca is a haven of gardens with fruit trees, flowering plants, and a secluded swimming pool. Both the rooms and the bungalow-style junior suites have colonial-style fittings and furnishings. The Calabaza Grill serves a buffet breakfast daily and has Mexican specialties for lunch and dinner. **Pros:** spacious; clean rooms; decent buffet. **Cons:** generic hotel brand occasionally comes through. *Blvd. Belisario Domínguez, Km 1080* *961/617–0000 or 800/780–7234* *www.bestwestern.com* *60 rooms, 20 suites* *In-room: Wi-Fi. In-hotel: restaurant, room service, bar, pool, laundry service, parking (free)* *AE, DC, MC, V.*

$$ ★ **Camino Real.** You might think you're in the Caribbean at this sprawling hotel set around a huge lagoon-style pool and a bar shaded with exotic vegetation. The amenities at this hilltop oasis—unmistakable for its purple-and-orange color scheme—are impressive. The Azulejos restaurant, open 24 hours, is enclosed in a sky-blue glass dome; its buffets are well worth the price. All the well-appointed rooms have mountain views. **Pros:** nice landscaping, beautifully laid-out, good value. **Cons:** takes on many large groups. *Blvd. Belisario Domínguez 1195* *961/617–7777 or 800/722–6466* *www.caminoreal.com* *174 rooms, 36 suites* *In-room: refrigerator, safe, Wi-Fi. In-hotel: restaurant, room service, bar, tennis courts, pool, gym, spa, no-smoking rooms* *AE, DC, MC, V.*

$$ **Hotel María Eugenia.** A few blocks from the main square, this high-rise that's a bit past its prime has rooms with balconies overlooking downtown. The cafeteria serves a scrumptious breakfast buffet of Mexican favorites. **Pros:** well-trained, helpful staff. **Cons:** looking a little ragged around the edges; rooms are pretty plain. *Av. Central Oriente 507, Col. Centro* *961/613–3767* *www.mariaeugenia.com.mx* *82 rooms* *In-room: Wi-Fi. In-hotel: restaurant, room service, bar, pool, laundry service, parking (free)* *AE, MC, V.*

CHIAPA DE CORZO

15 km (9 mi) southeast of Tuxtla Gutiérrez.

The town of Chiapa de Corzo (then known as Chiapa de los Indios) was founded in 1528 by Diego de Mazariegos, who one month later fled the heat and mosquitoes and settled instead in San Cristóbal de las Casas (then called Chiapa de los Españoles to avoid confusion).

EXPLORING

★ The **Cañón del Sumidero**, a canyon 38 km (24 mi) north of Chiapa de Corzo, came into being about 36 million years ago, with the help of the Río Grijalva, which flows north along the canyon's floor. The fissure, which meanders for some 23 km (14 mi), is perhaps the most interesting landscape in the region.

You can admire the Cañón del Sumidero from above, as there are five lookout points along the highway. But the best way to see it is from one of the dozens of boats that travel to the canyon from the Embarcadero in Chiapa de Corzo (two blocks south of the main square) between 8 and 4 daily. Two-hour rides cost about $12 per person, and for about $30 you can spend the day in the ecopark of the canyon. From the boat you can admire the nearly vertical walls that rise 3,500 feet at their highest point. As you coast along, consider the fate of the Chiapa people who reputedly jumped into the canyon rather than face slavery at the hands of the Spaniards during the 16th century.

TAMALE STANDS

The best food in Chiapa de Corzo can be bought for $1. As you walk down Mexicanidad de Chiapas toward the river, you'll pass numerous burger and hot dog stands; keep walking until you get to the row of three **tamale stands**, each of which serves 10 or so types of tamales, which are enjoyed at the little tables on the street. Don't miss the wonderful mole tamale. Wash it all down with a glass of *horchata* (almond milk). ✉ *Calle Mexicanidad de Chiapas* ☎ *No phone* 💳 *No credit cards.*

Life in this small town on the banks of the Río Grijalva revolves around the Plaza Angel Albino Corzo. In the center is the bizarre **Fuente Mudéjar**, or Moorish Fountain. The structure, built in 1562, once supplied the town with water. Said to be in the shape of the crown of the Spanish monarchs Ferdinand and Isabella, it is a mishmash of Moorish, Gothic, and Renaissance styles.

About a block south of Plaza Ángel Albino Corzo is a massive church called the Ex-Convento de Santo Domingo de Guzmán. It houses the **Museo de la Laca** *(Lacquerware Museum)*, which has a modest collection of carved and painted *jícaras* (gourds). The foreign examples are from as close as Guatemala and as far away as Asia. ✉ *Calle Mexicanidad de Chiapas 10* ☎ *961/616–0055* 🎫 *Free* ⏲ *Tues.–Sun. 10–5.*

WHERE TO EAT AND STAY

Restaurants serving fresh fish line the waterfront along the Río Grijavla. They are a great bet for a beer and ceviche at sunset.

$$ MEXICAN ✕ **Jardines de Chiapas.** Though it's touristy, this place serves a variety of regional dishes. Everything is buffet-style, so you can afford to experiment. Try the *tasajo* (sun-dried beef served with pumpkin-seed sauce) and the *chipilín con bolita,* a soup made with balls of ground corn paste cooked in a creamy herb sauce and topped with cheese. The restaurant closes at 6. ✉ *Av. Francisco I. Madero 395* ☎ *961/616–0070* 💳 *AE, MC, V* ⏲ *No dinner.*

$ MEXICAN ✕ **Los Corredores.** For fairly authentic *chiapaneca* cuisine in a lovely environment, try this restaurant on the corner of the main square. The best seats are in a cute garden in the back. The *tasajo* (a soup made of cured beef) is an interesting preparation. The food won't blow your mind, but it's pleasant. ✉ *Av. Francisco I. Madero 35* ☎ *961/616–0760* ▭ *AE, MC, V.*

$ **Hotel La Ceiba.** Billed as a hotel and spa, this is an old, but extremely well-kept hotel. You might fancy yourself in a miniature tropical paradise: the hotel is built around a lush tropical garden complete with a pair of toucans. Get a room in the back facing the garden, and you will awake to a rooster crowing and a view of palms. **Pros:** wonderful landscaping; a true escape; the best hotel rooms in town. **Cons:** service is spotty. ✉ *Av. Domingo Ruiz 300* ☎ *961/616–0389* *91 rooms* *In-hotel: restaurant, room service, bar, pool, spa, Internet terminal, parking (free)* ▭ *MC, V.*

THE ROAD TO PALENQUE

The road from San Cristóbal to Palenque veers slightly east on Carretera 190 upon leaving town, then links up to Carretera 199, which heads north to Palenque. You'll pass Ocosingo and the turnoff to Toniná along the first half of the journey, then Agua Azul and Misol-Há before reaching the ruins. It's sierra country until the valleys around Ocosingo; the climate will get progressively hotter and more humid as you descend from the highland and approach Palenque. The vegetation will also change, from mountain pine to thick, tropical foliage.

OCOSINGO

98 km (61 mi) northeast of San Cristóbal, 118 km (73 mi) south and east of Palenque.

8

Although Ocosingo is on the tourist trail, most people pass right by on their way to San Cristobál or Palenque. That's a shame, because Ocosingo sits in one of the prettiest valleys in Chiapas. It's a great place for horseback riding or bathing in waterfalls. It's also the best base for exploring the Mayan ruins of Toniná.

Like many other towns, Ocosingo is centered around a manicured square with a town hall on one end and a cathedral on the other. It hasn't caught up with the rest of the world, which is its charm.

GETTING HERE AND AROUND

If you're traveling from San Cristóbal de las Casas, follow the signs that read PALENQUE OCOSINGO along Carretera 190. Around km 12 (7 mi) in Rancho Nuevo, take the Carrertera 199 for 76 km (47 mi). Allow a little over an hour and a half for this trip.

ADO GL buses leave the San Cristóbal de las Casas station about four times a day, around every three hours. The trip costs around $4, and takes about 2 hours and 10 minutes.

WHERE TO EAT AND STAY

$ MEXICAN ✕ **El Desván.** Through a pair of graceful arches you can gaze down on the main square from this second-story restaurant. There's a certain rustic charm imparted by the wrought-iron wall sconces and the rough-hewn tables and chairs. The menu begins with simple dishes like quesadillas and enchiladas and moves on to more substantial fare like *pollo a la mexicana* (chicken simmered with tomatoes and onions). They also serve a number of different pizzas, which are thick, greasy, and ridiculously cheesy. ✉ *1 Av. Sur Oriente 10* ☎ *919/673–0117* ▭ *No credit cards.*

¢ MEXICAN ✕ **Las Delicias.** This restaurant, with a balcony overlooking the central plaza, serves home-style cooking daily 7 AM until 11 PM. Try the delicious *caldo tlalpeño,* a tasty broth with chicken, tortilla, avocado, and cheese, that comes with a plate of chili chipotle that you can use to spice up the soup. At dinner there's also a large plate—that's perfect for sharing—with grilled beef, fried chicken, fresh cheese, guacamole, and beans with tortilla chips. ✉ *Av. Central at Calle Central 5, Col. Centro* ☎ *919/673–0024* ▭ *MC, V.*

MARKET MADNESS

Ocosingo is primarily a market town, which is evident when you head to the market area called the Tianguis Campesino (2 Av. Sur Oriente and 4 Calle Oriente Sur—Ocosingo's addresses will make your brain dizzy). Brightly dressed Tzeltal and Lacandón women from the surrounding villages kneel on the ground or sit on tiny stools to sell vegetables and fruits from their gardens. Negotiations are often in whispers, making it one of the quietest markets you'll encounter.

¢ **Hotel Tierra Maya.** If your tour of area ruins leads you to Ocosingo, this hotel just a few blocks off the main square is one of the best spots in town to spend the night. You can't miss the yellow-and-blue exterior. Inside, accommodations are basic: the beds have cheerful yellow or blue headrests painted on the walls. All rooms have ceramic floors, and showers have ceramic tiling. **Pros:** good restaurant; affordable rates. **Cons:** three blocks from downtown; rooms are basic. ✉ *Calle 2da Oriente Norte 12* ☎ *919/673–0917* 🌐 *www.tierramayaocosingo.com* *42 rooms* *In-room: no phone, no TV. In-hotel: restaurant, bar, laundry service, Internet terminal* ▭ *MC, V.*

SHOPPING

Ocosingo is known throughout the region for its cheeses, so it's no surprise that truck drivers passing through call this town "Los Quesos." Delicious *queso botanero* (a creamy cheese with chilies, olives, and other additions mixed in) is available at **Quesos Laltic** (✉ *2 Av. Poniente Norte 1* ☎ *919/673–0231*).

TONINÁ

14 km (8 mi) east of Ocosingo.

GETTING HERE AND AROUND

Taxis from Ocosingo's main square cost about $8; for about twice that the driver will wait for you. Colectivos (shared minivans) headed to the ruins leave from the market as soon as they are full, which is usually every 20 minutes or so. They cost $1 per person each way.

EXPLORING

★ **Toniná.** Between San Cristóbal and Palenque, on a paved road running along the Río Jataté and through the Ocosingo Valley, is the ancient Mayan city of Toniná. The name means "house of stone" in Tzeltal, and you'll understand why it's named this once you glimpse this series of temples looming some 20 stories over the valley. Built on a steep hillside, Toniná is even taller than Palenque or Tikal.

Toniná is thought to be the last major Mayan ceremonial center to flourish in this area. It thrived for at least a century after the fall of Palenque and Yaxchilán. There is speculation as to whether it may have actually had a part in their downfall. Excavations indicate that the vanquished rulers of those cities were brought here as prisoners. Wonderfully preserved sculptures, including the *Mural de las Cuatro Eras* (*Mural of the Four Ages*) depict bloody executions. *$3* *Daily 9–4.*

TO DRIVE OR NOT TO DRIVE?

Is renting a car a worthwhile way to travel? If you plan on stopping between San Cristóbal and Palenque to visit the ruins at Toniná and the waterfalls at Agua Azul, you might want to consider it. If you're traveling straight through, take a bus or hire a tour company. Budget, Dollar, Hertz, and National have car-rental offices in the major cities of Chiapas and Tabasco. The national chain Excellent often has better prices and will deliver the car to your hotel.

AGUA AZUL

8

68 km (42 mi) northwest of Toniná.

GETTING HERE AND AROUND

Six-hour guided tours from Palenque, which include visits to Agua Azul and Misol-Há, cost about $10 per person. This is generally considered the safest way to travel in the area, because this is a curvy, mountainous road, and occasionally people stationed along the highway stop cars, and even ask for change.

Following signs on Carretera 199 that read PALENQUE, travel about 51 km (31.5 mi) northeast of Ocosingo to get to Agua Azul; the town is about 40 km (25 mi) before Palenque.

There's no public transportation to Agua Azul, but taxis from Ocosingo—it's difficult to get a taxi in Toniná—run about $40 round-trip.

EXPLORING

★ **Agua Azul.** The series of waterfalls and crystalline blue pools at Agua Azul is breathtaking, especially during the dry season (from about November through March), as wet-season waters are often churned up and brown with mud. You can swim in a series of interconnected pools.

If the single cascade at nearby Misol-Há is less grandiose than the series of falls and pools at Agua Azul, it's no less amazing. You can swim in the pool formed by the 100-foot cascade, or explore behind the falls, where a cave leads to a subterranean pool. (If there's a guide with flashlight in hand to help you, tip him $1 or so.)

PALENQUE AND ENVIRONS

Palenque is on the itinerary of almost every traveler to the region. But this magical city is only the beginning—there are other Mayan ruins in the area, such as Bonampak and Yaxchilán, which are astounding in their own ways. Palenque is easy to explore on your own, but it's best to visit Bonampak and Yaxchilán with a guide. They are so isolated that trying to get there on your own will be a headache.

PALENQUE TOWN

8 km (5 mi) north of the ruins.

Palenque Town's days as a sleepy little village are far behind. Locals have obliged the needs of travelers in search of the ruins at Palenque, Bonampak, and Yaxchilán by opening a string of restaurants and lodgings on and around Avenida Juárez, the main thoroughfare, and along La Cañada, a popular tourist destination west of downtown. Although Palenque is not a really cute place, it's colorful enough, with cinder-block buildings gussied up in coats of vivid yellow, orange, and blue paint. You can listen to a marimba band in the square or buy a sugary pastry from a vendor on a bicycle.

GETTING HERE AND AROUND

At this writing, the tiny international airport in Palenque was closed. If you want to fly here from the United States, your best bet is the daily flight between Houston and Villahermosa on Continental. Otherwise you're going to connect in Mexico City or another hub. Taxis from Villahermosa's airport can also drive you straight to Palenque for $80. ADO GL buses travel from Palenque to Ocosingo, San Cristóbal, and Tuxtla. If you can't get a first-class bus, many of the same destinations can be reached on the second-class buses operated by Transportes Rodolfo Figueroa, a few doors away from the main bus terminal. If driving from San Cristóbal, Carretera 199 heads north through Ocosingo to Palenque; this twisting, turning road nearly ties itself into a knot along the way.

ESSENTIALS

Bus Contacts **Palenque Bus Terminal** (*Estación Cristóbal Colón ⊠ Av. Juárez s/n ☎ 916/345–1344*).

Currency Exchange **Banamex** (*⊠ Av. Juárez 62 ☎ 916/345–0017*). **Bancomer** (*⊠ Av. Juárez 40 ☎ 916/345–0198*).

Medical Assistance **Clínica Santa Fe** (*⊠ Hidalgo 28 ☎ 916/345–0187*). **Hospital General de Palenque** (*⊠ Prolongación Juárez s/n ☎ 916/345–1433 or 916/325–0733*).

Visitor Info **Palenque Tourist Information Office** (*⊠ Av. Juárez at Calle Abasolo ☎ 916/345–0356*).

EXPLORING

The dominant landmark is the chalk-white **Cabeza Maya**, a giant sculpture of the head of a Mayan chieftain just west of downtown. It's in La Cañada, a quiet neighborhood with many great hotels and restaurants.

> **MAYA MESSAGE**
>
> The nonprofit Maya Exploration Center (MEC), dedicated to the study of Mayan civilization, has scholars who lead customized tours of Palenque, Toniná, Yaxchilán, Bonampak, Tikal, and other sites. The MEC also provides short on-site study-abroad programs that focus on Mayan architecture, astronomy, mathematics, and other aspects of culture. Visit www.mayaexploration.org to find out more or for details on how to support this worthy organization.

WHERE TO EAT

$ MEXICAN ✕ **Café de Yara**. There's something refreshing about this two-story corner café; maybe it's the doors flung open to catch the breeze, or the walls painted the colors of lemons and limes. Good choices include the *pollo a la pasilla con nopales* (boneless chicken breast cooked in a chili sauce and covered with bits of cactus) and the *filete de res a la pimienta* (beef simmered with peppers). Make sure to end your meal with a cup of organic coffee, the specialty of the house. ✉ *Av. Hidalgo 66, at Calle Abasolo* ☎ *916/345–0269* 🌐 *www.cafeyara.com* 💳 *MC, V.*

$ SEAFOOD ✕ **El Huachinango Feliz**. The location of this two-level restaurant, just next door to the Hotel Xibalba, has made it a favorite with tourists, but locals frequent the place too. The plates are big, and the food is varied and delicious. The freshness of the seafood is a big part of what makes dishes like the *chilpachole de mariscos* (a slightly spicy tomato-based seafood soup) delicious. The *filete de pescado* (a shrimp-stuffed fillet of fish baked in a banana leaf) is another delicious option. ✉ *Av. Hidalgo s/n* ☎ *916/345–4642* 💳 *MC, V.*

$$ MEXICAN ✕ **La Selva**. On the road to the ruins, this restaurant has an elaborate entrance inspired by the Temple of the Sun. Lamp shades fashioned from locally woven baskets add just the right touch of authenticity. Try the fish served *a la veracruzana* (in the Veracruz style, which means it's smothered with tomatoes, onions, garlic, green olives, and capers). There's a scrumptious Sunday brunch buffet, 1–5 PM. ✉ *Carretera Ruinas, Km 0.5* ☎ *916/345–0363* 💳 *MC, V.*

$ MEXICAN ✕ **Maya**. Billed as Palenque's oldest restaurant, Maya opened for business back in 1958. It sits so close to the main square that you can hear the birds that come home to roost each sunset. The tables in the dining room, swathed in magenta fabric, always seem to be crowded. The three-course set menus at lunch are a good deal. Dishes served à la carte include medallions of *robalo,* a local fish that is equally tasty fried or breaded. The coffee drinks are among the best in town. ✉ *Av. Independencia at Av. Hidalgo* ☎ *916/345–0042* 🌐 *www.mayarestaurante.com* 💳 *MC, V.*

$$ MEXICAN ★ ✕ **Maya Cañada**. This thatch-roof restaurant in La Cañada is one of the prettiest in Palenque. Grab a table amid the fragrant gardens, and listen to musicians play softly (evenings) as you choose one of the regional dishes like *pollo en mole chiapaneco* (chicken in a local version of

Continued on page 406

PALENQUE

Templo del Sol

91 km (118 mi) northeast of San Cristóbal de las Casas, 150 km (93 mi) southeast of Villahermosa.

Of all the Maya ruins, none is more sublime than Palenque, and only Tikal in Guatemala and Copán in Honduras are its equal. Arrive here during the morning when the fog still shrouds the surrounding hills and you'll know why it was considered a sacred place to the Maya rulers.

THE DISCOVERY Since the Spanish first heard tales of a colossal city shrouded by jungle, there has been no shortage of explorers—some hardy, others foolhardy—determined to uncover the secrets of Palenque. In 1831, an eccentric French count named Jean-Frédéric Maximilien de Waldeck set up house with his mistress for a year in what has become known as the Templo del Conde (Temple of the Count). Amateur archaeologist John Lloyd Stephens and Frederick Catherwood lived briefly in the sprawling Palacio (Palace) during their 1840 expedition. Serious excavations began in 1923 under the direction of Frans Blom, cofounder of the Na Bolom foundation in San Cristóbal. Work continued intermittently until 1952, when Alberto Ruz Lhuillier, a Mexican archaeologist, uncovered the tomb of the 7th-century ruler Pakal beneath the Templo de las Inscripciones (Temple of the Inscriptions).

A HAZY HISTORY Unraveling the story of Palenque has been difficult. Only around 800 of the thousands of glyphs found here have been deciphered, but they have already revealed the complex history of the Palenque dynasties. Exciting finds by archaeologists from the University of Texas in 1998 introduced a new character, Uc-Pakal-Kinich, into the lineage of Palenque rulers. Other clues unearthed at Templo 19 point to a probable liaison between rulers of Palenque and of Copán.

Maya glyphs adorn a stone tablet in the Palacio

Although it was inhabited as early as 1500 BC, Palenque's most important buildings date from the mid- to late-Classic period (AD 300–1000). At its zenith, between AD 600 and AD 700, the city dominated the greater part of what is today Tabasco and Chiapas. This period coincided with the reign of K'inich Hanab Pakal, the king who was buried beneath the Templo de las Inscripciones. But the city that thrived under Pakal's rule was abandoned around AD 900. The reasons for the Mayas' departure are currently still debated. Archaeologists think it likely relates to the fierce rivalry between Palenque and Toniná.

GREEKS OF THE NEW WORLD Palenque's elegance makes clear why archaeologist Sylvanus Morley called the Maya the "Greeks of the New World." The masters here shaped stone, stucco, and ceramics into ornate, lyrical designs. Instead of the freestanding stelae found at other Maya cities, at Palenque you find highly expressive relief sculptures and elaborate glyphs. In its heyday, Palenque encompassed an astonishing 128-plus square km (49-square mi). Hills were flattened to support the temples, which were surrounded by wide plazas, a ball court, and burial grounds. The temples themselves contained a complex array of twisting corridors, narrow subterranean stairways, and wide galleries. The design was more than just aesthetic, because the buildings also served as fortresses in time of war.

Engraving from John Lloyd Stephens' *Incidents of Travel in Central America, Chiapas, and Yucatan*, 1805-1852.

THE MAJOR SIGHTS

Palenque is enormous and you'd need weeks to really explore it all. The most stunning (and most visited) sights are around the Palacio, but if you have the stamina, it's worth winding your way up to the Northeastern Group, which is often deserted. The ruins are open daily from 8 to 5; admission is $4.00. Try to get here early when it's cooler and there may still be some clinging mist.

❶ **Templo de la Calavera.** As you enter the site, the first temple on your right is the reconstructed Temple of the Skull. A stucco relief, presumed to be in the shape of a rabbit or deer skull, was found at the entrance to the temple. It now sits at the top of the stairs. Like the rest of the buildings, the Templo de la Calavera is unadorned stone. When it was built, however, it was painted vivid shades of red and blue.

❷ **Templo de las Inscripciones.** At the eastern end of the cluster is this massive temple dedicated to Pakal. The temple's nine tiers correspond to the nine lords of the underworld. Atop this temple and the smaller ones surrounding it are vestiges of roof combs—delicate vertical extensions that are standard features of southern Mayan cities. You can descend the steep, damp flight of stairs to view the king's tomb. One of the first crypts found inside a Mexican pyramid, it contains a stone tube in the shape of a snake through which Pakal's soul was thought to have passed to the netherworld. The intricately carved sarcophagus lid weighs some 5 tons and measures 10 feet by 7 feet. It can be difficult to make out the carvings on the thick slab, but they depict the ruler, prostrate beneath a sacred ceiba tree. There's a reproduction in the site museum.

■TIP→ To enter the Templo de las Inscripciones, you must obtain a permit first thing in the morning at the site museum.

Templo de la Cruz

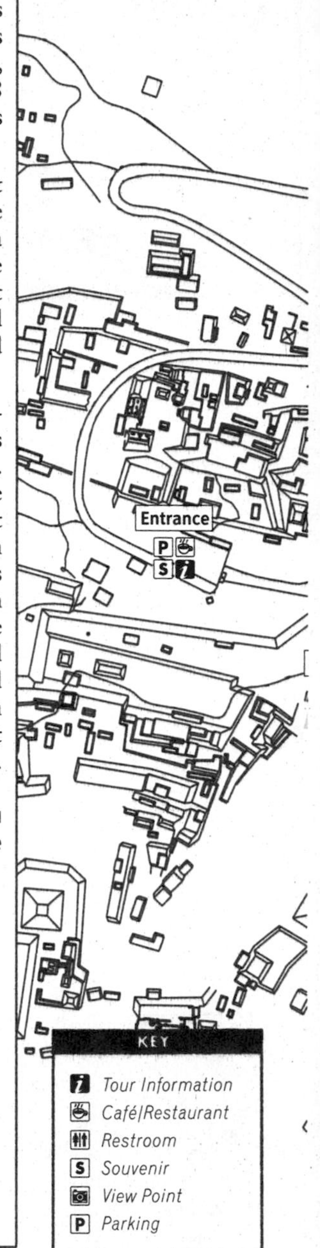

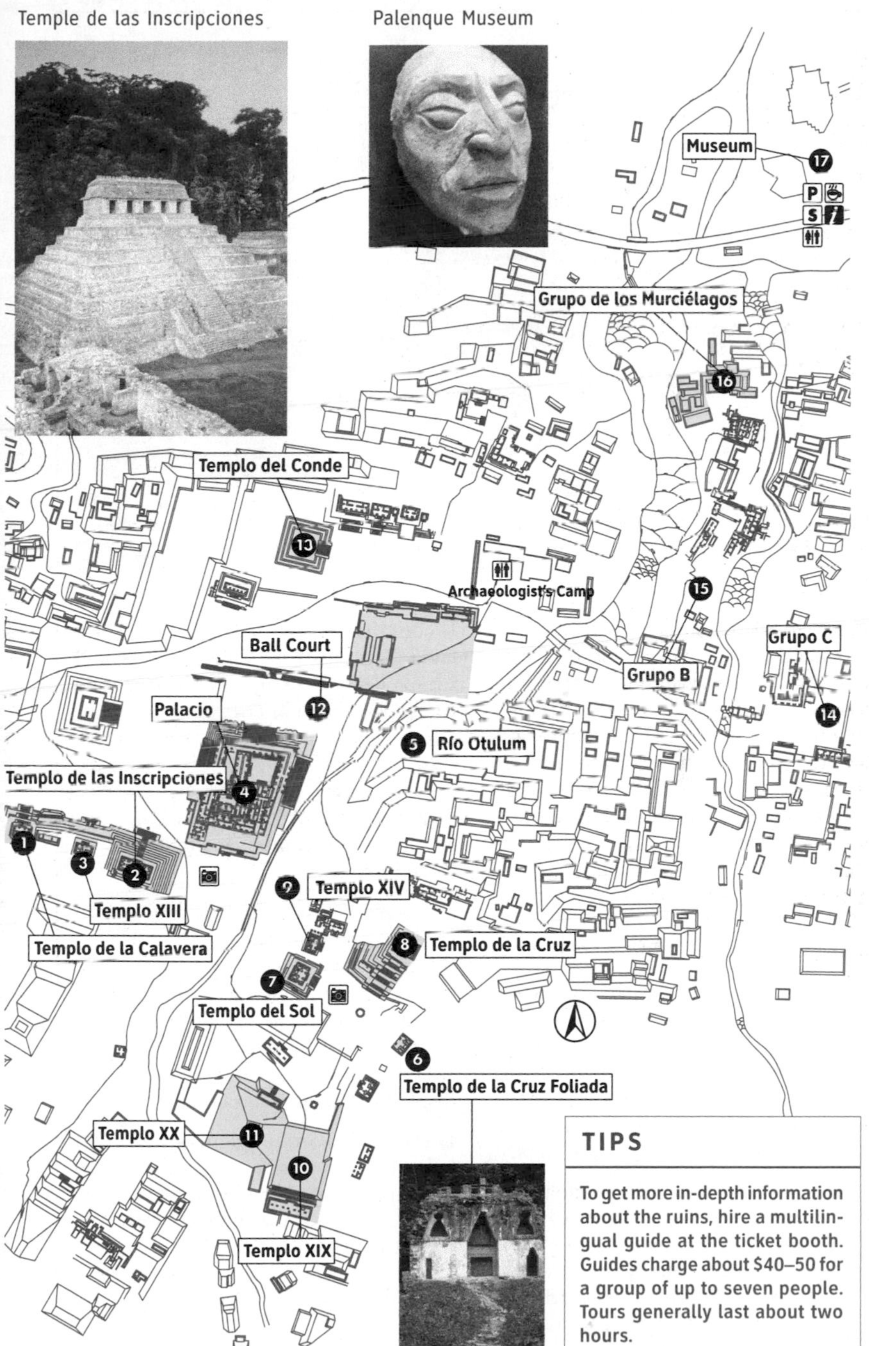

TIPS

To get more in-depth information about the ruins, hire a multilingual guide at the ticket booth. Guides charge about $40–50 for a group of up to seven people. Tours generally last about two hours.

Grupo Norte

❸ **Templo XIII.** If you can't secure a permit to enter the Templo de las Inscripciones, you can always visit the unassuming Templo XIII. Attached to the Temple of the Inscriptions, this structure has a royal tomb hidden in its depths, the Tumba de la Reina Roja, or Tomb of the Red Queen. The sarcophagus, colored with cinnabar, probably belonged to Pakal's wife or mother.

❹ **Palacio.** The smaller buildings inside the breathtaking Palacio are supported by 30-foot-high pillars. Stuccowork adorns the pillars of the galleries as well as the inner courtyards. Most of the numerous friezes inside depict Pakal and his dynasty. The palace's iconic tower was built on three levels, thought to represent the three levels of the universe as well as the movement of the stars.

❺ **Río Otulum.** To the east of the palace is the tiny Río Otulum, which in ancient times was covered over to form a 9-foot-high vaulted aqueduct. Cross the river and climb up 80 easy steps to arrive at the reconstructed Grupo de los Cruces. It contains the ❻ **Templo de la Cruz Foliada** (Temple of the Foliated Cross), ❼ **Templo del Sol** (Temple of the Sun), and the ❽ **Templo de la Cruz** (Temple of the Cross), the largest of the group. Inside the nearby ❾ **Templo XIV**, there's an underworld scene in stucco relief, finished 260 days after Pakal's death. The most exquisite roof combs are also found on these buildings.

❿ **Templo XIX.** This temple has yielded some exciting finds, including a large sculpted stucco panel, a carved stone platform with hundreds of hieroglyphics, and a limestone table (in pieces but now restored) depicting the ruler K'inich Ahkal Mo' Nahb' III. The latter is on display in the site museum.

⓫ **Templo XX.** Ground-penetrating radar helped locate a frescoed tomb covered in murals. Both temples are still being excavated and are only sporadically open to the public.

To reach the cluster called the Grupo Norte (Northern Group) walk north along the river, passing on your left the Palacio and the unexcavated ⑫ **Ball court**. There are five buildings here in various states of disrepair; the best preserved is the ⑬ **Templo del Conde** (Temple of the Count).

Ceremonial urn on display in the museum.

A short hike northeast of the Grupo Norte lies ⑭ **Grupo C** (Group C), an area containing remains of the homes of nobles and a few small temples shrouded in jungle. To maintain the natural setting in which the ruins were found, minimal restoration has been done. Human burials, funeral offerings, and kitchen utensils have been found here as well as in ⑮ **Grupo B** (Group B), which lies farther along the path through the jungle. On the way, you'll pass a small waterfall and pool called El Baño de la Reina (The Queen's Bath). By far the most interesting of these seldom-visited ruins is the ⑯ **Grupo de los Murciélagos** (Group of the Bats). Dark, twisting corridors beneath the ruins are ready to be explored. Just be aware that you might run into a few of the creatures that gave the spooky buildings their name.

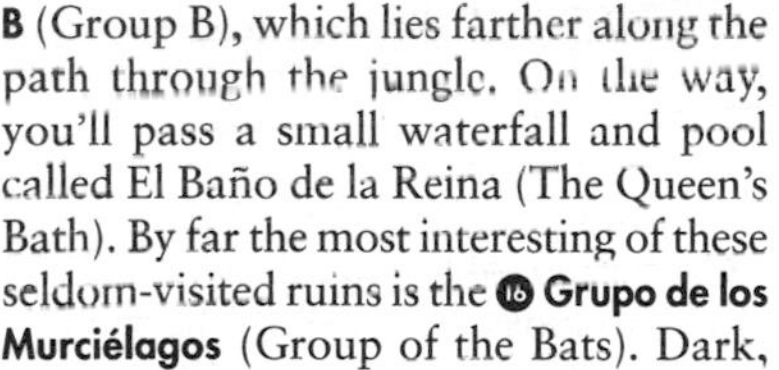

A path from the Grupo de los Murciélagos leads over a short extension bridge to the ⑰ **Museum**. You can also reach it by car or colectivo, as it's along the same road you took to the entrance. The museum has a remarkable stucco rendering of Mayan deities in elaborate zoomorphic headdresses, which was discovered in front of the Temple of the Foliated Cross. Also noteworthy are the handsome, naturalistic faces of Mayan men that once graced the facades. Displays here and in the rest of the site are labeled in English, Spanish, and the Maya dialect called Chol. There's also a snack bar and a crafts store. The museum is open Tuesday–Sunday from 9 to 4.

WHERE TO STAY

★ **$$** **Chan-Kah.** If you want to stay near the ruins, this is the place. Amid colorful wild ginger and aromatic jasmine, this cluster of spacious bungalows feels miles from anywhere. Your bungalow has a dressing room, sitting area, and a bedroom with floor-to-ceiling windows overlooking the gardens. If you aren't already close enough to nature, there is a pair of mahogany rocking chairs on your back porch. From many rooms you can see the nearby stream that fills the immense lagoon-style pool. Don't confuse this Chan-Kah with the hotel of the same name in town. This location is more charming and it's closer to the ruins. ✉ *Carretera Ruinas, Km 3.5, 29960* ☎ *916/345–1134* 🌐 *www.chan-kah.com.mx* *73 rooms, 6 suites* *In-room: Safe, no TV. In-hotel: Two restaurants, pools, bar, public Internet, parking (free).* ▭ *MC, V* 🍽 *EP* the dried-chili classic) and a soup of *chipilín* (a local herb). Skip the dry shrimp and go for the whole fried fish. Maya, the downtown restaurant *(listed above)*, is owned by the same people, but has a different vibe. ✉ *Calle Merle Green s/n, La Cañada* ☎ *916/345–0216* 🌐 *www.mayarestaurante.com* 💳 *MC, V.*

$ CAFÉ ✕ **Restaurant Las Tinajas.** The coffee is good at this sunny corner café, but it's also a great place to stop in for a meal. The menu includes a wide variety of Mexican dishes, including the delicious sopa de ajo (garlic soup). The *pechuga de pollo en chipotle al gratin* (chicken breast with chipotle and topped with cheese) is also tasty, but if you're looking for a simpler dish, you can also order international food—including burgers and fries. ✉ *Av. 20 de Noviembre* ☎ *916/345–4970* 💳 *No credit cards.*

$ MEXICAN ★ ✕ **Trotamundo.** This place is always packed, and usually with locals—a sign that the food is great. One woman makes tortillas at the entrance to the restaurant, while another slices fruit at a different station. A cheap 70-peso *comida corrida* (set-price lunch menu) is available. A *torta* (sandwich) of tender *cochinita pibil* (a pork dish) is excellent, and for breakfast, try the showstopping *chilaquiles con carne.* ✉ *Av. Juárez* ☎ *916/345–5127* 💳 *No credit cards.*

RUINS ON THE CHEAP

You'll find **Sitio Maya Pakal** (☎ *916/345–0379 or 916/345–2326*) taxis lined up along the main square. A ride to the ruins is $5; it's a bit more if you call for a cab from your hotel. Most tour operators run half-day guided tours of Palenque ruins for about $6, which includes a guide and transportation. Full-day tours costing $14 per person begin in Palenque, then move on to the waterfalls at Misol-Há and Agua Azul.

WHERE TO STAY

$$–$$$ 🏨 **Calinda Nututún Palenque.** A large natural pool forms in a bend in the Río Nututún, which runs through the grounds of this hotel. The rooms in the low-slung main building are plain but ample. Book a suite and you'll have a terrace overlooking the gardens. **Pros:** proximity to the river is great. **Cons:** the main drawback is location—far from town but not much closer to the ruins. ✉ *Carretera Palenque–Ocosingo, Km 3.5* 📫 *Apdo. 74 29960* ☎ *916/345–0100* 🌐 *www.nututun.com* 🛏 *57 rooms* 👍 *In-room: no TV (some). In-hotel: restaurant, room service, bar, pool, parking (free)* 💳 *AE, MC, V.*

$–$$ 🏨 **Ciudad Real Palenque.** This colonial-style hotel is surrounded by thriving gardens. A small waterfall and creek run through the grounds. All the rooms, with fabrics made by local artisans, have balconies facing the gardens. The palm-lined pool has several hammocks where you can spend a lazy afternoon. **Pros:** lovely landscaping; centrally located. **Cons:** overall character is a little bland. ✉ *Carretera Pakal-Na, Km 1.5* ☎ *916/345–1315* 🌐 *www.ciudadreal.com.mx* 🛏 *66 rooms, 6 suites* 👍 *In-hotel: restaurant, room service, bar, pool* 💳 *AE, MC, V.*

$ 🏨 **Hotel Lacandonia.** This comfortable, brand-new downtown hotel is most notable for Palenque ($), its pizzeria that serves really good pizza. Rooms are simple, but clean and pleasant in pastel pinks and oranges with reading lamps next to the wrought-iron bed and cable television.

Public areas are also decorated with orange details and lush plants, and you can buy bottled water and toiletries in the lobby. **Pros:** quite clean; good price; in town close to the shops. **Cons:** not close to the ruins. ✉ *Calle Allende 77* ☎ *916/345–0057* *27 rooms* *In-room: Wi-Fi. In-hotel: restaurant* *MC, V.*

$$ **Hotel Villas Kin-Ha.** This small hotel is made up of small cottages with palapa roofs grouped around two pools. Rooms are sparsely decorated, but the bright colors are cheerful and the rooms are clean and spacious. **Pros:** particularly close to the ruins; reasonable prices; tasty international food at the restaurant. **Cons:** tour groups occasionally crowd common areas. ✉ *Carretera Palenque-Zona Arqueológica, Km 2.7* ☎ *916/345–0954* *www.villaskinha.com* *120 villas, 3 suites* *In-room: safe. In-hotel: restaurant, pools* *MC, V.*

$ **Hotel Xibalba.** Quirky furniture and the only replica of the tomb of Pakal make this hotel unique. A newer section of the hotel has simple rooms without the character of the older ones, which have painted murals and an area where you can watch the street in hip chairs with treelike sculptures around you. **Pros:** solid air-conditioning; courteous staff; inexpensive rooms. **Cons:** no swimming pool; breakfast needs a little sprucing up. ✉ *Calle Merle Green 9* ☎ *916/345–0411* *www.hotelxibalba.com* *35 rooms* *In-room: kitchen (some), Wi-Fi. In-hotel: restaurant, room service, bar, laundry service, Internet terminal* *MC, V.*

$$ **Maya Tulipanes.** Although this hotel is uninspiring, it's quiet and well located on a posh suburban street, La Cañada. The spacious terrace is marked by a huge thatch-roofed sitting area where people meet for coffee in the morning or drinks in the afternoon. Nearby is the tree-shaded pool, which has a mosaic of a hibiscus blossom. Rooms are adequate, marred only by fluorescent lights. **Pros:** terrace get-togethers are a nice way to meet fellow travelers; package deals that include hotel and tours bring the price tag down considerably. **Cons:** a little pricey for what you get. ✉ *Cañada 6* ☎ *916/345–0201 or 01800/712–3560 toll-free in Mexico* *www.mayatulipanes.com* *72 rooms* *In-room: Wi-Fi. In-hotel: restaurant, room service, bar, pool, laundry service, Internet terminal, parking (free)* *AE, MC, V.*

$$$ **Villa Mercedes Hotel.** This comfortable hotel is one of the newest in the area. Spacious, modern, and clean rooms are distributed in 16 large buildings with thatch roofs that they call bungalows. The inviting lobby is also under a palapa roof, as is the large adjacent restaurant. You can access Wi-Fi in the lobby. **Pros:** one of the most comfortable options near the ruins. **Cons:** there are less expensive options. ✉ *Carretera Palenque-Ruinas, Km 2.9*

TRAVEL BY TOUR

Kichan Bajlum (✉ *Av. Juárez at Calle Abasolo, Palenque* ☎ *916/345–2452* *www.kichanbajlum.com*) has six-hour trips to Agua Azul and Misol-Há that cost about $12 per person. **Kukulcán** (✉ *Av. Juárez s/n at Calle 20 de Noviembre, Palenque* ☎ *916/345–1506 or 916/345–2778* *www.kukulcantravel.com*) has one- and two-day trips to Bonampak and Yaxchilán. A one-day trip costs $85, including transport by minivan and boat, a guide, and food.

8

☎ 916/345–5231 🌐 www.hotelesvillamercedes.com ⇨ 92 rooms, 2 suites ♨ In-hotel: restaurant, pools, spa, Wi-Fi hotspot, laundry service ▭ MC, V.

NIGHTLIFE

Palenque has more than its fair share of bars, but don't expect to be dancing until dawn. Things are *tranquilo* here, even on weekends. The second-floor **El Tapanco** (✉ *Av. Juárez 50* ☎ *916/345–0415*) has a happy hour that lasts from 3 until 11. The sound of local bands playing covers of U2's "With or Without You" and other rock clichés can be heard for blocks.

SHOPPING

Avenida Juárez has small crafts stores, but for the mother lode, head to the **Mercado de las Artesanías** just east of the main square.

BONAMPAK

183 km (113 mi) southeast of Palenque.

GETTING HERE AND AROUND

Until the 1990s few actually trekked out here. Now, however, you can take a three-hour bus ride from Palenque or drive on the paved Carretera 198. Buses or vans will take you to the ruins or drop you at Lacanjá so you can hike the last 3 km (2 mi).

EXPLORING

Bonampak, which means "painted walls" in Mayan, is renowned for its courtly murals of Mayan life. The settlement was built on the banks of the Río Lacanjá in the 7th and 8th centuries and was uncovered in 1946. Explorer Jacques Soustelle called it "a pictorial encyclopedia of a Maya city." In remarkable tones of blue, red, green, and yellow, the scenes in the three rooms of the fascinating Templo de las Pinturas recount such subjects as life at court and the aftermath of battle.

Wear sturdy shoes and bring insect repellent, good sunglasses, and a hat. Note that only four visitors are allowed in each room of the Templo de las Pinturas at a time, and you can't use a flash. *🎫 $8 includes transportation from park entrance to main structures ⏲ Daily 8–5.*

YAXCHILÁN

50 km (31 mi) northeast of Bonampak, 190 km (118 mi) southeast of Palenque.

GETTING HERE AND AROUND

Getting to Yaxchilán requires a one-hour riverboat ride; you must first drive or take a bus to the small town of Frontera Corozal, off Carretera 198, where boats depart for the ruins and for the Guatemalan border. It's best to arrange trips through travel agencies, tour operators, or tourist offices in Mexico City, Palenque, or San Cristóbal; they can arrange for you to stay at the wonderful indigenous Tzeltal cooperative, Escudo Jaguar.

EXPLORING

Fodor's Choice ★ Excavations at **Yaxchilán** (ya-shee- *lan*), on the banks of the Río Usumacinta, have uncovered stunning temples and delicate carvings. Spider monkeys and toucans are, at this point, more prolific than humans, and howler monkeys growl like lions from the towering gum trees and magnificent 100-year-old ceibas.

Yaxchilán, which means "place of green stones," reached its cultural peak during the Late Classic period, from about AD 800 to 1000. It's dominated by two acropolises that contain a palace, temples with finely carved lintels, and great staircases. Several generations ago the Lacandón made pilgrimages to this jungle-clad site to leave "god pots" (incense-filled ceramic bowls) in honor of ancient deities. They were awed by the headless sculpture of Yaxachtun (ya-sha- *tun*) at the entrance to the temple (called Structure 33) and believed the world would end when its head was replaced on its torso. *$3* *Daily 8–5.*

TABASCO

Graham Greene's succinct summation of Tabasco in *The Power and the Glory* as a "tropical state of river and swamp and banana grove" captures its essence. Although the state played an important role in Mexico's early history, its past is rarely on view. Instead, it's Tabasco's modern-day status as a supplier of oil that defines it. On a humid coastal plain and crisscrossed by 1,930 km (1,197 mi) of rivers, low hills, and unexplored jungles, the land is still rich in banana and cacao plantations. Refineries and related structures are, for the most part, invisible; what you're more apt to see are small ranches.

After the American Civil War, traders from the southern United States began operating in the region, hauling precious mahogany trees upstream from Chiapas and shipping them north from the small port of Frontera. After this prosperous era, Tabasco slumbered until the oil boom of the 1970s and 1980s. Although it has little infrastructure in place to help attract tourism, Tabasco has beaches, lagoons, caves, and nature reserves worthy of exploration. The fired-brick Mayan ruins of Comalcalco attest to the influence of Palenque, and the region southeast of the capital Villahermosa has rivers and canyons that are home to deer, alligators, and the occasional jaguar.

VILLAHERMOSA

227 km (173 mi) north of Tuxtla Gutiérrez.

The capital city of Villahermosa epitomizes the development of Tabasco, where the airplane arrived before the automobile. Thanks to oil and the money it brought in, the cramped and ugly neighborhoods—in the mosquito-ridden town of the 1970s—have largely been replaced by spacious boulevards, shady parks, and cultural centers. There is little of interest here, but as the city has the airport nearest Palenque, you may find yourself here for the night.

GETTING HERE AND AROUND

Villahermosa's tidy little Aeropuerto Capitán Carlos A. Rovirosa is 15 km (9 mi) south of the city in Ranchería dos Montes. Continental Express flies here daily from Houston. Aeroméxico, and Aviacsa have daily flights to Villahermosa from Mexico City. The only transportation from Villahermosa's airport is via taxi. A trip downtown costs $15. First-class bus service on ADO GL is available from Mexico City. If you're considering driving, Carretera 199 continues past Palenque until it reaches Carretera 186, which leads west to Villahermosa. There's frequent second-class service to nearby towns from the Central Camionera de Segunda Clase. Trips around Villahermosa are fixed at $1.50 in yellow colectivo taxis; the minimum fare is $2 in the white *especial* (special or private) taxis. **Creatur Transportadora Turística** (✉ *Av. Paseo Tabasco 1404, Villahermosa* ☎ *993/310–9900*) specializes in multiday excursions that take in Misol-Ha, Cañón de Sumidero, and other sights off the beaten path.

ESSENTIALS

Airlines Continental (☎ *01800/900–5000 toll-free in Mexico*).

Bus Contacts Villahermosa ADO (first class) (*Terminal Central de Primera Clase* ✉ *Calle F.J. Mina 297, at Calle Lino Merino* ☎ *993/312–1446*). **Villahermosa (second class)** (*Central Camionera de Segunda Clase* ✉ *Av. Ruíz Cortines s/n at Prolongación de Mina* ☎ *993/312–0863*).

Currency Exchange Scotiabank (✉ *Calle Zaragoza 607* ☎ *993/312–5803*).

Medical Assistance Hospital Cruz Roja de Villahermosa (✉ *Av. Sandino 716, Villahermosa* ☎ *993/315–5555 or 993/315–6263*).

Rental Cars Budget (✉ *Aeropuerto Capitán Carlos A. Rovirosa* ☎ *993/356–0118* 🌐 *www.budget.com* ✉ *Hotel Holiday Inn Express, Periférico Carlos Pellicer Camara 4000* ☎ *993/310–4650*). **Dollar** (✉ *Aeropuerto Villahermosa* ☎ *993/356–0211* 🌐 *www.dollar.com*). **Europcar** (✉ *Calle Vía 3 s/n* ☎ *993/356–0884* 🌐 *www.europcar.com*). **Hertz** (✉ *Aeropuerto Capitán Carlos A. Rovirosa* ☎ *993/356–0200* 🌐 *www.hertz.com* ✉ *Hotel Camino Real, Paseo Tabasco 1407* ☎ *993/310–0201*).

Visitor and Tour Info Villahermosa State Tourism Office (✉ *Av. de los Ríos at Calle 13, Villahermosa* ☎ *800/216–0842*).

EXPLORING

Covered with dazzlingly elaborate cobalt tiles, the building housing the **Museo de Historia de Tabasco** was originally called the Casa de los Azulejos (House of the Tiles). The mansion would be over the top even without the cherubs reclining along the roof. The museum's collection is a bit sparse, but the individual pieces—an anchor from the days that pirates patrolled the Gulf of Mexico, a carriage from the reign of dictator Porfirio Díaz—help bring the past to life. ✉ *Av. Juárez 402, at Calle 27 de Febrero* ☎ *No phone* 🎫 *$1.50* ⏲ *Tues.–Sun. 10–8.*

Fodor's Choice ★ Giant stone heads and other carvings were salvaged from the oil fields at La Venta, on Tabasco's western edge near the state of Veracruz. They're on display in the 20-acre **Parque-Museo La Venta**, a lush park founded by Carlos Pellicer Cámara in 1958. The views of the misty

Lago de las Ilusiones (Lake of Illusions) are stirring, which is probably why young lovers come here to smooch in quiet corners. The 6-foot-tall stone heads, which have bold features and wear what look like helmets, weigh up to 20 tons. The park also contains a zoo displaying animals from Tabasco and neighboring states. The jaguars—including one that is jet-black—always elicit screams from children. Sadly, many of the animals housed here are in danger of extinction. ✉ *Blvd. Ruíz Cortines s/n* ☎ *993/314–1652* *$3.50* ⏲ *Tues.–Sun. 8–5; ticket window closes at 4.*

Parque Yumká, which means "the spirit that looks after the forest" in Chontal Maya, is a nature reserve with jungle, savannah, and wetlands. Guided walking tours take you over a hanging bridge and past free-roaming endangered species such as spider monkeys, crocodiles, and native *tepezcuintles* (giant rodents). Boat tours allow for good bird-watching. The park is about 16 km (10 mi) east of Villahermosa. ✉ *Ranchería Las Barrancas s/n* ☎ *993/356–0107 or 993/356–0119* 🌐 *www.yumka.org* *$5* ⏲ *Daily 9–5; ticket window closes at 4.*

WHERE TO EAT

$$$ SPANISH ✕ **El Mesón del Angel.** You might think you've stumbled into a country inn when you make your way up the blue-tile steps. Inside are cheery lacy curtains and stained-glass windows. The owner is from Madrid, so the menu is full of dishes like *paella a la valenciana* (rice with seafood and sausage) and *arroz negro* (rice with squid ink). There's a wine list with plenty of Spanish vintages. ✉ *Av. Méndez 1604* ☎ *993/352–1138* 💳 *AE, MC, V.*

$$$ CONTEMPORARY ✕ **La Ceiba.** Polished wood, crimson carpets, and hanging lanterns are the backdrop at this restaurant inside the Hyatt; some entrées, like tamarind duck, have an Asian flair. But the food here is better termed international, especially on Wednesday and Thursday. On ordinary nights start with the paper-thin carpaccio before the garlic shrimp. ✉ *Av. Juárez 106, at Av. Ruíz Cortines* ☎ *993/310–1234* 💳 *AE, DC, MC, V.*

WHERE TO STAY

$$ **Calinda Viva Villahermosa.** This hotel is across from Parque-Museo La Venta. After a day exploring, head to the in-house spa. The low-slung building's gleaming white facade is softened by a Spanish tile roof. Rooms are simply furnished, quite comfortable, and complete with a small balcony. The nicest ones overlook the pool. **Pros:** tasty breakfasts; clean rooms. **Cons:** many business travelers; the restaurant and bar have bland interiors. ✉ *Av. Ruíz Cortines at Paseo Tabasco* ☎ *993/313–6000* 🌐 *www.hotelescalinda.com.mx* *239 rooms, 1 suite* *In-room: safe, Wi-Fi. In-hotel: restaurant, bars, pool, gym, spa, laundry service, Internet terminal, parking (free)* 💳 *AE, MC, V.*

$$ **Camino Real.** A stairway leads directly to the upscale Galería Tabasco, but other than that, this hotel is all work and no play. It's set up for conferences, so the sleek lines of the lobby are often obscured by people fiddling with their BlackBerrys. The restaurant, with floor-to-ceiling windows shaded with bamboo, is filled with executives. **Pros:** there's a gorgeous pool that often sits empty. **Cons:** scads of business travelers.

⊠ Paseo Tabasco 1407 ☎ 993/310–0201 or 800/722–6466 🌐 www.caminoreal.com 243 rooms, 24 suites In-room: safe, Internet. In-hotel: restaurant, room service, pool, gym, laundry service, Internet terminal, Wi-Fi hotspot, parking (free) ▭ AE, DC, MC, V.

LOCAL EATS

Tabascans eat lots of fresh fish from the sea as well as lakes and rivers. Local specialties include *pejelagarto*, an ugly fish with a head like an alligator's and a strong, sweet flavor. It's often served whole, so be prepared to face the beast. Also try *puchero* (boiled beef and other meats with vegetables and plantains) and *chaya*, a type of green similar to spinach. And make sure to try the region's fresh white cheese.

$–$$ **Cencali.** Overlooking the sparkling Laguna de las Ilusiones, this hotel is surrounded by coconut-palm, mango, and cacao trees that hide the neighboring hotels. The best rooms are in the newest wing beyond the lushly landscaped pool. A buffet breakfast is included in the rate. **Pros:** most of the big, cheerful rooms have small balconies; airport shuttle available. **Cons:** feels motel-ish. *⊠ Av. Juárez 105, at Paseo Tabasco ☎ 993/313–6611; 01800/112–5000 toll-free in Mexico 🌐 www.cencali.com.mx 151 rooms, 10 suites In-room: Wi-Fi. In-hotel: restaurant, room service, bar, pool, laundry service, Internet terminal, parking (free) ▭ AE, MC, V BP.*

$$ **Hyatt Regency Villahermosa.** Although it's stodgy on the outside, this luxury hotel lightens up once you pass through the front doors. The freshly remodeled Ceiba Café serves a superb breakfast buffet. With marble floors and polished modern wood furnishings, the guest rooms are some of the city's most luxurious. **Pros:** the young staff works hard at making you feel pampered. **Cons:** the restaurant is expensive. *⊠ Av. Juárez 106 ☎ 993/310–1234 🌐 www.villahermosa.regency.hyatt.com 198 rooms, 9 suites In-room: safe, Wi-Fi. In-hotel: restaurant, room service, bars, tennis courts, pool, gym, laundry service, Internet terminal, parking (free), no-smoking rooms ▭ AE, MC, V.*

$$ **Olmeca Plaza.** This graceful high-rise sits in the middle of the Zona Luz, not far from downtown. A waterfall sets the mood in the spacious marble lobby. Seemingly dozens of employees are ready at a moment's notice to bring a fresh towel or hail a taxi. The best of the tastefully decorated rooms are in the back. **Pros:** some rooms have a partial view of the river. **Cons:** style is a little outdated. *⊠ Av. Madero 418, at Calle Lerdo de Tejada ☎ 993/358–0102 or 01800/201–0901 toll-free in Mexico 🌐 www.hotelolmecaplaza.com 152 rooms In-room: refrigerator, safe, Internet, Wi-Fi (some). In-hotel: restaurant, room service, bar, pool, gym, laundry service, Internet terminal, parking (free) ▭ AE, MC, V.*

$ **Plaza Independencia.** The downtown location—on a quiet street near the main plaza—puts you close to everything in the Zona Luz. The lobby and common areas are painted in eye-popping bright pink, blue, and yellow. Ask for a room overlooking the river on one of the upper floors. **Pros:** the ground-floor restaurant serves regional cuisine and is popular with locals; the hotel has quirky artsy touches. **Cons:** popular

COMALCALCO TOWN

There's not much to see in this dusty little town 56 km (31 mi) northwest of Villahermosa, but it's the center of what's called the "Ruta del Cacao," or the Cocoa Route. Call ahead to arrange a free tour of **Hacienda de la Luz** (✉ *Blvd. Zovirosa Wade* ☎ *933/334–1126*), which is quite close to downtown Comalcalco. It's also known as Hacienda Hayer, because a German doctor named Otto Wolter Hayer bought it in the 1930s and turned it into the most profitable hacienda in the region. On the tour you'll learn everything about the production of cacao, from bean to chocolate.

A visit to Comalcalco is pretty much unavoidable if you are visiting the nearby ruins. From here you can take a taxi to the front gate. For about $10 the driver will wait for you while you explore.

with conventions and business travelers en masse. ✉ *Calle Independencia 123* ☎ *993/312–1299* 🌐 *www.hotelesplaza.com.mx* *90 rooms* *In-room: safe. In-hotel: restaurant, room service, bars, pool, laundry service, parking (free)* 💳 *AE, MC, V.*

SHOPPING

The pedestrian-only streets of the Zona Luz are great for window-shopping. But when locals want to spend money they head to **Galería Tabasco** (✉ *Paseo Tabasco* ☎ *993/316–1400*).

Near the main square, **Libros y Arte** (✉ *Calle Benito Juarez and Av. 27 de Febrero* ☎ *993/312–7323*) has a wonderful collection of books, including coffee-table volumes on the art and architecture of Tabasco. There are also plenty of maps and travel guides, some in English.

COMALCALCO

3 km (2 mi) northwest of Comalcalco Town.

GETTING HERE AND AROUND

EXPLORING

The region's abundant cacao trees provided food and a livelihood for a booming Mayan population during the Classic period (100 BC to AD 1000). **Comalcalco**, which was founded in about the 1st century BC, marks the westernmost reach of the Maya; descendants of its builders, the Chontal, still live in the vicinity. Its name means "place of the clay griddles" (bricks) in Nahuatl, and it is Tabasco's most important Mayan site, unique for its use of fired brick (made of sand, seashells, and clay), as the area's swamplands lacked the stone for building. The bricks were often inscribed and painted with figures of reptiles and birds, geometric figures, and drawings before being covered with stucco.

The major pyramid on the Gran Acrópolis del Este (Great Eastern Acropolis) is adorned with carvings as well as large stucco masks of the sun god, Kinich Ahau. The burial sites here also depart radically from Mayan custom: the dead were placed in cone-shape clay urns, in a fetal position. Some have been left *in situ,* and others are on display in the site museum along with many of the artifacts that were uncovered here. *$3* *Daily 10–5.*

PARAÍSO

19 km (12 mi) north of Comalcalco.

As you head toward the Gulf of Mexico coast and Paraíso, stop at one of the cacao plantations and chocolate factories. On the coast you'll get a glimpse of small-town life. Climb the Cerro Teodomiro (Teodomiro Hill) for a spectacular view of Laguna de las Flores (Las Flores Lagoon) and coconut plantations. Small seafood restaurants and several small hotels dot the shore here.

GETTING HERE AND AROUND

From Villahermosa, take Carretera 180 for 23 kilometers (14 miles) toward Heroica Cárdenas, where you will take Carretera 187, heading north to Comalcalco, for about 10 kilometers (6.2 miles). The entire trip is approximately 75 kilometers (46 miles), and takes around 45 minutes by car.

EXPLORING

The region's small, dark-sand beaches are not among Mexico's prettiest; the best place to spend your time is 5 km (3 mi) southeast of Paraíso, in **Puerto Ceiba**, a fishing community whose inhabitants breed and harvest oysters. You can take a two-hour boat tour aboard the *Puerto Ceiba I* around the mangrove-lined Laguna Mecoacán (Mecoacán Lagoon) and the coastal rivers. Tours, which cost about $5 for adults, leave from the small Puerto Ceiba Restaurant.

Sonora

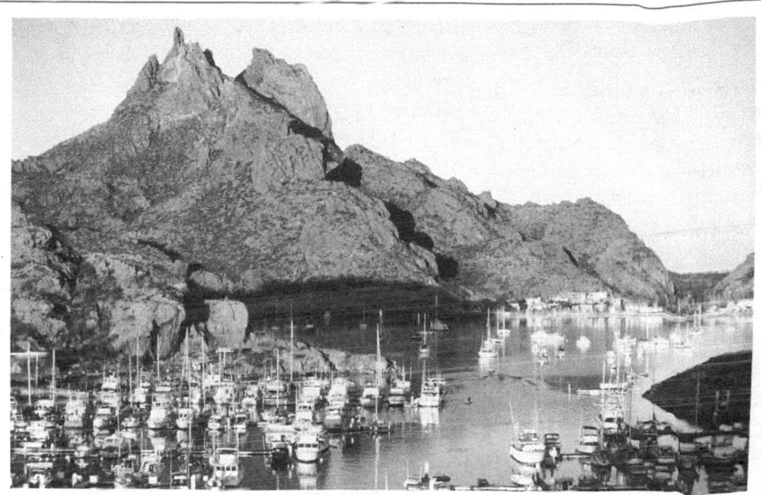

Guaymas marina

9

WORD OF MOUTH

"[Guaymas is] mostly a fishing and shrimping center. Nearby San Carlos is newer and built up for tourism. Most people from Phoenix who drive to a Mexican beach go to Rocky Point (Puerto Peñasco) because it's much closer."

—Bill_H

www.fodors.com/community

WELCOME TO SONORA

TOP REASONS TO GO

★ **The chance to visit a colonial city:** Wonderfully preserved Álamos has great hotels and restaurants and a friendly community of American expats.

★ **Having a beach all to yourself:** Resort towns provide plenty of creature comforts, but secluded beaches await those with a sense of adventure and a four-wheel drive.

★ **Experiencing ancient traditions:** Several indigenous groups here still live close to their roots—you might get a chance to see Yaqui and Mayo ceremonies.

★ **Going off the grid:** An otherworldly landscape of volcanic craters and towering sand dunes, El Pinacate is isolated, mysterious, and strictly for adventurous sorts.

★ **A drive along the Río Sonora:** Exploring this river route into the sleepy towns in the foothills of the Sierra Madre gives you a glimpse of traditional Mexican cowboy life.

1 El Pinacate. This biosphere reserve has a unique landscape of volcanic cones, lava formations, and desert plants that'll make you feel like you're on another planet.

2 The Sonoran Coast. Most visitors to Sonora come here, where desert collides with shimmering blue water. Puerto Peñasco, San Carlos, and Guaymas are developed, but you'll find miles of secluded beaches along the Mar de Cortés.

3 Nogales. Sonora's major gateway is the most logical border crossing. Given reports of gang-related violence here, it's best to drive through quickly (by day)—right on to the Ruta de la Misiones or the coastal resorts.

4 Hermosillo. This workaday state capital minds its own business, but is emerging as a major national-airline hub. A brand-new highway runs to lovely Bahía Kino, about an hour away.

5 Ruta de las Misiones. Just south of Nogales are a string of tiny mission towns that are important to the history of the region.

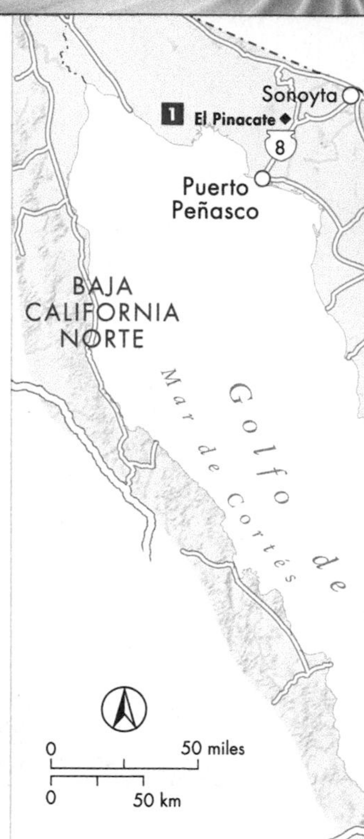

6 Ruta de Río Sonora. This gorgeous road trip takes you alongside the river and through small, unspoiled towns and old-fashioned ranches.

7 Álamos and Aduana. Northernmost of the major colonial cities, Álamos is the magical antidote to overdeveloped beach resorts. Aduana, a former mining town with one truly outstanding restaurant, is an easy trip from Álamos.

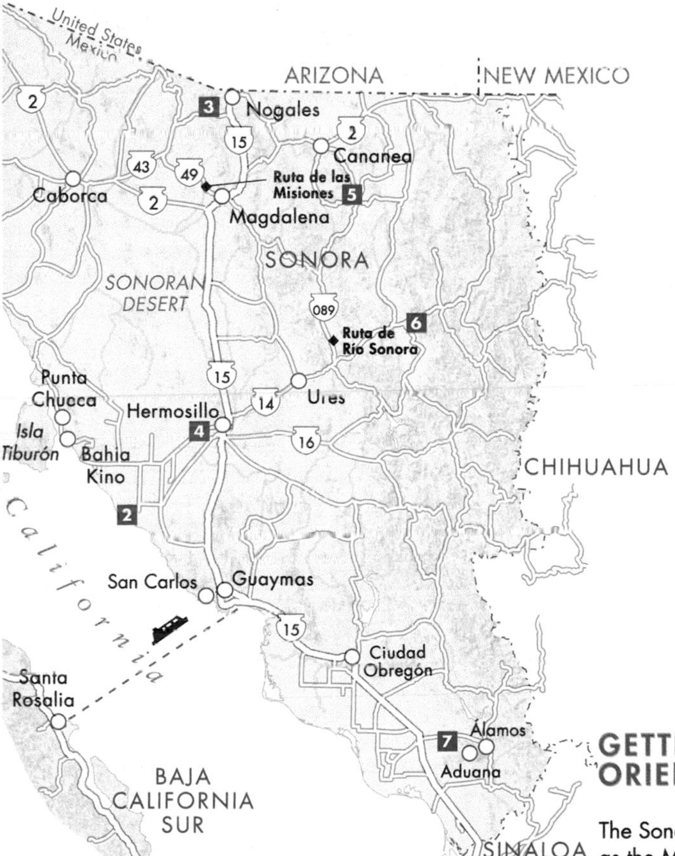

United States
Mexico
ARIZONA
NEW MEXICO
2
3 Nogales
15
2
Cananea
43
49
Caborca
2
Ruta de las Misiones 5
Magdalena
SONORA
SONORAN DESERT
089
6
Ruta de Río Sonora
15
Punta Chueca
14
Ures
Hermosillo
4
Isla Tiburón
Bahia Kino
16
CHIHUAHUA
2
Golfo de California
San Carlos
Guaymas
15
Ciudad Obregón
Santa Rosalia
Álamos
7
Aduana
BAJA CALIFORNIA SUR
SINALOA

GETTING ORIENTED

The Sonoran Desert—or as the Mexicans call it, El Desierto de Altar—dominates the northern part of this state, where long stretches of flat scrub are punctuated by brown hills, saguaros, and organ-pipe cacti. South of Guaymas, the desert gives way to a dry, tropical landscape.

SONORA PLANNER

A Simple Itinerary

Because it's a sprawling region, you'd need at least eight days to do justice to Sonora. If you have just a few days, start at beachfront San Carlos. (You can drive the entire way, or fly into Hermosillo and drive from there.) The next day, take the easier three-hour drive to lovely Álamos. Spend a night in Hermosillo before taking a leisurely drive along the Río Sonora, stopping for the night in Ures or Arizpe. Make sure to take the 4-km (2½-mi) hike along the rutted road out of Aconchi to soak in the hot springs.

If you only have the weekend, cross the border from the United States and explore the Ruta de los Misiones. Spend the night in Bahía Kino and come back up the Ruta de Río Sonora to catch the ruins of Padre Kino's adobe mission you missed at Imuris and head home.

Sea and Sun

If you want to skip the touristy areas around San Carlos and Puerto Peñasco, seek out the more secluded beaches around Bahía Kino and all along the Mar de Cortés. A coastal highway from Guaymas to Puerto Peñasco is underway: enjoy the solitude while you can.

Border Crossings

There are several border crossings, but most people cross at Nogales. Interstate 19 in Arizona travels south from Tucson and becomes Highway 15 beginning in Nogales, continues south through Hermosillo, and reaches the Mar de Cortés at Guaymas, 418 km (260 mi) from the Arizona border.

Owing to concerns about gang-related violence, some people are avoiding Nogales and instead taking Highway 85 from Phoenix or Highway 86 to Highway 85 from Tucson and crossing at Lukeville to the Mexican town of Sonoyta. From here Highway 8 runs to the coastal town of Puerto Peñasco; Highway 2 runs to Highway 15 and on to Hermosillo.

You no longer need a car permit (though you do need Mexico car insurance) unless you are traveling south of Ciudad Obregón. Permits cost $31 if you plan to travel elsewhere in Mexico. Make sure you check in with Mexican immigration to get your six-month tourist visa, which will cost $27.

The Baja Car Ferry

An alternative to the Arizona border crossings is to enter Mexico in Baja and take the car ferry from Santa Rosalía to Guaymas. The ferry departs every Tuesday and Wednesday at 9 AM and every Friday and Sunday at 8 PM, from the terminal (☎ *615/152–1246* 🌐 *www.ferrysantarosalia.com*) on the east side of the transpeninsular highway, near the bus station. Ferries from Guaymas to Santa Rosalía run every Monday, Tuesday, Thursday, and Saturday at 8 PM, from the ferry terminal on Avenida Serdán (☎ *622/222–0204*). The trip takes 9–10 hours; the fare is $65 for adults. Cars 18 feet or less in length are $248 and require at least a three-day advance notice. Check the times, too, as these are subject to change. Passenger tickets can be purchased the day of travel, though it's best to buy them a day in advance.

Safety

Before planning your trip to Nogales—or any other Mexican-American border town—check 🌐 *www.state.gov/travel* for updates on drug violence and security precautions.

Don't linger in Nogales, which has experienced some gang-related violence. If you must spend time here, stick to the touristed areas, and watch out for pickpockets and petty thieves. Remaining alert (and sober) will lessen your risk of becoming a victim.

Travel elsewhere in Sonora is generally not problematic. Though you really should plan to drive by day, know that roads here are good and help is easy to find in the populated areas.

What Time Is It?

Sonora is Mexico's only state that does not observe Daylight Saving Time with the rest of the country from early April to late October. It stays on Mountain Standard Time year-round in order to keep its clocks in sync with neighboring Arizona across the U.S. border.

Tour Companies

South of the Border Tours (✉ *7937 E. Coronado Rd., Tucson, AZ* ☎ *520/760–4000* 🌐 *www.southofthebordertours.com*) runs mostly senior-citizen package tours to Álamos, San Carlos, Puerto Peñasco, the Mission Route, Baja, and the Copper Canyon. **Solipaso** (✉ *Calle Obregon 3, Álamos* ☎ *647/428–0466* 🌐 *www.solipaso.com*) is run by an American expat couple based in Álamos; they sell set or custom itineraries and specialize in birding, soft adventure, and natural-history tours throughout Mexico.

WHAT IT COSTS IN DOLLARS

	¢	$	$$	$$$	$$$$
Restaurants	under $5	$5–$10	$10–$15	$15–$25	Over $25
Hotels	under $50	$50–$75	$75–$150	$150–$250	Over $250

Restaurant prices are per person for a main course at dinner. Hotel prices are for two people in a standard double room in high season. Hotel rates sometimes include the 17% tax; be sure to check this when you're quoted a price.

More Information

You can contact the Sonora Office of Conventions and Visitors (✉ *El Paseo del Canal at Comonfort, Edificio Sonora, 3rd fl., Hermosillo* ☎ *662/289–5800; 01800/716–2555 toll-free in Mexico* 🌐 *www.sonoraturismo.gob.mx or www.gotosonora.com*) while you plan your trip. They'll send you mounds of information and a helpful full-color booklet.

How's the Weather?

Summer temperatures in Sonora are as high as they are in southern Arizona, so unless you're prepared to broil, plan your trip for sometime between October and May. Even in winter, daytime temperatures can rise above 27°C (80°F), though at night the temperature does drop considerably. Winter on the coast can also bring strong, steady winds that make temperatures seem much cooler than they actually are. The foothill towns along the Río Sonora and Álamos are generally hot in the summer, but can drop to near freezing in the winter, even during the day. Snow is not unheard of in those places, either.

As the Sonoran weather varies, so does the landscape—from fertile cropland and arid desert to stretches of sandy beaches and mountain ranges.

NOGALES

109 km (68 mi) south of Tucson via Hwy. 19, on Arizona-Mexico border, 282 km (175 mi) north of Hermosillo on Hwy. 15.

Updated by Jeffrey Van Fleet

NOGALES SERVES AS THE ENTRY point for most Americans driving from Arizona into Sonora—generally to a beach community like Puerto Peñasco. Although it's considerably smaller than the border cities of Tijuana or Ciudad Juárez, Nogales can be chaotic, and it has had the same problems with drug cartel–related violence as its larger counterparts.

If you're driving down, consider heading along Highway 85 from Phoenix or Highway 86 to Highway 85 from Tucson and crossing at Lukeville to the Mexican town of Sonoyta. For the coast and Puerto Peñasco, pick up Mexican Highway 8; for Hermosillo, take Highway 2 to Highway 15. Always travel by car during the day; if you arrive in the region too late to drive onward before sunset, overnight on the Arizona side of the border.

As flights from Nogales to elsewhere in Mexico tend be expensive, consider flying into Hermosillo and traveling onward from there.

⚠ **At this writing, we don't recommend taking day trips to Nogales.**

SAFETY AND PRECAUTIONS

Before planning your trip to Mexican-American border towns, check 🌐 *www.state.gov/travel* for updates on drug violence and security precautions.

■ **TIP➔ Travel quickly through Nogales or bypass it altogether.**

GETTING HERE AND AROUND

Nogales International Airport is about 16 km (10 mi) south of the border. A taxi from the airport to downtown Nogales costs about $15.

You no longer need a car permit to drive south of Nogales. You only need a car permit if you're traveling farther than Ciudad Obregón (the permits can be obtained at Km 21, just south of Nogales). They are free (but must be returned) if you plan to stay in Sonora, and will cost $31 if you are going elsewhere in Mexico.

Most visitors to Sonora travel by car from Tucson via Interstate 19 to the border in Nogales, Arizona. Mexico's Highway 15, a divided four-lane toll road, begins in Nogales. This highway is the fastest way to get to Hermosillo and Guaymas–San Carlos, but expect to pay approximately $15 in tolls. The alternative *libre* (free) routes are generally slower and not as well maintained, though by no means problematic.

ESSENTIALS

Bus Contacts **Central de Autobuses** (☎ *631/313–1603*). **Greyhound Mexico** (☎ *01800/010–0600 toll-free in Mexico; 800/229–9424* 🌐 *www.greyhound.com.mx*).

Car Insurance **Arizona Automobile Association** (✉ *8204 E. Broadway, TucsonAZ* ☎ *520/296–7461* ✉ *6950 N. Oracle Rd., Phoenix* ☎ *520/885–0694 or 800/352–5382* 🌐 *www.aaaaz.com*). **Sanborn's Mexico Insurance** (✉ *105 W. Grant, TucsonAZ* ☎ *520/882–5000* 🌐 *www.sanbornsinsurance.com*).

Medical Assistance **Centro Hospitalario México** (✉ *Patras 123, at Prigos, Col. El Griego* ☎ *631/319–1637*).

HERMOSILLO

280 km (174 mi) south of Nogales on Hwy. 15.

Hermosillo, the state's on-and-off capital since 1831, is a hardworking city. Manufacturing and agriculture are its main concerns. But a few older plazas and 19th-century buildings hark back to a more gracious past. For travelers to Sonora, it's a transportation hub. Most visitors driving or flying into Sonora pass through this modern city.

GETTING HERE AND AROUND

Hermosillo's Aeropuerto Internacional General Ignacio L. Pesqueira (HMO) is a hub for flights between the United States and the rest of Mexico; both US Airways and Aeroméxico fly from Phoenix. It lies 15 minutes outside the city center, a journey that costs $20 by taxi. The Central de Autobuses, located just off Highway 15, serves all the major regional and national bus companies. A bus trip from Nogales, near the border, to Hermosillo takes approximately four hours. Greyhound Mexico has service to Hermosillo. Grupo Estrella Blanca has frequent service to Hermosillo from Nogales, Tijuana, and Mexicali. A taxi downtown should cost $5. Taxis can be flagged from just about anywhere, especially in front of the hotels.

ESSENTIALS

Airlines **Aeroméxico** (☎ *01800/021–4050 toll-free in Mexico*). **US Airways** (☎ *800/235–9292*).

Bus Contacts **Central de Autobuses** (✉ *Blvd. Encinas Luis Johnson 400, at Los Pinos y Jaffa, Col. El Coloso* ☎ *662/217–1522*). **Greyhound Mexico** (☎ *01800/710–8819 toll-free in Mexico; 800/231–2222* 🌐 *www.greyhound.com.mx*). **Grupo Estrella Blanca** (☎ *01800/507–5500 toll-free in Mexico; 662/212–5127* 🌐 *www.estrellablanca.com.mx*).

Currency Exchange **Banco Santander** (✉ *Blvd. Luis Encinas at Juárez, Centro* ☎ *662/259-1578*).

Medical Assistance **The Green Angels** (☎ *078 in Hermosillo; 01800/903–9200 toll-free in Mexico*). **Hospital CIMA de Hermosillo** (✉ *Paseo San Miguel de Río 39, Col. Vado del Río* ☎ *662/259–0900* 🌐 *www.cimahermosillo.com*).

Rental Cars **Hertz** (✉ *Blvd. Rodriguez 57 at Vera Cruz, Col. Centro* ☎ *662/210–1810 or 800/654–3030*).

EXPLORING

TOP ATTRACTIONS

The best viewpoint in the city is the top of Cerro de la Campana (Hill of Bells), where you'll also find the **Museo de Sonora**. The museum is in a former penitentiary; the cells hold 18 permanent exhibits on astronomy, anthropology, history, geology, geography, and culture, all with a Sonoran slant. The bulk of the exhibits are graphic displays, including charts

CLOSE UP

Ruta de las Misiones

Although most towns in northern Sonora have a link to a nearby mission, those founded by Padre Eusebio Francisco Kino, a prominent figure in early Sonoran history, seem to hold the most interest. Although none of the original missions is still standing—some were destroyed in the Pima Indian uprising of 1695, other were replaced with newer structures by the Franciscans, who took over after the Jesuits were expelled for defending the local people—the so-called "mission route" is still fascinating.

Most of the missions are closed to visitors, but their stolid presence and the mood of these tiny towns, basically unchanged for 400 years, make them worth a visit. The best way to see the mission route is to start on Highway 15 just south of Nogales. It takes around three hours to reach the city of Caborca, a decent-size city with many restaurants and a few hotels. Since most towns don't have much else to see, you could technically tour the missions in one day.

Start at the mission Kino named **Santa María de Magdalena,** in the town of Magdalena de Kino. Padre Kino died here in 1711, while dedicating the town's first church, and the town holds what are alleged to be Kino's surprisingly new-looking remains. The remains, discovered by archaeologists in 1966, can be viewed inside a special dome constructed for this purpose. The church, on the other side of the **Plaza Colosio**, honors St. Francis, the town's patron. Every October 4 the town hosts an extremely rowdy festival in his honor.

Heading south toward Santa Ana, turn west on Highway 2 toward Caborca. Detour north on Sonora Highway 43 toward Oquitoa to visit **San Antonio de Oquitoa** (meaning "white woman" in the Opata language) and **San Pedro y San Pablo de Tubutama,** (Opata for "the highest place"). The church at Oquitoa has the twin towers typical of the Franciscans, but also the flat roof favored by the Jesuits. Tubutama's facade has a working sundial, the church's most striking feature.

Back on Highway 2 you'll come to **San Diego de Pitiquito,** between the towns of Altar and Caborca. The whitewashed church (circa 1780) is famous for its didactic paintings, which are thought to have been created by Papago Indians in the late 1800s. Once painted over, they were rediscovered and restored in 1966.

The final mission you'll come to on this route is **La Purísima Concepción de Caborca,** built in 1809. The town is known for beating back the 1857 military expedition of Henry Alexander Crabb, a California state senator. After a six-day battle during which Crabb's 69 men exploded the doors of the church with dynamite, the Mexican commander, Hilario Gabilondo, came forward with terms of surrender. Crabb acquiesced, but he and his men were betrayed and executed the next morning. Crabb's was the last of the so-called "filibuster" incursions into Mexico that served as inspiration for Cormac McCarthy's novel *Blood Meridian.*

Tours of the mission route can be arranged through the compelling and extremely amiable local historian **José Jesús "Loco" Valenzuela Luna** (☎ *637/372–1989 or 637/107–0345*) The rates, based on your area of interest, range from $45 to $75.

and maps of trade routes and native populations. Each display has a short summary in English. ✉ *Jesús García Final s/n, Col. La Matanza* ☎ *662/217–2580* 🎟 *$2.50, free Sun.* ⏲ *Tues.–Sun. 9–5:30.*

At the center of town, look for alluring **Plaza Zaragoza**, a lovely square shaded by towering fig trees. At the center of the plaza stands a turn-of-the-century Florentine wrought-iron gazebo. Flanking the plaza are the contemporaneous **Palacio Gobierno and the Catedral de Nuestra Señora de la Asunción,** which was built between 1877 and 1912.

TOUR BY TROLLEY

Trolebús (☎ *662/213–8638* 🌐 *www.imcahermosillo.org* 🎟 *$2*), a faux-antique trolleybus, picks up passengers at Plaza Zaragoza. The trip is an exhilarating plunge into Hermosillo's urban pulse.

WORTH NOTING

From Plaza Zaragoza, cross the Río Sonora and walk south for several blocks until you reach the odd little neighborhood of **Villa de Seris.** Its small plaza and lovely church have much more charm than the modern city center. The coyota was first baked here. Eat your fill while exploring this elegant neighborhood.

WHERE TO EAT

$$ STEAKHOUSE ✕ **Sonora Steak.** Come to this sophisticated steak house for the finest cuts of the famous Sonoran beef. You won't break the bank, as the prices here are quite reasonable. The specialty, rib-eye steak, is aged for 28 days. Vegetarians can graze on a variety of salads or opt for cream of green chili soup. The restaurant is a good spot for a late-night meal—it's open until 1 AM. ✉ *Blvd. Kino 914, Zona Hotelera* ☎ *662/210–0313* 🌐 *www.sonorasteak.com* 💳 *AE, MC, V.*

$$ MEXICAN ✕ **Xochimilco.** This large restaurant is rather institutional-looking, but it's a great place to try regional specialties. There's a set menu—meals are designed for two or more, and typically include carne asada, ribs, tripe, vegetable salad, beans, and fresh flour tortillas. It's popular with both locals and visitors from across the border. ✉ *Av. Obregón 51, at Gutiérrez, Col. Villa de Seris* ☎ *662/220–4052* 💳 *AE, MC, V.*

9

WHERE TO STAY

$$–$$$ 🏨 **Fiesta Americana.** Hermosillo's top hotel, Fiesta Americana is especially popular among business executives. The guest rooms, with their tasteful beige-and-forest-green design, appeal to travelers as well. The adjacent disco is the biggest attraction in the town's sleepy nightlife scene. **Pros:** friendly staff; tasteful furnishings; modern gym. **Cons:** on an ugly street; uninspiring exterior. ✉ *Blvd. Kino 369, Zona Hotelera* ☎ *662/259–6000 or 800/154–5001* 🌐 *www.fiestaamericana.com* 🛏 *221 rooms* 👍 *In-room: refrigerator, Wi-Fi. In-hotel: 2 restaurants, room service, bar, tennis court, pool, gym, Wi-Fi hotspot, Internet terminal* 💳 *AE, MC, V.*

$–$$ 🏨 **Holiday Inn Hermosillo.** Most of the handsome rooms in this two-story hotel surround an expansive lawn and an inviting pool. The hotel is

CLOSE UP

Ruta de Río Sonora

The highways following the Río Sonora are a terrific way to see a less touristy side of Sonora. Between Hermosillo and Cananea, the riverbanks are speckled with small towns, each with its own appeal. Some are known for their thermal springs, others for their rich histories. As is typical of the area, each has a colonial church and a heart-of-town square. People come into town from the surrounding ranches, so you'll see plenty of cowboy boots and hats.

The region is known for its hospitality, and it's common for townspeople to wave as you pass by. The easiest drive is up the valley from Hermosillo, although it's also possible to drive south from Cananea. (This route passes over mountain roads, which are difficult in bad weather.) From Hermosillo, take Sonora Federal Highway 14 east to Mazocahui, where you'll pass through Ures, the first town on the route, and then continue north on Sonora Federal Highway 89. The whole route, without stopping, requires a little over three hours. Driving part of it, with stops, makes an easy day trip, especially in autumn.

The land along the Río Sonora was the region's first inhabited area; it was settled by the Pima and Opata people. The route is also linked to the arrival of the Europeans—the Spanish explorer Alvar Núñez Cabeza de Vaca followed the Río Sonora during his travels between central Mexico and what is now the United States in the mid-16th century, and the Coronado expeditions of the 1540s also followed the Río Sonora. The main towns along this route were founded and settled 100 years later. Signs at the entrance to each town give you the exact year.

Heading northeast on Highway 14 from Hermosillo, the first town that you'll come to is **Ures.** The former capital of the state, 45 minutes from Hermosillo, is the largest town on the Río Sonora. Its square is anchored by four bronze statues representing Greek mythological figures. There are some good country-style restaurants, and some of the 19th-century haciendas have been converted into hotels.

Continuing on Route 89, you'll pass through **Baviácora,** with its 19th-century church standing next to the 20th-century church built to replace it. **Aconchi,** about 15 minutes farther down the road, is a good base from which to explore the area. Make sure to visit the local hot springs, which range from tepid to really, really hot.

About two hours from Aconchi is **Arizpe,** the first place in Sonora to bear the title of "city." This was also the *first* capital of the province of Occidente, which encompassed Sonora and what is now part of California, Arizona, New Mexico, and Texas. Its magnificently worn church, built in 1646, contains the remains of Spanish Captain Juan Francisco de Anza, the founder of San Francisco, California. Arizpe's quiet central square, with its handsome brick clock tower, is a great place to soak up the peace of small-town life. If you decide to stay the night, there are some worthwhile local restaurants and hotels.

a bargain, given the fact that it has some amenities and is in the convenient and generally pricey Zona Hotelera. **Pros:** friendly staff; convenient location. **Cons:** on an ugly block; gives a chain-hotel impression. ✉ *Blvd. Kino and Ramón Corral, Zona Hotelera* ☎ *662/289–1700 or 888/465–4329* 🌐 *www.holidayinn.com* *116 rooms, 10 suites* *In-room: refrigerator (some). In-hotel: restaurant, room service, bar, pool, gym, Wi-Fi hotspot, Internet terminal, laundry service, parking (free)* 💳 *AE, MC, V.*

$ **Hotel Bugambilia.** This pleasant small property has a trio of assets: comfortable rooms, convenient location, and a good restaurant. The bougainvillea-covered bungalows facing the parking lot are most popular; other rooms surround the pool. Guests are free to use the facilities at the Holiday Inn across the street. **Pros:** nice accommodations; good-looking pool. **Cons:** on a noisy street. ✉ *Blvd. Kino 712, Zona Hotelera* ☎ *662/289–1600; 01800/623–3300 toll-free in Mexico* 🌐 *www.hotelbugambilia.com.mx* *79 rooms, 23 cabañas* *In-room: safe, Wi-Fi. In-hotel: restaurant, room service, pool, Wi-Fi hotspot, parking (free)* 💳 *AE, MC, V.*

LOCAL FOOD

Sonoran cuisine has all the makings for stellar surf and turf: It's distinguished by terrific steaks and fresh seafood. Steak is not the only specialty in Sonora; look for *machaca*, *carne asada*, and, if you can handle the concept, *tacos de cabeza* (pig's head tacos). Seafood lovers will find shrimp, scallops, octopus, clams, and fish (both freshwater and ocean species), as well as *cahuamanta*, a tasty and filling manta ray now eaten instead of the endangered sea turtles. There's an abundance of enchiladas, tacos, and tamales—the style of Mexican cooking with which most Americans are familiar derives from this region.

9

THE SONORAN COAST

Sonora's coastline is mostly known for resort towns such as Puerto Peñasco and San Carlos. Most of Sonora's main beaches have paved access roads, but some of the best—like pristine Playa San Nicolás just south of Bahía Kino—await the adventurous at the end of rutted, washed-out dirt tracks. Your lovable little hatchback isn't going to cut it, so make sure you're driving something sturdy, preferably with four-wheel drive.

PUERTO PEÑASCO

105 km (65 mi) southwest of the Lukeville, Arizona, border, on Mexico Hwy. 8.

Puerto Peñasco was dubbed Rocky Point by British explorers in the 18th century, and that's the name most Americans know it by today. The town itself was established about 1927, after Mexican fishermen found abundant shrimp beds in the area and American John Stone built the first hotel. Al Capone was a frequent visitor during the Prohibition era, when he was hiding from U.S. law.

CLOSE UP

Sonora Background

Mexico's second-largest state, Sonora, is also one of its richest. Ranch lands here feed Mexico's finest beef cattle, and rivers flowing west from the Sierra Madre are diverted by giant dams to irrigate this area. Sonora's many crops include wheat and other grains, cotton, vegetables, nuts, and fruit—especially melons, citrus, peaches, and apples. Hermosillo, Sonora's capital, bustles with agricultural commerce in the midst of the fertile lands that turn dry again toward the coast.

In 1540 Francisco Vázquez de Coronado, governor of the provinces to the south, became the first Spanish leader to visit the plains of Sonora. More than a century later, Father Eusebio Francisco Kino led a missionary expedition to Sonora and what is now southern Arizona—an area referred to as the Pimería Alta for the band of Pima Indians still living there. The Italian-born, German-educated priest is credited with founding more than 20 missions in what is now northern Sonora and southern Arizona, as well as introducing cattle, citrus, wheat, and peaches—all still important crops—to the region. Although Álamos, in the south of Sonora, boomed with silver-mining wealth in the late 17th century, no one paid much attention to the northern part of the region. When the United States annexed a giant chunk of Mexico's territory after the Mexican-American War (1846–48), northern Sonora suddenly became a border area—and a haven for Arizona outlaws. International squabbles bloomed and faded over the next decades as officials argued over such issues as the right to pursue criminals across the border. Porfirio Díaz, dictator of Mexico for most of the years between 1876 and 1911, finally moved to secure the state by settling it.

Settlers in Sonora, however, proved a hardy and independent bunch ill-suited to accepting the dictates of politicos in faraway Mexico City. Sonorans and their neighbors, the Chihuahenses, were major players in the Mexican Revolution, and the republic was ruled by three Sonorans: Plutarco Elías Calles, Adolfo de la Huerta, and Abelardo Rodríguez. Despite the enormous cost and destruction to railroads and other infrastructure, the Mexican Revolution brought prosperity to Sonora. With irrigation from the state's dams, inhabitants have been able to grow enough wheat and vegetables not only for Mexico but also for export. Today Sonora's economy continues to thrive, partly because of the *maquiladoras* (American factories that have moved across the border to take advantage of low wages and loose labor and environmental restrictions). The passage of the North American Free Trade Agreement (NAFTA), which relaxed tariffs on goods moving across North American borders, made the maquila a profitable tool for U.S. companies. Millions of people have flocked to Nogales, here in Sonora, and Tijuana, Ciudad Juárez, Nuevo Laredo, and Matamoros in search of employment. Critics decry the sweatshop conditions in many factories. On a happier note, state and federal governments are pouring money into tourist-oriented development, making it the fastest-growing part of the economy. Visitors enjoy not only Sonora's abundance of beaches, but also the seclusion and tranquillity of its mountains and deserts.

The real appeal of Puerto Peñasco, at the north end of the Mar de Cortés (Sea of Cortez), is the miles of sandy beaches punctuated by stretches of black volcanic rock. A remarkably high tide change—as much as 23 feet—makes for great exploring among countless tide pools. The town itself has already been discovered, as you'll know from all the neon signs advertising Subway, Century 21, and Thrifty. But the newly revamped malecón (waterfront boardwalk), illuminated by night in a wash of color, is a friendly gathering place for locals and travelers.

High-rise developments are already being built, which will add an eye-opening skyline to sleepy Puerto Peñasco. Even more dramatic changes to the landscape may result from the forthcoming coastal highway and the town's place at the top of the "Escalera Náutica" (Nautical Ladder), a series of high-end marinas along the coasts.

GETTING HERE AND AROUND

The airport at Puerto Peñasco has undergone significant changes in the past two years, and continues to expand and improve with the town's growth. If you arrive by bus, remember that the place is pretty spread out. Although cabs are available, you should always set a price with the driver before getting inside. Bus connections can be had from three stations on the main road into town, and buses to the rest of the state and country are plentiful.

ESSENTIALS

Currency Exchange **Banco Santander** (✉ *Av. Juárez 87, Carretera Internacional* ☎ *638/383–4288*).

Visitor and Tour Info **Puerto Peñasco tourism office** (✉ *Blvd. Juárez 320-B, at V. Estrella* ☎ *638/388–0444*).

9

EXPLORING

Though the desert to the north of Puerto Peñasco is one of the most barren-looking in the state, there is a complex and delicate ecosystem out in all that sand and scrub. The Gulf of California itself is one of the most vital marine ecosystems in North America, and its deep, nutrient-rich waters make it a breeding ground for whales and produce some of the biggest sportfishing trophies in the world.

The northern Gulf area forms an impressive desert-coast ecosystem, and scientists conduct research programs at the **Intercultural Center for the Study of Desert and Oceans** (known as CEDO, its acronym in Spanish), about 3 km (2 mi) east of town on Fremont Boulevard in the Fraccionamiento Las Conchas neighborhood. You can take an English-language tour of the facility to learn about the ecology of the area and its history, or just pick up a tide calendar (useful if you're planning beach activities) or field guide from the gift shop. Talks and nature outings—including tide-pool walks, Pinacate volcano excursions, and kayaking expeditions of area estuaries—are on offer. ✉ *Turn onto Blvd. Fremont at municipal building and follow signs for Las Conchas Beach and CEDO* ☎ *638/382–0113; 520/320–5473 in U.S.* 🌐 *www.cedointercultural.org* *Free natural history talks Tues. and Sat., donation for eco-tours* ⏲ *Mon.–Sat. 9–5, Sun. 10–2; tours Tues. at 2, Sat. at 4.*

CLOSE UP

El Pinacate

The somewhat difficult trip to **El Pinacate** is also one of the region's most rewarding. The reserve, midway between Puerto Peñasco and the Arizona border, is famous for volcanic rock formations and thousands of moonlike craters. Highlights include 4,000-foot-high **Santa Clara peak**, and the mile-wide **El Elegante crater**, created by a giant steam eruption 150,000 years ago.

With the addition of a solar-powered visitor center, which opened in 2009, exploring the area isn't quite as daunting. But you'll still need to plan ahead, bringing your own water, food, and extra gasoline. A high-clearance four-wheel-drive vehicle is also strongly advised. Since an unpopulated stretch of desert is a great place for drug trafficking and illegal border crossings, use common sense. Lastly, be mindful of the heat—summer temperatures can be blistering. The best time to visit is between November and March.

If all the "cons" listed above make you nervous, don't worry. Excellent naturalist-led tours can also be arranged through **La Ruta de Sonora** (☎ *520/886–6555 in U.S.* ⊕ *www.laruta.org*) in Tucson.

All visitors must register at the park entrance, where a ranger's station provides informative tips for visitors. For current park information, contact the International Sonoran Desert Alliance in Ajo, Arizona, at ☎ 520/387–6823 in U.S. ✉ *Hwy. 8, Km 51, Esperanza, near Ejido Nayarit* ☎ *638/384–9007* *$3* ⏲ *Daily 9–5.*

WHERE TO EAT

$$ SEAFOOD ✕ **Friendly Dolphin.** This bright blue-and-pink palace feels like a home, with its nicely stuccoed ceilings, hand-painted tiles, and upstairs porch with a harbor view. Unique family recipes include foil-wrapped shrimp or fish prepared *estilo delfín*—steamed in orange juice, herbs, and spices. Gaston, the operatic owner, can easily be coaxed into singing traditional rancheras in a baritone as rich and robust as the food. ✉ *Calle José Alcantar 44, Col. El Puerto* ☎ *638/383–2608* ⊕ *www.friendlydolphin.com* ▭ *MC, V.*

$$ MEXICAN ✕ **La Casa del Capitán.** Perched atop Puerto Peñasco's highest point, this restaurant has the best views over the bay and the town below. There's indoor dining, but the long outdoor terrace overlooking the sea is the place to be, especially at sunset, when it can be packed with locals and visitors alike. A wide-ranging menu includes everything from nachos and quesadillas to flaming, brandied jumbo shrimp. ✉ *Av. del Agua 1, Cerro de la Ballena* ☎ *638/383–5698* ▭ *MC, V.*

$$ MEXICAN ✕ **La Curva.** This friendly family restaurant with great Mexican food is easy to spot if you look for the large green-and-yellow building or the mermaid on the sign. Traditional Mexican dishes are the best bargain, but seafood lovers will have plenty to choose from: the menu lists 12 different shrimp dishes, such as Hawaiian-style shrimp wrapped in bacon and served in a sweet apple-and-pineapple sauce. ✉ *Blvd. Kino and Comonfort, Centro* ☎ *638/383–3470* ▭ *MC, V.*

WHERE TO STAY

$$–$$$ **Playa Bonita.** One of the first hotels in Puerto Peñasco, Playa Bonita is beginning to show its age, though rooms are clean and comfortable. Ask for one facing the hotel's broad, sandy beach. An RV park provides 300 hookups at $17–$20 a day. As the name of the Puesta del Sol restaurant ("setting of the sun") implies, this is a perfect place to see the sun set. Don't miss the divine margaritas. **Pros:** relaxed vibe; good security; talented bartender. **Cons:** pool isn't heated; maintenance is a bit slack. *Paseo Balboa 100, Playa Hermosa 638/383–2586 or 01800/426–6482 toll free in Mexico, 888/232–8142 www.playabonitaresort.com 120 rooms, 4 suites In-hotel: restaurant, bar, pool, beachfront, Internet terminal AE, MC, V.*

¢–$$ **Posada la Roca.** The oldest building in town, this 80-year-old stone villa is also the most winsome. Constructed by the current proprietor's grandfather, it has plenty of history. This is where gangster Al Capone hid out from the government in 1927, or so it's said. The rooms are small but expertly restored, with thick wooden doors and castlelike walls. **Pros:** atmospheric building; good downtown location; cozy rooms. **Cons:** rooms and bathrooms are quite small; no phones in rooms; need to make reservations well in advance. *Primero de Junio 2, Col. El Puerto 638/383–3199 hotelposadalaroca.blogspot.com 18 rooms In-room: no phone, Wi-Fi. In-hotel: Internet terminal No credit cards.*

$$–$$$ **Sonoran Spa Resort.** One of the first megacomplexes in Rocky Point, this massive pink resort operates much like a hotel, but it has one-, two-, and three-bedroom, fully furnished condominiums in place of standard rooms. The Sonoran Grill ($$–$$$) serves steaks and seafood, as well as a great spicy lasagna made with chipotle chilies. The beach in front is never crowded, and you can do plenty here without leaving the resort—a good thing, since it is a bit far from the center of town. **Pros:** good service; calm surroundings; excellent view. **Cons:** beach is rocky at low tide; need a car to get around. *Camino a La Cholla, Km 3.7 638/382–8060, 877/629–3750 in North America www.sonoran-spa-resort.com 202 condos In-room: kitchen. In-hotel: restaurant, room service, tennis court, pools, gym, spa, beachfront, Wi-Fi hotspot, Internet terminal MC, V.*

$–$$ **Viña del Mar Hotel.** Overlooking the ocean, this tidy hotel is the kind of place where you want to admire the sweeping views. That would be a shame, as it is steps away from the shops and restaurants of the town's waterfront walk. Rooms here are bright but sparsely decorated; some are excellent places to take in the sunset, but most of them actually don't have views, so take a look around first. **Pros:** convenient location; great pool area. **Cons:** not much charm; chilly staff; noise from motor homes coming and going. *Av. Primer de Junio, Col. Puerto 638/383–3600 or 01800/560–2123 toll free in Mexico www.vinadelmarhotel.com 110 rooms In-room: Wi-Fi. In-hotel: restaurant, bar, pool, beachfront, Internet terminal MC, V.*

9

NIGHTLIFE

BARS

Puerto Peñasco's nightlife centers around bars rather than big clubs.

The sports bar **Latitude 31** (⊠ *Blvd. Benito Juárez, en route to Col. Puerto* ☎ *638/383–4311* 🌐 *www.latitude31mex.com*) has a great view of the harbor and a host of TVs showing American sports.

The Lighthouse (⊠ *Lote 2, Fracc. el Cerro* ☎ *638/383–2389*), a pleasant place overlooking the harbor, appeals to a more sophisticated crowd. You can dance to live music between 7 and 10 on weekends.

Popular among the young and those who don't want to put too much distance between the water's edge and their next margarita is **Manny's Beach Club** (⊠ *Blvd. Matamoros s/n, Playa Miramar* ☎ *638/383–3605*). Recorded music blares constantly in this local landmark.

SPORTS AND THE OUTDOORS

WATER SPORTS

At **Sun N' Fun Dive and Activities Center** (⊠ *Blvd. Benito Juárez s/n, at Calle Lauro Contreras* ☎ *638/383–5450 or 888/381–7720* 🌐 *www.rockypointscuba.com*) you can rent fishing, diving, or snorkeling equipment or receive PADI and NAUI scuba instruction. Sunset cruises, fishing charters, and snorkeling trips can all be booked.

BAHÍA KINO

103 km (64 mi) southwest of Hermosillo on Sonora Hwy. 100.

On the eastern shore of the Mar de Cortés lies Bahía Kino, home to some of the prettiest beaches in northwest Mexico. For many years Bahía Kino was undiscovered except by RV owners and other aficionados of the unspoiled. In the past decade or so, great change has come at the hands of North Americans who have been building condos and beach houses here. More change is coming, as land has been acquired and designs submitted for a 100-acre golf course, three marinas, and, eventually, a series of hotels with 50,000 rooms.

The moniker "Bahía Kino" actually refers to twin towns: Kino Viejo (Old Kino, the Mexican village) and Kino Nuevo (New Kino), where facing a long strand of creamy beach you'll find private homes, condos, RV sites, and other tourist facilities.

GETTING HERE AND AROUND

If you want to catch a bus from Hermosillo to Bahía Kino, your best bet is La Costa. Public transportation is nearly nonexistent. If you want to stay in Bahía Kino, you pretty much need a car to get around.

ESSENTIALS

Bus Contacts **La Costa** (☎ *662/212–2556*).

Medical Assistance **Clinic Kino Viejo** (⊠ *Calle Tampico between Blvd. Kino and Calle Acapulco, Kino Viejo* ☎ *662/242–0297*).

CLOSE UP

Tribe on the Verge

A rustic Seri fishing village perched at the end of a long, bumpy, winding dirt road, Punta Chueca is 27 km (17 mi) north of Bahía Kino. To get there, you'll pass exquisite vistas of the bay, distant empty beaches, and rolling mountains. The inhabitants of this community live a subsistence lifestyle, relying on the sea and desert.

With fewer than 700 remaining members, the Seri tribe represents an ancient culture on the verge of dying out. The Seri love for their natural surroundings is evident in the necklaces that they have traditionally worn and now create to sell. Cute little shells are wound into the shape of flowers and strung with wild desert seeds and tiny bleached snake vertebrae. Seri women also weave elaborate *canastas* (baskets) of torote grass, which are highly prized and expensive.

As you get out of your car anywhere in town, be prepared to encounter an entourage of Seri women dressed in colorful ankle-length skirts, their heads covered with scarves, and their arms laden with necklaces for sale. The Seri are best known, however, for the carved *palofiero* (ironwood) figurines that represent the animal world around them, including dolphins, turtles, and pelicans. Many Mexican merchants have taken to machine-making large figures out of ironwood for the tourist trade, thereby seriously depleting the supply of the lilac-blossomed tree that grows only in the Sonoran Desert. (If the bottom of the statuette is smooth, it was cut with an electric saw and not made by the Seri.) For this reason, the Seri now carve figures out of several types of stone. In fact, those in the know suggest that few, if any, ironwood sculptures are being made by the Seri anymore. If you desire an original bit of Seri artwork, you're best off purchasing a necklace or one of the impressive grass baskets.

■ TIP→ **This is no place to hang out after dark, as there is some completely open drug trafficking on the part of local narcotraficantes.**

9

EXPLORING

For a crash ethnography lesson, poke around the interesting—if haphazard—collection of photographs, musical instruments, artwork, baskets, clothing, and dioramas in the **Museo de los Seris**. Be prepared to practice your Spanish, as there are no descriptions in English. ✉ *Blvd. Mar de Cortés at Calle Progreso* ☎ *662/213–4495* 🎫 *$2* ⏲ *Tues.–Sun. 9–5.*

WHERE TO EAT

$$$ SEAFOOD ✕ **El Pargo Rojo.** Fishnets and realistic reproductions of the fish you'll be eating decorate this restaurant, whose name means "red snapper." The catch of the day varies, but you can depend on consistent quality. Classics like a brimming shrimp cocktail could be followed by fish stuffed with shrimp, clams, squid, and octopus. Depending on your luck, you'll be serenaded either by Mexican musicians or by the ceaseless wailing of polkalike *norteña* music on MTV. The restaurant also delivers. ✉ *Blvd. Mar de Cortés 1426, Kino Nuevo* ☎ *662/242–0205* 💳 *D, MC, V.*

$$$ SEAFOOD **Jorge's Restaurant.** This clean, comfortable family restaurant overlooks the bay—a perfect spot for morning coffee and pancakes. At other meals, portions tend to be small, but the food is quite good, and the owner and his daughters play the guitar and sing in the evening. The outdoor patio is great for enjoying the giant margaritas that this place is known for. *Blvd. Mar de Cortés 519, at Alecantres, Kino Nuevo 662/242–0049 MC, V.*

$$ SEAFOOD **La Palapa del Pescador.** This palm-shaded spot is perched above a beach sprinkled with the thatch-topped palapas that give the place its name. In the summer, when Bahía Kino fills with travelers, the restaurant is the place to be. The kitchen churns out marlin, five kinds of shrimp, and a selection of excellent salads; this is where those in the know go for a juicy cheeseburger. *Blvd. Mar de Cortés and Wellington, on way into Kino Nuevo 662/242–0210 MC, V.*

$$ SEAFOOD ★ **Restaurant Marlin.** Though it may be a bit hard to locate, you may well find yourself returning, drawn by the clean, unpretentious environment and congenial service—not to mention margaritas as big as fishbowls. Superb seafood dishes include *sopa de siete mares* (soup of the seven seas) and *jaiba a la diabla* (a spicy hot crab dish). *Calles Tastiota and Guaymas, Kino Viejo 662/242–0111 MC, V Closed Mon.*

WHERE TO STAY

$$ **La Playa RV & Hotel.** This is the only hotel in Kino that's actually on the beach, making it quite a find. The rooms in the Mediterranean-style whitewashed buildings are simple, but tidy and extremely well maintained: all have views of the water. The owner is mercurial, however: to preserve the peace and quiet, he's likely to turn away young people and families with children. **Pros:** beachfront location; lovely building. **Cons:** two-night minimum stay; owner is quirky. *Av. Mar de Cortés and Beirut, Kino Nuevo 662/242–0273 www.laplayarvhotel.com 20 rooms In-room: kitchen Wi-Fi. In-hotel: pool No credit cards.*

GUAYMAS

128 km (79 mi) south of Hermosillo.

The buzz and bustle of Guaymas—one of Mexico's largest ports—has a pleasant backdrop of rusty red, saguaro-speckled bluffs that nudge the deep-blue waters of a sprawling bay on the Mar de Cortés. The Spanish arrived in this "port of ports" by the mid-16th century. In 1701 two Jesuit priests, Father Kino and his colleague Juan María Salvatierra, erected a mission base here intended to convert the native Guaimas, Seri, and Yaqui Indians.

Guaymas was declared a commercial port in 1814, and became an important center of trade. In 1847, during the Mexican-American War, U.S. naval forces attacked and occupied the town for a year. Bumbling filibuster William Walker also managed to take Guaymas for a short time in 1853, and in 1866, during Maximilian's brief reign, the French took control. Today's foreign invaders are mostly travelers passing through on their way somewhere else.

Hardworking Guaymas, unlike its more pristine twin San Carlos, takes Highway 15 right into its gritty heart, and has all the grime, noise, and traffic. But the town is undergoing a major makeover, with a malecón and a state-of-the-art cruise-ship terminal. The sweeping views across the old harbor are magically suggestive of the town's historic past.

The center of the city is **Plaza 13 de Julio,** a typical main square with thick fig trees, a Moorish-style bandstand, and ornate benches. Facing the park is the 19th-century church **Parroquia de San Fernando.**

GETTING HERE AND AROUND

Flying to Guaymas's airport, General José M. Yáñez International Airport (GYM), can be pricey; US Airways Express flies here from Phoenix. Buses bound for other cities stop in Guaymas; the trip here from Nogales is about seven hours. The bus company Grupo Estrella Blanca, which has a network that covers 27 of the 31 states of Mexico, has frequent service to Guaymas from Nogales, Tijuana, and Mexicali. And cabs can be hailed anywhere—a good thing, as the attractions are rather far-flung. The Ferry Santa Rosalía runs to and from Guaymas from Santa Rosalía four times a week. Tickets are $65.

ESSENTIALS

Bus Contacts **Grupo Estrella Blanca** (🌐 *www.estrellablanca.com.mx*).

Ferry Contacts **Ferry Santa Rosalía** (☎ *622/222-0204* 🌐 *www.ferrystantarosalia.com*).

Medical Assistance **Hospital General de Guaymas** (✉ *Calle 12 s/n, Centro* ☎ *622/224-2138*).

Visitor and Tour Info **Tourism Office** (✉ *Blvd. Manlio F. Beltrones 37, Sector Creston Norte, San Carlos* ☎ *622/226-0202* 🌐 *www.visitasonora.com*).

EXPLORING

There isn't much to see in Guaymas outside of the old harbor. The hills around the town are dramatic, but the outdoor activities are farther south. Relax here and enjoy the sunshine and the simple surroundings.

Follow the signs to Playa Miramar and take advantage of the free tours given by the pearl farm, **Perlas del Mar de Cortéz** (✉ *Bahía de Bacochibampo s/n* ☎ *622/221-0136* 🌐 *www.perlas.com.mx*), which has more than 200,000 native pearl oysters in cultivation—it's the only pearl farm of its scale in the Americas. Tours are conducted on the hour weekdays 9 to 3 and Saturday 9 to 11. After taking the tour, you will have an opportunity to buy jewelry made from the stunningly iridescent pearls they cultivate.

WHERE TO EAT AND STAY

$$ SEAFOOD ✕ **Los Arbolitos.** This palapa-shaded family restaurant is a great stopover on the highway to San Carlos. It has the lazy-day quality of a more rural place. It's all seafood here: fish fillets, scallops, oysters, and shrimp cooked to perfection. ✉ *Carretera Internacional, Km 198.2, Col. Lomalinda* ☎ *622/221-2601* ▭ *MC, V.*

¢–$$ **Hotel Armida.** This hotel has a well-kept pool and a popular coffee shop where locals gather for power breakfasts. At the steak house, El Oeste ($$–$$$), the stuffed and mounted heads of mountain goats, cougars, and buffalo gaze down. Large, bright accommodations are plain but serviceable, with comfortable beds; many have balconies overlooking the pool. Rooms at the back are a great bargain. **Pros:** excellent restaurants; lovely pool. **Cons:** on the ugliest strip in Guaymas; lots of traffic noise. ✉ *Carretera Internacional, Salida Norte (northern exit)* ☎ *622/225–2800* 🌐 *www.hotelarmida.com.mx* *124 rooms* *In-room: Wi-Fi. In-hotel: 2 restaurants, room service, bar, pool, gym, Internet terminal* 💳 *AE, MC, V.*

$–$$ **Hotel Playa de Cortes.** Built in 1928, this beachside villa is one of the most romantic lodgings in Sonora. The cute bungalows set amid bougainvillea-filled gardens have a 1920s-era quality. The common areas are decorated with antique furniture and heavy wooden chandeliers. The low-walled garden sweeps out to face the rocky shore of alluring Bahia Bacochibampo. **Pros:** sweeping views; scenic surroundings; attentive staff. **Cons:** beds are hard; isolated location. ✉ *Bahia Bacochibampo* ☎ *622/221–0135; 01800/623–4400 toll-free in Mexico* 🌐 *www.hotelesgandara.com.mx* *88 rooms, 20 suites, 9 bungalows* *In-room: Wi-Fi. In-hotel: restaurant, room service, bar, tennis court, pool, Wi-Fi hotspot* 💳 *AE, MC, V.*

SAN CARLOS

20 km (12 mi) northwest of Guaymas.

Long considered an extension of Guaymas, this resort town—on the other side of the rocky peninsula that separates Bahía de Bacochibampo from Bahía de San Carlos—has a personality of its own. Whitewashed houses with red-tile roofs snuggle together along the water where countless yachts and motorboats are docked. The town is a laid-back favorite among professional anglers, golfers, and the time-share crowd, as well as wealthy Mexican families from Hermosillo and Chihuahua. There are several good hotels, as well as two marinas and a country club with an 18-hole golf course.

The overlapping of desert and semitropical flora and fauna has created a fascinating diversity of species along this coast. More than 650 species of fish exist here, and the marlin and sailfish keep the charter sportfishing business healthy. Dolphins and pelicans frequent the bays, as do blue and gray whales and orcas. The water is calm and warm enough for swimming through October. Scuba, snorkeling, and fishing are popular, too.

The quiet 5-km (3-mi) stretch of sandy beach at **Los Algodones,** where the San Carlos Plaza Hotel and Paradiso reside, was in the 1960s a location for the film *Catch-22*. (In fact, it's still called Catch-22 Beach on many maps.) San Carlos lies in the shadow of the jagged twin-peak **Tetakawi mountain,** a sacred site where native warriors once gathered to gain spiritual strength. The **Mirador Escénico,** or scenic lookout, is the best place in San Carlos to view the Mar de Cortés. Take the steep road up here for a great photo op or just to get an idea of the lay of the land. While you're here you can browse the numerous trinket and souvenir stands set up every day. Just north of the Mirador is Zorro Cove, a great place to snorkel. An interesting day trip (by boat) is the pristine **Isla de San Pedro Nolasco,** an ecological reserve where sea lions claim the rocks.

GETTING HERE AND AROUND

The airfield in San Carlos is restricted to charter planes. Most people drive here, and refurbished roads are among the smoothest in the state. From nearby Guaymas, take a cab or local bus (you'll see the buses marked SAN CARLOS along the main drag).

ESSENTIALS

San Carlos is essentially a suburb of Guaymas; many folks here refer to it as "Nuevo Guaymas"). It is less developed in terms of infrastructure, and many essentials are available only in Guaymas.

Visitor and Tour Info **San Carlos Tourism Office** (✉ *Blvd. Manlio F. Beltrones 37, Sector Creston Norte* ☎ *622/226–0210* 🌐 *www.go2sancarlos.com*).

EXPLORING

Delfinario Sonora. On a pristine bay halfway between Bahia Bacochibampo and San Carlos, this facility affords a chance to interact with dolphins. There isn't much here other than getting close to the animals themselves, but it is an unforgettable experience for the kids. ✉ *Carretera a Las Tinajas, Km 5.5, Nuevo Guaymas* ☎ *622/225–2600* 🌐 *www.delfinariosonora.com.mx* ⏲ *Mon.–Sat. 9–5.*

WHERE TO EAT

$$ MEXICAN ✕ **Rosa's Cantina.** The walls at this cozy pink restaurant are decorated with historical photos from Mexico's past, including many of Mexican revolutionaries. Ask anyone in town, and they'll tell you Rosa's ample breakfasts are the best way to start the day. Try the *machaca* with eggs and salsa; the tortilla soup is great for lunch or dinner. Gringos who miss being pampered will appreciate the decaf coffee and salad bar. ✉ *Calle Aurora 297, Sector Creston* ☎ *622/226–1000* ▭ *MC, V.*

WHERE TO STAY

$$ **Fiesta Real Hotel San Carlos.** Every room in this small, beachfront, family-run hotel soaks up views of the Gulf. The rooms are clean and well maintained, with exceedingly comfortable beds. Some rooms with kitchens are available. **Pros:** gorgeous lawn; beachfront location. **Cons:** on a noisy road; busy singles' bar next door. ✉ *Blvd. Beltrones, Km 8.5, Carretera Escénico* ☎ *622/226–2054 or 866/673–8364* 🌐 *www.fiestareal-hotel.com* *33 rooms* *In-room: no phone, no TV. In-hotel: restaurant, bar, pool, Wi-Fi hotspot, Internet terminal, parking (free)* ▭ *MC, V* *BP.*

$$ **Hotel Hacienda Tetakawi.** This hotel and trailer park across from the beach on the town's main street is part of the Best Western chain. Rooms are generic but clean, and each has a balcony or patio, a few with a view of the sea. **Pros:** on one of the nicest stretches of beach in town. **Cons:** lacks charm. ✉ *Blvd. Beltrones, Km 10* ☎ *622/226–0248 or 01800/654–2172 toll free in Mexico* 🌐 *www.bwtetakawi.com*

9

22 rooms In-room: refrigerator, Wi-Fi. In-hotel: restaurant, room service, bar, pool, Internet terminal AE, MC, V.

$$–$$$ **Marinaterra Hotel & Spa.** This resort overlooks the San Carlos marina and has a commanding view of Cerro Tetakawi. Pastels soften the rooms, most of which have tiny kitchenettes. Some corner rooms have hot tubs on outdoor patios at no extra cost. A shuttle takes guests to the hotel beach club, which is a great place to hang out poolside or take a walk on the beach. El Embarcadero restaurant ($–$$) is a good place to try hearty, traditional Mexican soups like the *caldo Xochitl,* a steaming chicken consommé with white rice and avocado, garnished with chili. **Pros:** service of a luxury hotel; sophisticated character; great views. **Cons:** all your fellow guests are Americans. *Calle Gabriel Estrada s/n, Sector La Herradura 622/225–2020 or 01800/500–2040 toll free in Mexico, 888/688–5353 in North America www.marinaterra.com 92 rooms, 20 suites In-room: kitchen (some), refrigerator (some). In-hotel: restaurant, bar, pool, spa, Internet terminal AE, MC, V.*

$$–$$$ **San Carlos Plaza Hotel, Resort & Convention Center.** Rising from Bahía de San Carlos, this huge resort is the most luxurious lodging in Sonora. The arresting atrium lobby opens onto a large pool and beach. Pleasing rooms—all with at least a partial ocean view—have contemporary, if uninspiring, furnishings. Rooms on the first two floors have balconies overlooking the sea. Children love the swimming-pool slide and horseback riding on magnificent Algodones beach. **Pros:** elegant public areas; breathtaking beach. **Cons:** no flavor of the region; caters to many conventions. *Paseo Mar Barmejo Norte 4, Los Algodones 622/225–3000 www.sancarlosplaza.com.mx 132 rooms, 41 suites In-room: safe. In-hotel: 3 restaurants, bars, tennis courts, pools, gym, spa, beachfront, Wi-Fi hotspot, Internet terminal AE, MC, V.*

NIGHTLIFE

BARS

San Carlos has busy little clusters of bars around the marinas that are frequented by visitors.

The hottest gathering place for younger people is the bar of the restaurant **El Bronco** (*Manlio F. Beltrones 178, Sector Creston 622/226–1130*). There's a well-stocked bar at the center of the room.

Stop by the **Galería Bellas Artes** (*Villahermosa 111, Sector Villahermosa 622/226–0073*), where artwork is for sale. It's open Monday to Saturday 9:30 to 5.

Tequilas Bar (*Gabriel Estrada 1, Marina San Carlos 622/226–0545*) is a popular nightspot with a small dance floor, big crowd, and live music on weekends.

SHOPPING

Casa Kiamy (*Blvd. Beltrones, Km 10 622/226–0338*) is like a bazaar, with something for everyone: silver jewelry, woven and leather bags, ceramics, and Yaqui Indian masks.

Sagitario's Gift Shop (✉ *Blvd. Beltrones 132* ☎ *622/226–0090*) features clothing and a variety of crafts, including wood carvings, baskets, rugs, and Talavera tile.

SPORTS AND THE OUTDOORS

San Carlos may be small, but it's a big destination for anglers. Fishing outfitters are well equipped and knowledgeable about local waters.

Gary's Dive Shop (✉ *Blvd. Beltrones, Km 10* ☎ *622/226–0049 or 866/356–1236* 🌐 *www.garysdivemexico.com*) is run by American owners Gary and Donna Goldstein, who have been residents and business owners here for over 35 years. They run excellent fishing, snorkeling, and PADI-certified diving excursions. You can also book sunset cruises, whale-watching tours, and marine-biology trips.

Ocean Sports (✉ *San Carlos Marina #L-7* ☎ *622/226–0696 or 800/830–3483* 🌐 *www.desertdivers.com*) sells all types of diving and snorkeling equipment, as well as supplies for anglers.

ÁLAMOS

★ *257 km (160 mi) southeast of Guaymas.*

With its cobblestone streets, delightful central plaza, 250-year-old baroque church, and thoughtfully restored haciendas, Álamos is the most authentically revived colonial town in Sonora. Although Sonora has many historic areas from the Spanish colonial period, Álamos once held sway over a vast area, and is arguably the most historically important spot in the state. In the ecologically rich zone where the Sonoran Desert meets a dry tropical forest, the entire town is designated a national historic monument.

Coronado camped here in 1540, but Álamos really boomed when silver was discovered in the area during the 1680s. Wealth from the mines financed Spanish expeditions to the north—as far as Los Angeles and San Francisco during the 1770s and '80s—and the town became the capital of the state of Occidente from 1827 to 1832. A government mint was established here in 1864. The mines had closed by the beginning of the Mexican Revolution in 1910. All but abandoned for the first half of the 20th century, it retains it colonial character.

9

GETTING HERE AND AROUND

A bus ride from Nogales, near the border, to Álamos will take roughly nine hours. TUFESA (🌐 *www.tufesa.com.mx*) and Transportes del Pacifico run to nearby Navajoa, the closest large market town, where you can catch a TBC bus to Álamos. There is also a TBC bus that runs directly to Tucson and Phoenix nightly from the Álamos bus station.

ESSENTIALS

Bus Contacts **TBC** (☎ *647/428–0096*).

Currency Exchange **Banorte** (✉ *Calle Madero 27, Col. Centro* ☎ *647/428–0357*).

Visitor and Tour Info **Tourist Office** (✉ *Main Plaza, Calle Juárez 6* ☎ *647/428–0450*).

EXPLORING

Points of interest in Álamos include the impressive **Iglesia de la Purísma Concepción,** constructed on the site of a 17th-century adobe church destroyed in an Indian uprising. Fronting the parish church is the enchanting central square, the **Plaza de las Armas;** its ornate Moorish-style wrought-iron gazebo was brought from Mazatlán in 1904. From there head northwest to the rectangular **Alameda,** which is surrounded by promenades and flanked at night by food vendors. If you're in town on Sunday, cross the little arroyo (seasonal riverbed) north of the Alameda to the weekly market. Southeast of the main square is the **Cerro del Perico,** a hill that has awesome views of the city and the craggy forests surrounding it.

Every January Álamos hosts the 10-day **Festival Dr. Alfonso Ortiz Tirado** (🌐 *www.festivalortiztirado.com*), a celebration of classical music honoring one of its native sons. Named for the 20th-century's biggest Latin American opera star, the festival attracts musicians from around the world. Most of the performances are free.

Wealthy American expats who started coming here in the 1950s to restore the enormous haciendas turned some into luxurious private homes. If possible, time your trip to Álamos to include a Saturday **House and Garden Tour** ($10) of some of the superbly restored mansions and their interior patios and gardens. You can get a tour schedule from the tourist office or any of the local hotels; expat tour guides usually start the tours at Plaza de las Armas around 10 AM.

Don't miss the **Museo Costumbrista de Sonora** for an excellent overview of the history of the state of Sonora. The displays include antique wagons, artifacts from the nearby silver mines, and coins from the mints of Álamos and Hermosillo. There are also examples of the clothing and furnishings of prominent local families. ✉ *Calle Guadalupe Victoria 1, on Plaza de las Armas* ☎ *647/428–0053* 🎫 *$1* ⏲ *Wed.–Sun. 10–7.*

WHERE TO EAT

$ MEXICAN ★ ✕ **Las Palmeras.** This popular Mexican family restaurant sits on the west side of the Alameda. Here you might get homemade *rosca* bread (a sweet, round loaf) with your coffee and an assortment of daily specials. The made-fresh-daily corn tamales are hard to beat; other specialties include the chiles rellenos (cheese-stuffed chili peppers) and the *carne milanesa* (similar to chicken-fried steak). ✉ *Madero 48* ☎ *647/428–0065* 💳 *No credit cards.*

WHERE TO STAY

$$ 🏨 **Casa de los Tesoros.** This hotel, whose name means the "House of Treasures," is an idyllic and romantic converted 18th-century convent. The rooms were once nuns' cells, but they're no longer austere—they've now got fireplaces, tile baths, antique furnishings, and striking local art. The restaurant is excellent, and the in-house guitar trio provides the mood music. **Pros:** swanky vibe; perfectly located. **Cons:** austere courtyard; can feel a little too quiet. ✉ *Av. Obregón 10* ☎ *647/428–0010* 🌐 *www.tesoros-hotel.com* *12 rooms, 2 suites* *In-room: no phone, no TV. In-hotel: restaurant, bar, pool* 💳 *MC, V* 🍽 *BP.*

$$$$ Fodor's Choice ★ **Hacienda de los Santos.** Sonora's swankest hotel rambles across the grounds of five restored colonial mansions; you'll be entirely secluded from the outside world by the walls of these former haciendas. In gracious courtyards and lining long porticos are centuries-old pieces of religious art and hand-carved antique furniture, all collected by the American owners. The spacious bedrooms also have antiques, as well as fireplaces. A 100-year-old bar brought from Cuernavaca presents for your pleasure 400 different varieties of tequila, and a spa gives massage and beauty treatments. All rooms here are no-smoking. **Pros:** luxury on every level; personalized service; the feeling of complete seclusion. **Cons:** need a car to get around; noise from a nearby school. ✉ *Calle Molina 8* ☎ *647/428–0222 or 800/525–4800* 🌐 *www.haciendadelossantos.com* *8 rooms, 7 suites, 2 villas* *In-room: refrigerator (some), kitchen (some), no TV (some), DVDs (some), safe, Wi-Fi. In-hotel: 2 restaurants, bar, pools, gym, spa, no-smoking rooms, no kids under 18* *AE, MC, V* *BP, FAP.*

THE MEXICAN JUMPING BEAN

Both Álamos and Aduana claim to be the birthplace of the so-called "Mexican jumping bean." (Many communities in Sonora could make the same claim.) The phenomenon is not so much a bean as a seed, bored into by the larva of a moth. Slight increases in temperature activate the larva causing it to wiggle. Despite the name, they rarely jump.

$ **Hotel Solipaso.** The four rooms in this restored hacienda are gorgeous, with antique furnishings and wood-and-glass doors leading outdoors. A small courtyard holds a café and a tiny pool not much bigger than a hot tub. The American owners, a bird expert and a yoga teacher, are building El Pedregal, a 20-acre retreat just outside of town. **Pros:** cozy yet elegant; good location; on a quiet street. **Cons:** breakfast is a little pricey. ✉ *Calle Obregón 3* ☎ *647/428–0466* 🌐 *www.solipaso.com* *4 rooms* *In-room: no phone, no TV, Wi Fi. In-hotel: restaurant* *No credit cards* *Closed Sun. evening, Mon. and some of summer.*

$ **La Posada de Don Andrés.** Although it was built in the 1950s, this New Orleans–style hotel feels a century older. Facing the Alameda and just steps from the public market, the hotel's wrought-iron-and-marble courtyard calls to mind a more refined era. The owner, who named the place after his late father, plays acoustic guitar and violin in the comfortable wood-paneled lobby upstairs. **Pros:** great location; atmospheric building. **Cons:** interior sometimes resembles a second-hand store; noisy neighbors. ✉ *Calle Rosales 24-A* ☎ *647/428–1110* *16 rooms* *In-room: no phone, Wi-Fi. In-hotel: Internet terminal* *No credit cards.*

SHOPPING

Small stores lining the Alameda sell Mexican sweets, fabrics, belts, and hats, among other items. You'll find *tianguis* (market stalls) lining the Plaza de las Armas every day, but Sunday brings artisans and vendors from the surrounding area.

9

ADUANA

10 km (6 mi) west of Álamos, 251 km (156 mi) southeast of Guaymas.

A couple of miles off the main road to Álamos, tiny Aduana was once the site of one of the richest mines in the district. The tiny village is barely more than a church on the humblest of plazas, a country store and two local handicrafts cooperatives, and an abandoned silver mine on a hill. But it's worth a visit for a meal at Sonora's best restaurant.

EXPLORING

On the plaza is the **Iglesia de Nuestra Señora de Balvanera**. A cactus that grows out of one of the church's walls is said to mark the spot where the Virgin appeared to the Yaqui Indians in the 17th century.

WHERE TO STAY

$$ Fodor's Choice ★ **Casa la Aduana**. Though it's in an unlikely spot 3 km (2 mi) off the highway into Álamos, the restaurant here has a reputation as the best in the state. The restored 17th-century customhouse presents exceptional four-course, prix-fixe menus, with entrées such as tenderloin tips, pork tenderloin, beef medallions, and chicken in an apple-chipotle cream sauce. Although the walls and floors of the bed-and-breakfast here are the restored originals, modern luxuries haven't been overlooked: soft linens, comfortable beds, and thick bath towels add to the charm. Guest rooms have 4-foot-thick walls, which reflect their former duties as vaults for the riches that came from this area's mines. Your stay includes breakfast and four-course dinner. **Pros:** historic property; great meals. **Cons:** isolated location. ✉ *Frente a la Placita* ☎ *647/404–3473* 🌐 *www.casaladuana.com* *3 rooms* *In-room: no phone, Wi-Fi. In-hotel: restaurant, pool, no kids under 16* 💳 *No credit cards* 🍽 *MAP.*

The Copper Canyon

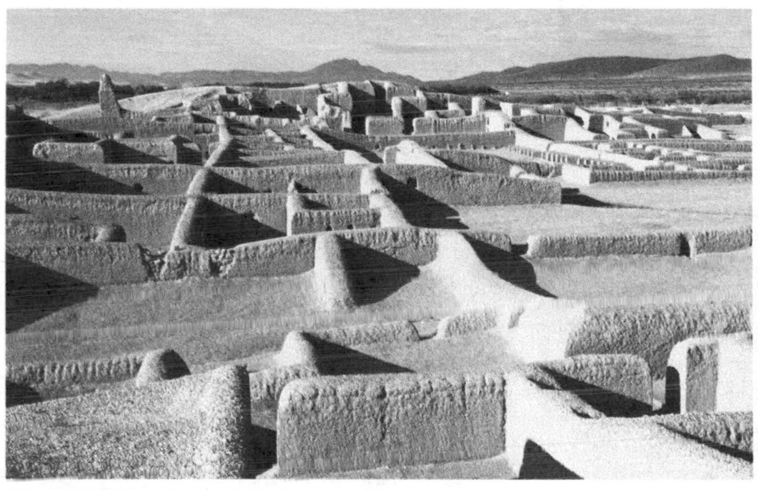

Paquimé. Casas Grandes

WORD OF MOUTH

"We did a Copper Canyon independent tour. We went to our local travel agent who booked our accommodation and train tickets. . . . The first day on the train was a long one, with our first night in the canyon at the Mirador Posada Barancas; over the following days we travelled on the train for a few hours per day and then finished up in Chihuahua. I highly recommend the trip independently. It was really an incredible journey and the scenery's just spectacular."

—SusieQ78

www.fodors.com/community

WELCOME TO THE COPPER CANYON

TOP REASONS TO GO

★ **The train ride:** The Chihuahua al Pacífico railroad allows you to cut a direct path through this dramatic landscape.

★ **Encountering the Tarahumara:** This indigenous community's culture has changed little in the last 1,000 years.

★ **Biking, hiking, or riding to Batopilas and Urique:** The rough roads to these towns are full of switchbacks, with incredible views around each turn.

★ **Communing with nature:** The backcountry Copper Canyon Sierra Lodge is a good place to start, with its tranquil backdrop amid pine trees, lack of electricity, and vegetarian meals.

★ **Exploring an ancient trading center:** The sea of roofless walls at World Heritage Site Casas Grandes, the ruins of Paquimé, looks like an adobe maze.

1 Western Terminus: Los Mochis. The train line begins at Los Mochis, near the ferry to Baja California, and convenient to the major highway skirting the Pacific coast.

2 The Mountain Towns. Most of the important towns in the region are along the train route. Cerocahui is a rugged mountain village with an excellent hotel. Urique is a tiny desert oasis on the floor of the deepest canyon in North America. Posada Barrancas is a whistle stop minutes from its more photogenic twin, Divisadero. Creel, the largest town, is the hub of most off-road expeditions. Batopilas, in its own canyon, has a storybook colonial center.

3 Eastern Terminus: Chihuahua City. It once made sense to end a train ride and canyon adventure in this modern metropolis. But Chihuahua City and nearby transit hub Cuidad Juárez have been affected by drug cartel–related violence in recent years. It's better to end a train journey in nearby Creel.

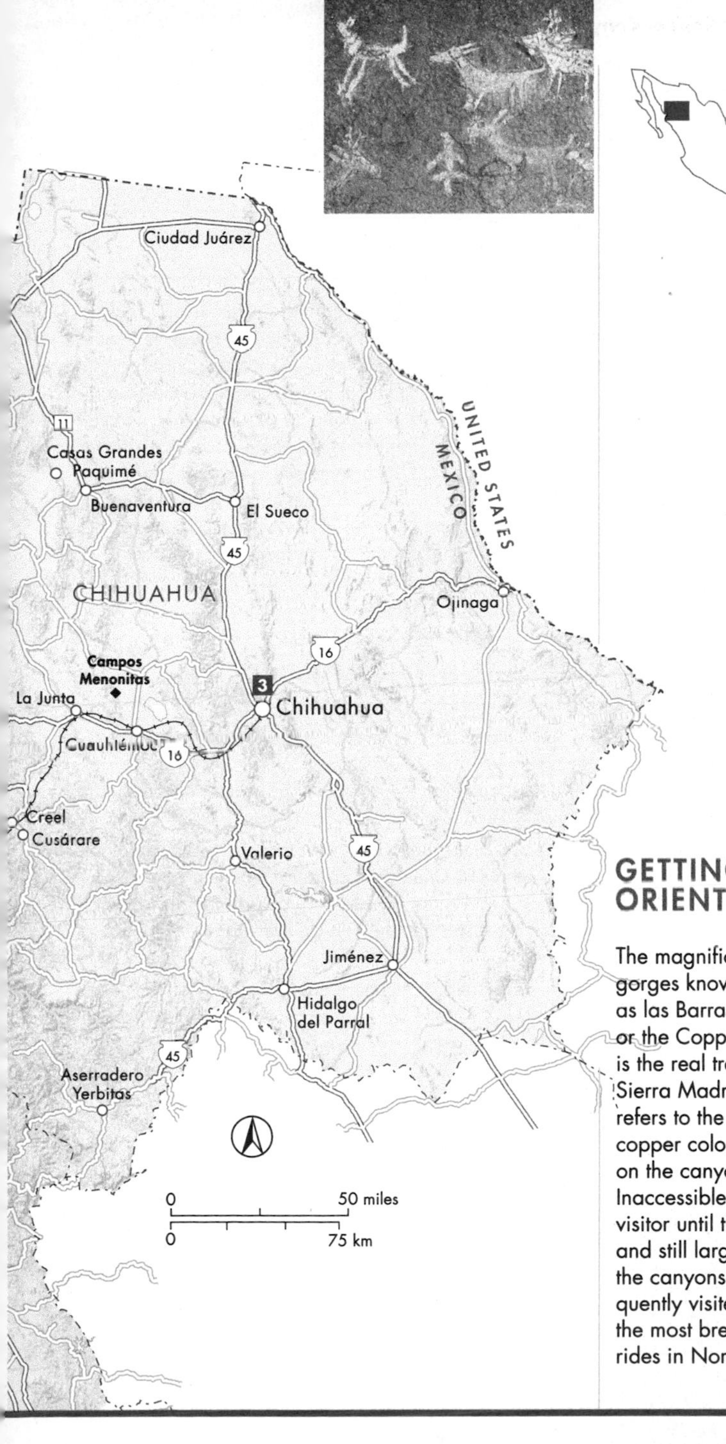

GETTING ORIENTED

The magnificent series of gorges known collectively as las Barrancas del Cobre, or the Copper Canyon, is the real treasure of the Sierra Madre. (The name refers to the tarnished-copper color of the lichen on the canyon walls.) Inaccessible to the casual visitor until the early 1960s and still largely uncharted, the canyons are most frequently visited via one of the most breathtaking train rides in North America.

10

THE COPPER CANYON PLANNER

A Little Rough Around the Edges

Imagine, if you will, visiting the Grand Canyon in the days before it was tamed by tourist facilities and you'll have some sense of what it's like to take a trip through the Barrancas del Cobre. And naturally it's to be expected that with the opportunity to encounter a relatively untouched natural environment come some of the discomforts of the rustic experience.

Outside small villages such as Creel and Batopilas there are few eateries except those connected to lodges; hearty meals are generally included in room rates. In Cerocahui, Divisadero, Posada Barrancas (*posada* means inn), and Creel, most hotels are pine-log types heated by gas furnaces or wood-burning stoves. The lodges send buses or cars to meet the train—which is extremely convenient. For this reason, reservations are essential.

Booking in Advance

From August to October, and around Christmas and Easter, it's important to book more than a month in advance. Many people come during Easter and Christmas, specifically to see the local take on church holidays. On these and other religious feast days, many Tarahumara communities dance throughout the night, fortified by *tesgüino,* a corn beverage fermented in clay pots. Villages challenge one another in races that can last for days. The men run in small groups for 161 km (100 mi) or more, all the while kicking a small wooden ball. It's not just fun and games—each village places a huge communal wager for this winner-take-all event.

Getting Here and Around

You can fly into Los Mochis connecting through several Mexican cities. The Los Mochis–Topolobampo airport (LMM) is about 30 minutes outside Los Mochis on the road to Topolobampo.

Most people make their way through the canyons by train, on the Ferrocarril Chihuahua al Pacífico, which stops in all the major towns in the region. You can arrange horseback riding or day hikes into the canyon from larger towns, such as Creel.

Bus service is limited, but there are buses between El Fuerte and Los Mochis at the western end of the train route. Getting on the train in El Fuerte makes sense, as the best scenery is between it and Creel. Such a journey also allows you to avoid Chihuahua City, which has seen some drug cartel–related violence.

Safety

Avoid Cuidad Juárez and Chihuahua City owing to problems with drug-related gang violence. If you must enter through either place, spend as little time there as possible and stay on the tourist path. Check www.state.gov/travel for updates on the violence and security precaustions.

Travel in and around the Barrancas del Cobre is generally safe, but off-road trips deep into the canyons should always be done with respectable, local guides who know the terrain. In addition to rock slides and other natural disasters, drug traffickers are sometimes a danger.

The Pros of Hiring a Pro

The complicated logistics of traveling in the region and the dearth of facilities and infrastructure mean that this is one place where a package tour really makes sense. But you can rest assured you won't see any megatour buses trundling along the canyon's dirt roads. The **California Native** (☎ *800/926–1140* 🌐 *www.calnative.com*) runs small group tours through the canyons. The 4- to 11-day self-guided trips start around $810; group trips last one to two weeks and begin at $2,330. **Copper Canyon Adventures** (☎ *800/732–3023* 🌐 *www.coppercanyonadventures.com*) provides private and group tours ranging from sedate to adventurous. **3 Amigos** (☎ *635/456–0179 in Creel; 698/893–5028 in El Fuerte* 🌐 *www.amigos3.com*) will plan tours based on your specific schedule, needs, and interests.Highly regarded **Caravan** (☎ *800/227–2826* 🌐 *www.cravan.com*) runs nine-day group tours through the canyons that begin and end in Phoenix, Arizona. Prices begin at $995.

Money Matters

WHAT IT COSTS IN DOLLARS					
	¢	$	$$	$$$	$$$$
Restaurants	under $5	$5–$10	$10–$15	$15–$25	over $25
Hotels	under $50	$50–$75	$75–$150	$150–$250	over $250

Restaurant prices are per person for a main course at dinner. Hotel prices are for two people in a standard double room.

How's the Weather?

The rainy season in this part of Mexico, which runs from late June to September, brings bursts of precipitation every day, but this normally won't interfere with your plans. May to August, the warmest months, are a great time to go hiking in the highlands, though the same doesn't hold true in the canyons, which are often broiling at this time of year.

Overall, the best months to visit are during the fall in September and October, when the weather at the top is starting to cool off the bottom. It's also when the rains of the previous months bring out all the colors of the region's flora.

The middle of winter—December through February—is not the best time to visit the high country. Although the scenery can be breathtaking in the snow, some of the hotels in the region are inadequately prepared for cold weather. However, temperatures on the canyon floors can be ideal for outdoor activities.

Updated by Jeffrey Van Fleet

THE CANYONS OF THE SIERRA Tarahumara, as this portion of the Sierra Madre Occidental is known, form part of the Pacific "Ring of Fire," a belt of seismic and volcanic activity ringing the globe. As a result of its massive geologic movement, a large quantity of the earth's buried mineral wealth was shoved toward the surface. The average height of the resulting peaks is 8,000 feet, and some rise to more than 10,000 feet.

The canyons were carved over eons by the Urique, Septentrión, Batopilas, and Chínipas rivers and further defined by wind erosion. Totaling more than 1,452 km (900 mi) in length and roughly four times the area of the Grand Canyon, the gorges are nearly a mile deep and wide in places. Four of the major canyons—Cobre, Urique, Sinforosa, and Batopilas—descend deeper than the Grand Canyon.

The unlikely idea of building a railroad line across this forbidding region was first conceived in 1872 by Albert Kinsey Owen, an idealistic American socialist. Owen met with some success initially. More than 1,500 people came from the States to join him in Topolobampo, his utopian colony on the Mexican west coast, and in 1881 he obtained a concession from Mexican president General Manuel Gonzales to build the railroad. Construction on the flat stretches near Los Mochis and Chihuahua presented no difficulties, but eventually the huge mountains of the Sierra Madre got in the way of Owen's dream, along with the twin scourges of typhoid and disillusionment within the community.

Owen abandoned the project in 1893, but it was taken up in 1900 by American railroad magnate and spiritualist Arthur Edward Stilwell. One of Stilwell's contractors in western Chihuahua was Pancho Villa, who ended up tearing up his own work during the Mexican Revolution in order to impede the movement of the government troops chasing him. By 1910, when the revolution began, the Mexican government had taken charge of building the rail line. Progress was painfully slow until 1940, when surveying the difficult Sierra Madre stretch finally began in earnest. Some 90 years and more than $100 million after it was started, the Ferrocarril Chihuahua al Pacífico was dedicated on November 23, 1961. Today the railroad runs between Los Mochis, near the original terminus of Topolobampo, and Chihuahua City.

WESTERN TERMINUS: LOS MOCHIS

Los Mochis is 761 km (473 mi) south of the U.S. border–Nogales via Hwy. 15, 80 km (50 mi) southwest of El Fuerte, and 653 km (405 mi) southwest of Chihuahua on the Chihuahua al Pacífico railway—the only direct route.

At the western end of the Chihuahua al Pacífico railway line, Los Mochis (population 335,000) sits near the Gulf of California. It's a friendly, but not terribly good-looking, town. Unless they're heading to the beach at Topolobampo, most travelers overnight here before boarding the morning train. El Fuerte is more historic and more scenic.

GETTING HERE AND AROUND

The Los Mochis–Topolobampo Airport (LMM) is about 30 minutes west of Los Mochis. The cost of a taxi to the city is less than $20. Baja Ferries between La Paz, Baja California, and Topolobampo leave daily, weather permitting. Travel time is about five hours. Tickets cost $75. If you're driving, Carretera 15, a four-lane toll road, connects the border town of Nogales, south of Tucson, Arizona, with Los Mochis. The trip is about 761 km (473 mi). The bus terminal is in the center of Los Mochis, a few blocks from most hotels.

ESSENTIALS

Bus Contacts **Terminal Los Mochis** (✉ *Zaragosa Sur 800, Col. Centro* ☎ *668/818–0357*).

Currency Exchange **Banamex** (✉ *Av. Guillermo Prieto at Calle Hidalgo, Col. Centro* ☎ *668/812–0116*).

Ferry Contacts **Baja Ferries** (✉ *Terminal Topolbampo* ☎ *668/862–1003*).

Medical Assistance **Centro Médico** (✉ *Blvd. Castro 30, Col. Centro* ☎ *668/812–0198*).

Rental Cars **Hertz** (✉ *Calle Leyva Norte 171, Col. Centro* ☎ *668/812–1122*).

Visitor and Tour Info **Flamingo Tours** (✉ *Calle Leyva at Av. Hidalgo, Col. Centro* ☎ *668/812–1613*). **Los Mochis Tourism Office** (✉ *Av. Allende at Calle Ordóñez, Col. Centro* ☎ *01800/508–0111 toll-free in Mexico*).

EXPLORING

In what was once a doctor's house, the **Museo Regional del Valle del Fuerte** is home to well-researched permanent exhibits covering the area's history. It also hosts rotating exhibits by local, regional, national, and international artists. Placards are in Spanish only, but you can pick up an English-language synopsis at the front office. Occasional music or poetry events are held on an outdoor patio. ✉ *Blvd. Rosales at Av. Obregón, Col. Centro* ☎ *668/812–4692* *$1, free Sun. and holidays* ⊙ *Mon.–Sat. 9–1 and 4–7, Sun. 10–1.*

Cottonwood trees and bougainvillea line the highway to **Topolobampo**. A century ago this was a socialist utopia built by the same man who dreamed up the railroad across the canyons. Today this seaside suburb is where travelers arrive on the ferry from La Paz. The beachfront is staked out by a sprinkling of open-air restaurants and budget motels. In the indigenous Mayo language, the name Topolobampo means "watering place of the sea lions"; Isla El Farallón, off the coast, is a breeding ground for the animals that gave the town its name. Tours of the bay, one of the largest in the Americas, can be arranged either through your hotel or tour operators at the dock. Your guide will almost certainly introduce you to Pechocho, the friendly bottlenose dolphin who lives in the bay. The 45-minute bus ride from Los Mochis costs $2; a taxi will take half the time but cost about $20.

CLOSE UP

Copper Canyon Train Ride

The Ferrocarril Chihuahua al Pacífico—"El Chepe"—passes through 86 tunnels and crosses 37 bridges on its journey through the canyon. The diverse landscapes include farmland, coastal plains, and the Sierra Madre, making this one of the world's most famous train trips.

From either direction, first-class trains depart dependably at 6 AM, or you can bypass Los Mochis and depart 1½ hours later from El Fuerte at 8:40 AM. A ticket costs $159 each way; arrange stopovers when you buy tickets. The first-class train has a restaurant and bar; food and beverages are not included in ticket prices. ⚠ **With increasing safety concerns about Chihuahua City, many passengers opt to begin or end their journeys in Creel; a Creel–Los Mochis ticket costs $87.**

Reserve ahead a week or more in July, August, and October, and a month or more around Christmas and Easter.

If you're departing on the first-class train from the western terminus of Los Mochis, you can expect to be in El Fuerte at 8:40 AM, Bahuichivo at 12:40 PM, Posada Barrancas at 1:55 PM, Divisadero at 2:05 PM, Creel at 3:40 PM, and Chihuahua finally at 9 PM that evening. From Chihuahua, you arrive in Creel at 11:20 AM, Divisadero at 12:35 PM, Posada Barrancas at 1 PM, Bahuichivo at 2:15 PM, El Fuerte at 6 PM, and Los Mochis at 8:40 PM that evening. Trains in both directions make a 20-minute stop at Divisadero for the best scenic views of the canyon.

The departure times for second-class trains are less certain, but they usually pull out of the station about an hour after the first-class trains. They make more stops along the way, arriving at their final destination about two hours after the first-class train. They're rarely crowded and quite comfortable; the cars were used on the first-class route until a few years ago. A snack car sells bad microwave burritos, sandwiches, and soft drinks. No reservations are needed; tickets are half the price of those on the first-class train. Cars on both trains contain air-conditioning and heating. All trains are no-smoking.

■ TIP→ **Delays of three hours or so aren't unusual, as cargo trains, which share the rails, break down frequently; don't count on reaching the route's scenic end before dark.**

TRAIN OPERATORS

The **Ferrocarril Chihuahua al Pacífico** (*Chepe ☎ 614/439–7211, 888/484–1623, 01800/122–4373 toll-free in Mexico 🌐 www.chepe.com.mx*) runs a first-class and a second-class train daily each way between Chihuahua and Los Mochis.

■ TIP→ **The most dramatic scenery is between El Fuerte and Creel. As the train ascends almost 6,000 feet from El Fuerte to Bahuichivo, the scenery shifts from cacti to the waterfalls and tropical foliage of the Río Septentrión canyon. Past Témoris, the surroundings shift to the oak and pine forest of higher elevations.**

WHERE TO EAT

$ SEAFOOD ✕ **El Farallón.** The food at this nautically themed restaurant has made it a hit for nearly half a century. The taquitos filled with marlin or shrimp are excellent, and you'll also find sushi and sashimi—rare in Mexico despite the abundance of seafood. For dessert, sample some pitalla (cactus-fruit) ice cream. ✉ *Av. Obregón 499 Poniente, at Calle Angel Flores* ☎ *668/812–1428 or 668/812–1273* 🌐 *www.retsurantefarallon.com* 💳 *AE, MC, V.*

$ SPANISH ✕ **España.** This downtown restaurant pulls in the local business crowd. The specialty is paella for two, with seafood, pork, and chicken. The $7 breakfast buffet, served until noon, lines up hearty Mexican favorites such as *chilaquiles* (tortilla strips cooked with cheese, mild chilies, and chicken) alongside the usual suspects, such as eggs cooked *al gusto* (as you like). ✉ *Av. Obregón 525 Poniente* ☎ *668/812–2221* 🌐 *www.espanarestaurante.com* 💳 *AE, MC, V.*

$ STEAKHOUSE ✕ **La Fuente.** This unpretentious colonial-style restaurant specializes in local and imported cuts of beef. The local favorite is *cabrería,* a thinly sliced, extremely tender fillet. Yummy *queso fundido* (cheese fondue) is served with flour tortillas. Corn tortillas are made on the premises throughout the day. ✉ *Blvd. López Mateos 1070 Norte, at Jiquilpán* ☎ *668/812–4770* 💳 *AE, MC, V.*

WHERE TO STAY

$$ 🏨 **Best Western Los Mochis.** This business-style hotel has a central location on the Plaza Central, yet it looks down on a large and ugly parking lot. The rooms are clean and comfortable. For many travelers returning from a canyon adventure the American-style restaurant is a welcome reminder of home. **Pros:** helpful staff; on the main square. **Cons:** bland personality; neighborhood is sketchy at night. ✉ *Av. Obregón 691* ☎ *668/816–3000* 🌐 *www.bestwestern.com* *112 rooms, 4 suites* *In-room: safe, refrigerator, Internet. In-hotel: restaurant, room service, bar, pool, gym, Wi-Fi hotspot, Internet terminal, parking (free)* 💳 *AE, MC, V.*

$–$$ 🏨 **Hotel Corintios.** Behind the huge white Corinthian columns that give the place its name, this centrally located hotel is a good budget option. Rooms are plain and worn, but have some amenities not often available in this price range, such as marble bathtubs. Junior suites differ from standard rooms only in that they have king-size beds and minibars. **Pros:** good budget option; unexpected amenities. **Cons:** cheesy interior; steps to climb. ✉ *Av. Obregón 580 Poniente, at Guerrero* ☎ *668/818–2300* 🌐 *www.hotelcorintios.com* *60 rooms* *In-room: Wi-Fi. In-hotel: restaurant, room service, bar, gym, laundry service, Internet terminal parking (free)* 💳 *AE, D, MC, V.*

$$–$$$$ 🏨 **Plaza Inn.** The town's only five-star hotel attracts a mix of busin executives and outdoors enthusiasts, many of them taking advanta the fishing trips led by the hotel's tour company. The standard roor spacious, but suffer from a disconcerting color palette combinir ous hues of pink, coral, and sea-foam green. Suites have amen kitchenettes. **Pros:** helpful staff; convenient location. **Cons:** u

10

style; neighborhood is deserted at night. ✉ *Calle Leyva at Cárdenas* ☎ *668/816–0809; 01800/672–6677 toll-free in Mexico, 800/862–9026 in North America* 🌐 *www.plazainnhotel.com.mx* ⇨ *122 rooms* ♁ *In-room: safe, Wi-Fi. In-hotel: 2 restaurants, room service, bar, pool, gym, laundry service, parking (free)* ▭ *AE, DC, MC, V.*

$$ **Santa Anita.** The hub of the ubiquitous Balderrama chain, this hotel can secure train tickets, book tours, and arrange accommodations in its sister hotels El Fuerte, Cerocahui, and Divisadero. In the city's commercial district, the hotel is near shops selling everything from cowboy boots to pirated CDs. The restaurant and bar are gathering places for local business executives. **Pros:** well-appointed rooms; lively neighborhood. **Cons:** staff can be uppity; labyrinthine public areas. ✉ *Calle Leyva at Hidalgo* ☎ *668/816–7046 or 01800/821–0000 toll-free in Mexico, 888/528–8401* 🌐 *www.santaanitahotel.com* ⇨ *105 rooms, 5 suites* ♁ *In-room: Wi-Fi. In-hotel: restaurant, bar, parking (free)* ▭ *AE, D, DC, MC, V.*

NIGHTLIFE

Los Mochis is full of cantinas where only locals will feel comfortable. There are, however, a few places where travelers can belly up to the bar. Part of the Plaza Inn, **Tabú Ultraclub** (✉ *Calle Leyva at Cárdenas* ☎ *668/812–8165*) is the city's most popular disco. Thursday through Saturday nights well-dressed locals take to the dance floor around 9 PM. The music, often live, ranges from techno to rock en español.

SHOPPING

The two-block stretch of Avenida Obregón between Calle Leyva and Calle Prieta has a number of small shops that sell everything. Here you can pick up any last-minute items you may need for your journey into the canyon. If you're headed to Divisadero, Creel, or beyond, snacks and reading material can help you survive the long train journey.

Librería Mochis (✉ *Av. Madero 402 Poniente, at Calle Leyva* ☎ *668/815–7242*) has maps and a small selection of English-language magazines.

Not far from the bus station is the **Mercado Independencia** (✉ *Av. Independencia between Calle Degollado and Calle Zapata* ☎ *No phone*), a typical Mexican market. Shops along the periphery sell cowboy hats and other apparel, while the stalls inside are piled high with fruits and vegetables, meats, and fish. ■ **TIP→ The restaurant stalls toward the back are great places to order cheap, tasty meals. Some are open 24 hours.**

VH (✉ *Av. Obregón at Calle Zaragoza* ☎ *668/815–7285*) is a large supermarket where you can stock up on provisions.

MOUNTAIN TOWNS

The towns between Creel and Bahuichivo (the train station for Cerocahui) are in the middle of the Sierra Madre, the reason most people are headed here in the first place. Creel is the largest town, and is connected to Chihuahua by a smooth highway that will seem even smoother if you ride it coming out of the canyons. Creel is also the best starting point if you want to take the six-hour trip to Batopilas or if you're intent on seeing high-country attractions such as the Cascada de Basaseachi. Southwest of Creel is Divisadero, the end of the line as far as paved roads are concerned. The view from Divisadero is the most famous in the canyon, and the train stops here for a full 15 minutes to allow passengers time to gaze into the depths of the Barranca de Urique. Beyond lies Posada Barrancas, where three tidy luxury hotels hold their breaths on the precipice.

EL FUERTE

82 km (51 mi) northeast of Los Mochis.

Smart travelers come to El Fuerte, a rather sleepy town of some 45,000 residents, to board the Ferrocarril Chihuahua al Pacífico. But tour operators also use El Fuerte as a base for hiking, birding, or fishing excursions. Some area hotels get in on the action by organizing float trips on the river near town. You'll see herons and egrets, as well as magpies, kingfishers, and many other birds as you drift downstream past willow trees, cacti, and lilac bushes. One popular tour is to Cerro de la Mascara, an interesting archaeological site where hundreds of rock paintings and petroglyphs have been preserved.

Conquistador Don Francisco de Ibarra and a small group of soldiers founded this small town as San Juan Bautista de Carapoa in 1564. It became known as El Fuerte for its 17th-century fort, built by the Spaniards to protect against attacks by the indigenous Mayo, Sinaloa, Zuaque, and Tehueco peoples.

GETTING HERE AND AROUND

If you're taking the train bound for Creel/Chihuahua, we recommend you depart from El Fuerte. Highway 124 takes you to El Fuerte from Los Mochis. To travel by bus from Los Mochis to El Fuerte, take Alianza de Transportes del Valle del Fuerte. These buses, which depart from in front of the Mercado Independencia, make the trip in 1½ hours. Instead of a terminal, buses pull up to the corner of Avenida Juárez and 16 de Deciembre.

ESSENTIALS

Bus Contacts Alianza de Transportes del Valle del Fuerte (✉ *Avs. Independencia and DegolladoCol. Centro* ☎ *No phone*).

Currency Exchange Banamex (✉ *Juárez 212, Col. Centro* ☎ *698/893–0151*).

Internet Cybermail (✉ *Rodolfo Romero 108, Col. Centro* ☎ *698/893–1558*).

Medical Assistance Farmacia Cosmos (✉ *Zaragosa s/n, Col. Centro* ☎ *698/893–1486*).

Visitor and Tour Info 3 Amigos Tours (✉ *Reforma 100, Col. Centro* ☎ *698/893–5028*).

EXPLORING

Situated on El Camino Real (literally, the "Royal Road"), El Fuerte was one of the frontier outposts from which the Spanish set out to explore and settle what are today New Mexico, Arizona, and California. For three centuries it was a major trading post for gold and silver miners from the nearby mountains. It was chosen as Sinaloa's capital in 1824, and remained so for several years. Some lovely colonial mansions face the cobblestone streets leading from the central plaza. The plaza itself is extremely appealing, and comes alive at night with food vendors, courting couples, and children playing games.

A replica of the original fort has been built on the Cerro de Las Pilas, not far from the main plaza. It houses the **Museo El Fuerte Mirador** (☎ *698/893–1501* *50¢* *Daily 9–7*), where several rooms have displays on the history of the fort and the regional flora and fauna, and works from local artists, past and present. **■ TIP→ The ramparts of the fort are a great vantage point over the river valley. At dusk you can catch a glimpse of hundreds of bats leaving their homes deep inside the walls of the fort.**

WHERE TO EAT

$$ MEXICAN **El Mesón del General.** Just a block off the main plaza, the General's Table is the best place to try the *lobina* (black bass) caught in local reservoirs or the *cauque* (crayfish) that thrive in nearby rivers. Beside a plant-filled courtyard, the blue-and-yellow dining room is decorated with pictures and documents from the town's past. If someone in your party is craving Chinese food, there's a restaurant in the back run by the same management. ✉ *Juárez 202* ☎ *698/893–0260* *www.elmesondelgeneral.com* *MC, V.*

WHERE TO STAY

$$ ★ **El Fuerte.** When hunting guide Robert Brand married a local woman, he and his bride decided to welcome guests to their 380-year-old mansion. Hand-stenciled furniture and antiques here and there add to its considerable charms. *Artesanía* (folk art) decorates the high-ceiling guest rooms; the beds have intricately carved and painted headboards but somewhat lumpy mattresses. Clusters of chairs and tables on wide verandas invite socializing. **Pros:** convenient location; lovely rooms. **Cons:** chilly staff; lumpy mattresses. ✉ *Montesclaros 37* ☎ *698/893–0226* *www.hotelelfuerte.com.mx* *45 rooms* *In-room: no phone, Wi-Fi. In-hotel: restaurant, bar* *AE, D, MC, V.*

¢ **Hotel Río Vista.** On the Cerro de las Pilas, the highest spot in El Fuerte, you'll find this adobe-and-wood posada. It's certainly rustic—the stone wall of one room is actually part of the hillside. Guest rooms are creatively decorated with antiques. It's called a "Bird Paradise" with good reason: hummingbirds frequent the feeders around the terrace. **Pros:** best value in the area; lovely views; family-friendly quality. **Cons:** tiny pool; hard to find. ✉ *Cerro de las Pilas* ☎ *698/893–0413* *www.hotelriovista.com.mx* *31 rooms* *In-room: no phone, no TV (some). In-hotel: restaurant* *MC, V.*

$$ **Posada del Hidalgo.** With its lovely courtyards and cobblestone paths, this restored hacienda dating from 1895 recalls a more gracious era.

It's difficult to choose between the larger rooms with balconies and the slightly more modern rooms that open onto the flower-filled gardens. No matter which you pick you'll find handcrafted furnishings. You can make reservations through Hotel Santa Anita in Los Mochis. **Pros:** splendid banquet hall; comfortable rooms. **Cons:** stuffy staff; stairs to climb. ✉ *Hidalgo 101* *Reservations: Hotel Santa Anita, Apdo. 159, Los Mochis 81200* ☎ *698/893-1194 or 01800/821-0000 toll-free in Mexico, 888/528-8401* 🌐 *www.hotelposadadelhidalgo.com* *69 rooms* *In-room: no phone, Wi-Fi. In-hotel: restaurant, bar, pool, Internet terminal* 💳 *AE, MC, V.*

$$-$$$ **Fodor'sChoice** ★ **Torres Del Fuerte.** This meticulously appointed hacienda has the style and service of a four-star hotel, minus the stuffy character. The owner, whose father was born in the house, has an eclectic assortment of furnishings from all over the world. The sometimes eccentrically decorated theme rooms are all unique, and often quite romantic (lovers should ask for the Moroccan Room). The courtyard, with hummingbirds flitting around the fruit trees, is a real charmer. **Pros:** fabulous design; romantic rooms. **Cons:** hard to locate; small rooms. ✉ *Rodolfo G. Robles 102* ☎ *698/893-1974* 🌐 *www.hotelestorres.com* *25 rooms* *In-room: no phone, no TV, Wi-Fi. In-hotel: restaurant, bar, Internet terminal* 💳 *MC, V.*

CEROCAHUI

Bahuichivo train station, the stop for Cerocahui, is 170 km (105 mi) northeast of El Fuerte.

Cerocahui is a quiet mountain village set amid towering pines. **TIP→ Cerocahui is a favorite stop for birders—nearly 200 species of birds have been spotted in this part of the Sierras.**

GETTING HERE AND AROUND

From the station at Bahuichivo, the village of Cerocahui is a 40-minute drive along a bumpy, mostly unpaved road. If you have reservations, a van from your hotel will pick you up. If not, drivers meet each train.

ESSENTIALS

Medical Assistance **Centro de Salud** (✉ *Cerocahui* ☎ *635/456-5297*).

Visitor and Tour Info **Albert López Ceniceros** (☎ *635/456-5275*).

EXPLORING

It's a lovely ride to **Cerro del Gallego**, with one of the region's most magnificent views. From there you can make out the slim thread of the Río Urique and the old mining town of Urique, a dot on the distant canyon bottom.

In Cerocahui you'll find the **Misión San Francisco Javier**, a graceful little temple established in 1680 by the Jesuits. Although the order arrived in the area in 1680, indigenous Tarahumara uprisings and other difficulties delayed construction of the church until 1741. It is said that this was th[e] favorite church of the founder, Padre Juan María de Salvatierra, becau[se] the Tarahumara were the most difficult people to convert. Nearby [is a] boarding school for Tarahumara children.

10

Paraíso del Oso (*Box 31089, El Paso, TX 79931* *614/421–3372 or 800/884–3107* *www.mexicohorse.com*) leads horseback tours into the Barranca de Urique. The company, run for more than a decade by Doug Rhodes, also rents mountain bikes and ATVs by the day.

At the bottom of the continent's deepest canyon—dropping 6,163 feet—**Urique** enjoys a semitropical climate. Orange, guava, sycamore, and fig trees dot the landscape. The Río Urique, which carved the great canyon, slides lazily along in the dry season but races briskly after the summer rains. Browse in the old general store, El Central, then have lunch at the town's best restaurant, La Plaza, on the main square.

The Tarahumara people eschew life in town, preferring to live in family enclaves scattered throughout the valley or in small communities such as Guadalupe, 7 km (4½ mi) from Urique. The most direct path to this town is across a 400-foot-long suspension bridge that rocks and sways above the river. It's not for the faint of heart.

You can visit Urique as a day trip from Cerocahui, two to three hours each way by car, or ride horses or hike down into the canyon. Tours are given through Paraíso del Oso Lodge and Hotel Misión in Cerocahui. The best lodgings in Urique are at Hotel Estrella del Río ($36 double), which has large rooms, hot water, and great river views.

WHERE TO STAY

$$ **Cabañas San Isidro Lodge**. Among the pine-covered hills outside Cerocahui, this cluster of ranch-style cabins feels like it's at the end of the earth. The rustic, wood-paneled rooms are surprisingly comfortable. The family running the place serves tasty meals in their homey kitchen. **Pros:** a romantic hideaway; transportation to and from train; more stars than you have ever seen. **Cons:** half-hour drive from anywhere else; the only heat is from wood stoves. ✉ *Rancho San Isidro, outside of Cerocahui* *635/456–5257, 866/989–8687 in North America* *www.coppercanyonamigos.com* *12 cabins* *In-room: no a/c, no phone, no TV* *No credit cards* *FAP.*

$$$ **Hotel Misión**. A cross between a ski lodge and a hacienda, the atmospheric main building of this hotel contains the reception area, a small shop, and a combined dining room and bar warmed by two fireplaces. Wide verandas draw you outside to sit in leather rocking chairs and sip a glass of house-made wine. The hotel is part of the Balderrama chain, so you can make reservations through Hotel Santa Anita in Los Mochis. **Pros:** colonial-style rooms; wood-burning stoves; lovely verandas. **Cons:** staff can be uppity; neighborhood isn't so hot. ✉ *Cerocahui* *Reservations: Hotel Santa Anita, Apdo. 159, Los Mochis 81200* *668/812–1616, 01800/821–0000 toll-free in Mexico, or 888/528–8401* *www.hotelmision.com* *41 rooms* *In-room: no a/c, no phone, no TV. In-hotel: restaurant, bar, pool, Wi-Fi hotspot* *AE, MC, V* *FAP.*

$$$ **Paraíso del Oso Lodge**. This down-to-earth lodge is perfectly situated for bird-watching, walking in the woods, or horseback riding into the canyons. Ranch-style rooms with rough-hewn furniture and wood-burning stoves face a grassy courtyard. A fireplace in the bar and kerosene lamps in the restaurant give the common areas a glow. Room price includes three meals, plus transfer to and from the train. Doug

Rhodes, a loquacious U.S. transplant, leads tours. **Pros:** amazing location; lots of charm. **Cons:** a little pricey; on a main road. ⊠ *5 km (3 mi) outside of Cerocahui* ✉ *Reservations: Box 31089, El Paso, TX 79931* ☎ *614/421–3372 or 800/884–3107* ⊕ *www.mexicohorse.com* ⇨ *21 rooms* ⌂ *In-room: no a/c, no phone, no TV. In-hotel: restaurant, bar, Internet terminal* ▭ *MC, V* ⊚ *FAP.*

DIVISADERO AND POSADA BARRANCAS

47 km northeast of Bahuichiva, 60 km (37 mi) southwest of Creel.

At these whistle stops five minutes apart on the Continental Divide, the views of the Copper Canyon are unforgettable. A couple of romantic hotels hug the rim of the canyon in Posada Barrancas; in Divisadero, 20 or so cooks working over oil-barrel stoves wait for the train to disgorge hungry travelers.

■TIP→ If you're staying in Posada Barrancas for one night, your hotel will arrange tours to the Tarahumara Caves that finish in time for you to catch the train. On longer stays you can book hiking or horseback-riding tours of the Copper Canyon.

GETTING HERE AND AROUND

Divisadero and Posada Barrancas are connected by a decent road, but it deteriorates as it continues beyond Posada Barrancas to the village of Areponapuchi, a favorite destination for hikers.

WHERE TO STAY

$$$ ★ **Hotel Posada Mirador.** On the edge of the canyon, this hotel has an enviable location. The views are spectular from every room. Although on the small side for a luxury hotel, the rooms are bright and comfortable, with lovely tile floors, old-fashioned chimneys, and small terraces with tables and chairs. The hotel is part of the Balderrama chain, so you can make reservations through Hotel Santa Anita in Los Mochis. **Pros:** great views; friendly staff; just steps from the train. **Cons:** smallish rooms; pushy souvenir vendors at the door. ⊠ *Posada Barrancas* ✉ *Reservations: Hotel Santa Anita, Apdo. 159, Los Mochis 81200* ☎ *668/812–1613; 01800/821–0000 toll-free in Mexico; 888/528–8401 in North America* ⊕ *www.hotelesbalderrama.com/mirador.htm* ⇨ *51 rooms, 14 suites* ⌂ *In-room: no a/c, no phone, no TV. In-hotel: restaurant, bar* ▭ *AE, MC, V* ⊚ *FAP.*

$$ ★ **Mansión Tarahumara.** It may be disconcerting at first to discover a red-turreted castle here in canyon country, but somehow this hotel does not seem out of place. The guest rooms have contemporary pine furnishings, stone walls, and exposed-beam ceilings. **Pros:** relaxing steam room; palatial common areas; authentic surroundings. **Cons:** quite a few stairs to climb; most of the rooms face away from the best views. ⊠ *Posada Barrancas* ✉ *Reservations: Av. Juárez 1602-A, Col. Centro, Chihuahu City Chihuahua 31000* ☎ *614/415–4721 or 01800/639–6845 toll-fr in Mexico, 888/790–5264* ⊕ *www.lasierratarahumara.com.mx* ⇨ *rooms, 1 suite* ⌂ *In-room: no a/c, no TV (some). In-hotel: restaur bar, pool, gym, Internet terminal* ▭ *MC, V* ⊚ *FAP.*

CLOSE UP

Beyond the Train Ride

Hiking in the Copper Canyon is fantastic if you take the proper precautions. *Mexico's Copper Canyon Country,* by M. John Fayhee, is a good source of information. But even the most experienced trekkers should enlist the help of local guides, who can be contacted through area hotels or through travel agents in Los Mochis, El Fuerte, and Chihuahua. Also, the presence of well-guarded marijuana plantations throughout the canyon makes it safer to travel with a local guide who knows which areas to avoid.

La Barranca de Urique is most easily reached—by horse, bus, truck, or on foot—from Cerocahui. Hotels in Creel, Divisadero, and Posada Barrancas lead tours ranging from easy rim walks to a 27-km (17-mi) descent to the bottom. If you're in Cusárare, a gentle and rewarding hike is the 6-km (4-mi) walk from the Copper Canyon Lodge to 100-foot-high Cusárare Falls. More challenging but also more impressive is a full-day trek to the base of the Cascada de Basaseachi. The descent to Batopilas—not for acrophobes—requires an overnight stay.

Hotels throughout the canyons can arrange for local guides and reasonably gentle horses; however, these trips aren't for couch potatoes. The trails into the canyon are narrow and rocky, also slippery if the weather is icy or wet. At rough spots you might be asked to dismount and walk part of the way. A fairly easy and inexpensive ride is to Wicochic Falls at Cerocahui, about two hours round-trip, including a half-hour hike at the end, where the trail is too narrow for the horses. From Divisadero, horses can be hired to the tiny settlement of Wakajípare, deep within the canyon.

CREEL

275 km (170 mi) northeast of El Fuerte, 296 km (183 mi) southwest of Chihuahua.

Surrounded by craggy, pine-covered bluffs, Creel is a mining, ranching, and logging town that grew up around the railroad station. The largest settlement in the area, it's also a gathering place for Tarahumara people who come to buy supplies and sell crafts. Creel is the hub of the Barrancas del Cobre, with a great tour company, a 24-hour medical clinic, and the only ATM between El Fuerte and Cuauhtemóc.

GETTING HERE AND AROUND

Creel sits at the crux of the region's highways, making it fairly easy to get around. Bus companies Grupo Estrella Blanca and Noroeste both have terminals immediately across the tracks from the train station.

ESSENTIALS

Currency Exchange **Banco Santander** (✉ *López Mateos, Col. Centro* ☎ *635/456–0060*). ■ **TIP→ The Banco Santander Serfín is open weekdays 9–4. The ATM sometimes runs out of cash, so use it during bank hours so that you can have a back-up plan. This is the only ATM between Cuauhtémoc and El Fuerte.**

Medical Assistance **Centro de Salud** (✉ *Tarahumara 113, Col. Centro* ☎ *635/456-0132*).

Rental Cars **3 Amigos Tours** (✉ *Av. López Mateos 46, Col. Centro* ☎ *635/456-0036* 🌐 *www.amigos3.com*).

Visitor and Tour Info **3 Amigos Tours** (✉ *Av. López Mateos 46, Col. Centro* ☎ *635/456-0036* 🌐 *www.amigos3.com*).

EXPLORING

TOP ATTRACTIONS

Across the tracks from the Museo de Paleontologia, the **Museo de las Tarahumaras** (✉ *Av. Ferrocarril 172* ☎ *635/456-0080* *$1* ⏲ *Mon.–Sat. 9–5, Sun. 9–1*) is actually two museums under one roof. One exhibit focuses on traditional Tarahumara life, including a stunning exhibit of black-and-white photographs. You'll also find dinosaur bones, Spanish-era artifacts, and mementos from the area's mining days.

WORTH NOTING

A popular way to spend the day is to hike to the **Balneario Manantial Termal de Recohuata**, or Recohuata Hot Springs. A trip here involves climbing down from the canyon rim into the Barranca de Tararecua. Some tour guides leave their clients at the rim to be guided down to the artificial pools by youngsters who station themselves at the trailhead. A little farther down the hill you'll find natural swimming holes.

Worthwhile stops along the way to the colonial town of Batopilas are **Basihuare**, where wide horizontal bands of color cross huge vertical outcroppings of rock, and **La Bufa**, a tiny settlement at the site of a former Spanish silver mine. In the opposite direction, about 73 km (45 mi) northwest of Creel, along an unpaved, winding road, the 806-foot **Cascada de Basaseachi** is among the highest cascades (seasonal waterfalls) in North America.

Don't pass up the easy 6-km (4-mi) hike through a lovely piñon forest to see the **Cascada Cusárare**, a 101-foot waterfall that is most impressive during the rainy months and after the snow melts.

In the middle of the main plaza a collective of tour guides specializes in day trips to areas of interest around Creel. Many half-day tours include a visit to **Cusárare**, whose Tarahumara name means "eagle's nest." Located 26 km (16 mi) from Creel, the village is the site of a Jesuit mission built in 1741, which still serves as a center for religious and community affairs for the Tarahumara people. Inside the simple whitewashed structure men and women stand for the Sunday service, women on one side, men on the other.

One of the most common day tours is a visit to **Lago Arareko**, about 7 km (4 mi) from Creel. The pine-ringed lake merits little more than a quick look. The **Valle de los Hongos** (Valley of the Mushrooms), where rocks perch atop each other precariously, is a scattering of formations among a distressingly poor Tarahumara settlement. In a bit of linguisti imperialism, nearby **Bisabirachi** (Tarahumara for "Valley of the Ere Penises") was renamed by the Spanish as **Valle de los Monjes** (Val of the Monks). The impressive stone monoliths, in marvelous rol countryside, don't care either way.

WHERE TO EAT

$ MEXICAN ★ **El Tungar.** "The Hangover Hospital," as it is nicknamed, is a no-nonsense Mexican café. The shacklike structure may be unnerving, but the food wins over most skeptics. The menu includes traditional morning pick-me-ups—and hangover cures—like *menudo* (tripe soup), *pozole* (hominy soup with chunks of spicy pork), and *ari*, a type of ant excrement that, when mixed with chili, is said to cure many ills. ✉ *Calle Francisco Villa s/n, next to train station* ☎ *635/456–0130* 💳 *No credit cards* ⊗ *No dinner.*

WHERE TO STAY

$$ **Best Western The Lodge at Creel.** Door handles fashioned from elk antlers give this hotel, the most luxurious in town, the character of a hunting lodge. Several wings of rooms resembling log cabins continue the theme. Gas heaters disguised as wood-burning stoves add a bit of character. All rooms are no-smoking, and small pets are allowed. **Pros:** clean and well-maintained rooms; convenient location. **Cons:** small and cramped bathrooms; motel-style layout; lacks local vibe. ✉ *Av. López Mateos 61* ☎ *635/456–0071 or 877/844–0409* 🌐 *www.thelodgeatcreel.com* *37 rooms, 1 suite* *In-room: no a/c. In-hotel: restaurant, bar, gym, spa, Wi-Fi hotspot, Internet terminal, parking (free), no-smoking rooms* 💳 *AE, MC, V* 🍽 *BP.*

$$ Fodor's Choice ★ **Copper Canyon Sierra Lodge.** On the edge of a peaceful piñon forest near the Cascada Cusárare, this lodge made of pine and stucco is a natural beauty. Rooms are romantically equipped with kerosene lamps and woodstoves or fireplaces. The vegetarian meals are served in a pleasant dining room. This spot is best for those with wheels; it's 26 km (16 mi) from Creel. **Pros:** excellent restaurant; lovely place. **Cons:** no electricity; cavelike rooms. ✉ *Cusárare* *Nichols Expeditions, 497 N. Main St., Moab, UT 84532* ☎ *435/259–3999 or 800/648–8488* 🌐 *www.coppercanyonlodges.com* *19 rooms* *In-room: no a/c, no phone, no TV. In-hotel: restaurant, bar, parking (free)* 💳 *MC, V* 🍽 *FAP.*

¢ **Margarita's.** A van awaits backpackers from the second-class train, and then drives them across the street to this international gathering place. The private rooms—with wrought-iron lamps and light-wood furnishings—compare favorably to anything at three times the price. **Pros:** excellent breakfast and dinner is included; friendly international clientele. **Cons:** dorm rooms are a little cramped; and fixtures are often broken or inappropriately placed. ✉ *Av. López Mateos 11* ☎ *635/456–0045* *26 rooms, 1 dorm room* *In-room: no a/c, no phone, no TV. In-hotel: restaurant, bicycles* 💳 *No credit cards* 🍽 *MAP.*

$ **Margarita's Plaza Mexicana.** This two-story hotel set around a courtyard is one of the town's best bargains. Each room has a television, a heater, and a different wall mural. The tequila-and-mariachi parties hosted for tour groups can get quite noisy, but don't run too late. **Pros:** friendly staff, and Margarita's properties are a magnet for interesting international travelers. **Cons:** the maintenance here is a bit subpar, and for a full-on hotel it's surprising that it still lacks a/c, phone, and the ability to take credit cards. ✉ *Calle Elfido Bautista s/n, off Av. López Mateos* ☎ *635/456–0245* *27 rooms* *In-room: no a/c, no phone. In-hotel: restaurant, bar* 💳 *No credit cards* 🍽 *MAP.*

CLOSE UP

The Tarahumara: People of the Land

Mexico's largest state was once heavily populated by the Tarahumara, close relatives of the Pima Indians of southern Arizona. They are renowned for their running ability and endurance—Tarahumara is a Spanish corruption of their word Rarámuri, which means "running people." Today winners of international marathon races, the Tarahumara in earlier times hunted deer by chasing them to the point of collapse. During festivals they still engage in a game called *rarajípame* in which Tarahumara men run while kicking a hand-carved wooden ball for up to 40 hours.

Like those of other native peoples, the Tarahumara's way of life was totally disrupted by the arrival of the Europeans. The Spanish forced them to labor in the mines, and later both Mexicans and Americans put them to work on the railroads. The threat of slavery and the series of wars that began in the 1600s and continued until the 20th century forced them to retreat deeper into the canyons, where they are still at the mercy of outsiders: nowadays it's loggers and drug lords. Their population has also diminished over the years because of disease, drought, and poverty.

Despite all this, the Tarahumara are also considered to have the most traditional lifestyles of any North American indigenous peoples. They live a life well adjusted to the canyon country—the majority live on small ranches, many of which are seemingly perched on ledges high up on the canyon walls. Housing may be small adobe or log shacks or even caves for at least part of the year. Many Tarahumara still practice transhumance, a form of migration where they live in the relative warmth of the canyon bottoms during the winter and move to cooler altitudes in summer. Primarily subsistence farmers, they rely on the corn, beans, and squash that they grow, supplemented with wild game, fish, and seasonal herbs they collect.

In cities you may encounter Tarahumara men wearing more modern clothing, but most of the women—and many of the men—still wear traditional attire. For men this consists of sandals, a white breechcloth, a flowing top cinched with a woven belt, and their ubiquitous headband. Attire for women is sandals, a long skirt, long-sleeved blouse, and a headband, all made of brightly colored printed fabric. The women are mostly encountered selling the crafts they create, which include baskets of pine needles and torote grass, woven belts, and beaded bracelets. Men are known for carving wooden figures and even more for the violins that they make from native woods—an art form they learned from the Spaniards.

Everyone who comes into close contact with Tarahumara culture comes away with a profound respect for these gentle people. That is not to say that all Tarahumara want to interact with you. When approaching their abodes, it is polite to stand at the outer edges of the property and wait quietly. If anyone wishes to greet you, they will eventually come out. If not, then you should move on. This same reserve is appropriate when encountering them in town. You should also take care not to photograph any Tarahumara without their express permission.

$ **Sierra Bonita.** Perched on a hillside just outside Creel, this self-contained lodging has a restaurant, bar, and even a disco (open on weekends). Rooms and suites have less of a rustic look than most in the canyon area. Vans—reserve one when you check in—make the five-minute jaunt to Creel. **Pros:** good breakfasts; excellent views; sprawling grounds. **Cons:** isolated location; need a car to get around. ✉ *Carretera Gran Visión s/n* ☎ *635/456–0615; 01800/713–4460 toll-free in Mexico* 🌐 *www.sierrabonita.com.mx* *21 cabanas, 2 suites* *In-room: no a/c, Wi-Fi. In-hotel: restaurant, room service, bar, Internet terminal, parking (free)* 💳 *MC, V* *BP.*

NIGHTLIFE

Tía Molca's (✉ *Avenida López Mateos 35, Col. Centro* ☎ *635/456–0033*) is a small, friendly hole-in-the-wall with a big fireplace. It's popular with expats and travelers.

SHOPPING

Avenida López Mateos, Creel's main drag, has undergone a considerable transformation, thanks to the influx of trekkers and tourists from the train. There are too many shops selling Tarahumara crafts to count, and individual women and children continually approach you with necklaces and baskets on the street. **Misión Tarahumara** (☎ *635/456–0097*), on the east side of the plaza sells only Tarahumara handiwork, including musical instruments, woven belts, and simple pots.

BATOPILAS

80 km (50 mi) southeast of Creel.

Veins of silver—mined on and off since the time of the conquistadors—made this remote village of fewer than 2,000 people one of the wealthiest towns in colonial Mexico. At one time it was the only community besides Mexico City that had electricity. Today this town has two postage-stamp plazas, bridges made of rope and river stones, and an aqueduct built in the 19th century by the mayor of Washington, D.C. Most of the entertainment comes from the canciòneros who perform for diners in the town's only restaurant and then sing their hearts out by the river. If this isn't actually the town that inspired Gabriel García Márquez's novel *One Hundred Years of Solitude,* as some locals claim, it might as well be.

GETTING HERE AND AROUND

There are just two ways to get to Batopilas: three days hiking overland from Urique, or four hours by torturous and sometimes frightening back-road switchbacks off Highway 35 from Creel. In Creel, 3 Amigos Tours (www.amigos3.com) provides trucks and a guided itinerary for the journey, but this is a route only for fearless drivers. A bus comes and goes from Creel daily, taking about six hours.

EXPLORING

The triple-dome 17th-century **Templo de San Miguel Arcángel** is mysteriously isolated in the Satevó Valley, a scenic 16-km (10-mi) round-trip hike from town. Although the mission church still serves the surrounding communities, it is usually locked. Obtain the key from the residents of a cluster of houses directly behind the church. Ask the townspeople to point you in the right direction.

TOURS BY TROLLEY

Sponsored by the state tourism office, the **Trolley Turístico El Tarahumara** (✉ *Palacio de Gobierno, Plaza Hidalgo, Centro, Chihuahua* ☎ *614/429–3596*) stops at every tourist sight in the city. The trolley departs every hour from 9 to noon and 3 to 6 daily except Monday. The $2.50 fare allows you to ride four times in the same day.

WHERE TO EAT AND STAY

$$ MEXICAN ★ **✕ Puente Colgante/Swinging Bridge.** Outdoor dining in the small courtyard over the river is the high point here, and the dinners are pricier than lunch but extremely good and authentic. The house guitar-and-bass trio is fronted by a terrific singer who could be the Mexican Joe Strummer. ✉ *Negromante and Pablo Ochoa* ☎ *649/456–9023* ▭ *No credit cards.*

$ MEXICAN ★ **✕ Restaurante Carolina.** Snuggled up against tiny Plaza Constitution, this old-fashioned dining room has tile floors, thick walls, and glass-panel doors that separate diners from the large kitchen and formal dining room reserved for special occasions. The machaca breakfast is some of the best and heartiest food in the canyons. ✉ *Plaza de la Constitutión 10* ☎ *649/456–9096* ▭ *No credit cards.*

¢ **Real de Minas.** Owner Martín Alcáraz worked as a hotel manager before opening his own small place. It's a delightful spot; each room has decent beds and rustic furnishings but no TV or phone. This is as it should be—you come to experience the mood of the place with few distractions. **Pros:** convenient location, near many restaurants; flower-filled courtyard. **Cons:** difficult to contact. ✉ *Donato Guerra at Pablo Ochoa* ☎ *649/456–9045* *10 rooms* *In-room: no a/c, no phone, no TV* ▭ *No credit cards.*

EASTERN TERMINUS: CHIHUAHUA CITY

375 km (233 mi) south of El Paso–Ciudad Juárez border, 653 km (405 mi) northeast of Los Mochis, 296 (183) km northeast of Creel.

For a city ringed with highways and pocked by parking lots, Chihuahua has a really pleasant center. Here you'll find a pair of lovely plazas and more trees than you will probably see in any northern city of comparable size. Chihuahua, with a population of 750,000, feels considerably smaller than it is. Its two good museums are tied to key figures in the nation's history: Pancho Villa, the mustachioed revolutionary who helped overthrow Dictator Porfirio Díaz in 1910, and Padre Miguel Hidalgo, the priest known as the father of Mexican independence.

⚠ **Given the problems with drug cartel–related violence in Chihuahua City and Cuidad Juárez, we strongly advise that you avoid using either as a transit hub or a base. Instead, use Los Mochis as a transit hub and travel from there or El Fuerte to Creel.**

If you must start and/or spend time in Chihuahua City, check with U.S. state department's Web site (🌐 *www.travel.state.gov*) for upd on the situation. Stay on the tourist path—or, better yet, sign on to an organized tour—and keep your wits about you.

GETTING HERE AND AROUND

Several airlines have daily direct flights to Chihuahua (CUU). American Eagle flies twice daily from Dallas. Continental Express flies daily from Houston. Aeroméxico Connect flies daily from Los Angeles. Aeroméxico and Interjet connect with all major Mexican destinations. The 20-minute taxi ride downtown costs less than $20. Most U.S. visitors drive to Chihuahua via Carretera 45 (Federal Highway 45). The trip from Ciudad Juárez, just across the border from El Paso, Texas, is about 375 km (233 mi). Parking can be hard to come by. Taxis are safe and can be flagged from anywhere.

Omnibus de México lines run clean, air-conditioned, first-class buses from Ciudad Juárez to Chihuahua City. The intercity bus station is inconveniently located on the ring highway called the Periférico. Getting downtown requires a 10-minute cab ride or a 40-minute journey on Circumvalación 2, a bus that drops you a block from the station. (Look for the ominous 1898 state penitentiary—you can't miss it. The station is on the other side.) Grupo Estrella Blanca bus lines, which includes Chihuahuense and Elite, connects Chihuahua City and Creel.

ESSENTIALS

Airlines **Aeroméxico** (☎ *01800/021–4010 toll-free in Mexico*). **American** (☎ *01800/904–6000 toll-free in Mexico*). **Continental** (☎ *01800/900–5000 toll-free in Mexico*).

Bus Contacts **Estación Central de Chihuahua** (✉ *Boulevard Juan Pablo II, Periférico Oeste* ☎ *614/429–0230*). **Grupo Estrella Blanca** (☎ *668/812–1757 in Los Mochis; 01800/507–5500 toll-free in Mexico* 🌐 *www.estrellablanca.com.mx*). **Omnibus de México** (☎ *01800/765–6636 toll-free in Mexico* 🌐 *www.odm.com.mx*)).

Medical Assistance **Consultorio Médico** (✉ *Victoria 416, Col. Centro* ☎ *614/415–5994*). **Hospital Central del Estado** (✉ *Calle 33 and Rosales, Col. Obrera* ☎ *614/415–6381*). **Red Cross (Cruz Roja)** (☎ *668/815–0808 in Los Mochis; 614/411–1619 in Chihuahua*).

Rental Cars **Hertz** (✉ *Avenida Revolución 514, Col. Centro* ☎ *614/416–9925*).

Visitor and Tour Info **Chihuahua Tourism Office** (✉ *Palacio de Gobierno, Plaza Hidalgo, Calle Juan Aldama at Venustiano Carranza, Col. Centro* ☎ *01800/508–0111 toll-free in Mexico* 🌐 *www.ah-chihuahua.com*).

EXPLORING

The regal **Casa Chihuahua** once held the main post office (and before that the telegraph office). All that has changed with a well-funded surge of civic pride that transformed it into this museum. The real treat is the *calabozo*, or dungeon, amazingly preserved despite the fact that the building has been rebuilt three times in the past two centuries. Revolutionary hero Padre Hidalgo was imprisoned here by the Spanish prior to his execution. His pistols, trunk, crucifix, and reproductions of his letters are on display. ✉ *Av. Juárez between Calles Neri Santos and*

Carranza, Centro ☎ *614/429–3300 Ext. 11724* $2 ⏲ *Wed.–Mon. 10–6.*

GET OUT OF TOWN

Turismo Al Mar (✉ *Calle Verna 2202, Col. Mirador, Chihuahua* ☎ *614/416–5950* 🌐 *www.copper-canyon.net*) offers city tours and canyon sojourns.

Fodor's Choice ★ Whatever you do, don't miss the **Museo de la Revolución Mexicana**, better known as La Casa de Pancho Villa. Villa lived in this 1909 mansion, also called the Quinta Luz (*quinta* means "manor," or "country house"), with his wife Luz Corral. Although Villa married dozens of women, Corral was considered his only legitimate wife, as the couple was married in both civil and church ceremonies. She lived in this house until her death on June 6, 1986. The 50 small rooms that used to house Villa's bodyguards now holds artifacts of Chihuahua's cultural and revolutionary history. In the courtyard is the bullet-ridden 1919 Dodge in which Villa was assassinated in 1923 at the age of 45. Don't be shocked by all the uniformed soldiers, as the museum is run by the Mexican Army. ✉ *Calle Décima 3010, near Calle Terrazas, Col. Santa Rosa* ☎ *614/416–2958* $1 ⏲ *Tues.–Sat. 9–1 and 3–7, Sun. and holidays 10–4.*

The **Palacio de Gobierno** was built by the Jesuits as a monastery in 1882. Converted into state government offices in 1891, it was destroyed by a fire and rebuilt in 1947. Murals around the courtyard depict famous episodes from the history of Chihuahua, and a plaque commemorates the spot where Father Hidalgo was executed on the morning of July 30, 1811. In addition, there are a pair of museums. The **Museo de Hidalgo** honors its namesake and his famous "grito de dolores," the rallying cry for Mexico's War of Independence. The **Galería de Armas** presents weapons from the colonial and independence eras. ✉ *Plaza Hidalgo, Centro* ☎ *614/429–3596* *Free* ⏲ *Daily 8–8, museum Tues.–Sun. 9–5.*

OFF THE BEATEN PATH

Casas Grandes. Some 300 km (186 mi) northwest of Chihuahua, the twin towns of Nuevo Casas Grandes and Casas Grandes are the gateways to the ancient area known as Paquimé, declared a UNESCO World Heritage Site in 1998.

Near the aspen-lined Casas Grandes River, Paquimé was inhabited by peoples of the Oasis America culture between AD 700 and 1500. The city was poised between the Pueblo cultures of today's Southwestern United States (to whom they were related) to the north and their Mesoamerican neighbors to the south. Paquimé was a commercial center whose residents manufactured jewelry and raised fowl and macaws from the tropics. Evidence of their engineering and architectural savvy still stands in the form of heat-shielding walls and intricate indoor plumbing systems. The high-tech on-site museum shows Paquimé artifacts and ceramics and has bilingual displays.

Omnibus de México makes the five-hour trip from Chihuahua t Nuevas Casas Grandes (about $20). To get to the ruins, it's easiest hail a taxi from the bus station in Nuevas Casas Grandes. Once the head for the *zócalo* (main square). Paquimé is a 10-minute walk f town—follow the PAQUIMÉ sign on Avenida Constitución. ☎ *636/692–4140* ☒ *Museum $2.60* ⊙ *Tues.–Sun. 8–5.*

If you want a quick bite, **Restaurante Constantino** (✉ *Minerva 110, Nuevo Casas Grandes* ☎ *636/694–1005*) makes great enchiladas.Family-style **Hotel Piñon** (✉ *Av. Juárez 605, Nuevo Casas Grandes* ☎ *636/694–0166*) has a swimming pool, restaurant, bar, and a private collection of ancient *ollas* (clay pots) from Paquimé.**Hotel Hacienda** (✉ *Av. Juárez 2603 Norte, Nuevo Casas Grandes* ☎ *636/694–1046* ⊕ *www.hotelhacienda.com.mx*), with a restaurant, bar, and swimming pool, is one of the best places to stay in town. Make reservations in advance.

WHERE TO EAT

$ MEXICAN ★ ✕ **Casa de los Milagros**. According to legend, the owner of this house fell in love with one of Pancho Villa's "girls." His wife's prayers to Saint Anthony were answered when her husband returned, so the villa was dubbed the "House of Miracles." Today it's *the* place for drinks, with a high-ceilinged room painted in electrifying colors. ✉ *Victoria 812, near Ocampo, Centro* ☎ *614/437–0693* ▭ *MC, V* ⊙ *No lunch.*

$ MEXICAN ✕ **Del Paseo Café**. Two doors down from Quinta Gameros, this casual restaurant is known for its good service. Original art decorates walls painted Santa Fe pinks, peaches, and ochers, and roving musicians sing romantic ballads Wednesday to Sunday after 9 PM. The specialty is *arrachera a la borracha,* tenderized beef marinated in beer and grilled with mushrooms and onions. It's open Sunday to Wednesday 8 AM to midnight and Thursday, Friday, and Saturday until 2 AM. ✉ *Bolívar 411, Centro* ☎ *614/410–3200* ⊕ *www.delpaseocafe.com.mx* ▭ *MC, V.*

$$ STEAKHOUSE ✕ **La Calesa**. With wood paneling and crimson tablecloths and curtains, La Calesa looks every bit the classic steak house. The filet mignon and rib-eye steaks are particularly good; try the former grilled with mushrooms. ✉ *Av. Juárez 3300, Centro* ☎ *614/416–0222* ⊕ *www.lacalesa.com.mx* ▭ *V.*

WHERE TO STAY

$$ **Hotel Posada Tierra Blanca**. Across the street from the Palacio del Sol, this modern motel charges considerably less. Rooms surrounding the gated swimming pool have firm mattresses and pseudo-antiques. ■ **TIP→ Even if you don't stay here, duck inside to see the impressive mural by Chihuahuan painter Aarón Piña Mora. Pros:** a swimming pool in an appealing courtyard; nice artwork. **Cons:** neighborhood is empty after dark; bland character. ✉ *Niños Héroes 102, Centro* ☎ *614/415–0000* *92 rooms, 2 suites* ⊕ *www.posadatierrablanca.com.mx* *In-room: Wi-Fi. In-hotel: restaurant, room service, bar, pool, Internet terminal, parking (free)* ▭ *AE, MC, V.*

$$–$$$ **Hotel Soberano**. Overlooking the city and surrounding mountains, Chihuahua's most elegant hotel couldn't have a more magnificent view. Designed around an atrium with a cascading waterfall, the sparkling hotel is quite a contrast to the rustic accommodations of the canyons. **Pros:** rooms are plush yet understated, with richly patterned textiles; televisions hidden in tall chests, and baths with tubs and showers.

Cons: far from the downtown attractions; not much charm. ✉ *Barranca del Cobre 3211, Fracc. Barrancas* ☎ *614/429–2929 or 01800/711–4099 toll-free in Mexico, 800/363–5997 in North America* 🌐 *www.hotelsoberano.com* 194 rooms, 10 suites *In-room: refrigerator, safe, Internet. In-hotel: 2 restaurants, bars, tennis court, pool, gym, parking (free), no-smoking rooms* 💳 *AE, MC, V.*

$$ **Palacio del Sol.** The high-rise hotel looks faded from the outside, but the rooms and common areas are redecorated on a regular basis. While lacking the luster of some higher-priced hotels, the Palacio del Sol is pleasant and understated. It's within walking distance of most of the downtown sights. The view from the upper floors is amazing. **Pros:** friendly staff; congenial mood; good mix of guests. **Cons:** building is charmless; surrounding blocks are desolate at night. ✉ *Independencia 116, Centro* ☎ *614/412–3456* 🌐 *www.hotelpalaciodelsol.com* *158 rooms, 25 suites* *In-room: refrigerator (some), Wi-Fi (some), Internet. In-hotel: 4 restaurants, room service, bar, gym, laundry service, Wi-Fi hotspot, parking (free)* 💳 *AE, MC, V.*

$–$$$ ★ **Quality Inn San Francisco.** A favorite of Mexican business travelers, this modern five-story hotel has a prime location behind the Plaza de las Armas. Rooms have firm beds, large TVs, and desks where you can finish that last-minute report. **Pros:** clean and comfortable; weekend rates are a bargain. **Cons:** no character; neighborhood is intimidating at night. ✉ *Victoria 409, Centro* ☎ *614/439–9000; 01800/364–6835 toll-free in Mexico* 🌐 *www.qualityinnchihuahua.com* *74 suites* *In-room: Wi-Fi. In-hotel: restaurant, bar, gym, Internet terminal, parking (free), no-smoking rooms* 💳 *AE, MC, V.*

Los Cabos and the Baja Peninsula

Cabo San Lucas

WORD OF MOUTH

"[Los Cabos is] one of the best places in the world for marlin fishing (January is good for striped marlin). There's also several scenic challenging golf courses and a wild party scene downtown most nights. Rent a car and visit the smaller, quieter towns on either the Pacific side (Todos Santos) or Cortez side (Los Barilles, etc), or go snorkeling or whale watching or various other water activities."

—Bill_H

www.fodors.com/community

WELCOME TO LOS CABOS AND THE BAJA PENINSULA

TOP REASONS TO GO

★ **Driving through starkly gorgeous landscapes:** Along the Pacific Coast, south of Tijuana, the Carretera Transpeninsular (Highway 1) is half the fun of getting to Baja's historic missions and remote beaches.

★ **Sampling the other California's finest wines:** The Valle de Guadalupe, near Ensenada, has vineyards and inns with unpretentious hosts.

★ **Making eye contact with a gray whale:** These gentle giants swim to Baja California every winter to mate and calve in three lagoons on the peninsula's west coast.

★ **Catching (and releasing) a feisty marlin:** Sportfishing aficionados flock to Cabo, East Cape, La Paz, Loreto, and San Felipe when temperatures are high and fish are abundant.

★ **Giving in to sybaritic pleasures:** Indulge in a massage, salt scrub, or seaweed wrap—maybe all three—at a Los Cabos spa.

1 San José del Cabo. Thirty-two kilometers (20 mi) east of Cabo San Lucas, San José, the eldest sister, has remained the smaller, quieter, and tamer of the two siblings. Its 18th-century colonial architecture, artsy vibe, and quality restaurants are great for those who like to be within driving distance—not right in the middle—of the action.

2 The Corridor. Along this stretch of road, which connects San José to Cabo, exclusive guard-gated resort complexes have taken over much of the waterfront with their sprawling villas, golf courses, and shopping centers such as Las Tiendas de Palmilla, an upscale, open-to-the-public mall.

3 Cabo San Lucas. Located to the west of the Corridor, Cabo holds the sportfishing fleet and the cruise ships terminal. Trendy restaurants and bars line the streets and massive hotels have risen all along the beachfront. Here you'll find Bahía Cabo San Lucas (Cabo Bay), the towering Land's End Rocks, and the famed arched landmark, El Arco.

4 Baja California Sur. La Paz, the capital of Baja California Sur, is a big little city, one of the most authentic on the peninsula. Smaller Loreto, beloved by sportfishermen, is developing an identity as construction on a huge planned community, Loreto Bay, wraps up. Along the Pacific lie three coves that fill with birthing gray whales and boats of whale-watchers from December to April.

5 Baja California Norte. Drive right on through the border towns of Tijuana, Tecate, and Mexicali—safety is questionable these days—and head to the beauty and charm of towns farther south. The beaches of Rosarito and Ensenada draw retirees, RVers, and, spring-breakers. The Valle de Guadalupe provides fantastic wine to those willing to stray from Napa. Farther south, Highway 1 traverses vacant landscapes of mountains and cacti, then enters Baja California Sur at Guerrero Negro.

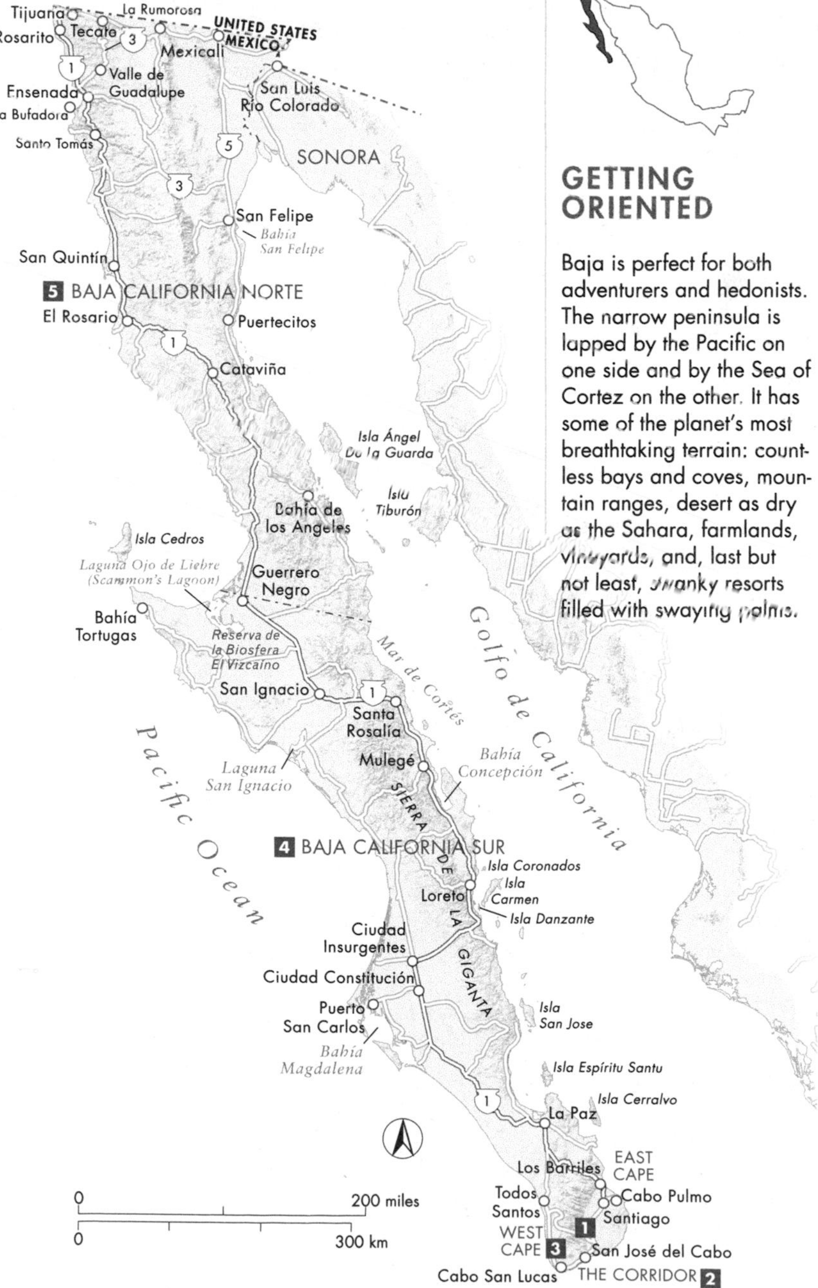

GETTING ORIENTED

Baja is perfect for both adventurers and hedonists. The narrow peninsula is lapped by the Pacific on one side and by the Sea of Cortez on the other. It has some of the planet's most breathtaking terrain: countless bays and coves, mountain ranges, desert as dry as the Sahara, farmlands, vineyards, and, last but not least, swanky resorts filled with swaying palms.

LOS CABOS AND THE BAJA PENINSULA PLANNER

Safety

Los Cabos is one of the safest areas in Mexico, but it's important to follow standard safety precautions and be aware of your surroundings. Pickpocketing and petty thievery are usually the biggest concerns. People have been victimized after imbibing drugged drinks in Los Cabos nightclubs. Like momma always said: don't drink alone or with strangers.

Mexican drug cartel activity has turned border areas into no-go areas the past couple of years. We've scaled coverage of the border cities back dramatically for this edition, but hope that will be only a temporary measure.

Getting Here

Once upon a time, the majority of Cabo's visitors were anglers primarily from Southern California and the west coast. These days, however, they fly in nonstop to Los Cabos from all over the United States, and to Loreto and La Paz from some U.S. cities. Via nonstop service, Los Cabos is about 2½ hours from Los Angeles, 2¾ hours from Houston, 2¾ hours from Dallas/Fort Worth, and 2 hours from Phoenix.

Flying time from New York to Mexico City, where you must switch planes to continue to Los Cabos, is five hours. Los Cabos is about a two-hour flight from Mexico City.

As far as Baja Norte is concerned, you have a few options other than flying in to Tijuana (which doesn't receive many international flights). Many people buy Mexican car insurance in San Diego and drive on in. If you don't live that close, you can fly into San Diego, rent a car, and drive down (be sure to check with rental companies, as their policies differ on this). Bring three copies of the following, plus the original: passport and vehicle registration. ⇨ *For more information on driving into Mexico, see Driving in Mexico below.*

IF THE BEACH BECKONS

If swimming is important to you, research beachside resorts, as many in this region are on stretches of beach where swimming is dangerous or forbidden due to strong currents. The Pacific side is notorious for rogue waves and intense undertows. Hotels will often post a red flag on the beach to alert swimmers to strong currents and undertows, but you won't see such warnings on the stretches of public beach. As a general rule, Los Cabos beaches are no-frills, with very few facilities.

An Active Life

Fishing is a main diversion, whether in *pangas* (small motorized skiffs) or yachts. International tournaments fill hotels from Loreto to Los Cabos from September through November. Golf is equally important, with some courses designed by the likes of Jack Nicklaus and Tom Weiskopf. Tour companies encourage clients to hike or bike through the Sierra de la Laguna, take ATV (all-terrain vehicle) trips along the beaches and into the desert, or hit the trails on horseback. December through April, multiday tours take you to such prime whale-watching places as Bahía Magdalena, Laguna San Ignacio, and Scammon's Lagoon.

A Taste of Baja

Baja's chefs rely on the vegetables and fruits grown in the region's fertile valleys. Beef, pork, and quail are all good here. And the seafood, which is often fried or grilled, is outstanding. You can also eat dorado, tuna, and snapper topped with *guajillo* and chipotle chilies, tomatillo salsa, or mango and papaya relishes. Mexico's best wines are nurtured in the Santo Tomás and Guadalupe valleys outside Ensenada, and a beloved beer, Tecate, comes from the Baja Norte border town of the same name.

Some say that fish tacos (*tacos de pescado*) originated in Ensenada, others insist it was San Felipe. No matter. They now appear on menus everywhere, and are made with hunks of battered and fried fish stuffed in a fresh corn tortilla and topped with such fixings as a mayonnaise-based sauce, cilantro, onions, and shredded cabbage.

Lobster gets special treatment in Puerto Nuevo. *Langosta Puerto Nuevo* is typically boiled in oil and served with beans, rice, melted butter, and steaming-fresh tortillas.

Try *ceviche,* which is fresh fish marinated in a mixture of lime, onions, and cilantro.

Eat, Drink and Be Merry

One of Los Cabos' most enjoyable celebrations is the Festival of Rhythms, Colors and Flavors (Festival de Ritmos, Colores y Sabores), which takes place in late November/early December. It's a weeklong celebration of food, drink, and music, and showcases the area's top restaurants.

Money Matters

Some restaurants add a 15% service charge to the tab. A few small hotels don't accept credit cards; some lavish places add a 10%–20% service charge. Most properties raise their rates December–April (and raise them even higher around Christmas).

WHAT IT COSTS IN DOLLARS

	¢	$	$$	$$$	$$$$
Restaurants	under $5	$5–$10	$10–$15	$15–$25	over $25
Hotels	under $50	$50–$75	$75–$150	$150–$250	over $250

Restaurant prices are for a main course excluding tax and tip. Hotel prices are for two people in a standard double room in high season.

How's the Weather

Although Los Cabos hotels are often busiest starting in mid-October for the sportfishing season, the high season doesn't technically begin until mid-December, running through the end of Easter week. Spring break is also a particularly crowded and raucous time in Cabo San Lucas and in the beach towns in Baja Norte. Downtown Cabo and the border towns up north are really busy, especially on weekend nights, throughout the year. Whale-watching season from mid-December to April really compounds the situation during high season, though whale-watchers tend to stay in La Paz and Loreto more often than Los Cabos.

The Pacific hurricane season mirrors that of the Atlantic and Caribbean, so there's always a slight chance of a hurricane from August through October. Although hurricanes rarely hit Los Cabos head-on, the effects can reverberate when a large hurricane hits Mexico's Pacific coast. Still, most summer tropical storms pass through quickly, even during the Cape's so-called short "rainy" season, from July through October.

Baja Norte's desert heat is tempered by low humidity and cool breezes off the water. Temperatures from June through September are searing. Winter sees chilly, stiff winds. Nights in Los Cabos December through April can be chilly (horrors—as low as 10°C/50°F). Daytime temp rise to 20°C (70°F) or higher.

LOS CABOS AND BAJA SUR

Updated by Jeffrey Van Fleet

IF HUMANS PULLED OUT OF Baja it would rapidly regress to its natural dry, brown, uninhabitable state. But man has wrought wonders here. Enormous swaths of desert and coast are carved into exclusive developments, and the demand for more marinas, golf courses, and private homes seems never-ending. In some locales, hotels command $500 or more a night for their enormous suites; restaurants and spas charge L.A. prices; and million-dollar vacation villas are all the rage.

With the completion in 1973 of the Carretera Transpeninsular (Mexico Carretera 1), travelers gradually found their way down the 1,700-km (1,056-mi) road, drawn by wild terrain and pristine beaches. Baja California Sur became a Mexican state in 1974, and the population and tourism have been growing ever since. Still, Baja Sur remains a rugged, largely undeveloped land. Many people opt to fly to the region rather than brave the often desolate (yet wildly adventurous) Carretera 1.

Whale-watching in Scammon's Lagoon, San Ignacio Lagoon, Magdalena Bay, and throughout the Mar de Cortés is a main attraction in winter. History buffs enjoy Loreto, where the first mission in the Californias was established. La Paz is a busy state capital and sportfishing hub. At the peninsula's southernmost tip, fishing aficionados, golfers, and sun worshippers gather in Los Cabos, which sits like a sun-splashed movie set where the desert and ocean collide.

San José del Cabo is a traditional Mexican town, albeit with a strong foreign influence. Massive all-inclusive resorts have consumed much of its coastline, making San José the favored destination for families who just want to stay put on a safe, self-contained vacation. Outrageous, excitement-packed Cabo San Lucas is the Cabo you see on MTV, with many of the hotels and restaurants and most of the action. It's spring break here year-round, making it the preferred home base for the let-it-all-hang-out crowd. Connecting the two towns is the Corridor—a strip of designer golf courses and superluxe resorts set in a desert landscape. Celebrities lounge poolside at Corridor hideaways, their privacy ensured by exorbitant room rates.

CABO SAN LUCAS

28 km (17 mi) southwest of San José del Cabo.

Cabo San Lucas is *in*—for its rowdy nightlife, its slew of trendy restaurants, and its lively beaches. The sportfishing fleet is headquartered here, cruise ships anchor off the marina, and there's a massive hotel on every available plot of waterfront turf. A pedestrian walkway lined with restaurants, bars, and shops anchored by the sleek Puerto Paraíso mall curves around Cabo San Lucas harbor, itself packed with yachts.

A five-story hotel complex at the edge of the harbor blocks the water view and sea breezes from the town's side streets, which are filled with a jarring jumble of structures. The most popular restaurants, clubs, and shops are along Avenida Lázaro Cárdenas (the extension of Highway 1 from the Corridor) and Boulevard Marina, paralleling the waterfront. The side streets closest to the marina are clogged with traffic, and their

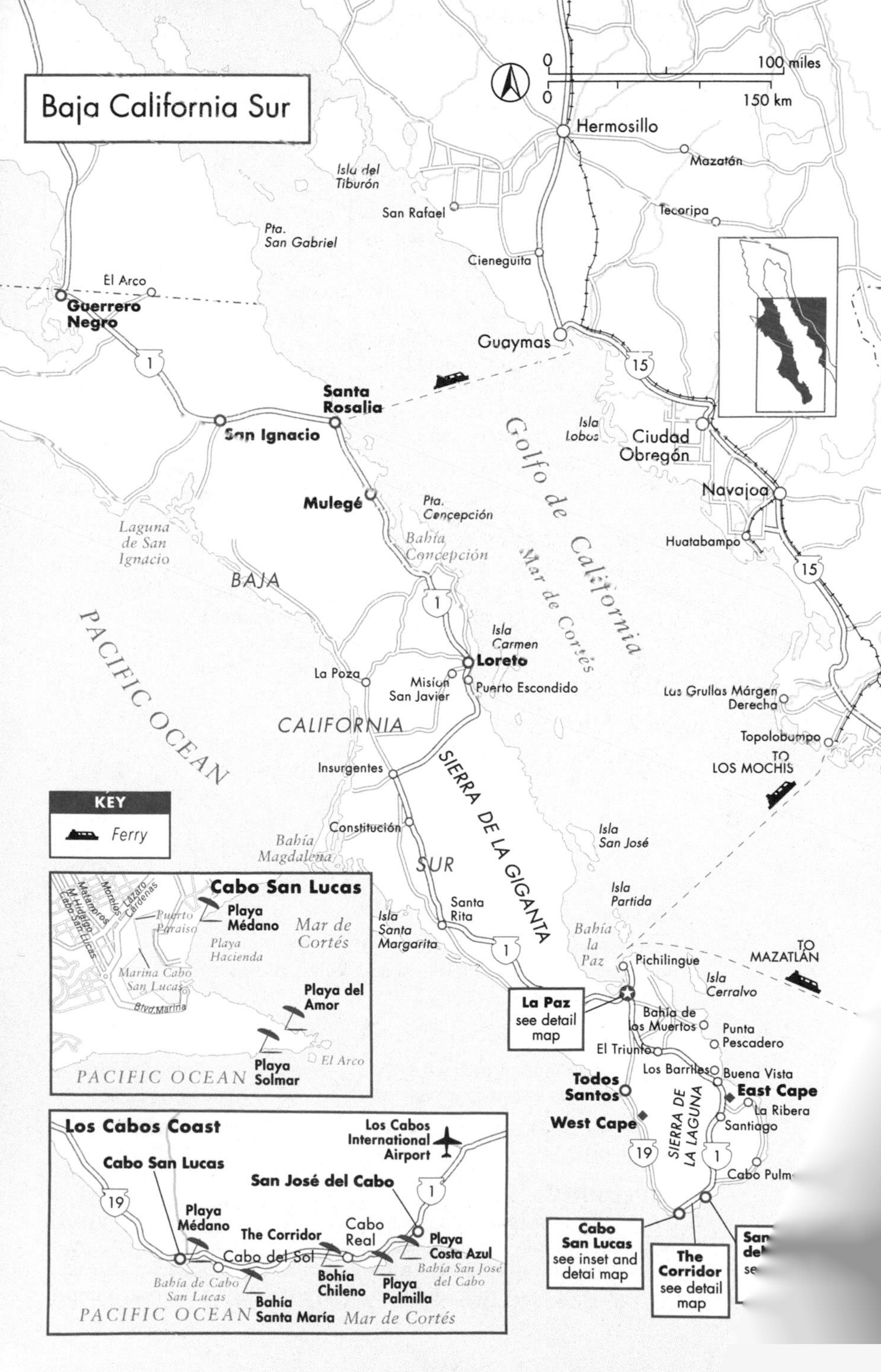

Baja California Sur
0
100 miles
0
150 km
Hermosillo
Mazatán
Isla del Tiburón
San Rafael
Tecoripa
Pta. San Gabriel
Cieneguita
El Arco
Guerrero Negro
Guaymas
1
15
Santa Rosalia
San Ignacio
Isla Lobos
Ciudad Obregón
Golfo de California
Navajoa
Mulegé
Pta. Concepción
Laguna de San Ignacio
Bahía Concepción
Huatabampo
Mar de Cortés
BAJA
PACIFIC OCEAN
Isla Carmen
Loreto
La Poza
Misión San Javier
Puerto Escondido
Los Grullas Márgen Derecha
CALIFORNIA
Topolobampo
TO LOS MOCHIS
Insurgentes
SIERRA DE LA GIGANTA
KEY
Ferry
Constitución
Isla San José
Bahía Magdalena
SUR
Isla Partida
Cabo San Lucas
Playa Médano
Puerto Paraiso
Mar de Cortés
Playa Hacienda
Marina Cabo San Lucas
Blvd. Marina
Playa del Amor
El Arco
PACIFIC OCEAN
Playa Solmar
Isla Santa Margarita
Santa Rita
Bahía la Paz
Pichilingue
TO MAZATLÁN
Isla Cerralvo
La Paz see detail map
Bahía de los Muertos
Punta Pescadero
El Triunfo
Los Barriles
Buena Vista
Todos Santos
East Cape
La Ribera
West Cape
SIERRA DE LA LAGUNA
Santiago
19
Cabo Pulmo
Los Cabos Coast
Los Cabos International Airport
Cabo San Lucas
San José del Cabo
Playa Médano
The Corridor
Cabo Real
Playa Costa Azul
Cabo del Sol
Bahía San José del Cabo
Bahía de Cabo San Lucas
Bohía Chileno
Playa Palmilla
Bahía Santa María
PACIFIC OCEAN
Mar de Cortés
Cabo San Lucas see inset and detai map
The Corridor see detail map

uneven, crumbling sidewalks front tourist traps jammed side by side. At Playa Médano, tanned bodies lie shoulder to shoulder on the sand, with every possible form of entertainment close at hand.

The short Pacific coast beach in downtown San Lucas is more peaceful, though huge hotels have gobbled up much of the sand. An entire new tourism area dubbed Cabo Pacifica by developers has blossomed on the Pacific, west of downtown. There's talk of a new international airport in San Lucas, along with golf courses and more resorts. San Lucas may soon be Mexico's gaudiest tourism capital.

POOR PITCH

Unless you want to tour a time-share, ignore the offers for free transfers at the airport in Los Cabos. Representatives from various properties compete vociferously for clients; often you won't realize you've been suckered into a sales presentation until you get in the van. To avoid this, go to the official taxi booths inside the baggage claim or just outside the final customs clearance area and pay for a ticket for a regular shuttle bus.

GETTING HERE AND AROUND

Aeropuerto Internacional de Los Cabos (Los Cabos International Airport, or SJD) is 1 km (½ mi) west of the Transpeninsular Highway (Hwy. 1) and 48 km (30 mi) northeast of Cabo San Lucas. Fares from the airport to hotels in Los Cabos are expensive. The least expensive transport is by shuttle buses that stop at various hotels along the route; fares run $12 to $25 per person. In Los Cabos, the main Terminal de Autobus (Los Cabos Bus Terminal) is about a 10-minute drive west of Cabo San Lucas. Express buses with air-conditioning and restrooms travel frequently from the terminal to Todos Santos (one hour), La Paz (three hours), and Loreto (eight hours). TransCabo can provide private transport for $60 between San José del Cabo and Cabo San Lucas. Taxi fares are exorbitant in Los Cabos, and the taxi union is definitely powerful. The fare between Cabo San Lucas and San José del Cabo runs about $45—more at night. Cabs from Corridor hotels to either town run about $25 each way.

ESSENTIALS

Bus Contacts Los Cabos Terminal de Autobus (✉ *Hwy. 19* ☎ *624/143–5020*). **TransCabo** (☎ *624/146–0888*).

Currency Exchange Banamex (✉ *Av. Cárdenas*).

Medical Assistance AmeriMed (✉ *Av. Cárdenas at Paseo Marina* ☎ *624/143–9670* 🌐 *www.amerimed-hospitals.com*).

Emergency Number for Medical Assistance (☎ *Dial 060 or 066*). **Police** (☎ *624/143–3977*).

EXPLORING

★ **El Arco,** the most spectacular sight in Cabo San Lucas, is a natural rock arch. It's visible from the marina and from some hotels, but it's more impressive from the water. To fully appreciate Cabo, take at least a short boat ride out to the arch and Playa del Amor, the beach underneath it.

Paved walkways run northeast from the busy Boulevard Marina to the hotels and beaches and southeast to the marina's main dock and **Mercado de Artesanías** *(Artisans Market)* that serve as the entryway to town for cruise passengers.

> **WORD OF MOUTH**
>
> "In the town of Cabo San Lucas, Medano Beach is a fun place. Typical Mexico set up of a line of various beach bars & restaurants, vendors, different activities, and a beautiful view out to the rock formations at the tip. —suze

The main downtown street, Avenida Lázaro Cárdenas, passes the **Plaza Amelia Wilkes**, aka Plaza San Lucas, with its white wrought-iron gazebo. The plaza is the loveliest patch of gardens in San Lucas. Many of the older buildings facing the plaza have been renovated as classy restaurants, hotels, and offices.

BEACHES

Fodor's Choice ★ **Playa del Amor.** Lovers have little chance of finding romantic solitude at Lovers' Beach. The azure cove on the Sea of Cortez at the tip of the peninsula may well be the area's most frequently photographed patch of sand. It's a must-see on every first-timer's list. Water taxis, glass-bottom boats, kayaks, and Jet Skis all make the short trip from Playa Médano to this small beach backed by cliffs streaked white with pelican and seagull guano. Snorkeling around the base of these rocks is fun when the water's calm; you may spot striped sergeant majors and iridescent green and blue parrot fish. Seals hang out on the rocks at the base of the arch. Walk along the sand to the Pacific side to see pounding white surf; just don't dive in ✉ *Just outside Cabo San Lucas, at El Arco.* **Amenities:** None.

Playa Médano. Foamy plumes of water shoot from Jet Skis and Wave Runners buzzing through the water off Médano, a 3-km (2-mi) span of grainy tan sand that's always crowded. When cruise ships are in town, it's mobbed. Bars and restaurants line the sand, waiters deliver ice buckets filled with beers to sunbathers in lounge chairs, and vendors sell everything from fake silver jewelry to henna tattoos. You can even have your hair braided into tiny cornrows or get a pedicure. Swimming areas are roped off to prevent accidents, and the water is calm enough for toddlers. Several hotels line Médano, which is just north of downtown off Paseo del Pescador. Construction is constant on nearby streets, and parking is virtually impossible. ✉ *Paseo del Pescador.* **Amenities:** Food concession.

Playa Solmar. Huge waves crash on the Pacific side of San Lucas. This wide, lovely beach stretches from Land's End north to the cliffs of El Pedregal, where mansions perch on steep cliffs. Swimming is impossible here because of the dangerous surf and undertow; stick to sunbathing and strolling. From December to March you can spot gray whales spouting just offshore; dolphins leap above the waves year-round. The beach is at the end of Avenida Solmar off Boulevard Marina. ✉ *Blvd. Marina to hotel entrances.* **Amenities:** None.

TAKE A TOUR

You may not be able to swim in Cabo's seas, but you can enjoy the sensations of being out on the water. Boat tours range from standard all-you-can-drink booze cruises to pirate-ship trips that kids love. The themes of Los Cabos boat tours vary, but most follow essentially the same route: through Bahía Cabo San Lucas, past El Arco, around Land's End into the Pacific Ocean, and then east through the Sea of Cortez along the Corridor.

Cruises on the remarkable *Pirate Ship* are ideal for families with children. Deckhands dressed in pirate garb let kids help hoist the sail and tie knots while they learn about the area's rich history of pirates. It sails from 10:30 to 1 and includes hot dogs and hamburgers. The two-hour sunset cruise departs at 5 Monday through Saturday. Kids under age 12 ride free. Pez Gato has two 42-foot catamarans, *Pez Gato I* and *Pez Gato II*. You can choose the romantic sunset cruise or the rowdier booze cruise. Sunset cruises depart every day but Tuesday, from 5 to 7. A whale-watching cruise sails daily from 10:30 AM to 1:30 and 2 PM to 4 PM, from January through March.

Tour Operators ***Pirate Ship*** (✉ *East end of Marina, Cabo San Lucas* ☎ *624/143–2714*). **Pez Gato** (✉ *El Tesoro hotel dock, Cabo San Lucas* ☎ *624/143–3797* 🌐 *www.pezgato.com*).

WHERE TO EAT

$ MEXICAN Fodor's Choice ★ ✕ **Crazy Lobster Bar & Grill.** Open for breakfast, lunch, and dinner, this typical Mexican sit-down locale has a happy hour that runs from 10 AM to 6 PM. Prices here are super-cheap: You can get a lobster tail for less than 10 bucks; Cuervo tequila shots are a mere 70¢; and Don Julio tequila shots are $2.80. And as you sit under the open-air palapa, strolling mariachis will pass by, providing your dining sound track. ✉ *Hidalgo and Zapata, Centro* ☎ *624/143–6535* 💳 *MC, V* ⊙ *Closed Sept.*

$$$ SEAFOOD ✕ **Edith's Restaurant.** The Caesar salad and flambéed banana crepes are prepared tableside at this colorful, classy, and popular restaurant. The Disca de Mariscos, with lobster, shrimp, and fish, is Baja's representative dish. Here even the simplest choices are special: quesadillas are homemade tortillas wrapped around Oaxacan cheese; meat and fish dishes are doused in chili or tropical fruit sauces. Edith's air-conditioned Wine Cellar offers a large selection of domestic and imported wines, and is ideal for hosting small intimate dinners for up to 10. Families dine in early evening, so come in later if you're looking for a more romantic atmosphere, when you'll hear soft, live Mexican music. ✉ *Paseo del Pescador near Playa Médano, Playa Médano* ☎ *624/143–0801* 🌐 *www.edithscabo.com* 💳 *MC, V* ⊙ *Closed Sept. No lunch.*

$$$ ECLECTIC ✕ **El Galeón.** Considered by some to be one of the most distinguished dining rooms in town, this eatery has been popular for more than 20 years. El Galeón serves traditional Italian, Mexican, and American fare. One enduring favorite is the Caesar salad prepared tableside, with all the proper flourishes. Dishes are expertly prepared, with an emphasis on thick, tender cuts of beef. The osso buco Milanese is a local favorite. The choice seats look out upon the marina, with heavy wooden

furnishings and white linens lending a sense of formality. Stop off at the piano bar afterwards, and enjoy Ronald Valentino's music over a late-night brandy. Or perhaps sip one last tequila with a dessert from the cart. ✉ *Across from marina by the road to Finisterra Hotel, Playa Médano* ☎ *624/143–0443, 624/145–7576 for reservations* ⊕ *www.restaurantgaleon.com* ▭ *AE, MC, V* ⊗ *No lunch Mon.–Sat.*

$$$$ SEAFOOD ✕ **Lorenzillo's.** Gleaming hardwood floors and polished brass give a nautical flair to this dining room, where fresh lobster is king. Lorenzillo's has long been a fixture in Cancún, where lobster is raised on the company's farm. That Caribbean lobster is shipped to Los Cabos and served in 14 ways (the simpler preparations—steamed or grilled with lots of melted butter—are best). Menu items are named after pirates and Caribbean marine history, so Sir Francis Drake is the rib-eye steak, El Barbolento is abalone sashimi with spicy diablo sauce, and El Doblón is a giant chop on the bone. If you desire a major lobster splurge, a 2-pounder served with spinach puree and linguine or potato sets you back more than $66. Other options—Alaska king crab, conch, coconut shrimp, or beef medallions—are more moderately priced. The dessert list is lengthy and mouthwatering. A less formal oyster bar with a limited selection from the same menu sits on the pier near the entrance. ✉ *Av. Cárdenas at Marina, Marina* ☎ *624/105–0212* ⊕ *www.lorenzillos.com.mx* ▭ *AE, MC, V.*

$$$ SEAFOOD ✕ **Mariscos Mocambo.** Veracruz—a region known for its seafood preparations—meets Los Cabos in an enormous dining room packed with appreciative locals. The menu has such regional dishes as octopus ceviche, shrimp empanadas, and a heaping mixed-seafood platter that includes sea snails, clams, octopus, lobster, and shrimp. Musicians stroll among the tables and the chatter is somewhat cacophonous, but you're sure to have a great local dining experience here. ✉ *Leona Vicario at Calle 20 de Noviembre, Centro* ☎ *624/143–2122* ⊕ *www.mariscosmocambo.com* ▭ *MC, V.*

$$ SEAFOOD Fodor's Choice ★ ✕ **Marisquería Mazatlán.** The crowds of locals lunching at this simple seafood restaurant are a good sign—as are the huge glass cases packed with shrimp, ceviche, and other seafood cocktails. You can dine inexpensively and quickly on wonderful seafood soup, or spend a bit more for tender *pulpo ajillo* (marinated octopus with garlic, chilies, onion, and celery) and enjoy some great people-watching as you eat. ✉ *Mendoza at Calle 16 de Septiembre, Centro* ☎ *624/143–8565* ▭ *MC, V.*

$$$ MEXICAN ✕ **Mi Casa.** One of Cabo's top restaurants is in a cobalt-blue adobe building painted with murals. The place is huge: Mi Casa can now seat up to 600. The fresh tuna and dorado, served with tomatillo salsa or Yucatecan achiote, both impress, as does the sophisticated *poblano chiles en nogada* (chilies stuffed with a meat-and-fruit mixture and covered with white walnut sauce and pomegranate seeds). If you're in the mood for something resembling a Mexican luau, try the *barbacoa borrego,* or barbecued goat. It's done à la Hawaii, cooked in the ground (luau olé?). Mi Casa also offers an incredible selection of 20 different fruit margaritas. The large back courtyard glows with candlelight at night, and mariachis provide entertainment. ✉ *Av. Cabo San Lucas at*

Lazaro Cardenas, Centro ☎ *624/143–1933* 🌐 *www.micasarestaurant.com* 💳 *MC, V.*

$$$ ECLECTIC Fodor's Choice ★ ✕ **Nick-San–Cabo.** Dare we make such a claim: That Nick-San may very possibly be Cabo San Lucas's top restaurant. Owner Angel Carbajal is an artist behind the sushi counter (he also has his own fishing boats that collect fish each day). A creative fusion of Japanese and Mexican cuisines truly sets his masterpieces apart. The sauce on the cilantro sashimi is so divine that some say diners sneak in bread to sop up the sauce (rice isn't the same). You can run up a stiff tab ordering sushi here. The mahogany bar and minimalist dining room are packed most nights, but the vibe is upbeat. Many diners eat here so frequently they've become family friends. There's also a second Nick-San on the Corridor in the Tiendas de Palmilla shopping center. Reservations are recommended, especially on weekend nights and during high season. Otherwise, be prepared for a wait. ✉ *Blvd. Marina, Plaza de la Danza next to Tesoro Hotel, Marina* ☎ *624/143–4484* 🌐 *www.nicksan.com* 💳 *MC, V.*

$$ ECLECTIC ✕ **The Office.** Playa Médano is lined with cafés on the sand, some with lounge chairs, others with more formal settings. At least once during your visit to Los Cabos, you must visit the Office, the original breakfast spot on Médano Beach. This place has a huge sign, blue umbrellas (the perfect photo backdrop), and a great view of Land's End. There's no better way to start out the morning in Cabo than by enjoying a *sabroso* (tasty) lobster omelet, fresh-fruit smoothie, and powerful cup of Mexican coffee, with your toes in the sand, of course. Another favorite menu item is the French toast. The service is friendly, the menu a bit expensive, but hey, amigo, you're on vacation. Cold beer (later in the day, of course), ceviche, nachos, fish tacos, french fries, and burgers are served in portions that somewhat justify the high prices. You can split most entrées. Dinners of grilled shrimp, fish with garlic, and steaks are popular. ✉ *Playa Médano* ☎ *624/143–3464* 🌐 *www.theofficeonthebeach.com* ✍ *Reservations essential* 💳 *MC, V.*

$$$ MEXICAN ✕ **Pancho's Restaurant & Tequila Bar.** Owner John Bragg has an enormous collection of tequilas, and an encyclopedic knowledge of the stuff. The restaurant is nothing short of a tequila museum, with a colorful display of many hundreds of the world's top tequilas—many no longer available—displayed behind the bar. Sample one or two of the nearly 1,000 labels available, and you'll appreciate the Oaxacan tablecloths, murals, painted chairs, and streamers even more than you did when you first arrived. Try regional specialties like tortilla soup, chiles rellenos, or *sopa de mariscos* (seafood soup). The breakfast and lunch specials are a bargain. Pancho's offers special and private tequila tastings; you'll leave with a greater appreciation of this piquant liquor from Jalisco. ✉ *Hidalgo between Zapata and Serdan, Centro* ☎ *624/143–0973* 🌐 *www.panchos.com* 💳 *AE, MC, V* ⊗ *Closed Sept.*

WHERE TO STAY

$ Fodor's Choice ★ 🏨 **Cabo Cush.** By far one of the most affordable hotels in Cabo, this little gem is reminiscent of courtyard hotels in mainland Mexico, with a central breezeway running between the low-slung two-story buildings. Owner Jeff Layton has created a serene little spot in the heart of town. Upon entering the rooms, you'll find top-of-the-line pillow-top

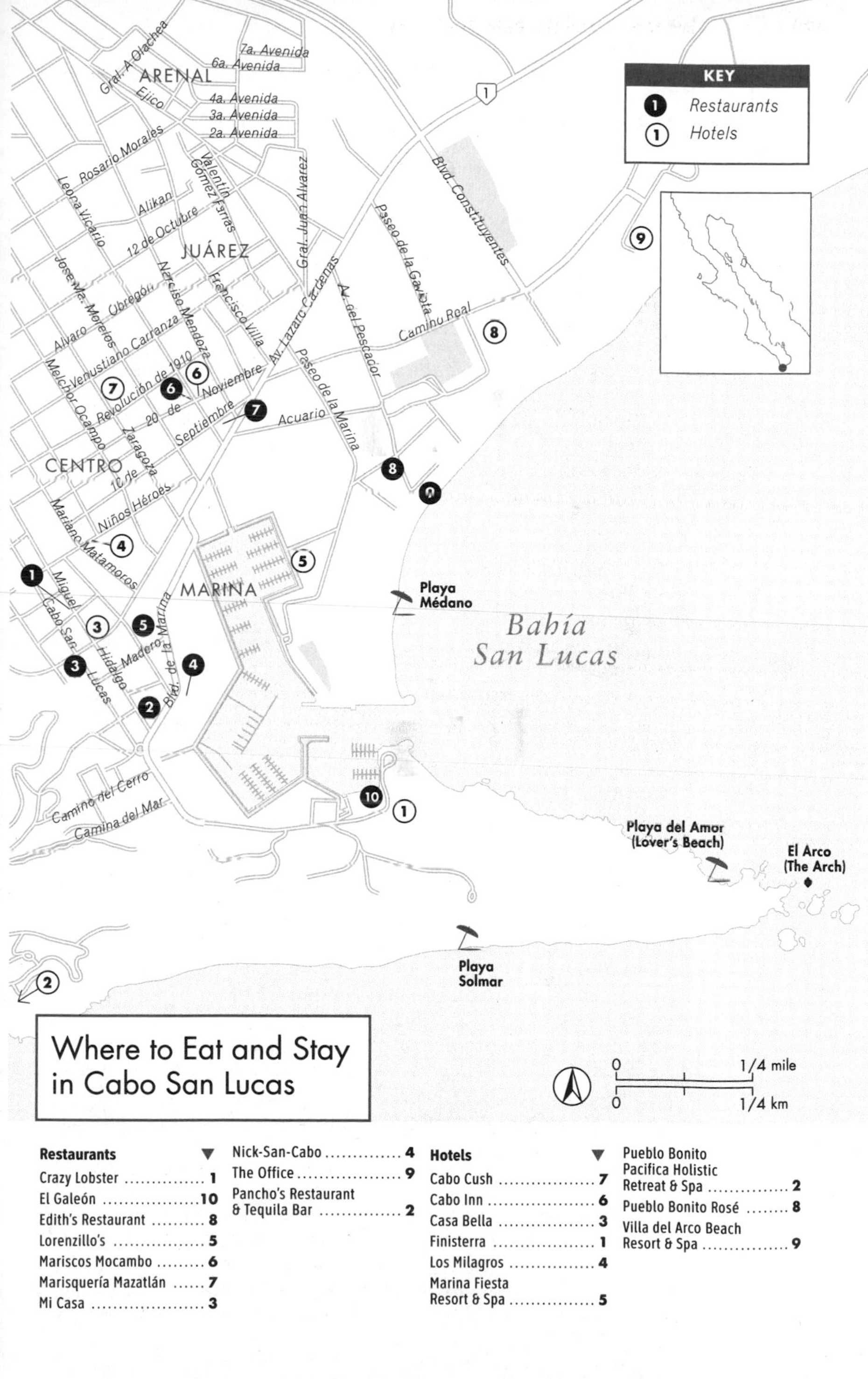
Where to Eat and Stay in Cabo San Lucas
KEY
Restaurants
Hotels
ARENAL
JUÁREZ
CENTRO
MARINA
7a. Avenida
6a. Avenida
4a. Avenida
3a. Avenida
2a. Avenida
Gral. A Olachea
Ejico
Rosario Morales
Leona Vicario
Alikan
12 de Octubre
Valentín Gómez Farías
Gral. Juan Alvarez
Blvd. Constituyentes
Paseo de la Gaviota
Jose Ma. Morelos
Alvaro Obregón
Narciso Mendoza
Francisco Villa
Av. Lazaro Cardenas
Av. del Pescador
Camino Real
Venustiano Carranza
Melchor Ocampo
Revolución de 1910
20 de Noviembre
Paseo de la Marina
Septiembre
Acuario
Zaragoza
10 de
Niños Héroes
Mariano Matamoros
Miguel
Cabo San Lucas
Hidalgo
Madero
Blvd. de la Marina
Camino del Cerro
Camina del Mar
Playa Médano
Bahía San Lucas
Playa del Amor (Lover's Beach)
El Arco (The Arch)
Playa Solmar
0 1/4 mile
0 1/4 km
Restaurants
Crazy Lobster 1
El Galeón 10
Edith's Restaurant 8
Lorenzillo's 5
Mariscos Mocambo 6
Marisquería Mazatlán 7
Mi Casa 3
Nick-San-Cabo 4
The Office 9
Pancho's Restaurant & Tequila Bar 2
Hotels
Cabo Cush 7
Cabo Inn 6
Casa Bella 3
Finisterra 1
Los Milagros 4
Marina Fiesta Resort & Spa 5
Pueblo Bonito Pacifica Holistic Retreat & Spa 2
Pueblo Bonito Rosé 8
Villa del Arco Beach Resort & Spa 9

mattresses with soft cotton sheets; sleek, contemporary furniture; and bathrooms with beautiful Talavera tiling. There is a midcentury-meets-Mexico feel to this place, and, though it's simple, it's quite comfortable. If you're in Cabo to get out and do things and you want an extremely comfortable and affordable rest when you finally lay your head down, this is the place for you. **Pros:** fantastic price for a simple, comfortable room; easygoing, friendly staff will offer all sorts of recommendations; cheap, tasty meals available from the on-site eatery. **Cons:** no swimming pool or gardens—not really a hangout spot; no view. ✉ *Calle Zaragoza between Revolucion and Carranza* ☎ *624/143–9300* 🌐 *www.cabocush.com* *19 rooms* *In-room: no phone, Wi-Fi. In-hotel: restaurant, gym, laundry service, Internet terminal, parking (free)* 💳 *MC, V.*

$–$$ **Cabo Inn.** The small, comfortable rooms at this affordable palapa-roof, cactus-lined, and jungle-like hotel have tangerine-and-cobalt sponge-painted walls and stained-glass windows above the headboards. The eight rooms on the lower level have refrigerators; and the two top-floor palapa suites are playful and funky, if a little bit noisy, due to their slightly open-air construction and the hotel's close proximity to downtown Cabo's festivities. Palapa No. 2 has a king bed and hot tub. A young, hip, international clientele frequents the Cabo Inn, with guests from Argentina, Germany, Ireland, Spain, and Sweden signing the guest book. **Pros:** very affordable hotel right in the thick of things and only a few minutes' walk to the beach; communal kitchen, barbecue, and dining area mean you can cook here and save on expensive meals out. **Cons:** some rooms are dark and cramped; upper rooms can get very noisy during high season, when downtown revelers are at their wildest. ✉ *Calle 20 de Noviembre and Vicario, Centro* ☎ *624/143–0819, 619/819–2727 in U.S.* 🌐 *www.caboinnhotel.com* *20 rooms* *In-room: refrigerator (some), no TV. In-hotel: spa* 💳 *MC, V.*

$ **Casa Bella.** The Ungson family had been in Cabo for more than four decades before turning their home across from Plaza San Lucas into a spacious, sedate inn. It's by far the classiest and friendliest place in the neighborhood, landscaped with meandering paths leading to the pool, gazebo, and terrace. It is indeed a *casa bella,* or beautiful house. Room furnishings are handcrafted and thoughtfully arranged. The open showers in the huge tiled bathrooms are works of art—some even have little gardens. **Pros:** no TVs in the rooms (pro or con? You decide); property feels totally secluded, though it's in the middle of town; ambience suggests a stay at a private home rather than a hotel. **Cons:** no TVs in the rooms (again, pro or con? Your call!); local roosters crow in the mornings. ✉ *Calle Hidalgo 10, Centro* ☎ *624/143–6400* 🌐 *www.casabellahotel.com* *11 rooms, 3 suites* *In-room: no TV. In-hotel: pool, laundry service, Wi-Fi hotspot* 💳 *MC, V* ⊗ *Closed Aug. and Sept.* *CP.*

$$$$ **Fodor's Choice** ★ **Finisterra.** One of the first hotels built in Cabo, the Finisterra, perched on a hill overlooking the marina and the Pacific, was an architectural marvel back in the 1960s. The hotel has grown over the years and the two towers of the newer Palapa Beach Club overlook their gorgeous pools and the Pacific. An eight-story palapa roof covers the restaurant and bar on the sand next to the hotel's three giant free-form swimming

pools and eight hot tubs. Rooms in the new Palapa Beach Club buildings are by far the nicest; they are large and have oceanfront balconies—where from the upper floors it's not uncommon to spot whales during the winter months. The stone buildings of the less expensive, older section of the hotel are simpler, and evoke the early days of Cabo's popularity. The Blue Marlin Restaurant is good, and the Whale Watcher bar that sits perched high atop the cliff behind the Finisterra has one of the best views in town, especially when the wintering whales are in town. A café-deli overlooking the marina side of Cabo San Lucas offers a great view of the Cabo Adventures Dolphin Experience below. **Pros:** fantastic location, short walk to the marina and Cabo's action, but very quiet, as well; great beach access for walking on the Pacific side; attentive but unobtrusive staff. **Cons:** restaurants (except at the pool) and older sections of the hotel are closed during the summer months; beach is not swimmable at all due to rough waves and undertow. ✉ *Blvd. Marina* ☎ *624/143–3333, 800/347–2252 in U.S.* 🌐 *www.finisterra.com* *286 rooms* *In-room: refrigerator (some), safe. In-hotel: 2 restaurants, bars, tennis courts, pools, gym, beachfront, Internet terminal, Wi-Fi hotspot* 💳 *AE, MC, V.*

$$ **Los Milagros.** A mosaic sign (crafted by co-owner Ricardo Rode) near the entrance hints at the beauty inside this small inn. Brilliant purple bougainvillea and orange lipstick vines line the patio, which showcases more of Rode's works by the fountain and small pool. *Bóveda*-style (arched brick) roofs top the rooms, which have terra-cotta tile floors and handmade Mexican furniture. Co-owner Sandra Scandiber dispenses budget travel tips while visiting with guests in the courtyard, and is always ready to lend books from her huge library. Checks or cash are accepted at the hotel; to use a credit card, you must pay prior to arrival through PayPal. **Pros:** quaint, quiet inn close to everything in Cabo; one room is accessible to travelers with disabilities. **Cons:** air-conditioning units in rooms can be loud; pool is small and not heated. ✉ *Matamoros 116* ☎ *718/928–6647 in U.S., 624/143–4566* 🌐 *www.losmilagros.com.mx* *12 rooms* *In-room: kitchen, InternetIn-hotel: pool, laundry service, Wi-Fi hotspot, parking (free)* 💳 *AE, D, MC, V.*

$$$ **Marina Fiesta Resort & Spa.** Though this colonial-style building is not ocean-side, most rooms have a pleasant view of the cloverleaf-shape pool and out to the yacht-filled marina. Rooms are designed for practicality, with stain-proof floral textiles, tile floors, and plenty of space to spread your stuff about. The hotel is on the Golden Zone walkway adjacent to the Puerto Paraíso Mall. **Pros:** close to popular bars and shops, and a quick walk from popular Playa Médano. **Cons:** staff is not trained to deal with problems or guest concerns; there is no buffer between guests and aggressive time-share salespeople. ✉ *Marina, Lot 37, Marina* ☎ *624/145–6020* 🌐 *www.marinafiestaresort.com* *155 rooms* *In-room: Safe, kitchen (some), refrigerator (some). In-hotel: restaurant, room service, bar, pools, gym, spa, laundry service, Wi-Fi hotspot* 💳 *AE, MC, V.*

$$$$ Fodor's Choice ★ **Pueblo Bonito Pacifica Holistic Retreat & Spa.** Soothing waterfalls, glass-domed ceilings, and pebbled floors bring nature indoors to complement this holistic approach to vacationing. The emphasis here is on health

and wellness, peace and tranquillity. No children are permitted. A physician who works with natural therapies oversees the Armonia spa, where treatments include *watsu* and an outdoor, beachside *temezcal,* or native Mayan sweat lodge. It's a refreshingly small hotel by Los Cabos standards, and rooms have minimalist decor with cream fabrics, cedar-and-straw accents, and ocean views. The designers incorporated feng shui elements throughout the resort and grounds, which are stunning, with patterned cactus gardens designed by the talented Cacti Mundo team from San José del Cabo. **Pros:** adults only; truly tranquil lodgings; entire hotel is no-smoking. **Cons:** the extremely sedate atmosphere can be shocking for guests; charges apply for use of beach beds and gym; beach is not swimmable; pushy time-share salespeople; you must have a car or take a cab to get to town. ✉ *Cabo Pacifica s/n* ☎ *624/142–9696, 800/990–8250 in U.S.* 🌐 *www.pueblobonitopacifica.com* *140 rooms, 14 suites* *In-room: safe, refrigerator, Internet. In-hotel: 2 restaurants, room service, bars, pools, gym, spa, beachfront, laundry service, Internet terminal, no kids under 16* 💳 *AE, MC, V.*

WHERE IT'S AT

You may have to run a gantlet of servers waving menus in your face, but the sidewalk bars along the marina between Plaza Bonita and Puerto Paraíso are great places to hang out at happy hour.

$$$–$$$$ **Pueblo Bonito Rosé.** Mediterranean-style buildings curve around elegant grounds; imitations of Roman busts guard reflecting pools, and Flemish tapestries adorn the lobby—this is definitely not your typical Cabo hotel. Even the Rosé's smallest suites can accommodate four people, and all have private balconies overlooking the grounds. Staff is gracious and attentive, and many guests return year after year because of this. **Pros:** there are two Pueblo Bonito hotels on El Médano Beach in San Lucas and two other properties, the Pueblo Bonito Pacifica Holistic Resort and Pueblo Bonito Sunset, out on the Pacific coast—a shuttle bus travels between them, and guests have signing privileges at all four; booking online often gets significant discounts on rates. **Cons:** pushy time-share salespeople; thin walls mean you may have to endure all the noises of your neighbors. ✉ *Playa Médano* ☎ *624/142–9898, 800/990–8250 in U.S.* 🌐 *www.pueblobonito.com* *260 suites* *In-room: safe, kitchen, refrigerator. In-hotel: 2 restaurants, room service, bars, pools, gym, spa, beachfront, laundry service, Internet terminal* 💳 *AE, MC, V.*

$$$$ **Villa del Arco Beach Resort & Spa.** Another resort opened by the Villa Group on El Médano Beach, the Villa del Arco is next to Villa La Estancia. As with its sister properties, del Arco offers comfortable, stylishly decorated one-, two- and three-bedroom suites and penthouses with all the amenities, including full kitchens. And for spa aficionados, the 31,000-square-foot Desert Spa is intoxicating—the largest in Los Cabos, offering treatments that utilize desert plants and herbs. Sign up for the Mexican Tequila Body Wrap or the Organic Succulent Cactus Facial. **Pros:** an on-property deli and market lets you stock up the kitchen, saving money on meals out; rooms are large and very comfortably furnished. **Cons:** service can be spotty, and is often geared more toward selling time-

shares than satisfying hotel guests. ✉ *Camino Viejo a San José, Km 0.5* ☎ *624/145–7000, 866/625–4502 in U.S.* 🌐 *www.villadelarcoloscabos.com* 221 *suites* *In-room: Safe, kitchen (some), Wi-Fi. In-hotel: 3 restaurants, room service, bars, pools* 💳 *MC, V* 🍽 *EP, AI.*

NIGHTLIFE

Classy, tranquil, and comfortable **Barómetro** (✉ *On Marina boardwalk, near Puerto Paraíso Mall* ☎ *624/143–1466* 🌐 *www.barometro.com.mx*) gives you a peaceful panoramic view of the fishing yachts in the Marina San Lucas. Inside, a giant screen shows sports, and tasty seafood is served.

The latest U.S. rock plays over an excellent sound system at **Cabo Wabo** (✉ *Calle Guerrero at Calle Lazaro Cardenas* ☎ *624/143–1188*), but the impromptu jam sessions with appearances by Sammy Hagar—an owner—are the real highlight.

Giggling Marlin (✉ *Blvd. Marina and Matamoros* ☎ *624/143–1182* 🌐 *www.gigglingmarlin.com*) has been around forever, but its gimmicks remain popular. Watch brave (and tipsy) souls be hoisted upside down at the mock fish-weighing scale or join in an impromptu moonwalk between tables.

Miami meets Cabo at **Nikki Beach** (✉ *ME by Meliá Hotel, Playa Médano* ☎ *624/145–7800* 🌐 *www.me-cabo.com*). White gauze canopies shade plush white sun beds and lounge chairs around swimming pools, while DJs spin all day long.

Despite the fact that the floor here is the sand, the oddly named **The Office** (✉ *Médano Beach* ☎ *624/143–3464* 🌐 *www.theofficeonthebeach.com*) is a tad more upscale than the other venues on Médano Beach. Sunday and Thursday nights mean a music show with traditional Mexican folk dances—a little cheesy, but always a crowd pleaser.

Fodor's Choice ★ There is no doubt that the hippest (and most expensive) spot in Los Cabos is the **Passion Club** (✉ *At ME by Meliá Hotel, on El Médano Beach* ☎ *624/145–7800 Ext. 745* 🌐 *www.me-cabo.com*). Top DJs from around the world come to spin the vinyl and light up the neon-cozy club. It has a great dance floor, and there are various VIP events throughout the year.

If you like martinis, the **Red Lounge/Cabo** (✉ *On Zaragoza near El Squid Roe* ☎ *624/143–5644*) is your kind of place. It's a classy spot where younger clientele enjoy a dizzying array of specialties.

SHOPPING

Cabo San Lucas has the widest variety of shopping options in the Los Cabos area, with everything from intriguing Mexican folk art and designer clothing to beer holsters and touristy T-shirts. Bargains on typical Mexican tourist items can be found in the dozens of shops between Boulevard Paseo de la Marina and Avenida Lazaro Cárdenas.

Fodor's Choice ★ **Arte de Origen** (✉ *Madero between Guererro and Blvd. Marina* ☎ *624/105–1965* 🌐 *www.artedeorigen.com*) is a standout among the shops on the increasingly hip Madero Street. Painting, ceramics, and inventive, painting-like collages are applied to a wide variety of objects like boxes, tables, and mirror frames.

★ **El Callejón** (✉ *Guerrero between Avs. Cárdenas and Madero* ☎ *624/143–1139*) is known for the gorgeous Mexican furniture, lamps, dishes, home decor, tableware, lamps, accessories, and pottery it sells.

Galería Gattamelata (✉ *Calle Gómez Farias, road to Hotel Hacienda* ☎ *624/143–1166*) specializes in colonial furniture and antiques. At **Golden Cactus Gallery** (✉ *Calle Guerrero at Madero, 2nd fl.* ☎ *624/143–6399* 🌐 *www.goldencactusgallery.com*), owner Marilyn Hurst exhibits paintings and sculptures by local artists.

DIVE IN!

One of the area's diving pioneers was none other than Jacques Cousteau, who explored the Sand Falls. Only 150 feet off Playa de Amor, this underwater sand river cascades off a steep drop-off into a deep abyss. It's just one of several excellent diving and snorkeling spots close to the Cabo San Lucas shore. There are also fantastic coral-reef sites in the Corridor and north of San José at Cabo Pulmo.

★ Consider visiting **Galería de Kaki Bassi** (✉ *Puerto Paraíso, Av. Cárdenas* ☎ *624/144–4510* 🌐 *www.kakibassi.com*), which has works by Kaki Bassi, one of Baja's leading painters.

Magic of the Moon (✉ *Calle Hidalgo near Blvd. Marina* ☎ *624/143–3161*) has handmade women's sundresses, skirts, and lingerie. Need a new bathing suit? Check out **H2O de los Cabos** (✉ *Av. Madero at Guerrero* ☎ *624/143–1219*).

The walk-in humidor at **J&J Casa de los Habanos** (✉ *Av. Madero, between Blvd. Marina and Guerrero* ☎ *624/143–6160*) is stocked with pricey cigars. The shop also sells expensive tequilas.

SPORTS AND THE OUTDOORS

DIVING

The area's oldest and most complete dive shop is **Amigos del Mar** (✉ *Blvd. Marina* ✣ *Near harbor fishing docks* ☎ *624/143–0505* 🌐 *www.amigosdelmar.com*). Their dive boats range from a 22-foot panga to a 25-foot runabout and 33- and 36-foot dive catamarans. The staff is courteous and knowledgeable, and all the guides speak English. **Cabo Acuadeportes** (✉ *In front of now-closed Hotel Hacienda, Playa Médano* ☎ *624/143–0117*) leads dive trips (prices start at $45), rents snorkel gear, and can outfit you for just about every other water sport imaginable.

FISHING

More than 800 species of fish teem in the waters off Los Cabos. It's easy to arrange charters online, through hotels, and directly with sportfishing companies along El Médano Beach and along the docks at Marina Cabo San Lucas. Indeed, to select a company yourself, consider hanging out at the marina between 1 PM and 4 PM when the boats come in, and asking the passengers about their experiences.

Prices range from $200 or $250 a day for a panga to $500 to $1,700 a day for a larger cruiser with a bathroom, a sunbathing deck, and possibly a few other amenities. The sky's the limit with the larger private yachts (think 80 feet); it's not unheard of for such vessels to cost $5,000 or $7,000 a day. All rates include a captain and crew, tackle, bait, fishing licenses, drinks, and—sometimes—lunch.

The **Jig Stop Tackle & Tours** (✉ *Docked between Gates 2 and 3 across from the Marina Fiesta Hotel* ☎ *624/145–8165 or 800/521–2281* 🌐 *www.jigstop.com*) provides charter cruisers and pangas. **Minerva's** (✉ *Av. Madero between Blvd. Marina and Guerrero* ☎ *624/143–1282* 🌐 *www.minervas.com*) is a renowned tackle store that also has a fleet of charter boats. Some of Cabo's top hotels use the extensive range of yachts from **Pisces Sportfishing Fleet** (✉ *Cabo Maritime Center, Blvd. Marina* ☎ *624/143–1288, 619/819–7983 in U.S.* 🌐 *www.piscessportfishing.com*). The fleet includes the usual 31-foot Bertrams and extraordinary 50- to 60-foot Hatteras cruisers with tuna towers and staterooms. **Solmar Sportfishing's** (✉ *Blvd. Marina, across from sportfishing dock* ☎ *624/145–7575 or 800/344–3349* 🌐 *www.solmar.com*) boats and tackle are always in good shape, and many regulars wouldn't fish with anyone else.

HORSEBACK RIDING

Cantering down an isolated beach or up a desert trail is one of Baja's great pleasures (as long as the sun isn't beating down on your head). Rates are about $25 per person for a 1¼-hour ride. Horses are available for rent in front of the Playa Médano hotels; contact **Rancho Collins Horses** (✉ *Playa Médano* ☎ *624/143–3652 or 624/127–0774*). **Red Rose Riding Stables** (✉ *Hwy. 1, Km 4* ☎ *624/143–4826*)has horses for all levels of riders as well as impressive tack.

WHALE-WATCHING

The gray whale migration doesn't end at Baja's Pacific lagoons. Plenty of whales of all sizes make it down to the warmer waters off Los Cabos. To watch whales from shore, go to the beach at the Solmar Suites, the Finesterra, or any Corridor hotel, or the lookout points along the Corridor highway. Several companies run trips (about $30–$50, depending on size of boat and length of tour) from Cabo San Lucas. **Cabo Expeditions** (✉ *El Tesoro hotel, Blvd. Marina* ☎ *624/143–2700* 🌐 *www.caboexpeditions.com.mx*) offers snorkeling and whale-watching tours in hard-bottom inflatable boats.

THE CORRIDOR

28 km (17 mi) between San José del Cabo and Cabo San Lucas.

Highway 1 dips into *arroyos* (riverbeds) and climbs onto a floodplain studded with boulders and cacti between San José del Cabo and Cabo San Lucas. This stretch of desert terrain, known as the Corridor, has long been the haunt of the rich and famous. In the 1950s a few fishing lodges and remote resorts with private airstrips attracted adventurers and celebrities. Today the region has gated communities, resorts, posh hotels, and championship golf courses.

BEACHES

The Corridor's coastline edges the Sea of Cortez, with long, secluded stretches of sand, tranquil bays, golf fairways, and huge resorts. Few areas are safe for swimming. Some hotels have man-made rocky breakwaters that create semi-safe swimming areas when the sea is calm. As a rule, the turnoffs for the beaches aren't well marked. Facilities are extremely limited and lifeguards are nonexistent, though many of the beaches now have portable toilets. ■ **TIP→ The four-lane Highway 1 has well-marked turnoffs for hotels, but it's not well lighted at night. Drivers tend to speed down hills, tempting vigilant traffic officers. Slow buses and trucks seem to appear from nowhere, and confused tourists switch lanes with abandon. Wait until you're safely parked to take in Sea of Cortez views.**

CAUTION

Remember that red flags warn of dangerous swimming conditions, yellow flags indicate that you should use caution, and green flags show safe areas.

★ **Bahía Chileno.** A private enclave with golf courses and residences is being developed at Bahía Chileno, roughly midway between San José and San Lucas. The beach skirts a small cove with aquamarine waters that are perfect for snorkeling. Getting here is easy, thanks to the well-marked access ramps on both sides of the road. As of this writing, construction on the new Chileno Bay project, a resort community on the rocky cliff at the east end of the beach, was well under way. Along the western edge of Bahía Chileno, some 200 yards away, are some good-size boulders that you can scramble up. ✣ *The turnoff for the beach is at Km 14.5 on Hwy. 1. Look for the signs whether driving west from San José or at Km 16 when driving east from Cabo San Lucas.* **Amenities:** Toilets, parking lot.

Fodor's Choice ★ **Bahía Santa María.** This wide, sloping, horseshoe-shape beach is surrounded by cactus-covered rocky cliffs; the placid waters here are a protected fish sanctuary. The bay is part of an underwater reserve and is a great place to snorkel: brightly colored fish swarm through chunks of white coral and golden sea fans. Unfortunately, this little slice of paradise offers no shade unless you sit in the shadows at the base of the cliffs, so you may want to bring a beach umbrella. In high season, from November to May, there's usually someone renting snorkeling gear for $10 a day or selling sarongs, straw hats, and soft drinks. It's best to bring your own supplies, though, including lots of drinking water, snacks, and sunscreen. Snorkel and booze-cruise boats from Cabo San Lucas visit the bay in mid-morning through about 1 PM. Arrive midafternoon if you want to get that total Robinson Crusoe feel. The parking lot is a quarter mile or so off the highway and is sometimes guarded; be sure to tip the guard. The bay is roughly 19 km (12 mi) west of San José and 13 km (8 mi) east of Cabo San Lucas. Heading east, look for the sign saying PLAYA SANTA MARÍA AND ACCESO A PLAYA. ✣ *19 km (12 mi) west of San José del Cabo, 13 km (8 mi) east of Cabo San Lucas.* **Amenities:** Toilets, parking lot.

Playa Costa Azul. Cabo's best surfing beach runs 3 km (2 mi) south from San José's hotel zone along Highway 1. Its Zippers and La Roca breaks (the point where the wave crests and breaks) are world famous. Surfers gather here year-round, but most come in summer, when waves are largest. Several condo complexes line the beach, which is popular with joggers and walkers. Swimming isn't advised unless the waves are small and you're a good swimmer. The turnoff to this beach is sudden, and only available to drivers coming from Cabo San Lucas (not from San José del Cabo). It's on the beach side of the highway, at Zipper's restaurant, which is on the sand by the surf breaks. ✣ *Just over 1 km (½ mi) southwest of San José.* **Amenities:** Toilets, food concession, picnic tables, parking lot.

Playa Palmilla. Check out the villas on the road to Playa Palmilla, the best swimming beach near San José. The entrance is from the side road through the ritzy Palmilla development; turn off before you reach the guardhouse at the star-studded One & Only Hotel Palmilla. There are signs, but they're not exactly large. The beach is protected by a grouping of rocks, and the water is almost always calm. A few palapas on the sand provide shade; there are trash cans, but no restrooms. Panga fishermen have long used this beach as a base, and they're still here, despite the swanky neighbors. Guards patrol the beach fronting the hotel, discouraging nonguests from entering. ✣ *Entrance on Hwy. 1, at Km 27, 8 km (5 mi) southwest of San José del Cabo.* **Amenities:** Parking lot.

WHERE TO EAT

$$$ ECLECTIC **✕ 7 Seas Restaurant.** It's quite soothing to sit in this restaurant, in the Cabo Surf Hotel, at the ocean's edge, smelling the sea breezes. Stop off after your morning surf session to munch on *machaca con huevos* (eggs scrambled with shredded beef) washed down with a fresh-fruit smoothie; or drop in after you've enjoyed the evening surf to dine on blue crab tostadas and tricolor shrimp ravioli. Your entertainment is simple: a wonderful view that never stops changing. ✉ *Cabo Surf Hotel, Km 28* ☎ *624/142–2666* 🌐 *www.7seasrestaurant.com* ▭ *MC, V.*

$$$ AMERICAN **✕ French Riviera.** Jacques Chretien's popular bistro has terrific views of El Arco and Land's End. The restaurant is upstairs, with the lounge-bar on the ground floor. The menu is airy and eclectic: a spinach, egg, and bacon burrito could be breakfast, and lunch and dinner might consist of a gourmet pizza, Cajun chicken salad, or sushi. For a special treat, ask the restaurant to pack you a picnic meal that you can bring to the beach. Though the dinner menu changes every day, look for braised red snapper with Provençale gratin potatoes and zucchini in a basil reduction. Finish with melt-in-your-mouth chocolate cake with pear puree or strawberries napoleon. ✉ *Hwy. 1, Km 27.5* ☎ *624/144–6013* 🌐 *www.frenchrivieraloscabos.com* ▭ *MC, V.*

$$$$ ECLECTIC Fodor's Choice ★ **✕ Market.** Charlie Trotter's now-closed "C" restaurant in the One&Only Palmilla resort was replaced in late 2008 by a new offering from three-star Michelin chef Jean-Georges Vongerichten—his first in Latin America. The roast veal chops with chipotle glaze, Chilean salmon with lemon and dill, crab-stuffed squash blossoms, and cornmeal ravioli with cherry tomatoes all exemplify the "European with Mexican flair" description that Market gives its menu. While the consensus is that Market's contemporary furnishings in warm, inviting earth tones are more casual than those of its predecessor, this could well be one of your more expensive dinners in already pricey Los Cabos. You can bring your bill down slightly by opting for a fine Baja wine from the extensive wine list rather than a European one. ✉ *One&Only Palmilla, Hwy. 1, Km*

27.5 ☎ 624/146–7000 🌐 www.oneandonlyresorts.com ✍ Reservations essential ▭ AE, D, MC, V ⊙ No lunch.

$$$ ASIAN Fodor's Choice ★ ✕ **Nick-San–Palmilla.** The sky's the limit here at this out-of-this-world-inventive sushi den in the Tiendas de Palmilla shopping mall. Pair each of your selections with an exceptional wine or liquor, and let chef Abel and floor manager Mauricio help you make the choices. Favorites include the lobster roll (with cilantro, mango, mustard, and roe) with a 2005 Chateau Montalena; lobster *sambal* (marinated in sake with soy, ginger, and garlic) with Kikusi sake; and the Hamachi belly cake and tuna tostadas with a Chilean Casas del Bosque Sauvignon Blanc. ✉ *Las Tiendas de Palmilla mall* ☎ *624/144–6262* 🌐 *www.nicksan.com* ▭ *MC, V* ⊙ *Closed Mon.*

$$$$ ASIAN Fodor's Choice ★ ✕ **Pitahayas.** In this elegant niche above the beach in the resort community Cabo del Sol, chef Volker Romeike blends Thai, Polynesian, and Chinese ingredients into artful, award-winning Asian fusion. He matches lobster with a vanilla-bean sauce, scallops with a sweet chili glaze, and the catch of the day with Thai curry. Soft jazz plays in the background, and the service is impeccable. The restaurant has been enlarged with a terrace and lounge, and now seats up to 500—it claims to be the largest restaurant in Los Cabos. On offer is one of the largest wine selections in all of Mexico. Dress to impress. ✉ *Sheraton Hacienda del Mar, Hwy. 1, Km 10* ☎ *624/145–8010* 🌐 *www.pitahayas.com* ▭ *AE, MC, V* ⊙ *No lunch.*

$$$ ITALIAN Fodor's Choice ★ ✕ **Sunset Da Mona Lisa.** Cocktail tables along the cliffs have panoramic views of El Arco, making this the best place to toast the sunset and another beautiful day in Los Cabos before moving to the candlelit dining room. Or remain outside, and enjoy dining alfresco. Italian chef Emanuele Olivero has paid his dues in Los Cabos, with time at La Dolce in San José, at C in the Palmilla, and also at Pitahayas. Now he has brought his ideas to full fruition here at the Mona Lisa. The restaurant's four seasonal menus all rely on ever-changing seasonal ingredients. How about ravioli filled with pumpkin, or La Paz blue crab covered with a cinnamon white sauce? Or seared halibut with crunchy polenta, sun-dried tomatoes, and asparagus tempura? You can also go all out with the Grand Mona Lisa Tasting Menu, which allows you to try just about everything on the extensive menu. The restaurant is not really in the Corridor, but not really in town either; it's just a couple of miles up the hill—a short and relatively inexpensive taxi ride, well worth the trip for a sunset cocktail and dinner. Make sure you appreciate the Mona Lisa tile artwork both close up and from a distance—it's an interesting optical illusion. ✉ *Hwy. 1, Km 5.5* ☎ *624/145–8160* ✍ *Reservations essential* ▭ *MC, V* ⊙ *No lunch.*

$$ AMERICAN ✕ **Zippers.** Home to the surfing crowd and those who don't mind a bit of sand in their burgers (well . . . not really), this casual palaparoof restaurant is on Costa Azul Beach, just south of San José. Come for the sea breezes, the delicious wafting smell of grilling lobster and tacos, and a sound track of surf tunes. Casual doesn't begin to describe the crowd, which can get downright raunchy. But hey, have fun, amigo, you've entered Los Cabos Surf Zone! There's no question that owner "Big Tony" feeds you well for your pesos. With half-pound burgers,

slabs of prime rib, or steak and lobster for two at just $40, you'll leave the beach a glutton, albeit a jolly one. Bring the kiddos in the daytime; they'll enjoy running from the dining table to the sand between every couple of bites. Sporting events sometimes blare on the TV, and Friday nights bring live music. ✉ *Hwy. 1, Km 18.5* ☎ *624/172–6162* ▭ *No credit cards.*

WHERE TO STAY

$$$$ **Cabo Surf Hotel.** Legendary and amateur surfers alike claim the prime break-view rooms in this small hotel on the cliffs above Playa Costa Azul. They mingle by the swimming pool and in the cozy Seven Seas restaurant (which is a great place to enjoy a wonderful meal and stunning views), and they schedule their day's activities around the daily surf report. Rooms are spacious enough for two wave-hounds to spread out their gear; some have French doors that open to the sea breezes. The hotel offers its own label of Cabo Surf Tequila, a surf school, and surfboard rentals. The small Sea Spa & Salon, adjacent to the lobby, offers massages developed specifically for surfers' wave-taxed muscles, with many other treatments for nonsurfers to enjoy, as well. Book early at this popular spot. **Pros:** if surfing is your thing, then you can't get any closer than this while having all your basic needs covered; celebrity sightings are frequent; in-room iPod players. **Cons:** traffic from the highway can be noisy; musty smells in the rooms. ✉ *Hwy. 1, Km 28* ☎ *624/142–2666, 858/964–5117 in U.S.* 🌐 *www.cabosurfhotel.com* *22 rooms* *In-room: kitchen (some), refrigerator, Wi-Fi. In-hotel: Restaurant, bar, pool, gym, spa, Internet terminal* ▭ *MC, V.*

$$$$ Fodor's Choice ★ **Esperanza.** This is an utterly polished inn with a focus on exquisite privacy and truly luxurious, but not over-the-top, accommodations. Some suites are right on a secluded beach; all have handcrafted furnishings, Frette linens, and dual-head showers. Even the smallest suite is still a heavyweight at 925 square feet. Villas take the luxe even further with private pools and butler service. The Penthouse Suite (which will run you a minimum of $2,500 per night) offers one of the most stunning views of El Arco imaginable. Californian and Mexican recipes get a Baja twist in the restaurants, which generally get high ratings. The spa, which is our favorite in the region, takes treatments to a whole new level, with 12 individual and two couples treatment cabins, steam caves, and a waterfall. Treatments with novel ingredients leave even the most sun-beaten skin soft and rejuvenated. An on-site art gallery showcases local painters and sculptors. **Pros:** service and amenities are virtually flawless; the physical setting is exquisite; every room has an ocean view; resort is for adults and children 16 and over only (families with younger children are welcome in the Villas). **Cons:** the high cost of everything at this property can get exhausting, even for guests used to luxury accommodations; wind can be fierce on the rocky cliffs that the resort is set on. ✉ *Hwy. 1, Km 7* ☎ *624/145–6400, 866/311–2226 in U.S.* 🌐 *www.esperanzaresort.com* *57 suites* *In-room: safe, refrigerator, DVD, Wi-Fi. In-hotel: 4 restaurants, room service, bar, pool, gym, spa, beachfront, laundry service* ▭ *AE, MC, V.*

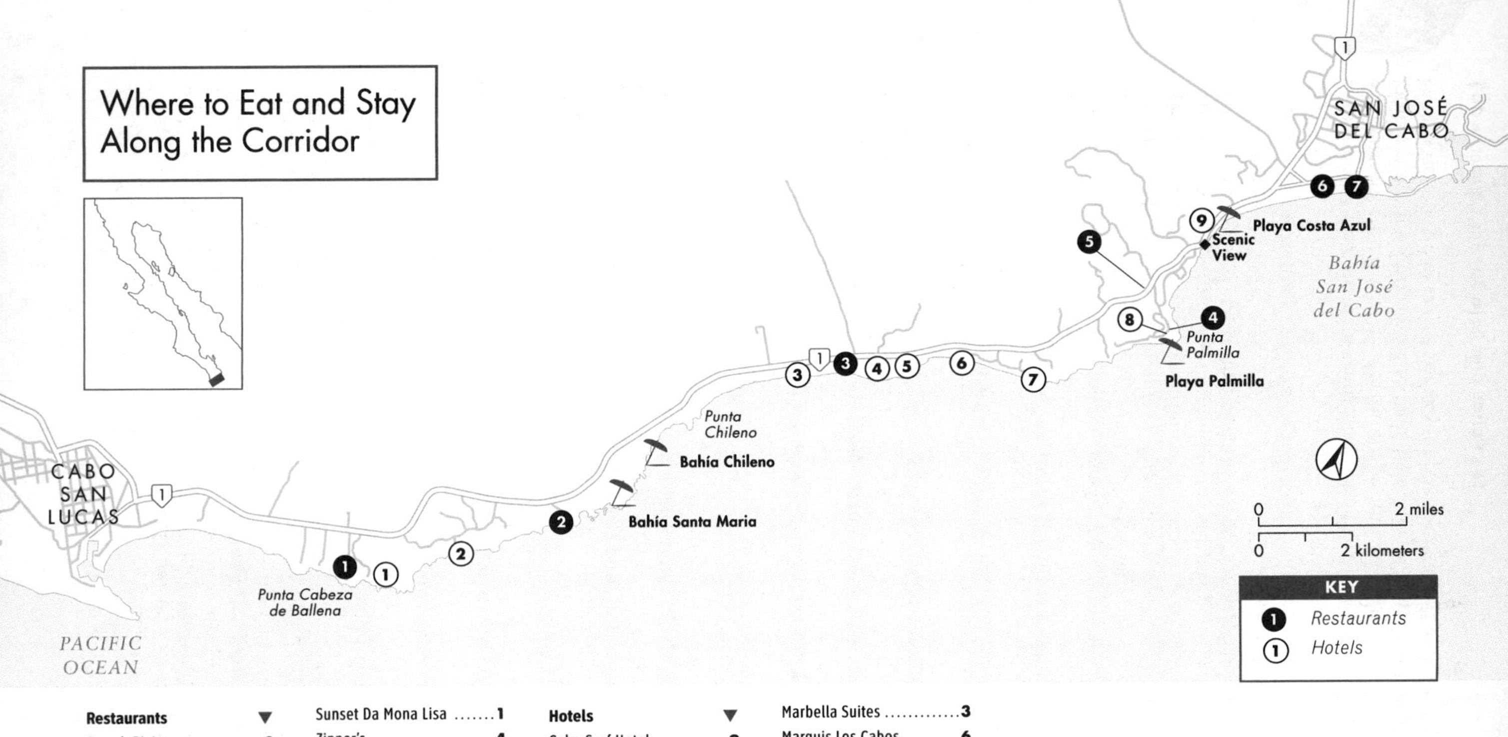

Restaurants ▼

- French Riviera 3
- Market 7
- Nick-San-Palmilla 5
- Pitahayas 2
- 7 Seas Restaurant 6
- Sunset Da Mona Lisa 1
- Zipper's 4

Hotels ▼

- Cabo Surf Hotel 9
- Esperanza 1
- Fiesta Americana Grand Los Cabos 2
- Hilton Los Cabos 5
- Las Ventanas al Paraíso 4
- Marbella Suites 3
- Marquis Los Cabos 6
- One&Only Palmilla 8
- Westin Resort & Spa, Los Cabos 7

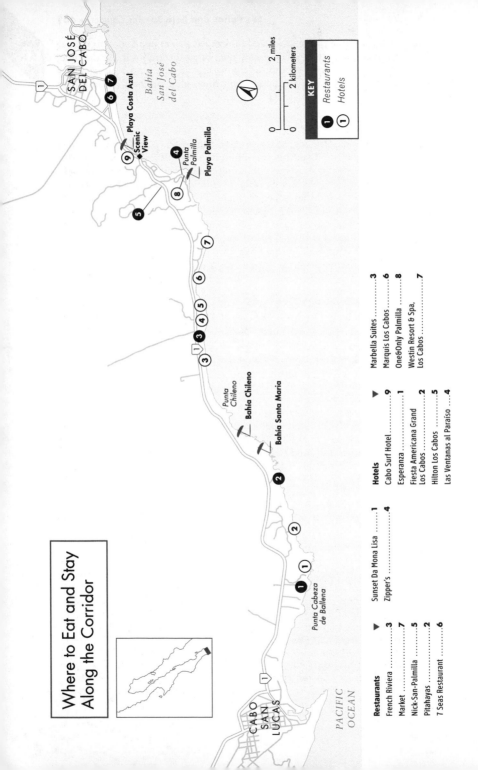

$$$$ **Fiesta Americana Grand Los Cabos.** The dramatic lobby of the Fiesta is eight stories above the beach, and every room looks out onto the Sea of Cortez. Stone walls, rich marble floors, and abundant art make for an elegant and contemporary atmosphere. As part of the Cabo del Sol development, the Fiesta also offers guests access to the 18-hole Jack Nicklaus Ocean Golf Course, in addition to the luxurious spa. **Pros:** a good choice for couples wanting a relaxing getaway; though the beach is rocky, this is one of the few hotels on a stretch of water that is safe to swim and snorkel in. **Cons:** not the place for people looking for Cabo's infamous party scene; expensive to get back and forth to town, whether in a cab or the resort's shuttle; food quality doesn't match expensive dining costs; service is notoriously spotty. *Hwy. 1, Km 10.3, Cabo del Sol* *624/145–6200, 800/345–5094, or 800/343–7821* *www.fiestamericanagrand.com* *288 rooms* *In-room: safe, refrigerator, Wi-Fi. In-hotel: 3 restaurants, bars, golf courses, pools, spa, beachfront, children's programs (ages 5–12)* *AE, DC, MC, V.*

$$$$ Fodor's Choice ★ **Hilton Los Cabos.** Rooms are spacious at this hacienda-style Hilton built on one of the Corridor's few swim-friendly beach lagoons. It's a multipurpose, business-friendly, wedding-friendly, kids-friendly hotel, with Hilton's famous high standard of service. Four meeting rooms will accommodate up to 600. In the guest rooms elaborate headboards, luxurious linens, and L'Occitane bath products are lovely touches to a resort that has an edge on most properties in this price category. **Pros:** professional, attentive staff stands out among Corridor hotels; the infinity pool is dramatic and relaxing; excellent golf concierge service can make arrangements at the area's best courses. **Cons:** spa services aren't up to par with the rest of the resort. *Hwy. 1, Km 19.5* *624/145–6500 or 800/522–2999* *www.hiltonloscabos.com* *309 rooms, 66 suites* *In-room: safe, refrigerator, Wi-Fi. In hotel: 5 restaurants, bars, tennis courts, pools, spa, beachfront, children's programs (ages 5–12), laundry facilities, parking (free)* *AE, D, DC, MC, V.*

$$$$ Fodor's Choice ★ **Las Ventanas al Paraíso.** Despite the high room rates at this ultraprivate, ultraluxe hotel, it's often hard to get a reservation. This hotel continues to garner awards in every category, making it a standout in the region. Guests luxuriate in suites that have hot tubs, fireplaces, and telescopes for viewing whales or stars. Newer hotels have attempted to copy such Ventanas touches as handcrafted lamps and doors, inlaid stone floors, and tequila service, but the original remains the best. Service is sublime, with a knowledgeable butler assigned to each suite; the restaurants are outstanding; and the spa treatments reflect the latest trends. The three spa suites (really more like individual villas) have private spa butlers and separate in-suite treatment rooms. **Pros:** this is the place to escape any semblance of the all-inclusive scene; restaurants are excellent and are worthy of a visit to the hotel even if you're not a guest; children under 12 not allowed. **Cons:** there can be a minimum night stay for weekends depending on the season; the resort is more formal than many in the area. *Hwy. 1, Km 19.5* *624/144–2800, 888/767–3966 in U.S.* *www.lasventanas.com* *68 suites, 3 spa suites* *In-room: safe, refrigerator, DVD, Internet. In-hotel: 3 restaurants, room service,*

bar, tennis courts, pools, gym, spa, beachfront, water sports, laundry service, some pets allowed, no kids under 12 ▭ *AE, MC, V.*

$$$ Fodor's Choice ★ **Marbella Suites.** With all the sophisticated properties in Los Cabos, it's a treat to discover little Marbella Suites, which still retains the flavor of the peaceful and romantic East Cape properties. A rental car is mandatory, though, if you wish to stay here and also explore Los Cabos and beyond. As stated on its brochure, Marbella is "located halfway between the shopping of San José and the nightlife of Cabo San Lucas." It's a good spot for inexpensive weddings, as wedding party, friends, and family can easily fill the hotel and have it to themselves. **Pros:** large rooms with kitchenettes; gracious, friendly staff; homey, relaxed atmosphere; hot tubs perched on a cliff above the beach. **Cons:** lobby is three floors above lowest level; not accessible for guests with wheelchairs; most rooms open onto a central garden courtyard with only minimal ocean views. ✉ *Hwy. 1, Km. 17* ☎ *624/144–1060* 🌐 *www.marbellasuites.com* *40 suites* *In-room: Safe, no phone, no TV, kitchen. In-hotel: Restaurant, bar, pool, gym, beachfront, Internet terminal, Wi-Fi hotspot* ▭ *AE, DC, MC, V.*

$$$$ Fodor's Choice ★ **One&Only Palmilla.** Built in 1956 by the son of the then-president of Mexico, the One&Only was the first resort built in Los Cabos area, and it retains an Old World ambience and elegance that is without match in the region. This world-class resort is home to renowned chef Jean-Georges Vongerichten's new Market restaurant. Also on offer are a Jack Nicklaus golf course and a top spa that offers such special treatments as an exclusive Bastien Gonzalez pedicure. The hotel also employs a Director of Celebrations in order to help guests further enjoy their stay. Two pools seem to flow over low cliffs into the sea, and each of the 13 beach casitas has its own infinity pool. Hand-painted tiles edge stairways leading to rooms and suites, where beds are overloaded with pillows, bathtubs are deep, and the water from the shower truly rains down upon you. Your quarters also have Bose sound systems, flat-screen TVs, and wireless Internet access. Some patios and terraces have daybeds and unobstructed sea views. **Pros:** from beginning to end, Palmilla has already thought of everything, even offering "Air to Go" meals: quality, custom-made box lunches to take along with you on the flight home. **Cons:** prices are exorbitant; increasing numbers of large, boisterous groups in the past few years mar the otherwise genteel atmosphere. ✉ *Hwy. 1, Km 27.5* ☎ *624/146–7000, 866/829–2977 in U.S.* 🌐 *www.oneandonlyresorts.com* *61 rooms, 91 junior suites, 20 one-bedroom suites* *In-room: safe, refrigerator, DVD, Internet, Wi-Fi. In-hotel: 2 restaurants, bars, golf course, tennis courts, pools, gym, spa, beachfront, water sports, laundry service* ▭ *AE, MC, V.*

$$$$ **Westin Resort & Spa, Los Cabos.** The stunning architecture of the Westin is a magnificent conglomeration of colors, shapes, and views. The rooms, some set high above a man-made beach, are among the best in this price range, and have Westin's trademark "Heavenly Beds," with cushy pillows and comforters. Villas have full kitchens and whirlpool tubs that face the sea. The hotel's dramatic setting means you'll get plenty of exercise moving from one area to another, which is good for some and less appealing for those not in good physical condition.

The restaurants receive mixed reviews, with most leaning toward the expensive but mediocre end—if you're a foodie, you'll need to make arrangements to get into Cabo or San José for satisfying meals. **Pros:** the children's center is clean and well staffed; great spa and gym; excellent pools. **Cons:** it's a trek from the parking lot and lobby to the rooms and pools, making this a poor choice for those with disabilities; cliff setting means the property has many steep stairs and precipitous walkways; time-share salespeople are pushy. ✉ *Hwy. 1, Km 22.5* ☎ *624/142–9000, 888/625–5144 in U.S.* 🌐 *www.starwood.com/westin* *243 rooms* *In-room: safe, refrigerator (some). In-hotel: 5 restaurants, room service, bars, tennis courts, pools, gym, spa, beachfront, children's programs (ages 5–12), laundry service* 💳 *AE, MC, V* *EP.*

SPORTS AND THE OUTDOORS

FISHING

Corridor hotels work with fishing fleets anchored at the Cabo San Lucas marina and a few with boats in Puerto Los Cabos. The major drawback of arranging a fishing trip from one of the Corridor hotels is the travel time involved in getting down to the water. It takes up to half an hour or more to reach the docks from Corridor hotels, and most boats depart at 6:30 AM.

GOLF

Los Cabos has become one of the world's top golf destinations, with championship courses that combine lush greens and desert terrain. Greens fees are exorbitant—more than $350 in winter and $200 in summer. **Cabo del Sol** (☎ *624/145–8200* 🌐 *www.cabodelsol.com*) has an 18-hole Jack Nicklaus course and an 18-hole Tom Weiskopf course. The Robert Trent Jones Jr.–designed **Cabo Real Golf Course** (✉ *Hwy. 1, Km 19.5* ☎ *624/173–9200 or 877/795–8727* 🌐 *www.caboreal.com*) has 18 holes on mountainous inland and flat oceanfront terrain. The 27-hole, Jack Nicklaus–designed **One&Only Palmilla Golf Course** (✉ *Hwy. 1, Km 7.5* ☎ *624/144–5250* 🌐 *www.palmillagc.com*) has wide fairways, gentle slopes, and large, challenging greens.

HORSEBACK RIDING

★ The **Cuadra San Francisco Equestrian Center** (✉ *Hwy. 1, Km 19.5, across from Casa del Mar and Las Ventanas al Paraíso hotels* ☎ *624/144–0160* 🌐 *www.loscaboshorses.com*) holds lessons and trail rides. Treks through back canyons are more interesting than those along the beach, and the horses and guides are both excellent. Reserve at least a day in advance and request an English-speaking guide, and note that you must query them for rates.

SAN JOSÉ DEL CABO

195 km (121 mi) south of La Paz, 28 km (17 mi) northeast of Cabo San Lucas.

San José's downtown is lovely, with adobe houses and jacaranda trees. Entrepreneurs have converted old homes into stylish restaurants and shops, and the government has enlarged the main plaza. An ambitious multiyear beautification process is underway. A 9-hole golf course and

Continued on page 501

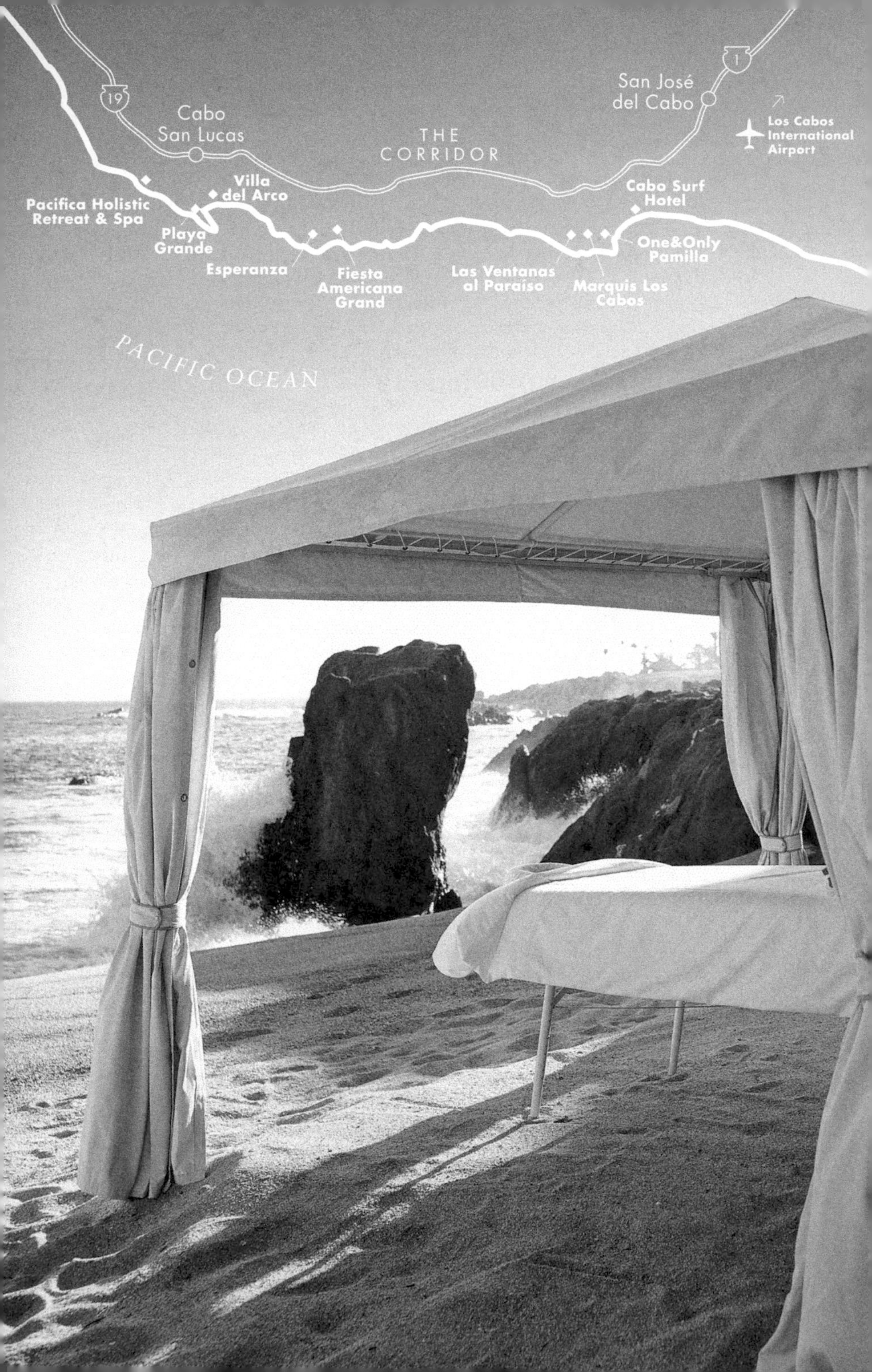
19
Cabo
San Lucas
THE
CORRIDOR
1
San José
del Cabo
Los Cabos
International
Airport
Pacifica Holistic
Retreat & Spa
Villa
del Arco
Playa
Grande
Esperanza
Fiesta
Americana
Grand
Las Ventanas
al Paraíso
Marquis Los
Cabos
One&Only
Pamilla
Cabo Surf
Hotel
PACIFIC OCEAN

BAJA REJUVENATION

Updated by Heidi Johansen and Georgia de Katona

A spa vacation—or even a single treatment—is the perfect way to kick-start a healthier lifestyle, slow a hectic routine, or simply indulge in a little pampering.

Los Cabos, the land of sybaritic pleasures, has no shortage of resorts where you can be smeared with rich mud, plunge into a series of hot and cold baths, or simply enjoy a traditional facial.

Although spas once drew upon European traditions, they now offer treatments from around the globe: Japanese shiatsu, Indonesian jasmine oil rubdowns, deep-tissue Thai massage, and the temazcal, or Maya sweat-lodge experience. Often you can follow an herbal wrap or mud bath with yoga or tension-relieving classes. The small Sea Spa at the Cabo Surf Hotel even offers a Surfer's Massage for those who've overdone it in the waves.

Self care is a growing trend, with custom prescriptions for upkeep between facials and massages and advice on holistic approaches to living to help keep you healthy and sane between spa visits.

All Los Cabos resort spas have packages—whether for a day of beauty or for a long weekend of treatments. Most spas are also open to nonguests of the resorts, and some properties allow you to use the fitness facilities if you've booked a spa treatment. Most impose minimum age requirements of 16 or 18. Always call ahead.

Resort Name	Body Treatments	Facials	Seaside Treatments	Treatments For Two	Fitness Day Pass	Sauna	Steam Room
Cabo Surf Hotel	\$60–\$125	\$80–\$120	yes	yes	yes	yes	no
Esperanza	\$160–\$335	\$185–\$295	yes	yes	no	no	yes
Fiesta Americana Grand	\$100–\$250	\$140–\$290	yes	yes	yes	yes	yes
Marquis Los Cabos	\$115–\$195	\$115–\$170	yes	yes	yes	no	yes
One&Only Palmilla	\$150–\$350	\$140–\$250	yes	yes	yes	yes	yes
Pacifica Holistic Retreat & Spa	\$120–\$275	\$165–\$275	yes	yes	yes	yes	yes
Playa Grande Resort	\$120–\$260	\$130–\$175	yes	yes	no	no	yes
Las Ventanas al Paraíso	\$145–\$300	\$180–\$215	yes	yes	yes	yes	yes
Villa del Arco	\$52–\$290	\$90–\$120	no	yes	yes	yes	yes

(opposite page) Esperanza Resort

TOP SPOTS

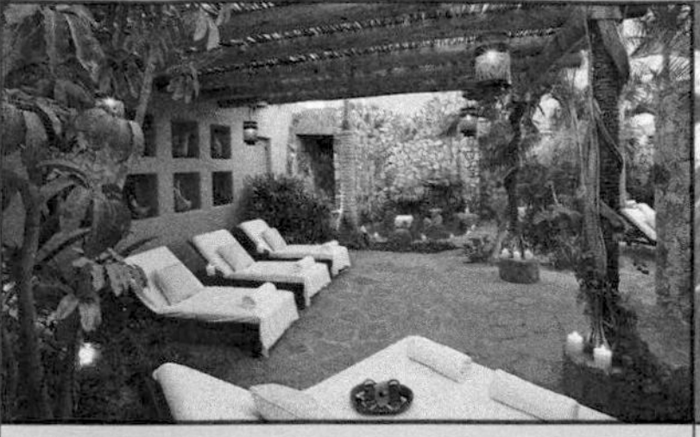

ESPERANZA

Luxury continues to soar to great heights at this exclusive 17-acre resort between the towns of Cabo San Lucas and San José del Cabo where the spa doubled its size in 2007. At check in you're presented with an *agua fresca*, a healthy drink made with papaya or mango, or other fruits and herbs.

Before your treatment, enjoy the *Pasaje de Agua* (water passage) therapy, which includes steam caves and a waterfall. Treatments incorporate local ingredients, tropical fruits, and ocean-based products. Look for such pampering as the papaya-mango body polish, the grated coconut and lime exfoliation, and the Corona beer facial. Two free yoga classes are offered at 9 and 10:15 each morning.

BODY TREATMENTS. Massage: Agua, hot stone, essential oil, Thai (stroke techniques vary). **Exfoliation:** Body polish, salt glow. **Wraps/baths:** Aloe wrap, floral bath, herbal bath, mud bath, thalassotherapy. **Other:** Outdoor shower, steam room, warm soaking pool, waterfall rinse.

BEAUTY TREATMENTS. Facials, hair/scalp conditioning, manicure, pedicure, peels.

PRICES. Body Treatments: $160–$335. **Facials:** $185–$295. **Mani/Pedi:** $45–$200.

*Hwy 1, Km 3.5. Tel. 624/145–6406, 866/311–2226. ⊕ www.esperanzaresort.com. **Parking:** Valet (free, but please tip). ▭ AE, MC, V.*

MARQUIS LOS CABOS

Known as the "Resort for All Senses," the Marquis is the only member of Leading Spas of the World in Los Cabos. You'll enjoy the open-air hot tubs that face the Cape's blue sky and overlook the Sea of Cortez. Lounge chairs draped with thick towels tempt you to linger by the hot tubs. Noteworthy is the Quetzalcoatl Oxygenating Experience: a eucalyptus foot bath, marine-salt exfoliation, herbal purification bath, and light massage with cucumber-milk lotion.

A hallway connects the spa with the Marquis' fitness center with its sky-high ceiling and wall-to-wall windows looking out to the pool slithering above the sand along the ocean.

BODY TREATMENTS. Massage: Aromatherapy, ayurvedic, deep tissue, essential oil, hot stone, pregnancy, reflexology, shiatsu, sports, Thai. **Exfoliation:** salt glow. **Wraps/baths:** herbal bath, mud wrap, thalassotherapy. **Other:** Ayurvedic treatments, hot tub, sauna, steam room.

BEAUTY TREATMENTS. Facials, manicure, pedicure, waxing.

PRICES. Body Treatments: $115–$195. **Facials:** $115–$170. **Mani/Pedi:** $39–$79.

*Hwy 1, Km 21.5. Tel. 624/144–20000, 877/238–9399. ⊕ www.marquisloscabos.com. **Parking:** Valet (free, but please tip). ▭ AE, MC, V.*

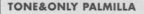

TONE&ONLY PALMILLA

Treatment villas are tucked behind white stucco walls, ensuring privacy. Therapists lead you through a locked gate into peaceful palm-filled gardens with a bubbling hot tub and a day bed covered with plump pillows.

Treatments blend Mexican, Asian, and other global accents; using cactus, lime, and a variety of Mexican spices. Each session begins with a Floral Footbath—a symbolic Balinese ritual, which represents a cleansing of life's tensions to prepare you for total relaxation. One signature treatment is the Aztec Aromatic Ritual, a spicy body wrap that uses an ancient village recipe of clove, ginger, and cinnamon.

BODY TREATMENTS. Massage: Aromatherapy, Balinese, chocolate synergy, deep tissue, essential oil, hot stone, pregnancy, reflexology, sports, Swedish, Thai, watsu. **Exfoliation:** Body polish, dry brush, salt glow. **Wraps/baths:** Floral bath, herbal wrap, milk bath. **Other:** Anticellulite, colon therapy, pools, sauna, steam.

BEAUTY TREATMENTS. Anti-aging, peels, facials, hair styling, scalp conditioning, makeup, manicure, pedicure, waxing.

PRICES. Body Treatments: $150–$350. **Facials:** $140–$250. **Mani/Pedi:** $55–$150.

*Hwy. 1, Km 7. S. Tel. 624/146–7000, 866/829–2977. ⊕ www.oneandonlyresorts.com. **Parking:** Valet (free, but please tip). ▭ AE, MC, V.*

LAS VENTANAS AL PARAÍSO

The resort's bi-level spa is surrounded by serene cactus gardens and has both indoor and outdoor facilities. It's known for innovative treatments—skin resurfacing facials, nopal (cactus) anticellulite and detox wrap, crystal healing massages, and raindrop therapy.

Some of the eight treatment rooms have private patios; and body wraps and massages are performed in a pavilion by the sea.

BODY TREATMENTS. Massage: Aromatherapy, ayurvedic, deep-tissue, hot stone, reflexology, Reiki, shiatsu, shirodhara, sports, Swedish, watsu. **Exfoliation:** Body polish, dry brush, loofah scrub, salt glow. **Wraps/baths:** Herbal wrap, milk bath, mud wrap, cactus wrap. **Other:** Acupuncture, anticellulite, aromatherapy, Ayurvedic treatments, crystal therapy, hydrotherapy pool, sauna, steam room, Mommy-to-Be treatments.

BEAUTY TREATMENTS. Facials, hair cutting/styling, manicure, pedicure, waxing.

PRICES. Body Treatments: $145–$300. **Facials:** $180–$275. **Mani/Pedi:** $45–$145.

*Hwy. 1, Km 19.5. Tel. 624/144–2800, 888/767–3966. ⊕ www.lasventanas.com. **Parking:** Valet (free, but please tip). ▭ AE, MC, V.*

TOP SPOTS

VILLA DEL ARCO

The Desert Spa on the beach in Los Cabos is also the area's largest, with 17 treatment rooms and two suites comfortably spread through three airy, sunny floors; the entire complex totals 31,000 square feet. With Los Cabos' largest hydrotherapy "wet" circuit, improve your circulation with dips in hot tubs followed by plunges in cold. The spa has the biggest fitness center in Cabo, and the beauty salon has a perfect view of the sea.

Treatments tend to utilize fruits, plants, and herbs that can be found in the area. Indulge in an organic succulent cactus facial or an after-sun soothing mint and eucalyptus treat.

BODY TREATMENTS. Massage: Deep tissue, reflexology, aromatherapy, couples. **Exfoliation:** Body scrub, fruit polish. **Wraps/baths:** Tequila wrap, fruit wrap, melon wrap, mineral bath. **Other:** Facials, hot-stone treatments Solo para Caballeros treatments for men.

BEAUTY TREATMENTS. Facials, hair/scalp conditioning, hair cutting/styling, manicure, pedicure, waxing.

PRICES. Body Treatments: $52–$290. **Facials:** $90–$120. **Mani/Pedi:** $36–$46.

*Camino Viejo a San José, Km 0.5. ☎ 624/145–7000, 866/625–4502. 🌐 www.villadelarcoloscabos.com. **Parking:** Valet (free, but please tip). 💳 MC, V.*

FIESTA AMERICANA GRAND

The Fiesta's SOMMA Wine Spa uses grapes from the up-and-coming Valle de Guadalupe wine region. It's an unusual experience blended with classical treatments, focusing on the calming, cosmetic, and antioxidant properties of grapes and wine, or vinotherapy.

The spa is the only one of its kind in Mexico, with only six others throughout the entire world. It towers high above the Sea of Cortez with 15 treatment rooms, both indoor and open-air, and offers more than 30 facial and body treatments.

BODY TREATMENTS. Massage: Classic, deep tissue, sports, aromatherapy, hot stone, relaxing, Swedish, Chardonnay foot. **Exfoliation:** Salt body scrub. **Wraps/baths:** Mud wrap, chocolate wrap, Chardonnay wrap, clay wrap, honey and fruit wrap, seaweed wrap, green coffee wrap, water lily wrap. **Other:** Facials, cellulite firming.

BEAUTY TREATMENTS. Hair/scalp conditioning, hair cutting/styling, manicure, pedicure, waxing.

PRICES. Body Treatments: $100–$250. **Facials:** $140–$290. **Mani/Pedi:** $40–$60.

*Hwy. 1, Km 10.3. ☎ 624/145–6200, 800/343–7821. 🌐 www.fiestaamericanagrand.com. **Parking:** Valet and self parking. 💳 MC, V.*

HONORABLE MENTIONS

PLAYA GRANDE RESORT

The meaning of the word thalassotherapy comes from the practice of using seawater baths and seaweed-based treatments for preventive and curative purposes. Playa Grande's spa is said to be the finest thalasso center in North America. They often use combinations of seaweed and seawater and the minerals in both will rejuvenate and renew your skin like you've never experienced.

BODY TREATMENTS. Massage: Hot stone, shiatsu, Swedish, four hands, foot reflexology. **Exfoliation:** Honey body polish, seaweed polish, sea-salt glow, cinnamon-sugar scrub, pomegranate/cranapple scrub. **Wraps/baths:** Thalassotherapy bath, seaweed bath, hydrotheraphy bath, seaweed body mask, honey/almond/buttermilk wrap.

PRICES. Body Treatments: $120–260. **Facials:** $130–175. **Mani/Pedi:** $30–$60.

Avenida Playa Grande No. 1, Playa Solmar ☎ 624/145-7575, 800/344-3349 🌐 www.playagranderesort.com ***Parking:*** *Valet (free, but please tip). 💳 MC, V.*

PACIFICA HOLISTIC RETREAT & SPA

This small, tranquil hotel on the Pacific side of Cabo is an adults-only property, filled with feng shui design, immaculately kept cactus gardens, and water, water, everywhere. The treatments at their Armonia (Harmony) Spa run the gamut from crystal reiki healing to a yogurt and violet exfoliation to temazcal.

BODY TREATMENTS. Massage: Hot stone, Swedish, sports, deep tissue, shiatsu, four hands, couples, expectant mother, ayurveda, shirobyhanga, Thai, reflexology, aromatherapy. **Exfoliation:** Honey sugar glow and amazing array of scrubs. **Wraps/baths:** Bamboo/alfalfa/aloe/chamomile, detox, Dead Sea mud, revitalizing.

PRICES. Body Treatments: $120–$275. **Facials:** $160–$275. **Mani/Pedi:** $35–$62.

Cabo Pacifica s/n ☎ 624/142-9696, 800/990-8250. 🌐 www.pueblobonitopacifica.com. ***Parking:*** *Valet, (free, but please tip). 💳 AC, MC, V.*

ALSO WORTH NOTING

The boutique Cabo Surf Hotel's Sea Spa caters to its athletic guests with, among others, a Surfer's Sports Package and Day at the Beach massage and facial. *Playa Acapulquito Km 28, San Jose del Cabo ☎ 624/142-2676. 🌐 www.seaspacabo.com.*

GLOSSARY

acupuncture. Painless Chinese medicine during which needles are inserted into key spots on the body to restore the flow of *qi* and allow the body to heal itself.

aromatherapy. Massage and other treatments using plant-derived essential oils intended to relax the skin's connective tissues and stimulate the flow of lymph fluid.

ayurveda. A traditional Indean medical practice that uses oils, massage, herbs, and diet and lifestyle modification to restore balance to the body.

body brushing. Dry brushing of the skin to remove dead cells and stimulate circulation.

body polish. Use of scrubs, loofahs, and other exfoliants to remove dead skin cells.

hot-stone massage. Massage using smooth stones heated in water and applied to the skin with pressure or strokes or simply rested on the body.

hydrotherapy. Underwater massage, alternating hot and cold showers, and other water-oriented treatments.

reflexology. Massage on the pressure points of feet, hands, and ears.

reiki. A Japanese healing method involving universal life energy, the laying on of hands, and mental and spiritual balancing. It's intended to relieve acute emotional and physical conditions. Also called radiance technique.

salt glow. Rubbing the body with coarse salt to remove dead skin.

shiatsu. Japanese massage that uses pressure applied with fingers, hands, elbows, and feet.

shirodhara. Ayurvedic massage in which warm herbalized oil is trickled onto the center of the forehead, then gently rubbed into the hair and scalp.

sports massage. A deep-tissue massage to relieve muscle tension and residual pain from workouts.

Swedish massage. Stroking, kneading, and tapping to relax muscles. It was devised at the University of Stockholm in the 19th century by Per Henrik Ling.

Swiss shower. A multijet bath that alternates hot and cold water, often used after mud wraps and other body treatments.

Temazcal. Maya meditation in a sauna heated with volcanic rocks.

THE TEMAZCAL TRADITION

Increasingly popular at Mexico spas is the traditional sweat lodge, or *temazcal*. Herb-scented water sizzles on heated lava rocks, filling the intimate space with purifying steam. Rituals blend indigenous and New Age practices, attempting to stimulate you emotionally, spiritually, and physically. For the sake of others, it's best to take a temazcal only if you're committed to the ceremony, or at least open-minded, and not claustrophobic.

Thai massage. Deep-tissue massage and passive stretching to ease stiff, tense, or short muscles.

thalassotherapy. Water-based treatments that incorporate seawater, seaweed and algae.

Vichy shower. Treatment in which a person lies on a cushioned, waterproof mat and is showered by overhead water jets.

Watsu. A blend of shiatsu and deep-tissue massage with gentle stretches—all conducted in a warm pool.

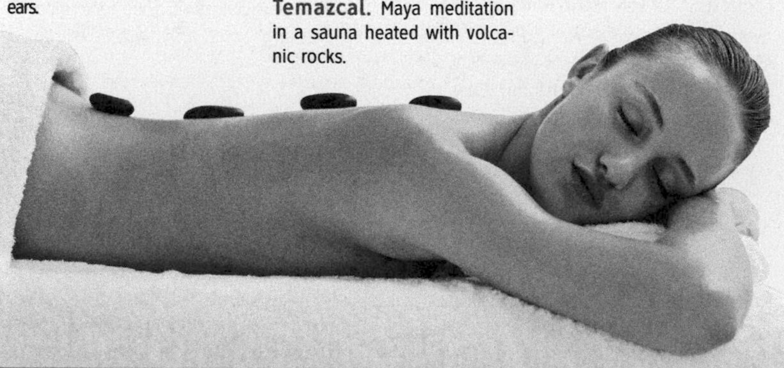

residential community are south of Centro (town center); farther south the ever-expanding Zona Hotelera (hotel zone) faces a long beach on the Sea of Cortez. Despite the development—and weekday traffic jams—San José is peaceful. If you want exciting nightlife and rowdy beaches, stay in Cabo San Lucas.

STARRY STARRY NIGHT

Every Friday night, customized desert vehicles transport One&Only Palmilla guests and the hotel's astronomer into the desert mountain region to enjoy the Baja desert at night under the star-filled sky. The unique mountain background sets the stage for an evening of exciting entertainment including fire dancing and song as well as a sumptuous Mexican feast.

GETTING HERE AND AROUND

Aeropuerto Internacional de Los Cabos (Los Cabos International Airport) is 1 km (½ mi) west of the Transpeninsular Highway (Highway 1), 13 km (8 mi) north of San José del Cabo. Fares from the airport to hotels in Los Cabos are expensive. The least expensive transport is by shuttle buses that stop at various hotels along the route; fares run $12 to $25 per person. TransCabo can provide private transport for $60 between San José del Cabo and Cabo San Lucas. Taxi fares are exorbitant in Los Cabos, and the taxi union is definitely powerful. The fare between Cabo San Lucas and San José del Cabo runs about $45—more at night. Cabs from Corridor hotels to either town run about $25 each way.

ESSENTIALS

Bus Contacts **TransCabo** (☎ *624/146–0888*).

Currency Exchange **Banamex** (✉ *Blvd. Mijares*).

Internet **Trazzo Digital** (✉ *Calle Zaragoza 24*).

Medical Assistance **Emergency Number for Medical Assistance** (☎ *Dial 060 or 066*). **Highway Patrol** (☎ *624/146–0573*). **Police** (☎ *624/142–2835*).

Visitor and Tour Info **Los Cabos Tourism Board** (✉ *Hwy. 1, Plaza San José* ☎ *624/146–9628* 🌐 *www.visitloscabos.org*).

EXPLORING

Boulevard Mijares, the main drag, runs roughly perpendicular to the sea. Its north end abuts Avenida Zaragoza, a spot marked by a long fountain and the modest yellow Palacio Municipal (City Hall). The boulevard's south end has been designated a tourist zone, with the Mayan Palace Golf Los Cabos as its centerpiece. A few reasonably priced hotels and large all-inclusives are on a long, marvelous beach with rough surf.

Fires, hurricanes, and neglect have harmed the **Estero San José,** which empties into the sea at the north end of Playa Hotelera, San José's beach. Over the years the estuary has served as a cultural center and a recreational area for kayakers and bird-watchers. This valuable natural resource is now the southern border of Puerto Los Cabos, a marina development that will eventually include several hotels, golf courses, and residential communities. The estuary is gradually coming back to life, and may once again harbor seabirds and migratory birds as well as all the flora and fauna it once had. ✉ *North end of Paseo Malecón San José* 🎫 *Free.*

Locals and travelers mingle at the central **Plaza Mijares,** on shaded green benches or in the white wrought-iron gazebo. The plaza is often the site of concerts and art shows. Be sure to walk up to the front of the nearby Iglesia San José, the town church, and see the tile mural of a priest being dragged toward a fire by Indians.

WORD OF MOUTH

"We stayed in both San Lucas and San Jose and walked around everywhere. Just watch out for bumpy sidewalks and drop offs; they don't make sidewalks there like they do at home. Remember, its the desert and very hot. It's not good for gringos to be traveling outside at high noon, that's siesta time, but mornings and evenings are wonderful for strolling around." —DGalley

BEACHES

Oh, the madness of it all. Here you are in a beach destination with gorgeous weather and miles of clear blue water, yet you dare not dive into the sea. Most of San José's hotels line **Playa Hotelera** on Paseo Malecón San José, and brochures and Web sites gleefully mention beach access. Although the long, level stretch of coarse brown sand is breathtaking, the current is dangerously rough, and the drop-offs are steep and close to shore. Swimming here is extremely dangerous, and signs warn against it all along the way. Feel free to walk along the beach to the Estero San José, or play volleyball on the sand. But for swimming, head to Playa Palmilla along the Corridor. **Amenities:** Parking lot.

WHERE TO EAT

$ THAI ✕ **Baan Thai.** The aromas alone are enough to bring you through the door, where you'll be greeted with visual and culinary delights. The small, comfortable, formal dining room has Asian antiques, and a fountain murmurs on a patio in the back. The chef blends Asian spices with aplomb, creating sublime pad thai, lamb curry, Thai lamb shank, and the catch of the day with lemon–black bean sauce. New favorites are mussels in a coconut broth, and wok-seared scallops. To wash it all down? Try the Ginger Martini. Prices are reasonable for such memorable food. ✉ *Morelos and Obregón, across from El Encanto Inn, Centro* ☎ *624/142–3344* 💳 *AE, MC, V* ⏲ *No lunch Sun.*

$$ AMERICAN ✕ **Baja Brewing Company.** Los Cabos has its own brewery, right in the middle of San José del Cabo. This fun, upbeat brewpub has great music, and serves up satisfying pub meals. Burgers, shepherd's pie, soups, salads, and pizza—and more elegant entrées such as filet mignon—should be washed down with a pint of any of the special San José cervezas, brewed within sight of the bar and restaurant. A branch opened in Cabo San Lucas in 2009. ✉ *Morelos 1277, Comonfort and Obregón, Centro* ☎ *624/146–9995* 🌐 *www.bajabrewingcompany.com* 💳 *MC, V.*

$$$$ ECLECTIC Fodor's Choice ★ ✕ **Casiano's.** A colorful interior of bold red-and-blue stripes and a very graphic-chic aesthetic beguile you as you enter this inventive restaurant. "No menu, no rules" is the way it describes the "spontaneous cuisine" dining experience you're about to enjoy here. If you're an open-minded, trusting, and adventurous eater, you'll enjoy this restaurant, which is

full of surprises. Give yourself up to top chef Casiano Reyes, who's worked at both Las Ventanas and El Chilar. Your waitperson will provide you with a general list of ingredients available for the day, such as Brie, goat cheese, heirloom tomatoes, shrimp, lobster, scallops, snapper, prime beef fillet, and foie gras. Give him or her an idea of your tastes, and let the kitchen create the perfect surprise dish. Five-course meals and food-wine pairings are the specialties. Reservations are strongly recommended. ✉ *Bahía de Palmas s/n, Local 2, 4 and 6, Plaza del Mar, Fonatur* ☎ *624/142–5928* 🌐 *www.casianos.com* ▭ *AE, MC, V.*

$$ CONTINENTAL ✕ **Damiana.** At this small hacienda beside San José's town plaza, bougainvillea wraps around tall pines that surround wrought-iron tables, and pink adobe walls glow in the candlelight. Start with mushrooms *diablo* (steeped in a fiery-hot sauce), then move on to tender chateaubriand steak or charbroiled lobster. For more traditional seafood preparations, order the shrimp *enfrijolladas*—in a creamy black-bean sauce—or the shrimp with a mild cactus sauce. If you like your dining experiences to come with a side of adventure, Damiana has created a "steak" out of ground shrimp in its signature Imperial Steak Shrimp. During peak season a trio of guitarists serenades the guests. ✉ *Blvd. Mijares 8, Centro* ☎ *624/142–0499* 🌐 *www.damiana.com.mx* ▭ *AE, MC, V* ⊗ *Closed Aug. and Sept.*

$$$$ MEXICAN Fodor'sChoice ★ ✕ **Don Emiliano.** One of the few woman chefs in Los Cabos area, Margarita Carrillo de Salinas is often considered one of the top chefs in Mexico. Carrillo de Salinas taps into the quality cooking that has run in the family for generations, and her menu shows it. The restaurant's signature dish is the complex Pescado Tikin-Xic (try to pronounce this Mayan recipe correctly after a shot or two of tequila). Tikin-Xic is the local catch of the day that is prepared in the Yucatecan style, with an achiote salsa and wrapped in banana leaves. For dessert, the simple grilled mangoes, filled with spices and nuts and smothered in a rich orange-juice reduction, is a delectable choice. ✉ *Blvd. Mijares 27, Centro* ☎ *624/142–0266* 🌐 *www.donemiliano.com.mx* ▭ *MC, V* ⊗ *No lunch.*

$$$ MEXICAN ✕ **El Chilar.** Set just a few blocks south of mainstream San José, this spot is worth the search. The fine selection of Mexican wines and tequilas suits the stylish menu in this small, bustling space, where murals of the Virgin of Guadalupe adorn bright orange walls. In his open kitchen, chef Armando Montaño uses chilies from all over Mexico to enhance traditional and continental dishes, coating rack of lamb with ancho chili and perking up lobster bisque with smoky *chiles guajillos*. The management refuses to stagnate, however, and changes the menu every month. One mainstay has been the Oaxacan *tlayudas* (similar to tostadas), possibly the most asked-for item of the last half-dozen years here. After dinner, retire to the wine-and-tequila tasting room, admiring the service that brought it the "Distintivo T" award for tequila knowledge. ✉ *Calle Juárez at Morelos, Centro* ☎ *624/142–2544* ▭ *No credit cards* ⊗ *No lunch.*

$$$$ MEXICAN ✕ **La Panga Antigua.** An ancient wooden *panga* (small skiff) hangs above the door at this intriguing restaurant just across from San José's historical mission. Tastefully decorated, La Panga has tables on a series of

patios, one with a faded mural, another with a burbling fountain. Chef Jacobo Turquie prepares a superb catch of the day, drizzled with basil-infused oil and served with sautéed spinach and mashed potatoes. His regional seafood dishes, *pollo con mole,* gazpacho, and creamed carrot soup are also exceptional. ✉ *Av. Zaragoza 20, Centro* ☎ *624/142–4041* 🌐 *www.lapanga.com* 💳 *AE, MC, V.*

$$$ ECLECTIC Fodor's Choice ★ **Mi Cocina.** Traveling foodies, visiting chefs, and locals in the know favor this chic outdoor restaurant at Casa Natalia, San José del Cabo's loveliest boutique hotel. Torches glow on the dining terrace, and the tables are spaced far enough apart so that you don't have to share your whispered sweet nothings with neighbors. Chef-owner Loic Tenoux plays with his ingredients, calling the new approach at Mi Cocina "Euro-Mexican Bistro-style." He mixes marinated octopus with Chinese noodles in a to-die-for salad, and stuffs poblano chilies with lamb and Oaxacan cheese. Tenoux also serves classic onion soup; the homemade focaccia bread is great for dipping. Fried Camembert goes well with many of the imported wines on the extensive list. ✉ *Casa Natalia, Blvd. Mijares 4, Centro* ☎ *624/146–7100* 🌐 *www.micocinaloscabos.com* 💳 *AE, MC, V* ⏲ *No lunch.*

WHERE TO STAY

$$$$ **Cabo Azul Resort & Spa.** A relative newcomer on the beach in San José del Cabo, the exceptional Cabo Azul is still partially under construction, but you would never know it. Azul seems destined to be one of Los Cabos' top hotels, with two restaurants on the premises: the gorgeous Javier's Cantina & Grill and the posh palapa-style Flor de Noche. This hotel-and-time-share hybrid, despite the sophistication and elegance, has a friendly, relaxed atmosphere, with spacious one- to three-bedroom villas and more than a dozen giant penthouses. The Paz Spa offers luxe indoor and outdoor treatments. You'll find that most of the action is centered on the giant asymmetrical pool, with a swim-up bar adjacent to the Flor de Noche Restaurant & Lounge. **Pros:** beautiful, distinctive rooms; professional and friendly staff keep it all running smoothly. **Cons:** the time-share aspect is difficult to avoid—with tours and salespeople nearly always present with hordes of prospective buyers; no shallow pool for kids. ✉ *Desarrollo Cabo Azul, Paseo Malecón 11, San José del Cabo, Zona Hotelera* ☎ *624/163–5100, 877/216–2226 in U.S.* 🌐 *www.caboazulresort.com* *332 villas* *In-room: Safe, kitchen, DVD. In-hotel: 2 restaurants, room service, bars, pools, gym, spa, laundry service, Internet terminal, parking (free)* 💳 *AE, MC, V.*

$$$$ Fodor's Choice ★ **Casa Natalia.** An intimate, graceful boutique hotel, Casa Natalia is in the heart of San José's downtown and opens onto the zócalo. Rooms are decorated in regional Mexican motifs and have king-size beds, soft robes, remote-controlled air-conditioning, and private patios screened by bamboo and bougainvillea. Suites have hot tubs and hammocks on large terraces. A free shuttle takes you to a beach club in the Corridor. Natalia's cozy little bar offers hotel guests afternoon happy-hour specials, including *dos por uno,* or two-for-ones. The in-patio restaurant, Mi Cocina, is fabulous. Staffers are helpful and welcoming. Casa Natalia is the most luxurious option for those who wish to spend time enjoying the culture of this tranquil town. **Pros:** lovely, oasis-like location in

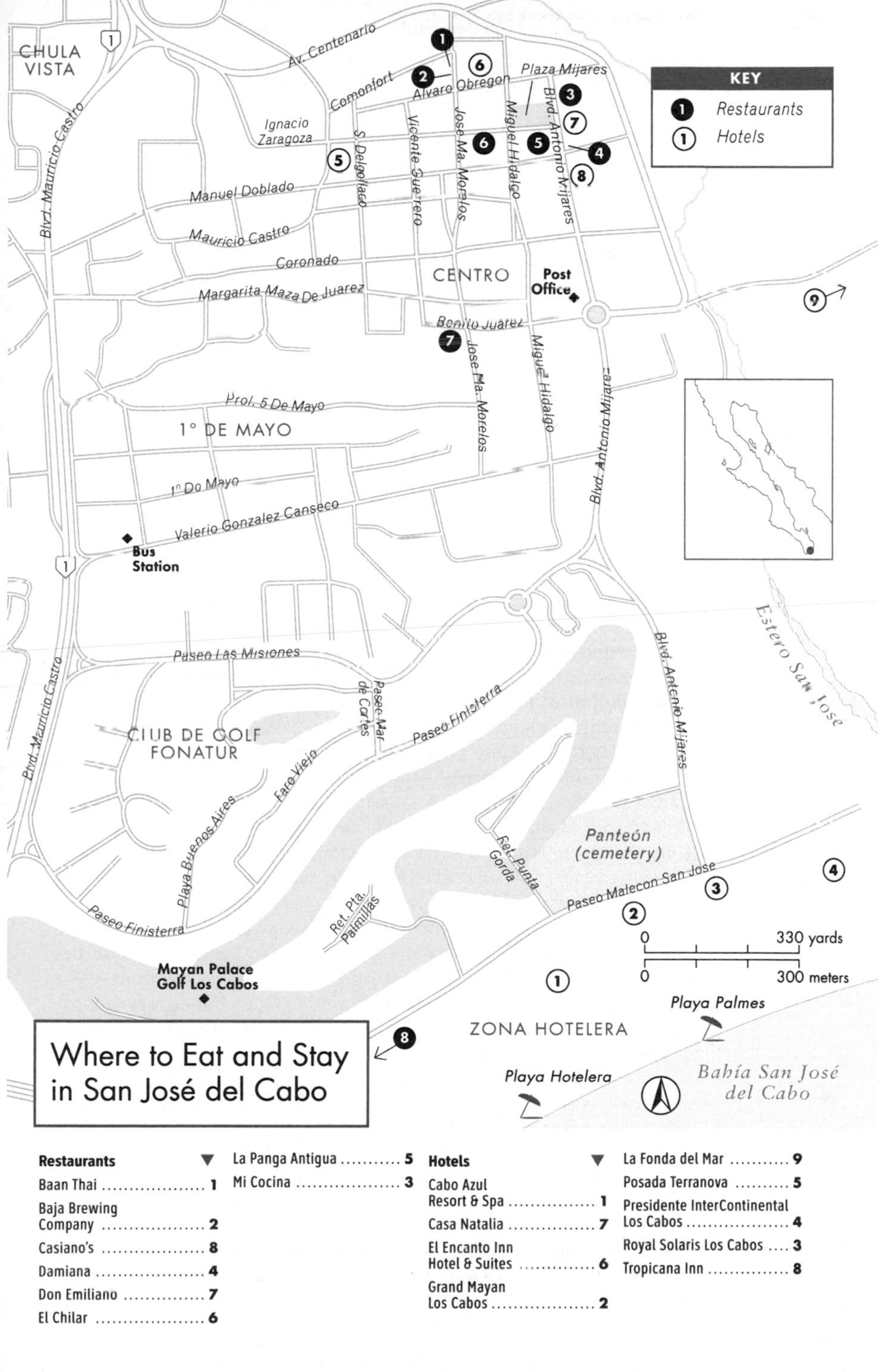

Where to Eat and Stay in San José del Cabo

Restaurants

- Baan Thai 1
- Baja Brewing Company 2
- Casiano's 8
- Damiana 4
- Don Emiliano 7
- El Chilar 6
- La Panga Antigua 5
- Mi Cocina 3

Hotels

- Cabo Azul Resort & Spa 1
- Casa Natalia 7
- El Encanto Inn Hotel & Suites 6
- Grand Mayan Los Cabos 2
- La Fonda del Mar 9
- Posada Terranova 5
- Presidente InterContinental Los Cabos 4
- Royal Solaris Los Cabos 3
- Tropicana Inn 8

the heart of downtown; fantastic complimentary breakfast; excellent staff. **Cons:** no bathtubs in the standard rooms; noise from music and fiestas on Plaza Mijares can be disturbing; beach shuttle only runs twice per day. ✉ *Blvd. Mijares 4, Centro* ☎ *624/146–7100, 888/277–3814 in U.S.* 🌐 *www.casanatalia.com* *14 rooms, 2 suites* *In-room: Safe. In-hotel: Restaurant, bar, pool, laundry service, Wi-Fi hotspot, no kids under 13* ▭ *AE, MC, V* 🍴 *CP.*

$$ **El Encanto Hotel & Suites.** In the heart of San José's Historic Arts District, and near many bars and great restaurants, this gorgeous and comfortable inn has two separate buildings—one looks onto the verdant gardens and pool; the other one, across the street, is in a charming, historic building with a narrow courtyard. All guest quarters are immaculate and impeccably decorated, and both buildings are surrounded by gardens and adorned with climbing vines. This intimate hotel makes for a great wedding property, and the on-property wedding chapel harks back to the Mexico of years gone by. **Pros:** lush, Mexican-hacienda feeling; sunny pool area; excellent location that is central but quiet. **Cons:** service may be friendly, but staffing is minimal. ✉ *Morelos 133, Centro* ☎ *624/142–0388* 🌐 *www.elencantoinn.com* *12 rooms, 14 suites* *In-room: Kitchen (some). In-hotel: Pool, laundry service* ▭ *AE, MC, V.*

$$$$ **Grand Mayan Los Cabos.** As soon as you see the enormous twin Mayan statues that stand in the dimly lighted lobby entrance, you'll feel as if you've entered another world. This ultraglitzy, exotic resort offers vibrant, spacious suites, all with a view of the enormous pool and the Sea of Cortez beyond. Water flows out of the mouths of giant rattlesnake sculptures into the pool, which is decked out with lights that change colors at night. Early-morning yoga classes greet the sunrise near the beach. **Pros:** children's programs; Grand Mayan golf course; guests can opt out of all-inclusive plan. **Cons:** no coffeemakers or refrigerators in standard rooms; views of sea vary from panoramic to none at all. ✉ *Paseo Malecón, San José del Cabo, Zona Hotelera* ☎ *624/163–4000* 🌐 *www.wyndham.com* *172 rooms, 86 suites* *In-room: Safe, kitchen (some). In-hotel: 2 restaurants, bars, gym, spa, beachfront, laundry services, Wi-Fi hotspot, parking (free)* ▭ *MC, V* 🍴 *AI.*

$$ **La Fonda del Mar.** If you're looking for a peaceful back-to-nature retreat, check out this hotel on a long, secluded beach that straddles the line between desert and ocean. And once the diners clear out of the adjacent and very popular Buzzard's Bar & Grill, La Fonda is even more tranquil. The three thatch-roof cabañas and one cabaña/suite are in heavy demand by both surfers and the more adventurous in high season. Cabañas have en-suite toilets and sinks but share a hot-water shower; the suite has standard in-room facilities. The whole operation runs on solar power. To get here, turn off Boulevard Mijares at the signs for Puerto Los Cabos, continue past PLC and follow the road up the hill, around the mini-circle, and continue out into the desert; it's about 5 km (3 mi; 10 minutes) outside town. **Pros:** fantastic location on the beach; excellent full breakfast included in room rate. **Cons:** not within walking distance to town; difficult to find; shared shower facilities. ✉ *Old East Cape Rd.* ☎ *624/113–6368 cell, 624/110–6454, 951/303–9384 in U.S.*

www.vivacabo.com 3 cabañas, 1 suite In-hotel: Restaurant, bar, pool, beachfront No credit cards Closed Aug. BP.

¢ **Posada Terranova.** People return to San José's best inexpensive hotel over and over again. Terranova's large rooms have two double beds, tile bathrooms, and Mexican art. Its restaurant serves quality Mexican cuisine for all three meals; the diverse clientele makes dining an international event. Yet, whether you congregate with other guests at the front patio tables or within the restaurant, it still feels like a private home. **Pros:** friendly staff; immaculate rooms; easy walk to Plaza Mijares. **Cons:** no pool; check the bed if a firm mattress is a necessity for you. *Calle Degollado at Av. Zaragoza, Centro 624/142–0534 www.hterranova.com.mx 25 rooms In-hotel: Restaurant, room service, bar AE, MC, V CP.*

$$$$ **Presidente InterContinental Los Cabos.** Cactus gardens surround this low-lying hotel, one of the originals in what has become a lineup of massive all-inclusives along the beach. There's an attentive, friendly, Old World Mexican attitude among the staff members, many of whom have been here for decades. Each of the hotel's three sections is centered on pools and lounging areas, and the ground-floor rooms, which have terraces, are the best; ask about the patio rooms with hammocks for tranquil, retreat-like stays. All accommodations have showers but no bathtubs. Try Napa, the property's top restaurant, part of the resort's all-inclusive plan. **Pros:** Chiqui Kids' Club (ages 5–12), adults-only restaurant and pool; generally mellow atmosphere is good for families and those looking for a getaway. **Cons:** rooms tend to be basic, without refrigerators; food is run-of-the-mill buffet style, except at Napa. *Paseo San José, at end of hotel zone, Zona Hotelera 624/142–0211, 800/424–6835 in U.S. www.ichotelsgroup.com 390 rooms, 7 suites In-room: safe, Internet. In-hotel: 6 restaurants, room service, bars, tennis courts, pools, gym, beachfront, children's programs (ages 5–12), laundry service AE, MC, V AI.*

$$$–$$$$ **Royal Solaris Los Cabos.** This was the first all-inclusive in Los Cabos—it runs smoothly, although the resort feels a bit like an amusement park. You'll be entertained with four major dinner shows per week in the Teatro (theater) Teotihuacan, a casino night, a Latin Show, and other themed nights. A complete Kids' Mini-Club area includes toboggan waterslides, dancing lessons, kites, and crayons. Adults can play tennis, basketball, and beach volleyball. **Pros:** Kids' Club entertains kids 4–12 years old from 9 to 9; there is something for everyone at this busy resort, from cooking classes to dancing lessons; this is the best value for the money of the all-inclusives. **Cons:** the accommodations and food veer toward only adequate here, despite the volume of options; this is not the place to go for romance-seeking couples; time-share salespeople are pushy. *Lote 10, Colonia Campo de Golf, San José del Cabo, Zona Hotelera 624/145–6800, 877/270–0440 in U.S. www.hotelessolaris.com 389 rooms In-hotel: 5 restaurants, room service, bars, gym, tennis courts, spa, children's programs (ages 4–12), Wi-Fi hotspot, parking (free) MC, V AI.*

$$ Fodor'sChoice ★ **Tropicana Inn.** It's not directly on the beach, but this hotel in a quiet enclave along one of San José's main boulevards is a delightful find. The hotel restaurant faces the street, with the guest quarters tucked away at the back of the property. The warm yellow buildings frame a pool and palapa bar in a quiet, verdant enclave. The rooms were all renovated in mid-2007 and outfitted with fine Mexican artwork and textiles. Two suites, El Troje and El Jacaranda, are situated poolside. In its previous life, El Troje was a hand-carved, dark wood, Tarascan Indian bungalow that the Tropicana transplanted here from Michoacán. Compared to the rates typical of Los Cabos properties, the rates for El Troje make for a very special and very romantic find. The hotel is steps from great shopping, across the street from several top restaurants (including Don Emiliano's), and a stone's throw from the zócalo. The Tropicana is clearly a favorite among locals, and it is common to see businesspeople having breakfast and lunch meetings in the restaurant. **Pros:** very good on-site restaurant and bar with live entertainment on the weekends; the bands pack in the dancers, but the music is not heard back in the hotel rooms; rooms are immaculate, and beds extremely comfortable; staff is attentive and courteous. **Cons:** kids are allowed, even though the hotel is clearly oriented to adults seeking peace and relaxation; Wi-Fi is only available around the pool. ✉ *Blvd. Mijares 30, Centro* ☎ *624/142–1580* 🌐 *www.tropicanainn.com* *37 rooms, 4 suites* *In-room: refrigerator. In-hotel: restaurant, room service, bar, pool, parking (free), Wi-Fi hotspot* 💳 *AE, MC, V* 🍽 *CP.*

NIGHTLIFE

★ The bar at the **Tropicana Inn** (✉ *Blvd. Mijares 30* ☎ *624/142–1580* 🌐 *www.tropicanainn.com*) is a great place to mingle and enjoy live music. Conversation is usually possible on the balcony overlooking the bar and stage, though when a really hot band gets going you'll be too busy dancing to talk.

SHOPPING

San José's shops and galleries carry gorgeous, high-quality folk art, jewelry, and housewares. Serious shoppers should plan on splurging here.

Thursday art walks occur November through June. Participating galleries and shops stay open until 9 PM and serve drinks and snacks, and many arrange for special events or openings. There is usually music on Plaza Mijares, and it's not uncommon for the streets to be full of people, locals and tourists alike. "Historic Art District" brochures are in most galleries and shops.

Copal (✉ *Plaza Mijares* ☎ *624/142–3070*) has carved animals from Oaxaca, masks from Guerrero Negro, and heavy wooden furnishings, along with woven rugs and beautiful Mexican crafts and jewelry.

★ **Frank Arnold Gallery** (✉ *1137 Calle Comonfort* ☎ *624/142–4422, 559/255–8273 in U.S.* 🌐 *www.frankarnoldart.com*) has two big draws: arguably the best gallery space in town, in a great new building by local architect Alfredo Gomez, and Frank Arnold's dramatic, widely acclaimed contemporary paintings.

★ **Galería Veryka** (✉ *Plaza Mijares 418* ☎ *624/142–0575*) is one of the best folk-art shops in the region, with gorgeous embroidered clothing, masks, wood carvings, jewelry, and hand-molded black and green pottery. Most of the goods are from Oaxaca. Check out the seasonal displays, especially the Day of the Dead altar.**Necri** (✉ *Blvd. Mijares 16* ☎ *624/130–7500* 🌐 *www.necri.com.mx*) is an offshoot of a longstanding San Lucas shop; it carries Talavera ceramics, handicrafts, pottery, and pewter pieces and hot sauce made by the owner.

Fodor'sChoice ★ **silvermoon gallery** (✉ *Plaza Mijares No. 10* ☎ *624/142–6077*) is known for the assortment and the quality of art contained within its walls. Mexican folk art makes up most of the inventory here. Treasures include Carlos Albert's whimsical papier-mâché sculptures, Mata Ortiz pottery from the Quezada family, Huichol yarn "paintings," Alebrijes (colorful wooden animal sculptures) from Oaxaca, and fine jewelry. Owner Armando Sanchez Icaza is gracious and knowledgeable; he knows volumes about the artists whose work he carries. His silversmiths can also make custom jewelry for you within a day or two.

El Mercado Municipal (✉ *Castro and Coronado, off Calle Doblado* ☎ *No phone*) is San José's traditional market area, where you can stock up on fresh meats and produce, or visit the market's **Viva Mexico** stand for clothes, belts, spices, jewelry, and other curios—all at excellent prices.

SPORTS AND THE OUTDOORS

BACKCOUNTRY

★ Longing to drive a Hummer? **Baja Outback** (☎ *624/142–9209* 🌐 *www.bajaoutback.com*) offers a variety of drive-yourself trips (with a guide in the passenger seat) that range from four hours to several days long. The routes run through Baja backcountry, where you have the opportunity to explore the Cape's rarely seen back roads while learning desert lore from a knowledgeable guide-cum-biologist. Day trips range from $165 to $220 per person.

★ **Baja Wild** (✉ *Hwy. 1, Km 28, s/n Local 5, Plaza Costa Azul* ☎ *624/172–6300* 🌐 *www.bajawild.com*) has a number of adventure packages, and its hikes to canyons, hot springs, fossil beds, and caves with rock paintings expose you to the natural side of Cabo. All-day backcountry Jeep tours cost about $420. Full-day kayak tours at Cabo Pulmo run $140 to $150. ATV tours in the desert with rappelling cost $98. Diving and rock climbing round out the options.

FISHING

Most hotels in San José can arrange fishing trips. The *pangas* of **Gordo Banks Pangas** (✉ *La Playa near San José del Cabo* ☎ *624/142–1147 or 800/408–1199* 🌐 *www.gordobanks.com*) are near some of the hottest fishing spots in the Sea of Cortez: the Outer and Inner Gordo Banks. The price for three anglers in a small *panga* runs from $210 to $290. Cruisers, which can accommodate four to six people, are available for $380 to $550 per day.

SURFING

For good surfing tips, rentals, and lessons, head to **Costa Azul Surf Shop** (✉ *Hwy. 1, Km 27.5* ☎ *624/142–2771 or 866/546–2102 in U.S.* 🌐 *www.costa-azul.com.mx*). Surfboard rentals are $20 a day and lessons are $85 and include the surfboard rental.

TODOS SANTOS

72 km (45 mi) north of Cabo San Lucas.

Artists from the Southwest (and a few from Mexico) have found a haven in this small town near the Pacific coast north of Los Cabos. Architects and entrepreneurs have restored early-19th-century adobe and brick buildings around the main plaza, and speculators have laid out housing tracts in the rocky hills between the town and the shore, contributing to a rapid rise in real-estate prices. In high season, tour buses on day trips from Los Cabos often clog the streets around the plaza. When the buses leave, the town is a peaceful place to wander.

Los Cabos visitors typically take day trips here, though several small inns provide a peaceful antidote to Cabo's noise and crowds. El Pescadero, the largest settlement before Todos Santos, is home to ranchers and farmers who grow herbs and vegetables. Business hours are erratic, especially in September and October.

GETTING HERE AND AROUND

Carretera 19 connects Cabo with Todos Santos. If you're only driving up for the day, be sure to head back to Cabo before dark, because Carretera 19 is unlighted and prone to high winds and flooding. And don't be tempted to try the dirt roads that intersect the highway unless you're in a four-wheel-drive vehicle. Sands on the beach or in the desert stop conventional vehicles in their tracks.

WHERE TO EAT

$$$ ITALIAN

✕ **Café Santa Fe.** The setting, with tables situated in an overgrown courtyard, is as appealing as the food, which includes salads and soups made with organic vegetables and herbs, homemade pastas, and fresh fish with light sauces. Many Cabo-area residents lunch here regularly. The marinated seafood salad is a sublime blend of shrimp, octopus, and mussels with olive oil and garlic, with plenty for two to share before dining on lobster ravioli. ✉ *Calle Centenario* ☎ *612/145–0340* 💳 *MC, V* ⏲ *Closed Tues. and Sept. and Oct.*

$$ ECLECTIC

✕ **Caffé Todos Santos.** Omelets, bagels, granola, and whole-grain breads delight the breakfast crowd at this small eatery; deli sandwiches, fresh salads, and an array of burritos, tamales, *flautas* (fried tortillas rolled around savory fillings), and combo plates are lunch and dinner highlights. Check for fresh seafood on the daily specials board. ✉ *Calle Centenario 33* ☎ *612/145–0787* 💳 *No credit cards* ⏲ *No dinner Mon.*

$$$$ ELCECTIC Fodor's Choice ★

✕ **El Gusto!** Even if you don't stay at the sumptuous Posada La Poza just outside town, lunch or dinner at its equally lovely restaurant will be one of the highlights of your Los Cabos vacation. Owners Jürg and Libusche Wiesendanger call their offerings "Swiss-Mex"—Mexican food with European touches, and careful attention to detail. Start with the vegetarian-based tortilla soup with three different types of dried chilies to give it just enough kick. Then sample the smoked-tuna flautas with raspberry-chipotle sauce, quesadillas with mushroom or shrimp, or marinated *arrachera* (flank steak) strips. You'll find dishes such as lamb shoulder in winter. Believe it or not, there is enough of an evening chill in the air that time of year that dining next to the fireplace feels cozy. Top your meal off with a sorbet, flan, or mousse, and possibly the best selection of wines in the region (all Mexican from northern Baja's Guadalupe Valley). Dinner is served from 6 to 8, which gives you time to catch the sunset. ✉ *Follow signs on Hwy. 19 and Benito Juárez to beach* ☎ *612/145–0400* 🌐 *www.lapoza.com* ✍ *Reservations essential* 💳 *MC, V* ⏲ *Closed Thurs.*

GET THE SCOOP

Be sure to pick up a copy of *El Calendario de Todos Santos*, a free English-language guide with events, available at many hotels and shops, for information on local events. Another good source is the Web site (🌐 *www.todossantos-baja.com*), which is maintained by local residents. Be sure to check out 🌐 *www.todossantos.cc*, an informative Web site about the area, as well.

$$ MEXICAN ✕ **Los Adobes.** Locals swear by the fried, cilantro-studded local cheese and the beef tenderloin with huitlacoche at this pleasant outdoor restaurant. The menu is ambitious, and includes tapas and several organic, vegetarian options—rare in these parts. At night the place sparkles with star-shape lights. An Internet café within the restaurant offers high-speed access. ✉ *Calle Hidalgo* ☎ *612/145–0203* 🌐 *www.losadobesdetodossantos.com* 💳 *MC, V* ⏲ *Closed Sun.*

$ MEXICAN ✕ **Miguel's.** Deliciously prepared chiles rellenos are the attraction at Miguel's. The sign out front says so, and it speaks the truth. Hearty bell peppers, almost any way you like them, stuffed with fish, lobster, shrimp, pork, beef, or veggies, make up the bulk of the lunch and dinner menu. Breakfast consists of burritos and eggs or Baja's ubiquitous fish tacos. A copy of *The New York Times* arrives later in the day for your perusal. Don't confuse this semi-outdoor place on the edge of town with Michael's, the Asian restaurant several blocks away near the church. ✉ *Degollado at Hwy. 19* ☎ *612/145–0733* 💳 *No credit cards* ⏲ *Closed Sun.*

WHERE TO STAY

$$$ 🏨 **Hotel California.** This handsome structure with two stories of arched terraces and rich, vibrant colors on the walls, is a testament to the artistic bent of owner Debbie Stewart. A deep-blue-and-ocher scheme runs throughout, and rooms, some with ocean views, are decorated with a mix of antiques and folk art reminiscent of Santa Fe, New Mexico. The Coronela restaurant and bar are local hot spots, and the Emporio shop is stuffed with curios, jewelry, and funky natural-fiber clothing from around the globe. **Pros:** the inn feels exotic and lush; great location in the heart of downtown Todos Santos. **Cons:** noise from town and cars can be disturbing; service not as smooth as at other hotels in town. ✉ *Benito Juárez at Morelos* ☎ *612/145–0525* 🌐 *www.*

EN ROUTE TO TODOS SANTOS

Playa Los Cerritos. This long, expansive beach on the Pacific Ocean, about 64 km (40 mi) north of Cabo San Lucas and on the way to the town of Todos Santos, is famous among surfers for its wonderful breaking waves in winter. Even if you don't ride the waves, you can watch them crash along the shore. The beach is wide, flat, and ideal for wading and swimming close to shore. Swimming farther out is not recommended because of the strong currents. ✣ *64 km (40 mi) north of Cabo San Lucas, 13 km (8 mi) south of Todos Santos.* **Amenities:** Toilets, showers (for restaurant patrons), food concession, parking lot, camping.

hotelcaliforniabaja.com *11 rooms* *In-room: no phone, no TV, Wi-Fi. In-hotel: restaurant, bar, pool* *MC, V.*

$$ Fodor'sChoice ★ **Hotelito.** This Mexican-modern hotel by local architect Jesús Fernando de Castro has been artfully decorated by British interior designer and owner Jenny Armit. Original art is found throughout, and has been mixed with contemporary and antique Mexican decorative pieces; the sculptural furniture is as comfortable as it is captivating. Each room has a private patio with lounge chairs and hammocks. A variety of activities can be planned with the assistance of the friendly, accommodating staff. Beds are incredibly comfortable, linens are dreamy, robes are fluffy, and fresh flowers are always present. There is also a three-bedroom home available for rent on the property, which is lush with palms, bougainvillea, and jasmine. **Pros:** saltwater swimming pool is fabulous; generous breakfasts are delicious (mangoes right off the tree!); boogie boards, beach towels, and umbrellas are available to use at the beach; five-minute walk to the beach. **Cons:** 10-minute walk to downtown; not recommended for families with young children—this is really a retreat-like property. ✉ *Rancho de la Cachora, take Topete north from downtown toward La Cachora* ☎ *612/145–0099* 🌐 *www.hotelitotodossantos.com* *4 rooms* *In-room: refrigerator, Wi-Fi. In-hotel: bar, pool, laundry service, Wi-Fi hotspot, parking (free)* *AE, D, DC, MC, V* *CP.*

$$$–$$$$ Fodor'sChoice ★ **Posada La Poza.** West of town, overlooking a bird-filled lagoon that gives way to the Pacific, this is the only Todos Santos property right on the water. The Swiss owners have taken great care to create a property that showcases the local flora, and the results are flawless. The handsome, spacious suites have terra-cotta–color walls, modern furniture, and sumptuous Swiss linens. You'll find a CD player and binoculars on hand, but there aren't any TVs or phones in the rooms. Even if you're not staying, stop by the excellent El Gusto! restaurant (closed Thursday) for spicy tortilla soup, local scallops, organic salads, and an impressive list of Mexican wines. **Pros:** very generous, delicious breakfasts; gorgeous saltwater pool and hot tubs. **Cons:** no children under 12; no TV or phones. ✉ *Follow signs on Carretera 19 and on Benito Juárez to beach* ☎ *612/145–0400* 🌐 *www.lapoza.com* *8 suites* *In-room:*

no phone, safe, refrigerator, no TV, Wi-Fi. In-hotel: restaurant, bar, pool, beachfront, no kids under 12 ⊟ *MC, V* 🍽 *BP.*

$$–$$$ Fodor's Choice ★ **Todos Santos Inn.** This converted 19th-century house, with only eight guest rooms, is unparalleled in design and comfort, owing to the loving care and attention of the owners, Todd and John. The pool deck is lined with hearty stone and brick; the painted walls of the foyer depict a fading, dusky scene; and gorgeous antiques are displayed throughout, completing the period feel in this hacienda that once belonged to a sugar baron. The absence of telephones and TVs allows for unencumbered relaxation. The attached Copa Wine Bar is open in the evening, and good restaurants are within easy walking distance. **Pros:** this is traditional Mexican elegance and hospitality at its best; the interior courtyard of this property is a verdant oasis. **Cons:** occasional noise from construction and renovation in the surrounding neighborhood; not ideal for families, as no children under 12 are allowed. ✉ *Calle Legaspi 33* ☎ *612/145–0040* 🌐 *www.todossantosinn.com* *8 rooms* *In-room: no phone, no TV. In-hotel: bar, pool, Wi-Fi hotspot, no kids under 12* ⊟ *MC, V* 🍽 *BP.*

THE REAL HOTEL CALIFORNIA?

Ignore rumors that everybody's favorite Eagles song originated at this Hotel California. It didn't. It hasn't stopped the establishment from playing up the ambiguity, and you can now buy T-shirts and tequila emblazoned with the iconic name.

SHOPPING

The annual Todos Santos Arts Fest (🌐 *www.elcalendariodetodossantos.com*), held at the end of January into early February, celebrates Mexican culture and performing arts as much as the art on display. If you visit on a Friday, there's an informal farmers' market on Camino Militar near Hidalgo, where you can find a surprising amount of organic produce. Don't hesitate to grab a taco or three at one of the carts by the corner if you get hungry.

Charles Stewart Gallery & Studio (✉ *Calle Centenario at Obregón* ☎ *612/145–0265* 🌐 *www.charlescstewart.com*) is a leader in the art scene here. Stewart moved from Taos, New Mexico, to Todos Santos in 1986, and is credited as one of the founders of the town's artist community. Baja and Mexican themes run through much of his work. The gallery is in one of the town's wonderful 19th-century buildings, and is surrounded by a wild, jungle-like garden.

The best bookstore in the Los Cabos region is **El Tecolote Bookstore** (✉ *Calle Juárez at Calle Hidalgo* ☎ *612/145–0295*)—it's the spot for Latin American literature, poetry, children's books, current fiction and nonfiction, and books on Baja.

Fénix de Todos Santos (✉ *Calle Juárez at Calle Topete* ☎ *612/145–0808*) has bowls and plates from Tonalá, handblown glassware, Talavera pottery, and cotton clothing by the designer Sucesos.

Galería de Todos Santos (✉ *Calle Topete and Calle Legaspi* ☎ *612/145–0040* 🌐 *www.galeriadetodossantos.com*), owned by Michael and Pat

Cope, displays Michael's modern art and exhibits works by international artists living in Baja.

At **Galería Santa Fe** (✉ *Calle Centenario 4* ☎ *612/145–0340*), in an 1850s adobe building, Paula and Ezio Colombo sell collector-quality folk art, including frames adorned with images of Frida Kahlo and her art, kid-size chairs decorated with bottle caps, Virgin of Guadalupe images, and *milagros* (small tin charms used as offerings to saints).

Fodor's Choice ★ **Mangos** (✉ *Calle Centenario across from Charles Stewart Gallery* ☎ *612/145–0451*) is filled with gorgeous Guatemalan textiles, Mexican folk art, belts, purses, wood carvings, and Day of the Dead figurine.

Fodor's Choice ★ **Joyeria Brilanti** (✉ *Centenario near Topete* ☎ *612/145–0799* 🌐 *www.brilanti.com*) showcases a number of contemporary-jewelry artists including famed Taxco silversmith Ana Brilanti.

BAJA SUR: THE EAST CAPE TO GUERRERO NEGRO

Los Barriles is 105 km (65 mi) south of La Paz, 64 km (40 mi) north of San José del Cabo.

The Sea of Cortez coast between La Paz and San José del Cabo is a favored hideaway for anglers and adventurers. The area consists of fast-growing gringo communities at Buena Vista and Los Barriles and beloved settlements at Cabo Pulmo and Punta Pescadero. Hotels and small lodges are scattered along the coast. Most present packages that include meals and activities—a good idea, since the properties can be quite isolated. The East Cape is renowned for its rich fishing grounds, good diving, and excellent windsurfing.

There's an outback quality to the East Cape, with a robust group of American "settlers" making their presence known. The East Cape is so Americanized it doesn't even have a Spanish name. It's the East Cape to everybody.

The first coastal settlement of note is Cabo Pulmo, site of one of the few coral reefs in the Sea of Cortez. You'll have to drive about 10 km (6 mi) on a dirt road to reach it, so a 4WD vehicle and some extra time are required. It's a magnet for serious divers, kayakers, and windsurfers. Power comes from solar panels, and drinking water is trucked in over dirt roads. Palapa-shaded restaurants on the sand serve fabulous fish tacos and cold drinks.

North of Cabo Pulmo, Buena Vista has more services and hotels, where you can join fishing and diving excursions. Next in line, Los Barriles has the most amenities, with Internet cafés, restaurants, gift shops, and plenty of eager real-estate agents. Devoted windsurfers roost in Los Barriles when the winter winds are high; anglers are happy year-round. You can rent water-sports equipment and organize boat trips through area hotels. If you're staying here, note that hotel airport transfers typically cost about $90 each way in an eight-person van.

GETTING HERE AND AROUND

Intrepid travelers can drive north of San José del Cabo on a dirt washboard road to the East Cape settlements, a dusty drive that takes about three hours to the first major town at Los Barriles. Some car-rental agencies don't allow their cars on these roads. Far easier is the drive north on paved Highway 1 through the Sierra de La Laguna.

WHERE TO STAY

You won't find much in the way of dining options in this remote area. Most people come here for the fishing—not the scene—and eat at their hotel's restaurants. If you'd rather cook your own food, you can stock up at **Tio's Tienda** (to get there, take the main road in town toward the beach until it dead-ends and turn left).

$$–$$$ **Cabo Pulmo Beach Resort.** Solar-powered cottages sit in even rows on the beach, much as in a trailer park. One of these, the Beach House, can accommodate up to eight guests at a time. No matter what your budget, you'll find something here, from basic rooms to more expensive cottages. The office is next to a PADI facility and a restaurant. It's the largest business in the neighborhood and the best place for newcomers to hang out for a few nights, meet a few people, and have some fun. The setting is idyllic, but the long road to get to the hotel is unpaved, and a little bumpy, so driving in before dark is recommended. Reservations are absolutely essential. **Pros:** good place to meet other travelers; great if you like diving. **Cons:** difficult to get to. ✉ *Hwy. 1 at La Ribera turnoff* ☎ *624/141–0885, 562/366–0398 in U.S.* 🌐 *www.cabopulmo.com* *11 rooms, 20 cottages* *In-room: no phone, kitchen (some), refrigerator (some), no TV. In-hotel: restaurant, beachfront, diving, water sports, Wi-Fi hotspot* *MC, V* *CP, FAP.*

$$$ **Hotel Buena Vista Beach Resort.** Flower-lined paths wrap around tile-roof bungalows, pools, fountains, and lawns. The rooms in the bungalows are simply decorated, and give you the feeling of stepping back a little in time, back to the '80s, when colors like bright orange and olive green were in fashion in textiles and furniture. Some rooms have private terraces. The fishing fleet is excellent, as are other diversions, such as diving, snorkeling, kayaking, horseback riding, and trips to natural springs. But it seems that most guests spend a good part of the day enjoying the pool and the hot tub, which is filled with water piped in from the hot springs. Many of the people at the swim-up bar seem to be regulars, swapping stories about Buena Vista's glory days, back when swim-up bars were novel, the furnishings were fashionable, and this was the place to be seen. Things are more laid-back today. A European plan (without meals) is available from November through March, which cuts the rate considerably. (And those months are a lovely time to be here.) Discounts are available for those who stay for three days or more. The food at the friendly Navegante Restaurant is decent, and they'll cook up the fish you caught earlier in the day. **Pros:** great place to kick back and relax; good restaurant. **Cons:** expensive during months with obligatory meal plan. ✉ *Hwy. 1, Km 105, Buena Vista* ☎ *624/141–0033, 800/752–3555 in U.S.* 🌐 *www.hotelbuenavista.com* *60 rooms* *In-room: No TV. In-hotel: Restaurant, bar, tennis court, pools, beachfront, spa, water sports, laundry service, Internet terminal* *AE, MC, V* *EP, FAP.*

$$$ **Hotel Palmas de Cortez.** The Palmas is the East Cape's social center. Often featured on sportfishing shows, the hotel is near the famed Cortez Banks—a submerged island that is famous for its fishing, diving,

and big-wave surfing. Palma's enormous pool has a swim-up bar, and there's also a 9-hole golf course and driving range where you can dedicate an afternoon or two. Some guest rooms have fireplaces and/or kitchens. Special events, including an arts festival in March and several fishing tournaments, are big draws. **Pros:** good food; lots of activities. **Cons:** can be difficult to find; not a good choice if you want solitude. ✉ *On the beach; take road north through Los Barriles and continue to beach* ☎ *624/141–0050, 888/241–1543 in U.S.* 🌐 *www.palmasdecortez.com* *22 rooms, 24 suites, 10 condos* *In-room: refrigerator, no TV (some). In-hotel: Restaurant, bar, golf course, tennis court, pool, gym, spa, water sports, Internet terminal* ▭ *MC, V* 🍽 *FAP.*

$ **Los Barriles Hotel.** Across the street from beachside businesses, this motel-like inn offers large, comfy, if somewhat basic, rooms. The two-story building wraps around a nicely landscaped central pool and lounging area with a palapa bar and hot tub; water and cold drinks are available at the front desk, as are tours and fishing trips. Reservations are highly recommended, since the hotel fills up fast. **Pros:** terrific value; spotless rooms. **Cons:** plain decor; fills up quickly; can be difficult to find. ✉ *Take road off Hwy. 1 north through Los Barriles and turn left when it ends at beach* ☎ *624/141–0024* 🌐 *www.losbarrileshotel.com* *20 rooms* *In-room: no TV, refrigerator. In-hotel: pool, water sports* ▭ *MC, V* 🍽 *EP.*

SPORTS AND THE OUTDOORS

Water-sports equipment and boat trips are available through area hotels, although veterans tend to bring their own gear and rent cars to reach isolated spots. Windsurfers take over the East Cape during winter months, when stiff breezes provide ideal conditions. Catch them flying over the waves at Playa Norte in Los Barriles. **Cabo Pulmo Divers** (✉ *On beach* 🌐 *www.baja.com/cabopulmodivers*) is another option if you want to dive. This family-run shop is right on the beach and provides full diving services, but it's most famous for excellent guided fishing trips that run $110 for three people for three hours.

Parque Marino Nacional Cabo Pulmo. The 25,000-year-old coral reef here has been legally protected since 1995, and it's home to more than 2,000 different kinds of marine organisms, including more than 230 species of tropical fish and a dozen kinds of petrified coral. The area is renowned among diving aficionados, whose favorite months to visit are June and July, when visibility is highest. The park isn't too difficult to access. It's just 8 km (5 mi) from the end of the paved road and is bordered by Playa Las Barracas in the north and Bahía Los Frailes to the south. Tourist facilities are still underdeveloped, so it's easiest if you bring your own gear.

If you happen to be traveling sans diving gear, you can get everything you need at **Pepe's Dive Center** (✉ *El Camino Rural Costero* 🌐 *www.cabopulmo.com.mx*). José Luis "Pepe" Murrieta and his knowledgeable crew of dive masters also give tours in English.

VelaWindsurf (☎ *800/223–5443* 🌐 *www.velawindsurf.com*) holds windsurfing and kite-boarding lessons and trips to Los Barriles in winter and fall; their center is in front of the Hotel Playa del Sol.

LA PAZ

188 km (117 mi) north of Los Cabos.

La Paz may be the capital of Baja Sur and home to about 250,000 residents, but it feels like a small town in a time warp. It's the most traditional Mexican city in Baja Sur, the antithesis of the gringolandia developments to the south. Granted, there are plenty of foreigners in La Paz, particularly during snowbird season. But in the slowest part of the off-season, during the oppressive late-summer heat, you can easily see how La Paz aptly translates as "the peace," and its residents can be called *paceños* (peaceful ones). The city sprawls inland from the curve of its *malécon* along the Bahía La Paz, which, through some strange feat of geography, angles west toward the sunset.

Travelers use La Paz as both a destination in itself and a stopping-off point en route to Los Cabos. There's always excellent scuba diving and sportfishing in the Sea of Cortez. La Paz is the base for divers and fishermen headed for Cerralvo, La Partida, and the Espíritu Santo islands, where parrot fish, manta rays, neons, and angels blur the clear waters by the shore, and marlin, dorado, and yellowtail leap from the sea. Cruise ships are more and more often spotted sailing toward the bay as La Paz emerges as an appealing port.

La Paz officially became the capital of Baja California Sur in 1974, and is the state's largest settlement, though Los Cabos is quickly catching up. There are few chain hotels or restaurants now, but the region, including parts of the coastline south of the city, is slated to have several large-scale, high-end resort developments with golf courses, marinas, and vacation homes.

GETTING HERE AND AROUND

Aeropuerto General Manuel Márquez de León serves La Paz. It's 11 km (7 mi) northwest of the Baja California Sur capital, which itself is 188 km (117 mi) north of Los Cabos. In La Paz taxis are readily available and inexpensive. Taxis between the La Paz airport and town are inexpensive (about $5) and convenient. A ride within town costs under $5; a trip to Pichilingue costs around $10. In La Paz the main Terminal de Autobus is on the malecón at Independencia. Bus companies extend service to Los Cabos (three hours), Loreto (five hours), and Guerrero Negro (the buses stop at the highway entrance to town). The Guerrero Negro trip takes anywhere from seven to nine hours, and buses stop in Santa Rosalia and San Ignacio.

ESSENTIALS

Airlines Aereo Calafia (☎ *612/135–2503*). **Horizon Air** (☎ *800/252–7522*).

Bus Contacts La Paz Terminal de Autobus (✉ *Calle Jalisco at Calle Gomez Farias* ☎ *612/122–7094*). **SuburBaja** (☎ *624/146–0888*).

Currency Exchange Banamex (✉ *Esquerro 110* ☎ *612/122–1011*).

Emergencies (☎ *Dial 065, 060, or 066*). **Highway Patrol** (☎ *612/122–0369*). **Police** (☎ *612/122–0477*).

Ferry Lines Baja Ferries (✉ *La Paz Pichilingue Terminal* ☎ *612/123–6600* 🌐 *www.bajaferries.com*).

Hospitals Centro de Especialidades Médicas (✉ *Calle Delfines 110* ☎ *612/124-0400*).

Internet Baja Net (✉ *Av. Madero 430* ☎ *612/125-9380*).

Pharmacies Farmacia Baja California (✉ *Calle Independencia at Calle Madero* ☎ *612/122-0240*).

WORD OF MOUTH

"How about a short flight to La Paz? It's truly a city of Peace & Serenity as it's name implies. It's a small city that is the capital of Baja Sur (South) on the Sea of Cortes. Lovely restaurants, an excellent museum, a great Malecon to stroll on & nearby wonderful beaches. Check it out." —Stewbear

EXPLORING

4 The downtown church, **Catedral de Nuestra Señora de la Paz,** is a simple, unassuming stone building with a modest gilded altar. The church was built in 1860 near the site of La Paz's first mission, which was established that same year by Jesuit priest Jaime Bravo. ✉ *Calle Juárez, Col. Centro* ☎ *No phone.*

1 ★ The **malecón** is La Paz's seawall, tourist zone, and social center all rolled into one. It runs for 5 km (3 mi) along Paseo Álvaro Obregón, and has a sidewalk as well as several park areas in the sand just off it. Paceños are fond of strolling the malecón at sunset. Teenagers slowly cruise the street in their spiffed-up cars, couples nuzzle on park benches, and grandmothers meander along while keeping an eye on the kids. (You will see people swimming here, and the water is possibly clean, but the beaches outside town are a far surer bet in that regard.) Marina La Paz, at the malecón's southwest end, is an ever-growing development with condominiums, vacation homes, and a pleasant café-lined walkway.

2 A two-story white gazebo is the focus of **Malecón Plaza,** a small concrete square where musicians sometimes appear on weekend nights. An adjacent street, Calle 16 de Septiembre, leads inland to the city.

OFF THE BEATEN PATH

The former governor's mansion is gradually being transformed into an aquarium called **Museo Acuario de las Californias,** on the road to Pichilingue. Featuring the marine life in the Sea of Cortez, the tanks containing lobster, corals, and rays are located inside the building, while the exterior has ponds and waterfalls. The house faces a coral reef; plans in the works include snorkeling programs and educational workshops. The facility has been a work in progress in recent years; expansion is still ongoing and likely will be for the near future. (Funds have materialized slowly.) No matter: an enthusiastic cadre of volunteers is happy to show you around what is in operation. ✉ *Hwy. to Pichilingue, Km 7* ☎ *No phone* *Donation requested* ⏲ *Daily 10–2.*

5 La Paz's culture and heritage are well represented at the **Museo de Antropología,** which has re-creations of indigenous Comondu and Las Palmas villages, photos of cave paintings found in Baja, and copies of Cortés's writings on first sighting La Paz. All exhibit descriptions are in Spanish only, but the museum's staff will help you translate. If you're a true Baja aficionado and want to delve into the region's history, this museum is a must; otherwise, a quick visit is all you need, if even

Catedral de Nuestra Señora de La Paz **4**
Malecón **1**
Malecón Plaza ...**2**
Museo de Antropología **5**
Plaza Constitución **3**

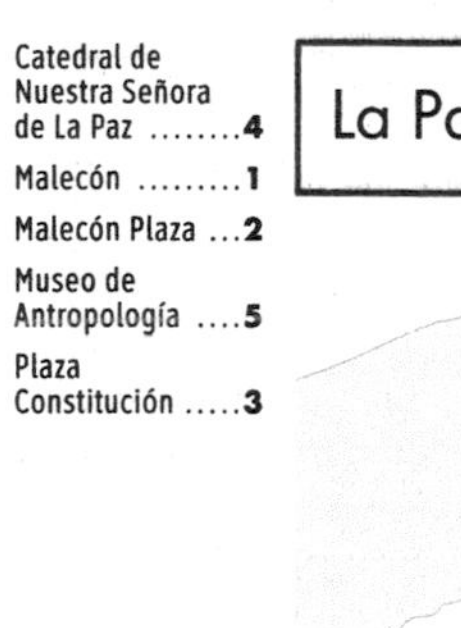

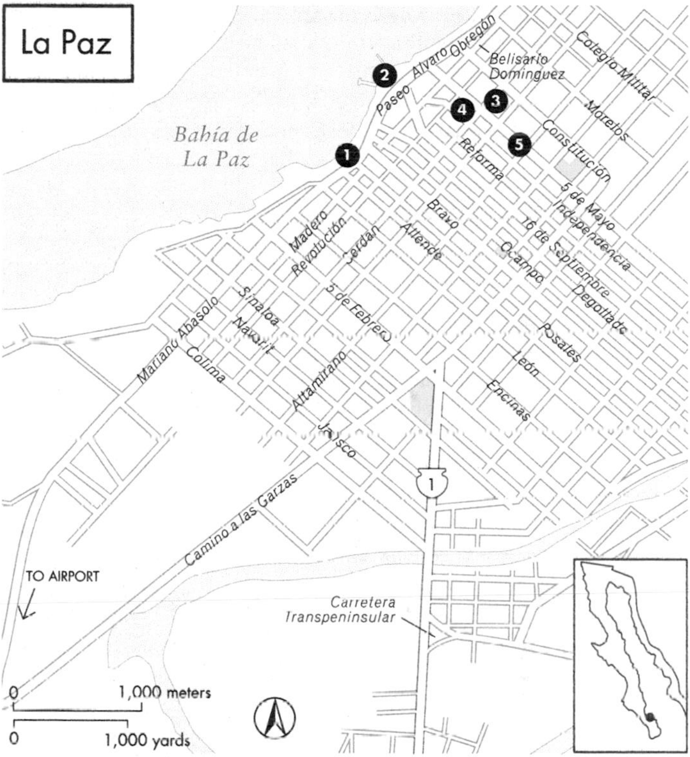

that. ✉ *Calle Altamirano at Calle 5 de Mayo, Centro* ☎ *612/122–0162* 🎟 *Donation requested* ⏲ *Daily 9–6.*

❸ **Plaza Constitución,** the true center of La Paz, is a traditional zócalo that also goes by the name Jardín Velazco. Concerts are held in the park's gazebo, and locals gather here for art shows and fairs.

BEACHES

Around the malecón, stick to ambling along the sand while watching local families enjoy the sunset. Just north of town the beach experience is much better; it gets even better north of Pichilingue. Save your swimming and snorkeling energies for this area. All facilities listed here are available on weekends. Their availability on weekdays, especially that of lifeguards, may be spottier.

Playa Balandra. A rocky point shelters a clear, warm bay at Playa Balandra, 21 km (13 mi) north of La Paz. Several small coves and pristine beaches appear and disappear with the tides, but there's always a calm area where you can wade and swim. Snorkeling is fair around Balandra's south end, where there's a coral reef. You may spot clams, starfish, and anemones. Kayaking and snorkeling tours usually set out from around here. If not on a tour, bring your own gear, as rentals aren't normally available. The beach has a few barbecue pits, trash cans, and palapas for shade. Camping is permitted but there are no hookups. The smallish beach gets crowded on weekends, but on a weekday morning you may have the place to yourself. Sand flies can be a nuisance here between July and October. **Amenities:** Lifeguard, toilets, showers, food concession, picnic tables, grills/fire pits, parking lot, camping.

Playa Caimancito. La Concha hotel takes up some of the sand at the beach 5 km (3 mi) north of La Paz. But you can enter the beach both north and south of the hotel and enjoy a long stretch of sand facing the bay and downtown. Locals swim laps here, as the water is almost always calm and salty enough for easy buoyancy. There aren't any public facilities here, but if you wander over to the hotel for lunch or a drink you can use its restrooms and rent water toys. **Amenities:** Toilets, food concession, parking lot.

Playa El Tecolote. Spend a Sunday at Playa El Tecolote, 24 km (15 mi) north of La Paz, and you'll feel like you've experienced the Mexico of old. Families set up house on the soft sand, kids race after seagulls and each other, and *abuelas* (grandmothers) daintily lift their skirts to wade in the water. Vendors rent out beach chairs, umbrellas, kayaks, and small, motorized boats; a couple of restaurants serve up simple fare such as freshly grilled snapper. These eateries are usually open throughout the week, though they sometimes close on wintery days. Facilities include public restrooms, fire pits, and trash cans. Camping is permitted, but there are no hookups. **Amenities:** Lifeguard, toilets, showers, food concession, picnic tables, grills/fire pits, playground, parking lot, camping.

Playa Pichilingue. Starting in the time of Spanish invaders, Pichilingue, 16 km (10 mi) north of La Paz, was known for its preponderance of oysters bearing black pearls. In 1940 a disease killed them off, leaving the beach deserted. Today it's a pleasant place to sunbathe and watch sportfishing boats haul in their daily catches. Locals set up picnics here on weekend afternoons and linger until the blazing sun settles into the bay. Restaurants consisting of little more than a palapa over plastic tables and chairs serve oysters *diablo,* fresh clams, and plenty of cold beer. Pichilingue curves northeast along the bay to the terminals where the ferries from Mazatlán and Topolobampo arrive and many of the sportfishing boats depart. If La Paz is on your cruise itinerary, you'll likely dock at Pichilingue, too. One downside to this beach: traffic buzzes by on the nearby freeway. The water here, though not particularly clear, is calm enough for swimming. **Amenities:** Lifeguard, toilets, showers, food concession, picnic tables, grills/fire pits, parking lot, camping.

WHERE TO EAT

¢ CAFÉ ✕ **Caffé Gourmet.** Not far from hotels, restaurants, and important downtown sights, this small air-conditioned café is a great place to recharge with a morning espresso, chai, or smoothie, along with great pastries. Wi-Fi is available here, so you can catch up on your e-mail. Credit cards are accepted with a minimum purchase of 100 pesos (about $7). ✉ *Esquerro at Calle 16 de Septiembre, Centro* ☎ *612/122–6037* ▭ *MC, V* ⊗ *Closed Sun.*

$$$ ITALIAN Fodor's Choice ★ **✕ Caffé Milano.** La Paz's hippest, hottest dining spot sits in a century-old restored building, painted ocher on the outside with a bright blue door, and with vaulted ceilings on the inside. Owners Lei Tam and Michele Milano, natives of Hong Kong and Italy, respectively, traveled the world, gathering knowledge of the world's cuisines, before setting down in La Paz. Tam has now established herself as one of Mexico's top woman chefs. At its core, the menu is standard Italian—the pastas and breads are made fresh here daily—with local touches, such as chipotle pepper in a seafood pasta, tossed in. You can see your creation being made: the kitchen is open to view. Best of all, prices here are reasonable for what you get. ✉ *Esquerro 15, at 16 de Septiembre, Centro* ☎ *612/125–9981* 🌐 *www.caffemilano.com.mx* ▭ *MC, V* ⏲ *Closed Sun.*

$$ MEXICAN **✕ El Bismark.** The original Bismark is a bit out of the way, but it attracts families who settle down for hours at long wood tables, while waitresses divide their attention between patrons and *telenovellas* on the TV above the bar. Tuck into seafood cocktails, enormous grilled lobsters, or carne asada served with beans, guacamole, and homemade tortillas. However, the restaurant is most loved for its seafood tacos, sold out of ice coolers that are set out in front of the restaurant before noon. The smaller Bismark on the malecón, called el Bismark-cito, is also popular. ✉ *Av. Degollado at Calle Altamirano, Centro* ☎ *612/122–4854* ✉ *Alvaro Obregón s/n, at the malecón* ▭ *MC, V.*

¢ VEGETARIAN **✕ El Quinto Sol Restaurante Vegetariano.** El Quinto Sol's brightly painted exterior is covered with snake symbols and smiling suns. The all-vegetarian menu includes fresh juices and herbal elixirs. The four-course prix-fixe *comida corrida* (daily special) is a bargain; it's served from noon to 4 PM. The back half of this space is a bare-bones store stocked with natural foods. ✉ *Blvd. Dominguez 60, at Av. Independencia, Centro* ☎ *612/122–1692* ▭ *No credit cards* ⏲ *Closed Sun.*

$$ ITALIAN **✕ La Pazta.** Locals who crave international fare rave about this trattoria with a sleek black-and-white interior and excellent homemade pastas and pizzas. Look for imported cheeses and wines and bracing espresso, though you can't enjoy an early morning coffee here, since La Pazta is only open for lunch and dinner. The adjacent café, however, is open for breakfast and lunch and also serves imported Italian *caffe*. Both eateries are at the Hotel Mediterrané, a small inn popular with Europeans. ✉ *Allende 36, at Hotel Mediterrane, Centro* ☎ *612/125–1195* 🌐 *www.hotelmed.com* ▭ *MC, V* ⏲ *No dinner Tues.*

$$ SEAFOOD **✕ Los Laureles.** A small stand that looks as if it might have been rolled along the street by a vendor is just the entryway decoration for this well-established restaurant. Whether you eat at a bench at the stand outside or dine within in the air-conditioning, if you like seafood, you will enjoy Los Laureles. It offers all sorts of *fruits de mer* served in many different ways, but the seafood cocktails are notable for their freshness (you can even try the shrimp raw) and variety (abalone is an option). ✉ *Paseo Alvaro Obregón s/n, Centro* ☎ *612/128–8532* ▭ *MC, V.*

$$ SEAFOOD ★ **✕ Mar y Peña.** The freshest, tastiest seafood cocktails, ceviches, and clam tacos imaginable are served in this nautical restaurant crowded with locals. If you come with friends, go for the *mariscada,* a huge platter of shellfish and fish for four. The shrimp *albondigas* (meatballs) soup

has a hearty fish stock seasoned with cilantro; and the crab *ranchero* is a savory mix of crabmeat, onions, tomatoes, and capers. Portions are huge. ✉ *Calle 16 de Septiembre between Isabel la Católica and Albáñez, Centro* ☎ *612/122–9949* ▭ *AE, MC, V.*

WHERE TO STAY

$$ **Club El Moro.** Possibly the best bargain on the malecón, although a bit away from the city center itself, this vacation-ownership resort has very reasonable suite rentals on a nightly and weekly basis. Within El Moro you'll find a palm-filled garden and a densely landscaped pool area, though the pool itself is a bit shallow for much serious swimming. You can recognize the building by its stark-white turrets and domes. Rooms are Mediterranean in style, with arched windows, Mexican tiles, and private balconies; some have ocean views. A small café serves breakfast and lunch. Fishing packages are available. **Pros:** good value; shallow pool great if you don't care to swim. **Cons:** some dated decor; rooms facing pool area can be noisy. ✉ *Hwy. to Pichilingue, Km 2* ☎ *612/122–4084* ⊕ *www.clubelmoro.com* *8 rooms, 20 suites* *In room: Wi-Fi, kitchen (some). In-hotel: restaurant, bar, pool, parking (free)* ▭ *MC, V* *CP.*

$$ Fodor's Choice ★ **el ángel azul.** Owner Esther Ammann converted La Paz's historic courthouse into a bed-and-breakfast that's a comfortable retreat in the center of the city. Rooms frame a central courtyard filled with palms and bougainvillea. Walls throughout are painted vivid yellow, coral, and blue, and rooms are decorated with original art and Mexican textiles. The rooftop suite overlooks the city. **Pros:** lovely owner; attentive service; historic building. **Cons:** street parking only. ✉ *Av. Independencia 518, at Guillermo Prieto, Centro* ☎ *612/125–5130* ⊕ *www.elangelazul.com* *10 rooms, 2 suites* *In-room: no TV, Wi-Fi. In-hotel: bar, no kids under 12* ▭ *MC, V* *CP.*

$$$ **Fiesta Inn La Paz.** As you approach this modern, bright-orange hotel, set apart from La Paz, you'll get the feeling that you are in an otherworldly place. From the towering columns that greet you as you drive up to the hotel to the size of the marble-floor lobby as you check in, the proportions in the hotel break from those of the world outside, and although you may feel a little like Alice in Wonderland at first, there is definitely room to put your feet up. Inside the rooms, many of which have views straight out over the water, things are a bit more standard. The decor is somewhat plain, much less shocking than the exterior, but the beige-and-gray interiors are agreeable. The service, which mainly caters to business travelers, is excellent. **Pros:** friendly staff; spacious rooms; stunning exterior. **Cons:** you'll need a car to stay here; ho-hum food in restaurant; plain rooms. ✉ *Hwy. to Pichilingue, Km 5, in Marina Costa* ☎ *612/123–6000* ⊕ *www.fiestamericana.com* *114 rooms, 6 suites* *In room: Wi-Fi, safe, refrigerator. In hotel: restaurant, room service, bar, pools, gym, beachfront, Internet terminal, laundry service, parking (free)* ▭ *D, MC, V* *EP.*

$$–$$$ **Hotel Marina.** The full-service marina offers fishing, scuba diving, and kayaking. Private charters are available. Most rooms have terraces or balconies with water views, gardens surround the pool and hot tub, and a seaside promenade lines the property. Naturally, it's popular with

boaters sailing the Sea of Cortez; they share tall tales and tips at the Dinghy Dock restaurant right on the harbor. **Pros:** good value and amenities for fishing vacations. **Cons:** you may feel out of place if you're not here on a fishing vacation. ✉ *Hwy. to Pichilingue, Km 2.5* ☎ *612/121–6254, 866/262–1787 in U.S.* 🌐 *www.hotelmarina.com.mx* *85 rooms, 5 suites* *In room: safe, refrigerator (some), Wi-Fi. In-hotel: restaurant, room service, bar, tennis court, pool, spa, Internet terminal, parking (free)* ▭ *AE, MC, V* *EP.*

$$ **Hotel Seven Crown.** This very reasonable, modern, minimalist hotel is perfectly situated to one side of the malecón's action. Take off from your hotel room for nearby cafés and restaurants, and prime people-watching. Other hotels are a little farther off. Hotel Seven Crown's rooms are comfortable, if a little plain, and come complete with a small refrigerator and extra sink. Other advantages here: there's a small bar on the roof from which you can enjoy a view of the bay; no one ever seems to use the small hot tub next to the bar; and rooms have petite, private balconies. Book your excursions with the travel-agency representative in the lobby. **Pros:** central location; affordable. **Cons:** very simple rooms; some rooms facing street can be noisy. ✉ *Paseo Alvaro Obregón 1710, Centro* ☎ *612/128–7788* 🌐 *www.sevencrownhotels.com* *55 rooms, 9 suites* *In-room: kitchen (some), refrigerator, Wi-Fi. In-hotel: restaurant, room service, bar, parking (free)* ▭ *MC, V* *EP.*

$$ **La Casa Mexicana Inn.** Arlaine Cervantes has created a lovely homelike ambience in her small bed-and-breakfast just one block from the malecón. The rooms are exquisite in calming pastels with niches and shelves full of folk art, beds with hand-carved headboards, wrought-iron work, Guatemalan textiles, and custom ceiling and door moldings. Some rooms overlook the bay, while others face the peaceful garden. Guests rave about the breakfasts (for an extra cost), with local fruit, Mexican pastries, crepes, frittatas, and home-baked breads. **Pros:** central location; friendly owner; attentive service. **Cons:** not right on malecón. ✉ *Calle Nicolas Bravo 106, Centro* ☎ *612/125–2748* 🌐 *www.casamex.com* *6 rooms* *In-room: no phone, no TV, kitchen (some), Wi-Fi, refrigerator. In-hotel: no kids under 10, parking (free)* ▭ *MC, V* *EP.*

$$–$$$ **La Concha Beach Resort.** On a long beach with calm water, this older resort has a water-sports center and a notable restaurant. Rooms can be dark and uninviting, but are gradually being renovated with white walls and cheery yellow-and-blue textiles. If you can, splurge on a condo unit with a separate bedroom and kitchen. These are in a separate apartment-style building with an elevator, within walking distance of the beach. There's also an infrequent shuttle to town. **Pros:** renovated rooms in good shape; lower priced rooms are good value. **Cons:** you'll need a car to stay here; some dark rooms. ✉ *Hwy. to Pichilingue, Km 5* ☎ *612/121–6161, 800/999–2252 in U.S.* 🌐 *www.laconcha.com* *107 rooms* *In-room: refrigerator. In-hotel: restaurant, room service, bar, pool, beachfront, diving, water sports, laundry service, Internet terminal, Wi-Fi hotspot, parking (free)* ▭ *AE, MC, V* *EP.*

NIGHTLIFE

El Teatro de la Ciudad (✉ *Av. Navarro 700, Centro* ☎ *612/125–0486*) is La Paz's cultural center.

The theater seats 1,500 and stages shows by visiting and local performers. **La Terraza** (✉ *Hotel Perla, Paseo Alvaro Obregón 1570, Malecón* ☎ *612/122–0777*) is the best spot for both sunset- and people-watching along the malecón. The hotel also has a disco called **La Cabaña,** where you can dance to Latin music on weekends.

★ **Las Varitas** (✉ *Av. Independencia 111, Centro* ☎ *612/123–1590* 🌐 *www.lasvaritas.com*), a Mexican rock club, heats up after midnight.

SHOPPING

Antigua California (✉ *Paseo Alvaro Obregón 220, Malecón* ☎ *612/125–5230*) has the nicest selection of Mexican folk art in La Paz, including wooden masks and lacquered boxes from the mainland state of Guerrero. **Artesanía Cuauhtémoc** (✉ *Av. Abasolo between Calles Nayarit and Oaxaca, south of downtown, Centro* ☎ *612/122–4575*) is the workshop of weaver Fortunado Silva, who creates and sells cotton place mats, rugs, and tapestries.

★ Julio Ibarra oversees the potters and painters at **Ibarra's Pottery** (✉ *Guillermo Prieto 625, Centro* ☎ *612/122–0404*). His geometric designs and glazing technique result in gorgeous mirrors, bowls, platters, and cups.

SPORTS AND THE OUTDOORS

BOATING AND FISHING

The considerable fleet of private boats in La Paz now has room for docking at three marinas: Fidepaz Marina at the north end of town, and the Marina Palmira and Marina La Paz south of town. Most hotels can arrange trips. Tournaments are held in August, September, and October.

The **Fishermen's Fleet** (☎ *612/122–1313, 408/884–3932 in U.S.* 🌐 *www.fishermensfleet.com*) has daylong fishing on pangas (skiffs). The **Mosquito Fleet** (☎ *612/121–6120, 877/408–6769 in U.S.* 🌐 *www.bajamosquitofleet.com*) has cabin cruisers with charters starting around $550 per person for up to four people, and superpangas at $399 per person for two people.

DIVING AND SNORKELING

Popular diving and snorkeling spots include the coral banks off Isla Espíritu Santo, the sea-lion colony off Isla Partida, and the seamount 14 km (9 mi) farther north (best for serious divers).

Baja Expeditions (✉ *2625 Garnet Ave., San Diego, CA* ☎ *612/125–3828, 800/843–6967 in U.S.* 🌐 *www.bajaex.com*) runs multiday dive packages in the Sea of Cortez. Seven-day excursions aboard the 80-foot *Don José* dedicated dive boat start at $1,595 for cabin, food, and nearly unlimited diving. Live-aboard trips run from June into November. You may spot whale sharks in June.

★ The **Cortez Club** (✉ *La Concha Beach Resort, Hwy. to Pichilingue, Km 5, between downtown and Pichilingue* ☎ *612/121–6120* 🌐 *www.cortezclub.com*) is a full-scale water-sports center with equipment rental and scuba, snorkeling, kayaking, and sportfishing tours. A two-tank dive costs about $125.

Fun Baja (✉ *Hwy. to Pichilingue, Km 2* ☎ *612/106–7148* 🌐 *www.funbaja.com*) offers scuba and snorkel trips with the sea lions. Two-tank scuba trips start at $135.

KAYAKING

The calm waters off La Paz are perfect for kayaking, and you can take
★ multiday trips along the coast to Loreto or out to the nearby islands. **Baja Expeditions** (✉ *2625 Garnet Ave., San Diego, CA* ☎ *612/125–3828, 800/843–6967 in U.S.* 🌐 *www.bajaex.com*), one of the oldest outfitters working in Baja (since 1974), offers several kayak tours, including multinight trips between Loreto and La Paz. A support boat carries all the gear, including ingredients for great meals. The seven-day trip in the Sea of Cortez with camping on remote island beaches starts at $1,395 per person, based on double occupancy.

Baja Quest (✉ *Sonora 174, Centro* ☎ *612/123–5320* 🌐 *www.bajaquest.com.mx*) has day and overnight kayak trips. Day trips cost $90 per person. **Fun Baja** (✉ *Hwy. to Pichilingue, Km 2* ☎ *612/121–5884, 800/667–5362 in U.S.* 🌐 *www.funbaja.com*) offers kayak trips around the islands, scuba and snorkel excursions, and land tours. A day of kayaking and snorkeling will run about $125. **Nichols Expeditions** (✉ *497 N. Main, Moab, UT* ☎ *800/648–8488 in U.S.* 🌐 *www.nicholsexpeditions.com*) arranges kayaking tours to Isla Espíritu Santo and between Loreto and La Paz, with camping along the way. A nine-day trip costs $1,350. It also offers a combination of sea kayaking in the Sea of Cortez with whale-watching in Magdalena Bay. A nine-day trip costs $1,400.

WHALE-WATCHING

La Paz is a good entry point for whale-watching expeditions to Bahía Magdalena, 266 km (165 mi) northwest of La Paz on the Pacific coast. Note, however, that such trips entail about six hours of travel from La Paz and back for two to three hours on the water. Only a few tour companies provide this as a daylong excursion, however, because of the time and distance constraints.

Many devoted whale-watchers opt to stay overnight in San Carlos, the small town by the bay. Most La Paz hotels can make arrangements for excursions, or you can head out on your own by renting a car or taking a public bus from La Paz to San Carlos, and then hiring a boat captain to take you into the bay. The air and water are cold during whale season from December to April, so you'll need to bring a warm windbreaker and gloves. Captains are not allowed to "chase" whales, but that doesn't keep the whale mamas and their babies from approaching your panga so closely that you can reach out and touch them.

An easier expedition is a whale-watching trip in the Sea of Cortez from La Paz, which involves boarding a boat in La Paz and motoring around until whales are spotted. They most likely won't come as close to the boats and you won't see the mothers and newborn calves at play, but it's still fabulous watching the whales breeching and spouting nearby.

Baja Expeditions (✉ *2625 Garnet Ave., San Diego, CA* ☎ *612/125–3828, 800/843–6967 in U.S.* 🌐 *www.bajaex.com*) runs adventure cruises around the tip of Baja between La Paz and Magdalena Bay. The eight-day cruises start at $1,995 per person, based on double occupancy.

Shorter trips including camping at Magdalena Bay are available through **Baja Quest** (✉ *Sonora 174, Centro* ☎ *612/123–5320* 🌐 *www.bajaquest.com.mx*). The two-night camping trip starts at $695 per person; the four-night trip starts at $1,050 per person. The water-sports center **Cortez Club** (✉ *La Concha Beach Resort, Hwy. to Pichilingue, Km 5, between downtown and Pichilingue* ☎ *612/121–6120* 🌐 *www.cortezclub.com*) runs extremely popular whale-watching trips in winter. The one-day excursion costs $150 per person.

LORETO

354 km (220 mi) north of La Paz.

Loreto's setting on the Sea of Cortez is spectacular: the gold and green hills of the Sierra de la Giganta seem to tumble into cobalt water. The desert climate harbors few bothersome insects, and according to local promoters, the skies are clear 360 days of the year.

The indigenous Kikiwa, Cochimí, Cucapa, and Kumiai peoples first inhabited the barren lands of Baja. Jesuit priest Juan María Salvatierra founded the first California mission at Loreto in 1697, and not long afterward the indigenous populations were nearly obliterated by disease and war. Seventy-two years later, a Franciscan monk from Mallorca, Spain—Father Junípero Serra—set out from here to establish a chain of missions from San Diego to San Francisco, in the land then known as Alta California.

Loreto has a population of around 13,000 full-time residents and an increasing number of part-timers who winter at hotels, homes, and trailer parks. It's still a good place to escape the crowds, relax, and go fishing or whale-watching. The Parque Maritímo Nacional Bahía de Loreto protects much of the Sea of Cortez in this area, but there are a few cruise ships that use Loreto as a port of call, and the marina at Puerto Escondido is central to the government's plans for a series of marinas.

GETTING HERE AND AROUND

The Aeropuerto Internacional Loreto (LTO) is 7 km (4½ mi) southwest of town. Alaska Airlines flies from Los Angeles to Loreto on Thursday and Sunday; its affiliate Horizon Air does the route on Tuesday and Friday. Aereo Calafia connects Loreto with Los Cabos daily. Several airlines connect Loreto with Mexico City and other domestic airports in Mexico. Taxis from the airport into town are inexpensive (about $5) and convenient. Loreto's Terminal de Autobus sits at the entrance to town and has service from La Paz, Los Cabos, and points north. In Loreto taxis are in good supply, and fares are inexpensive; it costs $5 or less to get anywhere in town and about $10 from downtown Loreto to Nopoló. Illegitimate taxis aren't a problem in this region. **■ TIP→ Don't go north from here without a full tank of gas; Pemex stations between Loreto and Guerrero Negro have been known to run out of gas on occasion.**

ESSENTIALS

Airlines Aereo Calafia (☎ *613/135–2503* 🌐 *www.aereocalafia.com.mx*). Alaska Airlines/Horizon Air (☎ *800/252–7522* 🌐 *www.alaskaair.com*).

Bus Contacts Loreto Terminal de Autobus (✉ *Calle Salvatierra at Calle Tamaral* ☎ *613/135–0767*). SuburBaja (☎ *624/146–0888*).

Visitor and Tour Info Loreto Tourist Information Office (✉ *Municipal Bldg. on Plaza Principal, Loreto* ☎ *613/135–0411* 🌐 *www.gotoloreto.com*).

EXPLORING

★ **El Museo de las Misiónes,** also called the Museo de Historia y Antropología (Missions Museum or Museum of History and Anthropology), contains religious relics, 19th-century leather saddles, and displays on Baja's history. A permit to take photos is an extra $2.50 beyond the admission price. ✉ *Calle Salvatierra s/n, next to La Misión de Nuestra Señora de Loreto* ☎ *613/135–0441* 💳 *$2.50* ⏲ *Tues.–Sun. 9–noon and 2–6.*

Loreto's main historic sight is **La Misión de Nuestra Señora de Loreto** (✉ *Calle Salvatierra at Calle Misioneros* ☎ *613/135–0005*). The stone church's bell tower is the town's main landmark, rising above the main plaza and reconstructed pedestrian walkway along Salvatierra.

The **malecón** along Calle de la Playa (also called Paseo Lopez Mateos) is a pleasant place to walk, jog, or sit on a cast-iron bench watching the sunset. A small marina shelters yachts and the panga fleet; the adjoining beach is popular with locals, especially on Sunday afternoons, when kids hit the playground.

Puerto Escondido, 25 km (15½ mi) down Highway 1 from Loreto, has an RV park, **Tripui** (☎ *613/133–0814* 🌐 *www.tripui.com*), with a good restaurant, a few motel rooms, a snack shop, a bar, stores, showers, a laundry, a pool, and tennis courts. There's a boat ramp at the small Puerto Escondido marina close to Tripui; you pay the fee required to launch here to the attendant at the parking lot. The **port captain's office** (☎ *613/135–0656*) is just south of the ramp, but it's rarely open.

Isla Danzante, 5 km (3 mi) southeast of Puerto Escondido, has good reefs and diving opportunities.

You can arrange picnic trips to **Isla Coronados,** inhabited only by seals, sea lions, and seabirds, from Loreto or Puerto Escondido. The snorkeling and scuba diving off the island are excellent. Danzante and other islands off Loreto are part of the Parque Maritímo Nacional Bahía de Loreto. Commercial fishing boats aren't allowed within the 60-square-km (23-square-mi) park.

★ A trip to **Misión San Javier,** 32 km (20 mi) southwest of Loreto, shows Baja at its best. A high-clearance vehicle is useful for the two-hour drive to the mission—don't try getting here if the dirt-and-gravel road is muddy. The road climbs past small ranches, palm groves, and the steep cliffs of the Cerro de la Giganta. Marked trails lead off the road to remnants of a small cluster of indigenous cave paintings. The mission village is a remote community of some 50 full-time residents, many of whom come outdoors when visitors arrive.

CLOSE UP

Baja's Gray Whales

A small boat glides through clear waters off Baja, its passengers bundled in jackets and scarves. Suddenly someone spots a dark shape slicing through the water like a submarine. Everyone sits still and silent as the creature moves closer, emitting gusts of air. And then, there she is: a 20-ton mama right by the boat. The interlopers tentatively reach out to touch the gray whale, her skin crusty with mollusks. She opens her enormous eyes, and slowly allows a small form to surface from beneath her fin and nuzzle a human hand. The scene repeats itself as the whale grows comfortable. Cheering and clapping, the enraptured passengers click photos, film videos, and generally perform as they would around any darling baby.

Every December through March, gray whales swim 8,000 km (nearly 5,000 mi) south from Alaska's Bering Strait to the tip of the Baja Peninsula. Up to 6,000 whales swim past and stop close to the shore at several spots to give birth to their calves. These newborns weigh about half a ton and consume nearly 50 gallons of milk a day.

The best places for close encounters are Bahía Magdalena (aka Mag Bay), which is about 266 km (165 mi) northwest of La Paz and 94 km (58 mi) southwest of Loreto, and Laguna San Ignacio, which is about 70 km (43 mi) southwest of San Ignacio. Less accessible is Parque Natural de la Ballena Gris (Gray Whale Natural Park) at Scammon's Lagoon near Guerrero Negro, about 227 km (141 mi) northwest of San Ignacio at the border with Baja Norte. There are no flights into this remote Pacific coast area, which is usually accessed by car or bus from the Tijuana border 720 km (447 mi) north. Several U.S. and Mexican companies provide multiday tours to the various whale-watching areas that include overnight stays in small hotels or camps.

Whale-watching boats—most of them *pangas*—must get permission from the Mexican government to enter the whale-watching areas. The experience itself entails a trip into the lagoons in a small boat. It's usually chilly, and passengers are bundled up but ready to take off their gloves if a whale comes near. But for a better view, and an easier stay in this rugged country, travel with an outfitter who will arrange your transportation, accommodations, and time on the water. Bring along a telephoto lens and lots of film or a high-capacity memory card if you're shooting digital. Binoculars come in handy as well.

The mission church (circa 1699), which is set in the middle of orchards, is built of blocks of gray volcanic rock and topped with domes and bell towers containing three bells from the 18th and 19th centuries. The side stained-glass windows are framed with wood. Inside, a gilded central altar contains a statue of Saint Xavier; side altars have statues of Saint Ignacio and the Virgen de los Dolores. Vestments from the 1700s are displayed in a glass cabinet. The church is often locked; ask anyone hanging about to find the person with the keys. Slip a few pesos into the contribution box as a courtesy to the village's inhabitants, who need all the help they can get to keep the church well maintained. Loreto residents make pilgrimages to the mission for the patron saint's festival, celebrated December 1–3. Although you can drive to San Javier on your own, it helps to have a guide along to lead you to the caves and indigenous paintings. Many hotels and tour companies can arrange trips. In San Javier you can spend the night at **Casa Ana** (☎ *613/135–1552*) in a little bungalow near the mission, to get a rare view into a small Baja community ($35 per night).

WHERE TO EAT

$ ECLECTIC ✕ **Café Olé.** Locals and gringos alike hang out at this casual spot for terrific breakfasts of scrambled eggs with chorizo (sausage), huevos rancheros, and other typical, delicious Mexican breakfasts. Later in the day (it's open until 10 PM most nights) it steers away from Mexican specialties and also serves good burgers, french fries, and ice cream. If you come on Sunday, make it breakfast or a very early lunch; it closes at 1 PM. ✉ *Calle Francisco Madero 14* ☎ *613/135–0496* 💳 *No credit cards* ⏲ *No dinner Sun.*

$ MEXICAN ★ ✕ **Canipole.** Sofía Rodríguez reigns over the open kitchen of this down-home, open-air Mexican restaurant. The 34 ingredients she uses in her savory mole are displayed in tiny bowls on one table, the ingredients for her homemade Mexican hot chocolate are in bowls on another. Pots of *pozole* (a hominy stew) and tortilla soup simmer over a gas fire on the patio while Sofia pats out fresh tortillas for each order. Specialties include *conejo* (rabbit), quesadillas with *flor de calabaza* (squash blossoms), and unusual carnitas made with lamb. Check out the view of the mission's dome from the restaurant's backyard. ✉ *Pino Suárez s/n beside mission* ☎ *613/133–0282* 💳 *No credit cards* ⏲ *Closed Sun.*

$$ STEAKHOUSE ✕ **El Nido.** If you're hungry for steak, chicken, and hearty Mexican combo plates, then this is your place. It's as close as you'll get to a steak house in these parts. The brass and woodwork and the courteous waiters make this a good place for a special night out or a big, satisfying meal after a hard day's fishing or kayaking. If you come for lunch, make it a late one; the restaurant opens at 1 PM. ✉ *Calle Salvatierra 154* ☎ *613/135–2445* 💳 *No credit cards.*

$$ ECLECTIC Fodor's Choice ★ ✕ **Pachamama.** The owners—she's from Argentina, he's from Mexico City—have combined their cultures and cuisines to create a restaurant worth repeat visits. Nibble on regional cheeses or empanadas, then move on to a salad of goat cheese and sliced homegrown tomatoes or a marinated *arrachera* (flank steak). Sandwiches on homemade bread make you wish the place were open for lunch. ✉ *Calle Zapata between Calles Salvatierra and Juárez* ☎ *613/135–2219* 💳 *MC, V* ⏲ *Closed Tues. No lunch.*

WHERE TO STAY

$$ 🏨 **Hotel Luna.** This Swiss-owned, modern hotel is clean and minimalist. There are only three rooms, and no lobby to speak of, only a small office. The rooms are air-conditioned and comfortable, with a small sofa and shelves to put away your things; the palette is mostly a stark white, decorated with beige, browns, and grays. Prices are reasonable. **Pros:** good value; comfortable, if spartan, rooms. **Cons:** few amenities; rooms can feel a bit claustrophobic. ✉ *Benito Juárez s/n* ☎ *613/135–2288* 🌐 *www.hotellunaloreto.com* *3 rooms* *In room: Wi-Fi. In hotel: bar, parking (free)* 💳 *MC, V* *EP.*

$$ **Hotel Oasis.** One of the original in-town hostelries, the Oasis remains an ideal base for those who want to be in town and spend plenty of time on the water. Rooms vary greatly in size and comfort; the best have coffeemakers, water views, and hammocks on the front terraces. Guests gather in the large bar to wish each other luck over breakfast or exchange fishing tales in the evening. Meal plans vary with the season and with packages. The hotel has its own fleet of skiffs. **Pros:** central location; friendly staff, knowledgeable about the fishing scene. **Cons:** some plain rooms; room quality varies greatly; you'll feel out of place if you're not here to fish. ✉ *Calle de la Playa, Apdo. 17* ☎ *613/135–0211, 866/482–0247 in U.S.* ⊕ *www.hoteloasis.com* *27 rooms, 12 suites* *In-room: no phone (some), refrigerator, Wi-Fi. In-hotel: restaurant, room service, bar, pool, Internet terminal, parking (free)* *MC, V* *BP, EP, FAP.*

$$$ **Hotel Posada de las Flores.** The rose-color walls of this surprisingly chic hotel rise beside downtown's plaza. The public areas are its forte. A glass-bottom pool doubles as a skylight above the atrium lobby, and the rooftop sundeck and restaurant have huge planters of bougainvillea. Exposed beams and locally crafted tiles adorn the lobby and hallways. Guest rooms, however, can be very dark and noisy, though they are also beautifully decorated. Have a drink at the rooftop bar for a good view of town and the mountains. There is also a tapas bar that is open in the evenings on the ground level. Sit outside and you can people-watch while you munch. **Pros:** beautiful public spaces; pool above lobby ceiling is novel to watch. **Cons:** some dark, noisy rooms. ✉ *Calle Salvatierra at Calle Francisco Madero* ☎ *613/135–1162* ⊕ *www.posadadelasflores.com* *10 rooms, 5 suites* *In-room: safe, refrigerator, Wi-Fi. In-hotel: restaurant, bar, pool, laundry service, no kids under 12, parking (free)* *MC, V* *CP.*

$ **Motel el Dorado.** Low rates, accessible parking, and a congenial bar are available at this spanking-clean motel. All that's missing is a pool, but the waterfront is a block away. Rooms are classic Baja basic, with thin mattresses, TVs anchored to the walls, and inexpensive dark-wood furnishings. The motel also offers motorbike rentals and fishing charters. A seven-hour trip on a 23-foot boat goes for $175. **Pros:** good value; immaculate rooms. **Cons:** no-frills rooms; a pool would be a nice addition in the heat. ✉ *Paseo Hidalgo at Calle Pipila* ☎ *613/135–1500 or 888/314–9023* ⊕ *www.moteleldorado.com* *11 rooms* *In-room: no phone, Wi-Fi. In-hotel: bar, laundry service, parking (free)* *MC, V* *EP.*

$–$$ **Sukasa.** Roomy air-conditioned bungalows with brick-and-stucco walls, palapa ceilings, and separate bedrooms are clustered in a compound just steps from the malecón. One sturdy, canvas-sided yurt is another affordable and definitely unique option. It's easy to imagine you've moved to Loreto, at least for a while, as you set up housekeeping in the kitchen and wander across the street, coffee in hand, to watch the sun rise and set. The manager is a delight, quick to make guests feel totally at home and set up excursions. Kayaks and bikes are also on hand for guest use. **Pros:** lovely owner; friendly service; yurt is a kick to stay in. **Cons:** some street noise. ✉ *Calle de la Playa at Calle*

Jordan ☎ 613/135–0490 🌐 www.loreto.com/sukasa *3 bungalows, 1 yurt* *In-room: kitchen, Wi-Fi. In hotel: water sports, parking (free)* *MC, V* *EP.*

SHOPPING

★ Loreto's shopping district is along the pedestrian zone on Calle Salvatierra, where there are several souvenir shops and stands, plus the town's only supermarket. **El Alacrán** (✉ *Calle Salvatierra 47* ☎ *613/135–0029*) has remarkable folk art, jewelry, and sportswear.

SPORTS AND THE OUTDOORS

FISHING

Fishing put Loreto on the map. You can catch cabrilla and snapper year-round, yellowtail in spring, and dorado, marlin, and sailfish in summer. If you're a serious angler, bring tackle. Some sportfishing fleets do update their equipment regularly. All Loreto-area hotels can arrange fishing, and many own skiffs. Local anglers congregate with their small boats on the beach at the north and south ends of town.

Arturo's Fishing Fleet (✉ *Paseo Hidalgo between plaza and marina* ☎ *613/135–0766* 🌐 *www.arturosport.com*) has several types of boats and fishing packages. The **Baja Big Fish Company** (✉ *Paseo Hidalgo 19, by plaza* ☎ *613/135–1603* 🌐 *www.bajabigfish.com*), which specializes in light tackle and fly-fishing, has packages from the United States that sometimes include free hotel nights and fishing trips from Loreto. Half-day fishing rates start at $270.

WATER SPORTS

Arrange kayaking excursions, whale-watching tours, scuba-certification courses, and dive and snorkeling trips through the **Baja Outpost** (✉ *Blvd. Mateos near Oasis Hotel* ☎ *613/135–1134, 888/649–5951 in U.S.* 🌐 *www.bajaoutpost.com*). The company specializes in sports packages. A three-day, two-night snorkeling package starts at $223 per person based on double occupancy in its hotels; with kayaking, the package starts at $307. The company also offers day tours to Misión San Javier.

Dolphin Dive Center (✉ *Calle Juárez between Calles Davis and Playa* ☎ *613/135–1914* 🌐 *www.dolphindivebaja.com*) is a PADI shop offering dives around the islands off Loreto and instruction. A two-tank trip costs $99–$120 depending on location; snorkeling excursions run $65. The company also has whale-watching and Misión San Javier tours.

Paddling South (📫 *Box 827, Calistoga, CA 94515* ☎ *800/398–6200 in U.S.* 🌐 *www.tourbaja.com*) runs guided kayaking trips starting at $1,045, including meals. The company also offers mountain-biking trips, and multiday mule pack trips with a historical focus.

The U.S.–based company **Sea Quest Expeditions** (☎ *888/589–4253 in U.S.* 🌐 *www.sea-quest-kayak.com*) has several trips that begin in Loreto. Options include kayaking with gray whales in Magdalena Bay or in the San Ignacio Lagoon. Weeklong trips start at $1,299.

MULEGÉ

134 km (83 mi) north of Loreto.

Mulegé (pronounced moo-lay-HAY) is a popular base for exploring the Sierra de Guadalupe mountains, the site of several prehistoric rock paintings of human and animal figures. Kayaking in Bahía Concepción, Baja's largest protected bay, is spectacular.

Once a mission settlement, this charming town of some 3,500 residents swells in winter, when Americans and Canadians fleeing the cold arrive in droves of motor homes. Amid an oasis of date palms on the banks of the Río Santa Rosalía, Mulegé looks and feels more tropical than other Baja Sur communities. Several narrow streets make up the business district, and dirt roads run from the highway to RV parks south of town.

Access to the rock paintings is good, though you must have a permit and be accompanied by a licensed guide. Tours typically involve a bumpy ride followed by an even bumpier climb on the backs of burros. **Mulegé Tours** (⊠ *Madero 50* ☎ *615/161–4987* 🌐 *www.mulegetours.com*) is run by Salvador Castro, a Mulegé native. He leads treks to the cave paintings and to working ranches in the mountains.

GETTING HERE AND AROUND

Mulegé's bus terminal sits 4 km (2½ mi) north of town. Informal taxis wait for each arriving bus and take you where you need to go. Services come and go from Loreto, Santa Rosalía, San Ignacio, and Guerrero Negro several times daily. ■ **TIP→ The one Pemex gas station in town periodically runs out of fuel.**

WHERE TO STAY

$$ ★ **Hotel Serenidad.** A Mulegé mainstay for Baja aficionados since the late 1960s, this delightful escape is owned by the Johnson family, longtime residents. The Serenidad's simple rooms in brick-and-stucco buildings are scattered under bougainvillea vines and fruit trees. Some suites have fireplaces and separate bedrooms. An expansive riverfront villa is set off from the complex and is fully furnished. (There's a minimum five-night stay in the villa.) The Saturday-night pig roast is a tradition. **Pros:** owners are a wealth of information about Baja; weekly pig roast is fun. **Cons:** lots of activity, so not a good option if you seek solitude. ✥ *2½ km (1½ mi) north of Mulegé, Hwy. 1* ☎ *615/153–0530* 🌐 *www.serenidad.com* *40 rooms 10 suites, 1 villa* *In-room: no phone, kitchen (some) Wi-Fi. In-hotel: restaurant, bar, pool* *MC, V* *EP.*

SANTA ROSALÍA

64 km (40 mi) north of Mulegé.

The architecture in this dusty mining town is a fascinating mix of French, Mexican, and American Old West styles. It's so different from other architecture in the area that you can easily forget you're in Baja California.

GETTING HERE AND AROUND

The Ferry Santa Rosalía makes four-times-weekly crossings between Santa Rosalía and Guaymas on the mainland, departing Tuesday and Wednesday at 9 AM and Friday and Sunday at 8 AM. The cost is $65 per person. The ferry terminal at the harbor also serves as Santa Rosalía's bus terminal, with services to Loreto, La Paz, San Ignacio, and Mulegé several times daily. The Pemex gas station in town has a reputation for overcharging and/or shortchanging tourists; fill up elsewhere if you can, although the spottiness of stations between Loreto and Guerrero Negro means you might need to do it here.

ESSENTIALS

Ferry Contacts **Ferry Santa Rosalía** (✉ *Marina Santa Rosalía* ☎ *615/152–0013* 🌐 *www.ferrysantarosalia.com*).

EXPLORING

Santa Rosalía is known for its **Iglesia Santa Bárbara** (✉ *Av. Obregón at Calle Altamirano*), a prefabricated iron church designed by Alexandre-Gustave Eiffel, creator of the Eiffel Tower. The iron panels of the little church are brightened by stained-glass windows.

WHERE TO EAT AND STAY

¢ CAFÉ ✕ **El Boleo.** Be sure to stop by this small shop where fresh breads tempt customers weekday mornings at 10 AM. The name, El Boleo, is taken from the French mining company that moved into town to exploit the mineral riches of the land here in the late 1800s. Try the *pitahaya,* an unexpected and very tasty combination of a sort of sugar cookie and bread roll in one. You won't find it anywhere else. ✉ *Av. Obregón at Calle 4* ☎ *615/152–0310* ▭ *No credit cards.*

$ **Hotel Francés.** The glory days of this well-kept 1886 French hillside mansion shine through. The lobby is decorated with framed embroidered flowers, old black-and-white photos of the town, and lace curtains. Many rooms open onto a second-story porch with views of town and the sea. There's a small pool and a classy restaurant in the courtyard. **Pros:** historic building; friendly staff. **Cons:** can be difficult to find (double-check your directions). ✉ *Av. 11 de Julio at Calle Jean M. Cousteau* ☎ *615/152–2052* *16 rooms* *In-room: Wi-Fi. In-hotel: restaurant, pool, laundry service, Internet terminal, parking (free)* ▭ *No credit cards* *EP.*

SAN IGNACIO

77 km (48 mi) west of Santa Rosalia.

Although San Ignacio is in the Desierto de Vizcaíno, date palms, planted by Jesuit missionaries in the late 1700s, sway gently, in sync with the town's laid-back rhythms. San Ignacio is primarily a place to organize whale-watching and cave-painting tours or to stop and cool off in the shady zócalo (town square).

GETTING HERE AND AROUND

San Ignacio has no bus terminal per se. Coaches head north to Guerrero Negro and south to Santa Rosalía and beyond several times a day and stop next to the Pemex station here. Buy your tickets when you board the bus. ■ **TIP→ The Pemex gas station here occasionally runs out of fuel. Fill up elsewhere to be on the safe side.**

WHERE TO STAY

$$ **Desert Inn.** This simple, functional hotel is a pleasant place to stay on your trans-peninsular journey—it's part of a six-hotel Baja-wide chain that has no connection to the famous, onetime Las Vegas lodging—although you may wish for a bit more for the money. White arches frame the courtyard and pool, and the rooms are decorated with folk art and wood furnishings. Both the river and town are within walking distance. **Pros:** good value; makes an effort to be more homey than other hotels in this chain. **Cons:** no-frills service; grounds are drab. *2 km (1 mi) west of Hwy. 1 on unnamed road into San Ignacio 615/157–1305, 619/275–4500, 800/542–3283 in U.S. www.desertinns.com 28 rooms In-room: No phone, Wi-Fi. In-hotel: restaurant, room service, bar, pool, laundry service, parking (free) MC, V EP.*

SPORTS AND THE OUTDOORS

San Ignacio is the base for trips to Laguna San Ignacio, 59 km (37 mi) from San Ignacio on the Pacific coast. The lagoon is one of the best places to watch the gray-whale migration.

★ Tours arranged through **Baja Discovery** (*Box 152527, San Diego, CA 92195 619/262–0700 or 800/829–2252 www.bajadiscovery.com*) include round-trip transport from San Diego to San Ignacio Lagoon, by van to Tijuana and private plane to the company's comfortable camp at the lagoon. Accommodations are in private tents facing the water, and there are solar-heated showers. The cost of a five-day package—including transportation, tours, and meals—is $2,375.

★ **Baja Expeditions** (*2625 Garnet Ave., San Diego, CA 612/125–3828 in La Paz, 800/843–6967 in U.S. www.bajaex.com*) operates a camp at San Ignacio Lagoon and runs five-day tours including air transportation from San Diego. The fee is $2,295 including transport, meals, and tours. **Ecoturísticos Kuyima** (*Av. Morelos 23 615/154–0070 www.kuyima.com*) in San Ignacio provides transportation between the town and San Ignacio Lagoon, operates a campground at an isolated area of the lagoon, and has adventure tours to caves with prehistoric paintings that include overnights in San Ignacio and at the lagoon. Whale-watching tours with camping and transportation from San Ignacio cost $165 per person per day. Day tours to area cave paintings from San Ignacio cost $50–$70 per person.

GUERRERO NEGRO

143 km (89 mi) northwest of San Ignacio.

Guerrero Negro, near the border with Baja Norte, is a good hub for whale-watching trips to Scammon's Lagoon. Near the Desierto de Vizcaíno (Vizcaíno Desert), on the Pacific Ocean, the area is best known for its salt pans, which produce one-third of the world's salt supply. Salt water collects in some 780 square km (301 square mi) of sea-level ponds and evaporates quickly in the desert heat, leaving great blocks of salt.

GETTING HERE AND AROUND

Guerrero Negro sits along the Carretera Transpeninsular (Highway 1) just south of the 28th parallel. That single highway provides the only access to and from the town, whether you're continuing on to Cataviña to the north or La Paz to the south. If you drive in from the north, you cross the state line into Baja California Sur as you enter Guerrero Negro. Officials at a police checkpoint at the edge of town will fumigate your vehicle's tires to protect the state from the entrance of pests that might have hitched a ride—one quick spray and you're on your way—and ask to see your passport, Mexican tourist card, and car-insurance papers. ■ **TIP→ Don't head south from here without a full tank of gas; Pemex stations between Guerrero Negro and Loreto have been known to run out of gas on occasion.** The small Aeropuerto Nacional de Guerrero Negro (GUB) sits 6 km (4 mi) north of town and offers reliable commercial flights provided by Aereoservicio Guerrero to Ensenada and Isla de Cedros.

TRUTH BE TOLD

If it weren't for the whales and the Carretera Transpeninsular, which passes nearby, few would venture into Guerrero Negro, a town of roughly 10,000. It's a dusty, windy, generally unpleasant place, except, it seems, to osprey, which are fond of roosting on area power poles.

Airlines Aereoservicio Guerrero (☎ *615/157–0137* 🌐 *www.aereoservicioguerrero.com.mx*).

EXPLORING

★ **Scammon's Lagoon** is about 27 km (17 mi) south of Guerrero Negro, down a rough but passable sand road that crosses salt flats. The lagoon got its name from U.S. explorer Charles Melville Scammon of Maine, who came here in the mid-1800s. On his first expedition Scammon and his crew collected more than 700 barrels of valuable whale oil, and the whale rush was on. Within 10 years nearly all the whales in the lagoon had been killed, and it took almost a century for the population to increase to what it had been before Scammon arrived. In the 1940s the U.S. and Mexican governments took measures to protect the whales. With a sturdy vehicle you can drive the washboard dirt road to Scammon's Lagoon and arrange a trip for about $25–$60 per person, depending on the type of boat and length of tour. Start early to take advantage of the calmest water and best viewing conditions.

WHERE TO STAY

$ ★ **Malarrimo Motel.** If you're looking for one-stop shopping, the staff at Malarrimo can wine and dine you and arrange your whale-watching expedition. The most comfortable place to stay along Boulevard Zapata, the main drag in Guerrero Negro, this motel has 18 rooms and 6 "Mex" rooms sometimes called cabañas, though they're not freestanding. The Mex rooms are a little larger, so they tend to stay cooler when the weather is warm, while the smaller rooms are better in winter. Rooms are spartan, although the hotel's miniature courtyard manages to enliven the ambience a bit. The hotel staff suggests making reservations around six months in advance if you are planning on visiting during whale-watching season. This is the largest, best-established hotel in the area, so rooms go quickly. The restaurant and bar, widely considered the best in town, are a great place to enjoy well-prepared seafood and delicious meats. The walls are covered in bric-a-brac including newspaper articles about the area, and found items like whale bones; buoys hang from the ceilings. The gift shop next door, Casa El Viejo Cactus, offers arts and crafts and a small selection of books. **Pros:** chilaquiles; fresh oysters; convenient tour operator. **Cons:** slow wait service; plain hotel rooms. ✉ *Blvd. Zapata s/n* ☎ *615/157–0250* 🌐 *www.malarrimo.com* *10 rooms, 6 "Mex" rooms* *In room: no phone, Wi-Fi. In hotel: restaurant, parking (free)* 💳 *AE, MC, V* *EP.*

SPORTS AND THE OUTDOORS

Malarrimo Eco-Tours (✉ *Blvd. Zapata s/n* ☎ *615/157–0100* 🌐 *www.malarrimo.com* 💳 *AE, MC, V*) is home to the original whale-watching tour in Guerrero Negro. You can arrange for a tour at the Malarrimo Restaurant, but to make sure that you can get a spot, reserve in advance, especially if you want to go out on a weekend. (A 50% deposit is necessary to make the reservation.) Owner Luis Enrique Achoy and his crew run two tours daily. One leaves at 8 AM and the other at 11 AM. Both tours last about four hours, and if the weather won't allow you to see the whales, Malarrimo will reschedule.

BAJA NORTE: BEACH TOWNS

The beaches of the northern peninsula are the stuff of dreams: fine sand, water that's refreshing but not too cold, excellent sunshine, and, for the surfer, some of the west coast's top waves. Part of that dream can evaporate, however, when you venture into the beach towns themselves.

More than a few of the stops along Highway 1 have been run down by years of American spring-breakers looking for a good time—and then leaving that good time's remnants behind. Ensenada is an exception: a charming fisherman's enclave, something larger than a village with a village's sleepy feel, complete with beachside trinket stores and fish taco stands (the town's beaches, conversely, are nothing special at all). Along this part of the peninsula, towns are close together, and the essentials (gas, food, lodging) are never far.

ENSENADA

75 km (47 mi) south of Rosarito.

In 1542 Juan Rodríguez Cabrillo first discovered the seaport that Sebastián Vizcaíno named Ensenada-Bahía de Todos Santos (All Saints' Bay) in 1602. Since then the town has drawn a steady stream of explorers and developers. After playing home to ranchers and gold miners, the harbor gradually grew into a major port for shipping agricultural goods, and today Baja's third-largest city (population over 369,000) is one of Mexico's largest sea- and fishing ports.

There are no beaches in Ensenada proper, but sandy stretches north and south of town are satisfactory for swimming, sunning, surfing,

DRIVING INTO MEXICO

Mexico Highway 1 (Carretera 1 or the Carretera Transpeninsular) runs 1,700 km (1,056 mi) from Tijuana to Cabo San Lucas—a weeklong journey one way. Few people go the distance, but many cross the border on their way south. A few points to ponder if you plan on driving into Mexico:

Many U.S. rental companies don't let you drive their cars into Mexico; those that do often charge fees atop the rental price and restrict how far south you can go.

You must have Mexican auto insurance, available at agencies near the border, which is sold by the day. Some reliable online outfitters that allow you to purchase insurance prior to your trip include Baja Bound (🌐 *www.bajabound.com*), Instant Mexico Auto Insurance (🌐 *www.instant-mex-auto-insur.com*), Mexico Insurance Professionals (🌐 *www.mexpro.com*), and Sanborn's Mexican Insurance (🌐 *www.sanbirnsinsurance.com*).

Plan your itinerary so that you avoid driving at night.

If you're going only as far as Ensenada or San Felipe, you don't need a tourist card unless you stay longer than 72 hours. Ask for cards at border customs offices.

You must cross the border with the following documents: vehicle title or registration, a passport or passport card, a credit card, and a valid driver's license with a photo. The names on these documents must match, if they don't, you won't be able to bring the car into the country. If the car is leased or rented, you must have a notarized letter of permission from the agency. Upon entry, you'll receive a car permit and sticker that's good for six months; be sure to turn these in before the expiration date to avoid heavy fines or restrictions on reentry

and camping. Estero Beach is long and clean, with mild waves; the Estero Beach Hotel takes up much of the oceanfront, but the beach is public. Surfers populate the strands off Carretera 1 north and south of Ensenada, particularly San Miguel, Tres Marías, and Salsipuedes; scuba divers prefer Punta Banda, by La Bufadora. Lifeguards are rare, so be cautious. The tourist office in Ensenada has a map that shows safe diving and surfing beaches.

Both the waterfront and downtown's main street are pleasant places to stroll. If you're driving, be sure to take the CENTRO exit from the highway, since it bypasses the commercial port area.

GETTING HERE AND AROUND

If you're flying into Tijuana, from Aeropuerto Alberado Rodriguez (TIJ) you can find buses that also serve Rosarito and Ensenada. Or you can hop on a bus at Tijuana Camionera de la Línea station, just inside the border, with service to Rosarito and Ensenada along with city buses to downtown. To head south from Tijuana by car, follow the signs for Ensenada Cuota, the toll road (i.e., Carretera Transpeninsular or Highway 1) along the coast. Tollbooths accept U.S. and Mexican currency; there are three tolls of about $2.50 each between Tijuana and Ensenada. Restrooms are available near toll stations. Ensenada is an hour south

CALIFORNIA
El Centro
UNITED STATES
MEXICO
Mexicali
Tijuana
Tecate
Yuma
ARIZONA
Playas de Rosarito
Laguna Salada
San Luis Río Colorado
Valle de Guadalupe
Puerto Nuevo
SIERRA DE JUÁREZ
Ensenada see detail map
La Bufadora
Punta Banda
Santo Tomás
Desierto de Altar
Nogales
BAJA
SIERRA SAN PEDRO MÁRTIR
Parque Nacional San Pedro Mártir
Colonet
San Felipe
Bahía San Felipe
Puerto Peñasco
San Quintín
CALIFORNIA
Golfo de California
Mar de Cortés
El Rosario
PACIFIC OCEAN
Puerto Sta. Catarina
Cataviña
NORTE
Isla Ángel de la Guarda
Bahía de Los Angeles
Punta Prieta
Rosarito
Bahía de Sebastián Vizcaíno
Isla Cedros
Parque Natural de Ballena Gris
Guerrero Negro
El Arco
Scammon's Lagoon
Desierto de Vizcaíno
BAJA
San Ignacio
CALIFORNIA
SUR
Laguna San Ignacio
0
100 miles
0
150 km
TO BAHÍA MAGDELENA
Baja California Norte

of Tijuana on this road. The alternative free road—Carretera 1D or Ensenada Libre—is curvy and not as well maintained. (Entry to it is on a side street in a congested area of downtown Tijuana.)

Highway 1 continues south of Ensenada to Guerrero Negro, at the border between Baja Norte and Baja Sur, and on to Baja's southernmost resorts; there are no tolls past Ensenada. Highway 1 is fairly well maintained and signposted.

> **WORD OF MOUTH**
>
> "Definitely go into Ensenada—hopefully not on a day the ships are in. [Check out the] shopping, fish market, social center, and Margaritas. The Guadalupe Valley is making a name as the wine country. Be sure to get to L A Cetto for tasting and ambiance." —camarg

Taxis are a reliable means of getting around Ensenada, and you can flag them down on the street.

ESSENTIALS

Internet **Equinoxio Internet Café** (✉ *Cárdenas 267* ☎ *646/174–0455*).

Medical Assistance **Emergencies** (☎ *Dial 066*). **Tourist Information and Assistance Hotline** (☎ *Dial 078*).

Visitor and Tour Info **Ensenada Tourist Information Office** (✉ *Lázaro Cárdenas 609, Centro* ☎ *01800/025–3991 toll-free in Mexico, 800/310–9687* ⊕ *www.enjoyensenada.com*).

EXPLORING

1 **Las Bodegas de Santo Tomás.** One of Baja's oldest wine producers gives tours and tastings at its downtown winery and bottling plant. Take a moment to see the satirical paintings in the main building, depicting the early days of the winery. Santo Tomás's best wines are the Alisio chardonnay, the cabernet, and the Sirocco syrah; avoid the overpriced Unico. The restaurant, La Embotelladora Vieja, is a marvel of modern design, and pairs dishes with the winery's picks. The winery also operates La Esquina de Bodegas, a café, shop, and gallery in a bright-blue building across the avenue. ■ **TIP→ The Santo Tomás Vineyards can be found on the eastern side of Highway 1 about 50 km (31 mi) south of Ensenada, fairly near the ruins of the Misión Santo Tomás de Aquino, which was founded by Dominican priests in 1791: only a few pieces of adobe remain of the old church.** ✉ *Av. Miramar 666, Centro* ☎ *646/174–0829* ⊕ *www.santo-tomas.com* *$5–$10, depending on wines* ⊙ *Tours, tastings daily 9–5; it's best to call first.*

2 ★ **Mercado de Mariscos.** At the northernmost point of Boulevard Costero, the main street along the waterfront, is an indoor-outdoor fish market where row after row of counters display piles of shrimp, tuna, dorado, and other fish caught off Baja's coasts. Outside, stands sell grilled or smoked fish, seafood cocktails, and fish tacos. The smoked salmon is excellent. You can pick up a few souvenirs, eat well for very little money, and take some great photographs. The original fish taco stands line the dirt path to the fish market; around lunchtime, cooks will stand outside to vie for your attention (and your pesos). If your stomach is delicate, try the fish tacos at the cleaner, quieter Plaza de Mariscos in

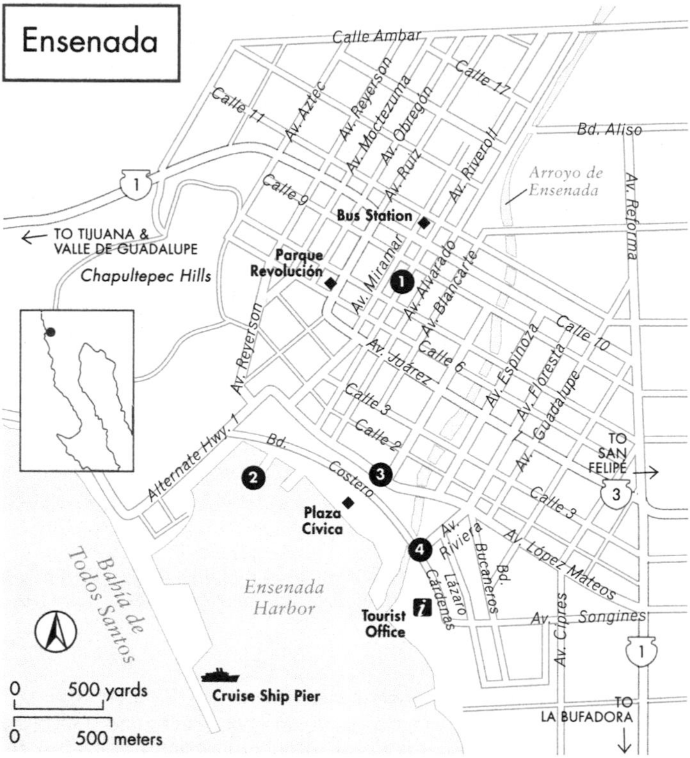

the shadow of the giant beige Plaza de Marina that blocks the view of the traditional fish market from the street.

3 **Paseo Calle Primera.** The renamed Avenida López Mateos is the center of Ensenada's traditional tourist zone. High-rise hotels, souvenir shops, restaurants, and bars line the avenue for eight blocks, from its beginning at the foot of the Chapultepec Hills to the dry channel of the Arroyo de Ensenada. The avenue also has cafés, American-style coffee shops, and most of the town's souvenir stores.

4 **Riviera del Pacífico.** Officially called the Centro Social, Cívico y Cultural de Ensenada, the Riviera is a rambling, white, hacienda-style mansion built in the 1920s. An enormous gambling palace, hotel, restaurant, and bar, the glamorous Riviera was frequented by wealthy U.S. citizens and Mexicans, particularly during Prohibition. You can tour some of the elegant ballrooms and halls, which occasionally host art shows and civic events. Many of the rooms are locked; check at the main office to see if someone is available to show you around. ✉ *Blvd. Costero at Av. Riviera, Centro* ☎ *646/177–0594* 🎟 *Building and gardens free; museum entry $2* ⏲ *Mon.–Sat. 9–5, Sun. 10–5.*

WHERE TO EAT

$$$ FRENCH **✕ El Rey Sol.** From its chateaubriand *bouquetière* (garnished with a bouquet of vegetables) to the savory chicken chipotle cooked with brandy, port wine, and cream, this French restaurant, family owned since 1947, sets a high standard. Louis XIV–style furnishings and an attentive staff make it both comfortable and elegant. The sidewalk tables are a perfect place to dine and people-watch. The small café in the front sells pastries that are made on the premises. ✉ *Av. López Mateos 1000, Centro* ☎ *646/178–1733* ▭ *AE, MC, V.*

$ MEXICAN Fodor's Choice ★ **✕ Hacienda Del Charro.** Hungry patrons hover over platters of chiles rellenos, enchiladas, and fresh chips and guacamole at heavy wooden picnic tables. Plump chickens slowly turn over a wood-fueled fire by the front window, and the aroma of simmering beans fills the air. ✉ *Av. López Mateos 454, Centro* ☎ *646/178–2351* ▭ *AE, MC, V.*

$$$ STEAKHOUSE ★ **✕ Sano's.** This elegant restaurant, along the highway heading out from Ensenada toward Tijuana, is the latest extension of the Hussong empire. It's also the best steak house in Baja California. The Sonora beef is juicy, flavorful, and tender, cooked just as beautifully rare (or done) as you order it, and it can be enjoyed on a wonderful outdoor patio. Throw in impeccable service and a wine list that rivals the best in the country, and you can justify the sky-high prices. ✉ *Carretera Tijuana–Ensenada, Km 108, just after Playitas Club del Mar if you're heading south to Ensenada* ☎ *646/174–4061* 🌐 *www.sanosrestaurant.com* ▭ *AE, DC, MC, V.*

WHERE TO STAY

$$–$$$ **Estero Beach Resort.** Families love this long-standing resort on Ensenada's top beach. The best rooms (some with kitchenettes) are by the sand. Be sure to check out the outstanding collection of folk art and artifacts in the resort's small museum. Midweek winter rates are a real bargain, and there are other frequent specials on the Web site. There's also an on-site RV park; its 38 sites have hookups for water, sewer, and electricity. **Pros:** wonderful breakfasts; right on the beach. **Cons:** rooms by parking lot aren't great; needs some updating. ✉ *Carretera Tijuana–Ensenada, 10 km (6 mi) south of Ensenada, Estero Beach* ☎ *646/176–6225* 🌐 *www.hotelesterobeach.com* *94 rooms, 2 suites* *In-room: kitchen (some). In-hotel: restaurant, bar, tennis courts, pool* ▭ *MC, V.*

$$$ **Hotel Coral & Marina.** This all-suites resort is enormous. It has a spa, tennis courts, a water-sports center, and a marina with slips for 350 boats and customs-clearing facilities. All guest quarters have refrigerators and coffeemakers. Suites in the two eight-story towers are done in burgundy and dark green; most have waterfront balconies, seating areas, and international phone service. **Pros:** affordable; spacious rooms. **Cons:** pool can get noisy with kids; can feel large and impersonal. ✉ *Carretera Tijuana-Ensenada, Km 103, Zona Playitas* ☎ *646/175–0000 or 800/862–9020* 🌐 *www.hotelcoral.com* *147 suites* *In-room: refrigerator, Wi-Fi. In-hotel: restaurant, room service, bar, tennis courts, pools, gym, spa, laundry service* ▭ *MC, V.*

$$$ Fodor's Choice ★ **Las Rosas Hotel & Spa.** All rooms in this intimate hotel north of Ensenada face the ocean and pool; some have fireplaces and hot tubs, and even the least expensive are lovely. The atrium lobby has marble floors, mint-green-and-pink couches that look out at the sea, and a glass ceiling that glows at night. **Pros:** boutique; laid-back; great ocean views from hot tub. **Cons:** no restaurants within walking distance. ✉ *Carretera Tijuana–Ensenada, just north of Ensenada, Zona Playitas* ☎ *646/174–4320* 🌐 *www.lasrosas.com* *48 rooms* *In-hotel: restaurant, bar, tennis courts, pool, gym, spa, laundry service* 💳 *MC, V.*

NIGHTLIFE

★ **Hussong's Cantina** (✉ *Av. Ruíz 113, Centro* ☎ *646/178–3210* 🌐 *www.cantinahussongs.com*) has been an Ensenada landmark since 1892, and has changed little since then. A security guard stands by the front door to handle the often-rowdy crowd—most of all local men. The floor is covered with sawdust, and the noise is usually deafening, pierced by mariachi and ranchera musicians and the whoops and hollers of the pie-eyed. **Papas & Beer** (✉ *Av. Ruíz 102, Centro* ☎ *646/174–0145*) attracts a collegiate crowd.

SHOPPING

Most of the tourist shops are found along Avenida López Mateos beside the hotels and restaurants. There are several two-story shopping arcades, some with empty spaces for rent. Dozens of curio shops line the street, all selling similar selections of pottery, sarapes, and the tackier trinkets and T-shirts.

Bazar Casa Ramírez (✉ *Av. López Mateos 496, Centro* ☎ *646/178–8209*) sells high-quality Talavera pottery and other ceramics, wrought-iron pieces, and papier-mâché figurines. Be sure to check out the displays upstairs.

★ The **Centro Artesanal de Ensenada** (✉ *Blvd. Costero 1094–39, Centro* ☎ *No phone*) has a smattering of galleries and shops.

La Esquina de Bodegas (✉ *Av. Miramar at Calle 6, Centro* ☎ *646/178–3557*) is an innovative gallery, shop, and café in a century-old winery building.

Los Globos (✉ *Calle 9, 3 blocks east of Av. Reforma, Centro* ☎ *No phone*) is a daily open-air swap meet. Vendors and shoppers are most abundant on weekends.

SPORTS AND THE OUTDOORS

SPORTFISHING

The best angling is from April through November, with bottom-fishing good in winter. Charter vessels and party boats are available from several outfitters along Avenida López Mateos and Boulevard Costero and off the sportfishing pier. Mexican fishing licenses for the day or year are available at the tourist office or from charter companies.

Sergio's Sportfishing (✉ *Sportfishing Pier, Blvd. Costero at Av. Alvarado, Centro* ☎ *646/178–2185* 🌐 *www.sergios-sportfishing.com*), one of the best sportfishing companies in Ensenada, has charter and group boats as well as boat slips for rent. The fee for a day's fishing is $50 per person on a group boat, plus the $12 cost of a license.

CLOSE UP

Detour to La Bufadora

Legend has it that **La Bufadora** (✉ *Carretera 23, 31 km [19 mi] south of Ensenada, Punta Banda*), an impressive tidal blowhole (*la bufadora* means "the buffalo snort") in the coastal cliffs at Punta Banda, was created by a whale or sea serpent trapped in an undersea cave; both these stories, and the less romantic scientific facts, are posted on a roadside plaque.

The road to La Bufadora along Punta Banda—an isolated, mountainous point that juts into the sea—is lined with olive, craft, and tamale stands; the drive gives you a sampling of Baja's wilderness. If you're in need of some cooling off, turn off the highway at the sign for La Jolla Beach Camp. The camp charges a small admission fee for day use of the beachside facilities, but it's a great place to do a few "laps" of lazy freestyle or breaststroke at La Jolla Beach.

At La Bufadora, expect a small fee to park, and then a half-mile walk past T-shirt hawkers and souvenir stands to the water hole itself. A public bus runs from the downtown Ensenada station to Maneadero, where you can catch a minibus labeled PUNTA BANDA that goes to La Bufadora.

VALLE DE GUADALUPE

The Valle de Guadalupe, northeast of Ensenada on Carretera 3, is filled with vineyards, wineries, and rambling hacienda-style estates. Although Mexican wines are still relatively unknown in the United States, the industry is exploding in Mexico, and the Valle de Gaudalupe is responsible for some 90% of the country's production.

With a region that combines the right heat, soil, and a thin morning fog, some truly world-class boutique wineries have developed in the Valle de Guadalupe, most in the past decade. Several of these are open to the public; most require appointments. Several tour companies, including Bajarama (☎ *646/178–3252)*, leave from Ensenada on tours that include visits to wineries, a historical overview, transportation, and lunch. Better yet is visiting the wineries yourself by car, as they all cluster in a relatively small area. Also worth a look is winemaker Hugo D'Acosta's new school, which brings in some 100 young winemakers to use common facilities to make their own blends. The facilities are on the site of an old olive-oil press (a few antique presses remain in the outlying buildings), and the grounds are augmented with artwork made from recycled wine bottles and other materials.

Several changes are in store, which may alter the isolation of the valley, and in five years the place may have a different, more upscale, feel. The Monte Xanic winery is constructing a 42-room resort and spa, a branch of the international Banyan Tree chain, on its property overlooking the vineyards; opening is planned for late 2011. Plus, the Baja state government has already begun paving some of the region's side roads. It seems that it's not only Mexican wine that's being discovered, but the potential of Guadalupe as a "wine destination," along with the mixed blessings that accompany such discovery.

GETTING HERE AND AROUND

If you're not on a tour, a private car (or hired taxi) is essential for touring the wine country. West of the town of Francisco Zarco (also called Guadalupe), the road is paved past Monte Xanic and the small village of Porvenir; after that, it is mainly gravel. The turnoffs for the major wineries are well marked; if you're looking for a smaller destination, you may end up doing a few loops or asking a friendly bystander. The general area is not too spread out; still, you will need to drive from one winery to the other. You can arrange a half- or full-day tour with many of the taxi drivers in Ensenada, and some drivers in Tecate may also be willing to take you.

ESSENTIALS

Banks are few and far between in this area, so get cash before arriving if you think you'll need it. There is a Pemex station in the town of Francisco Zarco, at the turnoff from Highway 3.

EXPLORING

Fodor's Choice ★ One of the most up-and-coming small wineries in Baja, **Adobe Guadalupe** (✉ *Off Carretera 3, turn at sign and drive 6 km [4 mi], Guadalupe* ☎ *646/155–2094, 949/733–2744 in U.S.* 🌐 *www.adobeguadalupe.com*) is making an array of fascinating high-end blends named after angels. Don't miss the Kerubiel, which is a blockbuster blend; the Serafiel, Gabriel, and Miguel are also excellent. Don and his wife Tru also run a bed-and-breakfast, and Tru's beautiful horses are available for riding tours of up to three days.

Casa de Piedra (✉ *Carretera Tecate–Ensenada, Km 93.5, San Antonio de las Minas* ☎ *646/155–3097 or 646/155–5267* 🌐 *www.vinoscasadepiedra.com*) is the brainchild of Hugo D'Acosta, who also consults for Adobe Guadalupe. The space is interesting and modern, designed by the winemaker's architect brother.

One of the larger and less personal wineries is **Domecq** (✉ *Carretera Tecate–Ensenada, Km 73.5* ☎ *646/165–2264 or 646/155–2254* 🌐 *www.vinosdomecq.com.mx*), which offers free wine tastings and tours weekdays 10–4 and Saturday 10–3. The operation is one of the most corporate of the Baja wineries—but it's estranged from the Allied Domecq worldwide liquor empire; don't expect to taste its top wines.

L. A. Cetto (✉ *Carretera 3, Km 73.5* ☎ *646/155–2179* 🌐 *www.cettowines.com*) is another giant, but this is the closest thing to the California wine country experience south of the border. When tasting or buying, avoid the cheaper wines, and go straight for the premiums. Free wine tastings and tours daily 10–5.

★ Call ahead if you want to get in **Monte Xanic** (✉ *Carretera 3, Km 70* ☎ *646/155–2080* 🌐 *www.montexanic.com.mx*). Most impressive is their consistency, right down to the cheapest table wines. Tastings and tours are available by appointment, and be sure to check out the impressively styled cellar.

★ Within **Vinisterra** (✉ *Carretera Tecate–Ensenada, Km 94.5, San Antonio de las Minas* ☎ *646/178–3350 or 646/178–3310* 🌐 *www.vinisterra.com*), expect to find Tempranillo and cabernet-merlot blends that are big and juicy. Call well ahead.

TIJUANA

29 km (18 mi) south of San Diego.

Over the course of the 20th century, Tijuana grew from a ranch populated by a few hundred Mexicans into a Prohibition retreat for boozing and gambling—then it morphed yet again into an industrial giant infamous for its proliferation of *maquiladoras* (sweatshops).

In recent years, as drug violence has boomed along the U.S.–Mexico border, Tijuana has taken the brunt of it. Until the wave of crime subsides, the town is best seen from behind windows, en route to other destinations of the Baja Peninsula.

GETTING HERE AND AROUND

Most visitors to Baja Norte arrive in San Diego: there are few international flights into Tijuana, Baja Norte's only major airport. Aeropuerto Alberado Rodriguez (TIJ) is on Tijuana's eastern edge, near the Otay Mesa border crossing. Private taxis and *colectivos* (shared vans) serve the airport. Greyhound buses head to Tijuana from downtown San Diego several times daily. Buses to San Diego and Los Angeles depart from the Greyhound terminal in Tijuana 14 times a day. Mexicoach runs buses from the trolley depot in San Ysidro and the large parking lot on the U.S. side of the border to the Tijuana Tourist Terminal at Avenida Revolución between Calles 6 and 7. If you are renting a car or meeting a bus on the Mexican side of the border, park in San Diego and walk across; this will save you the major waits in the automobile lines. You can pick up street food and cheap souvenirs from the artisan stands just across the border.

By car from San Diego, U.S. 5 and I–805 end at the San Ysidro border crossing; Highway 905 leads from U.S. 5 and I–805 to the Tijuana border crossing at Otay Mesa. The San Diego Trolley travels from the Santa Fe Depot in San Diego, at Kettner Boulevard and Broadway, to within 100 feet of the border in Tijuana every 15 minutes from 6 AM to midnight. The 45-minute trip costs $2.50; a day pass can be purchased for $5.

ESSENTIALS

Bus Contacts **Greyhound** (☎ *664/688–0165 in Tijuana, 01800/710–8819 toll-free in Mexico, 800/231–2222* 🌐 *www.greyhound.com*). **Mexicoach** (☎ *664/685–1440, 619/428–9517 in U.S.* 🌐 *www.mexicoach.com*). **San Diego Trolley** (☎ *619/233–3004* 🌐 *www.sdcommute.com*).

Medical Assistance **Emergencies** (☎ *Dial 066*). **Tourist Information and Assistance Hotline** (☎ *Dial 078*).

TECATE

62 km (38 mi) east of Tijuana.

For most Baja-bound Americans, Tecate serves as a convenient alternative to the northbound Tijuana–San Ysidro border crossing, and not much else. Although the town itself is sunny and pleasant—especially when compared to the sprawling jumbles of Tijuana and Mexicali—

CLOSE UP

Spa on the Border

More than seven decades since its 1940 opening, **Rancho La Puerta** continues to provide personalized service, with more than 350 employees seeing to the needs of up to 150 guests. Equally reliable is the climate, with an average of 341 dry, sunny days a year, and the lacto-ovo-vegetarian/seafood diet. The Cocina que Canta (kitchen that sings) cooking school teaches guests how to make the spa-cuisine-cum-healthy-Mex specialties for which La Puerta is famous, with both demonstration and hands-on classes taught by the ranch's star chefs.

Still managed by members of its founding family, the spa requires a weeklong Saturday-to-Saturday stay. Activities can include African dance, back care, spinning, labyrinth meditation, Feldenkrais technique, cardio-boxing, tai chi, and yoga. Mornings begin with guided hikes around the ranch's 40 km (25 mi) of trails at the base of sacred Mt. Kuchumaa. Backed by 3,000 acres of unspoiled foothills, the campus is a product of locally sourced landscaping, brick paths that meander in and out of secret gardens, and guest residences, which are hidden between yawning oaks and gorgeous swimming pools. An extensive range of à-la-carte spa treatments and salon services affords the chance to be pampered as well as engaged.

One-of-a-kind cottages contain studios and suites decorated with handmade rugs and furniture. Many have tile floors, fireplaces, and kitchenettes. All have safes, refrigerators and CD players. The studios and suites in the villas, which run more than the other cottages, give you the option of in-room massages (for a fee) and breakfast poolside or in-room. There's no air-conditioning or TV, and the entire property is no-smoking. ■ **TIP→ Inquire about reservations well before your stay; returning guests are known to rebook their same room—for the same week each year—up to a year in advance.**

Spa Services: Aromatherapy, body scrubs, facials, herbal wrap, hydrotherapy, hot-stone massage, manicure, pedicure, reflexology, scalp treatments, salt glow, seaweed wrap, sports massage, trigger-point massage.

Fitness Facilities: 11 gyms total. Elliptical machines, free weights, stair climbers, stationary bikes, treadmills, weight-training circuit; basketball court, labyrinth, Pilates studio, 4 pools, 4 lighted tennis courts, volleyball court; 5 whirlpools, 3 saunas.

Classes and Programs: Aerobics, bird walks, breathing techniques, cooking, crafts classes, creative writing, dance, drumming, Feldenkrais method, hiking, health lectures, meditation, photography, piano lessons, Pilates, personal finances, Spanish lessons, spinning, stretching, tai chi, tennis, yoga, volleyball.

Package: Rates $2,855–$4,510 for a seven-night package, per person, based on double occupancy, excluding tax (some rooms accommodate triples and quads). Space permitting, shorter stays can be arranged. This includes all meals, classes, and evening programs as well as use of all facilities. Spa treatments and cooking classes are extra. Ground transportation to and from San Diego International Airport is included in the weekly rate.

General Info: ✉ *Carretera Federal Tijuana, Km 5, Tecate* ☎ *858/764-5500 or 800/443-7565* 🌐 *www.rancholapuerta.com* *82 cottages* 💳 *AE, D, MC, V* 🍽 *AI.*

there isn't much here in the way of tourist infrastructure. A quick pit stop is probably the extent of many a traveler's stay.

GETTING HERE AND AROUND

Tecate is small and easy to navigate. Highway 2 becomes Benito Juárez as it passes through town. Follow Calle Cárdenas straight out of town to the U.S.–Mexico border. If you're heading south to Baja, there's rarely a delay at the San Diego–Tijuana border, and crossing at Tijuana allows you the scenic drive down Highway 3. Northbound travelers, however, might opt for the Tecate crossing, as multiple-hour backups are not uncommon heading north into the United States from Tijuana. Even the Tecate crossing can get crowded in the early morning, however.

ESSENTIALS

Medical Assistance **Emergencies (☎ *Dial 066*). Tourist Information and Assistance Hotline (☎ *Dial 078*).**

MEXICALI

146 km (91 mi) east of Tecate.

In some ways Tijuana's richer, more successful older brother, Mexicali is a border town founded on an economy that's less whimsical (agriculture, rather than tourism) and a seat of power that's real (the Baja statehouse). In place of trinket shops and taco stands, Mexicali's streetscape features Home Depots and Wal-Marts, and nary a luxury hotel is without its business center, conference rooms, Wi-Fi, and corporate stationery. Yet even with upscale digs and somewhat cleaner streets, Mexicali remains a border town, with all of the tensions and tragedies that accompany its walled divide from Calexico, California to the north.

GETTING HERE AND AROUND

ESSENTIALS

Medical Assistance **Emergencies (☎ *Dial 066*). Tourist Information and Assistance Hotline (☎ *Dial 078*).**

Puerto Vallarta and the Pacific Coast Resorts

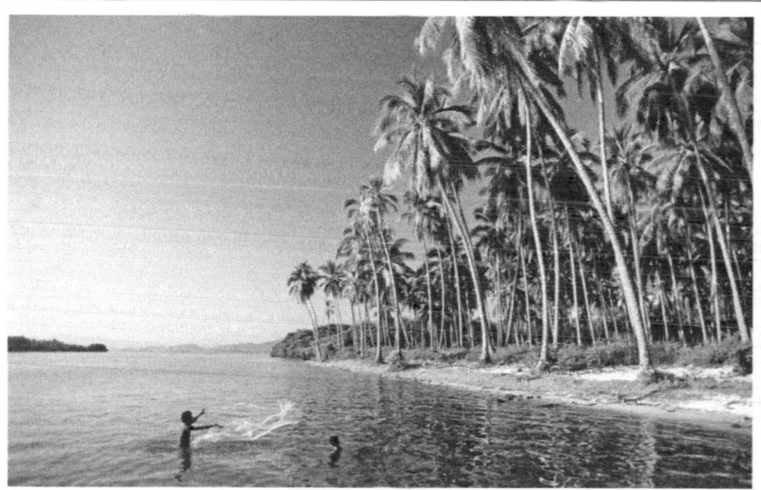

Coyuca de Benitez Lagoon

WORD OF MOUTH

"Muertos is PV's most popular beach and very swimable most days. You will be in the heart of shops, cafés, bars and much nightlife. About a half mile from the main Malecon where the more 'infamous' drinking spots are."

—stewbear

www.fodors.com/community

WELCOME TO PUERTO VALLARTA AND THE PACIFIC COAST RESORTS

TOP REASONS TO GO

★ **Snorkeling, surfing, kayaking:** Zihuatanejo Bay is all about water sports. And the warm Pacific is as appealing to orcas, humpback whales, and dolphins as it is to humans.

★ **Pitting your will against sport fish:** Sailfish, marlin, tuna, and yellowtail call these waters home. Fish from shore, small skiffs, or cruisers. In November, Mazatlán, Puerto Vallarta, and Manzanillo host tournaments.

★ **Partaking in PV's food scene:** Puerto Vallarta has great chefs in spades—many hailing from Mexico City, the United States, and Europe.

★ **Shopping till you drop:** Look for contemporary paintings and sculpture, blown-glass items, ceramic tiles, tin lamp shades and frames, distinctive pottery, and Huichol beadwork.

★ **Finding some peace:** Between resort towns are laid-back fishing villages and undeveloped beaches; inland are colonial towns, coffee plantations, and nature preserves.

1 Mazatlán. Many are content to party in Mazatlán's highly developed hotel zone (Zona Dorada). Others choose to stay in the revitalized Centro Histórico, which has brightly painted 19th-century buildings and small museums. The beaches here aren't the best, but there's some decent snorkeling.

2 Riviera Nayarit. The coast north of PV, dubbed the "Riviera Nayarit, " is being developed quickly. Nuevo Vallarta, on Bahía de Banderas and just over the border in Nayarit State is dominated by all-inclusives and golf courses. A long, sandy stretch runs north 12 km (7 mi) from Nuevo Vallarta to the growing town of Buceriás, followed by several engaging villages and beaches.

3 Puerto Vallarta. Ever-popular Puerto Vallarta (PV) fronts the big, blue Bahía de Banderas, and is backed by foothills covered in tropical forest. Ecotour opportunities abound, but most people come to party—outside of Acapulco, PV has the coast's most sophisticated nightlife.

4 La Costalegre. The "Happy Coast" south of PV between Cruz de Loreto and Manzanillo has several luxury

accommodations—including Hotelito Desconocido, Las Alamandas, El Careyes, and El Tamarindo—on pristine beaches.

5 Manzanillo. The twin bays of Manzanillo and Santiago—collectively called Manzanillo—are popular with Mexican families and snowbirds. On one end of town are two gorgeous peninsulas; on the other an unattractive working port that brings in most of the city's income. Sailfishing is a big sport here, and in-town beaches are nice.

6 Ixtapa and Zihuatenejo. Both of these laidback communities have lovely bays and beaches. But Ixta, a resort created by the Mexican government, has less personality than Zihua—a more authentic place.

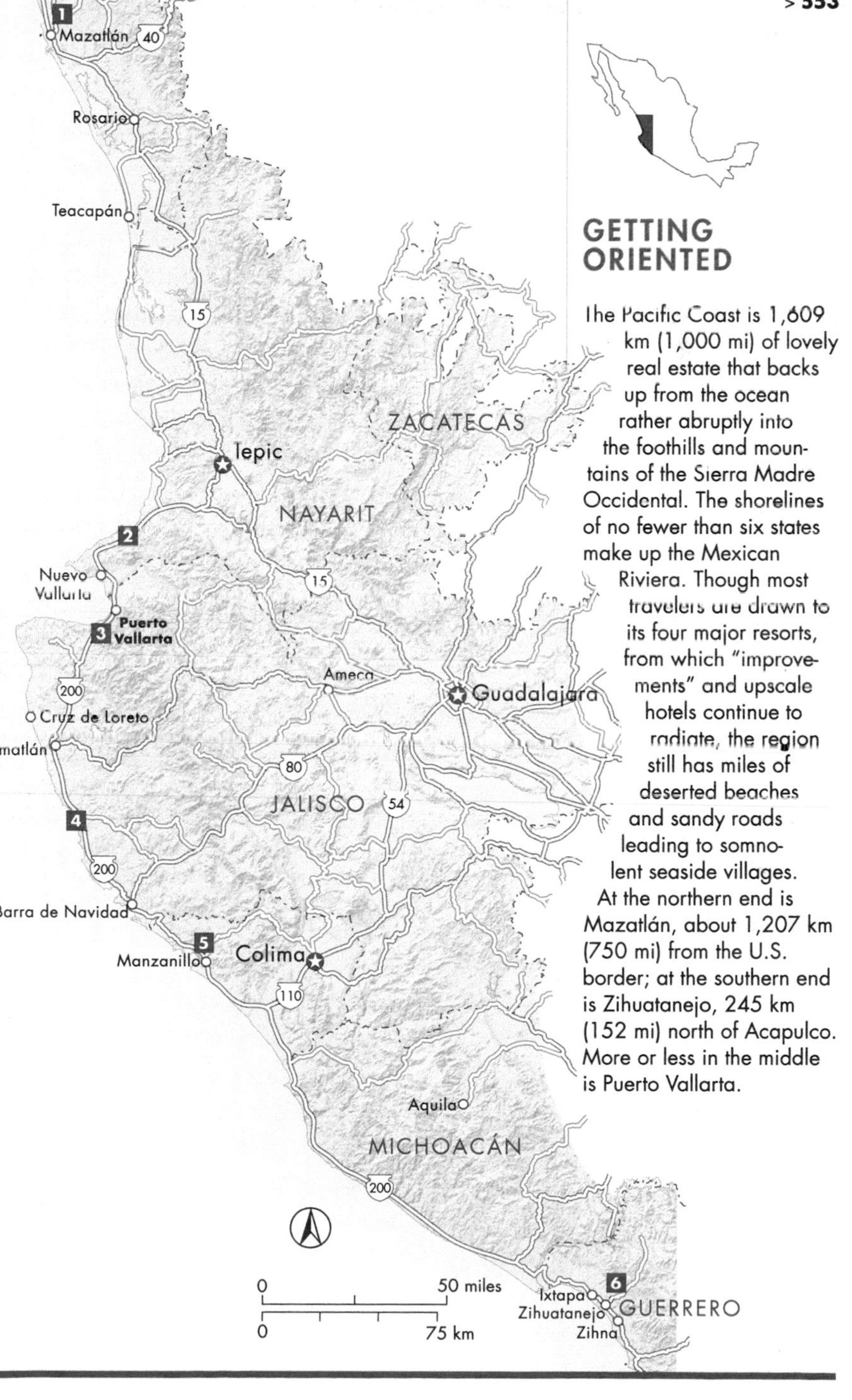

GETTING ORIENTED

The Pacific Coast is 1,609 km (1,000 mi) of lovely real estate that backs up from the ocean rather abruptly into the foothills and mountains of the Sierra Madre Occidental. The shorelines of no fewer than six states make up the Mexican Riviera. Though most travelers are drawn to its four major resorts, from which "improvements" and upscale hotels continue to radiate, the region still has miles of deserted beaches and sandy roads leading to somnolent seaside villages.

At the northern end is Mazatlán, about 1,207 km (750 mi) from the U.S. border; at the southern end is Zihuatanejo, 245 km (152 mi) north of Acapulco. More or less in the middle is Puerto Vallarta.

PUERTO VALLARTA AND THE PACIFIC COAST RESORTS PLANNER

Shopping List

In Puerto Vallarta, emporiums selling crafts from throughout Mexico vie with clothing and jewelry boutiques for your attention. Shops filled with home furnishings of carved wood, iron, tin, stone, blown glass, and brass may make you want to buy a house here or open an import–export enterprise. Look for bowls, masks, and less traditional statuettes made by the Huichol Indians. They embed tiny, colorful beads with beeswax and pine resin in hollowed-out gourds or carved wooden pieces.

Several Pacific Coast towns are also known for their utilitarian pottery, and you can buy place settings and individual pieces from Mazatlán to Ixtapa.

Throughout the region also look for silver jewelry from Taxco, masks and exquisitely rendered lacquerware from Michoacán and Guerrero, carved-wood animals and hand-dyed woven rugs from Oaxaca, and those ubiquitous embroidered dresses and blouses as well as more modern resort wear and bikinis.

Your Dream Vacation?

Aquamarine swells break upon sandy beaches. Waves are sliced by Boogie-boarders, Jet-Skiers, and surfers. Coves shelter schools of fish followed by curious snorkelers, and mangroves are a haven for birds of all stripes. Fishermen stand thigh deep in the surf, tossing their weighted nets, and each stretch of sand holds the promise of a glorious sunset. Lanky coconut trees shade huts thatched with palm leaves.

A Spot in the Sun

Mazatlán has its share of comfortable beachfront hotels and a few downtown inns. Puerto Vallarta accommodations range from tiny inns to high-rise chains to luxury resorts on secluded coves.

Many of Manzanillo's properties are laid-back, more functional than elegant. Beachfront high-rises are what's happening in Ixtapa. Zihuatanejo has budget hotels as well as a few exclusive spots on or above the bay. For stays mid-December through New Year's, or mid-March through Easter, reserve rooms up to a year in advance (especially at boutique hotels). The rest of the winter season and July and August are also extremely busy, especially in Puerto Vallarta.

Safety

Be aware of water-condition warning flags on the beach. Guard your belongings on the beach and in crowded places. Town squares and seaside promenades are often full of people until the wee hours, making them generally safe. Always avoid deserted beaches (even in front of large resorts) or other poorly lighted or desolate places at night.

Time-share vendors are a hassle—particularly in Puerto Vallarta and Mazatlán—but not a safety concern. Such people often begin their patter with an innocuous topic and then rope you into a sales pitch.

Getting Around

Highway 15 connects most of the coast, starting around Hermosillo and creating one doozy of a scenic drive—though the Pacific is an unwavering blue, the landscape around it shifts from rain forest to pine forest and back again.

Who Visits When

Visitors to this part of the country are primarily Americans and Canadians, especially between late November and Easter. The coast has become highly popular with the retired set and RVers. Surfers head to the small towns on the Costalegre and around Zihuatanejo.

Mexicans from Guadalajara, Mexico City, and other inland cities head to the beaches en masse during Christmas, New Year's, Easter, and school holidays in July and August.

Europeans make up some 20% to 25% of visitors, and they also tend to visit during the December holidays and in mid- to late summer.

Money Matters

Some hotel restaurants add 15% IVA (value-added tax) as well as a service charge to your tab. More humble establishments charge neither; check your bill and tip accordingly. Hotel prices drop by as much as 25% in off-season months such as May, June, September, or October; those latter two months, however, are part of hurricane season (late September–early November).

WHAT IT COSTS IN DOLLARS

	¢	$	$$	$$$	$$$$
Restaurants	under $6	$6–$12	$13–$19	$20–$25	over $25
Hotels	under $60	$60–$120	$121–$180	$181–$250	over $250

Restaurant prices represent the median price for a main course excluding tax and tip. Hotel prices are for two people in a standard double room in high season.

How's the Weather?

This coastal stretch is at its best in winter (December through February), with temperatures of 20°C–30°C (70°F–80°F) and a bit higher in Ixtapa and Zihuatanejo. The off-season brings humidity, mosquitoes, and heat, but also emptier beaches, warmer water (about 20°C (70°F), and less-crowded streets.

Brides who want to glow but not sweat like a sumo wrestler should avoid a June wedding. The rainy season here is June to October, and the heat just before and during it can be stifling.

Surfers, on the other hand, will love the turbulent waters at this time of year. What's more, the countryside, the Sierra Madre Occidental, and the Sierra Madre del Sur turn a brilliant green. Note, though, that hurricane season runs from late September to early November.

MAZATLÁN

460 km (286 mi) north of Puerto Vallarta.

Updated by Michele Joyce

MAZATLÁN, THE FIRST MAJOR RESORT town on the Pacific coastline, has a split personality. At the northern end of town is the Zona Dorada (Golden Zone), where the hotels (and the prices) rise high and the pace is frenetic. The streets are jammed with tour buses shuttling cruise-ship passengers to dozens of jewelry shops. At the southern end of the malecón (the seaside promenade) is Viejo Mazatlán (Old Mazatlán), the city's historic center, a gorgeous and low-key area of colorful post-colonial buildings—some restored, some still idyllic piles of chipped stucco—where you'll find a few hip restaurants, art galleries, and shops, and a totally different scene from the touristy Golden Zone.

Mazatlán's beaches are golden and wide, though they're not nearly as handsome as those south of Puerto Vallarta. There are, however, tons of beach activities here—this is the place for parasailing—and several nearby islands provide alternatives to the crowded sands in town. Overall, the town is a good choice for a quick getaway: it's cheaper than Puerto Vallarta, the party scene is there for those who want to partake, and unlike in many resort towns, the city has some sights to explore beyond the surf and sand.

GETTING HERE AND AROUND

Aeropuerto Internacional Rafael Buelna is about 25 km (18 mi) south of town—a good 30-minute drive. A private taxi from the airport will cost about $26. Mazatlán's main bus terminal offers connections north to the U.S. border, inland to Guadalajara and Mexico City, and south along the coast to Puerto Vallarta. When taking city buses, look for SÁBALO CENTRO above the front window to get from the Zona Dorada to Viejo Mazatlán. Fares range from 40¢ for the tanklike minibuses to 80¢ for bigger, air-conditioned models (look for the bright green buses). Taxis regularly cruise the Zona Dorada strip. Even easier to flag down (though usually more expensive) are the white, open-sided pulmonías; the fare starts at about $3 for a really short trip. It'll cost $6–$10 to get from the Zona Dorada to the Centro Histórico—always negotiate the fare before you get in.

ESSENTIALS

Bus Contacts **Estrella Blanca** (☎ *01800/507–5500 toll-free in Mexico* 🌐 *www.estrellablanca.com.mx*). **Transportes del Pacifico** (☎ *01800/001–1827 toll-free in Mexico* 🌐 *www.tap.com.mx*).

Medical Assistance **Balboa Hospital & Walk-In Clinic** (✉ *Av. Camarón Sábalo 4480, at Plaza Balboa, Zona Dorada* ☎ *669/916–5533* 🌐 *www.hospitalsinmexico.com*). **General Emergency Number** (☎ *065*). **Red Cross** (✉ *Calle Gral. I Zaragoza 1801, Centro Histórico* ☎ *669/981–1506*). **Sharp Hospital** (✉ *Av. Rafael Buelna at Dr. Jesus Kumate, Las Cruces* ☎ *669/986–7911* 🌐 *www.hospitalsharp.com*).

Visitor and Tour Info **Sinaloa State Tourism Office** (✉ *Calle Mariano Escobedo 1317, at Calle Carnaval, Centro Histórico* ☎ *669/981–8883 or 669/981–8889* 🌐 *www.vivesinaloa.com*).

EXPLORING

The Zona Dorada—the start of which is marked by a kitschy white castle that houses a dining and dancing complex—has blocks of high-rise hotels, shops (including car-rental offices and a few pharmacies), restaurants, and nightclubs, along with the city's best swimming beaches. The malecón connects this zone with the historic center to the south. The southern part of the city is where all of Mazatlán's charm lies, along with most of the museums and sights. There are some stunning viewpoints from the seaside promenade on this end, but there's virtually no beach access unless you want to do as the locals do and pick your way over rocks to catch the sunset from one of the jetties.

TOP ATTRACTIONS

2 **Acuario Mazatlán.** A perfect child-pleaser—and a lot of fun for adults, too—Mazatlán's homey little aquarium has more than 50 tanks with sharks, sea horses, and multicolor salt- and freshwater fish. Animal shows featuring kissing sea lions, skating macaws, and penny-pinching parrots are offered three times daily. Note that if you sit in the front, you will get splashed! The grounds aren't extensive, but there are two turtle and crocodile habitats and a small aviary, as well as a gift shop and snack bar. ✉ *Av. de los Deportes 111, Olas Altas* ☎ *669/981–7815* 🌐 *www.acuariomazatlan.gob.mx* 🎟 *$7.50* 🕒 *Daily 9:30–6.*

4 **Catedral de Mazatlán.** A new lighting scheme gives nighttime drama to the bright yellow spires of the Basilica of the Immaculate Conception, which have towered over downtown for more than a century. Church construction began in 1855 and took nearly 50 years, along the way embracing Moorish, Gothic, baroque, and neoclassical architectural styles. A recent restoration has the Italian marble, cedar fixtures, elaborate chandeliers, and Parisian organ shining brighter than ever. ✉ *Calles Juárez and 21 de Marzo, Centro Histórico* ☎ *No phone.*

10 ★ **El Faro (The Lighthouse).** The best view in Mazatlán gets you some exercise, too—a 30- to 45-minute climb along natural trails and rough-hewn stairs to the lighthouse that since 1571 has been warning ships from atop Cerro del Creston, 515 feet above the sea. Wear sturdy shoes, bring a bottle of water, and, if you go up to watch the sunset, maybe a flashlight for the trip back down. Note that it takes about 20 minutes to walk from the southern terminus of Paseo Claussen (the end of the malecón) to the start of the lighthouse trail, but it's a lovely route, most of which skirts the water. When Claussen ends just follow the signs for Paseo del Centenario for a few blocks through residential streets until you reemerge on the seaside road. ✉ *Southern terminus of Paseo del Centenario* ☎ *No phone.*

3 **Malecón.** A long, gorgeous waterfront makes Mazatlán a great city for walking, biking, or rollerblading. The *malecón,* a sidewalk atop the 10-km-long (6-mi-long) seawall, runs from the Zona Dorada south to Viejo Mazatlán. It bustles, especially in the evenings. The route is filled with a dozen quirky monuments, from a vat from the Pacífico Brewery to a bronzed *pulmonía,* Mazatlán's beloved open-air taxi. The centerpiece is the massive Monumento del Pescador (Fisherman's Monument), which seems to portray a man preparing to throw a net over a napping woman.

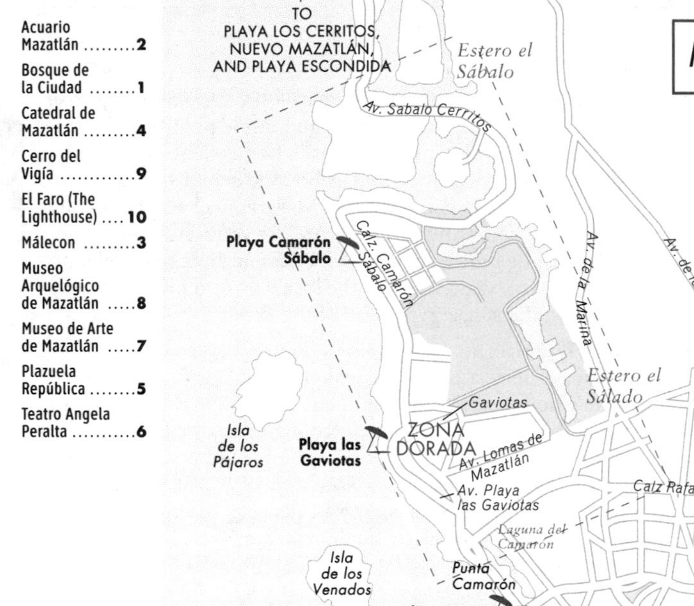
Mazatlán
Acuario Mazatlán 2
Bosque de la Ciudad 1
Catedral de Mazatlán 4
Cerro del Vigía 9
El Faro (The Lighthouse) 10
Málecon 3
Museo Arquelógico de Mazatlán 8
Museo de Arte de Mazatlán 7
Plazuela República 5
Teatro Angela Peralta 6
TO PLAYA LOS CERRITOS, NUEVO MAZATLÁN, AND PLAYA ESCONDIDA
Estero el Sábalo
Av. Sabalo Cerritos
Playa Camarón Sábalo
Calz. Camarón Sábalo
Av. de la Marina
Av. de las Torres
TO EL QUELITE
Estero el Sálado
Gaviotas
ZONA DORADA
Isla de los Pájaros
Playa las Gaviotas
Av. Lomas de Mazatlán
Av. Playa las Gaviotas
Calz Rafael Buelna
15
Laguna del Camarón
Carretera Internacional
Isla de los Venados
Punta Camarón
Playa Norte
Av. del Mar
Av. Reforma
Isla de los Lobos
Playa Isla de los Venados
TO AIRPORT, ESTRELLA DEL MAR GOLF COURSE
Av. Insurgentes
Av. de los Deportes
Estero del Infiernillo
Bahía de Puerto Viejo
Río Tamazula
Av. Juan Carrasco
Río Baluarte
Av. del mar
Fisherman's Beach
Playa Marlin
Punta Tiburón
Av. Rotarismo
Av. Pesqueira
Paseo Claussen
Gutiérrez Nájera
5 de Mayo
Juárez
A. Serdan
I. Zaragoza
Ocampo
Bahía Olas Altas
Paseo Olas Altas
M. Escobedo
Carbajal
Av. Emilio Barragan
Playa Olas Altas
Av. M. Alemán
Canal de Navegación
Paseo del Centenario
Observatorio
Carranza
Av. Carnaval
Camarena
Joel Montes Camarena
Cap. Joel Montes Camarena
Water taxis to Isla de la Piedra
0 1000 meters
0 1000 yards
Playa Isla de la Piedra
Isla de la Piedra

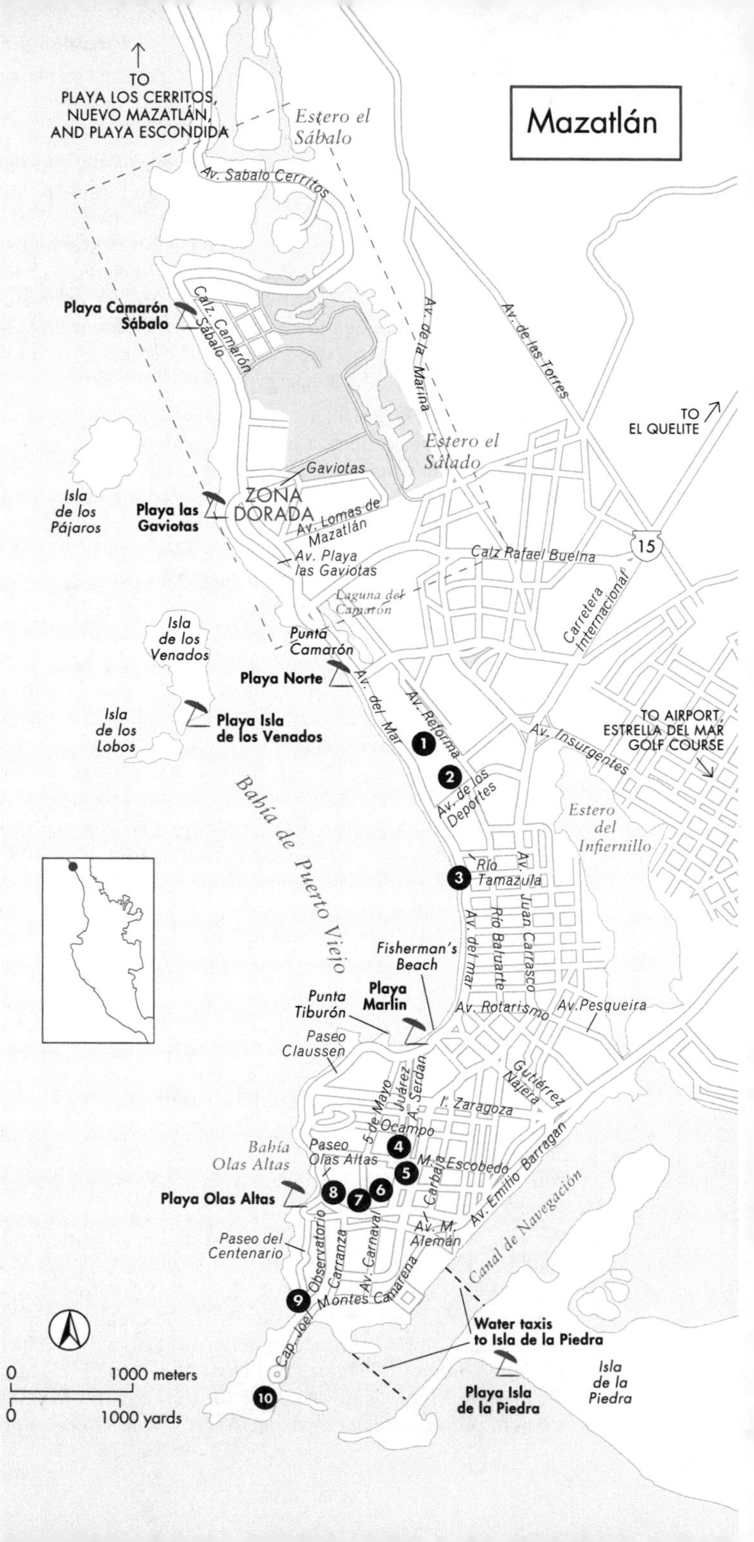

The road turns into Paseo Claussen, which continues past several more statues, including the Monumento a la Continuidad de la Vida (Monument to the Continuity of Life), a large fountain on which a bronze nude couple stand atop a large conch shell and a school of leaping porpoises. A few steps more bring you to a seaside plaza where you can buy snacks and kitschy souvenirs. If the crowd gets big enough, which it usually does when tour buses arrive around 11 AM, 3 PM, and sunset, young men will dive into the sea from a high white platform.

GOOD READING

Mazatlán's English-language monthly magazine, *Pacific Pearl* (*www.pacificpearl.com*), has ads and articles of interest to locals and visitors. *Viejo Mazatlán* is a monthly bilingual paper that focuses on art, culture, and activities in Centro Histórico. Both publications are free and widely distributed.

7 **Museo de Arte de Mazatlán.** The revival of the Centro Histórico has injected new relevance into this small museum. Beyond recognized Mexican artists like José Luis Cueva and Armando Nava, there are also debut exhibits by lesser-known artists in the burgeoning local scene, as well as eclectic concerts, films, and symposiums. *Calle Sixto Osuna and Av. Venustiano Carranza, Centro Histórico 669/985–3502 Free Tues.–Sat. 10–2 and 4–7, Sun. 10–2.*

5 **Plazuela Republica.** Also known as the zócalo or Plaza Revolución, this shaded square at the center of downtown—near the cathedral, city hall, and post office—is the perfect place to relax with a snack from the adjacent ice-cream and pizza shops or shaved-ice stands, get a shoeshine, or mail a letter home. Streets within a couple of blocks in any direction have small restaurants where fast, multicourse lunches (*comida corrida*) cost between $3 and $5. *Bounded by Calle 21 de Marzo to the north, Calle Flores to the south, Av. Benito Juárez to the east, and Av. Nelson to the west, Centro Histórico.*

WORTH NOTING

1 **Bosque de la Ciudad.** The city's best (read: only) real park is around the corner from the aquarium. With 29 acres of shaded playgrounds, trails, and a train to ride, it's a great place for kids to work off hotel-bound energy. It really gets moving on Sunday, frequently to the beat of a live band. *Av. Leonismo Internacional and Av. de los Deportes 111, Olas Altas No phone Free Daily dawn–dusk.*

9 **Cerro del Vigía.** The view from Lookout Hill is fantastic, but the road up from Paseo del Centenario is steep and confusing; take a pulmonía. At the top are a rusty cannon and the Centenario Pégola—built in 1848 to celebrate the end of the U.S. invasion (aka the Mexican–American War).

8 **Museo Arqueológico de Mazatlán.** The black-and-red pottery of the Totorame (an indigenous tribe that inhabited the area until 200 years before the Spanish arrived) highlights a small but interesting collection of regional artifacts here. Temporary exhibits fill the small main hall. Little of the information is in English. *Calle Sixto Osuna 76, at Av. Venustiano Carranza, Centro Histórico 669/981–1455 www.inah.gob.mx $3.10, free Sun. Mon-Fri 10–3.*

NEED A BREAK?

The unofficial heart of the old city is Plazuela Machado, next to Teatro Angela Peralta and bounded by Calles Libertad, Sixto Osuna, Carnaval, and Frias. Students gossip, locals chat on benches, and tourists tuck into affordable meals at the sidewalk cafés that ring the small, palm-shaded plaza. For a quick bite, check out Ta Café (🌐 *www.tacafe.com.mx*) on the quiet southwest corner; it has coffee and sandwiches and comfy orange- and brown-striped armchairs.

6 **Teatro Angela Peralta**. The restoration of this 1860s-era opera house—named for a touring diva who died of yellow fever before she could give her concert—ignited the revival of the Centro Histórico in 1990. Catch a performance by students at the adjacent contemporary dance school (schedule is outside the theater) or take a self-guided tour. ✉ *Plazuela Machado* ☎ *669/982–4446* 🌐 *www.culturamazatlan.com* 🎫 *Varies by performance; tour $2.*

BEACHES

★ **Playa Camarón Sábalo**. This beach is just north of Playa las Gaviotas on the map but a couple of notches lower on the energy scale. Although hotels and sports concessions back both stretches, there's more room to spread out on this beach. It's also well protected from heavy surf by offshore islands. Most of the hotels have lounge chairs and umbrellas that nonguests can often use if they order drinks.

Playa Escondida. Relentless condo construction is creeping along the 6 km (4 mi) stretch of sand between Marina Mazatlán and Punta Cerritos, so Hidden Beach no longer truly lives up to its name. Still, it is far calmer than the hotel zone. A few small hotel bars and restaurants sell food and drink; otherwise you're on your own. Note that the undertow is strong in places.

Playa las Gaviotas. Seagull Beach, Mazatlán's most popular, parallels the Zona Dorada hotel loop. Streams of vendors sell pottery, lace tablecloths, silver jewelry—even songs. Concessionaires rent boats, Boogie boards, and Windsurfers, and tout parasail rides. Food and drink are abundant, either at one of many beachfront hotel restaurants or from more of those vendors, who bear cups of freshly cut fruit, chilled coconuts, and even the odd pastry. If you're looking for relaxation, look elsewhere—between the constant solicitations from vendors and the endless renditions of "YMCA" blasting from the bars, you won't find a moment's peace here.

★ **Playa Isla de la Piedra**. Stone Island is where locals come on weekends, and it's a wonderful adventure for

UNCOVERING THE PAST

If you like archaeology, inquire about tours to mysterious petroglyphs and a pyramid. **Piedras Labradas** (Carved Rocks) is on the beach near Estación Dimas, 74 km (46 mi) north of Mazatlán. El Calón ruins—the site of a 99-foot pyramid made of seashells that probably took the Totorame Indians 100 years to build—are ensconced in a mangrove estuary southward near Rancho Los Angeles.

visitors—a short trip to a side of Mazatlán that seems worlds away. Stone Island is really a long peninsula and has 16 km (10 mi) of unspoiled sand fronting a coconut plantation and an adjacent village nestled in greenery. There's plenty of space for everyone, although most folks pack the northern end, where bands and boom boxes blare music, restaurants sell seafood, and outfitters rent water-sports gear. There's horseback riding, too. Tour operators sell party-boat trips for $35 and up, but inexpensive water taxis cross the same channel with departures nearly every 15 minutes from dawn to sunset (save your ticket for the return). You can catch them at two small piers: one near the Pacífico Brewery, the other at La Paz ferry terminal.

> **CHEAP BEACH READS**
>
> If you forgot your beach reading, the nonprofit **Mazatlán Membership Library** will lend you English-language books one at a time for a $15 annual membership fee ($30 for unlimited books). There are also used books for sale. ✉ *Sixto Osuna 115 E. Col. Centro* ☎ *669/982–3036* 🌐 *www.mazinfo.com/library/* ⏲ *Apr. 1–Oct. 31, weekdays 10–2; Nov. 1–Mar. 31, weekdays 9–5, Saturday 10–2.*

12

★ **Playa Isla de los Venados.** The most memorable way to get to Deer Island—one of three islands that form a channel off the Zona Dorada—is on an amphibious tank. The World War II relic departs regularly from El Cid hotel, in the Zona Dorada. It's a 20-minute ride. You can also get here on snorkeling and day cruises arranged through area tour operators. The beach is lovely and clean. For even better snorkeling, hike to small, secluded coves covered with shells.

Playa Marlin to Playa Norte. This 6-km (4-mi) arc of sand runs below a seawall walkway along the waterfront road known as Avenida del Mar, from Punta Camerón (Valentino's) to Punta Tiburón (south of the Fisherman's Monument). Palapas selling seafood, tacos, and cold drinks line the way. Fishermen land their skiffs at the sheltered cove at the south end; a bit farther south is Playa los Pinos, a calm inlet popular with families.

Playa Olas Altas. In this small cove, named for its high waves and edged by rocky hills, you can forget that the rest of Mazatlán exists. A couple of hotels—La Siesta, Belmar, Casa Lucila, and Posada Freeman—and several cafés line the waterfront. At the north end, a saltwater swimming pool is filled and drained by the tides. Excluding the one plaza where vendors hawk tacky souvenirs to tourists, this stretch is a favorite spot of locals.

WHERE TO EAT

$$$ ITALIAN ✕ **Angelo's.** With its fresh flowers, cream-and-beige color scheme, and small rooms flickering with candlelight, this Italian restaurant is truly elegant. A piano-accompanied singer stirs up the romance Thursday through Sunday after 7 PM. Try the veal scaloppine with mushrooms or the capellini with pesto and grilled scallops. The service is impeccable. ✉ *Pueblo Bonito Hotel, Av. Camarón Sábalo 2121, Zona Dorada* ☎ *669/989–8900* 💳 *AE, MC, V* ⏲ *No lunch.*

$ CAFÉ ★ **Café Bolero.** This small restaurant and gallery in an old building behind the Posada Freeman in the Centro Histórico lets you drink and dine, listen and talk so unhurriedly that it's almost meditative. The kitchen, which specializes in grilled meats and fish, serves until about 10:30 PM, but the bar is open long into the night. You're encouraged to listen to the music (nightly after 8 PM), consider the paintings, maybe read something in the small library, and engage in the lost art of conversation. ✉ *Venustiano Carranza 18, Centro Histórico* ☎ *669/985–0003* 🌐 *www.cafebolero1987.com* 💳 *V* ⊗ *Closed Mon. and Tues. No lunch.*

GET OUT OF THE GOLDEN ZONE

To find much greater seclusion than the city's main beaches will allow, head north (well past Camarón Sábalo) to the rocky **Playa los Cerritos** or **Playa las Brujas**. You can negotiate a taxi fare, but it's more economical to take the bus (from the Golden Zone look for ones marked CERRITOS JUÁREZ NORTH).

¢ MEXICAN **El Túnel.** The Tunnel—named for its long, narrow entrance across from the exit of the Teatro Angela Peralta—has been in business since 1945, and black-and-white photos of classic Mexican stars line the yellow-and-lavender-trimmed walls. You can taste its experience with faithful renditions of such famed regional snacks as *gorditas* (fried rounds of cornmeal topped with garnish), *tostadas*, meat or potato *tacos* and *pozole* (pork-and-hominy stew), and its specialty, *asada de la plaza de res* (chopped beef and cubed potatoes, spiced and smothered in lettuce, carrots, and onions). ✉ *Calle Carnaval 1207, Centro Histórico* ☎ *No phone* 🌐 *www.eltunelrestaurant.com* 💳 *No credit cards* ⊗ *Closed Wed.*

$$$ MEXICAN **La Casa Country.** The waiters that dance at night and the faux-rustic Western scheme can come across as a little too Disney, but the Mexican dishes from the kitchen's firewood grill are authentic and excellent. The *arrachera* (skirt steak) and other regional cuts arrive with kettle beans, quesadilla, and guacamole; the rib eye and American cuts have sides of corn on the cob and baked potato. Fresh-fruit margaritas and piña coladas are served by the pitcher. During the day, clowns come and go, offering children balloons. ✉ *Av. Camarón Sábalo s/n, Zona Dorada* 🌐 *www.lacasacountry.com* ☎ *669/916–5300* 💳 *AE, MC, V.*

$$$ ECLECTIC **La Concha.** It's a waterside palapa as large as a palace, but the character doesn't overshadow the menu: fish, beef, and pasta dishes are exquisitely prepared. A few old favorites come with a Mexican twist, perhaps a hint of cilantro or a spark of chili. There's an occasional outright adventure, such as stingray with black butter or calamari in its ink. Breakfast and lunch are served, too. The water views are hard to beat, especially at sunset. ✉ *El Cid Moro, Av. Camarón Sábalo s/n, Zona Dorada* ☎ *669/913–3333* 💳 *AE, MC, V.*

$$ SEAFOOD **La Costa Marinera.** The excellent seafood, reasonable prices, and tremendous beachfront view keep this family-owned spot thriving year-round with a clientele that's equal parts visitors and locals. Try the Sinaloa specialty *pescado zarandeado*, in which an entire fish is smothered with vegetables and spices, wrapped, and cooked slowly over a fire

until you can strip the meat with a touch of your fork. Request a song and maybe buy a CD from the singing waiter. Turn away the time-share sales pitch with a smile. ✉ *Privada del Camarón, at Privada de la Florida, Zona Dorada* ☎ *669/916–1599* 🌐 *www.lacostamarinera.com* 💳 *AE, MC, V.*

TACO ALLEY

The first three blocks of Calle Gutiérrez Nájera turn into a taco alley every evening after 5 PM, with 15 open-air restaurants serving up all kinds of tacos—including beef, pork, fish, and shrimp. Prices are less than a dollar per taco, depending on ingredients, and four or five make a good meal. It's mostly locals along this stretch, but menus are easy to read and waiters are gregarious as they serve the daily dose of what many call "Vitamina T" *(which stands for tacos, tortas, or Tecate, depending upon who you ask).* Just head east from the Fisherman's Monument.

12

$$ MEXICAN ✕ **Las Brasas**. It's one of the newer restaurants around the Plazuela Machado, with some of the most comfortable outdoor-fanned seating as well as air-conditioning inside. The menu is loaded with meat dishes, including a *carne rellena de champinones y queso* (beef stuffed with mushrooms and cheese), and the salsas and Spanish wines truly complement all the fare. After a meal, head to the small café on the corner and grab a piece of cake and a coffee. ✉ *Constitución at Herbierto Frias, Centro Histórico* ☎ *666/136–0916* 🌐 *www.lasbrasas.com.mx* 💳 *MC, V* ⊗ *Closed Mon.*

$$ MEXICAN ✕ **Las Lupitas**. It's only a block from the beach near the heart of the Golden Zone, but this chic and reasonably priced hotel restaurant provides a serene alternative to the ear-splitting beach-bar scene. There's a pleasant patio—if you don't mind looking at busy Avenida Playa Gaviotas—or a slightly mod dining room with wood-beam ceilings, polished stone floors, minimally dressed dark-wood tables, and a few red-and-white accents. At lunch you'll find simple, filling fare like ceviche, hamburgers, and fish tacos; at dinner the Mexican-Mediterranean menu is heavy on fresh fish specialties, like dorado in a honey glaze. ✉ *D'Gala Hotel, Calle Bugambillas 100, at Av. Playa Gaviotas, Zona Dorada* ☎ *669/913–4496* 🌐 *www.dgalamazatlan.com* 💳 *MC, V.*

$$ SEAFOOD ★ ✕ **Pancho's**. You can dine upstairs or down, inside or out, and sometimes even at tables on the sand at this bustling waterfront restaurant. Seafood is the specialty, and portions are as delicious as they are large. But the savvy come here for breakfast, when prices are lower, crowds are thinner, and the combination of coffee, *chilaquiles verdes con huevos* (tortilla chips sautéed with spices and served with green tomatillo sauce and eggs), and the crashing surf is an unbeatable way to start a day. ✉ *Av. Playa las Gaviotas 408, Centro Comercial las Cabanas, Local 11-B, Zona Dorada* ☎ *669/914–0911* 🌐 *www.restoranpanchos.com* 💳 *MC, V.*

$$ MEXICAN ★ ✕ **Pedro y Lola**. Memorializing two local kids who became Mexican legends—movie star Pedro Infante and ranchera singer Lola Beltrán—Pedro y Lola is the most upscale of several fine restaurants that ring the romantic Plazuela Machado. Its seafood dishes are as authentic and creative as the restored 19th-century building it inhabits. Shrimp is the

specialty, but try the *papillot,* the day's catch cooked in foil with white wine, shrimp, and mushrooms. Music is also on the menu. There's a piano bar inside and sometimes a harmless rock combo; a guitar soloist serenades diners outside. ✉ *Calle Carnaval 1303, at Plazuela Machado, Centro Histórico* ☎ *669/982–2589* 🌐 *www.restaurantpedroylola.com* 💳 *AE, MC, V* ⊗ *No lunch.*

WHERE TO STAY

$$ **Azteca Inn.** This three-story Zona Dorada low-rise is close to everything. Its straightforward accommodations are softened by white-and-yellow walls, colorful bedspreads, and a stand-alone bar called La Capilla (the chapel). Rates bounce up $15–$25 a night during Carnaval, Easter, and school vacations (Christmas through New Year's, July, and August). **Pros:** reasonable rates; beach access across the street. **Cons:** no-frills; extremely small pool area; motel-style configuration; ground-floor rooms are noisy. ✉ *Av. Playa las Gaviotas 307, Zona Dorada* ☎ *669/913–4477 or 888/777–0705* 🌐 *www.aztecainn.com.mx* *74 rooms* *In-room: Wi-Fi. In-hotel: restaurant, room service, bar, pool, laundry service, Internet terminal, parking (free)* 💳 *AE, MC, V.*

$$ **Best Western Posada Freeman.** The 12-story Freeman faces the ocean and fronts a delightful maze of narrow postcolonial streets that surround nearby Plazuela Machado. Other than the spacious and gleaming tiled bathrooms, the rooms don't deviate from the standard chain hotel look—don't expect colonial character—but they are bright and up-to-date and have some amenities (like free Wi-Fi and more than two English-language channels) that you won't find in many of the more expensive hotels. The rooftop bar and pool are marvelous spots to watch the sunset. **Pros:** many rooms have small balconies with ocean or nice city views; cool rooftop bar; great location. **Cons:** on-site restaurant is nothing special; some rooms get noise from creaking elevator; chain-hotel design; far from Golden Zone. ✉ *Av. Olas Altas 79 Sur, Centro Histórico* ☎ *669/985–6060 or 800/780–7234* 🌐 *www.bestwestern.com* *64 rooms, 8 junior suites* *In-room: safe, kitchen (some), refrigerator (some), Wi-Fi. In-hotel: bar, pool, laundry service, Wi-Fi hotspot, parking (free), no-smoking rooms* 💳 *AE, MC, V* 🍽 *BP.*

$$ **Casa Contenta.** An oasis of home-style tranquillity wedged among Zona Dorada's high-energy high-rises, Casa Contenta consists of two buildings: one with seven one-bedroom apartments (some with waterfront terraces) and the other a house that can accommodate up to eight people with its three bedrooms, three baths, and living-dining room. The live-like-a-local quality is authentic down to the cheerful Mexican furniture, well-stocked kitchens, and meticulously tended gardens. **Pros:** full kitchens, lots of space; good value for location; good for long-term stays. **Cons:** interiors could use updating; no activities or vacation-planning help. ✉ *Av. Playa las Gaviotas 224, Zona Dorada* ☎ *669/913–4976* 🌐 *www.casacontenta.com.mx* *7 units* *In-room: no phone, kitchen. In-hotel: pool, beachfront, parking (free)* 💳 *MC, V.*

$$ ★ **Casa de Leyendas.** The grand, old, Centro Histórico home of a prominent Mazatlán doctor and former mayor is now this excellent bed-and-breakfast. A stay here puts you across from two museums, a block

from the beach, and three blocks from Plazuela Machado. Each of its six rooms is dedicated to a different Mexican personage, Pancho Villa and Frida Kahlo among them. Rooms don't have TVs—more reason to head out and explore—but there's a media center with cable TV and a DVD. There's also a central courtyard and a rooftop terrace. **Pros:** historic building; tons of personality; great hosts. **Cons:** some rooms have small bathrooms; far from Golden Zone beaches; small service fee for paying with a credit card; strict cancellation policy. ✉ *Venustiano Carranza 4, Centro Histórico* ☎ *669/981–6180; 602/445–6192 in U.S* 🌐 *www.casadeleyendas.com* *6 rooms* *In-room: no phone, no TV. In-hotel: restaurant, bar, pool, laundry service, Internet terminal, Wi-Fi hotspot, no kids under 12* 💳 *MC, V.*

THE OTHER SPRING BREAK

Mazatlán's single most important event is **Carnaval** (🌐 *www.carnavalmazatlan.net*), celebrated each spring during the week before Lent. The city fills with music, parades, dances, fireworks, and a beauty pageant to crown the Carnaval queen. Book accommodations far in advance, and expect prices to rise significantly during the festival.

$$–$$$$ **Casa Lucila.** One of the Centro Histórico's nicest and newest hotels is in a remodeled mansion across from the Pedro Infante monument. Rooms are simple, but each has unique details and subdued colors as well as Italian ceramic floors, Mexican furniture, a plasma TV, plush robes, and windows so soundproof that you could sleep through a Carnaval procession in the street below. Most rooms also have terraces with views of the Olas Altas beach and the Pacific. The staff is friendly, and service is personalized. Dinners and other special functions are sometimes organized for guests during holidays and events in town. **Pros:** sleek, romantic getaway; beautiful ocean views from rooms and pool. **Cons:** no kids under 15, and older kids must have their own room, not within walking distance of most restaurants and shops. ✉ *Olas Altas 16* ☎ *669/982–1100* 🌐 *casalucila.com* *8 rooms* *In-room: safe. In-hotel: restaurant, room service, bar, pool, spa, no kids under 15* 💳 *AE, MC, V.*

$$–$$$$ **El Cid Megaresort.** Named after Spain's legendary medieval leader, Mazatlán's largest resort has four properties, three of which are together in the Zona Dorada. The most upscale are the all-inclusive La Castilla and El Moro. The Granada costs less because it's the oldest, has no beachfront, and operates on the European Plan (that is, no meals included). A free shuttle connects these to the upscale, all-inclusive Marina El Cid Hotel and Yacht Club, at the north end of town, overlooking the 100-slip marina. Staying at any El Cid property gets you access to the full-service spa and fitness center, the city's best golf school and course, tennis and racquetball courts, and the aquatics center. Among readers, the Marina seems to be the favorite of the properties for its friendly staff, superior upkeep, and serene mood. **Pros:** tons of activities; several price points, all-inclusive plans, good restaurants. **Cons:** time-share reps; about 1 mi from other resorts; some parts of complex feel dated. ✉ *Av. Camarón Sábalo s/n, Zona Dorada* ☎ *669/913–3333 or 800/525–1925* *www.elcid.com 1,320 rooms In-room: safe, kitchen (some), refrigerator (some), Wi-Fi (some). In-hotel: 9 restaurants, room service, bars, golf course, tennis courts, pools, gym, spa, beachfront, diving, water sports, children's programs (ages 4–12), laundry service, Internet terminal, Wi-Fi hotspot, parking (free), no-smoking rooms AE, MC, V AI.*

THEY GOT THE BEAT

A plaque at Hotel La Siesta's entrance reports that Jack Kerouac passed through this three-story hotel when he was writing *On The Road* in the 1950s, and there's still something rather Beat generation about the place.

¢–$ **Hotel La Siesta**. This small seaside inn is rich in history and low in price. Rooms are plain but comfortable; beds are firm, and the TVs have cable. Exterior halls and stairways are made of romantically creaking wood and surround a sweet-smelling courtyard where dieffenbachias grow to primeval proportions and doves roost in tropical almond trees. The first-floor patio is ringed by such nonaffiliated businesses as a car-rental office and a travel agency. El Shrimp Bucket restaurant provides room service. **Pros:** nice courtyard; small pool; cheap rates; ocean views from some rooms. **Cons:** rooms are extremely basic and not that attractive; far from Golden Zone beaches; no in-room safes. *Paseo Olas Altas 11 Sur, Olas Altas 669/981–2640 www.lasiesta.com.mx 57 rooms In-room: Wi-Fi. In-hotel: restaurant, room service, bar, pool, laundry service, Internet terminal AE, MC, V.*

$$ **Playa Mazatlán**. Accommodations are sunny, clean, and tasteful, and most open onto terraces or balconies. The well-kept grounds are mature but not dowdy, the pool is large, and there are palapas lining the beach. When you ask for an ocean-view room, specify that you want one away from Joe's Oyster Bar; also check that it's one of the refurbished rooms. **Pros:** lovely grounds; lots of activities including on-site rock-climbing wall; good value for location and amenities offered. **Cons:** a lot of noise from area bars; front-desk service slipping; pool area doesn't have enough seating. *Av. Playa las Gaviotas 202, Zona Dorada 669/989–0555 or 800/762–5816 www.playamazatlan.com.mx 408 rooms In-room: safe, kitchen (some), Wi-Fi (some). In-hotel: restaurant, room service, bars, pool, gym, beachfront, children's programs (ages 7–12), laundry service, Internet terminal, Wi-Fi hotspot, parking (free), no-smoking rooms AE, MC, V.*

$$$ ★ **Pueblo Bonito**. A sense of calm, confident service pervades this all-suites hotel. Colors in the garden are rich: deep terra-cotta, strolling pink flamingos, expansive green palms, pristine white umbrellas, and golden koi ponds. Chandeliers and beveled-glass doors sparkle in the imposing lobby. Guest quarters have cool aqua-tile floors, built-in sofas with earth-tone upholstery, beds with egg-crate-foam and pillow-top mattress pads, and pillow menus that let you choose the cushioning that's best for you. Kitchens are well equipped. It all opens out onto a glistening beach. **Pros:** close to marina and Golden Zone; great beachfront; less of a party scene than at hotels farther down the strip. **Cons:** so-so restaurants; room decoration is a little dated; street-side rooms are noisy. *Av. Camarón Sábalo 2121, Zona Dorada 669/989–8900 or 800/990–8250*

www.pueblobonito.com 247 suites In-room: safe, kitchen, refrigerator, Wi-Fi (some). In-hotel: 3 restaurants, room service, bar, tennis court, pools, gym, beachfront, water sports, children's programs (ages 4–11), laundry service, Internet terminal, Wi-Fi hotspot, parking (free) AE, MC, V.

SLICE OF LIFE

Take in the Mercado Central Pino Suarez's frenzy at a serene distance, from a table in one of the inexpensive restaurants upstairs.

$$$–$$$$ **Pueblo Bonito Emerald Bay.** The neoclassical elements of Mazatlán's most remote and luxurious resort feel so close to holy that you may find yourself whispering. Balconies protrude from all 425-square-foot suites, where you can contemplate gardens that undulate with the curves of spotless sidewalks, then seem to melt into the shifting sand and rippling ocean beyond. It's easy to enjoy the pillow-top mattresses or 350-foot-long shocking-blue pool. But if you don't like being marooned 10 km (6 mi) north of town, then choose another location. There is a driving range, and a golf course is planned for the future. **Pros:** splendid property; far from touristy Golden Zone; great pool areas. **Cons:** beachfront isn't impressive; obnoxious time-share pitches. *Av. Ernesto Coppel Campana 201, Nuevo Mazatlán 669/989–0525 or 800/990–8250 www.pueblobonitoemeraldbay.com 325 suites In-room: safe, kitchen, refrigerator. In-hotel: 2 restaurants, room service, bar, pools, gym, spa, beachfront, children's programs (ages 4–11), laundry service, Internet terminal, Wi-Fi hotspot, parking (free), no-smoking rooms AE, MC, V.*

$$$–$$$$ **Ramada Resort.** Bring on the partying at this beachfront high-rise just inside the southern entrance to the Zona Dorada. It's home to Joe's Oyster Bar, an open-air dance club–volleyball court that is popular with locals and tourists alike; things really rev up on weekends. Amenities are tasteful, however, with comfortable white-walled rooms highlighted by blue-and-green fabrics. **Pros:** great views; good staff. **Cons:** overpriced; beachfront is noisy and busy; rooms get noise from area bars. *Av. Playa las Gaviotas 100, Zona Dorada 669/983–5333 or 800/528–8760 www.lossabalos.com 155 rooms, 45 suites In-room: safe, kitchen (some), refrigerator (some). In-hotel: 5 restaurants, room service, bars, pool, gym, spa, beachfront, Internet terminal, Wi-Fi hotspot, parking (free) AE, MC, V.*

$$$ **Royal Villas Resort.** Everything feels supersize in this 12-story pyramid in the throbbing heart of the Zona Dorada, from the marble-heavy atrium lobby to the one- and two-bedroom suites that are done in bold blues and oranges. Even the glass elevators that take you to and fro offer amazing views. All rooms have balconies (be sure to request an ocean view, and if possible a room above the third floor). A delicate touch is the bridge to the pool, which spans a fishpond. **Pros:** good bar and restaurant; nice pool area; comfortable beds. **Cons:** not a place for a serene getaway (loud clubs nearby, kids at the pool); some junior suites are small for the price. *Av. Camarón Sábalo 500, Zona Dorada 669/916–6161 or 800/898–3564 www.royalvillas.com.mx 123 suites, 2 penthouses In-room: kitchen, Wi-Fi (some). In-hotel:*

BRING ON THE BANDA

Banda, which injects Latin energy into German oompah music, was born in southern Sinaloa when Bavarian immigrants showed up at the turn of the 20th century. It's more popular now than ever.

Mambocafe (✉ *Av. Reforma and Calz. Rafael Buelna, Zona Dorada* ☎ *669/986–6482* 🌐 *www.mambocafe.com.mx*) in Mazatlán's Gran Plaza mall is modeled after Caribbean-style clubs—it's heavy on the tropical vibe and large, live groups that pump out the best in modern and traditional Latin music. Free salsa lessons happen Thursday through Saturday at 7 PM. There's no cover Monday, and ladies enter free Thursday and Sunday; other times expect to pay around $6.

Banda music is everywhere in Mazatlán, including **Toro Bravo** (✉ *Av. del Mar 5500, Zona Costera* ☎ *669/985–0595*), but the mechanical bull is unique. The music starts after 11 PM. It's open Thursday through Sunday, or nightly during holiday seasons.

2 restaurants, room service, bar, pool, gym, beachfront, water sports, children's programs (ages 5–12), laundry facilities, laundry service, Internet terminal, Wi-Fi hotspot, parking (free), no-smoking rooms ▭ *AE, MC, V* 🍽 *AI.*

NIGHTLIFE

Mazatlán gets its share of spring-breakers, so much of its nightlife revolves around manic discos and loud beach bars. Head to the Centro Histórico for a quieter evening—there are a few low-key bars around Plazuela Machado. The bar at the restaurant Pedro y Lola is open nightly until 1 AM.

★ The **Fiesta Mexicana** (✉ *Playa Mazatlán hotel, Av. Playa las Gaviotas 202, Zona Dorada* ☎ *669/989–0555* 🌐 *www.laoriginalfiestamexicana.com*) is one of the city's oldest tourist traditions: the kitschy concept of a trip through Mexican history via a whirlwind of music and dance still draws and deserves big audiences for dinner shows Tuesday and Thursday (May through October only), and Saturday from 7 to 10:30 (doors open at 6). The $35 fee covers an all-you-can-eat buffet, open bar, the entertainment, and the chance to dance yourself.

Joe's Oyster Bar (✉ *Ramada Resort hotel, Av. Playa las Gaviotas 100, Zona Dorada* ☎ *669/983–5333*) has become perhaps Mazatlán's most popular club, although it's really not much more than a palapa and a volleyball court. Locals and tourists dance to pop and hip-hop. Get there early and watch the sunset over a couple of drinks, a plate of shrimp, and yes, some oysters.

SHOPPING

Zona Dorada is chockablock with shops, particularly along Avenidas Camarón Sábalo and Playa las Gaviotas. The area is essentially one big tourist trap, with busloads of cruise-ship passengers and package-tour travelers being dropped off every few minutes. That said, if you're looking for souvenirs, beachwear, delightfully tacky seashell art, and jewelry, you won't have to walk but a few blocks in this area to accomplish all your shopping. ⚠ **Be wary when purchasing jewelry in Mazatlán; stories of tourists paying $800 or more for a ring here only to have it appraised at $300 (or less) at home are all too common. Always demand certificates of authenticity for all pieces.**

OPEN HOUSE FOR ADULTS

The Centro Histórico's resident artists open up their studios to visitors on the first Friday of every month from 4 to 8 PM. Check out 🌐 *www.artwalkmazatlan.com* for information and maps.

The Centro Histórico has fewer shops, but it does have a handful of galleries that sell high-quality crafts that are much more interesting than what you'll find in the Golden Zone. Note that bargaining isn't the norm in shops, no matter where you are in the city, but it's worth a try in markets.

The **Mercado Central Pino Suárez** is a gigantic, turn-of-the-20th-century art nouveau structure between Calles Juárez, Ocampo, Serdán, and Leandro Valle. It's open daily and filled with produce, meat, fish, and bustle. The first few rows parallel to Calle Juárez have shell necklaces, huaraches (Mexican sandals), cowhide children's shoes, T-shirts, and gauzy dresses. Then comes the produce and grocery section, and finally the butcher stalls with the inevitable pigs' heads.

CRAFTS

Casa Antigua (✉ *Calle Mariano Escobedo 206, Centro Histórico* ☎ *669/982–5236*), in the former home of Mazatlán's first bishop, sells crafts from throughout Mexico in all price ranges and mediums—silver, ceramics, black clay, and papier-mâché.

★ **Casa Etnika** (✉ *Sixto Osuna 50, Centro Histórico* ☎ *669/136–0139* 🌐 *www.casaetnika.com* ⏲ *Closed Sun.*) sells a funky mélange of non-kitschy Mexican and world crafts, from jewelry to carved wood statuettes to nature photography of Sinaloa State. Some items are made from recycled materials.

Mexican artist **Elina Chauvet** (✉ *Calle Sixto Osuna 24, Centro Histórico* ☎ *No phone*) sells unique beaded necklaces and bracelets, casual beachwear, Guerrero masks, and embroidered cotton clothing. She's also a renowned painter who sells works by other artists alongside her own.

★ **La Querencia** (✉ *Calle Belisario Dominguez 1502, Centro Histórico* ☎ *669/981–1036*) is a colorful cavern of Latin American art, clothing, and furniture—from the playful to the sublime and with prices to match.

★ The stylish work at **Nidart** (✉ *Calle Libertad 45 and Calle Carnaval, Centro Histórico* ☎ *669/981–0002* 🌐 *www.nidart.com*) includes leather masks, ceramic sculptures, contemporary black-and-white photos, and other Mexican arts and crafts. Sometimes you can watch artisans in open workshops; it's normally open Monday through Saturday between 10 and 2 only.

JEWELRY

Casa Maya (✉ *Av. Playa las Gaviotas 411, Zona Dorada* ☎ *669/914–0491*) has silver and gold jewelry; silver tea sets, platters, and urns; and Talavera place settings. **Rubio Jewelers** (✉ *Costa de Oro hotel, Av. Camarón Sábalo L-1, Zona Dorada* ☎ *669/914–3167*) carries fine gold, silver, and platinum jewelry. It's also Mazatlán's exclusive distributor of Sergio Bustamante's whimsical ceramic and bronze sculptures.

SPORTS AND THE OUTDOORS

FISHING

You can arrange deep-sea charters through your hotel, or you can contact the companies directly. Charters include a full day of fishing, bait and tackle, and usually an ice chest with ice. Prices start at about $100 per person on a party boat or from $270 to $470 to charter a boat for one to six passengers.

For bass fishing in El Salto Reservoir, a lake northeast of Mazatlán off Carretera 40, contact **Amazing Outdoors Tours** (✉ *El Patio Restaurant, Camarón Sábalo 2601, Zona Dorada* ☎ *669/952–1442, 669/913–1719, or 866/245–1490* 🌐 *www.basselsalto.com*). Choose a half- or full-day trip, or stay overnight at their fishing lodge. The reputable **Aries Fleet** (☎ *669/916–3468*) is connected with El Cid Hotel and operates from Marina El Cid. The company has shared or charter boats for big-game fishing. **Bill Heimpel's Star Fleet** (☎ *669/982–2665 or 888/882–9614* 🌐 *www.starfleet.com.mx*), which has fast twin-engine boats, is well regarded.

GOLF

The last 9 holes of the spectacular 27-hole course at **El Cid Golf and Country Club** (✉ *Av. Camarón Sábalo s/n, Zona Dorada* ☎ *669/913–3333 Ext. 3261*) were designed by Lee Trevino. There's a putting green and driving range. Greens fees are $76 (nonguests) for 18 holes plus cart and caddy. The **Estrella del Mar Golf Club** (✉ *Camino Isla de la Piedra, Km 10* ☎ *01800/727–4653 toll-free in Mexico; 877/629–2852* 🌐 *www.estrelladelmar.com*) is an 18-hole waterfront course designed by Robert Trent Jones Jr., just south of Mazatlán proper on Isla de la Piedra (Stone Island). Transportation from some of Mazatlán's major hotels is free. Carts and transportation to and from the course are included in the $75–$110 greens fee.

WATER SPORTS

The two most popular activities are snorkeling tours to Deer Island and parasailing—nearly every hotel offers both, along with kayak and Jet Ski rentals. A few outfitters, including the Aqua Sport Center, offer scuba, but Mazatlán is not a popular diving area.

Aqua Adventures (✉ *Royal Villas Resort, Av. Camarón Sábalo 500, Zona Dorada* ☎ *669/916–6161*) rents kayaks ($12–$15 an hour) and WaveRunners ($60 an hour) and offers short parasailing and banana-boat rides.

AquaSport Center (✉ *Av. Camarón Sábalo s/n, next to Hotel La Puesta del Sol, Zona Dorada* ☎ *669/913–3333 Ext. 3341*) offers banana boat and parasailing rides and rents WaveRunners, kayaks, Boogie boards, and sailboats. Its staffers can also arrange half-day trimaran trips to Isla de los Venados aboard the *Kolonahe,* docked at El Cid Marina.

The 4-acre **Parque Acuático Mazagua** (✉ *Av. Sábalo Cerritos and Entronque Habal Cerritos, Nuevo Mazatlán* ☎ *669/988–0041* 🌐 *www.mazagua.com*) has slides, wading pools, and a wave pool as well as picnic facilities with barbecue grills. Entrance is about $12 per person; the park is open 10–6 Wednesday through Sunday for most of the year and daily in July, August, and during school holidays.

ECOVENTURING

EduVentura (☎ *669/940–8687* 🌐 *www.eduventura.com*) at the Playa Mazatlán hotel offers a grab bag of activities and ecotourism opportunities. After trying out the climbing wall and zip line, book a kayaking tour to Deer Island or a whale- or bird-watching excursion through one of several companies committed to sustainable tourism that supports local conservation efforts.

12

PUERTO VALLARTA

Updated by Jane Onstott

Although Puerto Vallarta (PV) has spread north and south over the years, every attempt has been made to keep the character of the original downtown village intact. City ordinances prohibit neon signs, require houses to be painted white, and dictate other architectural details downtown, where pack mules still occasionally clomp along a few blocks beyond the busy downtown scene.

PV the destination is much larger than PV the town. The original town sits smack dab at the center of a 42-km-long (26-mi-long) bay, Bahia de Banderas (Banderas, or Flags, Bay), Mexico's largest. On the same latitude as the Hawaiian Islands, PV is tropical. At Old Vallarta, in the center of the bay, the Sierra Madre foothills practically dive into the sea; numerous mountain-fed rivers and streams nourish tropical deciduous forest as far north as coastal San Blas. South of PV the hills recede from the coast and the drier tropical thorn forest predominates to Barra de Navidad.

The bay provides shelter from storms at sea, and has been attracting outsiders since the 16th century. Pirates and explorers paused here to relax—or maybe plunder and pillage—during long trips. Sir Francis Drake apparently stopped here. In the mid-1850s Don Guadalupe Sánchez Carrillo developed the bay as a port for the silver mines by the Río Cuale. Then it was known as Puerto de Peñas (Rocky Port) and had about 1,500 inhabitants. In 1918 it was made a municipality and renamed for Ignacio L. Vallarta, a governor of Jalisco State.

In the 1950s Puerto Vallarta was essentially a hideaway for the wealthy and a few hardy escapists. When it first entered the general public's consciousness, with John Huston's 1964 movie *The Night of the Iguana,* it was a quiet fishing and farming community. After the movie was released, tourism began to boom, and today PV has some 300,000 residents. Airports, hotels, and highways have supplanted palm groves and fishing shacks, and about 2 million people visit each year.

El Centro (downtown) rises abruptly from the sea; whitewashed homes and businesses line hilly cobblestone streets. South of the Cuale River, the Zona Romántica (Romantic Zone, aka Col. E. Zapata or South Side), bordering Los Muertos Beach, has the most restaurants and shops. Old Vallarta includes El Centro and the Zona Romántica.

Facing a busy avenue, the Zona Hotelera Norte (Northern Hotel Zone) has malls and businesses in addition to high-rise hotels. Additional shopping centers and deluxe hotels are in Marina Vallarta, sandwiched between a golf course and the city's main marina, 15 minutes north of downtown. At the southern edge of Nayarit State, the planned resort of Nuevo Vallarta has lots of all-inclusive hotels but few restaurants and shops outside the Paradise Plaza mall.

THE DISH

Although not cast in John Huston's *The Night of the Iguana*, Elizabeth Taylor accompanied Richard Burton during filming, and the gossip about their romance (both were married at the time, but not to each other) brought this tiny fishing village to the public's attention in the early '60s. Considering that Ava Gardner and Deborah Kerr were among the actresses in the film, it's no surprise that Liz felt compelled to be by Richard's side.

Part of what's now called the Riviera Nayarit, the beach towns north of Nuevo Vallarta are steadily gaining in popularity and tourist infrastructure. Once the private stomping grounds of local fishermen and surfers, Punta de Mita is now a super-exclusive gated community, but a sliver of paradise is still accessible to the hoi polloi. Bucerías, Sayulita, and other small communities are attracting more and more travelers while retaining their small-town appeal.

South of PV to Mismaloya, the condos and hotels of the Zona Hotelera Sur straddle the beach or overlook it from cliff-side aeries. Roughly 121 km (75 mi) south of PV en route to the city of Manzanillo, the Costalegre is a mixture of exclusive resorts and earthy little beach hamlets.

To fully explore the beaches and small towns outside downtown PV it really helps to have a car. However, cars are a serious hindrance in El Centro and the Río Cuale area, and you can see the sights there by taxi or on foot—as long as you wear comfortable shoes for the uneven cobblestone streets.

GETTING HERE AND AROUND

Many major U.S. airlines have flights to PV; some are nonstop. Private taxis and vans provide transportation from the airport to PV hotels; the airport is about 7½ km (4½ mi) north of downtown.

PV's Central Camionero, or Central Bus Station, is 1 km (½ mi) north of the airport, halfway between Nuevo Vallarta and downtown Puerto Vallarta. ETN has the most luxurious bus service to Guadalajara, Mexico City, and many other destinations. TAP serves Mexico City, Guadalajara, Puerto Vallarta, Tepic, and Mazatlán as well as lesser-known destinations.

City buses, around 50¢, serve downtown as well as points to the south and north. Buses and taxis are the way to get around downtown; rent a car for days when you'll be sightseeing outside the city center.

ESSENTIALS

Bus Contact **Central Camionero** (✉ *Puerto Vallarta–Tepic Hwy., Km 9, Las Mojoneras* ☎ *322/290–1009*).

Medical Assistance **Cornerstone Hospital** (✉ *Av. Los Tules 136, across from Plaza Caracol, Zona Hotelera* ☎ *322/226–3700* 🌐 *www.hospitalcornerstone.com*). **Hospital San Javier Marina** (✉ *Blvd. Francisco M. Ascencio 2760, at María Montessori, Zona Hotelera Norte* ☎ *322/226–1010*).

Visitor and Tour Info **Puerto Vallarta Tourism Board & Convention and Visitors Bureau** (✉ *Local 18 Planta Baja, Zona Comercial Hotel Canto del Sol, Zona Hotelera Norte, Las Glorias* ☎ *322/224–1175 or 888/384–6822* 🌐 *www.visitpuertovallarta.com*).

EXPLORING

❹ **Jardín Botánico de Puerto Vallarta.** On 20 acres of land 19 km (12 mi) south of town, the Puerto Vallarta Botanical Gardens features more than 3,000 species of plants. Set within the tropical dry forest at 1,300 feet above sea level, its trails lead to a stream where you can swim; palm, agave, and rose gardens; a tree fern grotto; an orchid house; and displays of Mexican wildflowers and carnivorous plants. There are free parking and a free guided tour daily at 1 PM December through Easter. The lovely, open-sided Hacienda de Oro restaurant serves an array of starters as well as pizza and Mexican dishes. Beverages include wine and a full bar. Go to its Web site to arrange a four-hour birding (via ATV) or hiking tour, with lunch, for $85 per person. A taxi here will cost about $20, but for less than a dollar you can take the "El Tuito" bus from the corner of Aguacate and Venustiano Carranza streets. Another tip: Slather on insect repellent before you go, and take some with you. This is the jungle, and *jejenes* (no-see-ums), mosquitoes, and other biting bugs can be counted on to attack. ✉ *Carretera a Barra de Navidad, Km 24, Las Juntas y Los Veranos* ☎ *322/223–6182* 🌐 *www.vallartabotanicalgardensac.org* 🎫 *$3* 🕑 *Mon.–Sat. 10–6.*

❶ **La Iglesia de Nuestra Señora de Guadalupe.** The Church of Our Lady of Guadalupe is dedicated to the patron saint of Mexico and of Puerto Vallarta. The holy mother's image, by Ignacio Ramírez, is the centerpiece of the cathedral's slender marble altarpiece. The brick bell tower is topped by a lacy-looking crown that replicates the one worn by Carlota, short-lived empress of Mexico. The wrought-iron crown toppled during an earthquake that shook this area of the Pacific Coast in October 1995, but was soon replaced with a fiberglass version, supported, as was the original, by a squadron of stone angels. This was replaced with a newer and larger rendition in October 2009. ✉ *Calle Hidalgo between Iturbide and Zaragoza, Centro* ☎ *No phone* 🕑 *7:30 AM–8 PM daily.*

❷ **Malecón.** This seaside walkway is the Champs Élysées of PV—only shorter, warmer, and less expensive. Every night and weekend along the mile-long concrete walkway bordering the sea is a spectacle, with locals

Fodor's Choice ★

and tourists out to stroll, and vendors and peddlers selling empanadas, corn on the cob, fried bananas, helium balloons, and cotton candy. Clowns, magicians, and musicians entertain in the Los Arcos amphitheater. Even those who have lived here all their lives come out to watch the red sun sink into the gray-blue water beyond the bay. Some of PV's most endearing art pieces are here *en plein air.* Along the sea walk is a series of bronze sculptures—including Puerto Vallarta's well-known seahorse icon—that are constantly touched, photographed, and climbed on. ✉ *Extending south from Calle 31 de Octubre south to Playa los Muertos, Centro.*

3 **Museo Arqueológico**. Pre-Columbian figures and Indian artifacts are on display at the Archaeological Museum. There's a general explanation of Western Pacific cultures and shaft tombs and abbreviated but attractive exhibits of Aztatlán and Purépecha cultures and the Spanish conquest. ✉ *Western tip of Isla Río Cuale, Centro* ☎ *No phone* 🎫 *By donation* ⏲ *Mon.–Sat. 10–6.*

La Tobara. Turtles sunning themselves on logs, crocodiles masquerading as logs, water-loving birds, and exotic orchids make the maze of green-brown canals that is La Tobara an out-of-town must for nature lovers. Launches putter along these waterways from El Conchal Bridge, at the outskirts of San Blas, about a three-hour drive from Marina Vallarta, or from the nearby village of Matanchén. After cruising along for about 45 minutes—during which you'll have taken *way* too many photos of the mangrove roots that protrude from the water and the turtles—you arrive at spring-fed freshwater pools for which the area is named. You can hang out at the restaurant overlooking the pool or play Tarzan and Jane on the rope swing. Most folks take the optional trip to a crocodile farm on the way back, stretching a two-hour tour into three hours. ✉ *El Conchal Bridge, entrance to/exit from San Blas, San Blas* ☎ *323/108–4174 (cell)* 🎫 *$9 per person; $28 for the whole boat* ⏲ *Daily 10–5.*

BEACHES

DOWNTOWN PUERTO VALLARTA

Playa los Muertos. PV's original happenin' beach has nice bay views, and as action central, it's definitely PV's most engaging beach. Facing Vallarta's South Side (south of the Río Cuale), this flat beach hugs the Zona Romántica and runs about 1½ km (1 mi) south to a rocky point called El Púlpito. **■ TIP→ The steps (more than 100) at Calle Púlpito lead to a lookout with a great view of the beach and the bay.**

Joggers cruise the cement boardwalk early morning and after sunset; vendors stalk the beach nonstop, hawking kites, jewelry, and serapes as well as hair braiding and alfresco massage. Their parade can range from entertaining (good bargainers can get excellent deals) to downright maddening. Bar-restaurants run the length of the beach; the bright blue umbrellas at the south end belong to Blue Chairs resort, the hub of PV's effervescent gay scene.

The surf ranges from mild to choppy with an undertow; the small waves crunching the shore usually discourage mindless paddling. Strapping

Sun-seekers kick back in wooden beach chairs, waiters serve up food and drink on the sand, massage techs offer their (so-so) services alfresco. Chico's Dive Shop sells dive packages and boat trips and rents snorkel gear, boogie boards ($10 for the day for either), and double sea kayaks ($20 per hour). Barceló La Jolla de Mismaloya has day passes for nonguests that are valid from 9 AM to 6 PM: $60 gets you use of facilities (pool, gym, game room, an hour of kayaking), plus food and drink. In the afternoon locals hang out at this beach, the kids playing in the sand while the moms wait for their men to return from fishing expeditions and touring gigs. The beach is about 13 km (8 mi) south of PV. The bus drops you on the highway, and it's a 200-yard walk from there down a dirt road to the beach. The tiny village of Mismaloya is on the east side of Carretera 200. **Facilities:** Boating, diving, kayaking, snorkeling; food concessions, toilets (Port-o-Potties on road to beach).

TURTLE RESCUE

In San Pancho, **Grupo Ecológico de la Costa Verde** (*Green Coast Ecological Group* ✉ *Av. Latino América 102, San Pancho* ☎ *311/258–4100* 🌐 *www.project-tortuga.org*) works to save the olive ridley, leatherback, and eastern Pacific green turtles. Volunteers patrol beaches, collect eggs, maintain the nursery, tabulate data, and educate the public. (Apply any time during the year, via the Web site, for an assignment June through November.) Call or check their Web site to see whether slide shows to raise awareness and funds are happening during your stay.

Boca de Tomatlán. This is the name of both a small village and a deep, V-shaped, rocky bay that lie at the mouth ("boca" means mouth) of the Río Horcones, about 5 km (3 mi) south of Mismaloya and 17 km (10½ mi) south of PV. Water taxis leave from Boca to the southern beaches; you can arrange snorkeling trips to Los Arcos. As far as most visitors are concerned, this is mainly the staging area for water taxis with nowhere else to hang out. However, this dramatic-looking bay fringed in palm trees does have a rustic appeal. Grocery stores sell chips, Cokes, and plastic water toys for tots; a handful of informal seaside cafés cluster at the water's edge. At very low tide only, it's possible for adventurers and cheapskates to walk south from Boca to Playa Las Animas (about 40 minutes) along a small path at waters' edge. You certainly don't want to be on this path, however, when the tide begins to come in, as the rocks behind it are steep and sharp. **Facilities:** Fishing; food concessions, toilets.

Playa las Ánimas. There's lots to do besides sunbathe at this beach and town 15 minutes south of Boca de Tomatlán. Framed in oak, coconut, and pink-flowering *amapa* trees, the brown-sand beach is named "The Souls" because pirate graves were reportedly located here many years ago. Along the 1-km-long (½-mi-long) beach are piles of smooth, strange rocks looking an awful lot like petrified elephant poo. Because of its very shallow waters, Las Animas is often referred to as *la playa de los niños* (children's beach), and it tends to fill up with families on weekends and holidays. They come by water taxi or as part of half- or full-day bay cruises. Five or six seafood eateries line the sand; a few will lend their clients volleyballs to use on sand courts out front. You can also rent Jet Skis, ride a banana boat, or soar up into the sky behind a speedboat while dangling from a colorful parachute. **Facilities:** Banana-boat rides, boating, Jet Skis, parasailing; food concessions.

Quimixto. Between the sandy stretches of Las Ánimas and Majahuitas, and about 20 minutes by boat from Boca de Tomatlán, Quimixto has a narrow, rocky shoreline that attracts few bathers. Tour boats stop here, and their clients usually have a meal at one of the seafood eateries facing the beach. Horses by the dozens are standing by to take passengers to Quimixto Falls (about $13 round-trip). It's only slightly longer than the 25-minute ride to walk there. You can bathe at the base of the energetic falls; the pool is enclosed by sheer rock walls. Be careful of the current during the rainy season, when the water crashing into the pool tends to push swimmers toward the rock walls. Before proceeding to the falls, have a cool drink at the casual restaurant; consuming something is obligatory to gain access. During stormy weather or a full moon there's a fun, fast wave at Quimixto's reef, popular with surfers but, because of its inaccessibility, rarely crowded. **Facilities:** Horseback riding, surfing; food concessions, toilets.

SNORKELING SANCTUARY

Protected area **Los Arcos** is an offshore group of giant rocks rising some 65 feet above the water, making the area great for snorkeling and diving. For reasonable fees, local men along the road to Mismaloya Beach run diving, snorkeling, fishing, and boat trips here and as far north as Punta Mita and Las Marietas or the beach villages of Cabo Corrientes. Recommended for all of these trips is Mis̆maloya Divers (☎ *322/228–0020*), with 23-foot skiffs and new, 75-horsepower, four-stroke motors. Restaurants and fishermen at Playa Mismaloya can also set you up.

★ **Yelapa.** This secluded village and ½-km-long (¼-mi-long) beach is about an hour southeast of downtown PV and a half-hour from Boca de Tomatlán—by boat, of course. A half-dozen seafood *enramadas* (thatch-roof huts) edge its fine, clean, grainy sand. Phones and electricity arrived in Yelapa around the turn of the 21st century. Believe it or not, it's the largest and most developed of the north Cabo Corrientes towns, with quite a few rustic rooms and houses for rent by the day, week, or month. That said, **bring all the money you'll need, as there's nothing as formal as a bank.**

The beach slopes down to the water, and small waves break right on the shore. In high season and during holidays, there are water-sports outfitters. From here you can hike 20 minutes into the jungle to see the small Cascada Cola del Caballo (Horse Tail Waterfall), with a pool at its base for swimming. (The falls are often dry near the end of the dry season, especially April–early June.) A more ambitious expedition of several hours brings you to less-visited, very beautiful Cascada del Catedral (Cathedral Falls). Beyond that, Yelapa is, for the most part, *tranquilisimo*: a place to just kick back in a beach chair and sip something cold. Seemingly right when you really need it, Cheggy or Agustina, the pie ladies, will show up with their homemade lime, coconut, or nut creations. **Facilities:** Boating, fishing, parasailing; food concessions.

WHERE TO EAT

PUERTO VALLARTA

ZONA ROMÁNTICA

$$ ASIAN

✕ **Archie's Wok.** Dishes at this extremely popular pan-Asian restaurant include Thai garlic shrimp, *pancit* (Filipino stir-fry with pasta), and Singapore-style (lightly battered) crispy fish. There are also several vegetarian dishes. The spinach and watercress salad with feta, pecans, and a hibiscus dressing is healthful, refreshing, and perfect for a late lunch (the restaurant opens only after 2 PM). Ceilings are high, and the decor is Asian tropical: dark wood, lacy potted palms, and Indonesian étagères. Thursday through Saturday from 7:30 to 10:30 PM, the soothing harp music of well-known local musician D'Rachel is the perfect accompaniment to your meal. ✉ *Calle Francisca Rodríguez 130, Col. E. Zapata* ☎ *322/222–0411* ✍ *Reservations not accepted* ▭ *MC, V* ⊙ *Closed Sun. and Sept.*

$ CLASSIC MEXICAN

✕ **Café de Olla.** Repeat visitors swear by the enchiladas and carne asadas at this earthy restaurant. It's also one of the few places in town where you can get a margarita made of *raicilla* (green-agave firewater as opposed to tequila, which comes from the blue agave) when available. A large tree extends from the dining-room floor through the roof, local artwork adorns the walls, and salsa music often plays in the background. Note that as soon as Café de Olla opens for the season, it fills up and seems to stay full: You may need to wait for a table, especially at breakfast and dinner. If you give up waiting, the taco shop next door is very good. ✉ *Calle Basilio Badillo 168–A, Col. E. Zapata* ☎ *322/223–1626* ✍ *Reservations not accepted* ▭ *No credit cards* ⊙ *Closed Tues. and Sept. 15–Oct. 15.*

$$$ INTERNATIONAL Fodor's Choice ★

✕ **Daiquiri Dick's.** Locals come over and over for breakfast (the homemade orange-almond granola is great), visitors for the good service and consistent Mexican and world cuisine. The lunch-dinner menu has fabulous appetizers, including superb lobster or shrimp tacos with a drizzle of béchamel sauce and perfect, tangy jumbo-shrimp wontons. On the menu since the restaurant opened almost 30 years ago is Pescado Vallarta, or grilled fish on a stick. The tortilla soup is popular, too. Start with a signature daiquiri; move on to the extensive wine list. The open patio dining room frames a view of Playa Los Muertos, creating a beautiful, simple scene to enjoy while you sip that drink. ✉ *Av. Olas Altas 314, Col. E. Zapata* ☎ *322/222–0566* 🌐 *www.ddpv.com* ▭ *MC, V* ⊙ *Closed Sept. and Tues. May–Aug.*

$ CLASSIC MEXICAN

✕ **El Brujo.** It's on a noisy street corner, but the seriously good food and generous portions mean that this is still an expat favorite. The *molcajete*—a sizzling black pot of tender flank steak, grilled green onion, and soft white cheese in a delicious homemade sauce of dried red peppers—is served with a big plate of guacamole, refried beans, and made-at-the-moment corn or flour tortillas. Try the breaded scallops, stuffed fish with shrimp and creamy *huitlacoche* (black corn fungus) sauce, or a grilled skirt steak with mushrooms and bell peppers bathed in tomato sauce. If you're into simpler fare, the unadorned grilled fish fillet is fresh and delicious, too. ✉ *Venustiano Carranza 510, at Naranjo, Col. Remance* ☎ *322/223–2036* *Reservations not accepted* ▭ *MC, V* ⊙ *Closed 2 wks in late Sept.–early Oct.*

$$ EUROPEAN ✕ **Kaiser Maximilian.** Viennese entrées dominate the menu, which is modified each year when the restaurant participates in PV's culinary festival. One favorite is herb-crusted rack of lamb served with horseradish and pureed vegetables au gratin; another is venison medallions in chestnut sauce served with braised white cabbage and steamed vegetables. The adjacent café (open 8 AM–midnight) has sandwiches, excellent desserts, and 20 specialty coffees—all of which are also available at the main restaurant. To avoid the stream of street peddlers off the patio, eat in the charming, European-style dining room, where handsome black-and-white-clad servers look right at home amid dark-wood framed mirrors, brightly polished brass, and lace café curtains. ✉ *Av. Olas Altas 380, Col. E. Zapata* ☎ *322/223–0760* ▭ *AE, MC, V* ⊙ *Closed Sun.*

$$$$ INTERNATIONAL ✕ **La Palapa.** This large, welcoming, thatched-roof eatery is open to the breezes of Playa Los Muertos and filled with wicker-covered chandeliers, art-glass fixtures, and lazily rotating ceiling fans. The menu meanders among international dishes with modern presentation: roasted stuffed chicken breast, pork loin, seared yellowfin tuna drizzled in cacao sauce. The seafood enchilada plate is divine. It's pricey, but the beachfront location and, in the evening, the low lights and Latin jazz combo (8 to 11 PM nightly) keep people coming back. Breakfast here (daily after 8 AM) is popular with locals as well as visitors. This is the sister property to Vista Grill, which has great views of the bay from the hills above town. ✉ *Calle Púlpito 103, Playa Los Muertos, Col. E. Zapata* ☎ *322/222–5225* 🌐 *www.lapalapapv.com* ▭ *AE, D, MC, V.*

$$$ INTERNATIONAL Fodor's Choice ★ ✕ **Vista Grill.** Sensational views of the sunset and sparkling city-light panoramas after dark make this one of the best restaurants in PV for a celebratory toast—of life, love, or the perfect vacation. Dedicated observers can spot whales spouting offshore almost any day during the winter months. An army of attentive waiters brings baskets of delicious, buttery rolls and whisks away plates. Try the stellar crab-and-sea-bass cakes, lobster tacos, or sashimi with truffle-and-soy vinaigrette and avocado coulis. The chef adds new dishes every very weeks; the barman stocks top-of-the-line spirits, and there is a large wine cellar representing several continents. ✉ *Calle Púlpito 377, near Calle Aguacate, Col. Alta Vista* ☎ *322/222–3570* 🌐 *www.vistagrill.com* ▭ *MC, V* ⊙ *No lunch.*

CENTRO AND ENVIRONS

$$$ SPANISH ✕ **Barcelona Tapas.** One of the few places in town with both good food and an excellent bay view, Barcelona Tapas has traditional Spanish tapas like garlicky roasted potatoes, spicy garlic shrimp, and grilled mushrooms. In addition to traditional paella, there's also a seafood-only version. To start you off, attentive waiters bring a free appetizer and delicious homemade bread. The "chef's surprise" six-course tasting menu lets you try soup, salad, and dessert as well as hot and cold tapas. The restaurant is air-conditioned in summer; the rest of the year the windows are taken off to let the breezes in. You pay for that patio view by having to walk up a few dozen stairs. ✉ *Calle Matamoros at 31 de Octubre,*

Centro ☎ *322/222–0510* 🌐 *www.barcelonatapas.net* ✍ *Reservations essential* ▭ *AE.*

$$$ INTERNATIONAL Fodor's Choice ★ **✕ Café des Artistes Bistro Gourmet.** Several sleek dining spaces make up the original, downtown restaurant Café des Artistes; the most beautiful and romantic is the courtyard garden with modern sculpture. The main restaurant achieves a contemporary Casablanca feel with glass raindrops and tranquil music. In either area, choose an appetizer, entrée, and dessert from the three-course bistro menu. We recommend the creamy soup of smoked chipotle chilies followed by a fresh fillet of fish cooked in one of several Mexican styles, and finishing with the crème brûlée. Also within these walls, Thierry Blouet's Cocina de Autor (closed Sunday and in September) is a limited-seating restaurant pairing four- to six-course tasting menus with or without wines. Decor is restrained, with a waterfall garden behind plate glass taking center stage. In these restaurants, drinks add significantly to the price of the meal. Many diners end the night at the clubby cigar bar or Constantini Wine Bar, which offers some 50 vintages by the glass as well as distilled spirits, appetizers, and live music most nights of the week. ✉ *Av. Guadalupe Sánchez 740, Centro* ☎ *322/222–3229* 🌐 *www.cafedesartistes.com* ▭ *AE, MC, V* ⊙ *No lunch.*

TACO PRIMER

In this region's informal eateries a taco is generally a diminutive corn tortilla heated on an oiled grill and filled with meat, shrimp, or batter-fried fish. If your server asks "*¿Preparadita?*" he or she is asking if you want it with cilantro and onions. Add-your-own condiments are *salsa mexicana* (chopped raw onions, tomatoes, and green chilies), liquidy guacamole made with green *tomatillos* (small green tomatoes), and pickled jalapeño peppers. Some restaurants also feature garnishes of chopped nopal cactus.

$$ CLASSIC MEXICAN **✕ Chez Elena.** Frequented in its heyday by Hollywood luminaries and the who's who of PV, this downtown restaurant still has a loyal following. The casual patio ambience is simple, but the wholesome food is satisfying, and the portions are generous. House specialties include fajitas and Yucatan-style pork. Elena's is also known for an eclectic signature dish, the Indonesian *sate mixto*, skewers of meat and chicken spiced with peanut sauce, as well as its killer handcrafted margaritas and its flaming coffee drinks. ✉ *Calle Matamoros 520, Centro* ☎ *322/222–0161* ▭ *MC, V* ⊙ *Closed June–Sept. No lunch.*

¢ CLASSIC MEXICAN **✕ Comedor de Sra. Heladia.** Here you can glimpse the real Old Vallarta. A short but steep walk up from the malecón is this neighborhood dining room, which serves construction workers and locals. It's in a typical one-story Vallarta house of whitewashed brick with a red-tile roof and a burnished-cement floor. The lady of the house serves breakfast from 8 to 11 AM and a limited later meal of two or three entrées, served between 1 and 5 PM. Choices like meatballs in tomato sauce, pork chops, or pig's feet are usually accompanied by rice, beans, homemade salsa, and a basket of hot tortillas. There's no menu, and you'll need to communicate in basic Spanish. ✉ *Calle Aldama at Calle Matamoros, Centro* ☎ *322/223–9612* ✍ *Reservations not accepted* ▭ *No credit cards* ⊙ *Closed Sun. No dinner.*

$$ SEAFOOD ✕ **Cueto's**. Teams of engaging waiters, all family members, squeeze past the trio that croons romantic tunes throughout the day to refill beer glasses, remove empty plates, or bring more fresh tostadas and hot, crusty garlic bread. But don't fill up on nonessentials, as the casseroles—with crab, clams, fish, shrimp, or mixed seafood—are so delicious you won't want to leave even one bite. We particularly recommend the cream-based casseroles. Enjoy a complimentary margarita with dinner or a free digestif later on. Cueto's is a few blocks behind the Unidad Deportivo complex of soccer fields and baseball diamonds. ☒ *Calle Brasilia 469, Col. 5 de Diciembre (Zona Hotelera)* ☎ *322/223–0363* ▭ *MC, V.*

$$ CLASSIC MEXICAN Fodor's Choice ★ ✕ **El Arrayán**. The oilcloth table covers, enameled tin plates, exposed rafters, and red roof tiles of this patio-restaurant conjure up nostalgia for the quaint Mexican home of less frenetic times. Here you can find the things *Abuelita* (Grandma) still loves to cook, with a few subtle variations. Highlights of classic Mexican dishes from around the country are rib-eye steak served with traditional cactus-pad salad, duck *carnitas* in a glaze of smoky chili and orange, and *cochinita pibil,* a dish from the Yucatan Peninsula of tender pork cooked in a banana leaf and served with black beans and fried plantain. For dessert, try caramel flan or a light tamarind-flavored ice. It's a bit pricey for Mexican comfort food, but it has a very dedicated fan club. ☒ *Calle Allende 344, at Calle Miramar, Centro* ☎ *322/222–7195* ⊕ *www.elarrayan.com.mx* ▭ *MC, V* ⊗ *Closed Tues. No lunch.*

¢ CLASSIC MEXICAN ✕ **El Campanario**. Fans swirl the air, doors are open to the street, and cheerful oilcloths cover wooden tables at this no-frills spot across from the cathedral. Egg dishes and chilaquiles are served 9 AM to 11 AM, and an inexpensive daily lunch menu is served 2 PM to 5 PM. For around $5, you get soup, a main dish, a drink, homemade tortillas, and dessert. Office workers come in for takeout or drift in between 6 PM and 10 PM for tacos, *tortas* (Mexican-style sandwiches on crispy white rolls), or pozole. A recipe for the last is given—along with a positive dining review—in a framed *Los Angeles Times* article from the 1980s. ☒ *Calle Hidalgo 339, Centro* ☎ *322/223–1509* ▭ *No credit cards* ⊗ *Closed Sun. and 5–6 PM.*

$$$ INTERNATIONAL ✕ **Le Bistro**. Start off with a classic tortilla soup or a combo appetizer plate of guacamole, quesadillas, and nachos before moving on to one of the Mexican or international main dishes: crab enchiladas, chicken-and-squash-blossom crepes, duck with blackberry sauce, or red snapper with red-pepper-studded crust and tequila-lime sauce. The romantic and exotic-looking restaurant is draped in ferns and tropical plants and overlooks the Cuale River; carved-stone columns, zebra chairs, and wicker settees are among the sophisticated touches. Breakfast is no longer served. ☒ *Isla Río Cuale 16–A* ☎ *322/225–9945* ⊕ *www.lebistro.com.mx* ▭ *AE, MC, V* ⊗ *Closed Sun. and mid-Aug.–Sept.*

$ CLASSIC MEXICAN ✕ **Los Alcatraces**. For a breakfast of chilaquiles that are crisp, not soggy, come to "The Calla Lilies." *Café de olla,* real Mexican coffee simmered with cinnamon and *panela* (unrefined brown sugar), is served in a keep-warm carafe; crumbly white cheese is delivered from a ranch in the nearby hills. All meals are economical, especially the combo plate: a quesadilla, chiles rellenos, skirt steak, rice, beans, and a taco. Weekdays, a fixed-price lunch for under $5 consists of soup, main dish, beans, and a fruit drink. This is a good, authentic-Mexican option for people staying in the Hotel Zone, although adjectives like "charming" and "picturesque" do not apply. ✉ *Blvd. Francisco M. Ascencio 1808, Col. Olímpica* ☎ *322/222–1182* ▭ *No credit cards* ⊙ *No dinner weekends.*

$ MODERN MEXICAN ✕ **Mamá Rosa.** Locals return over and over for the expansive breakfast buffet (served until 2 PM, but freshest before noon) and, in the evening, for budget gourmet meals. Recommended main dishes include the nut-crusted salmon served on a bed of asparagus and thin sliced potatoes, shrimp medallions in pineapple and chipotle chili sauce, lamb meatballs in red wine sauce, and Mamá Rosa special chicken, stuffed with chorizo and spinach on a bed of beans. Ingredients are reassuringly recognizable but uniquely combined. Presentation is also a work of art, proving that a beautifully designed dish isn't the sole province of restaurants with high prices and small portions. The setting is pleasant but not fancy; upper and lower patios are surrounded by plenty of plants. ✉ *Calle Leona Vicario 269, Centro* ☎ *322/222–4010* 🌐 *www.mamarosavallarta.com* ▭ *MC, V* ⊙ *Closed Mon. No lunch, no dinner May–mid-Oct.*

$ VEGETARIAN ✕ **Planeta Vegetariana.** Those who stumble upon this hogless heaven can "pig out" on tasty, meatless *carne asada* and a selection of main dishes that changes daily. Choose from at least three healthful yet unexciting main dishes, plus beans, several types of rice, and a soup at this unassuming buffet-only place. Though the selection of overdressed salads is good, the greens tend to be wilted or soggy. A healthful fruit drink, coffee, or tea, and dessert are included in the reasonable price. Eggs are not used; items containing milk products are labeled as such. ✉ *Iturbide 270, Centro* ☎ *322/222–3073* ▭ *No credit cards.*

$$$ INTERNATIONAL Fodor's Choice ★ ✕ **Trio.** Conviviality, hominess, and dedication on the part of chef-owners Bernhard Güth and Ulf Henriksson have made Trio one of Puerto Vallarta's best restaurants—hands down. Fans marvel at the kitchen's ability to deliver perfect meal after perfect meal. Popular demand guarantees rack of lamb with fresh mint and, for dessert, the warm chocolate cake. The kitchen often stays open until nearly midnight, and during high season the restaurant opens the back patio, second floor, and rooftop terrace. Waiters are professional yet unpretentious; either the sommelier or the maître d' can help you with the wine. But the main reason to dine here is the consistently fabulous food, which is also a great value. ✉ *Calle Guerrero 264, Centro* ☎ *322/222–2196* ▭ *AE, MC, V* ⊙ *No lunch.*

$$ FRENCH ✕ **Vitea.** When chefs Bernhard Güth and Ulf Henriksson, of Trio, needed a challenge, they cooked up this delightful seaside bistro. So what if your legs bump your partner's at the small tables? This will only make it easier to sneak bites from her plate. The decor of the open, casual venue is as fresh as the food. Appetizers include the smoked salmon roll with crème fraîche, or choose from the selection of "small plates" like the spicy shrimp tempura or the garlic-chili manicotti. Alternatively, make a meal of the bistro's soups, sandwiches, and salads. It's a nice place for breakfast overlooking the malecón. ✉ *Libertad 2, north*

of Cuale River on the malecón, Centro ☎ *322/222–8703* ▭ *MC, V* 🌐 *www.viteapv.com* ⏲ *Closed 1 wk in late Sept.*

$$$ INTERNATIONAL ✕ **Ztai.** Lounge music emanates from the cool, dark, modern interior and into the appealingly spare outdoor garden shaded by bamboo and fig trees. The food is quite good, and portions are large. Try the fresh and oh-so-lightly-fried calamari, the fruity shrimp ceviche, duck tacos, or the tender filet mignon. Asian flavors spice up the seafood recipes, while the meat dishes lean toward continental cuisine. After dinner you can recline with a cocktail on one of the beds, sofas, or bar stools of Ztai's upstairs lounge. ✉ *Calle Morelos 737, Centro* ☎ *322/222–0364* 🌐 *www.ztai.com* ▭ *AE, MC, V* ⏲ *No lunch.*

TIME IS OF THE ESSENCE

The state of Nayarit (Nuevo Vallarta and points north, i.e., la Riviera Nayarit) is in the Mountain Standard Time zone, while Jalisco (Marina Vallarta to Barra de Navidad) is on Central Standard Time. But because tourism in Bucerías and Nuevo Vallarta has always been linked to that of Puerto Vallarta, many Nayarit businesses run on Jalisco time. When making dinner reservations or checking restaurant hours, ask whether the place runs on *hora de Jalisco* (Jalisco time) or *hora de Nayarit.*

RIVIERA NAYARIT

$$ INTERNATIONAL ✕ **Cafe del Mar.** Chefs Eugene of Singapore and Amandine, a Belgian-Mexican, artfully blend Asian, Mediterranean, and Mexican cuisines to create a simple but sophisticated menu emphasizing seafood and chicken dishes. Try the sashimi of the day, Vietnamese spring rolls, smoked salmon linguini, or green curry chicken with jasmine rice. The setting itself is open and seductive in an earthy-chic, minimalist, Marin County sort of way. This is not the place for carnivores (no red meat), but the kitchen does creative things with fish, shrimp, and chicken dishes with a light, modern, and Asian touch. Tiny white lights and soft music bathe individual tables under a bower of purple and red flowering vines. There's usually a guitarist serenading during Friday dinner; the restaurant is open for lunch as well. Save room for a coconut rice dessert with flambéed tropical fruit. ✉ *Av. China 9, at Calle Asia, San Francisco* ☎ *311/258–4251* ▭ *No credit cards* ⏲ *Closed Wed. and Aug.–Sept.*

$$ INTERNATIONAL ✕ **Don Pedro's.** Sayulita institution Don Pedro's has wonderful pizzas baked in a wood-fire oven, prepared by European-trained chef and co-owner Nicholas Parrillo. Also on the menu are consistently reliable seafood dishes, yummy Niçoise salad, and tapenade. The mesquite-grilled filet mignon is just about the best around; it comes with baby vegetables, mashed potatoes, and pita bread. The pretty second-floor dining room, with the better view, is open when the bottom floor fills up, usually during the high season (November to May). During high season they also have dance classes and dancing to Latin tunes, currently on Monday, and live flamenco guitar on Thursday. This is a good spot for breakfast, too, after 8 AM. ✉ *Calle Marlin 2, at beach, Sayulita* ☎ *329/291–3090* 🌐 *www.donpedros.com* ▭ *MC, V* ⏲ *Closed Sept.*

$ CLASSIC MEXICAN Fodor's Choice ★ **El Brujo.** This newer Bucerías branch of El Brujo is right on the beach but with the same food and generous portions of the original location in Puerto Vallarta. The *molcajete*—a sizzling black pot of tender flank steak, grilled green onion, and soft white cheese in a delicious homemade sauce of dried red peppers—is served with a big plate of guacamole, refried beans, and made-at-the-moment corn or flour tortillas. Try the breaded scallops, stuffed fish with shrimp and creamy *huitlacoche* (black corn fungus) sauce, or a grilled skirt steak with mushrooms and bell peppers bathed in tomato sauce. If you're into simpler fare, the unadorned grilled fish fillet is fresh and delicious, too. ✉ *Av. del Pacífico 202 A, Bucerías* ☎ *329/298–0406* *Reservations not accepted* ▭ *MC, V* ⊗ *Closed 2 wks late Sept.–early Oct.*

$$ INTERNATIONAL Fodor's Choice ★ **La Ola Rica.** One of San Pancho's first upscale restaurants, "The Delicious Wave," has still got it goin'. Small, medium-crust, wood-fired pizzas are just right for an appetizer (we recommend the Brie pizza with caramelized onions) or, with a soup or salad, as a delicious dinner for one. Another good appetizer is the fresh white cheese round served with warm tomato sauce and fresh basil. The margaritas are lovely, and wine by the glass is a generous portion. All of the doe-eyed, wasp-waisted waitresses are relatives of the locally born and raised co-owner, Triny. Eat to the beat of a jazz-dominated sound track: overlooking the street on the covered patio or inside the home-cum-restaurant, artfully decorated with eclectic paintings, photographs of Old Mexico, and saints in niches. Summer hours vary each season, depending on tourist traffic; it's best to call during the off-season to double-check days and hours open. ✉ *Av. Tercer Mundo s/n, San Francisco* ☎ *311/258–4123* ▭ *MC, V* ⊗ *Closed Sun.; no lunch. Closed Sat.–Wed. June–July. Closed Aug.–Oct.*

$$$ INTERNATIONAL **Mark's Bar & Grill.** You can dine alone at the polished black-granite bar without feeling too lonely, or catch an important ball game. But seemingly a world away from the bar and (muted) TV is the charming restaurant known for its delightful decor and international cuisine. Both can be appreciated on the back patio, open to the stars, or in the softly lit dining room. Menu standouts include the homemade pizza, the salads, and the macadamia-crusted fresh fish fillets with Thai curry. The lamb is flown in from New Zealand; shrimp comes from San Blas; and the black Angus beef is from Monterrey. Mixed organic lettuces, chives, and basil come from the lady down the street. The restaurant is elegant yet warm and inviting, with a golden glow over everything and, sometimes, roving musicians. More than a dozen wines are offered by the glass. ✉ *Lázaro Cárdenas 56, Bucerías* ☎ *329/298–0303* 🌐 *www.marksbucerias.com* ▭ *MC, V* ⊗ *No lunch.*

$$ MEDITERRANEAN **Sandrina's.** The walls of this veteran, Canadian-owned restaurant and locals' favorite are covered in colorful paintings: portraits and tropical scenes and still lifes. Columns are adorned with bright broken-tile mosaics. The restaurant opens after 3 PM; it's very pleasant to dine on the back patio at night amid dozens of candles and tiny lights. The menu varies in accomplishment as well as cuisine: On our last visit we sampled tasty lentil soup and a nicely grilled hamburger as well as dry hummus and uninspired tzatziki. There are plenty of other choices, including

pizza, salads, pasta dishes, and such Mediterranean fare as chicken souvlaki and Greek-style chicken. Order a liqueur-laced coffee or dessert from the bakery counter. The café at the front has great espresso but is open in high season only, usually December through Easter. ✉ *Av. Lázaro Cárdenas 33, Bucerías* ☎ *329/298–0273* 🌐 *www.sandrinas.com* 💳 *MC, V* ⊙ *No lunch. Closed Tues. and 2 wks in Sept.*

SOUTH OF PUERTO VALLARTA

$$ INTERNATIONAL ✕ **La Playita de Lindo Mar.** Open to the ocean air, the wood-and-palm-front restaurant looks right at home on Conchas Chinas Beach. And there are wonderful views of waves crashing on or lapping at the shore. Enjoy breakfast or an expansive, inexpensive weekend brunch buffet (it runs 8 AM to 1 PM; come before 11 in the morning for the freshest food). Select from crepes, frittatas, omelets, and *huevos Felix* (eggs scrambled with fried corn tortillas, served with a grilled cactus pad, beans, and grilled serrano chilies). Lunch and dinner choices include crispy crab tacos, grilled burgers and chicken, shrimp enchiladas with spinach, and much, much more. If you're driving, look for the sign for HOTEL LINDO MAR on the coast highway; you can park in the small lot near the beach or in the hotel lot and take the elevator down to the beach. ✉ *Carretera a Barra de Navidad, Km. 2.5, Playa Conchas Chinas, at Hotel Lindo Mar* ☎ *322/221–5511* 🌐 *www.lindomarresort.com* 💳 *MC, V.*

WHERE TO STAY

PUERTO VALLARTA

ZONA ROMÁNTICA

$$ Fodor's Choice ★ **Hacienda Alemana Frankfurt.** Rooms here have king-size beds, 32-inch TVs, and double-pane windows to keep out noise. The decor and furnishings are original, modern, and warm—poured-cement floors, fine wood furniture, marble sink surrounds. Regular rooms are spacious; even more spacious are the three-room suites, which are also a steal in low season and well-priced year-round. On the large patio is a *Biergarten* and the hotel's restaurant, Café Frankfurt, which is well worth a meal or two. Although this is a comfortable, classy place to stay, it's better suited to self-sufficient guests, as there's no front-desk staff. A la carte breakfast at Langostino's Restaurant, facing Los Muertos Beach, is included. The free bottled water in your room's pint-sized fridge is replenished daily; guests pay for the beer or soft drinks stocked there. **Pros:** excellent on-site German restaurant; free access to gym, sauna, and steam room (off-site); DVDs and iPod stations upon request; great for couples. **Cons:** no real reception staff, so no one around when restaurant closed; possible noise from *Biergarten.* ✉ *Calle Basilio Badillo 378, Col. E. Zapata* ☎ *322/222–2071* 🌐 *www.haciendaalemana.com* *10 rooms* *In-room: a/c, safe, kitchen (some), refrigerator, Wi-Fi. In-hotel: restaurant, gym, parking (free), some pets allowed* 💳 *MC, V* *CP.*

$ Fodor's Choice ★ **Playa Los Arcos Beach Resort & Spa.** This hotel is recommended for its location: right on the beach and in the midst of Zona Romántica's restaurants, bars, and shops. Though the price is right, some longtime visitors report that quality has slipped in recent years. Still, yellow trumpet vines and lacy palms draped in tiny white lights enliven the pool and the bar-restaurant, which has music nightly and a Mexican fiesta on Saturday evening. Some rooms are larger than others and have a balcony with plastic lounge chairs; balcony rooms are the same price as those without, so ask for a balcony when booking. **Pros:** great Zona Romántica location; nightly entertainment with theme-cuisine buffet. **Cons:** small bathrooms; some rooms have tired furnishings; tour-group noise in high season. ✉ *Av. Olas Altas 380, Col. E. Zapata* ☎ *322/222–0583; 800/648–2403 in U.S.; 888/729–9590 in Canada; 01800/327–7700 toll-free in Mexico* 🌐 *www.playalosarcos.com* *158 rooms, 13 suites* *In-room: a/c, safe (some), kitchen (some), refrigerator (some). In-hotel: restaurant, bar, pool, spa, beachfront, parking (free)* *AE, MC, V* *AI, EP.*

12

¢ **Hotel Posada de Roger.** If you hang around the pool or the small shared balcony overlooking the street and the bay beyond, it's not hard to get to know the other guests—many of them savvy budget travelers from Europe and Canada. Rooms are spare and vaultlike—some are downright dark. Fredy's Tucan, the indoor-outdoor bar-restaurant (no dinner; $), is popular with locals—mainly for breakfast. The hotel is in a part of the Zona Romántica known for its restaurants and shops; Playa los Muertos is a few blocks away. **Pros:** great location; tinkling fountain and quiet courtyard; good bar-restaurant; free Wi-Fi. **Cons:** no in-room safes; cramped rooms; get-what-you-pay-for beds. ✉ *Calle Basilio Badillo 237, Col. E. Zapata* ☎ *322/222–0836 or 322/222–0639* 🌐 *www.hotelposadaderoger.com* *47 rooms* *In-room: a/c, Wi-Fi (some). In-hotel: restaurant, bar, pool, Wi-Fi, parking (free)* *AE, MC, V* *EP.*

Fodor's Choice ★

¢ **Hotel Yasmín.** Two-story and L-shaped, this budget baby has no pool, but it's just a block from the beach and joined at the hip to Café de Olla, a popular Mexican restaurant. It's also near Parque Lázaro Cárdenas, with underground parking, and dozens of bars, restaurants, and boutiques. Small, ho-hum rooms have low ceilings, firm beds, and open closets, but also floor fans and cable TV: not a bad deal for the price. About four bucks more buys you a/c, so go ahead and splurge. The front-desk staff can sometimes be brusque, but that doesn't really diminish the experience. **Pros:** very inexpensive; close to Zona Romántica action; pleasant courtyard garden with café, tables, and chaise longues. **Cons:** dark rooms; low ceilings; no pool. ✉ *Calle Basilio Badillo, Col. E. Zapata* ☎ *322/222–0087* *27 rooms* *In-room: a/c (some), no phone* *No credit cards* *EP.*

CENTRO AND ENVIRONS

$$ **Buenaventura Grand Hotel & Spa.** The location on downtown's northern edge is just a few blocks from the malecón, shops, hotels, and restaurants. The beach has gentle waves, but with brown sand and rocks. Views up and down the bay are great; it attracts more fishermen and people walking or jogging than bathers. There's a lively pool scene; the adults-only area, a shallow pool with submerged chaise longues facing the sea, is a big part of the draw. Rooms are cheerful, with wood furniture, bright white linens, and tastefully subdued accent colors. Ocean-facing balconies are tiny, and if you sit, you can't see a thing. Still, the sum of the whole makes up for any deficiencies, and the all-inclusive rate

is a good deal, especially for families. **Pros:** great place to socialize; good breakfast buffet; concierge service; five-minute walk to the malecón and downtown. **Cons:** balconies are small, no parking; fee to use next-door gym. ✉ *Av. México 1301, Col. 5 de Diciembre* ☎ *322/226–7000; 888/859–9439 in U.S. and Canada* 🌐 *www.hotelbuenaventura.com.mx* *216 rooms, 18 suites* *In-room: a/c, Wi-Fi. In-hotel: 3 restaurants, room service, bars, pools, spa, beachfront, water sports, laundry service, Internet, Wi-Fi hotspot* *AE, MC, V* *AI, EP.*

$$$$ **Hacienda San Angel**. Each room is unique and elegant at this pricey boutique hotel in the hills five blocks above the malecón. Public spaces also exude wealth and privilege: 16th- through 19th-century antiques are placed throughout, water pours from fonts into Talavera-tile-lined basins, mammoth tables grace open dining areas. The Celestial Room has a wondrous view of Bahía de Banderas and the cathedral's tower from its open-air, thatch-roof living room. You can call Canada or the United States for free and enjoy live music with complimentary cocktails in the early evening. There are fabulous views of the bay from the new second-floor restaurant, Hacienda San Angel Gourmet, which serves international food beginning at 6 PM. Non-guests are welcome by previous reservation. **Pros:** the most elegant lodging in downtown Puerto Vallarta; concierge service; excellent bay views; reasonably priced airport transfers. **Cons:** short but steep walk from the malecón; 5% service fee (in addition to taxes) plus 10% fee for using a credit card; three-night minimum; fewer amenities than hotels of comparable price point. ✉ *Calle Miramar 336, at Iturbide, Centro* ☎ *322/222–2692; 877/815–6594* 🌐 *www.haciendasanangel.com* *21 rooms* *In-room: a/c, safe, DVD. In-hotel: restaurant, pools, laundry service, Internet, Wi-Fi hotspot, no kids under 16* *AE, MC, V* *CP.*

MARINA VALLARTA

$$$ **CasaMagna Marriott Puerto Vallarta Resort & Spa**. The CasaMagna is hushed and stately in some places, lively and casual in others. Here's a classy property that nonetheless welcomes children. All of the restaurants—including a sleek Asian restaurant serving Thai, sushi, and teppanyaki and a large, pleasant sports bar—have kids' menus. The meandering grounds boast a large infinity pool as well as gardens of indigenous plants. Rooms have an upbeat, classy decor; each has a balcony, and most have an ocean view. Access to the excellent spa facilities is included with the purchase of any spa service. **Pros:** lovely spa; great concierge service; good Japanese restaurant. **Cons:** unimpressive beach; no business center or Internet terminals for guests. ✉ *Paseo de la Marina 455, Marina Vallarta* ☎ *322/226–0000; 888/236–2427 in U.S. and Canada* 🌐 *www.casamagnapuertovallarta.com* *404 rooms, 29 suites* *In-room: a/c, safe, Wi-Fi. In-hotel: 4 restaurants, room service, bars, pools, gym, spa, beachfront, children's programs (ages 4–12), laundry service, Wi-Fi hotspot, parking (free)* *AE, DC, MC, V* *EP.*

$$$$ **Velas Vallarta Suite Resort & Convention Center**. Silky sheets and cozy down duvets, multiple ceiling fans, and large flat-screen TVs are a few of the creature comforts that set Velas apart from the rest. Each large living area has two comfortably wide built-in couches in colorful prints

and a round dining table. Huichol cross-stitch tapestries and modern Mexican art decorate the walls. Studios and one-, two-, and three-bedroom suites have the same amenities except that the studios don't have balconies or beach views. Tall palms, pink bougainvillea, and wild ginger with brilliant red plumes surround the three enormous pools. This is a perfect destination for those who want to relax on-site, as the hotel offers tennis clinics, arts and crafts, theme nights, and lots of other activities. **Pros:** large suites; yoga; Spanish classes and other activities; pillow menu; special deals allowing kids to stay free are sometimes available. **Cons:** small spa; zealous time-share salespeople; high price point. ✉ *Av. Costera s/n LH2, Marina Vallarta* ☎ *322/226–9500 or 866/847–4609* 🌐 *www.velasvallarta.com* *339 suites* *In-room: a/c, safe, kitchen, refrigerator, Wi-Fi. In-hotel: 2 restaurants, room service, bars, tennis courts, pools, gym, spa, beachfront, children's programs (ages 4–12), laundry service, Internet, Wi-Fi hotspot, parking (free)* *AE, MC, V* *AI.*

$$$$ **Westin Resort & Spa, Puerto Vallarta.** Hot pink! Electric yellow! Color aside, the Westin's buildings evoke ancient temples and are about as mammoth in size. There's not a bad sightline anywhere, whether you're gazing out to the leafy courtyard or down an orange-tile, brightly painted corridor lined with Mexican art. The jarring echoes here are tempered by the rush of an enormous water feature. In the spacious, balconied rooms concrete-and-stone floors massage bare feet, and top-of-the-line mattresses with soft duvets make for heavenly siestas. Guest quarters above the sixth floor have ocean views; those below face the 600 palm trees surrounding four beautiful pools. **Pros:** fabulous beds and pillows; impressive architecture and landscaping; attentive but not overzealous staff; concierge service. **Cons:** small beach; no ocean views from lower floors. ✉ *Paseo de la Marina Sur 205, Marina Vallarta* ☎ *322/226–1100; 800/228–3000 in U.S. and Canada* 🌐 *www.starwoodhotels.com* *266 rooms, 14 suites* *In-room: a/c, safe, Wi-Fi. In-hotel: 2 restaurants, room service, bars, tennis courts, pools, gym, spa, beachfront, children's programs (ages 4–12), laundry service, Internet, Wi-Fi hotspot, parking (free), some pets allowed* *AE, DC, MC, V* *BP.*

RIVIERA NAYARIT

$$$$ **Casa de Mita.** Architect-owner Marc Lindskog has created a nook of nonchalant elegance, with updated country furnishings of wicker, leather, and wood; rock-floor showers without curtains or doors; and cheerful Pacific Coast architectural details. Mosquito netting lends romance to cozy, quilt-covered beds. Waves crashing onshore, their sound somehow magnified, create white noise that lulls you to sleep. In the morning, settle into a cushy chaise on your private patio to watch seabirds swim; at night watch the sunset behind Punta Mita. These simple pleasures make this hideaway a winner. It doesn't hurt that the food is truly delicious, the bar is well stocked with international labels, and it's all included in the room price. **Pros:** delicious food; nearly private beach; concierge service; free international phone calls. **Cons:** little nightlife in vicinity; three-night minimum stay; strict cancellation policy. ✉ *Playa Careyeros, Punta Mita, Nayarit* ☎ *329/298–4114 or*

Continued on page 597

SPAAAHH

The trend of luxury spas in Mexico, and particularly in vacation hot spots like Puerto Vallarta, shows no signs of slowing. From elegant resort spas scented with essence of orange and bergamot to Aztec-inspired day spas, each has its own personality and signature treatments. Competition keeps creativity high, with an ever-changing menu of new treatments, many using native products like sage, chocolate, aloe vera, and even tequila.

Four Seasons Resort, Punta Mita

Spa Savvy

All of the spas listed here are open to nonguests, but reservations are essential. Guests of the hotel may get discounts. Spa customers can sometimes use other facilities at a resort, such as the restaurant, beach, pool, or gym. Ask when you book. Prices are generally on par with those of resort spas worldwide, but some deals are to be had if you go with the less-expensive but still high-quality spas we list. Or scout out hotel-spa packages and specials.

RESORT NAME	BODY TREATMENTS	SEASIDE TREATMENTS	TREATMENTS FOR TWO	FITNESS DAY PASS	HOT TUB	TEMAZCAL
CasaMagna Marriot	$75–$135	yes	yes	yes*	yes	no
Four Seasons	$140–$255	yes	yes	yes**	yes	yes
Grand Velas	$80–$200	yes	yes	$40	yes	no
Paradise Village	$75–$170	yes	no	$12–$19	no	no
Terra Noble	$65	no	yes	yes	yes	yes

* Gym free for guests, $25 for nonguests; steam, sauna, and other spa areas $15 for guests, $50 for nonguests; both areas free for guests and nonguests with purchase of spa treatment.
** Nonguests pay day-use fee to get spa treatments and use spa facilities and golf course. Fee is half the cheapest room rate (often several hundred dollars).

TOP SPOTS

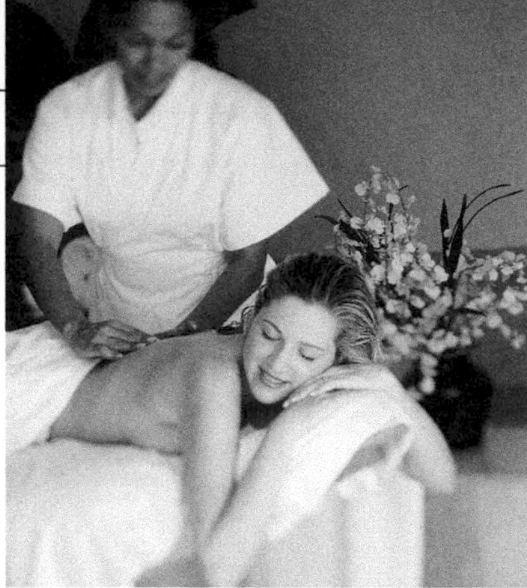

Indigenous Elegance

OHTLI SPA, CASAMAGNA MARRIOTT
The modern yet organic-looking Ohtli spa and its high-tech gym offer 22,000 square feet of elegant pampering. You can relax before or between treatments in the lounge, with a glass of water infused with love in the form of pink quartz crystals and messages of love in 13 languages. Come early to load up on this liquid love and to enjoy the cold pool, steam, sauna, and other elements of the separate men's and women's spa facilities.

Inspiration for this tasteful, soothing spa came from indigenous cultures. Treatment rooms are adorned with Huichol art and interior gardens to maintain a spiritual and nature-oriented mood. Many of the treatments—like the coconut exfoliation with deep-tissue massage—use local ingredients. The signature exfoliation treatment contains agave, cornmeal, and sea salt.

Body Treatments & Services: Exfoliation (9 kinds); wraps (8 kinds); massage (10 kinds).

Beauty Treatments: Facials (6 kinds); manicure; pedicure; waxing; children's treatments.

Prices: Body treatments $75–$135; facials $105–$145; hair $25–$95; manicure or pedicure $30–$72; waxing $18–$60.

Packages: Mother and daughter ice cream pedicure; other packages offered seasonally. *CasaMagna Marriott Puerto Vallarta, Paseo de la Marina 5, Marina Vallarta.* ☎ *322/226–0079* 🌐 *www.marriott.com* 💳 *AE, DC, MC, V.*

A Spa for All Seasons

APUANE SPA, FOUR SEASONS PUNTA MITA
Professional service is the hallmark of this exclusive spa. An inspirational experience is the Ha Waye healing waters treatment: a four-handed massage under a soothing Vichy bath complemented by aromatherapy.

Treatments are among the most expensive in the area, but everyting is top drawer. Native products are used almost exclusively; the Hakali massage, for example, employs catus pulque, which is applied to the skin using fresh cactus paddles.

Body Treatments & Services: Exfoliation; massage (18 types); Vichy hydrotherapy; wraps and scrubs (12 types).

Beauty Treatments: Facials (7 types); manicure; pedicure; hair/scalp treatment.

Prices: Body treatments $140–$265; facials $100–$230; hair $95–$145; manicure/pedicure $65–$95; waxing $27–$88.

Packages: Couples treatments such as Like Water for Chocolate—a chocolate scrub and facial; a hot-stone massage; and servings of fruit, chocolate fondue, and champagne. *Punta de Mita, Bahía de Banderas.* ☎ *329/291–6000* 🌐 *www.fourseasons.com/puntamita* 💳 *AE, DC, MC, V.*

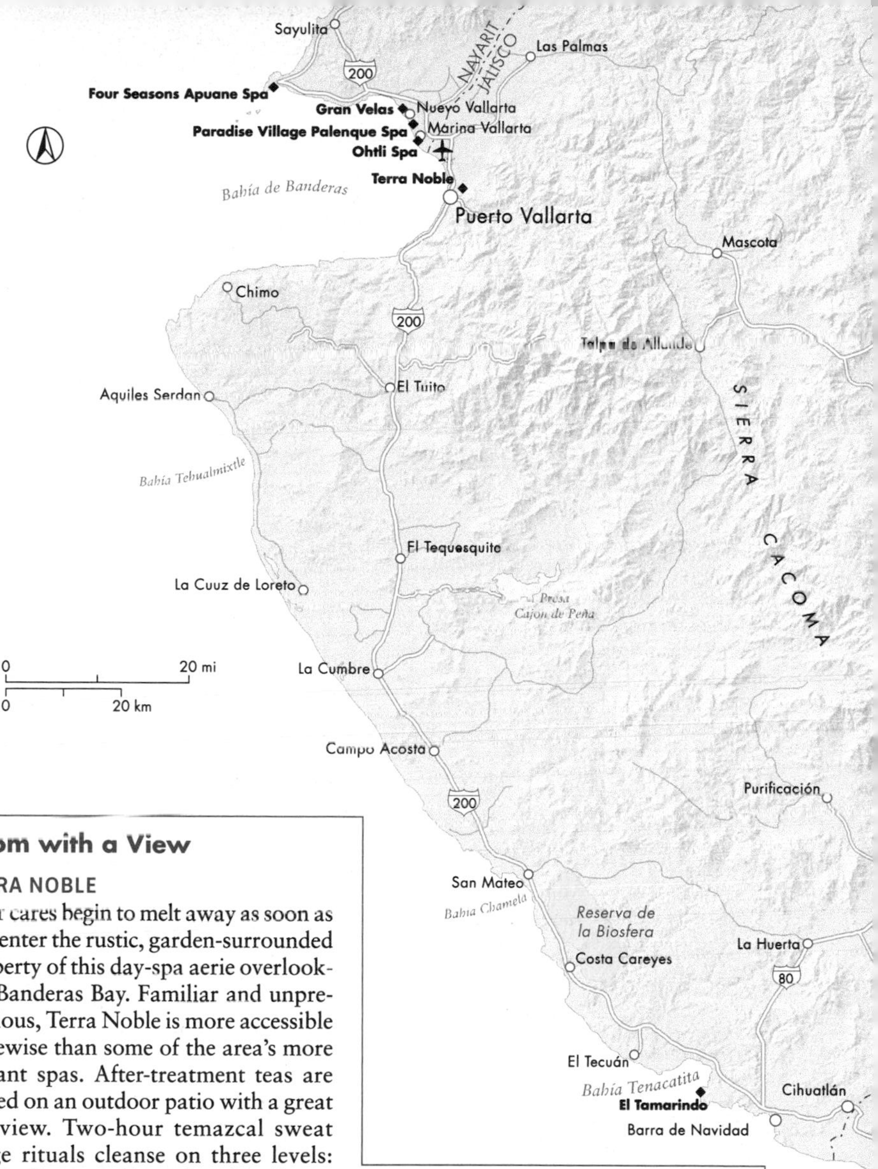

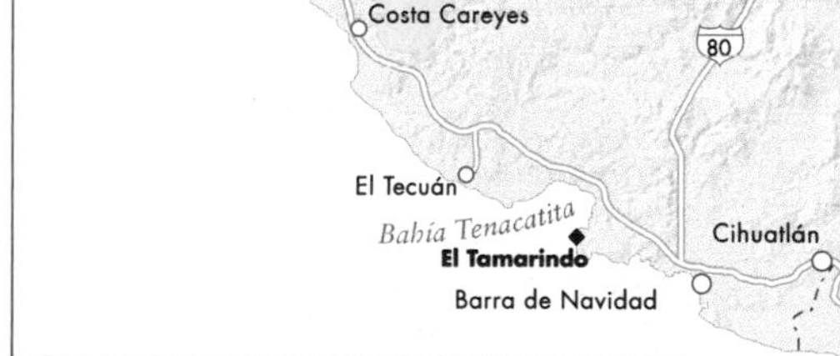

Room with a View

TERRA NOBLE

Your cares begin to melt away as soon as you enter the rustic, garden-surrounded property of this day-spa aerie overlooking Banderas Bay. Familiar and unpretentious, Terra Noble is more accessible pricewise than some of the area's more elegant spas. After-treatment teas are served on an outdoor patio with a great sea view. Two-hour temazcal sweat lodge rituals cleanse on three levels: physically, mentally, and spiritually. Or recharge with clay and painting classes, and Tarot readings.

Body Treatments: Reflexology; massage (5 types); several wraps and scrubs; temazcal sweat lodge; yoga/meditation.

Beauty Treatments: Facials.

Prices: Body treatments $65.

Packages: A few economical packages such as the Stress Recovery (a sea-salt body scrub, a massage, and a facial), for $145.

Av. Tulipanes 595, at Fracc. Lomas de Terra Noble, Col. 5 de Diciembre. Tel. 322/223–3530 www.terranoble.com AE, MC, V (through PayPal only).

MORE TOP SPOTS

Something for Every Body

PALENQUE SPA, PARADISE VILLAGE

On a peninsula between the beach and marina, this modern Maya temple of glass and marble is a cool, sweet-smelling oasis with separate wings for men and women; each is equipped with private hydrotherapy tubs, whirlpools, saunas, and steam rooms. The coed gym has state-of-the-art equipment and views of the ocean, plus aerobics classes in a separate studio and an indoor lap pool.

The reasonably priced therapy selections are extensive, from an anti-cellulite seaweed wrap to milk baths with honey, amaranth, and orange oil or the aromatherapy massage, employing clove, sage, bergamot, and other essential oils.

Body Treatments: Aromatherapy; facials; Reiki; exfoliation; hot-stone massage; hydrotherapy; wraps, scrubs, and body treatments (10 types); reflexology; shiatsu.

Beauty Treatments: Facials (8 types), manicure, pedicure.

Prices: Body treatments $75–$170; facials $46–$134; manicure/pedicure $46–$72; hair $39–$101; waxing $19–$69.

Packages: A wide variety of packages allow switching treatments in an equivalent price bracket. The basic plan combines three 50-minute treatments: marine body scrub, holistic massage, and hydrating facial.
Paseo de los Cocoteros 1 Nuevo Vallarta. Tel. 322/226-6770 ⊕ www.paradisevillage.com. ▭ AE, MC, V.

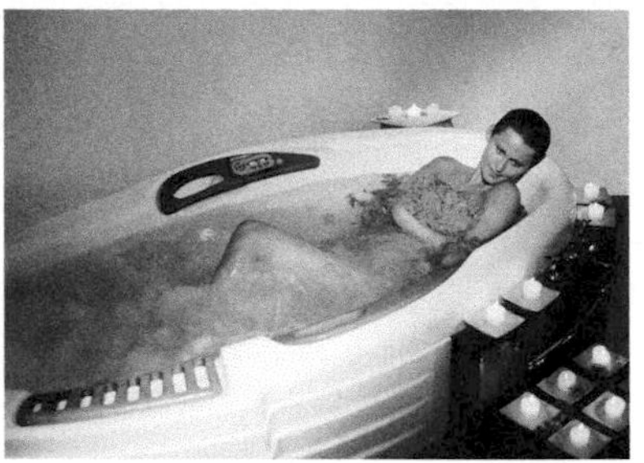

Drama Queen

GRAN VELAS

The spa at Nuevo Vallarta's most elegant all-inclusive resort has dramatic architectural lines and plenty of marble, stone, teak, and tile. The 16,500-square-foot facility has 20 treatment rooms, and ample steam, sauna, and whirlpools. Lounge in the comfortable chaises near the "plunge lagoon" (with warm and cold pools).

Highlights of the extensive treatments menu are the chocolate, gold, or avocado wraps; Thai massage; cinnamon-sage foot scrub; and the challenging buttocks sculpt-lift. There's even a kids spa menu with 15 treatments. Adjoining the spa is an impressive fitness facility.

Body Treatments: Reflexology; massage (18 types); shiatsu; Vichy shower; exfoliation; wraps, scrubs, baths, and body treatments (32 types).

Beauty Treatments: Facials (12+); manicure/pedicure; hair care; waxing; makeup.

Prices: Body treatments: $80–$200; facials: $135—$311; manicure/pedicure: $25–$100; hair care: $35–$110; waxing: $23–$63; makeup: $85.

Packages: Happy Bride, Just for Men, and Detox Ritual packages, plus 10% discount for three or more treatments; otherwise, no packages.
Av. de los Cocoteros 98 Sur, Nuevo Vallarta. Tel. 322/226-8000 ⊕ www.grandvelas.com. ▭ AE, MC, V.

866/740–7999 🌐 www.casademita.com 6 rooms, 2 suites In-room: a/c, no phone, safe, refrigerator, no TV, Wi-Fi (some). In-hotel: restaurant, bar, pool, spa, beachfront, water sports, Internet, Wi-Fi hotspot AE, MC, V AI.

$$ **Costa Azul.** What makes this place attractive are the many activities offered: horseback riding, kayaking, hiking, surfing (with lessons), and excursions to the Marietas Islands or La Tobara mangroves near San Blas. The all-inclusive plan, which includes activities, can be arranged through the U.S. office in San Clemente, California, but not in Mexico. But since San Pancho has a number of excellent restaurants, the European Plan is recommended. The sandy beach faces the open ocean, but the staff discourages guests from swimming there. Officially there's no Wi-Fi in guest rooms, but those closest to the restaurant may get access. **Pros:** great place to bond with kids of all ages; lots of planned outdoor activities and tours. **Cons:** mediocre food; some guests have complained of disorganized and unhelpful staff members; stringent cancellation policy. ✉ *Calle Amapas at Calle Las Palmas, Fracc. Costa Azul, San Francisco, Nayarit ☎ 311/258–4000; 800/365–7613 toll-free in U.S. 🌐 www.costaazul.com 18 rooms, 5 suites, 3 villas In-room: a/c, no phone, kitchen (some), refrigerator (some), no TV. In-hotel: restaurant, bars, pool, beachfront, water sports, laundry service, Wi-Fi hotspot, parking (free) MC, V EP, FAP.*

$$$$ **Four Seasons Resort, Punta Mita.** The hotel and its fabulous spa perch above a lovely beach at the northern extreme of Bahía de Banderas, about 45 minutes from the Puerto Vallarta airport and an hour north of downtown Puerto Vallarta. Spacious rooms occupy Mexican-style casitas of one, two, and three stories. Each room has elegant yet earthy furnishings and a private terrace or balcony—many with a sweeping sea view. The Jack Nicklaus–designed championship golf course has a challenging, optional 19th island hole; a second course opened in 2009. The gym is first-rate, and a good variety of sporting and beach equipment is on hand. Just offshore, the Marietas Islands are great for snorkeling, diving, whale-watching, and fishing. This is the place for indulging golf and spa fantasies or just using the luxurious, top-notch facilities. It's a great spot for kids, too, with fantastic beaches, a doughnut-shaped pool with current where you can float in inner tubes, and an excellent kids' playroom with Internet and lots of cool games. **Pros:** beautiful beach; concierge service; yoga on the point; excellent spa; private yacht for charter. **Cons:** staff trained to be overly solicitous (you'll be saying "hola" a lot); very expensive spa treatments; not all rooms have ocean view. ✉ *Bahía de Banderas, Punta Mita, Nayarit ☎ 329/291–6019; 800/819–5053 in U.S. and Canada 🌐 www.fshr.com/puntamita 141 rooms, 27 suites In-room: a/c, safe, refrigerator, DVD, Internet, Wi-Fi. In-hotel: 3 restaurants, room service, bars, golf courses, tennis courts, pools, gym, spa, beachfront, water sports, children's programs (ages 5–12), laundry service, Internet, Wi-Fi hotspot, parking (free) AE, MC, V BP, EP.*

$$$$ **Grand Velas All Suites & Spa Resort.** In scale and majesty, the public areas of this property outshine all other Nuevo Vallarta all-inclusive resorts. Ceilings soar overhead, and the structure and furnishings are

simultaneously minimalist and modern yet earthy, incorporating stucco, rock, polished teak, and gleaming ecru marble. The spa is excellent, and the views—with the garden-shrouded pool in the foreground and the beach beyond—are striking. Rooms are sleek, with elegant furnishings and appointments. The high price entitles you to top-of-the-line spirits in minibars and restaurants. **Pros:** exceptionally beautiful rooms and public spaces; lovely spa; extremely long beach great for walking. **Cons:** Nuevo Vallarta location is far from Puerto Vallarta (but 10 minutes by car from Bucerías); at more than $600 per night, you think they'd kick in free Wi-Fi. ✉ *Paseo de los Cocoteros 98 Sur, Nuevo Vallarta* ☎ *322/226–8000; 888/261–8436 in U.S. and Canada* 🌐 *www.grandvelas.com* *267 1-, 2-, and 3-bedroom suites* *In-room: a/c, safe, DVD, Wi-Fi. In-hotel: 4 restaurants, room service, bars, tennis court, pools, gym, spa, beachfront, children's programs (ages 4–12), laundry service, Internet, Wi-Fi hotspot, parking (free), some pets allowed* *AE, MC, V* *AI.*

$$ **Paradise Village Beach Resort & Spa.** This Nuevo Vallarta hotel and time-share property is perfect for families, with lots of activities geared to children. Many people love it, although the property's dedication to time-share guests makes some hotel guests feel short-shrifted. Most suites have balconies with either marina or ocean views. Furnishings are attractive as well as functional, with pretty cane sofa beds in a soothing palette and well-equipped kitchens. Locals like to visit the clean, well-organized spa, which smells divine and is noted for its massages and facials. The beach here is tranquil enough for swimming, although some small waves are suitable for bodysurfing. **Pros:** reasonably priced spa; can walk all the way to Bucerías on the beach; fully loaded kitchen in all suites; efficient a/c units; wide range of accommodations. **Cons:** big cats caged in depressing zoo; Internet room for time-share guests only; time-share oriented; guests must bring cable for Internet access. ✉ *Paseo de los Cocoteros 1, Nuevo Vallarta, Nayarit* ☎ *322/226–6770; 866/334–6080* 🌐 *www.paradisevillage.com* *702 suites* *In-room: a/c, safe, kitchen, refrigerator, Internet. In-hotel: 5 restaurants, room service, bars, golf course, tennis courts, pools, gym, spas, beachfront, children's programs (ages 4–11), Wi-Fi hotspot, parking (free)* *AE, MC, V* *EP, AI.*

SOUTH OF PUERTO VALLARTA

$$$$ **Barceló La Jolla de Mismaloya.** Guests consistently give this hotel high marks. Each of the classy suites here has an elegant feel, with a brown-and-taupe color scheme and an ample terrace with a table and four chairs. Separate sitting rooms have a second flat-screen TV, and there's even a pillow menu. The pools are surrounded by spacious patios, so there's plenty of room to find the perfect spot in the sun or the shade, whether you're on your honeymoon or with the kids. Given the elegance of the place, it's a shame to have to wear the usual wristbands required of All Inclusive guests. **Pros:** recently redecorated and remodeled; concierge service; lots of on-site dining and activity options. **Cons:** beach is small, least expensive rooms don't have ocean views; no bathtubs. ✉ *Zona Hotelera Sur, Km 11.5, Box 158B, Mismaloya* ☎ *322/226–0660; 800/227–2356* 🌐 *www.barcelo.com* *317 suites* *In-room:*

diving, water sports, bicycles, laundry service, Internet, Wi-Fi hotspot, parking (free) ▭ *AE, MC, V* 🍽 *EP.*

$$$$ 🏨 **Hotelito Desconocido Sanctuary Reserve & Spa.** A two-year renovation, during which time the resort was closed, has resulted in a more sedate, less whimsical decor that, like the original Hotelito, includes elements of hardwood, bamboo, and palm thatch designed by a group of young *tapatios* (artisans from Guadalajara). It's far from rustic, however: witness 600-thread-count sheets, Jacuzzi tubs, expansive furnished terraces, and private docks with personal canoes; the smallest palafito (house on wooden stilts) is more than 1,000 square feet. There are private butlers, too. The property is lit by torches, lanterns, candles, and low-wattage lamps. On a long stretch of beach, this isolated hotel is an idyllic escape for its discerning, high-end clientele. An integral part of the concept is health and self-improvement. Programs range from the 5-day "mom-to-be" to the 21-day "love the way you look" program; organic fruits and veggies make their way from the property's garden to guests' table, along with fish and seafood. **Pros:** isolated, unique, and charming; holistic spa with aromatherapy, yoga, and many other services; concierge service. **Cons:** rustic-chic it is, affordable it isn't; isolated. ✉ *Playón de Mismaloya s/n, Cruz de Loreto* ✣ *97 km (60 mi) south of Puerto Vallarta, 119 km (74 mi) north of Barra de Navidad* ☎ *800/851–1143* 🌐 *www.hotelito.com* *27 suites, 3 villas* *In-room: a/c (some), no phone, no TV. In-hotel: 2 restaurants, bar, pool, gym, spa, beachfront, water sports, bicycles, Internet terminal, parking (free)* ▭ *AE, MC, V* 🍽 *EP, FAP.*

$$$$ 🏨 **Las Alamandas.** Personal service and exclusivity lure movie stars and royalty to this low-key resort in a thorn-forest preserve about 1½ hours from both Puerto Vallarta and Manzanillo. Suites are filled with folk art; their indoor-outdoor living rooms have modern furnishings with deliciously nubby fabrics in bright, bold colors and Guatemalan-cloth throw pillows. Request a TV, DVD player, and movie from the library for an evening in; there's little else to do at night. There's lots more to do in the daytime, however, including picnics anywhere on the property and boat rides on the Río San Nicolás. There's a 10% service charge and a two-night minimum; the average stay is seven nights. **Pros:** stargazing from rooftop bar; stunning yet cozy architecture; one-hour horseback ride and use of bicycles; Boogie boards included; concierge service. **Cons:** open-style bungalows not pleasant in rainy season, with mosquitoes and high humidity; not close to any restaurants or nightlife; riptides. ✉ *Carretera 200, Km 85, Quemaro* ✣ *83 km (52 mi) south of Puerto Vallarta, 133 km (83 mi) north of Barra de Navidad* ☎ *322/285–5500 or 888/882–9616* 🌐 *www.lasalamandas.com* *14 suites* *In-room: a/c, refrigerator, DVD. In-hotel: restaurant, room service, bars, tennis court, pool, gym, spa, beachfront, water sports, bicycles, laundry service, Internet, parking (free)* ▭ *AE, MC, V* 🍽 *EP, FAP.*

NIGHTLIFE

BARS, PUBS, AND LOUNGES

Andale. Most nights, crowds spill out onto the sidewalk as party-hearty men and women shimmy out of the narrow saloon, drinks in hand, to the strains of Chubby Checker and other vintage tunes. For a laugh, intoxicated or less inhibited patrons sometimes take a bumpy ride on the burro just outside Andale's door (a handler escorts the burro). Andale opens at 8 AM. ✉ *Av. Olas Altas 425, Col. E. Zapata* ☎ *322/222–1054.*

★ **Apaches.** It's gay-friendly, lesbian-friendly, *people*-friendly. Heck, superwomen Mariann and her partner, Endra, would probably welcome you and your pet python with open arms and give you both a squeeze. PV's original martini bar, Apaches is the landing zone for expats reconnoitering after a long day, and a warm-up for late-night types. When the outside tables get jam-packed in high season, the overflow heads into the narrow bar and the adjacent, equally narrow bistro. It opens at 4 PM; happy hour is 5 to 7. If you're alone, this is the place to make friends of all ages. ✉ *Av. Olas Altas 439, Col. E. Zapata* ☎ *322/222–5235.*

★ **Encuentros.** At this darkly atmospheric gay lounge (which is open from 6 PM to 1 AM), take a seat at one of the comfortable faux-suede barstools surrounding the horseshoe-shaped bar; small tables face equally comfortable banquettes. The small pizzas are a perfect snack, or try the beef and chicken satay, chicken wings, or spring rolls. ✉ *Calle Lázaro Cárdenas 312, Col. E. Zapata* ☎ *322/222–0643* 🌐 *www.encuentrosbar.com.*

The Shamrock. At this Irish-owned pub, open daily after 11 AM, the Wi-Fi flows freely throughout the chummy bar, and the chips, batter-fried cod, cottage pies, and burgers are great. When the number of customers warrants it during busy season, the more sophisticated (and peaceful) upstairs lounge is opened. ✉ *Av. México 27, Bucerías* ☎ *329/298–3073.*

Tribu Bar Lounge. Locals decided that this was a bit out of the way to become a serious hot spot, but Mexicans and foreigners in the Marina district find it atmospheric. DJ-spun music pulses house, lounge, techno, disco, or '80s music—whatever the crowd demands, but only until 11 PM. There's also a billiards table. Wednesday is usually salsa night, though the music isn't live; head here Thursday for karaoke. In high season it's open Tuesday to Sunday from 5 PM, often earlier if there's an important ball game on. In low season (generally August through mid-November) it's open Thursday and Friday only. There's never a cover. ✉ *Paseo de la Marina 220, Mayan Palace Marina, Marina Vallarta* ☎ *322/226–6000 Ext. 4786.*

Victor's Place (Café Tacuba). This inexpensive restaurant doubles as a bar and is as casual as could be. Beer for a buck-fifty (or less, depending on the peso's fluctuations) and cheap tequila with beer chasers are practically a house rule. You can check it out nightly until 11 PM, a bit later on weekends. The outside deck overlooks the yachts in the marina. ✉ *Condominios Las Palmas, Local 9, Marina Vallarta* ☎ *322/221–2808.*

12

DANCE AND MUSIC CLUBS

Blanco y Negro. Here's a wonderful place for a quiet drink. The intimate café-bar is comfortable yet rustic, with *equipale* (leather-and-wood) love seats and traditional round cocktail tables. At around 10:30, *trova* (think Mexican Cat Stevens) by Latino legends Silvio Rodríguez and Pablo Milanés begins; songs composed and sung by the owner liven up the atmosphere. There's never a cover. It opens after 8 PM every night but Sunday (Sunday and Monday in low season). ✉ *Calle Lucerna at Calle Niza, behind Blockbuster Video store, Zona Hotelera* ☎ *322/293–2556.*

★ **Christine.** Christine has a spectacular light show set to bass-thumping music that ranges from techno and house to disco, rock, and Mexican pop. Most people (young boomers and Gen-Xers) come for the duration (it doesn't close until 6 AM), as this is the top of the food chain for the PV dancing experience. The dance club is open Wednesday through Sunday after 10 PM, and the cover is typically $20. Exceptions include ladies' nights (no set night), when women get in free. On open-bar nights the $36-per-person cover gets you unlimited drinks. ✉ *Krystal Vallarta, Av. de las Garzas s/n, Zona Hotelera* ☎ *322/224–6990.*

Fodor's Choice ★ **de Santos.** In addition to having a pretty good Mediterranean dinner in the ground-floor restaurant, you can start an evening here with chill-out and lounge music that appeals to an upscale, slightly older crowd of locals, gringos, local gringos, and Spanish-speaking travelers. Later, local and guest DJs spin the more danceable, beat-driven disco and house tunes that appeal to slightly younger folks. If the smoke and noise get to you, head upstairs to the rooftop bar, where you and your friends can fling yourselves on the giant futons for some stargazing. This is a see-and-be-seen place for locals, and the kitchen is generally open until 2 AM; the whole place shuts down at 4 AM, or 6 AM in high season. ✉ *Calle Morelos 771, at Leona Vicario, Centro* ☎ *322/223–3052.*

Hilo. Popular with young, hip *vallartenses,* Hilo attracts a mix of locals and visitors. It's mainly a young crowd, serving up house, techno, hip-hop, electronic, and Top 40. The ceiling is several stories high, and enormous bronze-color statues give an epic feeling. It's open from 4 PM to 6 AM but doesn't get rolling until midnight. The cover is $7–$10, or $30 with open bar. ✉ *Paseo Díaz Ordaz 588, Centro* ☎ *322/223–5361.*

★ **J&B Dance Club.** People call it "Hota Bay" (it's how you pronounce the letters "j" and "b" in Spanish), and it's the best club in town for salsa. The age of the crowd varies but tends toward thirty- and forty-somethings. J&B is serious about dancing, so it feels young at heart. There's usually a band Friday and Saturday nights, DJ music the rest of the week. Those with *dos patas zurdas* (two left feet) can attend salsa lessons Thursday and Friday 8 to 9 PM (50 pesos) or take tango lessons for the same price on Monday at 8 PM. The dance club's cover is $8 when there's live music, otherwise about $4 and free on Monday and Tuesday. ✉ *Blvd. Francisco M. Ascencio 2043, Zona Hotelera* ☎ *322/224–4616.*

La Bodeguita del Medio. It's a wonderful Cuban bar and restaurant with a friendly vibe. People of all ages come to salsa and drink mojitos made with Cuban rum. The small dance floor fills up as soon as the house sextet starts playing around 9:30 PM. There's no cover. ✉ *Paseo Díaz Ordaz 858, Centro* ☎ *322/223–1585.*

Philo's. It's the unofficial cultural center and meeting place of La Cruz, with music, food, a large-screen TV, and a pool table. The owner Philo, a former record producer, also has a small recording studio here. The space is plain, but there's excellent live music (a blend of Roots Rock, country, and blues) after 8:30 PM Thursday through Saturday year-round. Get down to the music or chow down on good pizza or barbecue. ✉ *Calle Delfín 15, La Cruz de Huanacaxtle* ☎ *329/295–5068.*

SHOPPING

ART

Galería 8 y Más. It started with eight Guadalajara artists and has expanded under new ownership to 45 artists from or residing in Jalisco. The large old building has glass, bronze, chalk, and oil paintings. The Miramar Street gallery is open 10–5 and the Calle Corona gallery 10–2 and 5–8. Both close after 2 on Saturday and all day Sunday. ✉ *Calle Miramar 237, Centro* ☎ *No phone* ✉ *Calle Corona 186, Centro* ☎ *322/223–9700* 🌐 *www.artismexico.com* ⊙ *Closed Sun.*

Fodor's Choice ★ **Gallería Dante.** Classical, contemporary, and abstract works are displayed and sold in this 6,000-square-foot gallery—PV's largest—and sculpture garden. Check out the marvelous large-format paintings of indigenous people in regional costumes by Juana Cortez Salazar, whimsical statues by Guillermo Gómez, and the startlingly realistic paintings of nature by James Knowles along with the work of nearly 50 other talented artists. ✉ *Calle Basilio Badillo 269, Col. E. Zapata* ☎ *322/222–2477.*

CLOTHING

★ **La Bohemia.** Some of the elegant clothing sold here was designed by the equally elegant owner, Toody. You'll find unique jewelry, accessories, and the San Miguel shoe—the elegant yet comfortable footwear designed for walking on cobblestone streets like those of San Miguel and Puerto Vallarta. ✉ *Calle Constitución, at Calle Basilio Badillo, Col. E. Zapata* ☎ *322/222–3164* ✉ *Plaza Neptuno, Av. Francisco M. Ascencio, Km 7.5, Marina Vallarta* ☎ *322/221–2160* ⊙ *Closed Sun. (both branches).*

★ **María de Guadalajara.** It's DIY chic here. You choose the colorful, cotton, triangular sash of your liking, miraculously transforming pretty but baggy dresses into flattering and stylish frocks. The color palette is truly inspired, although the selection for men is limited. ✉ *Puesta del Sol condominiums, Local 15–A, Marina, Marina Vallarta* ☎ *322/221–2566* ✉ *Calle Morelos 550, Centro* ☎ *322/222–2387* 🌐 *www.mariadeguadalajara.com.*

Serafina. This is the place to go for over-the-top ethnic clothing; stamped-leather purses from Guadalajara; belt buckles from San Miguel; and clunky necklaces and bracelets of quartz, amber, and turquoise. It also sells wonderful tchotchkes. The shop doubled in size in 2008, taking over the adjacent store. ✉ *Calle Basilio Badillo 260, Col. E. Zapata* ☎ *322/223–4594* ⊙ *Closed Sun.*

★ **Sirenas.** It's affiliated with Serafina and geared to women with eclectic tastes. Creative sisters from Tamaulipas State create chic and unusual, exuberant fantasy jewelry. Colorful clutches and makeup bags made from recycled packaging are an innovation from Mexico City. At this writing, the shop was filled with tight-fitting, ribbed T-shirts edged in sequins and an assortment of ethnically inspired yet edgy and contemporary blouses and skirts from Indonesia and elsewhere. ✉ *Calle Basilio Badillo 252B, Col. E. Zapata* ☎ *322/223–1925* ⏲ *Closed Sun.*

CRAFTS

Galería Indígena. The assortment of handicrafts here is huge: Huichol yarn paintings and beaded bowls and statuettes, real Talavera ceramics from Puebla, decorative pieces in painted wood, and many other items. The owner likes offering customers a drink of water or other refreshment, no strings attached. ✉ *Av. Juárez 628, Centro* ☎ *322/223–0800.*

Huichol Collection. Native artisans working on crafts and wearing their stunning and colorful clothing draw customers in. The shop has an excellent inventory, with some museum-quality pieces. Though the merchandise is genuine, the shop is also venue for timeshare sales—albeit with a soft sales pitch. ✉ *Paseo Diaz Ordaz 732, Centro, Puerto Vallarta* ☎ *322/223–0661* ✉ *Morelos 490, Centro, Puerto Vallarta* ☎ *322/223–2141.*

★ **Lucy's CuCú Cabana.** You can shop for inexpensive, one-of-a-kind folk art from Guerrero, Michoacán, Oaxaca, and elsewhere at this very small shop. Note that Lucy closes during lunch. ✉ *Calle Basilio Badillo 295, Col. E. Zapata* ☎ *322/222–1220* ⏲ *Closed Sun. and Sept.–mid-Oct.*

★ **Mundo de Azulejos.** Buy machine- or handmade tiles starting at about $1 each at this large shop. You can get mosaic tile scenes (or order your own design), a place setting for eight, hand-painted sinks, or any number of soap dishes, cups, saucers, plates, or doodads. Around the corner and run by family members, Mundo de Cristal has more plates and tableware in the same style. ✉ *Av. Venustiano Carranza 374, Col. E. Zapata* ☎ *322/222–2675* 🌐 *www.talavera-tile.com.*

JEWELRY

Fodor's Choice ★ **Cassandra Shaw Jewelry.** It's hard to ignore the huge, chunky rings, bracelets, and necklaces here. In the back of the shop are more delicate items of pure silver set with various stones in artful ways. All are unusual. There's a small selection of hats, handbags, tunics, and other items, and, up the spiral staircase the owner's oil paintings, mainly nonrepresentational portraits. ✉ *Calle Basilio Badillo 276, Col. E. Zapata* ☎ *322/223–9734.*

Joyería Yoler. Manager Ramon Cruz proudly shows off the store's collection of the Los Castillo family's silver jewelry made with lost-wax casting as well as hammering and burnishing techniques, small silver pitchers with lapis lazuli dragonfly handles, napkin rings, abalone pillboxes, and other lovely utilitarian pieces. The merchandise—which includes an extensive yet not overwhelming array of silver and semiprecious-stone jewelry—is nicely arranged in the ample shop. It's open daily from 9 AM to 10 PM (even on Sunday). ✉ *Calle Olas Altas 391, Col. E. Zapata* ☎ *322/222–8713 or 322/222–9051.*

★ **Joyería El Opalo.** It's a bright spot in a nearly abandoned mall that has stayed afloat through its cruise-ship contacts. Look for it near the northern entrance to the open-air mall, across the street from Gold's Gym. Silver jewelry ranges in price from $3 per gram for simpler pieces to $30 a gram for the lighter, finer-quality, more complex pieces. There's high-grade "950" silver jewelry in addition to the usual "925" sterling silver. Look for gold settings as well. Most of the semiprecious stones—amethyst, topaz, malachite, black onyx, and opal in 28 colors—are of Mexican origin. They sell blue diamond jewelry and increasingly rare tanzanite. The diamond-cut necklaces are magnificent. If you want to comparison-shop, there are three or four other jewelry stores in the immediate vicinity. ✉ *Local 13–A, Plaza Genovesa, Col. Las Glorias* ☎ *322/224–6584* ⏲ *Closed Sun.*

★ **Joyas Finas Suneson.** Some of Mexico's finest designers create the unusual silver jewelry and objets d'art that are sold here. Most items have modern rather than traditional motifs. ✉ *Calle Morelos 593, Centro* ☎ *322/222–5715* ⏲ *Closed Sun.*

SPORTS AND THE OUTDOORS

ATV, DUNE BUGGY, AND CANOPY TOURS

Fodor's Choice ★ **Canopy Tour de Los Veranos.** Los Veranos has the most zip lines (14), the longest zip line (1,300 feet), and the highest zip line (500 feet off the ground). It also has the most impressive scenery, crossing the Río Los Horcones half a dozen times on several miles of cables. Departures are from the office, across from the Pemex station at the south side of Puerto Vallarta, every hour on the hour between 9 and 2 (arrive 15 minutes early), with reduced hours in low season (June through November). After your canopy tour, there's time to scale the climbing wall, play in the Horcones River, eat at the restaurant, or hang out at the bar overlooking the river, but check to make sure that a ride back to town is available. There are shuttles from Marina Vallarta and Nuevo Vallarta, and discounts for groups. ✉ *Office: Calle Francisca Rodríguez 336, Col. E. Zapata* ☎ *322/223–0504; 877/563–4113 from U.S. and Canada* 🌐 *www.canopytours-vallarta.com.*

★ **Wild Vallarta.** Full- and half-day tours in Honda four-wheel ATVs and open-frame, five-speed "jungle buggies" with VW engines cost $80/$100 per day (single/double ATVs) to $110/$125 per day (dune buggy with or without lunch, respectively). The long and rugged ATV tour to San Sebastián, high in the Sierra Madre, requires some experience, but four-hour trips are fine for beginners. They offer a combined canopy and ATV tour ($140 for one, $215 for two people). ✉ *Manuel M. Dieguez 274–A, Col. E. Zapata* ☎ *322/222–8928* 🌐 *www.wildvallarta.com.*

GOLF

Fodor's Choice ★ **El Tamarindo.** About two hours south of Vallarta on the Costalegre is one of the area's best courses. At least six of the holes play along the ocean; some are cliff-side holes with fabulous views, while others go right down to the beach. On a slow day, golfers are encouraged at tee time to have a swim or a picnic on the beach during their round, or to play a hole a second time if they wish. Designed by David Fleming, the breathtaking course is the playground of birds, deer, and other wildlife. It's an awesome feeling to nail the course's most challenging hole, the 9th: a par 3 with a small green surrounded by bunkers. The greens fee is $240, including cart and tax. Resort guests get priority for tee times; call up to a week ahead to check availability. ✉ *Carretera Melaque–Puerto Vallarta, Carretera 200, Km 7.5, Cihuatlán* ☎ *315/351–5032 Ext. 113.*

El Tigre. At the Paradise Village hotel and condo complex is this 18-hole course with 12 water features. The greens fee of $150 includes a shared cart, bottled water, practice balls, and cold towels, but not tax. Don't be surprised if you see a guy driving around with tiger cubs in his truck: the course's namesake and mascot is the passion of the club's director, Jesús Carmona Jiménez. El Tigre has a par-3 hole played entirely on an island. ✉ *Paseo Paraíso 800, Nuevo Vallarta* ☎ *322/297–0773; 866/843–5951 from U.S.; 800/214–7758 from Canada* 🌐 *www.eltigregolf.com.*

★ **Four Seasons Punta Mita.** Nonguests are permitted to play the 195-acre, par-72, Jack Nicklaus–designed Pacifico course; however, they must pay the hotel's day-use fee of 50% of the room rate (approximately $300 plus 28% tax and service charge), which covers use of a guest room and hotel facilities until dark. Reservations are essential. The greens fee is $262, including tax and the golf cart. The club's claim to fame is that it has perhaps the only natural island green in golf. Drive your cart to it at low tide; otherwise hop aboard a special amphibious vessel (weather permitting) to cross the water. There are seven other oceanfront links. Opened in 2009, the Bahía is another stunning 18-hole course. It has more undulating fairways and greens than the first course, but similarly spectacular ocean views—and high price tag. ✉ *Punta Mita* ☎ *329/291–6000* 🌐 *www.fourseasons.com.*

Los Flamingos Country Club. Designed by Percy Clifford in 1978, PV's original course has been totally renovated. The 18-hole course in Los Flamingos development, at the northern extremity of Nuevo Vallarta, has new irrigation and sprinkler systems to maintain the rejuvenated greens. The high-season greens fee is $139, including a shared cart, tax, a bottle of water, and a bucket of balls. ✉ *Carretera 200, Km 145, 12 km (8 mi) north of airport, Nuevo Vallarta* ☎ *329/296–5006* 🌐 *www.flamingosgolf.com.mx.*

PUERTO VALLARTA ★ **Marina Vallarta.** Joe Finger designed this 18-hole course; the $129 greens fee includes practice balls, tax, and a shared cart. It's the area's second-oldest course, and is closest and most convenient for golfers staying in the Hotel Zone, downtown Puerto Vallarta, and Marina Vallarta. Although it's very flat, it's far more challenging than it looks, with lots of water hazards. Speaking of hazards, the alligators have a way of blending into the scenery. They might surprise you, but they supposedly don't bite. Go to the course's Web site to find hotels participating in their "Stay and Play" golf packages. ✉ *Paseo de la Marina s/n, Marina Vallarta* ☎ *322/221–0545 or 322/221–0073* 🌐 *www.marinavallartagolf.com.*

MULTISPORT OPERATORS

Ecotours (☎ *322/223-3130 or 322/222-6606* 🌐 *www.ecotoursvallarta.com*). It's a downtown PV–based operator (with a second office at Marina Vallarta) whoseofferings include hiking, diving, snorkeling, kayaking, bird-watching, whale-watching, and turtle tours.

Puerto Vallarta Tours (☎ *322/222-4935 or 01800/832-3632 in Mexico; 866/217-9704 or 866/464-6915 from U.S. or Canada* 🌐 *www.puertovallartatours.net*). This company offers tours that are available from other area operators, but we recommend it for its excellent Web site, English-speaking operators and crew, and the convenience factor: through this one operator, you can book everything from canopy tours, ATVs, deep-sea fishing, and mountain biking to cruise tours, cultural tours, and bullfighting.

Sociedad Cooperativa Corral del Risco (☎ *329/291-6298* 🌐 *www.puntamitacharters.com*). Local fishermen at Punta Mita (aka Punta de Mita) have formed this cooperative, which offers reasonably priced fishing trips, surfing, whale-watching excursions, and diving and snorkeling outings.

Tours Soltero (☎ *315/355-6777* ✉ *raystoursmelaque@yahoo.com*). Canadian expat Ray Calhoun and his wife Eva rent mountain bikes, snorkeling equipment, and Boogie boards ($10 per day) and lead active tours from their base in San Patricio Melaque, a town next to Barra de Navidad south of PV. Typical excursions are snorkeling in Tenacatita with Boogie boarding at Boca de Iguana, from 10 to 5 ($32), and a day trip to the state capital, Colima, which includes lunch and a stop at a typical hacienda-cum-museum ($60).

Vallarta Adventures (☎ *322/297-1212 in Nuevo Vallarta; 322/221-0657 in Marina Vallarta; 888/526-2238 from U.S. and Canada* 🌐 *www.vallarta-adventures.com*). It's a well-respected operator with 20 years' experience, two offices, dozens of tours, and a staff of some 350. It's often used by high-end hotel concierges and cruise-ship activity directors for canopy tours, hiking, sailing, dinner-show cruises, Sierra Madre expeditions, and dolphin- and whale-watching cruises.

Rancho Mi Chaparrita (✉ *Manuel Rodriguez Sanchez 14, Sayulita* ☎ *329/291-3112* 🌐 *www.michaparrita.com*). On his family ranch, Luis Verdin runs a 13-zip-line tour ($75) and horseback riding trips ($25 per hour). Or combine the two, accessing the ranch on Señor Verdin's lively, healthy horses via the beach and backcountry for a complete adventure ($95). The company rents Boogie boards, surfboards, and paddleboards and offers surfing lessons and four- to six-day surfing packages. They also provide snorkeling and whale- or wildlife-watching excursions around the Marietas Islands.

Wildlife Connection (☎ *322/225-3621* 🌐 *www.wildlifeconnection.com*). Based in downtown PV, this Mexican-owned company does what its name implies: It connects you with wildlife (specifically birds, turtles, dolphins, and whales) on seasonal trips. It also leads snorkeling and photography outings.

WATER SPORTS

FISHING

★ **Fishing with Carolina.** This Canadian expat has been sending out anglers for 25 years. Party-boat fishing is $150. Charter your own four-passenger boat to fish in the bay; $400 covers a four-hour trip, or pay a bargain $600 for eight hours. To access the farthest locations, plan on 12 hours and about $1,000. ✉ *Terminal Marítima, Los Peines Pier, Marina Vallarta* ☎ *322/224–7250* 🌐 *www.fishingwithcarolina.com.*

SCUBA DIVING AND SNORKELING

Chico's Dive Shop. This shop arranges PADI or NAUI certification, equipment rentals, and one- or two-tank dives. Trips to Los Arcos accommodate snorkelers ($40 per person) as well as those who want a one- or two-tank dive ($65 and $98, respectively). Book several days ahead for a night dive ($75 for one tank). From the Mismaloya shop you can also rent kayaks ($15 per hour). ✉ *Paseo Díaz Ordáz 772, Centro* ☎ *322/222–1895* ✉ *Mismaloya Beach, in Barceló La Jolla de Mismaloya hotel, Mismaloya* ☎ *322/228–0248* 🌐 *www.chicos-diveshop.com.*

★ **Ecotours.** This authorized equipment dealer has English-speaking PADI dive masters. Two-tank dives run $82 to $90. All two-tank trips include lunch, refreshments, and gear. Snorkeling trips to the Marieta Islands, where you may spot dolphins and, in season, whales, cost $85 per person, including lunch overlooking the beach. Hotel pickup, boat ride, and snorkel gear are included in the price. ✉ *Ignacio L. Vallarta 243, Col. E. Zapata* ☎ *322/223–3130 or 322/222–6606* 🌐 *www.ecotoursvallarta.com.*

★ **Sociedad Cooperativa Corral del Risco.** Tours with this co-op are a great deal if you have a group: two hours of snorkeling around the Marietas Islands, for up to eight people, cost just $95 on a one-motor boat, about $120 for the 2-motor vessel. This group represents local fishermen displaced when Punta Mita was developed by the Four Seasons and other associated establishments. ✉ *Av. El Anclote 1, Manzana. 17, Corral del Risco* ☎ *329/291–6298* 🌐 *www.puntamitacharters.com.*

SURFING

Captain Pablo. At this outfitter on the beach at Sayulita you can rent equipment or take surfing lessons with Patricia: $30 should get you to your feet (board included). Surf tours, gear included, cost $180 for four hours (up to four surfers). ✉ *Calle Las Gaviotas at beach, Sayulita* ☎ *329/291–2070 early morning and evenings only* ✉ *pandpsouthworth@hotmail.com.*

Sininen. Sininen rents surfboards ($5 per hour, $18 for the day) and paddleboards ($8/hour, $33 all day), gives lessons on both pieces of equipment, and sells surfboards and surf paraphernalia. Rent from the shop or head straight to its outpost a block away on the beach. ✉ *Calle Delfín 4–S, Sayulita* ☎ *329/291–3186.*

MANZANILLO

280 km (174 mi) south of Puerto Vallarta via Hwy. 200; 332 km (206 mi) southwest of Guadalajara via the Guadalajara–Colima autopista (toll road).

Updated by Michele Joyce

Manzanillo is the Pacific Coast's strangest resort city. The *Bahías Gemelas* (twin bays)—separated by a huge burl of craggy rocks and lush foliage—provide beaches of black-and-gold volcanic sand, so it ought to be a tourist's dream come true, times two. There's certainly no denying the fantastic quality of its fanciest resorts, nor the quirky cool that permeates some of its out-of-the-way places. But Manzanillo is mostly preoccupied with its other job—that of a working port—so shopping is uneventful, cultural sights are few, and tourism-related building seems to only happen in fits and starts.

Thanks to its geography, Manzanillo feels more like three towns than one. The breathtaking Peninsula de Santiago is covered with wealthy enclaves—epitomized by the anachronistic Moorish mini-city of Las Hadas resort—and is worlds away from the tightly packed, bustling downtown where there's nary a gringo in sight. The connective thread between the two is one long stretch of gold sand paralleled by a traffic-clogged road that is alternatively too built-up (if you need an Office Max or Home Depot, have no fear) and seemingly in decline.

With some lovely beaches and a minimum of faux-Mexicana, Manzanillo certainly does have its appeal. But perhaps the best way to enjoy the city is to not be too tied down to it. Along Highway 200 are dozens of low-key beaches easily toured using the city as a base.

GETTING HERE AND AROUND

Aeropuerto Internacional Playa de Oro is 32 km (20 mi), or 40 minutes, north of town. Taxis from the airport charge about $40; the shared vans that run to the major resorts are less expensive. First-class and executive-class buses connect Manzanillo's Central Nueva station with other Pacific Coast cities, Guadalajara, and Mexico City.

Having a car is a plus, since the city is extremely spread out. Driving from Guadalajara is a snap on the excellent four-lane toll road (54D), though not much faster than the scenic backcountry route on Highway 80 (via Barra). The trip from Puerto Vallarta on Highway 200 is slightly rough in patches but also really scenic.

Cabs are unmetered and are easy to hail on the streets. Agree on a price beforehand. The minimum fare is a little less than $2.

LOOKS DECEIVE

Although it hasn't the look of a colonial city, Manzanillo was founded soon after the Spanish conquest. Hernán Cortés envisioned it as a gateway to the Orient: from these shores Spanish galleons brought in the riches of Cathay to be trekked across the continent to Veracruz, where they filled vessels headed for Spain. But other ports received coveted, exclusive concessions, and Manzanillo was little developed in the colonial period.

$ ITALIAN **La Pergola**. At this little restaurant the pastas are made fresh, and the pizzas are tasty—especially the *cuatro queso* pie made with Gouda, mozzarella, Parmesan, and goat cheese. ✉ *Blvd. Costera Miguel de la Madrid, Km 11.5* ☎ *314/333–2265 or 314/334–2616* 🌐 *www.lapergolamanzanillo.com* 💳 AE, MC, V.

SUNSET SIGHTINGS

If you're visiting in cetacean season, come to L'Recif at 5 PM, when the restaurant opens, to watch for whales and hope for a glorious sunset.

12

$$$$ ITALIAN **Legazpi**. Maroon-and-white-stripe cushions adorn dark-wood chairs and banquettes, brass lamps hold thick white candles, and wide windows afford dramatic bay views. The menu is Italian, with an emphasis on Mediterranean dishes. Check out the cozy bar, where there's a mural depicting the history of Manzanillo. Some claim the food's not worth the high price, despite the dining room's personality. ✉ *Las Hadas Hotel, Av. De los Riscos and Av. Vista Hermosa, Fracc. Península de Santiago* ☎ *314/331–0101 Ext. 3512* 🌐 *www.brisas.com.mx* 💳 *AE, MC, V* ⏲ *No lunch.*

$$$ CONTINENTAL ★ **L'Recif**. Waves crash on the rocks below this lovely cliff-top spot a 15-minute drive from Manzanillo's Zona Hotelera toward Playa la Boquita. There's a little of everything on the menu—seafood, pasta, chicken, beef—but the signature dish is the camerón L'Recif (shrimp stuffed with cheese, wrapped in bacon, and broiled); it's served with mango sauce and sides of mashed potatoes and sautéed corn, zucchini, and carrots. ✉ *Cerro del Cenicero s/n, El Naranjo, Condominio Vida del Mar, Península de Juluapán* ☎ *314/335–0900* 🌐 *www.lrecif.com* 💳 *MC, V* ⏲ *Closed Easter–Oct. No lunch.*

$$ ECLECTIC **Toscana**. Reviews are good again for this longtime Manzanillo favorite, which has recovered from a stretch of inconsistency in its food and service. Service is now consistently friendly and fast. Specialties on the eclectic menu include seafood shish kebab served with rice and steamed vegetables, a three-lettuce salad with goat cheese, and a Caesar salad. For dessert, try the tiramisu. Most of the tables sit on the simple outdoor terrace overlooking the beach. People start using the dance floor nightly after 8:30. ✉ *Blvd. Costero Miguel de la Madrid 3177, Zona Hotelera* ☎ *314/333–2515* 🌐 *www.toscanamanzanillo.com* 💳 *MC, V* ⏲ *No lunch.*

WHERE TO STAY

You've got to pick your spots along the two sweeping bays of Manzanillo. Lots of people never leave the grand resorts on the Santiago Peninsula—and don't miss much. But you can secure comfortable waterfront accommodations in a pair of secondary Zonas Hoteleras (hotel zones)—Santiago and Las Brisas. More economical options can be found east along Manzanillo Bay, among a string of hotels on such quiet beaches as Playa Azul and Playa las Brisas. Backed by the Laguna de San Pedrito (San Pedrito Lagoon), this stretch is great for long walks on the beach. However, give the rooms a look before you check in for sure.

$$$$ **Barceló Karmina Palace.** Manzanillo's all-inclusive, all-suites hotel has grounds punctuated by cascades, fountains, and multitier lagoons. There's also a palapa restaurant at the ocean's edge. Each junior suite has marble floors, a balcony or terrace, a sofa bed, and a large tub with separate shower facilities. Corner suites have two bedrooms, a bath, a kitchen, and a dining room as well as a balcony with a plunge pool. **Pros:** lots of space; many activities for kids; rooms are s quiet. **Cons:** small restaurant selection for an all-inclusive; lots of families with small kids; beach isn't great for swimming; fee for in-room Wi-Fi access. ✉ *Av. Vista Hermosa 13, Fracc. Península de Santiago* ☎ *314/334–1313* 🌐 *www.barcelokarminapalace.com* *324 suites* *In-room: safe, refrigerator, Wi-Fi (some). In-hotel: 4 restaurants, room service, bars, pools, gym, spa, beachfront, water sports, children's programs (ages 4–12), laundry service, Internet terminal, Wi-Fi hotspot, parking (free), no-smoking rooms* 💳 *AE, MC, V* *AI.*

$$ **Blue Bay Los Angéles Locos.** This all-inclusive 45 minutes nort of Manzanillo is the kind of place where you might be tempted to stay for days without leaving the grounds. The major draw here is the lovely secluded bay with jungly mountain backdrop. You might catch a glimpse of turtles, dolphins, or whales while kayaking here or even just sitting on the beach. Things are in need of refurbishing; don't be surprised to see paint-chipped exteriors and furniture that's seen better days. Still, all rooms face the bay; the food is tasty; and there are activities for children, night shows, and a choice of water activities or tours. **Pros:** gorgeous beach; lots of activities; secluded grounds. **Cons:** far from town; dated buildings and room. ✉ *Carrertera Federal 200, Km 20, Tenacatita* ☎ *315/351–5411 or 800/713–3020* 🌐 *www.losangeloslocos.com* *204 rooms* *In-hotel: 3 restaurants, tennis court, pool, laundry service, Wi-Fi hotspot* 💳 *AE, MC, V* *AI.*

$$$$ **Camino Real Manzanillo.** Every detail has been well planned—from the oversized arch windows and entry to the marble floors and dark-wood furniture—and the service is exceptional. Suites have a minimalist style and two or three bedrooms, so they're perfect for families. Note that the beach here has rough sand and a strong current; the water isn't suitable for swimming, but it's lovely to look at from the pool. **Pros:** large suites; superb grounds; good service. **Cons:** beach isn't good for swimming; high prices. ✉ *Calzada Paraíso 11, Col. Residencial Salagua* ☎ *314/331–1740 or 866/543–1482* 🌐 *www.caminoreal.com/manzanillo* *50 suites* *In-room: safe, Wi-Fi. In-hotel: 2 restaurants, pools, gym, spa, beachfront* 💳 *AE, MC, V.*

$ **Hotel Colonial.** The classic appeal of this four-story, central hotel—frequently used in Mexican movies since its construction in 1944—extends from the stained-glass windows to the intricate curlicues of its brown woodwork to the tarnished little bell that sits on the receptionist's desk. Rooms are small but comfortable, and some include such architectural surprises as a split-level bathroom. The only downer is the artificial turf in the central courtyard. It's only a block from the waterfront zócalo, and the Wi-Fi in the restaurant usually works. **Pros:** cheap rates; close to restaurants and shops; away from resort scene. **Cons:** far from beaches. ✉ *Calle Bocanegra 28, at Av. Mexico* ☎ *314/332–1080*

WATER SPORTS

Except when the water is rough, the rocky points off Manzanillo's peninsulas and coves make for good snorkeling and scuba diving. **Colima Surf Academy** (✉ *Blvd. Costero 1509, Col. Infonavit* ☎ *314/333–2474* 🌐 *colimasurfacademy.com*) rents out boards and gives hour-long one-on-one surf lessons for $55 (promotional prices are often available).

You can rent snorkel and scuba gear as well as kayaks, Boogie boards, and Jet Skis at **Deportes Acuáticos el Pacífico** (✉ *Av. Audiencia s/n, Playa las Hadas, Península de Santiago* ☎ *314/331–0101 Ext. 3804* ✉ *Playa la Audiencia, Península de Santiago* ☎ *314/333–1848*).

Underworld Scuba (✉ *Blvd. Miguel de la Madrid, Km 15, near Juanito's restaurant, Santiago* ☎ *314/333–3678*) provides many services. The English-speaking instructors give resort classes and full PADI certification; sell single-day or multiday dive and hotel-dive packages; and rent snorkel and diving equipment.

IXTAPA AND ZIHUATANEJO

463 km (287 mi) south of Manzanillo via Hwy. 200, 247 km (154 mi) north of Acapulco via Hwy. 200.

Updated by Michele Joyce

Although they couldn't be more different, Ixtapa (eesh-*TAH*-pa) and Zihuatanejo (zee-wha-ta-*NEH*-ho) are marketed together as a single resort destination, and both have gorgeous bays and beaches. Zihua, as it's often called, was a remote fishing village with minimal tourist traffic for hundreds of years. Ixtapa was created in the 1970s when Mexico's National Fund for Tourism Development (FONATUR) cleared away a coconut plantation. Though both are still totally laid-back, they have attracted so much attention (and building) that "purists" are now heading 25 minutes north to the surfing enclave of Troncones or 35 minutes south to the more low-key fishing village of Barra de Potosí.

Although Ixtapa is quite pleasant, and self-sufficient in terms of services, its designers were unable to give it a heart and soul. A delightful marina with a few upscale seafood restaurants at the northern end of town is the only attraction (if you can call it that); other than that Ixtapa is simply a long line of beachfront resorts. Many visitors head 7 km (4 mi) south to enjoy the more authentic character of Zihua. There are plenty of beachfront hotels, and the cluster of pedestrian-only streets close to the marina is completely touristy. That said, tourism hasn't completely destroyed Zihua's small-town essence—it's one of the friendliest of the Pacific Coast's major resort areas.

GETTING HERE AND AROUND

Aeropuerto de Zihuatanejo is 12 km (8 mi) southeast of Zihua. Private cab fares range from $22 to $29. The bus station is in Zihua, with service to Manzanillo (8–9 hours), Acapulco (7 hours), Morelia (3½ hours), and Mexico City (7 hours). Driving south from Manzanillo on Carretera 200 is a gorgeous seven-hour trip that twists along mostly undeveloped coast.

🌐 *hotelcolonialmanzanillo.com* *40 rooms* *In-room: Wi-Fi. In-hotel: restaurant, room service, bar, laundry service, Wi-Fi hotspot, parking (free), some pets allowed* *MC, V.*

$$–$$$ **Hotel Riscos La Audiencia.** A sensible option for families and budget-conscious travelers, this small collection of accommodations clings to and cascades down the same hillside to Playa la Audiencia as the big resorts. With well-stocked kitchens as well as dining rooms, living rooms, and terraces, quarters are spacious enough to accommodate the two kids under 12 who can stay free in each room. Some rooms even have four beds. **Pros:** good deal for families; all rooms have kitchens. **Cons:** beach accessible only by car or a long stairway; signs of age throughout hotel. ✉ *Calle Los Riscos 27, Fracc. Península de Santiago* ☎ *314/334–1236* 🌐 *www.hotelriscoslaaudiencia.com* *9 rooms* *In-room: kitchen, Wi-Fi. In-hotel: pool, beachfront, laundry service* *MC, V.*

$$ **Hotel Villa Los Angeles.** Rooms are spacious; decorated simply with carved wooden furniture; and equipped with microwaves, refrigerators, and toasters. Master suites are outfitted with more complete kitchens, a Jacuzzi, and a large seating area. This is one of the most affordable hotels in Las Hadas Peninsula. **Pros:** accessible price; large rooms. **Cons:** short drive to beach; no Internet service. ✉ *Av. La Cima s/n, Fracc. Península de Santiago* ☎ *314/333–1702* 🌐 *www.villaslosangeles.com* *26 rooms* *In-room: kitchen (some). In-hotel: pool* *AE, MC, V.*

$$ **La Posada.** Only one of the famous old iron keys and antique locks remain, but the vibe that permeates this bright-pink beachfront lodging is as special as ever. Hoteliers Lisa and Juan Martinez have carefully applied their personal touch to a place that has been a favorite with North Americans since 1957. The large, open-air living-dining-bar area has rustic-color walls and *equipale* (pigskin and wood) furnishings. Only a few rooms have balconies, but all have screened windows. There's 24-hour e-mail access; an honor-system beer and soda bar; and a real sense of community among staff and guests, around the pool and over the complimentary morning breakfast. **Pros:** good value; great staff. **Cons:** far from swimming beaches; on an unattractive street (ask for water view); service too informal for some. ✉ *Av. Lázaro Cardenas 201, Zona Hotelera, Playa las Brisas* ☎ *314/333–1899* 🌐 *www.hotel-la-posada.info* *23 rooms* *In-room: no a/c (some), no phone, kitchen (some), no TV. In-hotel: bar, pool, beachfront, Internet terminal, parking (free)* *MC, V* *BP.*

$$$–$$$$ ★ **Las Hadas Golf & Marina.** The undulating roofs of the Moorish-style buildings glow pink in the afternoon sun. There's an almost hallucinogenic quality to the 15 acres of lacy palms, stylized geometric hedges, flamboyant orange-flowering trees, and white umbrellas on a small but virtually private beach. Las Hadas isn't as exclusive as it once was, but it still more than holds its own against the hotels that have followed it to Peninsula Santiago. White-on-white room decoration (even the TVs are white) is elegant and understated, and accented by pleasing touches like driftwood lamps; polished marble, fine sheets, and plush towels appear in both standard rooms and suites. The Legazpi restaurant is one

of the city's most exclusive. **Pros:** pleasant; semi-private beach; unique design and location; quiet. **Cons:** starting to show its age in places; understaffed; limited on-site dining options. ✉ *Av. Vista Hermosa s/n and Av. de los Riscos, Fracc. Península de Santiago* ☎ *314/331–0101 or 800/227–4727* 🌐 *www.brisas.com.mx* *102 rooms, 132 suites* *In-room: safe, DVD (some). In-hotel: 3 restaurants, room service, bars, golf course, tennis courts, pools, gym, beachfront, water sports, Internet terminal, Wi-Fi hotspot, parking (free), no-smoking rooms* 💳 *AE, MC, V* 🍽 *AI.*

$ **Marbella.** There's not much character in these blocks of basic motel-style rooms plunked down on the beach, but they're a good value, with cable TV, room service, and air-conditioning. The restaurant, El Marinero, as well as the buffet serve delicious Spanish, seafood, and Mexican fare. Ask to stay in the newer section (the cost is the same), where some standard rooms have ocean views and balconies. **Pros:** good food; great prices. **Cons:** nothing within walking distance; water too dangerous for swimming; exterior is run-down ✉ *Calle Marbella 7, at Blvd. Costero Miguel de la Madrid, Km 9.5, Zona Hotelera, Playa las Brisas* ☎ *314/333–1102 or 314/333–1222* 🌐 *www.hotelmarbella.com.mx* *92 rooms* *In-hotel: 2 restaurants, room service, bar, pool, beachfront, laundry service, Internet terminal, parking (free)* 💳 *AE, MC, V* 🍽 *MAP.*

SIP OF THE PAST

Bar Social has been downtown Manzanillo's main watering hole since 1941, owing to its location at Calle Juarez 101—just across from city hall. A circular bar surrounds a huge pedestal in the center of a high-ceiling room whirling with fans. Its walls are lined with tables and upholstered booths, and its windows are covered in Venetian blinds. An old red cash register rings up the cheap beers. *Botanas* (tortilla chips with assorted dips) are free through the afternoon, and a pianist plays most evenings. Note that the place goes dark on Sunday.

$$$$ **Suave Vida.** Suave Vida opened in December 2008, making it one of Manzanillo's newest properties. Its spacious rooms have such rustic details as carved wooden tables and tree trunks incorporated as pillars in the walls. The palapa-roofed restaurant serves international dishes, including pizzas baked in a pizza oven. Cuban dishes as well as the occasional Cuban dance reflect the owner's origins. **Pros:** large rooms for groups; attentive service. **Cons:** far from other hotels. ✉ *Av. Lázaro Cárdenas 1316, Col. Las Brisas* ☎ *312/333–2528* 🌐 *www.suavevidasuites.com* *8 suites* *In-room: kitchen. In-hotel: restaurant, bar, pool, beachfront* 💳 *AE, MC, V.*

$$$ **Tesoro Resort & Spa.** For a white-stucco link in a big hotel chain, this resort manages to exude some real personality. The rooms are handsome, the number of activities is dizzying, and the location on La Audiencia is sweet. A poolside snack bar doubles as a midnight disco; before that, hit the predictable floor show or the lounge, where the piano man sings corny-but-cool Mexican and American standards. All rooms have balconies, but not all have views. Take a look before you bring up the luggage. **Pros:** good activities desk; fun floor shows;

great play area for kids; tasty and varied buffets. **Cons:** pool crowded; rooms and some common areas get stuffy; spotty service. ✉ *Av. Audiencia 1, Playa la Audiencia* ☎ *314/333–20* 🌐 *www.tesororesorts.com* *289 rooms, 42 suites* *In-ro refrigerator. In-hotel: 4 restaurants, room service, bars, tenni pool, gym, spa, beachfront, children's programs (ages 4–12), service, Internet terminal, Wi-Fi hotspot, parking (free), no-s rooms* 💳 *AE, D, MC, V* 🍽 *AI.*

NIGHTLIFE

Bar de Félix (✉ *Blvd. Miguel de la Madrid 805, Zona Hotelera* 333–9277) is a large bar with crimson faux-velvet settees; a floor for Latin tunes, Spanish rock, some American oldies, an tronica; and a giant-screen TV. It's dark on Monday. People of a enjoy a night out at the lively **Colima Bay Café** (✉ *Blvd. Coster Fracc. Playa Azul* ☎ *314/333–1150*), with its whimsical style, background music, and variety of seating options—including pi barstools.

SPORTS AND THE OUTDOORS

FISHING

Manzanillo claims to be the world's sailfish capital; the season r from mid-October through March. The International Sailfish Tour ment (☎ *314/333–2770*) takes place during the last half of Novem and there's another in early February. Blue marlin and dorado are a abundant. Sportfishing boats are available at major hotels and throu tour agencies. Contact **Ocean Pacific Adventures** (☎ *314/335–0605*) charter a 26-foot boat (one to five people) for $225, or a 40-foot cruis (1 to 10 people) for $275. Both tours last five hours and include a fishi license and a case each of beer and soda as well as the usual ice, bai and tackle. A superb deal allows fisherpersons and their families to e their catch, along with side dishes, free at Colima Bay Café or Sunse Lounge, paying for drinks only.

GOLF

★ Robert Von Hagge mapped out the impressive 27-hole **Isla Navidad** (✉ *Paseo Country Club s/n* 🌐 *www.islanavidad.com*) course in the Grand Bay resort complex, about an hour north of Manzanillo. The expansive clubhouse has a pro shop where you can arrange lessons, a restaurant-bar, as well as men's and women's locker rooms with steam, sauna, and whirlpools. Greens fees are $230 for 18 holes, including cart. Caddies are mandatory and charge $30.

La Mantarraya (✉ *Av. De los Riscos and Av. Vista Hermosa, Fracc. Península de Santiago* ☎ *314/331–0101*), the 18-hole golf course at Las Hadas hotel, designed by Roy Dye, provides club rentals and caddies. The greens fee is $195, plus $45 for the cart.

The four-hour Zihua–Acapulco leg on Carretera 200 passes through small towns and coconut groves. Minibuses run every 10–15 minutes between the Ixtapa hotels and downtown Zihua until 10 PM; the fare is about 50¢. Cabs (unmetered) are easy to hail on the street in Zihua; the fare to Ixtapa is $4–$5. In town, a car only comes in handy if you plan to take day trips, as cab fares can be expensive (as much as $25 one way to Troncones from Ixtapa's resorts).

ESSENTIALS

Medical Assistance **Hospital General de Zihuatanejo** (✉ *Av. Morelos s/n, at Mar Egeo, Zihuatanejo* ☎ *755/554–3965*). **Police** (☎ *755/554–2040*).

Visitor and Tour Info **Guerrero State Tourism Office** (✉ *Paseo de las Golondrinas 1-A, Blvd. Ixtapa s/n, Ixtapa* ☎ *755/553–1967* 🌐 *www.guerrero.gob.mx*). **Oficina de Convenciones y Visitantes** (*Convention and Visitors' Bureau* ✉ *Paseo de las Gaviotas 12, Ixtapa* ☎ *755/553–1570* 🌐 *www.visit-ixtapa-zihuatanejo.org*).

EXPLORING

Ixtapa's primary hotel zone, the Zona Hotelera, extends along a 3-km (2-mi) strip of sandy beach called Playa del Palmar. It's fun to walk along the shore to check out the various hotel scenes and water-sports activities. Swimming is so-so because of how the small waves break close to shore. You can walk the length of the same zone on the landward side of the hotels, along Paseo Ixtapa. This landscaped thoroughfare—essentially, Ixtapa's only main street—is an access road that feeds the hotels on one side and strip malls filled with restaurants on the other. It includes a broad path for pedestrians and cyclists. The Zona Hotelera's southerly end is also home to the 18-hole Palma Real Golf Club; at the resort's northwest end is the anemic Marina Ixtapa development.

Everything in Zihuatenejo radiates out from the main beach. Although this stretch of sand is not the place for swimming, it's the best place to get a sense of the timeless local rhythm. Fishermen still set off in outboard-motorized skiffs and return a few hours later to sell their catch right there on the beach. A few blocks down, companies on and around the municipal pier, or *muelle,* take tourists on half- or full-day fishing adventures of their own, or on a 10-minute trip across the bay to one of the best swimming and snorkeling beaches, Playa las Gatas. The pier also marks the beginning of the Paseo del Pescador (Fishermen's Walk), or malecón. Follow this seaside path, only a third of a mile long, along the main beach, which is fronted by small restaurants and shops. Along the way you'll pass the basketball court that doubles as the town square.

Museo Arqueológico de la Costa Grande. The malecón ends at this archaeological museum, a gray stone building identified with a wooden shingle. A permanent display of pre-Hispanic murals, maps, and archaeological pieces traces the history of the so-called Costa Grande (Grand Coast) through the colonial era. Beyond the museum, a footpath cut into the rocks leads to Playa la Madera. ✉ *Paseo del Pescador 7, at Plaza Olof Palme, Zihuatanejo* ☎ *755/554–7552* 🎫 *$1* ⏲ *Mon.–Sun. 10–6.*

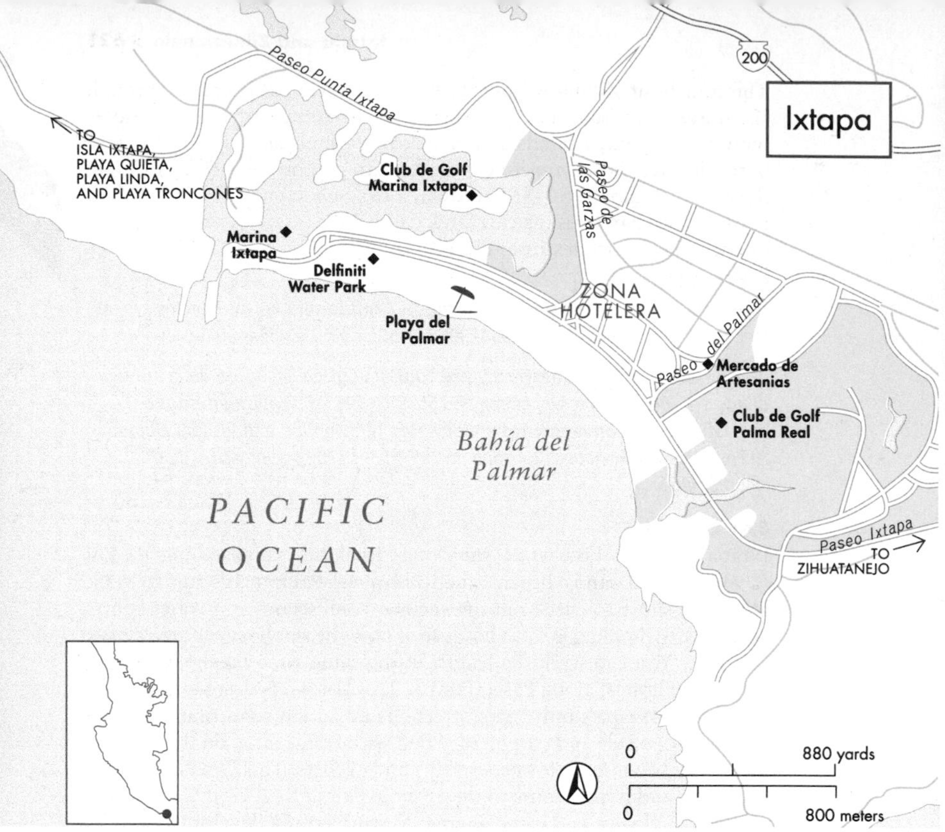

BEACHES

IXTAPA

Fodor's Choice ★ **Isla Ixtapa.** The most popular spot on Isla Ixtapa (and the one closest to the boat dock) is Playa Cuachalalate. An excellent swimming beach, it was named for a local tree whose bark has been used as a remedy for kidney ailments since ancient times. A short walk across the island, Playa Varadero hugs a rocky cove. Guides recommend snorkeling here, but watch for coral-covered rocks on both sides of the cove. Just behind is Playa Coral, whose calmer, crystal-clear water is more conducive to swimming. Each of the above beaches is lined with seafood eateries eager to rent snorkel equipment. Playa Carey, toward the island's south end, is small and has no services. Pangas ($4 round-trip) run between the boat landings at both Cuachalalate and Varadero beaches and Playa Linda on the mainland, where you'll find a few all-inclusive, high-rise hotels.

Playa del Palmar. Ixtapa's main beach, this broad, 3-km-long (2-mi-long) stretch of soft brown sand runs along the Zona Hotelera. Although you can swim here, small waves break right onshore and currents are sometimes strong. Each hotel offers shaded seating on the sand. Concessions rent Jet Skis ($40 per half hour) and Hobie Cats ($50 per day) and arrange banana-boat rides (15 minutes costs $5 per passenger with a four-person minimum) and parasail trips ($25 for a little more than 10 minutes). Licensed guides in white uniforms cruise up and down selling horseback-riding and boating tours. Women offer hair braiding and massage under open-sided tents.

GIDDYUP!

Most area tour operators arrange guided horseback excursions on Playa Linda and Playa del Palmar. Costs are high ($35–$40 for roughly 1½ hours), but they include transportation and usually a soft drink or beer after the ride.

Playa Linda. Thatch-roof restaurants dispense beer, soda, and the catch of the day just north of the Qualton Inn, in the Zona Hotelera II. Mexican families favor this long, coconut-palm-lined beach, which has marvelous views, is perfect for walking, and is bordered at one end by an estuary with birds and gators. You can rent horses (about half as much here as on Playa Ixtapa or from area tour operators), and a warren of identical stalls sells souvenirs and cheap plastic beach toys. Concessions arrange banana-boat rides and rent Jet Skis and Boogie boards. Water taxis depart here for Isla Ixtapa, and land taxis wait in the free parking lot for fares.

Playa Quieta. Club Med occupies the south end of tranquil Playa Quieta; the rest of the lovely cove is empty except for a cluster of tables and chairs that picnicking families rent for the day for a small fee, and the equally unobtrusive Restaurant Neptuno, which sells reasonably priced seafood all week.

ZIHUATANEJO

Playa la Madera. This is a small, flat, dark-sand beach with a sprinkling of restaurants on the sand (which provide just about the only shade, and facilities) and a few more hotels on or just above it. Bobbing boats and the green headlands make for stunning vistas. Waves are small or nonexistent, and as there's no drop-off it's a great place for the kiddies. Young locals always seem to be kicking a soccer ball around. Get there via a footpath cut into the rocks that separate it from Playa Principal, in downtown Zihua, or by car.

Fodor's Choice ★ **Playa la Ropa.** Clothing Beach apparently got its name hundreds of years ago when a textile-laden ship spilled its silks, which washed up on the sand. The area's most magnificent beach is a 20-minute walk from Playa la Madera and a five-minute taxi ride from town. Parasailers drift above the 1-km (½-mi) stretch of soft light sand; below, concessionaires rent Jet Skis ($40 for 30 minutes) and Hobie Cats (up to $50 an hour, depending on the size). Up and down the beach are open-air restaurants—some with hammocks for post-meal siestas—and a handful of hotels. Kids can splash in the calm, aquamarine water or toss a ball or Frisbee on the shore—but not too close to the little stream that empties into the southerly end: it's a crocodile refuge! There's free parking in a lot at the south end of the beach.

★ **Playa las Gatas.** Legend has it that a Tarascan king (from an indigenous, pre-Hispanic community) built the breakwater on Playa las Gatas to create a sheltered area for his daughter's exclusive use. Named for the

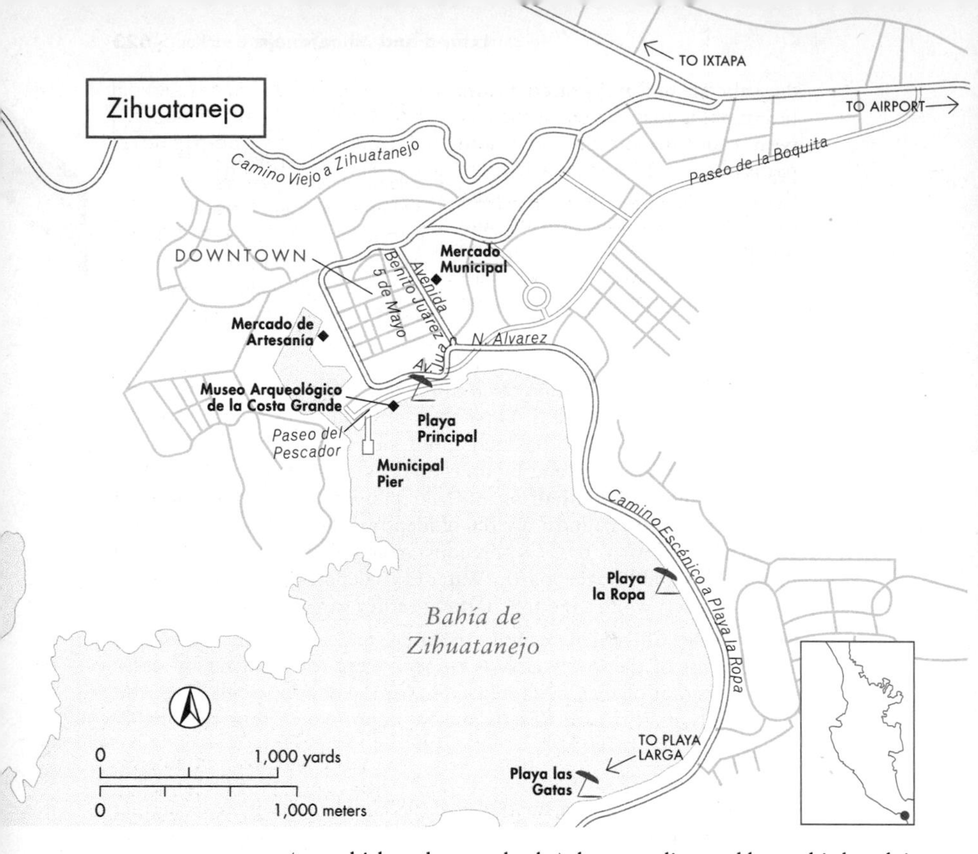

gatas (cat-whiskered nurse sharks) that once lingered here, this beach is bordered by a long row of hewn rocks that create a breakwater. Snorkelers scope out the rocky coves, and surfers spring to life with the arrival of small but fun summer swells. The beach is lined with simple seafood eateries that provide lounge chairs for sunning, as well as kayak and snorkeling-gear rentals, and guiding services. (You really can't go wrong with any of the concessionaires, but La Red del Pescador, at the far end of the beach, has the best setup with the hippest music; ask for Cruz if you need a kayak guide.) Overlooking the beach is *El Faro* (the lighthouse); the view from the top is marvelous, but the safe path up can be hard to find—ask any of the waiters to point it out. You can reach Playa las Gatas in about 20 minutes by climbing over the rocks that separate it from

LONG LEGS

To see pink flamingos and other wading birds, head for Barra de Potosí (20–25 minutes south of the airport), where a pleasant *laguna* (lagoon) is an unofficial bird sanctuary. You can go on a tour or take a bus or taxi—you'll pay less for the latter, and you'll be able to linger at one of the casual restaurants lining the beach. Or, hire a fisherman's boat from Zihuatanejo's municipal pier or Playa La Ropa for a trip to the scenic, remote Playa Manzanillo, which is great for snorkeling.

Playa la Ropa. But it's much more common and convenient to take one of the skiffs that run from the municipal pier every 10 or 15 minutes between 8 AM and a half hour before sunset. Buy your round-trip ticket (about $4) on the pier, and keep the stub for your return trip.

Playa Principal. The less-than-pristine water (water taxis and fishing boats hang out here) may keep you on the sand, but there's plenty going on. Check out the haggling over fish prices, settle into an umbrella-shaded chair with a cool drink and fresh seafood, or shop at makeshift stalls for trinkets and treasures, but save the bulk of your beach-going time for other shores.

WHERE TO EAT

IXTAPA

$$$ ITALIAN ★ ✕ **Beccofino**. This small, marina-side dining room and cozy bar has been a popular high-season hangout since 1992. Dark polished woods contrast with bright white linens, and bottles of wine are shelved on walls painted with trompe l'oeil scenes. A canopy-sheltered deck overlooks the marina. Among the best dishes on the northern Italian menu are minestrone soup, *caprese* salad (with tomatoes, basil, and mozzarella), fish fillet (usually red snapper or mahimahi) with a champagne sauce, and chicken cacciatore. Many of the pastas are made in-house, and breakfast is available after 9:30 AM. Enjoy the personalized attention of the owner and all-around excellent service. ✉ *Plaza Marina, Ixtapa* ☎ *755/553–1770* ✍ *Reservations essential* ▭ *AE, MC, V.*

$$$ MEXICAN ✕ **Casa Morelos**. The wooden bar, ocher walls, and handcrafted furnishings make this tiny restaurant seem like a true cantina, although it's in the middle of a shopping center. Patio tables are more elegant at night than during the day, with potted trees dressed in little white lights and lively tropical music at a level that doesn't drown out conversation. The *chiles rellenos de camarón* (egg-battered peppers stuffed with shrimp), fajitas, and tuna steak topped with three kinds of chilies are all filling and delicious, even if they cost slightly more than entrées at nearby restaurants. You can also come for a generous breakfast; this eatery opens at 7:30 AM. ✉ *La Puerta shopping center, Blvd. Ixtapa, Local 9 y 10* ☎ *755/553–0578* ▭ *AE, MC, V.*

$$$ MEXICAN ✕ **Laguna**. You can't beat the vibe at this restaurant where the tortillas are prepared fresh on a skillet over an open fire. A stairway leads you to a high palapa-ceiling dining area with a view of the open-air Señor Frogs; in the evening you can see people dancing as you eat. The seafood dishes, especially the *linguini del marinero* with shrimp and clam in a tomato sauce, are fresh and well prepared. Another standout is the *lechón entero al horno*, an entire baked suckling pig prepared for six people with a wine-based sauce and served with baked potatoes, mushrooms, and salad. ✉ *Plaza Marina, Ixtapa* ☎ *755/553–1103* ▭ *MC, V.*

$ CAFÉ ✕ **Nueva Zelanda**. Although it's open all day, this sparkling little coffee shop is best known for its breakfasts. This branch opened after the success of the original eatery in downtown Zihuatanejo. It's both more polished and more endearing, yet serves the same deli-style fresh Mexican food that's been served for 30 years at the original restaurant. Sit at the counter, at the varnished wood tables with six swivel chairs, or in the tiny booths. Options include fresh fruit juices, coconut milk shakes, banana splits, omelets, enchiladas, salads, soup, and *tortas* (sandwiches on large, crusty rolls with beans, avocado, and cheese). ✉ *Centro Comercial El Kiosko, behind bandstand, Blvd. Ixtapa s/n* ☎ *755/553–0838* *Reservations not accepted* *No credit cards.*

$ AMERICAN ✕ **Ruben's.** The delicious scent of grilling meats will entrance you from blocks away. Latin music blares from the jukebox inside, so after sundown most clients dine at the white plastic tables on the grassy front yard. The charcoal-grilled burgers, which are made of top sirloin, and the french fries, deep-fried zucchini, and baked potatoes are true-to-the-source American treats, but with a twist. The burgers are topped with cabbage, and delicious with the Benton's chipotle sauce that they bring out with the mustard and ketchup. Try the corn soup served with a generous dollop of sour cream. For dessert there are grilled bananas glazed with cinnamon and sugar and served with fresh cream. ✉ *Centro Comercial Flamboyant, next to Bancomer bank, Blvd. Ixtapa s/n* ☎ *755/553–0027* 🌐 *www.rubens-hamburgers.com.mx* *V.*

ZIHUATANEJO

$ SEAFOOD ✕ **Café America.** This small outdoor café is perfect for soaking up the boho vibe on a street lined with shops, small hotels, and huge potted plants. None of its hearty Mexican breakfasts costs more than $4. The lunch menu revolves around seafood plates and appetizers (try the *tiritas,* small strips of raw fish swimming in lime and onion) that don't top $5. Dinner is all about steak and lobster. There's an adjacent bar and rooms to rent upstairs. ✉ *Calle H. Galeana 16* ☎ *755/554–4337* *No credit cards.*

$$–$$$ MEXICAN ✕ **Casa Elvira.** This institution is right on the malecón, just a few steps from the fish market. It's not fancy, but the walls radiate bright orange, and a courtyard fountain splashes in a minor key. The staff is helpful yet unobtrusive, and the food habitually good. The fare consists of Mexican dishes and such simple seafood plates as fish steamed in foil and served with rice and french fries. Lobster is a specialty, though it and the well-loved seafood platter will push your tab into the $$$$ category. ✉ *Paseo del Pescador 32* ☎ *755/554–2061* *MC, V* *Closed Tues. during low season.*

$$$ ECLECTIC ★ ✕ **Coconuts.** Eat at the horseshoe-shape bar—especially if you happen to be by yourself—or out under the sky. Restored by owner Patricia Cumming's architect husband, Zihua's oldest house has a gorgeous patio open to the stars and surrounded by zillions of tiny white lights. The kitchen is consistent: try the roast pork loin, the sweet and zesty coconut shrimp, or one of the vegetarian offerings. Five different dessert coffees are prepared flaming at your table. In the evening a keyboarder or romantic duo playing bossa nova or jazz is sure to entertain. ✉ *Pasaje Agustín Ramírez 1* ☎ *755/554–2518* 🌐 *www.restaurantcoconuts.com* *AE, MC, V* *Closed June–mid-Oct.*

$ MEXICAN ✕ **Doña Licha.** Come for the authentic Mexican dining experience. Stay for the televised soccer game or beauty pageant. Traditional dishes include barbecued ribs, goat stew, tripe, and—on Thursday as Guerrero

State tradition dictates—pozole. The long list of daily specials might include pork chops, tacos, and enchiladas; all come with a drink and either rice or soup. On the extensive regular menu are seafood and breakfast items. ✉ *Calle de los Cocos 8, Centro* ☎ *755/554–3933* ▭ *No credit cards* ⏲ *Closes at 6* PM.

$$$ ECLECTIC ★ ✕ **Kau-Kan.** When was the last time you enjoyed a plate of stingray in black butter sauce? This unimposing restaurant encases the heart of Zihuatenejo's most deliciously inventive cuisine. Owner-chef Ricardo Rodriguez, who worked in Paris before returning to Mexico, applies deft Mexican and Mediterranean touches to seafood dishes in a beachcomber aura overlooking the bay. The melt-in-your-mouth abalone and exquisite grilled mahimahi under a sweet, spicy pineapple sauce are popular choices, but the house specialty remains *patata rellena*—potatoes stuffed with shrimp and lobster in a fresh basil-and-garlic sauce. ✉ *Carretera Escénica, Lote 7, en route to Playa la Ropa* ☎ *755/554–8446* 🌐 *www.casakaukan.com* ▭ *AE, MC, V* ⏲ *Closed last 2 wks of Sept. No lunch.*

$$$ SEAFOOD ✕ **La Perla.** The slightly more formal take on the typical toes-in-the-sand dining experience is evident in the fact this popular spot on Playa la Ropa accepts credit cards. Among the seafood specialties here are *filete* La Perla (fish fillet baked with cheese); lobster thermidor; and yummy fish or shrimp tacos made with homemade flour or corn tortillas and served with guacamole. There's a nice wine list and Havana cigars for after dinner. And you don't have to get your feet wet or sandy at all; you can sit in the palapa-covered restaurant under the trees or take a stool at the corner bar, where there's always a game on satellite TV. But plenty of customers just sit on the beach and sip a drink. ✉ *Playa la Ropa* ☎ *755/554–2700* 🌐 *www.laperlarestaurant.net* ▭ *AE, MC, V.*

$$–$$$ SEAFOOD ✕ **Rossy's.** Waterside dining doesn't get any purer than at this spot in the midst of several beachfront eateries. The extensive menu covers all the typical favorites—ceviches, shrimp dishes, and fish fillets served with rice and steamed vegetables. Make a feast of it and choose the mixed-grill selection, which feeds three. For dessert, indulge in the crispy fried bananas served with a scoop of coconut ice cream or bathed in cinnamon-laced cream. Walk it off with a stroll along the sand. The people-watching is great, whether they're wearing swimsuits or business suits. ✉ *South end of Playa la Ropa* ☎ *755/554–4004* 🌐 *www.hotelrossy.com* ▭ *MC, V.*

$ MEXICAN ★ ✕ **Tamales y Atoles Any.** The equivalent of a "soul food" restaurant for Los Guerrerense (the people of Guerrero state), this noisy, fun spot a few blocks from the beach, amid small shops and cafés, specializes in the traditional cuisine of the deep countryside. Tamales—16 different kinds—are the menu's most popular items. Ingredients ranging from pork and chicken to poblano peppers and squash blossoms are wrapped in *masa,* drenched in rich sauces, and baked in corn husks or banana leaves. Pozole, a pork-and-hominy stew that is traditionally eaten on Thursday, is a specialty of the house. There's also a restaurant in Ixtapa at Centro Comercial los Arcos in front of the kiosk. Breakfast is served daily at the downtown Zihua location (in Ixtapa, daily except Sunday). ✉ *Calle Vicente Guerrero 38, at Calle Ejido* ☎ *755/554–7373* 🌐 *restaurantesmexicanosany.blogspot.com* ▭ *MC, V.*

WHERE TO STAY

IXTAPA

Ixtapa is great for getting sticker shock, especially during December and in mid-March, but winter vacationers can get some great deals at its priciest resorts in January after the New Year and most weeks in February. It definitely pays to see what deals sites like Expedia are offering and to get a price quote directly from the hotel to see if they're offering better prices than their Web site might imply. Ixtapa has several gated communities with condo and villa rentals; a good place to start is *www.paradise-properties.com.mx*.

$$$$ **Barceló**. Once you get past its dull exterior, this high-rise turns out to be bright and lively. There's a subdued elegance to its marble-floor lobby and an irresistible cheerfulness to the skylighted inner courtyard—filled with a restaurant and shops—where long vines hang from the balconies of the surrounding rooms. The rooms are nothing special, but they are clean and comfortable; most have small balconies with ocean views (be sure to request one and opt for a higher floor to avoid noise from the pool area). The focus is on the outdoors, from the splendid pool and beach to a sprawling list of recreational options, all facilitated by a helpful staff. There's a quality live show six nights a week, and the hotel's Sanca Bar draws a nice crowd for dancing to Latin music. **Pros:** convenient to other hotels and restaurants; extraordinarily social; lots of amenities and activities; good service. **Cons:** rooms need updating; very busy; restaurants aren't spectacular. *Blvd. Ixtapa s/n 755/555–2000 or 800/227–2356 www.barcelo.com 341 rooms, 5 suites In-room: safe, refrigerator. In-hotel: 4 restaurants, room service, bars, tennis courts, pools, gym, spa, beachfront, children's programs (ages 5–12), laundry service, Internet terminal, Wi-Fi hotspot, parking (free), no-smoking rooms MC, V AI.*

$$–$$$ **Emporio Ixtapa**. Furnishings are an adroit mix of rustic and modern in this midsize, 11-story resort. Rooms are simple but bright, done in mostly white with a few earth-tone accents. Junior suites have views from both the living room and the bedroom. There aren't any private balconies, but windows that reach nearly from the floor to the ceiling open to the sea breezes. A children's pool with a slide lures kids away from the palm-shaded main pool, which has a swim-up bar. **Pros:** calmer than the megaresorts on the strip; good value; good spa services. **Cons:** not all rooms have ocean views; some rooms need updating; mediocre restaurants (avoid the all-inclusive plan). *Blvd. Ixtapa s/n 755/553–1066 or 866/936–7674 www.hotelesemporio.com 197 rooms, 23 suites In-room: safe, DVD (some), Wi-Fi (some). In-hotel: 3 restaurants, room service, bars, tennis courts, pools, gym, spa, laundry service, Internet terminal, Wi-Fi hotspot, parking (free), no-smoking rooms AE, MC, V AI, BP.*

$$$–$$$$ ★ **Las Brisas Ixtapa**. The balconies of this pyramid-shape resort are reason enough to stay here—sunbathe or sip cocktails from a deck chair during the day and stargaze from your hammock at night (junior-suite balconies also have hot tubs). Las Brisas is at the secluded southern end of Ixtapa away from the main strip, so there's nothing but blue water

to gaze at. The resort is built into a hill and has a bit of an awkward layout (it's a bit of a hike from the main building to the pool complex), but who needs gardens to stroll through when you're on the best stretch of beach in Ixtapa? Standard rooms have low ceilings and are a little narrow, but they have heavenly pillow-top beds and small sitting nooks with comfy window-seat-like couches. **Pros:** great balconies and views; great beachfront; away from the hodgepodge of hotels on the main strip. **Cons:** lobby area is cavernous and not that inviting; amenities and on-site restaurants are really expensive; not within walking distance of main strip ($4 cab ride away). ✉ *Playa Vista Hermosa* ☎ *755/553–2121 or 888/559–4329* 🌐 *www.brisas.com.mx* *390 rooms, 26 suites* *In-room: safe, refrigerator, Wi-Fi. In-hotel: 6 restaurants, room service, bars, pools, gym, beachfront, laundry service, Internet terminal, parking (free), no-smoking rooms* 💳 *AE, MC, V.*

> **CHOICES!**
>
> Zihua's singular hotels and gentle pace make for a more authentic Mexican experience. Ixtapa's brand-name resorts and compact hotel zone add up to a more predictable—some might say reassuring—vacation.

TRONCONES

This once-primitive surf spot along the rugged coast is still pretty remote, but a series of really comfortable—in some cases, luxurious—hostelries have sprung up along the road that traces the waterfront. Thankfully, most of these accommodations try to adapt themselves to the gorgeous environment, rather than the other way around. The focus is on the superb beaches and lush foliage. There is no high-end shopping district, and most of the restaurants are in the hotels.

$$ **Casa Ki.** Each bungalow at this homey haven in the wilds of Troncones has a patio with hammocks, table, and chairs. There's also a house with a full kitchen, two bedrooms, two baths, and a long porch looking right onto the sand and waves. All guests have access to a communal kitchen and dining room, as well as barbecue facilities. **Pros:** cute; colorful bungalows; pleasant beachfront; nice grounds. **Cons:** three-night minimum stay required; a little overpriced; no air-conditioning in most rooms; not many services. ✉ *Playa Troncones* *A.P. 405, Zihuatanejo 40880* ☎ *755/553–2815* 🌐 *www.casa-ki.com* *3 bungalows, 1 house* *In-room: no a/c (some), no phone, refrigerator, no TV, Wi-Fi. In-hotel: restaurant, beachfront, laundry service, Wi-Fi hotspot, parking (free)* 💳 *No credit cards* *BP.*

$$ ★ **Hacienda Eden.** Gorgeous views of Manzanillo Bay, a beach that has both a nice point break and calmer areas for swimming, and large, cheerful rooms have earned Hacienda Eden a loyal following. The property, which is surrounded by palm trees and gardens, has a two-story house with ocean-view rooms and hammock-filled terraces; one-room ocean-facing bungalows with patios; and newer air-conditioned suites that can accommodate families. Throughout, you'll see beamed ceilings, Talavera tile details, and splashes of purple, yellow, and turquoise. The restaurant is one of the best on the beach. **Pros:** nice beach that's good for swimming; great restaurant; boutique with unique items; great hosts.

a great value; hotel is equidistant from downtown and Playa la Ropa. **Cons:** popular with families; so can be noisy; pool is quite small. ✉ *Calle Adelita 11, Playa la Madera* ☎ *755/554–3794* 📠 *755/553–8213* 🌐 *www.laquintadedonandres.com* ⇨ *4 rooms, 8 suites* 🛎 *In-room: no a/c, kitchen (some), refrigerator (some). In-hotel: pool, beachfront, parking (free)* 💳 *No credit cards.*

$$$$ Fodor's Choice ★ **Tides Zihuatanejo.** The main draws are striking rooms with winning Mediterranean-Mexican architecture and the spectacular location on perfect Playa la Ropa. Paths meander through gardens, passing coconut palms and fountains en route to the beach. Rooms are artistically and individually designed with bright but not overpowering textiles and folk art; in some the adobe walls have been left white, while in others they've been painted pale shades of yellow or orange. All rooms have terraces or balconies; suites have private plunge pools. Service is downright deferential, with "beach butlers" delivering everything from sunscreen to pre-programmed iPods to your palapa. **Pros:** handsome semiprivate beachfront; outstanding service; standard rooms that actually stack up to the pricier suites. **Cons:** meal plan required in high season; four-night minimum stay required year-round; hosts many corporate events and weddings; pricey. ✉ *Playa la Ropa* ☎ *755/555–5500 or 866/905–9560* 🌐 *www.tideszihuatanejo.com* ⇨ *35 rooms, 35 suites* 🛎 *In-room: safe, DVD (some), Wi-Fi. In-hotel: 2 restaurants, room service, bars, tennis courts, pools, gym, spa, beachfront, Internet terminal, Wi-Fi hotspot, no-smoking rooms, some pets allowed* 💳 *AE, MC, V* 🍽 *MAP.*

NIGHTLIFE

Outside of the resort bars and discos, Ixtapa's nightlife options are limited—unless you like hanging out at Señor Frog's. Zihua's pedestrian-only core is great for barhopping; it has many casual spots, and most of the restaurants in this area serve drinks, too.

There's salsa, Cuban, or romantic music at **Bandidos** (✉ *Calle Pedro Ascencio 2, at Calle Cinco de Mayo, Zihuatanejo* ☎ *755/553–8072*) Monday through Saturday (in low season call to confirm schedule). It's smack in the middle of downtown and almost as popular with locals as with travelers—both foreign and domestic. In the afternoon and early evening you can get drinks, snacks, and full meals at the bar and outdoor patio. The TV is usually tuned to sports, though the volume is turned way down.

Head for **Blue Mamou** (✉ *Paseo Playa la Ropa s/n, near Hotel Irma, Zihuatanejo* ☎ *755/544–8025*) for live blues, swing, and jazz; it's open nightly except Sunday. The bar, which opens at 7 PM, sometimes hosts private events; call ahead for the schedule. Soak up the booze with some grub: ribs, chicken, fish, sausage, yams, and coleslaw.

Capricho's Grill (✉ *Cinco de Mayo 4, Zihuatanejo* ☎ *755/554–3019* 🌐 *www.caprichosgrill.com*) has live music Thursday, Friday, and Saturday—usually world, Latin, flamenco, or jazz—and occasionally hosts special events, such as concerts during March's Guitarfest. You can dine in a lovely courtyard with palm trees and hanging lanterns, or enjoy snacks, cocktails, and wine, and a front seat for the performances from the lounge.

El Sanka Grill (✉ *Calle Ejido 22, Zihuatanejo* ☎ *755/554–9358*) has musicians playing traditional Mexican songs from 7 PM to 9 PM to finish off a long day of serving delicious grilled meat and seafood.

Piano Bar Galería (✉ *Blvd. Ixtapa s/n, Ixtapa*), in the Hotel Dorado Pacifico, has a wonderful happy-hour pianist playing romantic songs nightly from December to April and July and August.

Sacbé (✉ *Calle Ejido at Guerrero, Zihuatanejo* ☎ *No phone*) is just far enough outside of the touristy downtown core to attract locals. The crowd at this trendy tri-level club is usually really young (it's a bit more mixed when hosting the odd live-music performance), but there are plenty of couches to lounge on if you're too intimidated to hit the dance floor. The music is a mix of the latest international and Mexican dance and pop hits. The cover is totally reasonable (never more than $5).

THE SIREN'S SONG

Though it's hardly a secret—it's one of the venues that hosts the Guitarfest in March— **El Canto de la Sirena** (✉ *Calle Colegio Militar, Zihuatanejo* ☎ *No phone*) is something of a hidden gem, if only because of its unlikely location outside of town by the main bus station. This local favorite is owned by a local legend, guitarist José Luis Cobo López, who performs most evenings. There's live music (and sometimes dancing) Tuesday through Saturday starting at 10 PM; jam sessions usually last until the wee hours.

SHOPPING

IXTAPA

Shopping in Ixtapa lacks traditional Mexican energy. Most stores are relegated to strip malls across from the hotels on Paseo del Palmar. There are boutiques, restaurants, pharmacies, self-service laundries, and grocery stores, but everything seems to blend together. A ban on street and beach vendors restricts small merchants to a large handicrafts zone, **Mercado de Artesanía Turístico**, on the right side of Boulevard Ixtapa across from the Hotel Barceló. It's open weekdays 10–9 and has some 150 stands, selling handicrafts, T-shirts, and souvenirs.

★ One of the few stores that stands out from the rest is **La Fuente** (✉ *Centro Comercial Los Patios* ☎ *755/553–0812* ✉ *Centro Comercial a Puerta* ☎ *755/553–1733*), with its huge assortment of women's resort wear as well as housewares and gifts.

For silver jewelry, check out **Santa Prisca** (✉ *Centro Comercial Los Patios* ☎ *755/553–0709*).

ZIHUATANEJO

Casa Marina (✉ *Paseo del Pescador 9, at main plaza* ☎ *755/554–2373*) houses excellent small shops selling Yucatecan hammocks, Oaxacan rugs, and a smattering of folk art. It's generally closed Sunday except when the cruise ships call.

★ The **Mercado de Artesanía Turístico** (✉ *Calle Cinco de Mayo between Paseo del Pescador and Av. Morelos*) has some 250 stands selling jewelry of shell, beads, and quality silver, as well as hand-painted bowls and plates, hammocks, gauzy blouses, T-shirts, and souvenirs.

Downtown Zihuatanejo has a compact but fascinating **Mercado Municipal** with a labyrinth of small stands on the east side of the town center, on Avenida Benito Juárez between Avenidas Nava and González.

> **JAVA FIX**
>
> The mountains of Guerrero State are home to many coffee plantations, and several shops in Zihuatanejo sell certified-organic, shade-grown blends. **Café Zihuatanejo** (✉ *Cuauhtémoc 170* ✉ *C. Galeana, between Bravo and Ejido*) is the best-known retailer in town; the Cuauhtémoc location sells beans, while the Galeana branch is a full café.

Zihua's tiny nucleus has several worthwhile shops; most are closed Sunday.Shop for wonderful silver and gold jewelry at **Alberto's** (✉ *Calle Cuauhtémoc 15, across from Cine* ☎ *755/554–2161*), which has a couple of branches.**Arte Mexicano Nopal** (✉ *Av. Cinco de Mayo 56* ☎ *755/554–7530*) sells Mexican handicrafts, reproductions of ancient art, candles, incense, and small gifts. **Fruity Keiko** (✉ *C. Guerrero 5a*) has a colorful yet tasteful selection of crafts from local artists, including jewelry and great handbags and beach bags.

Lupita's (✉ *Calle Juan N. Alvarez 5* ☎ *755/554–2238*) has been selling colorful women's apparel—including handmade pieces from Oaxaca, Yucatán, Chiapas, and Guatemala—for more than 20 years.

SPORTS AND THE OUTDOORS

DIVING AND SNORKELING

More than 30 dive sites in the area range from deep canyons to shallow reefs. The waters teem with sea life, and visibility is generally excellent.

Experienced, personable PADI dive masters run trips ($65 for one tank, $100 for two) and teach courses at **Carlo Scuba** (✉ *Playa las Gatas, Zihuatanejo* ☎ *755/554–6003* 🌐 *www.carloscuba.com*). **El Vigia** (✉ *South end of Playa la Ropa* ☎ *No phone*) rents snorkel gear and arranges boat trips to snorkel spots at Isla Ixtapa or Playa Manzanillo, about an hour's ride south. **Nautilus Divers** (✉ *Calle Juan N. Alvarez 30, Zihuatanejo* ☎ *755/544–6666* 🌐 *www.nautilus-divers.com*) is operated by students of famed local NAUI master diver and marine biologist Juan Barnard. They run one- and two-tank dives and night dives ($65, $75, and $60, respectively), as well as six-day certification courses.

FISHING

Right at the pier, **Cooperativo de Pescadores Azueta** (✉ *Paseo del Pescador 81, Zihuatanejo* ☎ *755/554–2056*) has a large fleet of boats with VHF radios; some have GPS. The outfit charges $180 for trips in small, fast skiffs with up to four passengers or $250 to $300 for larger, more comfortable, albeit somewhat slower, craft. **Cooperativo Triángulo del Sol**

(✉ *Paseo del Pescador 38, Zihuatanejo* ☎ *755/554–3758*) offers day trips in boats from 26 to 36 feet. Prices are in the $180 to $350 range.

VIPSA (✉ *Hotel Las Brisas, Paseo Vista Hermosa, Ixtapa* ☎ *755/553–2121 Ext. 3469*) is a reliable bet in the Ixtapa area, with boats that can handle four to six passengers; prices range from $300 to $500. **Whiskey Water World** (✉ *Paseo del Pescado 20, Zihuatanejo* ☎ *755/554–0147; 661/310–3298 in U.S.* 🌐 *www.ixtapa-sportfishing.com*) dispatches seven-hour expeditions in pangas ($190 for two people) and cruisers of 32 feet ($250–$350 for three–four people) and 38 feet ($350–$395 for six–eight people). It's run by Ed Garvis, an American expat in business here since 1997.

GONE FISHING

Anglers revel in the profusion of sailfish (November through March), black and blue marlin (May through January), yellowfin tuna (November through June), and mahimahi (November through January). Light-tackle fishing in the lagoons and just off the beach in *pangas* for *huachinango* (red snapper) is also popular.

GOLF

The **Campo de Golf Ixtapa (formerly Palma Real Golf Club)** (✉ *Blvd. Ixtapa s/n, Ixtapa* ☎ *755/553–1163 or 755/553–1062*) has an 18-hole, par-72 championship course designed by Robert Trent Jones Jr. It abuts a wildlife preserve that runs from a coconut plantation to the beach; you may glimpse a gator while you play. Greens fees are $75. You must use either a caddy ($25) or a cart ($35). Club rental is available. Part of the Marina Ixtapa complex, the challenging 18-hole, par-72 course at the **Club de Golf Marina Ixtapa** (✉ *Ixtapa* ☎ *755/553–1410*) was designed by Robert Von Hagge. Greens fees are $97 (including cart). Caddies charge $25, and you can rent clubs.

WATER PARK

At **Delfiniti Ixtapa** (✉ *Blvd. Ixtapa s/n, next to Best Western Posada del Real* ☎ *775/553–2707* 🌐 *www.delfiniti.com*), dolphins in a huge pool interact with paying customers—giving "kisses" and "hugs" and short rides (you hang onto their fins as they paddle around on their backs)—in exchange for food treats. Sessions are $160, and are organized by the age of customers (three–adult). Reservations are highly recommended—you can book online—especially if you have kids under 7, as there are limited time slots available.

Acapulco

WITH A SIDE TRIP TO TAXCO

Umbrellas on the beach, Acapulco

WORD OF MOUTH

"We stayed three nights . . . on the Costera. Admittedly we did not stray very far from there but we felt as safe in Acapulco as any place else. The sellers in the marketplaces can be aggressive, but a firm "no" will usually suffice if you're not looking to buy anything. Be very careful when crossing the street, especially the Costera. Cars don't stop at times even for the traffic officers at intersections. Use common sense and enjoy yourself."

—MAJ790HAN

www.fodors.com/community

WELCOME TO ACAPULCO

TOP REASONS TO GO

★ **Indulging in the most popular activity in town:** Eating out is all the rage. You can sample cuisines from around the world or feast on classics from throughout Mexico.

★ **The chance to see authentic, small-town life:** Pie de la Cuesta is a laid-back, coastal village northwest of Acapulco with some of the best seafood around.

★ **Standing in the middle of a history lesson:** The old Fort of San Diego overlooking Acapulco Bay houses one of the best museums in Mexico, illustrating the historical importance of this nearly 500-year-old city.

★ **Dancing the night away:** A sleepy village Acapulco is not. With big-city sophistication comes fabulous ocean-side restaurants, flashy hotel lounges, dance clubs with a sleek clientele, and laid-back surfer bars.

★ **Jewelry shopping in a spot where prices are still reasonable:** One of Mexico's prettiest towns, Taxco is also the place to buy silver jewelry.

1 Old Acapulco. Your trip to Acapulco would be incomplete without a few hours spent exploring the old section. The *zócalo* (town plaza) is filled with majestic banyan and rubber trees, providing shade for a wide cast of characters. The surrounding streets are crowded with small businesses and the elusive soul of the city. The beaches are favored by local families and fishermen, who now share the bay with gigantic cruise ships. The magnificent Fuerte de San Diego is nearby, as is La Quebrada, where otherwise sane men dive more than 30 meters (100 feet) into the surging and rocky Pacific.

2 Acapulco Bay. Acapulco is the world's largest U-shape outdoor amphitheater, and the Bahía de Acapulco is center stage. The inhabitants in the surrounding hills and beach resorts can admire the action of watercraft and people in the harbor. While the daytime performance is one of fun in the sun, the late-night show features twinkling lights reflected in the water and salsa music drifting on the breeze.

3 Costera. The heartbeat of Acapulco, Costera pulses with activity. There is nothing old-fashioned or serene about this busy 8-km (5-mi) stretch of commercial bay-front property along Avenida Costera Miguel Alemán. The thoroughfare is lined with resorts, shops, markets, banks, discos—even a park and a golf course. And within walking distance are the bay's golden beaches. You can land here and never find the need to leave, unless you crave peace and quiet.

4 Acapulco Diamante. As you head east from Acapulco Bay you enter Acapulco Diamante, which includes the smaller bay of Puerto Marqués and the long wide beaches of Revolcadero. This is where developments—mostly large, opulent resorts—crop up. Above, the hillside neighborhoods overlooking the water are dotted with many of Mexico's most spectacular private villas. If you like a little breathing room and miles of breezy beach walking, this is the place for you.

GETTING ORIENTED

The city of Acapulco is on the Pacific coast 433 km (268 mi) south of Mexico City. Warm water, nearly constant sunshine, and balmy year-round temperatures let you plan your day around the beach—whether you want to lounge in a hammock or go snorkeling, parasailing, fishing, or waterskiing. Attractions to lure you away from the sands include crafts markets, cultural institutions, and the amazing cliff divers at La Quebrada.

Updated by Michele Joyce

THE CENTER OF ACAPULCO IS on the western edge of the bay. The streets form a grid that's easy to explore on foot. Avenida Costera Miguel Alemán, a wide coastal boulevard, runs the length of the bay and is lined with hotels, restaurants, and malls. You can explore the strip by taxi, bus, or rental car, stopping along the way to shop.

You'll also need a vehicle to get to Acapulco Diamante, farther east along the coast. Running from Las Brisas Hotel to Barra Vieja beach, this 3,000-acre expanse encompasses exclusive Playa Diamante and Playa Revolcadero, with upscale hotels and residential developments, private clubs, breathtaking views, and pounding surf.

Pie de la Cuesta, 10 km (6.2 mi) northwest of Acapulco, is famous for its fabulous sunsets, small family-run hotels, and some of the wildest surf in Mexico. The village remains the flip side to the Acapulco coin—a welcome respite from the disco-driven big city. Only the main road is paved, and the town has no major resorts or late-night clubs. A beach chair, a bucket of cold beers, fresh fish and seafood, and a good book are about as much excitement as you'll get here.

For a break from beach life, you can travel north 300 km (185 mi) to the old silver-mining town of Taxco, a great place to buy silver from the country's finest metalwork artisans.

GETTING HERE AND AROUND

American, Continental, and US Airways have nonstop service to Acapulco's Aeropuerto Internacional Juan N. Alvarez, 20 minutes east of the city. Private taxis aren't permitted to carry passengers from the airport to town, so most people rely on Transportes Aeropuerto, a special airport taxi service.

Bus service from Mexico City to Acapulco is excellent. Grupo Estrella Blanca has first-class buses, which leave every hour on the hour from the Taxqueña station. Estrella de Oro also has deluxe service, called Servicio Diamante, which leaves four times a day.

Within Acapulco, one of the most useful buses runs from Puerto Marqués to Caleta, making stops along the way. Cabs that cruise the streets usually charge by zone, with a minimum charge of $2. A ride from Acapulco Diamante to downtown will run you about $15.

Rent a car only if you plan on being in town for more than a couple of days and/or want to take side trips to Taxco and the coastal villages. Rates average about $30 a day, including insurance and unlimited miles. And did we mention that the jeeps come in bright pink?

ESSENTIALS

Bus Contacts **Estrella de Oro** (✉ *Av. Cuauhtémoc 158, Old Acapulco, Acapulco* ☎ *744/485–8705 or 762/622–0648* 🌐 *www.estrelladeoro.com.mx*). **Grupo Estrella Blanca** (✉ *Calle Ejido 47, Old Acapulco* ☎ *744/469–2028* 🌐 *www.estrellablanca.com.mx*).

Currency Exchange **Banamex** (✉ *Av. Costera Miguel Alemán 63-A, Costera* ☎ *744/484–3381* 🌐 *www.banamex.com*). **Dollar Money Exchange** (✉ *Av. Costera Miguel Alemán 151, Local 6, Costera* ☎ *744/486–9688*).

Medical Assistance Hospital del Pacífico (✉ *Calle Nao 4 and Calle Fraile, Costera* ☎ *744/469–0300* 🌐 *www.starmedica.com*). **Hospital Privado Magallanes** (✉ *Calle Wilfrido Massieu 2, Fracc. Magallanes* ☎ *744/485–6194*). **Red Cross** (☎ *744/445–5912 or 744/445–5911* 🌐 *www.hospitalmagallanes.com*). **Tourist Police** (☎ *744/440–7020*).

Rental Cars Avis (☎ *800/288–8888* 🌐 *www.avis.com*). **Budget** (☎ *744/481–2433* 🌐 *www.budget.com*). **Hertz** (☎ *744/485–8947* 🌐 *www.hertz.com*).

Visitor and Tour Info Procuraduría del Turista (✉ *Acapulco International Center, Av. Costera Miguel Alemán 4455, Costera* ☎ *744/484–8555 or 744/484-8554* 🌐 *www.visitacapulco.com.mx*). **Taxco Tourism Office** (✉ *Av. de los Plateros 1, Taxco* ☎ *762/622–6616* 🌐 *www.guerrero.gob.mx*).

13

EXPLORING

Avenida Costera Miguel Alemán hugs the Bahía de Acapulco from the Carretera Escénica (Scenic Highway) in the east to Playa Caleta (Caleta Beach) in the southwest—a distance of about 8 km (5 mi). Most of the major beaches, shopping malls, and hotels are along or off this avenue, and locals refer to its most exclusive stretch—from El Presidente hotel to Las Brisas—simply as "the Costera." Since many addresses are listed as only "Costera Miguel Alemán," you'll need good directions from a major landmark to find specific shops and hotels.

COSTERA

❶ **Casa de la Cultura.** The city's cultural center has first-class regional and Mexican handicrafts for sale, the Ixcateopan art gallery, and a small sports hall of fame with photos of local athletes. The center also sponsors folk dancing and theater productions, and holds language workshops. ✉ *Av. Costera Miguel Alemán 4834, Costera* ☎ *744/484–2390* *Free* *Daily 8* AM*–9* PM.

❷ **CiCi.** A water park for children, the Centro Internacional para Convivencia Infantil, fondly known as CiCi, has dolphin shows, a freshwater pool with a wave machine, a waterslide, the Sky Coaster (a safe, low-key bungee jump for kids), and other attractions. If you book an hour-long swim with the dolphins, CiCi can have you picked up at your hotel. It's easy to catch a cab for the return trip. ✉ *Av. Costera Miguel Alemán, next to Planet Hollywood, Costera* ☎ *744/484–1970* 🌐 *www.cici.com.mx* *$12* *Daily 10–6.*

❸ **Parque Papagayo.** Named for the hotel that formerly occupied the grounds, this park is on 52 acres of prime Costera real estate, just after the underpass that begins at Playa Hornos. It has an aviary, a racetrack with mite-size race cars, a space-shuttle replica, a jogging path, a library, and bumper boats. Find some street food and a shady bench and do some people-watching. ✉ *Av. Costera Miguel Alemán, Costera* ☎ *744/485–2490* *No entrance fee; rides $1 each; $5 ride packages available* *Park: daily 6* AM*–8* PM*. Rides section: nightly 4–11.*

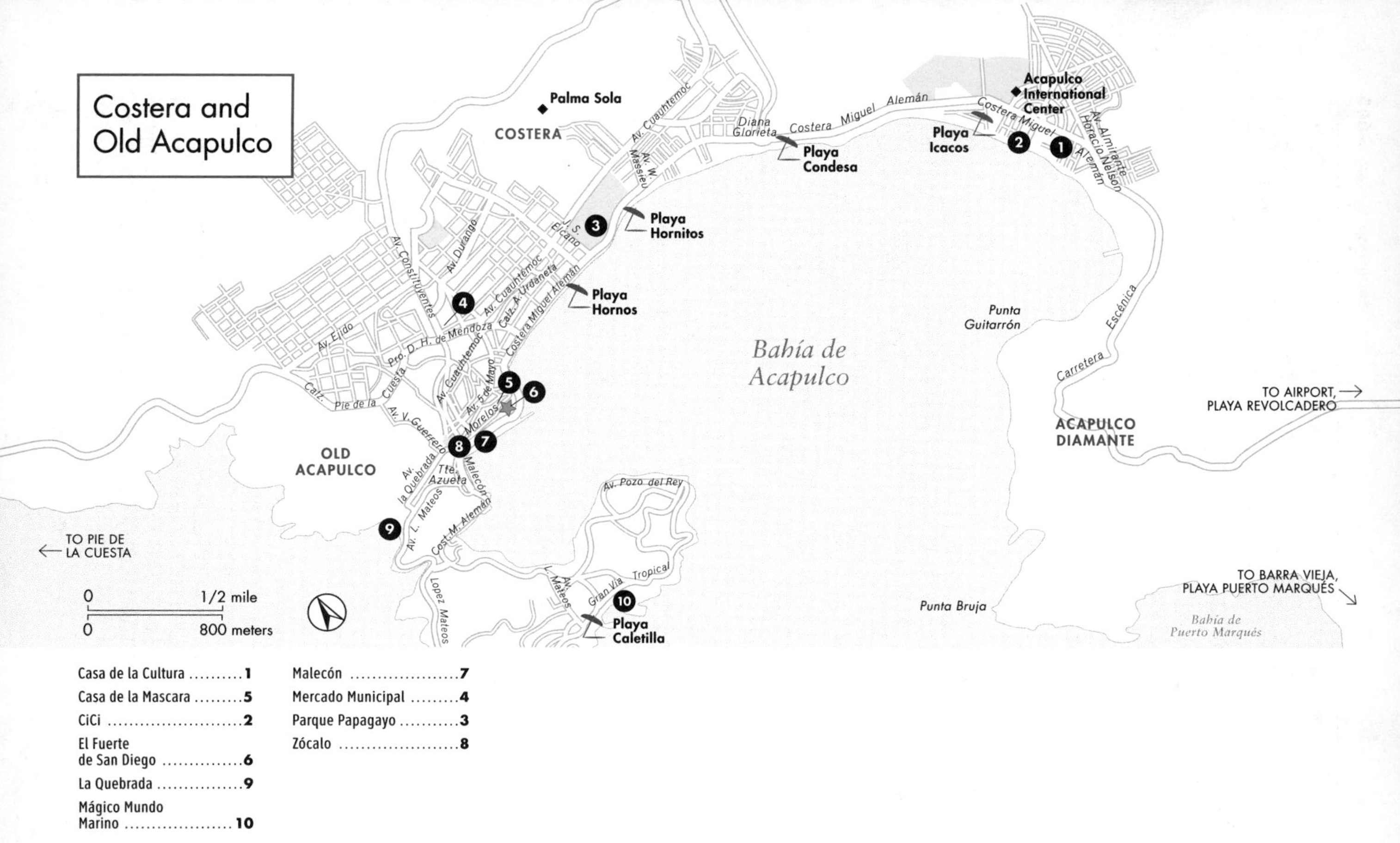
Costera and Old Acapulco
Palma Sola
COSTERA
Acapulco International Center
Av. Almirante Horacio Nelson
Costera Miguel Alemán
Diana Glorieta
Playa Icacos
Playa Condesa
Playa Hornitos
Playa Hornos
Playa Caletilla
Av. Cuauhtemoc
Av. W. Massieu
J. S. Elcano
Av. Durango
Av. Constituyentes
Av. Cuauhtemoc
Calz. A. Urdaneta
Costera Miguel Alemán
Av. Ejido
Pro. D. H. de Mendoza
Av. Cuauhtemoc
Av. 5 de Mayo
Morelos
Calz. Pie de la Cuesta
Av. V. Guerrero
Av. la Quebrada
Tte. Azueta
Malecón
Av. L. Mateos
Cost. M. Alemán
Lopez Mateos
Av. Pozo del Rey
Gran Via Tropical
Av. L. Mateos
OLD ACAPULCO
TO PIE DE LA CUESTA
Bahía de Acapulco
Punta Guitarrón
Punta Bruja
Carretera Escénica
ACAPULCO DIAMANTE
TO AIRPORT, PLAYA REVOLCADERO
TO BARRA VIEJA, PLAYA PUERTO MARQUÉS
Bahía de Puerto Marqués
0 1/2 mile
0 800 meters
Casa de la Cultura 1
Casa de la Mascara 5
CiCi 2
El Fuerte de San Diego 6
La Quebrada 9
Mágico Mundo Marino 10
Malecón 7
Mercado Municipal 4
Parque Papagayo 3
Zócalo 8

OLD ACAPULCO

Old Acapulco, an area that you can easily tour on foot, is where the locals go to dine, enjoy a town festival, run errands, and worship. Also known as El Centro, it's where you'll find the zócalo, the church, and El Fuerte de San Diego. Although a considerably old city, Acapulco retains little in the way of centuries-old buildings. When development took off here in the '40s and '50s, many of the old buildings were razed to make room for resort hotels.

OFF THE BEATEN PATH

Palma Sola. Taking the name of the neighborhood closest to it, this archaeological site juts up a mountainside northeast of Old Acapulco. The area is blanketed with 2,000-year-old petroglyphs executed by the Yopes, Acapulco's earliest known inhabitants. Stone steps with intermittent plazas for viewing the ancient art are set along a path through virgin vegetation. A cave used as a ceremonial center is atop the mountain, with wonderful city views at more than 1,000 feet above sea level, and definitely worth the visit. It's about a 25-minute taxi ride from Old Acapulco. ☎ *744/486–1514 for tours* *Free* *Daily 8–4.*

TOP ATTRACTIONS

9 **La Quebrada.** Just up the hill from Old Acapulco is the southern peninsula, where you'll find La Quebrada and its legendary cliff divers. The peninsula has remnants of Acapulco's golden era, the early- to mid-20th century. Although past its prime, this mostly residential area has been revitalized through the reopenings of the Caleta Hotel and the aquarium at Playa Caleta. And the inexpensive hotels here are still popular with travelers who want good deals and a slower pace.

7 **Malecón.** A stroll by the docks will confirm that Acapulco is a lively port. At night Mexicans bring their children to play on the tree-lined promenade. Farther west, by the zócalo, are docks for yachts and fishing boats. Vendors sell bait and even simple handmade fishing poles (a line attached to a bit of wood) for about a dollar if you'd like to stop and fish off the dock. ✉ *Av. Costera Miguel Alemán between Calle Escudero on the west and El Fuerte de San Diego on the east, Old Acapulco.*

8 **Zócalo.** Old Acapulco's hub is this shaded plaza overgrown with dense trees. All day it's filled with vendors, shoe-shine men, and tourists enjoying the culture. After siesta, the locals drift here to socialize. On Sunday evening there's often music in the bandstand. The zócalo fronts Nuestra Señora de la Soledad (Our Lady of Solitude), the town's modern but unusual church, with its stark-white exterior and bulb-shape blue-and-yellow spires. The church hosts the festive Virgin of Guadalupe celebration on December 12. ✉ *Bounded by Calle Felipe Valle on the north, Av. Costera Miguel Alemán on the south, Calle J. Azueta on the west, and Calle J. Carranza on the east, Old Acapulco.*

WORTH NOTING

5 **Casa de la Mascara.** This freshly remodeled private home has been turned into a gallery for a stunning collection of 550 handmade ceremonial masks, most from the state of Guerrero. Some are representative of those still used in such traditional ritualistic dances as "Moors and Christians" and "Battle of the Tigers." Call ahead to book a 30-minute

CLOSE UP

Acapulco Background

Archaeological evidence indicates that people first inhabited Acapulco around 3000 BC, growing crops and fishing. Around 1500 BC the area was settled by the Nahuas, a tribe related to the Nahuatl, who populated much of southern Mexico. The Nahuatl language provided the name Acapulco, meaning "place of canes" or "reeds." Although it is generally accepted that the first nonnatives to reach Acapulco were Spaniards led by Hernán Cortés, some local historians claim that a Chinese monk named Fa Hsein predated Cortés by 1,000 years.

From 1565 to 1815 the Spanish maintained a thriving port and trading center in Acapulco. Spanish galleons returning from Asia, primarily the Philippines and China, delivered silks, porcelain, jade, jasmine, and spices. These goods were then carried overland on a 6-foot-wide trail to the Mexico Gulf coast town of Veracruz for shipment to Spain. Many pirate ships lurked outside Acapulco Bay, making the Pacific voyages a risky business.

Acapulco became a town in 1799, but started to decline with the War of Independence, when locals sided with the Spanish Royalists. Insurgent leader José María Morelos showed his displeasure by burning much of the town in 1814. Independence from Spain and a changing world rendered the trade route obsolete.

The town remained in relative obscurity until 1927, when a road was built connecting the port to Mexico City and bringing the first tourists. It wasn't long before Hollywood celebrities and other wealthy world travelers started to arrive, and Acapulco began its transformation. One of the first to recognize the potential of the area was then Mexican President Miguel Alemán, who purchased miles of undeveloped coastline. He in turn sold a portion of the land to billionaire oil magnate J. Paul Getty, who built a lavish getaway for himself and his friends—now the Fairmont Pierre Marqués Hotel on Playa Revolcadero.

By the 1960s it seemed everyone in Hollywood was vacationing in Acapulco: Frank Sinatra, Bob Hope, Leslie Caron, Cary Grant, Lana Turner, John Wayne, Errol Flynn, Brigitte Bardot, Elvis Presley, Elizabeth Taylor—too many names to list. World leaders, artists, and writers were also frequent visitors, including John, Robert, and Edward Kennedy, Dwight Eisenhower, Richard Nixon, Ronald Reagan, the Reverend Billy Graham, Salvador Dalí, Tennessee Williams, and John Huston. To read about the long celebrity history of Acapulco, as well as a great account of how the town has grown, pick up a copy of the book *Mike Oliver's Acapulco.* Oliver, who died in 2004, published the English-language *Acapulco News* for decades, and knew and socialized with all of Acapulco's celebrity visitors.

Acapulco today, although not the Hollywood hangout of times past, is still a major tourist destination, especially with Mexican nationals, who make up about 80% of its visitors. Most people will acknowledge that early city planners allowed too much beachfront development, forever changing the visual and aesthetic landscape, but the sun, sand, and culture of this vibrant and historic city still attract fun-seekers by the millions.

tour in English or Spanish. ✉ *Calle Morelos s/n, Ex-Zona Militar B, a half-block from Fuerte de San Diego, Old Acapulco* ☎ *744/486–5577* *Free but donations requested* ⏲ *Tues.–Sat. 10–4.*

6 **El Fuerte de San Diego.** Acapulco's fort was built in 1616 to protect the city's lucrative harbor and wealthy citizens from pirate attacks. Although it was badly damaged by an earthquake in 1776, it was entirely restored by the end of that century. Today the fort houses the excellent **Museo Histórico de Acapulco** (Acapulco History Museum). Bilingual videos and text explain exhibits tracing the city's history from the first pre-Hispanic settlements 3,000 years ago through the exploits of pirates like Sir Francis Drake, the era of the missionaries, and up to Mexico's independence from Spain in 1821. There are also displays of precious silks, Talavera tiles, exquisitely hand-tooled wooden furniture, and delicate china. A visit to the fort is a wonderful way to learn about and appreciate the history of this old port city. ✉ *Calle Hornitos and Calle Morelos, Old Acapulco* ☎ *744/482–3828* *$4.10; free on Sun.* ⏲ *Tues.–Sun. 9:30–6.*

10 **Mágico Mundo Marino.** You can take in Magic Marine World's aquarium and free sea-lion show while the kids splash around in the swimming pools and fly down the waterslides. From nearby Playa Caleta you can take the glass-bottom boat to Isla la Roqueta—about 10 minutes each way—for snorkeling. ✉ *Islote de Caleta, Old Acapulco* ☎ *744/483–1193 or 744/483–9344* *$6 for adults, $3 for children* ⏲ *Daily 9–6.*

4 **Mercado Municipal.** Locals come to this municipal market to buy everything from candles and fresh vegetables to plastic buckets and love potions. In addition, you can buy baskets, pottery, hammocks—there's even a stand selling charms, amulets, and talismans. The stalls within the mercado are densely packed together and there's no air-conditioning, but things stay relatively cool. Come early to avoid the crowds. ✉ *Calle Diego Hurtado de Mendoza and Av. Constituyentes, a few blocks west of Costera, Old Acapulco* ⏲ *Daily 5 AM–7 PM.*

NEED A BREAK?

Cafetería Astoria is a little outdoor café on the zócalo where businesspeople stop for breakfast before work or meet mid-morning for a cappuccino and a sweet roll. It's always lively, and you can't beat the view of the passing parade of activity.

BEACHES

In the past few years city officials made a great effort to clean up the Bahía de Acapulco, and maintaining it is a priority. Although vending on the beach has been outlawed, you'll probably still be approached by snack vendors and souvenir hawkers. In Acapulco Bay watch for a strong shore break that can knock you off your feet in knee-deep water. It is wise to observe the waves for a few minutes before entering the water.

Barra Vieja. A pleasant drive 27 km (17 mi) east of Acapulco, between Laguna de Tres Palos and the Pacific, brings you to this long stretch of uncrowded beach. Most people make the trip for the solitude and

Continued on page 650

ACAPULCO'S CLIFF DIVERS

For many people the name Acapulco conjures up images of the *clavadistas,* or cliff-divers, brave local men (and womwn) who make their living by tempting death. The spectacle of these men swan-diving some 130 feet into ❾ **La Quebrada,** literally "gorge," and then splashing into 12 feet of rough surf is a sight not to be missed.

The practice of cliff diving began with local fishermen, who were known to dive from high up on the rocky cliffs in order to propel themselves deep enough into the water to free snagged lines. With the advent of tourism in the 1930s, however, the divers soon discovered that their sensational skill could earn them tips.

This is not a long-term occupation for most divers. New, young divers are trained continually to be accepted into what has become an elite association of daredevils. Amazingly, there have been no reported deaths associated with the dives.

Where to See the Divers

Unless you have recently trained with Sherpas, take a taxi to La Quebrada, high in the hills above downtown Acapulco. You can watch the dives from either the **observation area,** where you will be charged 35 pesos by the divers' union, or from the **Plaza Las Glorias at the El Mirador Hotel,** (☎ 744/483–1400, 🌐 www.hotelelmiradoracapulco.com.mx) for a cover charge of about 35 pesos. The hotel's **La Perla** supper club is the most comfortable viewing spot. Show times are 12:45, 7:30, 8:30, 9:30, and 10:30 PM. After the show the clavadistas mingle with the audience, posing for photos. This is a good time to offer a tip; most people give 10–50 pesos. Be sure to arrive early to get a spot with a good view. And if you can, try to make it to a night show, which often include hand-held torches carried by the divers—an unforgettable sight.

Clavadistas: 1 Tarzan: 0

A local legend has it that Johnny Weissmuller (1904–1984), the Olympic swimmer and original Hollywood Tarzan, was in attendance in 1947, when one of the divers, Raul Garcia, challenged him to make the dive. As Weissmuller contemplated the offer, the movie company executives called off the stunt, citing insurance risks. Weissmuller was filming *Tarzan and the Mermaids* at the time. He never returned to make the dive, but hey, aren't five Olympic gold medals and 67 world records enough?

The 130-Foot Plunge of the Clavadistas

❶ Divers precede their jumps with a prayer at a small shrine on the cliffs.

❷ They approach the edge—this is the part when most viewers hold their breath. The divers must time their jumps to coordinate with the wave and tide action below to ensure that they're landing in the maximum amount of water.

❸ The dive begins with a beautiful, horizontal takeoff in order to clear the uneven cliff face, and is followed by a plummet past the unforgiving boulders.

❹ After surfacing, hopefully without broken bones or dislocated limbs, the divers scale the steep rocky cliffs back to the top.

Showtimes: 12:45, 7:30, 8:30, 9:30 and 10:30 PM

to feast on *pescado à la talla* (red snapper marinated in spices and grilled over hot coals), available at all the seaside outdoor restaurants. The locals flock here on weekends.

> **CAUTION**
>
> Acapulco Bay is fairly well protected from the rough Pacific surf, but steep offshore drop-offs can produce waves large enough to knock you off your feet. Pay attention to the wave pattern before you go in. If you are not a strong swimmer, stay close to shore and other people. Some beaches, mostly those outside the bay such as Revolcadero and Pie de la Cuesta, have a strong surf and some have a rip current, so be careful. If you get caught in a rip current, which makes it hard to swim to shore, swim parallel to the sand. Above all, don't panic.

Fodor's Choice ★ **Pie de la Cuesta.** You can reach this relatively unpopulated spot by car, cab, or bus. It's about a 25-minute drive west of downtown. The bus runs every 15 minutes past the zócalo along the Costera, the last one departing at 8 PM. Simple thatch-roof restaurants and small, rustic inns border the wide beach, with straw palapas (palm frond roofs) providing shade. What attracts people to Pie de la Cuesta, besides the long expanse of beach and spectacular sunsets, is excellent Laguna Coyuca, a favorite spot for waterskiing, freshwater fishing, and boat rides. Boats ferry you to La Laguna restaurant, where, some people claim, the pescado à la talla is even better than at Barra Vieja.

Playa Caleta. On the southern peninsula in Old Acapulco, this beach and smaller Playa Caletilla (Little Caleta) to the south once rivaled La Quebrada as the main tourist area, and were quite popular with the early Hollywood crowd. Today their snug little bays and calm waters make them a favorite with Mexican families. Caleta has the Mágico Mundo Marino entertainment center for children and a large seafood restaurant. Caletilla has many small family-run restaurants serving good, cheap food. On both beaches vendors sell everything from seashells to peeled mangos; boats depart from both to Isla de Roqueta. Spend a day here to get a true taste of Mexico.

Playa Condesa. Referred to as "the strip," this stretch of sand facing the middle of Bahía de Acapulco has more than its share of visitors, especially singles. It's lined with lively restaurants and rockin' bars.

Playa Hornitos. Running from the Avalon Excalibur west to Las Hamacas, Hornitos (Little Hornos) and adjacent Playa Hornos are shoulder-to-shoulder with locals and visitors on weekends. Graceful palms shade the sand, and there are scads of casual eateries on the beach, especially on Playa Hornos. A slice of Playa Hornos and Playa Hornitos marks the beginning of the hotel zone to the east. The swimming is generally really safe in this area.

Playa Icacos. Stretching from the naval base to El Presidente hotel, away from the famous strip, this beach is less populated than others on the Costera. The morning surf is especially calm.

Playa Puerto Marqués. Tucked below the airport highway, this protected strand is popular with Mexican tourists, so it tends to get crowded on weekends. Beach shacks here sell fresh fish, and vendors sell silver and other wares.

Playa Revolcadero. This sprawling beach fronts the Fairmont Pierre Marqués and Fairmont Acapulco Princess hotels. People come here to surf and ride horses. The water is shallow, but the waves can be rough, and the rip current can be strong, so be careful while swimming.

WHERE TO EAT

Most people come to Acapulco for the sun, but dining comes in a close second. Fresh seafood is on every menu, supplied daily by local fishermen. You can also get top-quality beef brought in from the Mexican states of Sonora and Chihuahua.

As for location, you can have an utterly romantic meal high in the hills, with unparalleled views of the bay, or you can dine in a casual beachside restaurant. Night owls coming out of the clubs can even find a plate of flavorful tacos for less than $2 right before sunrise.

You can dine with the locals in Old Acapulco, or plan a half-day outing to rustic Barra Vieja, where you take a boat through the mangroves to one of many dining huts for fish grilled over hot coals. You can also head to Pie de la Cuesta, a laid-back area west of downtown. Here you can have lunch at a seaside eatery, go horseback riding, and then linger on the beach for a spectacular sunset.

ACAPULCO DIAMANTE

$$$–$$$$ SEAFOOD

✕ **Pool Bar** On a wharf that juts out into Bahía de Puerto Marqués, this casual open-air dining spot has wooden floors and a dramatic roof that simulates a huge white sail. It's particularly atmospheric after dark, when the lights of Puerto Marqués flicker in the distance. There are several fish and shellfish dishes on the menu, but the specialty is the red snapper *à la talla*. ✉ *Camino Real Acapulco Diamante, Carretera Escénica, Km 14, Acapulco Diamante* ☎ *744/466–1010* ▭ *AE, MC, V.*

COSTERA

Loud music blares from many restaurants along the Costera, especially those facing Playa Condesa, and proprietors will aggressively try to hustle you inside with offers of drink specials. If you're looking for a more sedate evening, avoid this area or decide in advance where to dine and head straight there.

$$$–$$$$ CONTEMPORARY ★

✕ **Baikal.** Modern, ultrachic Baikal is *the* place to see and be seen. The dining room has a white-on-white color scheme and 12-foot-high windows that frame the sparkling bay; sea-theme short films are shown from time to time on drop-down movie screens. The menu is small but select, with dishes that fuse French, Asian, and Mexican preparations and ingredients. Try the cold cream of cucumber soup spiced with mint and mild jalapeño; the sliced abalone with a chipotle (dried, smoked chilies) vinaigrette is also a good bet. Soft bossa nova and jazz play in the background. ✉ *Carretera Escénica 1622, Costera* ☎ *744/446–6867*

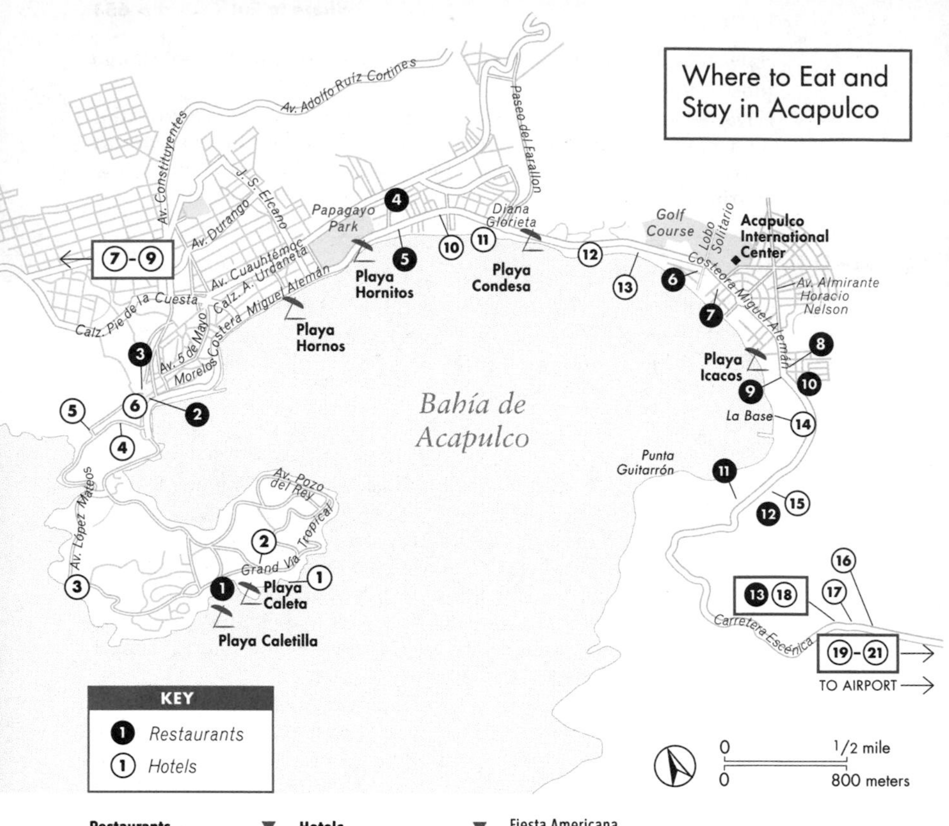

Restaurants ▼

Baikal **12**
El Amigo Miguel **2**
El Cabrito **7**
Hard Rock Cafe **6**
Julio's **4**
La Cabaña **1**
La Casa de Tere **3**
Los Navegantes **10**
Madeiras **11**
100% Natural **7, 9**
Pool Bar **13**
Suntory **8**
Zorrito's **5**

Hotels ▼

Alba Suites **2**
The Banyan Tree Cabo Marquês **20**
Boca Chica **1**
Camino Real Acapulco Diamante **18**
El Encanto **21**
El Mirador **5**
Elcano **13**
Etel Suites **4**
Fairmont Acapulco Princess **16**
Fairmont Pierre Marqués **17**
Fiesta Americana Villas Acapulco **12**
Grand Hotel Acapulco **14**
Hacienda Vayma **9**
Hotel Emporio **11**
Las Brisas **15**
Los Flamingos **3**
Misión **6**
Parador del Sol **7**
Park Hotel & Tennis Center **10**
Quinta Real **19**
Villas Ukae Kim **8**

🌐 *www.baikal.com.mx* ✍ *Reservations essential* 💳 *AE, MC, V* ⏲ *Closed Mon. May–Nov. No lunch.*

$–$$$ MEXICAN ✕ **El Cabrito.** As the name implies, young goat—served charcoal-grilled—is a specialty of this restaurant, open since 1963. You can also choose from among such truly Mexican dishes as chicken in *mole* (spicy chocolate-chili sauce); shrimp in tequila; and jerky with egg, fish, and seafood. Wash it down with a cold beer or glass of wine. ✉ *Av. Costera Miguel Alemán 1480, between CiCi and Centro Internacional, Costera* ☎ *744/484–7711* 💳 *AE, MC, V.*

$$–$$$ AMERICAN ✕ **Hard Rock Cafe.** This link in the international Hard Rock chain is one of Acapulco's most popular spots, among locals as well as visitors. The New York–cut steaks, hamburgers, and brownies, as well as the Southern-style fried chicken and ribs are familiar and satisfying. Taped rock music begins at noon, and a live group starts playing at 10 PM on Thursday, Friday, and Saturday. ✉ *Av. Costera Miguel Alemán 37, Costera* ☎ *744/484–6680* 🌐 *www.hardrock.com* 💳 *AE, D, MC, V.*

$–$$ SEAFOOD ★ ✕ **Julio's.** The locals rave about Julio's, where they know they'll get a great variety of fresh seafood at an affordable price. There is nothing fancy here except the fresh authentic Mexican dishes served by friendly folks. Try the shrimp tacos or the barbecued whole fish, preceded by a large seafood cocktail. A fish fillet dinner costs just under $7. Most tourists haven't found this place yet, so for a great cultural and dining experience that won't empty your wallet, this is the place. ✉ *Cristóbal Colón 56, Costera* ☎ *744/485–3289* 💳 *AE, MC, V.*

$–$$ MEXICAN ✕ **La Casa de Tere.** Hidden in a shopping district downtown (signs point the way), this spotless open-air eatery with pink walls is in a league of its own—expect beer-hall tables and chairs, colorful Mexican decorations, and photos of the Acapulco of yore. The varied menu includes outstanding *sopa de tortilla* (tortilla soup), chicken with mole, and flan. ✉ *Calle Alonso Martín 1721, 2 blocks from Av. Costera Miguel Alemán, Costera* ☎ *744/485–7735* 💳 *No credit cards* ⏲ *Closed Mon.*

$$–$$$$ SEAFOOD ✕ **Los Navegantes.** A line often goes out the door at this popular seafood restaurant on the second floor of El Tropicano Hotel. If you get a table by the window, you'll have views of the bustling Costera below. Most dishes, including the popular *filete habañero* (tilapia bathed in a creamy chili sauce), come accompanied with beans or rice and handmade tortillas. ✉ *Costera Miguel Alemán 20, Local A, Costera* ☎ *744/484–2101* 🌐 *www.eltropicano.com.mx* 💳 *AE, MC, V.*

$$$–$$$$ CONTINENTAL ★ ✕ **Madeiras.** All tables at this elegant restaurant have views of the bay, and the dishes and flatware were created by Taxco silversmiths. In the bar-reception area, groovy glass coffee tables rest on carved wooden animals. Dinner is a four-course, prix-fixe meal, and there are 15 menus from which to choose. Specialties include tasty chilled soups and red snapper baked in sea salt (a Spanish dish); there are also steak choices, lobster tail, chicken, and pork. ✉ *Carretera Escénica 33-Bis, just past La Vista shopping center, Costera* ☎ *744/446–5636* ✍ *Reservations essential* 💳 *AE, MC, V* ⏲ *No lunch.*

¢–$ MEXICAN ✕ **100% Natural.** Along the Costera Miguel Alemán are several of these 24-hour restaurants specializing in quick service and light, healthful food: sandwiches made with whole-wheat bread, soy burgers, chicken dishes, yogurt shakes, and fruit salads. You'll recognize these eateries by their green signs with white lettering. The original—the first, and best, in this now-national chain—is across from the Grand Hotel. ✉ *Av. Costera Miguel Alemán 200, Interior 34, near Acapulco Plaza, Costera* ☎ *744/485–3982* 🌐 *www.100natural.com.mx* 💳 *AE, MC, V.*

EXPAT ADVICE

Check out 🌐 *www.travel-acapulco.com*, a Web site that started as a travelogue by a Texas native named Rick, who moved to Acapulco in early 2003. His reviews, advice, and suggestions for activities are reliable and fun to read.

$$$–$$$$ JAPANESE ✕ **Suntory**. You can dine in the delightful Asian-style garden or in an air-conditioned room. Suntory is one of Acapulco's few Japanese restaurants, and one of the few deluxe places that's open for lunch. Many diners opt for the *teppanyaki* (thin slices of beef and vegetables seared on a hot grill), prepared at your table by skilled chefs. Rib eye and seafood are also on the menu, but not sushi. ✉ *Av. Costera Miguel Alemán 36, across from La Palapa hotel, Costera* ☎ *744/484–8088* 💳 *AE, MC, V.*

$–$$$ MEXICAN ★ ✕ **Zorrito's**. When Julio Iglesias is in town, he heads to this open-air street-side eatery after the discos close. It's open almost all the time, serving Acapulco's famous green-and-white *pozole* as well as such steak dishes as *filete tampiqueña* (a strip of tender grilled beef), which comes with tacos, enchiladas, guacamole, and beans. ✉ *Av. Costera Miguel Alemán and Calle Anton de Alaminos, next to Banamex, Costera* ☎ *744/485–3735* 💳 *AE, MC, V* ⏲ *Open 24 hrs except Tues., closed 7 AM–3 PM.*

OLD ACAPULCO

$–$$ SEAFOOD ★ ✕ **El Amigo Miguel**. Locals rave about this lively place. The seafood is fresh, the portions are ample and well priced, and it's in a convenient downtown location right off the zócalo. Feast on fish soup, whole grilled sea bass, fish fillet in a buttery garlic sauce, or lobster. All come with sides of rice and warm bread. ✉ *Calle Benito Juárez 31, at Calle Anzueta, Old Acapulco* ☎ *744/483–6981* 💳 *MC, V.*

¢–$$$$ SEAFOOD ✕ **La Cabaña**. In the 1950s this local favorite was a bohemian hangout that attracted renowned bullfighters along with Mexican songwriter Agustín Lara and his lady love, María Félix. You can see their photo over the bar and sample the same dishes that made the place famous back then: baby-shark tamales, seafood casserole, or shrimp prepared with sea salt, curry, or garlic. The restaurant is smack in the middle of Playa Caleta, and there are free lockers for diners who want to take a swim, as well as banana and wave-runner rentals. ✉ *Playa Caleta Lado Ote. s/n, Fracc. las Playas (5-min taxi ride east of town square), Old Acapulco* ☎ *744/482–5007* 🌐 *www.lacabanadecaleta.com* 💳 *AE, MC, V.*

WHERE TO STAY

ACAPULCO DIAMANTE

Most of the newer, more expensive resorts are in Acapulco Diamante and Playa Revolcadero. These are designed to keep you captive by providing the total vacation experience, including restaurants, clubs, spas, expansive grounds, splendid beaches, and in some cases golf courses. Acapulco proper is a $15 taxi ride away.

$$$$ **The Banyan Tree Cabo Marqués.** Well away from the crowds, the discos, and the oft-crowded beaches are Banyan Tree's romantic luxury villas, each with its own small infinity pool overlooking the bay. The architecture is Asian inspired, but there are plenty of Mexican touches. A glass wall faces the bay, providing stunning views from both the bed and the bathtub. The hotel spa, which is open to both guests and nonguests, is exceptional: massage therapists here must train for 300 hours in Thailand. Ninety-minute treatments run around $170. The dinner-only Saffron restaurant is a standout, with Thai food and incredible sunset views. Note that although families are welcome, the facilities seem designed with adults in mind, and some areas overlook cliffs (including the private room pools), making the property downright dangerous for small children. **Pros:** wonderful spa services, great room views, private pools, exceptional service. **Cons:** super expensive (we mean it), no beach access, far from attractions. ✉ *Blvd. Cabo Marqués, Lote 1, Col. Punta Diamante* ☎ *744/434–0100* 🌐 *www.banyantree.com* *47 villas, 1 presidential suite* *In-room: a/c, safe Internet, Wi-Fi. In-hotel: 3 restaurants, room service, 2 bars, pool, gym, spa, laundry service, Wi-Fi hotspot, parking (free).* 💳 *AE, MC, V.*

$$$–$$$$ ★ **Camino Real Acapulco Diamante.** This stunning hotel is at the foot of a lush hill on exclusive Playa Pichilingue, far from the madding crowd. All rooms are done in pastels and have tile floors, luxurious baths, and up-to-date amenities such as laptop-size safes outfitted with chargers; all rooms also have balconies or terraces with a view of peaceful Puerto Marqués bay. Eleven extra-spacious club rooms have their own concierge and extra amenities. **Pros:** good-size rooms; nice views. **Cons:** pool can be busy, nothing really within walking distance, extra charge to use Internet. ✉ *Calle Baja Catita off Carretera Escénica, Km 14, Acapulco Diamante* ☎ *744/435–1010 or 800/722–6466* 🌐 *www.caminoreal.com/acapulco* *156 rooms, 11 suites* *In-room: safe, Wi-Fi. In-hotel: 3 restaurants, room service, bars, pools, gym, spa, beachfront, water sports, children's programs (ages 5–15), laundry service, Internet terminal, no-smoking rooms, Wi-Fi.* 💳 *AE, MC, V.*

$$$$ **El Encanto.** Architect Miguel Angel Aragonés gave this hotel clean lines and his signature geometric cutouts in walls and floors. In the evening, the facade is dramatically lit in a changing array of colors, and the interior hallway is lit in amber. Rooms are as minimalist as public spaces, with white and beige marble, white linen bedspreads, and more geometric wall cutouts. All rooms have ocean views and are equipped with flat-screen TVs, iPod docks, and Wi-Fi. Standard rooms have a balcony with cushy cube-like sofas. For considerably more money a

night, you can have a room with small private outdoor pool. For a little more than the cost of a standard room, you can stay in a corner room, which won't have a private pool but will have a larger balcony and more expansive view. The hotel has one restaurant with a menu of Mexican and international dishes designed by noted chef Monica Patiño. Just off the restaurant is a large pool surrounded by comfortable beds and bean bags where you can relax to cool, lounge-style music. **Pros:** spectacular views; lighting inside and outside is striking, no children under 16. **Cons:** far from beach and other attractions, no children under 16. ✉ *Jacques Cousteau 51, Fracc. Risas del Marqués* ☎ *744/435–2555* ⊕ *www.hotelencanto.com.mx* *44 rooms* *In-room: a/c, safe (some), DVD (some), Wi-Fi (some). In-hotel: restaurant, room service, pool, gym, spa, laundry service, Wi-Fi hotspot, parking (free), no kids under 16.* *AE, MC, V.*

$$$$ ★ **Fairmont Acapulco Princess.** The 17-story Princess lures the rich and famous (Howard Hughes once hid away in a suite here). Near the reception desk, fantastic ponds with waterfalls and a slatted bridge hint at the luxury throughout. Large, airy rooms have cane furniture, marble floors, and wireless Internet access. You can dine in six excellent restaurants, then burn off the calories in a match at the tennis center, which hosts international tournaments. The superb Willow Stream spa, open to guests and nonguests, has aromatherapy, thalassotherapy, and body wraps, plus a fitness center, Swiss showers, a hair salon, and a Jacuzzi. A shuttle runs frequently to the adjacent Pierre Marqués, where you can use all facilities. **Pros:** elaborate pools; nice golf course. **Cons:** caters to conventions, so can be crowded; beach can be busy. ✉ *Playa Revolcadero, Granjas del Marqués* *AP 1351 39907* ☎ *744/469–1000; 800/441–1414; 01800/090–9900 in Mexico* ⊕ *www.fairmont.com* *927 rooms, 92 suites* *In-room: safe, Wi-Fi. In-hotel: 7 restaurants, room service, bars, golf course, tennis courts, pools, gym, spa, beachfront, water sports, children's programs (ages 2–13), laundry service, no-smoking rooms* *AE, DC, MC, V* *BP.*

$$$$ Fodor's Choice ★ **Fairmont Pierre Marqués.** This boutique-style hotel was built by J. Paul Getty in 1958 as a personal retreat. Longtime employees say that he never used it, instead making it available to his friends before eventually turning it into a hotel. After a multimillion-dollar renovation in 2004, the Pierre Marqués is one of Mexico's finest properties. The hotel provides the serenity and sophistication of a private hacienda but with the first-class services and amenities of an international resort, including a meandering pool overlooking the ocean. You can stay in a room or suite in the tower building or in one of the ultraluxe villas or bungalows, which have private plunge pools. A shuttle runs frequently to the adjacent Princess, where you can use all facilities. **Pros:** high-quality golf course; well-kept grounds. **Cons:** food is pricey; can't get anywhere without a taxi. ✉ *Playa Revolcadero, Granjas del Marqués* *AP 1351 39907* ☎ *744/466–1000; 800/441–1414; 01800/090–9900 toll-free in Mexico* ⊕ *www.fairmont.com* *220 rooms, 74 executive premier rooms, 25 suites, 10 villas, 4 bungalows* *In-room: safe, refrigerator (some). In-hotel: 2 restaurants, room service, bar, golf course, tennis courts, pools, beachfront, children's programs (ages 3–12), laundry service, Wi-Fi hotspot* *AE, MC, V* *BP.*

$$$$ **Las Brisas.** Perhaps Acapulco's signature resort, this hilltop haven is particularly popular with honeymooners. (The company motto is actually "Where children are seldom seen, but often created.") There are a variety of quarters, from one-bedroom units to deluxe private casitas complete with small private pools. Room interiors are a little dated, but nobody seems to mind because of the enchanting bay views. Since the property is extremely spread out (all rooms are at ground level), transportation is by pink-and-white Jeeps. The hotel also provides transportation to its private beach club. A continental breakfast is delivered to your room each morning. **Pros:** astounding views from almost everywhere; gracious service. **Cons:** room interiors dated; wait for Jeeps can be 20 minutes; pricey for what you get. ✉ *Carretera Escénica Clemente Mejia 5255, Las Brisas* ☎ *744/469–6900; 888/559–4329 in U.S. and Canada* 🌐 *www.brisas.com.mx* *263 units* *In-room: Wi-Fi (some). In-hotel: 3 restaurants, bars, 2 tennis courts, pools, water sports, laundry service, Internet terminal, no-smoking rooms, Wi-Fi.* *AE, MC, V* *CP.*

13

$$$$ ★ **Quinta Real.** A member of Mexico's most prestigious hotel chain, this low-slung hillside resort overlooks the sea, about a 15-minute drive from downtown. The 74 suites have balconies, Mexican-made hardwood furniture, and closet door handles shaped like iguanas—a signature motif. Six suites have private hot tubs and small pools on their balconies. **Pros:** nice facilities; great "world music" in the common areas. **Cons:** not much to do at night, and downtown's a bit of a drive; service is not up to snuff for the price you pay. ✉ *Paseo de la Quinta, Lote 6, Acapulco Diamante, Real Diamante* ☎ *744/469–1500 or 866/621–9288* 🌐 *www.quintareal.com* *74 suites In-room: safe (some).* *In-hotel: restaurant, room service, bar, pool, gym, spa, beachfront, water sports, laundry service, Internet terminal, Wi-Fi hotspot, no-smoking rooms* *AE, MC, V.*

COSTERA

The 8-km (5-mi) stretch of Avenida Costera Miguel Alemán known as the Costera is lined with beachfront, side-by-side high-rise hotels. Most were built in the '60s and '70s, forever changing one of the world's most exquisite bays. There are hotels in all price categories; the cheaper properties are on the north side of the avenue. Stay here if you want to be in the middle of the action, surrounded by restaurants, bars, discos, shops, malls, and food stores. For cheap transportation along the Costera, simply jump on one of the local buses that chug up and down the strip (a ride costs 4.50 pesos), or flag one of the many taxis.

$$$–$$$$ **Elcano.** Restored to its original 1950s glamour, this perennial favorite has snappy rooms with white-tile floors and modern bathrooms. There's a beachside restaurant with an outstanding breakfast buffet, a more elegant indoor restaurant, and a gorgeous pool that not only seems to float above the bay, but also has whirlpools built into its corners. **Pros:** ocean-facing rooms have balconies; located on good stretch of beach. **Cons:** pool fills up with parents and kids; exercise room extraordinarily small. ✉ *Av. Costera Miguel Alemán 75, Costera* ☎ *744/435–1500*

www.elcano-hotel.com 163 rooms, 16 suites In-room: safe, Wi-Fi. In-hotel: restaurant, room service, bar, pool, gym, beachfront, water sports, laundry service, no-smoking rooms AE, MC, V.

$$$$ **Fiesta Americana Villas Acapulco.** In the thick of the main shopping and restaurant district, this hotel is popular with tour groups and singles. It has a lively lobby bar and is on Playa Condesa, one of the most popular beaches in town. Pastel-color rooms have light-wood furniture and tile floors. **Pros:** bar can be loud after hours; good location. **Cons:** beach can fill up; rooms are average. *Av. Costera Miguel Alemán 97, Costera 744/435–1600 or 800/343–7821 www.fiestaamericana.com 492 rooms, 8 suites In-room: refrigerator, Wi-Fi (some). In-hotel: 2 restaurants, room service, bar, pools, beachfront, water sports, children's programs (ages 4–12), laundry service AE, MC, V.*

$$$ **Grand Hotel Acapulco.** Formerly a Hyatt, this large hotel is popular with business travelers, conventioneers, and—thanks to its bold Caribbean color schemes and striking design—TV producers, who have opted to use it as the backdrop for many a Mexican soap opera. It has four outstanding eateries (one is a kosher restaurant), a spa, and a deluxe shopping area. It's also the only hotel in Latin America with an on-site synagogue. The west side of the property insulates you from the noise of the nearby naval base. **Pros:** great service; spacious rooms. **Cons:** big hotel, so pools and bars can get crowded; children's programs only run during high season. *Av. Costera Miguel Alemán 1, Costera 744/469–1234; 800/633–7313 in U.S. and Canada www.grandhotelacapulco.com 640 rooms, 17 suites In-room: safe, refrigerator, Wi-Fi. In-hotel: 4 restaurants, room service, bars, tennis courts, pools, gym, spa, beachfront, children's programs (ages 8–12), laundry service, Wi-Fi hotspot, parking (free), no-smoking rooms AE, MC, V.*

$$$ **Hotel Emporio.** All of the rooms at this hotel, which used to be the Acapulco Hilton, are comfortably spacious, with marble floors and bathrooms, modern contemporary furniture, and balconies with ocean views. The marble-floored lobby, restaurant, and bar are comfortable for both guests dressed up for a night on the town and families in shorts and T-shirts. There are two pools with swim-up bars—one is geared to families, with a waterslide, while the other is for adults. (Really. Kids can't enter it.) The all-inclusive plan is a good deal, especially if you're planning to spend most of your time at the resort pools and beach, but there are some restrictions about what and when you can eat—each restaurant has a different schedule, not all are part of the AI plan, and not all dishes and drinks are covered, though many are. **Pros:** family options include a children's pool and supervised activities for kids. **Cons:** all-inclusive plans don't cover all foods at all times; lots of traffic in front of the hotel. *Av. Costera Miguel Alemán 121 744/469–0505 www.hotelesemporio.com 369 rooms, 50 suites In-room: safe, Wi-Fi. In-hotel: 3 restaurants, bars, pools, gym, spa, beachfront, children's programs (ages 2–11), no-smoking rooms AE, MC, V.*

$$ **Park Hotel & Tennis Center.** A helpful staff and a prime location make this an appealing place to stay. Rooms, which have colonial-style furnishings, are around a garden with a good-size pool. Some have

kitchenettes and balconies; all are spotlessly clean. The Park has a tennis center and is only a block from the beach. **Pros:** good location (close to a mall with an Internet café); fairly inexpensive. **Cons:** rooms are "economical"; hotel bar is tiny. ✉ *Av. Costera Miguel Alemán 127, Costera* 📫 *AP 269 39670* ☎ *744/485–5992* 🌐 *www.parkhotel-acapulco.com* *88 rooms* *In-hotel: bar, tennis courts, pool, Internet terminal, parking (free), no-smoking rooms* 💳 *AE, MC, V.*

OLD ACAPULCO

Old Acapulco is the place to find budget hotels and restaurants.

$$–$$$ **Alba Suites.** This all-white, all-suites hotel is popular with families, and comprises seven low-rise buildings—most four or five stories. Units sleep four, six, or eight and have terraces; some also have kitchenettes. There's a cable car to the hotel's beach club, which is on the bay and next to the Club de Yates and its 330-foot-long toboggan run. **Pros:** considerate service; cable car to beach club. **Cons:** noisy during the day from kids at pool; interior design is basic. ✉ *Grand Via Tropical 35, Caleta* ☎ *744/483–0073; 877/428–1327 in Canada* 🌐 *www.albasuites.com.mx* *300 suites* *In-room: safe, kitchen (some). In-hotel: restaurant, bar, pools, beachfront, laundry service, Wi-Fi hotspot, no-smoking rooms* 💳 *AE, MC, V.*

$$$–$$$$ **Boca Chica.** When this boutique hotel reopened in March 2010 it made headlines as one of Acapulco's coolest properties. It was originally built in the '50s (indeed, scenes from the Elvis movie *Fun in Acapulco* were actually shot here), and the remodel has a retro,'50s feel. An old refrigerator in the lobby is filled with Yoli sodas (a regional soda from the state of Guerrero), and there's vintage furniture and appointments throughout. The small rooms have a mint-green and-white color scheme and are simply furnished with comfortable beds, retro sinks and showers, flat-screen TVs, iPod docks, and ceiling fans. A beachy area within the hotel is a sort of natural swimming pool; the adjacent beach is probably Acapulco's most popular, so you get a look at how the locals enjoy the sun and sand. **Pros:** very cool vibe, great restaurant, nice perks (brief phone calls—even to United States—included in room price); great location. **Cons:** small gym, adjacent beach is often crowded and can be dirty. ✉ *Punta Caletilla, Fracc. Las Playas* ☎ *744/482–7879* 🌐 *www.hotel-bocachica.com* *30 rooms, 6 suites* *In-room: a/c, safe, Internet, Wi-Fi. In-hotel: restaurant, room service, pool, gym, spa, beachfront, diving, water sports, laundry service, Wi-Fi hotspot, parking (free).* 💳 *AE, MC, V.*

$$ **El Mirador.** Another '50s Hollywood hangout, El Mirador exudes nostalgia, with white walls, red-tile roofs, and hand-carved Mexican furnishings. It's on a hill with views of Bahía de Acapulco and La Quebrada, where the cliff divers perform. Many suites have refrigerators, hot tubs, and ocean vistas. **Pros:** close proximity to divers; nice views. **Cons:** food inconsistent; sense that its "heyday" has passed. ✉ *Av. Quebrada 74, Old Acapulco* ☎ *744/483–1155 or 866/765–0608* 🌐 *www.hotelelmiradoracapulco.com.mx* *133 rooms, 9 suites* *In-room: refrigerator (some). In-hotel: 2 restaurants, bar, pools, children's programs (ages 3–12), laundry service, parking (free)* 💳 *AE, MC, V.*

$$–$$$ **Etel Suites.** On Cerro Pinzona (Pinzona Hill), a five-minute walk from La Quebrada, the Etel has outstanding views of Bahía de Acapulco and spacious rooms with sturdy cedar furniture. All accommodations sleep three, and you can rent a full kitchen and dining room to turn your room into a suite. One studio has a kitchenette. There's a garden on the roof and a children's play area by the pool. The owner, gracious Señora Etel Alvarez, is the great-grandniece of John Augustus Sutter, whose gold mine launched the Gold Rush of 1849. **Pros:** near to cliff divers; reasonably priced; wonderful owner. **Cons:** accommodations basic (only one double room; need to call ahead if you don't have a large group). ✉ *Av. Pinzona 92, Old Acapulco* ☎ *744/482–2240* *12 rooms* *In-room: kitchen (some), Internet terminal. In-hotel: pool, no-smoking rooms* *AE, MC, V.*

$–$$$ ★ **Los Flamingos.** This hot-pink, cliff-side hotel was a favorite hangout of co-owners John Wayne and Johnny ("Tarzan") Weissmuller. A young busboy at the hotel in those days, Adolfo Santiago, is now the owner. He plays an amazing guitar and, if in the mood, will share some good stories. Today Los Flamingos draws an international clientele for its fine views and its *coco locos,* tequila drinks served in a green coconut. Rooms have bright pink walls and spartan, shower-only baths. Weissmuller liked to stay in the circular two-bedroom master suite. The hotel provides free transportation to the beach and downtown. **Pros:** history is intriguing; epic views. **Cons:** a little wear and tear in rooms; bathrooms need updating. ✉ *Av. López Mateos, Fracc. las Playas, Old Acapulco* ☎ *744/482–0690* 🌐 *www.hotellosflamingos.com* *30 rooms, 10 suites* *In-room: no a/c (some). In-hotel: restaurant, bar, pool, laundry service, Wi-Fi hotspot, parking (free), no-smoking rooms* *AE, MC, V.*

$ **Misión.** Two minutes from the zócalo, this enchanting, colonial-style hotel surrounds a greenery-rich courtyard with an outdoor dining area that's open only for breakfast. Rooms are small and by no means fancy, with painted brick walls, tile floors, wrought-iron beds, and ceiling fans. Every room has a shower, and there's plenty of hot water. The best rooms are on the second and third floors, as you can open the windows and fully appreciate the view; the top-floor room is large but hot in the daytime. **Pros:** artistic touches; delightful quality. **Cons:** tiny rooms; no lunch or dinner. ✉ *Calle Felipe Valle 12, Downtown* ☎ *744/482–3643* *20 rooms* *In-room: no a/c (some), no phone, no TV. In-hotel: no-smoking rooms* *No credit cards.*

PIE DE LA CUESTA

To the west of the bay, on the Pacific, is the laid-back beach town of Pie de la Cuesta, home to low- and mid-priced small hotels, usually family-run and on the beach. If you stay here, you'll get a good taste of Mexican beach-village life.

$$ Fodor's Choice ★ **Hacienda Vayma.** White stucco bungalows named for musicians and painters overlook the beach or interior courtyards. The sparse, contemporary rooms accommodate two, three, or five people. The bathrooms are tiny, however, and have no hot water. If you can opt for one of the

suites, which have plunge pools, air-conditioning, and terraces, you'll be a lot more comfortable. An excellent outdoor restaurant draws diners from miles around, and on weekends the hotel fills with an interesting array of guests, such as embassy personnel from Mexico City. **Pros:** animals allowed; some rooms have canopied beds. **Cons:** no credit cards accepted, no Internet access. ✉ *Av. Base Aerea Militar 378, Pie de la Cuesta* ☎ *744/460–2882* 🌐 *www.vayma.com.mx* *20 rooms, 4 suites* *In-room: no phone. In-hotel: restaurant, bar, pool, spa, beachfront, water sports, laundry service, parking (free), some pets allowed* 💳 *No credit cards.*

$$$$ **Parador del Sol.** Germans and Canadians favor this low-key, all-inclusive resort's white villas scattered throughout gardens along both the lagoon and the Pacific Ocean sides of Carretera Pie de la Cuesta. The ocean is particularly dramatic here, with towering waves. The spacious rooms have tile floors and fan-cooled terraces with hammocks. In addition to all meals, comprising Guerrero specialties served buffet-style, including red snapper and tamales, rates include the occasional on-site music and dance performance, aerobics classes, tennis, and nonmotorized water sports. Motorized water sports cost extra. **Pros:** peaceful, lovely beach; pricey for what you get. **Cons:** a trek to downtown by car; rough ocean limits swimming. ✉ *Carretera Pie de la Cuesta–Barra de Coyuca, Km 5, Pie de la Cuesta* *AP 1070 39300* ☎ *744/444–4050* 🌐 *www.paradordelsol.com.mx* *150 rooms* *In-hotel: restaurant, bars, tennis courts, pools, gym, laundry service, Wi-Fi hotspot, parking (free), no-smoking rooms, safe.* 💳 *MC, V* *AI.*

$–$$ **Villas Ukae Kim.** You can't miss this colorful, rustic seaside lodge. The large rooms are painted in bright Mexican hues, and all have terraces and mosquito nets slung over double beds; the honeymoon suite has a private hot tub. **Pros:** artistic touches. **Cons:** no credit cards accepted. ✉ *Av. Fuerza Aereo Mexicana 356, Pie de la Cuesta* ☎ *744/440–0186 or 744/460–2187* *21 rooms, 1 suite* *In-room: no a/c (some), no phone, no TV (some). In-hotel: restaurant, bar, pool, beachfront, water sports, laundry service, parking (free), no-smoking rooms* 💳 *No credit cards.*

NIGHTLIFE

Acapulco's clubs are open nearly 365 days a year from about 10:30 PM until they empty out. The minute the sun slips over the horizon, the Costera comes alive. People mill around, window-shopping, choosing restaurants, generally biding their time until the disco hour. Many casual beach restaurants on the strip have live music.

The resorts often have splashy entertainment, sometimes with big-name artists. At the least, such hotels have live music during happy hour, restaurant theme parties, dancing at a beach bar—or all three. For a more informal evening, head for the zócalo, where there's usually a band on weekend evenings.

The more expensive clubs have $20–$60 cover charges, sometimes including drinks and sometimes not. Women usually pay less than men. In general, a higher cover calls for dressier attire, that is, no shorts.

The more casual open-air bars are mostly free to enter, and shorts and T-shirts are common. Drinks cost $2–$5, and two-for-one drink specials during happy hour are common. The waiters depend on tips in the 15%–20% range. Note that Mexico's legal drinking age is 18.

Alebrije. This massive club can accommodate 5,000 people in its love seats and booths, and it attracts a younger (late teens, early twenties) crowd. When the club first opens at 11, the music is slow and romantic; afterward there's dance music and light shows until dawn. The music ranges from pop to tropical. ✉ *Av. Costera Miguel Alemán 3308, across from Hyatt Regency, Costera* ☎ *744/484–5902* *Cover: $33 women, $43 men, including drinks*

★ **Baby Lobster Bar.** Frequented primarily by tourists, this lively open-air bar is on the beach and not far from other bars. You will get two drinks when you order, and the mood is conducive to meeting other people. Tabletop dancing is not discouraged, especially late at night. There's no cover charge during the week, but on Saturday it's about $7 or $8 and Sunday it's around $5 and includes a drink. ✉ *Costera Miguel Alemán near Bungee Jump, La Condesa* ☎ *744/484–1096* *No cover during the week, Sat. and Sun. $5–$8*

Baby'O. Small, expensive, and exclusive, Baby'O caters to the local elite. The club has long had the reputation of being Acapulco's classiest, and the well-dressed clientele lounges and dances in a jungle-inspired interior. It can be hard to get in, and even harder to get a table, but this is *the* place to go to see and be seen. It's closed Sunday and Monday in low season (May through November). ✉ *Av. Costera Miguel Alemán 22, Costera* ☎ *744/484–7474* 🌐 *www.babyo.com.mx* *Cover: $30 women, $60–$100 men, not including drinks*

Disco Beach. As the name suggests, this relaxed nightspot is right on the sands. It's so informal that most people turn up in shorts. The waiters are young and friendly—some people find them overly so, and in fact, this is a legendary pickup spot. Every Wednesday is ladies' night, when all the women receive flowers. Foam parties reign on Friday. ✉ *Playa Condesa, Costera* ☎ *744/484–8230* *Cover: $30, including drinks.*

Fodor's Choice ★ **Palladium.** A waterfall cascades down from the dance floor, which is considered by many to be Acapulco's best. It's also surrounded by 50-foot-high windows, so dancers have a wraparound view of the city. The club is so popular that it may take awhile to get in. ✉ *Carretera Escénica, Costera* ☎ *744/446–5490* 🌐 *www.palladium.com.mx* *Cover: $33 women, $43 men, including drinks.*

★ **Paradise.** The restaurant downstairs has beach access, a swimming pool, and lively dance contests at night. The open-air bar upstairs affords a spectacular bay view and it's a great place to watch bungee jumpers as they plunge from the 165-foot platform right next door. ✉ *Av. Costera Miguel Alemán 101, Costera, near Fiesta Americana Hotel* ☎ *744/484–5988* *No cover.*

Salon Q. The so-called Cathedral of Salsa is a combination dance hall and disco, where the bands play salsas, merengues, and other Latin rhythms for young and old. Weekends see shows—mostly impersonations of Mexican entertainers. ✉ *Av. Costera Miguel Alemán 3117, Costera* ☎ *744/481–0114* 🎫 *Cover: $24*

SHOPPING

Guerrero State is known for hand-painted ceramics, objects made from *palo de rosa* wood, bark paintings depicting scenes of village life and local flora and fauna, and embroidered textiles. Although many of Acapulco's stores carry jewelry and other articles made of silver, aficionados tend to make the three-hour drive to the colonial town of Taxco—one of the world's silver capitals. Stands in downtown's sprawling municipal market are piled high with handicrafts, as well as fruit, flowers, spices, herbs, cheeses, seafood, poultry, and other meats. Practice your bargaining skills here or at one of the street-side handicrafts sellers, as prices are usually flexible.

Most shops are open Monday–Saturday 10–7. The main strip is along Avenida Costera Miguel Alemán from the Costa Club to El Presidente Hotel. Here you can find Guess, Peer, Aca Joe, Amarras, Polo Ralph Lauren, and other sportswear shops, as well as emporiums like Aurrerá, Gigante, Price Club, Sam's, Wal-Mart, Comercial Mexicana, and the upscale Liverpool department store, Fabricas de Francia. Old Acapulco has inexpensive tailors and lots of souvenir shops.

Sanborns. A countrywide institution, Sanborns is a good place to find English-language newspapers, magazines, and books; basic cosmetics and toiletries; and high-quality souvenirs. There are several branches; All are open 7 AM to 1:30 AM in high season and 7:30 AM–11 PM the rest of the year. ✉ *Av. Costera Miguel Alemán 3111, Costera* ☎ *744/484–2044.*

MARKETS

El Mercado de Artesanías El Parazal. It's a 15-minute walk from Sanborns downtown to this market. Look for fake ceremonial masks, the ever-present onyx chessboards, $20 hand-embroidered dresses, imitation silver, hammocks, and skin cream made from turtles (don't buy it, because turtle harvesting is illegal in both Mexico and the United States, and you won't get it through U.S. Customs). From Sanborns downtown, head away from Avenida Costera to Vásquez de León and turn right one block later. The market is open daily 9–9.

La Diana Mercado de Artesanías. One large flea market with a convenient location is a block from the Emporio hotel, close to the Diana monument in Costera.

Mercado Municipal. Don't miss the market where restaurateurs load up on produce early in the morning, and later in the day locals shop for piñatas, serapes, leather goods, baskets, hammocks, amulets to attract lovers or ward off enemies, and velvet paintings of the Virgin of Guadalupe.

SPECIALTY SHOPS

ART AND HANDICRAFTS

Arte Para Siempre. This shop in the Acapulco Cultural Center sparkles with handicrafts from the seven regions of Guerrero. Look for hand-loomed shawls, painted gourds, hammocks, baskets, Olinalá boxes, and silver jewelry. ✉ *Av. Costera Miguel Alemán 4834, near the Gran Hotel Acapulco, Costera* ☎ *744/484–2390*

> **SILVER SECRETS**
>
> Buy silver and jewelry made from semiprecious stones only in reputable establishments, or you might end up with cleverly painted paste or a silver facsimile called *alpaca*. Make sure that 0.925 is stamped on the silver piece; this verifies its purity.

Pal Kepenyes. The Hungarian artist Pal Kepenyes, who lives in Mexico, gets good press for his jewelry and sculpture (much of it racy and provocative), on display in his workshop. ✉ *Guitarrón 140, Lomas Guitarrón* ☎ *744/446–5287* 🌐 *www.pal-kepenyes.com*

SILVER AND JEWELRY

Maria Bonita. This shop has exquisite flatware, jewelry, and objets d'art. ✉ *Las Brisas hotel, Carretera Escénica 5255, Las Brisas* ☎ *744/469–6900*

Minette. Diamond jewelry of impeccable design by Charles Garnier and Nouvelle Bague is sold at Minette. There's also jewelry set with Caledonia stones from Africa as well as Emilia Castillo's exquisite line of brightly colored porcelainware inlaid with silver fish, stars, and birds. ✉ *Fairmont Acapulco Princess hotel arcade, Playa Revolcadero, Revolcadero* ☎ *744/469–1000*

SPORTS AND THE OUTDOORS

FISHING

Fishing is what originally drew many of the early tourists to Acapulco, and it is still an abundant area. Billfish, striped marlin, pompano, bonito, red snapper, and tuna are in the ocean year-round; and carp, mullet, and catfish swim in the freshwater lagoons. You can arrange fishing trips through your hotel or at the Pesca Deportiva near the *muelle* (dock) across from the zócalo. **Acapulco Scuba Center** (✉ *Paseo del Pescador 13 and 14, near zócalo, Old Acapulco* ☎ *744/482–9474* 🌐 *www.acapulcoscuba.com*) is an excellent place to sign up for deep-sea fishing excursions. The center's 40-foot boats accommodate up to six passengers. Trips depart at 9 AM, return at 2 PM, and cost $70 per person for scuba and $35 per person for snorkeling. We also recommend **Fish-R-Us** (✉ *Av. Costera Miguel Alemán 100, Fracc. Las Playas, Old Acapulco* ☎ *744/482–8282* 🌐 *www.fish-r-us.com*), which runs charter service for sailfish, tuna, and dorado fishing. Shared boats depart on Wednesday at 6 AM. You can share a boat for $87 per person, with a maximum of six people, or rent a private yacht for $380 to $450 per day.

For freshwater trips, try the companies along Laguna Coyuca. Boats accommodating 4–10 people cost $250–$500 a day, $45–$60 by chair. Excursions leave about 7 AM and return at 1 PM or 2 PM. At the docks you can hire a boat for $40 a day (two lines). You must get a license ($12, depending on the season) from the Secretaría de Pesca; there's a representative at the dock, but note that the office is closed during siesta, between 2 and 4.

GOLF

Club de Golf. There's a short, public, well-kept golf course at this club on the Costera next to the convention center. Greens fees are $50 for 9 holes, $70 for 18. ✉ *Av. Costera Miguel Alemán s/n* ☎ *744/484–0781*)

Fairmont Acapulco Princess and Pierre Marqués. Two championship courses—one designed by Ted Robinson, the other remodeled by Robert Trent Jones Sr. and then renovated under the supervision of Robert Trent Jones Jr.—are adjacent to the Fairmont hotels. Make reservations well in advance. Greens fees in high season, mid-December to mid-April, are $165 for hotel guests; nonguests should call for rates. Fees are lower after noon and in low season. ✉ *Playa Revolcadero* ☎ *744/469-1000*

Mayan Palace. A round on the 18-hole course at this time-share condo complex is $110 for guests who aren't members, $130 for nonguests. ✉ *Playa Revolcadero, domicilio conocido* ☎ *744/469-6000*

TENNIS

Court fees range from $9 to $26 an hour during the day and double that in the evening. At hotel courts, nonguests pay about $6 more per hour. Lessons start at about $15 an hour; ball boys get a $2 tip.

Fairmont Acapulco Princess. In addition to five outdoor courts, you'll find two air-conditioned synthetic-grass, lighted indoor courts and a stadium that hosts international tournaments. ✉ *Playa Revolcadero, Revolcadero* ☎ *744/469–1000*

Fairmont Pierre Marqués. This hotel has five synthetic-grass lighted courts. ✉ *Playa Revolcadero, Revolcadero* ☎ *744/466–1000*

Mayan Palace. There are 12 lighted clay courts at this condo complex. ✉ *Playa Revolcadero, domicilio conocido, Revolcadero* ☎ *744/469–6000*

WATER SPORTS

You can arrange to water-ski, rent broncos (one-person Jet Skis), parasail, and windsurf at outfitters on the beaches. Parasailing is an Acapulco highlight developed here in the 1960s; a five-minute trip costs $60. Waterskiing is about $40 an hour; broncos cost $40–$95 for a half hour, depending on the size. You can arrange to windsurf at Playa Caleta and most beaches along the Costera, but the best place to actually do it is at Bahía Puerto Marqués. The main surfing beach is Revolcadero.

Although visibility isn't as good as in the Caribbean, scuba diving is an option. It's best from November through February, when the water is the most transparent. (In summer, from June through October, rains bring mud from the hills down the rivers and into the bay.) A Canadian warship was scuttled in the bay to make a diving trip more appealing.

Acapulco Scuba Center. The center leads four-hour snorkeling and scuba outings for beginners and certified divers. All tours include gear and round-trip transportation from your hotel, and cost $70 with lessons and lunch included; snorkeling costs $35. The center also arranges deep-sea fishing excursions. ✉ *Paseo del Pescador 13 y 14, near zócalo, Old Acapulco* ☎ *744/482–9474* 🌐 *www.acapulcoscuba.com.*

Shotover Jet. The Shotover Jet is a wild boat ride that's an import from the rivers around Queenstown, New Zealand. An air-conditioned bus takes you to the Pierre Marqués Lagoon, about 20 minutes from downtown Acapulco. Twelve-passenger boats provide thrilling 30-minute boat rides on the lagoon, complete with 360-degree turns—one of the Shotover Jet's trademarks—and vistas of local flora and fauna. The cost for the ride and transportation to and from the site is $45. For more thrills, from July through January, you can shoot the rapids on 1½- to 2-hour guided trips for $55; there's a four-person minimum. ✉ *Centro Comercial Plaza Marbella, Local 17 and Av. Costera Miguel Aleman, Costera* ☎ *744/484–1154* 🌐 *www.shotoverjet.com.mx.*

SIDE TRIP TO TAXCO

275 km (170 mi) north of Acapulco.

In Mexico's premier "Silver City," marvelously preserved white-stucco, red-tile-roof colonial buildings hug cobblestone streets that wind up and down the foothills of the Sierra Madre. Taxco (pronounced *tahss*-ko) is a living work of art. For centuries its silver mines drew foreign mining companies. In 1928 the government made it a national monument. And today its charm, abundant sunshine, flowers, and silversmiths make it a popular getaway.

The town's name was derived from the Nahuatl word *tlacho* meaning "the place where ball is played." Spanish explorers first discovered a wealth of minerals in the area in 1524, just three years after Hernán Cortés entered the Aztec city of Tenochtitlán, present-day Mexico City. Soon Sovácon del Rey, the first mine in the New World, was established on the present-day town square. The first mines were soon depleted of riches, however, and the town went into stagnation for the next 150 years. In 1708 two Frenchmen, Francisco and Don José de la Borda, resumed the mining. Francisco soon died, but José discovered the silver vein that made him the area's wealthiest man. The main square in the town center is named Plaza Borda in his honor.

After the Borda era, however, Taxco's importance again faded, until the 1930s and the arrival of William G. Spratling, a writer-architect from New Orleans. Enchanted by the city and convinced of its potential as a center for silver jewelry, Spratling set up an apprentice shop. His talent and fascination with pre-Columbian design combined to produce silver jewelry and other artifacts that soon earned Taxco its worldwide reputation as the Silver City once more. Spratling's inspiration lives on in his students and their descendants, many of whom are today's famous silversmiths.

Taxco is on the side of a mountain, 5,800 feet above sea level, and many of its narrow, winding streets run nearly vertical. So bring some good walking shoes and be prepared to get some lung-gasping exercise.

GETTING HERE AND AROUND

The trip by car from Acapulco takes 3½ hours via the toll road and about 45 minutes longer on the more scenic free road. If you can start early, consider taking the scenic road to get there and the toll road to return. Warning: On the toll road there are extremely few opportunities to turn around. If you'd prefer not to rent a car, Estrella buses leave Acapulco for Taxco five times a day from 7 AM to 6:40 PM from the Terminal Central de Autobuses de Primera Clase (First-Class Bus Terminal). The cost for the approximately 4½-hour ride is about $18 one-way. Grupo Estrella Blanca buses depart from Acapulco several times a day from the Terminal de Autobuses. A first-class, one-way ticket is $18.

ESSENTIALS

Bus Contacts First-class **Estrella de Oro** (✉ *Av. Cuauhtémoc 1490, Acapulco* ☎ *744/485–8758* ✉ *Av. de los Plateros 386, Taxco* ☎ *762/485–8705 or 762/622–0648*). **Grupo Estrella Blanca** (✉ *Av. Ejido 47, Old Acapulco, Acapulco* ☎ *744/469–2017* ✉ *Av. de los Plateros 310, Taxco* ☎ *762/622–0131*).

EXPLORING

3 **Casa Humboldt.** The Museo de Arte Virreinal, as it is also known, was named for German naturalist Alexander von Humboldt, who stayed here in 1803. The Moorish-style 18th-century house has a finely detailed facade. It now contains a wonderful little museum of colonial art. ✉ *Calle Juan Ruíz de Alarcón 12* ☎ *762/622–5501* 💲 *$2* ⏲ *Tues.–Sun. 10–6.*

OFF THE BEATEN PATH

Grutas de Cacahuamilpa. Mexico's largest caverns are about 30 km (19 mi) northeast of Taxco. English-speaking guides will lead you along a 2-km (1 mi) illuminated walkway in large chambers with fascinating geological formations. A tour takes around two hours. 💲 *$6.50* ☎ *721/104–0155* ⏲ *Daily 9–5.*

1 ★ **Iglesia de San Sebastián y Santa Prisca.** This church has dominated Plaza Borda since the 18th century. Usually just called Santa Prisca, it was built by French silver magnate José de la Borda in thanks to the Almighty for his having literally stumbled upon a rich silver vein, although the expense nearly bankrupted him. According to legend, St. Prisca appeared to workers during a storm and prevented a wall of the church from tumbling. Soon after, the church was named in her honor. The style of the church—a sort of Spanish baroque known as churrigueresque—and its pale pink exterior have made it Taxco's most important landmark. Its facade, naves, and *bovedas* (vaulted ceilings), as well as important paintings by Mexican Juan Cabrera, are slowly

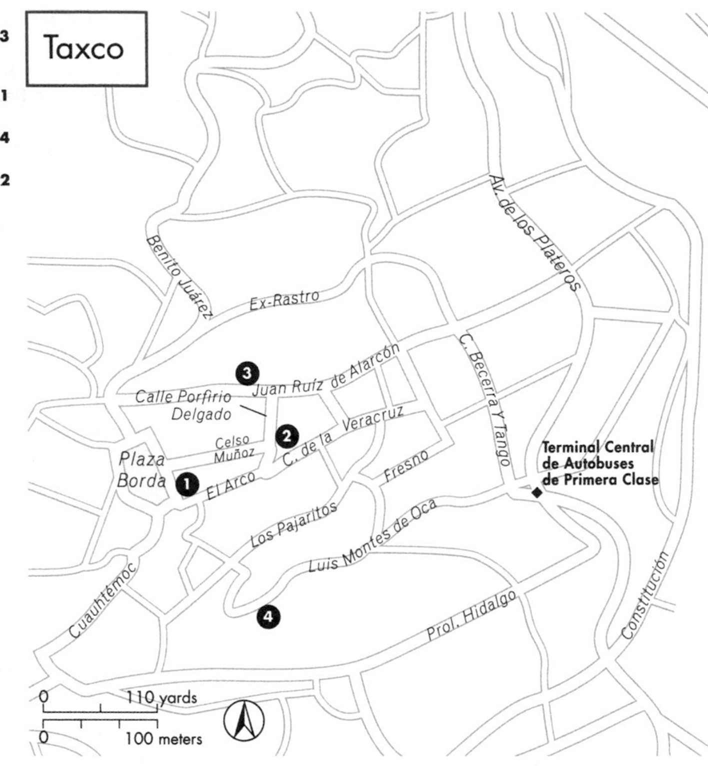

being restored. ✉ *Southwest side of Plaza Borda* ☎ *No phone* ⏲ *Daily 6 AM–9 PM.*

4 **Mercado Municipal.** Weekend mornings, locals from surrounding towns come to sell and buy produce, crafts, and everything from peanuts to electrical appliances at this market. It's directly down the hill from Santa Prisca. Look for the market's chapel to the Virgin of Guadalupe.

Fodor's Choice ★

2 **Museo Spratling.** The former home of William G. Spratling houses some 140 of the artist's original designs plus his collection of pre-Columbian artifacts. Exhibits also explain the working of colonial mines. ✉ *At Plazuela de Juan Ruíz de Alarcón on Calle Porfirio Delgado 1* ☎ *762/622–1660* 🎟 *$3.10* ⏲ *Tues.–Sun. 9–3.*

WHERE TO EAT

You can find everything from tagliatelle to iguana in Taxco restaurants, and meals are much less expensive than in Acapulco. Taxco has two main types of hotels: small inns nestled in the hills around the zócalo and larger, more modern hotels in the outskirts of town.

$–$$ ECLECTIC ★

✕ **El Mural.** You can eat indoors or out on a poolside terrace where there's a view not only of a Juan O'Gorman mural but of the stunning Santa Prisca church. The chef prepares international beef and seafood dishes as well as Mexican specialties like cilantro soup and crepes with

CLOSE UP

One Man's Metal

In less than a decade William Spratling transformed Taxco into a flourishing silver center not seen since colonial times. In 1929 the writer-architect from New Orleans settled in the then sleepy, dusty village because it was inexpensive and close to the pre-Hispanic Mexcala culture that he was studying in Guerrero Valley.

For hundreds of years Taxco's silver was made into bars and exported overseas. No one even considered developing a local jewelry industry. Journeying to a nearby town, Spratling hired a couple of goldsmiths and commissioned them to create jewelry, flatware, trays, and goblets from his own designs. Ever the artist with a keen mind for drawing, design, and aesthetics, Spratling decided to experiment with silver using his designs. Shortly afterward, he set up his own workshop and began producing highly innovative pieces. By the 1940s Spratling's designs were gracing the necks of celebrities and being sold in high-end stores abroad.

Spratling also started a program to train local silversmiths; they were soon joined by foreigners interested in learning the craft. It wasn't long before there were thousands of silversmiths in the town, and Spratling was its wealthiest resident. He moved freely in Mexico's lively art scene, befriending muralists Diego Rivera (Rivera's wife, Frida Kahlo, wore Spratling necklaces) and David Alfaro Siqueiros as well as architect Miguel Covarrubias. The U.S. ambassador to Mexico, Dwight Morrow, father of Anne Morrow who married Charles Lindbergh, hired Spratling to help with the architectural details of his house in Cuernavaca. American movie stars were frequent guests at Spratling's home; once, he even designed furniture for Marilyn Monroe.

When his business failed in 1946, relief came in the form of an offer from the U. S. Department of the Interior: Spratling was asked to create a program of native crafts for Alaska. This work influenced his later designs. Although he never regained the wealth he once had, he operated the workshop at his ranch and trained apprentices until he died in a car accident in 1969. A friend, Italian engineer Alberto Ulrich, took over the business and replicated Spratling's designs using his original molds. Ulrich died in 2002, and his children now operate the business.

Spratling bequeathed his huge collection of pre-Hispanic art and artifacts to the people of Taxco, and they're now displayed in a museum carrying his name. The grateful citizens also named a street after their much-beloved benefactor and put a bust of him in a small plaza off the main square.

huitlacoche (corn fungus, a pre-Hispanic delicacy that is counterintuitively delicious). The daily three-course, fixed-price meal is $27.50. For breakfast try the home-baked sweet rolls and marmalade from the fruit of nearby trees. ✉ *Posada de la Misión, Cerro de la Misión 32* ☎ *762/622–0063* ▭ *AE, MC, V.*

¢–$$ MEXICAN ★ ✕ **Hostería el Adobe.** This intimate place has excellent food and hanging lamps and masks. There are meat and fish dishes, but the favorites are garlic-and-egg soup and the *queso adobe,* fried cheese on a bed of

13

potato skins, covered with a green tomatillo sauce. ✉ *Plazuela de San Juan 13* ☎ *762/622–1416* ▭ *MC, V.*

$–$$ MEXICAN Fodor'sChoice ★ ✕ **La Parroquia.** The balcony at this pleasant café has an outstanding view of the plaza and cathedral. Enjoy a too-much-tequila cure—the $4 Mexican breakfast of *huevos parroquia*—and watch the town come to life. Or come in for a beer as the sun sets over the zócalo. ✉ *Plaza Borda* ☎ *762/622–3096* ▭ *MC, V.*

¢–$ MEXICAN ✕ **Santa Fe.** Mexican family-type cooking at its best is served in this simple restaurant a few blocks from the main square. Puebla-style mole, Cornish hen in garlic butter, and enchiladas in green or red chili sauce are among the offerings. There's a daily *comida corrida* (fixed-price) meal for $7. ✉ *Calle Hidalgo 2* ☎ *762/622–1170* ▭ *No credit cards.*

WHERE TO STAY

$$ **Hotel de la Borda.** It may be a bit worn, but the Borda is still a favorite with tour groups, and the staff couldn't be more hospitable. Ask for a room overlooking town or the suite that John and Jackie Kennedy occupied during their honeymoon in Mexico. **Pros:** view overlooking the Santa Prisca Cathedral. **Cons:** needs refurbishing. ✉ *Cerro del Pedregal 2* *AP 6 40200* ☎ *762/622–0025* 🌐 *www.taxcohotel.com* *110 rooms, 3 suites* *In-hotel: restaurant, room service, bar, pool, laundry service, parking (free), no-smoking rooms* ▭ *AE, MC, V.*

$ **Hotel Emilia Castillo.** Rooms at this straightforward hotel are simple but with carved-wood furniture and Mexican artwork that was clearly chosen with care. The brick-and-stone lobby has warm red-tile floors, cheerful murals, and its own silver shop. With a restaurant just outside the front door and attentive and friendly service, this lodging is as practical as it is an excellent value. **Pros:** appealing decor; intimate feeling. **Cons:** smallish rooms; overall quite compact; rooms near street can be noisy. ✉ *Juan Ruíz de Alarcón 7* ☎ *762/622–1396* 🌐 *www.hotelemiliacastillo.com* *14 rooms* *In-room: no phone. In-hotel: no-smoking rooms* ▭ *DC, MC, V.*

$ Fodor'sChoice ★ **Hotel Los Arcos.** This 1620 converted monastery is an island of historic tranquillity. Simple, ample-size rooms furnished with colonial hand-carved furniture provide a comfortable stay just a block from the plaza. The hotel doesn't have a restaurant or gift shop, but given its central location they aren't needed. **Pros:** lovely courtyard; intriguing history. **Cons:** no breakfast; rooms on the street can be noisy. ✉ *Juan Ruíz de Alarcón 4* ☎ *762/622–1836* 🌐 *www.hotellosarcos.net* *21 rooms* *In-room: no a/c, no phone. In-hotel: no-smoking rooms* ▭ *No credit cards.*

$–$$ **Hotel Victoria.** With its colonial-style architecture, the Victoria is a perfect fit for this adorable town. Its simple rooms are appealing and freshly painted. Most have balconies with great views of town and the distant hills. Furniture in the common areas was designed by William Spratling. **Pros:** dreamy architecture. **Cons:** sections are in disrepair. ✉ *Calle Carlos J. Nibbi 5* *AP 83 40200* ☎ *762/622–0004* 🌐 *www.victoriataxco.com* *63 rooms, 5 suites* *In-hotel: restaurant, bar, pool, parking (paid), no-smoking rooms* ▭ *AE, MC, V.*

$$$–$$$$ **Monte Taxco.** A colonial style predominates at this full-service hotel, which has a knockout view, a funicular, three restaurants, and a disco;

it's the fanciest hotel in Taxco. There are also rooms equipped for guests with disabilities. **Pros:** funicular is an amazing way to arrive at your digs. **Cons:** a few miles up a mountain from town, so plan to take taxis to get back and forth. ✉ *Lomas de Taxco* 📭 *AP 84 40210* ☎ *762/622–1300* 🌐 *www.montetaxco.com.mx* *153 rooms, 6 suites, 32 villas* *In-hotel: 3 restaurants, golf course, tennis courts, pools, gym, laundry service, parking (free), no-smoking rooms* 💳 *AE, MC, V.*

$$–$$$★ **Posada de la Misión.** Laid out like a colonial-style village, this hotel has well-kept doubles with beamed ceilings and two-bedroom suites; some come with fireplaces and terraces as well. The pool area has a mural by noted Mexican artist Juan O'Gorman, and there's a silver workshop and boutique that sells Spratling-designed silver jewelry. **Pros:** marvelous view; interesting architecture. **Cons:** too pricey for what you get; not kept up well. ✉ *Cerro de la Misión 32* 📭 *AP 88 40230* ☎ *762/622–0063* 🌐 *www.posadamision.com* *120 rooms, 30 suites* *In-room: no a/c, kitchen (some). In-hotel: restaurant, bar, pool, parking (paid), no-smoking rooms* 💳 *AE, MC, V* *MAP.*

¢–$$ **Posada San Javier.** The secluded San Javier sprawls haphazardly around a junglelike garden with a pool and a wishing well. In addition to guest rooms, there are seven one-bedroom apartments with living rooms and kitchenettes; however, these are often filled by visiting wholesale silver buyers. **Pros:** breakfast included, professionally run. **Cons:** no elevator. ✉ *Calle Estacadas 32* ☎ *762/622–3177* *posadasanjavier@hotmail.com* *18 rooms, 7 apartments* *In-room: kitchen (some). In-hotel: restaurant, room service, bar, pool, parking (free)* 💳 *MC, V.*

NIGHTLIFE

Acerto. This traditional favorite, also called Bar Paco, is a great place to meet fellow travelers. ✉ *Plaza Borda 12* ☎ *762/622–0064.*

Bertha's. At Taxco's oldest bar, a tequila, lime, and club soda concoction called a Bertha is the specialty. Watch out for Taxco's high curbs and ankle-turning cobblestones after a few Berthas. You can also sample local mescal here. ✉ *Plaza Borda 9* ☎ *762/622–0172.*

Windows. Much of Taxco's weekend nighttime activity is at the Monte Taxco hotel's discotheque. On Saturday night the hotel has a buffet and a fireworks display. ✉ *Lomas de Taxco* ☎ *762/622–1300.*

SHOPPING

Sidewalk vendors sell lacquered gourds and boxes from the town of Olinalá as well as masks, baskets, bark paintings, and other handicrafts. Sunday is market day, which means artisans from surrounding villages descend on the town, as do visitors from Mexico City.

Most people come to Taxco with silver in mind. Three types are available: sterling, which is always stamped 0.925 (925 parts in 1,000) and is the most expensive; plated silver; and the inexpensive *alpaca,* which is also known as German or nickel silver. Sterling pieces are usually priced by weight according to world silver prices. Fine workmanship will add to the cost. Bangles start at $4, and bracelets and necklaces cost $10 to $200 and higher.

Many of the more than 600 silver shops carry identical merchandise; a few are noted for their creativity. William Spratling, Andrés Mejía, and Emilia Castillo, daughter of renowned silversmith Antonio Castillo, are among the famous names. Designs range from traditional bulky necklaces (often inlaid with turquoise and other semiprecious stones) to streamlined bangles and chunky earrings.

CRAFTS

D'Elsa. Owned by Elsa Ruíz de Figueroa, This shop carries a selection of native-inspired clothing for women and a well-chosen selection of crafts ✉ *Plazuela de San Juan 13* ☎ *762/622–1683.*

La Tienda del Taller. You'll find a creativity running through the designs and unique pieces at this little shop. Necklaces and bracelets incorporate pieces of Mexican tile and miniature kitchen utensils like *mutates* (grinding stones) and *molinillos* (whisks for chocolate). In addition to jewelry and crafts, the shop carries bottles of local mescal and perfectly spiced *sal de jumil,* seasoning salt made from a local insect. Above the shop there's a small school. You can sign up for a class at the Escuela de la Platería Maestros de Taxco (Taxco Master's Silversmithing School), where some of Taxco's most experienced silversmiths teach jewelry making. ✉ *Calle Palma 2* ☎ *762/622–4320.*

SILVER

Fodor's Choice ★ **Emilia Castillo.** One of Taxco's most exciting silver shops is renowned for innovative designs and for combining silver with porcelain. ✉ *Juan Ruíz de Alarcón 7, in Hotel Emilia Castilla* ☎ *762/622–6716* 🌐 *www.emiliacastillojewelry.com.*

Galería de Arte en Plata Andrés. The stunning pieces sold here are created by the talented Andrés Mejía. He showcases his own designs and those of such promising young designers as Priscilla Canales, Susana Sanborn, Francisco Diaz, and Daniel Espinosa, whose jewelry has been loved by many a celebrity. ✉ *Av. de los Plateros 113A, near Posada de la Misión* ☎ *762/622–3778* 🌐 *www.andresartinsilver.com.mx.*

★ **Spratling Ranch.** This is where the heirs of William Spratling turn out designs using his original molds. You can shop only by appointment. ✉ *South of town on Carretera Taxco–Iguala, Km 177* ☎ *762/622–6108.*

Talleres de los Ballesteros. Expect a large collection of well-crafted silver jewelry and serving pieces. ✉ *Av. de los Plateros 68* ☎ *762/622–1076* 🌐 *www.ballesteros.net.*

Cancún and Isla Mujeres

Chac Mool, Cancún

WORD OF MOUTH

"Cancún is safe, but . . . use common sense. The bus system is easy, cheap and convenient. Walking is good also. We did the bar-hopping tour which ended at about 2 AM and we just walked back to our hotel. No problem. Please do not hibernate at your hotel. Get out, do some sightseeing, and check out some local bars/restaurants. If you don't, you're going to miss a lot."

—KVR

www.fodors.com/community

WELCOME TO CANCÚN AND ISLA MUJERES

TOP REASONS TO GO

★ **Dancing the night away:** Salsa, cumbia, reggae, mariachi, hip-hop, and electronic music dizzy the air of the Zona Hotelera's many nightclubs.

★ **Exploring the nearby Mayan ruins:** Trips to remarkable sites like Tulum, Cobá, and Chichén Itzá can easily be accomplished in a day.

★ **Getting wild on the water:** Rent Jet Skis, a Windsurfer, or a kayak and skim across the sea or Laguna Nichupté, or dive the caverns off Isla Mujeres to see "sleeping" sharks.

★ **Browsing for Mexican crafts:** The colorful stalls of Mercado Veintiocho will certainly hold something that catches your eye.

1 El Centro. More than 500,000 permanent residents live in Cancún's mainland commercial center; shops and cafés cater mainly to locals. Most hotels here are small and family-operated.

2 The Zona Hotelera Norte. Punta Sam, aka the Northern Hotel Zone, north of Puerto Juárez, is quieter than the main Zona, with smaller hotels and restaurants.

3 The Zona Hotelera. The Hotel Zone barrier island is Cancún's tourist heart, with huge luxury resorts, restaurants, nightclubs, malls, and golf courses—all just a stone's throw from the gorgeous white-sand beach.

4 Playa Norte. Waist-deep turquoise waters and wide soft sands make Isla Mujeres' most northerly beach its most beautiful one. Most of the island's hotels are here, just a short walk from El Pueblo.

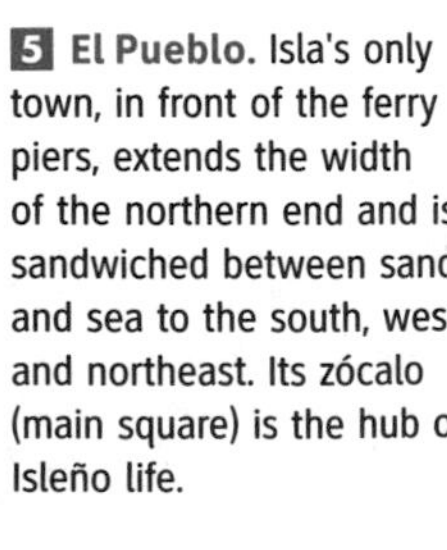

5 El Pueblo. Isla's only town, in front of the ferry piers, extends the width of the northern end and is sandwiched between sand and sea to the south, west, and northeast. Its zócalo (main square) is the hub of Isleño life.

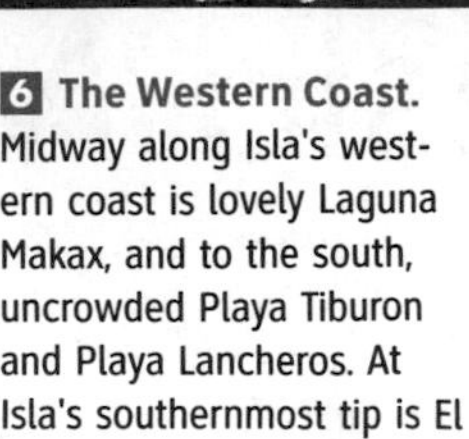

6 The Western Coast. Midway along Isla's western coast is lovely Laguna Makax, and to the south, uncrowded Playa Tiburon and Playa Lancheros. At Isla's southernmost tip is El Garrafón National Park.

GETTING ORIENTED

Cancún consists of the Zona Hotelera, a 22½-km (14-mi) barrier island with the Caribbean to the east and lagoons to the west, and El Centro, 4 km (2½ mi) west on the mainland. Sleepy Isla Mujeres is just 8 km (5 mi) long and 1 km (½ mi) wide, with flat sandy beaches in the north and steep rocky bluffs to the south.

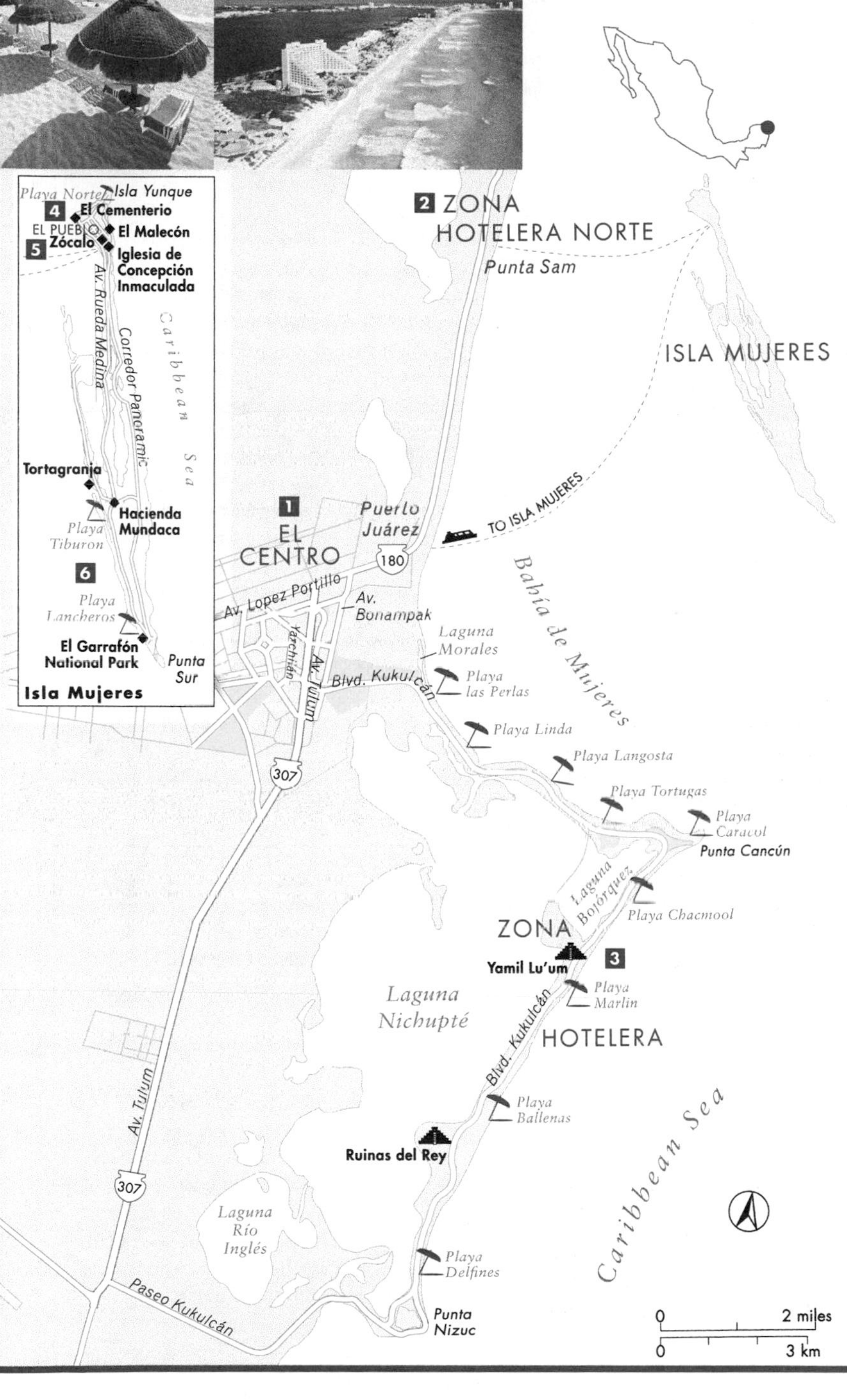
Playa Norte
Isla Yunque
4 El Cementerio
EL PUEBLO
El Malecón
5 Zócalo
Iglesia de Concepción Inmaculada
Av. Rueda Medina
Corredor Panoramic
Caribbean Sea
Tortagranja
Hacienda Mundaca
Playa Tiburon
6
Playa Lancheros
El Garrafón National Park
Punta Sur
Isla Mujeres
2 ZONA HOTELERA NORTE
Punta Sam
ISLA MUJERES
TO ISLA MUJERES
1 EL CENTRO
Puerto Juárez
180
Av. Lopez Portillo
Av. Bonampak
Yaxchilán
Av. Tulum
Blvd. Kukulcán
Bahía de Mujeres
Laguna Morales
Playa las Perlas
Playa Linda
Playa Langosta
Playa Tortugas
Playa Caracol
Punta Cancún
307
Laguna Bojórquez
Playa Chacmool
ZONA HOTELERA
3
Yamil Lu'um
Playa Marlin
Laguna Nichupté
Blvd. Kukulcán
Playa Ballenas
Ruinas del Rey
Caribbean Sea
Av. Tulum
307
Laguna Río Inglés
Playa Delfines
Paseo Kukulcán
Punta Nizuc
0
2 miles
0
3 km

14

CANCÚN AND ISLA MUJERES PLANNER

When to Go, How Long to Stay

There's a lot to see and do in Cancún and Isla Mujeres, though many visitors are happy to spend a week on the beach or at a resort. If you're game for exploring, allow an extra two or three days for day trips to nearby eco-parks and Mayan ruins like Tulum, Cobá, or even Chichén Itzá.

High season starts at the end of November and lasts until April. Between December 15 and January 5 hotel prices are highest—often as much as 30%–50% above regular rates. To visit during Christmas, spring break, or Easter, book at least three months in advance.

Safety

There have been reports of travelers being victimized after imbibing drinks that have been drugged in Cancún nightclubs. Never drink alone with strangers. Don't leave your drink unattended. Avoid driving on desolate streets, and don't travel at night, pick up hitchhikers, or hitchhike yourself.

Getting to Isla

The only way to get to Isla is by ferry from Puerto Juárez on the mainland, just north of Cancún. The trip lasts 30 minutes or less. Buy your ticket on board the boat; the people you see selling them on the docks aren't official ticket sellers, and will charge you more.

On Mexico Time

Mexicans are far more relaxed about time than their counterparts north of the border. Although *mañana* translates as "tomorrow," it is often used to explain why something is not getting done or not ready. In this context, mañana means, "Relax—it'll get taken care of eventually." If you make a date for 9, don't be surprised if everyone else shows up at 9:30. The trick to enjoying life on Mexican time is: don't rush. And be sure to take advantage of the siesta hour between 1 PM and 4 PM. How else are you going to stay up late dancing?

Tour Options

The companies listed here can book tours and arrange for plane tickets and hotel reservations. For more information about specific tour options and details, *see* "Tour Options" in Cancún Essentials *and* Isla Mujeres Essentials.

Intermar Caribe (✉ Av. Tulum 290, at Blvd. Pioneros, Sm 8 ☎ 998/881–0000 ⊕ www.travel2mexico.com) offers local tours such as snorkeling at Xel-ha, shopping on Isla Mujeres, or exploring the ruins at Chichén Itzá.

Mayaland Tours (✉ Av. Robalo 30, Sm 3 ☎ 998/887–2450) runs tours to Mérida, the Uxmal ruins, and the flamingo park at Celestún. Self-guided tours to local ruins such as Tulum and Cobá can also be arranged.

Olympus Tours (✉ Av. Yaxchilán, Lote 13, Sm 17, Mza 2 ☎ 998/881–9030 ⊕ www.olympustours.com) specializes in tours around Cancún, and can book you reservations to Xcaret, Xel-ha, and other local adventure parks.

Booking Your Hotel Online

A growing number of Cancún hotels are encouraging people to make their reservations online. Some allow you to book rooms right on their own Web sites, but even hotels without their own sites usually offer reservations via online booking agencies, such as www.docancun.com, www.cancuntoday.net, and www.travel-center.com. Since hotels customarily work with several different agencies, it's a good idea to shop around online for the best rates before booking with one of them.

Besides being convenient, booking online can often get you a 10%–20% discount on room rates. There are occasional breakdowns in communication, however, between booking agencies and hotels. You may arrive at your hotel to discover that your Spanish-speaking front desk clerk has no record of your Internet reservation, or has reserved a room that's different from the one you specified. To prevent such mishaps, print out copies of all your Internet transactions, including receipts and confirmations, and bring them with you.

Need More Information?

The **Cancún Visitors and Convention Bureau (CVB)** (✉ Blvd. Kukulcán, Km 9, Zona Hotelera ☎ 998/881–2745 🌐 www.cancun.info) has lots of information about area accommodations, restaurants, and attractions.

The **Cancún Travel Agency Association (AMAV)** (✉ Plaza Mexico, Av. Tulum 200, Sm 4, El Centro ☎ 998/887–1670) can refer you to local travel agents who'll help plan your visit to Cancún.

The **Isla Mujeres tourist office** (✉ Av. Rueda Medina 130 ☎ 998/877–0307 🌐 www.isla-mujeres.com.mx) is open weekdays 8–8 and weekends 8–noon, and has lots of general information about the island.

Dining and Lodging Prices

WHAT IT COSTS IN DOLLARS

	¢	$	$$	$$$	$$$$
Restaurants	under $5	$5–$10	$10–$15	$15–$25	over $25
Hotels	under $50	$50–$75	$75–$150	$150–$250	over $250

Restaurant prices are per person, for a main course at dinner, excluding tax and tip. Hotel prices are for a standard double room in high season.

When to Go

The sun shines an average of 253 days a year in Cancún. Isla and Cancún have nearly perfect weather between December and April, with daytime temperatures at around 29°C (84°F). May through September are much hotter and more humid; temperatures can reach upwards of 36°C (97°F). The rainy hurricane season starts mid-September and lasts until mid-November, bringing downpours in the afternoon, as well as the occasional hairy tropical storm such as Hurricane Wilma in October 2005.

Staying Awhile

There are several Internet-based rental agencies that can help you rent a home or apartment on Isla: www.islabeckons.com lists fully equipped properties (and also handles reservations for hotel rooms); www.morningsinmexico.com offers smaller and less expensive properties. Most rental homes have fully equipped kitchens, bathrooms, and bedrooms.

CANCÚN

Updated by Marlise Kast

CANCÚN IS A GREAT PLACE to experience 21st-century Mexico. There isn't much that's quaint or historic in this distinctly modern city, many of whose residents have embraced the accoutrements of urban middle-class life—cell phones, cable TV—that are found all over the world.

Most locals live on the mainland, in the part of the city known as El Centro, and work in the posh Zona Hotelera. Boulevard Kukulcán is the main drag in the Zona Hotelera. Kilometer markers alongside Boulevard Kukulcán indicate where you are, starting from Km 1 near El Centro to Km 20 at the southern tip of Punta Nizuc. The area in between consists entirely of hotels, restaurants, shopping complexes, marinas, and time-share condominiums. Most travelers are based within this 20 km stretch of paradise, unless the charm of El Centro's city life trumps the beach.

The party atmosphere of Zone Hotelera has inevitably earned it the title Spring Break Capital of the World. Catering to college students are dozens of bars and nightclubs just south of Punta Cancún at Km 9. Fortunately, this late-night/early-morning scene is contained within a small area, far from the larger resorts. Although Cancún is a magnet for youth on the loose, families are drawn to the island for the limitless water sports, pristine beaches, and children's activities, including theme parks, live entertainment, and dolphin programs.

For authentic Mexican food at some of the best hole-in-the-wall cantinas, travel west of Avenida Tulum (El Centro's main street) to Yaxchilán. The more upscale area of El Centro is east of Tulum to Avenida Bonampak. Although El Centro is less visited by travelers than Zona Hotelera, the downtown area holds cultural gems that will remind you that you really are in Mexico.

GETTING HERE AND AROUND

The Aeropuerto Internacional Cancún is 16 km (9 mi) southwest of the heart of Cancún and 10 km (6 mi) from the Zona Hotelera's southernmost point. While there are direct flights from some major U.S. cities, most flights transfer in Mexico City.

To get to or from the airport, you can take taxis or *colectivos* (vans). Taxi rides within the Zona Hotelera cost $6 to $10; between the Zona Hotelera and El Centro they run $8 and up; and to the ferries at Punta Sam or Puerto Juárez, fares are $15 to $20 or more. *Autobuses del Oriente,* or ADO, is one of the oldest bus lines in Mexico, and offers regular service to Puerto Morelos and Playa del Carmen every 15 minutes from 4 AM until midnight. Tickets, available outside Terminal 2 Baggage Claim, are less than $10 one-way. Playa Express has express buses that leave from a small terminal across from the main bus station every 10 minutes for Puerto Morelos and Playa del Carmen. Mayab Bus Lines has first- and second-class buses leaving for destinations along the Riviera Maya every hour.

Cancún is not the sort of place you can get to know on foot, although there's a bicycle-walking path that starts downtown at the beginning of the Zona Hotelera and continues through to Punta Nizuc. The beginning of the path parallels a grassy strip of Boulevard Kukulcán decorated with reproductions of ancient Mexican art.

South of Punta Cancún, Boulevard Kukulcán becomes a busy road and is difficult for pedestrians to cross. It's also punctuated by steeply inclined driveways that turn into the hotels, most of which are set back at least 100 yards from the road. The lagoon side of the boulevard consists of scrubby stretches of land alternating with marinas, shopping centers, and restaurants. **■ TIP→ Because there are so few sights, there are no orientation tours of Cancún: just do the local bus circuit to get a feel for the island's layout. The buses run 24 hours a day, and you'll rarely have to wait more than five minutes.**

When you first visit El Centro, the downtown layout might not be self-evident. It's not based on a grid but rather on a circular pattern. The whole city is divided into districts called Super Manzanas (abbreviated Sm in this book), each with its own central square or park. In general, walks through downtown are somewhat unpleasant, with whizzing cars, corroding pathways, and overgrown weeds. Sidewalks disappear for brief moments, forcing pedestrians to cross grassy inlets and thin strips of land separating four lanes of traffic. Few people seem to know exactly where anything is, even the locals who live in El Centro. When exploring on foot, expect to get lost at least once and enjoy it—you may just find yourself stumbling upon a courtyard café or a lively cantina.

BUSES MADE EASY

In conjunction with the Cancún tourist board, Autocar and Publicar have published an excellent pocket guide called "TheMAP" that shows all the bus routes to points of interest in Cancún and the surrounding area. The map is free and is easiest to find at the airport. Some of the mid-range hotels carry copies, and if you're lucky, you may find one on a bus.

14

ESSENTIALS

Bus Contacts **Autobuses del Oriente (ADO)** (☎ *998/884–5542*). **Playa Express** (☎ *998/887–6782*). **Mayab Bus Lines** (☎ *998/884–5542*). **Terminal de Autobuses** (✉ *Avs. Tulum and Uxmal, Sm 23* ☎ *998/884–5542* 🌐 *www.ticketbus.com.mx*).

Currency Exchange **Banamex** (✉ *Av. Tulum 19, next to City Hall, Sm 5* ☎ *998/881–6403*). **Banorte** (✉ *Av. Tulum 21, Sm 2* ☎ *998/887–6815* ✉ *Plaza Flamingos, Blvd. Kukulcán, Km 11, Zona Hotelera* ☎ *998/883–1653*). **HSBC** (✉ *Plaza Caracol, Blvd. Kukulcán, Km 8.5, Zona Hotelera* ☎ *998/883–4652*).

Mail and Shipping **Correos (Post Office)** (✉ *Avs. Sunyaxchén and Xel-Há, Sm 26* ☎ *998/884–1418*). **DHL** (✉ *Av. Tulum 29, Sm 5* ☎ *998/892–8449*). **Federal Express** (✉ *Av. Tulum 31, Sm 23* ☎ *998/887–4003*). **Mas Mail Center Inc.** (✉ *Av. Xpuhil 3, behind Mercado 28, Sm 27* ☎ *998/887–4918*).

Medical Assistance **Hospital Amat (emergency hospital)** (✉ *Av. Náder 13, Sm 2* ☎ *998/887–4422*). **Hospital Americano** (✉ *Retorno Viento 15, Sm 4* ☎ *998/884–6133*). **Hospital de las Americas** (✉ *Avs. Bonampak and Nichupté, next to Plaza las Américas, Sm 7* ☎ *998/881–3400; 998/881–3434 for emergencies*). **Municipal Police** (☎ *998/884–1913*). **Red Cross** (✉ *Avs. Xcaret and*

Labná, Sm 21 ☎ *998/884-1616*). **Tourist Assistance Office** (☎ *998/884-8073*). **Green Angels (for highway breakdowns)** (☎ *078*).

Rental Cars Avis (✉ *Aeropuerto Internacional Benito Juárez, Zona Hotelera* ☎ *998/886-0221 or 0222* 🌐 *www.avis.com*).**Adocar Rental** (✉ *Plaza Nautilus, Blvd. Kukulcán, Km 3.5, Zona Hotelera* ☎ *998/849-4233* 🌐 *www.adocarrental.com*). **Buster Renta Car** (✉ *Hotel Holiday Inn Arenas, Blvd. Kukulcán, Km 2.5, Zona Hotelera* ☎ *998/882-2800* 🌐 *www.busterrentacar.com*). **Caribetur Rent a Car** (✉ *Plaza Tropical, Av. Tulum 192, Local 16, Sm 4* ☎ *998/880-9167 or 01800/821-8854* 🌐 *www.caribetur.com*). **Mónaco Rent a Car** (✉ *Av. Yaxchilán 65, Lote 5, Sm 25* ☎ *998/884-7843* 🌐 *www.monacorentacar.com*).

EXPLORING

The best way to explore Cancún is by hopping on one of the public buses that run between Zona Hotelera and El Centro. The cost is 75¢ no matter the distance you travel. Don't be alarmed if a man in a clown suit roams the aisle in search of money. At night the buses come alive with all sorts of amateur performers, from accordionists to jugglers, hoping to earn a few pesos.

TOP ATTRACTIONS

El Centro. Nearly two decades ago, downtown Cancún was the place to be after a day at the beach. The once-barren Hotel Zone had very limited dining options, so tourists strolled the active streets of Avenida Tulum, Xachilan, and Parque de las Palapas. With the emergence of luxury resorts and mass tourism, a major shift brought the focus back to the Hotel Zone. Today many tourists are unaware that the downtown area even exists, while others consider "downtown" to be the string of flea markets near the Convention Center. In reality, El Centro's malls and markets offer a glimpse of Mexico's urban lifestyle. Avenida Tulum, the main street, is marked by a huge sculpture of shells and starfish in the middle of a traffic circle. This iconic Cancún sculpture, which many locals refer to as "el ceviche," is particularly dramatic at night when the lights are turned on. El Centro is also home to many restaurants and bars, as well as **Mercado Veintiocho** (Market 28)—an enormous crafts market just off avenidas Yaxchilán and Sunyaxchén. For bargain shopping, hit the stores and small strip malls along Avenida Tulum. While the Hotel Zone becomes increasingly dense and overcrowded, El Centro is booming with the development of Puerto Cancún. Construction of this downtown subset has been carefully designed to focus on the resident rather than the tourist. Shopping centers, marinas, golf courses, and over 2,500 condos are taking shape, making El Centro's bustling Avenida Bonampak the next Boulevard Kukulcán.

Ruinas del Rey. Large signs on the Zona Hotelera's lagoon side, roughly opposite Playa Delfines, point out the small Ruins of the King. Although much smaller than famous archaeological sites like Tulum and Chichén Itzá, this site, commonly called El Rey, is worth a visit, and makes for an interesting juxtaposition of Mexico's past and present.

First entered into Western chronicles in a 16th-century travelogue, then sighted in 1842 by American explorer John Lloyd Stephens and his draftsman, Frederick Catherwood, the ruins were finally explored by archaeologists in 1910, though excavations didn't begin until 1954. In 1975 archaeologists, along with the Mexican government, began restoration work on the 47 structures.

Dating from the 3rd to 2nd century BC, El Rey is notable for having two main plazas bounded by two streets—most other Mayan cities contain only one plaza. The pyramid here is topped by a platform, and inside its vault are paintings on stucco. Skeletons interred both at the apex and at the base indicate that the site may have been a royal burial ground. Originally named Kin Ich Ahau Bonil, Mayan for "king of the solar countenance," the site was linked to astronomical practices in the ancient Mayan culture. In 2006 workmen unearthed an ancient Mayan skeleton on the outskirts of the park. ✉ *Blvd. Kukulcán, Km 17, Zona Hotelera* ☎ *998/849–2880* 🌐 *www.inahqr.gob.mx/elrey/elrey.htm* 🎫 *$3.50; free on Sun.* ⏲ *Daily 8–5.*

BEACHES

Beaches that are not used by hotels have seaweed on their shores. All beaches can be reached by public transportation; just let the driver know where you are headed.

For those with young children, it is best to head to the beaches facing Bahía de Mujeres at the top of the "7." They tend to be less crowded and more sheltered than beaches on the Caribbean side. Wide beaches and shallow waters make the northern tip ideal for those wanting to snorkel or swim. Forming the right side of the "7" are beaches facing the Caribbean Sea. Here riptides and currents can be somewhat dangerous, especially when the surf is high. For snorkeling, it is best to head to the southern end of Boulevard Kukulcán near the Westin Hotel.

Although it is generally reserved for water sports, swimming is also allowed in the saltwater lagoon. Keep in mind that motorized Jet Skis and speedboats rule the waters by day and approximately 25 adult crocodiles wade the banks by night.

The beaches listed here are organized by location, beginning on the northwest side of the "7" facing Bahia de Mujeres, and continuing down along the Caribbean side toward Punta Nizuc.

■ TIP→ Don't swim when the red or black danger flags fly; yellow flags indicate that you should proceed with caution, and green or blue flags mean the waters are calm.

Playa las Perlas (Pearl Beach) is the first beach on the drive heading east from El Centro along Boulevard Kukulcán. Located at Km 2.5, between Cancún mainland and the bridge, it's a relatively small beach on the protected waters of the Bahía de Mujeres, and is popular with locals. There are several restaurants lining the beach; however, most of the water-sports activities are available only to those staying at the nearby resorts, such as Imperial las Perlas, Holiday Inn Cancun Arenas, or the Blue Bay Getaway. **Best For:** families with small children, accessibility to Isla Mujeres, swimming. **Amenities:** food concessions, lifeguard (in front of Holiday Inn Cancún).

At Km 4 on Boulevard Kukulcán, **Playa Linda** (Pretty Beach) is where the ocean meets the freshwater of Laguna Nichupté to create the Nichupté Channel. Restaurants and changing rooms are available near the Playa Linda launching dock. There's lots of boat activity along the channel, and the ferry to Isla Mujeres leaves from the adjoining Embarcadero marina, so the area isn't safe for swimming—although it's a great place to people-watch, and there's a 300-foot rotating scenic tower nearby that offers a 360-degree view. **Best For:** boating, people-watching, trips to Isla Mujers. **Amenities:** parking, restaurants, toilets (all located at El Embarcadero).

Small, placid **Playa Langosta** (Lobster Beach), which has an entrance at Boulevard Kukulcán's Km 5, has calm waters that make it an excellent place for a swim. There is a dock (mainly used by Dolphin Discovery) that juts out in the middle of the water, but swimming areas are marked off with ropes and buoys. The safe waters and gentle waves make this a popular beach with families as well as Spring Breakers. Next to the beach is a small building with a restaurant, an ice-cream shop, and an ATM. **Best For:** families with small children, swimming. **Amenities:** food concessions, ATM.

The calm surf and relaxing shallows of **Playa Pez Volador** make it an aquatic playground for families with young children. Marked by a huge Mexican flag at Km 5.5, the wide beach is popular with locals, as many tourists tend to head to the more active Playa Langosta. Occasionally sea grass washes ashore here, but by early morning it has already been cleared away by the staff of the neighboring Casa Maya Hotel. **Best For:** swimming, sunbathing. **Amenities:** none.

Playa Tortugas (Turtle Beach), eroded greatly after Hurricane Wilma. There's now a restored sand bank at the entrance located around Km 6.5 (next to Fat Tuesday) on Boulevard Kukulcán. The water is deep and the swimming is excellent; many people come here to sail, snorkel, kayak, paraglide, and use Wave Runners. The nicest section of this beach is on the far right, just past the rocks. Don't be fooled by the name—this spot is seldom frequented by *tortugas* (turtles). **Best For:** snorkeling, sailing, singles scene. **Amenities:** restaurants, toilets at Fat Tuesday's.

Playa Caracol (Snail Beach), the last "real" beach along the east–west stretch of the Zona Hotelera, is near Plaza Caracol and the Xcaret dock. Located at Km 8.5, the whole area has been eaten up by development—in particular the high-rise condominium complex next to the entrance. This beach is also hindered by the rocks that jut out from the water marking the beginning of Punta Cancún, where Boulevard Kukulcán turns south. There are several hotels along here and a few sports rental outfits. This is also the launching point for trips to Contoy Island. **Best For:** water sports, proximity to Contoy Island, sunbathing. **Amenities:** none.

At Km 10 on Boulevard Kukulcán, **Playa Chacmool** can be accessed through the beach entrance directly across the street from Señor Frog's. As at Playa Caracol, development has greatly encroached on Chacmool's shores. There are a lot of rocks, but the water is a stunning shade of turquoise and the beach is close to shopping centers and the party zone, so there are plenty of restaurants nearby. The short strand to the south has gentler waters and fewer rocks. Changing rooms are also available to the public. The shallow clear water makes it tempting to walk far out into the ocean, but be careful—there's a strong current and undertow. **Best For:** singles scene, proximity to shops and restaurants, color of the water. **Amenities:** restaurants, water-sport rentals on the west side of the beach, toilets, changing rooms.

Playa Marlin (Marlin Beach), at Km 13 along Boulevard Kukulcán, is a seductive beach in the heart of the Zona Hotelera, accessible via a road next to Kukulcán Plaza. Despite its turquoise waters and silky sands, the waves are strong and the currents are dangerous. If this beach is crowded, you can walk in either direction to find quieter spots. Sun umbrellas and beach chairs are available for $5 per day. There is also a small tent where one can rent Boogie boards, snorkel equipment, and motorized sports equipment. Although there are currently no public facilities, you can always walk over to Kukulcán Plaza if you need a restroom. **Best For:** Boogie boarding, Jet-Skiing, amenities. **Amenities:** beach umbrellas, chaise lounges, restrooms at Kukulcán Plaza.

14

Playa Ballenas (Whale Beach) is located at Km 14.5, between Le Meridien Cancún Resort & Spa and Cancún Palace. This stretch of sand and crystal-clear water between the two hotels is open to the public. There are often Jet-Skiiers zooming through the water here, and the strong wind makes the surf rough. Parking and beach access are available at Calle Ballenas. **Best For:** banana-boat rides, parasailing, Jet-Skiing. **Amenities:** parking at Calle Ballenas, water-sport rental.

Located near Ruinas del Rey at Km 18, where Boulevard Kukulcán curves into a hill, **Playa Delfines** (Dolphin Beach) is one of the last beaches before Punta Nizuc. Hotels have yet to dominate this small section of coastline, and there's an incredible lookout over the ocean; on a clear day you can see at least four shades of blue in the water, though swimming is treacherous unless one of the green flags is posted. Devoid of resorts, this area has plenty of sand and surfers. It's one of the few places in Cancún where you can take surfing lessons. Although decent waves roll in during hurricane season, seldom do they hit "epic" status. At best, you might find choppy, inconsistent surf at Playa Delfines, Playa Chacmool, and City Beach. Those seeking more than just a ripple should avoid the placid northern beaches, where Isla Mujeres lies just offshore. **Best For:** surfing, playing in the waves, flying a kite, isolation from resorts. **Amenities:** parking on Boulvard Kukulcán directly in front of the beach.

WHERE TO EAT

ZONA HOTELERA

$$$–$$$$ ITALIAN ✕ **Cenacolo**. Reliably good pizza and pasta, handmade in full view of patrons, have made this fine Italian restaurant a favorite. Appetizers include beef or octopus carpaccio that practically melts in your mouth and a light calamari. There are over fifteen pasta dishes to choose from, including the delicious lobster ravioli filled with ricotta cheese and served in a white-wine sauce. One of the restaurant's best features is

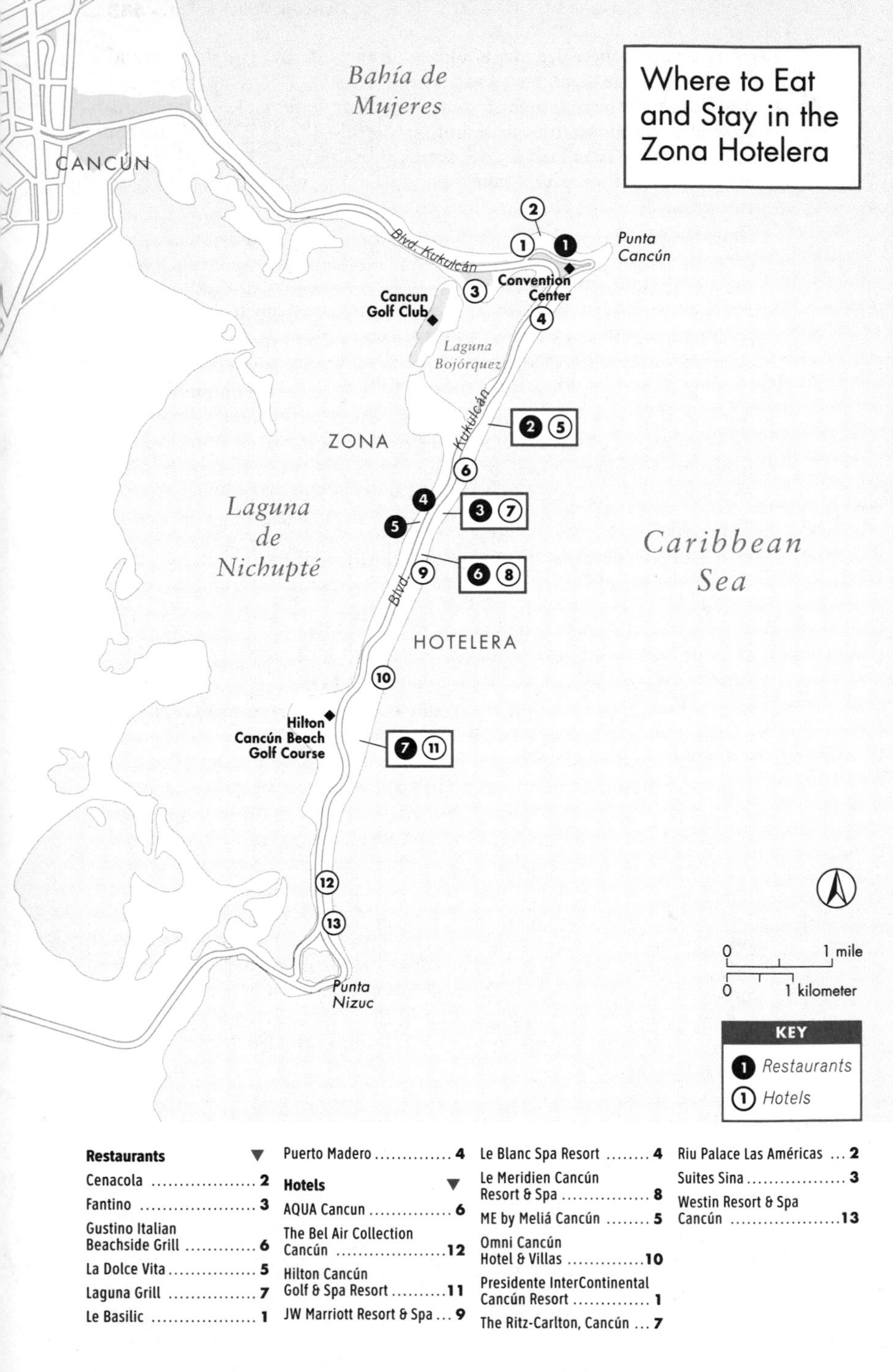
Where to Eat and Stay in the Zona Hotelera
Bahía de Mujeres
CANCÚN
Blvd. Kukulcán
Punta Cancún
Convention Center
Cancun Golf Club
Laguna Bojórquez
Kukulcán
ZONA
Laguna de Nichupté
Caribbean Sea
Blvd.
HOTELERA
Hilton Cancún Beach Golf Course
Punta Nizuc
0 1 mile
0 1 kilometer
KEY
Restaurants
Hotels
Restaurants
Cenacola 2
Fantino 3
Gustino Italian Beachside Grill 6
La Dolce Vita 5
Laguna Grill 7
Le Basilic 1
Puerto Madero 4
Hotels
AQUA Cancun 6
The Bel Air Collection Cancún 12
Hilton Cancún Golf & Spa Resort 11
JW Marriott Resort & Spa 9
Le Blanc Spa Resort 4
Le Meridien Cancún Resort & Spa 8
ME by Meliá Cancún 5
Omni Cancún Hotel & Villas 10
Presidente InterContinental Cancún Resort 1
The Ritz-Carlton, Cancún 7
Riu Palace Las Américas 2
Suites Sina 3
Westin Resort & Spa Cancún 13

its extensive wine cellar. Although it's inside a mall, the restaurant's main dining room is elegant, with stained-glass panels on the ceiling and live piano music. ✉ *Kukulcán Plaza, Blvd. Kukulcán, Km 13, Zona Hotelera* ☎ *998/885–3603* 🌐 *www.cenacolo.com.mx* 💳 *AE, MC, V.*

WORD OF MOUTH

"La Dolce Vita is excellent! A seafood Italian restaurant. They have great fresh seafood. They have this dish where they bake fish (snapper, I think) inside a puff pastry. It is to die for!" —egreen

$$$$ MEDITERRANEAN Fodor's Choice ★

✕ **Fantino.** Reflecting Mexico's rich Spanish heritage, this Mediterranean restaurant lives up to its reputation as one of the country's finest. Grandeur is at its peak in this ballroom setting, with long-stemmed roses and hand-painted ceiling frescoes that subtly match the fine English china. Each guest, referred to by name, is treated to the melodious sounds of live piano music. Velvet walls mounted with candelabras are only overshadowed by the red-satin curtains and ocean views. Each course is paired with its own wine, individually selected by Chef Andreas Schatzschneider. Designed to play with the senses, his appetizers moisten the palate in preparation for the seven-course tasting menu. Divine dishes include watermelon salad with buffalo mozzarella, sautéed foie gras with berries, and herb-crusted lamb with bell peppers and kalamata olive sauce. All ingredients are hand selected from local farms or air-freighted to the hotel. Just when you think you've seen it all, the waiter wheels over a candy cart, featuring 10 glass towers of handmade sweets. Reservations recommended. ✉ *Ritz-Carlton Cancún, Blvd. Kukulcán, Km 13.5, Zona Hotelera* ☎ *998/881–0822* 💳 *AE, D, DC, MC, V* ⊙ *Closed Sun. No lunch.*

$$$–$$$$ ITALIAN

✕ **Gustino Italian Beachside Grill.** From the moment you walk down the dramatic staircase to enter this restaurant, you know you're in for a memorable dining experience. The circular dining room has artistic lighting and views of the wine cellar and open-air kitchen. The *gamberetti al aglio* (sautéed shrimp with garlic) appetizer is a standout, as are the tagliatelle in truffle sauce and seafood risotto entrées. The service here is impeccable; the saxophone music adds a dash of romance. A private dinning area can hold up to 14 guests. ✉ *JW Marriott Resort, Blvd. Kukulcán, Km 14.5, Zona Hotelera* ☎ *998/848–9600 Ext. 6849 or 6851* ✍ *Reservations essential* 💳 *AE, MC, V* ⊙ *No lunch.*

$$$–$$$$ ITALIAN

✕ **La Dolce Vita.** This grande dame of Cancún restaurants delivers on the promise of its name (which means "the sweet life" in Italian). Whether you dine indoors or on the terrace overlooking the lagoon, the candlelit tables adorned with fine linen and china and discreet waiters will make you feel as if you've been transported to Italy. The Italian fare includes homemade pizzas and pastas such as bolognese-style lasagna, veal ravioli, and calamari steak in shrimp and lobster sauce. The wine list is excellent, and the truffle is a must for chocolate lovers. Be patient when waiting for your order, though—good food takes time to prepare. ✉ *Blvd. Kukulcán, Km 14.5, Zona Hotelera* ☎ *998/885–0161 or 998/885–0150* 🌐 *www.ladolcevitacancun.com* 💳 *AE, D, MC, V.*

$$$–$$$$ ECLECTIC

Laguna Grill. Intricate tile work adorns this restaurant's floors and walls, and a natural stream divides the open-air dining room, which overlooks the lagoon. Delectable menu options such as an Asian-inspired mojito shrimp entrée and fettuccini with lobster satays match the beautiful setting. The risotto, prepared with coconut milk and Thai curry, is sinfully creamy and mixed with vegetables, shrimp, chicken and beef. Grill favorites range from lamb and duck to chicken and beef. Their newly added vegetarian selections include organic soba pasta with teriyaki-sautéed vegetables. For dessert there's a Bailey's crème brûlée and coconut tempura ice cream with ginger and vanilla sauce. *Blvd. Kukulcán, Km 15.6, Zona Hotelera* *998/885–0267* *www.lagunagrill.com.mx* *AE, D, MC, V* *No lunch.*

$$$$ MEDITERRANEAN Fodor's Choice ★

Le Basilic. If heaven had a restaurant, this would be it. Arched bay windows, checkered marble floors, live classical music, and exquisite garden views create the backdrop for this ideal spot for couples. The 14 chestnut tables surround a sunken gazebo where long-stemmed orchids bloom under glass. The dishes here—created by French chef Henri Charvet—are served beneath silver domes by pleasant tuxedoed waiters. The menu changes every four months, but it is always comprised of French-Mediterranean cuisine, from fresh tuna and sea scallops to seared duck and roasted lamb. As a keepsake, guests are presented with a box of French truffles and elegant recipe cards recapping the bill of fare. The dress code is elegant, reservations are recommended, and children are not allowed. *Fiesta Americana Grand Coral Beach, Blvd. Kukulcán, Km 9.5, Zona Hotelera* *998/881–3200 Ext. 4220* *AE, D, DC, MC, V* *Closed Sun. No lunch.*

$$$–$$$$ STEAK Fodor's Choice ★

Puerto Madero. Modeled after the dock warehouses that have been converted into modern restaurants in the famed Argentine port city Puerto Madero, this steak and seafood house gets rave reviews from locals. It is the small touches—like fresh bread served in leather baskets, or martini reserves chilled in miniature ice buckets—that make this an unforgettable dining experience. The grilled octopus bathed in olive oil is exceptional, and the Big Rib Eye generously serves two people. The Alaskan halibut steak, also a crowd pleaser, is prepared with white wine, shallots, and fresh pepper. No matter what you order, be sure to request a side of *papas infladas,* inflated potatoes that crackle on your tongue. Adding to the cosmopolitan ambience is a fun-loving staff, most of whom have been there longer than 15 years. If the restaurant is too loud inside, ask for a table outside on the patio overlooking the lagoon. Reservations are recommended on weekends. *Blvd. Kukulcán, Km 14.1, Zona Hotelera* *998/885–2829* *www.puertomaderorestaurantes.com* *AE, MC, V, D.*

EL CENTRO

$$$ FRENCH

duMexique. Discreetly located on the bustling Avenida Bonampak, this hidden gem shows no resemblance to a restaurant. Chef Alain Grimond and his wife Sonya have converted their home into an intimate dinner-party setting to create a dining experience unlike any other. Doubling as a gallery, the dining room features modern art, a grand piano, and a crystal chandelier that casts spectrums of light onto the pristine ceiling. Accommodating only 20 guests per evening, the restaurant begins the ritual with martinis in the tropical garden, decorated with tiki torches, dark rattan furniture, glass lanterns, and micro-suede cushions. The French menu (featuring five appetizers, five entrées, and four desserts) changes daily and is never repeated. Selections might include duckling with risotto or entrecôte with wine sauce. By calling ahead, you can request soufflé *de huitlacoche,* a delicacy made from fungus that grows on cornstalks. A fusion for the eye and palate, each course is a masterpiece of presentation. Be sure to visit the kitchen, where the awards of master chef Grimond are on display. ⊠ *Av. Bonampak 109, Sm 3, El Centro* ☎ *998/884–5919* ✍ *Reservations essential* ▭ *MC, V* ⊗ *Closed Sun. No lunch.*

$ ITALIAN ✕ **El Principio.** Despite its rather simple decor, this small and rustic bistro restaurant, a lunch-hour favorite among Cancún execs, is arguably the best place in town for pasta. The owner, José Campos Frias, is a thirty-something cooking genius. His dishes fuse traditional Italian cuisine with his grandmother's Mexican recipes. The salmon and mango salad with cilantro dressing is a meal in itself. Those with hearty appetites should try the exotic oriental spaghetti or the meatball panini in chipotle sauce. The portions here are enormous (two people often share one entrée). There are only eight tables, so it gets crowded at times; takeout is also available. Lunch is served beginning at 1 PM. ⊠ *Ave. Bonampak 227, Sm 4, El Centro* ☎ *998/892–8499* ▭ *MC, V* ⊗ *Closed Mon.*

$$–$$$ ASIAN Fodor's Choice ★ ✕ **Iki Resto Bar.** Framing the town square of Parque de las Palapas, this chic, Zen-like utopia, from the owners of the renowned Laguna Grill, dares to go where few restaurants have gone before. The thatched temple beckons you into its velvet sanctuary, discreetly lit with beaded lamps, Buddha candles, and teardrop crystal globes. The main lounge features a glowing cobalt bar, antique Victorian furniture, and a wine wall complete with a sliding ladder. Slow-spinning palm fans twirl overhead while the sounds of chill music tie together this eclectic setting. Those seeking a bit more privacy can hide away in the Balinese cabaña, sinfully adorned with overstuffed pillows and bamboo flooring. Blending styles in both decor and cuisine, Iki showcases contemporary Asian-infused dishes like oriental potstickers and coconut cream soup, all with a pinch of Latin flavor. The shrimp siva wrap, rolled in spinach and topped with red curry, is deliciously exotic. The young, hip staff also serves sweet conclusions like chocolate cake with green-tea ice cream. ⊠ *Alcatraces 39, Sm 22, in front of Parque de las Palapas, El Centro* ☎ *998/884–7024* ✍ *Reservations essential* ▭ *AE, MC, V* ⊗ *Closed Sun. No lunch; open late.*

$$$–$$$$ ECLECTIC ★ ✕ **John Gray's Downtown.** This urban bistro, chef John Gray's fourth and newest eatery, brings a touch of New York into the heart of El Centro. Warehouse meets Zen in the informal yet sophisticated dining room, which has hardwood floors, exposed air ducts, dim light from dangling light bulbs, red velvet cushions, and a chicle tree enclosed in glass. Lack of detail on the chalkboard menu might deliver a pleasant surprise: the nondescript "duck" came on a bed of sweet potatoes, topped with chili, chipotle, and tequila sauce. The goat-cheese pizza and Portobello mushrooms are excellent starters—follow with swordfish in brandy and cream. You can watch the chefs at work in the open kitchen; there's

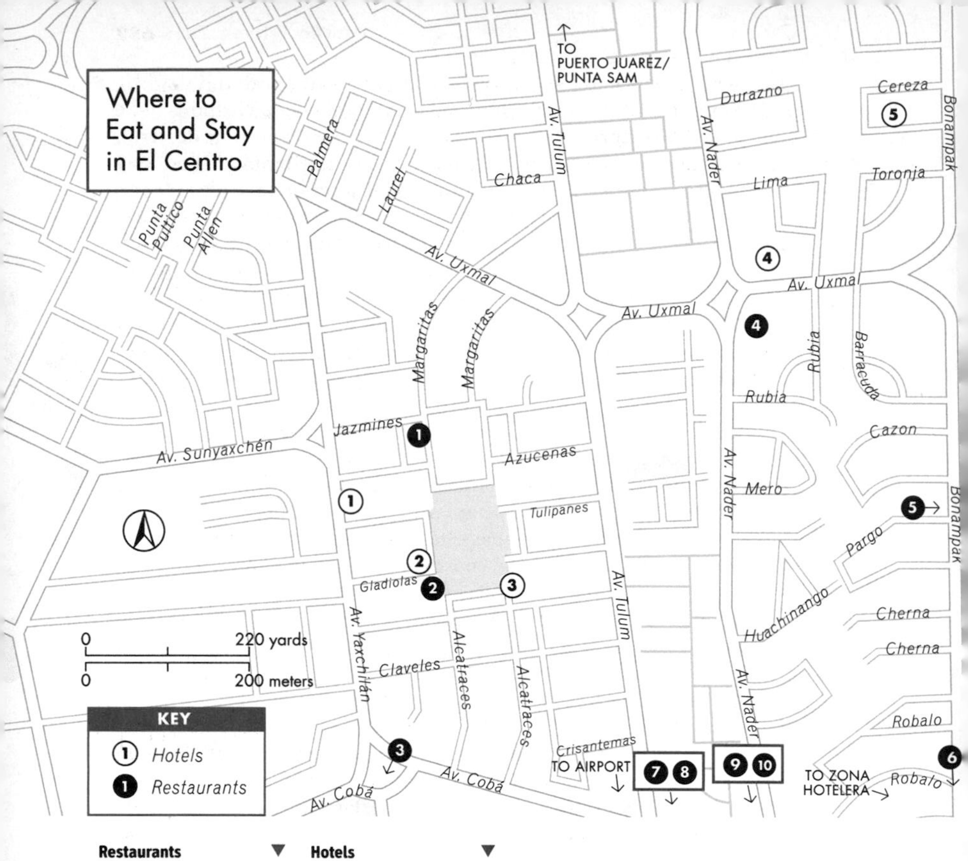

Restaurants ▼

duMexique 5
El Principio 6
Iki Resto Bar 2
John Gray's Downtown 7
La Guadalupana 9
La Habichuela 1
La Pasteleria-Crepería 3
La Troje 8
Rolandi's Pizzeria 10
Yamamoto 4

Hotels ▼

Cancún Inn El Patio 5
Hostel Chacmool 2
Hotel El Rey del Caribe 4
Hotel Sol Y Luna 3
Hotel Xbalamqué Resort & Spa 1

also a lounge area with chilled-out music and powerful martinis. ✉ *Av. Xpuhil, Sm 19, Mz 2, Lt 24, El Centro* ☎ *998/883–9800* ▭ *AE, MC, V* ⊗ *Closed Mon.*

$–$$ MEXICAN ✕ **La Guadalupana.** This lively cantina serves steak, fajitas, tacos, and other traditional Mexican dishes to an appreciative, if sometimes noisy, local crowd. Local favorites include cheese empanadas, grilled chilies, spicy shrimp, and of course cerveza. Those with brave appetites will want to try the *moronga*, sausage made from pig's blood. One wall is decorated with caricatures, mostly of political figures and famous bullfighters—very appropriate since it's on the bottom floor of Cancún's bullring. This is a good place to practice your Spanish. A mariachi band plays nightly at 6. ✉ *Av. Bonampak, Plaza de Toros, Sm 4, El Centro* ☎ *998/887–0660* ▭ *AE, MC, V* ⊗ *Closed Sun.*

14

$$$–$$$$ CARIBBEAN ★ ✕ **La Habichuela.** Elegant yet cozy, the much-loved Green Bean has an indoor dining room, as well as an outdoor area full of Mayan sculptures and local trees and flowers. Don't miss the famous *crema de habichuela* (a rich, cream-based seafood soup) or the *cocobichuela* (lobster and shrimp in a light curry sauce served inside a coconut). Seafood lovers will get their fix with Caribbean lobster tail or giant shrimp prepared ten different ways. The menu also features chicken, pasta, and shish kebab flambé. Finish off your meal with Xtabentun, a Mayan liqueur made with honey and anise. ✉ *Av. Margaritas 25, Sm 22, El Centro* ☎ *998/884–3158* 🌐 *www.lahabichuela.com* ▭ *AE, MC, V.*

$–$$ CAFÉ ✕ **La Pasteleteria-Crepería.** This cheery café and bakery has comfortable *equipales* (rustic Mexican chairs) to plop into as you sample terrific soups, salads, and pizzas. The crepes are what keep the locals coming back for more (the turkey-breast crepe makes a perfect lunch), as well as a variety of sumptuous pastries baked on-site. For travelers with a sweet tooth, this is the best place to buy a delectable dessert. Somewhat difficult to find, this downtown gem is on the bustling Cobá near Wal-Mart. ✉ *Av. Cobá 7, Sm 25, El Centro* ☎ *998/884–3420* ▭ *AE, MC, V.*

$–$$ ECLECTIC Fodor's Choice ★ ✕ **La Troje.** From the moment you enter the garden patio, you'll feel as if you've tapped into a local hideaway. Potted ferns hang from wooden beams in this charming setting that's fashioned around oak trees that pierce through the bamboo roof. A brick staircase leads into the main dining area, where Chef Ana Cano and her two daughters prepare homemade pastas, pizzas, baguettes, and crepes. The colorful menu features 21 different salads, all with the distinctive flavors of fruits, nuts, cheeses, and tangy dressings. For a local favorite, try the grilled chicken stuffed with spinach, apricots, and cream cheese. Early birds can enjoy the full breakfast menu, which includes blended smoothies and fresh-squeezed juices. Although the prices are unbeatable, the service tends to be somewhat brisk. ✉ *Av. Acanceh, Sm 15, El Centro* ☎ *998/887–9556* ▭ *AE, MC, V* ⊗ *Closed Sun.*

$–$$ PIZZA ✕ **Rolandi's Pizzeria.** A Cancún landmark for more than 30 years, Rolandi's continues to draw crowds with its scrumptious wood-fired pizzas. There are 20 varieties to choose from—if you can't make up your mind, try the one with Roquefort cheese, or the "Pizza Popeye" piled with spinach, tomato, basil, and fresh mozzarella. The calzones are smothered with olive oil and packed with fresh ingredients like asparagus, mushrooms, and ham. Homemade pasta dishes like the veal-stuffed ravioli or vegetable lasagna are also very good. Check their Web site for discounts on your next visit. ✉ *Av. Cobá 12, Sm 5, El Centro* ☎ *998/884–4047* 🌐 *www.rolandi.com* ▭ *AE, MC, V.*

$$–$$$ JAPANESE ✕ **Yamamoto.** As the oldest Japanese restaurant in Cancún, Yamamoto has some of the best sushi in the area. In addition to sashimi, there's a menu of traditional Japanese dishes (like chicken teriyaki and tempura) for those who prefer their food cooked. Large groups can order combination platters of sushi, sashimi, kushikatsu, and gyoza. The dining room is tranquil, with Japanese art and bamboo accents, but you can also call for delivery to your hotel room. ✉ *Av. Uxmal 31, Sm 3, El Centro* ☎ *998/887–3366; 998/860–0269 for delivery service* 🌐 *www.yamamoto-cancun.com* ▭ *AE, D, DC, MC, V.*

WHERE TO STAY

ZONA HOTELERA

$$$$ Fodor's Choice ★ **AQUA Cancún.** You won't find raucous Spring Breakers or screaming kids at this Mexican-owned Grupo Posadas property, which mostly attracts luxury-minded thirtysomething sun worshippers. Instead, expect soothing hues, large airy rooms, and resident DJ Gottardo Dorado's tunes perfecting the Zen vibe. MB Restaurant (by Michelle Bernstein) and Siete are both top-notch dining experiences. Splurge for a suite—they come equipped with freestanding circular Jacuzzi tubs and Aqua Lounge access, where you can enjoy complimentary continental breakfast, refreshments, and cocktails throughout the day, and hors d'oeuvres in the evening. Escape the sun in a beach or poolside cabana for a $100 fee, which includes a heavenly foot massage, use of an iPod, and dessert. **Pros:** huge suites, all rooms have oceanfront views, extensive spa services. **Cons:** aromatherapy scents in public spaces can be strong, sliding glass patio doors do not have screens, south-facing rooms had construction views at this writing. ✉ *Blvd. Kukulcán, Km 12.5, Zona Hotelera* ☎ *998/881–7600 or 888/782–9722* 🌐 *www.feel-aqua.com* *335 rooms, 36 suites* *In-room: safe, refrigerator, DVD, Wi-Fi. In-hotel: 3 restaurants, room service, bars, pools, gym, spa, beachfront, laundry service, Wi-Fi hotspot, parking (free)* ▭ *AE, MC, V.*

$$$–$$$$ **The Bel Air Collection Cancún.** The design scheme at this strikingly chic and tranquil resort is unlike that of any other hotel along Boulevard Kukulcán. White furniture is offset by red and black accents, giving the entire hotel a retro look. Billowing drapery creates a wall-less passage into the open-air lobby. Neon lights in the foil-lined elevators change every two seconds, triggering sensations of peace and relaxation. In addition to the sushi bar, there are two small dining sections where you can actually cool off your feet while eating or enjoying a drink, as the tables and chairs are sitting in a low pool of water. The spa here has a yoga–meditation room, light chambers, and high-tech machines from Europe that are used for aromatherapy and chromotherapy sessions, among other treatments. Children under the age of 12 are not permitted at this hotel, which is targeted at adults looking for a peaceful hideaway. All 19 suites have private, indoor Jacuzzis and ocean views. **Pros:** luxurious spa, aesthetically pleasing hotel. **Cons:** no

kids under 12, far from party zone. ✉ *Blvd. Kukulcán, Km 20.5, Zona Hotelera* ☎ *998/193–1770* 🛏 *136 rooms, 19 suites* ⚐ *In-room: safe, DVD, Wi-Fi. In-hotel: 2 restaurants, room service, bars, pool, gym, spa, beachfront, laundry service, Wi-Fi hotspot, parking (free), no kids under 12* 💳 *AE, MC, V* 🍽 *AI, BP, EP.*

$$$$ ★ **Hilton Cancún Golf & Spa Resort.** The Caribbean plays a central role at this resort, with ocean views from all standard guest rooms and junior suites. Set amid 150 lush acres, the tropical setting, with palapa huts and poolside hammocks, is luxurious without seeming overly ostentatious. The landscaping incorporates a series of lavish, interconnected swimming pools that wind through palm-dotted lawns, ending at the beach. Airy and vibrant, the rooms are pristine white with a splash of turquoise to match the sea. Some of the villas, however, offer only garden views, so make sure to specify oceanfront when booking. Guests who want to get more intimate with nature can participate in the resort's turtle-release program or work on their swing at the resort's championship 18-hole, par-72 course, where crocodile sightings are frequent. For the ultimate in pampering, the hotel's spa features a Zen-garden hot tub, a bamboo relaxation lounge, poolside yoga, and massages on the beach. The children's activities cost $45 for a full day, $32 for a half-day, or $10 per hour. **Pros:** outstanding beachfront villas, tasteful decor, angled pool area gets all-day sunshine. **Cons:** only one heated pool, food quality is inconsistent. ✉ *Blvd. Kukulcán, Km 17, Zona Hotelera* ☎ *998/881–8000* 🌐 *www.hiltoncancun.com* 🛏 *426 rooms, 23 suites, 82 villas* ⚐ *In-room: safe, DVD, Internet (some), Wi-Fi (some). In-hotel: 5 restaurants, room service, bars, golf course, tennis courts, pools, gym, spa, beachfront, diving, water sports, bicycles, children's programs (ages 4–11), laundry service, Internet terminal, Wi-Fi hotspot, parking (free)* 💳 *AE, D, DC, MC, V* 🍽 *EP.*

$$$$ Fodor's Choice ★ **JW Marriott Cancún Resort & Spa.** This is the best hotel for experiencing luxury Cancún style and service. Plush is the name of the game at the towering beach resort, where manicured lawns are dotted with an expansive maze of pools, and large vaulted windows let sunlight stream into a lobby decorated with marble floors and beautiful flower arrangements. All rooms have ocean views, private balconies, and wall-to-wall carpeting. Two of the hotel's best features are its three-level, 35,000-square-foot spa with indoor pool and its 20-foot dive pool with an artificial reef, where you can practice snorkeling and scuba diving. The hotel recently completed a beach recovery project which nearly tripled its width. Damage from the 2005 Hurricane Wilma resulted in major renovations, now making JW Marriott the only Cancún property able to withstand a level five hurricane. **Pros:** top-notch service, huge spa, iPod dock, artificial reef. **Cons:** lacks the festive mood of other hotels along the strip, breakfast buffet costs $25. ✉ *Blvd. Kukulcán, Km 14.5, Zona Hotelera* ☎ *998/848–9600 or 888/813–2776* 🌐 *www.marriott.com* 🛏 *448 rooms, 74 suites* ⚐ *In-room: safe, kitchen (some), refrigerator (some), Wi-Fi. In-hotel: 3 restaurants, room service, bars, tennis courts, pools, gym, spa, beachfront, diving, water sports, children's programs (ages 4–12), laundry service, Internet terminal, Wi-Fi hotspot, parking (free)* 💳 *AE, MC, V* 🍽 *EP.*

$$$$ **Le Blanc Spa Resort.** An airy and modern hotel with white and beige refined minimalist decor and lots of windows, Le Blanc Spa is the most upscale of the Palace Resorts properties in Cancún. Mainly couples stay in this resort, which is restricted to guests over 18. The spa is extremely large, with 17 indoor treatment rooms and services ranging from aroma foot reflexology to chocolate body wraps. Located along both the ocean and the lagoon, this resort offers some spectacular views. However, only about 50% of the rooms have full ocean views. **Pros:** aesthetically pleasing design, excellent spa, butler service. **Cons:** no kids, pricey. ✉ *Blvd. Kukulcán, Km 10, Zona Hotelera* ☎ *998/881–4740* 🌐 *www.leblancsparesort.com* *260 rooms* *In-room: safe, DVD (some), Wi-Fi. In-hotel: 5 restaurants, room service, bars, pools, gym, spa, beachfront, diving, laundry service, Wi-Fi hotspot, parking (free), no kids under 18* *AE, MC, V* *AI.*

$$$$ **Le Meridien Cancún Resort & Spa.** High on a hill and tucked away from the main boulevard, this refined yet relaxed hotel is an artful blend of art-deco and Mayan styles; there's lots of wood, glass, and mirrors. The beach is small, but rooms have partial ocean views. The many thoughtful details—such as different temperatures in each of the swimming pools—make a stay here truly special. The Spa del Mar offers the latest European treatments (including seaweed hydrotherapy) in 14 treatment rooms. Business groups are starting to book here, and account for about 40% of the hotel's clientele. **Pros:** near one of Cancún's best malls; large fitness center; all rooms with ocean or lagoon views, tastefully decorated. **Cons:** expensive considering that it's not all-inclusive; small beach; at this writing, south-facing rooms had construction views. ✉ *Blvd. Kukulcán, Km 14, Retorno del Rey, Lote 37, Zona Hotelera* ☎ *998/881–2200 or 800/543–4300* 🌐 *www.cancun.lemeridien.com* *213 rooms, 26 suites* *In-room: safe, refrigerator, DVD (some), Wi-Fi. In-hotel: 2 restaurants, bar, tennis courts, pools, gym, spa, beachfront, children's programs (ages 4–12), Wi-Fi hotspot, parking (free)* *AE, MC, V* *BP, CP, EP.*

$$$$ ★ **ME by Meliá Cancún.** The ME takes the chic flavor of a trendy boutique hotel and blows it up to the grand scale of a large resort. The aim here is to arouse all five senses; you'll find yourself inhaling soothing scents while listening to electronic lounge music that is played everywhere, even in the elevators. This hotel oozes hipness, from the sleek black mermaid sculptures by artist Marie France Porta to the slick bars created by nightlife gurus Rande and Scott Gerber. And if you want to literally bring a piece of ME back home with you, guest-room furnishings and artwork by Yuri Zatarain can be purchased from the on-site gallery. Also, pet owners take note—your furry friends are welcome here. **Pros:** great for young couples, amazing contemporary design, pet-friendly. **Cons:** not ideal for kids, lacks traditional Mexican flavor. ✉ *Blvd. Kukulcán, Km 12, Zona Hotelera* ☎ *998/881–2500 or 998/881–2506* 🌐 *www.mebymelia.com* *419 rooms, 41 suites* *In-room: safe, DVD (some), Internet, Wi-Fi. In-hotel: 4 restaurants, room service, bars, pools, gym, spa, beachfront, laundry service, Internet terminal, Wi-Fi hotspot, parking (free) some pets allowed* *AE, MC, V* *EP.*

$$$–$$$$ **Omni Cancún Hotel & Villas.** After undergoing a $15 million renovation in 2007, this 10-story hotel has definitely moved up a notch or two in Cancún's hotel hierarchy. Each standard room has a balcony with built-in benches, a marble bathroom, flat-screen TV, and radio with an MP3 docking station. If you decide to splurge on one of the three-floor villas that surround the hotel, you will not be disappointed. They each have a sunken living room, fully equipped kitchen, sun terrace off the third-floor bedroom, and parking space right outside. Your stay here will not be complete without paying a visit to the huge, adults-only hot-tub area with a swim-up sushi bar. If you'd rather be dry when drinking, then grab a table at the lobby bar and try one of the delicious martinis that are the house specialty. There are four handicapped-accessible rooms here. **Pros:** refurbished rooms, tons of scheduled activities. **Cons:** crowded pool area, time-share sales pitches in the lobby. ✉ *Blvd. Kukulcán, Km 16.5, Zona Hotelera* ☎ *998/881–0600* 🌐 *www.omnihotels.com* *259 rooms, 19 suites, 23 villas* *In-room: safe, kitchen (some), refrigerator (some), DVD (some), Wi-Fi. In-hotel: 3 restaurants, room service, bars, tennis courts, pools, gym, spa, beachfront, children's programs (ages 5–12), laundry service, Internet terminal, Wi-Fi hotspot, parking (free)* *AE, MC, V* *AI, EP.*

WORD OF MOUTH

"The Omni Cancún is about the best place for the money in Cancún." —Joe P.

$$$–$$$$ **Presidente InterContinental Cancún Resort.** This landmark hotel boasts arguably the best beach in Cancún. It gained at least 20 feet more sand after Hurricane Wilma. The entire hotel has a contemporary look to it, including the swanky lobby with a tequila bar. Adults looking for even more peace and quiet can take advantage of the adults-only, quiet pool or a beachfront massage. The atmosphere here is more conservative than at many of the other resorts along the Zona Hotelera, so you're likely to have a quiet, relaxed stay. **Pros:** short walk to shops and restaurants; virtually currentless beach is great for families. **Cons:** focus on business travelers and conventions. ✉ *Blvd. Kukulcán, Km 7.5, Zona Hotelera* ☎ *998/848–8700* 🌐 *www.intercontinental.com/cancun* *299 rooms, 7 suites* *In-room: safe, Wi-Fi. In-hotel: 3 restaurants, room service, bars, pools, gym, beachfront, diving, water sports, children's programs (ages 9–12), laundry service, Wi-Fi hotspot, parking (free)* *AE, MC, V* *EP.*

$$$$ Fodor's Choice ★ **The Ritz-Carlton, Cancún.** Outfitted with crystal chandeliers, beautiful antiques, and elegant oil paintings, this hotel's style is so European that you may well forget you're in Mexico. Rooms are done in understated shades of teal, beige, and rose, with wall-to-wall carpeting, large balconies overlooking the Caribbean, and marble bathrooms with separate tubs and showers. For families with small children, special rooms with cribs and changing tables are available. A great feature of this resort is its Culinary Center, where guests can participate in wine and tequila tastings or join in cooking classes. For an extra charge, guests can join Sunrise Boot Camp, a morning workout program that includes yoga, a power walk on the beach, and hydro-balance exercises in the pool.

The resort's overall atmosphere is fairly conservative, and it is one of few hotels that charges for children's activities ($45 for a half-day program and $65 for a full-day program). **Pros:** progressive dinner ($225) allows guests to sample three restaurants in one night, tennis center offers private lessons, hotel hosts full-moon parties year-round, large beach. **Cons:** conservative atmosphere for Hotel Zone, expensive, parking costs extra. ✉ *Blvd. Kukulcán, Km 13.5, Retorno del Rey 36, Zona Hotelera* ☎ *998/881–0808* 🌐 *www.ritzcarlton.com* *365 rooms, 50 suites* *In-room: safe, Wi-Fi. In-hotel: 6 restaurants, room service, bar, tennis courts, pools, gym, spa, beachfront, diving, children's programs (ages 4–12), laundry service, Internet terminal, Wi-Fi hotspot, parking (paid)* 💳 *AE, D, DC, MC, V* *EP.*

COOKING CLASSES

The Ritz-Carlton Culinary Center (✉ *Blvd. Kukulcán, Km 13.5, Retorno del Rey 36, Zona Hotelera* ☎ *998/881–0822* 🌐 *www.ritzcarlton.com* *$115* 🕒 *Mon.–Sat. 11–3 PM; wine and tequila tasting at 6:30*) offers two-hour cooking classes led by Chef Rory Dunaway. You can choose from six themed sessions, including Mexican grilling and Tuscan dinner parties. Courses are open to everyone but must be booked in advance.

$$$$ **Riu Palace Las Américas.** A colossal eight-story property at the north end of the Zona, the Palace is visually stunning and different from the modern, minimalist resorts that dot the Zona Hotelera. Here the decoration is a bit baroque. There are towering columns and cupolas in the lobby, and even the most basic guest rooms (all are suites) have ornate mahogany furniture and Victorian-print bedding. The daily origami ritual of swan towel folding can be rather vexing, as can the boisterous emcee directing poolside games. Each room has its own walk-in closet, sitting room, and four-bottle liquor dispenser. This resort mainly attracts guests over 40. **Pros:** spacious suites, access to sister properties Riu Cancún and Riu Caribe. **Cons:** small pools and tiny beach, not much sun by the pool or beach by late afternoon. ✉ *Blvd. Kukulcán, Km 8.5, Zona Hotelera* ☎ *998/891–4300* 🌐 *www.riu.com* *372 junior suites* *In-room: safe, refrigerator, Internet (some). In-hotel: 6 restaurants, room service, bars, pools, gym, spa, beachfront, water sports, children's programs (ages 4–12), laundry service, Wi-Fi hotspot* 💳 *AE, MC, V* *AI.*

$$ ★ **Suites Sina.** On a quiet residential street off Boulevard Kukulcán, these economical suites are in front of Laguna Nichupté and close to the Pok-Ta-Pok golf course. The lobby leads out to a lush garden, pool, and a small restaurant at the center. When it comes to accommodations, skip the standard rooms and upgrade to a junior or master suite, as they have lagoon views, kitchenettes, and spacious dining-living rooms. The atmosphere is relaxed and quiet, making it the perfect place to hide away from the craziness that is the Zona Hotelera; the hotel is actually between the Hotel Zone and El Centro, though it claims to be in the heart of the Hotel Zone. **Pros:** ideally situated on the lagoon, affordable. **Cons:** 10-minute walk from beach, no elevator. ✉ *Club de Golf, Calle Quetzal 33, turn right at Km 7.5 after golf course, Zona Hotelera/El Centro*

☎ *998/883–1017 or 877/883–1018* 🌐 *www.cancunsinasuites.com.mx* *4 rooms, 36 suites* *In-room: kitchen (some), refrigerator (some). In-hotel: restaurant, room service, bar, pool, Wi-Fi hotspot, parking (free)* ▭ *AE, MC, V* ǀ◎ǀ *EP.*

WORD OF MOUTH

"There are plenty of buses from Cancún airport into El Centro. This is a completely different area from the Zona Hotelera, where all the high-end hotels are. I stayed at a place right next to the bus station for less than $50 a night. Pool included." —gertie3751

$$$$ **The Westin Resort & Spa Cancún.** On the southern end of the Zona Hotelera, this hotel is quite secluded; you'll get privacy, but you'll have to drive to get to shops and restaurants. Subtle hints of pampering are what make this hotel so extraordinary, like the white tea mist that periodically sprays in the lobby and the "Heavenly Beds," so luxurious that many guests purchase them for their homes. Inside the resort, the modern is juxtaposed with the traditional, as sleek dark-wood furniture is offset by brightly colored rugs and the occasional blue or yellow wall. There are two beaches here—an expansive one on the Caribbean side and a smaller one facing Laguna Nichupté—so guests always have a place to sunbathe. Due to the quiet, isolated nature of the resort, it mainly attracts families with small children and adults in their 30s and 40s. This resort is one of the few in Cancún that allow pets. **Pros:** two beaches. **Cons:** extra charge for the use of amenities like Internet, gym, and spa. ✉ *Blvd. Kukulcán, Km 20, Zona Hotelera* ☎ *998/848–7400* 🌐 *www.westin.com/cancun* *379 rooms, 17 suites* *In-room: safe, DVD (some), Internet, Wi-Fi. In-hotel: 5 restaurants, room service, bars, tennis courts, pools, gym, spa, beachfront, diving, bicycles, children's programs (ages 4–12), laundry service, Wi-Fi hotspot, parking (free), some pets allowed* ▭ *AE, DC, MC, V* ǀ◎ǀ *AI, EP.*

EL CENTRO

$–$$ ★ **Cancún Inn El Patio.** This traditional, Mexican-style inn has been converted into a charming 15-room guesthouse. An iron gate leads off a busy street into a courtyard, delightfully landscaped with plants, flowers, and a tile fountain. Breakfast is served in a lower-level restaurant, creatively designed with arched doorways, brick walls, and wrought-iron chandeliers, giving it an intimate wine-cellar atmosphere. Upstairs, many of the large, airy rooms have Mexican rustic furniture and Talavera ceramics. An art gallery, small café, reading lounge, and business center have recently been added to the property. The helpful staff embraces the *mi casa es su casa* mentality, and offers expert advice on the area. **Pros:** clean and safe; great value; art gallery and Café d'Art promote a creative, cultural environment. **Cons:** high processing fee if you pay by credit card, major construction project across the street at this writing. ✉ *Av. Bonampak 51, El Centro* ☎ *998/884–3500* 🌐 *www.cancuninn.com* *15 rooms* *In-room: no phone, safe. In-hotel: Wi-Fi hotspot, Internet terminal, parking (free)* ▭ *MC, V* ǀ◎ǀ *CP.*

¢ **Hostel Chacmool.** One of the cheapest and hippest places to stay in downtown Cancún, this family-run hostel offers clean rooms, a complimentary continental breakfast, a trendy lobby bar, and a terrace with a

Continued on page 702

14

RIVIERA MAYA SPAS

by Marlise Kast

This area offers plenty of pampering, be it footbaths or facials, manicures or massages. Whether in a spa pavilion, on a soft white beach, or in a palapa nestled in the jungle, you'll experience the ultimate in relaxation of body, mind, and spirit.

Most spas in the region also have heated pools, steam rooms, beachside massages, and fitness facilities. Some even offer beauty salons, personal consultants, organic cafés, and natural cenotes.

A visit to the region is not complete without participating in a temazcal ritual based on traditional Mayan healing methods. Temazcal is a type of sweat lodge that's used to purify the body and cleanse mind and spirit. You can also indulge in one of the other Mayan-inspired spa remedies like chaya detoxification, chocolate body wraps, or ground corn and honey exfoliation. Most resorts also offer treatments from around the globe. Japanese shiatsu, Swedish massage, and deep-tissue Thai massage are just a few of the ways to rejuvenate your body.

There's a package for just about everyone: for men, for golfers, for expectant mothers. Send the kids to the teen spa for a Peppermint Patty foot massage or an ice cream pedicure. Newlyweds can indulge in candlelit massages for two or aroma baths brimming with floating petals.

Most spas are open to the public, but appointments are mandatory since walk-ins aren't the norm. Be sure to set aside extra time before or after your treatment and take advantage of all the facility has to offer.

Resort/ Spa name	Body Treatments	Facials	Outdoor Treatments	Couples Treatments	Fitness Day Pass	Sauna	Steam Room
Rosewood	\$85–\$195	\$165–\$255	Lagoon	yes	Free	yes	yes
Mandarin Oriental	\$145–\$205	\$205	Garden	yes	Free	yes	yes
JW Marriott	\$60–\$270	\$75–\$155	Pool	yes	no	yes	yes
Banyan Tree	\$90–\$210	\$180–\$190	Lagoon	yes	no	yes	yes
The Tides	\$70–\$240	\$85–\$180	Jungle or Ocean	yes	no	yes	yes
Fairmont	\$129–\$499	\$129–\$229	Jungle	yes	\$25	yes	yes
Azulik	\$73–\$165	\$66–\$90	Ocean	no	no	no	no
Maroma	\$125–\$215	\$125–\$210	Garden	yes	Free	yes	yes
Zoëtry Paraiso	\$129–\$220	\$129–\$250	Ocean	yes	Resort guests only	yes	yes
Hilton	\$109–\$199	\$119–\$179	Ocean	yes	\$15	yes	no

The Banyan Tree uses customized lotions and oils.

TOP SPOTS

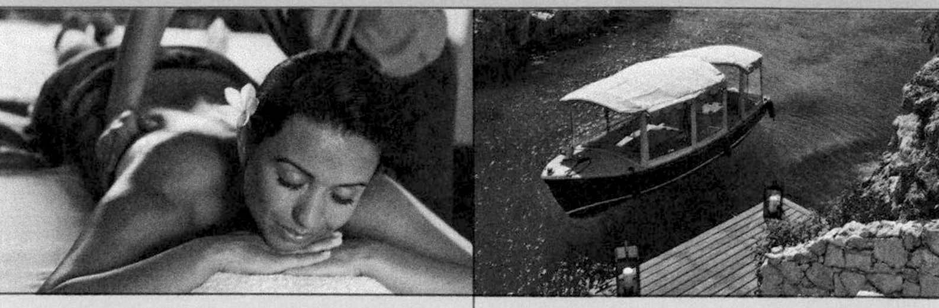

BANYAN TREE SPA, MAYAKOBA

Built over freshwater lagoons, the Banyan Tree Spa draws on centuries old Asian traditions. The therapists (80% of whom are from Thailand) begin with a heavenly footbath, followed by your choice of the healing treatments. Unique to Banyan Tree is its signature Rainmist Steam Bath and the 12-step Rainforest Experience that combines hydrotherapy with infrared light to release tension and revitalize the body.

BODY TREATMENTS: Massage: Sukhothai, Balinese, Swedish, Thai, Chinese footwork, lomi lomi, Indian head massage. **Wraps/Baths:** Tumeric and lemongrass scrub, green tea scrub, lulur scrub, yogurt splash, fresh milk bath, sandalwood and ginger scrub, marigold and honey scrub, footbath. **Other:** Rainmist Steam Bath, detox mud wrap, rain shower, 12-step Rainforest, Thai herbal compress, yoga lessons, men's treatments

BEAUTY TREATMENTS. Facials, hair/scalp conditioning, manicures, pedicures, waxing, makeovers

PRICES. Body Treatments: $90–$210. Facials: $180–$190. Hair: $50–$90. Manicure/Pedicure: $70–$90.

Banyan Tree Spa. ✉ *Carretera 307, Km 298. Mayakoba.* ☎ *984/877–3688* 🌐 *www.banyantree.com/mayakoba. Parking: Valet* 💳 *AE, MC, V*

SENSE, ROSEWOOD MAYAKOBA

Rosewood's 17,000-sq-ft spa is in a jungle on its very own island. Wooden walkways lead to a swimming pool and limestone cenote, which is fed by subterranean springs. Many treatments, such as the temazcal ritual and the Mayakoba ancient massage, incorporate the Mayan tradition of aligning the energies of the body in rhythmic harmony. Leave time to enjoy the spa facilities, including the gym, sauna, Jacuzzi, plunge pool and eucalyptus steam room.

BODY TREATMENTS. Massage: Swedish, deep tissue, hot stone, aromatherapy, reflexology, Asian. **Wraps/Baths:** Hydrating, chocolate, detox, revitalization, toning. **Other:** Natural cenote, temazcal ritual, 12 lagoon-side treatment rooms, 8 spa suites, Itzamná café, private yoga lessons, treatments for pregnant women.

BEAUTY TREATMENTS. Facials, hair cuts/style, manicures, pedicures, waxing, makeovers

PRICES. Body Treatments: $85–$195. Facials: $165–$255. Hair: $65–$85. Manicure/Pedicure: $75–$85.

Sense, Rosewood Spas. ✉ *Carretera 307, Km 298. Mayakoba* ☎ *984/875–8000* 🌐 *www.rosewoodmayakoba.com. Parking: Valet* 💳 *AE, MC, V*

THE TIDES, PUNTA BETE

Although not as grandiose as most spas in the area, the Tides is unique in its use of indigenous materials and local ingredients, such as chocolate, seaweed, aloe vera, and heated lava shells. It also offers a series of unusual treatments, like the Hammock Massage that allows the therapist to knead you through a hammock. Another massage uses a *manteada* (blanket stretch) to adjust posture and elongate muscles. The Sweet Honey and Rain Massage combine herbal bouquets, wild honey, and drops of water.

BODY TREATMENTS. Massage: Deep tissue, Thai, jantzu water massage, hot stone, reflexology, lunar, hammock. **Wraps/Baths:** Red seaweed wrap, aloe vera bath, mud wrap, Mayan bath. **Other:** Oceanfront yoga and Pilates, aromatherapy, fertility ceremony, temazcal ritual, men's treatments.

BEAUTY TREATMENTS. Facials, manicures, pedicures, waxing

PRICES. Body Treatments: $70–$240. Facials: $85–$180. Manicure/Pedicure: $85–$95.

The Tides. ✉ *Playa Xcalacoco Frac 7, Punta Bete* ☎ *984/877–3000* 🌐 *www.tides-rivieramaya.com. Parking: Valet* 💳 *AE, MC, V*

MANDARIN ORIENTAL

Both the design and philosophy of the spa are inspired by the Mayan healing elements of water, air, fire, and earth. Signature treatments include Oriental Harmony (four-hands massage), temazcal ceremony (guided by a Mayan shaman), and the Mayan Na Lu'Um massage (which opens blocked energy paths). For travelers who have spent too many days basking in the sun, the soothing Kinich Ahau program includes a sunburn remedy wrap, hair treatment, and hydrating facial.

BODY TREATMENTS. Massage: Shiatsu, hot stone, Thai, Oriental foot therapy, Swedish, deep tissue. **Wraps/Baths:** Yucatan mud wrap, Oriental salt scrub, herbal wrap, watsu pool, chocolate body treatment. **Other:** Aromatherapy, Kinesis fitness studio, yoga/pilates/meditation classes, temazcal, ice fountains.

BEAUTY TREATMENTS. Facials, manicures, pedicures

PRICES. Body Treatments: $145–$315. Facials: $205. Hair: $65–$85. Manicure/Pedicure: $80–$95.

The Spa at Mandarin Oriental. ✉ *Carretera 307, Km 298.8* ☎ *984/877–3888* 🌐 *www.mandarinoriental.com/rivieramaya Parking: Valet* 💳 *AE, MC, V*

HONORABLE MENTIONS

Fairmont Mayakoba

ZOËTRY PARAISO DE LA BONITA, PUNTA TANCHACTE

It's the only certified Thalassotherapy Spa and Anti-Aging Center in Riviera Maya, meaning many of it's treatments incorporate seawater. The extensive menu features body wraps, holistic treatments, saltwater hydrotherapy, and temazcal rituals. Although most treatments involve getting wet, you'll also find healing dry remedies like wraps, facials, massages, and acupuncture. To eliminate toxins, sea kelp and marine mud are infused into spa products.

Within the 22,000 sq-ft spa are facilities for yoga, Tai-Chi, acupuncture and Chinese medicine.

BODY TREATMENTS. Massage: Mayan, reflexology, pressotheraphy, Swedish, Thai, hot stone, therapeutic, regenerative, marine affusion shower massage, janzu massage. **Wraps/Baths:** Seaweed wrap, mud wrap, balneotherapy. **Other:** Temazcal, hydrotherapy, private yoga, Tai Chi, acupunture, Kinesiology, saltwater pool, fitness center, men's treatments.

BEAUTY TREATMENTS. Facials, manicures, pedicures, waxing, hair cut/style

PRICES. Body Treatments: \$129–\$220. Facials: \$129–\$250. Manicure/Pedicure: \$55–\$110.

Zoëtry Paraiso de la Bonia. ✉ *Carretera 307, Km 328* ☎ *984/872–8300* 🌐 *www.zoetryparaisodelabonita.com/Paraiso. Parking: Valet* 💳 *AE, MC, V*

WILLOW STREAM, FAIRMONT MAYAKOBA

It's easy to loose yourself (literally) within the enormous 37,000 sq-ft spa. Favorite treatments are the Mexican stone massage, the Cha Chac Rain Ritual (a massage that takes place on a seven-jet Vichy table), and Honey in the Heart (honey body mask and massage). Weary travelers will want to try the Jet Lag Recovery, an aromatherapy bath and massage that reverses the negative effects of flying and time zone changes. After a gym workout, ease your muscles in the rooftop vitality pool.

BODY TREATMENTS. Massage: hot stone, reflexology, aromatheraphy, deep tissue. **Wraps/Baths:** Seaweed bath, thermal mineral bath, chocolate wrap, rose bath, Mayan bath, clay purification. **Other:** Vichy shower, saltwater pool, fitness center, specialized wedding menu, men's treatments.

BEAUTY TREATMENTS. Facials, manicures, pedicures, waxing, hair cut/color/style, make-up application

PRICES. Body Treatments: \$129–\$499. Facials: \$129–\$229. Manicure/Pedicure: \$59–\$89.

Willow Stream at Fairmont Mayakoba. ✉ *Carretera 307, Km 298* ☎ *984/206–3039* 🌐 *www.willowstream.com. Parking: Valet* 💳 *AE, MC, V*

JW Marriott

Aventura Spa Palace

JW MARRIOTT, CANCUN

Located in Cancun proper, this 35,000 sq-ft spa should be included as one of the area's best. Choose from one of 13 invigorating facials including the pumpkin enzyme treatment or the cucumber green-tea facial. Women will enjoy Precious Stones and Flowers which begins with a detoxifying marine mask followed by flower petals and crystals placed over energy points to bring balance and harmony to the body. The JW Spa even offers specialized treatments for men, golfers, couples, and teens. For the ultimate Caribbean experience, take a dip in the ocean followed by a beachside massage.

BODY TREATMENTS. Massage: Swedish, Oriental, lomi lomi, deep tissue, shiatsu, hot stone. **Wraps/Baths:** Mayan herbal bath, chocolate body scrub. **Other:** Vichy shower, indoor/outdoor pool, fitness center, temezcal, teen spa menu (ages 6–17), men's treatments.

BEAUTY TREATMENTS. Facials, manicures, pedicures, waxing, hair cut/color/style, make-up application

PRICES. Body Treatments: $60–$270. Facials: $75–$155. Manicure/Pedicure: $10–$70.

JW Marriott Cancun Resort & Spa. ✉ *Blvd Kukulcan Km 14.5, Zona Hotelera, Cancun* ☎ *998/848–9700 Parking: Valet* 💳 *AE, MC, V*

ALSO WORTH NOTING

Several other Riviera Maya spas are also worth mentioning. The **Kinan Spa at Maroma Resort** (✉ *Carretera 307, Km 51* ☎ *998/872–8200* 🌐 *www.maromahotel.com*), has treatments based on ancient Mayan healing. **Aventura Spa Palace** (✉ *Carretera 307, Km 72, Puerto Aventuras* ☎ *984/875–1100* 🌐 *www.palaceresorts.com*) is known for its excellent hydrotherapy facilities. For treatments with a view, head to **Azulik Eco-Resort** in Tulum (✉ *Carretera Tulum Ruinas Km 5* ☎ *800/123–3278* 🌐 *www.azulik.com*).

Located in Cancun's Zona Hotelera, this impressive spa at **The Hilton** (✉ *Blvd. Kukulcan, Km 17, Zona Hotelera, Cancun* ☎ *998/881–8000* 🌐 *www.hiltoncancun.com*) has a Zen garden, relaxation lounge and treatments on the beach for men and women.

Also located in Cancun is the **Kayantá Spa at The Rtiz Carlton** (✉ Blvd. Kukulcan, Km 14, Zona Hotelera, Cancun ☎ 998/881–0808 🌐 www.ritzcarlton.com) where you can experience the "Deep Blue Peel." This massage and body-scrub combo consists of marine extracts, seaweed, bergamot and jojoba oil. The avocado and yogurt wrap will leave your skin feeling silky smooth.

At the **Ceiba del Mar Spa** (✉ Costera Norte, Puerto Morelos ☎ 998/872–8063 🌐 www.ceibadelmar.com) you can begin with a biotensor rod for testing vital energy. Based on the findings, specific treatments are then selected to help restore energy levels.

pool table. Live entertainment is just a stone's throw away at the Parque de las Palapas, and there's no curfew if you decide to make it a late night out. Mixed-gender and female-only dorms are available; if you decide to splurge, opt for the private room with two double beds and a private bath. There's a full kitchen with purified water that guests may use; towels, lockers, and padlocks are also included in the rate. **Pros:** excellent location, no curfew, one hour Internet free. **Cons:** not much privacy in dorms, young crowd. ✉ *Gladiolas 18, Sm 22, in front of Parque de las Palapas, El Centro* ☎ *998/887–5873* 🌐 *www.chacmool.com.mx* *40 beds* *In-room: no phone, no TV. In-hotel: restaurant, bar, laundry facilities, Internet terminal, Wi-Fi hotspot, parking (free)* *MC, V* *CP.*

$–$$ ★ **Hotel El Rey del Caribe.** Thanks to the use of solar energy, a water-recycling system, and composting toilets, this unique hotel has very little impact on the environment—and its luxuriant garden blocks the heat and noise of downtown. Hammocks hang poolside, and wrought-iron tables and chairs dot the grounds. There is artwork throughout the property, much of which was painted by the owner herself (who lives on-site). Standard rooms are small but pleasant, and have kitchenettes. The newest accommodations, known as the executive rooms, are larger and have wood floors. A great feature is the tiny spa, where you can book honey or chocolate massages that cost a third of what they do in the Zona Hotelera. El Centro's shops and restaurants are within walking distance. **Pros:** tranquil atmosphere, eco-friendly, affordable spa. **Cons:** simple and musty rooms, no elevator. ✉ *Av. Uxmal 24 at Náder, Sm 2A, El Centro* ☎ *998/884–2028* 🌐 *www.elreydelcaribe.com* *31 rooms* *In-room: safe, kitchen, Wi-Fi. In-hotel: restaurant, pool, spa, Wi-Fi hotspot, parking (free)* *MC, V* *BP.*

$$ **Hotel Sol Y Luna.** Reminiscent of an upscale European flat, this four-story hotel with tangerine shutters and signature cupolas is one of the jewels of Parque de las Palapas. Bearing names like Nova, Bamboo, Lotus, and Soleil, the themed rooms are uniquely designed to incorporate traces of nature. The artwork here is pure genius, ranging from rustic floor-plank paintings to plaster castings of sea life. Several bathrooms, inlaid with vibrant mosaic tiles, have freestanding stone basins and citrus-infused bath products. A small wooden bridge spans a swimming pool, which separates the main building from the hotel's check-in area. Each standard room comes with a private terrace and small lounging area. The two suites are more modern in design, with olive-toned walls, microsuede sofas, and teak furnishings; they offer stunning views of the town square below. **Pros:** thoughtful, creative details for a modest price. **Cons:** no elevator, loud and creaky wooden staircase might mean restless nights if you're on a lower floor, no restaurant. ✉ *Calle Alcatraces 33, Mz 9, Sm 22, in front of Parque de las Palapas, El Centro* ☎ *998/887–5528* *9 rooms, 2 suites* *In-room: safe, refrigerator (some), Wi-Fi. In-hotel: pool, parking (free)* *AE, V, MC* *EP.*

$$ Fodor's Choice ★ **Hotel Xbalamqué Resort & Spa.** A refreshing retreat from the bustling streets of El Centro, the hotel has a lobby adorned with palapa roofs, exquisite waterfalls, tropical birds, and stamped flooring. It forms part of a complex that also includes two restaurants and a snack shop which

are open to the general public. Guests can enjoy live music in Coffeebrary, a café–library with a bohemian atmosphere. The Xbalamqué is distinctively decorated, with Mayan-themed murals, statues, and reliefs throughout the hotel. The rooms are simply decorated with rustic Mexican furniture. **Pros:** only downtown hotel with (small) spa, beauty salon, and yoga studio on-site. **Cons:** street noise audible from front rooms, thin room doors offer limited security. ✉ *Av. Yaxchilan 31, Sm 22, Mz 18, El Centro* ☎ *998/884–9690* 🌐 *www.xbalamque.com* *80 rooms, 11 suites* *In-room: Internet. In-hotel: 2 restaurants, room service, bar, pool, spa, Wi-Fi hotspot, parking (free)* 💳 *AE, MC, V* 🍽 *BP.*

NIGHTLIFE

BARS

At **Carlos 'n Charlie's** (✉ *Blvd. Kukulcán, Km 9, Forum by the Sea Mall, Zona Hotelera* ☎ *998/883–4468* 🌐 *www.carlosandcharlies.com/cancun*) waiters will occasionally abandon their posts to start singing or performing comical skits. It's not unusual for them to roust everyone from their seats to join in a conga line before going back to serving food and drinks.

Fat Tuesday (✉ *Blvd. Kukulcán, Km 6.5, Zona Hotelera* ☎ *998/849–7201*), with its large daiquiri bar and live and piped-in disco music, is another place to dance the night away.

Pat O'Brien's (✉ *Plaza Flamingo, Blvd. Kukulcán, Km 11.5, Zona Hotelera* ☎ *998/883–0832* 🌐 *www.patobriens.com*) brings the New Orleans party scene to the Zona with live rock bands and its famous cocktails balanced on the heads of waiters as they dance through the crowd. The really experienced servers can balance up to four margaritas or strawberry daiquiris at once! It's always Mardi Gras here, so the place is decorated with lots of balloons, banners, and those infamous beads given out to brave patrons.

A relaxing alternative to the loud discos, **Resto-Bar Bling** (✉ *Blvd. Kukulcán, Km 13.5, in front of Plaza Kukulcán, Zona Hotelera* ☎ *998/840–6015* 🌐 *www.blingcancun.com* ⏲ *Opens at 6 PM*) has a chic open-air lounge bar with canopy-covered beds overlooking the lagoon. DJs spin house and chill-out tunes as the bartenders mix their famous kiwi, cucumber, or coffee martinis. The restaurant inside, which closes at 1 AM, specializes in Mediterranean cuisine and sushi.

Known for its over-the-top drinks, **Señor Frog's** (✉ *Blvd. Kukulcán, Km 9.5, Zona Hotelera* ☎ *998/883–1092* 🌐 *www.senorfrogs.com/cancun*) serves up foot-long funnel glasses filled with margaritas, daiquiris, or beer, which you can take home as souvenirs once you've chugged them dry. Needless to say, Spring Breakers simply adore this place and often stagger back night after night.

GAY BARS

Café D' Pa (✉ *Parque de las Palapas, Mz 16, Sm 22, El Centro* ☎ *998/884–7615* 🌐 *www.eldpa.com*) is a cheerful bar and restaurant offering a menu of specialty crepes; since it opens at 6 PM, it's a popular place to gather before the city's other gay bars open their doors.

A variety of drag shows with the usual lip-synching and dancing celebrity impersonations are put on every Wednesday and Thursday at **Karamba Bar** (✉ *Av. Tulum 9, Sm 22, El Centro* ☎ *No phone* 🌐 *www.karambabar.com*), a large open-air disco and club that's known for its stage performers. On Friday night the Go-Go Boys of Cancún entertain, and strip shows are on weekends. The bar opens at 10:30 PM and the party goes on until dawn. There's no cover charge.

The oldest gay bar in Cancún, **Picante Bar** (✉ *Plaza Galerias, Av. Tulum 20, Sm 5, El Centro* ☎ *No phone*) has been operating for 15 years. (It survived several raids and closures during less lenient times in the '90s.) The drag shows here tend to reflect local culture; for instance, during Carnival there is a special holiday beauty pageant followed by the crowning of "the Queen." The owner, "Mother Picante," emcees the floor show that includes Las Vegas–type dance revues, singers, and strippers. Doors open at 9 PM and close at 5 AM, and there's no cover.

SPORTS BARS

Champions Sports Bar & Grill (✉ *CasaMagna Marriott Cancún Resort, Blvd. Kukulcán, Km 14.5, Zona Hotelera* ☎ *998/881–2000 Ext. 6341*) has a giant TV screen and 26 smaller monitors on which to watch all kinds of sporting events. You can also play pool here and dig in to American-style bar grub.

WINE BARS

El Rincón del Vino (✉ *Alcatraces 29, Mz 10, Sm 22, in front of Parque de las Palapas, next to Los Huaraches de Alcatraces. El Centro* ☎ *998/898–3187*) is a popular wine and tapas bar where you can enjoy the sounds of live trova, rumba flamenco, and jazz music. The bar has 250 varieties of *vino* hailing from the world's top winemaking regions, and tapas like *tortilla española* (a potato omelet) and *chistorra* (a Spanish sausage). It's open from 6 to 12 Tuesday through Saturday.

DANCE CLUBS

Azúcar (✉ *Dreams Cancún Resort & Spa, Blvd. Kukulcán, Km 9.5, Zona Hotelera* ☎ *998/848–7000* 🎟 *$10*) showcases the very best Latin American bands. Go just to watch the locals dance (the beautiful people tend to turn up here really late). Proper dress is required—no jeans or sneakers.

The City (✉ *Blvd. Kukulcán, Km 9.5, Zona Hotelera* ☎ *998/848–8380* 🌐 *www.thecitycancun.com*) is a giant party complex with a daytime water park; at night there's a cavernous dance floor with stadium seating and several large bars selling overpriced drinks. Dancing and live shows are the main draw, as well as a Tuesday-night moonlight pool party and bikini contest. This is by far the loudest club in the Zona Hotelera, so don't be surprised if you go home with a ringing in your ears. Doors open at 10 PM.

The wild, wild **Coco Bongo** (✉ *Blvd. Kukulcán, Km 9.5, across street from Dady'O, Zona Hotelera* ☎ *998/883–5061* 🌐 *www.cocobongo.com.mx* 🎟 *$20, $60 for open bar*) has no chairs, but there are plenty of tables that everyone dances on. There's also a popular floor show billed as "Las Vegas meets Hollywood," featuring celebrity impersonators; and an amazing gravity-defying acrobatic show with an accompanying

12-piece orchestra. After the shows, the techno gets turned up to full volume and everyone gets up to get down.

AVOID TORTOISESHELL

Refrain from buying anything made from tortoiseshell. The *carey*, or hawksbill turtles from which most of it comes, is an endangered species, and it's illegal to bring tortoiseshell products into the United States and several other countries. Also be aware that there are some restrictions regarding black coral. You must purchase it from a recognized dealer.

14

Dady'O (✉ *Blvd. Kukulcán, Km 9.5, Zona Hotelera* ☎ *998/883–3333* 🌐 *www.dadyo.com.mx* 🎫 *$20 cover, $45 for open bar*) has been around for a while, but it is still very "in" with the younger set. A giant screen projects music videos about the always-packed dance floor, while laser lights whirl across the crowd. During spring break the place gets even livelier during the Hawaiian bikini contests.

Sweet Club (✉ *Blvd. Kukulcán, Km 9.5, Zona Hotelera* ☎ *998/883–3333 Ext. 138* 🌐 *www.sweetnightclub.com* 🎫 *$20, $45 for open bar*) draws a high-energy crowd that likes entertainment along with their drink. Live bands usually start off the action, followed by DJs spinning dance tracks into the wee hours of the morning. Girls drink free on Wednesday, wet body contests are on Thursdays, and hot male contests on Sundays. Winners take home $2,000 in cash and prizes. It's open daily from 8 PM on.

Mambo Café (✉ *Plaza Las Avenidas Sm 35, Mz 2, Lote 3, corner of Coba and Ave. Yaxchilan El Centro* ☎ *998/887–8761* 🌐 *www.mambocafe.com.mx* 🎫 *$10, $30 for open bar*) features some of the city's hottest live bands and DJs playing tropical music, making it the ideal disco in which to practice your salsa and merengue steps.

SHOPPING

GALLERIES

Serious collectors visit **Casa de Cultura** (✉ *Prolongación Av. Yaxchilán, Sm 25* ☎ *998/884–8364*) for regular art shows featuring Mexican artists.

Dorfman's Art Gallery (✉ *Inside the Royal Caribbean hotel, Blvd. Kukulcán, Km 17, Zona Hotelera* ☎ *998/881–0100 Ext. 63610*) features Mayan-inspired and environmentally themed sculptures and paintings by local artists and brothers Renato and Adán Dorfman.

El Pabilo (✉ *Av. Yaxchilán 3, Sm 7* ☎ *998/892–4553*) is a downtown café that showcases Mexican painters and photographers on a rotating basis.

MARKETS AND MALLS

ZONA HOTELERA

Coral Negro (✉ *Blvd. Kukulcán, Km 9, Zona Hotelera*), next to the Convention Center, is an open-air market that has about 50 stalls selling crafts and souvenirs. It's open daily until late evening. Everything here is overpriced, but bargaining does work. Stalls deeper in the market tend to have better deals than those around the market's periphery.

Forum-by-the-Sea (✉ *Blvd. Kukulcán, Km 9.5, Zona Hotelera* ☎ *998/883–4428*) is a three-level entertainment and shopping plaza in the Zona. This open-air mall features brand-name restaurants, upscale clothing boutiques, a food court, and chain stores, all in a circuslike atmosphere. For Spring Breakers, the main draws are the nightclubs, Coco Bongo and Hard Rock Cafe, which are identified by the massive guitar at the mall entrance. The bungee trampolines set up here during high season are especially popular with children.

★ The glittering, ultratrendy, and ultraexpensive **La Isla Shopping Village** (✉ *Blvd. Kukulcán, Km 12.5, Zona Hotelera* ☎ *998/883–5025*) is on the Laguna Nichupté under chic, white canopies. A series of canals and small bridges is designed to give the place a Venetian look. In addition to more than 200 shops, the mall has a marina, a disco, restaurants, and movie theaters. There is also an interactive aquarium where you can swim with the dolphins and feed the sharks. A fun, inexpensive activity here is the River Ride Tour, a 20-minute boat ride around the canals and out into the lagoon that costs only $4 per person (a great time to go is right at sundown, so you can watch the sun set over the lagoon).

North of the Convention Center, the two-story **Plaza Caracol** (✉ *Blvd. Kukulcán, Km 8.5, Zona Hotelera* ☎ *998/883–4760*) houses chain stores like Sunglass Island, Benetton, and Ultrafemme, along with souvenir and jewelry shops and pharmacies. Making up this contemporary mall are 150 shops, as well as a small food court, an enormous Starbucks, and the fine Italian restaurant Casa Rolandi. The Plaza is closed on weekends.

In from the Convention Center, **Plaza la Fiesta** (✉ *Blvd. Kukulcán, Km 9, Zona Hotelera* ☎ *998/883–2116*) has 20,000 square feet of showroom space and more than 100,000 different products for sale. Probably the widest selection of Mexican goods in the Hotel Zone, it includes leather goods, silver and gold jewelry, handicrafts, souvenirs, and swimwear. There are some good bargains here.

Plaza Flamingo (✉ *Blvd. Kukulcán, Km 11.5, across from Hotel Flamingo Resort & Plaza, Zona Hotelera* ☎ *998/883–2855*) is a small mall that houses around 80 different shops that sell mainly clothing, jewelry, and souvenirs. The main attractions here are the chain restaurants Jimmy Buffet's Margaritaville, Outback Steakhouse, Bubba Gump, and Pat O'Brien's, which fill up with partiers during spring break.

★ **Plaza Kukulcán** (✉ *Blvd. Kukulcán, Km 13, Zona Hotelera* ☎ *998/193–0161*) is a large, upscale mall with around 100 shops and six restaurants. Some highlights include a bar with a bowling alley and the Luxury Avenue section of the mall, which offers brand names from Cartier, Fendi, and Burberry to Coach. While parents shop, kids can enjoy the game arcade, a play area, and Chocolate City, a theme restaurant with table games, live music, and a weekly circus show. The mall hosts art exhibits and other cultural events. If you stop in any night at 8 PM, you can watch the 10-minute, English-language light show under the Mayan stained-glass dome. If you fell in love with the European clothing chain Mango on your last trip to Paris, swing by the branch here.

Plaza El Zócalo (✉ *Blvd. Kuckulcán, Km 9, Zona Hotelera* ☎ *998/883–3698*) may look small from the entrance, but it has about 60 stalls where you can find traditional Mexican handicrafts, silver jewelry, and handmade sandals. El Zócalo also houses four restaurants—including Mextreme, which still displays a banner announcing its claim to fame as a set in the 1980s movie *Cocktail.*

EL CENTRO

There are lots of interesting shops downtown along Avenida Tulum (between avenidas Cobá and Uxmal). The oldest and largest of Cancún's crafts markets is **Ki Huic** (✉ *Av. Tulum 17, between Bancomer and Bital banks, Sm 3* ☎ *998/884–3347*). It's open daily 9 AM to 10 PM and houses about 100 vendors. **Mercado Veintiocho** *(Market 28)*, just off avenidas Yaxchilán and Sunyaxchén, is the largest open-air market in Cancún. In addition to a few small restaurants, here you will find around 100 stalls selling many of the same items found in the Zona Hotelera but at half the price. **Ultrafemme** (✉ *Av. Tulum 111, at Calle Claveles, Sm 21* ☎ *998/884–1402*) is a popular downtown store that carries duty-free perfume, cosmetics, and jewelry. It also has branches in the Zona Hotelera at Plaza Caracol, Plaza las Américas, Plaza Kukulcán, and La Isla Shopping Village. The downtown store is open daily 9:30 AM to 9 PM.

14

Cancún Gran Plaza (✉ *Av. Nichupté, Mz 18, Lote 1, Locales 24, 30 y 62A, Sm 51, El Centro* ⏲ *9–9*) offers jewelry shops, fashion boutiques, and major department stores such as Sanborns and Wal-Mart. There are also cinemas, cafés, and restaurants in the shopping mall, which is mainly frequented by El Centro residents.

Paseo Cancún (✉ *Av. Andrés, Sm 39 El Centro* ☎ *998/872–3735*) was developed by the same company that owns La Isla in the Zona Hotelera, so it has the same open-air design with modern white canopies throughout. Here you'll find a small ice-skating rink, a movie theater, a bowling alley, a pet store, a food court, several cafés, and around 60 stores.

Parque Lumpkul (✉ *Between Av. Margaritas and Calle Azucenas, Sm 22 El Centro*) is a small park with a hippy vibe. Vendors sell their wares here Wednesday through Sunday, but Friday and Saturday are the best nights to go. There are only about 20 tables, but you can find bargains on beautiful handmade jewelry with unusual stones, as well as hand-painted clothes. There are sometimes music and artistic performances on market days.

Plaza las Américas (✉ *Av. Tulum, Sm 4 and Sm 9* ☎ *998/887–3863*) is the largest shopping center in downtown Cancún. Its 50-plus stores, three restaurants, two movie theaters, video arcade, fast-food outlets, and several large department stores will—for better or worse—make you feel right at home. This mall is intolerably crowded on weekends.

Plaza Las Avenidas (✉ *Av. Yaxchilán, Sm 35, N.C-2, El Centro* ☎ *998/887–7552*) has gift shops, fast-food restaurants, cafés, nightclubs, and a karaoke bar. There are also a drugstore and a bakery on the premises. Far from Hotel Zone, this shopping area is most convenient for those staying in El Centro.

Plaza Bonita (✉ *Av. Xel-Há 1 and 2, Sm 28* ☎ *998/884–6812*) is a small outdoor plaza attached to Mercado Veintiocho (Market 28). It has many wonderful specialty shops carrying Mexican goods and crafts.

Plaza Chinatown (✉ *Sm 35, Mza. 2, Lote 6, between Labná and Av. Xcaret, El Centro* ☎ *998/887–6315*) commonly referred to as Plaza Hong Kong, seems strikingly out of place with it massive pagoda structure. Here you will find Mexican handicrafts, souvenir shops, and a restaurant appropriately named Hong Kong. There is also a babysitting service available in the mall.

Plaza Hollywood (✉ *Av. Xcaret at Rubi Cancún, El Centro* ☎ *998/887–3187*) is one of the newest strip malls to join El Centro. Here you will find several small boutiques and restaurants as well as a bank, post office, and Starbucks. For the wine connoisseur, there is La Europe Wine Market, which carries a wide selection of imported cheeses and meats, as well as Mexican reds.

Plaza Nayandei (✉ *Av. Bonampak 200, Mz 1, Lote 4B-2, Sm 4-A, El Centro* ☎ *998/898–3743*) is a local favorite with its bars, cafés, gym, and eight restaurants. This plaza also has several good furniture stores and a yoga club for kids.

SPORTS AND THE OUTDOORS

BOATING AND SAILING

AquaWorld (✉ *Blvd. Kukulcán, Km 15.2, Zona Hotelera* ☎ *998/848–8300* 🌐 *www.aquaworld.com.mx*) rents boats and water toys like Aqua Twister, a high-speed boat that fishtails 270 degrees. They also offer parasailing and submarine tours.

Delta Tours (✉ *Playa Tortugas, Blvd. Kukulcán, Km 6.5, Zona Hotelera* ☎ *998/849–4995*) has banana boats, snorkeling gear, Wave Runners, and parasails. Willing to match competitive prices, they also offer night cruises, paddy boats, catamarans, and all-inclusive tours to Isla Mujeres.

El Embarcadero (✉ *Blvd. Kukulcán, Km 4, Zona Hotelera* ☎ *998/849–7343*), the marina complex at Playa Linda, is the departure point for ferries to Isla Mujeres and several tour boats.

Marina Barracuda (✉ *Blvd. Kukulcán, Km 14, in front of Ritz-Carlton, Zona Hotelera* ☎ *998/885–3444*), **Marina Punta del Este** (✉ *Blvd. Kukulcán, Km 10.3, Zona Hotelera* ☎ *998/883–1210*), and **Marina del Rey** (✉ *Blvd. Kukulcán, Km 15.6, in front of Grand Oasis Cancún, Zona Hotelera* ☎ *998/885–0363*) all rent out Wave Runners and offer jungle tours that leave several times a day. Marina Punta del Este also has jungle tours that leave every hour from 9 AM to 3 PM.

FISHING

Asterix Tours (✉ *Blvd. Kukulcán, Km 5.5, Zona Hotelera* ☎ *998/886–4847* 🌐 *www.contoytours.com*) offers nighttime "party fishing" trips that cost $78 per person and include dinner and drinks. With an emphasis on nature conservation, Asterix is the only tour company permitted to visit Isla Contoy and the underwater gardens of Isla Mujeres. Tours to Isla Contoy ($100 per person) depart at 9 AM and return at 5 PM on Tuesday, Thursday, and Saturday.

FISHING AND DIVING COMBOS

Mundo Marino (✉ *Blvd. Kukulcán, Km 5.5, Zona Hotelera* ☎ *998/849–7257 or 998/849–7258*) is the marina closest to downtown, and specializes in diving and fishing, including deep-sea fishing expeditions. Prices range from $380 to $940, depending on the size of the boat and the length of the trip. They also offer small game-fishing trips that cost $250 for four hours or $350 for six hours.

Scuba Cancún (✉ *Blvd. Kukulcán, Km 5, Zona Hotelera* ☎ *998/849–7508, 998/849–4736, or 998/849–5225* 🌐 *www.scubacancun.com*) also offers deep-sea fishing and diving. Prices are $550 for a four-hour fishing trip, $650 for six hours, and $800 for an eight-hour expedition.

GOLF

Many hotels offer golf packages that can considerably reduce your greens fees at Cancún golf courses. Cancún's main golf course is at **Cancún Golf Club at Pok-Ta-Pok** (✉ *Blvd. Kukulcán, Km 7.5, Zona Hotelera* ☎ *998/883–1230* 🌐 *www.cancungolfclub.com*). The club has fine views of both sea and lagoon; its 18 holes were designed by Robert Trent Jones Jr. It also has two practice greens, three tennis courts, a pro shop, and a restaurant. The greens fees go from $145 to $175, and include your cart, food, and beverages; club rentals are $40, shoes $18.

The 9-hole executive course **Gran Sol Meliá** (✉ *Gran Melia Cancún Resort, Blvd. Kukulcán, Km 16.5, Zona Hotelera* ☎ *998/881–1100* 🌐 *www.solmelia.com*) forms a semicircle around the property and looks out onto the lagoon. The greens fee is $35, but the course is for the exclusive use of hotel guests.

There's an 18-hole championship golf course at the **Hilton** (✉ *Hilton Cancún Golf & Spa Resort, Blvd. Kukulcán, Km 17, Zona Hotelera* ☎ *998/881–8016* 🌐 *www.hiltoncancun.com/golf.htm*). Lying along the Nichupté Lagoon, the course has a practice facility with driving range and putting green. The 16th hole overlooks the Mayan Ruinas del Rey. Greens fees are $199 ($159 for hotel guests), carts included.

The newest course in Cancún is the **Playa Mujeres Golf Club** (✉ *Playa Mujeres Beach Resort, Prolongación Bonampak, Punta Sam* ☎ *998/887–7322 or 998/892–0874*). Designed by Greg Norman, this 18-hole, par-72 course is within the 930-acre Playa Mujeres Resort that is currently being developed in Punta Sam. Practice facilities include a driving range, two putting greens, and a short game area. You can also arrange for individual and group instruction. Greens fees run from $185 to $253.

Riviera Cancun Golf. Designed by Jack Nicklaus, this 18-hole golf course has ocean views and a Mexican-style clubhouse surrounded by mangroves. A 30% discount is available for guests of all Palace Resorts properties. All others pay $200 greens fees. ✉ *Blvd. Kukulkán, Km. 25, Zona Hotelera* ☎ *998/193–2010 Ext. 8760* 🌐 *www.palaceresorts.com.*

SNORKELING AND SCUBA DIVING

Aqua Fun (✉ *Blvd. Kukulcán, Km 16.5, Zona Hotelera* ☎ *998/885–0195 or 1682*) offers a two-hour tour of the mangroves that costs $66 per person and includes snorkeling at the Punta Nizuc reef.

AquaWorld (✉ *Blvd. Kukulcán, Km 15.2, Zona Hotelera* ☎ *998/848–8300* 🌐 *www.aquaworld.com.mx*) has a day-trip snorkeling excursion to Isla Mujeres that costs $77 per person. This operation also offers diving; a one-tank dive costs $72, and two-tank dives start at $77. Dive explorations of boat wrecks cost $85, and three-day dive packages cost $266.

Marina Barracuda (✉ *Blvd. Kukulcán, Km 14, Zona Hotelera* ☎ *998/885–2444* 🌐 *www.marinabarracuda.com*) has a two-hour jungle boat tour through the mangroves, which ends with snorkeling at the Punta Nizuc coral reef. The fee (starting at $66) includes snorkeling equipment, life jackets, and refreshments.

Marina Punta del Este (✉ *Blvd. Kukulcán, Km 10.3, Zona Hotelera* ☎ *998/883–1210*) is right in front of the Cancún Caribe Park Royal Grand. They have dives that last from 3½ to 4 hours; $72 if you are certified and $88 for a lesson. Daily lessons begin at 8 AM and 1 PM.

Mundo Marino (✉ *Blvd. Kukulcán, Km 5.5, Zona Hotelera* ☎ *998/849–7257 or 998/849–7258*) has a 2½-hour snorkeling excursion that costs $28 per person. They also offer a single-tank dive ($55), two-tank dive ($70), night dive ($70), and diving instruction course ($90).

Solo Buceo (✉ *Blvd. Kukulcán, Km 9.5, Zona Hotelera* ☎ *998/883–3979* 🌐 *www.solobuceo.com*) charges $55 for one-tank dives, $70 for two-tank dives, and $90 for twilight diving every Tuesday and Thursday. They also have NAUI, FMAS, CMAS, and PADI instruction (lesson prices range from $90 to $240).

ISLA MUJERES

Updated by Marlise Kast

Once a small fishing village, this colorful destination has become a favorite for travelers seeking natural beauty, island serenity, and a slower pace of life. Without compromising its cultural traditions, Isla Mujeres is one of the most relaxing and affordable places to vacation.

During high season boatloads of visitors pop over from Cancún to have a taste of the island life. This midday rush is a boon for vendors and hagglers offering every kind of service from braided hair to beach massages. By late afternoon the masses disappear and return to their big-city nightlife and the comforts of the mainland. Those who stay behind discover that on Isla Mujeres concerns fade with the sinking of the sun and are washed away by the cool breezes of the Caribbean morning.

Embracing its rewards are Isla's permanent residents, including nearly 100 Canadian and American expats (most operating hotels and restaurants) and 15,000 friendly Maya, many of whom earn a living selling fish at the docks or plates of food outside their homes. There are plenty of opportunities to practice your Spanish, and you'll find that most locals beam when you try. Taxi drivers are genuinely interested in sharing details of the island's history, or telling you about their families who were born and raised on Isla Mujeres.

The minute you step off the boat, you'll get a sense of how small Isla is. The sights and properties on the island are strung along the coasts. There's not much to the interior except the two saltwater marshes, Salina Chica and Salina Grande, where Maya harvested salt centuries ago.

EXPLORING

To get your bearings, try thinking of the island as a long, narrow fish: the head is the southeastern tip, the tail is the northwest prong. Five miles long and half a mile wide, Isla Mujeres can easily be explored in a single day. If you take your time, however, you'll discover that the island is not a destination to be rushed. Virtually car-free, the dirt roads of this quaint fishing village are best traveled by golf cart, by scooter, or by bike.

⚠ **Before leaving the rental agency, check your scooter and golf cart for scratches and dings. You may even want to take a photo for additional proof of the original condition. Otherwise, you will pay dearly for any damage that was not noted prior to your rental agreement.**

If you're staying at one of the remote hotels on the southern tip, a taxi will take you from one end of the island to the other for $6.

TOP ATTRACTIONS

7 **El Garrafón National Park.** Despite participation in the much-publicized "Garrafón Reef Restoration Program," much of the coral reef at this national marine park remains dead (the result of hurricanes, boat anchors, and too many careless tourists). There are still colorful fish, but many of them will only come near if bribed with food. Although there's no longer much for snorkelers, the park does have kayaks and a diving platform, as well as a three-floor facility with restaurants, bathrooms, and gift shops. Be prepared to spend $69 for the basic package called "Garrafón Discovery," which includes gear, breakfast, lunch, activities, open bar, and even transportation from Cancún. An additional $30 includes a bicycle tour, zip-lining, and access to a climbing tower. Another option is Dolphin Discovery ($149–$199), where you can use the park's amenities and swim with dolphins or bull sharks. ■ **TIP→ The Beach Club Garrafón de Castilla next door is a much cheaper alternative; the snorkeling is at least equal to that available in the park. The club is open to everyone, and the entrance fee is $4. You can take a taxi from town.** The park is home to the **Santuario Maya a la Diosa Ixchel,** the sad vestiges of a Mayan temple once dedicated to the goddess Ixchel. A lovely walkway around the area remains, but the natural arch beneath the ruin has been blasted open and "repaired" with concrete badly disguised as rocks. The views here are spectacular, though: you can look to the open ocean where waves crash against dramatic cliffs on one side, and the Bahía de Mujeres (Bay of Women) on the other. On the way to the temple there's a cutesy Caribbean-style shopping center selling overpriced jewelry and souvenirs, as well as a park with abstract sculptures painted in bright colors. There's also an old lighthouse, which you can enter for free. Climb to the top for an incredible

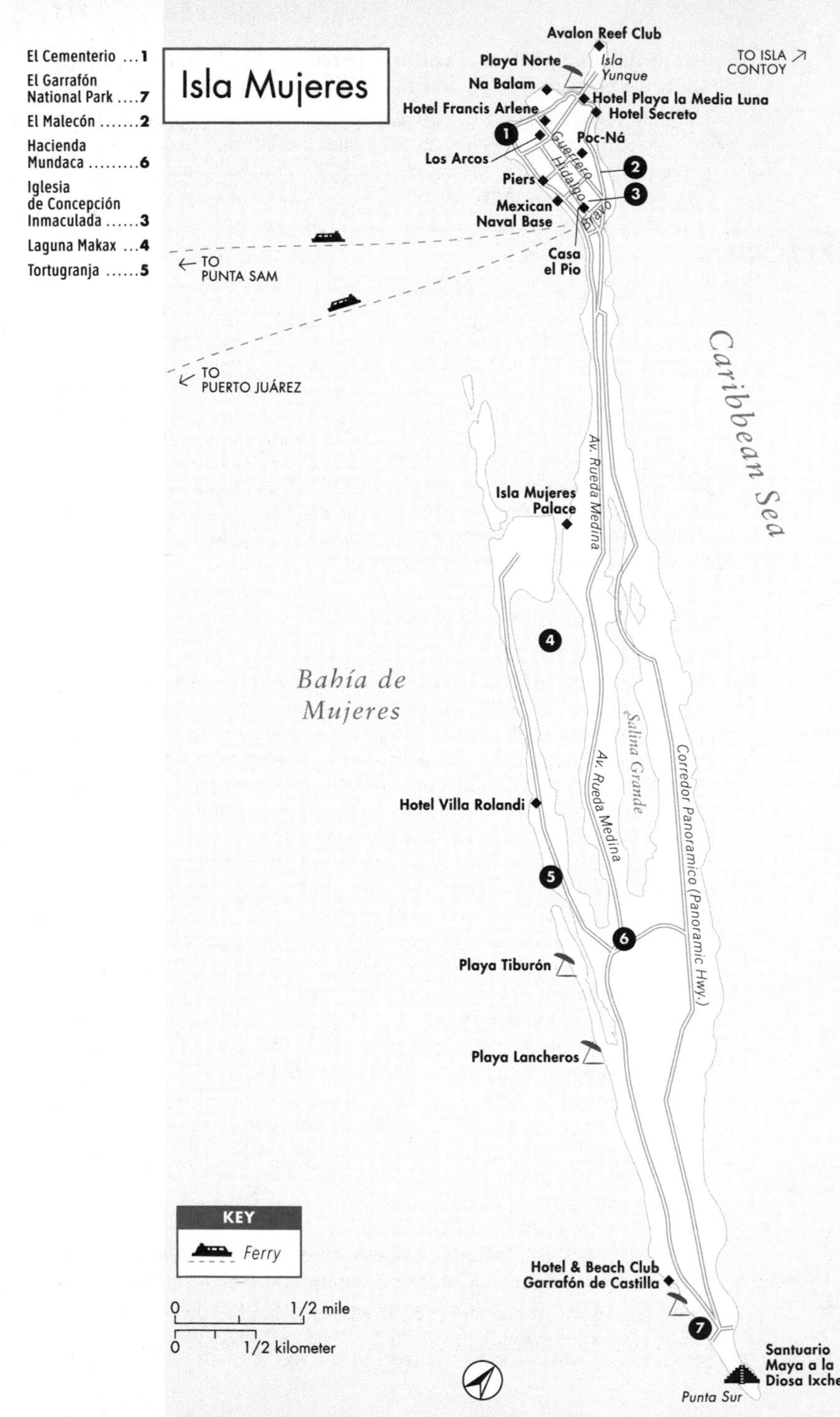
Isla Mujeres
El Cementerio ...1
El Garrafón National Park 7
El Malecón 2
Hacienda Mundaca 6
Iglesia de Concepción Inmaculada 3
Laguna Makax ...4
Tortugranja 5
Avalon Reef Club
Playa Norte
Isla Yunque
TO ISLA CONTOY
Na Balam
Hotel Playa la Media Luna
Hotel Francis Arlene
Hotel Secreto
Poc-Ná
Los Arcos
Guerrero
Hidalgo
Piers
Mexican Naval Base
Bravo
Casa el Pio
TO PUNTA SAM
TO PUERTO JUÁREZ
Caribbean Sea
Av. Rueda Medina
Isla Mujeres Palace
Bahía de Mujeres
Salina Grande
Corredor Panoramico (Panoramic Hwy.)
Hotel Villa Rolandi
Playa Tiburón
Playa Lancheros
KEY
Ferry
Hotel & Beach Club Garrafón de Castilla
0
1/2 mile
0
1/2 kilometer
Santuario Maya a la Diosa Ixchel
Punta Sur

CLOSE UP

Who Was Ixchel?

Ixchel (ee-*shell*) is a principal figure in the pantheon of Mayan gods. Originally married to the earth god Voltan, Ixchel fell in love with the moon god Itzamna, considered the founder of the Maya because he taught them how to read, write, and grow corn. When Ixchel became his consort, she gave birth to four powerful sons known as the Bacabs, who continue to hold up the sky in each of the four directions. Sometimes called Lady Rainbow, Ixchel is the goddess of childbirth, fertility, and healing. She controls the tides and all water on earth.

Often portrayed as a wise crone, she is seen wearing a skirt decorated with crossbones and a crown of serpents while carrying a jug of water. The crossbones are a symbol of her role as the giver of new life and keeper of dead souls. The serpents represent her wisdom and power to rejuvenate. The water jug alludes to her dual role as both a benign and destructive delty. Although she gives mankind the continual gift of water—the most essential element of life—according to Mayan myth, Ixchel also sent floods to cleanse the earth of wicked men who had stopped thanking the gods. She is said to give special protection to those making the sacred pilgrimage to her sites on Cozumel and Isla Mujeres.

14

view to the south; the vista in the other direction is marred by a tower from a defunct amusement-park ride (Ixchel would not be pleased). The ruin, which is open daily 9 to 5, is at the point where the road turns northeast into the Corredor Panorámico. To visit just the ruins and sculpture park, the admission is $3. Admission to the village is free. ✉ *Carretera El Garrafón, 6 km (3¾ mi), Mz 41, Lote 12, Sm 9, Punta Sur, southeast of Playa Lancheros* ☎ *998/877–1100 or 998/193–3360* 🌐 *www.garrafon.com* 💵 *Tours from Cancún $69–$99; tours from Isla $55* 🕑 *Daily 10 AM–5 PM. Closed Sat.*

3 **Iglesia de Concepción Inmaculada** *(Church of the Immaculate Conception).* In 1890 local fishermen landed at a deserted colonial settlement known as Ecab, where they found three identical statues of the Virgin Mary, each carved from wood with porcelain face and hands. No one knows for certain where the statues originated, but it's widely believed that they were gifts from the Spanish during a visit in 1770. One statue went to the city of Izamal in the Yucatán, and another was sent to Kantunikin in Quintana Roo. The third remained on the island. It was housed in a small wooden chapel while this church was being built; legend has it that the chapel burst into flames when the statue was removed. Some islanders still believe that the statue walks on the water around the island from dusk until dawn, looking for her sisters. You can pay your respects daily from 10 AM until 11:30 AM and then from 7 PM until 9 PM. ✉ *Avs. Morelos and Bravo, south side of the zócalo.*

QUICK BITES

It's a small island, but there are several small shops selling gelato. Gelateria Monte Bianco (✉ *Av. Matamoros 20* ☎ *998/149–3109* 💳 No credit cards) is run by an Italian couple who have lived on the island for a few years. Cool Gelato (✉ *Av. Hidalgo, next to Plaza Los Almendros,*

☎ *998/167–6351*) has over a dozen flavors, and is the only island gelateria to make 100% natural ice cream.

> **WORD OF MOUTH**
>
> "If you want a quiet place to go where the kids will be welcome, it's a nice place—just not as fancy or crowded or rowdy as the mainland in Cancún."
>
> —woodbutcherl

2 **El Malecón**. To enjoy the drama of Isla's eastern shore while soaking up some rays, stroll along this mile-long boardwalk. It's the beginning of a long-term improvement project and will eventually encircle the island. Currently, it runs from Half Moon Bay to El Colonia, with several benches and lookout points. Visit El Monumento de Tortugas (Turtle Monument) along the way.

5 **Tortugranja** *(Turtle Farm)*. This scientific station is run by the Mexican government in partnership with private funding. Its mission is to continue conservation efforts on behalf of the endangered sea turtle. You can see rescued turtle hatchlings in three large pools or watch the larger turtles in sea pens. There is also a small museum with an excellent display about turtles and the ecosystem. From May through August you can make arrangements to join the staff in collecting and hatching eggs, and in the fall you can assist in releasing the baby turtles. ✉ *Take Av. Rueda Medina south of town; about a block southeast of Hacienda Mundaca, take right fork (smaller road that loops back north called Sac Bajo); entrance is about ½ km (¼ mi) farther, on left* ☎ *998/877–0595* 🎟 *$5* ⏲ *Daily 9–5.*

WORTH NOTING

1 **El Cementerio**. Isla's unnamed cemetery, with its century-old colorful gravestones, is on Avenida López Mateos, the road that runs parallel to Playa Norte. Many of the tombstones are covered with carved angels and flowers; the most elaborate and beautiful mark the graves of children. Hidden among them is the tomb of the notorious Fermín Mundaca de Marechaja. This 19th-century slave trader—who's often billed more glamorously as a pirate—carved his own skull-and-crossbones gravestone with the ominous epitaph: AS YOU ARE, I ONCE WAS; AS I AM, SO SHALL YOU BE. Mundaca's grave is empty, however; his remains lie in Mérida, where he died. The monument is tough to find—ask a local to point out the unidentified marker.

6 **Hacienda Mundaca**. A dirt drive where vendors sell mobiles, mermaid figurines, and other crafts made out of local shells marks the entrance to what's left of a mansion constructed by 19th-century slave trader–turned–pirate Fermín Mundaca de Marechaja. When the British navy began cracking down on slavers, Mundaca settled on the island. He fell in love with a local beauty nicknamed La Trigueña (The Brunette). To woo her, Mundaca built a sprawling estate with verdant gardens. Apparently unimpressed, La Trigueña instead married a young islander—and legend has it that Mundaca went slowly mad waiting for her to change her mind. He ended up dying in a brothel in Mérida.

This place is more about learning the history than it is about seeing the actual sights. The actual hacienda has vanished. All that remain are a rusted cannon and a ruined stone archway with a triangular pediment carved with the following inscription: HUERTA DE LA HACIENDA DE VISTA ALEGRE (Orchard of the Happy View Hacienda). The gardens are also suffering from neglect, and the animals in a small on-site zoo seem as tired as the rest of the property. Mundaca would, however, approve of the admission charge; considering what little there is to see, it's piracy. ✉ *East of Av. Rueda Medina; take main road southeast from town to S-curve at end of Laguna Makax, turn left onto dirt road* ☎ *No phone* 🎟 *$2* ⏲ *Daily 9 AM–4 PM.*

4 **Laguna Makax.** Pirates are said to have anchored their ships in this lagoon while waiting to ambush hapless vessels crossing the Spanish Main (the area in which Spanish treasure ships sailed). These days the lagoon houses a local shipyard and provides a safe harbor for boats during hurricane season. It's off Avenida Rueda Medina, about 2½ km (1½ mi) south of town, about two blocks south of the naval base and some *salinas* (salt marshes).

SAFETY FIRST

Unlike Cancún and Cozumel, Isla Mujeres does not use the colored safety flag system, and there are no lifeguards to keep watch over swimmers. Therefore, it is best to only venture out near familiar beaches like Playa Norte, Playa Lancheros, and Playa Tiburón on calm days when winds are light. Be wary of strong currents and riptides, especially on the east side of the island. If you plan on spending a day at the beach, apply sunscreen or wear protective clothing to avoid overexposure. Bring fresh drinking water to keep you hydrated, and above all, use common sense.

BEACHES

★ **Playa Norte (North Beach)** is easy to find: simply head north on any of the north–south streets in town until you hit this superb beach. The turquoise sea is as calm as a lake here, though developers have arrived on the scene and the area no longer has a secluded feel. The small cove between Avalon Reef Club and the Caribbean is the nicest section of Playa Norte. Although relatively shallow, the water flows directly from the open sea, making this protected area cool and clean. Play a game of beach volleyball, or enjoy a drink at one of the area's palapa bars, where wooden swings take the place of bar stools; **Buho's** is especially popular with locals and tourists who gather to chat, eat fresh seafood, drink cold beer, and watch the sunset. Lounge chairs and hammocks at **Sergio's** are free for customers, but to relax in front of **Maria del Maria** in a lounge chair will cost you $3. **Na Balam** charges a whopping $10 for one chair and umbrella. **Best For:** swimming, kayaking, relaxing, beach volleyball. **Amenities:** toilets, umbrellas, and chaise lounges available at beach bars.

There are two beaches between Laguna Makax and El Garrafón National Park.

Playa Lancheros (Boatman's Beach) is a popular spot with an open-air restaurant where locals gather to eat freshly grilled fish. The beach has grittier sand than Playa Norte, but more palm trees. The calm water makes it the perfect spot for children—although it's best if they stay close to shore, since the ocean floor drops off steeply. The souvenir stands, renting kayaks, canoes, and beach toys, are fairly low-key and run by local families. Most bars and restaurants will give you access to beach chairs, umbrellas and facilities provided you order a drink. There is a small pen with domesticated and quite harmless *tiburones gatos*—nurse sharks. (These sharks are much friendlier than the *tintoreras,* or blue sharks, which live in the open seas, have seven rows of teeth, and weigh up to 1,100 pounds.) You can swim with the nurse sharks or get your picture taken with them for $1. **Best For:** snorkeling, families with children. **Amenities:** toilets, food concessions, umbrellas, beach chairs.

NOT ALL BEACHES ARE FOR SWIMMING!

Although the beaches on the eastern side of the island (often referred to as the Caribe side) are quite beautiful, they're not safe for swimming because of the dangerous undertows; several drownings have occurred at these beaches. Another gorgeous but dangerous beach is found northeast, just kitty-corner to Playa Norte. **Playa Media Luna** (Half Moon beach) is very tempting, but the strong currents make it treacherous for swimmers.

Playa Tiburón (Shark Beach), like Playa Lancheros, is on the west coast facing Bahía de Mujeres, and so its waters are also exceptionally calm. It's a more developed beach, with a large, popular seafood restaurant (through which you actually enter the beach), serving burgers, hot dogs, and fish. There are several souvenir stands selling the usual T-shirts as well as handmade seashell jewelry. On certain days there are women who will braid your hair or give you a henna tattoo. This beach also has two sea pens with the sleepy and relatively tame nurse sharks. Swim with them for $2. **Best For:** snorkeling, swimming, sunbathing. **Amenities:** food concessions, toilets at restaurants.

WHERE TO EAT

EL PUEBLO

$$$ ITALIAN ✕ **Angelo.** Named for Angelo Sanna, its Italian chef, this charming bistro is done up with soft lighting and a wood-fired oven. The pizzas are decent, but the meat dishes are even tastier. Try their famous wood-oven lasagna or mussels steamed in white wine. Angelo, who has lived and worked in Isla Mujeres for more than 15 years, is also a great source of local information. ✉ *Av. Hidalgo 14* ☎ *998/877–1273* ▭ *MC, V.*

$$–$$$ ECLECTIC ✕ **Bamboo.** This casual restaurant, with its bamboo-covered walls, offers seafood, steak, Asian, and Mexican dishes prepared by two different chefs. Starting at 7 AM, the first chef cooks up hearty breakfasts of omelets and hash browns with freshly brewed coffee. Later in the day, the second chef switches to steaks, tacos, and Asian-fusion-style lunches and dinners, including knockout shrimp tempura, vegetable stir-fry, and chicken satay in a spicy peanut sauce. During high season Bamboo's split personality continues: two bands play each evening,

attracting locals who linger until around midnight. This restaurant has an ATM for those who are short on cash. ✉ *Plaza Los Almendros No. 4* ☎ *998/877–1355* ▭ *MC, V.*

$ CAFÉ ✕ **Café Cito.** This cheery, seashell-decorated café was opened in 1988 as one of Isla's first cafés—and it's still one of the best places to breakfast on the island. The breakfast menu includes fresh waffles, fruit-filled crepes, and egg dishes, as well as great cappuccino and espresso; lunch specials are also available daily. After your meal, be sure to head to the Soñadores del Sol shop next door; the proprietor gives great tarot readings daily from 11 to 2. ✉ *Avs. Juárez and Matamoros* ☎ *998/877–1470* ▭ *No credit cards,* ⊙ *No dinner.*

$$ MEXICAN ✕ **Don Chepo.** Mexican-style grilled meats (tacos, fajitas, and steaks) are the draw at this lively restaurant that resembles a small hacienda. Inside, the focal point is the large and well-stocked bar, where you can chat with other visitors or enjoy the (sometimes live) mariachi music. Tables outside are perfect for watching all the downtown action on Hidalgo Street. The *arrachera,* a fine cut of beef grilled to perfection and served with rice, salad, baked potato, warm tortillas, and beans, is a reliably excellent choice, as is the chile relleno. ✉ *Avs. Hidalgo and Francisco Madero* ☎ *998/877–0165* ▭ *MC, V.*

$$$ MEXICAN ✕ **Fayne's.** The vibe at this brightly painted spot is hip and energetic. Best known for its terrific cocktails (don't miss the mango margaritas), this funky restaurant serves good island fare such as garlic shrimp, ceviche enchiladas, calamari stuffed with seafood and spinach, and grilled snapper. There's live music nightly starting at 10:30. ✉ *Av. Hidalgo 12A, between Avs. Mateos and Matamoros* ☎ *998/877–0528* ▭ *MC, V.*

$$ ECLECTIC ✕ **Jax Bar & Grill.** The downstairs of this hot spot is a lively sports bar that serves huge, thick, perfectly grilled burgers and cold beer. If you're not in the mood for a burger, you can choose from over 70 items on the menu, including fish tacos, corn dogs, and filet mignon. The satellite TV is always turned to the big game, and there's a table for those who want to shoot some pool. Upstairs is a terrace where you can enjoy dishes like fresh grilled seafood and the house "bucket of beer" (five Coronas for $6) while watching the sunset. The friendly staff caters to kids, and is often able to procure their favorite dishes, even if they aren't on the menu. ✉ *Av. Adolfo Mateos 42* ☎ *998/887–1218* 🌐 *www.jaxsportfishing.com* ▭ *MC, V.*

¢ CAFÉ ✕ **Los Aluxes Cafe.** The perfect spot for an early-morning or late-night cappuccino (it opens at 7 AM and closes at 10 PM), this place also has terrific desserts and baked goods. The New York–style cheesecake and triple-fudge brownies are especially decadent. There's also a great selection of exotic teas, and locally made jewelry is for sale. If you want the café's famous banana bread, get here early—the loaves usually sell out by 10 AM. ✉ *Av. Matamoros 87* ▭ *No credit cards* ⊙ *Closed Tues.*

$ CAFÉ ✕ **Mañana Restaurant & Bookstore.** It's hard to miss this bright fuchsia restaurant with a yellow sun stretching its rays over the front door. But you won't want to miss the great breakfasts, with excellent egg dishes, fresh baguettes, and Italian coffee. Salads, homemade burgers (meat or vegetarian), and fresh fruit shakes are served at lunch. If you're in a hurry, you can grab a quick snack at the outdoor counter with its

14

palapa roof—but since Cosmic Cosas bookstore is also here, you may want to lounge on the couch and read after your meal. ✉ *Av. Guerrero 17* ☎ *998/877–0555* ▭ *No credit cards* ⊗ *No dinner. Closed Sun.*

$ MEDITERRANEAN Fodor's Choice ★ ✕ **Olivia**. The delightful dishes at this Mediterranean restaurant are fusions of Moroccan, Greek, and Turkish flavors based on owners Lior and Yaron Zelzer's old family recipes. Everything from the freshly baked spanakopita to the flaky baklava is made from scratch in the open-air kitchen. House favorites include the *shawarma* pita wrap filled with grilled chicken, hummus, tahini, and fried eggplant, or the *mafrum* (a blend of potatoes stuffed with ground beef in Moroccan red sauce). The setting is casual yet romantic, with tiki torches lighting the way to a tropical garden where rustic tables sit beneath a palapa roof. A visit to Oliva's isn't complete without a bowl of homemade cherry ice cream. ✉ *Av. Matamoros between Juárez and Medina, El Pueblo* ☎ *998/877–1765* ⊕ *www.olivia-isla-mujeres.com* ▭ *No credit cards* ⊗ *No lunch. Closed Sun. and Mon.*

$$ SEAFOOD ✕ **Picus Cocktelería**. Kick off your shoes and settle back with a cold beer at this charming beachside restaurant right near the ferry docks. You can watch the fishing boats come and go while you wait for some of the freshest seafood on the island. The grilled fish and grilled lobster with garlic butter are both magnificent, as are the shrimp fajitas—but the real showstopper is the mixed seafood ceviche, which might include conch, shrimp, abalone, fish, or octopus. ✉ *Av. Rueda Medina, 1 block northwest of ferry docks* ☎ *998/129–6011* ▭ *MC, V.*

$ CUBAN Fodor's Choice ★ ✕ **Qubano.** One of the main draws to this delightful Cuban restaurant is its vivacious owner and chef, Vivian Reynaldo. Her Hungarian potatoes (a recipe from her mother) have been known to leave customers speechless. Many of the grilled sandwiches, like the "Toston," creatively use fried plantain instead of bread. Try the juicy hamburger stuffed with goat cheese, or the roasted pork served with yucca fries, rice, and beans. Salads are topped with the freshest ingredients, like garbanzo beans, avocado, blue cheese, and jicama. There are also several vegetarian dishes as well as fresh-squeezed juices—the watermelon is divine. The simple setting, with four tables inside a turquoise-colored shack, is cozy, pleasant, and welcoming. ✉ *Av. Abasolo, between Hidalgo and Vicente Guerrero* ☎ *998/214–2118* ▭ *No credit cards* ⊗ *12–5 PM. No dinner.*

$ MEXICAN ✕ **Sergio's Playa Sol**. Delicious chicken nachos, creamy guacamole, and savory fish kebabs are on the menu at this great beach bar at Playa Norte. You can easily spend the whole day here and stay for the sunset; there are free hammocks, beach chairs, and umbrellas for customers. ✉ *North end of Rueda Medina on Playa Norte* ☎ *No phone* ▭ *No credit cards.*

$$$ MEXICAN ★ ✕ **Sunset Grill**. The perfect place to savor the sunset, this spot has a covered dining terrace with large picture windows that overlook the sea. Soft music and candlelight add to the romantic ambience. Grab a table outside and you can take a dip in the ocean between your appetizer and main course. The dinner menu has a wide range of dishes, including favorites like fried calamari, coconut shrimp, and fried snapper. The kitchen offers a lunch of Mexican favorites like tacos and quesadillas, but also fries up a great burger. Service is very good, and there's live

music nightly. ✉ *Av. Rueda Medina, North End, Condominios Nautibeach, Playa Norte* ☎ *998/877–0785* ▭ *AE, MC, V.*

> **WORD OF MOUTH**
>
> "It really IS easy to get around Isla—just turn left at the ferry docks and walk right into Playa Norte about six blocks ahead. Most of the bars and beach clubs are around on the north/east portion of the wide beach. Downtown shops and eateries are straight ahead from the dock a few blocks and run north toward the North beach. Even more fun—get a golf cart or take a cab to Playa Lancheros—pretty beach, cold beer, and the best grilled fish you'll ever eat!" jw2

14

ELSEWHERE ON THE ISLAND

$ FRENCH ✕ **Bistro Français.** This casual café, with menu items painted on the walls in bright colors, serves up tasty French dishes at reasonable prices. Breakfast is particularly nice, with tasty fruit salads and practically perfect waffles. Later on in the day, try French dishes like chicken cordon bleu or coq au vin. The deck overlooks the street, so you can watch the world go by. ✉ *Av. Matamoros 29* ☎ *No phone* ▭ *No credit cards.*

$$$ ECLECTIC Fodor's Choice ★ ✕ **Casa Rolandi.** This hotel restaurant is casually sophisticated, with an open-air dining room leading out to a deck that overlooks the water. Tables are set with beautiful linens, china, and cutlery. The northern Italian menu here includes the wonderful carpaccio *di tonno alla Giorgio* (thin slices of tuna with extra-virgin olive oil and lime juice), along with excellent pastas—even the simplest dishes such as angel-hair pasta in tomato sauce are delicious. For something different, try the saffron risotto or the *costolette d'agnello al forno* (lamb chops with a thyme infusion). The sunset views are spectacular. ✉ *Hotel Villa Rolandi, Fracc. Laguna Mar, Sm 7, Mz 75, Lotes 15 and 16* ☎ *998/999–2000* ▭ *AE, MC, V.*

$ MEXICAN ✕ **Playa Lancheros Restaurant.** If you want to savor one of the island's most authentic meals, take a short taxi ride to this casual eatery under a big palapa roof. It's right on the beach, so it's no surprise that the kitchen takes pride in serving the freshest fish. The house specialty is the Yucatecan *tikinchic* (fish marinated in a sour-orange sauce and cooked in a banana leaf over an open flame). There are also delicious tacos, fresh guacamole, and spicy salsa. The food may take a while to arrive, so bring your swimsuit and take a dip while you wait. On Sunday there's music, dancing, and the occasional shark wrestler. ✉ *Playa Lancheros, where Av. Rueda Medina splits into Sac Bajo and Carretera El Garrafón* ☎ *998/274–0018* ▭ *MC, V.*

WHERE TO STAY

EL PUEBLO

$$$$ **Avalon Reef Club.** This all-inclusive resort sits on a tiny island at the northern tip of Isla Mujeres. The location is gorgeous, and the seaside suites take advantage of this with balconies overlooking the ocean. Regular rooms in the hotel tower are small without balconies. Be warned: this is a time-share resort, and preference is given to those who bought

into the "Paradise Found" program. Sales pitches are relentless, but if you can be stalwart in your refusal, you may be able to enjoy this lovely property. You can choose to pay just for your room or go with the all-inclusive option if you prefer to stay in. **Pros:** beautiful location, stunning beaches. **Cons:** constant sales pitches, some rooms lack views. ✉ *Calle Zazcil-Ha s/n 7, Isla Yunque* ☎ *998/999–2050* 🌐 *www.avalonvacations.com* *74 rooms, 6 suites, 49 villas* *In-room: a/c, kitchen (some), safe. In-hotel: 2 restaurants, room service, pool, gym, beachfront, spa, Wi-Fi hotspot* 💳 *AE, MC, V* *AI, EP.*

$ Fodor'sChoice ★ **Casa el Pio.** Off the town square, this boutique hotel—owned by a graphic designer and hair stylist—is bursting with character, charm and creativity. It's ideally suited for independent travelers who do not require 24-hour service, but appreciate value, comfort, and modern design. Inspired by the owners' trips to Greece, the property is stark white with hints of aqua. The sound of crashing waves can be heard from every room, each with its own reading nook, kitchenette, and lounge area with an extra daybed. There is also a large courtyard where guests can watch the sunset while drinking an evening cocktail. **Pros:** unlimited fresh drinking water, spotless property, MP3 audio tour available detailing sites of Isla Mujeres. **Cons:** no restaurant, no housekeeping on Sundays, lacks 24-hour service. ✉ *Av. Hidalgo between Bravo and Allende* ☎ *No phone* 🌐 *www.casaelpio.com* *4 rooms* *In-room: a/c, no phone, safe, kitchen, refrigerator, no TV, Wi-Fi. In-hotel: beachfront, pool, Wi-Fi hotspot, no kids under 18* 💳 *AE, MC, V (via PayPal only)* *EP.*

$–$$ **Hotel Francis Arlene.** This small hotel is a perennial favorite. Rooms surround a pleasant courtyard and are outfitted with double beds, bamboo furniture, and refrigerators. Some have kitchenettes. The Magaña family takes great care to maintain the property—signs everywhere remind you to save electricity and keep noise to a minimum. Playa Norte is a few blocks north, and downtown is a block away. This is one of the few hotels that can accommodate wheelchairs. **Pros:** reasonable rates, friendly staff. **Cons:** some street noise, not all rooms have balconies. ✉ *Av. Guerrero 7* ☎ *998/877–0310* 🌐 *www.francisarlene.com* *26 rooms* *In-room: a/c (some), kitchen (some), refrigerator. In-hotel: Wi-Fi hotspot* 💳 *MC, V* *EP.*

$$–$$$ **Hotel Playa la Media Luna.** This breezy palapa-roofed bed-and-breakfast lies along Half Moon Beach, just south of Playa Norte. Guest rooms here are done in bright Mexican colors, with king-size beds and balconies or terraces that look out over the pool and the ocean beyond; some have Jacuzzis. Continental breakfast is served in a sunny dining room. The hotel also has small, spartan rooms, with no view and no breakfast, for $60 per night. **Pros:** rooms have balconies, nearby beach is calm and shallow. **Cons:** thin towels, no bar, no elevator. ✉ *Sección Rocas, Punta Norte, Lote 9/10* ☎ *998/877–0759* 🌐 *www.playamedialuna.com* *18 rooms* *In-room: a/c, safe, refrigerator. In-hotel: restaurant, room service, pool, beachfront, Wi-Fi hotspot* 💳 *MC, V* *CP.*

$$$ **Hotel Secreto.** It's beautiful. It's famous. It's très, très chic. But if you're looking for a warm, inviting atmosphere, this may not be the place for you. Although the sense of reserve makes it perfect for honeymoon

couples that want to be alone, singles may find it too quiet, and families with children are not made to feel welcome. Rooms have floor-to-ceiling windows, veiled king-size four-poster beds, and balconies overlooking Half Moon Bay. Mexican artwork looks bold against the predominantly white color scheme, and a small, intimate dining room sits alongside a small ocean-side pool. This place isn't much of a secret anymore, so it's sometimes hard to get a reservation. **Pros:** in-room massage and facials, pool overlooks ocean, peace and quiet. **Cons:** not good for children, books up in advance, no restaurant. ✉ *Sección Rocas, Lote 11, Half Moon Beach* ☎ *998/877–1039* 🌐 *www.hotelsecreto.com* *12 rooms* *In-room: a/c, safe, refrigerator, Wi-Fi. In-hotel: bar, pool, water sports, gym, parking (free)* ▭ *AE, MC, V* *CP.*

WORD OF MOUTH

"We have stayed at Na Balam and it is lovely, with beautiful beach right out your door. You can easily walk the 'downtown' portion of the island. Renting a golf cart is the best way to explore the rest of the island. Be sure to have breakfast or lunch at Cafe Cito (Calle Matamoros). Fabulous waffles and freshly made marmalade!"

—AJMelheim

14

$–$$ ★ **Los Arcos.** In the heart of downtown, this hotel is a terrific value. The comfortable suites are all cheerfully decorated with Mexican-style furnishings. Each has a small kitchenette with a microwave and fridge, a fully tiled bathroom with great water pressure, a small sitting area, and a king-size bed. The large and sunny balconies on the front have views of the street, whereas those at the back are more private. The pleasant and helpful staff is an added bonus. The hotel management encourages online booking. **Pros:** reasonable rates, spacious rooms, near restaurants and shops. **Cons:** some linens feel worn, sparse furnishings, no elevator. ✉ *Av. Hidalgo 58, between Abasolo and Matamoros* ☎ *998/877–1343* 🌐 *www.suites-los-arcos.myislamujeres.com* *12 rooms* *In-room: a/c, safe, kitchen. In-hotel: Wi-Fi hotspot* ▭ *MC, V* *EP.*

$$$–$$$$ ★ **Na Balam.** Elegant without being pretentious, this tranquil hotel is a true sanctuary. Each guest room in the main building has a thatched palapa roof, Mexican folk art, a large bathroom, an eating area, and a spacious balcony or patio facing the ocean. The beach here is private, with its own bar serving snacks and drinks. Although somewhat pricy, the restaurant serves delicious seafood, shrimp tacos, and salads with the freshest ingredients. Across the street are eight more spacious rooms surrounding a pool, a garden, and a meditation room where yoga classes are held. Great for families is the on-site scuba center with its own dive master. **Pros:** excellent restaurant, beautiful beach. **Cons:** not all rooms are on the beach, mosquitoes at night. ✉ *Calle Zazil-Ha 118* ☎ *998/881–4770* 🌐 *www.nabalam.com* *35 rooms* *In-room: a/c, no phone, safe, no TV. In-hotel: spa, restaurant, bar, pool, beachfront, diving, Wi-Fi hotspot* ▭ *AE, MC, V* *EP, CP.*

¢ **Poc-Ná.** This coed youth hostel is one of El Pueblo's best deals. Half the rooms are dorm-style and have fans; the others are private and air-conditioned. To promote community spirit, the hostel hosts movie nights, board and card games, and regular parties. There is also a "beach bar," which is not actually on the beach but is open to the public nightly. The hostel is within walking distance of Playa Norte and all the downtown shops, restaurants, and bars. **Pros:** convivial, unbeatable price. **Cons:** party atmosphere, rooms not that clean, no elevator. ✉ *Av. Matamoros 15* ☎📠 *998/877–0090* 🌐 *www.pocna.com* *187 beds* *In-room: a/c (some), no phone, no TV (some). In-hotel: restaurant, bar, Internet terminal, Wi-Fi hotspot* 💳 *MC, V* 🍽 *CP.*

WORD OF MOUTH

"This was such a wonderfully small island—with everything we wanted. We did a wreck dive, found affordable accommodations, had great food, and found a nice place on the beach to spend our afternoons." —alovesa

ELSEWHERE ON THE ISLAND

$ **Hotel & Beach Club Garrafón de Castilla.** The snorkeling at this small family-owned hotel is better than what you're likely to experience at El Garrafón National Park next door; the reef is less crowded, and there are more fish. Rooms have double beds and balconies overlooking the water; some have refrigerators. Decorations are minimal, but the overall effect is bright, cheery, and comfortable. **Pros:** one of the best locations on the island, great for snorkeling and diving. **Cons:** taxi ride away from downtown, no Internet, no elevator. ✉ *Carretera Punta Sur, Km 6* ☎ *998/877–0107* *12 rooms* *In-room: a/c, no phone, refrigerator (some), no TV. In-hotel: beachfront, diving, water sports* 💳 *No credit cards* 🍽 *CP.*

$$$$ Fodor's Choice ★ **Hotel Villa Rolandi.** A private yacht delivers you to the hotel's lagoon dock from Cancún's Embarcadero Marina. Each elegant suite has an ocean view, a king-size bed (pillow menu available), and a sitting area that leads to a balcony with a heated whirlpool bath. Italian marble floors, vaulted ceilings, and stained-glass archways create a feeling of decadence. Showers have *six* adjustable heads and can be converted into saunas. Both the restaurant and the infinity pool overlook the Bahía de Mujeres; a path leads down to an intimate beach. For additional pampering, try thalassotherapy, an ancient form of natural healing that uses hot sea water, at the spa. The hotel runs on-site cooking classes and can arrange whale shark swimming expeditions. For the best view, ask for a second- or third-floor room. **Pros:** attentive staff, great ocean views, luxurious touches like fragrant towels and bathrobes. **Cons:** expensive, pool and beach can get crowded, young children not allowed. ✉ *Fracc. Laguna Mar, Sm 7, Mz 75, Lotes 15 and 16, Carretera Sac-Bajo* ☎ *998/999–2000* 🌐 *www.villarolandi.com* *35 suites* *In-room: a/c, safe. In-hotel: restaurant, room service, pool, gym, spa, beachfront, water sports, laundry service, no kids under 13* 💳 *AE, MC, V* 🍽 *MAP.*

$$$$ **Isla Mujeres Palace.** At this all-inclusive hotel you can forget about ever leaving the property and take advantage of the restaurants, the beach, and the pool. Each room has its own Jacuzzi, either inside the room or on the balcony, from which you can view the ocean below. The service is excellent; each building has its own attentive butler. Included in the price is a tour of the island, fishing, or a snorkeling trip. In the evening

there are music and dance performances. **Pros:** family-friendly environment, comfortable rooms. **Cons:** far from downtown. ✉ *Carretera Garrafón, Km 4.5, Mz 62, Sm 8* ☎ *998/999–2020; 800/346–8225 in U.S.* 🌐 *www.islamujerespalace.com* *62 rooms* *In-room: a/c, safe, refrigerator, Wi-Fi. In-hotel: restaurant, room service, bar, pool, spa, beachfront, bikes, water sports, Internet terminal, Wi-Fi hotspot, parking (free)* *AE, MC, V* *AI.*

NIGHTLIFE

BARS

Buho's (✉ *Avenida Carlos Lazo 1, at Cabanas Marina del Mar on Playa Norte* ☎ *998/877–0179* ⏲ *10 AM–midnight*) has three palapa beach bars with swings and hammocks where you can pass away the day with a tropical drink or ice-cold beer. From 5–7, take a seat at the bar and enjoy happy-hour sunset.

Designed by renowned architect Lluis Güell, **Café del Mar** (✉ *Av. Adolfo Lopez Mateos, at Privilege Aluxes in front of Playa Norte,* ☎ *998/848–8470*) is an Ibiza-inspired beach bar that plays chill-out music from 10 AM to 10 PM daily. The fish tacos are a perfect cerveza accompaniment.

Jax Bar & Grill (✉ *Av. Adolfo Mateos 42, near lighthouse* ☎ *998/887–1218* ⏲ *9 AM–11 PM*) has live music, cold beer, good bar food, and satellite TV that's always turned to whatever game happens to be on at the time.

La Adelita (✉ *Av. Hidalgo Norte 12A* ☎ *998/877–0528*) is a popular spot for enjoying reggae, salsa, and Caribbean music while trying out a variety of tequilas and cigars.

Romi's (✉ *Av. Rueda Medina at Posada del Mar* ☎ *998/877–0044*) has happy-hour specials including piña coladas, margaritas, and cold beers. The thatched roof and swings (instead of bar stools) have made this one of the island's most festive bars for more than 25 years (open 9 AM–11 PM).

DANCE CLUBS

Bar OM (✉ *Av. Matamoros, Lote 19, Mz 15* ☎ *998/820–4876*) is an eclectic lounge bar offering wine, organic teas, and self-serve draft-beer taps at each table. Chill out to the sounds of acid jazz, bossa nova, and reggae.

You can dance the night away with the locals at **Nitrox** (✉ *Av. Guerrero 11* ☎ *998/887–0568*). Wednesday night is ladies' night, Friday is Latin night, and the weekend is a blend of disco, techno, and house. It's open Wednesday through Sunday from 9 PM until 3 AM.

La Luna (✉ *Av. Guerreo s/n Centro, opposite church square* ☎ *998/845–7384*), just across from the downtown main square, is the only downtown bar that overlooks the Caribbean. There's a lovely terrace bar that serves a variety of sinful cocktails and a DJ who sets the mood with techno, reggae, and dance music. Salsa Saturdays are popular with the locals. The owners recently added a courtyard restaurant to the lively scene.

SHOPPING

CRAFTS

Artesanías Arcoiris (✉ *Avs. Hidalgo and Juárez* ☎ *No phone*) has Mexican blankets and other handicrafts. The staffers here also braid hair. Look for Mexican ceramics and onyx jewelry at **Artesanías Lupita** (✉ *Av. Hidalgo 13* ☎ *No phone*). Many local artists display their works at the **Artesanías Market** (✉ *Avs. Matamoros and Arq. Carlos Lazo* ☎ *No phone*), where you can find plenty of bargains. For custom-made clothing, visit Hortensia—the last stall on the left after you come through the market entrance. You can choose from bright Mexican fabrics and then pick a pattern for a skirt, shirt, shorts, or a dress; Hortensia will sew it up for you within a day or two. You can also buy off-the-rack designs. **Casa del Arte Mexicano** (✉ *Av. Hidalgo 16* ☎ *No phone*) has a large selection of Mexican handicrafts, including ceramics and silver jewelry. **De Corazón** (✉ *Av. Abasolo between Avs. Hidalgo and Guerrero* ☎ *998/877–1211*) has a wide variety of jewelry, T-shirts, and personal-care products. **Gladys Galdamez** (✉ *Av. Hidalgo 14* ☎ *998/877–0320*) carries Isla-designed and -manufactured clothing and accessories for both men and women, as well as bags and jewelry.

JEWELRY

Jewelry on Isla ranges from tasteful creations to junk. Bargains are available, but beware of street vendors—most of their wares, especially the amber, are fake. **Gold and Silver Jewelry** (✉ *Av. Hidalgo 58* ☎ *No phone*) specializes in precious stones such as sapphires, tanzanite, and amber in a variety of settings. **Joyería Maritz** (✉ *Av. Hidalgo between Avs. Morelos and Francisco Madero* ☎📠 *998/877–0526*) sells jewelry from Taxco (Mexico's silver capital) and crafts from Oaxaca at reasonable prices. **Van Cleef & Arpels** (✉ *Avs. Juárez and Morelos* ☎ *998/877–0331*) stocks rings, bracelets, necklaces, and earrings with precious stones set in 18K gold. Many of the designs are innovative; prices are often lower than in the United States. You can also check out the Van Cleef sister store, the **Silver Factory** (✉ *Avs. Juárez and Morelos* ☎ *998/877–0331*), which has a variety of designer pieces at reduced prices.

SPORTS AND THE OUTDOORS

BOATING

Villa Vera Puerto Isla Mujeres (✉ *Puerto de Abrigo, Laguna Makax* ☎ *998/287–3340* 🌐 *www.puertoislamujeres.com*) is a full-service marina for vessels up to 175 feet. Services include a fuel station, a 150-ton lift, customs assistance, 24-hour security, and laundry and cleaning services. Docking prices depend on the size of your boat and how long you stay. If you prefer to sleep on land, the Villa Vera Puerto Isla Mujeres resort is steps away from the docks.

Serious Diving (✉ *DigaMe Internet, Av. Guerrero between Matamoros and Abasolo* ☎ *No phone* 🌐 *www.islawhalesharks.com*) will take you into the heart of whale shark territory, where you can swim with these gentle creatures. Owner Ramon Guerrero Garcia is a professional diver who has dedicated more than 20 years to researching whale sharks.

Included in the six-hour boat trip are beverages, a light snack, and snorkel gear. Tours are approximately five hours long, cost $125, and must be prebooked online. Ramon is available to answer questions nightly from 7 to 8 at DigaMe Internet.

FISHING

Captain Anthony Mendillo Jr. (✉ *Av. Arq. Carlos Lazo 1* ☎ *998/877–0759*) provides specialized fishing trips from December to June aboard his 41-foot vessel, the *Keen M.* He charges $1,000 for a daylong trip for four people. **Jax Sport Fishing** (✉ *Av. Adolfo Mateos 42, near lighthouse* ☎ *998/877–1218*) offers a 29-foot custom charter boat for $850 per full day. Captain Michael has more than 20 years experience in offshore fishing. **Sea Hawk Divers** (✉ *Av. Arq. Carlos Lazo* ☎ *998/877–1233* 🌐 *www.sea-hawk-divers.myislamujeres.com*) runs fishing trips—for barracuda, snapper, and smaller fish—that start at $250 for a half day. **Sociedad Cooperativa Turística** (✉ *Av. Rueda Medina at Contoy Pier* ☎ *998/887–0800*) is a fishermen's cooperative that rents boats for a maximum of four hours and six people ($150). An island tour with lunch costs $55 per person.

14

SNORKELING AND SCUBA DIVING

Isla is a good place for learning to dive, since the snorkeling is close to shore. Offshore, there is excellent diving and snorkeling at Xlaches (pronounced *ees*-lah-chayss) Reef, due north on the way to Isla Contoy. One of Contoy's most alluring dives is the **Cave of the Sleeping Sharks,** east of the northern tip. The cave was discovered by an island fisherman, Carlos García Castilla, and extensively explored by Ramón Bravo, a local diver, cinematographer, and Mexico's foremost expert on sharks. The cave is a fascinating 150-foot dive for experienced divers only.

At 30 feet to 40 feet deep and 3,300 feet off the southwestern coast, the coral reef known as **Los Manchones** is a good dive site. During the summer of 1994 an ecological group hoping to divert divers and snorkelers from El Garrafón commissioned the creation of a 1-ton, 9¾-foot bronze cross, which was sunk here. Named the Cruz de la Bahía (Cross of the Bay), it's a tribute to everyone who has died at sea. Another option is the Barco L-55 and C-58 dive, which takes in sunken World War II boats just 20 minutes off the coast of Isla.

DIVE SHOPS

Most dive shops offer a variety of dive packages, with rates depending on the time of day, the reef visited, and the number of tanks. A PADI-affiliated dive shop, **Aqua Adventures** (✉ *Plaza Almendros 10* ☎ *998/877–1615* 🌐 *www.diveislamujeres.com*) offers dives to shipwrecks and sleeping shark caves. A one-tank dive goes for $40, and a two-tank dive costs $64. **Coral Scuba Dive Center** (✉ *Av. Matamoros 13A* ☎ *998/877–0763* 🌐 *www.coralscubadivecenter.com*) has a variety of dive packages. Fees start at $55 for one-tank dives and go up to $65 for two-tank dives and shipwreck dives. The PADI-affiliated shop also offers snorkeling trips. **Cruise Divers** (✉ *Avs. Rueda Medina and Matamoros* ☎ *998/877–1190*) offers two-tank reef dives starting at $49 and a resort course (a quickie learn-to-scuba course) for $69. The company also organizes nighttime dives. **Sea Hawk Divers** (✉ *Av. Arq.*

CLOSE UP

Shhh . . . Dont Wake the Sharks

The underwater caverns off Isla Mujeres attract a dangerous species of shark—though nobody knows exactly why. Stranger still, once the sharks swim into the caves, they enter a state of relaxed nonaggression seen nowhere else. Naturalists have two explanations, both involving the composition of the water inside the caves—it contains more oxygen, more carbon dioxide, and less salt. According to the first theory, the decreased salinity causes the parasites that plague sharks to loosen their grip, allowing the remora fish (the sharks' personal vacuum cleaner) to eat the parasites more easily. Perhaps the sharks relax in order to facilitate the cleaning, or maybe their deep state of relaxation is a side effect of having been scrubbed clean. Another theory is that the caves' combination of freshwater and saltwater may produce euphoria, similar to the effect scuba divers experience on extremely deep dives. Whatever the sharks experience while "sleeping" in the caves, they pay a heavy price for it: a swimming shark breathes automatically and without effort (water is forced through the gills as the shark swims), but a stationary shark must laboriously pump water to continue breathing. If you dive in the Cave of the Sleeping Sharks, be cautious: many are reef sharks, the species responsible for the largest number of attacks on humans. Dive with a reliable guide, and be on your best diving behavior.

Carlos Lazo ☎ *998/877–1233* 🌐 *www.sea-hawk-divers.myislamujeres.com*) runs reef dives from $50 (for one tank) to $65 (for two tanks). Special excursions to the more exotic shipwrecks cost from $75 to $95. The PADI courses taught here are highly regarded. For non-divers there are snorkel trips that depart at 9:30 and 2:30 daily.

Cozumel and the Riviera Maya

15

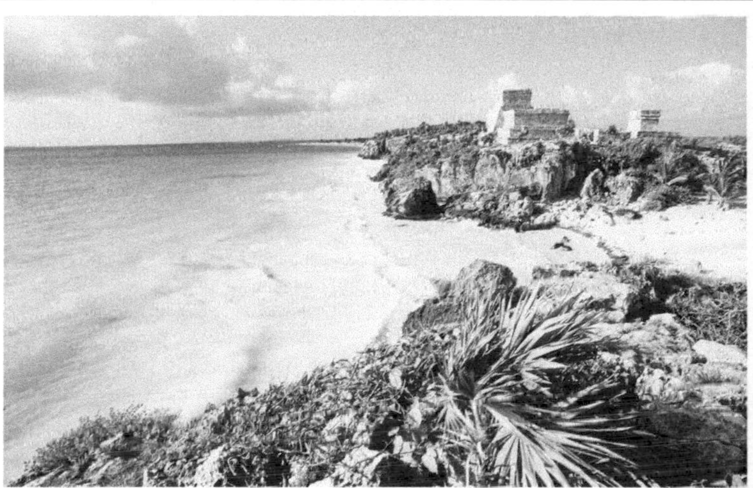

Tulum, Riviera Maya

WORD OF MOUTH

"Cozumel is not really a party place like Cancún. It's more relaxed and laid-back. Most people that go to Cozumel are divers and people looking to chill out, so partying to wee hours of the night is not a priorty."

—KVR

www.fodors.com/community

WELCOME TO COZUMEL AND THE RIVIERA MAYA

TOP REASONS TO GO

★ **Scuba diving along the Great Maya Reef:** A Technicolor profusion of fish, coral, and other creatures resides in this 600-mi-long reef.

★ **Indulging in a body treatment:** The Riviera Maya is flush with spa resorts that will make you say ooh and aah.

★ **Tasting local flavor:** On Sunday nights at San Miguel's Plaza Central, on Cozumel, join the people who gather for music and dancing. Visit during Carnival, the spring Fería del Cedral, or any national holiday, and you'll find processions and seasonal treats sold at food stands.

★ **Exploring the inland jungle:** South of Rio Bec the forests grow thick, and you might glimpse howler monkeys, coatimundis, and Yucatán parrots.

★ **Contemplating the Maya:** Explore the temples dedicated to Ixchel, goddess of fertility and the moon, at San Gervasio on Cozumel, and visit Tulum, on the mainland, overlooking the Caribbean.

1 San Miguel. Cozumel's only town, where cruise ships loom from the piers and endless souvenir shops line the streets, still retains some of the flavor of a Mexican village. On weekend nights musical groups and food vendors gather in the main square, attracting a lively crowd.

2 Coastal Cozumel. White beaches with calm waters line Cozumel's leeward (western) side. Parque Marino Nacional Arrecifes de Cozumel encompasses the reefs along the southwest edge. The windward (eastern) side facing the Caribbean has rocky strands and powerful surf. To the northwest broad beaches sometimes give way to limestone shelves over the water.

3 The Riviera Maya. The coastal communities along the Caribbean vary widely: some are sleepy fishing villages, others are filled with glitzy resorts, and one—Tulum—is an ancient Mayan port city. The beaches along this stretch are stunning, and beloved by scuba divers, snorkelers, anglers, bird-watchers, and beachcombers.

GETTING ORIENTED

A 490-square-km (189-square-mi) island 19 km (12 mi) east of the Yucatán peninsula, Cozumel is mostly flat, with an interior covered by parched scrub, low jungle, and marshy lagoons. Beaches, above all else, are what define the Riviera Maya. Powdery white sands embrace clear turquoise Caribbean lagoons, and vibrant marine life lies beneath. Inland, scrub and jungle are punctuated by Mayan ruins.

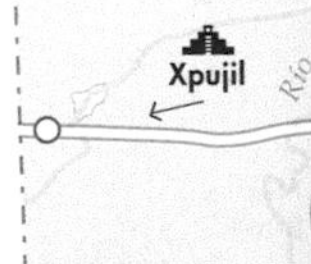

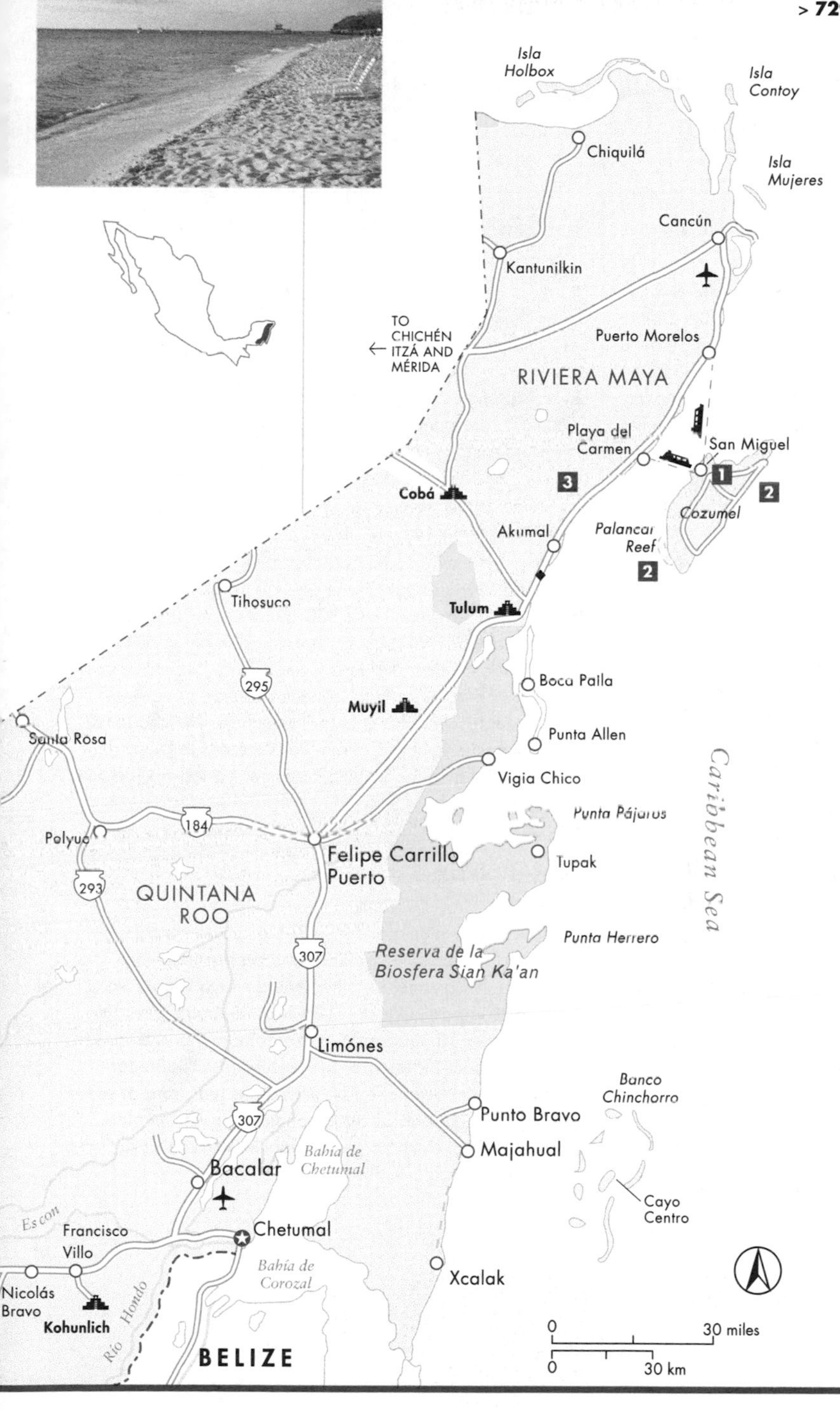
Isla Holbox
Isla Contoy
Chiquilá
Isla Mujeres
Cancún
Kantunilkin
TO CHICHÉN ITZÁ AND MÉRIDA
Puerto Morelos
RIVIERA MAYA
Playa del Carmen
San Miguel
Cobá
Cozumel
Akumal
Palancar Reef
Tihosuco
Tulum
295
Boca Palla
Muyil
Santa Rosa
Punta Allen
Vigia Chico
Caribbean Sea
Punta Pájaros
184
Polyuc
Felipe Carrillo Puerto
Tupak
293
QUINTANA ROO
Punta Herrero
307
Reserva de la Biosfera Sian Ka'an
Limónes
Banco Chinchorro
Punto Bravo
307
Bahía de Chetumal
Majahual
Bacalar
Cayo Centro
Francisco Villo
Chetumal
Bahía de Corozal
Xcalak
Nicolás Bravo
Kohunlich
Río Hondo
BELIZE
0
30 miles
0
30 km

COZUMEL AND THE RIVIERA MAYA PLANNER

Stay for a While

Cozumel is perfect for a week-long vacation—though some people wind up hanging around for months. It's all about the water here—the shimmering, clear-as-glass sea that makes you want to kick off your shoes, slip on your fins, and dive in. Come up for air, though, and you'll find that it's fun to explore on land, too. The island's paved roads are, for the most part, excellent. Dirt roads, however, are too deeply rutted for most rental cars, and flash floods in rainy season make them even tougher to navigate. Many have been closed since Hurricane Wilma in 2005.

Beaches and towns aren't visible from the Riviera Maya's well-paved main highway. The stretch from Cancún to Tulum is 1–2 km (½–1 mi) from the coast, so there's little to see but dense vegetation, billboards, roadside markets, and signs marking hotel entrances. The white-sand beaches and beautiful Maya ruins are here, though. A stay of five to seven days will allow you to visit Tulum and Cobá, spend a day kicking around Playa del Carmen, and still have time to work on your tan.

Booking Hotels

Many Cozumel hotels encourage you to make reservations online though booking agencies such as www.cozumel-hotels.net, www.comeetocozumel.com, or cozumel-mx.com, or their own Web sites. Since hotels customarily work with several agencies, shop around. Booking online can mean 10%–20% discounts. It can also mean occasional breakdowns in communication. You may arrive only to discover that your Spanish-speaking desk clerk has no record of your reservation. To prevent such mishaps, bring printouts of all receipts and confirmations.

Peak season on Cozumel and along the Riviera Maya is November through April, with availability plummeting and rates spiking—as much as $100 a night—at Christmas, Easter, and Carnival seasons. Book well in advance for these periods. Direct flights to Cozumel are expensive year-round. It's cheaper to fly to Cancún and hop a regional flight (though schedules change frequently). The cheapest alternative is to fly into Cancún, take the bus to Playa del Carmen, and then the ferry to Cozumel—a tedious journey that only costs about $16.

Water World

All manner of water sports—Jet-Skiing, scuba diving, snorkeling, waterskiing, sailing, and parasailing—are embraced in Cozumel and the Riviera Maya. Underwater enthusiasts in particular are drawn to the area's clear turquoise waters, abundant tropical marine life, and exquisite coral formations. There are dive excursions suitable for veterans and neophytes—to both famous reefs and offshore wrecks—and currents allow for drift diving. Freshwater cenotes (natural sinkholes) and underwater caverns provide still more dive opportunities.

Tour Options

Tours of Cozumel's sights, including the San Gervasio ruins, El Cedral, Parque Chankanaab, and the Museo de la Isla de Cozumel, cost about $50 a person; you can arrange them through travel agencies. Private taxi tours are also an option; they run about $70 a day. Fiesta Holidays (✉ Calle 11 Sur 598, between Avs. 25 and 30 ☎ 987/872–0923), which has representatives in many hotels, sells several tours.

Although it's easy to visit many of the Riviera Maya's sights on your own, it's also nice to have someone else do everything for you. After all, you're on vacation. Maya Sites Travel Services (☎ 719/256–5186 or 877/620–0715 🌐 www.mayasites.com) offers inexpensive personalized tours.

Akumal local Hilario Hiller (✉ La Jolla, Casa Nai Na, 3rd fl. ☎ 984/875–9066) is famous for his custom tours of Mayan villages, ruins, and the jungle. Trips typically cost about $100 a day, plus transportation expenses, and Hiller is fluent in Spanish, English, and Maya.

Need More Info?

The Web site www.cozumelmycozumel.com, edited by full-time residents of the island, has insider tips on activities, sights, and places to stay and eat. There's a bulletin board, too, where you can post questions.

For additional information on attractions, lodging, dining, and other services on the Caribbean Coast (and the rest of Quintana Roo), these Web sites can be very helpful: www.locogringo.com and www.playamayaews.com.

Money Matters

WHAT IT COSTS IN DOLLARS

	¢	$	$$	$$$	$$$$
Restaurants	under $5	$5–$10	$10–$15	$15–$25	over $25
Hotels	under $50	$50–$75	$75–$150	$150–$250	over $250

Restaurant prices are per person, for a main course at dinner, excluding tax and tip. Hotel prices are for a standard double room in high season.

How's the Weather?

Cozumel's weather is more extreme than you might expect on a tropical island.

Nortes—winds from the north—blow through in December, making air and water temperatures drop. If you visit during this time, bring a shawl or jacket for the chilly 18°C (65°F) evenings. Summers, on the other hand, can be beastly hot and humid.

The windward side is calmer in winter than the leeward side, and the interior is warmer than the coast.

From November to April, the Riviera Maya is heavenly, with temperatures hovering around 27°C (80°F) and near-constant ocean breezes.

In July and August the breezes disappear and humidity soars, especially inland, where temperatures reach 35°C (95°F).

September and October bring the worst conditions—mosquitos, rains, and the risk of hurricanes.

15

COZUMEL

Updated by Maribeth Mellin

IT'S ALL ABOUT THE WATER here—the shimmering, clear-as-glass aquamarine sea that makes you want to kick off your shoes, slip on your fins, and dive right in. Once you come up for air, though, you'll find that Mexico's largest Caribbean island is pretty fun to explore on land, too.

Cozumel has been a popular diving site ever since a 1961 Jacques Cousteau documentary catapulted the island's underwater wonders into the international spotlight. And even though Hurrican Wilma seriously damaged the reefs around the island, it's still, rightfully, a popular destination for snorkelers and divers of all skill levels. Cozumel is also the peninsula's favored cruise-ship destination, so you'll find plenty of diversions on land. If you're up for a little souvenir shopping, join the throngs on the waterfront promanade, where you'll find plenty of little trinkets at not-so-little prices.

Just 19 km (12 mi) off the coast, Cozumel is 53 km (33 mi) long and 15 km (9 mi) wide, making it the the country's largest island. Plaza Central, or *la plaza,* the heart of San Miguel, is directly across from the docks. Residents congregate here in the evening, especially on weekends, when free concerts begin at 8. Shops and restaurants abound in the square. Heading inland (east) takes you away from the tourist zone and toward the residential sections. The heaviest commercial district is concentrated between Calle 10 Norte and Calle 11 Sur to beyond Avenida Pedro Joaquin Coldwell.

The island's main paved roads are excellent, but the dirt roads are another story; take care as you explore, because they're too deeply rutted for most rental cars. Streets in congested neighborhoods and remote areas flood quickly in heavy rains, and are tough to navigate in heavy traffic no matter the weather. The island's windward side and rapidly developing interior lack the infrastructure to handle severe storms.

GETTING HERE AND AROUND

Cozumel's main road is Avenida Rafael E. Melgar, which runs along the island's western shore. South of San Miguel, the road is known as Carretera Chankanaab or Carretera Sur; it runs past hotels, shops, and the international cruise-ship terminals. South of town, the road splits into two parallel lanes, the right lane reserved for slower motor-scooter and bicycle traffic. After Parque Chankanaab, the road passes several excellent beaches and a cluster of resorts. At Cozumel's southernmost point the road turns northeast; beyond that point, it's known simply as "the coastal road." North of San Miguel, Avenida Rafael E. Melgar becomes Carretera Norte along the North Hotel Zone and ends near the Cozumel Country Club.

Alongside Avenida Rafael E. Melgar in San Miguel is the 14-km (9-mi) walkway called the *malecón.* The sidewalk by the water is relatively uncrowded; the other side, packed with shops and restaurants, gets clogged with crowds when cruise ships are in port. Avenida Juárez, Cozumel's other major road, stretches east from the pier for 16 km (10 mi), dividing town and island into north and south.

ESSENTIALS

Currency Exchange **American Express** (✉ *Punta Langosta, Av. Rafael E. Melgar 599* ☎ *987/869–1389*). **Promotora Cambiaria del Centro** (✉ *Av. 5 between Calles 1 Sur and Adolfo Rosado Salas* ☎ *987/872–2165*).

Medical Assistance **Air Ambulance** (☎ *987/872–4070*). **Centro Médico de Cozumel** (*Cozumel Medical Center* ✉ *Calle 1 Sur 101 and Av. 50* ☎ *987/872–9400*). **Police** (✉ *Anexo del Palacio Municipal* ☎ *987/872–0092; 065 for emergencies*). **Red Cross** (✉ *Calle Adolfo Rosada Salas and Av. 20 Sur* ☎ *987/872–1058; 065 for emergencies*).

Recompression Chambers **Buceo Médico Mexicano** (✉ *Calle 5 Sur 21B* ☎ *987/872–1430 24-hr hotline*). **Cozumel Recompression Chamber** (✉ *San Miguel Clinic, Calle 6 Norte between Avs. 5 and 10* ☎ *987/872–3070*).

Visitor and Tour Info **Fidecomiso and the Cozumel Island Hotel Association** (✉ *Calle 2 Norte and Av. 15* ☎ *987/872–7585* 🌐 *www.islacozumel.com.mx*).

EXPLORING

TOP ATTRACTIONS

2 ★ **Museo de la Isla de Cozumel.** Cozumel's island museum is housed on two floors of a former hotel. It has displays on natural history—with exhibits on the island's origins, endangered species, topography, and coral-reef ecology—as well as the pre-Columbian and colonial periods. The photos of the island's transformation over the 20th and 21st centuries are especially fascinating, as is the exhibit of a typical Mayan home. Guided tours are available. ✉ *Av. Rafael E. Melgar, between Calles 4 and 6 Norte* ☎ *987/872–1475* *$3* *Daily 9–5.*

5 ★ **Parque Chankanaab.** Chankanaab (which means "small sea") is a national park with a saltwater lagoon, an archaeological park, and a botanical garden. Scattered throughout are reproductions of a Mayan village, and of Olmec, Toltec, Aztec, and Mayan stone carvings. You can enjoy a cool walk along pathways leading to the sea, where parrotfish and sergeant majors swarm around snorkelers.

You can swim, scuba dive, or snorkel at the beach. There's plenty to see: underwater caverns, a sunken ship, crusty old cannons and anchors, and a sculpture of la Virgen del Mar (Virgin of the Sea). To preserve the ecosystem, park rules forbid touching the reef or feeding the fish.

Dive shops, restaurants, gift shops, a snack stand, and dressing rooms with lockers and showers are right on the sand. A small museum has exhibits on coral, shells, and the park's history, as well as some sculptures. ✉ *Carretera Sur, Km 9* ☎ *987/872–2940* *$16* *Daily 8–5.*

1 **San Gervasio.** Surrounded by a forest, these temples make up Cozumel's largest remaining Mayan and Toltec site. San Gervasio was the island's capital and ceremonial center, dedicated to the fertility goddess Ixchel. Its classic- and postclassic-style buildings and temples were continuously occupied from AD 300 to 1500. Typical architectural features include limestone plazas and arches atop stepped platforms, as well as stelae and bas-reliefs. Be sure to see the temple "Las Manitas," with red handprints all over its altar. Plaques clearly describe each structure

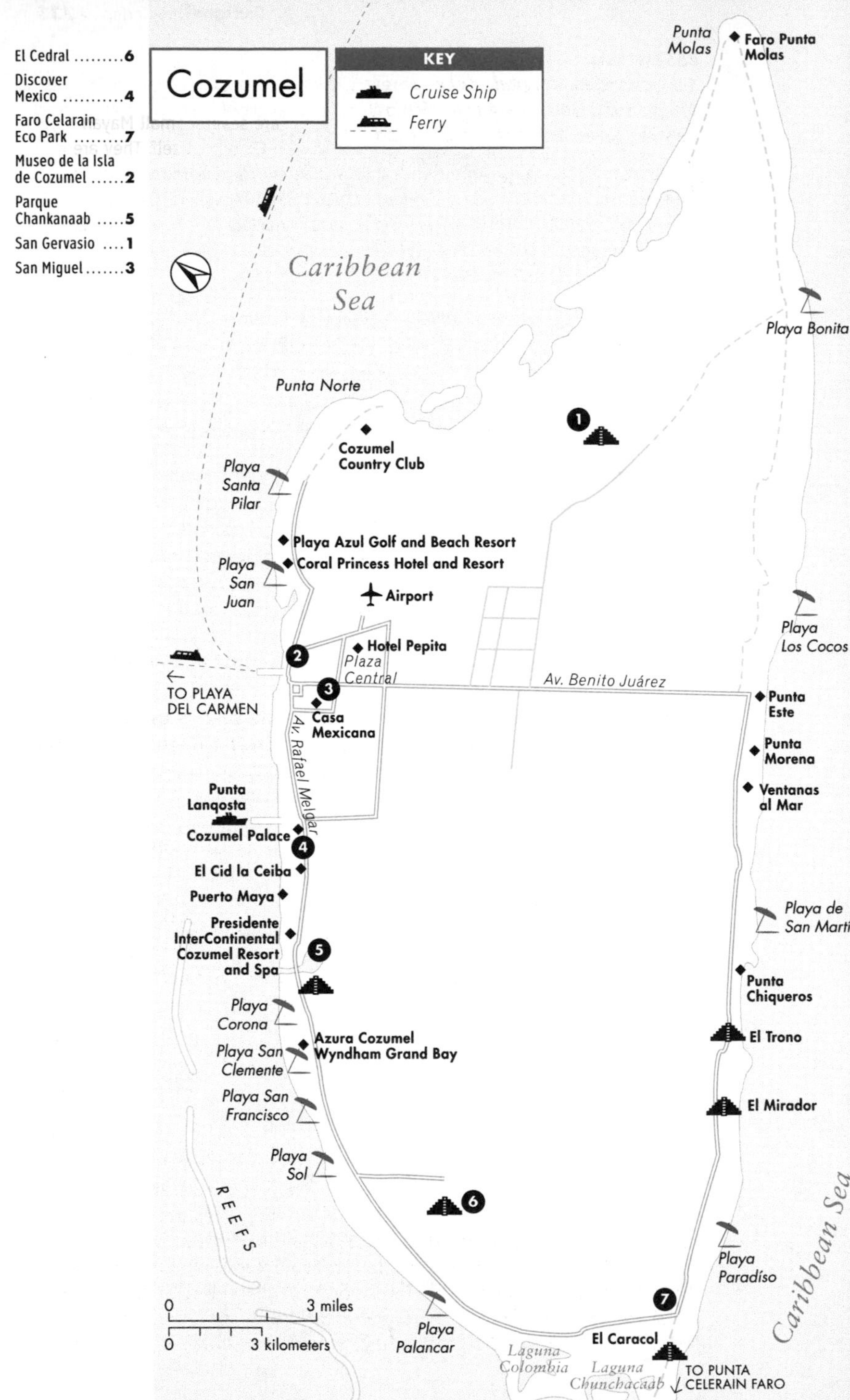

El Cedral 6
Discover Mexico 4
Faro Celarain Eco Park 7
Museo de la Isla de Cozumel 2
Parque Chankanaab 5
San Gervasio 1
San Miguel.......3
Cozumel
KEY
Cruise Ship
Ferry
Punta Molas
Faro Punta Molas
Caribbean Sea
Playa Bonita
Punta Norte
Cozumel Country Club
Playa Santa Pilar
Playa Azul Golf and Beach Resort
Coral Princess Hotel and Resort
Playa San Juan
Airport
Playa Los Cocos
Hotel Pepita
Plaza Central
Av. Benito Juárez
TO PLAYA DEL CARMEN
Casa Mexicana
Av. Rafael Melgar
Punta Este
Punta Morena
Ventanas al Mar
Punta Lanqosta
Cozumel Palace
El Cid la Ceiba
Puerto Maya
Presidente InterContinental Cozumel Resort and Spa
Playa de San Martín
Punta Chiqueros
Playa Corona
El Trono
Azura Cozumel Wyndham Grand Bay
Playa San Clemente
Playa San Francisco
El Mirador
Playa Sol
REEFS
Caribbean Sea
Playa Paradíso
0
3 miles
0
3 kilometers
Playa Palancar
El Caracol
Laguna Colombia
Laguna Chunchacaab
TO PUNTA CELERAIN FARO

in Mayan, Spanish, and English. ⊠ *From San Miguel, take cross-island road (follow signs to airport) east to San Gervasio access road; turn left and follow road 7 km (4½ mi)* *$7* *Daily 8–4.*

> **WORD OF MOUTH**
>
> "There are several small Mayan Ruins in Cozumel itself. They are small in comparison to Tulum or Cobá. San Gervasio is probably your best bet. " —Eschew

3 ★ **San Miguel.** Wait until the cruise ships sail toward the horizon before visiting San Miguel, Cozumel's only town. Then stroll along the *malecón* (boardwalk) and take in the ocean breeze. The waterfront has been taken over by large shops selling jewelry, imported rugs, leather boots, and souvenirs to cruise-ship passengers. The northern end of the malecón, past Calle 10 Norte, is a pleasant area lined with sculptures of Mayan gods and goddesses that draws more locals than tourists. The town feels more traditional as you head inland to the pedestrian streets around the plaza, where family-owned restaurants and shops cater to locals and savvy travelers. The plaza and surrounding buildings are the heart of San Miguel, with plenty of benches for watching he action. The central *kiosko* (bandstand) and clock tower are local landmarks—and a good place to rendezvous with the shoppers in your group. There's live music most Sunday nights, and families gather to dance, chat, and watch the children race around after pigeons. Behind the bright yellow Plaza del Sol building facing the plaza an artisans' market is packed with tacky and desirable souvenirs.

WORTH NOTING

4 **Discover Mexico.** This ingenious attraction allows visitors to learn about Mexico's archaeological sites, important architectural landmarks, and cultures. A gorgeous film about Mexico runs continuously, and exhibits display collector-quality textiles, pottery, and painted figurines. Outdoors are scale models of temples, pyramids, monasteries, and Mexico City's main square, the Zócalo. An outdoor café serves tasty fruit sorbets and light meals. The gift shop has the island's finest array of Mexican folk art. Expect to spend about two hours to fully experience the entire exhibit. A combo entry ticket includes admissions to Discover Mexico and Parque Chankanaab. The price is $34 for adults and $24 for children. ⊠ *Carretera Sur, Km 5.5* ☎ *987/875–2820* *www.discovermexico.org* *$10 adults and children* *Mon.–Sat. 8–6.*

6 **El Cedral.** Spanish explorers discovered this site, once the hub of Mayan life on Cozumel, in 1518. Later it became the island's first official city, founded in 1847. Today it's a farming community with small well-tended houses and gardens. Conquistadors tore down much of the Mayan temple, and during World War II the U.S. Army Corps of Engineers destroyed the rest to make way for the island's first airport. All that remains of the Mayan ruins is one small structure with an arch. Nearby is a green-and-white cinder-block church, decorated inside with crosses shrouded in embroidered lace; legend has it that Mexico's first Mass was held here. Vendors display embroidered blouses, hammocks, and other souvenirs at stands around the main plaza. ⊠ *Turn at Km 17.5 off Carretera Sur or Av. Rafael E. Melgar, then drive 3 km (2 mi) inland to site* ☎ *No phone* *Free* *Daily dawn–dusk.*

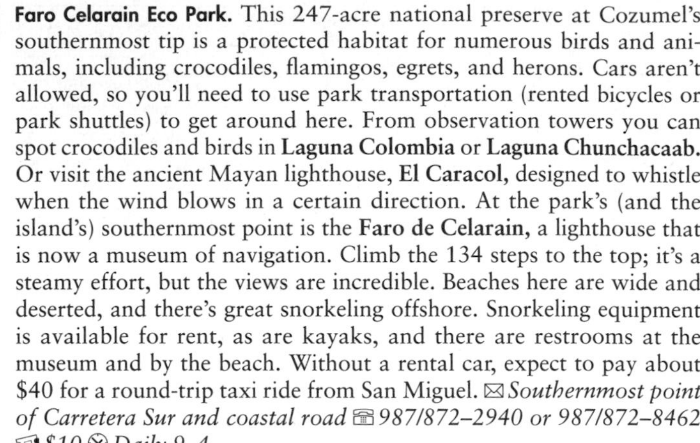

7 **Faro Celarain Eco Park.** This 247-acre national preserve at Cozumel's southernmost tip is a protected habitat for numerous birds and animals, including crocodiles, flamingos, egrets, and herons. Cars aren't allowed, so you'll need to use park transportation (rented bicycles or park shuttles) to get around here. From observation towers you can spot crocodiles and birds in **Laguna Colombia** or **Laguna Chunchacaab.** Or visit the ancient Mayan lighthouse, **El Caracol,** designed to whistle when the wind blows in a certain direction. At the park's (and the island's) southernmost point is the **Faro de Celarain,** a lighthouse that is now a museum of navigation. Climb the 134 steps to the top; it's a steamy effort, but the views are incredible. Beaches here are wide and deserted, and there's great snorkeling offshore. Snorkeling equipment is available for rent, as are kayaks, and there are restrooms at the museum and by the beach. Without a rental car, expect to pay about $40 for a round-trip taxi ride from San Miguel. ⊠ *Southernmost point of Carretera Sur and coastal road* ☎ *987/872–2940 or 987/872–8462* *$10* *Daily 9–4.*

BEACHES

LEEWARD BEACHES

Playa Santa Pilar runs along the northern hotel strip and ends at Punta Norte. Long stretches of sand and shallow water encourage leisurely swims. The privacy diminishes as you swim south past hotels and condos. Hotels along the beach have all the facilities you would need, but most are all-inclusive and don't allow nonguests on the premises. **Best for:** families with small children, easy snorkeling. **Amenities:** parking, showers (at hotels).

Playa San Juan, south of Playa Santa Pilar, has a rocky shore with no easy ocean access. You can park on the roadside just south of the fence surrounding the ruins of the Sol Cabañas del Caribe hotel, which was destroyed by Hurricane Wilma. The winds can be strong here, so it's popular with kiteboarders. **Best for:** solitude, snorkeling. **Amenities:** none.

★ The club at **Paradise Beach** (⊠ *Carretera Sur, Km 14.5* ☎ *987/871–9010* *www.paradise-beach-cozumel.net*) has cushy lounge chairs and charges $12 per person for full-day use of kayaks, snorkel gear, a trampoline, and a climbing wall that looks like an iceberg in the water. There's no charge to enter, and there are restrooms at the facility. Food is expensive, though. **Best for:** families, swimming, singles scene. **Amenities:** chaise lounges, food concession, lockers, parking lot, playground, showers.

★ **Mr. Sancho's Beach Club** (⊠ *Carretera Sur, Km 15* ☎ *987/876–1629* *www.mrsanchos.com*) always has a party going on: scores of holidaymakers come here to swim, snorkel, and drink buzz-inducing concoctions out of pineapples. Seemingly every water toy known to man is here; kids shriek happily as they hang onto banana boats dragged behind speedboats. Guides lead horseback and ATV rides into the jungle and along the beach, and the restaurant holds a lively, informative tequila seminar at lunchtime. Grab a swing seat at the beach bar and sip a mango margarita, or settle into the 30-person hot tub. Showers, lockers, and restrooms are available, and there are souvenirs aplenty for sale. **Best for:** ATV rides, banana-boat rides, families, horseback riding, shopping, swimming. **Amenities:** lifeguard, chaise lounges, food concession, lockers, parking lot, playground, showers.

★ South of the resorts lies the mostly ignored (and therefore serene) **Playa Palancar** (✉ *Carretera Sur* ☎ *987/878–5238*). The deeply rutted and pot-holed road to the beach is a sure sign you've left the tourist hot spots. Offshore is the famous Palancar Reef, easily accessed by the on-site dive shop. There's also a water-sports center, a bar-café, and a long beach with hammocks hanging under coconut palms. Playa del Palancar keeps prices low and rarely feels crowded. **Best for:** diving, snorkeling, sunbathing, swimming. **Amenities:** food concession, parking lot.

WINDWARD BEACHES

Punta Chiqueros, a half-moon-shaped cove sheltered by an offshore reef, is the first popular swimming area as you drive north on the coastal road (it's about 12 km [8 mi] north of Faro Celarain Eco-Park). Part of a longer beach that some locals call Playa Bonita, it has fine sand, clear water, and moderate waves. This is a great place to swim, watch the sunset, and eat fresh fish at the restaurant, also called Playa Bonita. **Best for:** families, sunbathing, swimming. **Amenities:** food concession, parking on road.

15

Not quite 5 km (3 mi) north of Punta Chiqueros, a long stretch of beach begins along the Chen Río Reef. Turtles come to lay their eggs on the section known as **Playa de San Martín.** During full moons in May and June the beach is sometimes blocked by soldiers or ecologists to prevent poaching of the turtle eggs. Directly in front of the reef is a small bay with clear waters and surf that's relatively mild, thanks to a protective rock formation. When the wind is blowing from the south, however, the water is best for kiteboarders. This is a particularly good spot for swimming when the water is calm. A restaurant, also called **Chen Río,** serves cold drinks and decent seafood. **Best for:** swimming, kiteboarding, solitude. **Amenities:** parking on road.

Surfers and Boogie-boarders have adopted **Punta Morena,** a short drive north of Ventanas al Mar, as their official hangout. The pounding surf creates great waves, and the local restaurant serves typical surfer food (hamburgers, hot dogs, and french fries). Vendors sell hammocks by the side of the road. The owners allow camping here. **Best for:** surfing. **Amenities:** food concession, parking on road.

The beach at **Punta Este** has been nicknamed Mezcalitos, after the much-loved restaurant here. **Mezcalito Café** serves seafood and beer, and can get pretty rowdy. Punta Este is a typical windward beach—great for beachcombing but unsuitable for swimming. **Best for:** drinking and dining with a fun-loving crowd. **Amenities:** food concession, parking on road.

WHERE TO EAT

ZONA HOTELERA SUR

$$$ ITALIAN

Alfredo di Roma. The opportunity to dine graciously amid crystal and candlelight (and blessedly cool air-conditioning) is just one reason to book a special dinner at Alfredo's. The pastas are made fresh daily, and cheeses are flown in from Italy so the chef can prepare authentic fettuccine Alfredo tableside. The octopus salad, pasta puttanesca, and sea bass with capers are all superb, and the wine cellar is the largest on the island. Book a table for early evening and enjoy the sunset view through wall-length windows. Diners not staying at the hotel must have advance reservations. ✉ *Presidente InterContinental Cozumel, Carretera Chankanaab, Km 6.5* ☎ *987/872–9500* *Reservations essential* *AE, MC, V* ⏲ *No lunch.*

SAN MIGUEL

$ MEXICAN ★

Casa Denis. This little yellow house near the plaza has been satisfying cravings for Yucatecan *pollo pibíl* (spiced chicken baked in banana leaves) and other local favorites since 1945. *Tortas* (sandwiches) and tacos are a real bargain, and you'll start to feel like a local if you spend an hour at one of the outdoor tables watching shoppers dash about. ✉ *Calle 1 Sur 132, between Avs. 5 and 10* ☎ *987/872–0067* *No credit cards.*

$$ MEXICAN

Casa Mission. Part private home and part restaurant, this estate evokes a country hacienda in mainland Mexico. The on-site botanical garden has mango and papaya trees and a small zoo with caged birds. The setting, with tables lining the veranda, outshines the food. Stalwart fans rave about huge platters of fajitas and grilled fish. It's out of the way, so you'll need to take a cab. ✉ *Av. Juárez and Calle 55A* ☎ *987/872–1641* *www.missioncoz.com* *AE, MC, V* ⏲ *No lunch.*

$$–$$$ ITALIAN ★

Guido's. Chef Yvonne Villiger works wonders with fresh fish—if the wahoo with capers and black olives is on the menu, don't miss it. But Guido's is best known for its pizzas baked in a wood-burning oven, which makes sections of the indoor dining room rather warm. Sit in the pleasant, recently expanded courtyard instead, and order a pitcher of sangria to go with the puffy garlic bread. ✉ *Av. Rafael E. Melgar 23, between Calles 6 and 8 Norte* ☎ *987/872–0946* *MC, V* ⏲ *Closed Sun.*

$–$$ MEXICAN Fodor's Choice ★

Kinta. Both locals and visitors rave about this little café, which is owned by former Guido's chef Kris Wallenta. It's easy to overlook the entrance (look for a bright orange facade on the west side of the street), but once you've discovered the blissfully air-conditioned dining room, romantic outdoor garden, and impressive menu, you'll likely return. Wallenta rushes about the open kitchen, whipping up savory black-bean soup, a chile relleno filled with vegetable ratatouille and Chihuahua cheese, chicken breast stuffed with *chaya* (like spinach) and mushrooms with a Gorgonzola sauce, and a tender filet mignon with *huitlaoche* (a corn truffle) and cheese. Hand-crushed mojitos, fruity sangria, and virgin *limomenta* (lemonade with mint) add a refreshing lilt, and the bread pudding with Mexican chocolate and *cajeta* (caramel sauce) is a fitting end to a stellar meal. ✉ *Av. 5 between Calles 2 and 4* ☎ *987/869–0544* ▭ *MC, V* ⊙ *Closed Mon.*

$ MEXICAN ★ ✕ **La Choza.** Locals get together for breakfasts of *migas* (scrambled eggs with bits of bacon and tortilla) and the daily lunchtime *comida corrida*, a set-priced meal of the day (about $4.50–$6) with a choice of appetizers and entrées. Favorite dishes include *pollo con mole poblano* (chicken in chocolate, cinnamon, and chiles) and chile relleno *de camarón* (chile stuffed with shrimp). Leave room for the chilled avocado pie. ✉ *Av. 10 between Calle Adolfo Rosado Salas and Av. 3* ☎ *987/872–0958* ▭ *AE, MC, V.*

$$$ ECLECTIC Fodor'sChoice ★ ✕ **La Cocay.** This casually sophisticated dining room is one of the most exciting culinary venues on the island, thanks to the creative chef. The menu changes frequently, but you can expect to find salad with mixed baby lettuces, salmon pâté, and entrées like seared sashimi-grade tuna. Such fare may be the norm in L.A. or Honolulu, but is hard to find on Cozumel. Consider sharing several small plates, such the blue-cheese phyllo rolls, the *empanaditas* (tiny empanadas) with goat cheese and caramelized apple, and the figs with prosciutto. There are reasonably priced wines by the glass from Argentina, Chile, and Mexico. ✉ *Calle 8 Norte between Avs. 10 and 15* ☎ *987/872–5533* 🌐 *www.lacocay.com* ▭ *AE, MC, V* ⊙ *No lunch. Closed Sun.*

$$–$$$ MEXICAN ★ ✕ **Pancho's Backyard.** Marimbas play beside the bubbling fountain in this gorgeous courtyard behind one of Cozumel's best folk-art shops. Though Pancho's is always busy, the waitstaff is amazingly patient and helpful. Cruise-ship passengers seeking a taste of Mexico pack the place at lunch; dinner is a bit more serene. The menu is definitely geared toward tourists (written in English with detailed descriptions and prices in dollars), but regional ingredients make even the standard steak stand out when it's flavored with smoky chipotle chilies. Other stellar dishes include the cilantro cream soup and shrimp flambéed with tequila. ✉ *Av. Rafael E. Melgar between Calles 8 and 10 Norte* ☎ *987/872–2141* 🌐 *www.panchosbackyard.com* ▭ *AE, MC, V* ⊙ *Dinner only on Sun.*

WINDWARD COAST

$–$$ MEXICAN ★ ✕ **Coconuts.** The T-shirts and bikinis hanging from the palapa roof at this windward-side hangout are a good indication of its party-time atmosphere. Jimmy Buffett tunes play in the background while crowds down *cervezas* (beers). The scene is more peaceful if you choose a palapa-shaded table on the rocks overlooking the water. The calamari and garlic shrimp are good enough to write home about. Assign a designated driver and hit the road home before dark (remember, there are no streetlights). ✉ *East-coast road near junction with Av. Benito Juárez* ☎ *No phone* ▭ *No credit cards* ⊙ *No dinner.*

WHERE TO STAY

ZONA HOTELERA NORTE

$$$ 🏨 **Coral Princess Hotel and Resort.** Good snorkeling off the rocky shoreline and a relaxed family feel make this a north coast favorite. The suites have one or two bedrooms, a kitchen, and a balcony or terrace. These

15

large rooms are often taken by time-share owners, though there's no pressure to attend a sales demo. Most of the studio-size hotel rooms overlook the jungle; try to get an ocean-view room on an upper floor for the best views and sea breezes. Management goes out of its way to make guests comfortable, providing inexpensive large jugs of purified water in-room (upon request) and other friendly touches. **Pros:** excellent snorkeling right off beach; decent, well-priced meals; family-friendly. **Cons:** can be noisy, some rooms lack bathtubs. ✉ *Carretera Costera Norte, Km 2.5* ☎ *987/872–3200 or 800/253–2702* 🌐 *www.coralprincess.com* *110 rooms, 26 suites* *In-room: a/c, safe, kitchen (some), refrigerator. In-hotel: restaurant, room service, bar, pools, gym, diving, water sports, laundry service, parking (free)* 💳 *AE, MC, V* 🍽 *BP.*

$$$$ ★ **Playa Azul Golf and Beach Resort.** This romantic boutique hotel has bright and airy rooms facing the ocean or the gardens. Inside the rooms are mirrored niches, wicker and pale-wood furnishings, and sun-filled terraces. None of the rooms have bathtubs, and the best are the corner suites on the upper floors. Small palapas shade lounge chairs on the beach, and you can arrange snorkeling and diving trips at the hotel's own dock. Golf fees are included in the room rates, and the hotel sponsors an annual golf tournament. Some guests hit the course daily, often with the hotel's owners. A freestanding spa at the hotel's entrance offers body and beauty treatments. The small Chan Ka'an dinner restaurant is a lovely spot for a quiet evening. Make reservations in advance in case there's a reception or other function taking place. The beach club next door serves excellent ceviche and sandwiches and has live salsa on Sunday afternoons. **Pros:** small and intimate feel, excellent spa, no greens fees. **Cons:** unheated pool and no hot tub, may be too quiet for some, rocky beach. ✉ *Carretera Costera Norte, Km 4* ☎ *987/869–5160* 🌐 *www.playa-azul.com* *34 rooms, 16 suites, 1 house* *In-room: a/c, safe, Wi-Fi. In-hotel: 2 restaurants, room service, bars, pool, spa, beachfront, diving, water sports, laundry service, parking (free)* 💳 *AE, MC, V* 🍽 *BP.*

ZONA HOTELERA SUR

$$$$ **Aura Cozumel Wyndham Grand Bay.** Opened in 2008, this elegant, all-inclusive boutique hotel raises the standard for the southern coast's string of all-inclusive resorts. Four low-rise buildings face a meandering pool with separate areas linked by a lazy river. Swim-up suites have direct patio access to the ground-level pool, while third-story solarium suites have narrow rooftop lap pools. The design throughout the seven suite categories is sleekly contemporary, with dark-wood furnishings and contrasting sea-blue textiles, flat-screen TVs, iPod docks, and Egyptian cotton sheets. The hotel is adjacent to the 402-room Wyndham Cozumel Resort and Spa; both face a long beach with shallow water. Aura guests have use of the spa, restaurants, and facilities at both hotels. **Pros:** high-tech, luxurious suite amenities (rare on Cozumel); intimate, sophisticated ambience. **Cons:** far from town, offshore snorkeling not very good, no kids. ✉ *Carretera Costera Sur, Km 12.9* ☎ *987/872–9300 or 877/999–3223* 🌐 *www.auraresorts.com* *87 suites* *In-room: a/c, safe, refrigerator, DVD, Wi-Fi. In-hotel: 2 restaurants, room service, bars, pools, gym, beachfront, diving, water sports, laundry service,*

Wi-Fi hotspot, parking (free), no kids under 18 ▭ *MC, V* 🍽 *AI.*

$$$$ **Cozumel Palace.** This gorgeous all-inclusive hotel is part of the popular Palace Resorts chain. Within walking distance of San Miguel, the hotel faces the water but lacks a beach. Instead, an infinity pool seems to flow into the sea, and stairs lead from the property into a fairly good snorkeling area. The romantic rooms are airy, white enclaves with double whirlpool tubs and hammocks on most balconies. The chain has vacation ownership and club programs, so you may feel a bit hassled by sellers. Owners can use the facilities at the Palace Resort in Playa del Carmen on the mainland. The rate includes spa and golf discount vouchers and unlimited free calls to the U.S. and Canada. **Pros:** in-room hot tubs, good honeymoon hideaway. **Cons:** sales pressure, slow elevators. ✉ *Av. Rafael E. Melgar, Km 1.5* ☎ *987/872–9430 or 800/635–1836* 🌐 *www.palaceresorts.com* ⇨ *175 rooms* 👍 *In-room: a/c, safe, refrigerator, Wi-Fi. In-hotel: 3 restaurants, room service, bars, pools, gym, spa, diving, water sports, children's programs (ages 4–12), laundry service, Wi-Fi hotspot, parking (free)* ▭ *AE, DC, MC, V* 🍽 *AI.*

> **WORD OF MOUTH**
>
> "This may be on the higher end of reasonable, but I've gone there twice for the snorkeling—Presidente Intercontinental. I've booked it through Apple or Funjet or similar and stayed in one of the less expensive room options to get the great snorkeling right from the beach, which is right out of your hotel door. The resident iguanas are photogenic, too." —atravelynn

15

$$$ **El Cid la Ceiba.** A favorite among divers and frequent Cozumel visitors, this compact property was originally built in 1978 beside a shady ceiba (a tree sacred to the Maya). The hotel was completely remodeled in 2006 with an eye to casual comfort (lots of towels, fold-out couches facing TVs, large dining tables). Most rooms overlook the ocean; the best have separate living rooms, kitchenettes, and enormous bathrooms with deep tubs and separate showers. The lobby and a small pool area separate the two towers, one facing a generous beach and the other above a smaller patch of sand bordering a shallow saltwater lagoon with a waterfall and a *temazcal* (outdoor sauna) on a small lawn. The Puerto Maya cruise pier and shopping center is next door, and has branches of most of San Miguel's best restaurants and shops. **Pros:** great Mexican food in restaurant and reasonably priced all-inclusive option available, good snorkeling offshore. **Cons:** massive cruise ships nearby mar sea view, pool scene can be rowdy. ✉ *Carretera Chankanaab, Km 4.5* ☎ *987/872–0844 or 866/796–5571* 🌐 *www.elcid.com* ⇨ *60 rooms* 👍 *In-room: a/c, safe, refrigerator, kitchen (some). In-hotel: 2 restaurants, room service, bars, tennis court, pools, gym, spa, beachfront, diving, water sports, Wi-Fi hotspot, parking (free)* ▭ *MC, V* 🍽 *AI, EP.*

$$$$ Fodor's Choice ★ **Presidente InterContinental Cozumel Resort and Spa.** Cozumel's loveliest resort is a thoroughly modern, sophisticated property. The expansive lawns and beaches are bordered by a marina to the north and undeveloped jungle to the south, making the hotel feel ultraprivate and secluded. Soft sand covers the limestone shelf beside a small cove and the shores in front of the two hotel wings. There are several room

designs with touches that make guests favor one over the other. On the north side, ground-level suites facing the sea have large terraces, outdoor rain showers, and indoor bathtubs, whereas some of those in the upper floors have whirlpool tubs with sea views (and separate showers in the large bathrooms), and garden rooms have rain showers and hammocks on wide terraces. In the south wing, ground-floor rooms have rain showers and hammocks; second-floor rooms have hammock chairs on balconies. Rooms have sleek dark-wood furnishings and a calm cream-and-brown color scheme. Special touches include gourmet coffeemakers, iPod docks, and complimentary Wi-Fi. The main palapa-covered restaurant is best for breakfast and lunch by the sea. The Mandara Spa is the island's best, with sublime treatments and a *temazcal* (sweat lodge). Bellmen greet you like an old friend, waiters quickly learn your preferences, and housekeepers are quick to provide whatever you need. **Pros:** secluded and spacious feel, high-quality beds and linens, professional service. **Cons:** may be too quiet for partyers, far from town. ✉ *Carretera Chankanaab, Km 6.5* ☎ *987/872–9500 or 800/327–0200* 🌐 *www.intercontinentalcozumel.com* *183 rooms, 37 suites* *In-room: a/c, safe, DVD, Wi-Fi. In-hotel: 3 restaurants, room service, bars, tennis courts, pools, gym, spa, beachfront, diving, water sports, children's programs (ages 4–12), laundry service, Wi-Fi hotspot, parking (free)* 💳 *AE, MC, V* *EP.*

SAN MIGUEL

$$ Fodor's Choice ★ **Casa Mexicana.** A dramatic staircase leads up to this hotel's windswept lobby, and distinctive rooms are decorated in subtle blues and yellows. Some face the ocean and Avenida Rafael E. Melgar; others overlook the town's rooftops and trees behind the hotel or the indoor terrace, where breakfast is served. Splurge on a waterfront room if you can, as the balcony is a great place to hang out and enjoy the sea view and malecón scene. Rooms have bathtubs (hard to find downtown) and are immaculate and comfy. The rate includes a full breakfast buffet with eggs cooked to order, and the lobby bar overlooking the street is a great place for sunset drinks. There isn't a more efficient, pleasant place to stay in San Miguel, and the rates are surprisingly low for all you get—large rooms, balconies, free Wi-Fi, breakfast. It's popular with visitors doing business on the island and return guests who prefer walking to everything they need. Two sister properties, Hotel Bahía and Suites Colonial, offer less expensive suites with kitchenettes (the Bahía has some ocean views; the Colonial is near the square). **Pros:** great downtown location near restaurants and shops, friendly staff (especially bartenders), substantial breakfast. **Cons:** no beach, tiny pool, some street noise. ✉ *Av. Rafael E. Melgar Sur 457, between Calles 5 and 7* ☎ *987/872–9090 or 877/228–6747* 🌐 *www.casamexicanacozumel.com* *90 rooms* *In-room: a/c, safe, Internet. In-hotel: bar, pool, gym, laundry service, Wi-Fi hotspot* 💳 *AE, D, MC, V* *BP.*

¢ **Hotel Pepita.** Despite being more than 50 years old, the Pepita is one of the best budget hotels on the island. The blue-and-white facade is painted frequently, as are the rooms. Wooden shutters cover screened windows that keep out the bugs (who thrive happily among the courtyard's many plants and shrubs). Cable TV, refrigerators, and air-conditioning are surprising pluses given the low room rates. Shelves in the lobby are stacked high with novels in several languages, and German and Dutch are as common as Spanish and English during conversations over free coffee around the long wooden table in the courtyard. There are no kitchen facilities, but plenty of small markets and cafés nearby. **Pros:** untouristy neighborhood, amiable staff. **Cons:** buggy (keep doors closed), no phones in rooms, some staff speak Spanish only. ✉ *Av. 15 Sur 120* ☎ *987/872–0098* 🌐 *www.hotelpepitacozumel.com* *20 rooms* *In-room: a/c, no phone, refrigerator.* *No credit cards* *EP.*

WINDWARD COAST

$$ ★ **Ventanas al Mar.** The lights of San Miguel are but a distant glow on the horizon when you look west from the only hotel on the windward coast. Turn east, though, and you can watch shooting stars flash through the nighttime sky over the foaming sea. Escape is complete at this small, eco-friendly inn that runs on solar power; there are no phones, no computer hookups. The rooms are commodious and comfortable, and have kitchenettes with sinks and coffeemakers; mini-refrigerators are available on request. Two-story suites have a bedroom and full bath upstairs and a trundle sleeper sofa and half-bath downstairs. Rates ($164–$184) are significantly higher, but a bargain when shared by four people. A full breakfast is served in the open-air lobby; lunches and early dinners are available at Coconuts, next door. Sea turtles nest on the long beach beside the hotel in summer, and tropical fish and anemones gather by the rocky point in front of the rooms. **Pros:** blissful solitude, long beach great for sunset walks. **Cons:** limited food and drink options, driving at night not advisable, as coastal road is not lighted. ✉ *East-coast road north of Coconuts* ☎ *987/105–2684* 🌐 *www.ventanasalmar.com.mx* *14 rooms* *In-room: a/c, no phone, kitchen, refrigerator (some), no TV. In-hotel: beachfront, water sports, parking (free)* *No credit cards* *BP.*

15

NIGHTLIFE

BARS

Carlos 'n Charlie's and Señor Frog's (✉ *Av. Rafael E. Melgar at Punta Langosta* ☎ *987/872–0191*) are members of the Carlos Anderson chain of rowdy restaurant-bars that attract crowds. The *Animal House* ambience includes loud rock music and a libertine, anything-goes dancing scene that seems to have special allure to the cruising set.

Lively, rowdy **Fat Tuesdays** (✉ *Av. Juárez between Av. Rafael E. Melgar and Calle 3 Sur* ☎ *987/872–5130*) draws crowds day and night for frozen daiquiris, ice-cold beers, and blaring rock.

For a more sophisticated scene with mojitos and great cigars, check out **Havana Blue** (✉ *Av. Rafael E. Melgar and Calle 10 Norte, 2nd fl.* ☎ *987/869–1687*) in the flashy Forum shopping mall.

Martinis and high-end tequilas are on order at **1.5 Tequila Lounge** (✉ *Av. Rafael Melgar at Calle 11 Sur* ☎ *987/872–4421*) on the south end of downtown. The waterfront location and classy lounge ambience set it apart from the rowdier bars, though the scene does get pretty wild here as well.

Viva Mexico (⊠ *Av. Rafael E. Melgar* ☎ *987/872–0799*) sometimes has a DJ who spins Latin and American dance music into the wee hours. There's also an extensive snack menu. This place is wildly popular any time of day or night. The best seats are near the second-story railing overlooking the waterfront.

DANCE CLUBS

Cozumel's oldest disco, **Neptune Dance Club** (⊠ *Av. Rafael E. Melgar and Av. 11* ☎ *987/872–1537*), underwent a complete makeover in 2008. It now has dance floors and bars on two levels and upgraded sound systems. The music ranges from disco to salsa. The remodel hasn't been as successful as the original disco; seems it got too fancy for locals.

SHOPPING

MARKETS

★ There's a **crafts market** (⊠ *Calle 1 Sur, behind Plaza del Sol building*) in town that sells a respectable assortment of Mexican wares. It's the best place to practice your bartering skills while shopping for blankets, T-shirts, hammocks, and pottery.

For fresh produce, fish, chilies, and a taste of local life, try the **Mercado Municipal** (⊠ *Calle Adolfo Rosado Salas between Avs. 20 and 25 Sur* ☎ *No phone*), open Monday–Saturday 8–5.

SHOPPING MALLS

Forum Shops (⊠ *Av. Rafael E. Melgar and Calle 10 Norte* ☎ *987/869–1687*) is a flashy marble-and-glass mall with jewels glistening in glass cases and an overabundance of eager salesclerks. Diamonds International and Tanzanite International have shops in the Forum and all over Avenida Rafael E. Melgar, as does Roger's Boots, a leather store. There's a Havana Blue bar upstairs, where shoppers select expensive cigars.

Puerto Maya (⊠ *Carretera Sur at southern cruise dock*) is a mall geared to cruise-ship passengers, with branches of many of downtown's most popular shops, restaurants, and bars. It's close to the ships at the end of a huge parking lot.

Punta Langosta (⊠ *Av. Rafael E. Melgar 551, at Calle 7*), a fancy multilevel shopping mall, is across the street from the cruise-ship dock. An enclosed pedestrian walkway leads over the street from the ships to the center, which houses several jewelry and sportswear stores. The center is designed to lure cruise-ship passengers into shopping in air-conditioned comfort and has reduced traffic for local businesses.

SPECIALTY STORES

CLOTHING

Several trendy sportswear stores line Avenida Rafael E. Melgar between Calles 2 and 6. **Exotica** (⊠ *Av. Juárez at plaza* ☎ *987/872–5880*) has high-quality sportswear and shirts with nature-theme designs.

Island Outfitters (⊠ *Av. Rafael E. Melgar, at plaza* ☎ *987/872–0132*) has high-quality sportswear, beach towels, and sarongs.

Mr. Buho (✉ *Av. Rafael E. Melgar between Calles 6 and 8* ☎ *987/869–1601*) specializes in white-and-black clothes and has well-made guayabera shirts and cotton dresses.

CRAFTS

At **Balam Mayan Feather** (✉ *Av. 5 and Calle 2 Norte* ☎ *987/869–0548*) artists create intricate paintings on feathers from local birds.

Bugambilias (✉ *Av. 10 Sur between Calles Adolfo Rosado Salas and 1 Sur* ☎ *987/872–6282*) sells handmade Mexican linens.

★ **Los Cinco Soles** (✉ *Av. Rafael E. Melgar and Calle 8 Norte* ☎ *987/872–0132* 🌐 *www.loscincosoles.com*) is the best one-stop shop for crafts from around Mexico. Several display rooms, covering almost an entire block, are filled with clothing, furnishings, home-decor items, and jewelry. They also have a shop at the Puerto Maya cruise pier.

At Cozumel's best art gallery, **Galería Azul** (✉ *449 Av. 15 N (between Calles 8 and 10)* ☎ *987/869–0963* 🌐 *www.cozumelglassart.com*), artist Greg Deitrich displays his engraved blown glass along with paintings, jewelry, and other works by local artists. Deitrich recently moved the gallery to his home, where you can see him working with his glassware and silk paintings. It's open Monday–Friday 11–7 and by appointment.

El Porton (✉ *Av. 5 Sur and Calle 1 Sur* ☎ *987/872–5606*) has a collection of masks and unusual crafts.

JEWELRY

Look for silver, gold, and coral jewelry—especially bracelets and earrings—at **Joyería Palancar** (✉ *Av. Rafael E. Melgar Norte 15* ☎ *987/872–1468*).

One of Mexico's most famous jewelry designers, **Tanya Moss** (✉ *Av. Rafael E. Melgar at Punta Langosta* ☎ *987/869–1612*) creates original silver and gold necklaces and earrings that have become collectibles for those in the know. There's also a shop at the Hotel Presidente InterContinental.

SPORTS AND THE OUTDOORS

Most people come to Cozumel for the water sports—especially scuba diving, snorkeling, and fishing. Services and equipment rentals are available throughout the island, especially through major hotels and water-sports centers at the beach clubs.

If you're curious about what's underneath Cozumel's waters but don't like getting wet, **Atlantis Submarine** (✉ *Carretera Sur, Km 4, across from Hotel Casa del Mar* ☎ *987/872–5671 or 866/546–7820* 🌐 *www.atlantisadventures.com*) runs 1½-hour submarine rides that explore the Chankanaab Reef and surrounding area; tickets for the tours are $89 for adults and $59 for children. Even divers enjoy going down 100 feet below sea level. Claustrophobes may not be able to handle the sardine-can conditions.

FISHING

The waters off Cozumel swarm with more than 230 species of fish, making this one of the world's best deep-sea fishing destinations. During billfish migration season, from late April through June, blue marlin, white marlin, and sailfish are plentiful, and world-record catches aren't uncommon.

Most sportfishing boats are located in the Puerto Abrigo marina just north of San Miguel. Fishing boats are also located at **La Caleta**, the marina on the south side, beside the Presidente Intercontinental resort. At this writing, La Caleta was being refurbished. Most sportfishing companies are affiliated with dive shops, and offer a full range of water activities.

CHARTERS

You can charter high-speed fishing boats for about $420 per half-day or $600 per day (with a maximum of six people). Your hotel can help arrange daily charters—some offer special deals, with boats leaving from their own docks.

Albatros Deep Sea Fishing (☎ *987/872–7904 or 888/333–4643* 🌐 *www.albatroscharters.com*) offers full-day trips that include boat and crew, tackle and bait, and lunch with beer and soda starting at $575 for up to six people.

All equipment and tackle, lunch with beer, and the boat and crew are also included in **Ocean Tours'** (☎ *987/872–9530 Ext. 8*) full-day rates, which start at $550.

3 Hermanos (☎ *987/872–6417; 651/755-4897 in the U.S.* 🌐 *www.cozumelfishing.com*) specializes in deep-sea and fly-fishing trips. Their rates for a half-day deep-sea fishing trip start at $350; a full day is $450. They also offer scuba-diving trips, and their boats are available for group charters (a great way to snorkel and cruise around at your own pace) for $400 for up to six passengers.

GOLF

The **Cozumel Country Club** (✉ *Carretera Costera Norte, Km 5.8* ☎ *987/872–9570* 🌐 *www.cozumelcountryclub.com.mx*) has an 18-hole championship golf course. The gorgeous fairways amid mangroves and a lagoon are the work of the Nicklaus Design Group, and have been declared an Audubon nature reserve. The greens fees are $169 before 12:30 PM and $105 after, and include a shared golf cart. Some hotels, including Playa Azul, offer golf packages here.

If you're not a fan of miniature golf, the challenging **Cozumel Mini-Golf** (✉ *Calle 1, Sur 20* ☎ *987/872–6570*) might turn you into one. The jungle-theme course has banana trees, birds, two fountains, and a waterfall. You can choose your music from a selection of more than 800 CDs and order your drinks via walkie-talkie; they'll be delivered as you try for that hole in one. Admission is $7 for adults, $5 for kids; it's open Monday through Saturday 10 AM to 11 PM and Sunday 5 PM to 11 PM.

HORSEBACK RIDING

Aventuras Naturales (✉ *Av. 35, No. 1081* ☎ *987/872–1628 or 858/366–4632* 🌐 *www.aventurasnaturalascozumel.com*) runs a two-hour guided horseback tour through the jungle to El Cedral. Prices start at $35. Groups are small, and the guides fun and informative. The company also has Jeep tours and an action tour combining biking, horseback riding, and snorkeling for $65 per person.

Rancho Buenavista (✉ *Carretera Perimetral, Km 32.5* ☎ *987/872–1537* 🌐 *www.buenavistaranch.com*) provides four-hour rides through the jungle starting at $65 per person.

SNORKELING AND SCUBA DIVING

Aqua Safari (✉ *Av. Rafael E. Melgar 429, between Calles 5 and 7 Sur* ☎ *987/872–0101*) is among the island's oldest and most professional shops. Owner Bill Horn has long been involved in efforts to protect the reefs and stays on top of local environmental issues. The shop provides PADI certification, classes on night diving, deep diving and other interests, and individualized dives.

Sergio Sandoval of **Aquatic Sports and Scuba Cozumel** (✉ *Calle 21 Sur and Av. 20 Sur* ☎ *987/872–0640*) gets rave reviews from his clients, many of them guests at the Flamingo Hotel. His boats carry only six to eight divers, so the trips are extremely personalized.

Dive magazines regularly rate **Scuba Du** (✉ *at the Presidente Inter-Continental hotel* ☎ *987/872–9505, or 310/684–5556 from the U.S.*) among the best dive shops in the Caribbean. Along with the requisite Cozumel dives, the company offers an advanced divers trip to walls off Punta Sur.

THE RIVIERA MAYA

Updated by Marlise Kast

It takes patience to discover the treasures along this part of the coast. Beaches and towns aren't easily visible from the main highway—the road from Cancún to Tulum is 1 to 2 km (½ to 1 mi) from the coast. Thus there's little to see but dense vegetation, lots of billboards, many roadside markets, and signs marking entrances to various hotels and attractions.

Still, the treasures—which include spectacular white-sand beaches and some of the peninsula's most beautiful Mayan ruins—are here, and they haven't been lost on resort developers. In fact, the Riviera Maya, which stretches from Punta Tanchacté in the north down to Punta Allen in the south, currently has about 23,512 hotel rooms. This frenzy of building has affected many beachside Mayan communities, which have had to relocate to the inland jungle. The residents of these settlements, who mainly work in the hotels, have managed to keep Yucatecan traditions—including food, music, and holiday celebrations—alive in the area.

PLAYA DEL CARMEN

68 km (42 mi) south of Cancún

Playa has become one of Latin America's fastest-growing communities, with a population of more than 135,000 and a pace almost as hectic as that of Cancún. Hotels, restaurants, and shops multiply here faster than you can say "Kukulcán." Some are branches of Cancún eateries whose owners have taken up permanent residence in Playa, while others are owned by American and European expats (predominately Italians) who came here years ago. It makes for a varied, international community.

Considered the South Beach of Mexico, the club scene (raging night and day) is one of the main draws here. In fact, you may have trouble sleeping if you are staying in the heart of downtown. By day, Playa's lively beach clubs are packed with travelers lounging in sun or dancing to the sounds of a live DJ. By night the action moves to Calle 12, where a cluster of nightclubs line the street.

GETTING HERE AND AROUND

Almost everyone who arrives in this region by air flies into Cancún's Aeropuerto Internacional. Buses traveling south from Cancún stop at Playa del Carmen's bus terminal at Avenida 20 and Calle 12. Buses headed to Cancún from Playa del Carmen use the main bus terminal at Avenida Juárez and Avenida 5. ADO runs express, first-class, and second-class buses to major destinations. You can hire taxis in Cancún to go as far as Playa del Carmen, but the price is steep—about $55 for the one-hour drive. Shared vans from Cancún airport generally cost $80 for a six-person van, or $120 for a 10-person van; if you're traveling with a group or even find some other Playa-bound travelers at the airport, a van can be a good way to go.

ESSENTIALS

Bus Contacts **ADO** (☎ *983/832-5110* 🌐 *www.ado.com.mx*).

Car Rental **Avis** (✉ *Carretera 307, Lote 4, Mz 73, next to fire station, Playa del Carmen* ☎ *984/873-3843* 🌐 *www.avis.com.*)

Police **Police Department.** (✉ *Playa del Carmen* ☎ *984/877-3340*). **Federal Police.** (✉ *Playa del Carmen* ☎ *998/884-1107*).

Medical Assistance **Centro de Salud** (✉ *Av. Juárez and Av. 15* ☎ *984/873-1230 Ext. 147*). **Clinica Medica del Carmen.** ✉ *Av 25 between Calle 2 and Juarez, Playa del Carmen* ☎ *984/873-0885*).

Visitor and Tour Info **Playa del Carmen tourist information booth** (✉ *Av. Juárez by police station, between Calles 15 and 20* ☎ *984/873-2804 in Playa del Carmen; 888/955-7155 in U.S.; 604/990-6506 in Canada*). **Tierra Maya Tours** (✉ *Av. 5 and Calle 6* ☎ *984/873-1385*).

EXPLORING

La Casa del Arte Popular Mexicano. This entrancing folk-art museum is a must for anyone interested in Mexican culture and handicrafts. It is brimming with original works by the country's finest artisans, which are arranged in fascinating tableaux. The collection represents different regions of Mexico—from nativity scenes sculpted out of Oaxaca's clays

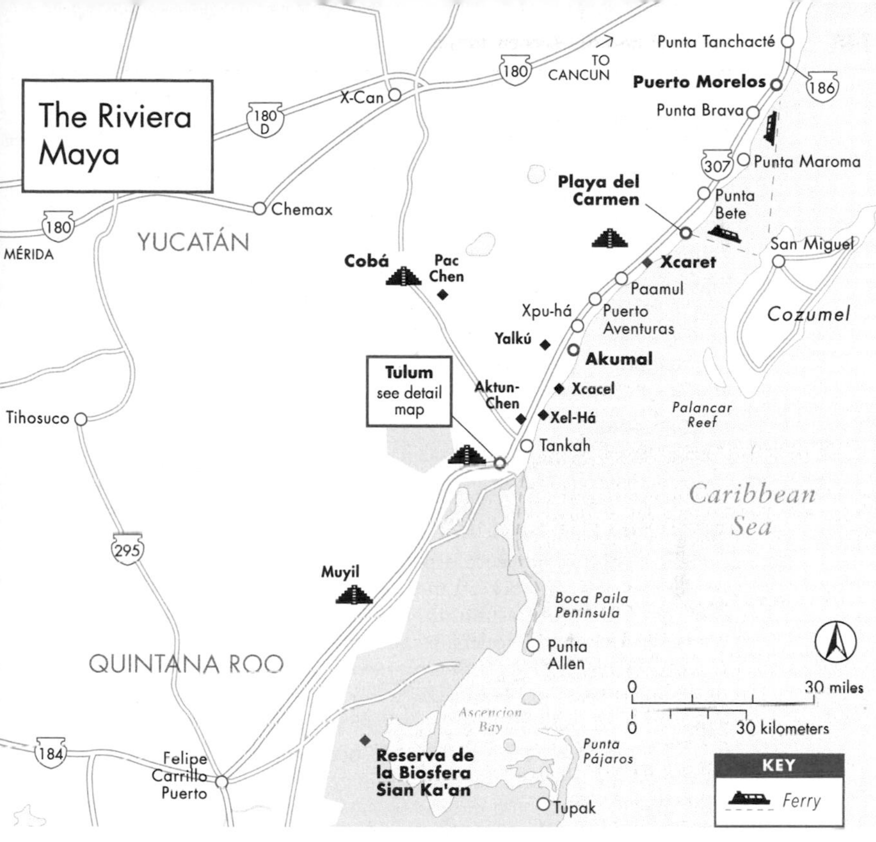

to the intricate *arbol de la vida* (tree of life) sculptures crafted in Metepec, Estado de México. Children will love the toy room, which includes an impressive display of *alebrijes* (dreamworld animals). In addition to the handicrafts, there are scenes set up throughout the museum to give visitors an idea of traditional Mexican life. The mannequins used in these re-creations, which include a church and a market setting, were actually modeled on real people that the museum director met during her trips through Mexico. ✉ *Carretera 307, Km 282, 6 miles south of Playa del Carmen* ☎ *984/871–5200 Ext. 399* 🌐 *www.xcaret.com* 🎫 *Free (museum only)* 🕓 *Weekdays 8:30 AM–10 PM.*

The excellent 32-acre **Xaman Ha Aviary** (✉ *Paseo Xaman-Ha, Mz 13-A Lote 1, Playacar* ☎ *984/873–0330* 🌐 *www.aviarioxamanha.com*), in the middle of the Playacar development, is home to more than 30 species of native birds. It's open daily 9 to 5, and admission is $20.

BEACHES

Playa del Carmen is as famous for its pristine beaches as it is for its thriving nightlife. This charming coastal city has managed to blend the two into one with its trendy beach clubs, offering everything from cabanas and cocktails to dancing and DJ's. Although the beaches themselves are pleasant, the focus is more on what the clubs have to offer than what's happening on the water. The music, combined with cocktails and bikinis, makes these open-air bars extremely popular with young singles. They are also the only places (other than resorts) you'll find beach amenities.

Main Beach. Stretching from the ferry docks to Calle 14, Main Beach is the most central beach in Playa del Carmen. You'll find clean, white sand, but it's not as powdery as the coastline further north. Within walking distance are countless bars and restaurants lining Fifth Avenue, and it's easy to find a dive shop ready to take you out to sea. The closer you get to the ferry docks, the more people you'll find. If you're looking for seclusion, head farther north outside of Playa del Carmen. **Best for:** swimming, sunbathing. **Amenities:** none. ✉ *Calle 14 and the beach, Playa del Carmen*

BEACH CLUBS

Canibal Royal. With 1950s Brazilian-inspired architecture, this funky beach club has incredible food (braised octopus, tarte flambé, fish ceviche), breathtaking views, and a wide selection of genre-crossing eclectic music. The beach area is equipped with plenty of lounge chairs, and there is a rooftop bar with a plunge pool and sundeck. There is also a juice bar and full cocktail menu featuring their signature rosemary caipiroska. **Best for:** restaurant, singles scene, amenities, music. **Amenities:** chaise lounges, toilets, restaurant. ✉ *Calle 48 and the beach; in front of Elements Condominiums next to Grand Coco Bay, Playa del Carmen* ☎ *984/859–1443* ⏲ *Daily 10–10.*

Zenzi. This beach club and restaurant is one of the only spots open everyday until late. Take a dip in the ocean and then catch some rays on one of the sun beds or chaise lounges. When the sun goes down, they offer live music and movies on the beach. The fish tacos and daily happy-hour specials make it difficult to ever leave. **Best for:** singles scene, amenities, live music, nightly entertainment. **Amenities:** umbrellas, chaise lounges, toilets, restaurant. ✉ *Calle 10 and the beach, Playa del Carmen* ☎ *984/876–2191 or 984/125–3074* 🌐 *www.zenzi-playa.com* ⏲ *Daily 7:30 AM–2 AM.*

WHERE TO EAT

$$ THAI ★ ✕ **Babe's Noodles & Bar.** Photos and paintings of Old Hollywood pinup models decorate the walls and are even laminated onto the bar of this Swedish-owned Thai restaurant, known for its fresh and interesting fare. Everything is cooked to order—no prefab dishes here. Try the spring rolls with peanut sauce, or the sesame noodles made with chicken or pork, veggies, lime, green curry, and ginger. In the Buddha Garden you can sip a mojito or sit at the bar and watch the crowds on nearby 5th Avenue. The lemonade, blended with ice and mint, is incredibly refreshing. If the place is crowded, head to their second location on Avenida 5 between calles 28 and 30. ✉ *Calle 10 between Avs. 5 and 10* ☎ *984/120–2592* 🌐 *www.babesnoodlesandbar.com* ✉ *Av. 5 between Calles 28 and 30* ☎ *984/803–0056* 💳 *No credit cards.*

$$$–$$$$ SEAFOOD ✕ **Blue Lobster.** You can choose your dinner live from a tank here, and if it's grilled, you pay by the weight—a small lobster costs $20, while a monster will set you back $100. At night the candlelit dining room draws a good crowd. People come not only for the lobster but also for

the ceviche, mussels, and jumbo shrimp. Ask for a table on the terrace overlooking the street. ✉ *Calle 12 and Av. 5* ☎ *984/873–1360* 💳 *AE, MC, V.*

¢–$ CAFÉ ✕ **Café Sasta.** This sweet little café serves fantastic coffee drinks (cappuccino, espresso, mocha blends), teas, bagel sandwiches, and baked goods. The flan is sinfully delicious, and the staff is very pleasant. ✉ *Av. 5 between Calles 8 and 10* ☎ *984/125–3516* 💳 *No credit cards.*

$–$$ VEGETARIAN ✕ **Casa Tucan.** The refined Italian, Swiss, and Greek dishes at this sidewalk restaurant are top-notch. Everything on the menu is fresh; even the herbs are homegrown. The spanakopita and lasagna are especially good. There's additional seating on the rooftop terrace. ✉ *Calle 4 between Avs. 10 and 15* ☎ *984/873–0283* 💳 *MC, V.*

$$$$ MEDITERRANEAN ✕ **Glass Bar.** Centrally located in the heart of 5th Avenue, this Italian restaurant serves food inspired by the regional cuisines of Naples, Rome, Milan, and Venice. The *gelato* lends an authentic touch, as do the rough brick walls, wooden floors, square umbrellas, and chalkboard inscribed with the daily specials. All breads and pastas, which include potato ravioli and linguine with mussels and clams, are made from scratch. The scallops au gratin are delicious, as is the Chilean sea bass served with grape and ginger reduction. The desserts here are said to be the best in Playa, especially the chocolate mousse and bitter chocolate cake with homemade ice cream. Large groups can reserve the Imperial Table for 18; the street-level patio is the best place to sit if you want to people-watch. There's a buffet breakfast from 7 to 11 daily, and the bar is open until 2 AM. ✉ *Av. 5 and Calle 12, Playa del Carmen* ☎ *984/803–1270* 🌐 *www.theglassbar.com.mx* 💳 *AE, MC, V.*

15

¢–$ CAFÉ ✕ **Java Joe's.** In business since 1997, this is one of Playa's favorite coffee spots, where you can buy your joe by the cup or by the kilo. You can also indulge in Joe's "hangover special"—an English muffin, Canadian bacon, and a fried egg—if you've had a Playa kind of night. There are also 16 types of bagels to choose from, along with other baked goodies and pastries. ✉ *Calle 10 between Avs. 5 and 10* ☎ *984/876–2694* 🌐 *www.javajoes.net* 💳 *No credit cards.*

$$$ ECLECTIC **Fodor's Choice** ★ ✕ **John Gray's Place.** This sophisticated and inviting bistro is tucked away at the end of Calle Corazón near 5th Avenue. Large picture windows offer a glimpse into the bustling kitchen, where Chef John Gray prepares such dishes as pork loin with Roquefort crust and salmon fillet wrapped in crispy potatoes. Offering a gourmet touch to ordinary food, the menu features macaroni and cheese with grilled shrimp and black truffle oil, as well as Gray's famous "snails and beans." After dinner, you can head across the way to The Den at John Gray's Place. This quaint bar serves cocktails, appetizers, and wines, including John Gray's private barrel selection, El Corazón. The menu is constantly changing, so ask about the daily specials. ✉ *Calle Corazón, just off Av. 5, between Calles 12 and 14* ☎ *984/803–3689* 🌐 *www.johngrayrestaurantgroup.com* 💳 *AE, MC, V* ⏲ *Open 1–11 PM. Closed Sun.*

$$$$ SEAFOOD ✕ **La Casa del Agua.** This eatery features four separate levels, each with its own atmosphere. From the street-level bistro a dramatic staircase leads to a small cocktail bar where candelabras drip onto the wooden floors. A stone waterfall is the focal point in the dining rooms illuminated by

wrought-iron chandeliers. The open layout provides nearly every table with an ocean breeze. Among the favorites are grilled grouper with goat cheese, blue-fin tuna with Portobello mushrooms, and seafood risotto. Remarkably flavorful is the shredded pork, which is cooked for eight hours in black beer, Dijon mustard, red wine, and honey. ✉ *Av. 5 and Calle 2* ☎ *984/803–0232* 🌐 *www.lacasadelagua.com* 💳 *MC, V.*

$$$$ ECLECTIC ✕ **Negrosal**. An isolated location and alluring atmosphere make "Black Salt" a local favorite. Inspired by the female form, the decor integrates damask chairs cinched by corsets, candles wrapped in black lace, and table legs shaped to resemble those of a ballerina. The restaurant's lighting subtlety changes color every few minutes, and a glass flooring allows you to peek down at the extensive wine cellar. Playing with contradictions, the menu features sweet and salty combinations like lobster tail topped with a corn and pineapple sauce, and cheese tempura with apricot marmalade. Every dish, including the tequila duck tacos and the grilled sea bass, is served under a silver dome. Be sure to try the house cocktail: black champagne covered with floating rose petals. ✉ *Calle 16 between Avs. 1 and 5* ☎ *984/803–2448* 🌐 *www.negrosal.com* 💳 *AE, MC, V* ⏲ *No lunch.*

$$$–$$$$ ECLECTIC ✕ **Ula-Gula**. As original as its name, this rooftop restaurant boldly experiments with a variety of textures, colors, and flavors. Sushi, tapas, and spring rolls make the perfect martini companions, with portions large enough to satisfy without leaving you stuffed. Unusual combinations in the entrées include grilled salmon with cucumber tagliatelle and ravioli mascarpone with mushroom sauce. For dessert, don't miss the liquid chocolate cake served with vanilla ice cream and peach marmalade—a truly exceptional dish. Livelier than the secluded restaurant is the street-level bar of the same name. ✉ *Av. 5 and Calle 10* ☎ *984/879–3727* 🌐 *www.ula-gula.com* 💳 *AE, MC, V* ⏲ *No lunch.*

$$–$$$ MEXICAN ✕ **Yaxche**. One of Playa's best restaurants has reproductions of stelae (stone slabs with carved inscriptions) from famous ruins, and murals of Mayan gods and kings. Mayan dishes such as *halach winic* (chicken in a spicy four-pepper sauce) are superb, and you can finish your meal with a Café Maya (made from Kahlúa, brandy, vanilla, and Xtabentun, the local liqueur flavored with anise and honey). Watching the waiter pour and light Café Maya from its silver demitasse is almost as seductive as the drink itself. For a romantic setting, request a table on the garden terrace. ✉ *Calle 8 between Av. 5 and 10* ☎ *984/873–2502* 🌐 *www.mayacuisine.com* 💳 *AE, MC, V.*

WHERE TO STAY

PLAYA DEL CARMEN

¢–$ 🏨 **Casa Tucan**. For the price, it's hard to beat this warm, eclectic hotel a few blocks from the beach. Mexican fabrics decorate the cheerful rooms and apartments, and the property has a yoga palapa, a TV bar, a book exchange, and a specially designed pool that's used for on-site diving instruction. Guest rooms have Wi-Fi access, and there's also an Internet café. This is one of the only hotels in Playa del Carmen to offer parking. **Pros:** multilingual staff, on-site car-rental agency, exceptional restaurant. **Cons:** some rooms lack a/c. ✉ *Calle 4 between Avs. 10 and 15* ☎ *984/873–0283* 🌐 *www.casatucan.de* 🛏 *24 rooms, 4 apartments,*

10 cabanas *In-room: no a/c (some), no phone, no TV. In-hotel: restaurant, bar, pool, diving, parking (free)* *MC, V* *EP.*

$$$ Fodor's Choice ★ **Deseo Hotel & Lounge.** This adults-only hotel is known for its cutting-edge design. A great stone stairway cuts through the stark modern main building; the steps lead to a minimalist, white-on-white open-air lobby, with huge daybeds for sunning, a trendy bar (with a DJ), and a pool illuminated with purple lights. Each of the soundproof rooms has a king-size bed, soft lighting, and clothesline hung with flip-flops, bananas, and a beach bag. Suites have large balconies with draping hammocks. Each room is outfitted with a noisemaker, so you can fall asleep to the sound of chirping crickets and awake to the sound of whistling birds. Although this is not a beachfront property, guests have free access to Mamitas Beach Club. **Pros:** contemporary decor, friendly staff, comfortable beds, films shown nightly. **Cons:** small pool, kids not allowed. *Av. 5 and Calle 12* *984/879–3620* *www.hoteldeseo.com* *12 rooms, 3 suites* *In-room: safe, Wi-Fi. In-hotel: room service, bar, pool, no kids under 18* *AE, MC, V* *CP.*

15

$$$ **Hotel Básico.** This ultrahip hotel has won awards for its innovative design. You'll find ingenious materials throughout the hotel—70% of which is recycled—from the used tires on the spongy lobby floor to the rooftop lounge chairs made from boxes that were once pickup truck beds. The roof also has two small pools made of recycled oil tanks, and a small bar where Playa's young and trendy meet up with hotel guests for late-night drinks. Guest rooms, though equipped with plasma TVs and DVD players, are designed to look very basic, with plain cement walls, exposed plumbing, and rubber curtains made from inner tubes. All come with retro amenities like beach balls, swim fins, and Polaroid cameras. **Pros:** innovative and eco-friendly design, great rooftop lounge, showers have strong water pressure, huge beds. **Cons:** limited storage space in rooms, not family-friendly, late-night noise, thin walls. *Av. 5 at Calle 10 Norte* *984/879–4448* *www.hotelbasico.com* *In-room: refrigerator, DVD. In-hotel: restaurant, room service, bar, laundry service, Wi-Fi hotspot* *AE, MC, V* *CP.*

$$–$$$ Fodor's Choice ★ **La Tortuga Hotel & Spa.** European couples often choose this inn, which is on a quiet side street. Mosaic stone paths wind through the gardens, and colonial-style hardwood furnishings gleam throughout. At the center of the property are a botanical garden and stunning pool area where tiki torches and illuminated palm trees guide your way to two-story adobe buildings. Rooms are small but have balconies, and are well equipped with flat-screen TVs, minibars, and iPod docks. There is a common area with a bar and pool table. Guests are given passes to the nearby Mamitas Beach Club. **Pros:** some rooms have rooftop terraces, gorgeous grounds, outstanding breakfast. **Cons:** late-night street noise, flat pillows, kids not allowed. *Calle 14 and Av. 10* *984/873–1484 or 800/822–3274* *www.hotellatortuga.com* *45 rooms, 6 junior suites* *In-room: safe. In-hotel: restaurant, room service, pool, spa, Wi-Fi hotspot, no kids under 16* *AE, MC, V* *BP.*

$$$–$$$$ **Mosquito Blue Hotel.** Modern, exotic, and elegant, this hotel has Indonesian decor, mahogany furniture, and soft lighting. Standard rooms have king-size beds, marble bathrooms, and patios that open onto the

pool or garden area. The courtyard bar, near one of the pools, is a soothing spot—it's sheltered by a thatch roof and pastel walls. The 4,000-square-foot spa offers services like Mayan healing baths and an aromatherapeutic oxygen bar. For some beach time, spend a day at sister property Mosquito Beach Hotel, where sun beds, showers, and service are on hand. **Pros:** access to Mosquito Beach Hotel, spotless rooms, access to nearby fitness center. **Cons:** billiards area tends to get loud at night, kids not allowed. ✉ *Calle 12 between Avs. 5 and 10* ☎ *984/873–1245* 🌐 *www.mosquitoblue.com* *44 rooms, 1 suite* *In-room: safe, refrigerator, Internet, Wi-Fi. In-hotel: restaurant, room service, bar, pools, spa, laundry service, Wi-Fi hotspot, some pets allowed, no kids under 16* ▭ *AE, MC, V* 🍽 *CP.*

PLAYACAR

$$$$ **Iberostar Tucan and Quetzal.** This unique all-inclusive resort has preserved its natural surroundings—among the resident animals are flamingos, turtles, toucans, and monkeys. Landscaped pool areas surround the open-air restaurant and reception area. Spacious rooms have cheerful color schemes and patios overlooking dense vegetation. **Pros:** oceanfront rooms, tropical setting, separate areas for families and singles. **Cons:** food lacks variety, small beach, water at swim-up bar can be chilly. ✉ *Fracc. Playacar, Playacar* ☎ *984/877–2000* 🌐 *www.iberostar.com* *700 rooms* *In-room: safe, refrigerator. In-hotel: 5 restaurants, room service, bars, tennis courts, pools, gym, spa, beachfront, diving, water sports, children's programs (ages 4–12), laundry service, Wi-Fi hotspot, parking (free)* ▭ *AE, D, MC, V* 🍽 *AI.*

$$$$ **Royal Hideaway.** Located on a stretch of beach, this 13-acre resort has exceptional amenities and superior service. Art and artifacts from around the world fill the lobby, and streams, waterfalls, and fountains dot the grounds. Rooms are in two- and three-story colonial-style villas, each with its own concierge. Gorgeous rooms have two queen-size beds, sitting areas, and ocean-view terraces. **Pros:** romantic setting, attentive service, the ultimate in pampering. **Cons:** not family-friendly, cold pool, roaming beach vendors can be bothersome. ✉ *Fracc. Playacar, Lote 6, Playacar* ☎ *984/873–4500 or 800/858–2258* 🌐 *www.royalhideaway.com* *176 rooms, 24 suites* *In-room: Wi-Fi. In-hotel: 6 restaurants, bars, tennis courts, pools, spa, beachfront, water sports, bicycles, laundry service, Wi-Fi hotspot, parking (free), no kids under 13* ▭ *AE, MC, V* 🍽 *AI.*

NIGHTLIFE

Bali (✉ *Calle 12 Norte between Avs. 5 and 10, Playa del Carmen* ☎ *984/803–2864*) is one of the area's largest dance clubs, accommodating up to 800 people. The multilevel club offers the latest hits mixed by resident spinmaster DJ Carlos. The cover charge is $10.

Bar Ranita (✉ *Calle 10 between Avs. 5 and 10* ☎ *984/873–0389*), a cozy alcove, is run by a Swedish couple who really know how to party. The prices are unbeatable, and the margaritas pack a powerful punch.

Following the success of its sister property in Cancún, **CoCo Bongo,** (✉ *Av. 10 Norte* ☎ *984/803–3232* 🌐 *www.cocobongo.com.mx* *$50* ⏲ *Closed Sun.*) has flying acrobats, bar-top conga lines, live bands, and

DJs mixing everything from rock to hip-hop. The $50 cover charge includes unlimited drinks.

Classic films are projected on the wall as DJs spin disco nightly at the **Deseo Lounge** (✉ *Av. 5 at Calle 12, Playa del Carmen* ☎ *984/879–3620* 🌐 *www.hoteldeseo.com*), a rooftop bar and local hot spot.

Diablito Cha Cha Cha (✉ *Calle 12 between Avs. 5 and 1, Playa del Carmen* ☎ *984/803–3695* 🌐 *www.diablitochachacha.com*) is a popular palapa bar. The open-air setting is the perfect place to grab sushi, a cocktail, and people-watch while a DJ spins until 2 AM.

Kartabar (✉ *Calle 12 at Av. 1, Playa del Carmen* ☎ *984/873–2228*) has a laid-back vibe. The sweet scents of strawberry, mint, apple, and rose waft from the hookah pipes as belly dancers weave between the tables. The house martini is sinfully divine.

★ **La Santanera** (✉ *Calle 12 between Avs. 5 and 10, Playa del Carmen* ☎ *984/803–4771* 🌐 *www.lasantanera.com* 🎫 *$8* ⏲ *Closed Sun.*). In Studio 54–like fashion, this "clubsito" has patent-leather sofas and a distinctive retro-tropical Mexican essence. To escape the dance floor, head upstairs to the rooftop lounge, where a DJ spins chill-out music.

15

At **Mambo Cafe** (✉ *Calle 6 between Avs. 5 and 10, Playa del Carmen* ☎ *984/879–2304*) a dance review begins at 9:30 every night, followed by live salsa music. A younger crowd of locals and tourists typically fills the dance floor.

Mandala (✉ *Calle 12 between Avs. 1 and 5, Playa del Carmen* ☎ *984/879–4189*) is the area's newest party spot. This trendy venue is divided into a street-level bar, a rooftop terrace, and a dance club. Each section has its own DJ spinning everything from house and hip-hop to disco and techno. The patent-leather sofas are great places to chill out.

SHOPPING

Avenida 5 between Calles 4 and 10 is the best place to shop along the coast. Boutiques sell folk art and textiles from around Mexico, and clothing stores carry lots of sarongs and beachwear made from Indonesian batiks. A shopping area called Calle Corazón, between Calles 12 and 14, has a pedestrian street, art galleries, restaurants, and boutiques.

CLOTHING

The retro '70s-style fashions at **Blue Planet** (✉ *Av. 5 between Calles 10 and 12* ☎ *984/803–1504*) are great for a day at the beach.

Crunch (✉ *Av. 5 between Calles 6 and 8* ☎ *984/873–1240*) sells high-style evening gowns, swimsuits, and sportswear for women. **Xbaal** (✉ *Av. 5 and Calle 14* ☎ *984/803–4107*) is filled with attractive men's and women's cotton shirts, woven skirts, and stylish sundresses.

CRAFTS

★ **Hacienda Tequila** (✉ *Av. 5 and Calle 14, Playa del Carmen* ☎ *984/873–1202*) sells traditional Mexican crafts and clothing, as well as 480 different types of tequila. Free tastings are available, and there is a small museum displaying the various stages of tequila production. At **La Hierbabuena Artesanía** (✉ *Av. 5 between Calles 8 and 10*

☎ *984/873–1741*), owner Melinda Burns offers a collection of fine Mexican clothing and crafts.

La Calaca (✉ *Av. 5 between Calles 12 and 14* ☎ *984/873–0174*) has an eclectic selection of wooden masks, whimsically carved angels and devils, and other crafts. **Maya Arts Gallery** (✉ *Av. 5 between Calles 6 and 8* ☎ *984/879–3389*) has an extensive collection of *huipiles*, the embroidered cotton dresses worn by Mayan women in Mexico and Guatemala.

JEWELRY

Ambar Mexicano (✉ *Av. 5 between Calles 4 and 6* ☎ *984/873–2357*) has amber jewelry crafted by a local designer who imports the amber from Chiapas. The **Opal Mine** (✉ *Av. 5 between Calles 4 and 6* ☎ *984/879–5041* ✉ *Av. 5 and Calle 12* ☎ *984/803–3658*) has fire, white, pink, and orange opals from Jalisco State. You can buy loose stones or commission pieces of custom jewelry. **Santa Prisca** (✉ *Av. 5 between Calles 2 and 4* ☎ *984/873–0960*) has silver jewelry, flatware, trays, and decorative items from the town of Taxco. Some pieces are set with semiprecious stones.

MALLS

Centro Maya (✉ *Carretera Federal 2100* ☎ *984/803–9057*) has Soriana, Mexico's large retail outlet, and more than 50 other stores. **Paseo del Carmen** (✉ *Av. 10 and Calle 1* ☎ *984/803–3789*) is an open-air shopping mall with a number of boutiques, including Diesel, Ultrafemme, and American Apparel. Caffeine junkies can get their fix at the Starbucks that dominates the center of the mall. A cobblestone path makes this mall one of the area's most popular and pleasant shopping destinations. **Plaza Las Américas** (✉ *Carretera Federal* ☎ *984/109–2161*) is a family-friendly mall featuring restaurants, shops, and cinemas.

SPORTS AND THE OUTDOORS

ADVENTURE TOURS

Alltournative (✉ *Carretera Federal 307, Km 287, in front of Playacar development, Playa del Carmen* ☎ *984/803–9999* 🌐 *www.alltournative.com*) will have you feeling like Indiana Jones in no time. Trips, which range in price from $82 to $125, focus on ecological preservation and Mexican culture. You can kayak through a lagoon, snorkel in a cenote, or zip-line above a lush jungle. The company also organizes trips to Mayan communities.

South of Playa del Carmen, **Punta Venado** (✉ *Carretera Federal 307, Km 278, Calica* ☎ *998/887–1191 or 800/503–0046* 🌐 *www.puntavenado.com*) offers adventure tours in all-terrain vehicles, on mountain bikes, or in jeeps. The 2.5 mi of isolated coastline are perfect for horseback riding, snorkeling, and kayaking. Packages range from $48 to $90.

Yucatán Sky Explorer (✉ *Playa del Carmen Airport, Playa del Carmen* ☎ *984/873–1626* 🌐 *www.playatoursdirect.com*) will take you on an exhilarating aerial tour above the Caribbean's turquoise waters. The ultralight airplane comfortably seats one person plus the licensed pilot. The 25-minute trips cost $99 per person.

GOLF

Playa del Carmen's golf course is an 18-hole, par-72 championship course designed by Robert von Hagge. The greens fee is $180; there's also a special twilight fee of $120. Information is available from the **Casa Club de Golf** (☎ *984/873–0624 or 998/881–6088*). The **Golf Club at Playacar** (✉ *Paseo Xaman-Ha and Mz 26, Playacar* ☎ *984/873–4990* 🌐 *www.palaceresorts.com*) has an 18-hole course; the greens fee is $190 and the twilight fee $130.

SCUBA DIVING

The PADI and SSI-affiliated **Abyss** (✉ *Av. 1 between Calles 10 and 12* ☎ *984/873–2164* 🌐 *www.abyssdiveshop.com*) offers introductory courses and dive trips ($50 for one tank, $70 for two tanks). The friendly staff at **Diversity Diving** (✉ *Calle 24, between Avs. 5 and 10, Playa del Carmen* ☎ *984/803–1042* 🌐 *www.diversitydiving.com*) takes you snorkeling at three different locations: open ocean, cenote, and lagoon. The trips cost $85 per person and include lunch, beverages, snorkeling gear, park entrance, and a guide.

15

Mexico Blue Dream (✉ *Between Av. 1 and Mamitas Beach, Playa del Carmen* ☎ *984/803–0660* 🌐 *www.mexicobluedream.com*) provides custom tours to Cozumel, Yal-Ku, Akumal, and nearby cenotes. Four-tank dives start at $136; boats depart five times daily. The oldest shop in town, **Tank-Ha Dive Center** (✉ *Calle 10 between Avs. 5 and 10, Playa del Carmen* ☎ *984/873–0302* 🌐 *www.tankha.com*) has PADI-certified teachers and runs diving and snorkeling trips to the reefs and caverns. A one-tank dive costs $45; for a two-tank trip it's $75. Dive packages are also available, as well as trips to Cozumel.

★ **Yucatek Divers** (✉ *Av. 15 Norte between Calles 2 and 4, Playa del Carmen* ☎ *984/803–2836* 🌐 *www.yucatek-divers.com*), which is affiliated with PADI, specializes in cenote dives, dive packages, and dives for those with disabilities. Introductory courses start at $95 for a one-tank dive and go as high as $390 for a four-day beginner course in open water.

SKYDIVING

Thrill seekers can take the plunge high above Playa in a tandem sky dive (where you're hooked up to the instructor the whole time). **Sky-Dive** (✉ *Plaza Marina 32,Playa del Carmen* ☎ *984/873–0192* 🌐 *www.skydive.com.mx*) even videotapes your trip so you have proof that you did it. Jumps take place every hour, and cost $230. Reserve at least one day in advance.

PUERTO MORELOS

32 km (20 mi) north of Playa del Carmen.

The sleeping beauty is awakening. For years Puerto Morelos was known only for being the coastal town where the car ferry departed for Cozumel. Over the past decade this cargo port has morphed into the gateway to the Riviera Maya. About halfway between Cancún and Playa del Carmen, Puerto Morelos makes a great base for exploring the region. The town itself is quaint and colorful, with a central plaza surrounded by shops and restaurants. Its trademark is a leaning lighthouse.

The pace is slow, the vibe is relaxed, and the atmosphere bohemian enough to attract a cluster of artists, painters, and poets. Many of the residents are Americans and Canadians who own local businesses or commute daily to Cancún.

EXPLORING

The biologists running the **Croco-Cun** (✉ *Carretera 307, Km 31* ☎ *998/850–3719* 🌐 *www.crococunzoo.com*), an animal farm just north of Puerto Morelos, have collected specimens of many of the reptiles and some of the mammals indigenous to the area. They offer immensely informative tours—you may even get to handle a baby crocodile or feed a monkey. Be sure to wave hello to the 500-pound crocodile secure in his deep pit. The farm is open daily 9 AM to 5 PM. Admission is $20.

South of Puerto Morelos, the 150-acre **Yaax Che Jardín Botánico del Dr. Alfredo Barrera Marín** (*Dr. Alfredo Barrera Marín Botanical Garden* ✉ *Carretera 307, Km 33* ☎ *983/832–1666 or 998/206–9233* 🌐 *www.ecosur.mx/jb/yaaxche*) is the largest botanical garden in Mexico. Named for a local botanist, the garden exhibits the peninsula's plants and flowers, which are labeled in English, Spanish, and Latin. The park features a 40-meter suspension bridge, three observation towers, and a library equipped with reading hammocks. There's also a tree nursery, a remarkable orchid and epiphyte garden, an authentic Mayan house, and an archaeological site. A nature walk goes directly through the mangroves for some great birding. More than 220 species have been identified here (be sure to bring the bug spray, though). Spider monkeys can usually be spotted in the afternoon, and a tree-house lookout offers a spectacular view—but the climb isn't for those afraid of heights. The park is open daily, 8 to 4. Closed Sundays May through November. Admission is $10.

WHERE TO EAT

$$$ MEXICAN

✕ **El Pirata**. A popular spot for breakfast, lunch, dinner, or just a drink from the bar, this open-air restaurant seats you at the center of the action on Puerto Morelos's town square. If you have a hankering for American food, you can get a good hamburger with fries here; there are also great daily specials. If you're lucky, they might include *pozole,* a broth made from cracked corn, chicken, chilies, and bay leaves and served with tostada shells. The tacos are delicious. ✉ *Av. Rafael E Melgar, Lote 4* ☎ *998/251–7948* 💳 *MC, V.*

$$$ INTERNATIONAL Fodor's Choice ★

✕ **John Gray's Kitchen**. This former Ritz-Carlton chef's current restaurant, which is right next to the jungle, draws a regular crowd of Cancún and Playa locals. Using only the freshest ingredients—from local fruits and vegetables to seafood right off the pier—Gray works

WORD OF MOUTH

"You might also want to consider Puerto Morelos—it's less touristy and the beaches are gorgeous. Lots of awesome snorkeling and diving. It's also just across the highway from some great cenotes, lesser known, but one of them even has a zip line that's a blast for teenagers. There's also a jungle spa that's helping the local people. The town is really nice and has great restaurants."

—Debiky

his magic in a comfortable and contemporary setting that feels more Manhattan than Mayan. Don't miss the delicious tender roasted duck breast with tequila, chipotle, and honey. Another great option is Coronado, a local whitefish grilled to perfection and served with mango salsa. ✉ *Av. Niños Heroes, Lote 6* ☎ *998/871–0665* 🌐 *www.johngrayrestaurantgroup.com* ▭ *MC, V* ⏲ *Closed Sun. No lunch.*

A SACRED JOURNEY

In ancient times Puerto Morelos was a point of departure for pregnant Mayan women making pilgrimages by canoe to Cozumel, the sacred isle of the fertility goddess, Ixchel. Remnants of Mayan ruins survive along the coast here, although none of them have been restored.

$$ MEXICAN ★ **Posada Amor.** This restaurant, the oldest in Puerto Morelos, has retained a loyal clientele for nearly three decades. In the palapa-covered dining room with its picnic-style wooden tables and benches, the gracious staff serves up terrific Mexican and seafood dishes, including a memorable whole fish dinner and a rich seafood bisque. The Sunday buffet is also delicious. Live music, including Spanish guitar, can be heard every night at the patio bar. ✉ *Avs. Javier Rojo Gómez and Tulum* ☎ *998/871–0033* ▭ *MC, V.*

15

WHERE TO STAY

$$$$ Fodor's Choice ★ **Ceiba del Mar Hotel & Spa.** Rooms at this secluded beach resort north of town are in eight thatch-roofed buildings, all with ocean-view terraces. Arching palms shade meandering paths that lead directly to the Caribbean waters. Painted tiles, stone floors, white duvets, and bamboo details in the rooms complement the hardwood furnishings from Guadalajara. **Pros:** delicious coconut ice cream, excellent service, romantic setting. **Cons:** few restaurants nearby, cold pool, no children's activities. ✉ *Costera Norte* ☎ *998/872–8060 or 877/545–6221* 🌐 *www.ceibadelmar.com* *88 rooms, 7 suites* *In-room: safe, DVD, Wi-Fi. In-hotel: 2 restaurants, bar, room service, tennis court, pools, gym, spa, beachfront, diving, water sports, laundry service, Wi-Fi hotspot, parking (free)* ▭ *AE, MC, V* *EP, MAP.*

¢–$ **Posada Amor.** In the early 1970s the founder of this small, cozy downtown hotel dedicated it to the virtues of love (*amor*). Although he's since passed away, the founding philosophy has been upheld by his wife and children, who now run the property. Rooms are clean, small, and simple; all have private baths. The on-site restaurant serves delicious meals, the specialty being fresh fish, and on Sunday the breakfast buffet is not to be missed. The helpful staff makes you feel right at home. **Pros:** excellent food, friendly staff, family-run business. **Cons:** no towels, rooms can get musty, and some lack a/c. ✉ *Avs. Javier Rojo Gómez and Tulum* ☎ *998/871–0033* *13 rooms* *In-room: no a/c (some), no phone, no TV. In-hotel: restaurant, bar, Wi-Fi hotspot* ▭ *MC, V* *EP.*

SHOPPING

CRAFTS AND FOLK ART

The **Colectivo de Artesanos de Puerto Morelos** (*Puerto Morelos Artists' Cooperative* ✉ *Avs. Javier Rojo Gómez and Isla Mujeres* ☎ *No phone*) is a series of palapa-style buildings where local artisans sell their jewelry, hand-embroidered clothes, hammocks, and other items. You can sometimes find real bargains. It's open daily from 8 AM until dusk.

SPORTS AND THE OUTDOORS

ADVENTURE TOURS

Selvática (✉ *Carretera 307, Km 321, 19 km from turnoff* ☎ *998/898–4312* 🌐 *www.selvatica.com.mx*), just outside the center of Puerto Morelos, offers tours over the jungle on more than 3 km (2 mi) of zip lines. The entire tour will take you a little over two hours, so you'll be glad to have a snack afterward in the on-site cafeteria. Mountain-biking tours are also available. If you want a taste of all the activities, you can go on a four-hour zip-line, biking, and swimming tour for $95. Advance reservations are required.

SCUBA DIVING

Almost Heaven Adventures (✉ *Av. Javier Rojo Gómez, Mz 2, Lote 10* ☎ *998/871–0230* 🌐 *www.almostheavenadventures.com*), the oldest dive shop in the area, is the only one owned and operated by locals. Snorkeling trips cost $55, and two-tank reef dives cost $75. Night tours are especially popular in the summer, so book at least a day in advance. **Diving Dog Tours** (☎ *998/201–9805 or 998/848–8819* 🌐 *www.puertomorelosfishing.com*) runs snorkeling trips at various sites on the Great Mesoamerican Reef for $30 per person.

XCARET

11 km (6½ mi) south of Playa del Carmen.

Fodor's Choice ★

Once a sacred Mayan city and port, Xcaret (pronounced *ish*-car-et) is now home to two theme parks on a gorgeous stretch of coastline. The 250-acre ecological theme park, simply known as "Xcaret," is the coast's most heavily advertised attraction. Billed as "nature's sacred paradise," it has a network of buses, its own published magazines, and a collection of stores. Just 2 km from Xcaret is the new adventure park, Xplor. This sister property is designed especially for extreme adventure seekers.

Among the most popular attractions are the Paradise River raft tour that takes you on a winding, watery journey through the jungle; the Butterfly Pavilion, where thousands of butterflies float dreamily through a botanical garden while New Age music plays in the background; and an ocean-fed aquarium where you can see local sea life drifting through coral heads and sea fans.

The park has a Wild Bird Breeding Aviary, nurseries for both abandoned flamingo eggs and sea turtles, and a series of underwater caverns that you can explore by snorkeling or snuba (a hybrid of snorkeling and scuba). A replica Mayan village includes a colorful cemetery with catacomb-like caverns underneath; traditional music and dance ceremonies (including performances by the famed *Voladores de Papantla*—the Flying Birdmen of Papantla) are performed here at night. But the star show is the evening "Spectacular Mexico Night Show," which tells the history of Mexico through song and dance.

The list of Xcaret's attractions goes on and on: you can visit a dolphinarium, a bee farm, a manatee lagoon, a bat cave, an orchid and bromeliad greenhouse, an edible-mushroom farm, and a small zoo. You can also visit a scenic tower that takes you 240 feet up in the air for a spectacular view of the park.

■ **TIP→ Although Xcaret has 11 restaurants, many visitors bring their own lunches and take advantage of picnic tables scattered throughout the park.** The entrance fee covers only access to the grounds and the exhibits; all other activities and equipment—from sea treks and dolphin tours to lockers and swim gear—are extra. The $99 Plus Pass includes park entrance, lockers, snorkel equipment, food, and drinks. You can buy tickets from any travel agency or major hotel along the coast. *☎ 984/871–5200; 998/883–0470 in Cancún ⊕ www.xcaret.com ✉ $69 Basic Pass; $99 Plus Pass ⊙ Daily 8:30 AM–10 PM.*

AKUMAL

37 km (23 mi) south of Playa del Carmen; 104 km (65 mi) south of Cancún.

In Mayan, Akumal (pronounced ah-koo-*maal*) means "place of the turtle," and for hundreds of years this beach has been a nesting ground for turtles. The season is June through August, and the best place to see them is on Half Moon Bay. Akumal first attracted international attention in 1926, when explorers discovered the *Mantanceros,* a Spanish galleon that sank there in 1741.

Today Akumal is probably the most Americanized community on the coast. It consists of three areas: Half Moon Bay, with its pretty beaches, terrific snorkeling, and large number of rentals; Akumal proper, a large resort with a market, grocery stores, laundry facilities, and a pharmacy; and Akumal Aventuras, to the south, with more condos and homes. The original Mayan community has been moved to a planned location across the highway.

EXPLORING

Fodor's Choice ★ **Aktun-Chen** is Mayan for "the cave with cenote inside." These amazing underground caves, estimated to be about 5 million years old, are the area's largest. You walk through the underground passages, past stalactites and stalagmites, until you reach the cenote with its various shades of deep green. There is also a canopy tour and one cenote where you can swim. You don't want to miss this one. *✉ Carretera 307, Km 107 ☎ 984/109–2061 ⊕ www.aktunchen.com ✉ $25 cave tour, $36 canopy tour ⊙ Daily 9–4.*

Brought to you by the people who manage Xcaret, **Xel-Há** (pronounced shel-*hah*) is a natural aquarium made from coves, inlets, and lagoons cut from the limestone shoreline. The name means "where the water is born," and a natural spring here flows out to meet the salt water, creating a perfect habitat for tropical marine life. There's still enough here to impress novice snorkelers, although there seem to be fewer fish each year, and the mixture of fresh and salt water can cloud visibility.

Scattered throughout the park are small Mayan ruins, including Na Balaam, known for a yellow jaguar painted on one of its walls. Low wooden bridges over the lagoons allow for leisurely walks around the park, and there are spots to rest or swim.

Xel-Ha gets overwhelmingly crowded, so come early. The grounds are well equipped with bathrooms, restaurants, and a shop. At the entrance you will receive specially prepared sunscreen that won't kill the fish; other sunscreens are prohibited. For an extra charge you can "interact" (not swim) with dolphins. There's also an all-inclusive package with a meal, a towel, a locker, and snorkel equipment for $79. Other activities like scuba diving and an underwater walk, are available at an additional cost and should be reserved at least a day in advance. ☎ *984/875–6000, 998/884–7165, or 800/009–3542* ⊕ *www.xelha.com* ⊙ *Daily 8:30–6.*

Devoted snorkelers may want to walk the unmarked dirt road to **Yalkú**, a couple of miles north of Akumal in Half Moon Bay. A series of small lagoons that gradually reach the ocean, Yalkú is an ecopark that's home to schools of parrot fish in superbly clear water with visibility to 160 feet. The entrance fee is about $7.50. You can rent snorkeling equipment in the parking lot for $10 and a locker for $2. The park is open daily 8 to 5:30.

WHERE TO EAT

$$–$$$ SEAFOOD ✕ **La Cueva del Pescador.** Dig your toes in the sand floor at this simple restaurant and enjoy the catch of the day. Their *ceviche,* a mix of shrimp, octopus, and fish "cooked" with lime juice and flavored with cilantro, is one of the best around because the ingredients are so fresh. All the servings are generous, so a soup and an entrée might be perfect for two. If you really have a big appetite, try the seafood medley of lobster, octopus, and shrimp. ✉ *Akumal Rd., at plaza* ☎ *984/875–9002* ▭ *No credit cards.*

$$–$$$ ITALIAN ✕ **Que Onda.** A Swiss-Italian couple created this northern Italian restaurant at the end of Half Moon Bay. Dishes are served under a palapa and include great homemade pastas, shrimp flambéed in cognac with a touch of saffron, and vegetarian lasagna. The Nutella crepes are to die for. Que Onda also has a neighboring seven-room hotel that's creatively furnished with Mexican and Guatemalan handicrafts. ✉ *Caleta Yalkú, Lotes 97–99; enter through Club Akumal Caribe, turn left, and go north to end of road at Half Moon Bay* ☎ *984/875–9101* ⊕ *www.queondaakumal.com* ▭ *MC, V* ⊙ *Closed Tues.*

¢–$ CAFÉ ✕ **Turtle Bay Café & Bakery.** This funky café has delicious (and healthy) breakfasts, lunches, and dinners; the smoothies, homemade ice cream, and fresh baked goods are especially yummy. It has a garden where you can sit and drink coffee, and its location by the ecological

> **WORD OF MOUTH**
>
> "I absolutely love Akumal, although it can be crowded at times. They have great restaurants, bars and shops all within walking distance and it's just a great friendly atmosphere. I was there about a month ago and it was much more crowded than it was in previous trips, so I guess it's becoming a lot more popular, but who can blame people for that?"
>
> —ewesthoff

center makes it the closest thing Akumal has to a downtown. ✉ *Half Moon Bay Rd., at Plaza* ☎ *984/875–9138* ▭ *MC, V* ⊙ *Closed Sept.*

SHOPPING

Galería Lamanai Carribean Arts & Crafts (✉ *Carrertera 307, Km 104* ☎ *984/875–9055*) is a laid-back gallery under a palapa roof. There's a real mix of folk art and fine art from Mexican and international artists.

Mexicarte (✉ *Carrertera 307* ☎ *984/875–9115*) is a little shop that sells high-quality crafts from around the country.

SPORTS AND THE OUTDOORS

★ The **Akumal Dive Center** (✉ *About 10 min north of Club Akumal Caribe* ☎ *984/875–9025* 🌐 *www.akumaldivecenter.com*) is the area's oldest and most experienced dive operation, offering reef or cenote diving, fishing, and snorkeling. Dives cost from $40 (one tank) to $120 (four tanks); a three-hour fishing trip for up to four people runs $150. Take a sharp right at the Akumal arches and you'll see the dive shop on the beach.

TSA Travel Agency and Bike Rental (✉ *Carretera 307, Km 104, next to Ecology Center* ☎ *984/875–9030* 🌐 *www.akumaltravel.com*) rents bikes for a 3½-hour jungle-biking adventure. The cost is $45 per person.

EN ROUTE

Hidden Worlds Cenotes Park. This park was made semi-famous when it was featured in a 2002 IMAX film, *Journey into Amazing Caves,* which was shown at theaters across North America. The park, which was founded by Florida native Buddy Quattlebaum in 1998, contains some of the Yucatán's most spectacular cenotes. You can explore these startlingly clear freshwater sinkholes, which are full of fantastic stalactites, stalagmites, and rock formations, on guided diving or snorkeling tours. To get to the cenotes, you ride in a jungle buggy through dense tropical forest from the main park entrance. You can also ride the skycycle, a cable bicycle that glides over the abundant Mayan rain forest. Prices start at $25 for snorkeling tours ($13 for children) and go up to $100 for two-tank diving tours. Canopying on the 600-foot zip line will set you back $35. Be sure to bring your bug spray. ✉ *1.5 km (0.9 mi) south of Xel-Há on Carretera 307* ☎ *984/115–4514 or 984/120–1977* 🌐 *www.hiddenworlds.com* ⊙ *Mon.–Sun. 9–5; snorkeling tours at 9, 11, 1, and 3.*

TULUM

Fodor's Choice ★

61 km (38 mi) southwest of Playa del Carmen.

Tulum, which means "wall" in Mayan, is a quickly growing town built near the spectacular ruins that draw most visitors here. But its charm extends past the famous ruins: pristine beaches, $10 cabanas, and open-air markets explain the town's increasing popularity with travelers. The town is divided into three main sections: the archaeological site, the Pueblo (town), and the Zona Hotelera (hotel zone).

The Tulum site itself is the Yucatán Peninsula's most-visited Mayan ruin, attracting more than 2 million people annually. Though most of the architecture is of unremarkable postclassic (1000–1521) style, the amount of attention that Tulum receives is not entirely undeserved. Its location—on a beach known for its sugar-white sand, by the blue-green Caribbean—is breathtaking.

GETTING HERE AND AROUND

Tulum is a 10-minute drive from Akumal and a 45-minute drive from Playa del Carmen. You can hire taxis in Cancún to go as far as Tulum, but the price is approximately $75 unless you have many passengers.

To reach Tulum's Zona Hotelera, head south on Carretera 307 and turn left (east) at the second stoplight in Tulum. Shortly after passing a fire station, you'll come to a "T" in the road. There you will find dozens of signs directing travelers to both north- and south-end resorts.

ESSENTIALS

Currency Exchange **Asesores Turísticos Cambiarios del Caribe** (✉ *Av. Tulum s/n, Pueblo Tulum* ☎ *984/871–2078*).

Bus **Bus Terminal.** (✉ *The main bus station for ADO, Mayab, OCC, ATS, and Oriente is in the center of town next to Charlie's Restaurant, Tulum* ☎ *800/702–8000*).

Police A police station is next to the HSBC bank on the east side of Tulum Ave.

EXPLORING

Tulum is one of the few Mayan cities known to have been inhabited when the conquistadores arrived in 1518. In the 16th century it functioned as a safe harbor for trade goods from rival Mayan factions; it was considered neutral territory, where merchandise could be stored and traded in peace. The city reached its height when traders, made wealthy through the exchange of goods, for the first time outranked Mayan priests in authority and power. When the Spaniards arrived, they forbade the Mayan traders to sail the seas, and commerce among the Maya died.

Tulum has long held special significance for the Maya. A key city in the League of Mayapán (AD 987–1194), it was never conquered by the Spaniards, although it was abandoned about 75 years after the conquest. For 300 years thereafter it symbolized the defiance of an otherwise subjugated people; it was one of the last outposts of the Maya during their insurrection against Mexican rule in the War of the Castes, which began in 1846. Uprisings continued intermittently until 1935, when the Maya ceded Tulum to the Mexican government.

■ **TIP→ At the entrance to the ruins you can hire a guide for $25, but keep in mind that some of their information is more entertainment than historical accuracy. (Disregard that stuff about virgin sacrifices atop the altars.)** Although you can see the ruins in two hours, you might want to allow extra time for a swim or a stroll on the beach.

The first significant structure is the two-story **Templo de los Frescos,** to the left of the entryway. The temple's vault roof and corbel arch are examples of classic Mayan architecture. Faint traces of blue-green frescoes outlined in black on the inner and outer walls refer to ancient Mayan beliefs (the clearest frescoes are hidden from sight now that you aren't allowed to enter the temple). Reminiscent of the Mixtec style, the frescoes depict the three worlds of the Maya and their major deities, and are decorated with stellar and serpentine patterns, rosettes, and ears of maize and other offerings to the gods. One scene portrays the rain god seated on a four-legged animal—probably a reference to the Spaniards on their horses.

The largest and most famous building, the **Castillo** (Castle), looms at the edge of a 40-foot limestone cliff just past the Temple of the Frescoes. Atop it, at the end of a broad stairway, is a temple with stucco ornamentation on the outside and traces of fine frescoes inside the two chambers. (The stairway has been roped off, so the top temple is inaccessible.) The front wall of the Castillo has faint carvings of the Descending God and columns depicting the plumed serpent god, Kukulcán, who was introduced to the Maya by the Toltecs. To the left of the Castillo is the **Templo del Díos Descendente**—so called for the carving of a winged god plummeting to earth over the doorway.

A few small altars sit atop a hill at the north side of the cove with a good view of the Castillo and the sea. ✉ *Carretera 307, Km 133, Tulum* ☎ *983/837–2411* 🎫 *$5 entrance, $3 parking, $3 video fee, $1 shuttle from parking to ruins* ⏲ *Daily 8–5.*

WHERE TO EAT

$–$$ MEXICAN ✕ **Charlie's.** This eatery is a happening spot where local children display their artwork. Wall murals are made from empty wine bottles, and painted chili peppers adorn the dining tables. There's a charming garden in back with a stage for live salsa and rock. The chicken tacos and black-bean soup are especially good here, and the chiles rellenos are a house favorite. Attached to the restaurant is a wonderful boutique selling jewelry, clothing, and souvenirs. ✉ *Avs. Tulum and Jupiter, next to bus station, downtown* ☎ *984/871–2573* 💳 *MC, V* ⏲ *Closed Mon.*

$$–$$$ ECLECTIC Fodor's Choice ★ ✕ **Ginger.** With its red walls, exotic menu, martini bar, and metropolitan vibe, this chic restaurant has taken Tulum dining to a whole new level. Flavorful starters include tropical ceviche, goat-cheese tart, and spinach salad with camembert and green apple. Select from entrées like the coconut-crusted salmon with mango ginger sauce or grouper fillet topped with passion fruit. Save room for the sweet fruit flambé and vanilla ice cream. This is a great spot to relax with a martini, listen to chill-out music, and meet some locals. ✉ *Av. Polar Poniente between Satelite and Centauro, downtown Tulum* ☎ *984/116–4033* 💳 *MC, V* ⏲ *Closed Tues.*

WHERE TO STAY

$$$$ ★ 🏨 **Blue Tulum.** From the lush tropical plants and crashing waterfall at the hotel entrance to the gorgeous rooms with private hot tubs, this all-inclusive offers luxury and relaxation everywhere you look. There are nearly 100 rooms, but the hotel is divided into smaller buildings that give it a very personal atmosphere. Rooms are spacious, and have high-tech touches like flat-screen TVs, iPod docks, DVD players, and a selection of DVDs (just fill out the request form). The restaurants feature international chefs who will prepare whatever suits you, whether or not it is on the menu. Pampering can be found in the glass-walled spa

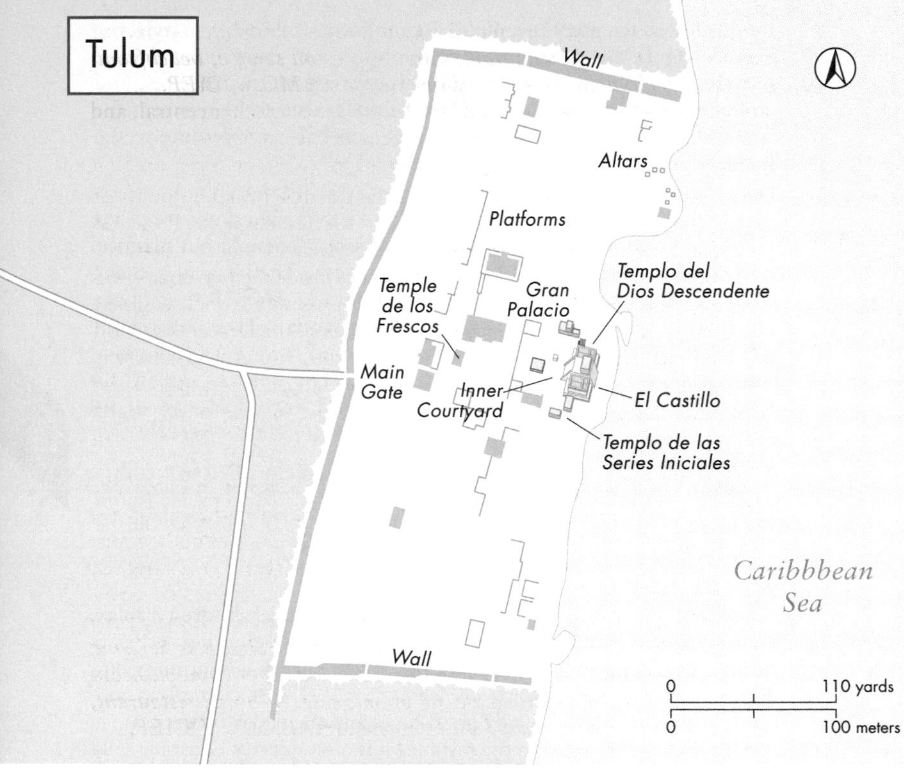

that overlooks the ocean; there are even treatment rooms for kids. The staff is happy to provide different kinds of pillows and bath products upon request. **Pros:** incredible service and attention to detail, beautiful grounds, airport shuttle. **Cons:** rocky beach, uncomfortable sheets, not as environmentally friendly as other Tulum hotels. ✉ *Carretera Tulum Ruinas, Lote 47* ☎ *984/871–1000* 🌐 *www.bluetulumresorts.com* *96 rooms* *In-room: safe, refrigerator, DVD, Wi-Fi. In-hotel: 3 restaurants, room service, bar, pool, gym, spa, beachfront, water sports, laundry service, Wi-Fi hotspot* *AE, MC, V* *AI, CP, EP.*

$$$ **Fodor's Choice** ★ **Mezzanine**. Music lovers will enjoy this small, hip hotel where DJs mix lounge and house music on the patio. On Friday evenings this is the place to be, as guest musicians entertain until 2 AM. Stylish rooms have vaulted ceilings, onyx lamps, dark-wood furnishings, and adobe floors inlaid with stones. Splashes of red brighten the cream-colored rooms, four of which have spacious lofts and ocean views. The suites have Jacuzzis and balconies facing the Caribbean, but the other rooms (on the ground floor) have no view. Environmentally sound, the hotel operates on solar energy and recycled rainwater. There's Wi-Fi access throughout the entire property. **Pros:** incredible Thai restaurant, helpful staff, two-for-one margaritas daily from 1 to 4. **Cons:** pool area gets crowded, some rooms lack view, noisy on weekends. ✉ *Carretera Tulum–Boca Paila, Km 1.5, Zona Hotelera* ☎ *984/131–1596* 🌐 *www.*

mezzanine.com.mx 9 *rooms, 2 suites* *In-room: no a/c, no phone, safe, Wi-Fi. In-hotel: restaurant, bar, pool, room service, beachfront, bicycles, no children under 16, Wi-Fi hotspot* *MC, V* *EP.*

¢ **Weary Traveler Hostel, Cafe and Bar.** Tulum is backpacker central, and if you're roughing it, this is one of the cheapest, most convenient spots to hang your hat. Most rooms are shared, with either bunk or twin beds and a private bath. Furnishings are basic but neat. You have use of a communal television, pool table, and kitchen, and there are picnic tables in a central area for eating and meeting. A simple but plentiful breakfast is included in the price of the room. There's also a cheap Internet café, and the bus station is one block away. The staff can organize snorkeling and diving tours upon request. **Pros:** reasonable rates, friendly atmosphere, great location. **Cons:** rustic furniture, noise from bar. *Av. Tulum, between Avs. Jupiter and Acuario, downtown* *984/871–2390* *20 rooms, 66 beds* *In-room: no a/c (some), no phone, kitchen, no TV. In-hotel: restaurant, bar, Internet terminal* *No credit cards* *BP.*

15

$$–$$$ **Zamas.** On the wild, isolated *Punta Piedra* (Rock Point), this hotel has ocean views as far as the eye can see. The romantically rustic cabanas—with mosquito nets over comfortable beds, spacious tile bathrooms, and bright Mexican colors—are nicely distanced from one another. The restaurant, one of the area's best, has an eclectic Italian-Mexican-Yucatecan menu. **Pros:** great restaurant, unspoiled views. **Cons:** rocky beach, on noisy street. *Carretera Tulum–Boca Paila, Km 5, Zona Hotelera* *984/877–8523; 415/387–9806 in U.S.* *www.zamas.com* *24 cabanas* *In-room: no a/c, no phone, safe. In-hotel: restaurant, bar, beachfront, water sports, Wi-Fi hotspot* *AE, MC, V* *EP.*

COBÁ

50 km (31 mi) northwest of Tulum.

Fodor's Choice ★ Mayan for "water stirred by the wind," **Cobá** flourished from AD 800 to 1100, with a population of as many as 55,000. Now it stands in solitude, and the jungle has overgrown many of its buildings. Cobá exudes stillness, the silence broken only by the occasional shriek of a spider monkey or the call of a bird. Unlike Tulum's, Cobá's ruins are spread out and best explored by bike. Most of the trails here are pleasantly shaded by overgrown jungle. Processions of huge army ants cross the footpaths as the sun slips through openings between the tall hardwood trees, ferns, and giant palms.

■ TIP→ Cobá is often overlooked by visitors who opt for better-known Tulum. This site is less crowded, giving you a chance to immerse yourself in ancient culture. If you plan on walking (rather than exploring by bike), expect to cover anywhere between 3 and 4 miles. Cobá is open daily from 8 to 5, and costs $4.50 to enter. (use of video camera $4; taxi-bike tours $8; bike rental $3).

Near five lakes and between coastal watchtowers and inland cities, Cobá (pronounced ko-*bah*) exercised economic control over the region through a network of at least 16 *sacbéob* (white-stone roads), one of which measures 100 km (62 mi) and is the longest in the Mayan world. The city once covered 70 square km (27 square mi), making it a noteworthy sister state to Tikal in northern Guatemala, with which it had close cultural and commercial ties. It is noted for its massive temple-pyramids, one of which is 138 feet tall, the largest and highest in northern Yucatán. The main groupings of ruins are separated by several miles of dense vegetation, so the best way to get a sense of the immensity of the city is to scale one of the pyramids. Don't be tempted by the narrow paths that lead into the jungle unless you have a qualified guide with you. ■ **TIP→ It's easy to get lost here, so stay on the main road, wear comfortable shoes, and bring insect repellent and drinking water.**

WORD OF MOUTH

"At Cobá you can rent bikes and ride to all the ruins, which is very fun. We have been twice and once you get away from the main areas, you feel like you are in the jungle all alone. Cobá is also next to a lake full of crocodiles and you can eat at a really good restaurant located across the street and watch the crocs swim around." —Suru11

GETTING HERE AND AROUND

Cobá is a 45-minute drive northwest of the city of Tankah, where most of the accommodations are located, along a road that leads straight through the jungle. Buses depart to and from Cobá for Playa del Carmen and Tulum at least twice daily. Taxis from Tulum are about $20.

OFF THE BEATEN PATH

Pac Chen is a Mayan jungle settlement of 125 people who still live in round thatch huts. There's no electricity or indoor plumbing, and the roads aren't paved. The inhabitants, who primarily make their living farming pineapple, beans, and plantains, still pray to the gods for good crops.

■ **TIP→ You can only visit Pac Chen (pronounced "*pak chin*") on trips organized by Alltournative, an ecotour company based in Playa del Carmen. The unusual, soft-adventure experience is definitely worth your while.** Alltournative pays the villagers by the number of tourists it brings in, though no more than 80 people are allowed to visit on any given day. This money has made the village self-sustaining, and has given the people an alternative to logging and hunting, which were their main means of livelihood before.

The half-day tour starts with a trek through the jungle to a cenote, where you grab onto a harness and zip-line to the other side. Next is the Jaguar cenote, set deeper into the forest, where you must rappel down the cavelike sides into a cool underground lagoon. You'll eat lunch under an open-air palapa overlooking another lagoon, where canoes await. The food includes such Mayan dishes as grilled *achiote* (annatto seed) chicken, fresh tortillas, beans, and watermelon.

Triolesa Kukikan Zipline. The best way to view Lago Cobá (and the 10-foot crocodiles below) is by soaring over the water on a 500 meter zip line. The lookout tower is also a great place to photograph the ruins poking out of the treetops. ✉ *At the entrance to the* Cobá ruins, Cobá ☎ *984/106–2768* 🎫 *$4 lookout tower; $12 zip line* ⏲ *Daily 10–6.*

WHERE TO EAT

¢–$ MEXICAN **El Bocadito.** The restaurant near the Cobá ruins is run by a gracious Mayan family that serves simple, traditional cuisine. A three-course fixed-price lunch costs $6. Look for such classic dishes as *pollo pibíl* and *cochinita pibíl*. There are also a few bare-bones rooms for $10 a night for those who want to stay close to the ruins. *On road to Cobá ruins, ½ km from ruin-site entrance 985/106–9822 No credit cards.*

$ MEXICAN **Ki-Janal.** You can't get any closer to the Cobá ruins than this two-story restaurant. Adding color to the palapa setting are colorful Mexican blankets draped over wooden tables. Some of the more traditional selections include fish prepared Yucatán style, chicken in banana leaves, and cochinita pibíl (slow-roasted pork). You can also find soups, salads, and pastas. *To the right of the Cobá ruins entrance, Cobá 984/745–8529 No credit cards Daily 10–5*

15

RESERVA DE LA BIOSFERA SIAN KA'AN

15 km (9 mi) south of Tulum to Punta Allen turnoff and within Sian Ka'an; 252 km (156 mi) north of Chetumal.

Fodor's Choice ★ The **Sian Ka'an** ("where the sky is born," pronounced see-*an* caan) region was first settled by the Maya in the 5th century AD. In 1986 the Mexican government established the 1.3-million-acre Reserva de la Biosfera Sian Ka'an as a protected area. The next year it was named a UNESCO World Heritage Site. The Riviera Maya and Costa Maya split the biosphere reserve; Punta Allen and north belong to the Riviera Maya, and everything south of Punta Allen is part of the Costa Maya.

The Sian Ka'an reserve constitutes 10% of the land in Quintana Roo, and covers 100 km (62 mi) of coastline. Hundreds of species of local and migratory birds, fish, other animals and plants, and fewer than 1,000 residents (primarily Maya) share this area of freshwater and coastal lagoons, mangrove swamps, cays, savannas, tropical forests, and a barrier reef. There are approximately 27 ruins (none excavated) linked by a unique canal system—one of the few of its kind in the Mayan world in Mexico. This is one of the last undeveloped stretches of North American coast. There's a $4 entrance charge. To visit the sites, you must take a guided tour.

Many species of the once-flourishing wildlife have fallen into the endangered category, but the waters here still teem with rooster fish, bonefish, mojarra, snapper, shad, permit, sea bass, and crocodiles. Fishing the flats for wily bonefish is popular, and the peninsula's few lodges also run deep-sea fishing trips.

Most fishing lodges along the way close for the rainy season in August and September, and accommodations are hard to come by. The road ends at Punta Allen, a fishing village whose main catch is spiny lobster, which was becoming scarce until ecologists taught the local fishing cooperative how to build and lay special traps to conserve the species. There are several small, expensive guesthouses. If you haven't booked ahead, start out early in the morning so you can get back to civilization before dark.

Visitors Information **Sian Ka'an Visitor Center** is 11 mi south of Tulum, on Punta Allen toward Boca Paila Village by the coastal road. (☎ *998/884–3667, 998/884–9580,* 🌐 *www.ecotravelmexico.com*)

Several kinds of tours, including bird-watching by boat and night kayaking to observe crocodiles, are offered on-site through the **Sian Ka'an Visitor Center** (☎ *998/884–3667, 998/884–9580,* 🌐 *www.ecotravelmexico.com*), which also offers five rooms with shared bath and one private suite for overnight stays. Prices range from $70 to $100, and meals are separate. For the more adventurous, there are also three- and five-day camping trips, which include kayaking, hiking, snorkeling, bicycling and wildlife observation in the reef, wetlands, and jungle.

The visitor center's observation tower offers the best view of the Sian Ka'an Biosphere from high atop their deck and wood bridge. It is 11 mi south of Tulum on Punta Allen toward Boca Paila Village.

This photogenic archaeological site at the northern end of the *Reserva de la Biosfera Sian Ka'an* is underrated. Once known as Chunyaxché, it's now called by its ancient name, **Muyil** (pronounced mool-*hill*). It dates from the late preclassic era, when it was connected by road to the sea and served as a port between Cobá and the Mayan centers in Belize and Guatemala. A 15-foot-wide *sacbé,* built during the postclassic period, extended from the city to the mangrove swamp and was still in use when the Spaniards arrived.

Structures were erected at 400-foot intervals along the white limestone road, almost all of them facing west, but there are only three still standing. At the beginning of the 20th century the ancient stones were used to build a chicle (gum arabic) plantation, which was managed by one of the leaders of the War of the Castes. The most notable site at Muyil today is the remains of the 56-foot **Castillo**—one of the tallest on the Quintana Roo coast—at the center of a large acropolis. During excavations of the Castillo, jade figurines representing the moon and fertility goddess Ixchel were found. Recent excavations at Muyil have uncovered some smaller structures.

The ruins stand near the edge of a deep-blue lagoon, and are surrounded by almost impenetrable jungle—so be sure to bring insect repellent. You can drive down a dirt road on the side of the ruins to swim or fish in the lagoon. The bird-watching is also exceptional here. 🌐 *muyil.smv.org* 🎫 *$3* 🕑 *Daily 8–5.*

Mérida and Environs

WITH CHICHÉN ITZÁ

Tourists climbing El Castillo (Pyramid of Kukulcán). Chichén Itzá

WORD OF MOUTH

"The best part of Mérida was just getting out and walking downtown. We met some wonderful people, had great food, and found some really interesting and eclectic shops."

—CozAnnie

"Merida en Domingo (Sundays) turns the entire downtown into an open air concert with dancing and many bands playing in different parks and streets."

—Cimbrone

www.fodors.com/community

WELCOME TO MÉRIDA AND ENVIRONS

TOP REASONS TO GO

★ **Visiting spectacular Mayan ruins:** Chichén Itzá and Uxmal are two of the largest, most beautiful sites in the region.

★ **Living like a wealthy hacendado:** You can stay in a restored henequen (sisal) plantation-turned-hotel and delight in its Old World charm.

★ **Browsing at fantastic craft markets:** This region is known for its handmade *hamacas* (hammocks), piñatas, and other local handicrafts.

★ **Swimming in the secluded, pristine freshwater cenotes:** These sinkholes, like portals to the underworld, are scattered throughout the inland landscape.

★ **The chance to taste the diverse flavors of Yucatecan food:** Mérida has 50-odd restaurants, which serve up local specialties like fish stews and Mayan-originated dishes like *pollo pibíl* (chicken cooked in banana leaves).

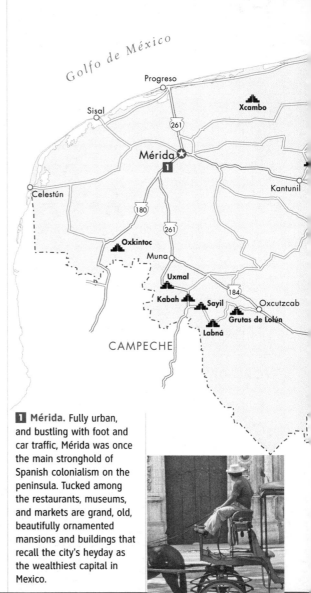

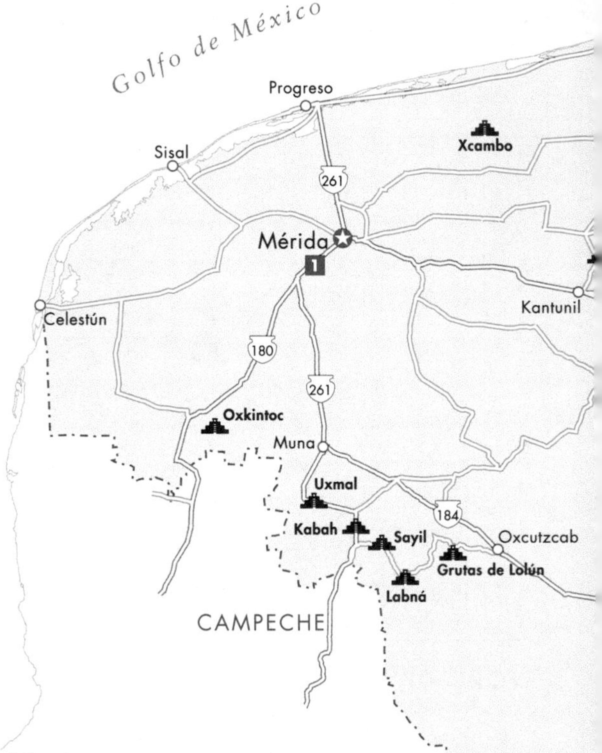

Golfo de México
Progreso
Xcambo
Sisal
261
Mérida
1
Kantunil
Celestún
180
261
Oxkintoc
Muna
Uxmal
184
Kabah
Sayil
Oxcutzcab
Grutas de Lolún
Labná
CAMPECHE

1 Mérida. Fully urban, and bustling with foot and car traffic, Mérida was once the main stronghold of Spanish colonialism on the peninsula. Tucked among the restaurants, museums, and markets are grand, old, beautifully ornamented mansions and buildings that recall the city's heyday as the wealthiest capital in Mexico.

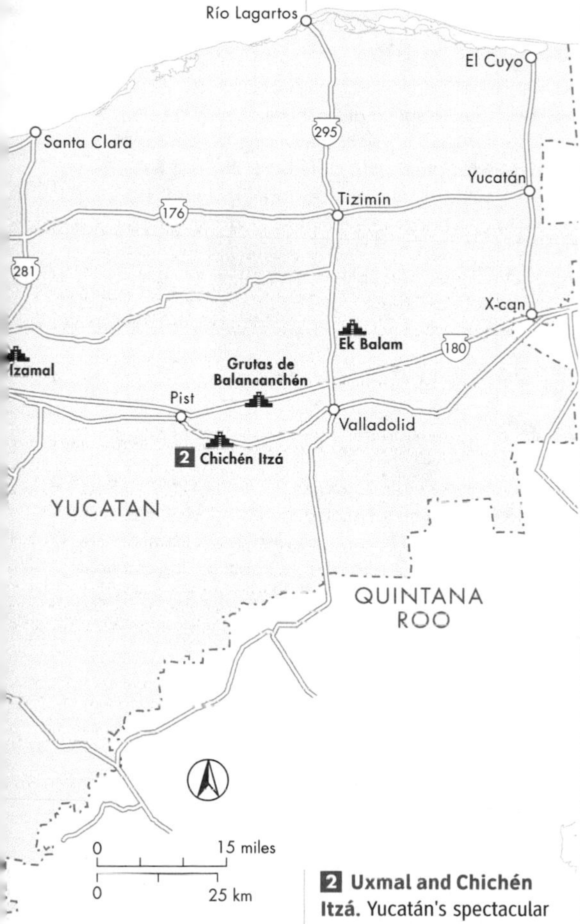

Río Lagartos
El Cuyo
Santa Clara
295
Yucatán
Tizimín
176
281
X-can
Ek Balam
180
Izamal
Grutas de Balancanchén
Pist
Valladolid
2 Chichén Itzá
YUCATAN
QUINTANA ROO
0 15 miles
0 25 km

GETTING ORIENTED

Yucatán State's topography has more in common with that of Florida and Cuba—with which it was probably once connected—than with central Mexico. Exotic plants like wild ginger and spider lilies grow in the jungles; vast flamingo colonies nest at coastal estuaries. Human history is evident everywhere here—in looming Franciscan missions, thatch-roofed adobe huts, and the majestic ruins of ancient Mayan cities.

16

2 Uxmal and Chichén Itzá. Yucatán's spectacular Mayan ruins are famous all over the world. The best-known, Chichén Itzá, draws thousands of visitors every year. Farther south is the less-known but beautiful site of Uxmal. Many smaller archaeological sites—some hardly visited—lie along the Ruta Puuc south of Mérida.

MÉRIDA AND ENVIRONS PLANNER

When to Go

As with many other places in Mexico, the weeks around Christmas and Easter are peak times for visiting Yucatán State. Making reservations up to a year in advance is not over the top.

If you like music and dance, Mérida hosts its Otoño Cultural, or Autumn Cultural Festival, during the last week of October and first week of November. Free and inexpensive classical-music concerts, dance performances, and art exhibits take place almost nightly at theaters and open-air venues around the city.

Thousands of people, from international sightseers to Maya shamans, swarm Chichén Itzá on the vernal equinox (the first day of spring). On this particular day the sun creates a shadow that looks like a snake—meant to evoke the ancient Maya serpent god, Kukulcán—that moves slowly down the side of the main pyramid. If you're planning to witness it, make your travel arrangements many months in advance.

How Long to Stay

You should plan to spend at least five days in Yucatán. It's best to start your trip with a few days in Mérida; the weekends, when streets are closed to traffic and there are lots of free outdoor performances, are great times to visit. You should also budget enough time to take day trips to the sites of Chichén Itzá and Uxmal; visiting Mérida without traveling to at least one of these sites is like going to the beach and not getting out of the car.

Mérida Carriage Tours

One of the best ways to get a feel for the city of Mérida is to hire a *calesa*—a horse-drawn carriage. You can hail one of these at the main square or, during the day, at Palacio Cantón, site of the archaeology museum on Paseo de Montejo. Some of the horses look dispirited, but others are fairly well cared for. Drivers charge about $13 for an hour-long circuit around downtown and up Paseo de Montejo, and $22 for an extended tour.

How's the Weather?

Rainfall and humidity are greatest between June and October. The coolest months are December–February, when it can get chilly in the evenings. April and May are usually the hottest, as both heat and humidity begin to build unbearably prior to rainy season. Hurricane season is late September through early November.

WHAT IT COSTS IN DOLLARS

	¢	$	$$	$$$	$$$$
Restaurants	under $5	$5–$10	$10–$15	$15–$25	over $25
Hotels	under $50	$50–$75	$75–$150	$150–$250	over $250

Restaurant prices are per person, for a main course at dinner, excluding tax and tip. Hotel prices are for a standard double room in high season.

MÉRIDA

Updated by Michele Joyce

TRAVELERS TO MÉRIDA ARE A loyal bunch, who return again and again to their favorite restaurants, neighborhoods, and museums. The hubbub of the city can seem frustrating—especially if you've just spent a peaceful few days on the coast or visiting Mayan sites—but as the cultural and intellectual hub of the peninsula, Mérida is rich in art, history, and tradition.

If you need extra orientation, be sure to stop in at the tourism offices, where you will find friendly, helpful staff. After recent scandals involving scam artists who hang official-looking "tourist guide" badges around their necks, the tourism office staff warns tourists not to trust people offering themselves as guides. A two- to three-hour group tour of the city, including museums, parks, public buildings, and monuments, costs $20 to $35 per person. Free guided tours are offered daily by the Municipal Tourism Department. These last about an hour and 45 minutes and depart from City Hall, on the main plaza, at 9:30 AM Monday through Saturday. More information is available at ☎ *999/942–0000*.

There have also been recent reports of vendors increasing the prices of their art and crafts by the hundreds, claiming that the value of their wares is far greater than it really is. Most vendors are honest, so just be sure to shop around and acquaint yourself with the kinds of crafts, and the levels of quality, that are available. Once you have an idea of what's out there, you'll be much better able to spot fraud, and you may even have some fun bargaining.

GETTING HERE AND AROUND

Mérida's airport, Aeropuerto Manuel Crescencio Rejón, is 7 km (4½ mi) west of the city on Avenida Itzáes. Getting there from the downtown area usually takes 20 to 30 minutes by taxi. For travel outside the city, ADO and UNO have direct buses to many coastal cities and ruins, they depart from the first-class CAME bus station. Regional bus lines to intermediate or more out-of-the-way destinations leave from the second-class terminal. City buses charge about 60¢ (6 pesos); having the correct change is helpful but not required.

Regular taxis in Mérida charge beach-resort prices, and most don't use meters. Taxis that do use meters have a sign that reads TAXIMETRO on the roof. These are recommended, since they offer a fair price.

TOURS

Mérida has more than 50 tour operators, and it could be said that they generally take you to the same places. Since there are so many reputable and reasonably priced operators, there's no reason to opt for the less-predictable *piratas* ("pirates") who sometimes stand outside tour offices offering to sell you a cheaper trip and don't necessarily have much experience or your best interests at heart. If you enjoy walking, the Mérida English-Language Library (⇨ *see the Shopping section, below*) conducts home and garden tours (2½ hours costs $20) every Wednesday morning. Meet at the library about 15 minutes before 10 AM. More information is available on the Mérida English Library Web site at 🌐 *www.meridaenglishlibrary.com*.

ARCHAEOLOGICAL TOURS

Amigo Travel is a reliable operator offering group and private tours to the major archaeological sites and also to Celestún, the town known for the massive flamingo colonies living in its river. Amigo has transfer–accommodation packages and well-crafted tours, like their Campeche and Yucatán combo, and have adopted a pace that allows you to actually enjoy the sites you visit.

WORD OF MOUTH

"I should add here that Mérida is totally genuine and not particularly touristy. Or perhaps a better way of saying it is that the size of the city makes tourists less noticeable." —robertino

If you don't have your own wheels, but like the freedom afforded by traveling in your own, a great option for seeing the ruins of the Ruta Puuc is the unguided **ATS** tour that leaves Mérida at 8 AM from the second-class bus station (Terminal 69, ATS line). The tour stops for a half hour each at the ruins of Labná, Xlapak, Sayil, and Kabah, giving you just enough time to scan the plaques, poke your nose into a crevice or two, and pose before a pyramid for your holiday card picture. You get almost two hours at Uxmal before heading back to Mérida at 2:30 PM. The trip costs $10 per person (entrance to the ruins isn't included) and is worth every penny.

EcoTurismo Yucatán has a good mix of day and overnight tours. Their Calakmul tour includes several nights camping in the biosphere reserve for nature spotting, as well as visits to Calakmul, Chicanná, and other area ruins. The one-day biking adventure packs in biking as well as brief visits to two archaeological sites, a cave, and two cenotes.

CITY TOURS BY BUS

Within Mérida, a fun way to get around, to get a feel for the city layout—and to hear some of its history—is to spend some time on the red, open-roof, double-decker **Turibus**. You buy your ticket ($10) onboard the bus, and you can get on and off at the seven bus stops as you please. The complete bus route is 1 hour and 45 minutes. Buses operate from 9:05 AM until 9 PM, and stop at the Holiday Inn, Fiesta Americana, and Hyatt hotels, clustered near one another on Paseo Montejo, the Museo de Antropología e Historia, the old barrio of Izimná, the Gran Plaza mall (with its 250 stores), the Monument to the Flag, and finally the Parque de las Américas.

A second, smaller tour-bus operator is the Carnavalito, which visits many of the same sites. The advantage to this tour is that it's given by real people (in both Spanish and English) as opposed to a recording, so you can ask questions. The disadvantage is that you cannot get on and off the bus at will. The tour lasts around two hours, with a 20-minute break at a small shopping center where you can stretch your legs or buy something to drink. The colorful Carnavalito bus takes off from Parque Santa Lucia Monday through Saturday at 10 AM, 1 PM, and 7 PM.

CITY TOURS BY CARRIAGE

One of the best ways to get a feel for the city of Mérida is to hire a *calesa*—a horse-drawn carriage. The gentle clip-clop of hooves is transporting. You can hail one of these at the main square or, during the day, at Palacio Cantón, site of the archaeology museum on Paseo Montejo. Choose your horse and driver carefully, as some of the horses look dispirited, but others are fairly well cared for. Drivers charge about $15 for an hour-long circuit around downtown and up Paseo de Montejo, pointing out notable buildings and providing a little historic background along the way, and $22 for an extended tour.

ESSENTIALS

Bus Contacts **Autobuses de Occidente** (✉ *Calle 70, between 79 and 71, Centro* ☎ *999/924-8391 or 999/924-9741* 🌐 *www.ado.com.mx*). **CAME** (✉ *Calle 71 No. 555, between Calles 69 and 71, Centro* ☎ *999/924-9130*).

Currency Exchange **Banamex** (✉ *Calle 59 No. 485, Centro* ☎ *01800/021-2345 toll-free in Mexico* 🌐 *www.banamex.com*). **Banorte** (✉ *Prolongación Paseo de Montejo No. 497, Itzimna* ☎ *999/926-6060* 🌐 *www.banorte.com*). **HSBC** (✉ *Paseo Montejo 467A Centro* ☎ *999/942-2378* 🌐 *www.hsbc.com*).

Medical Assistance **Star Médica** (✉ *Calle 26 No. 199, between Avs. 15 and 16, Alta Brisa* ☎ *999/930-2800* 🌐 *www.starmedica.com*). **Centro Médico de las Américas** (✉ *Calle 54 No. 365, between Calle 33A and Av. Pérez Ponce, Centro* ☎ *999/926-2111* 🌐 *www.centromedicodelasamericas.com.mx*). **Clínica Santa Helena** (✉ *Calle 14 No. 81, between Calles 5 and 7, Col. San Antonio Cinta* ☎ *999/943-1334 or 999/943-1335*).

16

Rental Cars **Avis** (✉ *Fiesta Americana, Calle 60 No. 319-C, near Av. Colón, Centro* ☎ *999/925-2525 or 999/920-1101* 🌐 *www.avis.com*). **Budget** (✉ *Holiday Inn, Av. Colón 498, at Calle 60, Centro* ☎ *999/920-4395 or 999/925-6877 Ext. 516* ✉ *Airport* ☎ *999/946-1323* 🌐 *www.budget.com*).

Visitor and Tour Info **Amigo Travel** (✉ *Av. Colón 508C, Col. García Ginerés, Mérida* ☎ *999/920-0104 or 999/920-0103* 🌐 *www.amigoyucatan.com*). **ATS** (✉ *Calle 69 No. 544, between Calles 68 and 70, Centro, Mérida* ☎ *999/923-2287*). **Carnavalito** (☎ *999/927-6119 and 999/928-7916* 🌐 *www.citytouryucatan.com*). **EcoTurismo Yucatán** (✉ *Calle 3 No. 235, between Calles 32A and 34, Col. Pensiones, Mérida* ☎ *999/920-2772* 🌐 *www.ecoyuc.com*). **Municipal Tourism Department** (✉ *Calles 61 and 60, Centro* ☎ *999/930-3101*). **Municipal Tourist Information Center** (✉ *Calle 62, ground floor of Palacio Municipal, Centro* ☎ *999/928-2020 Ext. 133*).**Turibus** (☎ *999/946-2424 and 55/5563-6693 in Mexico City* 🌐 *www.turibus.com.mx*)

EXPLORING

Every Sunday, from 8 AM to 12:30 PM, downtown streets are closed for pedestrians and cyclists. The route begins at the Parque de la Ermita, and travels through the Plaza Grande and out onto the Paseo Montejo (🌐 *www.merida.gob.mx/biciruta*).

TOP ATTRACTIONS

2 **Casa de Montejo.** The two Franciscos de Montejo—father and son—conquered the Peninsula and founded Mérida in January of 1542, they built their stately "casa" 10 years later. In the late 1970s it was restored by banker Agustín Legorreta, converted to a branch of Banamex bank, and now sits on the south side of the plaza. It is the city's finest—and oldest—example of colonial plateresque architecture, a Spanish architectural style popular in the 16th century and typified by the kind of elaborate ornamentation you'll see here. A bas-relief on the doorway—the facade is all that remains of the original house—depicts Francisco

de Montejo the younger, his wife, and daughter, as well as Spanish soldiers standing on the heads of the vanquished Maya. ✉ *Calle 63, Centro* ⏲ *Weekdays 9–5 and Saturdays 9–1.*

6 **Catedral de San Ildefonso.** Begun in 1561 and completed 38 years later, St. Ildefonso is the oldest cathedral on the American continent (though an older one can be found in Dominican Republic). It took several hundred Maya laborers, working with stones from the pyramids of the ravaged Mayan city, 36 years to complete it. Designed in the somber Renaissance style by an architect who had worked on the Escorial in Madrid, its facade is stark and unadorned, with gunnery slits instead of windows, and faintly Moorish spires. Inside, the black *Cristo de las Ampollas* (Christ of the Blisters) occupies a side chapel to the left of the main altar. At 7 meters (23 feet) tall, it's the tallest Christ in Mexico inside a church. The statue is a replica of the original, which was destroyed during the revolution in 1910, this is also when the gold that typically decorated Mexican cathedrals was carried off. According to one of many legends, the Christ figure burned all night yet appeared the next morning unscathed—except that it was covered with the blisters for which it is named. You can hear the pipe organ play at the 11 AM Sunday mass. ✉ *Calles 60 and 61, Centro* ☎ *No phone* ⏲ *Daily 7–11:30 and 4:30–8.*

3 **Centro Cultural de Mérida Olimpo.** Referred to as simply Olimpo, this is the best venue in town for free cultural events. The beautiful porticoed cultural center was built adjacent to City Hall in late 1999, occupying what used to be a parking lot. The marble interior is a showcase for top international art exhibits, classical-music concerts, conferences, and theater and dance performances. The adjoining 1950s-style movie house shows classic art films by directors like Buñuel, Fellini, and Kazan. There is also a planetarium with 90-minute shows explaining the solar system ($3, Tuesday through Saturday at 6 PM and Sunday at 11, noon, and 6; be sure to be there 15 minutes early, since nobody is allowed to sneak in once the show has begun), a bookstore, and a wonderful cybercafé-restaurant. ✉ *Calle 62 between Calles 61 and 63, Centro* ☎ *999/942–0000* 🌐 *www.merida.gob.mx/planetario* 🎟 *Free* ⏲ *Tues.–Sun. 10–10.*

12 **Paseo Montejo.** North of downtown, this 10-block-long street was *the* place to reside in the late 19th century, when wealthy plantation owners sought to outdo each other with the opulence of their elegant mansions. Mansion owners typically opted for the decorative styles popular in New Orleans, Cuba, and Paris—imported Carrara marble, European antiques—rather than any style from Mexico. The broad boulevard, lined with tamarind and laurel trees, has lost much of its former panache; some of the mansions have fallen into disrepair. Many are now used as office buildings, others have been or are being restored as part of a citywide, privately funded beautification program. The street is a lovely place to explore on foot or in a horse-drawn carriage.

10 **Teatro Peón Contreras.** This 1908 Italianate theater was built along the same lines as grand turn-of-the-20th-century European theaters and opera houses. In the early 1980s the marble staircase, dome, and frescoes

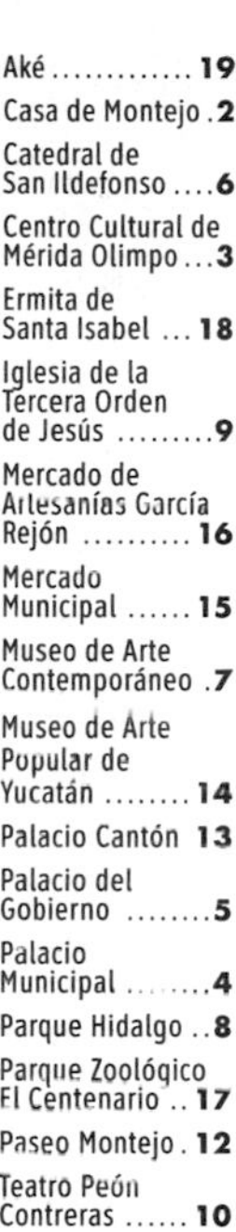

Aké **19**
Casa de Montejo . **2**
Catedral de San Ildefonso **6**
Centro Cultural de Mérida Olimpo . . . **3**
Ermita de Santa Isabel . . . **18**
Iglesia de la Tercera Orden de Jesús **9**
Mercado de Artesanías García Rejón **16**
Mercado Municipal **15**
Museo de Arte Contemporáneo . **7**
Museo de Arte Popular de Yucatán **14**
Palacio Cantón **13**
Palacio del Gobierno **5**
Palacio Municipal **4**
Parque Hidalgo . . **8**
Parque Zoológico El Centenario . . **17**
Paseo Montejo . **12**
Teatro Peón Contreras **10**
Universidad Autónoma de Yucatán **11**
Zócalo **1**

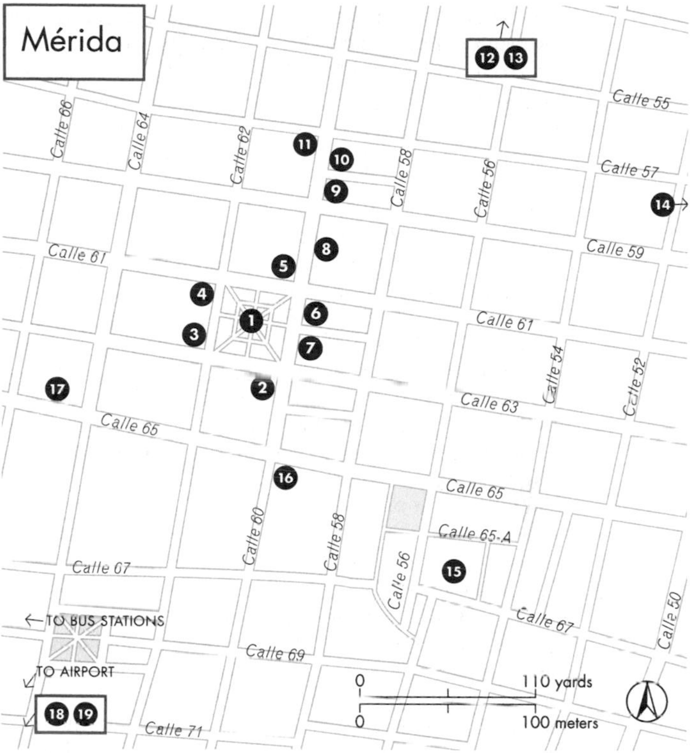

were restored. Today, in addition to performing arts, the theater houses the **Centro de Información Turística** (Tourist Information Center), which provides maps, brochures, and details about attractions in the city and state. The theater's most popular attraction, however, is the café-bar spilling out into the street facing Parque de la Madre. It's crowded every night with people enjoying the balladeers singing romantic and politically inspired songs. ✉ *Calle 60 between Calles 57 and 59, Centro* ☎ *999/924–9290 Tourist Information Center, 999/923–7344, 999/924–9290 theater* ⏲ *Tourist Information Center daily 8 AM–9 PM.*

11 **Universidad Autónoma de Yucatán.** Pop into the university's main building—which plays a major role in the city's cultural and intellectual life—to check the bulletin boards just inside the entrance for upcoming cultural events. The folkloric ballet performs on the patio of the main building most Fridays between 9 and 10 PM ($5). You'll easily find this imposing Moorish-inspired building, which dates from 1711, with its crenellated ramparts and arabesque archways. ✉ *Calle 60 between Calles 57 and 59, Centro* ☎ *999/924–8000 operator, 999/924–6429 art and culture programming* 🌐 *www.uady.mx/sitios/cultura/ballet.html.*

1 **Zócalo.** Méridians traditionally refer to this main square as the Plaza de la Independencia, or the Plaza Principal. Whichever name you prefer, it's a good spot from which to begin a tour of the city, in which to watch

music or dance performances, or in which to chill in the shade of a laurel tree when the day gets too hot. The plaza was laid out in 1542 on the ruins of T'hó, the Mayan city demolished to make way for Mérida, and is still the focal point around which the most important public buildings cluster. *Confidenciales* (S-shape benches) invite intimate tête-à-têtes, and lampposts keep the park beautifully illuminated at night. ✉ *Bordered by Calles 60, 62, 61, and 63, Centro.*

> **WORD OF MOUTH**
>
> "[Our] last day in Mérida was a Sunday, the best day in the city because the streets are closed—activities and vendors are all over the zócalo. The zócalo has free Wi-Fi which was pretty cool, so I was able check e-mail on my iPhone and use Internet." —Nicci

WORTH NOTING

19  **Aké**, a compact archaeological site 35 km (22 mi) southeast of Mérida, offers the unique opportunity to see architecture spanning two millennia in one sweeping vista. Standing atop a ruined Mayan temple built more than a thousand years ago, you can see the incongruous nearby sight of workers processing sisal in a rusty-looking factory, which was built in the early 20th century. To the right of this dilapidated building are the ruins of the old Hacienda and Iglesia de San Lorenzo Aké, both constructed of stones taken from the Mayan temples.

Experts estimate that Aké was populated between around 200 BC and AD 900; today many people in the area have Aké as a surname. The city seems to have been related to the very important and powerful one at present-day Izamal; in fact, the two cities were once connected by a *sacbé* (white road) 13 meters (43 feet) wide and 33 km (20 mi) long. All that's excavated so far are two pyramids, one with rows of columns (35 total) at the top, very reminiscent of the Toltec columns at Tula, north of Mexico City. *$3.70* ⏲ *Daily 9–5.*

18 **Ermita de Santa Isabel.** At the southern end of the city stands the restored and beautiful Hermitage of St. Isabel. Built circa 1748 as part of a Jesuit monastery also known as the Hermitage of the Good Trip, it served as a resting place for colonial-era travelers heading to Campeche. It is one of the most peaceful places in the city, with an interesting, inlaid-stone facade (although the church itself is almost always closed), and is a good destination for a ride in a horse carriage. Behind the hermitage are its huge and lush tropical gardens, with a waterfall and footpaths; they're usually unlocked during daylight hours. ✉ *Calles 66 and 77, La Ermita* ☎ *No phone* *Free* ⏲ *Church open only during mass.*

9 **Iglesia de la Tercera Orden de Jesús.** Just north of Parque Hidalgo is one of Mérida's oldest buildings and the first Jesuit church in the Yucatán. It was built in 1618 from the limestone blocks of a dismantled Mayan temple, and faint outlines of ancient carvings are still visible on the west wall. Although a favorite place for society weddings due to its antiquity, the church interior is not ornate.

The former convent rooms in the rear of the building now host the **Pinoteca Juan Gamboa Guzmán,** a small but interesting art collection. The most engaging pieces here are the striking bronze sculptures of indigenous Maya crafted by celebrated 20th-century sculptor Enrique Gottdiener Soto. On the second floor are about 20 forgettable oil paintings—mostly of past civic officials of the area. ✉ *Calle 59 between Calles 58 and 60, Centro* ☎ *999/924–5233* 🌐 *www.inah.gob.mx* 🎫 *$3* ⏲ *Tues.–Sat. 9–5, Sun. 10–5.*

16 **Mercado de Artesanías García Rejón.** Although many deal in the same wares, the shops or stalls of the García Rejón Crafts Market sell some quality items, and the shopping experience here can be less of a hassle than at the municipal market. You'll find reasonable prices on palm-fiber hats, hammocks, leather sandals, jewelry, and locally made liqueurs. Persistent but polite bargaining may get you even better deals. ✉ *Calles 60 and 65, Centro* ☎ *No phone* ⏲ *Weekdays 9–6, Sat. 9–4, Sun. 9–1.*

15 **Mercado Municipal.** Sellers of chilies, herbs, crafts, trinkets, and fruit fill this pungent and labyrinthine municipal market. In the early morning the first floor is jammed with housewives and restaurateurs shopping for the freshest seafood and produce. The stairs at Calles 56 and 57 lead to the second-floor Bazar de Artesanías Municipales, on either side, where you'll find local pottery, embroidered clothes, men's guayabera dress shirts, hammocks, and straw bags. Note that most prices are inflated, and vendors expect you will bargain—one way to begin is to politely request a discount. ✉ *Calles 56 and 67, Centro* ☎ *No phone* ⏲ *Mon.–Sat. dawn–dusk, Sun. 8–3.*

7 **Museo de Arte Contemporáneo.** Originally designed as an art school and used until 1915 as a seminary, this enormous, light-filled building now showcases the works of contemporary Yucatecan artists such as Gabriel Ramírez Aznar and Fernando García Ponce, as well as a variety of temporary exhibits. If you want to explore beyond the outside plaza, be sure to sign in first. ✉ *Pasaje de la Revolución 1907, between Calles 58 and 60 on main square, Centro* ☎ *999/928–3236 or 999/928–3258* 🎫 *Free* ⏲ *Wed. and Thurs. 10–6, Fri. and Sat. 10–8.*

14 **Museo de Arte Popular de Yucatán.** Facing the Plaza Mejorada, this museum is funded by the Banamex Cultural Foundation, and offers a comprehensive introduction to the different kinds of Mexican art craft including ceramics, textiles, stone work, cardboard art, woodwork, and glass. Even if you don't want to see the whole museum, take a look in the gift shop, which sells all sorts of crafts like shawls, baskets, dolls, and masks. Prices are a bit high, but so is the quality of the crafts; even if you don't buy anything here, a look around will inform your purchases at area markets. ✉ *Calle 50 No. 487, between 57 and 59* ☎ *999/928–5263* 🎫 *$3* ⏲ *Tues.–Sat. 9:30–6:30.*

13 **Palacio Cantón.** The most compelling of the mansions on **Paseo Montejo**, this stately palacio was built as the residence for a general between 1909 and 1911. Designed by Enrique Deserti, who also did the blueprints for the Teatro Peón Contreras, the building has a grandiose air that seems more characteristic of a mausoleum than a home: there's marble everywhere, as well as Doric and Ionic columns and other Italianate Beaux-Arts flourishes. The building also houses the air-conditioned **Museo de Antropología e Historia,** which introduces visitors to ancient Mayan culture. Temporary exhibits sometimes brighten the standard collection.

⊠ *Paseo Montejo 485, at Calle 43, Paseo Montejo* ☎ *999/923–0469* 🌐 *www.inah.gob.mx* 🎟 *$4* ⏲ *Tues.–Sun. 8–5.*

5 **Palacio del Gobierno.** Visit the seat of state government to see Fernando Castro Pacheco's murals of the bloody history of the conquest of the Yucatán, painted in bold colors in the 1970s and influenced by the Mexican muralists José Clemente Orozco and David Alfaro Siquieros. On the main balcony (visible from outside on the plaza) stands a reproduction of the Bell of Dolores Hidalgo, on which Mexican independence rang out on the night of September 15, 1810, in the town of Dolores Hidalgo in Guanajuato. On the anniversary of the event, the governor rings the bell to commemorate the occasion. ⊠ *Calle 61 between Calles 60 and 62, Centro* ☎ *999/930–3101* 🎟 *Free* ⏲ *Daily 9 AM–9 PM.*

4 **Palacio Municipal.** The west side of the main square is occupied by City Hall, a 17th-century building trimmed with white arcades, balustrades, and the national coat of arms. Originally erected on the ruins of the last surviving Mayan structure, it was rebuilt in 1735 and then completely reconstructed along colonial lines in 1928. It remains the headquarters of the local government, and houses the municipal tourist office. ⊠ *Calle 62 between Calles 61 and 63, Centro* ☎ *999/928–2020* ⏲ *Palacio daily 9–8, Tourist Information Center weekdays 8–8, Sat. 9–1.*

NEED A BREAK?

The homemade ice cream and sorbet at El Colón have been a tradition since 1907. It's one way that locals keep cool. The tropical fruit flavors, like *chico zapote* (a brown fruit native to Mexico that has a flavor a little like cinnamon and comes from a tree that is used in chewing-gum production), served up in a pyramid-shaped scoop are particularly delicious and refreshing. The shop also sell cookies and fresh candies—the meringues are exceptional. The Paseo Montejo branch has the same menu with both outdoor and indoor seating. The tables inside are under whirling fans that make it a comfortable spot to cool off on a hot afternoon, and the Paseo Montejo location makes it a great place to watch people walking by. ⊠ ***Calle 62 No. 500, at Calles 59 and 61, Centro*** ☎ ***999/928-1497*** 💳 ***No credit cards*** ⊠ ***Paseo de Montejo No 474, at Calles 39 and 41, Mérida*** ☎ ***999/927-6443.***

8 **Parque Hidalgo.** A half block north of the main plaza is this small cozy park, officially known as Plaza Cepeda Peraza. Historic mansions, now reincarnated as hotels and sidewalk cafés, line the south side of the park, at night the area comes alive with marimba bands and street vendors. On Sunday the streets are closed to vehicular traffic, and there's free live music performed throughout the day. ⊠ *Calle 60 between Calles 59 and 61, Centro* ☎ *No phone.*

17 **Parque Zoológico El Centenario.** Mérida's greatest children's attraction, this large amusement complex features playgrounds, inexpensive rides like motorized cars for rent and small electric merry-go-round style rides, pony rides, a small train ($1) that circles the park, a rollerblading rink, and cages with more than 300 native animals as well as exotics such as lions, tigers, and bears. At the exit, there are snack bars and

vendors. It also has picnic areas, pleasant wooded paths, and a small lake where you can rent rowboats. The French Renaissance–style arch (1921) commemorates the 100th anniversary of Mexican independence. ✉ *Av. Itzáes between Calles 59 and 65, entrances on Calles 59 and 65, Centro* ☎ *No phone* 🌐 *www.merida.gob.mx/centenario* 🎫 *Free* ⏲ *Zoo Tues.–Sun. 6–6.*

WHERE TO EAT

$ MEXICAN ✕ **Café La Habana.** A gleaming wood bar, white-jacketed waiters, and the scent of cigarettes contribute to the Old European feel at this overwhelmingly popular spot, a branch of a Mexico City café that has been around since the 1950s. Overhead, brass-studded ceiling fans swirl the air-conditioned air. Sixteen specialty coffees are offered (some spiked with spirits like Kahlúa or cognac), and the menu has light snacks as well as some entrées, including tamales, fajitas, and enchiladas. The waiters are friendly, and there are plenty of them, although service is not always brisk. Both the café and upstairs Internet joint are open 24 hours a day; free Wi-Fi is available downstairs for laptop-toting customers. ✉ *Calle 59 No. 511A, at Calle 62, Centro* ☎ *999/928–6502* 💳 *MC, V.*

16

$$ ITALIAN ✕ **Café Lucía.** Opera music floats above black-and-white tile floors in the dining room of this century-old restaurant in the Hotel Casa Lucía near the main plaza. Pizzas and calzones are the linchpins of the Italian menu, luscious pecan pies, cakes, and cookies beckon from behind the glass dessert case. The original art on the walls is for sale, however the paintings by the late Oaxacan artist Rodolfo Morales are not, so don't bother asking. ✉ *Calle 60 No. 474A, Centro* ☎ *999/928–0704* 🌐 *www.casalucia.com.mx* 💳 *AE, MC, V.*

$$ MEXICAN Fodor's Choice ★ ✕ **Hacienda Teya.** Once a henequen-producing site, this beautiful hacienda just outside the city serves some of the best regional food around. It has attracted some big names, like Vicente Fox (back when he was president, and would order the *queso relleno* to go) and even Hillary Clinton. Most patrons are well-to-do Méridians enjoying a leisurely lunch, so you don't want to wear your beach clothes, in fact, men wearing tank tops are asked to change. It's open from noon to 6 daily (though most Mexicans don't show up until after 3), and a guitarist serenades the tables between 2 and 5 on weekends. After a fabulous lunch like *cochinita pibíl* (pork baked in banana leaves), take a stroll through the surrounding orchards and botanical gardens. If you find yourself wanting to spend the night, you can. The hacienda has six handsome suites ($$), which are often available on short notice, although they need to be reserved in advance over long weekends and holidays. ✉ *12.5 km (8 mi) east of Mérida on Carretera 180, Kanasín* ☎ *999/988–0800* 🌐 *www.haciendateya.com* 💳 *AE, MC, V* ⏲ *No dinner.*

$$ ECLECTIC ✕ **La Bella Epoca.** The coveted, tiny private balconies at this elegantly restored mansion overlook Parque Hidalgo. You'll need to call in advance to reserve one for a 7 PM or 10 PM seating, tables that overlook the park go especially fast. On weekends, when the street below is closed to traffic and tables are set up outside, it's especially pleasant to survey the park while feasting on Mayan dishes like *sikil-pak*

(a dip with ground pumpkin seeds, charbroiled tomatoes, and onions) or succulent *pollo pibíl* (chicken baked in banana leaves). ✉ *Calle 60 No. 497, between Calles 57 and 59, Centro* ☎ *999/928–1928* 💳 *AE, MC, V* ⏲ *No lunch.*

$ MEXICAN Fodor's Choice ★ ✕ **La Casa de Frida.** Chef-owner Gabriela Praget puts a healthful, cosmopolitan spin on Mexican fare at her restaurant. This is a great place to sample foods from around Mexico. Praget prepares all the dishes herself, and is usually on hand to greet guests. Traditional dishes like duck in a dark, rich mole sauce (made with chocolate and chilies) share the menu with gourmet vegetarian cuisine: potato and cheese tacos, ratatouille in puff pastry, and crepes made with *cuitlachoche* (a delicious truffle-like corn fungus). The flavors here are so divine that diners have been known to hug Praget after a meal. The dining room—a casual covered patio decorated with plants, copies of Frida Kahlo self-portraits, several Frida dolls, and other art—is a comfortable place to enjoy a leisurely meal. ✉ *Calle 61 No. 526, at Calle 66, Centro* ☎ *999/928–2311* 🌐 *www.lacasadefrida.com.mx* 💳 *No credit cards* ⏲ *No lunch Mon.–Fri.*

WORD OF MOUTH

"I chose to dine at La Casa de Frida specifically because I had read a review that praised its *chiles en nogada*... and I found it praiseworthy indeed! I began with an appetizer of crepes with *cuitlachoche* that was so delicious that I couldn't bring myself to stop eating... unfortunately, I was too full to do proper justice to the chiles en nogada. Even so, just thinking of that evening brings back memories of that entrée and its intensely flavorful and rich walnut sauce—wow! My server always seemed to appear out of nowhere at exactly the right time." —kja

$ ITALIAN ✕ **Ristorante & Pizzería Bologna.** You can dine alfresco or inside at this beautifully restored old mansion a few blocks off Paseo Montejo. Tables have fresh flowers and cloth napkins, walls are adorned with pictures of Italy, and there are plants everywhere. Most menu items are ordered à la carte; among the favorites are the shrimp pizza and pizza *diabola*, topped with salami, tomato, and chilies. The beef fillet—served solo or covered in cheese or mushrooms—is served with baked potato and a medley of mixed sautéed vegetables. ✉ *Calle 21 No. 117A, between Calles 24 and 28, Col. Izimná* ☎ *999/926–2505* 💳 *AE, MC, V.*

WHERE TO STAY

$$ 🏨 **Casa Mexilio.** This eclectic B&B is four blocks from the main square. French tapestries, and colorful tile floors crowd the public spaces. Individually decorated rooms have tile sinks and folk-art furniture. Some find this inn private and romantic, although others may find it a bit too intimate and quiet for their liking. The grottolike pool is surrounded by ferns, and the light-filled rooftop room, up four-dozen steps, has an excellent city view from its oversize balcony. **Pros:** pleasant courtyard, easy walk to downtown attractions, excellent room prices, nice breakfasts. **Cons:** small bathrooms, some linens look dated. ✉ *Calle 68 No. 495, between Calles 57 and 59, Centro* ☎📠 *999/928–2505* ☎ *800/538–6802 in U.S. and Canada* 🌐 *www.mexicoholiday.com* ⇨ *9 rooms* 👍 *In-*

room: no phone, a/c, no TV, Wi-Fi (some). In-hotel: restaurant, bar, pool, Wi-Fi hotspot, no kids under 12 ▭ *AE, MC, V* ⊚ *CP.*

$$ **Gran Hotel.** Cozily situated on Parque Hidalgo, this legendary 1901 hotel does look its age, with extremely high ceilings, wrought-iron balcony and stair rails, and ornately patterned tile floors. The period decor is so classic that you expect a mantilla-wearing Spanish señorita to appear, fluttering her fan, at any moment. The old-fashioned sitting room has formal seating areas and lots of antiques and plants. A renovation in 2004 enlarged some guest rooms and replaced tiny twin beds with doubles. Wide interior verandas on the second and third floors provide pretty outside seating. Porfirio Díaz, a former Mexican president, stayed in one of the corner suites, which have small living and dining areas. The downstairs boutique sells high-quality clothes, including wedding dresses made from natural fibers. **Pros:** beautiful antique decorations (especially in public areas); in the middle of downtown bustle, sights, and shops. **Cons:** downtown noise, no elevator makes upstairs rooms quite a hike; not easy to park in front, and parking is sometimes unavailable (check ahead if you are driving). ✉ *Calle 60 No. 496, Centro* ☎ *999/923–6963* 🌐 *www.granhoteldemerida.com.mx* *25 rooms, 7 suites* *In-room: a/c. In-hotel: restaurant, room service, laundry service, parking (free), some pets allowed* ▭ *MC, V* ⊚ *EP.*

MARKET SNACKS

The simple market in **Parque Santa Ana** (✉ *Calle 60, between 45 and 47, Centro* ☎ *No phone*) is a popular breakfast spot where you will find locals happily starting their day with regional dishes and fresh juices at plastic tables. The *tamales* are good. The *tortas de cochinita,* pork sandwiches flavored with a few drops of sour-orange chili sauce are heavenly. Most vendors here close around 1:30 in the afternoon, but some reopen to sell snacks between 7 PM and midnight.

$$$$ ★ **Hacienda Xcanatun.** The furnishings at this beautifully restored 18th-century henequen hacienda include African and Indonesian antiques, locally made lamps, and comfortable, oversized couches and chairs from Puebla. The cool and spacious rooms come with cozy sleigh beds, fine sheets, and fluffy comforters, and are impeccably decorated with art from Mexico, Cuzco, Peru, and other places the owners have traveled. Bathrooms are luxuriously large. The restaurant serves a standard breakfast as well as French and Caribbean dishes with Yucatán accents and ingredients for lunch and dinner, while the hacienda's spa cooks up innovative treatments such as cacao-and-honey massages. **Pros:** good restaurant, expansive gardens, poolside bar service. **Cons:** a drive from the city, pricey. ✉ *Carretera 261, Km 12, 13 km (8 mi) north of Mérida* ☎ *999/941–0213 or 888/883–3633* 🌐 *www.xcanatun.com* *18 suites* *In-room: a/c, safe, no TV. In-hotel: restaurant, room service, bars, pools, spa, laundry service, Wi-Fi hotspot, parking (free)* ▭ *AE, MC, V* ⊚ *CP.*

$$ ★ **Hyatt Regency Mérida.** The city's first deluxe hotel is still among its most elegant. Rooms are regally decorated, with russet-hue quilts and rugs set off by blond-wood furniture and cream-color walls. There's a

16

top-notch business center, and a beautiful marble lobby. Upper-crust Méridians recommend Spasso Italian restaurant as a fine place to have a drink in the evening, for an amazing seafood extravaganza, don't miss the $20 seafood buffet at Peregrina bistro on Friday afternoons from 1 to 5. **Pros:** attentive service, reasonably priced compared to neighboring hotels, popular restaurant. **Cons:** just off the Paseo Montejo but far from downtown, Internet access only included in some rooms. ✉ *Calle 60 No. 344, at Av. Colón, Paseo Montejo* ☎ *999/942–0202, 999/942–1234, or 800/233–1234* 🌐 *merida.regency.hyatt.com.mx* *296 rooms, 4 suites* *In-room: a/c, safe, Internet, Wi-Fi. In-hotel: 2 restaurants, room service, bars, tennis courts, pool, gym, laundry service, Wi-Fi hotspot, parking (free)* ▭ *AE, DC, MC, V* *BP, EP.*

$$ ★ **Marionetas.** Attentive proprietors Daniel and Sofija Bosco, who are originally from Argentina and Macedonia, have created this lovely B&B on a quiet street seven blocks from the main plaza. From the Macedonian lace dust ruffles and fine cotton sheets and bedspreads to the quiet, remote-controlled air-conditioning and pressurized showerheads (there are no tubs), every detail and fixture here is of the highest quality. You'll delight in the carefully chosen folk-art decoration throughout. You'll need to book your reservation well in advance. You can pick up the Wi-Fi signal in some rooms but not others, so let the staff know if you'll be bringing a laptop when you book. **Pros:** intimate feel, personal attention from proprietors and staff, courtyard and pool area are a calm escape from the bustling Mérida streets. **Cons:** reservations can be hard to come by in high season, restaurant only serves breakfast. ✉ *Calle 49 No. 516, between Calles 62 and 64, Centro* ☎ *999/928–3377 or 999/923–2790* 🌐 *www.hotelmarionetas.com* *8 rooms, 1 suite* *In-room: a/c, safe. In-hotel: restaurant, bar, Internet terminal, Wi-Fi hotspot* ▭ *MC, V* *BP.*

$ **Posada Toledo.** This beautiful centuries-old house has retained its elegance with high ceilings, floors of patterned tile, and carved, colonial-style furniture. The guest rooms themselves are less impressive, and the furnishings (and their condition) vary more than the rates reflect, so be sure to inspect your shabby-chic room before checking in. Room 5 is an elegant two-room suite that was originally the mansion's master bedroom. Rooms on the second floor are newer and somewhat more modern. If you're a light sleeper, ask for a room away from the courtyard. The restaurant only serves breakfast. **Pros:** inexpensive, friendly staff. **Cons:** room quality varies, sound from courtyard audible from nearby rooms, small bathrooms. ✉ *Calle 58 No. 487, at Calle 57, Centro* ☎ *999/923–1690* *21 rooms, 2 suites* *In-hotel: restaurant, parking (paid)* ▭ *MC, V* *EP.*

NIGHTLIFE

Mérida has an active and diverse cultural life, which features free government-sponsored music and dance performances many evenings, as well as sidewalk art shows in local parks. Thursday at 9 PM Méridians enjoy an evening of outdoor entertainment at the **Serenata Yucateca**. At **Parque Santa Lucía** (calles 60 and 55) you'll see trios, the local orchestra, and soloists performing compositions by Yucatecan composers.

On Saturday evenings after 7 PM the **Noche Mexicana** (corner of Paseo Montejo and Calle 47) hosts different musical and cultural events. More free music, dance, comedy, and regional handicrafts can be found at the **Corazón de Mérida,** on Calle 60 between the main plaza and Calle 55. Between 8 PM and 1 AM multiple bandstands throughout this area (which is closed to traffic) entertain locals and visitors with an ever-changing playbill, from grunge to classical.

MAKING YOURSELF AT HOME

There are a few Internet agencies that can help you rent a home if you plan on staying in the area for a while. At 🌐 *www.bestofyucatan.com,* you can find some stunningly remodeled old Mérida homes, and haciendas remodeled by artists John Powell and Josh Ramos.

BARS AND DANCE CLUBS

★ Popular with the local *niños fresa* (which translates as "strawberry children," meaning upper-class youth) as well as some middle-age professionals, the indoor-outdoor lounge **El Cielo** (✉ *Prolongación Paseo Montejo between Calles 15 and 17, Col. México* ☎ *999/944–5127* 🌐 *www.elcielobar.com*) is one of the latest minimalist hot spots where you can drink and dance to party or lounge-music videos. It's open Wednesday through Saturday nights after 9:30 PM. Their first-floor restaurant, Sky, serves sushi beginning at 1 daily, except on Mondays when it's closed.

Mambo Café (✉ *Calle 21 No. 327, between Calles 50 and 52, Plaza las Américas, Fracc. Miguel Hidalgo* ☎ *999/987–7533* 🌐 *www.mambocafe.com.mx*) is the best place in town for dancing to DJ-spun salsa, merengue, cumbia, and disco tunes. You might want to hit the john during their raunchy audience-participation acts between sets. It's open from 9 PM until 3 AM Wednesday, Friday, and Saturday. Admission is free on Wednesdays.

El Nuevo Tucho (✉ *Calle 60 No. 482, between Calles 55 and 57, Centro* ☎ *999/924–2323*) has cheesy cabaret-style entertainment beginning at 4 PM, with no drink minimum and no cover. In fact, despite the music and comedy, this is not just a place for young people or for dancing. Families dine here as well. There's music for dancing in this cavernous—sometimes full, sometimes empty—venue. Drinks come with free appetizers.

Pancho's (✉ *Calle 59 No. 509, between Calles 60 and 62, Centro* ☎ *999/923–0942* 🌐 *www.panchosmerida.com*), open daily 6 PM–2:30 AM, has a lively bar and a restaurant. It also has a small dance floor that attracts locals and visitors for a mix of live salsa and English-language pop music.

If dancing to the likes of Los Panchos and other romantic trios of the 1940s is more your style, don't miss this Tuesday-night ritual at **Parque de Santiago** (✉ *Calles 59 and 72, Centro* ☎ *No phone*), where old folks and the occasional young lovers gather for dancing under the stars at 8:30 PM.

Fodor's Choice ★ Enormously popular and rightly so, the red-walled **Slavia** (✉ *Calle 29 No. 490, at Calle 58* ☎ *999/926–6587*) is an exotic Middle Eastern beauty. There are all sorts of nooks where you can be alone yet together with upscale Méridians, most of whom simply call this "the Buddha Bar." Arabian music in the background, low lighting, beaded curtains, embroidered tablecloths, mirrors, and sumptuous pillows and settees surrounding low tables produce a fabulous Arabian-nights vibe you won't find anywhere else in Mérida. It's open daily 7 PM–2 AM.

Tequila Rock (✉ *Prolongación Paseo Montejo at Av. Campestre* ☎ *999/883–3147*) is a disco where salsa and Mexican and American pop are played Wednesday through Saturday. It's popular mainly with young people between 18 and 25.

FOLKLORIC SHOWS

Paseo Montejo hotels such as the Fiesta Americana, Hyatt Regency, and Holiday Inn stage dinner shows with folkloric dances, check with concierges for schedules.

★ The **Ballet Folklórico de Yucatán** (✉ *Calles 57 and 60, Centro* ☎ *999/923–1198* 🌐 *www.uady.mx/sitios/cultura/ballet.html*) presents a combination of music, dance, and theater every Friday at 9 PM at the university; tickets are $5. (Performances are every other Friday in the off-season, and there are no shows from August 1 to September 22 and the last two weeks of December.)

SHOPPING

MALLS

Mérida has several shopping malls, but the largest and nicest, **Gran Plaza** (✉ *Calle 50 Diagonal 460, Fracc. Gonzalo Guerrero* ☎ *999/944–7657* 🌐 *www.granplaza.com.mx*), has more than 200 shops and a multiplex theater. It's just outside town, on the highway to Progreso (called Carretera a Progreso beyond the Mérida city limits). Tiny **Pasaje Picheta** is on the north side of the town square on Calle 61. It has a bus-ticket information booth and an upstairs art gallery, as well as souvenir shops and a food court. **Plaza Américas** (✉ *Calle 21 No. 331, Col. Miguel Hidalgo* ☎ *No phone*) is a pleasant mall where you'll find the Cineopolis movie theater complex.

MARKETS

The **Mercado Municipal** (✉ *Calles 56 and 67Centro*) has lots of things you won't need, but which are fascinating to look at: songbirds in cane cages, mountains of mysterious fruits and vegetables, dippers made of hollow gourds (the same way they've been made here for a thousand years). There are also lots of crafts for sale, including hammocks, sturdy leather huaraches, and piñatas in every imaginable shape and color. ■ **TIP→ Guides often approach tourists near this market. They expect a tip and won't necessarily bring you to the best deals. You're better off visiting some specialty stores first to learn about the quality and types of hammocks, hats, and other crafts, then you'll have an idea of what you're buying—and what it's worth—if you want to bargain in the market. Also be wary of pickpockets within the markets.**

Sunday brings an array of wares into Mérida, starting at 9 AM, the Handicrafts Bazaar, or **Bazar de Artesanías** (✉ *At main square, Centro*), sells lots of *huipiles* (traditional, white embroidered dresses) as well as hats and costume jewelry. As its name implies, popular art, or handicrafts, are sold at the **Bazar de Artes Populares** (✉ *Parque Santa Lucía, at Calles 60 and 55, Centro*) beginning at 9 AM on Sunday. If you're interested in handicrafts, **Bazar García Rejón** (✉ *Calles 65 and 62, Centro*) has rows of indoor stalls that sell items like leather goods, palm hats, and handmade guitars.

SPECIALTY STORES

CLOTHING

You might not wear a guayabera to a business meeting as some men in Mexico do, but the shirts are cool, comfortable, and attractive. For a good selection, try **Camisería Canul** (✉ *Calle 62 No. 484, between Calles 57 and 59, Centro* ☎ *999/923–0158* 🌐 *www.camiseriacanul.com.mx*). Custom shirts take a week to construct, in sizes 4 to 52.

Guayaberas Jack (✉ *Calle 59 No. 507A, between Calles 60 and 62, Centro* ☎ *99/928–6002*) has an excellent selection of guayaberas (18 delicious colors to choose from!) and typical women's cotton *filipinas* (house dresses), blouses, dresses, classy straw handbags, and lovely rayon *rebozos* (shawls) from San Luis Potosí. Guayaberas can be made to order, allegedly in less than a day, to fit anyone from a year-old baby to a 240-pound man, and anything in the shop can be altered or custom made. Everything here is of fine quality, and is often quite different from the clothes sold in neighboring shops. Prices are higher than in neighboring shops. The store has a small branch near the Fiesta Americana Mérida, but the branch does not have as much variety as the downtown location. You can browse and make purchases on their Web site as well. **Mexicanísimo** (✉ *Calle 60 No. 496, at Parque Hidalgo, Centro* ☎ *999/923–8132* 🌐 *www.mexicanisimobymasud.com*) sells sleek, clean-lined clothing made from natural fibers for both women and men.

JEWELRY

Shop for malachite, turquoise, and other semiprecious stones set in silver at **Joyería Kema** (✉ *Calle 60 No. 502-B, between Calles 61 and 63, at main plaza, Centro* ☎ *999/923–5838*). Beaders and other creative types flock to **Papagayo's Paradise** (✉ *Calle 62 No. 488, between Calles 57 and 59, Centro* ☎ *999/993–0383*), where you'll find loose beads and semiprecious stones, lovely necklaces and earrings, and Brussels-lace-trimmed, hand-embroidered, tatted, and crocheted blouses. This small but exceptional store also sells men's handkerchiefs and place mats. **Tane** (✉ *Centro Comercial Galerias, Carretera Mérida–Progreso, Km. 5, local 6, Paseo Montejo* ☎ *999/941–5862* 🌐 *www.tane.com.mx*) is an outlet for exquisite (and expensive) silver earrings, necklaces, and bracelets, some incorporating ancient Mayan designs.

LOCAL GOODS AND CRAFTS

A great place to purchase hammocks is **El Aguacate** (✉ *Calle 58 No. 604, at Calle 73, Centro* ☎ *999/928–6425* 🌐 *www.hamacaselaguacate.com.mx*), a family-run outfit with many sizes and designs. Closed Sunday. Visit the government-run **Casa de las Artesanías Ki-Huic** (✉ *Calle 63 No.*

16

CLOSE UP

Hamacas: A Primer

Yucatecan artisans are known for creating some of the finest *hamacas,* or hammocks, in the country. For the most part, the shops of Mérida are the best places in Yucatán to buy these beautiful, practical items—although if you travel to some of the outlying small towns, like Tixkokob, Izamal, and Ek Balam, you may find cheaper prices—and enjoy the experience as well.

One of the first decisions you'll have to make when buying a hamaca is whether to choose one made from cotton or nylon: nylon dries more quickly and is therefore well suited to humid climates, but cotton is softer and more comfortable (though its colors tend to fade faster). You'll also see that hamacas come in both double-threaded and single-threaded weaves; the double-threaded ones are sturdiest because they're more densely woven.

Hamacas come in a variety of sizes, too. A *sencillo* (cen-*see*-oh) hammock is meant for just one person (although most people find it's a rather tight fit), a *doble* (*doh*-blay), on the other hand, is very comfortable for one but crowded for two. *Matrimonial* or king-size hammocks accommodate two, and *familiares* or *matrimoniales especiales* can theoretically sleep an entire family. (Yucatecans tend to be smaller than Anglos are, and also lie diagonally in hammocks rather than end-to-end.)

For a good-quality king-size nylon or cotton hamaca, expect to pay about $35, sencillos go for about $22. Unless you're an expert, it's best to buy a hammock at a specialty shop, where you can climb in to try the size. The proprietors will also give you tips on washing, storing, and hanging your hammock. There are lots of hammock stores near Mérida's municipal market on Calle 58, between Calles 69 and 73.

503A, between Calles 64 and 62, Centro ☎ *999/928–6676*) for folk art from throughout Yucatán. There's a showcase of hard-to-find traditional filigree jewelry in silver, gold, and gold-dipped versions. **Casa de los Artesanos** (✉ *Calle 62 No. 492, between Calles 59 and 61, Centro* ☎ *999/923–4523*), half a block from the main plaza, sells mainly small ceramic pieces, including more modern, stylized takes on traditional designs. The **Casa de Cera** (✉ *Calle 74A No. 430E, between Calles 41 and 43, Centro* ☎ *999/920–0219*) is a small shop selling signed collectible indigenous beeswax figurines. Closed afternoons after 5 PM. **El Hamaquero** (✉ *Calle 58 No. 572, between Calles 69 and 71, Centro* ☎ *999/923–2117*) has knowledgeable personnel who let you try out the hammocks before you buy. Closed Sundays. **El Mayab** (✉ *Calle 58 No. 553-A, at Calle 71, Centro* ☎ *999/924–0853*) has a multitude of hammocks and is open on Sundays until 2 PM. **Miniaturas** (✉ *Calle 59 No. 507A, between Calles 60 and 62, Centro* ☎ *999/928–6503*) sells a delightful and diverse assortment of different crafts, but specializes in miniatures. **Tequilería Ajua** (✉ *Calle 59 No. 506, at Calle 62, Centro* ☎ *999/924–1453*) sells tequila, brandy, and mezcal as well as Xtabentún—a locally made liqueur flavored with anise and honey, which some claim is a aphrodisiac—and thick liqueurs made of local fruit from 10 AM to 9 PM.

You can get hammocks made to order—choose from standard nylon and cotton, super-soft processed sisal, Brazilian-style (six-stringed), or crocheted—at **El Xiric** (✉ *Calle 57-A No. 15 y 16, Pasaje Congreso, Centro* ☎ *999/924–9906*). You can also get Xtabentún, as well as jewelry, black pottery, woven goods from Oaxaca, T-shirts, and souvenirs.

SPORTS AND THE OUTDOORS

BASEBALL

Baseball is played with enthusiasm between February and July at the **Centro Deportivo Kukulcán** (✉ *Calle 6 No. 315, Circuito Colonias, Col. Granjas* ✢ *Across street from Pemex gas station and next to Santa Clara brewery* ☎ *999/940–0676 or 999/940–4261*). There are also tennis courts, soccer courts, and an Olympic pool. It's most common to buy your ticket at the on-site ticket booth the day of the game. A-league volleyball and basketball games and tennis tournaments are also held here.

GOLF

The 18-hole championship golf course at **Club de Golf de Yucatán** (✉ *Carretera Mérida–Progreso, Km 14.5* ☎ *999/922–0053* 🌐 *www.golfyucatan.com*) is open to the public. It is about 16 km (10 mi) north of Mérida on the road to Progreso; greens fees are about $125, carts are an additional $40, and clubs can be rented. The pro shop is closed Monday, but the golf course is open seven days a week.

16

UXMAL AND CHITZÉN ITZÁ

Ruta Puuc, or hilly route, is a series of secondary roads that wind through one of the Yucatán's least populated areas, leading you from one fantastic Mayan ruin to another. The roads are well marked and easy to navigate, since sites line up one right after another. ■ **TIP→ It's important to fill up on gas and visit an ATM before entering the area, since both gas stations and ATMs are hard to come by.**

Uxmal, meaning thrice built city, is the largest site along the Ruta Puuc. Several smaller satellite sites—including Kabah, Sayil, and Labná—are all well worth a visit. Another memorable Ruta Puuc site is the Grutas de Loltún, Yucatán's most mysterious and extensive cave system. Here you can still see evidence of ancient Mayan ritual. If you plan on exploring the cave, take along sturdy shoes and a flashlight.

If you want to use your video camera at any of the sites, expect a $3 charge.

TIMING

It's possible to visit the sites on the Ruta Puuc in one long day or over the course of two days. To do Uxmal justice, you'll want to spend anywhere from three to five hours exploring the ruins. Smaller area sites like Labná, Xlapak, Sayil, and Kabah can easily be explored in twenty minutes to a half an hour. Plan on spending a couple of hours at the Grutas de Loltún; be aware that guided tours through the cave are mandatory.

Uxmal is a good place to grab lunch. Snacks are sold on-site, and hotel restaurants are within walking distance; food is a little harder to come by at the other sites. We also recommend the hotels around Uxmal, since it's easy to catch the nightly light and sound show.

GETTING HERE AND AROUND

There's daily transportation on the ATS bus line to Uxmal, Labná, Xlapak, Sayil, and Kabah. $10 buys you a ride to each of these places with 20 to 30 minutes to explore the lesser sites and nearly two hours to see Uxmal. In addition to standard tours, Mayaland Tours also offers "self-guided tours," which means that you set out on your own, but they provide a road map, itinerary, rental car, and arrange lodgings at the archaeological sites. When you consider the price of lodgings and a rental car, this is a pretty sweet deal.

If you plan on spending the night in Uxmal, you may want to start the trip off at Grutas de Loltún and work your way toward Uxmal. To get to Grutas de Loltún from Mérida, take Highway 261 to Muná. Turn left on Highway 184. From there, it is about 65 km (40 miles) to Oxkutzcab. Once in Oxkutzcab, simply follow the signs to the Grutas de Loltún.

ESSENTIALS

Tours and Visitors Information **Mayaland Tours** (✉ *Calle Robalo 30, Sm 3, Cancún* ☎ *998/887–2495 in Cancún, 01800/719–5465 toll-free from elsewhere in Mexico, 800/235–4079* 🌐 *www.mayaland.com*).

UXMAL

78 km (48 mi) south of Mérida on Carretera 261.

If Chichén Itzá is the most expansive Mayan ruin in Yucatán, Uxmal is arguably the most elegant. The architecture here reflects the late classical renaissance of the 7th to 9th centuries, and is contemporary with that of Palenque and Tikal, among other great Mayan cities of the southern highlands.

The site is considered the finest and most extensively excavated example of Puuc architecture, which embraces such details as ornate stone mosaics and friezes on the upper walls, intricate cornices, rows of columns, and soaring vaulted arches.

You could easily spend a couple of days exploring the ruins, though keep in mind that the only entertainment offered outside the ruins is provided by hotels and the odd restaurant.

GETTING HERE AND AROUND

If you plan to drive yourself, take Highway 180 south out of Mérida, and then get on Highway 261 in Umán. This will take you south all the way to Uxmal.

EXPLORING

Fodor's Choice ★ **Uxmal.** Although much of Uxmal hasn't been restored, the following buildings in particular merit attention:

At 125 feet high, the **Pirámide del Adivino** is the tallest and most prominent structure at the site. Unlike most other Mayan pyramids, which are stepped and angular, the Temple of the Magician has a softer and more refined round-corner design. This structure was rebuilt five times over hundreds of years, each time on the same foundation, so artifacts found here represent several different kingdoms. The pyramid has a stairway on its western side that leads through a giant open-mouthed mask to two temples at the summit. During restoration work in 2002 the grave of a high-ranking Mayan official, a ceramic mask, and a jade necklace were discovered within the pyramid. Continuing excavations have revealed exciting new finds that are still being studied.

West of the pyramid lies the **Cuadrángulo de las Monjas**, considered by some to be the finest part of Uxmal. The name was given to it by the conquistadors, because it reminded them of a convent building in Old Spain (*monjas* means nuns). You may enter the four buildings, each comprises a series of low, gracefully repetitive chambers that look onto a central patio. Elaborate and symbolic decorations—masks, geometric patterns, coiling snakes, and some phallic figures—blanket the upper facades.

16

Heading south, you'll pass a small ball court before reaching the **Palacio del Gobernador**, which archaeologist Victor von Hagen considered the most magnificent building ever erected in the Americas. Interestingly, the palace faces east, while the rest of Uxmal faces west. Archaeologists believe this is because the palace was built to allow observation of the planet Venus. Covering five acres and rising over an immense acropolis, it lies at the heart of what may have been Uxmal's administrative center.

Apparently the house of an important person, the recently excavated **Cuadrángalo de los Pájaros** (Quadrangle of the Birds), located between the above-mentioned buildings, is composed of a series of small chambers. In one of these chambers archaeologists found a statue of the royal, by the name of Chac (as opposed to Chaac, the rain god), who apparently dwelt there. The building was named for the repeated pattern of birds, which decorates the upper part of the building's frieze.

Today you can watch a sound-and-light show at the site that recounts Mayan legends. The colored light brings out details of carvings and mosaics that are easy to miss when the sun is shining. The show is performed nightly in Spanish, earphones ($2.50) provide an English translation. ■ **TIP→ In the summer months tarantulas are a common sight at the ruins and around the hotels that surround the ruins.** *Site, museum, and sound-and-light show $19.50, parking $1, use of video camera $2 (keep this receipt if visiting other archaeological sites along the Ruta Puuc on the same day)* *Daily 8–5, sound-and-light show just after dusk (at 7 PM in winter or 8 PM in summer, tickets to only the show $3), official English language tour guide $55.*

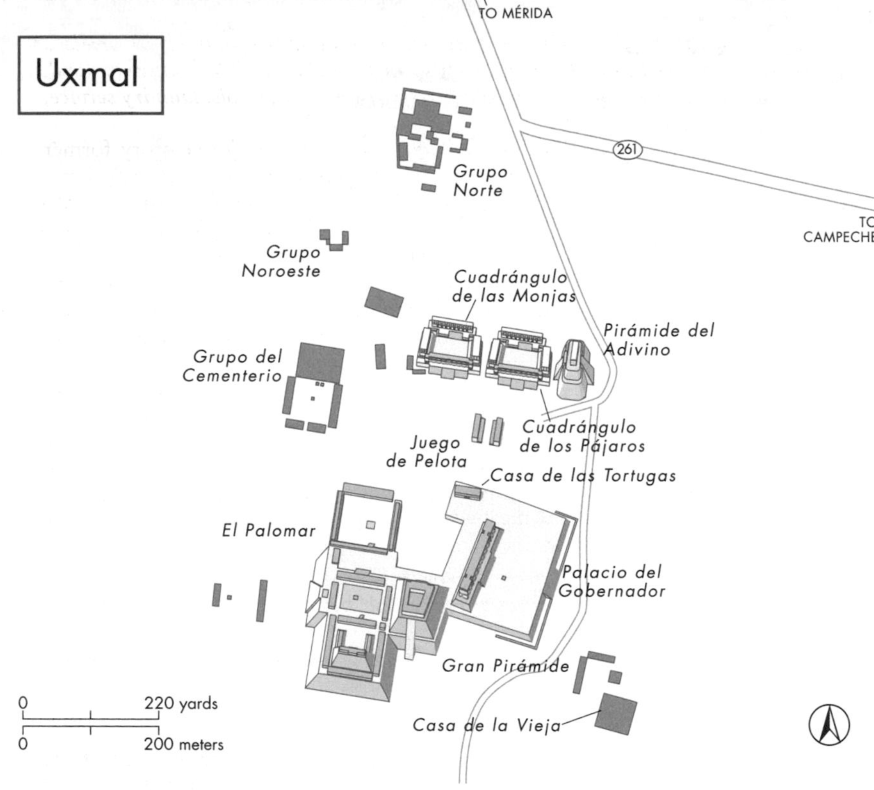

WHERE TO EAT

$ MEXICAN **Cana Nah.** Although this large, recently remodeled roadside spot mainly caters to the groups visiting Uxmal, locals recommend it as the most formally established and hygienic eatery in the area, and the friendly owners are happy to serve small parties. The basic menu includes local dishes like lime soup and *pollo pibíl,* and such universals as fried chicken and vegetable soup. Approach the salsa on the table with a bit of caution: it's made almost purely of habanero chilies. After your meal you can laze in one of the hammocks out back under the trees or dive into the property's large rectangular swimming pool. There's a small shop as well, selling pieces of popular art including figurines of *los aluxes,* the mischievous "lords of the jungle" that Mayan legend says protect farmers' fields. ✉ *Carretera Muna–Uxmal, 4 km (2½ mi) north of Uxmal* ☎ *997/971–0102* ▭ *No credit cards.*

WHERE TO STAY

$$$ **Lodge at Uxmal.** The outwardly rustic, thatch-roof buildings here have red-tile floors, doors and rocking chairs carved from polished hardwood, and local weavings. The effect is comfortable yet luxuriant, the property feels sort of like a peaceful ranch. All rooms have bathtubs and screened windows, suites have king-size beds and spa baths. **Pros:** directly across from Uxmal entrance, simple, beautiful rooms, big pools.

Cons: no room phones, mediocre restaurant, expensive. ✉ *Carretera Uxmal, Km 78* ☎ *997/976–2031 or 800/235–4079* 🌐 *www.mayaland.com* ⇨ *40 suites* ♨ *In-hotel: 2 restaurants, bar, pools, laundry service, parking (free)* ▭ *AE, MC, V.*

$$ Fodor's Choice ★ **Villas Arqueológicas Uxmal.** Rooms at this pretty two-story former Club Med property are small, like hobbit holes, but bright and functional, with wooden furniture and cozy twin beds that fit nicely into alcoves, and a number of them have garden views. Since rooms are petite, guests tend to hang out in the comfy library with a giant-screen TV and lots of reading material, or at thatch-shaded tables next to the pool. The indoor restaurant ($), which may seem classy or Old Europe fussy depending on your taste, serves both regional fare and international dishes. With museum-quality reproductions of Mayan statues throughout (even in the pool), it's several times less expensive than, and equally as charming as, the other options, which are just a stone's throw from the ruins. While you can't connect a laptop to the Internet, you can borrow a computer in the hotel office for a couple of dollars an hour. **Pros:** upgraded beds and other improvements, walking distance to ruins, nice pool. **Cons:** rooms could be more spacious, restaurant food is just OK. ✉ *Carretera 261, Km 76* ☎ *997/974–6020 or 800/258–2633* 🌐 *www.villasarqueologicas.com.mx* ⇨ *40 rooms, 3 suites* ♨ *In-room: a/c, safe, no TV. In-hotel: restaurant, bar, tennis court, pool, laundry service, parking (free)* ▭ *AE, MC, V.*

16

KABAH

23 km (14 mi) south of Uxmal on Carretera 261.

The most important buildings at Kabah, which means "lord of the powerful hand" in Mayan, were built between AD 600 and 900, during the later part of the classic era. A ceremonial center of almost Grecian beauty, it was once linked to Uxmal by a sacbé, at the end of which looms a great independent arch—now across the highway from the main ruins. The 151 foot-long **Palacio de los Mascarones,** or Palace of the Masks, boasts a three-dimensional mosaic of 250 masks of inlaid stones. On the central plaza you can see ground-level wells called *chultunes,* which were used to store precious rainwater. The site officially opens at 8 AM, but the staff doesn't usually show up until 9. 🎫 *$3.50* ⏲ *Daily 8–5.*

SAYIL

9 km (5½ mi) south of Kabah on Carretera 31 E.

Experts believe that Sayil, or "place of the red ants," flourished between AD 800 and 1000. It's renowned primarily for its majestic **Gran Palacio.** Built on a hill, the three-story structure is adorned with decorations of animals and other figures, and contains more than 80 rooms. The structure recalls Palenque in its use of multiple planes, columned porticoes, and sober cornices. Also on the grounds is a stela in the shape of a phallus—an obvious symbol of fertility. 🎫 *$3.50* ⏲ *Daily 8–5.*

Continued on page 804

The towering **El Castillo** pyramid, nearly 80-feet high, is the most striking structure at Chichén Itzá. Each side of the pyramid has 91 steps, which, with the addition of the topmost platform, equal 365, one for each day of the calendar year. At the vernal and autumnal equinoxes, thousands of people gather to watch as the shadow of the serpent god Kukulcán seems to slither down the side of the pyramid.

CHICHÉN ITZÁ

Carvings of ball players adorn the walls of the *juego de pelota*.

One of the most dramatically beautiful of the ancient Maya cities, Chichén Itzá draws some 3,000 visitors a day from all over the world. Since the remains of this once-thriving kingdom were discovered by Europeans in the mid 1800s, many of the travelers who make the pilgrimage here have been archaeologists and scholars, who study the structures and glyphs and try to piece together the mysteries surrounding them. While the artifacts here give fascinating insight into the Maya civilization, they also raise many, many unanswered questions.

The name of this ancient city, which means "the mouth of the well of the Itzás," is a mystery in and of itself. Although it likely refers to the valuable water sources at the site (there are several sinkholes here), experts have little information about who might have actually founded the city—some structures, likely built in the 5th century, pre-date the arrival of the Itzás who occupied the city starting around the late 8th and early 9th centuries. The reason why the Itzás abandoned the city, around 1224, is also unknown. The role that this center then took is still being evaluated.

Of course, most of the visitors that converge on Chichén Itzá come to marvel at its beauty, not ponder its significance. This ancient metropolis, which encompasses 6 square km (2½ square mi), is known around the world as one of the most stunning and well-preserved Maya sites in existence.

The sight of the immense ❶ **El Castillo** pyramid, rising imposingly yet gracefully from the surrounding plain, has been known to produce goose pimples on sight. El Castillo (The Castle) dominates the site both in size and in the sym-

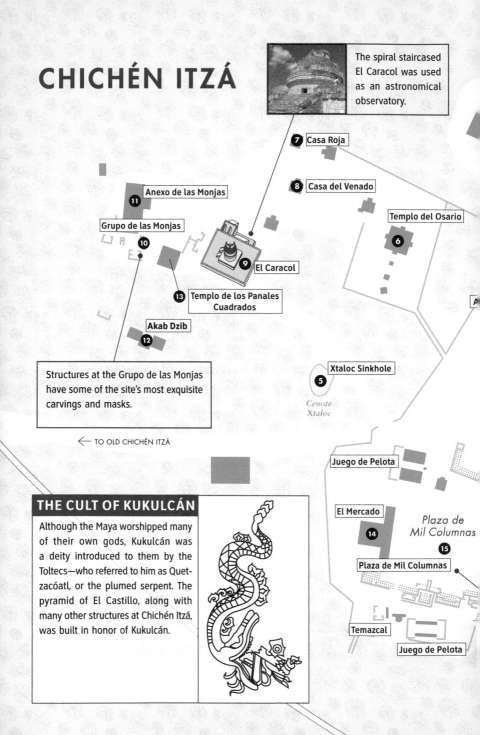

CHICHÉN ITZÁ

The spiral staircased El Caracol was used as an astronomical observatory.

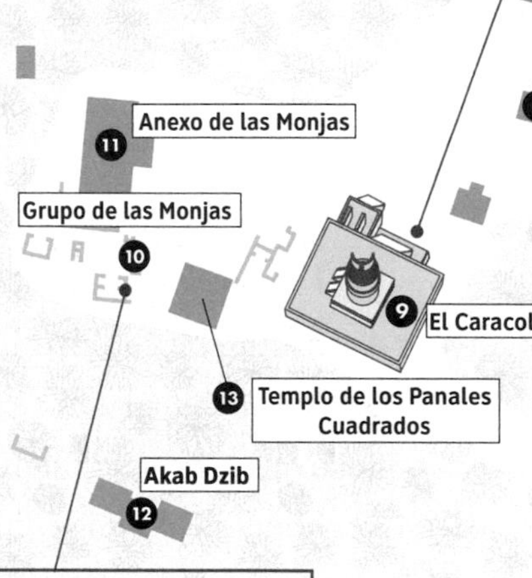

Structures at the Grupo de las Monjas have some of the site's most exquisite carvings and masks.

← TO OLD CHICHÉN ITZÁ

THE CULT OF KUKULCÁN

Although the Maya worshipped many of their own gods, Kukulcán was a deity introduced to them by the Toltecs—who referred to him as Quetzacóatl, or the plumed serpent. The pyramid of El Castillo, along with many other structures at Chichén Itzá, was built in honor of Kukulcán.

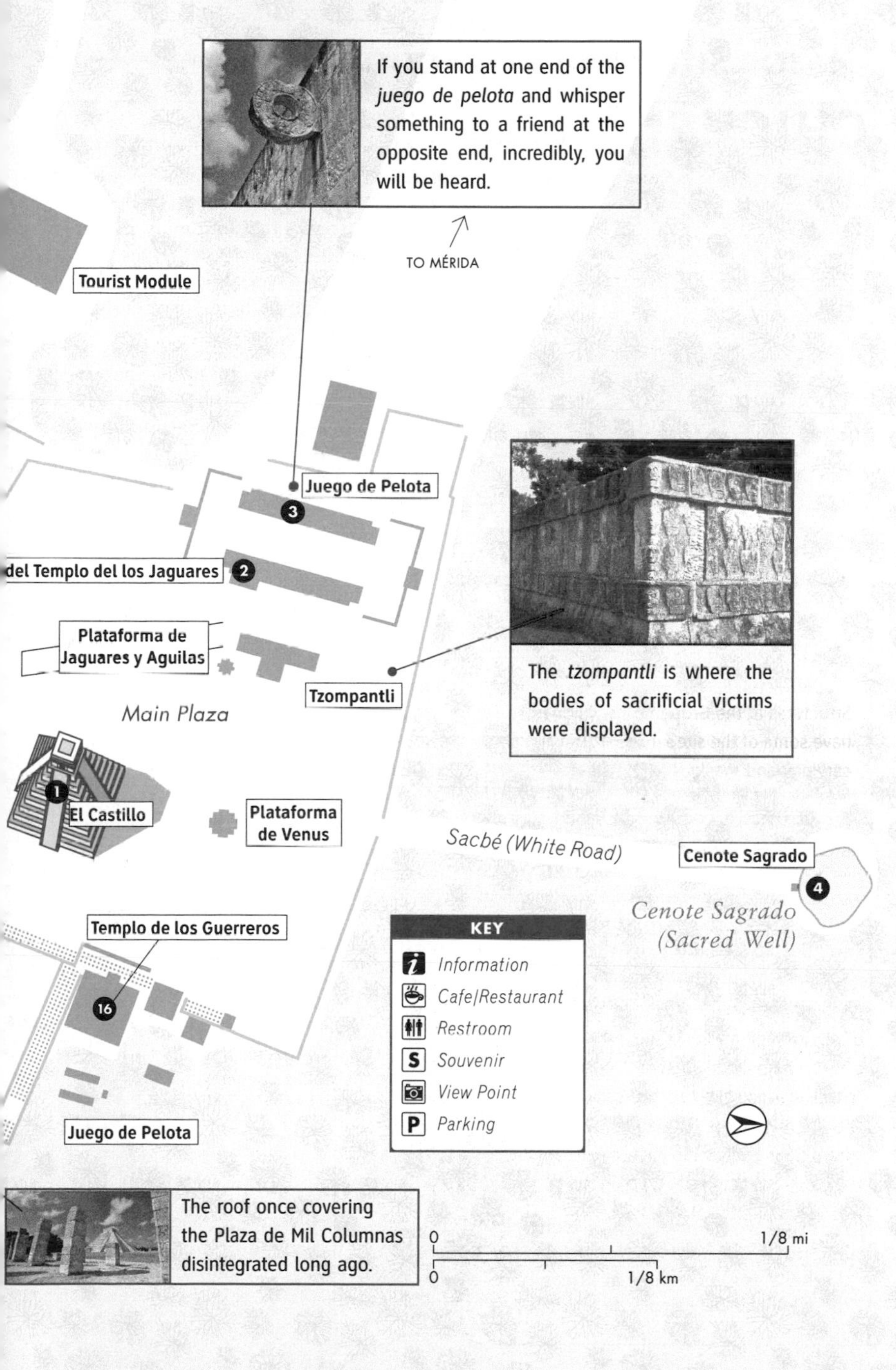
If you stand at one end of the *juego de pelota* and whisper something to a friend at the opposite end, incredibly, you will be heard.
TO MÉRIDA
Tourist Module
Juego de Pelota
3
del Templo del los Jaguares
2
Plataforma de Jaguares y Aguilas
Tzompantli
The *tzompantli* is where the bodies of sacrificial victims were displayed.
Main Plaza
1
El Castillo
Plataforma de Venus
Sacbé (White Road)
Cenote Sagrado
4
Cenote Sagrado (Sacred Well)
Templo de los Guerreros
16
KEY
Information
Cafe/Restaurant
Restroom
Souvenir
View Point
Parking
Juego de Pelota
The roof once covering the Plaza de Mil Columnas disintegrated long ago.
0
1/8 mi
0
1/8 km

MAJOR SITES AND ATTRACTIONS

Rows of freestanding columns at the site have a strangely Greek look.

metry of its perfect proportions. Open-jawed serpent statues adorn the corners of each of the pyramid's four stairways, honoring the legendary priest-king Kukulcán (also known as Quetzalcóatl), an incarnation of the feathered serpent god. More serpents appear at the top of the building as sculpted columns. At the spring and fall equinoxes, the afternoon light strikes the trapezoidal structure so that the shadow of the snake-god appears to undulate down the side of the pyramid to bless the fertile earth. Thousands of people travel to the site each year to see this phenomenon.

At the base of the temple on the north side, an interior staircase leads to two marvelous statues deep within: a stone jaguar, and the intermediate god Chacmool. As usual, Chacmool is in a reclining position, with a flat spot on the belly for receiving sacrifices. On the **❷Anexo del Templo de los Jaguares** (Annex to the Temple of the Jaguars), just west of El Castillo, bas-relief carvings represent more important deities. On the bottom of the columns is the rain god Tlaloc. It's no surprise that his tears represent rain—but why is the Toltec god Tlaloc honored here, instead of the Maya rain god, Chaac?

That's one of many questions that archaeologists and epigraphers have been trying to answer, ever since John Lloyd Stephens and Frederick Catherwood, the first English-speaking explorers to discover the site, first hacked their way through the surrounding forest in 1840. Scholars once thought that the symbols of foreign gods and differing architectural styles at Chichén Itzá proved it was conquered by the Toltecs of central Mexico. (As well as representations of Tlaloc, the site also has a *tzompantli*—a stone platform decorated with row upon row of sculpted human skulls, which is a distinctively Toltec-style structure.) Most experts now agree, however, that Chichén Itzá was only influenced—not conquered—by Toltec trading partners from the north.

Just west of the Anexo del Templo de los Jaguares is another puzzle: the auditory marvel of Chichén Itzá's main ball court. At 490 feet, this **❸ Juego de Pelota**

The flat part of a reclining Chacmool statue is where sacrificial offerings were laid.

Although the rules of the game that were played on the ball court aren't known, it's thought that players had to pass some sort of ball through high stone loops.

The walls of the ball field are intricately carved.

is the largest in Mesoamerica. Yet if you stand at one end of the playing field and whisper something to a friend at the other end, incredibly, you will be heard. The game played on this ball court was apparently something like soccer (no hands were used), but it likely had some sort of ritualistic significance. Carvings on the low walls surrounding the field show a decapitation, blood spurting from the victim's neck to fertilize the earth. Whether this is a historical depiction (perhaps the losers or winners of the game were sacrificed?) or a symbolic scene, we can only guess.

On the other side of El Castillo, just before a small temple dedicated to the planet Venus, a ruined *sacbé,* or white road leads to the ❹ **Cenote Sagrado** (Holy Well, or Sinkhole), which was also probably used for ritualistic purposes. Jacques Cousteau and his companions recovered about 80 skeletons from this deep, straight-sided, subsurface pond, as well as thousands of pieces of jewelry and figures of jade, obsidian, wood, bone, and turquoise. In direct alignment with this cloudy green cenote, on the other side of El Castillo, the ❺**Xtaloc sinkhole** was kept pristine, undoubtedly for bathing and drinking. Adjacent to this water source

TIPS

To get more in-depth information about the ruins, hire a multilingual guide at the ticket booth. Guides charge about $35 for a group of up to 7 people. Tours generally last about two hours. ***$9.80*** **Ruins daily 8–5, museum Tues.–Sun. 9–4.**

is a steam bath, its interior lined with benches along the wall like those you'd see in any steam room today. Outside, a tiny pool was used for cooling down during the ritual.

The older Mayan structures at Chichén Itzá are south and west of Cenote Xtaloc. Archaeologists have been restoring several buildings in this area, including the ❻ **Templo del Osario** (Ossuary Temple), which, as its name implies, concealed several tombs with skeletons and offerings. Behind the smaller ❼ **Casa Roja** (Red House) and ❽ **Casa del Venado** (House of the Deer) are the site's oldest structures, including ❾ **El Caracol** (The Snail), one of the few round buildings built by the Maya, with a spiral staircase within. Clearly built as a celestial observatory, it has eight tiny windows precisely aligned with the points of the compass rose. Scholars now know that Maya priests studied the planets and the stars; in fact, they were able to accurately predict the orbits of Venus and the moon, and the appearance of comets and eclipses. To modern astronomers, this is nothing short of amazing.

The Maya of Chichén Itzá were not just scholars, however. They were skilled artisans and architects as well. South of El Caracol, the ❿ **Grupo de las Monjas** (The Nunnery complex) has some of the site's most exquisite façades. A combination of Puuc and Chenes styles dominates here, with playful latticework, masks, and gargoylelike serpents. On the east side of the ⓫ **Anexo de las Monjas** (Nunnery Annex), the Chenes facade celebrates the rain god Chaac. In typical style, the doorway represents an entrance into the underworld; figures of Chaac decorate the ornate façade above.

The doorway of the Anexo de las Monjas represents an entrance to the underworld.

South of the Nunnery Complex is an area where field archaeologists are still excavating (fewer than a quarter of the structures at Chichén Itzá have been fully restored). If you have more than a superficial interest in the site—and can convince the authorities ahead of time of your importance, or at least your interest in archaeology—you can explore this area, which is generally not open to the public. Otherwise, head back toward El Castillo past the ruins of a housing compound called ⓬ **Akab Dzib** and the ⓭ **Templo de los Panales Cuadrados** (Temple of the Square Panels). The latter of these buildings shows more evidence of Toltec influence: instead of weight-bearing Mayan arches—or "false arches"—that traditionally supported stone roofs, this structure has stone columns but no roof. This means that the building was once roofed, Toltec-style, with perishable materials (most likely palm thatch or wood) that have long since disintegrated.

Beyond El Caracol, Casa Roja, and El Osario, the right-hand path follows an ancient sacbé, now collapsed. A mud-and-straw hut, which the Maya called a **na,** has been reproduced here to show the simple implements used before and after the Spanish conquest. On one side of the room are a typical pre-Hispanic table, seat, fire pit, and reed baskets; on the other, the Christian cross and colonial-style table of the post-conquest Maya.

Behind the tiny oval house, several unexcavated mounds still guard their secrets. The path meanders through a small grove of oak and slender bean trees to the building known today as ⓮ **El Mercado.** This market was likely one end of a huge outdoor market whose counterpart structure, on the other side of the grove, is the ⓯ **Plaza de Mil Columnas.** (Plaza of the Thousand Columns). In typical Toltec-Maya style, the roof once covering the parallel rows of round stone columns in this long arcade has disappeared, giving the place a strangely Greek—and distinctly non-Maya—look. But the curvy-nosed Chaacs on the corners of the adjacent ⓰ **Templo de los Guerreros** are pure Maya. Why their noses are pointing down, like an upside-down "U, " instead of up, as usual, is just another mystery to be solved.

The Templo de los Guerreros shows the influence of Toltec architecture.

WHERE TO STAY AT CHICHÉN ITZÁ

★ **$$$–$$$$** **Mayaland.** This charming property is in a large garden, and close enough to the ruins to have its own entrance (you can even see some of the older structures from the windows). The large number of tour groups that come here, however, will make it less appealing if you're looking for privacy. Colonial-style guest rooms have decorative tiles; ask for one with a balcony, which doesn't cost extra. Bungalows have thatched roofs as well as wide verandas with hammocks. The simple Maya-inspired "huts" near the front of the property, built in the 1930s, are the cheapest option, but are for groups only. ✉ *Carretera 180, Km 120* ☎ *985/851–0100 or 800/235–4079* 📠 *985/851–0128* ☎📠 *985/851–0129* 🌐 *www.mayaland.com* *60 bungalows, 30 rooms, 10 suites* *4 restaurants, room service, bars, tennis court, pools, laundry service, parking (free), no-smoking rooms* 💳 *AE, D, MC, V.*

★ Fodor's Choice **$$$** **Hacienda Chichén.** A converted 16th-century hacienda with its own entrance to the ruins, this hotel once served as the headquarters for the Carnegie expedition to Chichén Itzá. Rustic-chic, soap-scented cotes are simply but beautifully furnished in colonial Yucatecan style, with bedspreads and dehumidifiers; all of the ground-floor rooms have verandas, but only master suites have hammocks. There's a satellite TV in the library. An enormous (and deep) old pool graces the gardens. Meals are served on the patio overlooking the grounds, or in the air-conditioned restaurant. A big plus is the hotel's intimate size; it's a place for honeymoons and silver anniversaries, not tour groups. ✉ *Carretera 180, Km 120* ☎ *985/851–0045, 999/924–2150 reservations, 877/631–4005* ☎📠 *999/924–5011* 🌐 *www.haciendachichen.com* *24 rooms, 4 suites* *In-room: no phone, no TV. In-hotel: 2 restaurants, bar, pool, laundry service, parking (free), no-smoking rooms* 💳 *AE, DC, MC, V.*

LABNÁ

9 km (5½ mi) south of Sayil on Carretera 31 E.

The striking monumental structure at Labná (which means "old house" or "abandoned house") is a fanciful corbeled arch (also called the Mayan arch, or false arch), with elaborate latticework and a small chamber on each side. One theory says the arch was the entrance to an area where religious ceremonies were staged. The site was used mainly by the military elite and royalty. *$3.50 Daily 8–5.*

GRUTAS DE LOLTÚN

19 km (12 mi) northeast of Labná.

★ The Loltún ("stone flower" in Mayan) is one of the largest and most fascinating cave systems on the Yucatán Peninsula. Long ago, Mayan ceremonies were routinely held inside these mysterious caves, artifacts found inside date as far back as 800 BC. The topography of the caves themselves is fascinating: there are stalactites, stalagmites, and limestone formations known by such names as Ear of Corn and Cathedral. Illuminated pathways meander a little over a kilometer through the caverns, most of which are quite spacious and well ventilated (claustrophobics needn't worry). Nine different openings allow air and some (but not much) light to filter in. **■ TIP→ You can enter only with a guide. Although these guides were once paid a small salary, they are now forced to work for tips only—so be generous.** Scheduled tours are at 9:30, 12:30, 3, and 4 (in Spanish), and 11 and 2 (in English). *$6.70, parking $1 Daily 9–5.*

UNDERSTANDING MEXICO

Chronology

Vocabulary

CHRONOLOGY

PRE-COLUMBIAN MEXICO

ca. 40,000 BC Asian nomads cross land bridge over the Bering Strait to North America, gradually migrate south.

ca. 7000 BC–**2000** BC Archaic period, which marked the beginnings of agriculture and village life.

ca. 2000 BC–AD **100** Formative or Preclassic period: development of pottery, incipient political structures. (The late Preclassic period runs from 400 BC to AD 100.)

500 BC–**900** BC The powerful and sophisticated Olmec civilization develops primarily along the Gulf of Mexico in the present-day states of Veracruz and Tabasco. Olmec culture, the "mother culture" of Mexico, flourishes along Gulf Coast.

AD **100**–AD **1000** Classic period: height of Mesoamerican culture. Totonac-speaking people build the city of Teotihuacán (near Mexico City); the powerful and cultured Zapotec rule in Oaxaca, and the Maya advance math and astronomy in the Yucatán. Ruling dynasties produce impressive art and architecture; powerful priests perform elaborate ceremonies based on their interpretation of signs and celestial events. (The Late Classic period runs from 800 to 1000.)

650–900 Fall of Teotihuacán circa 650 leads to competition among other city-states, exacerbated by migrations of tribes from the harsh northern deserts.

ca. 900–1150 The Toltec, a northern tribe, establish a flourishing culture at their capital of Tula under the legendary monarch Topiltzin-Quetzalcóatl.

1000–1521 Postclassic period: with the decline of the monarchy, rule passes to tribal councils. Cultural achievements wane; many once-flourishing cities have by now been abandoned.

1111 The unlettered Aztecs migrate to mainland from island home off the Nayarit coast. They are not welcomed by the peoples of central Mexico.

ca. 1200 Rise of Mixtec culture at Zapotec sites of Monte Albán and Mitla; notable for production of picture codices, which include historical narratives.

1150–1350 Following the fall of Tula, the Chichimec and then the Tepanec assert hegemony over central Mexico. The Tepanec tyrant Tezozómoc (1320–1426), like his contemporaries in Renaissance Italy, establishes his power with murder and treachery.

1320 The Aztec city of Tenochtitlán is built in the middle of Lake Texcoco.

1420–1519 Aztecs extend their rule to much of central and southern Mexico. A warrior society, they build a great city at Tenochtitlán.

1502 Moctezuma II (1502–20) assumes throne at the height of Aztec culture and political power.

1517 Spanish expedition under Francisco Hernandez de Córdoba (1475–1526) lands on Yucatán coast.

1519 Hernán Cortés (1485–1547) lands in Cozumel, founds Veracruz, and is determined to conquer. Steel weapons, horses, and smallpox, combined with a belief that Cortés was the resurrected god Quetzalcóatl, minimize Aztec resistance. Cortés and his men stay for months as somewhat captive guests at Tenochtitlán before taking Moctezuma hostage.

THE COLONIAL PERIOD

1521 Tenochtitlán falls to Cortés after Moctezuma is killed in 1520. The last Aztec emperor, Cuauhtémoc, is tortured to reveal hidden gold; he doesn't, and is later executed.

1528 Juan de Zumárraga (1468–1548) arrives as bishop of Mexico City, gains title "Protector of the Indians"; conversions to Catholicism increase.

1535 First Spanish viceroy arrives in Mexico.

1537 Pope Paul III issues a papal bull declaring that Mesoamerica's indigenous people are indeed human and not beasts. First printing press arrives in Mexico City.

1546–48 Silver deposits discovered at Zacatecas.

1547 Spanish conquest of Aztec Empire—now known as "New Spain"—completed, at enormous cost to native peoples.

1553 Royal and Pontifical University of Mexico, first university in the New World, opens.

1571 The Spanish Inquisition established in New Spain; it is not abolished until 1820.

1609 Northern capital of New Spain established at Santa Fe (New Mexico).

1651 Birth of Sor (Sister) Juana Inés de la Cruz, greatest poet of colonial Mexico (d. 1695).

1718 Franciscan missionaries settle in Texas, which becomes part of New Spain.

1765 Charles III of Spain (1716–88) sends José de Galvez to tour New Spain and propose reforms.

1769 Franciscan Junípero Serra establishes missions in present-day California, extending Spanish hegemony.

1788 Death of Charles III; his reforms improve administration, but also raise social and political expectations among the colonial population that are not fulfilled.

1808 Napoléon invades Spain, leaving a power vacuum in New Spain.

THE WAR OF INDEPENDENCE

1810 September 16: Father Miguel Hidalgo y Costilla (1753–1811) and co-conspirators launch the War of Independence against the Spanish crown.

1811 Hidalgo is captured and executed; leadership of the movement passes to Father José María Morelos y Pavón (1765–1815).

1813 Morelos calls a congress at Chilpancingo, which drafts a Declaration of Independence.

1815 Morelos is captured and executed.

THE EARLY NATIONAL PERIOD

1821 Vicente Guerrero, a rebel leader, and Agustín de Iturbide (1783–1824), a Spanish colonel, sign a peace accord, rejuvenating the independence movement. Spain soon recognizes Mexican independence with the Treaty of Córdoba.

1822 Agustín de Iturbide is named Emperor of Mexico, which stretches from California to Central America.

1823 After 10 months in office, de Iturbide is turned out.

1824 A new constitution creates a federal republic, the Estados Unidos Mexicanos; modeled on the U.S. Constitution, the Mexican version retains the privileges of the Catholic Church and gives the president extraordinary "emergency" powers.

1829 President Vicente Guerrero abolishes slavery. A Spanish attempt at reconquest is halted by General Antonio López de Santa Anna (1794–1876), already a hero for his role in the overthrow of de Iturbide.

1833 Santa Anna is elected president by a huge majority; by 1855, he has held the office for 11 of its 36 changes of hands.

1836 Although voted in as a liberal, Santa Anna abolishes the 1824 constitution. Already dismayed at the abolition of slavery, Texas—whose population is largely American—declares its independence. Santa Anna successfully besieges the Texans at the Alamo. But a month later he is captured by Sam Houston following the Battle of San Jacinto. Texas gains its independence as the Lone Star Republic.

1846 The U.S. decision to annex Texas leads to war.

1848 The treaty of Guadalupe Hidalgo reduces Mexico's territory by half, ceding present-day Texas, New Mexico, Arizona, California, Nevada, Utah, and part of Colorado to the United States.

1853 Santa Anna agrees to the Gadsden Purchase, ceding a further 48,000 square km (18,500 square mi) to the United States.

THE REFORM AND FRENCH INTERVENTION

1855 The Revolution of Ayutla topples Santa Anna and leads to the period of the Reform.

1857 The liberal Constitution of 1857 disestablishes the Catholic Church, among other measures.

1858–61 The Civil War of the Reform ends in liberal victory. Benito Juárez (1806–72) is elected president. France, Spain, and Britain agree jointly to occupy the customhouse at Veracruz to force payment of Mexico's huge foreign debt.

1862 Spain and Britain withdraw their forces; the French, seeking empire, march inland. On May 5 General Porfirio Díaz repulses the French at Puebla.

1863 Strengthened with reinforcements, the French occupy Mexico City. Napoléon III of France appoints Archduke Ferdinand Maximilian of Austria (1832–67) as Emperor of Mexico.

1864 Maximilian and his empress, Charlotte, known as Carlotta, land at Veracruz.

1867 With U.S. assistance, Juárez overthrows Mexico's second empire. Maximilian is executed; Carlotta, pleading his case at the Vatican, goes mad.

1872 Juárez dies in office. The Mexico City–Veracruz railway is completed, symbol of the new progressivist mood.

THE PORFIRIATO

1876 Porfirio Díaz (1830–1915) comes to power in the revolution of Tuxtepec; he holds office nearly continuously until 1911. With his advisers, the *cientificos,* he forces modernization and balances the budget for the first time in Mexican history. But the social cost is high.

1886 Birth of artist Diego Rivera (d. 1957).

1890 José Schneider, who is of German ancestry, founds the Cerveceria Cuauhtémoc, brewer of Carta Blanca beer.

1900 Jesús, Enrique, and Ricardo Flores Magón publish the anti-Díaz newspaper *La Regeneración.* Suppressed, the brothers move their campaign to the United States, first to San Antonio, then to St. Louis.

1906 The Flores Magón group publish their Liberal Plan, a proposal for reform. Industrial unrest spreads.

THE SECOND REVOLUTION

1907 Birth of the renowned painter Frida Kahlo (d. 1954).

1910 On the centennial of the Revolution, Díaz wins yet another rigged election. Encouraged by Francisco Madero's campaigning and publications, revolt breaks out.

1911 Rebels under Pascual Orozco and Francisco (Pancho) Villa (1878–1923) capture Ciudad Juárez; Díaz resigns. Francisco Madero is elected president; calling for land reform, Emiliano Zapata (1879–1919) rejects the new regime. Violence continues.

1913 Military coup: Madero is deposed and murdered. In one day Mexico has three presidents, the last being General Victoriano Huerta (1854–1916). Civil war rages.

1914 American intervention leads to dictator Huerta's overthrow. Villa and Zapata briefly join forces at the Convention of Aguascalientes, but the revolution goes on. Birth of poet-critic Octavio Paz.

1916 Villa's border raids lead to an American punitive expedition under Pershing. Villa eludes capture.

1917 Under a new constitution, Venustiano Carranza, head of the Constitutionalist Army, is elected president. Zapata continues his rebellion, which is brutally suppressed.

1918 CROM, the national labor union, is founded.

1919 On order of Carranza, Zapata is assassinated.

1920 Carranza is assassinated; Alvaro Obregón (1880–1928), who helped overthrow dictator Huerta in 1914, is elected president, beginning a period of reform and reconstruction. Schools are built and land is redistributed. In the next two decades, revolutionary culture finds expression in the art of Diego Rivera and José Clemente Orozco (1883–1949), the novels of Martin Luis Guzmán and Gregorio López y Fuentes, and the music of Carlos Chávez (1899–1978).

1923 Pancho Villa is assassinated. The United States finally recognizes the Obregón regime.

1926–28 Catholics react to government anticlericalism in the Cristero Rebellion.

1934–40 The presidency of Lázaro Cárdenas (1895–1970) leads to the fullest implementation of revolutionary reforms.

1938 Cárdenas nationalizes the oil companies, removing them from foreign control.

1940 On August 20, exiled former Soviet leader Leon Trotsky is murdered in his Mexico City home.

POSTREVOLUTIONARY MEXICO

1951 Mexico's segment of the Pan-American Highway is completed, confirming the industrial growth and prosperity of postwar Mexico. Culture is increasingly Americanized; writers such as Octavio Paz and Carlos Fuentes express disillusionment with the post-revolution world.

1968 The Summer Olympics in Mexico City showcase Mexican prosperity, but hundreds of student activists are murdered or jailed during a massive demonstration. The government denies and suppresses this information.

1981–82 Recession and a drop in oil prices severely damage Mexico's economy. The peso is devalued.

1985 Thousands die in the Mexico City earthquake.

1988 American-educated economist Carlos Salinas de Gortari is elected president; for the first time since 1940, support for the PRI, the national political party, seems to be slipping.

1993 North American Free Trade Agreement (NAFTA) is signed with United States and Canada.

1994 Uprising by the indigenous peoples of Chiapas, led by the Zapatista National Liberation Army and their charismatic ski-masked leader, Subcomandante Marcos; election reforms promised as a result. Popular PRI presidential candidate Luis Donaldo Colosio assassinated while campaigning in Tijuana. Ernesto Zedillo, generally thought to be more of a technocrat and "old boy" PRI politician, replaces him and wins the election. Zedillo, blaming the economic policies of his predecessor, devalues the peso in December.

1995 Recession sets in as a result of the peso devaluation. Ex-President Carlos Salinas de Gortari is linked to scandals surrounding the assassinations of Colosio and another high-ranking government official; Salinas moves to the United States.

1996 Mexico's economy, bolstered by a $28 billion bailout program led by the United States, turns upward, but the recovery is fragile. The opposition National Action Party (PAN), which is committed to conservative economic policies, gains strength. New details of scandals of the former administration continue to emerge.

1997 Mexico's top antidrug official is arrested on bribery charges. Nonetheless, the United States recertifies Mexico as a partner in the war on drugs. The Zedillo administration faces midterm party elections.

1998 Death of Octavio Paz.

1999 Raúl Salinas, brother of the former president Carlos Salinas de Gortari, sentenced to prison for the murder of a PRI leader.

2000 Spurning the long-ruling PRI, Mexicans elect opposition candidate Vicente Fox president.

2001 U.S.-Mexico relations take on increased importance as Fox meets repeatedly with George W. Bush to discuss immigration reform and economic programs. President Fox frees imprisoned Zapatista rebel sympathizers and signs into law a controversial Indian rights bill in hopes of bringing peace to southern Chiapas state; however, peace talks remain stalled. Human-rights attorney Digna Ochoa is assassinated, opening the country to accusations of failing to investigate human-rights abuses by the military and police. The case is unsolved.

2002 Under President Fox's orders, the federal Human Rights Commission investigates and confirms that hundreds of people, most suspected leftist rebels, disappeared at the hands of the state after being arrested in the 1960s, '70s, and '80s. Fox also signs into law a freedom of information act and releases nearly 80 million secret intelligence files collected by the government.

2003 High hopes for NAFTA erode as hundreds of factories relocate from Mexico to the Far East, where labor is even cheaper.

2004 In his autobiography *Change of Course,* former president Miguel de la Madrid admits that the government rigged the 1988 presidential election in favor of PRI candidate Carlos Salinas de Gortari and that opposition candidate Cuauhtémoc Cárdenas, son of agrarian reformist Lázaro Cárdenas, was likely to win according to an early count of electronic ballots.

2005 During state elections in February, residents of Guerrero vote in the PRD's favor, dealing a blow to the PRI party, which had been making steady progress since its momentous defeat with the election of President Fox in 2000. Left-wing Mexico City mayor Andrés Manuel López Obrador, a 2006 presidential front-runner, loses his immunity from prosecution by order of congress. The PRD-affiliated mayor faces charges because of a building violation, though he claims it is purely political scheming. The scandal sends Mexico's stock market down 14%.

2006 This is a landmark year for discussions about Mexico–U.S. border security, as well as illegal-immigrant status in the United States. Many people view the issue of closing off the border as a hypocritical move, considering the dependency of the U.S. economy on illegal workers. Others believe that securing the border may help illegal immigrants already in the United States obtain legal status, and also create a more organized system for future immigrants.

2007 Left-wing presidential candidate Andres Manuel Lopez Obrador is defeated by less than one percentage point by Felipe Calderón of the governing National Action Party (PAN). Widespread protests and political unrest ensue. Picturesque Oaxaca City is the site of months-long protests instigated by a teachers' union. Protesters seeking higher wages and the ouster of the state governor take hold of the downtown area of the city, with riot police eventually using drastic tactics to break up the protest. Though the city is calmer and recuperating, lack of tourism to this part of the country is a huge blow to the local economy, while the national economy enjoys great stability.

President Bush visits Mexico in early spring for bilateral talks with President Calderón. Having failed to act on his promise of allowing more guest workers, and for entertaining the idea of constructing a large wall between the United States and Mexico, Bush is met with considerable hostility.

2008 Gang-related violence escalates on both sides of the U.S.-Mexican border, with the fatality count reaching into the thousands by year's end.

2009 In April, U.S. President Barack Obama and President Calderón meet to discuss ways to curb gang violence on both sides of the border. Late April also sees outbreaks of H1N1 influenza (Swine flu), with Mexico City as the epicenter. By late May the U.S. Centers for Disease Control have downgraded the threat level of H1N1 and Mexico scrambles to attract travelers.

2010 This year marks the dual anniversary of the Mexican bicentennial and centennial. September 15 is the 200-year anniversary of the beginning of the independence movement from Spain. The Mexican Revolution began 100 years later on November 20. In August of this year, the World Health Organization declares the H1N1 pandemic officially over.

2012 The end of the universe, at least according to the Mayans. On December 21, 2012 the Maya long-count calendar reaches the end of its cycle and a new one begins . . . hopefully.

SPANISH VOCABULARY

	ENGLISH	SPANISH	PRONUNCIATION
BASICS			
	Yes/no	Sí/no	see/no
	Please	Por favor	pore fah-**vore**
	May I?	¿Me permite?	may pair-**mee**-tay
	Thank you (very much)	(Muchas) gracias	(**moo**-chas) **grah**-see-as
	You're welcome	De nada	day **nah**-dah
	Excuse me	Con permiso	con pair-**mee**-so
	Pardon me	¿Perdón?	pair-**dohn**
	Could you tell me?	¿Podría decirme?	po-dree-ah deh-**seer**-meh
	I'm sorry	Lo siento	lo see-**en**-toh
	Good morning!	¡Buenos días!	**bway**-nohs **dee**-ahs
	Good afternoon!	¡Buenas tardes!	**bway**-nahs **tar**-dess
	Good evening!	¡Buenas noches!	**bway**-nahs **no**-chess
	Good-bye!	¡Adiós!/¡Hasta luego!	ah-dee-**ohss/ah** -stah **lwe**-go
	Mr./Mrs.	Señor/Señora	sen-**yor**/sen-**yohr**-ah
	Miss	Señorita	sen-yo-**ree**-tah
	Pleased to meet you	Mucho gusto	**moo**-cho **goose**-toh
	How are you?	¿Cómo está usted?	**ko**-mo es-**tah** oo-**sted**
	Very well, thank you.	Muy bien, gracias.	**moo**-ee bee-**en**, **grah**-see-as
	And you?	¿Y usted?	ee oos-**ted**
	Hello (on the telephone)	Diga	**dee**-gah
NUMBERS			
	1	un, uno	oon, **oo**-no
	2	dos	dos
	3	tres	tress
	4	cuatro	**kwah**-tro
	5	cinco	**sink**-oh

ENGLISH	SPANISH	PRONUNCIATION
6	seis	saice
7	siete	see-**et**-eh
8	ocho	**o**-cho
9	nueve	new-**eh**-vey
10	diez	dee-**es**
11	once	**ohn**-seh
12	doce	**doh**-seh
13	trece	**treh**-seh
14	catorce	ka-**tohr**-seh
15	quince	**keen**-seh
16	dieciséis	dee-**es**-ee-**saice**
17	diecisiete	dee-**es**-ee-see-**et**-eh
18	dieciocho	dee-**es**-ee-**o**-cho
19	diecinueve	**dee-es**-ee-new-**ev**-eh
20	veinte	**vain**-teh
21	veinte y uno/ veintiuno	**vain**-te-**oo**-noh
30	treinta	**train**-tah
32	treinta y dos	train-tay-**dohs**
40	cuarenta	kwah-**ren**-tah
43	cuarenta y tres	kwah-**ren**-tay-**tress**
50	cincuenta	seen-**kwen**-tah
54	cincuenta y cuatro	seen-**kwen**-tay **kwah**-tro
60	sesenta	sess-**en**-tah
65	sesenta y cinco	sess-**en**-tay **seen**-ko
70	setenta	set-**en**-tah
76	setenta y seis	set-**en**-tay **saice**
80	ochenta	oh-**chen**-tah
87	ochenta y siete	oh-**chen**-tay see-**yet**-eh
90	noventa	no-**ven**-tah

ENGLISH	SPANISH	PRONUNCIATION
98	noventa y ocho	no-**ven**-tah-**o**-choh
100	cien	see-**en**
101	ciento uno	see-**en**-toh **oo**-noh
200	doscientos	doh-see-**en**-tohss
500	quinientos	keen-**yen**-tohss
700	setecientos	set-eh-see-**en**-tohss
900	novecientos	no-veh-see-**en**-tohss
1,000	mil	meel
2,000	dos mil	dohs meel
1,000,000	un millón	oon meel-**yohn**

COLORS

ENGLISH	SPANISH	PRONUNCIATION
black	negro	**neh**-groh
blue	azul	ah-**sool**
brown	café	kah-**feh**
green	verde	**ver**-deh
pink	rosa	**ro**-sah
purple	morado	mo-**rah**-doh
orange	naranja	na-**rahn**-hah
red	rojo	**roh**-hoh
white	blanco	**blahn**-koh
yellow	amarillo	ah-mah-**ree**-yoh

DAYS OF THE WEEK

ENGLISH	SPANISH	PRONUNCIATION
Sunday	domingo	doe-**meen**-goh
Monday	lunes	**loo**-ness
Tuesday	martes	**mahr**-tess
Wednesday	miércoles	me-**air**-koh-less
Thursday	jueves	hoo-**ev**-ess
Friday	viernes	vee-**air**-ness
Saturday	sábado	**sah**-bah-doh

	ENGLISH	SPANISH	PRONUNCIATION
MONTHS			
	January	enero	eh-**neh**-roh
	February	febrero	feh-**breh**-roh
	March	marzo	**mahr**-soh
	April	abril	ah-**breel**
	May	mayo	**my**-oh
	June	junio	**hoo**-nee-oh
	July	julio	**hoo**-lee-yoh
	August	agosto	ah-**ghost**-toh
	September	septiembre	sep-tee-**em**-breh
	October	octubre	oak-**too**-breh
	November	noviembre	no-vee-**em**-breh
	December	diciembre	dee-see-**em**-breh
USEFUL PHRASES			
	Do you speak English?	¿Habla usted inglés?	**ah**-blah oos-**ted** in-**glehs**
	I don't speak Spanish	No hablo español	no **ah**-bloh es-pahn-**yol**
	I don't understand (you)	No entiendo	no en-tee-**en**-doh
	I understand (you)	Entiendo	en-tee-**en**-doh
	I don't know	No sé	no seh
	I am American/ British	Soy americano (americana)/inglés(a)	soy ah-meh-ree- **kah**-no (ah-meh-ree- **kah**-nah)/in-**glehs(ah)**
	What's your name?	¿Cómo se llama usted?	koh-mo seh **yah**-mah oos-**ted**
	My name is . . .	Me llamo . . .	may **yah**-moh
	What time is it?	¿Qué hora es?	keh **o**-rah es
	It is one, two, three . . . o'clock.	Es la una./Son las dos, tres . . .	es la **oo**-nah/sohnahs dohs, tress
	Yes, please/No, thank you	Sí, por favor/No, gracias	**see** pohr fah-**vor**/no **grah**-see-us
	How?	¿Cómo?	**koh**-mo

ENGLISH	SPANISH	PRONUNCIATION
When?	¿Cuándo?	**kwahn**-doh
This/Next week	Esta semana/ la semana que entra	**es**-teh seh-**mah**- nah/ lah seh-**mah**-nah keh **en**-trah
This/Next month	Este mes/el próximo mes	**es**-teh mehs/el **proke**-see-mo mehs
This/Next year	Este año/el año que viene	**es**-teh **ahn**-yo/el **ahn**-yo keh vee-**yen**-ay
Yesterday/today/ tomorrow	Ayer/hoy/mañana	ah-**yehr**/oy/mahn-**yah**-nah
This morning/ afternoon	Esta mañana/ tarde	**es**-tah mahn-**yah**- nah/ **tar**-deh
Tonight	Esta noche	**es**-tah **no**-cheh
What?	¿Qué?	keh
What is it?	¿Qué es esto?	keh es **es**-toh
Why?	¿Por qué?	pore **keh**
Who?	¿Quién?	kee-**yen**
Where is . . . ?	¿Dónde está . . . ?	**dohn**-deh es-**tah**
the train station?	la estación del tren?	la es-tah-see-on del trehn
the subway station?	la estación del tren subterráneo?	la es-ta-see-**on** del trehn la es-ta-see-**on** soob-teh-**rrahn**-eh-oh
the bus stop?	la parada del autobus?	la pah-**rah**-dah del ow-toh-**boos**
the post office?	la oficina de correos?	la oh-fee-**see**- nah deh koh-**rreh**-os
the bank?	el banco?	el **bahn**-koh
the hotel?	el hotel?	el oh-**tel**
the store?	la tienda?	la tee-**en**-dah
the cashier?	la caja?	la **kah**-hah
the museum?	el museo?	el moo-**seh**-oh
the hospital?	el hospital?	el ohss-pee-**tal**
the elevator?	el ascensor?	el ah-**sen**-sohr
the bathroom?	el baño?	el **bahn**-yoh

ENGLISH	SPANISH	PRONUNCIATION
Here/there	Aquí/allá	ah-**key**/ah-**yah**
Open/closed	Abierto/cerrado	ah-bee-**er**-toh/ ser-**ah**-doh
Left/right	Izquierda/derecha	iss-key-**er**-dah/ dare-**eh**-chah
Straight ahead	Derecho	dare-**eh**-choh
Is it near/far?	¿Está cerca/lejos?	es-**tah** **sehr**-kah/ **leh**-hoss
I'd like . . .	Quisiera . . .	kee-see-ehr-ah
a room	un cuarto/una habitación	oon **kwahr**-toh/ **oo**-nah ah-bee- tah-see-**on**
the key	la llave	lah **yah**-veh
a newspaper	un periódico	oon pehr-ee-**oh**- dee-koh
a stamp	un sello de correo	oon **seh**-yo deh korr-ee-oh
I'd like to buy . . .	Quisiera comprar . . .	kee-see-**ehr**-ah kohm-**prahr**
cigarettes	cigarrillos	ce-ga-**ree**-yohs
matches	cerillos	ser-**ee**-ohs
a dictionary	un diccionario	oon deek-see-oh- **nah** ree-oh
soap	jabón	hah-**bohn**
sunglasses	gafas de sol	**ga**-fahs deh sohl
suntan lotion	Loción bronceadora	loh-see-**ohn** brohn- seh-ah-**do**-rah
a map	un mapa	oon **mah**-pah
a magazine	una revista	**oon**-ah reh-**veess**-tah
paper	papel	pah-**pel**
envelopes	sobres	**so**-brehs
a postcard	una tarjeta postal	**oon**-ah tar-**het**-ah post-**ahl**
How much is it?	¿Cuánto cuesta?	**kwahn**-toh **kwes**-tah
It's expensive/ cheap	Está caro/barato	es-**tah** **kah**-roh/ bah-**rah**-toh

ENGLISH	SPANISH	PRONUNCIATION
A little/a lot	Un poquito/ mucho	oon poh-**kee**-toh/ **moo**-choh
More/less	Más/menos	mahss/**men**-ohss
Enough/too	Suficiente/	soo-fee-see-**en**-teh/
much/too little	demasiado/ muy poco	deh-mah-see-**ah**- doh/ **moo**-ee **poh**-koh
Telephone	Teléfono	tel-**ef**-oh-no
Telegram	Telegrama	teh-leh-**grah**-mah
I am ill	Estoy enfermo(a)	es-**toy** en-**fehr**- moh(mah)
Please call a doctor	Por favor llame a un medico	pohr fah-**vor ya**-meh ah oon **med**-ee-koh

ON THE ROAD

Avenue	Avenida	ah-ven-**ee**-dah
Broad, tree-lined boulevard	Bulevar	boo-leh-**var**
Fertile plain	Vega	**veh**-gah
Highway	Carretera	car-reh-**ter**-ah
Mountain pass	Puerto	poo-**ehr**-toh
Street	Calle	**cah**-yeh
Waterfront promenade	Rambla	**rahm**-blah
Wharf	Embarcadero	em-bar-cah-**deh**-ro

IN TOWN

Cathedral	Catedral	cah-teh-**dral**
Church	Templo/Iglesia	**tem**-plo/ ee-**glehs**- see-ah
City hall	Casa de gobierno	kah-sah deh go-bee-**ehr**-no
Door, gate	Puerta portón	poo-**ehr**-tah por-**ton**
Entrance/exit	Entrada/salida	en-**trah**-dah/sah-**lee**- dah
Inn, rustic bar, or restaurant	Taverna	tah-**vehr**-nah

ENGLISH	SPANISH	PRONUNCIATION
Main square	Plaza principal	plah-thah prin- see-**pahl**

DINING OUT

Can you recommend a good restaurant?	¿Puede recomendarme un buen restaurante?	**pweh**-deh rreh-koh-mehn-**dahr**-me oon bwehn rrehs-tow- **rahn**-teh?
Where is it located?	¿Dónde está situado?	**dohn**-deh ehs-**tah** see-**twah**-doh?
Do I need reservations?	¿Se necesita una reservación?	seh neh-seh-**see**-tah **oo**-nah rreh-sehr- bah-**syohn**?
I'd like to reserve a table . . .	Quisiera reservar una mesa . . .	kee-**syeh**-rah rreh-sehr-**bahr** **oo**-nah **meh**-sah . . .
for two people.	para dos personas.	**pah**-rah dohs pehr- **soh**-nahs
for this evening.	para esta noche.	**pah**-rah **ehs**-tah **noh**-cheh
for 8 PM	para las ocho de la noche.	**pah**-rah lahs **oh**-choh deh lah **noh**-cheh
A bottle of . . .	Una botella de . . .	**oo**-nah bo-**teh**-yah deh
A cup of . . .	Una taza de . . .	**oo**-nah **tah**-thah deh
A glass of . . .	Un vaso de . . .	oon **vah**-so deh
Ashtray	Un cenicero	oon sen-ee-**seh**-roh
Bill/check	La cuenta	lah **kwen**-tah
Bread	El pan	el pahn
Breakfast	El desayuno	el deh-sah-**yoon**-oh
Butter	La mantequilla	lah man-teh-**key**-yah
Cheers!	¡Salud!	sah-**lood**
Cocktail	Un aperitivo	oon ah-pehr-ee-**tee**-voh
Dinner	La cena	lah **seh**-nah
Dish	Un plato	oon **plah**-toh
Menu of the day	Menú del día	meh-**noo** del **dee**-ah
Enjoy!	¡Buen provecho!	bwehn pro-**veh**-cho

ENGLISH	SPANISH	PRONUNCIATION
Fixed-price menu	Menú fijo o turistico	meh-**noo** **fee**-hoh oh too-**ree**-stee-coh
Fork	El tenedor	el ten-eh-**dor**
Is the tip included?	¿Está incluida la propina?	es-**tah** in-cloo-**ee**-dah lah pro-**pee**-nah
Knife	El cuchillo	el koo-**chee**-yo
Large portion of savory snacks	Raciónes	rah-see-**oh**-nehs
Lunch	La comida	lah koh-**mee**-dah
Menu	La carta, el menú	lah **cart**-ah, el meh-**noo**
Napkin	La servilleta	lah sehr-vee-**yet**-ah
Pepper	La pimienta	lah pee-me-**en**-tah
Please give me	Por favor déme	pore fah-**vor** **deh**-meh
Salt	La sal	lah sahl
Savory snacks	Tapas	**tah**-pahs
Spoon	Una cuchara	**oo**-nah koo-**chah**-rah
Sugar	El azúcar	el ah-**thu**-kar
Waiter!/Waitress!	¡Por favor Señor/ Señorita!	pohr fah-**vor** sen- **yor**/ sen-yor-**ee**-tah

Travel Smart Mexico

WORD OF MOUTH

"I lived in Belize for 14 years and traveled over the border into Mexico at least twice a month. I've been to Cancún and throughout Quintana Roo, both by bus and car. I've driven from Florida to Belize through Mexico. . . . Yes, there are the reports about *mordidas* (bribes) and violence, but using common sense and being courteous will go a long way in helping you enjoy your stay. Go Mexico!"

—rdesabatino

www.fodors.com/community

GETTING HERE AND AROUND

AIR TRAVEL

Air travel to Mexico is better than ever, with major carriers running more nonstop flights to resorts on both coasts and foregoing layovers at gateway Aeropuerto Internacional Benito Juárez in Mexico City. Prices on flights to the country are getting better, too.

Plane travel within Mexico, however, still costs two to four times as much as bus travel, though you can sometimes save money by buying domestic tickets at a Mexican travel agency. Still, if time is of the essence, flying is you best option—particularly if you can avoid a Mexico City layover.

AIRLINES

The country's flagship carriers are Aeroméxico and Mexicana. Note that Mexicana experienced financial difficulties and, in mid 2010, was forced to file for bankruptcy and reorganization. At this writing, all efforts are being made to ensure that the airline and its domestic line, Click, remain up and flying. Still, before booking with the company, you might want to check on its status.

Major U.S. carriers with service to and from myriad hubs include American, Continental, and Delta.

JetBlue flies into Cancún from New York, Boston, D.C. (Dulles), Orlando, and Fort Lauderdale. Alaska/Horizon Airlines flies from Los Angeles, San Francisco, and Seattle to Los Cabos and Puerto Vallarta; it also serves Mazatlán from Seattle and Loreto, Guadalajara, Mexico City, Manzanillo, and Ixtapa/Zihuatanejo from Los Angeles.

Aeroméxico, Mexicana's Click Mexicana, Aerolitoral, Aeromar, and Volaris are among the carriers with domestic service.

FLYING TIMES

Mexico City is 5 hours from New York, 4½ hours from Chicago, and 3½ hours from Los Angeles. Cancún is 3½ hours from New York and Chicago, 4½ hours from Los Angeles. Acapulco is 6 hours from New York, 4 hours from Chicago, and 3½ hours from Los Angeles.

Airlines and Airports **Airline and Airport Links.com** (🌐 *www.airlineandairportlinks.com*) has links to many of the world's airlines and airports.

Major Carriers **Aeroméxico** (☎ *800/237-6639, 01800/021-1400 toll-free in Mexico, 55/5133-4000 in Mexico* 🌐 *www.aeromexico.com*). **American** (☎ *800/433-7300* 🌐 *www.aa.com*). **Continental** (☎ *800/523-3273 for U.S. and Mexico reservations, 800/231-0856 for international reservations* 🌐 *www.continental.com*). **Delta** (☎ *800/221-1212 for U.S. reservations, 800/241-4141 for international reservations* 🌐 *www.delta.com*). **Mexicana** (☎ *800/531-7921, 866/281-3049 in Canada, 01800/502-2000 in Mexico* 🌐 *www.mexicana.com*).

Smaller Carriers **Aeroliteral** (☎ *01800/800-2376 toll-free in Mexico* 🌐 *www.aeroliteral.com*). **Alaska Airlines/Horizon** (☎ *800/252-7522* 🌐 *www.alaskaair.com*). **JetBlue** (☎ *800/538-2583* 🌐 *www.jetblue.com*). **Volaris** (☎ 866/988-3527 🌐 *www.volaris.com.mx*).

Security Issues **Transportation Security Administration** (🌐 *www.tsa.gov*) has answers for questions about security and travel.

AIRPORTS

The main gateway to the country is Mexico City's Aeropuerto Internacional Benito Juárez (airport code: MEX), a large, well-equipped, modern airport, though infamous for pickpocketing and taxi scams; be careful and discreet with your possessions; be especially watchful when exchanging money or withdrawing it from ATMs. You can easily exchange money here as well as buy last-minute gifts (although at high prices) on your way out of the country.

Regional airports vary greatly in size and efficiency, though most coastal hubs are really nice and have plenty of services and facilities catering to tourists.

Most airports in Mexico are easy to navigate. For flights within Mexico originating at Benito Juárez, arrive 1½ hours before the scheduled departure time; for flights originating at small airports, arrive an hour before departure. You may need to arrive earlier if you're flying from one of the busier airports, during peak air-traffic times, or during peak seasons. Arrive 2½ to 3 hours before international flights.

Airport Information **Aeropuerto Internacional Benito Juárez** (☎ *55/2482-2424* 🌐 *www.aicm.com.mx*).

BOAT TRAVEL

Certain islands in Mexico are connected to the mainland by ferry, such as speedboats that run between Playa del Carmen and Cozumel or from Puerto Juárez, Punta Sam, and Isla Mujeres, all in the Yucatán.

Boats also connect Isla Tiburón near Bahía Kino in northwest Mexico, Chiquila, and Isla Holbox, and car ferries connect Baja California with the mainland on three key routes: Guaymas, Sonora, is connected with Santa Rosalía, Baja California Sur; and La Paz, Baja California Sur, is connected with both Los Mochis and Mazatlán in the state of Sinaloa.

BUS TRAVEL

Getting to Mexico by Greyhound is no longer for just the adventurous or budget-conscious. In the past, bus travelers were required to change to Mexican vehicles at the border, and vice versa. Now, however, in an effort to bring more American visitors to off-the-beaten-track markets and attractions, the Mexican government has removed this obstacle, and more transborder bus tours are available.

Within Mexico the bus network is extensive. Though there's a trend toward consolidation, some towns have different stations for each bus line. In Mexico City, there's an ADO luxury bus station at the Mexico City airport, directly across the street from the national arrival terminal.

CLASSES

First-class Mexican buses are air-conditioned coaches with bathrooms, movies, reclining seats with seat belts, and refreshments (first class or deluxe, known as *primera clase* and *de lujo* or *ejecutivo*). They take the fastest route (usually on safer, well-paved toll roads) and make few stops.

Second-class vehicles (*segunda clase*) connect smaller, secondary routes; they also run along long-distance routes, often taking slower, local roads. They're tolerable (and air-conditioned), even for long distances, but are usually cramped and make many stops.

The class of travel will be listed on your printed ticket—if you see economico printed next to servicio, you've been booked on a second-class bus. At many bus stations one counter will represent several lines and classes of service, and mistakes do happen.

For comfort's sake, if you're planning a long-distance haul, buy tickets for first class or better when traveling by bus within Mexico. Bring snacks, a sweater, and toilet paper. Smoking is prohibited.

LINES

There are several first-class and deluxe bus lines, including ADO and ADO GL (deluxe service), Estrella de Oro, ETN, Omnibus de Mexico, and Primera Plus. Some lines have more comprehenisve service than others; combined, they cover just about cover all of Mexico. Greyhound travels between the United States and Mexico.

TICKETS AND BOOKING

Although most of the deluxe bus services have started accepting credit cards such as Visa and MasterCard, plan to pay in pesos.

Tickets for first-class or better—not for the other classes—can be reserved in advance; this is advisable during peak periods or on routes that only have one or two daily departures. You can make reservations for many first-class bus lines through the Ticketbus central reservations agency.

If you're unable to reserve online, buy your tickets at the station the day before you travel. The day of travel, ask your hotel desk to confirm that your bus still is still scheduled—even executive-class buses can be canceled at the last minute.

Bus Information **ADO** and **ADO GL** (☎ *55/5133–2424, 01800/702–8000 toll-free in Mexico* 🌐 *www.ticketbus.com.mx*). **Estrella de Oro** (☎ *55/5484–1400, 01800/900–0105 toll-free in Mexico* 🌐 *www.estrelladeoro.com.mx*). **ETN** (☎ *55/5089–9200, 01800/800–0386 toll-free in Mexico* 🌐 *www.etn.com.mx*). **Greyhound** (*800/231–2222, 800/661–8747 in Canada* ☎ *01800/010–0600 toll-free in Mexico* 🌐 *www.greyhound.com, www.greyhound.com.mx*). **Omnibus de México** (☎ *01800/765–6636 toll-free in Mexico* 🌐 *www.odm.com.mx*). **Primera Plus** (☎ *55/5567–7176, 01800/375–7587 toll-free in Mexico* 🌐 *secure.primeraplus.com.mx*). **Ticketbus** (☎ *55/5133–2424, 01800/702–8000 toll-free in Mexico* 🌐 *www.ticketbus.com.mx*).

TRAVEL TIMES FROM MEXICO CITY

To	By Air	By Car or Bus
Guadalajara	1¼ hours	7–8 hours
San Miguel	45 minutes	3½ hours
Veracruz City	1 hour	5 hours
Oaxaca City	1 hour	5½ hours
Puerto Vallarta	1½ hours	12 hours
Acapulco	1 hour	5–6 hours
San Cristóbal	1¼ hours	16 hours
Villahermosa	1½ hours	11 hours
Cancún	2 hours	23 hours
Mérida	1¾ hours	19 hours

CAR TRAVEL

There are two absolutely essential points to remember about driving in Mexico. First and foremost is to carry Mexican auto insurance. If you injure anyone in an accident, you could well be jailed unless you have insurance. Second, if you enter Mexico with a car you must leave with it. In recent years the high rate of U.S. vehicles being sold illegally in Mexico has caused the Mexican government to enact stringent regulations on bringing cars into the country.

BORDER CROSSINGS

You must cross the border with the following documents: title or registration for your vehicle; a passport or passport card; a credit card (AE, DC, MC, or V); a valid driver's license with a photo. The title-holder, driver, and credit-card owner must be one and the same—that is, if your spouse's name is on the title or registration of the car and yours isn't, you cannot be the one to bring the car into the country.

For financed, leased, rental, or company cars you must bring a notarized letter of permission from the bank, lien holder, rental agency, or company. When you submit your paperwork at the border and pay the $27 charge on your credit card, you'll receive a car permit and a sticker to put on your vehicle, all valid for up to 180 days, to be used within a year. If you do not plan on using your permit further, be sure to turn it in along with the sticker at the border prior to their expiration date; otherwise you could incur high fines or even be barred from entering Mexico if you try to visit again.

If you do plan on returning, and there are still days left on your permit, let the border agent know that you would like to leave, and use the remaining days at a later time (before the permit expires).

The fact that you drove in with a car is stamped on your tourist card (visa), which you must give to immigration authorities at departure. If an emergency arises and you must fly home, there are complicated customs procedures to face. Additionally, if you bring a car into the country you must be in the vehicle at all times when it is driven. Technically, you may not use valet parking.

INSURANCE

You must carry Mexican auto insurance, which you can purchase near border crossings on the U.S. side, by mail, or via the Internet. It's sold by the day ($10 per day and up), and if your trip is shorter than your original estimate, some companies might issue a prorated refund for the unused time upon application after you exit the country.

Baja Bound, Mexico Insurance Professionals, and Instant Mexico Auto Insurance are a few of the many online outfits that allow you to buy the insurance beforehand, but if you're approaching the border at almost any U.S.–Mexico crossing, you'll be overwhelmed by companies where you can buy the insurance on the spot. Sanborn's is a reliable company, has offices in almost every border town, and has online options, too.

Be sure that you have been provided with proof of such insurance; if you drive without it, you're not only liable for damages, but you're also breaking the law. You could be jailed during investigations after an accident unless you have Mexican insurance. For this reason, after an accident many Mexicans simply pull over, discuss things, arrive at an impromptu cash settlement on the spot if necessary, and continue on their way.

Contacts **Baja Bound** (☎ *888/552–2252* 🌐 *www.bajabound.com*). **Instant Mexico Auto Insurance** (☎ *800/345–4701* 🌐 *www.instant-mex-auto-insur.com*). **Mexico Insurance Professionals** (☎ *888/467–4639* 🌐 *www.mexpro.com*). **Sanborn's Mexican Insurance** (☎ *800/222–0158* 🌐 *www.sanbornsinsurance.com*).

GASOLINE

Pemex (the government petroleum monopoly) franchises all of Mexico's gas stations, which you'll find at most junctions and in cities and towns. Gas is measured in liters. Some stations accept credit cards and a few have ATMs, but don't count on it—make sure you have pesos handy. Overall, prices run slightly cheaper (around 30% less) than in the United States (at this writing, about 8 cents a liter or $2.40 a gallon).

Premium unleaded gas (called *premium*), the red pump, and regular unleaded gas (*magna*), the green pump, are available nationwide, but it's still best to fill up whenever you can. Fuel quality is generally lower than that in the United States and Europe, but it has improved enough so that your car will run acceptably.

Attendants pump the gas and will also wash your windshield and check your fluids and tire air pressure on request. A 5- or 10-peso tip is customary, depending on the number of services rendered (even if they just pump the gas). Make sure the attendant resets the pump to "0" and that you're charged the correct price. For a receipt, ask for a *recibo*. To ask the attendant to fill the tank, say "Lleno (YAY-noh), por favor."

PARKING

A circle with a diagonal line superimposed on the letter *E* (for *estacionamiento*) means "no parking." Illegally parked cars are either towed or have wheel blocks placed on the tires, which can require a trip to the traffic-police headquarters for payment of a fine. When in doubt, park in a lot instead of on the street; your car will probably be safer there anyway.

Lots are plentiful although not always clearly marked, and fees are reasonable—as little as $1 for a half day or up to $1 or more an hour. Sometimes you park your own car; more often, though, you hand the keys over to an attendant. There are a few (extremely few) parking meters in larger cities; the cost is usually about 10¢ per 15 minutes.

RENTAL CARS

As a rule, avoid local agencies; stick with the major companies, because they tend to be more reliable. With the exception of Volkswagen, you can get the same kind of midsize and luxury cars in Mexico that you can rent in the United States. Economy usually refers to a Volkswagen Beetle or another small car barely fitting four passengers, which may or may not come with air-conditioning.

It can really pay to shop around: in Mexico City, rates for a compact car with a/c, manual transmission, and unlimited mileage range from $16 a day and $116 a week to $50 a day and nearly $300 a week, excluding taxes. At resort towns in high season, expect the higher prices.

By far the best option is booking ahead. Although consolidators like Travelocity.com may give great deals, it's a good idea to book directly through a major rental company's Web site, as consolidator sites will sometimes allow you to make a booking even when there aren't any available cars.

Basic accident insurance averages $18 a day and is compulsory; additional theft and personal injury policies are optional. This doesn't include 10%–15% tax, or the additional 12% concession fee charged at all airport rental facilities. Surcharges for additional drivers are around $5 per day plus tax. Children's car seats run about the same, but not all companies have them.

The minimum driving age is 18, but most rental-car agencies have a minimum-age requirement ranging from 21 to 25; some have a surcharge for drivers under 25. Your own driver's license is acceptable.

Major Agency Contacts **Alamo** (☎ *800/222-9057* 🌐 *www.alamo.com*). **Avis** (☎ *800/331-1212* 🌐 *www.avis.com*). **Budget** (☎ *800/472-3325* 🌐 *www.budget.com*). **Dollar** (☎ *800/800-3665* 🌐 *www.dollar.com*). **Hertz** (☎ *800/654-3001* 🌐 *www.hertz.com*). **National Car Rental** (☎ *800/227-7368* 🌐 *www.nationalcar.com*). **Thrifty** (☎ *877/283-0898* 🌐 *www.thrifty.com*).

CAR AND DRIVER

You can also hire a car with a driver (who generally doubles as a tour guide) through your hotel. The going rate is about $22–$25 an hour within a given town. Limousine service runs about $65 an hour and up, with a three- to five-hour minimum. Rates for out-of-town trips may be higher.

Negotiate a price beforehand if you'll need the service for more than one day. If your hotel can't arrange limousine or car service, ask the concierge to refer you to a reliable *sitio* (cab stand); the rate will be lower.

ROAD CONDITIONS

The most dangerous thing about driving in Mexico is the actual road conditions—like the potholes and inexplicable placement of speed bumps. That said, there are several well-kept toll roads in Mexico—most of them two lanes wide; a few have four lanes. These *carreteras de cuota* (toll highways) are numbered and connect major cities or border areas. (*Cuota* means "toll road"; *libre* means "free," and such roads are often one lane, slower, and usually not as smooth.)

Most newer highways have either designated lanes for slower vehicles or a paved shoulder that's wide enough for you to cruise in while letting the speed demons pass. There are highways in good condition connecting Acapulco and Mexico City; Cancún and Mérida; Nogales and Mazatlán; León and Aguascalientes; Guadalajara and Tepic; Mexico City, Morelia, and Guadalajara; Mexico City, Puebla, Teotihuacán, and Oaxaca; Mexico City and Veracruz; and Nuevo Laredo and Monterrey. However, tolls as high as $40 one way (most tolls start at $6–$8) can make using these thoroughfares expensive.

In rural areas, roads range from good to poor: use caution, especially during the rainy season, when rock slides, flooding, and potholes may pose problems.

Note that driving in Mexico's central highlands may also necessitate adjustments to your carburetor.

Topes (speed bumps, also called reductores de velocidad) are common and are extremely large; occasionally, you'll see one that's actually been painted or fitted with reflectors, but usually they're just announced by a single yellow sign. Other road signs follow the widespread system of international symbols.

CITY DRIVING

Big-city driving is—as it is in many parts of the world—harrowing. The worst parts are negotiating four-way stops (where seemingly no rules except those of machismo apply), and trying to find street signs (which are nearly impossible to spot and hard to read even if you do see them) while keeping up with traffic.

In Mexico City, watch out for *Hoy no Circula* notices. Because of pollution, all cars in the city without a Verification "0" rating (usually those built before 1994) are prohibited from driving one day a week (two days a week during high-alert periods).

Posted signs show certain letters or numbers paired with each day of the week, indicating that vehicles with those letters or numbers in their license plates aren't allowed to drive on the corresponding day. Cars with license plate numbers ending in 5 or 6 are prohibited on Monday; 7 or 8 on Tuesday; 3 or 4 on Wednesday; 1 or 2 on Thursday; and cars with permits as well as 9 or 0 on Friday. Cars whose license plates have only letters, not numerals, can't drive on Friday.

Cars are also restricted on Saturday between 5 AM and 11 PM. On the first Saturday of each month, license plates ending in 5 or 6 are restricted; on the second Saturday, licenses ending in 7 or 8; on the third Saturday, those that end in 3 or 4; on the fourth Saturday, those that end in 1 or 2. When there is a fifth Saturday in the month, those that end in 9, 0, or those that have permits may not drive.

Foreigners' cars aren't exempt. In fact, not only do foreign cars need to follow the *Hoy no Circula* program, but they're also only allowed to move about the city on weekdays from 5 AM to 11 PM. That said, foreigners' cars with emissions-test results might be given either a sticker with a "0" or a "00," which makes them exempt from the *Hoy no Circul*" program. One-way traffic is indicated by an arrow; two-way, by a double-pointed arrow. Look for these signs in cities and towns; they are sometimes oddly placed or otherwise hard to see.

HAZARDS

Be alert to animals, especially untethered cattle and dogs, and to dangerous, unrailed curves.

Slow down when approaching a village, where you'll find the most *topes*, though you may also encounter them on straight stretches of highway, where there are no visible hazards or reasons to reduce speed.

The utter lack of visibility on rural routes, even well-traveled highways, will make even the most confident driver white-knuckled after a few hours. And, unless you're totally familiar with the terrain, avoid driving at night outside the city, where you can run into—literally—wandering cows, horses, or dogs, or unforeseen speed bumps at the entrance to small towns.

Bandits are generally run off if they start staking out cars or buses along major routes, where tourists with expensive cameras and cash are known to pass by, but their rare presence is another reason to avoid night travel.

MEXICAN DRIVERS

Mexicans are generally skilled drivers, but they do drive quite fast, even on twisting or extraordinarily dark roads. That said, Mexicans are in some ways more courteous than U.S. drivers—it's customary, for example, for drivers to put on their hazard lights to warn the cars behind them of poor road conditions, slow-downs, or upcoming speed bumps; oncoming cars may flash their lights at you for the same reasons.

THE POLICE

Checks for weapons and drugs are commonplace; customarily, police at these checkpoints ask to see the car's registration and look in the backseat, the trunk, and at the undercarriage with a mirror. Basic Spanish does help during these stops, though a smile and polite demeanor will go a long way.

Some of the biggest hassles might be from police who pull you over for supposedly breaking the law, or for being a good prospect for a scam.

Be polite—displays of anger will only make matters worse—and be aware that a police officer may be pulling you over for something you didn't do. Although efforts are being made to fight corruption, the officer who pulls you over might have no intention of following the proper protocol by taking you down to police headquarters and might, instead, ask you to pay to get your license back.

If you dispute a charge, do so with a smile, and tell the officer that you would like to talk to the police captain when you get to the station. The officer will usually let you go rather than make that trip.

If you find yourself in a really difficult situation with police, call your embassy. If, for example, they may hold you for any reason, your embassy can probably give you a list of local English-speaking attorneys and other assistance based on your situation.

ROADSIDE EMERGENCIES

The Mexican Tourism Ministry operates a fleet of more than 350 pickup trucks, known as the Angeles Verdes, or Green Angels, easily reachable by phone throughout Mexico by simply dialing 078. The bilingual drivers provide mechanical help, first aid, radio-telephone communication, basic supplies and small parts, towing, tourist information, and protection.

Services are free, and spare parts, fuel, and lubricants are provided at cost. Tips are always appreciated (figure $5–$10 for big jobs, $3–$5 for minor repairs).

The Green Angels patrol certain sections of the major highways twice daily 8–6 (usually later on holiday weekends). If you break down, pull off the road as far as possible, lift the hood of your car, hail a passing vehicle, and ask the driver to notify the patrol. Most bus and truck drivers will be quite helpful.

Emergency Services **Angeles Verdes** (☏ *078, nationwide 3-digit Angeles Verdes and tourist emergency line*). **Ministry of Tourism hotline** (☏ *55/3002–6300*).

WORD OF MOUTH

"...The speed limit changes frequently; if you're not paying close attention, you'll miss it. [When I was pulled over], I was polite, used very little Spanish, and basically told the officer to go ahead and write me a ticket. He told me the ticket would be 1,200 pesos. I acted sad and told him I was sorry and that he should just write me the ticket. He acted sad also, walked to his squad car, [seemingly] pretended to call someone and to write down my tag number, came back to the car, and repeated the bit about 1,200 pesos. When he realized that I was firm about receiving the ticket, he gave a big sigh, and told me to slow down.... [The hotel] said I did the right thing by telling him to just write the ticket...." —stotz

RULES OF THE ROAD

When you sign up for Mexican car insurance, you should receive a booklet on Mexican rules of the road.

On the road itself, lines delineating the various lanes are most often totally ignored; horns are leaned on constantly; and you must either pass or be passed.

To pass a slower-moving vehicle, put on your left blinker. If the slower driver notices, often he or she will signal you with the left blinker when it's safe for you to pass. When you do pass, check that none of the cars behind you have gotten the same idea first—it's not uncommon for someone to speed up from the back of a long line of cars.

If an oncoming vehicle flicks its lights at you in daytime, slow down: it could mean trouble ahead. When approaching a narrow bridge, the first vehicle to flash its lights has right-of-way.

There's no right on red.

Seat belts are required by law throughout Mexico.

SPEED LIMITS

Mileage and speed limits are given in kilometers: 100 kph and 80 kph (62 mph and 50 mph, respectively) are the most common maximums, which are regularly exceeded by most drivers. A few of the toll roads allow 110 kph (68 mph). However, speed limits can change from curve to curve, so watch the signs carefully. In cities and small towns, posted limits are as low as 20 kph (12 mph).

If you're stopped for speeding, the officer is supposed to take your license and hold it until you pay the fine at the local police station. Local officers might ask for a *mordida* (bribe) rather than make a trip to the station; highway patrol officers aren't likely to attempt bribery.

DRUNK DRIVING

If you're caught driving while intoxicated, you'll go to jail immediately. It's hard to know what the country's blood-alcohol limit really is. Everyone seems to have a different idea about it; this means it's probably being handled in a discretionary way, which is nerve-racking, to say the least. The best way to avoid any problems is to simply not drink and drive.

CRUISE SHIP TRAVEL

Cozumel and Playa del Carmen have become increasingly popular ports of call for Caribbean/Riviera Maya cruises; some lines also go down as far as the Panama Canal on such itineraries. Many vessels also run along Baja California and farther down the Pacific Coast, along the so-called Mexican Riviera. Ports of embarkation include Miami, Galveston, Los Angeles, Long Beach, San Diego, San Francisco, and Vancouver.

Cruise lines with Mexico routes include Carnival, Cunard, Holland America, Norwegian, Princess, Royal Caribbean International, and Silversea.

Cruise Lines **Carnival Cruise Line** (☎ *305/406–4779 or 877/885–4856* 🌐 *www.carnival.com*). **Cunard Line** (☎ *661/753–1000 or 800/728–6273* 🌐 *www.cunard.com*). **Holland America Line** (☎ *206/281–3535 or 877/932–4259* 🌐 *www.hollandamerica.com*). **Norwegian Cruise Line** (*866/234–7350* 🌐 *www.ncl.com*). **Princess Cruises** (☎ *661/753–0000 or 800/774–6237* 🌐 *www.princess.com*). **Royal Caribbean International** (☎ *316/526–9723 or 866/562–7625* 🌐 *www.royalcaribbean.com*). **Silversea Cruises** (☎ *954/522–4477 or 877/356–9052* 🌐 *www.silversea.com*).

TAXI TRAVEL

Taxis are ubiquitous in both big cities and midsize towns. The standard taxi is a midsize, four-door sedan. Drivers generally speak English, either enough to negotiate the fare or, in some cases, excellent enough for a lively discussion of national politics.

Street taxis might be the cheapest, but an alarming increase in crime involves them, particularly in Mexico City. Play it safe and use radio taxis or those hired at hotels and stands *(sitios)*. Note that in Mexico City, regulations for taxis have recently changed: street taxis are orange and red while the safer sitio taxis are white. Further, VW Bugs are being phased out since crimes are more often committed in these cars than in four-door sedans.

In addition to private taxis, many cities have bargain-price collective taxi services using minibuses and sedans. The service is called *colectivo* or *pesero*. Such vehicles run along fixed routes, and you hail them on the street and tell the driver where you are going. He charges you based on distance. Note that drivers often run out of change, so being able to pay the exact amount can make the experience smoother.

AIRPORT TAXIS

For safety, you should only take the authorized taxi service from most airports. Whenever possible, purchase the taxi vouchers sold at stands inside or just outside the terminal, which ensure that your fare is established beforehand. Check the taxi-zone map (it should be posted on or by the ticket stand) before you purchase your ticket and make sure your ticket is properly zoned.

FARES

A metered taxi has a *taximetro*, and if a cab has one, ask the driver what the rates are. Most taxis, particularly those in resort areas, are unmetered. Always confirm the fare before setting out. Major hotels post rate sheets, or you can ask a concierge or front-desk person what the rates should be. Note that even the posted rates are inflated, so always try to negotiate a slightly better price. Clearly, if any cabbie asks for more than the posted fare you're being grossly overcharged.

A surcharge of 20% to 40% may be added at night, usually after 11 PM.

If a driver doesn't know the address you give him, he'll radio either a dispatcher or other cabbie to get the info, or drive to the neighborhood and ask around. When you've negotiated the fare before starting, you needn't pay extra if the cabbie has to drive around a bit to find the address.

Tipping isn't customary, especially since you've negotiated the rate.

ESSENTIALS

ACCOMMODATIONS

TIP→ Find hotel and restaurant price charts in individual chapters.

The price and quality of accommodations in Mexico vary from superluxurious hotels and all-inclusive resorts to modest budget properties, down-at-the-heel places with shared bathrooms, and cabanas. There are far fewer *casas de huéspedes* (guesthouses) and youth hostels in Mexico than, say, Europe, because there are so many options for budget travelers. You may find appealing bargains while you're on the road, but if your comfort threshold is low, look for an English-speaking staff, guaranteed dollar rates, and toll-free reservation numbers. **TIP→ Assume that hotels operate on the European Plan (EP, no meals) unless we specify that they use the Breakfast Plan (BP, with full breakfast), Continental Plan (CP, continental breakfast), Full American Plan (FAP, all meals), Modified American Plan (MAP, breakfast and dinner), or are all-inclusive (AI, all meals and most activities).**

APARTMENT AND HOUSE RENTALS

Contacts **Akumal Villas** (☎ *984/875-9088 or 866/535-1324 in Akumal* 🌐 *www.akumal-villas.com*). **San Miguel Rentals** (☎ *415/259-4807* 🌐 *www.sanmiguelrentals.com*). **Turquoise Waters** (☎ *877/254-9791* 🌐 *www.turquoisewater.com*). **Villanet** (☎ *206/417-3444 or 800/964-1891* 🌐 *www.rentavilla.com*). **Villas and Apartments Abroad** (☎ *212/213-6435* 🌐 *www.vaanyc.com*). **Villas International** (☎ *415/499-9490 or 800/221-2260* 🌐 *www.villasintl.com*). **Villas of Distinction** (☎ *707/778-1800 or 800/289-0900* 🌐 *www.villasofdistinction.com*). **Wimco** (☎ *866/850-6140* 🌐 *www.wimco.com*).

BOUTIQUE HOTELS AND B&BS

Mexico has many unique properties that put you in close touch with the country's essence *and* cater to your need for pampering. Hoteles Boutique de México (Mexico Boutique Hotels) is a private company that represents 45 such properties. Most have fewer than 50 rooms; each is not only selected for its small size, service, and allure, but is inspected annually to ensure it continues to meet the set high standards.

The bed-and-breakfast craze hasn't missed Mexico, although there are fewer than in Europe and the United States. San Miguel de Allende and other heartland cities have their share of delightful places, as do Mexico City and parts of the Yucatán.

Reservation Services **Bed & Breakfast.com** (☎ *512/322-2710* 🌐 *www.bedandbreakfast.com/mexico.html*) also sends out an online newsletter. **Hoteles Boutique de México** (☎ *01800/508-7927 toll-free in Mexico, 800/728-9098* 🌐 *mexicoboutiquehotels.com*). **Internet San Miguel** (🌐 *www.internetsanmiguel.com/bed_and_breakfasts.html*). **Mexperience Guide to Boutique Hotels** (🌐 *www.mexperience.com/mexicoboutiquehotels* ☎ *01800/725-2522 toll-free in Mexico, 877/372-5123*). **Oaxaca Bed and Breakfast Association** (🌐 *www.oaxacabedandbreakfast.org*).

HOSTELS

Mexico, while it has many cheap hotels, has few hostels. High-school and college students are more often the norm than older travelers at the few hostels that do exist. Hostelling International (HI) has locations in Acapulco, Guanajuato, Guadalajara, Jalapa, Mexico City, and Puebla.

Information **Hostelling International—USA** (☎ *301/495-1240* 🌐 *www.hihostels.com*).

HOTELS

It's essential to reserve in advance if you're traveling to the resort areas during high season or holiday periods, and it's recommended to do so elsewhere during low season. Overbooking is a common practice in some parts of Mexico, such as

Cancún, Puerto Vallarta, and Acapulco. Get a confirmation in writing, via fax or e-mail.

Hotel rates are subject to the 15% value-added tax (it's 10% in the states of Quintana Roo, Baja California, and Baja California Sur, and anywhere within 20 km [12½ mi] of the border). In addition, many states charge a 2 to 3% hotel tax. Service charges and meals generally aren't included in rates.

The Mexican government categorizes hotels, based on qualitative evaluations, into *gran turismo*; five star down to one star. Anything less than two stars generally doesn't advertise the fact, and even budget travelers are unlikely to stay at a one-star lodging. Keep in mind that many hotels that might otherwise be rated higher have opted for a lower category to avoid higher interest rates on loans and financing.

High- versus low-season rates can vary significantly. Hotels in this guide have private bathrooms with showers, unless stated otherwise; bathtubs aren't common in inexpensive hotels in smaller towns. Hotels have private baths, phones, TVs, and air-conditioning unless otherwise noted.

COMMUNICATIONS

INTERNET

Connections are fast in major cities and many smaller towns as well. Wi-Fi is widely available in large hotels, at least in public areas. The cost for in-room connection can run from $15 to $25 per day—quite high, especially when Wi-Fi can sometimes be a free perk at other hotels.

Many coffee shops in larger cities provide free Wi-Fi. Most charge 10 to 40 pesos for one hour, though some charge in 10- or 15-minute increments (usually 5 to 10 pesos). Many Internet cafés are equipped with Skype connections, too.

If you're bringing a laptop with you, check with the manufacturer's technical support line to see what service or repair affiliates they have in the areas you plan to visit. Larger cities have repair shops that service Compaq, Dell, Macintosh, Sony, Toshiba, and other major brands, though parts tend to be more expensive than in the United States. Carry a spare battery to save yourself the expense and headache of having to hunt down a replacement on the spot.

Contacts **Cybercafes** (🌐 *www.cybercafes.com*) lists some 173 internet cafes in Mexico.

PHONES

The good news is that you can now make a direct-dial telephone call from virtually any point on earth. The bad news? You can't always do so cheaply. Calling from a hotel is almost always the most expensive option; hotels usually add huge surcharges to all calls, particularly international ones. In some countries you can phone from call centers or even the post office.

Calling cards usually keep costs to a minimum, but only if you purchase them locally. And then there are mobile phones (⇨ *below*), which are sometimes more prevalent—particularly in the developing world—than landlines; as expensive as mobile phone calls can be, they are still usually a much cheaper option than calling from your hotel.

CALLING MEXICO

The country code for Mexico is 52. Dial any necessary international access code, then the country code, and then all of the numbers listed for the entry.

CALLING WITHIN MEXICO

Directory assistance is 040 nationwide. For assistance in English, dial 090 first for an international operator; tell the operator in what city, state, and country you require directory assistance, and he or she will connect you.

If you're calling long distance within Mexico, dial 01 before the area code and number. For local calls, just dial the number; no other prefix is necessary.

For local or long-distance calls, you can use either a standard public pay phone or

LOCAL DO'S AND TABOOS

CUSTOMS OF THE COUNTRY

In the United States and elsewhere in the Western world, being direct, efficient, and succinct is highly valued. But Mexican communication tends to be more subtle, and the direct style of Americans, Canadians, and Europeans is often perceived as curt and aggressive. Mexicans are extremely polite, so losing your temper over delays or complaining loudly will get you branded as rude and make people less inclined to help you.

Remember that things move at a slow pace here and that there's no stigma attached to being late; be gracious about this and other local customs and attitudes. In restaurants, for example, a waiter would never consider bringing you the check before you ask for it; that would be pushy. It's customary to inquire about a colleague's family or general health, and perhaps some other banal subject (such as the beauty of the town you're visiting, or the weather), before launching into a request or mundane business. Mexicans love to discuss politics and ethics, so don't be afraid to ask questions or discuss these issues in friendly and general terms.

Learning basic phrases in Spanish such as *por favor* (please) and *gracias* (thank you) will make a big difference in how people respond to you. Also, being deferential to those who are older than you will earn you lots of points.

GREETINGS

Mexicans are extremely polite and ceremonious. Businesspeople and strangers shake hands upon greeting each other or being introduced, while friends (women to women or women to men) may give a kiss on one cheek, or an "air kiss." Male friends or acquaintances may give each other, and sometimes women, a stiff hug with a triple pat on the back. When in doubt, shake hands.

It's traditional to use the formal form of you (*usted*) rather than the informal *tu* when addressing elders, subordinates, superiors, and strangers. However, so few gringos speak Spanish that any courteous attempt to speak Spanish is acceptable (although using the correct pronoun is, naturally, best). When taking your leave, say "adios" (good-bye) or "hasta luego" (see you later).

SIGHTSEEING

Although shorts are permissible in churches, short shorts and skimpy tops are frowned upon. Don't sightsee during church services, although you can stand at the back and look. If photography or flash photography is prohibited, there's usually a sign at the front of the church; otherwise, taking pictures is not a problem. Old women and men or people with disabilities often beg at the entrance to churches; it's common to give them a few coins.

Say *"con permiso"* (pardon me) to get past people in a crowd.

Giving up one's seat on a bus for the elderly, the blind, and pregnant women is common courtesy.

OUT ON THE TOWN

Mexicans call waiters "joven" (literally, young man) no matter how old they are. Call a female waitress "señorita" (miss) or "señora" (ma'am). Ask for "la cuenta, por favor" (the check, please) when you want the bill; it's usually considered rude for a server to bring it before a customer asks for it. Mexicans tend to dress nicely for a night out, but in tourist areas, dress codes are mainly upheld only at the more sophisticated discotheques. Some restaurants have separate smoking sections, but it is increasingly common to not allow smoking in smaller establishments.

a *caseta de larga distancia,* a telephone service usually operated out of a small business. Tell the person on duty the number you'd like to call, and she or he will give you a rate and dial for you. Rates, which are generally higher than those of pay phones, vary widely, so shop around. If using a pay phone, you'll probably need a prepaid phone card.

When they allow collect calls, casetas generally charge 50¢–$1.50 to place them (some charge by the minute). It's usually better to call *por cobrar* (collect) from a pay phone.

CALLING OUTSIDE MEXICO

To make an international call, dial 00 before the country code, area code, and number. The country code for the United States and Canada is 1, the United Kingdom 44, Australia 61, New Zealand 64, and South Africa 27.

Avoid phones near tourist areas that advertise, in English, "Call the U.S. or Canada here!" They charge an outrageous fee per minute. If in doubt, dial the operator and ask for rates.

CALLING CARDS

AT&T, MCI, and Sprint calling cards are useful, although infrequently, hotels block access to their service numbers.

Most pay phones, which are predominantly operated by Telmex, accept only prepaid cards (tarjetas Lada), sold in 30-, 50-, or 100-peso denominations at newsstands, pharmacies, and grocery stores; coin-only pay phones are few and far between. There are pay phones all over the place—on street corners, in bus stations, and so on. They usually have two unmarked slots, one for a Ladatel (a Spanish acronym for "long-distance direct dialing") card and the other for a credit card. These are primarily for Mexican bank cards, but some accept Visa or MasterCard, though *not* U.S. phone credit cards.

To use a Ladatel card, simply insert it in the appropriate slot with the computer chip insignia forward and right-side up, and dial. Credit is deleted from the card as you use it, and your balance is displayed on a small screen on the phone. You'll be charged 1 peso per minute for local calls and more for long-distance and international calls. Most pay phones display a price list and dialing instructions.

Access Codes **AT&T Direct** (☎ *01800/112-2020 toll-free in Mexico*). **MCI WorldPhone** (☎ *01800/674-7000 toll-free in Mexico*). **Sprint International Access** (☎ *01800/877-8000 toll-free in Mexico*).

MOBILE PHONES

If you have a multiband phone (some countries use different frequencies than what's used in the United States) and your service provider uses the world-standard GSM network (as do T-Mobile, Cingular, and Verizon), you can probably use your phone in Mexico. Even semi-remote coastal areas seem to get excellent reception, though don't expect the same to be true in out-of-the-way mountain towns.

Roaming fees can be steep, however: 99¢ a minute is considered reasonable. And overseas you normally pay the toll charges for incoming calls. It's almost always cheaper to send a text message than to make a call, since text messages have a low set fee (often less than 5¢).

To just make local calls, consider buying a new SIM card (note that your provider may have to unlock your phone for you to use a different SIM card) and a prepaid service plan in the destination. You'll then have a local number and can make local calls at local rates. ■TIP→ **If you travel internationally frequently, save one of your old mobile phones or buy a cheap one on the Internet; ask your cell phone company to unlock it for you, and take it with you as a travel phone, buying a new SIM card with pay-as-you-go service in each destination.**

There are now many companies that rent cell phones with or without SIM cards. Receive the phone, charger, and carrying case in the mail and return it in the mailer. EZ Wireless, Daystar, and other companies rent phones: charges vary for incoming and outgoing calls, depending on the plan you choose.

Contacts Daystar (☎ *888/908–4100* 🌐 *www.daystarwireless.com*) rents cell phones at about $3.95 per day, with incoming calls at aproximately 22¢ a minute and outgoing at $1.19.

TOLL-FREE NUMBERS

Mexico-only toll-free numbers appear as follows: 01800/123–4567. The toll-free numbers listed simply as 800/123–4567 are U.S. numbers, and generally work north of the border only (though some calling cards will allow you to dial them from Mexico, charging you minutes as for a toll call). Note that Mexican toll-free numbers are billed as local calls if dialed from a private phone. In this guide, numbers listed as 001800/123–4567 are toll-free numbers that connect you from Mexico to the United States and are charged as international calls.

CUSTOMS AND DUTIES

Upon entering Mexico, you'll be given a baggage declaration form—you can fill out one per family. Most airports have random bag-inspection schemes. You'll approach something that looks like a stoplight; hand your form to the attendant, press the button, and if you get a green light you (and the rest of your family) may proceed. If you get a red light, you may be subject to further questioning or inspection.

Some regional airports have heightened security, and all passengers are required to undergo a cursory bag inspection.

GENERAL GUIDELINES

You can bring in 3 liters of spirits or wine for personal use; 400 cigarettes, 50 cigars, or 250 grams of tobacco; a reasonable amount of perfume for personal use; one video camera and one regular camera and 12 rolls of film for each; and gift items not to exceed a total of $300 (except if you're driving in, in which case the limit is $50).

You can also bring in one of each of the following items without paying taxes: a cell phone, a beeper, a radio or tape recorder, a musical instrument, a laptop computer, and portable copier or printer. Compact discs and audio cassettes are limited to 20 total and DVDs to five.

You aren't allowed to bring in firearms or ammunition, meat, vegetables, plants, fruit, or flowers. Mexico also allows you to bring one cat or dog, if you have two things: 1) a pet health certificate signed by a registered veterinarian in the United States and issued not more than 72 hours before the animal enters Mexico; and 2) a pet vaccination certificate showing that the animal has been treated (as applicable) for rabies, hepatitis, distemper, and leptospirosis.

INFORMATION

Aduana Mexico (Mexican Customs) has an informative Web site. You can also get customs information from the Mexican consulate, which has branches in many major American cities as well as border towns. To find one, check the Ministry of Foreign Affairs Web site, http://portal.sre.gob.mx/usa, select Consular Services from the menu on the left, and scroll down.

Customs Contacts Aduana Mexico (🌐 *www.aduanas.sat.gob.mx*).

U.S. Information U.S. Customs and Border Protection (🌐 *www.cbp.gov*).

EATING OUT

MEALS AND MEALTIMES

Restaurants are plentiful and have long hours, though seafood places often close by late afternoon, and traditional restaurants may close on Sunday. Reduced hours aren't a problem in major tourist areas, where plenty of eateries are open daily. If you're visiting a small town, however, check with locals or the hotel staff to avoid going hungry. Unless otherwise noted, the restaurants listed in this guide are open daily for lunch and dinner.

During the day, rely on standard regional dishes served in the hot food area of the local market, or *mercado.* Most of the archaeological sites have a café; some have surprisingly good restaurants.

To save money, look for the fixed-menu lunch known as *comida corrida* or *menú del día,* which is served from about 1 to 4 almost everywhere in Mexico.

For information on food-related health issues, see Health below.

BREAKFAST

You can get *desayuno* (breakfast) in *cafeterías* (coffee shops) as well as snack bars and other establishments. Choices range from hefty egg-and-chorizo, ham, or beef dishes, to *chilaquiles* (a layered casserole with fried tortilla strips, tomato sauce, spices, crumbled white cheese, and sometimes meat or eggs) to lighter fare like bread rolls, yogurt, and fruit.

Some cafés don't open until 8 or 8:30, in which case hotel restaurants are the best bets for early risers. *Panaderías* (bakeries) open early and provide the cheapest breakfast you'll find—a bag of assorted rolls and pastries will likely cost less than $1.

LUNCH

Comida (lunch) is traditionally the big meal of the day, and set menus usually consist of soup and/or salad, bread or tortillas, a main dish, one or two side dishes, and dessert. Restaurants geared toward travelers often serve lighter fare, and cafés and restaurants serve soups, salads, sandwiches, and pizza for those who don't want a full spread. Lunch is usually served from 2 PM to 4 PM

DINNER

Cena (dinner) tends to be lighter; in fact, many people just have milk or hot chocolate and a sweet roll; *tamales* are also traditional evening fare. Many restaurants, however, including both tourist-oriented and local spots serve substantial, multicourse dinners. Mexicans rarely go out to dinner before 8 PM.

PAYING

Small restaurants generally don't accept credit cards. Larger restaurants and those catering to tourists take credit cards, but their prices reflect the fee placed on all credit-card transactions. Credit cards most often accepted are MasterCard and Visa, and to a slightly lesser extent, American Express.

For guidelines on tipping see Tipping below.

■TIP→ Find hotel and restaurant price charts in individual chapters.

RESERVATIONS

Make a reservation whenever you can. In some places they're expected. We mention them specifically only when reservations are essential (there's no other way you'll ever get a table) or when they are not accepted.

For popular restaurants, book as far ahead as you can (often two weeks), and reconfirm as soon as you arrive. (Large parties should always call ahead to check the reservations policy.) Some restaurants have online reservations, but it's again wise to call ahead. We mention dress only when men are required to wear a jacket or a jacket and tie.

ELECTRICITY

For U.S. and Canadian travelers, electrical converters aren't necessary, because Mexico operates on the 60-cycle, 120-volt system; however, many Mexican outlets have not been updated to accommodate three-prong and polarized plugs (those with one larger prong), so to be safe bring an adapter. Blackouts and brownouts—often lasting an hour or so—are fairly common everywhere, particularly during the rainy season.

Consider making a small investment in a universal adapter, which has several types of plugs in one lightweight, compact unit. Most laptops and mobile phone chargers are dual voltage (i.e., they operate equally well on 110 and 220 volts), and require only an adapter. These days the same is true of small appliances such as hair dryers. Always check labels and manufacturer instructions to be sure. Don't use 110-volt outlets marked FOR SHAVERS ONLY for high-wattage appliances such as hair dryers.

Contacts **Steve Kropla's Help for World Travelers** (🌐 *www.kropla.com*) has information on electrical and telephone plugs around the world.

EMERGENCIES

The emergency number ☎ 060 works best in Mexico City and environs. In other areas, call ☎ 080 or ☎ 066. For roadside assistance, contact the Angeles Verdes.

If you get into a scrape with the law, you can call your nearest consulate; the U.S. Embassy Web site has links to all consular offices. U.S. citizens can also call the Overseas Citizens Services Center in the United States.

The Mexican Ministry of Tourism also has Infotur, a 24-hour toll-free hotline, and local tourist boards may be able to help as well.

Foreign Embassies **U.S. Embassy** (✉ *Paseo de la Reforma 305, Col. Cuauhtémoc, Mexico City* ☎ *55/5080–2000* 🌐 *mexico.usembassy.gov/eng*).

General Emergency Contacts **Angeles Verdes, Mexico City** (☎ *078*). **Mexico Ministry of Tourism** (☎ *800/446–3942* 🌐 *www.sectur.gob.mx*). **U.S. Overseas Citizens Services Center** (☎ *202/501–4444* 🌐 *www.state.gov/travel*).

HEALTH

FOOD AND DRINK

Despite concerns raised by the H1N1 influenza outbreak of early 2009, in Mexico the biggest health risk is *turista* (traveler's diarrhea) caused by consuming contaminated fruit, vegetables, water, or ice. In places not geared to foreigners, don't eat raw vegetables that haven't been, or can't be, peeled (e.g., lettuce and raw chili peppers or piles of fresh cilantro, a common cause of turista); ask for your plate *sin ensalada* (without salad). Avoid uncooked food and unpasteurized milk and other dairy products.

Although fresh *ceviche* (raw seafood) cured in lemon juice can be delicious, wary travelers heed the Mexican Department of Health, which warns that marinating in lemon juice does not constitute the "cooking" that would make contaminated shellfish safe to eat.

If you eat food from street stands, check that utensils and dishes are properly washed and dried (plastic sleeves cover plates at the most hygienic street stalls), and that the food is hot and fresh-looking. Although much street food is healthful and tasty, err on the side of caution.

Hotels with water-purification systems post signs to that effect in the rooms; even then, be wary. Play it safe by drinking bottled water (or water that has been boiled for at least 10 minutes) even when you're brushing your teeth. *Agua mineral* means mineral water, and *agua purificada* means purified water.

Stay away from ice, unless you're sure it was made from purified water; commercially made purified ice usually has a uniform shape and a hole in the center. When in doubt, especially when ordering cold drinks at untouristed establishments, skip the ice: *sin hielo*.

REMEDIES

Mild cases of *turista* may respond to Imodium (known generically as loperamide), Lomotil, or Pepto-Bismol (not as strong), all of which you can buy over the counter; keep in mind, though, that these drugs can complicate more serious illnesses.

Replace fluids by drinking plenty of purified water or tea; chamomile tea (*té de manzanilla*) is a good, readily available folk remedy. In severe cases, rehydrate yourself with Gatorade or a salt-sugar solution (½ teaspoon salt and 4 tablespoons sugar per quart of water). If your fever and diarrhea last longer than three days, see a doctor—you may have picked up a parasite that requires prescription medication.

AIR POLLUTION

Air pollution in Mexico City can pose a health risk. The sheer numbers of cars and industries in the capital, thermal inversions, and the inability to process sewage have all contributed to the high levels of lead, carbon monoxide, and other pollutants.

Children, the elderly, and those with respiratory problems should avoid outdoor activities—including sightseeing—on days of high smog alerts. Information on smog is often published in the daily papers and mentioned on the radio. If Spanish isn't one of your languages, ask a hotel staffer for an update.

If you have heart problems, keep in mind that Mexico City is at 7,556 feet, so altitude sickness can be a concern. This, compounded with the smog, may pose a serious health risk, so check with your doctor before planning a trip.

SMOKING

Smoking is prohibited in offices, restaurants, and public spaces, restricting lighting up to those areas where special ventilation equipment has been installed. Whether or not these restrictions are stringently enfored is another issue. The governors of tobacco-growing states like Nayarit have been opposed to the ban and have said they will not enforce it.

WATER POLLUTION

In the last few years Mexico has had to make tough choices between much-needed development and protecting the environment. In some places the rate of development has exceeded the government's ability to keep the environment safe. Polluted waters, which can give you gastrointestinal and other problems, are among the issues.

Some cleanup action is under way, after studies released in early 2003 indicated that waters near 16 resort areas contained high levels of pollution from trash, sewage, or industrial waste. Of the resorts—which included Acapulco, Puerto Vallarta, Puerto Escondido, and Huatulco—Zihuatanejo was considered the most polluted. Two factors reportedly contributed to the problem: the waters off its shores are in a bay where pollution is more apt to accumulate than it would in open waters, and this area in particular had difficulties properly treating its wastewater.

Cleanup efforts have a long way to go. Ask locals about where it's best to swim.

ALTITUDE

The higher you go, the lower the oxygen levels in the air—and the oxygen deficiency in your breathing intake can cause *mal de alturas* (altitude sickness). It usually sets in at 8,000 feet, though some people are affected at 6,000 feet (at 7,556 feet, Mexico City is in the altitude-sickness zone for many travelers).

Headache, insomnia, and shortness of breath are the most common symptoms. More severe symptoms include nausea, vomiting, dry cough, confusion, and difficulty walking a straight line; at worst, altitude sickness can cause pulmonary and cerebral edema. Altitude sensitivity varies, but in general you can expect symptoms to abate after two or three days.

PRECAUTIONS AND REMEDIES

Stay hydrated; go easy on diuretics, like coffee, tea, and alcoholic beverages; and scale back physical activity until you're acclimated. Mild pain relievers, such as aspirin or aspirin substitutes, should help with headaches. Stronger drugs, such as acetazolamide, should be taken only after consulting a doctor. If your symptoms don't go away, get to a lower altitude and consult a doctor.

SUNBURN

Sunbathers lulled by a slightly overcast sky or the sea breezes can be burned badly in just 20 minutes. To avoid overexposure, use strong sunscreens and avoid the peak sun hours of noon to 2 PM. Sunscreen, including many American brands, can be purchased in pharmacies, supermarkets, and resort gift shops.

PESTS

Mosquitoes are most prevalent in tropical coastal areas and in the south—particularly in the jungle areas of Campeche, Quintana Roo, and the Yucatán peninsula, where it's best to be cautious and go indoors at dusk (called the "mosquito hour" by locals).

An excellent brand of *repelente de insectos* (insect repellent) called Autan is readily available; do not use it on children under age two. Sprays (*aerosoles repelentes contra mosquitos*) don't always have the effective ingredients; make sure they do. If you want to bring a mosquito repellent from home, make sure it has at least 10% DEET or it won't be effective.

If you're hiking in the jungle (or near standing water or even a patio restaurant edged in tropical plants), wear repellent and long pants and long sleeves; if you're camping in the jungle, use a mosquito net and invest in a package of *espirales contra mosquitos*, mosquito coils, which are sold in *ferreterías* or *tlalpalerías* (hardware stores) and also in some corner stores. Malaria and dengue fever are carried by mosquitoes, so be sure to use enough repellent as necessary to keep mosquitoes away.

TRIP INSURANCE

Consider buying trip insurance with medical-only coverage. Neither Medicare nor some private insurers cover medical expenses anywhere outside of the United States. Medical-only policies typically reimburse you for medical care (excluding that related to preexisting conditions) and hospitalization abroad, and provide for evacuation. You still have to pay the bills and await reimbursement from the insurer, though.

Another option is to sign up with a medical-evacuation assistance company. A membership in one of these companies gets you doctor referrals, emergency evacuation or repatriation, 24-hour hotlines for medical consultation, and other assistance. International SOS Assistance Emergency and AirMed International provide evacuation services and medical referrals. MedjetAssist provides medical evacuation.

TIP→ If you're staying in Mexico City, you will receive free health-insurance coverage upon check-in at a hotel. It's all part of the tourist board's initiative to make people feel more secure about visiting the captial.

Medical Assistance Companies **AirMed International** (*www.airmed.com*). **International SOS Assistance Emergency** (*www.internationalsos.com*). **MedjetAssist** (*www.medjetassist.com*).

Medical-Only Insurers **International Medical Group** (*www.imglobal.com*). **International SOS** (*www.internationalsos.com*). **Wallach & Company** (*www.wallach.com*).

HOLIDAYS

Banks and government offices close on January 1, February 5 (Constitution Day), March 21 (Benito Juárez's birthday), May 1 (Labor Day), September 16 (Independence Day), November 20 (Revolution Day), and December 25. They may also close on unofficial holidays, such as Day of the Dead (November 1–2), Virgin of Guadalupe Day (December 12), and during Holy Week (the days leading to Easter Sunday). Government offices usually have reduced hours and staff from Christmas through New Year's Day.

MAIL

The Mexican postal system is notoriously slow and unreliable; avoid sending packages through it, and don't expect to receive them. It's much better to use a courier service. If you're an American Express cardholder, you may be able to receive packages at a branch office, but check beforehand with customer service.

Post offices (*oficinas de correos*) are found in even the smallest villages. International postal service is all airmail, but even so, your letter will take anywhere from 10 days to six weeks to arrive. Service within Mexico can be equally slow.

It costs 9.50 pesos to send a postcard or letter weighing under 20 grams to the United States; it's 10.50 to Canada.

Information **American Express** (🌐 *www.americanexpress.com/travel*).

SHIPPING PACKAGES

Federal Express, DHL, Estafeta, AeroMexpress, and United Parcel Service are available in major cities and many resort areas. These companies provide office or hotel pickup with 24-hour advance notice (sometimes less, depending on when you call), and are completely reliable. From Mexico City to anywhere in the United States, the minimum charge is around $30 for a package weighing about 1 pound.

Express Services **AeroMexpress** (☎ *01800/398–2700 toll-free in Mexico, 55/5133–0275 in Mexico City* 🌐 *www.aeromexpress.com.mx*). **DHL** (☎ *01800/765–6345 toll-free in Mexico, 55/5345–7000 in Mexico City* 🌐 *www.dhl.com*). **Estafeta** (☎ *01800/903–3500 toll-free in Mexico, 55/5270–8300 in Mexico City* 🌐 *www.estafeta.com*). **Federal Express** (☎ 01800/900–1100 toll-free in Mexico, 55/228–9904 in Mexico City 🌐 *www.fedex.com*). **United Parcel Service** (☎ *01800/902–9200 toll-free in Mexico, 55/5228–7900 in Mexico City* 🌐 *www.ups.com*).

MONEY

The prices given in this book have nearly always been converted to U.S. dollars, because high-end hotels and heavily touristed areas often quote prices in U.S. dollars. Admissions and meal prices outside these areas will likely be quoted in pesos.

As a rule when traveling in Mexico, pay in pesos. Hotels almost always accept dollars but usually do not give a good exchange rate. Many businesses, most restaurants (unless they're high-end or in major resort areas), market vendors, and most highway tollbooths do not accept dollars. If you run out of pesos, pay with a credit card or make a withdrawal from an ATM.

TIP→ Unlike their U.S. counterparts, Mexican banks may refuse torn bills, and for this reason merchants also may refuse them.

Cancún, Cozumel, Isla Mujeres, Playa del Carmen, Puerto Vallarta, Mexico City, Monterrey, Acapulco, Ixtapa, Los Cabos, Manzanillo, and, to a lesser extent, Mazatlán and Huatulco are the most expensive places to visit. All the beach towns, however, have budget accommodations; lodgings are even less expensive in less accessible areas such as the Chihuahua and Sonora states of northwest Mexico, the Gulf Coast and northern Yucatán parts of Quintana Roo, some of the less-developed spots north and south of Puerto Vallarta in the states of Jalisco and Nayarit, and the smaller Oaxacan coastal towns as well as those of Chiapas and Tabasco.

Probably the best value for your travel dollar is in smaller, inland cities such as Mérida, Morelia, Guanajuato, and Oaxaca.

WHAT IT COSTS	
Cup of Coffee	80¢ to $1.50
Bottle of Beer	$2.50–$5
Sandwich	$1.50–$2.50
One-Mile Taxi Ride	$1.50–$3.50
Museum Admission	Free–$10 (average $8)

Prices throughout this guide are given for adults. Substantially reduced fees are almost always available for children, students, and senior citizens.

ATMS AND BANKS

ATMs (*cajeros automáticos*) are widely available, with Cirrus and Plus the most frequently found networks. Unless you're in a major city, though, treat ATMs as you would gas stations—don't assume you'll be able to find one in a pinch (in smaller towns, even when they're present, machines are often out of order or out of cash). Many, but not all, gas stations have ATMs. All airports have them, but many bus stations do not.

Before you leave home, alert your bank's customer-protection division to let them know you will be using your card in Mexico—otherwise they may assume that the card's been stolen and put a hold on your account.

Many Mexican ATMs can't accept PINs (personal identification numbers, *número de identificación personal* or NIP in Spanish) with more than four digits. If yours is longer, ask your bank about changing your PIN before you leave home. If your PIN is fine yet your transaction still can't be completed, chances are that the computer lines are busy or that the machine has run out of money or is being serviced. Don't give up.

CREDIT CARDS

Throughout this guide, the following abbreviations are used: **AE,** American Express; **D,** Discover; **DC,** Diners Club; **MC,** MasterCard; and **V,** Visa.

Credit cards are accepted in most tourist areas. Smaller, less expensive restaurants and shops, however, tend to take only cash. In general, credit cards aren't accepted in small towns and villages, except in hotels. The most widely accepted cards are MasterCard and Visa. When shopping, you can often get better prices if you pay with cash, particularly in small shops.

In Mexico the decision to pay cash or use a credit card might depend on whether the establishment in which you are making a purchase finds bargaining for prices acceptable, as well as whether you want the safety net of your card's purchase protection. To avoid fraud, it's wise to make sure that "pesos" is clearly marked on all credit-card receipts.

CURRENCY AND EXCHANGE

CURRENCY

Mexican currency comes in denominations of 20-, 50-, 100-, 200-, and 500-peso bills. Coins come in denominations of 1, 2, 5, 10, and 20 pesos, and 10, 20, and 50 centavos (10 and 20 centavos pieces are rarely seen, however). Many of the coins and bills are decidedly similar, so check carefully.

U.S. dollar bills (but not coins) are widely accepted in border towns and in many parts of the Yucatán, particularly in Cancún and Cozumel, where you'll often find prices in shops quoted in dollars. Still, in the majority of the country, even in other resort areas, pesos are the preferred (and many times, only) accepted currency.

EXCHANGE

At this writing, the exchange rate was approximately 12.70 pesos to the U.S. dollar.

ATM transaction fees may be higher abroad than at home, but ATM currency-exchange rates are the best of all because they're based on wholesale rates obtained only by major banks. And if you take out a fair amount of cash per withdrawal, the transaction fee becomes less of a strike against the exchange rate (in percentage terms). However, most ATMs allow only up to $300 per transaction. Banks and *casas de cambio* (money-exchange bureaus) have the second-best exchange rates. The difference from one place to another is usually only a few pesos. Some banks change money on weekdays only until 3 (though they stay open until 5 or later).

Casas de cambio generally stay open until 6 and often operate on weekends also; they usually have competitive rates and much shorter lines. Some hotels exchange money, but for providing you with this convenience they help themselves to a bigger commission than banks.

You can do well at most airport exchange booths, though not as well as at the ATMs. You'll do even worse at rail and bus stations, in hotels, in restaurants, or in stores.

Count your bills before leaving the bank or casa de cambio, and don't accept any partially torn or taped-together notes as they won't be accepted anywhere. Also, many shop and restaurant owners are unable to make change for large bills, so request *billetes chicos* (small bills).

Currency Conversion **Google** (*www.google.com*). **Oanda.com** (*www.oanda.com*). **XE.com** (*www.xe.com*).

PACKING

For resorts, bring lightweight sportswear, bathing suits, and cover-ups for the beach. Bathing suits and immodest clothing are inappropriate for shopping and sightseeing, both in cities and, to a lesser extent, in beach resorts. Keep in mind that Mexican men do not generally wear shorts except in beach cities and resorts, even in extremely hot weather.

Mexico City, Queretaro, and the other capital cities are more formal than the resorts, and many are cooler because of their high elevation. Men will want to bring lightweight suits or slacks and blazers; women should pack dresses or pants suits. Many high-end Mexico City restaurants require jacket and tie.

Jeans are acceptable for shopping and sightseeing, but shorts are rarely worn by local men or women.

In winter the resort areas along the Pacific Coast can get particularly cool at night; make sure you have at least one pair of long pants and sweater or light jacket. Elsewhere you many need a lightweight topcoat for winter and an all-weather coat and umbrella in case of sudden rainstorms.

The sun anywhere in Mexico can be fierce; bring a sun hat and sunscreen for the beach and for sightseeing. You'll need a sweater or jacket to cope with hotel and restaurant air-conditioning. **TIP→ Bring tissue packs in case you hit a place where the toilet paper has run out.**

PASSPORTS AND VISAS

You need a valid passport to reenter the United States via air, land, or sea. If, however, you frequently travel between Mexico and the United States by land—as many border-area residents do—or sea, the U.S. passport card is also acceptable. It's smaller (think wallet size) and cheaper than a passport and valid for just as long, but you can't use it for travel by air.

A tourist visa is required for all visitors to Mexico. You're allowed to stay 180 days as a tourist; frequently, though, immigration officials will give you less. Be sure to ask for as much time as you think you'll need up to 180 days; going to a Mexican immigration office to extend a visa can easily take a whole day; plus, you'll have to pay an extension fee.

If you're arriving by plane, the standard tourist visa forms will be given to you on the plane. They're also available through travel agents and Mexican consulates, and at the border if you're entering by land. You're supposed to keep a portion of the form. *Be sure that you do.* You'll be asked to present it, your ticket, and your passport at the gate when boarding for departure.

A tourist visa costs about $20. The fee is generally tacked on to the price of your airline ticket; if you enter by land or boat you'll have to pay the fee separately. You're exempt from the fee if you enter by sea and stay less than 72 hours, or by land and do not stray past the 26–30-km (16–18-mi) checkpoint into the interior.

Minors traveling with one parent need notarized permission from the absent parent.

U.S. Passport Information **U.S. Department of State** (877/487–2778 *www.state.gov/travel*).

U.S. Passport and Visa Expediters
A. Briggs Passport & Visa Expeditors (☎ *800/806-0581 or 202/338-0111* 🌐 *www.abriggs.com*). **American Passport Express** (☎ *800/455-5166 or 800/841-6778* 🌐 *www.americanpassport.com*). **Passport Express** (☎ *800/362-8196* 🌐 *www.passportexpress.com*). **Travel Document Systems** (☎ *800/874-5100 or 202/638-3800* 🌐 *www.traveldocs.com*). **Travel the World Visas** (☎ *866/886-8472* 🌐 *www.world-visa.com*).

GENERAL REQUIREMENTS FOR MEXICO	
Passport	Required for Americans traveling by air, land, or sea.
Passport Card	Valid in place of a passport for Americans traveling by land or sea, but not by air.
Visa	Required for stays of longer than 72 hours ($20, included in price of airline or cruise ticket); valid for 180 days
Vaccinations	Typhoid and hepatitis A recommended by the CDC
Driving	U.S. or Canadian driver's license suffices, no international license is necessary; but Mexican auto insurance is required
Departure Tax	US$18–$29, almost always included in the price of airline ticket

RESTROOMS

Expect to find reasonably clean flushing toilets and running water at public restrooms in the major tourist destinations and at tourist attractions; toilet paper, soap, hot water, and paper towels are not always available, though. Keep a packet of tissues with you at all times.

Although many markets, bus and train stations, and the like have public facilities, you usually have to pay about 5 pesos for the privilege. Gas stations have public bathrooms—some tidy and others not so tidy. You're better off popping into a restaurant, buying a little something, and using its restroom, which will probably be simple but clean and adequately equipped.

Unless otherwise indicated you should put your used toilet paper in the wastebasket next to the toilet; many plumbing systems in Mexico still can't handle accumulations of toilet paper.

The Bathroom Diaries is a Web site flush with unsanitized info on restrooms the world over—each one located, reviewed, and rated. Sit or Squat is another site with ratings, features, and location information for restrooms around the world.

Find a Bathroom The Bathroom Diaries (🌐 *www.thebathroomdiaries.com*). **SitorSquat** (🌐 *www.sitorsquat.com*).

SAFETY

Since roughly 2003 there has been a significant spike in violent crime, most of it drug-trafficking related. The states of Chihuahua, Sinaloa, Baja California, Tamaulipas, Guerrero, Michoacan, and Nuevo León have seen the most trouble.

In 2008 there were several firefights in Tijuana, Chihuahua City, and Ciudad Juarez. The situation in Ciudad Juarez is particularly dire, with increases in shootouts, carjackings, and robberies.

Acapulco has also been plagued by gang violence in recent years, though the police presence in tourist areas of the city has also increased. In fact, expect to find increased police presence elsewhere as well as greater security measures in regional airports and more checkpoints along roads in northern Mexico. President Felipe Calderón has sent roughly 20,000 soldiers and federal police throughout the country to battle the cartels.

CRIME

In Mexico City, abductions and robberies in taxicabs hailed from the street (as opposed to hired from a hotel or taxi stand) or on city buses have overshadowed the age-old problem of pickpocketing. But petty theft—here and elsewhere—is still the greatest threat to travelers.

The patronage system is a well-entrenched part of Mexican politics and industry, and workers in the public sector (notably police and customs officials) are notoriously underpaid. Everyone has heard some horror story about highway assaults, pickpocketing, bribes, or foreigners languishing in Mexican jails. These reports apply in large part to Mexico City and more remote areas of Oaxaca and Chiapas. Cancún, which has traditionally been a safe haven, has also seen an increased incidence of taxi robberies and extortion; be particularly careful that your cab from the airport is associated with a reputable company.

So far, crime isn't such a problem in the heartland (cities like San Miguel de Allende) and much of the rest of the country.

Reporting a crime to the police will be frustrating unless you speak excellent Spanish and have a great deal of patience. If you're victimized, contact your local consular agent or the consular section of the embassy in Mexico City.

SCAMS

Reports indicate that there's a growing problem with people impersonating police officers, pulling over motorists, and extorting money from or robbing them.

In cities, especially Mexico City, people selling trinkets, washing windows, and asking for handouts often victimize drivers at stoplights. If someone approaches you, shake your index finger or head to indicate that you don't want what they're selling, roll up your windows, and lock your doors.

Big-city shakedown artists may take advantage of you using a convincing sob story. A common ruse is for a woman with multiple children in tow and tears in her eyes to approach a victim saying that she's just been robbed and needs bus fare to get home. It's hard to resist when there are little ones involved, but these and other similar stories are, sadly, often made up.

Women on their own—particularly in the cities—may be subjected to *piropos* (flirtatious comments). Dressing conservatively may deflect some of the attention, but don't count on it. Your best strategy is to ignore the offender.

PRECAUTIONS

Use common sense everywhere, but exercise particular caution in Mexico City.

When registering at your hotel, use only your first initial and last name, particularly if you're on your own. Don't wear expensive jewelry, and carry only enough money to cover casual spending. Distribute your cash or credit cards between a deep front pocket, an inside jacket or vest pocket, and a hidden money pouch (which you never reach for in public).

If you carry a purse, choose one with a zipper and a thick strap that you can drape across your body; adjust the length so that the purse sits in front of you—at or above hip level. Carry your own baggage whenever possible.

Keep your passport and all valuables in hotel-room safes or hotel safety-deposit boxes.Use ATMs during the day and in big, enclosed commercial areas. Avoid the glass-enclosed street variety of banks where you're vulnerable to thieves who force you to withdraw money for them.

Avoid driving on desolate streets, and don't travel at night, pick up hitchhikers, or hitchhike yourself.

Use luxury buses whenever possible; these take the safer toll roads.

In big cities, avoid hailing taxis on the street. Use only registered hotel taxis, or have a concierge call a radio taxi or *sitio* (cab stand).

Think twice about getting away from it all on your own (even as a couple) to go hiking in remote national parks; women in particular shouldn't venture alone onto uncrowded beaches.

General Information and Warnings U.S. Department of State (*www.state.gov/travel*).

TAXES

Mexico has a value-added tax of 15% (10% in the states of Quintana Roo, Baja California Norte, and Baja California Sur, as well as areas that are up to 20 km, or 12½ mi, from the border), called IVA (*impuesto al valor agregado*). It's often waived for cash purchases, or incorporated into the price. When comparing hotel prices, it's important to know if yours includes or excludes IVA and any service charge. Other taxes and charges apply for phone calls made from your room. Many states are charging a 2% tax on accommodations that is used for tourism promotion.

TIME

Mexico has three time zones; most of the country falls in Central Standard Time (in line with Chicago), including Mexico City. Baja California Norte is on Pacific Standard Time—the same as California. Baja California Sur, Sonora, Chihuahua, Sinaloa, and most of Nayarit are on Mountain Standard Time.

If you're staying in southern Nayarit and flying out of the Puerto Vallarta airport, note that clocks in Puerto Vallarta, in Jalisco state, are an hour later than those in Nayarit. Mexico switches to and from daylight saving time on the same schedule as the United States.

TIPPING

TIPPING GUIDELINES FOR MEXICO	
Bartender	10 pesos per drink
Bellhop	10–20 pesos per bag
Coat-check Personnel	10 pesos per item checked unless there is a fee
Hotel Concierge	20–50 pesos or more
Hotel Doorman	10 pesos if he helps you get a cab
Hotel Maid	10–20 pesos per day
Hotel Room Service	10–20 pesos per meal
Parking Attendant	5–10 pesos
Porter or Skycap at Airport or Bus Station	10–20 pesos per bag
Restroom Attendant	5–10 pesos
Tour Guide	10% of the cost of the tour or 50 pesos per half day
Valet Parking Attendant	10–20 pesos, but only when you get your car
Waiter	10%–15%

Remember that the minimum wage is just under $5 a day and that maids, bellhops, and others in the tourism industry earn minimum wage. Waiters and bellmen in international chain hotels, for example, think in dollars and know that in the United States porters are tipped about $2 a bag; they tend to expect the equivalent. That said, tip using local currency whenever possible, so that service personnel aren't stuck going to the bank to exchange dollars for pesos.

We've provided some guidelines. Naturally, larger tips are always welcome.

VISITOR INFORMATION

The Mexico Tourism Board has branches in New York, Chicago, Los Angeles, Houston, Miami, Montréal, Toronto, Vancouver, and London.

Mexico Tourism Board United States (*800/446–3942 [44-MEXICO] www.visitmexico.com*).

INDEX

D

K

L

M

PHOTO CREDITS

5, Peter Purchia viestiphoto.com. Chapter 1: Experience Mexico: 9, Sexto Sol/Photodisc. 10, GUILLERMO ALDANA/Mexico Tourism Board. 11 (left), Corbis. 11 (right), GUILLERMO ALDANA/Mexico Tourism Board. 12, Joe Viesti/Viestiphoto.com. 13 (left), Corbis.13 (right), Joe Viesti/Viestiphoto.com. 16, Mexico Tourism Board. 17, Peter Purchia/viestiphoto.com. 18, CARLOS SANCHEZ/Mexican Tourism Board. 19, Doug Scott/age fotostock. 20, Corbis. 21, (left), Joe Viesti/Viestiphoto.com. 21, (right), GUILLERMO ALDANA/Mexico Tourism Board. 22 (left), GUILLERMO ALDANA/Mexico Tourism Board. 22 (right), Joe Viesti/Viestiphoto.com. 24, S. Murphy-Larronde/age fotostock. 27 (left), Corbis. 27 (right), Juan Carlos Calvin/age fotostock. 29 (left), Walter Bibikow/viestiphoto.com. 29 (right), José Fuste Raga/age fotostock. Chapter 2: Mexico City: 31, Martin Siepmann/age fotostock. 32, Corbis. 33 (top left), CARLOS SANCHEZ/Mexican Tourism Board. 33 (top right), José Fuste Raga/age fotostock. 33 (bottom), BRUCE HERMAN/Mexican Tourism Board. 44–45, Walter Bibikow/ age fotostock. 47 (top), Peter Purchia/viestiphoto.com. 47 (bottom), George And Audrey DeLange. 61, Peter Purchia/viestiphoto.com. 62 (top), Yale Collection of American Literature, Beinecke Rare Book and Manuscript Library (Photograph by Carl Van Vechten). 62 (bottom), Planet Art. 63 (top), Yale Collection of American Literature, Beinecke Rare Book and Manuscript Library (Photograph by Carl Van Vechten). 63 (bottom), Flat Earth. 64, Museo Dolores Olmedo Patiño. 65 (top left, center, and right), Russell Gordon/viestiphoto.com. 65 (bottom), George And Audrey DeLange. Chapter 3: Around Mexico City: 115, Ken Welsh/age fotostock. 116, José Fuste Raga/age fotostock. 117 (top left), GUILLERMO ALDANA/Mexico Tourism Board. 117 (top right), GUILLERMO ALDANA/Mexico Tourism Board. 117 (bottom), José Fuste Raga/age fotostock. 136 (full page), BRUCE HERMAN/Mexico Tourism Board. 136 (inset), José Fuste Raga/age fotostock. 137 (top), Marco/viestiphoto.com. 137 (bottom), J.D. Heaton/Picture Finders/age fotostock. 138, Russell Gordon/age fotostock. 139, Toño Labra/age fotostock. 140, José Fuste Raga/age fotostock. Chapter 4: San Miguel de Allende & the Heartland: 153, José Fuste Raga/age fotostock. 154 (top left), PABLO DE AGUINACO/Mexico Tourism Board. 154(top right), Angelo Cavalli/age fotostock. 154 (bottom), CARLOS SANCHEZ/Mexico Tourism Board. 155, Bruno Perousse/age fotostock. 210, Joe Viesti/Viestiphoto.com. 211 (top), Joe Viesti/Viestiphoto.com. 211 (bottom), Bruno Perousse/age fotostock. 212 (top), Joe Viesti/Viestiphoto.com. 212 (bottom), Joe Viesti/Viestiphoto.com. 213 (top), Joe Viesti/Viestiphoto.com. 213 (center), Joe Viesti/viestiphoto.com. 213 (bottom), Corbis. Chapter 5: Guadalajara: 217, BRUCE HERMAN/Mexico Tourism Board. 218 (left), Corbis. 218 (right), BRUCE HERMAN/Mexico Tourism Board. 219 (left and right), PABLO DE AGUINACO/Mexico Tourism Board. 235 and 236 (top left), folkart.com/Sullivan. 236 (bottom left), Corbis. 236 (top right), Colonial Arts, San Francisco. 236 (bottom right), Andrew J. Morris. Chapter 6: Veracruz: 263 and 264 (top), GUILLERMO ALDANA/Mexico Tourism Board. 264 (middle), Joe Viesti/Viestiphoto.com. 264 (bottom), NADINE MARKOVA/Mexico Tourism Board. 265 (left and right), GUILLERMO ALDANA/Mexico Tourism Board. 294 and 295 (top and 2nd from top), Joe Viesti/Viestiphoto.com. 295 (3rd from top and bottom), GUILLERMO ALDANA/Mexico Tourism Board. Chapter 7: Oaxaca: 303, S. Murphy-Larronde/age fotostock. 304, BRUCE HERMAN/Mexico Tourism Board. 305 (top left), GUILLERMO ALDANA/Mexico Tourism Board. 305 (top right), Don Klumpp/age fotostock. 305 (bottom), GUILLERMO ALDANA/Mexico Tourism Board. 331, Joe Viesti/Viestiphoto.com. 332, Peter Purchia/viestiphoto.com. 333 (all), folkart.com/oaxaca. 336-337, Oaxaca Ministry of Tourism. 338, marco/viestiphoto.com. Chapter 8: Chiapas & Tabasco: 365, Corbis. 366, Jaime Boites/Viestiphoto.com. 367 (top left), Sergio Pitamitz/age fotostock. 367 (top right), Corbis. 367 (bottom), GUILLERMO ALDANA/Mexico Tourism Board. 400, Wojtek Buss/age fotostock. 401 (top), SuperStock/age fotostock. 401 (bottom), Beinecke Rare Book and Manuscript Library, Yale University. 402, Jean Pierre Lebras/Viestiphoto.com. 403 (top left), GUILLERMO ALDANA/Mexico Tourism Board. 403 (top right), George & Audrey DeLange. 403 (bottom), Philip Baird/www.anthroarcheart.org. 404, Sergio Pitamitz/age fotostock. 405, GUILLERMO ALDANA/Mexico Tourism Board. Chapter 9: Sonora: 415, NADINE MARKOVA/Mexico Tourism Board. 416, GUILLERMO ALDANA/Mexico Tourism Board. 417 (left), Joe Viesti/Viestiphoto.com. 417 (right), Ken Ross/Viestiphoto.com Inc. Chapter 10: Barrancas del Cobre: 441, Gonzalo Azumendi/age fotostock. 442 (top), Ann Duncan/viestiphoto.com. 442 (bottom), Peter Purchia/viestiphoto.com. 443, Peter Purchia/viestiphoto.com. Chapter 11: Los Cabos & the Baja Peninsula: 467, Mexico Tourism Board. 468, Vicki Sills/Casa Del Mar Beach Golf & Spa Resort. 494, Esperanza Resort. 496 (left), Esperanza Resort. 496 (right), Marquis Los Cabos. 497 (left), One & Only Palmilla. 497 (right), Las Ventanas Al Paraiso. 498 (left), Villa Group Resorts. 498 (right), Fiesta Americana Grand Los Cabos. 499 (left), Solmar Hotels & Resorts. 499 (right), Larry Dunmire. 500, George Doyle/iStockphoto. Chapter 12: Puerto Vallarta & the Pacific Coast Resorts: 551, Corbis. 552, Mexico Tourism Board. 592, El Careyes Beach Resort. 593 (left and right) and 594, Four Seasons Resort, Punta Mita. 596, Grand Velas. Chapter 13: Acapulco - With a Side Trip to Taxco: 637, Corbis. 638, Walter Bibikow/age fotostock. 639 (left), CARLOS SANCHEZ/Mexico Tourism Board. 639 (right), Ken Welsh/age fotostock. 648, Everett Collection. 649 (all), Joe Viesti/Viestiphoto.com. Chapter 14: Cancún & Isla Mujeres: 673, Chris Cheadle/age fotostock. 674 (top), Jimmy Buffett's Margaritaville. 674 (bottom), Frank Lukasseck/age fotostock. 675 (left), Philip Coblentz/Brand X Pictures. 675 (right), Corbis. 696 and 698 (left), Banyan Tree Hotels & Resorts. 698 (right), Rosewood Hotels & Resorts. 699 (left), Viceroy Hotel Group. 699 (right), George Apostolidis. 700, Fairmont Hotels & Resorts. 701 (left), Marriott International. 701 (right), Palace Resorts. Chapter 15: Cozumel and the Riviera Maya: 727, Bruno Morandi/age fotostock. 728 (top), cancuncd.com. 728 (bottom), Richard Cummins/viestiphoto.com. 729, Robert inslow/viestiphoto.com. Chapter 16: Mérida & Environs with Chichén Itzá: 771, Mark Newman/age fotostock. 772 (top), Corbis. 772 (bottom), GUILLERMO ALDANA/Mexico Tourism Board. 773, J. D. Heaton/Picture Finders/age fotostock. 796, David Davis/Shutterstock. 797, Corbis. 798 (top), José A. Granados/Cancun CVB. 798 (bottom), William Wu. 799 (top), Gonzalo Azumendi/age fotostock. 799 (center), Philip Baird/anthroarcheart.org. 799 (bottom), Mexico Tourism Board. 800 (top), Corbis. 800 (bottom), Bruno Perousse/age fotostock. 801 (top inset), Luis Castañeda/age fotostock. 801 (top image), José A. Granados/Cancun CVB. 801 (bottom), Joe Viesti/Viestiphoto.com. 802, Marco/viestiphoto.com. 803, Joe Viesti/viestiphoto.com.

NOTES